DATE DUE

JUL 2 4 2008	
SEP 1 7 2008	MAY 1 5 2011
OCT 0 7 2008	NOV 2 8 2012
NOV 0 5 2008	NOV 2 8 2012
MAR 2 9 2009	MAR 2 2 2016
MAY 0 5 2009	
	APR 2 6 2016
JUL 2 7 2009	
SEP 1 8 2009	NOV 0 3 2016
APR 1 7 2010	
MAY 1 6 2010	
FEB 1 6 2011	NOV 2 2 2016
FEB 1 6 2011	
	N. Dees
FEB 2 8 2011	Dec. 12, 2016

Psychology
IN THE NEW MILLENNIUM

SEVENTH EDITION

Psychology
IN THE NEW MILLENNIUM

SEVENTH EDITION

SPENCER A. RATHUS
Montclair State University

HARCOURT BRACE COLLEGE PUBLISHERS

FORT WORTH   PHILADELPHIA   SAN DIEGO   NEW YORK   ORLANDO   AUSTIN   SAN ANTONIO
TORONTO   MONTREAL   LONDON   SYDNEY   TOKYO

Publisher: Earl McPeek

Acquisitions Editor: Carol Wada

Market Strategist: Don Grainger/Kathleen Sharp

Development Editor: steve Norder

Project Editor: Michele Tomiak

Art Director: Carol Kincaid

Production Manager: Andrea A. Johnson

ISBN: 0-15-508215-9
Library of Congress Catalog Card Number: 98-85704

Address for orders:
Harcourt Brace College Publishers
6277 Sea Harbor Drive
Orlando, FL 32887-6777
1-800-782-4479

Address for editorial correspondence:
Harcourt Brace College Publishers
301 Commerce Street, Suite 3700
Fort Worth, TX 76102

Web site address:
http://www.hbcollege.com

Harcourt Brace & Company will provide complimentary supplements or supplement packages to those adopters qualified under our adoption policy. Please contact your sales representative to learn how you qualify. If as an adopter or potential user you receive supplements you do not need, please return them to your sales representative or send them to: Att: Returns Department, Troy Warehouse, 465 South Lincoln Drive, Troy, MO 63379.

Printed in the United States of America

0 1 2 3 4 5 6 7 048 9 8 7 6 5

To my daughter Jill,
who has become a psychologist

Brief Contents

TO THE INSTRUCTOR   xxv

BECOMING A SUCCESSFUL STUDENT   xlv

CHAPTER 1   WHAT IS PSYCHOLOGY?   1

CHAPTER 2   RESEARCH METHODS IN PSYCHOLOGY   32

CHAPTER 3   BIOLOGY AND BEHAVIOR   66

CHAPTER 4   LIFESPAN DEVELOPMENT   106

CHAPTER 5   SENSATION AND PERCEPTION   154

CHAPTER 6   CONSCIOUSNESS   206

CHAPTER 7   LEARNING   240

CHAPTER 8   MEMORY   280

CHAPTER 9   THINKING AND LANGUAGE   318

CHAPTER 10   INTELLIGENCE   358

CHAPTER 11   MOTIVATION AND EMOTION   390

CHAPTER 12   PERSONALITY   428

CHAPTER 13   GENDER AND SEXUALITY   466

CHAPTER 14   STRESS AND HEALTH   510

CHAPTER 15   PSYCHOLOGICAL DISORDERS   552

CHAPTER 16   METHODS OF THERAPY   594

CHAPTER 17   SOCIAL PSYCHOLOGY   632

APPENDIX A   STATISTICS   A1

APPENDIX B   ANSWER KEYS FOR QUESTIONNAIRES   B1

GLOSSARY   G1

REFERENCES   R1

CREDITS   C1

NAME INDEX   NI1

SUBJECT INDEX   SI1

CONTENTS

TO THE INSTRUCTOR	xxv
BECOMING A SUCCESSFUL STUDENT	xlv
CHAPTER 1 WHAT IS PSYCHOLOGY?	**1**
PSYCHOLOGY AS A SCIENCE	3
WHAT PSYCHOLOGISTS DO	5
Fields of Psychology	5
WHERE PSYCHOLOGY COMES FROM: A HISTORY	9
Structuralism	10
Functionalism	10
Behaviorism	11
Gestalt Psychology	13
Psychoanalysis	15
Psychology's "Top Ten"—The "Golden Oldies"	17
PSYCHOLOGY IN A WORLD OF DIVERSITY: THE DIVERSITY OF PSYCHOLOGISTS	17
HOW TODAY'S PSYCHOLOGISTS VIEW BEHAVIOR	18
The Biological Perspective	18
The Cognitive Perspective	19
The Humanistic-Existential Perspective	20
The Psychodynamic Perspective	20
Learning Perspectives	21
The Sociocultural Perspective	21
CRITICAL THINKING AND PSYCHOLOGY	24
Principles of Critical Thinking	25
PSYCHOLOGY AND MODERN LIFE: THINKING CRITICALLY ABOUT SELF-HELP BOOKS: ARE THERE ANY QUICK FIXES?	26
PSYCHOLOGY IN THE NEW MILLENNIUM: PSYCHOLOGY—HOT, HOT, HOT	28
Common Errors in Arguments	29
SUMMARY	30
CHAPTER 2 RESEARCH METHODS IN PSYCHOLOGY	**32**
THE MILGRAM STUDIES: SHOCKING STUFF AT YALE	34
THE SCIENTIFIC METHOD: PUTTING IDEAS TO THE TEST	37
SAMPLES AND POPULATIONS: REPRESENTING HUMAN DIVERSITY	39
Problems in Generalizing From Psychological Research	40
PSYCHOLOGY IN A WORLD OF DIVERSITY: INCLUDING WOMEN AND MEMBERS OF DIVERSE ETHNIC GROUPS IN RESEARCH	41
METHODS OF OBSERVATION: THE BETTER TO SEE YOU WITH	42
Case Study	43
The Survey	44

CONTENTS

PSYCHOLOGY IN A WORLD OF DIVERSITY: A SEX SURVEY THAT ADDRESSES
SOCIOCULTURAL FACTORS   45
Testing   46
Naturalistic Observation   47
Laboratory Observation   48
CORRELATION   49
THE EXPERIMENTAL METHOD: TRYING THINGS OUT   52
Independent and Dependent Variables   52
Experimental and Control Groups   53
Blinds and Double Blinds   53
PSYCHOLOGY IN THE NEW MILLENNIUM: IN THE GLOBAL RESEARCH LAB   56
METHODS OF STUDYING THE BRAIN   57
ETHICAL ISSUES IN PSYCHOLOGICAL RESEARCH
AND PRACTICE   59
Research With Humans   59
Research With Animals   61
PSYCHOLOGY AND MODERN LIFE: THINKING CRITICALLY ABOUT TEA LEAVES,
BIRD DROPPINGS, PALMS, AND THE STARS   62
SUMMARY   64

CHAPTER 3   BIOLOGY AND BEHAVIOR   66

NEURONS: INTO THE FABULOUS FOREST   69
The Makeup of Neurons   69
The Neural Impulse: Let Us "Sing the Body Electric"   71
The Synapse   73
Neurotransmitters   73
THE NERVOUS SYSTEM   76
The Central Nervous System   77
The Peripheral Nervous System   81
THE CEREBRAL CORTEX   83
The Geography of the Cerebral Cortex   83
Thought, Language, and the Cortex   85
Left Brain, Right Brain?   86
Handedness: Is It Gauche or Sinister to Be Left-Handed?   87
Split-Brain Experiments: When Hemispheres Stop Communicating   88
THE ENDOCRINE SYSTEM   89
The Hypothalamus   90
The Pituitary Gland: The Pea-Sized Governor   90
The Pancreas: How Sweet It Is (or Isn't)   91
The Thyroid Gland: The Body's Accelerator   92
The Adrenal Glands: Coping With Stress   92
The Testes and the Ovaries   92
PSYCHOLOGY IN A WORLD OF DIVERSITY: CROSS-CULTURAL PERSPECTIVES
ON MENSTRUATION   93
PSYCHOLOGY AND MODERN LIFE: COPING WITH PMS   94

CONTENTS

HEREDITY: THE NATURE OF NATURE 96
  Genes and Chromosomes 98
  Kinship Studies 99
PSYCHOLOGY IN THE NEW MILLENNIUM: HOW MANY OF YOU ARE THERE?
  HOW MANY WILL THERE BE? 100
PSYCHOLOGY AND MODERN LIFE: HEALTH APPLICATIONS OF THE
  HUMAN GENOME PROJECT 102
SUMMARY 104

CHAPTER 4   LIFESPAN DEVELOPMENT 106

CONTROVERSIES IN DEVELOPMENTAL PSYCHOLOGY 108
  Does Development Reflect Nature or Nurture? 108
  Is Development Continuous or Discontinuous? 109
PRENATAL DEVELOPMENT 109
PSYCHOLOGY AND MODERN LIFE: AVERTING GENETIC AND CHROMOSOMAL
  ABNORMALITIES 112
PHYSICAL DEVELOPMENT 113
  Reflexes 113
  Perceptual Development 113
SOCIAL DEVELOPMENT 116
  Erik Erikson's Stages of Psychosocial Development 116
  Attachment: Ties That Bind 117
  Parenting Styles: Rearing the Competent Child 120
  Day Care 122
PSYCHOLOGY AND MODERN LIFE: BECOMING AN AUTHORITATIVE PARENT 122
  Child Abuse 123
COGNITIVE DEVELOPMENT 125
  Jean Piaget's Cognitive-Developmental Theory 125
  Information-Processing Approaches to Cognitive Development 131
  Lawrence Kohlberg's Theory of Moral Development 133
PSYCHOLOGY IN A WORLD OF DIVERSITY: ARE THERE GENDER DIFFERENCES IN
  MORAL DEVELOPMENT? 136
ADOLESCENCE 136
  Physical Development 137
  Social and Personality Development 138
ADULT DEVELOPMENT 140
  Young Adulthood 140
  Middle Adulthood 141
PSYCHOLOGY IN THE NEW MILLENNIUM: WHAT BIOLOGICAL CLOCK? 144
  Late Adulthood 145
PSYCHOLOGY IN A WORLD OF DIVERSITY: GENDER, ETHNICITY, AND AGING 146
QUESTIONNAIRE: HOW LONG WILL YOU LIVE? THE LIFE-EXPECTANCY SCALE 148
SUMMARY 152

CHAPTER 5   SENSATION AND PERCEPTION   154

SENSATION AND PERCEPTION: YOUR TICKET OF ADMISSION
TO THE WORLD OUTSIDE   157
Absolute Threshold: Is It There or Isn't It?   157
Difference Threshold: Is It the Same or Is It Different?   158
Signal-Detection Theory: Is It Enough to Be Bright?   159
Feature Detectors   160
Sensory Adaptation: Where Did It Go?   160

VISION: LETTING THE SUN SHINE IN   161
Light: What Is This Stuff?   161
The Eye: The Better to See You With   162
Color Vision: Creating an Inner World of Color   166
Psychological Dimensions of Color   166
Theories of Color Vision   169
Color Blindness   171

VISUAL PERCEPTION   171
Perceptual Organization   172
Perception of Movement   175
Depth Perception   177
Problems in Visual Perception   181
Perceptual Constancies   182
Visual Illusions   183

HEARING   185
Pitch and Loudness   185
The Ear: The Better to Hear You With   187
Locating Sounds   188
Perception of Loudness and Pitch   189
Deafness   190

PSYCHOLOGY IN A WORLD OF DIVERSITY: THE SIGNS OF THE TIMES ARE CHANGING   191

SMELL   193

TASTE   193

PSYCHOLOGY IN THE NEW MILLENNIUM: WILL WE USE "A SIXTH SENSE FOR SEX"
IN THE 21ST CENTURY?   194

THE SKIN SENSES   195
Touch and Pressure   195

PSYCHOLOGY IN THE NEW MILLENNIUM: SENSATION, PERCEPTION, AND
VIRTUAL REALITY   196
Temperature   197
Pain: The Often Unwanted Message   197

PSYCHOLOGY AND MODERN LIFE: COPING WITH PAIN   198

KINESTHESIS   200

THE VESTIBULAR SENSE: ON BEING UPRIGHT   200

EXTRASENSORY PERCEPTION   201

SUMMARY   203

CONTENTS

CHAPTER 6   CONSCIOUSNESS   206

JUST WHAT *IS* CONSCIOUSNESS?   208
SLEEP AND DREAMS   210
   The Stages of Sleep   211
   Functions of Sleep   213
   Dreams   213
PSYCHOLOGY AND MODERN LIFE: COPING WITH INSOMNIA   216
   Sleep Disorders   217
ALTERING CONSCIOUSNESS THROUGH DRUGS   219
   Substance Abuse and Dependence   220
   Causal Factors in Substance Abuse and Dependence   221
DEPRESSANTS   222
   Alcohol   222
PSYCHOLOGY IN A WORLD OF DIVERSITY: ALCOHOLISM, GENDER, AND ETHNICITY   222
QUESTIONNAIRE: WHY DO YOU DRINK?   224
   Opiates   225
   Barbiturates and Methaqualone   226
STIMULANTS   226
   Amphetamines   226
   Cocaine   226
   Cigarettes (Nicotine)   227
PSYCHOLOGY AND MODERN LIFE: QUITTING SMOKING   228
PSYCHOLOGY IN THE NEW MILLENNIUM: WILL WE FIND THAT NICOTINE CAN BE (GASP!)
   GOOD FOR YOU?   230
HALLUCINOGENICS   230
   Marijuana   230
   LSD and Other Hallucinogenics   231
MEDITATION   233
BIOFEEDBACK: GETTING IN TOUCH WITH THE
   UNTOUCHABLE   233
PSYCHOLOGY AND MODERN LIFE: TRYING MEDITATION   234
HYPNOSIS: ON BEING ENTRANCED   235
   Changes in Consciousness Brought About by Hypnosis   236
   Theories of Hypnosis   236
SUMMARY   238

CHAPTER 7   LEARNING   240

CLASSICAL CONDITIONING   244
   Ivan Pavlov Rings a Bell   244
   Stimuli and Responses in Classical Conditioning   246
   Types of Classical Conditioning   247
   Taste Aversion   248
   Extinction and Spontaneous Recovery   249
   Generalization and Discrimination   250

CONTENTS

Higher-Order Conditioning 252

Applications of Classical Conditioning 252

OPERANT CONDITIONING 254

Edward L. Thorndike and the Law of Effect 255

B. F. Skinner and Reinforcement 255

Types of Reinforcers 258

Extinction and Spontaneous Recovery in Operant Conditioning 260

Reinforcers Versus Rewards and Punishments 260

Discriminative Stimuli 262

Schedules of Reinforcement 262

Applications of Operant Conditioning 265

PSYCHOLOGY AND MODERN LIFE: USING CONDITIONING TO HELP CHILDREN OVERCOME FEARS 266

PSYCHOLOGY IN THE NEW MILLENNIUM: VIRTUAL CLASSROOMS DRAW CHEERS, FEARS 268

COGNITIVE FACTORS IN LEARNING 269

Contingency Theory: What "Really" Happens During Classical Conditioning? 269

Latent Learning: Forming Cognitive Maps 270

Observational Learning: Monkey See, Monkey May Choose to Do 271

PSYCHOLOGY IN A WORLD OF DIVERSITY: CULTURE, ETHNICITY, AND ACADEMIC ACHIEVEMENT 274

PSYCHOLOGY AND MODERN LIFE: TEACHING CHILDREN NOT TO IMITATE MEDIA VIOLENCE 275

SUMMARY 277

CHAPTER 8   MEMORY 280

FIVE CHALLENGES TO MEMORY 282

THREE KINDS OF MEMORY 283

Episodic Memory 283

Semantic Memory 284

Procedural Memory 284

THREE PROCESSES OF MEMORY 284

Encoding 285

Storage 285

Retrieval 286

THREE STAGES OF MEMORY 286

Sensory Memory 288

Short-Term Memory 290

Long-Term Memory 294

THE LEVELS-OF-PROCESSING MODEL OF MEMORY 302

FORGETTING 304

Memory Tasks Used in Measuring Forgetting 305

Interference Theory 307

Repression 308

CONTENTS

Infantile Amnesia 308

Anterograde and Retrograde Amnesia 309

PSYCHOLOGY AND MODERN LIFE: USING PSYCHOLOGY TO IMPROVE YOUR MEMORY 310

THE BIOLOGY OF MEMORY: FROM ENGRAMS TO ADRENALINE 312

Changes at the Neural Level 312

Changes at the Structural Level 313

PSYCHOLOGY IN THE NEW MILLENNIUM: WHAT DOES RESEARCH ON THE BIOLOGY OF
MEMORY HOLD IN STORAGE? 314

SUMMARY 316

CHAPTER 9   THINKING AND LANGUAGE 318

CONCEPTS AND PROTOTYPES: BUILDING BLOCKS OF
THOUGHT 321

PROBLEM SOLVING 322

Approaches to Problem Solving: Getting from Here to There 323

Factors That Affect Problem Solving 326

CREATIVITY 330

Creativity and Academic Ability 331

Factors That Affect Creativity 332

QUESTIONNAIRE: THE REMOTE ASSOCIATES TEST 333

REASONING 334

Types of Reasoning 334

JUDGMENT AND DECISION MAKING 335

Heuristics in Decision Making: If It Works, Must It Be Logical? 336

The Framing Effect: Say That Again? 337

PSYCHOLOGY IN A WORLD OF DIVERSITY: ACROSS THE GREAT DIVIDE?

DIVERSE PERSPECTIVES ON THE O. J. SIMPSON VERDICTS 338

Overconfidence: Is Your Hindsight 20–20? 340

LANGUAGE 341

Basic Concepts of Language 342

LANGUAGE DEVELOPMENT 344

Development of Vocabulary 345

Development of Syntax 345

Development of More Complex Language 346

Theories of Language Development 347

PSYCHOLOGY AND MODERN LIFE: BILINGUAL EDUCATION 350

Bilingualism 351

PSYCHOLOGY IN A WORLD OF DIVERSITY: EBONICS 352

LANGUAGE AND THOUGHT 353

The Linguistic-Relativity Hypothesis 354

SUMMARY 356

CONTENTS

CHAPTER 10 INTELLIGENCE 358

THEORIES OF INTELLIGENCE 360
Factor Theories 361
Gardner's Theory of Multiple Intelligences 362
Sternberg's Triarchic Theory 363
The Theory of Emotional Intelligence 364
PSYCHOLOGY IN THE NEW MILLENNIUM: ARTIFICIAL INTELLIGENCE 366

THE MEASUREMENT OF INTELLIGENCE 367
Individual Intelligence Tests 367
Group Tests 370
PSYCHOLOGY IN A WORLD OF DIVERSITY: SOCIOECONOMIC AND ETHNIC
  DIFFERENCES IN INTELLIGENCE 371

EXTREMES OF INTELLIGENCE 373
Mental Retardation 373
Giftedness 375
PSYCHOLOGY AND MODERN LIFE: FACILITATING DEVELOPMENT OF THE GIFTED CHILD 376

THE TESTING CONTROVERSY: JUST WHAT DO INTELLIGENCE
TESTS MEASURE? 377
Is It Possible to Develop Culture-Free Intelligence Tests? 377

DETERMINANTS OF INTELLIGENCE: WHERE DOES
INTELLIGENCE COME FROM? 378
Genetic Influences on Intelligence 379
Environmental Influences on Intelligence 381
PSYCHOLOGY IN THE NEW MILLENNIUM: WILL MUSIC PROVIDE CHILDREN WITH
  THE SWEET SOUNDS OF SUCCESS? 382
PSYCHOLOGY AND MODERN LIFE: ENHANCING INTELLECTUAL FUNCTIONING 386
Ethnicity and Intelligence: A Concluding Note 387

SUMMARY 388

CHAPTER 11 MOTIVATION AND EMOTION 390

COMING TO TERMS WITH MOTIVATION 393
THEORIES OF MOTIVATION: THE *WHYS* OF BEHAVIOR 394
Instinct Theory: "Doing What Comes Naturally" 394
Drive-Reductionism and Homeostasis: "Steady, Steady . . ." 394
Humanistic Theory: "I've Got to Be Me" 395
Cognitive Theory: "I Think, Therefore I Am Consistent" 396
PSYCHOLOGY IN A WORLD OF DIVERSITY: SOCIOCULTURAL PERSPECTIVES ON MOTIVATION 397
Evaluation of Theories of Motivation 397

HUNGER: DO YOU GO BY "TUMMY-TIME"? 399
Obesity—A Serious and Pervasive Problem 400
PSYCHOLOGY AND MODERN LIFE: CONTROLLING YOUR WEIGHT 402

STIMULUS MOTIVES 404
Sensory Stimulation and Activity 404

CONTENTS

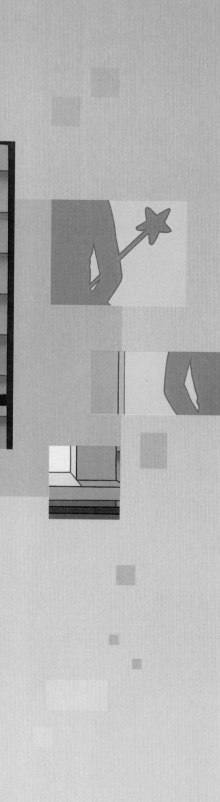

QUESTIONNAIRE: THE SENSATION-SEEKING SCALE 405
Exploration and Manipulation 406
COGNITIVE-DISSONANCE THEORY: MAKING THINGS FIT 407
Effort Justification: "If I Did It, It Must Be Important"? 407
THE THREE A'S OF MOTIVATION: ACHIEVEMENT, AFFILIATION, AND AGGRESSION 408
Achievement 409
Affiliation: "People Who Need People" 411
Aggression: Some Facts of Life and Death 411
PSYCHOLOGY AND MODERN LIFE: ENHANCING PRODUCTIVITY AND JOB SATISFACTION 412
EMOTION: ADDING COLOR TO LIFE 416
Arousal, Emotions, and Lie Detection 416
How Many Emotions Are There? Where Do They Come From? 418
The Expression of Emotions 419
The Facial-Feedback Hypothesis 420
Theories of Emotion: Is Feeling First? 420
SUMMARY 425

CHAPTER 12   PERSONALITY 428

INTRODUCTION TO PERSONALITY: "WHY ARE THEY SAD AND GLAD AND BAD?" 430
THE PSYCHODYNAMIC PERSPECTIVE 430
Sigmund Freud's Theory of Psychosexual Development 431
Other Psychodynamic Theorists 435
Evaluation of the Psychodynamic Perspective 437
PSYCHOLOGY IN A WORLD OF DIVERSITY: INDIVIDUALITY VERSUS RELATEDNESS 438
THE TRAIT PERSPECTIVE 439
From Hippocrates to the Present 440
Hans Eysenck 440
The Five-Factor Model 441
Evaluation of the Trait Perspective 443
THE LEARNING PERSPECTIVE 443
Behaviorism 443
Social-Cognitive Theory 444
QUESTIONNAIRE: WILL YOU BE A HIT OR A MISS? THE EXPECTANCY FOR SUCCESS SCALE 446
Evaluation of the Learning Perspective 448
THE HUMANISTIC-EXISTENTIAL PERSPECTIVE 449
QUESTIONNAIRE: DO YOU STRIVE TO BE ALL THAT YOU CAN BE? 450
Abraham Maslow and the Challenge of Self-Actualization 451
Carl Rogers' Self-Theory 451
PSYCHOLOGY AND MODERN LIFE: ENHANCING SELF-ESTEEM 452
Evaluation of the Humanistic-Existential Perspective 453

CONTENTS

THE SOCIOCULTURAL PERSPECTIVE   454
Individualism Versus Collectivism   455
Sociocultural Factors and the Self   456
Acculturation and Self-Esteem   456
Evaluation of the Sociocultural Perspective   456
MEASUREMENT OF PERSONALITY   458
Objective Tests   458
PSYCHOLOGY AND MODERN LIFE: USING PSYCHOLOGICAL TESTS TO FIND A
CAREER THAT FITS   460
PROJECTIVE TESTS   462
SUMMARY   463

CHAPTER 13   GENDER AND SEXUALITY   466

GENDER POLARIZATION: GENDER STEREOTYPES AND
THEIR COSTS   469
PSYCHOLOGY IN A WORLD OF DIVERSITY: MACHISMO/MARIANISMO
STEREOTYPES AND HISPANIC CULTURE   471
Costs of Gender Polarization   472
PSYCHOLOGICAL GENDER DIFFERENCES: VIVE LA
DIFFÉRENCE OR VIVE LA SIMILARITÉ?   474
Cognitive Abilities   475
Social Behavior   476
GENDER-TYPING: ON BECOMING A WOMAN OR A MAN   478
Biological Influences   478
Psychological Influences   478
ATTRACTION: ON LIKING, LOVING, AND RELATIONSHIPS   482
Factors Contributing to Attraction   482
Love: Doing What Happens . . . Culturally?   486
QUESTIONNAIRE: THE LOVE SCALE   487
Sexual Orientation   488
PSYCHOLOGY IN A WORLD OF DIVERSITY: ETHNICITY AND SEXUAL ORIENTATION:
A MATTER OF BELONGING   489
PSYCHOLOGY IN THE NEW MILLENNIUM: THE GAY GLOBAL VILLAGE   490
SEXUAL COERCION   492
Rape   492
QUESTIONNAIRE: CULTURAL MYTHS THAT CREATE A CLIMATE THAT SUPPORTS RAPE   493
PSYCHOLOGY AND MODERN LIFE: PREVENTING RAPE   495
PSYCHOLOGY AND MODERN LIFE: RESISTING SEXUAL HARASSMENT   496
Sexual Harassment   497
SEXUAL RESPONSE   498
The Sexual Response Cycle   499
Sexual Dysfunctions and Sex Therapy   500
AIDS AND OTHER SEXUALLY TRANSMITTED DISEASES   501
AIDS   504

CONTENTS

PSYCHOLOGY AND MODERN LIFE: PREVENTING STDS   506
SUMMARY   507

CHAPTER 14   STRESS AND HEALTH   510

HEALTH PSYCHOLOGY   512
STRESS: PRESSES, PUSHES, AND PULLS   513
   Sources of Stress: Don't Hassle Me?   514
QUESTIONNAIRE: THE SOCIAL READJUSTMENT RATING SCALE   516
   Psychological Moderators of Stress   522
QUESTIONNAIRE: ARE YOU TYPE A OR TYPE B?   524
PSYCHOLOGY AND MODERN LIFE: ALLEVIATING THE TYPE A BEHAVIOR PATTERN   526
   The General Adaptation Syndrome   529
QUESTIONNAIRE: THE LOCUS OF CONTROL SCALE   530
   Effects of Stress on the Immune System   532
PSYCHOLOGY AND MODERN LIFE: COPING WITH STRESS   534
A MULTIFACTORIAL APPROACH TO HEALTH AND ILLNESS   538
   "An Opportunity to Keep Those Nasty Genes from
     Expressing Themselves"   538
PSYCHOLOGY IN A WORLD OF DIVERSITY: HUMAN DIVERSITY AND HEALTH:
   NATIONS WITHIN THE NATION   540
   Headaches   542
   Coronary Heart Disease   543
   Cancer   544
PSYCHOLOGY IN THE NEW MILLENNIUM: HEALTH PSYCHOLOGY IN THE 21ST CENTURY   546
PSYCHOLOGY AND MODERN LIFE: REDUCING THE RISK OF BREAST CANCER   548
SUMMARY   550

CHAPTER 15   PSYCHOLOGICAL DISORDERS   552

WHAT ARE PSYCHOLOGICAL DISORDERS?   555
CLASSIFYING PSYCHOLOGICAL DISORDERS   556
PSYCHOLOGY IN THE NEW MILLENNIUM: WILL YOUR PROBLEMS BE DIAGNOSED
   BY COMPUTER?   558
ANXIETY DISORDERS   560
   Types of Anxiety Disorders   560
   Theoretical Views   562
DISSOCIATIVE DISORDERS   564
   Types of Dissociative Disorders   564
   Theoretical Views   566
SOMATOFORM DISORDERS   567
MOOD DISORDERS   568
   Types of Mood Disorders   568
   Theoretical Views   569

CONTENTS

PSYCHOLOGY IN A WORLD OF DIVERSITY: THE CASE OF WOMEN AND DEPRESSION   569

PSYCHOLOGY AND MODERN LIFE: ALLEVIATING DEPRESSION (GETTING OUT OF THE DUMPS)   572

Suicide   574

PSYCHOLOGY AND MODERN LIFE: SUICIDE PREVENTION   576

SCHIZOPHRENIA   577

Types of Schizophrenia   579

Theoretical Views   579

PERSONALITY DISORDERS   582

Types of Personality Disorders   582

Theoretical Views   583

EATING DISORDERS   585

Types of Eating Disorders   585

PSYCHOLOGY IN THE NEW MILLENNIUM: WILL WE BE COMPETING WITH "CYBERBABES" AND "CYBERHUNKS" IN THE NEW MILLENNIUM?   586

PSYCHOLOGY IN A WORLD OF DIVERSITY: EATING DISORDERS: WHY THE GENDER GAP?   588

Theoretical Views   589

SUMMARY   591

CHAPTER 16   METHODS OF THERAPY   594

WHAT IS THERAPY? THE SEARCH FOR A "SWEET OBLIVIOUS ANTIDOTE"   596

The History of Therapies   597

PSYCHODYNAMIC THERAPIES   599

Traditional Psychoanalysis: "Where Id Was, There Shall Ego Be"   599

Modern Psychodynamic Approaches   601

HUMANISTIC-EXISTENTIAL THERAPIES   602

Client-Centered Therapy: Removing Roadblocks to Self-Actualization   602

Gestalt Therapy: Getting It Together   603

BEHAVIOR THERAPY: ADJUSTMENT IS WHAT YOU DO   604

Fear-Reduction Methods   604

PSYCHOLOGY IN THE NEW MILLENNIUM: GETTING HIGH (AND KEEPING COOL) WITH VIRTUAL REALITY   606

Aversive Conditioning   607

Operant Conditioning Procedures   607

QUESTIONNAIRE: THE RATHUS ASSERTIVENESS SCHEDULE   608

PSYCHOLOGY AND MODERN LIFE: BECOMING MORE ASSERTIVE   610

Self-Control Methods   611

COGNITIVE THERAPIES   613

Cognitive Therapy: Correcting Cognitive Errors   613

Rational-Emotive Therapy: Overcoming "Musts" and "Shoulds"   615

GROUP THERAPIES   615

Encounter Groups   617

Couple Therapy   618

Family Therapy   618

CONTENTS

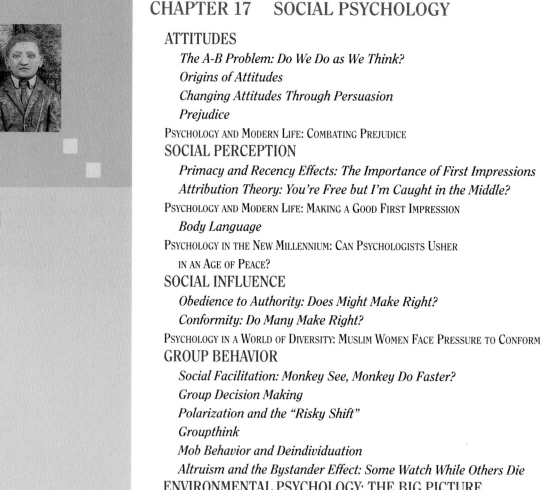

DOES PSYCHOTHERAPY WORK?	619
Problems in Conducting Research on Psychotherapy	619
Analyses of Therapy Effectiveness	620
PSYCHOLOGY IN A WORLD OF DIVERSITY: PSYCHOTHERAPY AND HUMAN DIVERSITY	622
BIOLOGICAL THERAPIES	625
Drug Therapy	625
PSYCHOLOGY IN THE NEW MILLENNIUM: LOOKING AHEAD FROM THE "DECADE OF THE BRAIN"	626
Electroconvulsive Therapy	627
Psychosurgery	628
Does Biological Therapy Work?	628
SUMMARY	629

CHAPTER 17   SOCIAL PSYCHOLOGY   632

ATTITUDES	635
The A-B Problem: Do We Do as We Think?	636
Origins of Attitudes	637
Changing Attitudes Through Persuasion	637
Prejudice	641
PSYCHOLOGY AND MODERN LIFE: COMBATING PREJUDICE	642
SOCIAL PERCEPTION	645
Primacy and Recency Effects: The Importance of First Impressions	645
Attribution Theory: You're Free but I'm Caught in the Middle?	646
PSYCHOLOGY AND MODERN LIFE: MAKING A GOOD FIRST IMPRESSION	648
Body Language	650
PSYCHOLOGY IN THE NEW MILLENNIUM: CAN PSYCHOLOGISTS USHER IN AN AGE OF PEACE?	650
SOCIAL INFLUENCE	653
Obedience to Authority: Does Might Make Right?	653
Conformity: Do Many Make Right?	656
PSYCHOLOGY IN A WORLD OF DIVERSITY: MUSLIM WOMEN FACE PRESSURE TO CONFORM	658
GROUP BEHAVIOR	659
Social Facilitation: Monkey See, Monkey Do Faster?	660
Group Decision Making	661
Polarization and the "Risky Shift"	661
Groupthink	662
Mob Behavior and Deindividuation	663
Altruism and the Bystander Effect: Some Watch While Others Die	664
ENVIRONMENTAL PSYCHOLOGY: THE BIG PICTURE	666
Noise: Of Muzak, Rock 'n' Roll, and Low-Flying Aircraft	667
Temperature: Getting Hot Under the Collar	667
Of Aromas and Air Pollution: Facilitating, Fussing, and Fuming	668
Crowding and Personal Space: "Don't Burst My Bubble, Please"	669
SUMMARY	671

CONTENTS

APPENDIX A   STATISTICS   A1

APPENDIX B   ANSWERS   B1

GLOSSARY   G1

REFERENCES   R1

CREDITS   C1

NAME INDEX   NI1

SUBJECT INDEX   SI1

FEATURES CONTENTS

PSYCHOLOGY IN A WORLD OF DIVERSITY

The Diversity of Psychologists 17

Including Women and Members in Diverse Ethnic Groups in Research 41

A Sex Survey That Addresses Sociocultural Factors 45

Cross-Cultural Perspectives on Menstruation 93

Are There Gender Differences in Moral Development? 136

Gender, Ethnicity, and Aging 146

The Signs of the Times Are Changing 191

Alcoholism, Gender, and Ethnicity 222

Culture, Ethnicity, and Academic Achievement 274

Across the Great Divide? Diverse Perspectives on the O. J. Simpson Verdicts 338

Ebonics 352

Socioeconomic and Ethnic Differences in Intelligence 371

Sociocultural Perspectives on Motivation 397

Individuality Versus Relatedness 438

Machismo/Marianismo Stereotypes and Hispanic Culture 471

Ethnicity and Sexual Orientation: A Matter of Belonging 489

Human Diversity and Health: Nations Within the Nation 540

The Case of Women and Depression 569

Eating Disorders: Why the Gender Gap? 588

Psychotherapy and Human Diversity 622

Muslim Women Face Pressure to Conform 658

PSYCHOLOGY AND MODERN LIFE

Thinking Critically About Self-Help Books: Are There Any Quick Fixes? 26

Thinking Critically About Tea Leaves, Bird Droppings, Palms, and the Stars 62

Coping With PMS 94

Health Applications of the Human Genome Project 102

Averting Genetic and Chromosomal Abnormalities 112

Becoming an Authoritative Parent 122

Coping With Pain 198

Coping With Insomnia 216

Quitting Smoking 228

Trying Meditation 234

Using Conditioning to Help Children Overcome Fears 266

Teaching Children Not to Imitate Media Violence 275

Using Psychology to Improve Your Memory 310

Bilingual Education 350

Facilitating Development of the Gifted Child 376

Enhancing Intellectual Functioning 386

Controlling Your Weight 402

Enhancing Productivity and Job Satisfaction 412

Enhancing Self-Esteem 452

Using Psychological Tests to Find a Career That Fits 460

Preventing Rape 495

Resisting Sexual Harassment 496

Preventing STDs 506

Alleviating the Type A Behavior Pattern 526

Coping With Stress 534

Reducing the Risk of Breast Cancer 548

Alleviating Depression (Getting Out of the Dumps) 572

Suicide Prevention 576

Becoming More Assertive 611

Combating Prejudice 642

Making a Good First Impression 648

PSYCHOLOGY IN THE NEW MILLENNIUM

Psychology—Hot, Hot, Hot 28

In the Global Research Lab 56

How Many of You Are There? How Many Will There Be? 100

What Biological Clock? 144

Will We Use "a Sixth Sense for Sex" in the 21st Century? 194

Sensation, Perception, and Virtual Reality 196

Will We Find That Nicotine Can Be (Gasp!) Good for You? 230

Virtual Classrooms Draw Cheers, Fears 268

FEATURES CONTENTS

What Does Research on the Biology of Memory Hold in Storage? 314

Artificial Intelligence 366

Will Music Provide Children With the Sweet Sounds of Success? 382

The "Gay Global Village" 490

Health Psychology in the 21st Century 546

Will Your Problems Be Diagnosed by a Computer? 558

Will We Be Competing with "Cyberbabes" and "Cyberhunks" in the New Millennium" 586

Getting High (and Keeping Cool) with Virtual Reality 606

Looking Ahead from the "Decade of the Brain" 626

Can Psychologists Usher in an Age of Peace? 650

IN PROFILE

Aristotle 9

Wilhelm Wundt 10

William James 11

Mary Whiton Calkins 17

Kenneth B. Clark 18

"Genie" 44

Phineas Gage 57

Paul Broca 86

Charles Darwin 97

Jean Piaget 125

Lawrence Kohlberg 133

Gustav Theodor Fechner 158

Ernst Heinrich Weber 159

Hermann von Helmholtz 170

John B. Watson 209

Franz Anton Mesmer 235

Ivan Pavlov 245

Little Albert 252

B. F. Skinner 256

George Miller 292

Hermann Ebbinghaus 305

Noam Chomsky 349

Robert Williams 352

Alfred Binet 367

Sir Francis Galton 377

Claude Steele 381

Leon Festinger & Stanley Schachter 408

Henry A. Murray 409

Sigmund Freud 431

Karen Horney 436

Erik Erikson 437

Hermann Rorschach 462

Sandra Lipsitz Bem 469

The Hammer of Witches 556

Philippe Pinel 598

Carl Rogers 603

Aaron Beck 614

Beverly A. Greene 623

Gustave Le Bon 663

John Darley & Bibb Latané 665

QUESTIONNAIRE

How Long Will You Live? The Life-Expectancy Scale 148

Why Do You Drink? 224

The Remote Associates Test 333

The Sensation-Seeking Scale 405

Will You Be a Hit or a Miss? The Expectancy for Success Scale 446

Do You Strive to Be All That You Can Be? 450

The Love Scale 487

Cultural Myths that Create a Climate That Supports Rape 493

The Social Readjustment Rating Scale 516

Are You Type A or Type B? 524

The Locus of Control Scale 530

The Rathus Assertiveness Schedule 608

There is a joy of psychology. I felt it when I was a student. I feel it when I am teaching and when I am writing. The joy in psychology is the joy of learning about ourselves, and it is a constant in my life.

When I was an undergraduate student, my life was quite different. I was the first member of my family to go to college. College at first seemed strange and frightening, and I felt detached. Professors and textbooks seemed cold and aloof. I dropped out once, and I flunked out once. But I returned each time. All in all, it took me six years to earn my bachelor's degree.

I eventually realized that the problem lay not in the subjects I studied, but in the way the subjects were presented, both in the classroom and in the textbooks. Subjects that seemed dry and remote could be made interesting and relevant to students' lives. I experimented with drawing my own students into psychology by telling them stories about psychologists and my own family, and by showing them how to apply psychological principles to their own lives. When the opportunity arose for me to write my own introductory psychology textbook, I determined that it would be warm, engaging, and relevant—not frightening, cold, and aloof. I determined to write a book that presented psychology as the rigorous science that it is and that also motivated and helped students understand and appreciate psychology. I also attempted to communicate the joy that psychology had added to my own life.

In writing this seventh edition, I turned to my fellow instructors to share their experiences to help me bring my vision of the joy of psychology into the new millennium.

■ *PSYCHOLOGY IN THE NEW MILLENNIUM,* SEVENTH EDITION

Before a single word for the seventh edition was typed out on my computer, before any decisions for content changes, additions, or deletions were made, I spent time with instructors and students on college campuses to learn what they need from an introductory textbook. Such trips included visits to Lewis University, Moraine Valley Community College, and Olive Harvey College. Even with the work on the seventh edition well underway, I continued to visit with psychology instructors and their students to listen to the exciting things they are doing in the classroom, to hear what it is that makes psychology interesting for them. Among others, stops were made at Austin Community College, Eastfield College, and McLennan Community College.

Ideas and opinions also were solicited through a survey of instructors across the country and followed up by selected, direct telephone interviews. Helpful advice concerning the ancillary package came from a group of dedicated instructors at Navarro College. Specific comments were given by more than 20 reviewers who carefully scrutinized the first-draft text, helping me in innumerable ways to shape the chapters as you see them here.

The seventh edition of *Psychology in the New Millennium,* therefore, is a collaborative work with the instructors who are in the classroom every day. We considered ideas such as including a chapter on human diversity and expanding lifespan development into two chapters (one on child development and the second on adolescent and adult development). But instructors informed us that they did not want diversity to be segregated. Instead, they want diversity integrated throughout the text, wherever topics appear "naturally." They also expressed the preference that development should remain succinct—presented in one chapter that covers the lifespan.

Instructors also informed us of two other desires. First, they wanted the chapter on development moved forward to help set the stage for other topics. Second, they wanted full-chapter coverage of gender and sexuality. Moreover, they wanted sexual behavior explicated within the contexts of attraction and relationships. In fact, one instructor remarked that the introductory psychology class might be the only time in students' lives when they are acquainted with gender and sexual issues from a scientific perspective. Otherwise, students might find themselves relying completely on friends' ideas and the popular media. The seventh edition of *Psychology in the New Millennium* therefore shows students that there are bodies of research evidence about topics such as the nature of gender-role stereotypes; the differences between males and females and how those differences develop; attraction, love, and sexual orientation (sexual orientation is discussed within the context of interpersonal attraction); sexual coercion (including rape and sexual harassment); biological aspects of sexual response and sexual dysfunctions; and AIDS and other sexually transmitted diseases.

Instructors also said they wanted more interim review sections. We thus developed the "In Review" charts to meet this need. Moreover, they liked the descriptions of important people in psychology from earlier editions of the text and wanted more of these. We therefore developed the "In Profile" features found in the seventh edition. These features motivate students and teach them by providing absorbing tidbits of information about psychologists and other important figures and case studies in psychology. These profiles present psychologists and others as interesting flesh-and-blood people.

Yet the instructors did not want us to "throw out the baby with the bath water." Therefore, much in your textbook is traditional and familiar. The text continues to recount psychology's rich tradition, the philosophical and methodological roots that can be traced beyond the ancient Greeks. A century ago, William James wrote, "I wished, by treating Psychology like a natural science, to help her become one." Psychology, as we enter the new millennium, is very much that science of which he spoke. Your textbook explores psychology's tradition as an empirical science. It explores the research methods innovated in 19th century Germany and brought to the shores of the New World in the 20th century. It also provides comprehensive coverage of the traditional areas of subject matter in psychology.

Instructors also found many useful and enjoyable learning aids and features from earlier editions and asked us to keep them. These include:

- "Truth or Fiction" items that stimulate students to delve into the subject matter by challenging folklore and common sense (which is often common *non*sense)
- Running glossary items that provide quick access to the meanings of key terms so that students can maintain their concentration on the flow of material in the chapter
- "Psychology in a World of Diversity" features that help students perceive why people of different backgrounds and genders behave and think in different ways, and how the science of psychology is enriched by addressing those differences
- Questionnaires that stimulate student interest by helping them satisfy their curiosities about themselves and enhance the relevance of the text to students' lives

- "Psychology and Modern Life" features that apply psychology to help students cope with the challenges in their own lives
- "Psychology in the New Millennium" features that help students prepare for life in the new millennium by exploring the interfaces between technological advances, psychology, and our styles of life
- "Reflections" items at the end of every major section that promote learning and stimulate critical thinking by having students relate the subject matter to things they already know

■ COVERAGE

Chapter-by-chapter coverage of the seventh edition is as follows:

Chapter 1 (What Is Psychology?) introduces psychology as a science. It discusses the specialties, history, and schools of psychology, along with critical thinking. There is **new** coverage of "Thinking Critically About Self-Help Books" and the future of psychology: "Psychology—Hot, Hot, Hot."

Chapter 2 (Research Methods in Psychology) covers the ways in which psychologists expand and refine knowledge. There is **new** coverage of "Including Women and Members of Diverse Ethnic Groups in Research," and "A Sex Survey That Addresses Sociocultural Factors."

Chapter 3 (Biology and Behavior) addresses three "things borrowed" from biology that are of interest to psychologists: the nervous system, the endocrine system, and heredity. There is **new** coverage of "Health Applications of the Human Genome Project."

Chapter 4 (Lifespan Development) covers development from conception through death. There is **new** coverage of theories of aging and "successful aging," along with **new** features: "Becoming an Authoritative Parent," "What Biological Clock?," "Gender, Ethnicity, and Aging," and "How Long Will You Live? The Life-Expectancy Scale."

Chapter 5 (Sensation and Perception) covers vision, visual perception, hearing, and the other senses. There is **new** coverage of "Sensation, Perception, and Virtual Reality."

Chapter 6 (States of Consciousness) covers sleep and dreams, psychoactive drugs, meditation, biofeedback, and hypnosis. The "Psychology and Modern Life" features help students cope with insomnia, quit smoking, and try meditation. There is a **new** feature, "Will We Find That Nicotine Can Be (Gasp!) Good for You?"

Chapter 7 (Learning) addresses classical conditioning, operant conditioning, and cognitive factors in learning. There is **new** coverage of virtual classrooms and "Culture, Ethnicity, and Academic Achievement." There are **new** "Psychology and Modern Life" features: "Using Conditioning to Help Children Overcome Fears" and "Teaching Children Not to Imitate Media Violence."

Chapter 8 (Memory) covers kinds of memory, processes of memory, the stage model of memory, the levels-of-processing model of memory, and high-interest topics such as flashbulb memories and infantile amnesia. There is **new** coverage of the biology of memory: "What Does Research on the Biology of Memory Hold in Stor*age*?"

Chapter 9 (Thinking and Language) covers problem solving, creativity, reasoning, judgment and decision making, and language. There is **new** coverage of "Across the Great Divide? Diverse Perspectives on the O. J. Simpson Verdicts" and of Ebonics.

Chapter 10 (Intelligence) covers theories, measurement, and determinants of intelligence. There is **new** coverage of the theory of "emotional intelligence" and new applications: "Facilitating the Development of the Gifted Child" and "Enhancing Intellectual Functioning."

Chapter 11 (Motivation and Emotion) addresses theories of emotion, hunger, stimulus motives, achievement motivation, affiliation, aggressions, and emotion. There is **new** coverage of "Enhancing Productivity and Job Satisfaction" in the section on achievement motivation.

Chapter 12 (Personality) discusses five major perspectives in the study of personality—psychodynamic, trait, learning, humanistic–existential, and sociocultural—and personality measurement. **New** questionnaires encourage students to assess their self-efficacy expectancies and whether they are self-actualizers. **New** applications include "Enhancing Self-Esteem" and "Using Psychological Tests to Find a Career That Fits."

New Chapter 13 (Gender and Sexuality) covers gender-role stereotypes; gender differences and their development; attraction, love, and sexual orientation; sexual coercion, sexual response, and sexual dysfunctions; and AIDS and other sexually transmitted diseases.

Chapter 14 (Stress and Health) covers stress, psychological factors, and other factors in health and illness. The chapter contains questionnaires that permit students to assess the stress they are experiencing and whether they believe that they are in control of that stress. It also includes important applications, including features on "Coping With Stress" and "Reducing the Risk of Breast Cancer."

Chapter 15 (Psychological Disorders) covers diagnostic issues and a variety of psychological disorders. There is **new** coverage on women and depression and a **new** application on "Alleviating Depression (Getting Out of the Dumps)."

Chapter 16 (Methods of Therapy) explores psychological and biological methods of therapy. It contains two **new** cutting-edge features on "Getting High (and Keeping Cool) With Virtual Reality" and "Looking Ahead From the 'Decade of the Brain.'" There is **new** coverage of issues concerning psychotherapy and human diversity, such as therapy and women, and therapy and gay people. There is also a **new** application, "Becoming More Assertive."

Chapter 17 (Social Psychology) discusses attitudes, social perception, social influence, group behavior, and environmental issues. Applications are timely: "Combating Prejudice" and (**new**) "Making a Good First Impression."

■ SUPPORT FOR *PSYCHOLOGY IN THE NEW MILLENNIUM*

A full package of support materials is available to help the student learn and the instructor teach. These ancillaries are available to qualified adopters. Special "kitted" packages are available for the student, such as the textbook with *Thinking and Writing About Psychology in the New Millennium*, the Study Guide, The *Explorer* CD-ROM, or any combination thereof. Interested instructors should contact their Harcourt Brace representative for more information.

• *Thinking and Writing About Psychology in the New Millennium by Spencer A. Rathus, Montclair State University*

As its name implies, *Thinking and Writing About Psychology in the New Millennium* is designed to promote two aspects of contemporary college education: critical thinking and writing across the curriculum. To this end, this ancillary contains a discussion of what critical thinking is, a comprehensive guide to writing about psychology using the American Psychological Association style, and dozens of writing exercises. Writing exercises may be assigned as a way of encouraging the development of thinking and writing skills, as a way of providing an opportunity for class participation, and, perhaps, as a way of earning part of the grade for the course.

ISBN: 0-15-507171-8

• *Student Study Guide*
  by Gary King, Rose State College; Spencer A. Rathus, Montclair State University; and Robbye N. Nesmith, Navarro College

The Study Guide is designed as a tool to help the student learn and understand what he or she reads in the textbook. It reinforces each chapter's topics and acts as the initial "test" of knowledge. From the Study Guide, the student will learn the major points of the textbook's chapter, follow the outline of the chapter's topics (with room added to take lecture notes right on the Study Guide pages), reinforce key points through simple exercises, review and think about the chapter's topics, and test that understanding. In addition, two special sections are included in the Study Guide. "Effective Studying Ideas" will help students to focus their study habits. "Knowing the Language" will help students of diverse cultures understand the language of psychology, while giving English-speaking students an understanding of the challenges faced by non-native speakers.

ISBN: 0-15-508221-3

• *Instructor's Manual With Video Instructor's Guide*
  by James E. Tremain, Midland Lutheran College and Lynn Haller Augsbach, Morehead State University

The function of an effective *Instructor's Manual* is to provide the instructor (a first-timer or a veteran) with a variety of methods to present information to the student during the class period. The *Instructor's Manual for Psychology in the New Millennium* does that through a listing of teaching objectives for each chapter, corresponding to the student's learning objectives in the Study Guide, followed by additional information on people in psychology; lecture suggestions with references to other resources; classroom demonstrations created exclusively by Lawrence Weinstein, Cameron University; and reproducible in-class activities, quizzes, and figures.

The *Video Instructor's Guide* portion of the *Instructor's Manual* lets the instructor know about the Harcourt Brace psychology video and videodisk library. Also included are specific teaching suggestions for using the Teaching Modules of the *Discovering Psychology* video series. The suggestions are abundant with activities and discussions, and are customized to correspond with material covered in *Psychology in the New Millennium* (includes textbook page references). Finally, the updated and expanded annotated Film Guide lists more than 175 psychology-related films, many of them produced within the past five years. Included is distribution-contact information for each film.

ISBN: 0-15-508223-X

• *Test Bank*
by George P. Zimmar, Nan Taylor Balser, Rosstyslaw W. Robak,
and Linda English, all of Pace University

A unique team of authors has revamped the set of test bank questions to provide instructors with a great tool for evaluating the progress of their students. The author team's goal is to provide a means for the instructor and the student to discover what the student knows, not what the student does not know. A strong attempt was made to write valid and reliable questions, not "trick" questions.

Each textbook chapter has between 100 and 175 multiple-choice items plus additional questions relating to the book's statistical appendix. Test questions appear in the order of the presentation in the textbook, are keyed to teaching/learning objectives, and are coded in terms of correct answer, question type (recall, applied, and conceptual), difficulty level, and textbook page number. Often a question on the same topic is given in more than one way, providing the instructor with a choice.

Approximately a third of the test items is designated as "recall," testing knowledge of factual material. Another third of the items is designated as "applied," measuring the student's abilities to understand and apply the learned material in real-life situations. The remaining third of the questions is "conceptual," showing how well the student understands the overall concepts presented in the chapter and their relationship to one another.

ISBN: 0-15-508222-1

• *EXAMaster+™ Computerized Test Bank*

EXAMaster+™ offers easy-to-use options for computerized test creation:

EasyTest creates a test from a single screen in just a few easy steps. Instructors choose the parameters, then select questions from the database or let *EasyTest* randomly select them.

FullTest offers a range of options that includes selecting, editing, adding, or linking questions or graphics; random selection of questions from a wide range of criteria; creating criteria; blocking questions; and printing up to 99 different versions of the same test and answer sheet.

On-Line Testing allows instructors to create a test in *EXAMaster+*™, save it to the OLT subdirectory or diskette, and administer the test online. The results of the test can then be imported to *ESAGrade*.

ESAGrade can be used to set up new classes, to record grades from tests or assignments utilizing scantron, and to analyze grades and produce class and individual statistics. *ESAGrade* comes packaged with *EXAMaster+*™.

DOS 3.5" ISBN: 0-15-508220-5
Macintosh® ISBN: 0-15-508216-7
MS Windows™ ISBN: 0-15-508218-3

RequesTest is a service for instructors without access to a computer. A software specialist will compile questions according to the instructor's criteria and mail or fax the test master within 48 hours. Call 1-800-447-9457 between the hours of 8:30 a.m. and 5 p.m. Central Time. Or you may e-mail your request to requestest@harbrace.com.

The *Technical Support Line* is available to answer questions during normal business days from 7 a.m. to 6 p.m. Central Time at 1-800-447-9457, or a specialist may be reached by e-mail (tsc@hbtechsupport.com). Also, access is available 24 hours a day, seven days a week through the Harcourt Brace technical support interactive Web site (www.hbtechsupport.com) and by fax on demand at 1-800-352-1680.

• *The Explorer CD-ROM*
by John Mitterer, Brock University

The Explorer is an innovative learning tool that allows students to explore and understand the realm of psychology in an interactive, multimedia environment. In PsychLinks, at the end of each chapter in the main textbook, the student will find a listing of each *Explorer* topic found on the CD-ROM. By using *The Explorer,* the student will be able to interactively view the dynamic processes illustrated graphically in the text. In addition, the student will have access to short film clips that will visually enhance the reader's understanding of many major topics. Also available is an *Instructor's Explorer* (CD-ROM), which allows the instructor to integrate elements from *The Explorer* into the lecture. Projection quality simulations, demonstrations, and experiments from *The Explorer* enhance the teaching of key concepts in psychology.

The Explorer ISBN: 0-15-507184-X

• *Discovering Psychology*

Once again, Harcourt Brace offers its support for alternative learning methods through the ongoing partnership with WGBH Boston and Annenberg/CPB. *Discovering Psychology,* a video series for introductory psychology, is divided into 26 half-hour segments covering the full range of topics. Hosted by Philip Zimbardo, the series is perfect for a telecourse when integrated with reading from *Psychology in the New Millennium.*

A telecourse Faculty Guide, updated by David Gersh and Felecia Moore-Davis (both of Houston Community College) to match the seventh edition of *Psychology in the New Millennium,* is available. This Faculty Guide (ISBN: 0-15-508219-1) contains the telecourse study guide plus faculty notes.

For the telecourse student, there is the Study Guide (ISBN: 0-15-508217-5), also updated by Gersh and Moore-Davis to be compatible with the textbook. This guide includes activities, questions, readings, and illustrations to help reinforce what the student sees on the series programs and reads in *Psychology in the New Millennium.*

An edited version of the *Discovering Psychology* series provides brief segments designed for easy classroom use. The *Video Instructor's Guide* in the *Instructor's Manual* provides descriptions and teaching suggestions for the 15 modules (84 total segments). These modules are available on videodisk and videocassette.

• *Introductory Psychology Overhead Transparencies*

A full package of overhead transparencies has been developed exclusively for *Psychology in the New Millennium.* Not only does this package include almost every figure found in the main textbook, but it also has every chapter outline (something asked for by instructors). A new feature of the Overhead Transparencies is the inclusion of selected figures whose labels are replaced with blanks. These overheads correspond to the reproducible pages found in the *Instructor's Manual,* allowing the instructor to discuss and fill in the blanks on the overhead while students do the same at their seats.

ISBN: 0-15-507172-6

Also available is a set of 130 generic transparencies for introductory psychology, both in acetate form and as PowerPoint® templates for Windows™ 3.1 and better computers. These transparencies, all full color and including a user's guide, cover the full range of topics typical to an introductory psychology course.

Psychology Transparencies ISBN: 0-15-501456-0

• *Other Multimedia*

- ***Dynamic Concepts in Psychology II,*** a highly successful videodisk developed by John Mitterer (Brock University), covers every major concept of introductory psychology. Media include animated sequences, video footage, still images, and demonstrations of well-known experiments. A modular format allows instructors to tailor the program to their individual course. *Lecture-Active* presentation software (for Windows™ and Macintosh®) accompanies *Dynamic Concepts*. This software gives instructors the ability to pre-program classroom presentations as well as to import material from other multimedia sources, such as videodisks, CD-ROMs, or a hard drive.
- ***Psychology MediaActive***™, a CD-ROM-based psychology image bank, is designed to be used with commercially available presentation packages like *PowerPoint*® and *Astound*™, as well as Harcourt Brace's *LectureActive*™ for Windows™ and Macintosh®.
- ***The Whole Psychology Catalog: Instructional Resources to Enhance Student Learning, 1997,*** by Michael B. Reiner, Kennesaw State College. Instructors can easily supplement course work and assignments with this updated manual. It has perforated pages containing experiential exercises, questionnaires, and visual aids. Each activity is classified by one of eight learning goals central to the teaching of psychology. Also included in the new version is an informative section on using the Internet and the World Wide Web.
- ***The Harcourt Brace Multimedia Library*** provides additional media for instructors to use in the classroom. The Library includes videos from Films for the Humanities and Sciences and Pyramid Films, as well as series such as *The Brain* Teaching Modules, *The Mind* Video Modules, *Childhood, Seasons of Life,* and *Time to Grow.* Contact your local Harcourt Brace representative for qualifying details and further information.
- ***World Wide Web*** on psychology is available through Harcourt Brace's website at **http://www.hbcollege.com.** At this site are up-to-date instructor's resources, student's resources, and maintained links to dynamic web sites that will enhance the teaching and understanding of psychology.

■ ACKNOWLEDGMENTS

Think about the development of psychology from the philosophical speculations of the ancients, to the firm grounding of the field as a scientific study in the 19th century, to the full-blown diverse theories and research of the beginning of a new millennium. Without the contributions of many individuals, psychology as a discipline would not and will not continue to progress. Those individuals, of course, include those who do the research in the laboratory or in the field, those who pass on the knowledge gained through the time devoted to students, and those who do both.

A textbook of psychology, any such textbook, relies upon all those contributions. While I, as author, am responsible for what appears in *Psychology in the New Millennium,* I could not have created this seventh edition and its earlier editions without the help of many of my colleagues in the discipline. My sincere thanks goes out to the following individuals who contributed to the development of the seventh edition.

In those early trips, I listened to the concerns and comments from Anne Barich, John C. Greenwood, Chwan-Shyang Jih, Ed Kearney, and Mary Vandendrope at Lewis University; Mary Rita Freudenthal, Bob Freudenthal, and Michael Goodstein at Moraine Valley Community College; William Bell at Olivet Nazarene University; Ambrose Akinkunle, Lydia Guerra, Bernard Rechlicz, and Victoria Reid at Olive Harvey College; Ed James, Dwight Kirkpatrick, and Rose Ray at Purdue University–Calumet; James McCaleb and Frank Stanicek at South Suburban College; Ron Gilkerson and Dave Murphy at Waubonsee Community College; and John Clark and James Roll at William Rainey Harper College.

Later I met with Evelyn Brown, Carol Burk-Braxton, Gloria Foley, Adam Maher, and Carole Pierce at Austin Community College; Michael Garza at Brookhaven College; Alylene Hegar, A. W. Massey, Ursula Palmer, and Adolph Streng at Eastfield College; Nancy Grayson, Jim Hail, Juan Mercado, Sharon Sexton, Susan Spooner, Doris Stevens, and Rob Winningham at McLennan Community College; and Judith Keith and Michael M. Mayall at Tarrant County Junior College.

I thank these instructors for taking the time to provide valuable responses through a mail survey: Lynn Haller Augsbach (Morehead State University), Lucy B. Champion (Southern Union State Community College), Gene Douglas (Cameron University), Jeanette Engles (Southeastern Oklahoma State University), David Gersh (Houston Community College), Vincent Greco (Weschester Community College), Lisa R. Hempel (Columbia Basin College), Elaine Mawhinney (Horry-Georgetown Technical College), Jim McCaleb (South Suburban College), Richard E. Miller (Navarro College), Patricia Slocum (College of DuPage), and Larry M. Till (Fullerton College/Cerritos College).

Those graciously giving of their time for telephone interviews are Connie Beddingfield (Jefferson State Community College), Samuel Clay (Morehead State University), Terry Daniel (University of Arizona), Robert DeStefano (Rockland Community College), Mary Dezindolet (Cameron University), Eve Efird (Johston Community College), Algea Harrison (Oakland University), Marliss Lauer (Moraine Park Technical College), Ricardo A. Machon (Loyola Marymount University), and George Rotter (Montclair State College).

Richard Miller, Robbye Nesmith, Terrie Potts, Ron Smith, and Hugh Stroube at Navarro College provided many helpful comments concerning the ancillary package.

Finally, with the first draft of the manuscript completed, the following reviewers helped shape the final text: Lynn Haller Augsbach (Morehead State University), Charles M. Bourassa (University of Alberta), Thomas Brothen (University of Minnesota), Lucy B. Champion (Southern Union State Community College), Samuel L. Clay II (Morehead State University), Miki A. Cook (Gadsden State Community College), Gene Douglas (Cameron University), Warren Fass (University of Pittsburgh at Bradford), Lawrence A. Fehr (Widener University), David A. Gersh (Houston Community College), Vincent J. Greco (Westchester Community College), Algea O. Harrison (Oakland University), Gayle Y. Iwamasa (Oklahoma State University), Mary Ann Larson (Fullerton College and Rancho Santiago College), Charles A. Levin (Baldwin-Wallace College), Richard E. Miller (Navarro College), Luis Montesinos (Montclair State University), Carol Pandey (L.A. Pierce College), George S. Rotter (Montclair State University), Patricia J. Slocum (College of DuPage), Larry Till (Fullerton College and Cerritos College), Benjamin Wallace (Cleveland State University), and Cathrine Wambach (University of Minnesota).

My sincere thanks also to the reviewers of earlier editions: Mark H. Ashcraft (Cleveland State University), Gladys J. Baez-Dickreiter (St. Phillip's College), Patricia Barker (Schenectady County Community College), Barbara Basden (California State University), Melita Bauman (Glendale Community College), James Beaird (Western Oregon State University), Thomas L. Bennett (Colorado State University), John Benson (Texarkana College), Otto Berliner (SUNY-Alfred), Tom Billimek (San Antonio College), Joyce Bishop (Golden West College), Richard A. Block (Montana State University), C. Robert Boresen (Wichita State University), Theodore N. Bosack (Providence College), Betty Bowers (North Central Technical Institute), Peter J. Brady (Clark Technical College), Jack Brennecke (Mount San Antonio College), Donald Buckley (Cumberland Community College), Robert Cameron (Fairmont State College), Garvin Chastain (Boise State University), John Childers (East Carolina University), Michael Connor (Long Beach Community College), Lauren Coodley (Napa Valley College), Richard Day (Manchester Community College), Donald L. Daoust (Southern Oregon State College), Carl L. Denti (Dutchess County Community County), Carol Doolin (Henderson County Junior College), Wendy L. Dunn (Coe College), John Foust (Parkland College), Morton P. Friedman (University of California at Los Angeles), William Rick Fry (Youngstown State University), Marian Gibney (Phoenix College), Bernard Gorman (Nassau County Community College), Richard Gottwald (Indiana University at South Bend), Peter Gram (Pensacola Junior College), Beverly Greene (St. John's University), Gloria Griffith (Tennessee Technological University), Richard Griggs (University of Florida), Sandra L. Groeltz (DeVry Institute of Technology at Chicago), Arthur Gutman (Florida Institute of Technology), Jim Hail (McClennan Community College), Robert W. Hayes (Boston University), George Herrick (SUNY-Alfred), Sidney Hochman (Nassau Community College), Morton Hoffman (Metropolitan State College), Betsy Howton (Western Kentucky University), John H. Hummel (University of Houston), Sam L. Hutchinson (Radford University), Jarvel Jackson (McClellan Community College), Rafael Art. Javier (St. John's University), Robert L. Johnson (Umpqua Community College), Timothy Johnston (University of North Carolina at Greensboro), Eve Jones (Lost Angeles City College), Karen Jones (University of the Ozarks), Kenneth Kallio (SUNY-Genesco), Charles Karis (Northwestern University), Kevin Keating (Broward Community College), Mary Louise Keen (University of California at Irvine), Richard Kellogg (SUNY-Alfred), Dan Kimble (University of Oregon), Gary King (Rose State College), Richard A. King (University of North Carolina at Chapel Hill), Mike Knight (Central State University), Wolanyo Kpo (Chicago State University), Velton Lacefield (Prairie State College), Alan Lanning (College of DuPage), Daniel Lapsley (University of Notre Dame), Patsy Lawson (Volunteer State Community College), John D. Lawry (Marymount College), Charles Levinthal (Hofstra University), William Levy (Manchester Community College), Robert G. Lowder (Bradley University), Robert MacAleese (Spring Hill College), Daniel Madsen (University of Minnesota-Duluth), John Malone (University of North Carolina at Greensboro), George Martin (Mount San Antonio College) , S. R. Mathews (Converse College), Juan Mercado (McClellan Community College), Richard McCarbery (Lorain College), Joseph McNair (Miami-Dade Community College), Leroy Metze (Western Kentucky University), Joseph Miele (East Stroudsberg University), Richard E. Miller (Navarro College), Thomas Minor (SUNY-Stony Brook), Thomas Moeschl (Broward Community College), Christopher F. Monte (Manhattanville College), Joel Morgovsky (Brookdale Community College), Walena C. Morse (Westchester University), Basil Najjar (College of DuPage), Jeffrey S. Nevid (St. John's University), John W. Nichols (Tulsa Junior College), Nora Noel (University of North Carolina at Wilmington), Joseph Paladino (Indiana State University at Evansville), Carol

Pandey (L.A. Pierce College), Fred Patrizi (East Central University), John Pennachio (Adirondack Community College), Terry Pettijohn (Ohio State University-Marion), Gregory Pezzetti (Rancho Santiago College), Walter Pieper (Georgia State University), Donis Price (Mesa Community College), Rosemary Price (Rancho Santiago College), Gerald Pudelko (Olympic College), Richard A. Rare (University of Maine), Beth Rienzi (California State University, Bakersfield), Ross Robak (Pace University), Valda Robinson (Hillsborough Community College), Laurie Rotando (Westchester Community College), Patrick J. Ryan (Tompkins-Cortland Community College), H. R. Schiffman (Rutgers University), Joseph Shaver (Fairmont State College), Larry J. Siegel (University of Lowell), Paul Silverstein (L.A. Pierce College), Pamela Simon (Baker College), William Sproull (Texas Christian University South), Jacob Steinberg (Fairleigh Dickinson University), Valierie Stratton (Pennsylvania State University-Altoona), Elizabeth Street (Central Washington University), Ann Swint (North Harris County College), Sherrill Tabing (Los Angeles Harbor College), Robert S. Tacker (East Carolina University), Francis Terrell (North Texas State University), Harry A. Tiemann (Mesa State College), Linda Truesdale (Midland Technical College), Frank J. Vattano (Colorado State University), Douglas Wallen (Mankato State University), Cathrine Wambach (University of Minnesota) Glen Weaver (Calvin College), Charles Weichert (San Antonio College), Paul Wellman (Texas A&M University), Richard Whinery (Ohio University-Chillicothe), Kenneth Wildman (Ohio Northern University), Robert Williams (William Jewel College), Keith A. Wollen (Washington State University), and Walter Zimmerman (New Hampshire College).

I am also pleased to have had the opportunity to work with a fine group of publishing professionals at Harcourt Brace College Publishers. Earl McPeek, formerly executive editor for psychology and now publisher, conceived of the idea of touring the country and assembling focus groups to develop the plan for the seventh edition. Carol Wada, current executive editor for psychology, picked up the ball when Earl received his well-deserved promotion and quickly added her own imagination and work ethic to the project. I had the good fortune to have two developmental editors for this edition: and steve Norder, the Harcourt editor, who showed an endless capacity for piecing concepts together (and for being at his desk 24 hours a day). Michele Tomiak, senior project editor, oversaw the myriad matters that were involved in transforming my manuscript into a bound book. Carol Kincaid, the art director, created the seventh edition's original and stunning design. Cindy Young, senior production manager, and Andrea Johnson, production manager, provided perspective for the production of the book and made certain that things fell into place. I thank Don Grainger, senior product manager, for his marketing acumen and his choice of restaurants. ("Moo," Don.) Several people were involved in obtaining photographic and literary permissions—my gratitude to Sandra Lord, Annette Coolidge, Elsa Peterson, and Aimé Merizon. I am also extremely grateful to the following district managers and field representatives for shepherding me around the country: Brad Balaban, Craig Gagstetter, Tom Hall, Brian Hickman, Melinda Horan, Ann Rayner, Fritz Schanz, Jain Simmons, and Jill Yuen. Finally, I want to thank two old friends for being there for me at Harcourt Brace: Ted Buchholz, President, and Chris Klein, Senior Vice-President, Editorial.

SPENCER A. RATHUS
Short Hills, New Jersey
Rathus@aol.com
PsychLinks@aol.com

*T*he central task of a
textbook is to provide
students with informa-
tion in a format that
promotes learning.
PSYCHOLOGY IN THE
NEW MILLENNIUM
provides learning aids
that are designed to
meet this goal.

"All the world's a stage," wrote William Shakespeare, "and all the men and women merely players."
Miriam Schapiro's *Escape Me Never* (1984) captures some of the zest and playfulness of players on a stage. Psychology is about
those players, in all their complexity and diversity. Psychology is the scientific study of behavior and mental processes. It seeks
to understand why people think as they do and act as they do—whether alone or with others.

MIRIAM SCHAPIRO

Chapter 1
What Is Psychology?

TRUTH OR FICTION?

✓ T F

☐ ☐ Psychologists attempt to control behavior.

☐ ☐ A book on psychology, whose contents are similar to those of the book you are now holding, was written by Aristotle more than 2,000 years ago.

☐ ☐ The ancient Greek philosopher Socrates suggested a research method that is still used in psychology.

☐ ☐ Some psychologists look upon our strategies for solving problems as "mental programs" operated by our very "personal computers"—our brains.

☐ ☐ Even though she had completed all the degree requirements, the first female president of the American Psychological Association turned down the Ph.D. that was offered to her.

☐ ☐ Men receive the majority of doctoral degrees in psychology.

OUTLINE
PSYCHOLOGY AS A SCIENCE
WHAT PSYCHOLOGISTS DO
    Fields of Psychology
WHERE PSYCHOLOGY COMES FROM:
    A HISTORY
    Structuralism
    Functionalism
    Behaviorism
    Gestalt Psychology
    Psychoanalysis
    Psychology's "Top Ten"—The "Golden Oldies"
    Psychology in a World of Diversity:
        The Diversity of Psychologists
HOW TODAY'S PSYCHOLOGISTS VIEW
    BEHAVIOR
    The Biological Perspective
    The Cognitive Perspective
    The Humanistic-Existential Perspective
    The Psychodynamic Perspective
    Learning Perspectives
    The Sociocultural Perspective
CRITICAL THINKING AND PSYCHOLOGY
    Principles of Critical Thinking
    Psychology and Modern Life:
        Thinking Critically About Self-Help
        Books: Are There Any Quick Fixes?
    Psychology in the New Millennium:
        Psychology—Hot, Hot, Hot
    Common Errors in Arguments

"*W*HAT A PIECE OF WORK IS MAN," wrote William Shakespeare. He was writing about you: "How noble in reason! How infinite in faculty! In form and moving how express and admirable! In action how like an angel! In apprehension how like a god! The beauty of the world! The paragon of animals!"

You probably had no trouble recognizing yourself in this portrait—"noble in reason," "admirable," godlike in understanding, head and shoulders above other animals. That's you to a *tee*, isn't it? Consider some of the noble and admirable features of human behavior:

• The human abilities to think and solve problems have allowed us to build cathedrals and computers and to scan the interior of the body without surgery. Yet what exactly is thinking? How do we solve problems?

• The human ability to create led to the writing of great works of literature and the composition of glorious operas. Yet what exactly is creativity?

• Human generosity and charity have encouraged us to care for older people, people who are ill, and people who are less advantaged than we are—even to sacrifice ourselves for those we love. Why do we care for others? What motivates us to care for our children and protect our families?

Some human behavior is not as noble or admirable as these examples suggest. In fact, human behavior varies greatly. Some of it is downright puzzling. Consider some more examples:

• Although people can be generous, most adults on crowded city streets will not stop to help a person lying on the sidewalk. Why?

• Most people who overeat or smoke cigarettes know that they are jeopardizing their health. Yet they continue in their bad habits. Why?

• A person claims to have raped, killed, or mutilated a victim because of insanity. The person was overcome by an irresistible impulse, or "another personality" took control. What is insanity? What is an irresistible impulse? How can we know if someone is insane? Should people who are found to be insane be judged guilty or not guilty of their crimes?

Human behavior has always fascinated people. Sometimes we are even surprised at ourselves. We have thoughts or impulses that seem to be out of character, or we can't recall something that seems to be hovering on the "tip of the tongue." Most people try to satisfy their curiosity about behavior, if at all, in their spare time. Perhaps they ask a friend for an opinion, or make some casual observations. Psychologists, like other people, are also intrigued by the mysteries of behavior, but for them the scientific study of behavior is their life's work. **Psychology** is the scientific study of behavior and mental processes. Topics of interest to psychologists include the nervous system, sensation and

PSYCHOLOGY • (sigh-KOLL-oh-gee). The science that studies behavior and mental processes.

"Truth or Fiction?" Sections

Each chapter begins with a "Truth or Fiction?" section. "Truth of Fiction?" sections are one of the text's most prominent pedagogical features. They help give the book its unique stamp. They contain items that stimulate students to delve into the subject matter by challenging folk lore and common sense (which is often "common nonsense").

Many students consider themselves psychologists. Psychology involves the study of human behavior, and even by the age at which students first attend college, they have observed people for many years. The "Truth or Fiction?" items prod them to reflect upon the accuracy of their observations and to reconsider conclusions they may have drawn about human nature. Many students find themselves reading the chapters to learn what the research evidence has to say about these items.

Chapter Outlines

Chapter outlines are found in the left-hand column of the first page within each chapter. They provide students with "advance organizers"—that is, expectations about what is to come. One of the themes of the text is that predictability helps us manage events.

The "To the Student" section highlights the PQ4R study method, in which students are encouraged to preview the subject matter, phrase questions, and read to answer them. The chapter outlines offer one kind of preview. Students are encouraged to transform them into questions about the subject matter. They can thus engage in more active learning.

LEARNING AIDS

"Truth or Fiction Revisited" Items

"Truth or Fiction Revisited" inserts are found throughout the chapters, where the "Truth or Fiction?" items are discussed in the text. The inserts provide students with feedback as to whether their assumptions about psychology were accurate.

Running Glossary

Key terms are boldfaced and defined in the margins, near where they occur in the text. Ready access to glossary items permits students to maintain their concentration on the flow of material in the chapter. Students need not flip back and forth between different sections of the book to decode the vocabulary.

In many cases, word origins and pronunciations are also provided. Etymology always helped me decode the meanings of new words, and I wanted to share this benefit with students. Pronunciation guides help students avoid embarrassing errors and encourage usage of new terms.

Kinesthesis. This young acrobat receives information about the position and movement of the parts of his body through the sense of kinesthesis. Information is fed to his brain from sensory organs in the joints, tendons, and muscles. This allows him to follow his own movements without looking at himself.

Truth or Fiction Revisited

It is true that we have a sense that keeps us upright. The sense — the vestibular sense — keeps us physically upright. It apparently takes more than the vestibular sense to keep us morally upright.

Therefore, it may well be that the analgesic effects of acupuncture can be linked to the morphinelike endorphins.

THE PLACEBO EFFECT Interestingly, some scientists have also credited endorphins with the so-called **placebo** effect, in which the expectation of relief sometimes leads to relief from pain and other problems. They speculate that a positive attitude may lead to release of endorphins.

■ KINESTHESIS

Try a brief experiment. Close your eyes, then touch your nose with your finger. If you weren't right on target, I'm sure you came close. But how? You didn't see your hand moving, and you didn't hear your arm swishing through the air.

Kinesthesis is the sense that informs you about the position and motion of parts of the body. The term is derived from the ancient Greek words for "motion" *(kinesis)* and "perception" *(aisthesis)*. In kinesthesis, sensory information is fed back to the brain from sensory organs in the joints, tendons, and muscles. You were able to bring your finger to your nose by employing your kinesthetic sense. When you "make a muscle" in your arm, the sensations of tightness and hardness are also provided by kinesthesis.

Imagine going for a walk without kinesthesis. You would have to watch the forward motion of each leg to be certain that you had raised it high enough to clear the curb. And if you had tried our brief experiment without the kinesthetic sense, you would have had no sensory feedback until you felt the pressure of your finger against your nose (or cheek, or eye, or forehead), and you probably would have missed dozens of times.

Are you in the mood for another experiment? Close your eyes again. Then "make a muscle" in your right arm. Could you sense the muscle without looking at it or feeling it with your left hand? Of course you could. Kinesthesis also provides information about muscle contractions.

■ THE VESTIBULAR SENSE: ON BEING UPRIGHT

Your **vestibular sense** tells you whether you are upright (physically, not morally). Sensory organs located in the **semicircular canals** (Figure 5.33) and elsewhere in the ears monitor your body's motion and position in relation to gravity. They tell you whether you are falling and provide cues to whether your body is changing speed such as when you are in an accelerating airplane or automobile.

PLACEBO • A bogus treatment that controls for the effect of expectations.
KINESTHESIS • The sense that informs us about the positions and motion of parts of our bodies.
VESTIBULAR SENSE • The sense of equilibrium that informs us about our bodies' positions relative to gravity.
SEMICIRCULAR CANALS • Structures of the inner ear that monitor body movement and position.

REFLECTIONS
- Has food ever seemed to lose its flavor when you had a cold or an allergy attack? Why?
- Why do older people often spice their food heavily?
- How can a drink that is 70 degrees Fahrenheit be either warming or cooling, depending on the weather?
- Has rubbing or scratching a painful area ever reduced the pain? How do you explain the experience?

"Reflections"

"Reflections" items are found at the end of every major section and serve a dual function: They (1) help students learn the subject matter and (2) stimulate critical thinking.

Psychologists and educators have shown that students learn effectively when they reflect on what they are learning. Reflecting on a subject means relating it to things they already know. Relating the material to things known makes it meaningful and easier to remember. Relating also makes it more likely that students will be able to use the new information in their own lives.

Extrasensory Perception **201**

In Review The Senses

SENSE	WHAT IS SENSED	RECEPTOR ORGANS	NATURE OF SENSORY RECEPTORS
Vision	Visible light (part of the spectrum of electromagnetic energy; different colors have different wavelengths)	The Eyes	Photoreceptors in the retinas (*rods*, which are sensitive to the intensity of light; and *cones*, which are sensitive to color)
Hearing	Changes in air pressure (or in another medium, such as water) that result from vibrations called *sound waves*	The Ears	"Hair cells" in the organ of Corti, which is attached to a membrane (the *basilar membrane*) within the inner ear (the *cochlea*)
Smell	Molecules of the substance	The Nose	Receptor neurons in the olfactory membrane high in each nostril
Taste	Molecules of the substance	The Tongue	Taste cells located on taste buds on the tongue
Touch, Pressure	Pushing or pulling of the body surface	The Skin	Nerve endings in the skin, some of which are located around the hair follicles
Kinesthesis	Muscle contractions	Sensory organs in joints, tendons, and muscles	Receptor cells in joints, tendons, and muscles
Vestibular Sense	Movement and position in relation to gravity	Sensory organs in the ears (e.g., in the *semicircular canals*)	Receptor cells in the ears

■ EXTRASENSORY PERCEPTION

Imagine the wealth you could amass if you had *precognition,* that is, if you were able to perceive future events in advance. Perhaps you would check next month's stock market reports and know what to buy or sell. Or you could bet with confidence on who would win the next Superbowl or World Series.

Or think of the power you would have if you were capable of *psychokinesis,* that is, of mentally manipulating or moving objects. You may have gotten a glimpse of the possibilities in films like *Carrie* and *The Fury.*

Precognition and psychokinesis are two concepts associated with *extrasensory perception* (ESP) or psi communication. ESP by definition refers to the perception of objects or events through means other than sensory organs. Psi communication refers to the transfer of information through an irregular or unusual process—not through the usual senses. Two other theoretical forms of ESP are *telepathy,* or direct transmission of thoughts or ideas from one person to another, and *clairvoyance,* or the perception of objects that do not stimulate the sensory organs. An example of clairvoyance is "seeing" what card will be dealt next, even though it is still in the deck and unseen even by the dealer.

Many psychologists do not believe that ESP is an appropriate area for scientific inquiry. Scientists study natural events, but ESP smacks of the supernatural,

"In Review" Charts

"In Review" charts—new to the 7th edition—provide easy-to-follow descriptions of many of the key concepts throughout the text.

Chapter Summaries

Chapter summaries are presented in a distinct question-and-answer format that fosters active learning. The PQ4R method of learning suggests that students preview the subject matter of chapter, phrase questions about it, and read to answer those questions. Learning thus becomes active rather than passive. *Psychology in the New Millennium's* summaries aid students learning actively by posing key questions and providing the answers. However, they do not attempt to cover every concept in the chapter. Thus they point the way to active learning but intentionally leave the student some work to do.

SUMMARY

1. **What are the parts of the nervous system?** The nervous system consists of neurons, which transmit information through neural impulses, and glial cells, which serve support functions. Neurons have a cell body, dendrites, and axons. Neurotransmitters transmit messages across synapses to other neurons.

2. **What is myelin?** Many neurons have a myelin coating that insulate axons, allowing for more efficient conduction of neural impulses.

3. **What are afferent and efferent neurons?** Afferent neurons transmit sensory messages to the central nervous system. Efferent neurons conduct messages from the central nervous system that stimulate glands or cause muscles to contract.

4. **How are neural impulses transmitted?** Neural transmission is electrochemical. An electric charge is conducted along an axon through a process that allows sodium ions to enter the cell and then pumps them out. The neuron has a resting potential of -70 millivolts and an action potential of $+30$ to $+40$ millivolts.

5. **How do neurons fire?** Excitatory neurotransmitters stimulate neurons to fire. Inhibitory neurotransmitters cause them not to fire. Neurons fire according to an all-or-none principle. They may fire hundreds of times per second. Each firing is followed by a refractory period, during which neurons are insensitive to messages from other neurons.

6. **What are some important neurotransmitters?** These include acetylcholine, which is involved in muscle contractions; dopamine, imbalances of which have been linked to Parkinson's disease and schizophrenia; and noradrenaline, which accelerates the heartbeat and other body processes. Endorphins are naturally occurring painkillers.

7. **What is the central nervous system?** The brain and spinal cord make up the central nervous system. Reflexes involve the spinal cord but not the brain. The somatic and autonomic systems make up the peripheral nervous system.

8. **What are the parts of the brain?** The hindbrain includes the medulla, pons, and cerebellum. The reticular activating system begins in the hindbrain and continues through the midbrain into the forebrain. Important structures of the forebrain include the thalamus, hypothalamus, limbic system, and cerebrum. The hypothalamus is involved in controlling body temperature and regulating motivation and emotion.

9. **What are the other parts of the nervous system?** The somatic nervous system transmits sensory information about skeletal muscles, skin, and joints to the central nervous system. It also controls skeletal muscular activity. The autonomic nervous system (ANS) regulates the glands and activities such as heartbeat, digestion, and dilation of the pupils. The sympathetic division of the ANS helps expend the body's resources, such as when fleeing from a predator, and the parasympathetic division helps build the body's reserves.

10. **What are the parts of the cerebral cortex?** The cerebral cortex is divided into the frontal, parietal, temporal, and occipital lobes. The visual cortex is in the occipital lobe, and the auditory cortex is in the temporal lobe. The somatosensory cortex lies behind the central fissure in the parietal lobe, and the motor cortex lies in the frontal lobe, across the central fissure from the somatosensory cortex.

11. **What parts of the brain are involved in thought and language?** The language areas of the cortex lie near the intersection of the frontal, temporal, and parietal lobes in the dominant hemisphere. For right-handed people, the left hemisphere of the cortex is usually dominant. The notion that some people are left-brained whereas others are right-brained is exaggerated and largely inaccurate.

12. **How do people who have had split-brain operations behave?** For the most part, their behavior is perfectly normal. However, although they may verbally be able to describe a screened-off object such as a pencil that is held in the hand connected to the dominant hemisphere, they cannot do so when the object is held in the other hand.

13. **What is the endocrine system?** The endocrine system consists of ductless glands that secrete hormones.

14. **What are some pituitary hormones?** The pituitary gland secretes growth hormone; prolactin, which regulates maternal behavior in lower animals and stimulates production of milk in women; and oxytocin, which stimulates labor in pregnant women.

15. **What is the function of insulin?** Insulin enables the body to metabolize sugar. Diabetes, hyperglycemia, and hypoglycemia are all linked to imbalances in insulin.

16. **What hormones are produced by the adrenal glands?** The adrenal cortex produces steroids, which promote the development of muscle mass and increase activity level. The adrenal medulla secretes adrenaline (epinephrine), which increases the metabolic rate and is involved in general emotional arousal.

17. **What hormones are secreted by the testes and ovaries?** These are sex hormones such as testos-

104

PSYCHOLOGY IN THE NEW MILLENNIUM *also has a number of features that spur motivation, highlight certain material, and underscore the relevance of psychology to students' lives. The features thus also function as another group of learning aids.*

The Writing Style

Through its style, *Psychology in the New Millennium* communicates the excitement of psychology. The text was deliberately written to be user friendly—to meet the needs of students. It uses humor and personal anecdotes to motivate students and help them understand the subject matter. The "personalized" approach is exemplified in the way that the text "walks students through" the Milgram studies on obedience to authority in Chapter 2. The Milgram studies are used as a thread to tie together the material on research methods. Students vicariously experience Milgram's methods. As a result, motivation, comprehension, and retention are enhanced.

The goal of the style is lofty: to engage and motivate students without descending into frivolity and condescension. Even the most abstract and difficult concepts are presented with energetic prose and concrete examples.

There is also a logic to the building of concepts and vocabulary. Every paragraph, every section is designed to assure that concepts are adequately defined and that prerequisites are in place for further learning.

"Psychology in the New Millennium"

"Psychology in the New Millennium" features explore the interfaces among technological advances, psychology, and our styles of life. Some, such as those on artificial intelligence and virtual reality, consider the increasing roles of electronics in our daily lives. Others concern societal trends and suggest new ways of looking at the behavior and mental processes of the individual. Each of these features is very much on the cutting edge. In some cases, the topics may seem to have the flavor of science fiction, but today's science fiction has a way of becoming tomorrow's science—or even tomorrow's household appliance.

144 CHAPTER 4 *Lifespan Development*

doubles. The eardrums thicken, as do the lenses of the eyes, resulting in some loss of hearing and vision. There is also loss of endurance as the cardiovascular system and lungs become less capable of responding effectively to exertion.

Some of these changes can be slowed or even reversed. Exercise helps maintain muscle tone and keep the growth of fatty tissue in check. A diet rich in calcium and Vitamin D can help ward off bone loss in men as well as in women. Hormone replacement may also help, but is controversial. Although testosterone replacement appears to boost strength, energy, and the sex drive, it is connected with increased risks of prostate cancer and cardiovascular disease (Cowley, 1996).

Even though sexual interest and performance decline, men can remain sexually active and father children at advanced ages. For both genders, attitudes toward the biological changes of aging—along with general happiness—may affect sexual behavior as much as biological changes do.

THE EMPTY-NEST SYNDROME In earlier decades, psychologists placed great emphasis on a concept referred to as the **empty-nest syndrome**. This concept was applied most often to women. It was assumed that women experience a

What Biological Clock?

As we stand at the edge of the new millennium, we find more and more parents with gray hair at Little League games and PTA meetings—even while most of the other parents are still trying to cope with their acne (Matus, 1996). The trend is clear. Bearing children is no longer defined as an event of young adulthood. Although fertility declines with age (Rathus and others, 1997), fathers have traditionally had children in middle and late adulthood. But today increasing numbers of women in the United States are bearing children in middle age. The birthrate for women aged 40 to 44 doubled between 1974 and 1994 (Clay, 1996a). In 1997, a 63-year-old woman gave birth. The trend to bear children at later ages continues.

MOTHERS IN THEIR FORTIES What kinds of mothers do middle-aged women make? According to Los Angeles psychologist Renee Cohen (1996), they make good ones. These mothers are usually settled in their work and marriage. Their decisions to bear children are well thought out. Because they have usually completed their education, established their career, and traveled, they are less likely to resent children for interfering with their lives.

"By the time older people decide to become parents," notes Cohen (1996, p. 37), "nothing is haphazard. Everything is planned. By having a baby, they're opening a new chapter in their lives."

OLDER FATHERS Older men also tend to be more involved as fathers, whether they are having their first child or parenting a second family (Clay, 1996b). Younger fathers tend to get embroiled in power struggles and physical discipline with their children, but "All of the studies on parenting show that the older the parent, the more nurturing, laid back, flexible, and supportive they are" (Pollack, 1996, p. 37).

Unlike younger men, men who choose fatherhood in their forties are less likely to view themselves as distant breadwinners whose major role in the home is to provide discipline. More mature fathers are more likely to see themselves as "team players" who share parenting with their wives. Moreover, they are likely to have more time and patience for fatherhood because they have already established themselves in their careers. ■

136 CHAPTER 4 *Lifespan Development*

views on women reflected the ignorance and prejudice of his times. In more recent years, researchers using Heinz's dilemma have also reported gender differences in moral development, as we see in the following section.

Psychology in a World of
DIVERSITY

Are There Gender Differences in Moral Development?

Some studies using Heinz's dilemma have found that boys reason at higher levels of moral development than girls. However, Carol Gilligan (1982; Gilligan and others, 1989) argues that this gender difference is illusory and reflects different patterns of socialization for boys and girls.

Gilligan makes her point through two examples of responses to Heinz's dilemma. Eleven-year-old Jake views the dilemma as a math problem. He sets up an equation showing that life has greater value than property. Heinz is thus obligated to steal the drug. Eleven-year-old Amy vacillates. She notes that stealing the drug and letting Heinz's wife die would both be wrong. Amy searches for alternatives, such as getting a loan, stating that it would profit Heinz's wife little if he went to jail and were no longer around to help her.

According to Gilligan, Amy's reasoning is as sophisticated as Jake's, yet she would be rated as showing a lower level of moral development. Gilligan asserts that Amy, like other girls, has been socialized to focus on the needs of others and forgo simplistic judgments of right and wrong. As a consequence, Amy is more likely to exhibit stage 3 reasoning, which focuses in part on empathy for others. Jake, by contrast, has been socialized to make judgments based purely on logic. To him, clear-cut conclusions are to be derived from a set of premises. Amy was aware of the logical considerations that influenced Jake, but she saw them as one source of information—not as the only source. It is ironic that Amy's empathy, a trait that has "defined the 'goodness' of women," marks Amy "as deficient in moral development" (Gilligan, 1982, p. 18). Prior to his death, Kohlberg had begun to correct the sexism in his scoring system.

REFLECTIONS
- Think of children you know or have known. (You were a child yourself once!) How do their behavior and some of the things they say seem to reflect the stages described by Piaget?
- Can you provide some examples of assimilation and accommodation in your own learning about the various areas of psychology?
- How would you characterize your current level of cognitive development in terms of Piaget's and Kohlberg's theories? Why?

ADOLESCENCE • The period of life bounde
and the assumption of adult r

QUESTIONNAIRE

WHY DO YOU DRINK?

Do you drink? If so, why? To enhance your pleasure? To cope with your problems? To help you in your social encounters? Half of all Americans use alcohol for a variety of reasons. Perhaps as many as 1 user in 10 is an alcoholic.

To gain insight into your reasons for using alcohol, respond to the following items by circling the *T* if an item is true or mostly true for you, or the *F* if an item is false or mostly false for you. Then turn to the answer key in Appendix B. ■

T F	1. I find it very unpleasant to do without alcohol for some time.	
T F	2. Alcohol makes it easier for me to talk to other people.	
T F	3. I drink to appear more grown-up and more sophisticated.	
T F	4. When I drink, the future looks brighter to me.	
T F	5. I like the taste of what I drink.	
T F	6. If I go without a drink for some time, I am not bothered or uncomfortable.	
T F	7. I feel more relaxed and less tense about things when I drink.	
T F	8. I drink so that I will fit in better with the crowd.	
T F	9. I worry less about things when I drink.	
T F	10. I have a drink when I get together with the family.	
T F	11. I have a drink as part of my religious ceremonies.	
T F	12. I have a drink when a toothache or some other pain is disturbing me.	
T F	13. I feel much more powerful when I have a drink.	
T F	14. You really can't blame me for the things I do when I have been drinking.	
T F	15. I have a drink before a big test, date, or interview when I'm afraid of how well I'll do.	
T F	16. I find I have a drink for the taste alone.	
T F	17. I've found a drink in my hand when I can't remember putting it there.	
T F	18. I'll have a drink when I feel "blue" or want to take my mind off my cares and worries.	
T F	19. I can do better socially and sexually after having a drink or two.	
T F	20. Drinking makes me do stupid things.	

T F	21. Sometimes when I have a few drinks, I can't get to work.	
T F	22. I feel more caring and giving after having a drink or two.	
T F	23. I drink because I like the look of a drinker.	
T F	24. I like to drink more on festive occasions.	
T F	25. When a friend or I have done something well, we're likely to have a drink or two.	
T F	26. I have a drink when some problem is nagging away at me.	
T F	27. I find drinking pleasurable.	
T F	28. I like the "high" of drinking.	
T F	29. Sometimes I pour a drink without realizing I still have one that is unfinished.	
T F	30. I feel I can better get others to do what I want when I've had a drink or two.	
T F	31. Having a drink keeps my mind off my problems at home, at school, or at work.	
T F	32. I get a real gnawing hunger for a drink when I haven't had one for a while.	
T F	33. A drink or two relaxes me.	
T F	34. Things look better when I've had a drink or two.	
T F	35. My mood is much better after I've been drinking.	
T F	36. I see things more clearly when I've been drinking.	
T F	37. A drink or two enhances the pleasure of sex and food.	
T F	38. When I'm out of alcohol, I immediately buy more.	
T F	39. I would have done much better on some things if it weren't for alcohol.	
T F	40. When I have run out of alcohol, I find it almost unbearable until I can get some more.	

"Psychology in a World of Diversity"

People differ not only as individuals, but also in terms of their culture, gender, age, sexual orientation, and other factors. The United States alone is a nation of hundreds of different ethnic and religious groups. This diversity extends to the "global village" of nearly 200 nations and to those nations' own distinctive subcultures.

Psychology students cannot understand people's behavior and mental processes without reference to their diversity. Studying perspectives other than their own helps students understand the role of a culture's beliefs, values, and attitudes on behavior and mental processes. It helps students perceive why people from diverse cultures behave and think in different ways and how the science of psychology is enriched by addressing those differences. The "Psychology in a World of Diversity" features explore and celebrate the rich variety of behavior and mental processes found worldwide and especially in the multicultural United States.

Questionnaire

"Know thyself," said Socrates. The questionnaires found throughout the text truly help students know themselves. They also stimulate student interest by helping them satisfy their curiosities about their own motives, attitudes, and personality traits. Moreover, questionnaires make the text more user friendly by enhancing its relevance to students' lives. For example, when I raise the topic of life changes as a source of stress, I provide students with a questionnaire that permits them to assess the extent of stress connected with changes in their own lives.

Moreover, the inclusion of questionnaires actually used by psychologists gives students insight into how psychologists conceptualize research variables, collect data, and obtain norms for tests.

"In Profile"

"In Profile" features—new to the 7th edition—motivate and teach by providing fascinating tidbits of information about psychologists and other key figures and case studies in psychology. In many cases, the profiles stimulate student interest by making psychologists and other notable figures into flesh-and-blood people. For example, the profile of Mary Whiton Calkins, first female president of the American Psychological Association, recounts that she turned down the PhD that was offered her by Harvard University because it would have been issued by Harvard's sister college, Radcliffe College. Harvard did not officially accept women students at the time, and even though Calkins completed all the requirements for the degree at Harvard, the university would not grant her the degree.

Other profiles include important case studies in the history of psychology, such as those on Phineas Gage, "Little Albert," and "Little Hans." There is even a profile on "The Hammer of Witches," which is important in the history of psychological disorders. "The Hammer" is the 15th century guide to identifying witches that contributed to the deaths of hundreds of thousands of disturbed people in Europe.

"Psychology and Modern Life"

One or more "Psychology and Modern Life" features is found within each chapter. These features apply psychological knowledge to help students cope with the challenges in their own lives.

IN PROFILE

Lawrence Kohlberg

His car was found parked beside Boston Harbor. Three months later his body washed up onto the shore. He had discussed the moral dilemma posed by suicide with a friend, and perhaps Lawrence Kohlberg (1927–1987) had taken his own life. He was suffering from a painful parasitic intestinal disease that he had acquired 40 years earlier while smuggling Jewish refugees from Europe past the British blockade into Palestine (now Israel). There had also been recent disappointments in his work. Nevertheless, Carol Gilligan wrote that he had "almost singlehanded established moral development as a central concern of developmental psychology" (Hunt, 1993, p. 381).

Kohlberg was born into a wealthy family in suburban New York. He graduated from Phillips Academy as World War II came to an end. Rather than go on immediately to college, he became a merchant mariner and helped save people who had been displaced by the war. He was captured and imprisoned on the Mediterranean island of Cyprus. He soon escaped, but not before acquiring the disease that would bring him a lifetime of pain. Between high school and college, Kohlberg had already decided that one must attend more to one's own conscience than to law and authority figures in determining what was right and wrong. ■

If you were trying to remember a new phone number, you would know to rehearse it several times or to write it down before doing a series of math problems. Ten-year-olds are also aware that new mental activities (math problems) can interfere with old ones (rehearsing the telephone number), and they usually suggest jotting down the number before trying the problems. Few 5-year-olds see the advantage of jotting down the number before doing the math problems.

Let us now turn our attention to Lawrence Kohlberg's theory of moral development and see how children process information that leads to judgments of right and wrong.

• *Lawrence Kohlberg's Theory of Moral Development*

Psychologist Lawrence Kohlberg (1981) originated a cognitive-developmental theory of children's moral reasoning. Before we describe Kohlberg's views, read the following tale, which he used in his research, and answer the questions that follow.

In Europe a woman was near death from a special kind of cancer. There was one drug that the doctors thought might save her. It was a form of radium that a druggist in the same town had recently discovered. The drug was expensive to make, but the druggist was charging ten times what the drug cost him to make. He paid $200 for the radium and charged $2,000 for a small dose of the drug. The sick woman's husband, Heinz, went to everyone he knew to borrow the money, but he could only get together about $1,000, which was half of what it cost. He told the druggist that his wife was dying and asked him to sell it cheaper or let him pay later. But the druggist said: "No, I discovered the drug and I'm going to make money from it." So Heinz got desperate and broke into the man's store to steal the drug for his wife. (Kohlberg, 1969)

What do you think? Should Heinz have tried to steal the drug? Was he right or wrong? The answer is more complicated than a simple yes or no. Heinz is caught up in a moral dilemma in which a legal or social rule (in this case, the law forbidding stealing) is pitted against a strong human need (his desire to save his wife). According to Kohlberg's theory, children and adults arrive at yes or no answers for different reasons. These reasons can be classified according to

According to Kohlberg,
are based largely on

133

---

112   CHAPTER 4   *Lifespan Development*

pass through the placenta. They include some microscopic disease organisms—such as those that cause syphilis and German measles—and some chemical agents, including acne drugs, aspirin, narcotics, alcohol, and tranquilizers. Because these and other agents may be harmful to the baby, pregnant women are advised to consult their physicians about the advisability of using any drugs, even those that are sold over the counter.

THE FETAL STAGE The fetal stage lasts from the beginning of the third month until birth. By the end of the third month, the major organ systems and the fingers and toes have been formed. In the middle of the fourth month, the mother usually detects the first fetal movements. By the end of the sixth month, the fetus moves its limbs so vigorously that the mother may complain of being kicked. The fetus opens and shuts its eyes, sucks its thumb, alternates between periods of wakefulness and sleep, and perceives light. It also turns somersaults, which can be clearly perceived by the mother. The umbilical cord is composed so that it will not break or become dangerously wrapped around the fetus, no matter how many acrobatic feats the fetus performs.

During the last 3 months, the organ systems of the fetus continue to mature. The heart and lungs become increasingly capable of sustaining independent life.

psychology and modern life

AVERTING GENETIC AND CHROMOSOMAL ABNORMALITIES

Genetic counselors obtain information about a couple's medical background to assess the risk that they might pass along genetic defects to their children. Some couples who face a high risk of doing so choose to adopt instead of having their own children. Other couples choose to have an abortion if the fetus is found to have certain abnormalities.

Various procedures are used to learn whether the fetus has these disorders. *Amniocentesis* is usually performed about four months into pregnancy. In this procedure, fluid containing fetal cells is drawn from the amniotic sac (or "bag of waters") with

a syringe. The cells are then grown in a culture and examined for the presence of abnormalities. *Chorionic villus sampling* (CVS) is performed several weeks earlier. A narrow tube is used to snip off material from the chorion, a membrane that contains the amniotic sac and fetus, and the material is analyzed. CVS is somewhat riskier than amniocentesis, so most obstetricians prefer to use the latter. These tests are used to detect the presence of Down syndrome, sickle cell anemia, Tay-Sachs disease, spina bifida, muscular dystrophy, Rh incompatibility, and other disorders. They also reveal the gender of the fetus.

Ultrasound bounces high-pitched sound waves off the fetus, revealing a picture of the fetus on a monitor and allowing the obstetrician to detect certain abnormalities. Obstetricians also use ultrasound during amniocentesis to locate the fetus in order to avoid hitting it with the syringe.

Parental blood tests can suggest the presence of problems such as sickle cell anemia, Tay-Sachs disease, and neural tube defects. Still other tests examine fetal DNA and can indicate the presence of Huntington's chorea, cystic fibrosis, and other disorders. ■

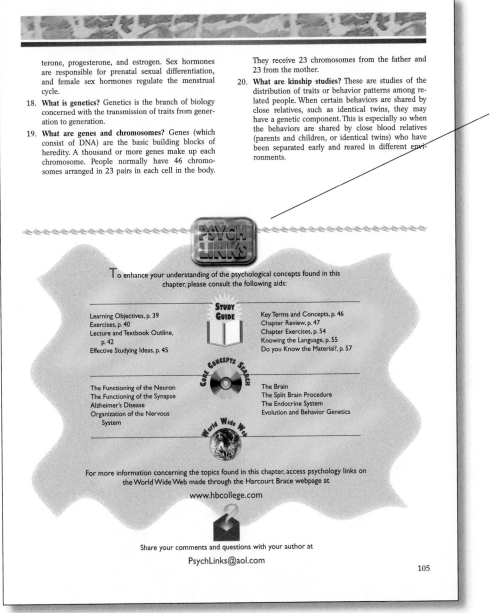

terone, progesterone, and estrogen. Sex hormones are responsible for prenatal sexual differentiation, and female sex hormones regulate the menstrual cycle.

18. **What is genetics?** Genetics is the branch of biology concerned with the transmission of traits from generation to generation.

19. **What are genes and chromosomes?** Genes (which consist of DNA) are the basic building blocks of heredity. A thousand or more genes make up each chromosome. People normally have 46 chromosomes arranged in 23 pairs in each cell in the body.

They receive 23 chromosomes from the father and 23 from the mother.

20. **What are kinship studies?** These are studies of the distribution of traits or behavior patterns among related people. When certain behaviors are shared by close relatives, such as identical twins, they may have a genetic component. This is especially so when the behaviors are shared by close blood relatives (parents and children, or identical twins) who have been separated early and reared in different environments.

To enhance your understanding of the psychological concepts found in this chapter, please consult the following aids:

STUDY GUIDE

Learning Objectives, p. 39
Exercises, p. 40
Lecture and Textbook Outline, p. 42
Effective Studying Ideas, p. 45

Key Terms and Concepts, p. 46
Chapter Review, p. 47
Chapter Exercises, p. 54
Knowing the Language, p. 55
Do you Know the Material?, p. 57

CORE CONCEPTS SEARCH

The Functioning of the Neuron
The Functioning of the Synapse
Alzheimer's Disease
Organization of the Nervous System

The Brain
The Split Brain Procedure
The Endocrine System
Evolution and Behavior Genetics

World Wide Web

For more information concerning the topics found in this chapter, access psychology links on the World Wide Web made through the Harcourt Brace webpage at

www.hbcollege.com

Share your comments and questions with your author at

PsychLinks@aol.com

105

"PsychLinks"

PsychLinks features, new to the 7th edition, are a guide at the end of every chapter designed to link students to more information. The links include the printed Study Guide, the core concepts on The Explorer CD-ROM, the World Wide Web through the Harcourt Brace Web page, and even a direct link via e-mail to Spence Rathus at PsychLinks@aol.com.

One of the wonderful things about psychology is that it is relevant to so many aspects of life. Psychology, for example, can help you become a successful student. This introduction is written to help you do well not only in psychology, but in all your college courses.

■ THE PSYCHOLOGY OF STUDYING PSYCHOLOGY

When I first went off to college, I had little idea of what to expect. New faces, a new locale, responsibility for doing my own laundry, new courses—it added up to an overwhelming assortment of changes. Perhaps the most stunning change of all was the new-found freedom. Nobody told me what to read or when to study. It was up to me to plan ahead to do my course work but somehow manage to leave time for socializing and playing bridge.

Another surprise was that it was no longer enough to enroll in a course and sit in class. I learned that I was not a sponge and would not passively soak up the knowledge. Active measures were required to take in the subject matter.

The problems of soaking up knowledge from this and other textbooks are not entirely dissimilar. Psychological theory and research have taught us that an active approach to learning results in better grades than a passive approach. It is better to look ahead and seek the answers to specific questions than to read the subject matter page by page "like a good student." We tend to remember material better when we attend to it and when it is meaningful. Reading in order to answer questions boosts our attention to it and renders it meaningful. It is also helpful not to try to do it all in one sitting, as in cramming before tests. Learning takes time.

• *Pay Attention*

Pay close attention to your professors in class and to your reading assignments. It is easier to remember things when you pay close attention to them in the first place (Scruggs & Mastropieri, 1992).

• *Plan Ahead*

Modern college life makes conflicting demands on students' time. Classes, studying, writing papers, extracurricular activities, athletic events, and the desire to socialize all compete for the precious hours you devote to your course work. Therefore, it is helpful to begin your active approach to studying by assessing the amount of material you must master during the term and relating it to your rate of learning. How long does it take you to learn the material in a chapter or in a book? How many hours do you spend studying each day? How much material is there? Does it add up right? Will you make it? It may be that you will not be able to determine the answers until you have gotten into the book for a week or two. Once you have, be honest with yourself about the mathematics of how you are doing. Be willing to revise initial estimates.

Once you have determined the amount of study time you will need, try to space it out fairly evenly. For most of us, spaced or distributed learning is more efficient than massed learning or cramming. Outline a study schedule that will provide nearly equal time periods each weekday. Leave weekends relatively open so that you can have some time for yourself and your friends as well as some extra hours to digest topics or assignments that are not going down so smoothly.

The following suggestions are derived from Rathus and Fichner-Rathus (1997):

1. Determine where and when the next test will be and what material will be covered.

2. Ask your instructor what will be most important for you to know, and check with students who have already taken the course to determine the sources of test questions—chapters in the textbook, lecture notes, student study guides, old exams, and so on.

3. Determine the number of chapters to be read between now and the test.

4. Plan to read a specific number of chapters each week and try to "psych out" your instructor by generating possible test questions from the chapters.

5. In generating possible test questions, keep in mind that good questions often start with phrases such as:

   Give several examples of . . .

   Which of the following is an example of . . .

   Describe the functions of . . .

   What is most important about . . .

   List the major . . .

   Compare and contrast . . .

   Describe the structure of . . .

   Explain how psychologists have determined that . . .

   Why do psychologists advise clients to . . .

   Identify the parts of . . .

6. Plan specific study periods each week during which you will generate questions from lecture notes, old exams, the student study guide, and so on.

7. Plan for weekly study periods during which you will compose and take practice tests.

8. Take the practice quizzes in the student study guide. Many instructors reinforce the use of the study guide by occasionally taking some exam questions directly from it.

9. Keep a diary or log in which you record your progress, including when, where, and how long you study and how well you perform on practice tests.

• *Study a Variety of Subjects Each Day*

Variety is the spice of life: We are more responsive to novel stimulation. Don't study psychology all day Monday, physics all day Tuesday, and literature all day Wednesday. Study each for a little while each day so that you won't feel bored or dulled by too lengthy an immersion in one subject.[1]

---

[1] Here, of course, I am referring to those other subjects. Obviously, you could study psychology endlessly without becoming bored.

TABLE 1	SOME DO'S AND DON'TS OF CLASS PARTICIPATION

Do's	*Don'ts*
Come with good questions that you want answered. Ask them. If you are shy and uncomfortable in group discussions, ask something early—break the ice.	*Argue for the sake of arguing.* Aim, instead, for honest expression of ideas.
Answer questions on topics about which you are knowledgeable.	*Show off.* If you know more than most other students, you can afford to express yourself diplomatically and intermittently. Your expertise will show without your making a point of it.
Share information when appropriate. Be concrete: Provide dates, statistics, and names. (There is no harm in checking through your notes to do so.) Show how to solve problems. Point out, diplomatically, the errors of others. Do so in a helpful way. Otherwise, you seem nasty and picky.	*Monopolize discussion.* Give others a chance. The point of group discussions is to afford everyone an opportunity to participate.
Share your opinions. In math and chemistry there is frequently (but not always!) one correct answer to a problem and, sometimes, one proper way to arrive at that answer. But in literature, philosophy, and behavioral and social sciences, it is usually appropriate to share opinions as to what a passage or a behavior pattern means.	*Go on and on with personal stories.* Your personal life may be more interesting to you than to others. Ask yourself whether you're really making a contribution or talking to hear yourself talk.
	Interrupt. Wait until others have finished what they have to say or until the instructor cuts them off.
Listen to others when they speak. Make eye contact. Nod your head when you agree with them. It is the decent thing to do and will also be appreciated by your instructor.	*Chat with a neighbor, or hum, or tap your foot while another person is talking.*
	Accept remarks that you believe are wrong, prejudiced, or foolish. Wait for an opportunity and voice your opinions.

Reprinted with permission from *The Right Start,* by S. A. Rathus and L. Fichner-Rathus, 1997, New York: Longman Publishers.

• Accept Your Concentration Span

If you can't push yourself at first into studying enough each day, start at a more comfortable level and build toward the amount of study time you'll need by adding a few minutes every day. See what your concentration span is like for your subjects—how long you can continue to focus on course work without your attention slipping away and, perhaps, lapsing into daydreaming. Plan to take brief study breaks before you reach your limit. Get up and stretch. Get a sip of water.

• Cope With Distractions

Find a study place that is comfortable and free from distractions. Environmental stimuli compete for our attention. A quiet place will help you screen out the background noise. To better understand how distractions work, consider the case of Melinda:

> All through high school, Melinda withdrew to her bedroom to study—the one room where she had complete privacy—and studied in her bed. She assumed that it would be easy to do the same thing in college. But in college, she has two roommates, and they very often want to chat while Melinda is hitting the books. Or, if they're not talking together, one of them may be on the phone. Or, if no one's on the phone, someone is

likely to come knocking at the door. Melinda has put a sign up on the door that says "No knocking between 7:00 and 10:00 P.M.—This means you!" Nevertheless, someone's always coming by and saying, "Oh, but I wanted to see if Nicky or Pam was in. I didn't mean to disturb you."

Pam, it happens, likes to study with the stereo on—soft, but on, nevertheless. Nicky eats in bed—incessantly. While Melinda is trying to concentrate on the books, she's assailed by the chomping of potato chips or pretzels.

Finally, Melinda gets disgusted and gets up to go for a brief walk to clear her head. She passes the lounge and is intrigued by glimpses of a new hit series. A friend calls her over to pass the time. Before she knows it, it's 8:30 and she hasn't really begun to get to work. (Adapted from Rathus & Fichner-Rathus, 1997)

Avoid Melinda's pitfalls by letting your spot for studying—your room, a study lounge, a place in the library—come to mean studying to you. Do nothing but study there—no leafing through magazines, no socializing, no snacking. But after you have met a goal, such as finishing half of your studying, you may want to reward yourself with a break and do something like people watching in a busier section of the library.

Here are some other ways of handling distractions:

MAKE ARRANGEMENTS WITH ROOMMATES Arrange for certain times of the day to be quiet study periods. Negotiate: Try something like, "I'll stay out of the room from 3:00 to 6:00 on Monday afternoons, if you'll honor a quiet study period from 7:00 to 10:00 on Mondays, Tuesdays, and Thursdays." If you live at home, try asking your family for quiet time in the house. Tell them specifically what hours you need for yourself.

HANDLE INTERNAL DISTRACTIONS If you're hungry, get a small snack. If you're uncomfortable, move to another spot. If some important ideas come to you, jot them down so that you can think about them when you have some free time. Then let them go.

PLACE A "DO NOT DISTURB!" SIGN ON YOUR DOOR You'd be surprised. Many people actually honor these signs. Of course, someone occasionally barges in and says, "Did you put up the sign now or leave it up from before?" or "Listen, I'll only take a minute of your time." (Be assertive!)

JUST SAY NO Say, "I'm in the middle of something and can't get distracted. You'll have to stop back later." It's better to give a specific time than to say "later," because people are more likely to follow concrete suggestions and instructions. If you have a hard time saying no, consider why. Are you afraid the intruder won't approve of your saying no or won't like you anymore? Psychologist Albert Ellis (see Chapter 15) notes that many of us hold the mistaken belief that we cannot survive unless other people approve of us all the time. You don't need everybody's approval all the time! Be polite but firm with intruders.

• Use Self-Reward

Use rewards for meeting daily study goals. Rewards inspire repetition of desired behavior. Don't be a martyr and try to postpone all pleasures until the end of the term. Some students can do this, but it isn't necessary. And, if you have never spent much time in nonstop studying, you may be demanding too much of yourself.

• *PQ4R: Preview, Question, Read, Reflect, Recite, and Review*

Don't question some of your instructors' assignments. Question all of them. By so doing, you can follow the active PQ4R study technique originated by educational psychologist Francis P. Robinson. In PQ4R, you phrase questions about your assignments, and then you seek to answer them. There are six steps to PQ4R: previewing, questioning, reading, reflecting, reciting, and reviewing.

PREVIEW

Skipping through the pages of a "whodunit" to identify the killer is a sure-fire way to destroy the impact of a mystery novel, but previewing can help you learn textbook material. In fact, many textbooks are written with devices that stimulate you to survey the material before reading it. This book has chapter outlines, "Truth or Fiction?" sections, major and minor section headings throughout each chapter, and chapter summaries. If drama and suspense are your goals, begin with the outlines, then read the chapters page by page. But if learning the facts is more important, it may be more effective to examine the chapter outlines first, skim the minor headings not covered in the outlines, and read the summaries—before you get to the meat of the chapters. Familiarity with the skeletons or advance organizers of the chapters will provide you with frameworks for learning the meat of the chapters as you ingest them page by page.

QUESTION

Generating questions about textbook material has been shown to promote retention (R. J. Hamilton, 1985). Phrase questions for each heading in the chapter. Write them down in a notebook. Some questions can also be based on material within sections. For courses in which the textbooks do not have helpful major and minor headings, get into the material page by page and phrase questions as you proceed. With practice, you will develop questioning skills, and your questions will help you perceive the underlying structure of each chapter. The following questions are recastings of some of the major and minor headings in Chapter 14. Notice that they are indented according to the outlined chapter structure, providing an instant sense of how the material is organized:

A. What is stress?
  B. What are the sources of stress?
  B. What psychological factors moderate the effects of stress?
  B. What is the general adaptation syndrome?
  B. What are the effects of stress on the immune system?
A. What factors contribute to physical illness?
  B. How do patterns of health and illness vary among different ethnic groups?
  B. How are psychological factors related to headaches?
    C. What are muscle-tension headaches?
    C. What are migraine headaches?
  B. How are psychological factors related to coronary heart disease?

The questions you would have phrased from these headings might have been different, but they might have been as useful as these or more useful. As you study, you will learn what works for you.

Do You Choke Up During Tests?
The Suinn Test Anxiety
Behavior Scale (STABS)

How about you? Do you look upon tests as an opportunity to demonstrate your knowledge and test-taking ability, or do you drive yourself bananas by being overly self-critical and expecting the worst? How does your level of test anxiety compare with that of others? To find out, take the Suinn Test Anxiety Behavior Scale (STABS) items listed below.

Directions: The items in the questionnaire refer to experiences that may cause fear or apprehension. For each item, place a checkmark under the column that describes how much you are frightened by it nowadays. Work quickly but be sure to consider each item individually.

	Not at all	A little	A fair amount	Much	Very much
1. Rereading the answers I gave on the test before turning it in.	_____	_____	_____	_____	_____
2. Sitting down to study before a regularly scheduled class.	_____	_____	_____	_____	_____
3. Turning in my completed test paper.	_____	_____	_____	_____	_____
4. Hearing the announcement of a coming test.	_____	_____	_____	_____	_____
5. Having a test returned.	_____	_____	_____	_____	_____
6. Reading the first question on a final exam.	_____	_____	_____	_____	_____
7. Being in class waiting for my corrected test to be returned.	_____	_____	_____	_____	_____
8. Seeing a test question and not being sure of the answer.	_____	_____	_____	_____	_____
9. Studying for a test the night before.	_____	_____	_____	_____	_____

READ Once you have phrased questions, read the subject matter with the purpose of answering them. This sense of purpose will help you focus on the essential points of the material. As you answer each question, write down in your notebook a few key words that will telegraph that answer to you when you recite and review later on. Many students find it helpful to keep two columns in their notebooks: questions in the column to the left and key words (to the answer) in the column to the right.

	Not at all	A little	A fair amount	Much	Very much
10. Waiting to enter the room where a test is to be given.	_____	_____	_____	_____	_____
11. Waiting for a test to be handed out.	_____	_____	_____	_____	_____
12. Waiting for the day my corrected test will be returned.	_____	_____	_____	_____	_____
13. Discussing with the instructor an answer I believed to be right but which was marked wrong.	_____	_____	_____	_____	_____
14. Seeing my standing on the exam relative to other people's standing.	_____	_____	_____	_____	_____
15. Waiting to see my letter grade on the test.	_____	_____	_____	_____	_____
16. Studying for a quiz.	_____	_____	_____	_____	_____
17. Studying for a midterm.	_____	_____	_____	_____	_____
18. Studying for a final.	_____	_____	_____	_____	_____
19. Discussing my approaching test with friends a few weeks before the test is due.	_____	_____	_____	_____	_____
20. After the test, listening to the answers my friends selected.	_____	_____	_____	_____	_____

To attain your total STABS score, assign points to your check marks according to the following code:

Not at all	=	1
A little	=	2
A fair amount	=	3
Much	=	4
Very much	=	5

Add the numbers to obtain your total score. (You may want to include items on which you scored a 4 or a 5 in your cognitive restructuring program.)

Norms for the 20-item STABS were attained with Northeastern University students (see Table 3). There were no gender differences.

If the material you are reading happens to be fine literature, you may wish to read it once just to appreciate its poetic features. When you reread it, however, use PQ4R to tease out the essential information it contains.

REFLECT Reflecting on subject matter is a key way to understanding and remembering it (Simpson and others, 1994). As you are reading, think of examples or create mental images of the subject matter. One way of reflecting is to relate new information to old information. We can reflect on information about whales by relating whales to other mammals. Then we will better remember that whales are warm-blooded, breathe air rather than water, bear their young live (rather than lay eggs), and nurse their young. Another strategy for reflecting is to relate new information to events in our personal lives. The media (and sometimes our personal lives) are replete with stories about people with psychological disorders. To help learn about the psychological disorders outlined in Chapter 15, think of media portrayals of characters who had the problem. Or perhaps a friend or family member has one of the problems. Consider how the behavior patterns displayed by these people are consistent (or inconsistent) with the descriptions given in the text and by your professor.

RECITE   Once you have read a section and jotted down the key words to the answer, recite each answer aloud if possible. (Doing so may depend on where you are, who's around, and your level of concern over how you think they'll react to you.) Reciting answers aloud helps us to remember them and provides an immediate check on the accuracy of the key words.

REVIEW   Review the material according to a reasonably regular schedule such as once weekly. Relearning material regularly is much easier than initial learning. Moreover, by reviewing material regularly, we foster retention.

Cover the answer column and read the questions as though they were a quiz. Recite your answers and check them against the key response words. Reread the subject matter when you forget an answer. Forgetting too many answers may mean that you haven't phrased the questions efficiently for your own use or that you haven't reviewed the material frequently enough. (Maybe you didn't learn it well enough in the first place.) By taking a more active approach to studying, you may find that you are earning higher grades and gaining more pleasure from the learning process.

■ COPING WITH TEST ANXIETY

Are these complaints familiar? "I just know I'm going to flunk." "I study hard and memorize everything, but when I get in there my mind goes blank." "I don't know what's wrong with me—I just can't take tests." "The way I do on standardized tests, I'll never get into graduate school." When we study diligently, test anxiety seems a particularly cruel hurdle.

WHY DO SOME OF US ENCOUNTER TEST ANXIETY?   We are not born with test anxiety. Test-anxious students show high arousal, as shown, for example, by dryness in the mouth and rapid heart rate. They also have more negative thoughts and are more self-critical than people with low or moderate test anxiety, even when they are performing just as well (Galassi and others, 1981). Moreover, they allow self-criticisms and negative thoughts of the sort shown in Table 2 to *distract* them from the test (Bandura, 1977).

COGNITIVE RESTRUCTURING OF TEST ANXIETY   Since test anxiety is often linked to catastrophic, irrational thoughts that distract test takers, it is fitting to cope with test anxiety by challenging these thoughts and returning your attention to the test (Goldfried, 1988). College students on several campuses have

TABLE 2	PERCENT OF POSITIVE AND NEGATIVE THOUGHTS FOR UNIVERSITY STUDENTS WITH LOW OR HIGH TEST ANXIETY		
	Thought	*Low Test Anxiety*	*High Test Anxiety*
Positive Thoughts	Will do all right on test	71%	43%
	Mind is clear, can concentrate	49	26
	Feel in control of my reactions	46	23
Negative Thoughts	Wish I could get out or test was over	46	65
	Test is hard	45	64
	Not enough time to finish	23	49
	Work I put into studying won't be shown by my grade	16	44
	Stuck on a question and it's making it difficult to answer others	13	34
	Mind is blank or can't think straight	11	31
	Going to do poorly on test	11	28
	Think how awful it will be if I fail or do poorly	11	45

High test-anxious students report fewer positive thoughts and more negative thoughts while taking tests. Moreover, their negative thoughts are linked to signs of sympathetic arousal such as dryness in the mouth and rapid heart rate. Source of data: Galassi, Frierson, & Sharer, 1981, pp. 56, 58.

TABLE 3	NORMS FOR THE STABS
STABS Score	*Percentile*
68	95
61	80
57	75
52	60
49	50
45	35
41	25
38	20
32	10

TABLE 4	RATIONAL ALTERNATIVES TO IRRATIONAL COGNITIONS CONCERNING TEST TAKING

Irrational, Catastrophizing Thoughts	*Rational Alternatives*
"I'm the only one who's going so bananas over this thing."	"Nonsense, lots of people have test anxiety. Just don't let it take your mind off the test itself.
"I'm running out of time!"	"Time is passing, but just take it item by item and answer what you can. Getting bent out of shape won't help."
"This is impossible! Are all the items going to be this bad?"	"Just take it item by item. They're all different. Don't assume the worst."
"I just can't remember a thing!"	"Just slow down and remember what you can. Take a few moments and some things will come back to you. If not, go on to the next item."
"Everyone else is smarter than I am!"	"Probably not, but maybe they're not distracting themselves from the test by catastrophizing. Just do the best you can and take it easy. Breathe easy, in and out."
"I've got to get out of here! I can't take it anymore!"	"Even if I feel that I need to leave now and then, I don't have to act on it. Just focus on the test items, one by one."
"I just can't do well on tests."	"That's only true if you believe it's true. Back to the items, one by one."
"There are a million items left!"	"Quite a few, but not a million. Just take them one by one and answer as many as you can. Focus on each item as it comes, not on the number of items."
"Everyone else is leaving. They're all finished before me."	"Fast work is no guarantee of good work. Even if most of them do well, it doesn't have to mean that you won't do well. Take all the time you need. Back to the items, one by one."
"If I flunk, everything is ruined!"	"You won't be happy if you fail, but it won't be the end of the world either. Just take it item by item and don't let worrying distract you. Breathe easy, in and out."

reduced test anxiety and improved their test grades through such a method of cognitive restructuring.

Participants in one study of this method (Goldfried and others, 1978) selected 15 anxiety-evoking items from the Suinn Test Anxiety Behavior Scale (STABS). Three of the items were presented for four one-minute trials during each of five treatment sessions. During these trials, subjects first pinpointed the irrational or catastrophizing thoughts that were evoked. Then they restructured their responses to them by constructing rational alternative thoughts.

One student's irrational thoughts included, "I'm going to fail this test, and then everyone's going to think I'm stupid." Restructuring of these catastrophizing ideas might be as follows: "Chances are I probably won't fail. And even if I do, people probably won't think I'm stupid. And even if they do, that doesn't mean I *am* stupid" (Goldfried and others, 1978, p. 34).

You can use these four steps to restructure your own cognitions concerning test-taking:

1. Pinpoint irrational, catastrophizing thoughts,

2. Construct incompatible, rational alternatives,

3. Practice thinking the rational alternatives, and

4. Reward yourself for doing so.

You can pinpoint irrational thoughts by studying the STABS items. Jot down several items that cause you concern. Include other items that come to mind as you review the STABS. Sit back, relax, imagine yourself in each situation. After a while, jot down the irrational thoughts that have come to mind.

Examine each thought carefully. Is it rational and accurate, or is it irrational? Does it catastrophize? Construct rational alternatives for each thought that is irrational, as in Table 4.

In order to restructure your cognitions concerning test taking, prepare rational alternatives to your irrational thoughts and rehearse them. Don't let catastrophizing distract you from the test items.

Arrange practice tests that resemble actual tests. Time yourself. If the tests are GRE's or civil service exams, buy the practice tests and make testing conditions as realistic as possible.

Attend to your thoughts while you take the practice tests. Can you find additional irrational thoughts? If so, prepare additional rational alternatives.

Whenever an irrational thought comes to mind, think the rational alternative firmly. If you are alone, say it out loud. If no irrational thoughts pop into mind, mentally rehearse the ones that you usually think in such a situation. For each one, think the rational alternative firmly.

Reward yourself for thinking rational alternatives. Say to yourself, for example, "That's better, now I can return to the test," or, "See, I don't have to be at the mercy of irrational thoughts. I can decide what I'm going to say to myself." When the test is over, think something like, "Well, I did it. What's done is done, but I certainly got through that feeling much better, and I may have done better as well."

Additional hints: Practice progressive relaxation (see Chapter 14). If you feel uptight during a test, allow feelings of relaxation to drift in, especially into your shoulders and the back of your neck. Take a deep breath, tell yourself to relax, and let the breath out. Also, try overlearning the material you're studying. Study it even after you feel you know it fully. Overlearning aids retention of material and increases your belief in your ability to recall it. Finally, when a test is over, *let it be over.* Check answers to help master important material, if you wish, but not just to check your score. Do something that's fun. (Go ahead. You've earned it.)

"All the world's a stage," wrote William Shakespeare, "and all the men and women merely players." Miriam Schapiro's *Escape Me Never* (1984) captures some of the zest and playfulness of players on a stage. Psychology is about those players, in all their complexity and diversity. Psychology is the scientific study of behavior and mental processes. It seeks to understand why people think as they do and act as they do—whether alone or with others.

MIRIAM SCHAPIRO

Chapter *1*

What Is Psychology?

TRUTH OR FICTION?

✔ **T F**

☐ ☐ Psychologists attempt to control behavior.

☐ ☐ A book on psychology, whose contents are similar to those of the book you are now holding, was written by Aristotle more than 2,000 years ago.

☐ ☐ The ancient Greek philosopher Socrates suggested a research method that is still used in psychology.

☐ ☐ Some psychologists look upon our strategies for solving problems as "mental programs" operated by our very "personal computers"—our brains.

☐ ☐ Even though she had completed all the degree requirements, the first female president of the American Psychological Association turned down the Ph.D. that was offered to her.

☐ ☐ Men receive the majority of doctoral degrees in psychology.

OUTLINE

PSYCHOLOGY AS A SCIENCE

WHAT PSYCHOLOGISTS DO
Fields of Psychology

WHERE PSYCHOLOGY COMES FROM: A HISTORY
Structuralism
Functionalism
Behaviorism
Gestalt Psychology
Psychoanalysis
Psychology's "Top Ten" — The "Golden Oldies"
Psychology in a World of Diversity: The Diversity of Psychologists

HOW TODAY'S PSYCHOLOGISTS VIEW BEHAVIOR
The Biological Perspective
The Cognitive Perspective
The Humanistic-Existential Perspective
The Psychodynamic Perspective
Learning Perspectives
The Sociocultural Perspective

CRITICAL THINKING AND PSYCHOLOGY
Principles of Critical Thinking
Psychology and Modern Life: Thinking Critically About Self-Help Books: Are There Any Quick Fixes?
Psychology in the New Millennium: Psychology — Hot, Hot, Hot
Common Errors in Arguments

"*W*HAT A PIECE OF WORK IS MAN," wrote William Shakespeare. He was writing about you: "How noble in reason! How infinite in faculty! In form and moving how express and admirable! In action how like an angel! In apprehension how like a god! The beauty of the world! The paragon of animals!"

You probably had no trouble recognizing yourself in this portrait—"noble in reason," "admirable," godlike in understanding, head and shoulders above other animals. That's you to a *tee,* isn't it? Consider some of the noble and admirable features of human behavior:

- The human abilities to think and solve problems have allowed us to build cathedrals and computers and to scan the interior of the body without surgery. Yet what exactly is thinking? How do we solve problems?

- The human ability to create led to the writing of great works of literature and the composition of glorious operas. Yet what exactly is creativity?

- Human generosity and charity have encouraged us to care for older people, people who are ill, and people who are less advantaged than we are— even to sacrifice ourselves for those we love. Why do we care for others? What motivates us to care for our children and protect our families?

Some human behavior is not as noble or admirable as these examples suggest. In fact, human behavior varies greatly. Some of it is downright puzzling. Consider some more examples:

- Although people can be generous, most adults on crowded city streets will not stop to help a person lying on the sidewalk. Why?

- Most people who overeat or smoke cigarettes know that they are jeopardizing their health. Yet they continue in their bad habits. Why?

- A person claims to have raped, killed, or mutilated a victim because of insanity. The person was overcome by an irresistible impulse, or "another personality" took control. What is insanity? What is an irresistible impulse? How can we know if someone is insane? Should people who are found to be insane be judged guilty or not guilty of their crimes?

Human behavior has always fascinated people. Sometimes we are even surprised at ourselves. We have thoughts or impulses that seem to be out of character, or we can't recall something that seems to be hovering on the "tip of the tongue." Most people try to satisfy their curiosity about behavior, if at all, in their spare time. Perhaps they ask a friend for an opinion, or make some casual observations. Psychologists, like other people, are also intrigued by the mysteries of behavior, but for them the scientific study of behavior is their life's work.

Psychology is the scientific study of behavior and mental processes. Topics of interest to psychologists include the nervous system, sensation and

PSYCHOLOGY • (sigh-KOLL-oh-gee). The science that studies behavior and mental processes.

"What a piece of work is man," wrote William Shakespeare. "How noble in reason! How infinite in faculty!" Chinese American artist Hung Liu, seen here with one of her paintings, illustrates the creativity that humans are capable of. Psychologists are interested in all aspects of human behavior and mental processes.

perception, learning and memory, intelligence, language, thought, growth and development, personality, stress and health, psychological disorders, ways of treating those disorders, sexual behavior, and the behavior of people in social settings such as groups and organizations.

Psychologists test their ideas with carefully designed research methods such as the survey and the experiment. Although most psychologists are interested primarily in human behavior, many others focus on the behavior of animals ranging from sea snails and pigeons to rats and gorillas. Some psychologists believe that the findings of research using lower animals can be applied, or generalized, to humans. Others argue that humans are so distinct from other animals that we can learn about humans only by studying humans. Each view holds some merit. For example, laboratory studies of the nerve cells of squids have given us some insight into the workings of human nerve cells. Experiments in teaching sign language to chimpanzees and gorillas have led to innovations in teaching language to severely retarded people. Only by studying people, however, can we learn about human qualities such as morality, values, and romantic love.

■ PSYCHOLOGY AS A SCIENCE

Psychology, like other sciences, seeks to describe, explain, predict, and control the events it studies. Psychology thus seeks to describe, explain, predict, and control behavior and mental processes.

When possible, descriptive terms and concepts are interwoven into **theories.** Theories are formulations of apparent relationships among observed events. Psychological theories are based on assumptions about behavior and mental processes. They contain statements about the principles and laws that may govern them, and they allow us to derive explanations and predictions. Many psychological theories combine statements about behavior (such as eating or aggression), mental processes (such as attitudes and mental images), and

THEORY • A formulation of relationships underlying observed events.

anatomical structures or biological processes. For instance, many of our responses to drugs such as alcohol and marijuana can be measured as overt behavior, and they are presumed to reflect the biochemical actions of these drugs and our (mental) expectations about their effects.

A satisfactory psychological theory allows us to predict behavior and mental processes. For instance, a satisfactory theory of hunger will allow us to predict when people will or will not eat. A broad, comprehensive theory should have a wide range of applicability. A broad theory of hunger might apply to human beings and lower animals, to normal-weight and overweight people, and to people who have been deprived of food for differing lengths of time. If our observations cannot be adequately explained by, or predicted from, a given theory, we should consider revising or replacing it.

In psychology, many theories have been found to be incapable of explaining or predicting new observations. As a result, they have been discarded or revised. For example, the theory that hunger results from stomach contractions may be partially correct for normal-weight individuals, but it is inadequate as an explanation for feelings of hunger among the overweight. In Chapter 11 we shall see that stomach contractions are only one of many factors, or variables, involved in hunger. Contemporary theories also focus on biological variables (such as the body's muscle-to-fat ratio) and situational variables (such as the time of day and the presence of other people who are eating).

The notion of controlling behavior and mental processes is controversial. Some people erroneously think that psychologists seek ways to make people do their bidding, like puppets on strings. This is not so. Psychologists are committed to a belief in the dignity of human beings, and human dignity demands that people be free to make their own decisions and choose their own behavior. Psychologists are learning more about the influences on human behavior all the time, but they implement this knowledge only upon request and in order to help an individual or organization.

The remainder of this chapter presents an overview of psychology and psychologists. You will see that psychologists have diverse interests and fields of specialization. We discuss the history of psychology and the major perspectives from which today's psychologists view behavior. Finally, we explore the impacts of human diversity and critical thinking on the science of psychology.

Truth or Fiction Revisited

It is true that psychologists attempt to control behavior. In practice, however, "controlling behavior" means helping clients engage in behavior that will help them meet their own goals.

REFLECTIONS

To *read without reflecting is like eating without ingesting.*

EDMUND BURKE

The research shows that if students are going to remember something, they have to think about it. They need to put it in their own heads in their own words, not just sit back passively and absorb it.

WILBERT MCKEACHIE, 1994, P. 39

Psychologists and educators have shown that you learn more effectively when you *reflect* on what you are learning. Reflecting on a subject means *relating* it to things you already know about (Willoughby and others, 1994). This process makes the material meaningful and easier to remember (Woloshyn and others, 1994). It also makes it more likely that you will be able to *apply* the information to your own life (Kintsch, 1994).

Things you already know include your own life experiences and other academic subjects. As you read through this book, you will notice that I tell you many things about my family (including many things my family would rather keep to themselves). My reasons for doing so are to arouse your interest (which also promotes learning) and to help you relate the subject matter to real-life experiences. The "Reflections" that appear at the end of every major section further stimulate you to relate the subject matter to your life experiences and academic knowledge. They ask you to pause and consider some questions before going on to the following section.

For example, now that you have read the section on "Psychology as a Science," reflect on the following questions:

- How would you have defined psychology before you began this course or opened your book? How does the true scientific nature of psychology differ from your expectations?

- Do you have theories as to why people act and think as they do? What are they? What is the evidence for them?

- Do you believe that it is possible to understand people from a scientific perspective? Why or why not?

■ WHAT PSYCHOLOGISTS DO

Psychologists share a keen interest in behavior, but in other ways, they may differ markedly. Some psychologists engage primarily in basic, or **pure research.** Pure research has no immediate application to personal or social problems and therefore has been characterized as research for its own sake. Other psychologists engage in **applied research,** which is designed to find solutions to specific personal or social problems. Although pure research is sparked by curiosity and the desire to know and understand, today's pure research frequently enhances tomorrow's way of life (Leibowitz, 1996; N. E. Miller, 1995). For example, pure research on learning and motivation in lower animals done early in the century has found widespread applications in today's school systems. Pure research into the workings of the nervous system has enhanced knowledge of disorders such as epilepsy, Parkinson's disease, and Alzheimer's disease.

Many psychologists do not conduct research. Instead, they apply psychological knowledge to help people change their behavior so that they can meet their own goals more effectively. Many psychologists engage primarily in teaching. They disseminate psychological knowledge in classrooms, seminars, and workshops.

Many psychologists are involved in research and consultation as well as teaching. For example, professors of psychology usually conduct pure or applied research and consult with individuals or industrial clients. Full-time researchers may be called on to consult with industrial clients and to organize seminars or workshops to help clients develop skills. Practitioners, such as clinical and industrial psychologists, may also engage in research—which is usually applied—and teach in the classroom or workshop. Unfortunately for psychologists who teach, conduct research, and also do consulting work, researchers have not yet found a way to expand the week to 250 hours.

• *Fields of Psychology*

Let us now explore some of the specialties of psychologists. Although psychologists tend to wear more than one hat, most of them carry out their functions in the following fields.

PURE RESEARCH • Research conducted without concern for immediate applications.
APPLIED RESEARCH • Research conducted in an effort to find solutions to particular problems.

Clinical psychologists help people with psychological disorders adjust to the demands of life. People's problems may range from anxiety and depression to sexual dysfunctions to loss of goals. Clinical psychologists evaluate these problems through structured interviews and psychological tests. They help their clients resolve their problems and change self-defeating behavior. Clinical psychologists work in institutions for mentally ill or mentally retarded people, in outpatient clinics, in college and university clinics, and in private practice. They are the largest subgroup of psychologists (see Figure 1.1). In fact, when they hear the term *psychologist,* most people think of clinical psychologists. Clinical psychologists differ from psychiatrists. A *psychiatrist* is a medical doctor who specializes in the study and treatment of psychological disorders.

Counseling psychologists, like clinical psychologists, use interviews and tests to define their clients' problems. Their clients typically have adjustment problems but not serious psychological disorders. Clients may have trouble making academic or vocational decisions, or making friends in college. They may experience marital or family conflicts, have physical handicaps, or have adjustment problems such as those encountered by people who lose their jobs because of mergers or downsizing. Counseling psychologists use counseling methods to help clients clarify their goals and overcome obstacles. Counseling psychologists are often employed in college and university counseling and testing centers. They are also found in rehabilitation agencies. As suggested by Figure 1.1, more than half of psychologists are clinical or counseling psychologists.

School psychologists are employed by school systems to identify and assist students who have problems that interfere with learning. Such problems range from social and family problems to emotional disturbances and learning disorders. School psychologists define students' problems through interviews with teachers and parents; psychological tests; and classroom observation. They consult with teachers, school officials, parents, and other professionals to help students overcome obstacles to learning. They help make decisions about placement of students in special classes. School psychologists also help children and adolescents obtain psychological health care when they need it (Kubiszyn, 1996).

FIGURE 1.1

RECIPIENTS OF DOCTORATES IN THE VARIOUS SUBFIELDS OF PSYCHOLOGY

Nearly 40% of the doctorates in psychology are awarded in clinical psychology. The next most popular subfield is counseling psychology. Source: Office of Demographic, Employment, and Educational Research (1994). Table WO4846, Summary report doctorate recipients from United States universities. Washington, DC: American Psychological Association.

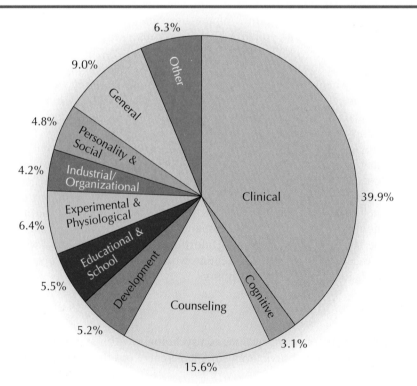

Environmental Psychology. Environmental psychologists focus on the ways in which people affect and are affected by their physical environment. How are city dwellers like these subway riders in Japan affected by crowding and "stimulus overload"?

Educational psychologists, like school psychologists, optimize classroom conditions so as to facilitate learning. But they usually focus on course planning and instructional methods for a school system rather than on individual children. Educational psychologists do research on theoretical issues related to learning, measurement, and child development. For example, they study how learning is affected by psychological factors such as motivation and intelligence, sociocultural factors such as poverty and acculturation, and teacher behavior. Some educational psychologists prepare standardized tests such as the Scholastic Aptitude Tests (SATs).

Developmental psychologists study the changes—physical, emotional, cognitive, and social—that occur throughout the life span. They attempt to sort out the influences of heredity (nature) and the environment (nurture) on development. Developmental psychologists conduct research on issues such as the effects of maternal use of drugs on an embryo, the outcomes of various patterns of child rearing, children's concepts of space and time, conflicts during adolescence, and problems of adjustment among older people.

Personality psychologists attempt to define human traits; to determine influences on human thought processes, feelings, and behavior; and to explain psychological disorders. They are particularly concerned with human issues such as anxiety, aggression, and gender roles.

Social psychologists are concerned primarily with the nature and causes of individuals' thoughts, feelings, and overt behavior in social situations. Whereas personality psychologists tend to look within the person for explanations of behavior, social psychologists tend to focus on external or social influences. Behavior is influenced both from within and from without.

Environmental psychologists focus on the ways in which behavior influences, and is influenced by, the physical environment. They are concerned with the ways in which buildings and cities serve, or fail to serve, human needs. They investigate the effects of extremes of temperature, noise, and air pollution.

Psychologists in all specialties may conduct experiments. However, those called *experimental psychologists* specialize in basic processes such as the nervous system, sensation and perception, learning and memory, thought, motivation, and emotion. Compared to other psychologists, experimental psychologists are more likely to engage in pure research. Their findings are often applied by other specialists. Pure research in motivation, for example, has helped clinical and counseling psychologists devise strategies for helping people control their weight. Pure research in learning and memory has helped school and educational psychologists enhance learning conditions in schools.

Industrial psychology and organizational psychology are closely related fields. *Industrial psychologists* focus on the relationships between people and work. *Organizational psychologists* study the behavior of people in organizations such as business firms. However, many psychologists are trained in both areas. *Human factors psychologists* make technical systems such as automobile dashboards and computer keyboards more user-friendly. *Consumer psychologists* study the behavior of shoppers in an effort to predict and influence their behavior. They advise store managers how to lay out the aisles of a supermarket in ways that will boost impulse buying and how to arrange window displays in ways that will attract customers. They devise strategies for making newspaper ads and television commercials more persuasive.

Forensic psychologists work within the criminal justice system. They may serve as expert witnesses, testifying about the competence of defendants to stand trial or explaining how psychological disorders may affect criminal behavior. Psychologists are employed by police departments to assist in the selection of officers; to counsel officers on how to cope with stress; and to train police in the handling of suicide threats, hostage crises, and family disputes.

Health psychologists examine the ways in which behavior and mental processes such as attitudes are related to physical health. They study the effects of stress on health problems such as headaches, cardiovascular disease, and cancer. Health psychologists also guide clients toward more healthful behavior patterns such as exercising, quitting smoking, and eating a more healthful diet.

Sports psychologists help people improve their performance in sports (Hays, 1995; Petrie & Diehl, 1995). Many teams have psychologists as well as coaches. Sports psychologists deal with issues such as the following:

- How athletes can concentrate on their performance and not on the crowd
- How athletes can use cognitive strategies such as positive visualization (imagining themselves making the right moves) to enhance performance
- The role of emotions in sports. For example, does it help or hurt performance to become angry with one's opponent?
- The relationships between sports and psychological well-being
- Handling choking up because of anxiety

Psychologists continue to apply their knowledge and skills in new areas. For example, as the new millennium approaches we can expect to see more psychologists involved in designing user-friendly computer systems and in helping health professionals improve their "bedside manner."

REFLECTIONS
- Which fields of psychology are most in keeping with your own interests? Why?
- What characteristics or interests are shared by all psychologists? What sets apart the various kinds of psychologists?
- If a friend had a problem, would it be adequate to advise him or her to see a psychologist? Why or why not?

■ WHERE PSYCHOLOGY COMES FROM: A HISTORY

Psychology is as old as history and as modern as today. Knowledge of the history of psychology allows us to appreciate its theoretical conflicts, its place among the sciences, the evolution of its methods, and its social and political roles (McGovern and others, 1991).

Did you know that the outline for this book could have been written by the ancient Greek philosopher Aristotle? One of Aristotle's works is *Peri Psyches,* which translates as "About the Psyche." Like this book, *Peri Psyches* begins with a history of psychological thought and historical perspectives on the nature of the mind and behavior. Aristotle argued that human behavior, like the movements of the stars and the seas, was subject to rules and laws. Then he delved into his subject matter topic by topic: personality, sensation and perception, thought, intelligence, needs and motives, feelings and emotion, and memory. This book presents these topics in a different order, but each is here.

Aristotle also declared that people are motivated to seek pleasure and avoid pain. This view has been employed in modern psychodynamic and learning theories.

Other ancient Greek philosophers also contributed to psychology. Around 400 B.C., Democritus suggested that we could think of behavior in terms of a body and a mind. (Contemporary psychologists still talk about the interaction of biological and cognitive processes.) He pointed out that our behavior is influenced by external stimulation. He was one of the first to raise the question of whether there is such a thing as free will or choice. Putting it another way, where do the influences of others end and our "real selves" begin?

Plato (ca. 427–347 B.C.) was a disciple of the great philosopher Socrates. He recorded Socrates' advice to "Know thyself," which has remained a motto of psychology ever since. Socrates claimed that we could not attain reliable self-knowledge through our senses because the senses do not exactly mirror reality. Today's psychologists still note that there are differences between the stimuli that act on our senses and our perceptions and memories, which are often distorted. Because the senses provide imperfect knowledge, Socrates suggested that we should rely on processes such as rational thought and **introspection**—careful examination of one's own thoughts and emotions—to achieve self-knowledge. He also pointed out that people are social creatures who influence one another greatly.

Had we room enough and time, we could trace psychology's roots to thinkers even farther back in time than the ancient Greeks, and we could trace its development through the great thinkers of the Renaissance. We could point to 19th-century influences such as theories about evolution, the movements of the atoms, transmission of neural messages in the brain, and the association of thoughts and memories. We could also describe the development of statistics, which is used by psychologists to help judge the results of their research.

Truth or Fiction Revisited

It is true that a book on psychology, whose contents are similar to those of the book you are now holding, was written by Aristotle more than 2,000 years ago. Its title is *Peri Psyches.*

Truth or Fiction Revisited

It is true that the ancient Greek philosopher Socrates suggested a research method that is still used in psychology. That method is introspection.

INTROSPECTION • Deliberate looking into one's own mind to examine one's own thoughts and feelings.

Wilhelm Wundt

The German psychologist Wilhelm Wundt was born in 1832, in a time when people used candles to light their homes and horses for travel. Several of Wundt's brothers died when he was young, and Wundt left home to live with a village pastor. At first he did poorly in school—his mind would wander—and he had to repeat a grade. Eventually he attended medical school because he wanted to earn a good living. He did not like working with patients, however, and dedicated himself to philosophy and psychology. He became such a workaholic that his wife and family received only one paragraph in his autobiography. During a serious illness, his main preoccupation lay in analyzing the experience of dying. He went on to live a long life, however. He died in 1920, in a time when people lit their homes with electricity and traveled by automobile and airplane. ■

As it is, we must move on to the development of psychology as a laboratory science during the second half of the 19th century. Some historians set the marker date at 1860. It was then that Gustav Theodor Fechner (1801–1887) published his landmark book *Elements of Psychophysics*, which showed how physical events (such as lights and sounds) are related to psychological sensation and perception. Fechner also showed how we can scientifically measure the effect of these events. Most historians set the debut of modern psychology as a laboratory science in the year 1879, when Wilhelm Wundt established the first psychological laboratory in Leipzig, Germany.

• Structuralism

Like Aristotle, Wilhelm Wundt claimed that the mind is a natural event and can be studied scientifically, just like light, heat, and the flow of blood. Wundt used the method of introspection recommended by Socrates to try to discover the basic elements of experience. When presented with various sights and sounds, he and his colleagues tried to look inward as objectively as possible to describe their sensations and feelings.

Wundt and his students founded the school of psychology known as **structuralism.** Structuralism attempted to break conscious experience down into **objective** sensations such as sight or taste, and **subjective** feelings such as emotional responses, will, and mental images such as memories or dreams. Structuralists believed that the mind functions by combining the elements of experience.

One of Wundt's American students was G. Stanley Hall (1844–1924), whose main interests lay in developmental psychology. Hall is usually credited with originating the discipline of child psychology, and he founded the American Psychological Association.

• Functionalism

I wished, by treating Psychology like a natural science, to help her become one.

WILLIAM JAMES

STRUCTURALISM • The school of psychology that argues that the mind consists of three basic elements—sensations, feelings, and images—that combine to form experience.

OBJECTIVE • Of known or perceived objects rather than existing only in the mind; real.

SUBJECTIVE • Of the mind; personal; determined by thoughts and feelings rather than by external objects.

FUNCTIONALISM • The school of psychology that emphasizes the uses or functions of the mind rather than the elements of experience.

HABIT • A response to a stimulus that becomes automatic with repetition.

Toward the end of the 19th century, William James was a major figure in the development of psychology in the United States. James adopted a broad view of psychology that focused on the relation between conscious experience and behavior. He argued, for example, that the stream of consciousness is fluid and continuous. Introspection convinced him that experience cannot be broken down into units as the structuralists maintained.

James was a founder of the school of **functionalism,** which dealt with behavior as well as consciousness. Functionalism addressed the ways in which experience permits us to function more adaptively in our environments—for example, how the development of **habits** allows us to cope with commonly occurring situations. It used behavioral observation in the laboratory to supplement introspection. The structuralists tended to ask, "What are the parts of psychological processes?" The functionalists tended to ask, "What are the *purposes* (functions) of behavior and mental processes? What difference do they make?"

James was influenced by the English naturalist Charles Darwin's (1809–1882) theory of evolution. Earlier in the 19th century, Darwin had argued that organisms with adaptive features survive and reproduce. Those without such features are doomed to extinction. This doctrine is known as the "survival of the fittest." It suggests that as the generations pass, organisms whose behavior and physical traits (weight, speed, coloring, size, and so on) are best suited to their environments are most likely to survive until maturity and to transmit these traits to future generations.

Functionalists adapted Darwin's theory in the study of behavior and proposed that adaptive behavior patterns are learned and maintained. Maladaptive behavior patterns tend to drop out. They are discontinued, while the "fittest" behavior patterns survive. Adaptive actions tend to be repeated and become habits. James wrote that "habit is the enormous flywheel of society." It is habit that keeps civilization going from day to day.

The formation of habits is seen in acts such as lifting a fork to our mouth and turning a doorknob. At first, these acts require our full attention. If you are in doubt, stand by with paper towels and watch a baby's first efforts at self-feeding. Through repetition, the acts that make up self-feeding become automatic, or habitual. The multiple acts involved in learning to drive a car also become routine through repetition. We can then perform them without much attention, freeing ourselves to focus on other matters such as our clever conversation and the CD player. The idea of learning by repetition is also basic to the behavioral tradition in psychology.

• *Behaviorism*

Imagine that you have placed a hungry rat in a maze. It meanders down a pathway that ends in a T. It can then turn left or right. If you consistently reward the rat with food for turning right at this choice point, it will learn to turn right when it arrives there, at least when it is hungry. But what does the rat *think* when it is learning to turn right? "Hmm, last time I was in this situation and turned to the right, I was given some food. Think I'll try that again"?

Does it seem absurd to try to place yourself in the "mind" of a rat? So it seemed to John Broadus Watson (1878–1958), the founder of American behaviorism. But Watson was asked to consider just such a question as one of the requirements for his doctoral degree, which he received from the University of Chicago in 1903. Functionalism was the dominant view of psychology at the University of Chicago, and functionalists were concerned with the stream of consciousness as well as observable behavior. Watson was unimpressed by their introspective struggles to study consciousness, especially the consciousness of lower animals. He asserted that if psychology was to be a natural science, like physics or chemistry, it must limit itself to observable, measurable events—that is, to behavior—hence, **behaviorism.** Observable behavior includes activities such as pressing a lever; turning left or right; eating and mating; even involuntary body functions such as heart rate, dilation of the pupils of the eyes, blood pressure, and emission of brain waves. These behaviors are *public.* They can be measured by simple observation or by laboratory instruments. Even the emission of brain waves is made public by scientific instruments (see Chapters 3 and 6), and diverse observers would readily agree about their existence and features. From this perspective, psychology must not concern itself with "elements of consciousness" that are accessible only to the organism perceiving them. It should be concerned only with observable behavior. (Behaviorists define psychology as the scientific study of *behavior,* not of *behavior and mental processes.*)

Watson agreed with the functionalist focus on the importance of learning, however. He suggested that psychology should address the learning of measurable responses to environmental stimuli (see Chapter 7). He pointed to the laboratory experiments being conducted by Ivan Pavlov in Russia as a model. Pavlov had found that dogs will learn to salivate when a bell is rung if ringing the bell has been repeatedly associated with feeding. He explained the salivation in terms of the laboratory conditions, or conditioning, that led to it, not in terms of the imagined mental processes of the dogs. Moreover, the response that Pavlov chose to study, salivation, was a public event that could be measured by laboratory instruments. It was absurd to try to determine what a dog, or person, was thinking.

In 1908, Watson began teaching at Johns Hopkins University. Behaviorism took root there and soon was firmly planted in American psychology. In 1920 Watson got a divorce so that he could marry a former student, and the resulting scandal forced him to leave academic life. For a while he sold coffee and worked as a clerk in a department store. Then he undertook a second career in advertising, eventually becoming vice president of a New York agency.

Harvard University psychologist B. F. Skinner (1904–1990) was another major contributor to behaviorism. Organisms, he believed, learn to behave in certain ways because they have been **reinforced** for doing so—that is, their behavior has had a positive outcome. He demonstrated that laboratory animals will carry out behaviors, both simple and complex, because of reinforcement. They will peck buttons (Figure 1.2), turn in circles, climb ladders, and

BEHAVIORISM • The school of psychology that defines psychology as the study of observable behavior and studies relationships between stimuli and responses.
REINFORCEMENT • A stimulus that follows a response and increases the frequency of the response.

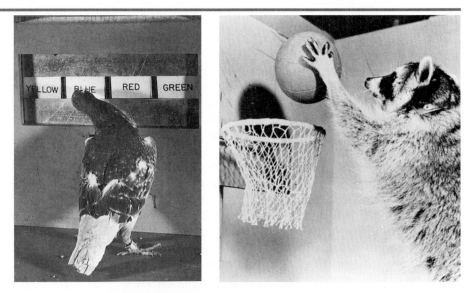

FIGURE 1.2
A COUPLE OF EXAMPLES OF THE POWER OF REINFORCEMENT

In the photo on the left, we see how our feathered gift to city life has earned its keep in experiments on reinforcement. Here, the pigeon pecks the blue button because pecking it has been followed (reinforced) with food. In the photo on the right, "Air Raccoon" shoots a basket. Behaviorists teach animals complex behaviors such as shooting baskets by first reinforcing approximations to the goal (or target behavior). As time progresses, closer approximations are demanded before reinforcement is given.

push toys across the floor. Many psychologists adopted the view that, in principle, one could explain complex human behavior in terms of thousands of instances of learning through reinforcement. Nevertheless, as a practical matter, they recognized that trying to account for all of a person's behaviors by enumerating her or his complete history of reinforcement episodes would be a hopeless task.

• Gestalt Psychology

In the 1920s, another school of psychology—**Gestalt psychology**—was prominent in Germany. In the 1930s, the three founders of the school—Max Wertheimer (1880–1943), Kurt Koffka (1886–1941), and Wolfgang Köhler (1887–1967)—left Europe to escape the Nazi threat. They carried on their work in the United States, giving further impetus to the growing American ascendance in psychology.

Wertheimer and his colleagues focused on perception and on how perception influences thinking and problem solving. In contrast to the behaviorists, Gestalt psychologists argued that one cannot hope to understand human nature by focusing only on clusters of overt behavior. In contrast to the structuralists, they claimed that one cannot explain human perceptions, emotions, or thought processes in terms of basic units. Perceptions were *more* than the sums of their parts: Gestalt psychologists saw our perceptions as wholes that give meaning to parts.

Gestalt psychologists illustrated how we tend to perceive separate pieces of information as integrated wholes, including the contexts in which they occur. Consider Figure 1.3. The dots in the centers of the configurations at the left are the same size, yet we may perceive them as being of different sizes because of the contexts in which they appear. The inner squares in the central figure are equally bright, but they may look different because of their contrasting backgrounds. The second symbol in each line at the right is identical, but in the top row we may

GESTALT PSYCHOLOGY • (gesh-TALT). The school of psychology that emphasizes the tendency to organize perceptions into wholes and to integrate separate stimuli into meaningful patterns.

FIGURE 1.3
THE IMPORTANCE OF CONTEXT
Gestalt psychologists have shown that our perceptions depend not only on our sensory impressions but also on the context of our impressions. You will interpret a man running toward you very differently depending on whether you are on a deserted street at night or at a track in the morning.

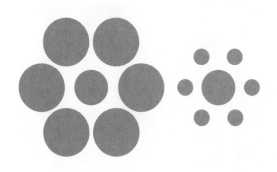

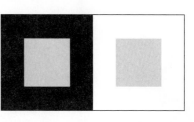

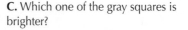

A. Are the circles in the center of the configurations the same size? Why not take a ruler and measure their diameters?

B. Is the second symbol in each line the letter B or the number 13?

C. Which one of the gray squares is brighter?

perceive it as a B and in the bottom row as the number 13. The symbol has not changed, only the context in which it appears. There are many examples of this in literature and everyday life. In *The Prince and the Pauper*, Mark Twain dressed a peasant boy as a prince, and the kingdom bowed to him. Do clothes sometimes make the man or woman? Try wearing cutoffs for a job interview!

Gestalt psychologists believed that learning could be active and purposeful, not merely responsive and mechanical as in Pavlov's experiments. Wolfgang Köhler and the others demonstrated that much learning, especially in learning to solve problems, is accomplished by **insight,** not by mechanical repetition. Köhler was marooned by World War I on one of the Canary Islands, where the Prussian Academy of Science kept a colony of apes, and his research while there gave him, well, insight into the process of learning by insight.

Have you ever pondered a problem for quite a while and then, suddenly, seen the solution? Did the solution seem to come out of nowhere? In a "flash"? Consider the chimpanzee in Figure 1.4. At first, it is unsuccessful in reaching for bananas suspended from the ceiling. Then it suddenly stacks the boxes and climbs up to reach the bananas. It seems that the chimp has experienced a sudden reorganization of the mental elements of the problem—that is, it has had a "flash of insight." Köhler's findings suggest that we often manipulate the elements of problems until we group them in such a way that we believe we will be able to reach a goal. The manipulations may take quite some time as mental trial and error proceeds. Once the proper grouping has been found, however, we seem to perceive it all at once.

INSIGHT • In Gestalt psychology, the sudden reorganization of perceptions, allowing the sudden solution of a problem.

FIGURE 1.4
SOME INSIGHT INTO INSIGHT

At first, the chimpanzee cannot reach the bananas hanging from the ceiling. After some time has passed, it has an apparent "flash of insight" and piles the boxes on top of one another to reach the fruit.

• *Psychoanalysis*

Psychoanalysis, the school of psychology founded by Sigmund Freud, is very different from the other schools in both background and approach. Freud's theory, more than the others, has invaded popular culture, and you may already be familiar with a number of its concepts. For example, on at least one TV crime show each season, an unstable person goes on a killing spree. At the end of the show, a psychiatrist explains that the killer was "unconsciously" doing away with his own mother or father. Or perhaps a friend has tried to "interpret" a slip of the tongue you made or has asked you what you thought might be the symbolic meaning of an especially vivid dream.

The notions that people are driven by hidden impulses and that verbal slips and dreams represent unconscious wishes largely reflect the influence of Freud (1856–1939), a Viennese physician who fled to England in the 1930s to escape the Nazi tyranny. Academic psychologists conducted their research mainly in the laboratory. Freud, however, gained his understanding of people through clinical interviews with patients. He was astounded at how little insight his patients seemed to have into their motives. Some patients justified, or rationalized, the most abominable behavior with absurd explanations. Others seized the opportunity to blame themselves for nearly every misfortune that had befallen the human species.

Freud came to believe that unconscious processes, especially sexual and aggressive impulses, were more influential than conscious thought in determining human behavior. He thought that most of the mind was unconscious—a seething cauldron of conflicting impulses, urges, and wishes. People were motivated to gratify these impulses, ugly as some of them were. But at the same time, people were motivated to see themselves as decent, and hence might delude themselves about their true motives. Because Freud proposed that the motion of underlying forces of personality determines our thoughts, feelings, and behavior, his theory is referred to as **psychodynamic.**

Freud devised a method of psychotherapy called psychoanalysis. Psychoanalysis aims to help patients gain insight into many of their deep-seated conflicts and find socially acceptable ways of expressing wishes and gratifying needs. It is a process that can extend for years. We describe psychoanalysis at length (but not for years) in Chapter 16.

PSYCHOANALYSIS • (sigh-coe-an-AL-uh-sis). The school of psychology that emphasizes the importance of unconscious motives and conflicts as determinants of human behavior.
PSYCHODYNAMIC • (sigh-coe-die-NAM-ick). Referring to Freud's theory, which proposes that the motion of underlying forces of personality determines our thoughts, feelings, and behavior. (From the Greek *dynamis,* meaning "power".)

TABLE 1.1	HISTORIANS' RANKINGS OF THE IMPORTANCE OF FIGURES IN THE HISTORY OF PSYCHOLOGY	
RANK	***FIGURE***	***AREA OF CONTRIBUTION***
1.	Wilhelm Wundt	Structuralism
2.	William James	Functionalism
3.	Sigmund Freud	Psychoanalysis
4.	John B. Watson	Behaviorism
5.	Ivan Pavlov	Conditioning
6.	Hermann Ebbinghaus	Memory
7.	Jean Piaget	Cognitive Development
8.	B. F. Skinner	Operant Conditioning
9.	Alfred Binet	Assessment of Intelligence
10.	Gustav Theodor Fechner	Psychophysics

Note: Rankings based on data from "Historians' and chairpersons' judgments of eminence among psychologists," by J. H. Korn, R. Davis, & S. F. Davis, 1991, *American Psychologist, 46,* pp. 789–792.

In Review   Historic Schools of Psychology

SCHOOL	KEY FIGURES	KEY POINTS
Structuralism	Wilhelm Wundt (1832–1920)	Proposed that the mind was a natural event that could be studied scientifically. Used introspection to break conscious experience down into objective sensations, subjective feelings, will, and mental images. Believed that the mind functioned by combining the elements of experience.
Functionalism	William James (1842–1910)	Studied the functions rather than the structure of thought; dealt with behavior as well as consciousness. Adapted evolutionary theory to behavior, proposing that adaptive behavior patterns are learned and become habits.
Behaviorism	John B. Watson (1878–1958) B. F. Skinner (1904–1990)	Argued that if psychology were to be a natural science, it must limit itself to observable behavior. Proposed that psychology address the learning of measurable responses to stimuli.
Gestalt Psychology	Max Wertheimer (1880–1943) Kurt Koffka (1886–1941) Wolfgang Köhler (1887–1967)	Focused on how perception influences thinking and problem solving. Saw perceptions as wholes that give meaning to parts. Studied learning by insight.
Psychoanalysis	Sigmund Freud (1856–1939)	Argued that unconscious processes, especially sexual and aggressive impulses, are more influential than conscious thought in determining human behavior. Developed methods of mental detective work and psychotherapy called *psychoanalysis*.

• Psychology's "Top Ten"—The "Golden Oldies"

Table 1.1 lists psychology's "top 10"—the field's golden oldies. They are ranked according to their importance in the eyes of historians of psychology (Korn and others, 1991). Do the top ten seem to have anything in common? We consider this question further in the following World of Diversity feature.

Today we no longer find psychologists who describe themselves as structuralists or functionalists. Although the school of Gestalt psychology gave birth to current research approaches in perception and problem solving, few would consider themselves Gestalt psychologists. The numbers of orthodox behaviorists and psychoanalysts have also been declining. Many contemporary psychologists in the behaviorist tradition look on themselves as social-cognitive[1] theorists, and many psychoanalysts consider themselves neoanalysts rather than traditional Freudians. Still, many of the historical traditions of psychology find expression in contemporary perspectives on psychology.

REFLECTIONS
- Which school of psychology is most consistent with your own views of people? Why?
- Why do behaviorists object to schools of psychology that use introspection? Do you agree with the behaviorist point of view? Why or why not?

---

[1] Formerly termed social-learning theorists.

- Had you heard of Sigmund Freud before you began this course? What had you heard? Were your impressions accurate? Why or why not?
- Psychology's "top 10," as selected by historians of psychology, are all White males. Why do you think this is so?

Psychology in a World of
DIVERSITY

The Diversity of Psychologists

Have another look at psychology's "golden oldies," as listed in Table 1.1. What have they in common? They are all White males. Such lists may create the impression that women and people of color have not contributed to psychology (DeAngelis, 1996; Guthrie, 1990). This is an erroneous assumption, however.

Consider some of the women. Christine Ladd-Franklin (1847–1930) was born during an era in American history in which women were expected to remain in the home and were excluded from careers in science (Furumoto, 1992). She nevertheless pursued a career in psychology, taught at Johns Hopkins and Columbia Universities, and formulated a theory of color vision. Margaret Floy Washburn (1871–1939) was the first woman to receive a Ph.D. in psychology. Washburn also wrote *The Animal Mind,* a work that contained many ideas that would later become part of behaviorism.

Numerous early psychologists came from different ethnic backgrounds. Back in 1901, Gilbert Haven Jones, an African American, received his Ph.D. in psychology in Germany. J. Henry Alston engaged in research on perception of heat and cold and was the first African American psychologist to be published in a major psychology journal (the year was 1920).

Hispanic American and Asian American psychologists have also made their mark. Jorge Sanchez, for example, was among the first to show how intelligence tests are culturally biased—to the disadvantage of Mexican American children. Asian American psychologist Stanley Sue (see Chapter 10) has engaged in research on racial differences in intelligence and academic achievement and has discussed these differences in terms of adaptation to discrimination, among other factors.

True—psychology was once the province of White males. Today, however, more than half of the Ph.D.s in psychology are awarded to women. African Americans and Hispanic Americans each receive 3% to 4% of the Ph.D.s awarded in psychology (ODEER, 1994). This percentage is far below their representation in the general population, unfortunately. In a recent year, only one tenth of 1 percent of the 65,000 members of the American Psychological Association were Native Americans (DeAngelis, 1993). Even so, fewer than two psychology Ph.D.s in five are now awarded to White males. Psychology, like the societies in which it flourishes, is becoming increasingly diverse.

Mary Whiton Calkins

She just said no. Mary Whiton Calkins (1863–1930) had completed all the requirements for the Ph.D., but accepting the degree would endorse prejudice against women. So she turned it down. Calkins studied psychology at Harvard University. However, she had to attend Harvard as a "guest student," because Harvard was not yet admitting women. It did not matter that William James considered Calkins to be his brightest student. When she completed her degree requirements, Harvard would not award her the degree because of her gender. Instead, Harvard offered to grant her a doctorate from its sister school, Radcliffe. She declined the offer.

Even without a doctorate, Calkins went on to pioneer research in memory at Wellesley College, where she founded a psychology laboratory in 1891. She introduced the method of paired associates and discovered the primacy and recency effects. In 1905 she became the first female president of the American Psychological Association—doctorate or no. ■

Truth or Fiction Revisited

It is not true that men receive the majority of degrees in psychology. Women actually receive the majority of Ph.D.s in psychology today.
    Put it another way: Psychology is for everyone.

Kenneth B. Clark

Kenneth Bancroft Clark was born in the Panama Canal Zone in 1914, the son of West Indian parents. His mother brought her children to the United States for their education, and they settled in New York City's Harlem district. He earned his bachelor's degree from Howard University in Washington, DC, where he also met and married Mamie Phipps. The couple then earned their doctorates in psychology at Columbia University.

In the 1940s, the Clarks founded the Northside Center for Child Development and conducted research that showed the negative effects of school segregation on African American children. In one such study, African American children were shown white and brown dolls and asked to "Give me the pretty doll," or "Give me the doll that looks bad." Most children's choices showed that they preferred the white dolls over the brown ones. The Clarks concluded that the children had swallowed the larger society's preference for White people.

In the 1950s, Kenneth Clark began working with the NAACP to end school segregation. Clark's research was cited by the Supreme Court when it overturned the "separate but equal" schools doctrine in 1954. Clark went on to study the quality of education and juvenile delinquency. He was among the first to recommend preschool classes, afterschool programs, and community participation. ■

GENES • (jeans). The basic building blocks of heredity.
COGNITIVE • Having to do with mental processes such as sensation and perception, memory, intelligence, language, thought, and problem solving.
HUMANISM • The philosophy and school of psychology that asserts that people are conscious, self-aware, and capable of free choice, self-fulfillment, and ethical behavior.
EXISTENTIALISM • (egg-ziss-TEN-shall-izm). The view that people are completely free and responsible for their own behavior.

■ HOW TODAY'S PSYCHOLOGISTS VIEW BEHAVIOR

First a new theory is attacked as absurd; then it is admitted to be true, but obvious and insignificant; finally it is seen to be so important that its adversaries claim that they themselves discovered it.

WILLIAM JAMES

The history of psychological thought has taken many turns, and contemporary psychologists also differ in their approaches. Today there are six broad, influential perspectives in psychology: the biological, cognitive, humanistic-existential, psychodynamic, learning, and sociocultural perspectives. Each emphasizes different topics of investigation. Each tends to approach its topics in its own ways.

• *The Biological Perspective*

Psychologists assume that our thoughts, fantasies, and dreams are made possible by the nervous system and especially by the brain. Biologically oriented psychologists seek the links between events in the brain—such as the activity of brain cells—and mental processes. They use techniques such as CAT scans and PET scans to show what parts of the brain are involved in thoughts, emotions, and behavior (see Chapter 3). It has been shown that specific parts of the brain are highly active when we listen to music, solve math problems, or experience certain kinds of psychological disorders. We have learned how the production of chemical substances in certain parts of the brain is involved in the formation of memories. Among some lower animals, electrical stimulation of parts of the brain prompts the expression of innate, or built-in, sexual and aggressive behaviors.

Biological psychologists are also concerned with the influences of hormones and genes. In people, for instance, the hormone prolactin stimulates production of milk. In rats, however, prolactin also gives rise to maternal behavior. In lower animals, sex hormones determine whether mating behavior will follow stereotypical masculine or feminine behavior patterns. In people, hormones play a subtler role, as we see in Chapter 13.

Genes are the basic units of heredity. Psychologists are interested in genetic influences on behavior and mental processes such as psychological disorders, criminal behavior, and thinking. Generally speaking, genetic factors provide a broad range of behavioral and mental possibilities. Environmental factors interact with genetic factors to determine behavior and mental processes.

• *The Cognitive Perspective*

Cognitive psychologists venture into the realm of mental processes to understand human nature (Sperry, 1993). They investigate the ways in which we perceive and mentally represent the world, how we learn, remember the past and plan for the future, solve problems, form judgments, make decisions, and use language (Basic Behavioral Science Task Force, 1996b). Cognitive psychologists, in short, study all the things that we refer to as the *mind.*

The cognitive tradition has roots in Socrates' advice to "Know thyself" and in his suggested method of introspection. We also find cognitive psychology's roots in structuralism, functionalism, and Gestalt psychology, each of which, in its own way, addressed issues that are of interest to cognitive psychologists.

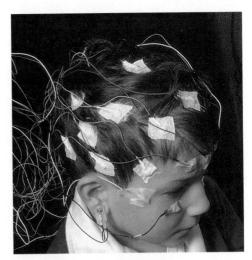

A

COGNITIVE-DEVELOPMENTAL THEORY Today the cognitive perspective has many faces. One is the cognitive-developmental theory advanced by the Swiss zoologist Jean Piaget (1896–1980). Piaget studied how people mentally represent and reason about the world. According to Piaget, the child's conception of the world grows more sophisticated as the child matures (see Chapter 4). Although experience is essential to children, children's perception and understanding unfolds as if guided by an inner clock.

INFORMATION PROCESSING Another face of the cognitive perspective is information processing. Psychological thought has always been influenced by the physical sciences of the day. For example, Freud's psychodynamic theory was related to the development of thermodynamics in the last century. (Freud saw the mind as a sort of steam engine that could explode if some of the "steam"— that is, primitive impulses—were not "vented," or released.) Similarly, many of today's cognitive psychologists have been influenced by computer science. Computers process information to solve problems. Information is first fed into the computer (encoded so that it can be input). Then it is placed in *memory*— or working memory—while it is manipulated. You can also store the information more permanently in *storage* on a floppy disk, a hard drive, or another device. In Chapter 8 we shall see that many psychologists also speak of people as having working memories (short-term memories) and storage (long-term memories). If information has been placed in *storage* (or in long-term memory), it must be retrieved before we can use it to solve problems (output). To retrieve information from computer storage, we must know the code or name for the data file and the rules for retrieving data files. Similarly, note psychologists, we must have the right cues to retrieve information from our own long-term memories or the information may be lost. The data in a computer's storage is usually retrieved in a more exact state than human memories. Our memories tend to be colored by our biases and our expectations.

Our strategies for solving problems are sometimes referred to as our "mental programs" or "software." In this computer metaphor, our brains are translated into the "hardware" that runs our mental programs. Our brains, that is, become *very* personal computers.

Behaviorists argue that cognitions are not directly observable and that cognitive psychologists do not place enough emphasis on the situational determinants of behavior. Cognitive psychologists counter that the richness of human behavior cannot be understood without reference to cognition.

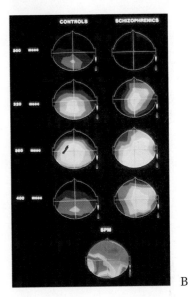

B

The Biological Perspective. Psychologists with a biological perspective investigate the connections among biological processes, behavior, and mental processes. They use methods such as brain electrical activity mapping (BEAM), in which electrodes measure the electrical activity of parts of the brain while people are exposed to various stimuli (photo A). The left-hand column of photo B shows the average level of electrical activity of the brains of 10 normal people at four time intervals. The right-hand column shows the average activity of 10 people diagnosed with schizophrenia, a severe psychological disorder. The more intense the activity, the brighter the color (white is most intense). The bottom diagram summarizes similarities and differences between people not diagnosed with schizophrenia and people diagnosed with schizophrenia: areas in blue reflect smaller differences; white areas reflect larger differences.

• *The Humanistic-Existential Perspective*

The humanistic-existential perspective is related to Gestalt psychology and is cognitive in flavor. **Humanism** stresses the human capacity for self-fulfillment and the central roles of consciousness, self-awareness, and decision making. Consciousness is seen as the force that unifies our personalities. **Existentialism** views people as free to choose and responsible for choosing ethical conduct.

Humanistic psychology considers personal, or subjective experience to be the most important event in psychology. Humanists believe that self-awareness, experience, and choice permit us, to a large extent, to "invent ourselves" and our ways of relating to the world as we progress through life.

There is a debate in psychology about whether we are free to choose or whether our behavior is determined by external factors. Behaviorists like John Watson assumed that our behavior reflects the stimuli acting upon us. The humanistic-existential approach of American psychologists such as Carl Rogers, Rollo May, and Abraham Maslow asserts that we are free to determine our own behavior. Humanistic-existential psychologists suggest that we are engaged in quests to discover our personal identities and the meanings of our lives.

The goals of humanistic-existential psychology have been more applied than academic. Humanistic-existential psychologists have devised ways to help people get in touch with their feelings and realize their potentials, for example.

Critics, including some behaviorists, insist that psychology must be a natural science and address itself to observable events. They argue that subjective experiences are poorly suited to observation and measurement. Humanistic-existential psychologists such as Carl Rogers may admit that the observation methods used by humanists have sometimes been less than scientific. They argue, however, that subjective experience remains the key to understanding human nature.

• *The Psychodynamic Perspective*

In the 1940s and 1950s, psychodynamic theory dominated the practice of psychotherapy and was influential in scientific psychology and the arts. Most psychotherapists were psychodynamically oriented. Many renowned artists and writers consulted psychodynamic therapists as a way to liberate the expression of their unconscious ideas.

Today the influence of psychoanalytic thought continues to be felt, although it no longer dominates psychology. Psychologists who follow Freud are likely to call themselves **neoanalysts.** Neoanalysts such as Karen Horney, Erich Fromm, and Erik Erikson focus less on unconscious processes and more on conscious choice and self-direction.

Many Freudian ideas are retained in watered-down form by the population at large. For example, sometimes we have ideas or inclinations that seem atypical to us. We may say that it seems as if something is trying to get the better of us. In the Middle Ages, such thoughts and impulses were usually attributed to the Devil or to demons. Dreams, likewise, were thought to enter us magically from the spirit world. Today, largely because of Sigmund Freud, many people ascribe dreams and atypical ideas or inclinations to unconscious processes.

Research and philosophical analysis have been somewhat hard on psychodynamic theory. Many psychoanalytic concepts cannot be confirmed by scientific means (see Chapter 12). On the other hand, reviews of psychoanalytic forms of psychotherapy have been generally positive (see Chapter 16).

• *Learning Perspectives*

NEOANALYSTS • (knee-oh-AN-al-lists). Contemporary followers of Freud who focus less on the roles of unconscious impulses and more on conscious choice and self-direction.

Many psychologists study the effects of experience on behavior. Learning, to them, is the essential factor in describing, explaining, predicting, and controlling behavior. The term *learning* has different meanings to psychologists of different persuasions, however. Some students of learning find roles for consciousness and insight. Others do not. This distinction is found among those who adhere to the behavioral and social-cognitive perspectives.

THE BEHAVIORAL PERSPECTIVE For John B. Watson, behaviorism was an approach to life as well as a broad guideline for psychological research. Not only did Watson despair of measuring consciousness and mental processes in the laboratory, he also applied behavioral analysis to virtually all situations in his daily life. He viewed people as doing things because of their learning histories, their situations, and rewards rather than because of conscious choice.

Learning, for Watson and his followers, is exemplified by experiments in conditioning. The results of conditioning are explained in terms of laboratory procedures, not in terms of changes within the learner.

THE SOCIAL-COGNITIVE PERSPECTIVE Since the 1960s, **social-cognitive theorists** (previously termed *social-learning theorists*) have gained influence in the areas of personality development, psychological disorders, and methods of therapy. Theorists such as Albert Bandura, Julian Rotter, and Walter Mischel see themselves as part of the behaviorist tradition because of their focus on the importance of learning. Yet they also return to their functionalist roots by giving cognition a key role. Behaviorists emphasize environmental influences and the learning of habits through repetition and reinforcement. Social-cognitive theorists, in contrast, suggest that people can modify or create their environments. People also engage in intentional learning by observing others. Through observational learning, we acquire a storehouse of responses to life's situations. Social-cognitive theorists are also humanistic in that they believe that our expectations and values help determine whether we *choose* to do what we have learned how to do.

• *The Sociocultural Perspective*

The profession of psychology focuses mainly on the individual and is committed to the dignity of the individual. However, psychology students cannot understand people's behavior and mental processes without reference to their diversity (Basic Behavioral Science Task Force, 1996c). Studying perspectives other than their own helps students understand the role of a culture's beliefs, values, and attitudes on behavior and mental processes. It helps students perceive why people from diverse cultures behave and think in different ways, and how the science of psychology is enriched by addressing those differences (Denmark, 1994; Reid, 1994).

People differ in many ways. The **sociocultural perspective** addresses the influences of ethnicity, gender, culture, and socioeconomic status on behavior and mental processes (Allen, 1993; Lewis-Fernández & Kleinman, 1994). For example, what is often seen as healthful, self-assertive outspoken behavior by most U.S. women may be interpreted as brazen behavior in Hispanic American or Asian American communities (Lopez & Hernandez, 1986).

ETHNICITY One kind of diversity involves people's ethnicity. Members of an **ethnic group** are united by their cultural heritage, race, language, and common history. The experiences of various ethnic groups in the United

SOCIAL-COGNITIVE THEORY • A school of psychology in the behaviorist tradition that includes cognitive factors in the explanation and prediction of behavior. Formerly termed *social-learning theory.*
SOCIOCULTURAL PERSPECTIVE • The view that focuses on the roles of ethnicity, gender, culture, and socioeconomic status in behavior and mental processes.
ETHNIC GROUP • A group characterized by common features such as cultural heritage, history, race, and language.

Human Diversity. How can psychologists understand the hopes and problems of people from a particular ethnic group without understanding that group's history and cultural heritage? The study of human diversity helps us understand and appreciate the scope of behavior and mental processes.

States highlight the impact of social, political, and economic factors on human behavior and development (Basic Behavioral Science Task Force, 1996c; Phinney, 1996).

The probing of human diversity enables students to appreciate the cultural heritages and historical problems of various ethnic groups. This textbook considers many psychological issues related to ethnicity, including:

- The representation of ethnic minority groups in psychological research studies
- Alcohol and substance abuse among adolescents from various ethnic minority groups
- Bilingualism
- Ethnic differences in intelligence test scores—their implications and possible origins
- The prevalence of suicide among members of different ethnic minority groups
- Ethnic differences in vulnerability to various physical problems and disorders, ranging from obesity to hypertension and cancer
- Ethnic differences in the utilization of health care
- Multicultural issues in the practice of psychotherapy
- Prejudice

GENDER   **Gender** is the state of being male or being female. Gender is not simply a matter of anatomic sex. It involves a complex web of cultural expectations and social roles that affect people's self-concepts and hopes and dreams as well as their behavior. How can sciences such as psychology and medicine hope to understand the particular viewpoints, qualities, and problems of women if most research is conducted with men and by men (Matthews and others, 1997)?

GENDER • The state of being female or being male.

TABLE 1.2	PERCENTAGE OF DOCTORAL DEGREES AWARDED TO WOMEN IN VARIOUS MAJOR FIELDS AND PROFESSIONS		
	Percentage of Women Receiving Doctorates		
Major Field (degree awarded)	1971	1981	1991
Biology (Ph.D.)	14.5	25.5	38.7
Dentistry (D.D.S. or D.M.D.)	1.1	14.0	32.1
Education (Ph.D.)	21.9	47.2	58.1
Engineering (Ph.D.)	0.4	3.9	8.7
Humanities (Ph.D.)	24.2	41.3	46.5
Law (J.D.)	7.1	32.0	42.9
Mathematics (Ph.D.)	7.8	15.4	18.7
Medicine (M.D.)	9.1	25.0	35.9
Physical sciences	5.9	11.8	18.3
Psychology (Ph.D.)	24.7	43.9	61.2
Sociology and Anthropology (Ph.D.)	19.7	40.0	49.5
Veterinary Medicine (D.V.M.)	7.8	36.4	57.2

Note. From Pion, G. M., and others (1996). The shifting gender composition of psychology: Trends and implications for the discipline. *American Psychologist, 51*, pp. 509–528.

Just as members of ethnic minority groups have experienced prejudice, so too have women. Even much of the scientific research on gender roles and gender differences assumes that male behavior represents the norm (Ader & Johnson, 1994; Matlin, 1996; Walsh, 1993). Women have traditionally been channeled into domestic pursuits, regardless of their wishes as individuals. Not until relatively modern times were women generally considered suitable for higher education (and they are still considered unsuited to education in many parts of the world!). Women have attended college in the United States only since 1833, when Oberlin College opened its doors to women. Today, however, more than half (54.5%) of U.S. postsecondary students are women. Other gains by women are suggested by the numbers of women who received doctoral degrees in various areas in the 1970s, 1980s, and 1990s (see Table 1.2).

Contemporary psychologists continue to view behavior and mental processes from various perspectives. The influence of the cognitive and biological perspectives appears to be increasing (Boneau, 1992). Yet there is little or no falloff in interest in the behavioral and psychodynamic perspectives, as measured by the number of journal articles that address these views (Friman and others, 1993). It remains to be seen which perspectives will dominate psychology in the new millennium.

REFLECTIONS
- Which psychological perspectives seem to support the view that people are free to choose their own destinies? Which perspectives do not?
- How does knowledge of human diversity contribute to our understanding of behavior and mental processes?
- Does it seem reasonable to compare human mental processes to computer information processing? Why or why not?

Critical Thinking. Critical thinking means being skeptical and taking nothing for granted. It means analyzing arguments by examining their definitions of terms, their premises, and their logic.

■ CRITICAL THINKING AND PSYCHOLOGY

A great many people think they are thinking when they are merely rearranging their prejudices.

WILLIAM JAMES

Higher education is a broadening experience not only because it exposes students to intellectual disciplines and human diversity, but also because it encourages them to learn to think critically. By thinking critically, people can challenge widely accepted but erroneous beliefs, including some of their own. **Critical thinking** helps make us active, astute judges of other people and their points of view, rather than passive recipients of the latest intellectual fads and tyrannies.

Critical thinking fosters skepticism so that we no longer take certain "truths" for granted (Murray, 1997b). People often assume that authority figures like doctors and government leaders usually provide us with factual information and are generally best equipped to make the decisions that affect our lives (Kimble, 1994). But when doctors disagree as to whether surgery is necessary to cure a health problem, how can they all be correct? When political leaders who all claim to have the "best interests" of the nation at heart fling accusations and epithets at one another, how can we know whom to trust? If we are to be conscientious, productive citizens of the nation and of the world, we need to seek pertinent information to make our own decisions and rely on our analytical abilities to judge its accuracy. This book will help you learn how to seek and analyze information that lies within the province of psychology, but the critical thinking skills you acquire can be applied in all of your courses and other adult undertakings.

Critical thinking helps students evaluate other people's claims and arguments. It encourages students to evaluate and, when necessary, dispute widely held beliefs (Murray, 1997b). Critical thinking has many meanings. On one level, it means taking nothing for granted. It means not believing things just because they are in print or because they were uttered by authority figures or celebrities. On another level, critical thinking refers to carefully evaluating the questions, statements, and arguments of others. It means examining the definitions of terms, and examining the premises and logic of arguments.

A group of psychologists (McGovern, 1989) defined the goals of critical thinking as fostering the following thinking skills:

- Development of skepticism about explanations and conclusions
- The ability to inquire about causes and effects
- Increased curiosity about behavior
- Knowledge of research methods
- The ability to analyze arguments critically

Your college education is intended to do more than provide you with a data bank of useful knowledge. It is also meant to supply intellectual tools that allow you to analyze information independently. With these tools, you can continue to educate yourself for the rest of your life.

Many of the "Truth or Fiction?" items in this book are intended to encourage you to apply principles of critical thinking to the subject matter of psychology. Some of them reflect "truisms," or beliefs that are often taken for granted. Consider a sampling of "Truth or Fiction?" items from several chapters:

- Alcohol causes aggression.
- We tend to act out our forbidden fantasies in our dreams.
- We must make mistakes in order to learn.

CRITICAL THINKING • An approach to thinking characterized by skepticism and thoughtful analysis of statements and arguments—for example, probing arguments' premises and the definitions of terms.

- We value things more when we have to work for them.
- Misery loves company.
- You can never be too rich or too thin.
- People who threaten to commit suicide are only seeking attention.
- Beauty is in the eye of the beholder.

• *Principles of Critical Thinking*

Let us consider some principles of critical thinking:

1. *Be skeptical.* Keep an open mind. Politicians and advertisers try to persuade you. Even research reported in the media or in textbooks may take a certain slant. Extend this principle to yourself. If you examine them critically, you might discover that some of your own attitudes and beliefs are superficial or unfounded. Accept nothing as true until you have examined the evidence.

2. *Examine definitions of terms.* Some statements are true when a term is defined in one way but not when it is defined in another way. Consider the statement "Head Start programs have raised children's IQs." Although I won't drop the answer in your lap, I'll tell you that the correctness of the statement depends on the definition of "IQ." (In Chapter 10, you will see that *IQ* has a specific meaning and is not exactly the same as *intelligence*.)

3. *Examine the assumptions or premises of arguments.* Consider the statement that one cannot learn about human beings by engaging in research with animals. One premise in the statement seems to be that human beings are not animals. We are, of course—and thoroughly delightful animals, I might add. (Would you rather be a plant?)

4. *Be cautious in drawing conclusions from evidence.* For many years studies had shown that most clients who receive psychotherapy improve. It was therefore generally assumed that psychotherapy worked. Some 40 years ago, however, a psychologist named Hans Eysenck pointed out that most psychologically troubled people who did *not* receive psychotherapy also improved! The question thus becomes whether people receiving psychotherapy are *more* likely to improve than those who do not. Current research on the effectiveness of psychotherapy therefore carefully compares the benefits of therapy techniques to the benefits of other techniques or of no treatment at all. Be skeptical, moreover, when a friend swears by the effectiveness of megavitamin therapy for colds. What is the nature of the "evidence"? Is it convincing?

    Correlational evidence is also inferior to experimental evidence as a way of determining cause and effect. Consider the statement "Alcohol causes aggression" in the following principle.

5. *Consider alternative interpretations of research evidence.* Does alcohol cause aggression? Is the assertion that it does so truth or fiction? Evidence certainly shows a clear *connection,* or "correlation," between alcohol and aggression. That is, many people who commit violent crimes have been drinking. Does the evidence show that this connection is *causal,* however? Tune into Chapter 2's discussion of the differences between the correlational and experimental methods to find out.

6. *Do not oversimplify.* Most human behavior involves interactions of genetic and environmental influences. Also consider the issue of whether

psychotherapy helps people with psychological problems. In Chapter 16 you will see that a broad answer to this question—a simple yes or no—might be oversimplifying. It is more worthwhile to ask, What *type* of psychotherapy, practiced by *whom,* is most helpful for *what kind of problem?*

7. *Do not overgeneralize.* Consider the statement "Misery loves company." In Chapter 11 you will see that the statement is accurate under certain circumstances. Again, consider the statement that one cannot learn about human beings by engaging in research with animals. Is the truth of the matter an all-or-nothing issue? Are there certain kinds of information we can obtain about people from research with animals? What kinds of things are you likely to be able to learn only through research with people?

psychology and modern life

THINKING CRITICALLY ABOUT SELF-HELP BOOKS: ARE THERE ANY QUICK FIXES?

*C*hicken Soup for the Soul; The Road Less Traveled; The 7 Habits of Highly Effective People; The Seven Spiritual Laws of Success; Don't Say Yes When You Want to Say No; Our Bodies Our Selves; The 8-Week Cholesterol Cure; Treating Type A Behavior and Your Heart; Feeling Good—The New Mood Therapy. . . .

These are just a few of the self-help books that have flooded the marketplace in recent years. Every day, shy people, anxious people, heavy people, stressed people, and confused people scan bookstores and supermarket checkout racks in hope of finding the one book that will provide the answer. How can they evaluate the merits of these books? How can they separate the helpful wheat from the useless and sometimes harmful chaff?

Unfortunately, there are no easy answers. Many of us believe the things we see in print, and anecdotes about

how chubby John lost 60 pounds in 60 days and shy Joni blossomed into a social butterfly in a month have a powerful allure. Especially when we are needy.

Be on guard. A price we pay for freedom of speech is that nearly anything can wind up in print. Authors can make extravagant claims with little fear of punishment. They can lie about the effectiveness of a new fad diet as easily as they can lie about communicating with the departed Elvis Presley or being kidnapped by a UFO.

How can you protect yourself? How could you know, for example, that *Mind Power* and *Toilet Training in a Day* are authored by respected psychologists? How could you know that *Looking Out for Number One* was written by a professional writer and publisher? How would you know that *The Relaxation Response* is well researched, whereas many books are not.

Try some critical thinking:

1. First, don't judge the book by its cover or its title. Good books as well as bad books can have catchy titles and interesting covers. Dozens, perhaps hundreds of books are competing for your attention. It is little wonder, then, that publishers try to do something sensational with the covers.

2. Avoid books that make extravagant claims. If it sounds too good to be true, it probably is. No method helps everyone who tries it. Very few methods work overnight (*Toilet Training in a Day* might be an exception). Yet people want the instant cure. The book that promises to make you fit in ten days will outsell the book that says it will take ten weeks. Responsible psychol-

8. *Apply critical thinking to all areas of life.* A skeptical attitude and a demand for evidence are not simply of use in college. They are of value in all areas of life. Be skeptical when you are bombarded by TV commercials, when political causes try to sweep you up, when you see the latest cover stories about Elvis and UFOs in supermarket tabloids. How many times have you heard the claim "Studies have shown that . . ."? Perhaps such claims sound convincing, but ask yourself: Who ran the studies? Were the researchers neutral scientists, or were they biased toward obtaining certain results?

As noted by the educator Robert M. Hutchins, "The object of education is to prepare the young to educate themselves throughout their lives." One of the primary ways of educating yourself is through critical thinking.

ogists and health professionals do not make lavish claims.

3. Check authors' educational credentials. Be suspicious if the author's title is just "Dr." and is placed before the name. The degree could be a phony doctorate bought through the mail. It could be issued by a religious cult rather than a university or professional school. It is better if the "doctor" has an M.D., Ph.D., Psy.D., or Ed.D. after her or his name, rather than "Dr." in front of it.

4. Check authors' affiliations. There are no guarantees, but psychologists who are affiliated with colleges and universities may have more to offer than those who are not.

5. Consider authors' complaints about the conservatism of professional groups to be a warning. Do the authors boast that they are ahead of their time? Do they berate professional health organizations as pigheaded or narrow-minded? If so, be suspicious. Most psychologists and other scientists are open-minded. They just ask to see evidence before they jump on the bandwagon. Enthusiasm is no substitute for research and evidence.

6. Check the *evidence* reported in the book. Bad books usually make extensive use of *anecdotes*, unsupported stories about fantastic results with a few individuals. Responsible psychologists and other health professionals check the effectiveness of techniques with large numbers of people. They carefully measure the outcomes. They use qualified language. For example, they say "It appears that . . ." or "It may be that . . ."

7. Check the reference citations for the evidence. Legitimate psychological research is reported in the journals you will find in the reference section of this book. These journals report only research methods and outcomes that seem to be scientifically valid. If there are no reference citations, or if the list of references seems suspicious, you should be suspicious, too.

8. Ask your instructor for advice. Ask for advice on what to do, whom to talk to, what to read.

9. Read textbooks and professional books, like this book, rather than self-help books. Search the college bookstore for texts in fields that interest you. Try the suggested readings at the end of textbook chapters.

10. Stop by and chat with your psychology professor. Talk to someone in your college or university health center.

In sum, there are few, if any quick fixes to psychological and health problems. Do your homework. Become a critical consumer of self-help books. ■

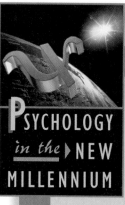

Psychology— Hot, Hot, Hot

Psychology is a hot field—very hot. It is growing rapidly, both as a college major and as a profession. As noted by psychologist Thomas McGovern (1996) of Arizona State University West, "Psychology is inherently interesting to our family lives and to ourselves, . . . The psychological implications of behavior have become part of the fabric of American culture."

THE SECOND MOST POPULAR UNDERGRADUATE MAJOR

Just how interesting is psychology to people in the United States? It turns out that psychology is the second most popular undergraduate major—behind business administration and management (Murray, 1996a). Moreover, the numbers of psychology majors are growing at a rapid pace. Nearly 70,000 students each year graduate with degrees in psychology in the 1990s. If current trends continue, that number could well surpass 100,000 students per year early in the new millennium.

Other popular majors include engineering, teacher education, accounting, and nursing. Notice that each of these majors leads to a job in the chosen field. But most psychology majors, like most majors in literature and history, have chosen this major because of the intellectual pleasure it provides. Jobs in the field are usually a secondary consideration. Of the 70,000 students who earn undergraduate degrees in psychology each year, only about 4,000 go on to receive doctoral degrees in psychology.

JOB GROWTH FOR PSYCHOLOGISTS IN THE NEW MILLENNIUM

Yet the new millennium will have room for more psychologists. According to "Money Guide, 1995" (American Psychological Association, 1996), in 2005 there will be about 64% more jobs in psychology than there were in the mid 1990s. Only the fields of computer science and physical therapy are growing more rapidly, with projected increases in jobs of 79% and 76%, respectively. By contrast, only 47% more jobs are anticipated in marketing and advertising, 40% in financial services, 35% in law, and 34% in engineering. Psychology thus promises to remain an area of relatively hot growth.

WHERE PSYCHOLOGISTS WILL WORK

In the 1970s, according to the National Science Foundation (American Psychological Association, 1996, 1997), more than half of psychologists were employed in colleges, universities, and medical schools. That number dropped to under 40% in the 1990s as jobs for psychologists in business and industry increased rapidly. The trend seems clear: in the new millennium, relatively fewer psychologists will be employed in educational settings. Greater numbers will be helping businesses and organizations in such areas as:

- devising psychological tests for recruitment of personnel
- interviewing people being recruited for jobs
- measuring performance on the job
- motivating workers to enhance productivity
- increasing job satisfaction
- helping organizations function more efficiently

WOMEN ENTERING PSYCHOLOGY

Psychology was originally a domain of men. In fact, Freud was one of those who believed that a woman's place was in the home. However, today about 40% of the psychologists in the United States are women, and the percentage is growing.

The trend is clear. In 1975, women received 27,103 (53%) of the 51,435 bachelor's degrees awarded in psychology. In 1993, women received 48,820 (73%!) of the 66,728 bachelor's degrees awarded in psychology (Murray, 1996a).

My daughter Jill recently graduated from a program in clinical psychology at a university in New York. She was one of 13 graduates in clinical psychology. Twelve of them were women. By the mid 1990s, 63% of the doctoral degrees in clinical psychology were being awarded to women (American Psychological Association, 1996, 1997), along with

- 77% of the degrees in developmental psychology
- 74% of the degrees in educational psychology
- 69% of the degrees in school psychology
- 58% of the degrees in counseling psychology
- 54% of the degrees in the personality and social psychology
- 48% of the degrees in experimental psychology
- 46% of the degrees in industrial/organizational psychology

Psychology, thus, is hot, hot, hot—for both men and women. ■

• *Common Errors in Arguments*

Another aspect of critical thinking is learning to recognize the errors in other people's claims and arguments. Consider the following examples:

1. *Arguments directed to the person:* The views of Sigmund Freud, the founder of psychodynamic theory, were assaulted almost as soon as they were publicized both by members of his circle, such as Carl Jung, and by psychologists of other schools, such as behaviorists. Freud has been alternately referred to as an ingenious, compassionate scientist and as an elitist fakir who based his theories on the fantasy lives of bored, wealthy women. Freud's personality and motives may be of historic interest, but they do not affect the accuracy of his views. Theories should be judged on the evidence, not on the character of the theorist.

2. *Appeals to force:* In the 17th century Galileo invented the telescope and discovered that the Earth revolved around the sun, rather than vice versa. The Catholic church, however, taught that the Earth was at the center of the universe. Galileo was condemned for heresy and warned that he would be burned at the stake if he did not confess the error of his ways. Galileo apparently agreed with Shakespeare that "The better part of valor is discretion" and retracted his views. But the facts are what they are. Social approval or threats of violence do not make arguments correct or incorrect.

3. *Appeals to authority:* You have probably often heard arguments like this one: "Well, my mother/teacher/minister says this is true, and I think that he/she knows more about it than you do." Appeals to authority can be persuasive or infuriating, depending on whether or not you agree with them. It matters not *who* makes an assertion, however—even if that person is a psychological celebrity like Sigmund Freud, William James, or John B. Watson. An argument is true or false on its own merits. Consider the evidence presented in arguments, not the person making the argument, no matter how exalted.

4. *Appeals to popularity:* The appeal to popularity is cousin to the appeal to authority. The people making the pitches in TV commercials are usually very popular—either because they are good looking or because they are celebrities. Again, evaluate the evidence being presented and ignore the appeal of the person making the pitch.

   The argument that you should do something or believe something because "everyone's doing it" is another type of appeal to popularity—one that gets some people involved in activities they later regret.

In sum, be skeptical. Examine evidence critically. Acquiring an education means more than memorizing information and learning how to solve chemistry and math problems. It also means acquiring the tools to think critically so that you can continue to educate yourself throughout your life.

We have concluded this chapter by urging students to examine the evidence before accepting the truth or falseness of other people's claims and arguments. In the next chapter, we explain how psychologists gather evidence to support their points of view.

REFLECTIONS
- Have you experienced arguments directed to the person or appeals to authority, force, or popularity? Did you recognize these arguments for what they were? How did you respond to them? Why?
- Why is learning to think critically an essential part of higher education? How might critical thinking protect the individual from dictators, advertisers, and other tyrants of the mind?

1. **What is psychology?** Psychology is the scientific study of behavior and mental processes.

2. **What are the goals of psychology?** Psychology seeks to describe, explain, predict, and control behavior and mental processes. Psychologists do not attempt to control the behavior of other people against their wills. Instead, they help clients modify their behavior for their own benefit.

3. **What is the role of psychological theory?** Behavior and mental processes are explained through psychological theories, which are sets of statements that involve assumptions about behavior. Explanations and predictions are derived from theories. Theories are revised, as needed, to accommodate new observations. If necessary, they are discarded.

4. **What is the difference between pure and applied research?** Basic or pure research has no immediate applications. Applied research seeks solutions to specific problems.

5. **What do clinical and counseling psychologists do?** Clinical psychologists help people with psychological disorders adjust to the demands of life. Counseling psychologists usually work with individuals who have adjustment problems.

6. **What do school and educational psychologists do?** School psychologists assist students with problems that interfere with learning. Educational psychologists are more concerned with theoretical issues involving human learning.

7. **What do developmental psychologists do?** Developmental psychologists study the changes that occur throughout the life span.

8. **What do personality and social psychologists do?** Personality psychologists study influences on our thought processes, feelings, and behavior. Social psychologists focus on the nature and causes of behavior in social situations.

9. **What do experimental psychologists do?** Experimental psychologists conduct research into basic psychological processes such as sensation and perception, learning and memory, and motivation and emotion.

10. **What do industrial and organizational psychologists do?** Industrial psychologists focus on the relationships between people and work. Organizational psychologists study the behavior of people in organizations.

11. **What do some other kinds of psychologists do?** Forensic psychologists work within the criminal justice system, serving as expert witnesses, training police in the handling of suicide threats, and so on. Health psychologists study the effects of stress on health problems and guide clients to undertake more healthful behavior patterns such as exercising, quitting smoking, and eating a more nutritious diet. Sports psychologists help people improve their performance in sports, as in showing them how to handle "choking."

12. **What contributions did the ancient Greek philosophers make to psychological thought?** The Greek philosopher Aristotle was among the first to argue that human behavior is subject to rules and laws. Socrates proclaimed "Know thyself" and suggested the use of introspection to gain self-knowledge.

13. **Where did psychology begin as a laboratory science?** Wilhelm Wundt established the first psychological laboratory in Leipzig, Germany, in 1879.

14. **What is structuralism?** Structuralism is the school of psychology founded by Wundt. It used introspection to study the objective and subjective elements of experience.

15. **What is functionalism?** Functionalism is the school of psychology founded by William James. It dealt with observable behavior as well as conscious experience and focused on the importance of habit.

16. **What is behaviorism?** Behaviorism is the school of psychology founded by John B. Watson. It argues that psychology must limit itself to observable behavior and not attempt to deal with subjective consciousness. Behaviorism focuses on learning by conditioning, and B. F. Skinner introduced the concept of reinforcement as an explanation of how learning occurs.

17. **What is Gestalt psychology?** Gestalt psychology is the school of psychology founded by Wertheimer, Koffka, and Köhler. It is concerned with perception and argues that psychologists must focus on the wholeness of human experience.

18. **What is psychoanalysis?** Sigmund Freud founded the school of psychoanalysis, which asserts that people are driven by hidden impulses and that they distort reality to protect themselves from anxiety.

19. **What are the major contemporary perspectives in psychology?** They are the biological, cognitive, humanistic-existential, psychoanalytic, learning, and sociocultural perspectives. Biologically oriented psychologists study the links between behavior and biological events such as brain activity and the release of hormones. Cognitive psychologists study the ways in which we mentally represent the world and process information. Humanistic-existential psychol-

ogists stress the importance of subjective experience and assert that people have the freedom to make choices. The sociocultural perspective focuses on the roles of matters of ethnicity, gender, culture, and socioeconomic status in behavior and mental processes.

20. **What is critical thinking?** Critical thinking is associated with skepticism. It involves thoughtfully analyzing the questions, statements, and arguments of others. It means examining the definitions of terms, examining the premises or assumptions behind arguments, and scrutinizing the logic with which arguments are developed.

21. **How is critical thinking applied to the science of psychology?** Critical thinking refers to the ability to inquire about causes and effects, as well as knowledge of research methods. Critical thinkers are cautious in drawing conclusions from evidence. They do not oversimplify or overgeneralize.

22. **What logical fallacies are recognized by critical thinkers?** Critical thinkers recognize the fallacies in arguments directed to the person, arguments employing force, appeals to authority, and appeals to popularity.

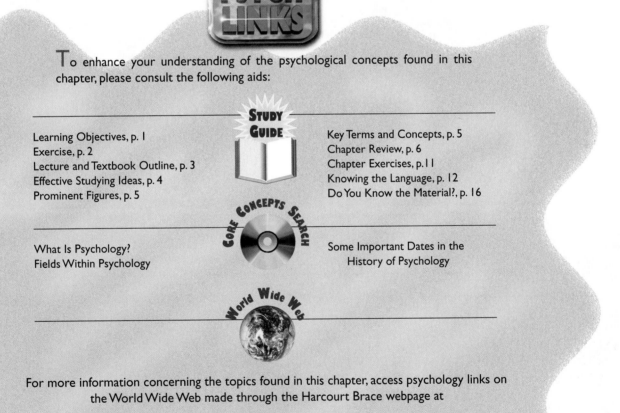

To enhance your understanding of the psychological concepts found in this chapter, please consult the following aids:

STUDY GUIDE

Learning Objectives, p. 1
Exercise, p. 2
Lecture and Textbook Outline, p. 3
Effective Studying Ideas, p. 4
Prominent Figures, p. 5

Key Terms and Concepts, p. 5
Chapter Review, p. 6
Chapter Exercises, p. 11
Knowing the Language, p. 12
Do You Know the Material?, p. 16

CORE CONCEPTS SEARCH

What Is Psychology?
Fields Within Psychology

Some Important Dates in the
History of Psychology

World Wide Web

For more information concerning the topics found in this chapter, access psychology links on the World Wide Web made through the Harcourt Brace webpage at

www.hbcollege.com

Share your comments and questions with your author at

PsychLinks@aol.com

Psychology is a science, and scientists insist that statements be supported by research evidence. Researchers attempt to piece together their observations into meaningful theories or wholes. Quilt making is a traditional form of artistic expression in which designs are pieced together. This quilt—*Young Man's Fancy* (1985)—has special meaning for the artist, Dora Lee Simons, a quilt maker from Fort Worth, Texas. She writes that it was made "during a very troubled time for me. Working on this quilt was my only consolation. As I lay each block in my own colors and hand-pieced them, it was like putting together a jigsaw puzzle."

Chapter 2

Research Methods in Psychology

TRUTH OR FICTION?

✔ **T F**

☐ ☐ You could survey 20 million voters and still not predict the outcome of a presidential election accurately.

☐ ☐ Only a small minority of people would be willing to deliver agonizing electric shocks to an innocent party.

☐ ☐ Americans in their forties have had more sex partners than Americans in their twenties.

☐ ☐ Only humans use tools.

☐ ☐ In many experiments, neither the subjects nor the researchers know who is taking the real treatment and who is not.

☐ ☐ Psychologists would not be able to carry out many kinds of studies without deceiving subjects as to the purposes and methods of the studies.

☐ ☐ A psychologist could write a believable personality report about you without interviewing you, testing you, or even knowing who you are.

OUTLINE

THE MILGRAM STUDIES: SHOCKING
STUFF AT YALE
THE SCIENTIFIC METHOD: PUTTING
IDEAS TO THE TEST
SAMPLES AND POPULATIONS: REPRE-
SENTING HUMAN DIVERSITY
Problems in Generalizing From Psycho-
logical Research
Psychology in a World of Diversity:
Including Women and Members of
Diverse Ethnic Groups in Research
METHODS OF OBSERVATION: THE
BETTER TO SEE YOU WITH
Case Study
The Survey
Psychology in a World of Diversity:
A Sex Survey That Addresses
Sociocultural Factors
Testing
Naturalistic Observation
Laboratory Observation
CORRELATION
THE EXPERIMENTAL METHOD: TRYING
THINGS OUT
Independent and Dependent Variables
Experimental and Control Groups
Blinds and Double Blinds
Psychology in the New Millennium:
In the Global Research Lab
METHODS OF STUDYING THE BRAIN
ETHICAL ISSUES IN PSYCHOLOGICAL RE-
SEARCH AND PRACTICE
Research With Humans
Research With Animals
Psychology and Modern Life:
Thinking Critically About Tea Leaves,
Bird Droppings, Palms, and the Stars

*P*SYCHOLOGY IS THE SCIENTIFIC STUDY of behavior and mental processes. Consider some questions of interest to psychologists: Do only humans use tools? Does alcohol cause aggression? Why do some people hardly ever think of food, while others are obsessed with it and snack all day long? Why do some unhappy people attempt suicide, whereas others seek other ways of coping with their problems? Does having people of different ethnic backgrounds collaborate in their work serve to decrease or increase feelings of prejudice?

Many of us have expressed opinions on questions like these at one time or another. Different psychological theories also suggest a number of possible answers. Psychology is an empirical science, however. In an **empirical** science, assumptions about the behavior of cosmic rays, chemical compounds, cells, or people must be supported by evidence. Strong arguments, reference to authority figures, even tightly knit theories are not adequate as scientific evidence. Psychologists and other scientists make it their business—literally and figuratively—to be skeptical.

Psychologists use research to study behavior and mental processes empirically. To undertake our study of research methods, let us recount some famous research undertaken at Yale University more than 30 years ago.

■ THE MILGRAM STUDIES: SHOCKING STUFF AT YALE

People are capable of boundless generosity and of hideous atrocities. Throughout history, people have sacrificed themselves for the welfare of their families, friends, and nations. Throughout history, people have maimed and destroyed other people to vent their rage or please their superiors.

Let us follow up on the negative side. Soldiers have killed civilians and raped women in occupied areas to obey the orders of their superiors or to win the approval of their comrades. Millions of Native Americans, Armenians, and Jews have been slaughtered by people who were obeying the orders of officers.

Obeying the orders of officers . . . How susceptible are people—how susceptible are you and I—to the demands of authority figures such as military officers? Is there something unusual or abnormal about people who follow orders and inflict pain and suffering on their fellow human beings? Are they very much unlike you and me? Or *are* they you and me?

It is easy to imagine that there must be something terribly wrong with people who would hurt a stranger without provocation. There must be something abnormal about people who would slaughter innocents. But these are assumptions, and scientists are skeptical of assumptions. Psychologist Stanley Milgram also wondered whether normal people would comply with authority figures

EMPIRICAL • Emphasizing or based on observation and experiment.

who made immoral demands. But rather than speculate on the issue, he undertook a series of classic experiments at Yale University that have become known as the Milgram studies on obedience.

In an early phase of his work, Milgram (1963) placed ads in New Haven (Connecticut) newspapers for people who would be willing to serve as subjects in studies on learning and memory. He enlisted 40 people ranging in age from 20 to 50—teachers, engineers, laborers, salespeople, people who had not completed elementary school, people with graduate degrees.

Let's suppose that you've answered the ad. You show up at the university in exchange for a reasonable fee ($4.50, which in the early 1960s might easily fill your gas tank) and to satisfy your own curiosity. You may be impressed. After all, Yale is a venerable institution that dominates the city. You are no less impressed by the elegant labs, where you meet a distinguished behavioral scientist dressed in a white coat and another person who has responded to the ad. The scientist explains that the purpose of the experiment is to study the *effects of punishment on learning.* The experiment requires a "teacher" and a "learner." By chance, you are appointed the teacher and the other recruit the learner.

You, the scientist, and the learner enter a laboratory room where there is a rather threatening-looking chair with dangling straps. The scientist straps the learner in. The learner expresses some concern, but this is, after all, for the sake of science. And this is Yale University, is it not? What could happen to a person at Yale?

You follow the scientist to an adjacent room, from which you are to do your "teaching." This teaching promises to have an impact. You are to punish the learner's errors by pressing levers marked from 15 to 450 volts on a fearsome-looking console (see Figure 2.1). Labels describe 28 of the 30 levers as running the gamut from "Slight Shock" to "Danger: Severe Shock." The last two levers are simply labeled "XXX." Just in case you've no idea what electric shock feels like, the scientist gives you a sample 45-volt shock. It stings. You pity the person who might receive more.

Your learner is expected to learn pairs of words, which are to be read from a list. After hearing the list once, the learner is to produce the word that pairs

FIGURE 2.1
THE "AGGRESSION MACHINE"
In the Milgram studies on obedience to authority, pressing levers on the "aggression machine" was the operational definition of aggression.

FIGURE 2.2
THE EXPERIMENTAL SETUP IN THE
MILGRAM STUDIES
When the "learner" makes an error, the experimenter prods the "teacher" to deliver a painful electric shock.

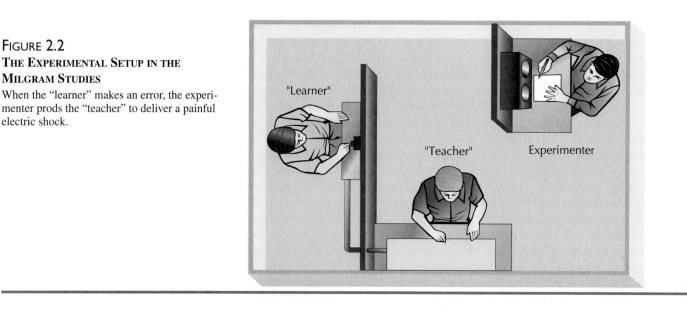

with the stimulus word from a list of four alternatives. This is done by pressing a switch that lights one of four panels in your room. If it is the correct panel, you proceed to the next stimulus word. If not, you are to deliver an electric shock. With each error, you are to increase the voltage of the shock (Figure 2.2).

You probably have some misgivings. Electrodes have been strapped to the learner's wrists, and the scientist has applied electrode paste "to avoid blisters and burns." You have also been told that the shocks will cause "no permanent tissue damage," although they might be extremely painful. Still, the learner is going along. And after all, this is Yale.

The learner answers some items correctly and then makes some errors. With mild concern you press the levers up through 45 volts. You've tolerated that much yourself. Then a few more mistakes are made. You press the 60-volt lever, then 75. The learner makes another mistake. You pause and look at the scientist, who is reassuring: "Although the shocks may be painful, there is no permanent tissue damage, so please go on." The learner makes more errors, and soon you are up to a shock of 300 volts. But now the learner is pounding on the other side of the wall! Your chest tightens and you begin to perspire. 'Damn science and the $4.50!' you think. You hesitate and the scientist says, "The experiment requires that you continue." After the delivery of the next stimulus word, the learner chooses no answer at all. What are you to do? "Wait for 5 to 10 seconds," the scientist instructs, "and then treat no answer as a wrong answer." But after the next shock the pounding on the wall resumes! Now your heart is racing, and you are convinced that you are causing extreme pain and discomfort. Is it possible that no lasting damage is being done? Is the experiment that important, after all? What to do? You hesitate again, and the scientist says, "It is absolutely essential that you continue." His voice is very convincing. "You have no other choice," he says, "you *must* go on." You can barely think straight, and for some unaccountable reason you feel laughter rising in your throat. Your finger shakes above the lever. *What are you to do?*

SCIENTIFIC METHOD • A method for obtaining scientific evidence in which research questions or hypotheses are formulated and tested.
THEORY • A formulation of the relationships and principles that underlie observed events. Theories allow us to explain and predict behavior.
HYPOTHESIS • In psychology, a specific statement about behavior or mental processes that is tested through research.

Milgram (1963, 1974) found out what most people in his sample would do. The sample was a cross section of the male population of New Haven. Of the 40 men in this phase of his research, only five refused to go beyond the 300-volt level, the level at which the learner first pounded the wall. Nine other "teachers" defied the scientist within the 300-volt range. But 65% of the subjects complied with the scientist throughout the series, believing that they were delivering 450-volt, XXX-rated shocks.

Were these subjects unfeeling? Not at all. Milgram was impressed by their signs of stress. They trembled, they stuttered, they bit their lips. They groaned, they sweated, they dug their fingernails into their flesh. Some had fits of laughter, though laughter was inappropriate. One salesperson's laughter was so convulsive that he could not continue with the experiment.

We return to the Milgram studies later in the chapter. They are a rich mine of information about human nature. They are also useful for our discussions of research issues such as replication, the experimental method, and ethics.

REFLECTIONS
- How would you have felt if you had been a "teacher" in the Milgram study? What would you have done? Are you sure?
- What would you do if you heard that such an experiment was being conducted at your own college or university? Why?

■ THE SCIENTIFIC METHOD: PUTTING IDEAS TO THE TEST

The **scientific method** is an organized way of using experience and testing ideas in order to expand and refine knowledge. Psychologists do not necessarily follow the steps of the scientific method as one might follow a cookbook recipe. However, their research endeavors are guided by certain principles.

Psychologists usually begin by *formulating a research question*. Research questions can have many sources. Our daily experiences, psychological **theory,** even folklore all help generate questions for research. Consider some questions that may arise from daily experience. Daily experience in using day care centers may motivate us to conduct research on whether day care influences the development of social skills or the bonds of attachment between children and their mothers.

Or consider questions that might arise from psychological theory (see Figure 2.3). Social-cognitive principles of observational learning may prompt research on the effects of TV violence. Sigmund Freud's psychoanalytic theory may prompt research on whether the verbal expression of feelings of anger helps relieve feelings of depression.

Research questions may also arise from common knowledge. Consider familiar adages such as "Misery loves company," "Opposites attract," and "Beauty is in the eye of the beholder"—statements that we consider in Chapters 11 and 13. Psychologists may ask, *Does* misery love company? *Do* opposites attract? *Is* beauty in the eye of the beholder?

A research question may be studied as a question or reworded as a hypothesis (see Figure 2.3). A **hypothesis** is a specific statement about behavior or mental processes that is tested through research. One hypothesis about day care might be that preschoolers who are placed in day care will acquire greater social skills in relating to peers than preschoolers who are cared for in the home. A hypothesis about TV violence might be that elementary schoolchildren who watch more violent TV shows tend to behave more aggressively toward their peers. A hypothesis that addresses Freudian theory might be that verbally expressing feelings of anger will decrease feelings of depression.

Psychologists next examine the research question or *test the hypothesis* through controlled methods such as naturalistic or laboratory observation and

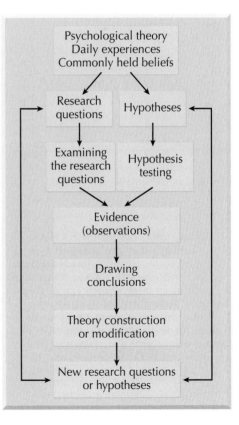

FIGURE 2.3
THE SCIENTIFIC METHOD
The scientific method is a systematic way of organizing and expanding scientific knowledge. Daily experiences, common beliefs, and scientific observations all contribute to the development of theories. Psychological theories explain observations and lead to hypotheses about behavior and mental processes. Observations can confirm the theory or lead to its refinement or abandonment.

the experiment. For example, we could introduce children who are in day care and children who are not to a new child in a college child research center and observe how children in each group interact with the new acquaintance.

To undertake research we must provide **operational definitions** for the variables under study. Concerning the effects of TV violence, we could have parents help us tally which TV shows their children watch and rate the shows for violent content. Each child could receive a composite "exposure-to-TV-violence score." We could also operationally define aggression in terms of teacher reports on how aggressively the children act toward their peers. Then we could determine whether more aggressive children also watch more violence on television.

Testing the hypothesis that verbally expressing feelings of anger decreases feelings of depression might be more complex. Researchers would have to decide, for example, whether they should use feelings of anger that people already have or use a standardized set of angry statements that address common areas of parent-child conflict. Would the people they study include people who are undergoing psychoanalysis or, say, students in introductory psychology courses? What would be the operational definition of feelings of depression? Self-ratings of depression according to a numerical scale? Scores on psychological tests of depression? Reports of depressive behavior by informants such as spouses? Psychologists frequently use a combination of definitions to increase their chances of tapping into targeted behavior patterns and mental processes.

Psychologists draw conclusions about their research questions or the accuracy of their hypotheses on the basis of their observations or findings. When their observations do not bear out their hypotheses, they may modify the theories from which the hypotheses were derived (see Figure 2.3). Research findings often suggest refinements to psychological theories and, consequently, new avenues of research.

In our research on day care, we would probably find that children in day care show greater social skills than children who are cared for in the home (Clarke-Stewart, 1991; Field, 1991). We would probably also find that more aggressive children spend more time watching TV violence (see Chapter 7). Research on the effectiveness of psychoanalytic forms of therapy is usually based on case studies, as we see in Chapter 16.

As psychologists draw conclusions from research evidence, they are guided by principles of critical thinking. For example, they try not to confuse correlations between findings with cause and effect. Although more aggressive children apparently spend more time watching violent TV shows, it may be erroneous to conclude from this kind of evidence that TV violence *causes* aggressive behavior. Perhaps a **selection factor** is at work. Perhaps more aggressive children are more likely than less aggressive children to tune into violent TV shows.

To better understand the effects of the selection factor, consider a study on the relationship between exercise and health. Imagine that we were to compare a group of people who exercised regularly with a group of people who did not. We might find that the exercisers were physically healthier than the couch potatoes. But could we conclude that exercise is a causal factor in good health? Perhaps not. The selection factor—the fact that one group chose to exercise and the other did not—could also explain the results. Perhaps healthy people are more likely to *choose* to exercise.

As critical thinkers, psychologists also attempt to avoid oversimplifying or overgeneralizing their results. The effects of day care, for example, apparently are very complex. Although children who are in day care usually exhibit better social skills than children who are not, they also tend to be more aggressive. If we conducted our research on the benefits of expressing feelings of anger with

OPERATIONAL DEFINITION • A definition of a variable in terms of the methods used to create or measure that variable.
SELECTION FACTOR • A source of bias that may occur in research findings when participants are allowed to determine for themselves whether or not they will partake of a certain treatment in a scientific study. Do you think, for example, that there are problems in studying the effects of a diet or of smoking cigarettes when we allow subjects to choose whether or not they will try the diet or smoke cigarettes? Why or why not?

people who are undergoing psychoanalysis, do you think we could generalize the results to the population at large? Why or why not?

Some psychologists include publication of research reports in professional journals as a crucial part of the scientific method. Researchers are obligated to provide enough details of their work that others will be able to repeat or **replicate** it. Psychologists may replicate a study in every detail in order to corroborate the findings, especially when the findings are significant for people's health or general welfare. Sometimes psychologists replicate studies with different kinds of subjects to determine, for example, whether findings of research with women can be generalized to men, or whether findings of research with people who have sought psychotherapy can be generalized to people at large.

Publication of research also permits the scientific community at large to evaluate the methods and conclusions of other scientists. A bruised ego here and there is a reasonable price to pay for the advancement of knowledge.

REFLECTIONS

- Have you heard the expressions "Misery loves company," "Opposites attract," or "Beauty is in the eye of the beholder"? Is there evidence for them? Is the evidence scientific? Why or why not?
- People who exercise are generally healthier than people who do not. Does this fact show that exercise is a causal factor in good health? Why or why not?

■ SAMPLES AND POPULATIONS: REPRESENTING HUMAN DIVERSITY

Consider a piece of history that never quite happened: The Republican candidate Alf Landon defeated the incumbent president, Franklin D. Roosevelt, in 1936. Or at least Landon did so in a poll conducted by a popular magazine of the day, the *Literary Digest.* In the actual election, however, Roosevelt routed Landon by a landslide of 11 million votes. How, then, could the *Digest* predict a Landon victory? How was so great a discrepancy possible?

The *Digest,* you see, had surveyed voters by phone. Today telephone sampling is a widely practiced and reasonably legitimate polling technique. But the *Digest* poll was taken during the Great Depression, when people who had telephones were much wealthier than those who did not. People at higher income levels are also more likely to vote Republican. No surprise, then, that the overwhelming majority of those sampled said that they would vote for Landon.

The principle involved here is that samples must accurately *represent* the population they are intended to reflect. Only representative samples allow us to **generalize** from research samples to populations.

In surveys such as that conducted by the *Literary Digest,* and in other research methods, the individuals who are studied are referred to as a **sample.** A sample is a segment of a **population.** Psychologists and other scientists need to ensure that the people they observe *represent* their target population, such as U.S. voters, and not subgroups such as southern Californians or non-Hispanic White members of the middle class.

Science is a conservative enterprise. Scientists therefore are cautious about generalizing experimental results to populations other than those from which their samples were drawn.

Truth or Fiction Revisited

It is true that you could survey 20 million voters and still not predict the outcome of a presidential election accurately. Sample size alone does not guarantee that a sample will accurately represent the population from which it was drawn.

REPLICATE • Repeat, reproduce, copy. What are some reasons that psychologists replicate the research conducted by other psychologists?

GENERALIZE • To extend from the particular to the general; to apply observations based on a sample to a population.

SAMPLE • Part of a population.

POPULATION • A complete group of organisms or events.

A Population? Psychologists and other scientists attempt to select their research samples so that they will represent target populations. What population is suggested by the people in this photograph? How might you go about sampling them? How do people who agree to participate in research differ from those who refuse?

• *Problems in Generalizing From Psychological Research*

All generalizations are dangerous, even this one.

ALEXANDRE DUMAS

Truth or Fiction Revisited

It is not true that only a small minority of people would be willing to deliver agonizing electric shocks to an innocent party. The Milgram studies reveal that when people are placed under strong social pressure, many, even most, will deliver such shocks. What does this research finding say to you about "human nature"?

Many factors must be considered in interpreting the accuracy of the results of scientific research. One is the nature of the research sample.

Milgram's initial research on obedience was limited to a sample of New Haven men. Could he generalize his findings to other men or to women? Would college students, who are considered to be independent thinkers, show more defiance? A replication of Milgram's study with a sample of Yale men yielded similar results. What about women, who are supposedly less aggressive than men? In subsequent research women, too, administered shocks to the learners. All this took place in a nation that values independence and free will.

Later in the chapter we consider research in which the subjects were drawn from a population of college men who were social drinkers. That is, they tended to drink at social gatherings but not when alone. Whom do college men represent, other than themselves? To whom can we extend, or generalize, the results? For one thing, the results may not extend to women, not even to college women. In Chapter 6, for example, we will learn that alcohol goes more quickly to "women's heads" than to men's.

College men also tend to be younger and more intelligent than the general adult population. We cannot be certain that the findings extend to older men of average intelligence, although it seems reasonable to assume that they do. Social drinkers may also differ biologically and psychologically from alcoholics, who have difficulty controlling their drinking. Nor can we be certain that college social drinkers represent people who do not drink at all.

Psychology in a World of
DIVERSITY

Including *Women and Members of Diverse Ethnic Groups in Research*

There is a historic bias in favor of conducting research with men (Matthews and others, 1997). Inadequate resources have been devoted to conducting health-related research with women (Matthews and others, 1997). For example, most of the large sample research on the relationships between lifestyle and health has been conducted with men (see Chapters 6 and 14). There is a crucial deficiency of research into women's health (including disease prevention), women and depression, and women and chemical dependence.

More research with women is also needed in other areas. One of these is the effects of violence on women. One fifth to one third of U.S. women will be physically assaulted—slapped, beaten, choked, or attacked with a weapon—by a partner with whom they share an intimate relationship (Browne, 1993). As many as one woman in four has been raped (Koss, 1993). Many psychologists believe that the epidemic of violence against women will only come to an end when people in the United States confront and change the social and cultural traditions and institutions that give rise to violence (Goodman and others, 1993). (Some of these traditions are discussed in Chapter 13.)

Another area in which more research is needed is the impact of work on women's lives. For example, how does working outside the home affect the division of labor within the home? Numerous studies have found that women are more likely than men to put in a "double shift." Women, that is, tend to put in a full day of work along with an equally long "shift" of shopping, mopping, and otherwise caring for their families (Chitayat, 1993; Keita, 1993). Even so, research shows that women who work outside the home have lower cholesterol levels and fewer illnesses than women who are full-time homemakers (Weidner and others, 1997).

It is now fairly widely accepted that findings of research with men cannot be generalized to women (Ader & Johnson, 1994). However, psychology may now be in danger of overgeneralizing findings of research with White, privileged women to *all* women (Yoder & Kahn, 1993). When women of color and of lower socioeconomic status are not included in research studies, or when their responses are not sorted out from those of non-Hispanic White women, issues of interest to them tend to get lost.

Research samples have also tended to underrepresent minority ethnic groups in the population. For example, personality tests completed by non-Hispanic White Americans and by African Americans may need to be interpreted in diverse ways if accurate conclusions are to be drawn (Nevid and others, 1997). The well-known Kinsey studies on sexual behavior (Kinsey and others, 1948, 1953) did not adequately represent African Americans, poor people, older people, and numerous other groups. The results of the National Health and Social Life Survey (NHSLS), reported later in the chapter, *do* reflect the behavior of diverse groups.

RANDOM AND STRATIFIED SAMPLING One way to achieve a representative sample is by means of **random sampling.** In a random sample, each member of a population has an equal chance of being selected to participate. Researchers can also use a **stratified sample,** which is selected such that identified subgroups in the population are represented proportionately in the sample. For instance, 12% of the American population is African American (U.S. Bureau of the Census, 1995). A stratified sample would thus be 12% African American. As a practical matter, a large, randomly selected sample will show reasonably accurate stratification. A random sample of 1,500 people will represent the general U.S. population reasonably well. A haphazardly drawn sample of 20 million, however, might not.

Large-scale magazine surveys of sexual behavior have asked readers to fill out and return questionnaires. Although many thousands of readers completed the questionnaires and sent them in, did they represent the general U.S. population? Probably not. These studies and similar ones may have been influenced by **volunteer bias.** People who offer or volunteer to participate in research studies differ systematically from people who do not. In the case of research on sexual behavior, volunteers may represent subgroups of the population—or of readers of the magazines in question—who are willing to disclose intimate information (Rathus and others, 1997). Volunteers may also be more interested in research than nonvolunteers, as well as have more spare time. How might such volunteers differ from the population at large? How might such differences slant or bias the research outcomes?

> ## REFLECTIONS
> * Were you surprised that women in the Milgram study obeyed orders and shocked "learners" just as men did? Why or why not?
> * Would a random sample of students from your own school represent the general U.S. population? Why or why not?
> * Why do you think that women who work outside the home have lower cholesterol levels and fewer illnesses than full-time homemakers do?

RANDOM SAMPLE • A sample that is drawn so that each member of a population has an equal chance of being selected to participate.

STRATIFIED SAMPLE • A sample that is drawn so that identified subgroups in the population are represented proportionately in the sample. How can stratified sampling be carried out to ensure that a sample represents the ethnic diversity we find in the population at large?

VOLUNTEER BIAS • A source of bias or error in research that reflects the prospect that people who offer to participate in research studies differ systematically from people who do not.

■ METHODS OF OBSERVATION: THE BETTER TO SEE YOU WITH

Many people consider themselves experts on behavior and mental processes. How many times, for example, have grandparents told us what they have seen in their lives and what it means about human nature?

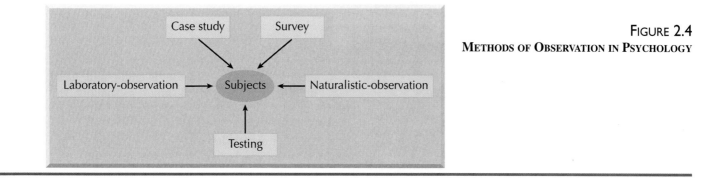

FIGURE 2.4
METHODS OF OBSERVATION IN PSYCHOLOGY

We see much indeed during our lifetimes. Our personal observations tend to be fleeting and uncontrolled, however. We sift through experience for the things that interest us. We often ignore the obvious because it does not fit our assumptions about the way things ought to be. Scientists, however, have devised more controlled ways of observing others. In this section we consider the case study, survey, testing, naturalistic observation, and laboratory observation methods (see Figure 2.4).

• *Case Study*

We begin with the case study method because our own informal ideas about human nature tend to be based on **case studies,** or information we collect about individuals and small groups. But most of us gather our information haphazardly. We often see only what we want to see. Unscientific accounts of people's behavior are referred to as *anecdotes.* Psychologists attempt to gather information about individuals more carefully.

Sigmund Freud developed psychodynamic theory largely on the basis of case studies. He studied people who sought his help in great depth, seeking the factors that seemed to contribute to certain patterns of behavior. He followed some people for many years, meeting with them several times a week.

However, there are gaps and factual inaccuracies in memory (Azar, 1997; Brewin and others, 1993). People may also distort their pasts to please the interviewer or because they want to remember things in certain ways. Interviewers may also have certain expectations and may subtly encourage subjects to fill in gaps in ways that are consistent with these expectations. Bandura (1986) notes, for example, that psychoanalysts have been criticized for guiding people who seek their help into viewing their own lives from the psychodynamic perspective. No wonder, then, that many people provide "evidence" that is consistent with psychodynamic theory. However, interviewers and other kinds of researchers who hold *any* theoretical viewpoint run the risk of indirectly prodding people into saying what they want to hear.

Case studies are often used to investigate rare occurrences, as in the cases of "Eve" and "Genie." "Eve" (in real life, Chris Sizemore) was an example of a person with dissociative identity disorder (see Chapter 15). "Eve White" was a mousy, well-intentioned woman who had two other "personalities" living inside her. One of them was "Eve Black," a promiscuous personality who now and then emerged to take control of her behavior. The case of Genie is discussed in the "In Profile" feature.

The case study method is also used in psychological consultation. Psychologists learn whatever they can about individuals, agencies, and business firms so that they can suggest ways in which these clients can meet their challenges more effectively.

Self-Portrait. "Genie" drew herself as a small child being held by her mother.

CASE STUDY • A carefully drawn biography that may be obtained through interviews, questionnaires, and psychological tests.

"Genie"

Young children seem to soak up languages. It seems that children are more "sensitive" to language than adults are. The disturbing case history of "Genie" offers insights into the issue of whether there is a sensitive period for learning language (Rymer, 1993). *Genie* is the name that was given to a girl who had been locked in a small room at the age of 20 months and kept there until she was 13. Genie's social contacts during her captivity were limited to her mother, who entered the room only to feed her, and to beatings by her father. When Genie was rescued, she weighed only about 60 pounds, did not speak, was not toilet trained, and could barely stand.

Genie was placed in a foster home, where she was exposed to language for the first time in nearly 12 years. What is of interest to psychologists who study language is that Ge-

nie's language development followed a normal pattern of development that is usually followed by much younger children. Nevertheless, Genie never acquired the mastery shown by most children. Five years after she was found, Genie's language remained largely *telegraphic.* That is, she would use one or a few words to try to express complex ideas. (An infant may telegraphically say *cat* but mean "I want to hold the cat.")

Genie also showed problems with grammar. For example, she did not reverse subjects and verbs to phrase questions. She had trouble using the past tense (adding *-ed* to words) and using negative helping verbs such as *isn't* and *haven't.* Her efforts to acquire English after puberty were clearly laborious. The results were substandard when compared even to the language of many 2- and 3-year-olds. ▪

SURVEY • A method of scientific investigation in which a large sample of people answer questions about their attitudes or behavior.

• *The Survey*

In the good old days, one had to wait until the wee hours of the morning to learn the results of local and national elections. Throughout the evening and early morning hours, suspense would build as ballots from distant neighborhoods and states were tallied. Nowadays, one is barely settled in with an after-dinner cup of coffee on election night when reporters announce that a computer has examined the ballots of a "scientifically selected sample" and predicted the next president of the United States. All this may occur with less than 1% of the vote tallied.

Just as computers and pollsters predict election results and report national opinion on the basis of scientifically selected samples, psychologists conduct **surveys** to learn about behavior and mental processes that cannot be observed in the natural setting or studied experimentally. Psychologists conducting surveys may employ questionnaires and interviews or examine public records. By distributing questionnaires and analyzing answers with a computer, psychologists can survey many thousands of people at a time.

We alluded earlier to the "Kinsey studies." Alfred Kinsey of Indiana University and his colleagues published two surveys of sexual behavior, based on interviews, that shocked the nation. These were *Sexual Behavior in the Human Male* (1948) and *Sexual Behavior in the Human Female* (1953). Kinsey reported that masturbation was virtually universal in his sample of men at a time when masturbation was still widely thought to impair physical or mental health. He also reported that about one woman in three who was still single at age 25 had engaged in premarital intercourse.

Interviews and questionnaires are not foolproof, of course. People may recall their behavior inaccurately or purposefully misrepresent it. Some people try to ingratiate themselves with their interviewers by answering in what they perceive to be the socially desirable direction. The Kinsey studies all relied on male interviewers, for example. It has been speculated that female interviewees might have been more open and honest with female interviewers. Similar problems may occur when interviewers and the people surveyed are from different ethnic or socioeconomic backgrounds. Other people may falsify their attitudes and exaggerate their problems in order to draw attention to themselves or foul up the results.

Humphrey Taylor (1993), president of Louis Harris & Associates (the company that takes the Harris Polls), recounts examples of survey measurement errors caused by inaccurate self-reports of behavior. For example, if people brushed their teeth as often as they claimed, and used the amount of toothpaste they indicated, three times as much toothpaste would be sold in the United States as is actually sold. People also appear to overreport church attendance and to underreport abortions (Espenshade, 1993). The following "Psychology in a World of Diversity" feature reports the results of a survey on sexual behavior.

Psychology in a World of
DIVERSITY

A Sex Survey That Addresses Sociocultural Factors

How Do Researchers Learn About People's Sex Lives? Can scientists gather accurate information about people's sex lives by means of a survey? Would you participate in such a survey? Why or why not?

Is it possible for scientists to describe the sex lives of people in the United States? There are many difficulties in gathering data, such as the refusal of many individuals to participate in research. Moreover, we must specify *which* people we are talking about. Are we talking, for example, about the behavior of women or men, younger people or older people, White Americans or African Americans?

The National Health and Social Life Survey (NHSLS) sample included 3,432 people (Laumann and others, 1994). Of this number, 3,159 people were English-speaking adults aged 18 to 59. The other 273 respondents were obtained by purposefully oversampling African American and Hispanic American households in order to obtain more information about these ethnic groups. While the sample probably represents the overall U.S. population aged 18–59 quite well, it may include too few Asian Americans, Native Americans, and Jews to offer much information about these groups.

The NHSLS research team identified sets of households in various locales—addresses, not names. They sent a letter to each household describing the purpose and methods of the study. An interviewer visited each household one week later. The people targeted were assured that the purposes of the study were important and that their identities would be kept confidential. Incentives of up to $100 were offered to obtain a high completion rate of close to 80%.

The NHSLS considered the sociocultural factors of gender, age, level of education, religion, and race/ethnicity in the numbers of sex partners people have (Laumann and others, 1994; see Table 2.1). Males in the survey report having higher numbers of sex partners than females do. For example, one male in three (33%) reports having 11 or more sex partners since the age of 18. This compares with fewer than one woman in 10 (9%). One the other hand, most people in the United States appear to limit their numbers of sex partners to a handful or fewer.

Note that the numbers of sex partners appears to rise with age into the forties. Why? As people gain in years, have they had more opportunity to accumulate life experiences, including sexual experiences? But reports of the numbers of partners fall off among people in their fifties. People in this age group entered adulthood when sexual attitudes were more conservative.

Level of education is also connected with sexual behavior. Generally speaking, it would appear that education is a liberating influence. People with some college, or who have completed college, are likely to report having more sex partners than those who attended only grade school or high school. But if education has a liberating influence on sexuality, conservative religious experience appears to be a restraining factor. Liberal Protestants (for example, Methodists, Lutherans, Presbyterians, Episcopalians, and United Churches of Christ) and people who say they have no religion report higher numbers of sex partners than Catholics and conservative Protestants (for example, Baptists, Pentecostals, Churches of Christ, and Assemblies of God).

Ethnicity is also connected with sexual behavior. The research findings in Table 2.1 suggest that White (non-Hispanic) Americans and African Americans have the highest numbers of sex partners. Hispanic Americans are mostly Catholic. Perhaps Catholicism provides a restraint on sexual behavior. Asian Americans would appear to be the most sexually restrained ethnic group. However, the sample sizes of Asian Americans and Native Americans are relatively small.

Truth or Fiction Revisited

It is true that Americans in their forties have had more sex partners than Americans in their twenties. Perhaps they have had more opportunity to have sexual relationships.

TABLE 2.1	NUMBER OF SEX PARTNERS SINCE AGE 18 AS FOUND IN THE NHSLS* STUDY					
SOCIOCULTURAL FACTORS	**0**	**1**	**2–4**	**5–10**	**11–20**	**21+**
GENDER						
Male	3	20	21	23	16	17
Female	3	32	36	20	6	3
AGE						
18–24	8	32	34	15	8	3
25–29	2	25	31	22	10	9
30–34	3	21	29	25	11	10
35–39	2	19	30	25	14	11
40–44	1	22	28	24	14	12
45–49	2	26	24	25	10	14
50–54	2	34	28	18	9	9
55–59	1	40	28	15	8	7
EDUCATION						
Less than high school	4	27	36	19	9	6
High school graduate	3	30	29	20	10	7
Some college	2	24	29	23	12	9
College graduate	2	24	26	24	11	13
Advanced degree	4	25	26	23	10	13
RELIGION						
None	3	16	29	20	16	16
Liberal, moderate Protestant	2	23	31	23	12	8
Conservative Protestant	3	30	30	20	10	7
Catholic	4	27	29	23	8	9
RACE/ETHNICITY						
White (non-Hispanic)	3	26	29	22	11	9
African American	2	18	34	24	11	11
Hispanic American	3	36	27	17	8	9
Asian American[†]	6	46	25	14	6	3
Native American[†]	5	28	35	23	5	5

Note. Adapted from *The Social Organization of Sexuality: Sexual Practices in the United States* (Table 5.1C, p. 179), by E. O. Laumann, J. H. Gagnon, R. T. Michael, & S. Michaels, 1994, Chicago: University of Chicago Press.
*National Health and Social Life Survey, conducted by a research team centered at the University of Chicago.
[†]These sample sizes are quite small.

• *Testing*

Psychologists also use psychological tests—such as intelligence, aptitude, and personality tests—to measure various traits and characteristics in a population. There is a wide range of psychological tests, and they measure traits ranging from verbal ability and achievement to anxiety, depression, the need for social dominance, musical aptitude, and vocational interests.

Because important decisions are made on the basis of psychological tests, they must be *reliable* and *valid*. The **reliability** of a measure is its consistency. A measure of height would not be reliable if a person appeared to be taller or shorter every time a measurement was taken. A reliable measure of personality or intelligence, like a good tape measure, must yield similar results under different testing occasions.

There are different ways of showing a test's reliability. One of the most commonly used ways is **test-retest reliability.** This involves comparing scores on tests taken on different occasions. The closer the scores, the higher the reliability. In tests of intelligence and **aptitude,** measurement of test-retest reliability may be confused by the fact that people often improve their scores from one occasion to the next because of familiarity with the test items and the testing procedure.

The **validity** of a test is the degree to which it measures what it is supposed to measure. To determine whether a test is valid, we see whether it actually predicts an outside standard, or external criterion. An appropriate criterion for determining the validity of a test of musical aptitude is the ability to learn to play a musical instrument. Tests of musical aptitude therefore should predict ability to learn to play a musical instrument. Similarly, most psychologists assume that intelligence is one of the factors responsible for academic prowess. Thus, scores on intelligence tests should predict school grades, and indeed they do so moderately well (Neisser and others, 1996).

Results of psychological tests, like those of surveys, can be distorted by respondents who answer in a socially desirable direction or attempt to exaggerate problems. For these reasons, some commonly used psychological tests have items called **validity scales** built into them. The answers to these items are sensitive to misrepresentations and alert the psychologist when test results may be deceptive. An example of such an item might be "I never tell a lie."

• *Naturalistic Observation*

You use **naturalistic observation**—that is, you observe people in their natural habitats—every day. So do psychologists. The next time you opt for a fast-food burger lunch, look around. Pick out slender people and overweight people and observe whether they eat their burgers and fries differently. Do the overweight people eat more rapidly? Chew less frequently? Leave less food on their plates? Psychologists have used this method to study the eating habits of normal weight and overweight people. In fact, while you're at McDonald's, if you notice people peering over sunglasses and occasionally tapping the head of a partly concealed microphone, perhaps they are recording their observations of other people's eating habits.

In naturalistic observation, psychologists and other scientists observe behavior where it happens, or "in the field." They try to avoid interfering with the behaviors they are observing by using **unobtrusive** measures. For example, Jane Goodall has observed the behavior of chimpanzees in their natural environment to learn about their social behavior, sexual behavior, use of tools, and other facts of chimp life (see Figure 2.5). Her observations have shown us that (1) we were incorrect to think that only humans use tools; and (2) kissing, as a greeting, is used by chimpanzees as well as by humans.

Truth or Fiction Revisited

It is not true that only humans use tools. Other animals also do so, including apes and otters. (Did you know that otters use rocks to open the shells of mollusks?)

RELIABILITY • Consistency.
TEST-RETEST RELIABILITY • A method for determining the reliability of a test by comparing (correlating) test takers' scores from separate occasions.
APTITUDE • An ability or talent to succeed in an area in which one has not yet been trained.
VALIDITY • The degree to which a test measures what it is supposed to measure.
VALIDITY SCALES • Groups of test items that suggest whether the test results are valid (measure what they are supposed to measure).
NATURALISTIC OBSERVATION • A scientific method in which organisms are observed in their natural environments.
UNOBTRUSIVE • Not interfering.

FIGURE 2.5

THE NATURALISTIC-OBSERVATION METHOD
Jane Goodall has observed the behavior of chimpanzees in the field, "where it happens." She has found that chimps use sticks to grub for food, and that they apparently kiss each other as a social greeting. Scientists who use this method try not to interfere with the animals or people they observe, even though this sometimes means allowing an animal to be mistreated by other animals or to die from a curable illness.

• *Laboratory Observation*

I first became acquainted with the laboratory observation method when, as a child, I was given tropical fish. My parents spent a small fortune to keep my new dependents in sound health. My laboratory for observation—my tank—was an artificial sea world. I filtered impurities out of the water with an electric pump. I warmed the water and regulated its acidity (pH). All this enabled me to while away the hours watching the fish swim in and out of protecting leaves, establish and defend territories, and, sometimes, court mates and breed. I even noted how the fish became conditioned to swim to the surface of the water when the light was turned on in the room. They apparently came to associate the light with the appearance of food.

By bringing the fish into my home, I did not have to voyage to the reefs of the Caribbean or to the mouth of the Amazon to make my observations. I also created just the conditions I wished, and I observed how my subjects reacted to them.

Somewhat like wondering children, psychologists at times place lower animals and humans in controlled laboratory environments where they can be readily observed and where the effects of specific conditions can be discerned. Figure 1.2 on page 12 shows one such environment, which is constructed so that pigeons receive reinforcers for pecking buttons.

With human subjects, the **laboratory** takes many forms. Do not confine your imagination to rows of Bunsen burners and the smell of sulfur or to rats and pigeons in wire cages being reinforced with food pellets from heaven. Figure 2.2 (see p. 36), for example, diagrams the laboratory setup used in Milgram's studies at Yale University, where subjects (the "teacher" in the diagram) were urged to deliver electric shocks to other people (so-called learners) as a way of signaling them that they had made errors on a learning task. This study was inspired by the atrocities committed by apparently typical German citizens during World War II, and its true purpose was to determine how easy it would be to induce normal people to hurt others. In studies on sensation and perception, subjects may be placed in dark or quiet rooms in order to learn how bright or loud a stimulus must be before it can be detected.

LABORATORY • A place in which theories, techniques, and methods are tested and demonstrated.

REFLECTIONS

• What methods of observation do your family and friends use to learn about human behavior? How do their methods overlap with those described in this section? How scientific are they?
• Why do you think people tend to overreport how often they brush their teeth and go to church?

■ CORRELATION

Are people with higher intelligence more likely to do well in school? Are people with a stronger need for achievement likely to climb higher up the corporate ladder? What is the relationship between stress and health?

Correlation follows observation. By using the **correlational method,** psychologists investigate whether observed behavior or a measured trait is related to, or correlated with, another. Consider the variables of intelligence and academic performance. These variables are assigned numbers such as intelligence test scores and academic averages. Then the numbers are mathematically related and expressed as a **correlation coefficient.** A correlation coefficient is a number that varies between + 1.00 and − 1.00. Psychologists use correlation coefficients to determine the reliability and validity of psychological tests.

For a test to be considered reliable, correlations between a group's test results on separate occasions should be positive and high—about + 0.90 (see Table 2.2). Studies report **positive correlations** between intelligence and achievement. People's scores on intelligence tests are also positively correlated with their grades. Generally speaking, the higher people score on intelligence tests, the better their academic performance is likely to be. The scores attained on intelligence tests tend to be positively correlated (about + 0.60 to + 0.70) with academic achievement (see Figure 2.6). As noted in Table 2.2, a correlation of about + 0.60 to + 0.70 is generally considered to be adequate for purposes of test validity. However, such a correlation does not approach a perfect positive

CORRELATIONAL METHOD • A scientific method that studies the relationships between variables.
CORRELATION COEFFICIENT • A number between + 1.00 to − 1.00 that expresses the strength and direction (positive or negative) of the relationship between two variables.
POSITIVE CORRELATION • A relationship between variables in which one variable increases as the other also increases.

Intelligence and Achievement. Correlations between intelligence test scores and academic achievement—as measured by school grades and achievement tests—tend to be positive and strong. Does the correlational method allow us to say that intelligence *causes* or *is responsible for* academic achievements? Why or why not?

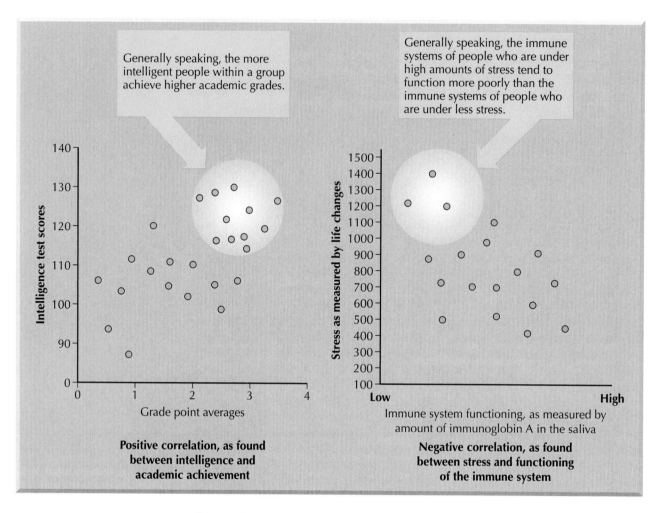

Generally speaking, the more intelligent people within a group achieve higher academic grades.

Generally speaking, the immune systems of people who are under high amounts of stress tend to function more poorly than the immune systems of people who are under less stress.

Positive correlation, as found between intelligence and academic achievement

Negative correlation, as found between stress and functioning of the immune system

FIGURE 2.6
POSITIVE AND NEGATIVE CORRELATIONS
When there is a positive correlation between variables, as there is between intelligence and achievement, one increases as the other increases. By and large, the higher people score on intelligence tests, the better their academic performance is likely to be, as in the diagram to the left. (Each dot represents an individual's intelligence test score and grade point average.) On the other hand, there is a negative correlation between stress and health. As the amount of stress we experience increases, the functioning of our immune systems tends to decrease. Correlational research may suggest but does not demonstrate cause and effect.

relationship. This finding suggests that factors *other* than performance on intelligence tests contribute to academic and occupational success. Achievement motivation, adjustment, and common sense are three of them (Collier, 1994; Sternberg and others, 1995).

What of the need for achievement and getting ahead? The need for achievement can be assessed by rating subjects' stories for the presence of this need (see Chapter 11). Getting ahead can be assessed in many ways—the amount of one's salary and the prestige of one's occupation or level within the corporation are just two of them.

There is a **negative correlation** between stress and health. As the amount of stress affecting us increases, the functioning of our immune systems decreases (see Chapter 14). Under high levels of stress, many people show poorer health.

Correlational research may suggest possible causes, but it does not demonstrate causality. For instance, it may seem logical to assume that high intelli-

NEGATIVE CORRELATION • A relationship between two variables in which one variable increases as the other decreases.

TABLE 2.2 INTERPRETATIONS OF SOME CORRELATION COEFFICIENTS

CORRELATION COEFFICIENT	INTERPRETATION
+ 1.00	Perfect positive correlation, as between temperature in Fahrenheit and centigrade
+ 0.90	High positive correlation, adequate for test reliability
+ 0.60 to + 0.70	Moderate positive correlation, usually considered adequate for test validity
+ 0.30	Weak positive correlation, unacceptable for test reliability or validity
0.00	No correlation between variables (no association indicated)
− 0.30	Weak negative correlation
− 0.60 to − 0.70	Moderate negative correlation
− 0.90	High negative correlation
− 1.00	A perfect negative correlation

gence makes it possible for children to profit from education. Research has also shown, however, that education contributes to higher scores on intelligence tests. Preschoolers who are placed in stimulating Head Start programs later attain higher scores on intelligence tests than age-mates who did not have this experience. The relationship between intelligence and academic performance may not be as simple as you might think. What of the link between stress and health? Does stress impair health, or is it possible that people in poorer health encounter higher levels of stress? (See Figure 2.7.)

FIGURE 2.7
CORRELATIONAL RELATIONSHIPS, CAUSE, AND EFFECT

Correlational relationships may suggest but does not demonstrate cause and effect. In part A, there is a correlation between variables X and Y. Does this mean that either variable X causes variable Y or that variable Y causes variable X? Not necessarily. Other factors could affect both variables X and Y. Consider the examples of academic grades (variable X) and juvenile delinquency (variable Y) in part B. There is a negative correlation between the two. Does this mean that poor grades contribute to delinquency? Perhaps. Does it mean that delinquency contributes to poor grades? Again, perhaps. But there could also be other variables—such as a broken home, lack of faith in the educational system, or peer influences—that contribute both to poor grades and delinquency.

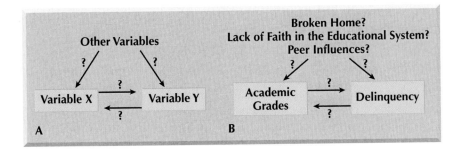

■ THE EXPERIMENTAL METHOD: TRYING THINGS OUT

The people who signed up for the Milgram studies participated in an elaborate experiment. The subjects received an intricate *treatment*—one that involved a well-equipped research laboratory. The experiment also involved deception. Milgram had even foreseen subjects' objections to the procedure. He had therefore conceived standardized statements that his assistants would use when subjects balked—for example: "Although the shocks may be painful, there is no permanent tissue damage, so please go on." "The experiment requires that you continue." "It is absolutely essential that you continue." "You have no other choice, you *must* go on." These statements, the bogus "aggression machine," the use of the "learner" (who was actually a confederate of the experimenter)—all these things were part of the experimental treatment.

Although we can raise many questions about the Milgram studies, most psychologists agree that the preferred method for answering questions about cause and effect is the experiment. In an **experiment,** a group of subjects obtains a **treatment,** such as a dose of alcohol, a change in room temperature, perhaps an injection of a drug. The subjects are then observed carefully to determine whether the treatment makes a difference in their behavior. Does alcohol alter the ability to take tests, for example? What about differences in room temperatures and level of background noise?

Experiments are used whenever possible because they allow psychologists to control the experiences of subjects and draw conclusions about cause and effect. A psychologist may theorize that alcohol leads to aggression because it reduces fear of consequences or because it energizes the activity levels of drinkers. She or he may then hypothesize that a treatment in which subjects receive a specified dosage of alcohol will lead to increases in aggression. Let us follow the example of the effects of alcohol on aggression to further our understanding of the experimental method.

• *Independent and Dependent Variables*

EXPERIMENT • A scientific method that seeks to confirm cause-and-effect relationships by introducing independent variables and observing their effects on dependent variables.

TREATMENT • In experiments, a condition received by subjects so that its effects may be observed.

INDEPENDENT VARIABLE • A condition in a scientific study that is manipulated so that its effects may be observed.

In an experiment to determine whether alcohol causes aggression, subjects would be given an amount of alcohol and its effects would be measured. In this case, alcohol is an **independent variable.** The presence of an independent variable is manipulated by the experimenters so that its effects may be determined. The independent variable of alcohol may be administered at different levels, or doses, from none or very little to enough to cause intoxication or drunkenness.

The measured results, or outcomes, in an experiment are called **dependent variables.** The presence of dependent variables presumably depends on the independent variables. In an experiment to determine whether alcohol influences aggression, aggressive behavior would be a dependent variable. Other dependent variables of interest might include sexual arousal, visual-motor coordination, and performance on intellectual tasks such as defining words or doing numerical computations.

In an experiment on the relationships between temperature and aggression, temperature would be an independent variable and aggressive behavior would be a dependent variable. We could use temperature settings ranging from below freezing to blistering hot, and study the effects of each. We could also use a second independent variable such as social provocation. That is, we could insult some subjects but not others. This method would allow us to study the interaction between temperature and social provocation as they affect aggression.

Experiments can be complex, with several independent and dependent variables. Psychologists often use complex experimental designs and sophisticated statistical techniques to determine the effect of each independent variable, acting alone and in combination with others.

• Experimental and Control Groups

Ideal experiments use experimental and control groups. Subjects in **experimental groups** obtain the treatment. Members of **control groups** do not. Every effort is made to ensure that all other conditions are held constant for both groups. This method enhances the researchers' ability to draw conclusions about cause and effect. The researchers can be more confident that outcomes of the experiment are caused by the treatments and not by chance factors or chance fluctuations in behavior.

In an experiment on the effects of alcohol on aggression, members of the experimental group would ingest alcohol and members of the control group would not. In a complex experiment, different experimental groups might ingest different dosages of alcohol and be exposed to different types of social provocations.

• Blinds and Double Blinds

One experiment on the effects of alcohol on aggression (Boyatzis, 1974) reported that men at parties where beer and liquor were served acted more aggressively than men at parties where only soft drinks were served. But we must be cautious in interpreting these findings because the subjects in the experimental group *knew* that they had drunk alcohol, and those in the control group *knew* that they had not. Aggression that appeared to result from alcohol might not have reflected drinking per se. Instead, it might have reflected the subjects' *expectations* about the effects of alcohol. People tend to act in stereotypical ways when they believe that they have been drinking alcohol. For instance, men tend to become less anxious in social situations, more aggressive, and more sexually aroused.

A **placebo,** or "sugar pill," often results in the kind of behavior that people expect. Physicians sometimes give placebos to demanding, but healthy, people, many of whom then report that they feel better. When subjects in psychological experiments are given placebos—such as tonic water—but think that they have drunk alcohol, we can conclude that changes in their behavior stem from their beliefs about alcohol, not from the alcohol itself.

Well-designed experiments control for the effects of expectations by creating conditions under which subjects are unaware of, or **blind** to, the treatment. Yet

DEPENDENT VARIABLE • A measure of an assumed effect of an independent variable.
EXPERIMENTAL GROUPS • In experiments, groups whose members obtain the treatment.
CONTROL GROUPS • In experiments, groups whose members do not obtain the treatment, while other conditions are held constant.
PLACEBO • A bogus treatment that has the appearance of being genuine.
BLIND • In experimental terminology, unaware of whether or not one has received a treatment.

What Are the Effects of Alcohol? Psychologists have conducted numerous studies to determine the effects of alcohol. Questions have been raised about the soundness of research in which people *know* that they have drunk alcohol. Why is this research questioned?

researchers may also have expectations. They may, in effect, be "rooting for" a certain treatment. For instance, tobacco company executives may wish to show that cigarette smoking is harmless. In such cases, it is useful if the people measuring the experimental outcomes are unaware of which subjects have received the treatment. Studies in which neither the subjects nor the experimenters know who has obtained the treatment are called **double-blind studies.**

The Food and Drug Administration requires double-blind studies before it will allow the marketing of new drugs (Carroll and others, 1994). The drug and the placebo look and taste alike. Experimenters assign the drug or placebo to subjects at random. Neither the subjects nor the observers know who is taking the drug and who is taking the placebo. After the final measurements have been made, an impartial panel judges whether the effects of the drug differed from those of the placebo.

In one double-blind study on the effects of alcohol, Alan Lang and his colleagues (1975) pretested a highball of vodka and tonic water to determine that it could not be discriminated by taste from tonic water alone. They recruited college men who described themselves as social drinkers to participate in the study. Some of the men drank vodka and tonic water. Others drank tonic water only. Of the men who drank vodka, half were misled into believing that they had drunk tonic water only (Figure 2.8). Of those who drank tonic water only, half were misled into believing that their drink contained vodka. Thus, half the subjects were blind to their treatment. Experimenters who measured the men's aggressive responses were also blind concerning which subjects had or had not drunk vodka.

The research team found that men who believed that they had drunk vodka responded more aggressively to a provocation than men who believed that they had drunk tonic water only. The actual content of the drink was immaterial. That is, men who had actually drunk alcohol acted no more aggressively than men who had drunk tonic water only. The results of the Lang study differ dramatically from those reported by Boyatzis, perhaps because the Boyatzis study did not control for the effects of expectations or beliefs about alcohol.

Truth or Fiction Revisited

It is true that in many experiments, neither the subjects nor the researchers know who is receiving the real treatment and who is receiving a placebo ("sugar pill"). Such double-blind studies control for the effects of subjects' and researchers' expectations.

DOUBLE-BLIND STUDY • A study in which neither the subjects nor the observers know who has received the treatment.

In Review Research Methods

METHOD	WHAT HAPPENS	COMMENTS
Case Study	The researcher uses interviews and records to gather in-depth information about an individual or a small group.	The accuracy of case studies is compromised by gaps and mistakes in memory, and by subjects' tendency to present themselves in a socially desirable manner.
The Survey	The researcher uses interviews, questionnaires, or public records to gather information about large numbers of people.	Surveys can include thousands of people but are subject to the same problems as case studies. People who volunteer to participate in surveys may also differ from people who do not. There may thus be problems in generalization of results to people who do not participate.
Testing	The researcher uses psychological tests to measure various traits and characteristics among a population	Good psychological tests are reliable and valid. The *reliability* of a measure is its consistency. The *validity* of a test is the degree to which it measures what it is supposed to measure.
Naturalistic Observation	The researcher observes behavior where it happens—"in the field."	Researchers try to avoid interfering with the behaviors they are observing by using *unobtrusive* measures.
Laboratory Observation	The researcher observes behavior in a controlled environment.	This method allows researchers to control conditions to which subjects are subjected. It is unclear whether behavior observed in the laboratory is the same as behavior in "real life."
Correlation	The researcher uses statistical (mathematical) methods to reveal positive and negative relationships between variables.	The correlational method does not show cause and effect. Correlation coefficients vary between $+1.00$ (a perfect positive correlation) and -1.00 (a perfect negative correlation).
Experiment	The researcher manipulates independent variables and observes their effects on dependent variables.	Experimental groups obtain the treatment; control groups do not. Researchers use *blinds* to control for the effect of expectations. With *double blinds*, neither the subjects nor the observers know which subject has received which treatment. The experimental method allows researchers to draw conclusions about cause and effect.

		Participants' Beliefs	
		Vodka and Tonic Water	Tonic Water only
Participants' Actual Drinks	Vodka and Tonic Water	drank vodka/ believed vodka	drank vodka/ believed tonic water only
	Tonic Water only	drank tonic water only/believed vodka	drank tonic water only/believed tonic water only

FIGURE 2.8

THE EXPERIMENTAL CONDITIONS IN THE LANG STUDY

The taste of vodka cannot be discerned when vodka is mixed with tonic water. For this reason, it was possible for subjects in the Lang study on the effects of alcohol to be kept "blind" as to whether or not they had actually drunk alcohol. Blind studies allow psychologists to control for the effects of subjects' expectations.

Note that in the Lang study on alcohol and aggression, alcohol was operationally defined as a certain dose of vodka. Other types of drinks and other dosages of vodka might have had different effects. Research evidence does show that drunkenness is connected with verbal and physical aggression (Bushman & Cooper, 1990; Lau and others, 1995). In the Lang study, aggression was operationally defined the same way as in the Milgram studies on obedience: as selecting a certain amount of electric shock to administer to another subject in a psychological experiment. College men might behave differently when they drink in other situations—for example, when they are insulted by a fan of an opposing football team or threatened outside a bar.

REFLECTIONS

- Can you devise a method whereby researchers can use placebos and double blinds to investigate the effects of a new drug on the urge to smoke cigarettes? Can you think of various ways in which the researchers can measure the "urge" to smoke?

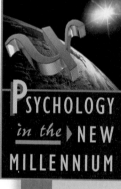

PSYCHOLOGY
in the ▶ NEW
MILLENNIUM

In the Global Research Lab

Imagine that you are a psychologist in Australia and that you have complex data from studies of twins on the subject of, say, sexual orientation. A question arises and you would like to confer with a colleague in, say, Chicago. Using a high-speed, long-distance telephone line, the data are transferred from your computer to your colleague's within minutes. Your colleague then analyzes the data and the two of you compare results.

This example of transfer of information may sound familiar enough. It is used every day. The example just given refers to an exchange of information between Nick Martin at the Queensland Institute of Medical Research and J. Michael Bailey at Northwestern University (Azar, 1994d).

But electronic developments are linking the world's researchers yet more closely. Psychologist Gary Olson and his colleagues at the University of Michigan are studying the ways in which electronic equipment can be used to match the ways in which researchers do their work (Azar, 1994c). One finding is that researchers are frequently inspired to strike out in new directions as they observe the work of other researchers thousands of miles away. Researcher B may access Researcher A's data, analyze it, and suggest modifications to Researcher A's study before Researcher A has completed the first phase of the study!

Graduate students and veterans alike stand to profit from the new global computer linkages. Graduate students are, in effect, apprentices who can learn by observing the interactions of other scientists (Azar, 1994c). They can also participate in research that is under way, providing fresh insights. Electronic interactions tend to be more candid and democratic than face-to-face interactions. Thus, the barriers between revered, established researchers and novices may be brought tumbling down—all to the betterment of psychological knowledge. ■

■ METHODS OF STUDYING THE BRAIN

The Brain—is wider than the Sky—
 For—put them side by side—
The one the other will contain
 With ease—and You beside—

EMILY DICKINSON

Just where is that elusive piece of business you think of as your "mind"? Thousands of years ago, it was not generally thought that the mind had a place to hang its hat within the body. It was common to assume that the body was inhabited by demons or souls that could not be explained in terms of physical substance. After all, if you look inside a human being, the biological structures you find do not look all that different from those of many lower animals. Thus, it seemed to make sense that those qualities that made us distinctly human—such as abstract thought, poetry, science, and the composition of music—were unrelated to substances that you could see, feel, and weigh on a scale.

Ancient Egyptians attributed control of the human being to a little person, or **homunculus,** who dwelled within the skull and regulated behavior. The Greek philosopher Aristotle thought that the soul had set up living quarters in the heart. After all, serious injury to the heart could be said to cause the soul to take flight from the body.

Today, however, we recognize that the mind, or consciousness, dwells within the brain (Goldman-Rakic, 1995; Sperry, 1993). Our knowledge of the brain is based on the effects of accidents and on research methods that are designed to allow us to discover the links between the psychological and the biological. Some of these methods involve methods of observation. Other methods involve experimentation.

ACCIDENTS Consider the accidents that have taught us about the brain. From injuries to the head—some of them minimal, some horrendous—we have learned that brain damage can impair consciousness and awareness. Brain damage can result in loss of vision and hearing, confusion, or loss of memory. In some cases, the loss of large portions of the brain may result in little loss of function. Ironically, the loss of smaller portions in particularly sensitive locations can result in language problems, memory loss, or death.

ELECTRICAL STIMULATION OF THE BRAIN (ESB) Experiments in electrical stimulation of areas in animal and human brains have shown that portions of the surface of the brain are associated with specific types of sensations (such as sensation of light or a touch on the torso) or motor activities (such as movement of a leg). ESB has shown that a tiny group of structures near the center of the brain (the hypothalamus) is involved in sexual and aggressive behavior patterns. It has also shown that a rectangular structure that rises from the back part of the brain into the forebrain (the reticular activating system) is involved in wakefulness and sleep.

HOMUNCULUS • (hoe-MONK-you-luss). Latin for "little man." A homunculus within the brain was once thought to govern human behavior.

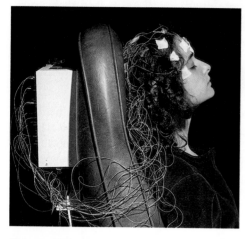

FIGURE 2.9
THE ELECTROENCEPHALOGRAPH (EEG)

LESION • (LEE-shun). An injury that results in impaired behavior or loss of a function.
ELECTROENCEPHALOGRAPH • (el-eck-trow-en-SEFF-uh-lo-graf). An instrument that measures electrical activity of the brain. Abbreviated *EEG*. ("Cephalo-" derives from the Greek *kephale,* meaning "head.")
COMPUTERIZED AXIAL TOMOGRAPHY • (AX-ee-al toe-MOG-raf-fee). Formation of a computer-generated image of the anatomical details of the brain by passing a narrow X-ray beam through the head and measuring from different angles the amount of radiation that passes through. Abbreviated *CAT scan.*
POSITRON EMISSION TOMOGRAPHY • (POZZ-I-tron). Formation of a computer-generated image of the neural activity of parts of the brain by tracing the amount of glucose used by the various parts. Abbreviated *PET scan.*
MAGNETIC RESONANCE IMAGING • (REZZ-oh-nants). Formation of a computer-generated image of the anatomy of the brain by measuring the signals emitted when the head is placed in a strong magnetic field.

FIGURE 2.10
THE COMPUTERIZED AXIAL TOMOGRAPH
(CAT) SCAN

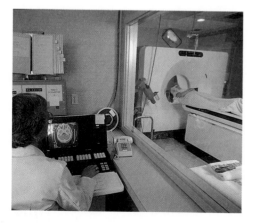

LESIONS Accidents have shown us how destruction of certain parts of the brain is related to behavioral changes in humans. Intentional **lesions** in the brains of laboratory animals have led to more specific knowledge. For example, destroying one part of the limbic system causes rats and monkeys to behave gently. Destruction of another part of the limbic system causes monkeys to become enraged at the slightest provocation. Destruction of yet another area of the limbic system prevents animals from forming new memories.

THE ELECTROENCEPHALOGRAPH (EEG) The **electroencephalograph** records the electrical activity of the brain. When I was an undergraduate psychology student, I first heard that psychologists studied sleep by "connecting" people to the EEG. I had a gruesome image of people somehow being plugged in. Not so. As suggested in Figure 2.9, electrodes are simply attached to the scalp with tape or paste. Later, once the brain activity under study has been duly recorded, the electrodes are removed. A bit of soap and water and you're as good as new.

The EEG detects minute amounts of electrical activity—called brain waves—that pass between the electrodes. Certain brain waves are associated with feelings of relaxation and with various stages of sleep (see Chapter 6). Researchers and physicians use the EEG to locate the areas of the brain that respond to certain stimuli, such as lights or sounds, and to diagnose some kinds of abnormal behavior. The EEG also helps locate tumors.

THE CAT SCAN The computer's capacity to generate images of the parts of the brain from various sources of radiation has led to the development of imaging techniques that have been useful to researchers and physicians (Goleman, 1995; Posner & Raichle, 1994). In one technique, **computerized axial tomography** (the CAT scan), a narrow X-ray beam is passed through the head. The amount of radiation that passes through is measured simultaneously from multiple angles (see Figure 2.10). The computer integrates these measurements into a three-dimensional view of the brain. As a result, brain damage and other abnormalities that years ago could be detected only by surgery can now be displayed on a video monitor.

THE PET SCAN A second method, **positron emission tomography** (the PET scan), forms a computer-generated image of the activity of parts of the brain by tracing the amount of glucose used (or metabolized) by these parts. More glucose is metabolized in the parts of the brain in which activity is greater. To trace the metabolism of glucose, a harmless amount of a radioactive compound, called a *tracer,* is mixed with glucose and injected into the bloodstream. When the glucose reaches the brain, the patterns of activity are revealed by measurement of the positrons—positively charged particles—that are given off by the tracer. The PET scan has been used by researchers to see which parts of the brain are most active when we are, for example, listening to music, working out a math problem, using language, or playing chess ("Pinpointing Chess Moves," 1994; Sarter and others, 1996). As shown in Figure 2.11, patterns of activity in the brains of people diagnosed with schizophrenia appear to differ from patterns of other people. Researchers are exploring the meanings and potential applications of these differences.

MRI A third imaging technique is **magnetic resonance imaging (MRI).** In MRI, the person lies in a powerful magnetic field and is exposed to radio waves that cause parts of the brain to emit signals, which are measured from multiple angles. The PET scan assesses brain activity in terms of metabolism of glucose. MRI relies on subtle shifts in blood flow. (More blood flows to more active parts of the brain, supplying them with oxygen.) As with the CAT scan, the signals are integrated into an anatomic image (see Figure 2.12).

In *functional* or *fast MRI*, computer programs in effect turn static images into movies. Fast MRI yields sharper pictures than the PET scan (Raichle, 1994). Researchers are using fast MRI to pinpoint parts of the brain that are active when people engage in activities such as viewing objects with various shapes (for example, moving dots or colored stripes), pressing a lever when the name of a dangerous animal is mentioned, or reporting the first verb that comes to mind when researchers say a noun (Raichle, 1994).

All these methods make it clear that the mind is a manifestation of the brain. Without the brain, there is no mind. Within the brain lies the potential for self-awareness and purposeful activity. Somehow, the brain gives rise to the mind. Today it is generally agreed that for every mental event such as a thought or a feeling there are underlying biological events.

The use of some research methods, such as lesioning, raises ethical issues. To study behavior properly, psychologists must not only be skilled in the uses and limitations of research methods but must also treat research subjects in an ethical manner.

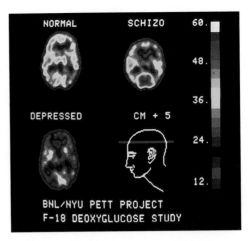

FIGURE 2.11
THE POSITRON EMISSION TOMOGRAPH (PET) SCAN

These PET scans of the brains of normal, schizophrenic, and depressed individuals are computer-generated images of neural activity as indicated by the amount of glucose metabolized by parts of their brains. More active parts metabolize more glucose. Metabolic activity ranges from low (blue) to high (red).

REFLECTIONS

- Before reading this section, did you believe that your mind, or sense of consciousness, dwelled within your brain? Why or why not?
- Are you aware of anyone who has had a scan by one of the techniques discussed in this section? What was the experience like? What was the purpose of the scan?

ETHICAL • Moral; referring to one's system of deriving standards for determining what is moral.

■ ETHICAL ISSUES IN PSYCHOLOGICAL RESEARCH AND PRACTICE

It is in the area of ethics that we raise the most serious questions about the Milgram studies. The Milgram studies on obedience made key contributions to our understanding of the limits of human nature. In fact, it is difficult for professional psychologists to imagine a history of psychology without the knowledge provided by such studies. But the subjects experienced severe psychological anguish. Were the Milgram studies **ethical**?

Psychologists adhere to a number of ethical standards that are intended to promote individual dignity, human welfare, and scientific integrity (McGovern and others, 1991). They also ensure that psychologists do not undertake research methods or treatments that are harmful to subjects or clients (American Psychological Association, 1992a). Let us look at these ethical standards as they apply to research with humans and with other animals.

• *Research With Humans*

Lang and his colleagues (1975) gave small doses of alcohol to college students who were social drinkers. Other researchers, however, have paid alcoholics—people who have difficulty limiting their alcohol consumption—to drink in the laboratory so that they could study their reactions and those of family members

FIGURE 2.12
MAGNETIC RESONANCE IMAGING (MRI)
An MRI image of the brain.

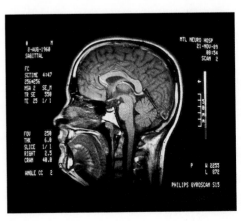

(e.g., Jacob and others, 1991). Practices such as these raise ethical questions. For example, paying the alcoholics to drink in the laboratory, and providing the alcohol, could be viewed as encouraging them to engage in self-destructive behavior (Koocher, 1991).

Recall the signs of stress shown by the subjects in the Milgram studies on obedience. They trembled, stuttered, groaned, sweated, bit their lips, and dug their fingernails into their flesh. In fact, if Milgram had attempted to run his experiments in the 1990s rather than in the 1960s, he might have been denied permission to do so by a university ethics review committee. In virtually all institutional settings, including colleges, hospitals, and research foundations, **ethics review committees** help researchers consider the potential harm of their methods and review proposed studies according to ethical guidelines. When such committees find that proposed research might be unacceptably harmful to subjects, they may withhold approval until the proposal has been modified. Ethics review committees also weigh the potential benefits of research against the potential harm.

Today individuals must also provide **informed consent** before they participate in research programs. Having a general overview of the research and the opportunity to choose not to participate apparently gives them a sense of control and decreases the stress of participating (Dill and others, 1982). Is there a way in which subjects in the Milgram studies could have provided informed consent? What do you think?

Psychologists treat the records of research subjects and clients as **confidential.** This is because they respect people's privacy and also because people are more likely to express their true thoughts and feelings when researchers or therapists keep their disclosures confidential. Sometimes conflicts of interest arise, however, as when a client threatens a third party and the psychologist feels an obligation to warn that person (Nevid and others, 1997).

Ethics limit the types of research that psychologists may conduct. For example, how can we determine whether early separation from one's mother impairs social development? One way would be to observe the development of children who have been separated from their mothers at an early age. It is difficult to draw conclusions from such research, however, because of the selection factor. That is, the same factors that led to the separation—such as family tragedy or irresponsible parents—and *not* the separation, may have led to the outcome. Scientifically, it would be more sound to run experiments in which researchers separate children from their mothers at an early age and compare their development with that of other children. But psychologists would not undertake such research because of the ethical issues they pose. Yet, they do run experiments with lower animals in which infants are separated from mothers.

THE USE OF DECEPTION Many psychological experiments cannot be run without deceiving the people who participate. However, the use of deception raises ethical issues. You are probably skeptical enough to wonder whether the "teachers" in the Milgram studies actually shocked the "learners" when the teachers pressed the levers on the console. They didn't. The only real shock in this experiment was the 45-volt sample given to the teachers. Its purpose was to make the procedure believable.

The learners in the experiment were actually confederates of the experimenter. They had not answered the newspaper ads but were in on the truth from the start. The "teachers" were the only real subjects. They were led to believe that they had been chosen at random for the teacher role, but the choosing was rigged so that newspaper recruits would always become teachers.

As you can imagine, many psychologists have debated the ethics of deceiving subjects in the Milgram studies (Fisher & Fyrberg, 1994). According to the

ETHICS REVIEW COMMITTEE • A group found in an institutional setting that helps researchers consider the potential harm of their methods and reviews proposed studies according to ethical guidelines.
INFORMED CONSENT • The term used by psychologists to indicate that a person has agreed to participate in research after receiving information about the purposes of the study and the nature of the treatments.
CONFIDENTIAL • Secret; not to be disclosed.

American Psychological Association's (1992a) *Ethical Principles of Psychologists and Code of Conduct,* psychologists may use deception only when

- they believe that the benefits of the research outweigh its potential harm,
- they believe that the individuals might have been willing to participate if they had understood the benefits of the research, and
- subjects receive an explanation afterward.

Regardless of the ethics of Milgram's research, we must acknowledge that it has highlighted some hard truths about human nature.

Return to the Lang (Lang and others, 1975) study on alcohol and aggression. In this study, the researchers (1) misinformed subjects about the beverage they were drinking and (2) misled them into believing that they were giving other subjects electric shock when they, like the subjects in the Milgram studies, were actually only pressing switches on a dead control board. (*Aggression* was defined as pressing these switches in the study.) In the Lang study, students who believed they had drunk vodka were "more aggressive"—that is, selected higher levels of shock—than students who believed they had not. The actual content of the beverages was immaterial.

The Lang study, like the Milgram studies, could not have been carried out without deception. Foiling subjects' expectations was crucial to the experiment. One can debate whether the potential benefits of the research outweigh the possible harm of deception.

Psychological ethics require that research subjects who are deceived be **debriefed** afterward. Debriefing helps eliminate misconceptions and anxieties about the research and leave subjects with their dignity intact. After the Lang study was completed, for example, the subjects were informed of the deceptions and of the rationale for them. Subjects who had actually drunk alcohol were given coffee and a breathalyzer test so that the researchers could be sure they were not leaving the laboratory while intoxicated.

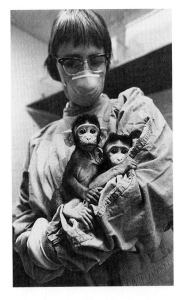

Ethics and Animal Research. Is it ethical for researchers to harm animals in order to obtain knowledge that may benefit humans?

Truth or Fiction Revisited

It is true that psychologists would not be able to carry out certain kinds of research without deceiving subjects as to the purposes and methods of the studies.

• *Research With Animals*

Psychologists and other scientists frequently use animals to conduct research that cannot be carried out with humans. For example, experiments on the effects of early separation from the mother have been done with monkeys and other animals. Such research has helped psychologists investigate the formation of attachment bonds between parent and child (see Chapter 4).

Experiments with infant monkeys highlight some of the dilemmas faced by psychologists and other scientists who contemplate potentially harmful research. Psychologists and biologists who study the workings of the brain destroy sections of the brains of laboratory animals to learn how they influence behavior. For instance, a lesion in one part of a brain structure will cause a rat to overeat (see Chapter 11). A lesion elsewhere will cause the rat to go on a crash diet. Psychologists generalize to humans from experiments such as these in the hope of finding solutions to problems such as eating disorders. Proponents of the use of animals in research argue that major advances in medicine and psychology could not have taken place without them (Fowler, 1992; Pardes and others, 1991).

The majority of psychologists disapprove of research in which animals are exposed to pain or killed (Plous, 1996). According to the ethical guidelines of the American Psychological Association (1992c), animals may be harmed only when there is no alternative and when researchers believe that the benefits of the research will justify the harm.

DEBRIEF • To elicit information about a just-completed procedure.

THINKING CRITICALLY ABOUT TEA LEAVES, BIRD DROPPINGS, PALMS, AND THE STARS

This chapter explores the methods used by psychologists. We have seen that psychologists are critical thinkers. They are skeptical. They insist on seeing the evidence before they will accept people's claims and arguments as to what is truth and what is fiction. The same procedures can be applied to pseudosciences (false sciences) such as astrology. Pseudoscience beckons us from magazines and tabloids at supermarket checkout counters. Each week, there are 10 new sightings of Elvis and 10 new encounters with extraterrestrials. There are 10 new "absolutely proven effective" ways to take off weight and 10 new ways to beat stress and depression. There are 10 new ways to tell if your partner has been cheating and, of course, 10 new predictions by astrologers and psychics.

Let's focus on one example of pseudoscience. Begin with this personality test: Circle the letter that shows whether each item is mostly true or false for you. Then read the report that follows to learn everything you always wanted to know about your personality but were too intelligent to ask.

T F 1. I can't unclasp my hands.

T F 2. I often mistake my hands for food.

T F 3. I never liked room temperature.

T F 4. My throat is closer than it seems.

T F 5. Likes and dislikes are among my favorites.

T F 6. I've lost all sensation in my throat.

T F 7. I try to swallow at least three times a day.

T F 8. My squirrels don't know where I am tonight.

T F 9. Walls impede my progress.

T F 10. My toes are numbered.

T F 11. My beaver won't go near the water.

Total Number marked true (T): _____
If your total number of items marked true was between 0 and 11, the following personality report applies to you:

> The personality test you have taken has been found to predict inner potential for change. . . . In the past it has been shown that people with similar personality scores . . . have a strong capacity for change. . . . You have a great deal of unused potential you have not yet turned to your advantage. . . .
>
> The test also suggests that you display ability for personal integration and many latent strengths, as well as the ability to maintain a balance between your inner impulses and the demands of outer reality. Therefore, your personality is such that you have a strong potential for improvement (Halperin & Snyder, 1979, pp.142–143).

That's you all right, isn't it? I shouldn't be surprised if you thought it sounded familiar. Psychologists Keith Halperin and C. R. Snyder (1979) administered a phony 50-item personality questionnaire to women in an introductory psychology course at the University of Kansas. The items weren't as silly as the ones you answered, which were thrown together by Daniel Wegner (1979) and some friends during their graduate school days. Still, the test was meaningless. The students then rated the same personality report, which included the paragraphs just cited, for accuracy. The average rating was "quite accurate"!

Truth or Fiction Revisited

It is true that a psychologist could write a believable personality report about you without interviewing you, testing you, or even knowing who you are. Such reports are generalized; they have "something for everyone." The tendency to believe them has been termed the Barnum effect.

Women who had read the phony report and women who had not then participated in a therapy program conducted by the researchers. Believe it or not, women who had obtained the report, which underscored their capacity for change, showed greater improvement from the treatment than women who had not. When you believe that you have the capacity to improve your lot—when your self-efficacy expectations are raised—you are apparently more likely to succeed.

The tendency to believe a generalized (but phony) personality report has been labeled the Barnum effect after circus magnate P. T. Barnum, who once declared that a good circus had a "little something for everybody." It is probably the Barnum effect—the tendency for general personality reports to have a "little something for everybody"—that allows fortune-tellers to make a living. That is, most of us have enough characteristics in common so that a fortune-teller's "revelations" about our personalities may have the ring of truth.

IS THERE A "SUCKER BORN EVERY MINUTE?"
Most of us have personality traits in common. But what do tea leaves, bird droppings, palms (of your

hands, not on the tropical sands), and the stars have in common? Let us see.

P. T. Barnum once declared, "There's a sucker born every minute." The tendency to believe generalized personality reports has made people vulnerable to fakirs and phonies throughout history. It enriches the pocketbooks of people who offer to "read their personalities" and predict their futures based on patterns of tea leaves or bird droppings. These particular phony methods of "personality measurement" and forecasting are not all that fashionable today, but reading palms, consulting ghosts through "spiritualists," and studying the movements of the stars and planets through astrology are (Browne, 1995). Now and then we also hear of "psychics" who are recruited by police departments to help find missing persons or criminals. (We don't usually hear that they have found them.)

Astrology has been popular for centuries (Maher & Maher, 1994). Gallup and Newport (1991) report that one person out of four in the United States believes in astrology. Another one in four to five are not sure. Put it this way: In an age in which science has proved itself capable of making significant contributions to people's daily lives and health, more people are likely to check their horoscope than to seek scientific information when they have a decision to make.

Astrology is based on the notion that the positions of the sun, the moon, and the stars affect human temperament and human affairs (Maher & Maher, 1994). For example, people born under the sign of Jupiter are believed to be jovial, or full of playful good humor. People born under the sign of Saturn are thought to be gloomy and morose (saturnine). And people born under the sign of Mars are believed to be warlike (martial). One supposedly can also foretell the future by studying the positions of these bodies.

Astrologers maintain that the positions of the heavenly bodies at the time of our birth determines our personality and our destiny. They prepare forecasts called *horoscopes* that are based on the month during which we were born and which indicate whether it is safe for us to undertake various activities on various days. If you get involved with someone who asks for your "sign" (for example, Aquarius or Taurus), he or she is inquiring about your birthdate in astrological terms. Astrologers claim that your sign, which reflects the month during which you were born, indicates whom you will be compatible with. You may have been wondering whether you should date someone of another religion. If you start to follow astrology, you may also be wondering whether it is safe for a Sagittarius to be dating a Pisces or a Gemini.

Although psychologists consider astrology to be a pseudoscience, it has millions of followers. How do we account for its allure? What can we tell people who believe in it?

Supporters of astrology tend to provide arguments such as the following:

- Astrology has been practiced for many centuries and is a time-honored aspect of human history, tradition, and culture (Crowe, 1990).
- Astrology seems to provide a path to the core of meaning in the universe for people who are uneducated, and for a fortunate few with limited means, a road to riches.
- People in high positions in government have followed the advice of astrologers. (Nancy Reagan, wife of former president Ronald Reagan, is reported to have consulted an astrologer in arranging her husband's schedule.)
- One heavenly body (the moon) is powerful enough to sway the tides of the seas. The pulls of heavenly bodies are therefore easily capable of affecting people's destinies (Crowe, 1990).
- Astrology is a special art and not a science. Therefore, it is inappropriate to subject astrology to the rigors of scientific testing (Crowe, 1990).
- Astrology has been shown to work (Crowe, 1990).

Refer to the principles of critical thinking outlined in Chapter 1 as you consider the claims of astrologers. For example, does the fact that there may be a long-standing tradition in astrology affect its scientific credibility? Does Nancy Reagan's (or anyone else's) possible belief in astrology affect its scientific credibility? Are the tides of the seas comparable to human personality and destiny?

Psychology is an empirical science. In an *empirical* science, beliefs about the behavior of cosmic rays, chemical compounds, cells, people—or the meaning of bird droppings or the movements of the stars—must be supported by evidence. Persuasive arguments and reference to authority figures are *not* scientific evidence (Kimble, 1994).

Astrologers have made specific forecasts of events, and their accuracy—or lack of it—provides researchers with a means of evaluating astrology. It turns out that astrological predictions are no more likely to come true than predictions based on pure chance (Crowe, 1990; Dean, 1987; Kelly and others, 1989). That is scientific fact, but let me ask you a question: Will followers of astrology be dissuaded by facts? Perhaps some will. But cognitive dissonance theory (discussed in Chapter 11) suggests that the faith of some followers of astrology will be *strengthened* when predictions are not borne out. (Perhaps your instructor will permit you to glance ahead for an explanation.) ∎

SUMMARY

1. **What is the scientific method?** The scientific method is an organized way of going about expanding and refining knowledge. Psychologists usually begin by formulating a research question, which may be reworded as a hypothesis. They reach conclusions about their research questions or the accuracy of their hypotheses on the basis of their research observations or findings.

2. **How do psychologists use samples to represent populations?** The individuals who are studied are referred to as a sample. A sample is a segment of a population. Samples must accurately represent the population they are intended to reflect. Women's groups and health professionals argue that there is a historic bias in favor of conducting research with men. Research samples have also tended to underrepresent minority ethnic groups in the population.

3. **What kinds of sampling are undertaken to ensure that samples represent populations?** In a random sample, each member of a population has an equal chance of being selected to participate. Researchers can also use a stratified sample, which is selected so that identified subgroups in the population are represented proportionately in the sample.

4. **What is volunteer bias?** The concept behind volunteer bias is that people who offer to participate in research studies differ systematically from people who do not.

5. **What methods of observation are used by psychologists?** The methods used include the case study, survey, testing, naturalistic observation, and laboratory observation. Case studies gather information about the lives of individuals or small groups. The survey method uses interviews, questionnaires, or public records to gather information about behavior that

cannot be observed directly. Psychological tests are used to measure various traits and characteristics among a population. The naturalistic observation method observes behavior where it happens—"in the field," while the laboratory-observation method observes behavior in a controlled environment.

6. **What is a correlation?** Correlations reveal relationships between variables, but do not determine cause and effect. In a positive correlation, variables increase simultaneously. A correlation coefficient of about 10.90 is considered adequate for test reliability (that is, consistency from one occasion to another). A correlation coefficient of about 10.60 to 10.70 is considered adequate for test validity (that is, whether it measures what it is supposed to measure). In a negative correlation, one variable increases while the other decreases.

7. **What is the experimental method?** Experiments are used to discover cause and effect—that is, the effects of independent variables on dependent variables. Experimental groups receive a specific treatment, while control groups do not. Blinds and double blinds may be used to control for the effects of the expectations of the subjects and the researchers. Results can be generalized only to populations that have been adequately represented in the research samples.

8. **What are the ethical standards of psychologists?** Ethical standards are intended to prevent mistreatment of humans and animals in the course of research. Limits are set on the discomfort that may be imposed on animals. Records of human behavior are kept confidential. Human subjects are required to give informed consent prior to participating in research.

To enhance your understanding of the psychological concepts found in this chapter, please consult the following aids:

STUDY GUIDE

Learning Objectives, p. 19
Exercise, p. 20
Lecture and Textbook Outline,
    p. 22
Effective Studying Ideas, p. 24

Key Terms and Concepts, p. 25
Chapter Review, p. 25
Chapter Exercises, p. 32
Knowing the Language, p. 33
Do You Know the Material?, p. 34

CORE CONCEPTS SEARCH

Correlations
Research Ethics
The Experimental Method

WORLD WIDE WEB

For more information concerning the topics found in this chapter, access psychology links on the World Wide Web made through the Harcourt Brace webpage at

www.hbcollege.com

Share your comments and questions with your author at

PsychLinks@aol.com

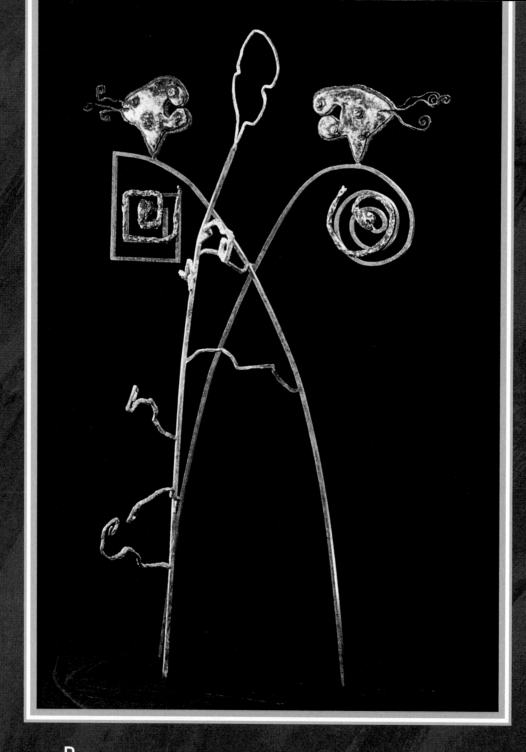

Psychology is the scientific study of behavior and mental processes. The nervous system that makes our mental processes and behavior possible does not at all resemble our experience of them. This sculpture by Grace Bakst Wapner, *Shall Be as Numerous as Grains of Sand II* (1992), is reminiscent of parts of the nervous system. One of the great mysteries of science is how the nervous system allows us to be aware of ourselves and our experiences.

GRACE BAKST WAPNER

Chapter 3
Biology and Behavior

TRUTH OR FICTION?

T F

☐ ☐ A single cell can stretch all the way down your back to your big toe.

☐ ☐ Messages travel in the brain by means of electricity.

☐ ☐ Alzheimer's disease is a normal part of growing old.

☐ ☐ The human brain is larger than that of any other animal.

☐ ☐ Fear can give you indigestion.

☐ ☐ If a surgeon were to stimulate a certain part of your brain electrically, you might swear in court that someone had stroked your leg.

☐ ☐ PMS impairs the academic, occupational, or social functioning of the majority of college women.

☐ ☐ Women can do little about menstrual discomfort other than "tough it out."

☐ ☐ You can't buy happiness.

OUTLINE

NEURONS: INTO THE FABULOUS FOREST
The Makeup of Neurons
The Neural Impulse: Let Us "Sing the Body Electric"
The Synapse
Neurotransmitters

THE NERVOUS SYSTEM
The Central Nervous System
The Peripheral Nervous System

THE CEREBRAL CORTEX
The Geography of the Cerebral Cortex
Thought, Language, and the Cortex
Left Brain, Right Brain?
Handedness: Is It Gauche or Sinister to Be Left-Handed?
Split-Brain Experiments: When Hemispheres Stop Communicating

THE ENDOCRINE SYSTEM
The Hypothalamus
The Pituitary Gland: The Pea-Sized Governor
The Pancreas: How Sweet It Is (or Isn't)
The Thyroid Gland: The Body's Accelerator
The Adrenal Glands: Coping With Stress
The Testes and the Ovaries
Psychology in a World of Diversity: Cross-Cultural Perspectives on Menstruation
Psychology and Modern Life: Coping With PMS

HEREDITY: THE NATURE OF NATURE
Genes and Chromosomes
Kinship Studies
Psychology in the New Millennium: How Many of You Are There? How Many Will There Be?
Psychology and Modern Life: Health Applications of the Human Genome Project

*A*CCORDING TO THE BIG BANG THEORY, our universe began with an enormous explosion that sent countless particles hurtling outward through space. For billions of years, these particles have been forming immense gas clouds. Galaxies and solar systems have been condensing from the clouds, sparkling for some eons, and then winking out. Human beings came into existence only recently on an unremarkable rock circling an average star in a standard spiral galaxy.

Since the beginning of time, the universe has been changing. Change has brought life and death and countless challenges. Some creatures have adapted successfully to these challenges. Others have not met the challenges and have become extinct. Some have left fossil records. Others have disappeared without a trace.

At first, human survival required a greater struggle than it does today. We fought predators such as leopards. We foraged across parched lands for food. We might have warred with creatures very much like ourselves—creatures who have since become extinct. We prevailed. The human species has survived and continues to transmit its unique traits through the generations by means of genetic material whose chemical codes are only now being cracked.

Yet, exactly what is handed down through the generations? The answer is biological, or physiological, structures and processes. Our biology serves as the material base for our observable behaviors, emotions, and cognitions (our thoughts, images, and plans). Biology gives rise to specific behavioral tendencies in some organisms, such as the chick's instinctive fear of the hawk's shadow (Knight, 1994). But most psychologists believe that human behavior is flexible and is influenced by learning and choice as well as by heredity.

Biological psychologists (or psychobiologists) work at the interface of psychology and biology. They study the ways in which our mental processes and behaviors are linked to biological structures and processes. In recent years, biological psychologists have been exploring these links in several areas:

1. *Neurons.* Neurons are the building blocks of the nervous system. There are billions upon billions of neurons in the body—perhaps as many as there are stars in the Milky Way galaxy.

2. *The nervous system.* Neurons combine to form the structures of the nervous system. The nervous system has branches that are responsible for muscle movement, perception, automatic functions such as breathing and the secretion of hormones, and psychological events such as thoughts and feelings.

3. *The cerebral cortex.* The cerebral cortex is the large, wrinkled mass inside your head that you think of as your brain. Actually, it is only one part of the brain—the part that is the most characteristically human.

4. *The endocrine system.* Through secretion of hormones, the endocrine

system controls functions ranging from growth in children to production of milk in nursing women.

5. *Heredity.* Within every cell of your body there are about 100,000 genes. These chemical substances determine just what type of creature you are, from the color of your hair to your body temperature to the fact that you have arms and legs rather than wings or fins.

■ NEURONS: INTO THE FABULOUS FOREST

Let us begin our journey in a fabulous forest of nerve cells, or **neurons,** that can be visualized as having branches, trunks, and roots—something like trees. As in other forests, many nerve cells lie alongside one another like a thicket of trees. Neurons can also lie end to end, however, with their "roots" intertwined with the "branches" of neurons that lie below. Trees receive water and nutrients from the soil. Neurons receive "messages" from a number of sources such as light, other neurons, and pressure on the skin, and they can pass these messages along to one another.

Neurons communicate by means of chemicals called **neurotransmitters.** They release neurotransmitters, which are taken up by other neurons, muscles, and glands. Neurotransmitters cause chemical changes in the receiving neuron so that the message can travel along its "trunk," be translated back into neurotransmitters in its "branches," and then travel through the small spaces between neurons to be received by the "roots" of yet other neurons. Each neuron transmits and coordinates messages in the form of neural impulses.

We are born with more than 100 billion neurons. Most of them are found in the brain. The nervous system also contains **glial cells.** These nourish and insulate neurons, direct their growth, and remove waste products from the nervous system. But neurons occupy center stage in the nervous system. The messages transmitted by neurons somehow account for phenomena ranging from the perception of an itch from a mosquito bite to the coordination of a skier's vision and muscles to the composition of a concerto to the solution of an algebraic equation.

• *The Makeup of Neurons*

Neurons vary according to their functions and their location. Some neurons in the brain are only a fraction of an inch in length, whereas others in the legs are several feet long. Every neuron is a single nerve cell with a cell body, dendrites, and an axon (see Figure 3.1). The cell body contains the nucleus of the cell. It uses oxygen and nutrients to generate the energy needed to carry out the work of the cell. Anywhere from a few to several hundred short fibers, or **dendrites,** extend like roots from the cell body to receive incoming messages from thousands of adjoining neurons. Each neuron has one **axon** that extends like a trunk from the cell body. Axons are very thin, but those that carry messages from the toes to the spinal cord extend for several feet.

Like tree trunks, axons too can divide and extend in different directions. Axons end in small bulb-shaped structures which are aptly named called **terminals.** Neurons carry messages in one direction only: from the dendrites or cell body through the axon to the axon terminals. The messages are then transmitted from the terminals to other neurons.

As a child matures, the axons of neurons become longer and the dendrites and terminals proliferate, creating vast interconnected networks for the

---

Truth or Fiction Revisited

It is true that a single cell can stretch all the way down your back to your big toe. These cells are neurons. Question: How can cells that are this long be "microscopic"?

NEURON • (NEW-ron). A nerve cell.
NEUROTRANSMITTERS • (new-row-tranz-MIT-ters). Chemical substances involved in the transmission of neural impulses from one neuron to another.
GLIAL CELLS • (GLEE-al). Cells that nourish and insulate neurons, direct their growth, and remove waste products from the nervous system.
DENDRITES • Rootlike structures, attached to the cell body of a neuron, that receive impulses from other neurons. (Derived from the Greek word for "tree.")
AXON • (AX-on). A long, thin part of a neuron that transmits impulses to other neurons from branching structures called *terminals.*
TERMINALS • Bulb-shaped structures at the tips of axons.

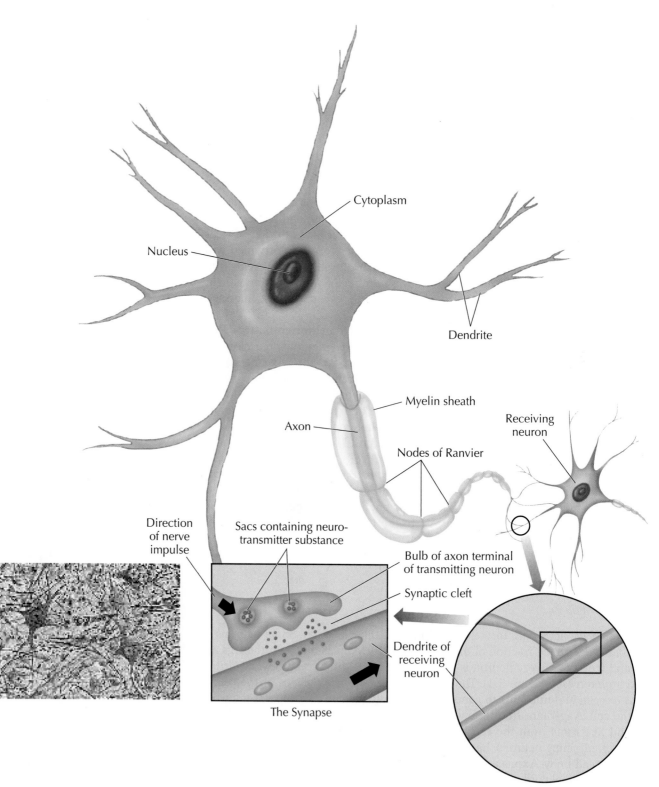

FIGURE 3.1

THE ANATOMY OF A NEURON

"Messages" enter neurons through dendrites, are transmitted along the trunklike axon, and then are sent from axon terminals to muscles, glands, and other neurons. Axon terminals contain sacs of chemicals called *neurotransmitters*. Neurotransmitters are released into the synaptic cleft, where many of them are taken up by receptor sites on the dendrites of receiving neuron. Dozens of neurotransmitters have been identified.

transmission of complex messages. The number of glial cells also increases as the nervous system develops, contributing to its dense appearance.

MYELIN The axons of many neurons are wrapped tightly with white, fatty **myelin** that makes them look like strings of sausages under the microscope (bratwurst, actually). The fat insulates the axon from electrically charged atoms, or ions, found in the fluids that surround the nervous system. The myelin sheath minimizes leakage of the electric current being carried along the axon, thereby allowing messages to be conducted more efficiently.

Myelination is part of the maturation process that leads to the child's ability to crawl and walk during the first year. Infants are not physiologically "ready" to engage in visual-motor coordination and other activities until the coating process reaches certain levels. In people with the disease multiple sclerosis, myelin is replaced with a hard fibrous tissue that throws off the timing of nerve impulses and disrupts muscular control. Affliction of the neurons that control breathing can result in suffocation.

AFFERENT AND EFFERENT NEURONS If someone steps on your toes, the sensation is registered by receptors or sensory neurons near the surface of your skin. Then it is transmitted to the spinal cord and brain through **afferent neurons,** which are perhaps 2 to 3 feet long. In the brain, subsequent messages might be buffeted by associative neurons that are only a few thousandths of an inch long. You experience the pain through this process and perhaps entertain some rather nasty thoughts about the perpetrator, who is now apologizing and begging for understanding. Long before you arrive at any logical conclusions, however, motor neurons **(efferent neurons)** send messages to your foot so that you withdraw it and begin an impressive hopping routine. Other efferent neurons stimulate glands so that your heart is now beating more rapidly, you are sweating, and the hair on the back of your arms has become erect! Being a good sport, you say, "Oh, it's nothing." But considering all the neurons involved, it really *is* something, isn't it?

In case you think that afferent and efferent neurons will be hard to distinguish because they sound pretty much the SAME to you, remember that they *are* the "SAME." That is, *S*ensory = *A*fferent, and *M*otor = *E*fferent. But don't tell your professor I let you in on this secret.

• *The Neural Impulse: Let Us "Sing the Body Electric"*[1]

In the 18th century, the Italian physiologist Luigi Galvani (1737–1798) conducted a shocking experiment in a rainstorm. While his neighbors had the sense to remain indoors, Galvani and his wife were out on the porch connecting lightning rods to the heads of dissected frogs whose legs were connected by wires to a well of water. When lightning blazed above, the frogs' muscles contracted. This is not a recommended way to prepare frogs' legs. Galvani was demonstrating that the messages **(neural impulses)** that travel along neurons are electrochemical in nature.

Neural impulses travel somewhere between 2 (in nonmyelinated neurons) and 225 miles an hour (in myelinated neurons). This speed is not impressive when compared with that of an electric current in a toaster oven or a lamp, which can travel at the speed of light—over 186,000 miles per second. Distances in the body are short, however, and a message will travel from a toe to the brain in perhaps 1/50th of a second.

---

[1] From a poem by Walt Whitman.

MYELIN • (MY-uh-lin). A fatty substance that encases and insulates axons, facilitating transmission of neural impulses.
AFFERENT NEURONS • Neurons that transmit messages from sensory receptors to the spinal cord and brain. Also called *sensory neurons.*
EFFERENT NEURONS • Neurons that transmit messages from the brain or spinal cord to muscles and glands. Also called *motor neurons.*
NEURAL IMPULSE • (NEW-ral). The electrochemical discharge of a nerve cell, or neuron.

AN ELECTROCHEMICAL PROCESS The process by which neural impulses travel is electrochemical. Chemical changes take place within neurons that cause an electric charge to be transmitted along their lengths. In a resting state—that is, when a neuron is not being stimulated by its neighbors—there are relatively more positively charged sodium (Na+) ions and negatively charged chloride (Cl−) ions in the body fluid outside the neuron than in the fluid within the neuron. Positively charged potassium (K+) ions are more plentiful inside, but there are many other negative ions inside that are not balanced by negative ions on the outside. This gives the inside an overall negative charge in relation to the outside. The difference in electrical charge **polarizes** the neuron with a negative **resting potential** of about − 70 millivolts in relation to the body fluid outside the cell membrane.

When an area on the surface of the resting neuron is adequately stimulated by other neurons, the cell membrane in the area changes its permeability to allow sodium ions to enter. As a consequence, the area of entry becomes positively charged, or **depolarized** with respect to the outside (Figure 3.2). The permeability of the cell membrane then changes again, allowing no more sodium ions to enter.

The inside of the cell at the disturbed area has an **action potential,** of 110 millivolts. This action potential, added to the − 70 millivolts that characterize the resting potential, brings the membrane voltage to a positive charge of + 40 millivolts. This inner change causes the next section of the cell to become permeable to sodium ions. At the same time, potassium ions are being pumped out of the area of the cell that was previously affected, which then returns to its resting potential. In this way, the neural impulse is transmitted continuously along an axon that is not myelinated. Because the impulse is created anew as it progresses, its strength does not change.

The conduction of the neural impulse along the length of a neuron is what is meant by "firing." Some neurons fire in less than 1/1,000th of a second. In firing, neurons attempt to transmit the message to other neurons, muscles, or glands. However, other neurons will not fire unless the incoming messages combine to reach an adequate *threshold.* A weak message may cause a temporary shift in electrical charge at some point along a neuron's cell membrane, but this charge will dissipate if the neuron is not stimulated to its threshold.

Truth or Fiction Revisited

It is true that messages travel in the brain by means of electricity. However, this is not the whole story. Messages also travel from neurons to other neurons, muscles, or glands via chemical messengers termed neurotransmitters.

POLARIZE • To ready a neuron for firing by creating an internal negative charge in relation to the body fluid outside the cell membrane.

RESTING POTENTIAL • The electrical potential across the neural membrane when it is not responding to other neurons.

DEPOLARIZE • To reduce the resting potential of a cell membrane from about −70 millivolts toward zero.

ACTION POTENTIAL • The electrical impulse that provides the basis for the conduction of a neural impulse along an axon of a neuron.

FIGURE 3.2

THE NEURAL IMPULSE

When a section of a neuron is stimulated by other neurons, the cell membrane becomes permeable to sodium ions so that an action potential of about + 40 millivolts is induced. This action potential is transmitted along the axon. The neuron fires according to the all-or-none principle.

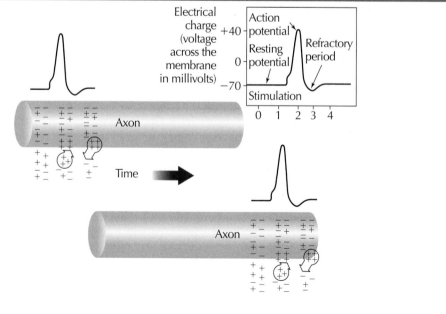

A neuron may transmit several hundred such messages in a second. Yet, in accordance with the **all-or-none principle,** each time a neuron fires, it transmits an impulse of the same strength. Neurons fire more frequently when they have been stimulated by larger numbers of other neurons. Stronger stimuli cause more frequent firing.

For a few thousandths of a second after firing, a neuron is insensitive to messages from other neurons and will not fire. It is said to be in a **refractory period.** This period is a time of recovery during which sodium is prevented from passing through the neuronal membrane. When we realize that such periods of recovery might take place hundreds of times per second, it seems a rapid recovery and a short rest indeed.

• The Synapse

A neuron relays its message to another neuron across a junction called a **synapse.** A synapse consists of a "branch," or an axon terminal from the transmitting neuron; a dendrite ("root"), or the body of a receiving neuron; and a fluid-filled gap between the two that is called the *synaptic cleft* (see Figure 3.1). Although the neural impulse is electrical, it does not jump across the synaptic cleft like a spark. Instead, when a nerve impulse reaches a synapse, axon terminals release chemicals into the synaptic cleft like myriad ships being cast into the sea.

• Neurotransmitters

In the axon terminals are sacs, or synaptic vesicles, that contain neurotransmitters. When a neural impulse reaches the axon terminal, the vesicles release varying amounts of neurotransmitters into the synaptic cleft. From there, they influence the receiving neuron.

Dozens of neurotransmitters have been identified. Each has its own chemical structure, and each can fit into a specifically tailored harbor, or **receptor site,** on the dendrite of the receiving cell. The analogy of a key fitting into a lock is often used to describe this process. Once released, not all molecules of a neurotransmitter find their ways into receptor sites of other neurons. "Loose" neurotransmitters are usually either broken down or reabsorbed by the axon terminal (a process called reuptake).

Some neurotransmitters act to *excite* other neurons—that is, to cause other neurons to fire. Other neurotransmitters act to *inhibit* receiving neurons. That is, they prevent them from firing. The additive stimulation received from all these cells determines whether a particular neuron will fire and which neurotransmitters will be released in the process.

Neurotransmitters are involved in processes ranging from muscle contraction to emotional response. Excesses or deficiencies of neurotransmitters have been linked to psychological disorders such as depression and schizophrenia.

ACETYLCHOLINE **Acetylcholine (ACh)** is a neurotransmitter that controls muscle contractions. It is excitatory at synapses between nerves and muscles that involve voluntary movement but inhibitory at the heart and at some other locations.

The effects of curare highlight the functioning of ACh. Curare is a poison that is extracted from plants by South American Indians and used in hunting. If an arrow tipped with curare pierces the skin and the poison enters the body, it prevents ACh from lodging within receptor sites in neurons, resulting in

ALL-OR-NONE PRINCIPLE • The fact that a neuron fires an impulse of the same strength whenever its action potential is triggered.
REFRACTORY PERIOD • A phase following firing during which a neuron is less sensitive to messages from other neurons and will not fire.
SYNAPSE • (SIN-apps). A junction between the axon terminals of one neuron and the dendrites or cell body of another neuron.
RECEPTOR SITE • A location on a dendrite of a receiving neuron tailored to receive a neurotransmitter.
ACETYLCHOLINE • (uh-SEE-till-COE-lean). A neurotransmitter that controls muscle contractions. Abbreviated ACh.

paralysis. The victim is prevented from contracting the muscles used in breathing and therefore dies from suffocation. Botulism, a disease that stems from food poisoning, prevents the release of ACh and has the same effect as curare.

ACh is also normally prevalent in a part of the brain called the **hippocampus,** a structure involved in the formation of memories. When the amount of ACh available to the brain decreases, memory formation is impaired.

Alzheimer's disease is a case in point. **Alzheimer's disease** is a progressive form of mental deterioration that affects about 10% of people over the age of 65. The risk increases dramatically with advanced age. Although Alzheimer's is connected with aging, it is a disease and not part of the normal aging process.

Alzheimer's disease is characterized by general, gradual deterioration in mental processes such as memory, language, and problem solving. As the disease progresses, people may fail to recognize familiar faces or forget their names (Mendez and others, 1992). In the most severe cases, people with Alzheimer's disease become helpless. They become unable to communicate or walk and require help in toileting and feeding. More isolated memory losses (for example, forgetting where one put one's glasses) may be a normal feature of aging (Abeles, 1997b). Alzheimer's, in contrast, seriously impairs vocational and social functioning.

In Alzheimer's disease, there is a loss of synapses in the hippocampus and the frontal cortex (Tanzi, 1995). Acetylcholine (ACh) is normally prevalent in the hippocampus, but people with Alzheimer's have reduced levels of ACh in their brains. Because Alzheimer's is connected with reductions in ACh, drug therapy has aimed at heightening ACh levels. Current drugs achieve modest benefits with many people by inhibiting the breakdown of ACh ("FDA Approves," 1996).

DOPAMINE **Dopamine** is primarily an inhibitory neurotransmitter. It is involved in voluntary movements, learning and memory, and emotional arousal. Deficiencies of dopamine are linked to Parkinson's disease, in which people progressively lose control over their muscles. They develop muscle tremors and jerky, uncoordinated movements. The drug L-dopa, a substance that stimulates the brain to produce dopamine, helps slow the progress of Parkinson's disease.

Schizophrenia (see Chapter 15) has also been linked to dopamine. People with schizophrenia may have more receptor sites for dopamine in an area of the brain that is involved in emotional responding. For this reason, they may *overutilize* the dopamine available in the brain. This leads to hallucinations and disturbances of thought and emotion. The phenothiazines, a group of drugs used in the treatment of schizophrenia, block the action of dopamine by locking some dopamine out of these receptor sites (Carpenter & Buchanan, 1994). Not surprisingly, phenothiazines may have Parkinson-like side effects, which are usually treated by prescribing additional drugs, lowering the dose of phenothiazine, or switching to another drug.

NORADRENALINE **Noradrenaline** is produced largely by neurons in the brain stem. It acts both as a neurotransmitter and as a hormone. It speeds up the heartbeat and other body processes and is involved in general arousal, learning and memory, and eating. Excesses and deficiencies of noradrenaline have been linked to mood disorders (see Chapter 15).

The stimulants cocaine and amphetamines ("speed") facilitate the release of dopamine and noradrenaline and also impede their reabsorption by the releasing synaptic vesicles—that is, reuptake. As a result, there are excesses of these neurotransmitters in the nervous system, vastly increasing the firing of neurons and leading to persistent arousal.

Truth or Fiction Revisited

Alzheimer's disease is not a normal part of growing old.

Runner's High? Why have thousands of people taken up long-distance running? Running promotes cardiovascular conditioning, muscle strength, and weight control. But many long-distance runners also experience a "runner's high" that appears to be connected with the release of endorphins. Endorphins are naturally occurring substances that are similar in function to the narcotic morphine.

In Review Neurotransmitters

NEUROTRANSMITTER	TYPE	FUNCTIONS	COMMENTS
Acetylcholine (ACh)	Generally excitatory (causes receiving neurons to fire) at synapses between nerves and muscles	Controls muscle contractions and is involved in memory formation	Deficiencies are connected with paralysis and with Alzheimer's disease.
Dopamine	Inhibitory (causes receiving neurons *not* to fire)	Involved in voluntary movements, learning and memory, and emotional response	Deficiencies are linked to Parkinson's disease. Overutilization is connected with schizophrenia.
Noradrenaline	Excitatory	Acts as neurotransmitter and hormone; speeds up body processes and is involved in arousal, learning and memory, and eating	Imbalances are connected with mood disorders.
Serotonin	Inhibitory	Involved in emotional arousal, mood, sleep, and eating.	Deficiencies have been linked to depression, aggression, eating disorders, and insomnia.
Endorphins	Inhibitory	Inhibits pain	May increase self-confidence and be linked with "runner's high."

SEROTONIN Also primarily an inhibitory transmitter, **serotonin** is involved in emotional arousal and sleep. Deficiencies of serotonin have been linked to overeating, alcoholism, depression, aggression, and insomnia (Azar, 1997b). The drug LSD (see Chapter 6) decreases the action of serotonin and may also influence the utilization of dopamine. With LSD, "two no's make a yes." By inhibiting an inhibitor, it increases brain activity, in this case frequently producing hallucinations.

ENDORPHINS The word *endorphin* is the contraction of *endogenous morphine*. *Endogenous* means "developing from within." **Endorphins** occur naturally in the brain and in the bloodstream and are similar to the narcotic morphine in their functions and effects.

Endorphins are inhibitory neurotransmitters. They lock into receptor sites for chemicals that transmit pain messages to the brain. Once the endorphin "key" is in the "lock," the pain-causing chemicals are locked out. Endorphins may also increase our sense of competence and be connected with the pleasurable "runner's high" reported by many long-distance runners (Grady, 1997b).

There you have it—a fabulous forest of neurons in which billions upon billions of vesicles are pouring neurotransmitters into synaptic clefts at any given time: when you are involved in strenuous activity, now as you are reading this page, even as you are passively watching television. This microscopic picture is

HIPPOCAMPUS • A part of the limbic system of the brain that is involved in memory formation.

ALZHEIMER'S DISEASE • (AHLTS-high-mers). A progressive disorder characterized by loss of memory and other cognitive functions.

DOPAMINE • (DOPE-uh-mean). A neurotransmitter that is involved in Parkinson's disease and that appears to play a role in schizophrenia.

NORADRENALINE • (nor-uh-DRENN-uh-lin). A neurotransmitter whose action is similar to that of the hormone adrenaline and that may play a role in depression.

SEROTONIN • (ser-oh-TONE-in). A neurotransmitter, deficiencies of which have been linked to affective disorders, anxiety, and insomnia.

ENDORPHINS • (en-DOOR-fins). Neurotransmitters that are composed of amino acids and that are functionally similar to morphine.

repeated several hundred times every second. The combined activity of all these neurotransmitters determines which messages will be transmitted and which ones will not. Your experience of sensations, your thoughts, and your sense of control over your body are very different from the electrochemical processes we have described. Yet somehow, these processes are responsible for your psychological sense of yourself and of the world (Greenfield, 1995).

REFLECTIONS

- How does the text use the term *message* in referring to neural transmission? Does this use of the term agree with your own sense of the meaning of the word?
- Had you heard that the brain operates means of electricity? How are messages actually transmitted in the nervous system?
- Psychology is the study of behavior and mental processes. Why, then, are psychologists interested in biological matters such as the nervous system, the endocrine system, and heredity?

■ THE NERVOUS SYSTEM

As a child, I did not think it was a good thing to have a "nervous" system. After all, if your system were not so nervous, you might be less likely to jump at strange noises.

Later I learned that a nervous system is not a system that is nervous. It is a system of nerves involved in thought processes, heartbeat, visual-motor coordination, and so on. I also learned that the human nervous system is more complex than that of any other animal and that our brains are larger than those of any other animal. Now, this last piece of business is not quite true. A human brain weighs about 3 pounds, but the brains of elephants and whales may be four times as heavy. Still, our brains account for a greater part of our body weight than do those of elephants or whales. Our brains weigh about 1/60th of our body weight. Elephant brains weigh about 1/1,000th of their total weight, and whale brains are a paltry 1/10,000th of their weight. So, if we wish, we can still find ways to look at ourselves that make us proud.

Truth or Fiction Revisited

It is not true that the human brain is larger than that of any other animal. Elephants and whales have larger brains.

FIGURE 3.3

THE DIVISIONS OF THE NERVOUS SYSTEM

The nervous system contains two main divisions: the central nervous system and the peripheral nervous system. The central nervous system consists of the brain and spinal cord. The peripheral nervous system contains the somatic and autonomic systems. In turn, the autonomic nervous system has sympathetic and parasympathetic divisions.

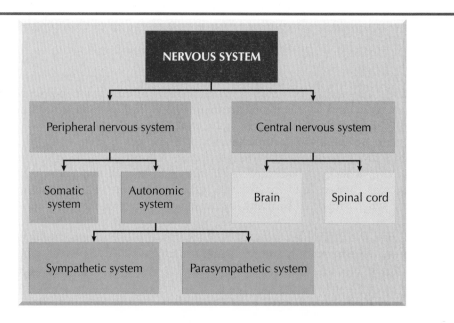

The brain is only one part of the nervous system. A **nerve** is a bundle of axons and dendrites. The nervous system consists of the brain, the spinal cord, and the nerves linking them to receptors in the sensory organs and effectors in the muscles and glands. As shown in Figure 3.3, the brain and spinal cord make up the **central nervous system.** The sensory (afferent) neurons, which receive and transmit messages to the brain and spinal cord, and the motor (efferent) neurons, which transmit messages from the brain or spinal cord to the muscles and glands, make up the **peripheral nervous system.**

• *The Central Nervous System*

The central nervous system consists of the spinal cord and the brain. Let us take a closer look at each of these.

THE SPINAL CORD The **spinal cord** is a column of nerves about as thick as a thumb. It transmits messages from receptors to the brain and from the brain to muscles and glands throughout the body. The spinal cord is also capable of some "local government." That is, it controls some responses to external stimulation through **spinal reflexes.** A spinal reflex is an unlearned response to a stimulus that may involve only two neurons—a sensory (afferent) neuron and a motor (efferent) neuron (Figure 3.4). In some reflexes, a third neuron, called an **interneuron,** transmits the neural impulse from the sensory neuron through the spinal cord to the motor neuron.

NERVE • A bundle of axons and dendrites from many neurons.
CENTRAL NERVOUS SYSTEM • The brain and spinal cord.
PERIPHERAL NERVOUS SYSTEM • (pair-IF-uh-ral). The part of the nervous system consisting of the somatic nervous system and the autonomic nervous system.
SPINAL CORD • A column of nerves within the spine that transmits messages from sensory receptors to the brain and from the brain to muscles and glands throughout the body.
SPINAL REFLEX • A simple, unlearned response to a stimulus that may involve only two neurons.
INTERNEURON • A neuron that transmits a neural impulse from a sensory neuron to a motor neuron.

FIGURE 3.4
THE REFLEX ARC
A cross section of the spinal cord, showing a sensory neuron and a motor neuron, which are involved in the knee-jerk reflex. In some reflexes, interneurons link sensory and motor neurons.

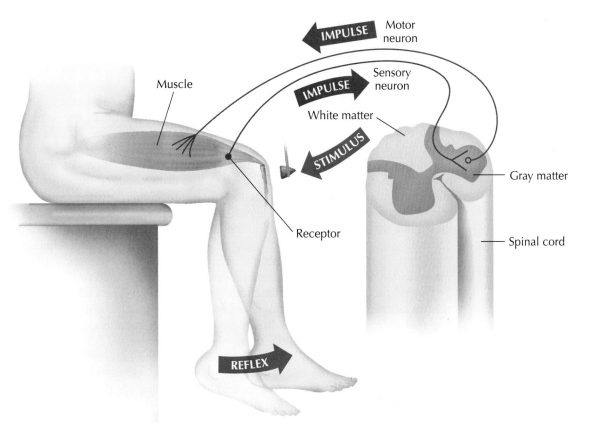

The spinal cord (and the brain) consists of gray matter and white matter. The **gray matter** is composed of nonmyelinated neurons. Some of these are involved in spinal reflexes, whereas others send axons to the brain. The **white matter** is composed of bundles of longer, myelinated (and thus whitish) axons that carry messages to and from the brain. As you can see in Figure 3.4, a cross section of the spinal cord shows that the gray matter, which includes cell bodies, is distributed in a butterfly pattern.

We engage in many reflexes. We blink in response to a puff of air. We swallow when food accumulates in the mouth. A physician may tap the leg below the knee to elicit the knee-jerk reflex, a sign that the nervous system is operating adequately. Urinating and defecating are reflexes that occur in response to pressure in the bladder and the rectum. Parents typically spend weeks or months toilet-training infants—in other words, teaching them to involve their brains in the process of elimination. Learning to inhibit these reflexes makes civilization possible.

Sexual response also involves many reflexes. Stimulation of the genital organs will lead to erection in the male, vaginal lubrication in the female (both are reflexes that make sexual intercourse possible), and the involuntary muscle contractions of orgasm. As reflexes, these processes need not involve the brain, but most often they do. Feelings of passion, memories of an enjoyable sexual encounter, and sexual fantasies usually contribute to sexual response by transmitting messages from the brain to the genitals through the spinal cord (Rathus and others, 1997).

THE BRAIN Every show has a star, and the brain is the undisputed star of the human nervous system. The size and shape of your brain are responsible for your large, delightfully rounded head. In all the animal kingdom, you (and about 6 billion other people) are unique because of the capacities for learning and thought residing in the human brain. The brains of men are about 15% larger than those of women, on average (Blum, 1997), which, feminists might argue, shows that bigger isn't necessarily better. In the human brain it may well be that how well-connected one is (in terms of synapses) is more important than size. Moreover, women's brains "run hotter" than men's. Women metabolize more glucose and appear to use more of their brains on a given task (Blum, 1997).

Let us take a closer look at the brain (see Figure 3.5). We begin with the back of the head, where the spinal cord rises to meet the brain, and work our way forward. The lower part of the brain, or hindbrain, consists of three major structures: the medulla, the pons, and the cerebellum.

Many pathways that connect the spinal cord to higher levels of the brain pass through the **medulla.** (*Medulla* is a Latin word meaning "marrow.") The medulla regulates vital functions such as heart rate, blood pressure, and respiration. It also plays a role in sleep, sneezing, and coughing. The **pons** is a bulge in the hindbrain that lies forward of the medulla. *Pons* is the Latin word for "bridge." The pons is so named because of the bundles of nerves that pass through it. The pons transmits information about body movement and is also involved in functions related to attention, sleep and alertness, and respiration.

Behind the pons lies the **cerebellum** ("little brain" in Latin). The two hemispheres of the cerebellum are involved in maintaining balance and in controlling motor (muscle) behavior. Injury to the cerebellum may lead to lack of motor coordination, stumbling, and loss of muscle tone.

The **reticular activating system (RAS)** begins in the hindbrain and ascends through the region of the midbrain into the lower part of the forebrain. It is vital in the functions of attention, sleep, and arousal. Injury to the RAS may leave an animal in a coma. Stimulation of the RAS causes it to send messages to the

GRAY MATTER • In the spinal cord, the grayish neurons and neural segments that are involved in spinal reflexes.
WHITE MATTER • In the spinal cord, axon bundles that carry messages from and to the brain.
MEDULLA • (meh-DULL-ah). An oblong area of the hindbrain involved in regulation of heartbeat and respiration.
PONS • (ponz). A structure of the hindbrain involved in respiration, attention, and sleep and dreaming.
CEREBELLUM • (ser-uh-BELL-um). A part of the hindbrain involved in muscle coordination and balance.
RETICULAR ACTIVATING SYSTEM • (reh-TICK-you-lar). A part of the brain involved in attention, sleep, and arousal.

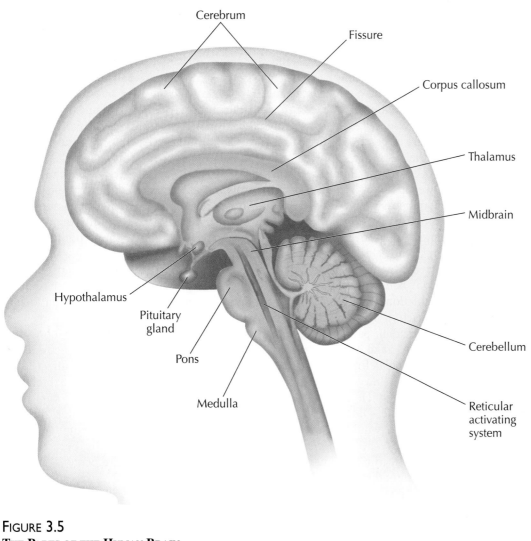

Cerebrum

Fissure

Corpus callosum

Thalamus

Midbrain

Hypothalamus

Cerebellum

Pituitary gland

Pons

Reticular activating system

Medulla

FIGURE **3.5**

THE PARTS OF THE HUMAN BRAIN

This view of the brain, split top to bottom, shows some of the most important structures.

cortex, making us more alert to sensory information. Electrical stimulation of the RAS awakens sleeping animals. Drugs known as central nervous system depressants, such as alcohol, are thought to work, in part, by lowering RAS activity.

Sudden, loud noises stimulate the RAS and awaken a sleeping animal or person. But the RAS may become selective through learning. That is, it comes to play a filtering role. It may allow some messages to filter through to higher brain levels and awareness while screening others out. For example, the parent who has primary responsibility for child care may be awakened by the stirring sounds of an infant, while the sounds of traffic or street noise are filtered out, even though they are louder. The other parent, in contrast, may sleep through even loud crying by the infant. If the first parent must be away for several days, however, the second parent's RAS may quickly become sensitive to noises produced by the child. This sensitivity may rapidly fade again when the first parent returns.

Also located in the midbrain are areas involved in vision and hearing. These include the area that controls eye reflexes such as dilation of the pupils and eye movements.

FIGURE 3.6

A "PLEASURE CENTER" OF THE BRAIN

A rat with an electrode implanted in a section of the hypothalamus that has been termed a pleasure center learns to press a lever to receive electrical stimulation.

THALAMUS • (THAL-uh-muss). An area near the center of the brain involved in the relay of sensory information to the cortex and in the functions of sleep and attention.

HYPOTHALAMUS • (HIGH-poe-THAL-uh-muss). A structure below the thalamus involved in body temperature, motivation, and emotion.

LIMBIC SYSTEM • A group of structures involved in memory, motivation, and emotion that forms a fringe along the inner edge of the cerebrum.

AMYGDALA • (uh-MIG-dull-uh). A part of the limbic system that apparently facilitates stereotypical aggressive responses.

Key areas of the forward-most part of the brain, or forebrain, are the thalamus, the hypothalamus, the limbic system, and the cerebrum. The **thalamus** is located near the center of the brain. It consists of two joined egg- or football-shaped structures. The thalamus serves as a relay station for sensory stimulation. Nerve fibers from the sensory systems enter from below; the information carried by them is then transmitted to the cerebral cortex by way of fibers that exit from above. For instance, the thalamus relays sensory input from the eyes to the visual areas of the cerebral cortex. The thalamus is also involved in controlling sleep and attention in coordination with other brain structures, including the RAS.

The **hypothalamus** lies beneath the thalamus and above the pituitary gland. It weighs only 4 grams, yet it controls the autonomic nervous system and the endocrine system. Thus, it is vital in the regulation of body temperature, concentration of fluids, storage of nutrients, and various aspects of motivation and emotion. Experimenters learn many of the functions of the hypothalamus by implanting electrodes in parts of it and observing the effects of an electrical current. They have found that the hypothalamus is involved in hunger, thirst, sexual behavior, caring for offspring, and aggression. Among lower animals, stimulation of various areas of the hypothalamus can trigger instinctual behaviors such as fighting, mating, or even nest building.

Canadian psychologists James Olds and Peter Milner (1954) made a wonderful mistake in the 1950s. They were attempting to implant an electrode in a rat's reticular formation to see how stimulation of the area might affect learning. Olds, however, was primarily a social psychologist and not a biological psychologist. He missed his target and found a part of the animal's hypothalamus instead. Olds and Milner dubbed this area the "pleasure center" because the animal would repeat whatever it was doing when it was stimulated (see Figure 3.6). The term *pleasure center* is not used too frequently, because it appears to attribute human emotions to rats. Yet the "pleasure centers" must be doing something right, because rats will stimulate themselves in these centers by pressing a pedal several thousand times an hour, until they are exhausted (Olds, 1969).

The hypothalamus is just as important to humans as it is to lower animals. Unfortunately (or fortunately), our "pleasure centers" are not as clearly defined as those of the rat. Then, too, our responses to messages from the hypothalamus are less instinctual and relatively more influenced by cognitive functions such as thought, choice, and value systems. It's all a part of being human.

The **limbic system** is made up of several structures, including the amygdala, hippocampus, and parts of the hypothalamus (Figure 3.7). The limbic system lies along the inner edge of the cerebrum and is fully evolved only in mammals. It is involved in memory and emotion, and in the drives of hunger, sex, and aggression. People in whom operations have damaged the hippocampus can retrieve old memories but cannot permanently store new information. As a result, they may reread the same newspaper day in and day out without recalling that they read it before. Or they may have to be perpetually reintroduced to people they have met just hours earlier (Squire, 1996).

The **amygdala** looks like two little almonds. Studies using lesioning and electrical stimulation show that the amygdala is connected with aggressive behavior in monkeys, cats, and other animals. Early in the 20th century Heinrich Klüver and Paul Bucy (1939) lesioned part of the amygdala of a rhesus monkey. Rhesus monkeys are normally a scrappy lot and try to bite or grab at intruders, but destruction of this animal's amygdala made it docile. No longer did it react aggressively to people. It even allowed people to poke and pinch it. On the other hand, electrical stimulation of the part of the amygdala that Klüver and Bucy had destroyed will trigger a so-called rage response. For example, it

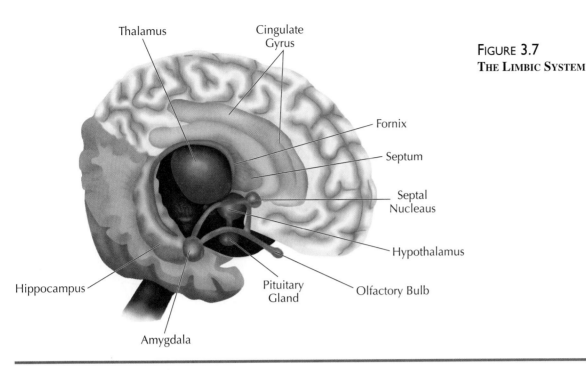

Thalamus

Cingulate
Gyrus

Fornix

Septum

Septal
Nucleaus

Hypothalamus

Olfactory Bulb

Pituitary
Gland

Hippocampus

Amygdala

FIGURE **3.7**
THE LIMBIC SYSTEM

will cause a cat to hiss and arch its back in preparation for an attack. Yet, if you electrically stimulate another part of the amygdala, the cat will cringe in fear when you cage it with a mouse. Not very tigerlike.

The **cerebrum** is the crowning glory of the brain. Only in human beings does the cerebrum account for such a large proportion of the brain (Figure 3.5). The surface of the cerebrum is wrinkled, or convoluted, with ridges and valleys. This surface is termed the **cerebral cortex.** The convolutions allow a great deal of surface area to be packed into the brain.

Valleys in the cortex are called *fissures.* One of the most important of these almost divides the cerebrum in half, creating two hemispheres. The hemispheres of the cerebral cortex are connected by the **corpus callosum** (Latin for "thick body" or "hard body"), a thick bundle of some 200 million nerve fibers.

• *The Peripheral Nervous System*

The peripheral nervous system consists of sensory and motor neurons that transmit messages to and from the central nervous system. Without the peripheral nervous system, our brains would be isolated from the world: They would not be able to perceive it, and they would not be able to act on it. The two main divisions of the peripheral nervous system are the somatic nervous system and the autonomic nervous system.

THE SOMATIC NERVOUS SYSTEM The **somatic nervous system** contains sensory (afferent) and motor (efferent) neurons. It transmits messages about sights, sounds, smells, temperature, body positions, and so on, to the central nervous system. As a result, we can experience the beauties and the horrors of the world, its physical ecstasies and agonies. Messages transmitted from the brain and spinal cord to the somatic nervous system control purposeful body movements such as raising a hand, winking, or running, as well as breathing and movements that we hardly attend to—movements that maintain our posture and balance.

CEREBRUM • (ser-REE-brum). The large mass of the forebrain, which consists of two hemispheres.
CEREBRAL CORTEX • (ser-REE-bral CORE-tecks). The wrinkled surface area (gray matter) of the cerebrum.
CORPUS CALLOSUM • (CORE-puss cal-LOSS-sum). A thick fiber bundle that connects the hemispheres of the cortex.
SOMATIC NERVOUS SYSTEM • (so-MAT-tick). The division of the peripheral nervous system that connects the central nervous system with sensory receptors, skeletal muscles, and the surface of the body.

PARASYMPATHETIC BRANCH

SYMPATHETIC BRANCH

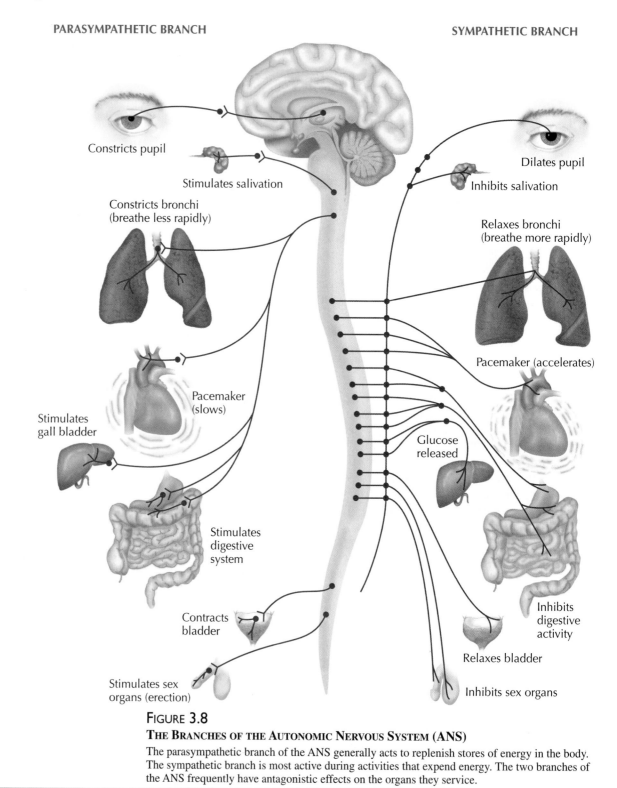

Constricts pupil

Stimulates salivation

Constricts bronchi
(breathe less rapidly)

Pacemaker
(slows)

Stimulates
gall bladder

Stimulates
digestive
system

Contracts
bladder

Stimulates sex
organs (erection)

Dilates pupil

Inhibits salivation

Relaxes bronchi
(breathe more rapidly)

Pacemaker (accelerates)

Glucose
released

Inhibits
digestive
activity

Relaxes bladder

Inhibits sex organs

FIGURE 3.8

THE BRANCHES OF THE AUTONOMIC NERVOUS SYSTEM (ANS)

The parasympathetic branch of the ANS generally acts to replenish stores of energy in the body. The sympathetic branch is most active during activities that expend energy. The two branches of the ANS frequently have antagonistic effects on the organs they service.

AUTONOMIC NERVOUS SYSTEM • (aw-toe-NOM-ick). The division of the peripheral nervous system that regulates glands and activities such as heartbeat, respiration, digestion, and dilation of the pupils. Abbreviated ANS.

THE AUTONOMIC NERVOUS SYSTEM *Autonomic* means "automatic." The **autonomic nervous system (ANS)** regulates the glands and the muscles of internal organs. Thus, the ANS controls activities such as heartbeat, respiration, digestion, and dilation of the pupils of the eyes. These activities can occur automatically, while we are asleep. But some of them can be overridden by conscious control. You can breathe at a purposeful pace, for example. Methods like biofeedback and yoga also help people gain voluntary control of functions such as heart rate and blood pressure.

The ANS has two branches, or divisions: **sympathetic** and **parasympathetic.** These branches have largely opposing effects. Many organs and glands are stimulated by both branches of the ANS (Figure 3.8). When organs and glands are simultaneously stimulated by both divisions, their effects can average out to some degree. In general, the sympathetic division is most active during processes that involve the spending of body energy from stored reserves, such as in a fight-or-flight response to a predator or when you find out that your rent is going to be raised. The parasympathetic division is most active during processes that replenish reserves of energy, such as eating. When we are afraid, the sympathetic division of the ANS accelerates the heart rate. When we relax, the parasympathetic division decelerates the heart rate. The parasympathetic division stimulates digestive processes, but the sympathetic branch inhibits digestion. Since the sympathetic division predominates when we feel fear or anxiety, these feelings can cause indigestion.

The ANS is of particular interest to psychologists because its activities are linked to various emotions such as anxiety and love. Some people seem to have overly reactive sympathetic nervous systems. In the absence of external threats, their bodies still respond as though they were faced with danger (see Chapter 15).

> **Truth or Fiction Revisited**
> ....
> *It is true that fear can give you indigestion.* Fear predominantly involves sympathetic ANS activity, whereas digestive processes involve parasympathetic activity. Since sympathetic activity can inhibit parasympathetic activity, fear can prevent digestion.

REFLECTIONS

- Does it seem possible that sexual responses are reflexive? Why or why not?
- Before taking this course, had you heard of "nerves"? How do the definitions of *neurons* and *nerves* agree with your earlier ideas?
- Have you ever lost your appetite or thrown up because of anxiety or fear? What biological processes caused fear to produce indigestion?

■ THE CEREBRAL CORTEX

Sensation and muscle activity involve many parts of the nervous system. The essential human activities of thought and language, however, involve the hemispheres of the cerebral cortex.

• *The Geography of the Cerebral Cortex*

Each of the two hemispheres of the cerebral cortex is divided into four parts, or lobes, as shown in Figure 3.9. The **frontal lobe** lies in front of the central fissure and the **parietal lobe** behind it. The **temporal lobe** lies below the side, or lateral, fissure—across from the frontal and parietal lobes. The **occipital lobe** lies behind the temporal lobe and behind and below the parietal lobe.

When light strikes the retinas of the eyes, neurons in the occipital lobe fire, and as a result, we "see" (that is, the image is projected in the brain). Direct artificial stimulation of the occipital lobe also produces visual sensations. If neurons in the occipital region of the cortex were stimulated with electricity, you would "see" flashes of light even if it were pitch black or your eyes were covered. The hearing or auditory area of the cortex lies in the temporal lobe along the lateral fissure. Sounds cause structures in the ear to vibrate (see Chapter 5).

SYMPATHETIC • The branch of the ANS that is most active during emotional responses such as fear and anxiety that spend the body's reserves of energy.
PARASYMPATHETIC • The branch of the ANS that is most active during processes such as digestion that restore the body's reserves of energy.
FRONTAL LOBE • The lobe of the cerebral cortex that lies to the front of the central fissure.
PARIETAL LOBE • (par-EYE-uh-tal). The lobe that lies just behind the central fissure.
TEMPORAL LOBE • The lobe that lies below the lateral fissure, near the temples of the head.
OCCIPITAL LOBE • (ox-SIP-it-all). The lobe that lies behind and below the parietal lobe and behind the temporal lobe.

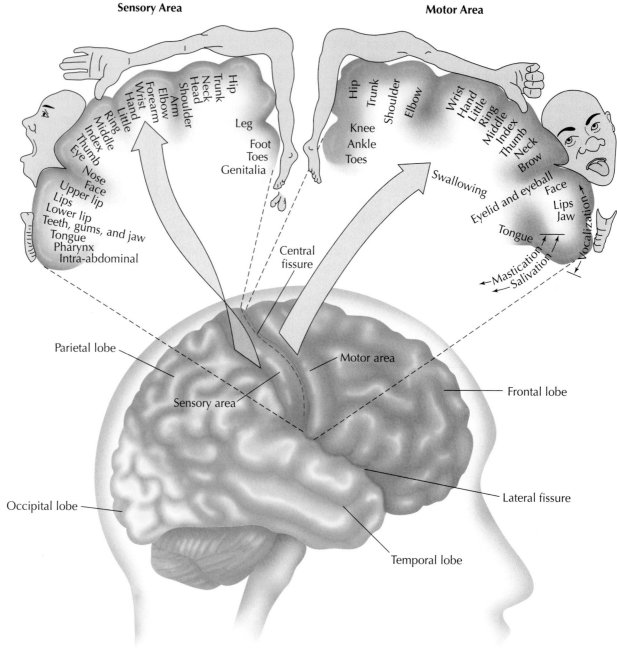

Cross-sections of motor
and sensory areas
of the cerebral cortex,
as seen from the front

Sensory Area

Motor Area

Central
fissure

Parietal lobe

Motor area

Sensory area

Frontal lobe

Occipital lobe

Lateral fissure

Temporal lobe

FIGURE 3.9

THE GEOGRAPHY OF THE CEREBRAL CORTEX

The cortex is divided into four lobes: frontal, parietal, temporal, and occipital. The visual area of the cortex is located in the occipital lobe. The hearing or auditory cortex lies in the temporal lobe. The sensory and motor areas face each other across the central fissure. What happens when a surgeon stimulates areas of the sensory or motor cortex during an operation?

SOMATOSENSORY CORTEX • (so-mat-toe-SENSE-or-ree). The section of cortex in which sensory stimulation is projected. It lies just behind the central fissure in the parietal lobe.

Messages are relayed from those structures to the auditory area of the cortex, and when you hear a noise, neurons in this area are firing.

Just behind the central fissure in the parietal lobe lies an area of **somatosensory cortex,** which receives messages from skin senses all over the body. These sensations include warmth and cold, touch, pain, and movement. Neurons in different parts of the sensory cortex fire, depending on whether you wiggle your finger or raise your leg. If a brain surgeon were to stimulate the proper area of your somatosensory cortex with an electric probe, it might seem as if someone were touching your arm or leg.

Figure 3.9 suggests how our face and head are overrepresented on this cortex compared with, say, our trunk and legs. This overrepresentation is one of the reasons that our face and head are more sensitive to touch than other parts of the body.

Many years ago it was discovered that patients with injuries to one hemisphere of the brain would show sensory or motor deficits on the opposite side of the body below the head. This led to the recognition that sensory and motor nerves cross in the brain and elsewhere. The left hemisphere controls acts on, and receives inputs from, the right side of the body. The right hemisphere controls acts on, and receives inputs from, the left side of the body.

How do you make a monkey smile? One way is by inserting an electrical probe in its motor cortex and giving it a burst of electricity. Let us see what we mean by this.

The **motor cortex** lies in the frontal lobe, just across the valley of the central fissure from the somatosensory cortex. Neurons firing in the motor cortex cause parts of our body to move. More than 100 years ago, German scientists electrically stimulated the motor cortex in dogs and observed that muscles contracted in response (Fritsch & Hitzig, 1870). Since then, neuroscientists have mapped the motor cortex in people and lower animals by inserting electrical probes and seeing in which parts of the body muscles contract. For example, José Delgado (1969) caused one patient to make a fist even though he tried to prevent his hand from closing. The patient said, "I guess, doctor, that your electricity is stronger than my will" (Delgado, 1969, p. 114). Delgado also made a monkey smile in this manner, many thousands of times in a row. If a surgeon were to stimulate a certain area of the right hemisphere of the motor cortex with an electric probe, you would raise your left leg. This action would be sensed in the somatosensory cortex, and you might have a devil of a time trying to figure out whether you had intended to raise that leg!

• *Thought, Language, and the Cortex*

Areas of the cerebral cortex that are not primarily involved in sensation or motor activity are called **association areas.** They make possible the breadth and depth of human learning, thought, memory, and language. The frontal region of the brain, near the forehead, appears to be the brain's executive center, where we make plans and decisions (Gazzaniga, 1997; Goldman-Rakic, 1995).

Areas in the frontal lobes are involved in the memory functions required for problem solving and decision making (Goldman-Rakic, 1992; Goleman, 1995b). These areas are connected with different sensory areas and therefore tap different kinds of sensory information. They retrieve visual, auditory, and other kinds of memories and manipulate them—similar to the way in which a computer retrieves information from files in storage and manipulates it in working memory (Hilts, 1995).

Certain neurons in the visual area of the occipital lobe fire in response to the visual presentation of vertical lines. Others fire in response to presentation of horizontal lines. Although one group of cells may respond to one aspect of the visual field and another group of cells may respond to another, association areas put it all together. As a result, we see a box or an automobile or a road map and not a confusing array of verticals and horizontals.

MOTOR CORTEX • The section of cortex that lies in the frontal lobe, just across the central fissure from the sensory cortex. Neural impulses in the motor cortex are linked to muscular responses throughout the body.
ASSOCIATION AREAS • Areas of the cortex involved in learning, thought, memory, and language.

Paul Broca

One of French Surgeon Paul Broca's (1824–1880) hobbies was *craniometry,* or measurement of the skull. He believed that the size of the brain was related to intelligence. (Generally speaking, it isn't.) He argued that the brains of mature people were larger than those of older people, in "superior" races than in "inferior" ones, in men than in women, and in accomplished men than in run-of-the-mill men. Broca was well aware of evidence that contradicted his views. He knew that the brains of Asians were generally smaller than those of Europeans, although Asians were at least as bright. He knew of extremely intelligent women and of criminals with large brains. Nevertheless, he and his fellow craniometrists touted their views. Upon his death, it was discovered that Broca's own brain was but a bit above average in size— nothing to brag of.

Despite his only slightly-above-average-sized brain, Broca was the first to observe a behavior problem and then locate the area of the brain that caused it. In 1861, Leborgne, a 51-year-old patient at La Bicêtre, the Paris asylum, came down with gangrene in the leg and was admitted to the surgical ward. The patient could apparently understand what was said to him, but he could only utter the meaningless sound "tan" and sometimes blurt out "Sacred name of God!" in frustration. Leborgne had entered the asylum 21 years earlier, when he had lost the ability to speak.

Leborgne died six days later and Broca performed an autopsy. He discovered that an egg-sized area on the left side of the brain, which we now call *Broca's area,* had deteriorated. Broca concluded that this part of the brain was the seat of speech. ∎

LANGUAGE FUNCTIONS In some ways, the left and right hemispheres of the brain duplicate each other's functions. In other ways, they are very different. The left hemisphere contains language functions for nearly all right-handed people and for two out of three left-handed people (Pinker, 1994a). Sensory pathways cross over in the brain. Thus, dominance by the left hemisphere is associated with dominance by the right ear, and vice versa. However, the brain remains "plastic" through about the age of 13. As a result, children who lose the left hemisphere of the brain because of surgery to control epilepsy, usually transfer speech functions to the right hemisphere (Zuger, 1997b).

Two key language areas lie within the dominant hemisphere of the cortex (usually the left hemisphere): Broca's area and Wernicke's area (see Figure 3.10). Damage to either area is likely to cause an aphasia—that is, a disruption of the ability to understand or produce language.

Wernicke's area lies in the temporal lobe near the auditory cortex. It responds mainly to auditory information. As you are reading this page, however, the visual information is registered in the visual cortex of your occipital lobe. It is then recoded as auditory information as it travels to Wernicke's area. If you are "subvocalizing"—saying what you are reading "under your breath"—that is because Wernicke's area transmits information to Broca's area via nerve fibers. Broca's area is located in the frontal lobe, near the section of the motor cortex that controls the muscles of the tongue, throat, and other areas of the face that are used when speaking (Pinker, 1994a; Raichle, 1994). Broca's area processes the information and relays it to the motor cortex. The motor cortex sends the signals that cause muscles in your throat and mouth to contract.

People with damage to Wernicke's area may show **Wernicke's aphasia,** which impairs their abilities to comprehend speech and to think of the proper words to express their own thoughts. Ironically, they usually speak freely and with proper syntax. Wernicke's area thus is essential to understanding the relationships between words and their meanings. When Broca's area is damaged, people speak slowly and laboriously, in simple sentences. This pattern is termed **Broca's aphasia.**

• Left Brain, Right Brain?

It has become popular to speak of people as being "left-brained" or "right-brained." The notion is that the hemispheres of the brain are involved in very different kinds of intellectual and emotional functions and responses, along the lines suggested in Figure 3.11. According to this view, left-brained people would be primarily logical and intellectual. Right-brained people would be intuitive, creative, and emotional. Those of us who are fortunate enough to have our brains "in balance" would presumably have the best of it—the capacity for logic combined with emotional richness.

WERNICKE'S APHASIA • (WER-nick-key). A language disorder characterized by difficulty comprehending the meaning of spoken language.

BROCA'S APHASIA • A language disorder characterized by slow, laborious speech.

Like so many other popular ideas, the left-brain–right-brain notion is at best exaggerated. Research does suggest that in right-handed individuals, the left hemisphere is relatively more involved in intellectual undertakings that require logical analysis and problem solving, language, and mathematical computation (Gazzaniga, 1995). The nondominant hemisphere (usually the right hemisphere) is usually superior in spatial functions (it's better at putting puzzles together), recognition of faces, discrimination of colors, aesthetic and emotional responses, understanding metaphors, and creative mathematical reasoning.

Despite these differences, it would be erroneous to think that the hemispheres of the brain act independently—that some people are truly left-brained and others right-brained (Gazzaniga, 1995). The functions of the left and right hemispheres overlap to some degree, and the hemispheres tend to respond simultaneously as we focus our attention on one thing or another. The hemispheres are aided in their "cooperation" by the corpus callosum, the bundle of 200 million axons that connects them.

• *Handedness: Is It Gauche or Sinister to Be Left-Handed?*

What do Michelangelo, Leonardo da Vinci, Pablo Picasso, and Steve Young all have in common? No, they are not all artists. Only one is a football player. But they are all left-handed. Yet being a lefty is often looked on as a deficiency. The language swarms with slurs on lefties. We speak of "left-handed compliments," of having "two left feet," of strange events as "coming out of left field." The word *sinister* means "left-hand or unlucky side" in Latin. *Gauche* is a French word that literally means "left," though in English it is used to mean awkward or ill-mannered. Compare these usages to the positive phrases "being righteous" or "being on one's right side."

Yet, 8–10% of us are lefties. We are usually labeled right-handed or left-handed on the basis of our handwriting preferences, yet some people write with one hand and pass a football with the other. Some people even swing a tennis racket and pitch a baseball with different hands. Left-handedness is more common in boys than girls.

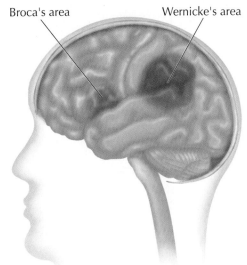

FIGURE 3.10

BROCA'S AND WERNICKE'S AREAS OF THE CEREBRAL CORTEX

The areas of the dominant hemisphere that are most involved in speech are Broca's area and Wernicke's area. Damage to either area can produce an *aphasia*—a disruption of the ability to understand or produce language.

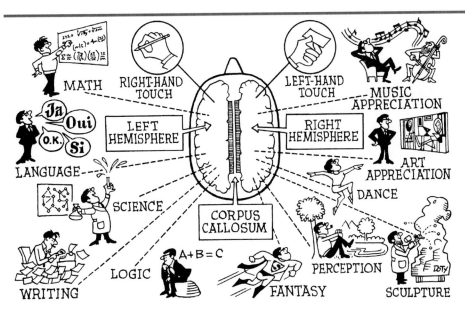

FIGURE 3.11

SOME "SPECIALIZATIONS" OF THE LEFT AND RIGHT HEMISPHERES OF THE CEREBRAL CORTEX

This cartoon, which appeared in a popular magazine, exaggerates the "left brain–right brain" notion. The dominant (usually left) hemisphere appears to be more involved in intellectual undertakings that require logic and problem solving, while the nondominant (usually right) hemisphere is relatively more concerned with decoding visual information, aesthetic and emotional responses, and imagination. However, each hemisphere has some involvement with logic and with creativity and intuition.

Left-Handed Quarterback Steve Young Passes a Football. Is it gauche to be left-handed, or are lefties as competent (or incompetent) as righties?

Being left-handed may not be gauche or sinister, but it appears to be connected with learning disabilities (especially in reading), and health problems such as migraine headaches and allergies (Geschwind & Galaburda, 1987). But there may also be some advantages to being left-handed. According to a British study, left-handed people are twice as likely as right-handed people to be numbered among the ranks of artists, musicians, and mathematicians (Kilshaw & Annett, 1983).

The origins of handedness are likely to have a genetic component. If both of your parents are right-handed, your chances of being left-handed are about 1 in 50. If one of your parents is left-handed, your chances of being left-handed are about 1 in 6. And if both of your parents are left-handed, your chances of also being left-handed are about 1 in 2 (Springer & Deutsch, 1993). In any event, handedness comes early. A study employing ultrasound found that about 95% of fetuses suck their right thumbs rather than their left (Hepper and others, 1990).

• *Split-Brain Experiments: When Hemispheres Stop Communicating*

A number of people with severe cases of **epilepsy** have split-brain operations in which much of the corpus callosum is severed (Engel, 1996). The purpose of the operation is to try to confine epilepsy to one hemisphere of the cerebral cortex rather than allowing a reverberating neural tempest to continue. These operations do seem to help. People who have undergone them can be thought of as winding up with two brains, yet under most circumstances their behavior remains ordinary enough. Still, some aspects of hemispheres that have stopped talking to one another are intriguing.

As reported by pioneering brain surgeon Joseph Bogen (1969), each hemisphere may have a "mind of its own." One split-brain patient reported that her hemispheres frequently disagreed on what she should be wearing. What she meant was that one hand might undo her blouse as rapidly as the other was buttoning it. A man reported that one hemisphere (the left hemisphere, which contained language functions) liked reading but the other one did not. If he shifted a book from his right hand to his left hand, his left hand would put it down. The left hand is connected with the right hemisphere of the cerebral cortex, which in most people—including this patient—does not contain language functions.

Michael Gazzaniga (1995) showed that people with split brains whose eyes are closed may be able to verbally describe an object such as a key when they hold it in one hand, but not when they hold it in the other hand. As shown in Figure 3.12, if a person with a split brain handles a key with his left hand behind a screen, tactile impressions of the key are projected into the right hemisphere, which has little or no language ability. Thus, he will not be able to describe the key. If he holds it in his right hand, he will have no trouble describing it because sensory impressions are projected into the left hemisphere of the cortex, which contains language functions. To further confound matters, if the word *ring* is projected into the dominant (left) hemisphere while the person is asked what he is handling, he will say "ring," not "key."

However, this discrepancy between what is felt and what is said occurs only in people with split brains. Most of the time the two hemispheres work together, even when we are playing the piano or solving math problems.

In our discussion of the nervous system, we have described naturally occurring chemical substances—neurotransmitters—that facilitate or inhibit the transmission of neural messages. Let us now turn our attention to other naturally occurring chemical substances that influence behavior: hormones. We shall see that some hormones also function as neurotransmitters.

EPILEPSY • (EP-pea-lep-sea). Temporary disturbances of brain functions that involve sudden neural discharges.

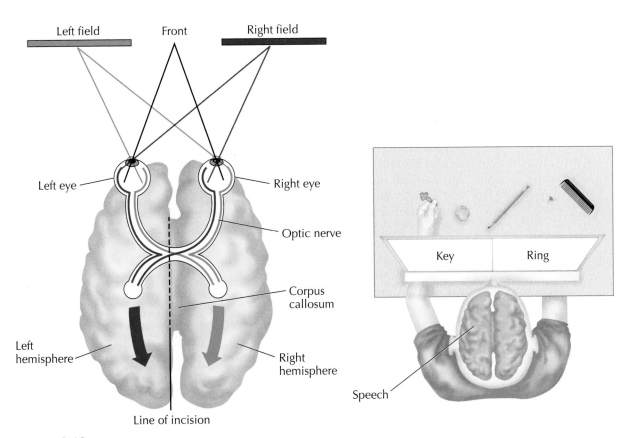

FIGURE 3.12
A DIVIDED-BRAIN EXPERIMENT

In the drawing on the left, we see that visual sensations in the left visual field are projected in the occipital cortex of the right hemisphere. Visual sensations from the right visual field are projected in the occipital cortex in the left hemisphere. In the divided-brain experiment diagramed on the right, a person with a severed corpus callosum handles a key with his left hand and perceives the written word *key* in his left visual field. The word "key" is projected in the right hemisphere. Speech, however, is usually a function of the left (dominant) hemisphere. The written word "ring," perceived by the right eye, is projected in the left hemisphere. So, when asked what he is handling, the divided-brain subject reports "ring," not "key."

REFLECTIONS

- As you read the words on this page, neurons in your brain are firing. Where are the neurons whose firing results in your seeing the words?
- Do you think of yourself as predominantly "left-brained" or "right-brained"? Why?

■ THE ENDOCRINE SYSTEM

Here are some things you may have heard about hormones and behavior. Are they truth or fiction?

____ Some overweight people actually eat very little; their excess weight is caused by "glands."

____ A woman who becomes anxious and depressed just before menstruating is suffering from "raging hormones."

___ Women who "pump iron" frequently use hormones to achieve the muscle definition that is needed to win bodybuilding contests.

___ People who receive injections of adrenaline may report that they feel as if they are about to experience some emotion, but they're not sure which one.

Let us consider each of these items. Some overweight people *do* eat relatively little, but they are "sabotaged" in their weight loss efforts by hormonal changes that lower the rate at which they metabolize food. Women may become somewhat more anxious or depressed at the time of menstruation, but the effects of hormones have been exaggerated. Many top bodybuilders (both women and men) *do* use steroids (hormones that are produced by the **adrenal cortex**) and growth hormone to achieve muscle mass and definition. Steroids and growth hormone promote resistance to stress and muscle growth in both genders. Finally, adrenaline, a hormone produced by the **adrenal medulla**, *does* heighten emotional responsiveness. The specific emotion may depend in part on the person's situation (see Chapter 11).

The body contains two types of glands: glands with ducts and glands without ducts. A duct is a passageway that carries substances to specific locations. Saliva, sweat, tears (a new rock group?), and milk all reach their destinations through ducts. Psychologists are interested in the substances secreted by ductless glands because of their behavioral effects. The ductless glands constitute the **endocrine system,** and they secrete **hormones** (from the Greek *horman*, meaning "to stimulate" or "to excite").

Hormones are released directly into the bloodstream and circulate through the body. Like neurotransmitters, hormones have specific receptor sites. They act only on hormone receptors in certain locations. Some hormones released by the hypothalamus influence only the **pituitary gland.** Some hormones released by the pituitary influence the adrenal cortex, others influence the testes and ovaries, and so on. Let us consider the hormones produced by several glands.

• *The Hypothalamus*

The hypothalamus secretes a number of releasing hormones, or factors, that influence the pituitary gland to secrete corresponding hormones. For example, growth hormone–releasing factor (hGRF) causes the pituitary to produce growth hormone. A dense network of blood vessels between the hypothalamus and the pituitary gland provides a direct route of influence for these factors.

• *The Pituitary Gland: The Pea-Sized Governor*

The pituitary gland lies just below the hypothalamus (see Figure 3.13). Although it is only about the size of a pea, it is so central to the body's functioning that it has been referred to as the "master gland." Despite this designation, today we know that the hypothalamus regulates a good deal of pituitary activity.

Much hormonal action helps the body maintain steady states, as in fluid levels, blood sugar levels, and so on. Bodily mechanisms measure current levels, and when these levels deviate from optimal, they signal glands to release hormones. The maintenance of steady states requires feedback of bodily information to glands. This type of system is referred to as a *negative feedback loop.* That is, when enough of a hormone has been secreted, the gland is signaled to stop. With a negative feedback system in effect, even the master gland must serve a master—the hypothalamus. In turn, the hypothalamus responds to information coming to it from various parts of the body.

ADRENAL CORTEX • (ad-DREE-nal). The outer part of the adrenal glands located above the kidneys. It produces steroids.

ADRENAL MEDULLA • The inner part of the adrenal glands that produces adrenaline.

ENDOCRINE SYSTEM • (END-oh-krinn). Ductless glands that secrete hormones and release them directly into the bloodstream.

HORMONE • A substance secreted by an endocrine gland that regulates various body functions.

PITUITARY GLAND • (pit-TOO-it-tar-ree). The gland that secretes growth hormone, prolactin, antidiuretic hormone, and other hormones.

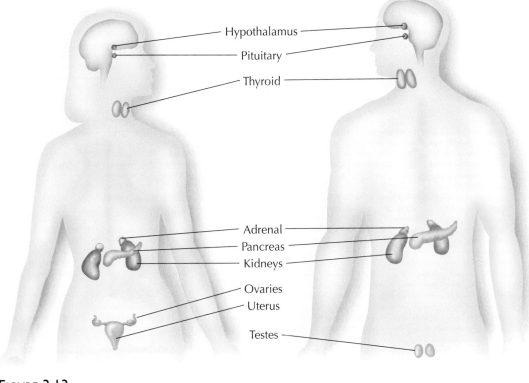

FIGURE 3.13
MAJOR GLANDS OF THE ENDOCRINE SYSTEM

The anterior and posterior (back) lobes of the pituitary gland secrete many hormones. **Growth hormone** regulates the growth of muscles, bones, and glands. Children whose growth patterns are abnormally slow may catch up to their age-mates when they obtain growth hormone.

Prolactin largely regulates maternal behavior in lower mammals such as rats and stimulates production of milk in women. As a water conservation measure, **antidiuretic hormone (ADH)** inhibits production of urine when fluid levels in the body are low. ADH is also connected with stereotypical paternal behavior patterns in some mammals. For example, it transforms an unconcerned male prairie vole (a mouselike rodent) into an affectionate and protective mate and father. **Oxytocin** stimulates labor in pregnant women and is connected with maternal behavior (cuddling and caring for young) in some mammals. Obstetricians may induce labor by injecting pregnant women with oxytocin. During nursing, stimulation of nerve endings in and around the nipples sends messages to the brain that cause oxytocin to be secreted. Oxytocin then causes the breasts to eject milk.

• *The Pancreas: How Sweet It Is (or Isn't)*

The **pancreas** regulates the level of sugar in the blood and the urine by releasing **insulin** and other hormones. One form of diabetes (diabetes mellitus) is characterized by excess sugar in the blood—a condition termed *hyperglycemia*—and in the urine. This condition can lead to coma and death. Diabetes stems from the presence of too little insulin. People whose pancreas does not secrete enough insulin may need to inject themselves with insulin to control diabetes.

GROWTH HORMONE • A pituitary hormone that regulates growth.

PROLACTIN • (pro-LACK-tin). A pituitary hormone that regulates production of milk and, in lower animals, maternal behavior.

ANTIDIURETIC HORMONE • A pituitary hormone that conserves body fluids by increasing reabsorption of urine and is connected with paternal behavior in some mammals. Also called *vasopressin.*

OXYTOCIN • (OX-see-TOE-sin). A pituitary hormone that stimulates labor and lactation.

PANCREAS • (PAN-kree-as). An organ behind the stomach; endocrine cells in the pancreas secrete hormones that influence the blood sugar level.

INSULIN • (IN-sue-lin). A pancreatic hormone that stimulates the metabolism of sugar.

Psychologists are interested in the condition, *hypoglycemia,* which is caused by too little sugar in the blood. The symptoms of hypoglycemia—shakiness, dizziness, and lack of energy—resemble those of anxiety. Many people who seek help for anxiety find that they actually have hypoglycemia. The problem can generally be controlled by changing one's diet.

• The Thyroid Gland: The Body's Accelerator

Thyroxin is produced by the thyroid gland. It affects the body's *metabolism,* the rate at which it uses oxygen and produces energy. Some people are overweight because of *hypothyroidism,* a condition that results from too little thyroxin. Thyroxin deficiency in children can lead to *cretinism,* a condition characterized by stunted growth and mental retardation. Adults who secrete too little thyroxin may feel tired and sluggish and may put on weight. People who produce too much thyroxin may develop *hyperthyroidism,* which is characterized by excitability, insomnia, and weight loss.

• The Adrenal Glands: Coping With Stress

The adrenal glands, located above the kidneys, have an outer layer, or cortex, and an inner core, or medulla. The adrenal cortex is regulated by pituitary ACTH. It secretes hormones known as **corticosteroids,** or cortical steroids (*cortisol* is one). These hormones increase resistance to stress; promote muscle development; and cause the liver to release stored sugar, making more energy available in emergencies, as when you see another car veering toward your own.

Anabolic steroids (synthetic versions of the male sex hormone testosterone) have been used, sometimes in tandem with growth hormone, to enhance athletic prowess. Steroids increase the muscle mass, heighten resistance to stress, and increase the body's energy supply by signaling the liver to release sugar into the bloodstream (Bagatell & Bremner, 1996). Steroids may also spur sex drive and raise self-esteem. Steroids are generally outlawed in amateur and professional sports.

The lure of steroids is understandable. Sometimes the difference between an acceptable athletic performance and a great one is rather small. Thousands of athletes try to make it in the big leagues, and the "edge" offered by steroids—even if minor—can spell the difference between a fumbling attempt and success. If steroids help, why the fuss? Some of it is related to the ethics of competition—the notion that athletes should "play fair." Part of it is related to the fact that steroid use is linked to liver damage and other health problems.

Adrenaline and noradrenaline are secreted by the adrenal medulla. **Adrenaline,** also known as epinephrine, is manufactured exclusively by the adrenal glands, but noradrenaline (norepinephrine) is also produced elsewhere in the body. The sympathetic branch of the autonomic nervous system causes the adrenal medulla to release a mixture of adrenaline and noradrenaline that helps arouse the body to cope with threats and stress. Adrenaline is of interest to psychologists because it has emotional as well as physical effects. It intensifies most emotions and is crucial to the experience of fear and anxiety. Noradrenaline raises the blood pressure, and in the nervous system it functions as a neurotransmitter.

• The Testes and the Ovaries

Did you know that, were it not for the secretion of the male sex hormone **testosterone** about 6 weeks after conception, we would all develop into

THYROXIN • (thigh-ROCKS-sin). The thyroid hormone that increases metabolic rate.

CORTICOSTEROIDS • (CORE-tick-oh-STAIR-oids). Steroids produced by the adrenal cortex that regulate carbohydrate metabolism and increase resistance to stress by fighting inflammation and allergic reactions. Also called *cortical steroids.*

ADRENALINE • (ad-RENN-uh-lin). A hormone produced by the adrenal medulla that stimulates sympathetic ANS activity. Also called *epinephrine.*

TESTOSTERONE • (tess-TOSS-ter-own). A male sex hormone produced by the testes that promotes growth of male sexual characteristics and sperm.

females? Testosterone is produced by the testes and, in smaller amounts, by the ovaries and adrenal glands. A few weeks after conception, testosterone causes the male sex organs to develop. (The amount produced by the ovaries and adrenal glands is normally not enough to foster development of male sex organs.)

During puberty, testosterone promotes the growth of muscle and bone and the development of primary and secondary sex characteristics. *Primary sex characteristics* such as the increased size of the penis and the sperm-producing ability of the testes are directly involved in reproduction. *Secondary sex characteristics* such as presence of a beard and a deeper voice differentiate males from females but are not directly involved in reproduction.

The ovaries produce **estrogen** and **progesterone.** Estrogen is also produced in smaller amounts by the testes. Estrogen fosters female reproductive capacity and secondary sex characteristics such as accumulation of fat in the breasts and hips. Progesterone stimulates growth of the female reproductive organs and prepares the uterus to maintain pregnancy.

THE MENSTRUAL CYCLE Whereas testosterone levels remain fairly stable, estrogen and progesterone levels vary markedly and regulate the woman's menstrual cycle. Following menstruation—the monthly sloughing off of the inner lining of the uterus—estrogen levels increase, leading to the ripening of an ovum (egg cell) and the growth of the lining of the uterus. The ovum is released by the ovary when estrogens reach peak blood levels. Then the lining of the uterus thickens in response to the secretion of progesterone, gaining the capacity to support an embryo if fertilization should occur. If the ovum is not fertilized, estrogen and progesterone levels drop suddenly, triggering menstruation once more.

Psychology in a World of DIVERSITY

Cross-Cultural Perspectives on Menstruation

In Peru, they speak of a "visit from Uncle Pepé." In Samoa, menstruation is referred to as "the boogie man." One of the more common epithets given to the menstrual period throughout history is "the curse." The Fulani of Burkina Faso in Africa use a term for it that translates as "to see dirt." Some nations even blame "the curse" on their historic enemies. In earlier times, the French referred to menstruation as "the English" and to its onset as "the English are coming." Iranians used to say "The Indians have attacked" to announce menstrual bleeding.

A common folk belief in preliterate societies is that menstrual blood is tainted (Rathus and others, 1997). Men avoid contact with menstruating women for fear of their lives. To avoid contamination, menstruating women are sent to special huts on the fringe of the village. In the traditional Navajo Indian culture, for instance, menstruating women would be consigned to huts that were set apart from other living quarters.

The Old Testament (Leviticus 15:19) warns against physical contact with a menstruating woman—including of course, sexual contact: "And if a woman have an issue, and her issue in her flesh be blood, she shall be put apart seven days; and whosoever toucheth her shall be unclean." Orthodox Jews still abstain from sex during menstruation and the week afterward. Prior to resuming sexual relations, the woman must attend a *mikvah*—a ritual cleansing.

ESTROGEN • (ESS-trow-jen). A generic term for several female sex hormones that promote growth of female sex characteristics and regulate the menstrual cycle.
PROGESTERONE • (pro-JESS-ter-own). A female sex hormone that promotes growth of the sex organs and helps maintain pregnancy.

Fears of contamination by menstruating women are nearly universal and persist today (Rathus and others, 1997). As late as the 1950s, women were not allowed in some European breweries for fear that the beer would turn sour. Some Indian castes still teach that a man who touches a woman during her period is contaminated and must be purified by a priest.

We might laugh off these misconceptions as folly were it not for their profound effects on women. Women who suffer from premenstrual syndrome may be responding to negative cultural attitudes toward menstruation as well as to menstrual symptoms themselves. The traditional view of menstruation as a time of pollution may make women highly sensitive to internal sensations at certain times of the month as well as concerned about how to dispose of the menstrual flow discreetly.

PREMENSTRUAL SYNDROME (PMS) Menstruation is a source of concern to psychologists because of stereotypes about menstruating women and because of the physical discomfort experienced by many women during their periods. For several days prior to and during menstruation, according to the stereotype, "raging hormones" doom women to irritability and poor judgment—two facets of the condition known as *premenstrual syndrome* (PMS). (The following "Psychology in a World of Diversity" section shows how misconceptions about menstruation may contribute to stereotypes about menstruating women.)

Women have historically been assumed to be more likely to commit suicide

Truth or Fiction Revisited

It is not true that PMS impairs the academic, occupational, or social functioning of most college women.

psychology and modern life

COPING WITH PMS

Only a generation ago, PMS was seen as something a woman had to put up with. No longer. Many treatment options are available today. Women with PMS may profit from the following suggestions.

1. Don't blame yourself! PMS was once erroneously attributed to women's "hysterical" nature. This is nonsense! Menstrual problems largely reflect variations in levels of certain hormones and neurotransmitters.

2. Develop strategies for dealing with days when you experience the most distress. Pick activities that will help enhance your pleasure and minimize stress, or simply relax. Go to a movie or get into the novel you've been meaning to begin.

3. Consider whether you have self-defeating attitudes toward menstruation that may compound your discomfort. Do relatives or friends see menstruation as an

illness or "pollution"? Do you harbor any of these attitudes?

4. See a doctor about your symptoms, especially if they are severe. Severe symptoms may be caused by medical conditions such as endometriosis and pelvic inflammatory disease (PID).

5. Develop nutritious eating habits—and continue them throughout the entire cycle (that means always). Consider limit-

or crimes, call in sick at work, or develop physical and emotional problems during the eight-day period prior to and during menstruation. Moreover, the ability of college women to focus on academic tasks during this period has been called into question. Three out of four women report *some* psychological and physical problems, such as depression, anxiety, and headaches, during the four to six days that precede menstruation (Brody, 1996a). However, fewer than one woman in 10 has symptoms severe enough to impair her academic, occupational, or social functioning (Brody, 1996a). Symptoms of PMS are shown in Table 3.1.

The symptoms of PMS appear to be linked to levels of hormones and serotonin (Steiner and others, 1995). For instance, prostaglandins cause many women to experience strong, unrelieved uterine contractions. The nearby "Psychology and Modern Life" feature offers advice on coping with PMS.

REFLECTIONS
- Do you know anyone with hormonal problems? What are those problems?
- Have you heard of athletes who were using steroids? What are the effects of the hormones?
- What hormones are involved in reproductive behavior? Has anyone you know been given any of these hormones by a physician? For what reason?
- Why are psychologists interested in the endocrine system?

TABLE 3.1 SYMPTOMS OF PMS*
Depression
Anxiety
Mood swings
Anger and irritability
Loss of interest in usual activities
Difficulty concentrating
Lack of energy
Overeating or cravings for certain foods
Insomnia or too much sleeping
Feelings of being out of control or over-whelmed
Physical problems such as headaches, tenderness in the breasts, joint or muscle pain, weight gain or feeling bloated

* Most women experience only a few of these symptoms, if any at all.

ing your intake of alcohol, caffeine, fats, salt, and sweets.

6. Eat several small meals (or nutritious snacks) a day, rather than filling up.

7. Get more exercise. Some women find that vigorous exercise—jogging, swimming, bicycling, fast walking, dancing, skating, even jumping rope—helps relieve PMS. Women who exercise are not taking menstruation discomfort "lying down"! They remain the masters of their physical fates.

8. Check with your doctor about vitamin and mineral supplements (such as calcium and magnesium). Vitamin B$_6$ appears to have helped some women who experience menstrual discomfort.

9. Do you have cramps? Prostaglandin-inhibiting drugs such as ibuprofen and indomethacin help relieve cramps in many women. Ask your doctor for a recommendation.

10. Many women are also helped by antianxiety or antidepressant medication (Brody, 1996a). Serotonin-enhancing antidepressants such as Effexor, Paxil, Prozac, and Zoloft can take up to three weeks to be effective in treating depression. However, they frequently help women with PMS when they are taken for a week or two prior to menstruation (Brody, 1996a).

11. Remember that menstrual problems are time limited. Don't worry about getting through life or a career. Focus on getting through the next few days. ■

Truth or Fiction Revisited
It is no longer true that women can do little about menstrual discomfort other than *"tough it out."* Many measures can help relieve the discomfort.

In Review The Endocrine System

GLAND	HORMONE	FUNCTIONS
Hypothalamus	Releasing hormones, or factors (e.g., Growth-hormone releasing factor, corticotrophin-releasing hormone)	Influences the pituitary gland to secrete corresponding hormones (e.g., growth hormone, adrenocorticotrophic hormone)
Pituitary *Anterior Lobe*	Growth hormone	Causes growth of muscles, bones, and glands
	Adrenocorticotrophic hormone (ACTH)	Regulates adrenal cortex
	Thyrotrophin	Causes thyroid gland to secrete thyroxin
	Follicle-stimulating hormone	Causes formation of sperm and egg cells
	Leutinizing hormone	Causes ovulation, maturation of sperm and egg cells
	Prolactin	Stimulates production of milk
Posterior Lobe	Antidiuretic hormone (ADH)	Inhibits production of urine
	Oxytocin	Stimulates uterine contractions during delivery and ejection of milk during nursing
Pancreas	Insulin	Enables body to metabolize sugar; regulates storage of fats
Thyroid	Thyroxin	Increases metabolic rate
Adrenal *Cortex*	Steroids (e.g., cortisol)	Increases resistance to stress; regulates carbohydrate metabolism
Medulla	Adrenaline (epinephrine)	Increases metabolic activity (heart and respiration rates, blood sugar level, etc.)
	Noradrenaline (norepinephrine)	Raises blood pressure; acts as neurotransmitter
Testes	Testosterone	Promotes development of male sex characteristics
Ovaries	Estrogen	Regulates menstrual cycle; promotes development of female sex characteristics
	Progesterone	Promotes development of the uterine lining to maintain pregnancy

■ HEREDITY: THE NATURE OF NATURE

Consider some facts of life:

HEREDITY • The transmission of traits from one generation to another through genes.
GENETICS • (jen-NET-ticks). The branch of biology that studies heredity.
BEHAVIORAL GENETICS • The study of the genetic transmission of structures and traits that give rise to behavior.

- People cannot breathe underwater (without special equipment).
- People cannot fly (again, without rather special equipment).
- Fish cannot learn to speak French or do an Irish jig even if you rear them in enriched environments and send them to finishing school.
- Chimpanzees and gorillas can use sign language but cannot speak.

People cannot breathe underwater or fly (without oxygen tanks, airplanes, or other devices) because of their **heredity.** Their heredity defines their nature—which is based in their biological structures and processes. Fish are limited in other ways by the natural traits that have been passed down from one generation to another. Chimpanzees and gorillas can understand many spoken words and express some concepts through nonverbal symbol systems such as American Sign Language. However, apes cannot speak. They have probably failed to inherit the humanlike speech areas of the cerebral cortex. Their nature differs from ours.

Heredity is basic to the transmission of physical traits such as height, hair texture, and eye color. Animals can be selectively bred to enhance desired physical and psychological traits. We breed cattle and chickens to be bigger and fatter so that they provide more food calories for less feed. We breed animals to enhance psychological traits such as aggressiveness and intelligence. For example, poodles are relatively intelligent. Golden retrievers are gentle and patient with children. Border collies show a strong herding instinct. Even as puppies, Border collies will attempt to corral people who are out on a stroll.

Heredity both makes behaviors possible and places limits on them. The subfield of biology that studies heredity is called **genetics. Behavioral genetics** bridges the sciences of psychology and biology. It is concerned with the transmission of structures and traits that give rise to patterns of behavior.

Heredity is involved in almost all human traits and behavior (Rutter, 1997). Examples include sociability, shyness, social dominance, aggressiveness, leadership, thrill seeking, effectiveness as a parent or a therapist, even interest in arts and crafts (Angier, 1996; Carey & DiLalla, 1994; Goldsmith, 1993; Lykken and others, 1992). Genetic influences are also involved in most behavioral problems, including anxiety and depression, schizophrenia, bipolar disorder, alcoholism, even criminal behavior (DiLalla and others, 1996; Plomin and others, 1997). However, most behavior patterns also reflect life experiences and personal choice (Rose, 1995).

According to Charles Darwin, there is a struggle for survival as various species and individuals compete for the same territories. Adaptive features or traits that contribute to the ability of an organism to survive and reproduce are more likely to be transmitted to the next generation. Some biologists, known as sociobiologists, believe that many adaptive social behaviors—ranging from altruism to aggression and mate-selection strategies—can be inherited (Archer, 1996).

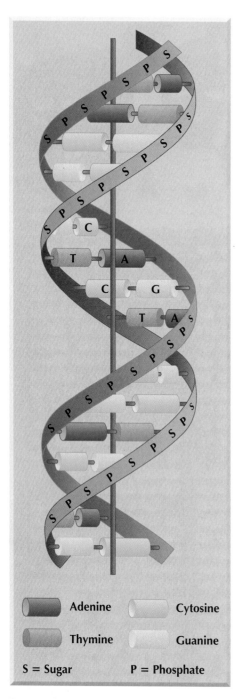

Adenine   **Cytosine**

Thymine   **Guanine**

S = Sugar   P = Phosphate

FIGURE 3.14
THE DOUBLE HELIX OF DNA

GENES • (jeans). The basic building blocks of heredity, which consist of DNA.
CHROMOSOMES • (CROW-moe-soams). Structures consisting of genes that are found in the nuclei of the body's cells.
SEX CHROMOSOMES • The 23rd pair of chromosomes, which determine whether the child will be male or female.

• *Genes and Chromosomes*

Genes are the building blocks of heredity. They are the biochemical materials that regulate the development of specific traits. Some traits, such as blood type, are controlled by a single pair of genes. (One gene is derived from each parent.) Other traits are determined by combinations of genes. The inherited component of complex psychological traits, such as intelligence, is believed to be determined by combinations of genes (Solomon and others, 1993). We have about 100,000 genes in every cell in our bodies.

Genes are segments of **chromosomes,** each of which consists of more than 1,000 genes. Each cell in the body contains 46 chromosomes arranged in 23 pairs. Chromosomes are large, complex molecules of deoxyribonucleic acid, which has several chemical components. (You can breathe a sigh of relief, for this acid is usually referred to simply as DNA.) The tightly wound structure of DNA was first demonstrated in the 1950s by James Watson and Francis Crick. It takes the form of a double helix—a twisting ladder (see Figure 3.14). In all living things, the sides of the ladder consist of alternating segments of phosphate (P) and a kind of sugar (S). The "rungs" of the ladder are attached to the sugars and consist of one of two pairs of bases, either *adenine* with *thymine* (A with T) or *cytosine* with *guanine* (C with G). A single gene can contain hundreds of thousands of base pairs. The sequence of the rungs is the *genetic code* that will cause the unfolding organism to grow arms or wings, skin or scales.

We normally receive 23 chromosomes from our father's sperm cell and 23 chromosomes from our mother's egg cell (ovum). When a sperm cell fertilizes an ovum, the chromosomes form 23 pairs (Figure 3.15). The 23rd pair consists of **sex chromosomes,** which determine whether we are female or male. We all receive an X sex chromosome (so called because of the X shape) from our mother. If we also receive an X sex chromosome from our father, we develop into a female. If we receive a Y sex chromosome (named after the Y shape) from our father, we develop into a male.

Gender is not determined by sex chromosomes throughout the animal kingdom. Reptiles such as crocodiles, for example, do not have sex chromosomes. The crocodile's sex is determined by the temperature at which the egg develops (Crews, 1994). Some like it hot. That is, hatchlings are usually male when the eggs develop at temperatures in the mid-90s Fahrenheit or above. Some like it . . . well not cold perhaps, but certainly cooler. When crocodile eggs develop at temperatures below the mid-80s Fahrenheit, the hatchlings are usually female.[2]

When people do not have the normal complement of 46 chromosomes, physical and behavioral abnormalities may result. The risk of these abnormalities rises with the age of the parents. Most persons with Down syndrome, for example, have an extra, or third, chromosome on the 21st pair. The extra chromosome is usually contributed by the mother, and the condition becomes increasingly likely as the mother's age at the time of pregnancy increases (Rathus and others, 1997). Persons with Down syndrome have a downward-sloping fold of skin at the inner corners of the eyes, a round face, a protruding tongue, and a broad, flat nose. They are mentally retarded and usually have physical problems that cause death by middle age.

_____

[2] This does not mean that male crocodiles are hot-blooded. Reptiles are cold-blooded animals.

Behavior geneticists are attempting to sort out the relative importance of **nature** (heredity) and **nurture** (environmental influences) in the origins of behavior. Psychologists are especially interested in the roles of nature and nurture in intelligence and psychological disorders. They have found that behavior in general reflects the influences of both nature and nurture (Azar, 1997c). Organisms inherit structures that set the stage for certain behaviors. But none of us is the result of heredity alone. Environmental factors such as nutrition, learning opportunities, cultural influences, exercise, and (unfortunately) accident and illness also determine whether genetically possible behaviors will be displayed. Behavior thus represents the interaction of nature and nurture. A potential Shakespeare who is reared in poverty and never taught to read or write will not create a *Hamlet*.

• *Kinship Studies*

The more *closely* people are related, the more *genes* they have in common. Parents and children have a 50% overlap in their genetic endowments, and so do siblings (brothers and sisters). Aunts and uncles related by blood have a 25% overlap with nieces and nephews. First cousins share 12.5% of their genetic endowment. If genes are involved in a trait or behavior pattern, people who are more closely related should be more likely to show similar traits or behavior. Psychologists therefore conduct kinship studies to help determine the role of genetic factors in traits and behavior. They are especially interested in twins and adopted individuals.

Twin Studies The fertilized egg cell (ovum) that carries genetic messages from both parents is called a *zygote*. Now and then, a zygote divides into two cells that separate, so that instead of developing into a single person, it develops into two people with the same genetic makeup. Such people are

MR. BERGH TO THE RESCUE.

The Defrauded Gorilla. "That *Man* wants to claim my Pedigree. He says he is one of my Descendants."

Mr. Bergh. "Now, Mr. Darwin, how could you insult him so?"

Ridicule of Darwin's Theory. Darwin's theory of evolution was originally met with ridicule. It was one thing to be "a monkey's uncle." It was much less to the public's liking to think of themselves as monkey's nephews and nieces.

NATURE • In behavior genetics, heredity.
NURTURE • In behavior genetics, environmental influences on behavior, such as nutrition, culture, socioeconomic status, and learning.

FIGURE 3.15

THE 23 PAIRS OF HUMAN CHROMOSOMES

People normally have 23 pairs of chromosomes. Whether one is female or male is determined by the 23rd pair of chromosomes. Females have two X sex chromosomes (part A), whereas males have an X and a Y sex chromosome (part B).

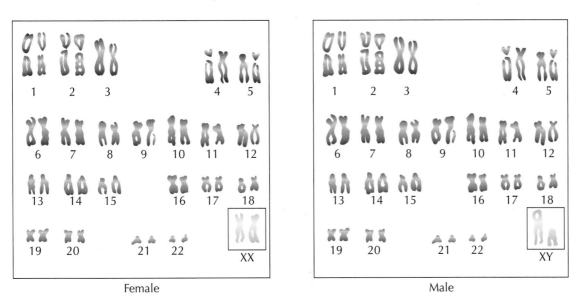

Female   Male

identical or **monozygotic (MZ) twins.** If the woman releases two ova in the same month and they are both fertilized, they develop into fraternal or **dizygotic (DZ) twins.** DZ twins are related in the same way that other siblings are. They share 50% of their genes. MZ twins are important in the study of the relative influences of nature (heredity) and nurture (the environment) because differences between MZ twins are the result of nurture. (They cannot differ in heredity or nature because their genetic makeup is identical.)

Physically speaking, MZ twins are more likely to look alike and to be similar in height, even to have more similar cholesterol levels than DZ twins (Heller and others, 1993). Psychologically speaking, MZ twins resemble one another more strongly than DZ twins in traits such as shyness and activity levels (Emde,

MONOZYGOTIC (MZ) TWINS • (MON-oh-zy-GOT-tick). Identical twins. Twins who develop from a single zygote, thus carrying the same genetic instructions.

DIZYGOTIC (DZ) TWINS • (die-zy-GOT-tick). Fraternal twins. Twins who develop from separate zygotes.

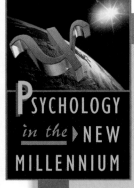

PSYCHOLOGY *in the* **NEW MILLENNIUM**

How Many of You Are There? How Many Will There Be?

How valuable would your individual existence be if a copy of you could be developed on demand? What if a dozen or more of you could be brought to life?

Some fear that our increasing control of genetics will make possible scenarios like that portrayed by Aldous Huxley in his still-powerful 1939 novel *Brave New World.* Through a science fiction method called "Bokanovsky's Process," egg cells from parents who were ideally suited to certain types of labor were made to "bud." From these buds, up to 96 people with identical genetic makeups were developed—easily meeting the labor needs of society.

In the novel, the director of a "hatchery" leads a group of students on a tour. One student is foolish enough to question the advantage of Bokanovsky's Process:

"My good boy!" The Director wheeled sharply round on him. "Can't you see? Can't you see?"

He raised a hand; his expression was solemn. "Bokanovsky's Process is one of the major instruments of social stability!"

Major instruments of social stability (wrote the student).

Standard men and women; in uniform batches. The whole of a small factory staffed with the products of a single Bokanovskied egg.

"Ninety-six identical twins working 96 identical machines!" The voice was almost tremulous with enthusiasm. "You really know where you are. For the first time in history." He quoted the planetary motto. "Community, Identity, Stability." Grand words. "If we could Bokanovskify indefinitely the whole problem would be solved."

Bokanovsky's Process was science fiction when Huxley wrote *Brave New World.* Today, however, cloning technology has made the creation of genetically identical people possible. Techniques similar to that described by Huxley have been developed for making identical cattle. For example, an ovum (egg cell) would be fertilized with sperm in the laboratory (*in vitro*). The fertilized ovum would begin to divide. The dividing mass of cells would be separated into clusters so that each cluster develops into a separate organism. The embryos would then be implanted in one or more "mothers" to develop to maturity. Or else some embryos would be frozen to be implanted if the natural parents (or adoptive parents) desired a genetically identical offspring.

1993), irritability (Goldsmith, 1993), sociability, and cognitive development (DeFries and others, 1987). MZ twins show more similarity than DZ twins in their early signs of attachment, such as smiling, cuddling, and expression of fear of strangers (Scarr & Kidd, 1983). MZ twins are also more likely than DZ twins to share psychological disorders such as autism, anxiety, substance dependence, and schizophrenia (DiLalla and others, 1996).

Twin studies carried out by psychologist David Lykken (1996) at the University of Minnesota suggest that people even inherit a tendency toward a certain level of happiness. Despite the ups and downs of experience, people tend to drift back to their usual levels of cheerfulness or grumpiness. Factors such as availability of money, level of education, and marital status are much less influential than heredity when it comes to human happiness.

Truth or Fiction Revisited

It is apparently true that you can't buy happiness. Heredity is a more important determinant of happiness than money and other social factors.

In an approach that has been used successfully with sheep, a DNA-containing cell nucleus would be surgically extracted from an egg cell donated by a woman. The nutrients that will nourish the development of the egg would be retained. A DNA-containing cell from another person (male or female, child or adult) would be fused with the egg cell. An electric charge might "jump start" cell division, and the embryo would be implanted in a woman's uterus. There it would develop into a person with the genetic traits determined by the nucleus.

These technologies have been used successfully with cattle and sheep (Kolata, 1997), but they would raise many ethical concerns if they were applied to people. One involves human dignity, a core concern for psychologists. One reason that we consider people to be dignified and valuable is their uniqueness. Imagine a world, however, in which every child and adult had one or more frozen identical twins in embryo form:

- If a child died by accident, would the parents develop a frozen embryo to replace the lost child? *Would* this method "replace" the lost child?

- Would some frozen embryos be developed to term to provide donor organs for people who were ill?

- Would society desire that a dozen twins be developed to maturity when a Toni Morrison, a Wolfgang Amadeus Mozart, a Mary Cassatt, or an Albert Einstein was discovered?

- Would society, on the other hand, attempt to lower the incidence of certain genetic disorders or antisocial behavior by *preventing* the twins of less fortunate individuals from being developed to maturity?

- Would parents "invest" frozen embryos that were the twins of their children in embryo banks? As their children developed, would they take photographs and administer psychological tests? Could it happen that the twins of the brightest, most attractive children would be sold to the highest bidder?

- What would happen in societies that valued brawny soldiers? In societies that valued dull workers of the sort envisioned by Huxley? In societies that valued boys more than girls or girls more than boys?

Some ethicists argue that parents' embryos are their own and that it is not society's place to prevent parents from cloning them. Others argue that cloning would devalue the individual and change society in ways that we cannot foresee. Today, nearly three out of five people in the United States say that cloning is a bad thing (Berke, 1997). Only one in four or five say it is a good thing. As we head into the new millennium, the development of many technologies is outpacing ethical considerations. As citizens, it is our duty to keep abreast of technical innovations and to ensure that their applications are beneficial. ■

ADOPTEE STUDIES The interpretation of kinship studies can be confused when relatives share similar environments as well as genes (Coon and others, 1990; Segal, 1993). This is especially true of identical twins, who may be dressed identically and encouraged to follow similar interests. Adoptee studies, in which children are separated from their parents at an early age (or in which identical twins are separated at an early age) and reared in different environments provide special opportunities for sorting out nature and nurture. Psychologists look for similarities between children and their adoptive and natural parents. When children reared by adoptive parents are more similar to their natural parents in a particular trait, strong evidence exists for a genetic role in the appearance of that trait.

GENOME • (JEE-nome). All the DNA contained within the set of human chromosomes. The sum of the genetic material that controls the processes that define the human being.

psychology and
modern life

HEALTH APPLICATIONS OF THE HUMAN GENOME PROJECT

If you had only four letters with which to work, how would you spell *human being?* In a sense, the answer to this question is a key quest of the government-funded Human Genome Project that is expected to be completed early in the new millennium. Using only C, A, T, and G (which stand for *cytosine, adenine, thymine,* and *guanine*), one goal of the project is to sequence the 3 billion letters that compose human DNA.

Another goal of the project is to identify all the genes that make up the human **genome** (that is, all the DNA contained within the set of 23 pairs of human chromosomes). By so doing, researchers will be able to determine whether individuals have the genes that contribute to disorders ranging from physical disorders such as cancer to psychological disorders

such as bipolar mood disorder and schizophrenia.

HEALTH APPLICATIONS Part of the promise of the Human Genome Project is revealed in methods of genetic diagnosis and genetic engineering. We have already developed DNA screening methods for the fatal hereditary diseases Huntington's chorea and cystic fibrosis (Baum and others, 1997; Marteau and others, 1997). Genetic engineering promises to give couples with genetically abnormal embryos a chance to correct the problem in the uterus. In gene replacement therapy, for example, abnormal genes are replaced with normal genes. In other cases, genes are added to encourage organisms to grow in new ways (Kolata, 1996).

The following developments are in the offing or, in some cases, here:

- Ways of detecting predispositions for physical disorders such as cancer, heart disease, and emphysema by studying a newborn's (or fetus's) genetic code (Lerman, 1997).

- Ways of detecting predispositions for psychological disorders such as serious mood disorders and schizophrenia.

- Ways of detecting predispositions for psychological traits such as activity level and shyness.

- "Behavior transplants"(!). Could it be that importing brain cells from other organisms will help people with brain injuries regain lost functions ("A behavior trans-

REFLECTIONS

- Agree or disagree and support your answer: "Since psychological traits such as introversion, intelligence, and aggressiveness are influenced by heredity, there is no point to trying to encourage introverted people to be more sociable, to help poor students do better in school, or to teach aggressive people other ways of getting what they want."
- Which family members seem to be like you physically or psychologically? Which seem to be very different? How do you explain the similarities and differences?
- Are you aware of any people with genetic or chromosomal disorders?

plant," 1997)? Perhaps. In one study, embryonic quail brain cells were implanted in chickens, and the chickens bobbed their heads like quails when they crowed. People with brain injuries may be able to regain lost behavior patterns from implants of working brain cells that regulate those behaviors.

- Understanding how "spelling errors" in the genetic code cause hereditary diseases. For example, sickle cell anemia, a health problem prevalent among African Americans, is connected with an abnormal sequence in the genetic code. The normal sequence is CCTGAGG, but sickle cell anemia occurs when the sequence is misspelled CCTGTGG.

- New vaccines for diseases like hepatitis and herpes.

- Modification of the genetic codes of unborn children through gene replacement therapy to prevent certain diseases.

- Inserting healthy genes into white blood cells to enhance the cells' ability to combat cancer and other diseases.

- Inserting normal genes into fertilized egg cells, so that future generations will not develop genetic disorders. Such an approach would be a true genetic cure.

- Fighting cardiovascular disease by inserting genes into clogged arteries so that people will grow new blood vessels and thus in-

crease their blood flow (Kolata, 1996).

- Creation of wonder drugs from DNA.

- Use of artificial chromosomes to transport healthy genes into human cells (Wade, 1997).

In the new millennium, the genetic code that makes up the human being will be held in the memories of computers. What applications will occur when we have all the genetic information necessary to define a human being? Can you begin to speculate on the ethical and religious debates that are likely to take place? Can you sketch out a science fiction story in which researchers use this information to create superhumans in the laboratory? ■

1. **What are the parts of the nervous system?** The nervous system consists of neurons, which transmit information through neural impulses, and glial cells, which serve support functions. Neurons have a cell body, dendrites, and axons. Neurotransmitters transmit messages across synapses to other neurons.

2. **What is myelin?** Many neurons have a myelin coating that insulate axons, allowing for more efficient conduction of neural impulses.

3. **What are afferent and efferent neurons?** Afferent neurons transmit sensory messages to the central nervous system. Efferent neurons conduct messages from the central nervous system that stimulate glands or cause muscles to contract.

4. **How are neural impulses transmitted?** Neural transmission is electrochemical. An electric charge is conducted along an axon through a process that allows sodium ions to enter the cell and then pumps them out. The neuron has a resting potential of -70 millivolts and an action potential of $+30$ to $+40$ millivolts.

5. **How do neurons fire?** Excitatory neurotransmitters stimulate neurons to fire. Inhibitory neurotransmitters cause them not to fire. Neurons fire according to an all-or-none principle. They may fire hundreds of times per second. Each firing is followed by a refractory period, during which neurons are insensitive to messages from other neurons.

6. **What are some important neurotransmitters?** These include acetylcholine, which is involved in muscle contractions; dopamine, imbalances of which have been linked to Parkinson's disease and schizophrenia; and noradrenaline, which accelerates the heartbeat and other body processes. Endorphins are naturally occurring painkillers.

7. **What is the central nervous system?** The brain and spinal cord make up the central nervous system. Reflexes involve the spinal cord but not the brain. The somatic and autonomic systems make up the peripheral nervous system.

8. **What are the parts of the brain?** The hindbrain includes the medulla, pons, and cerebellum. The reticular activating system begins in the hindbrain and continues through the midbrain into the forebrain. Important structures of the forebrain include the thalamus, hypothalamus, limbic system, and cerebrum. The hypothalamus is involved in controlling body temperature and regulating motivation and emotion.

9. **What are the other parts of the nervous system?** The somatic nervous system transmits sensory information about skeletal muscles, skin, and joints to the central nervous system. It also controls skeletal muscular activity. The autonomic nervous system (ANS) regulates the glands and activities such as heartbeat, digestion, and dilation of the pupils. The sympathetic division of the ANS helps expend the body's resources, such as when fleeing from a predator, and the parasympathetic division helps build the body's reserves.

10. **What are the parts of the cerebral cortex?** The cerebral cortex is divided into the frontal, parietal, temporal, and occipital lobes. The visual cortex is in the occipital lobe, and the auditory cortex is in the temporal lobe. The somatosensory cortex lies behind the central fissure in the parietal lobe, and the motor cortex lies in the frontal lobe, across the central fissure from the somatosensory cortex.

11. **What parts of the brain are involved in thought and language?** The language areas of the cortex lie near the intersection of the frontal, temporal, and parietal lobes in the dominant hemisphere. For right-handed people, the left hemisphere of the cortex is usually dominant. The notion that some people are left-brained whereas others are right-brained is exaggerated and largely inaccurate.

12. **How do people who have had split-brain operations behave?** For the most part, their behavior is perfectly normal. However, although they may verbally be able to describe a screened-off object such as a pencil that is held in the hand connected to the dominant hemisphere, they cannot do so when the object is held in the other hand.

13. **What is the endocrine system?** The endocrine system consists of ductless glands that secrete hormones.

14. **What are some pituitary hormones?** The pituitary gland secretes growth hormone; prolactin, which regulates maternal behavior in lower animals and stimulates production of milk in women; and oxytocin, which stimulates labor in pregnant women.

15. **What is the function of insulin?** Insulin enables the body to metabolize sugar. Diabetes, hyperglycemia, and hypoglycemia are all linked to imbalances in insulin.

16. **What hormones are produced by the adrenal glands?** The adrenal cortex produces steroids, which promote the development of muscle mass and increase activity level. The adrenal medulla secretes adrenaline (epinephrine), which increases the metabolic rate and is involved in general emotional arousal.

17. **What hormones are secreted by the testes and ovaries?** These are sex hormones such as testos-

terone, progesterone, and estrogen. Sex hormones are responsible for prenatal sexual differentiation, and female sex hormones regulate the menstrual cycle.

18. **What is genetics?** Genetics is the branch of biology concerned with the transmission of traits from generation to generation.

19. **What are genes and chromosomes?** Genes (which consist of DNA) are the basic building blocks of heredity. A thousand or more genes make up each chromosome. People normally have 46 chromosomes arranged in 23 pairs in each cell in the body.

They receive 23 chromosomes from the father and 23 from the mother.

20. **What are kinship studies?** These are studies of the distribution of traits or behavior patterns among related people. When certain behaviors are shared by close relatives, such as identical twins, they may have a genetic component. This is especially so when the behaviors are shared by close blood relatives (parents and children, or identical twins) who have been separated early and reared in different environments.

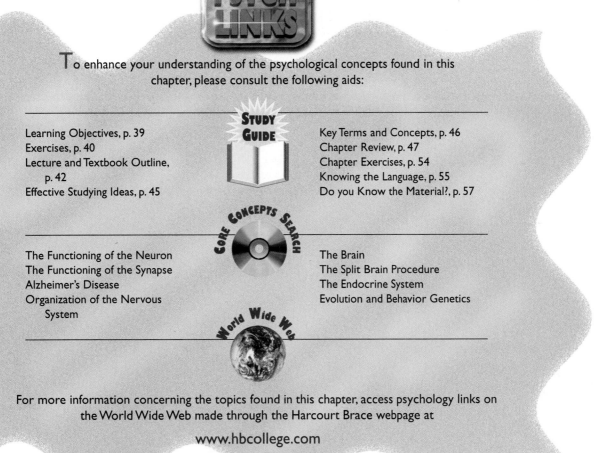

To enhance your understanding of the psychological concepts found in this chapter, please consult the following aids:

STUDY GUIDE

Learning Objectives, p. 39
Exercises, p. 40
Lecture and Textbook Outline, p. 42
Effective Studying Ideas, p. 45

Key Terms and Concepts, p. 46
Chapter Review, p. 47
Chapter Exercises, p. 54
Knowing the Language, p. 55
Do you Know the Material?, p. 57

CORE CONCEPTS SEARCH

The Functioning of the Neuron
The Functioning of the Synapse
Alzheimer's Disease
Organization of the Nervous System

The Brain
The Split Brain Procedure
The Endocrine System
Evolution and Behavior Genetics

World Wide Web

For more information concerning the topics found in this chapter, access psychology links on the World Wide Web made through the Harcourt Brace webpage at

www.hbcollege.com

Share your comments and questions with your author at

PsychLinks@aol.com

Many psychologists study human development through the lifespan. This family portrait by Chinese American artist Hung Liu—*Branches: Three Generations of the Wong Family (detail panel #3) (1988)*—portrays people in various stages of life. It is, in a sense, a snapshot of the United States of the new millennium. We are a nation made up mainly of immigrants, who often marry the offspring of previous generations of immigrants and thus provide vigorous new directions for growth and development. Much of Liu's work deals with acculturation in the United States.

HUNG LIU

Chapter 4
Lifespan Development

TRUTH OR FICTION?

✔ **T F**

☐ ☐ Fertilization takes place in the uterus.

☐ ☐ Your heart started beating when you were only one-fifth of an inch long and weighed a fraction of an ounce.

☐ ☐ The way to a baby's heart is through its stomach—that is, babies become emotionally attached to those who feed them.

☐ ☐ Children with strict parents are most likely to become competent.

☐ ☐ Children placed in day care are more aggressive than children cared for in the home.

☐ ☐ Child abusers frequently were abused themselves as children.

☐ ☐ A girl can become pregnant when she has her first menstrual period.

☐ ☐ Menopause signals the end of a woman's sexual interest.

☐ ☐ Mothers suffer from the "empty-nest syndrome" when their youngest child leaves home.

☐ ☐ Older people who blame health problems on aging rather than on specific factors such as a virus are more likely to die in the near future.

OUTLINE

CONTROVERSIES IN DEVELOPMENTAL PSYCHOLOGY
Does Development Reflect Nature or Nurture?
Is Development Continuous or Discontinuous?

PRENATAL DEVELOPMENT
Psychology and Modern Life:
Averting Genetic and Chromosomal Abnormalities

PHYSICAL DEVELOPMENT
Reflexes
Perceptual Development

SOCIAL DEVELOPMENT
Erik Erikson's Stages of Psychosocial Development
Attachment: Ties That Bind
Parenting Styles: Rearing the Competent Child
Day Care
Psychology and Modern Life:
Becoming an Authoritative Parent
Child Abuse

COGNITIVE DEVELOPMENT
Jean Piaget's Cognitive-Developmental Theory
Information-Processing Approaches to Cognitive Development
Lawrence Kohlberg's Theory of Moral Development
Psychology in a World of Diversity:
Are There Gender Differences in Moral Development?

ADOLESCENCE
Physical Development
Social and Personality Development

ADULT DEVELOPMENT
Young Adulthood
Middle Adulthood
Psychology in the New Millennium:
What Biological Clock?
Late Adulthood
Psychology in a World of Diversity:
Gender, Ethnicity, and Aging
Questionnaire:
How Long Will You Live? The Life-Expectancy Scale

There is no cure for birth or death save to enjoy the interval.

GEORGE SANTAYANA

O̶N A SUMMERLIKE DAY IN OCTOBER, LING Chang and her husband Patrick rush out to their jobs as usual. While Ling, a buyer for a New York department store, is arranging for dresses from the Chicago manufacturer to arrive in time for the spring line, a very different drama is unfolding in her body. Hormones are causing a follicle (egg container) in one of her ovaries to rupture and release an egg cell, or ovum. Ling, like other women, possessed from birth all the egg cells she would ever have. How this particular ovum was selected to ripen and be released this month is unknown. But in any case, Ling will be capable of becoming pregnant for only a couple of days following ovulation.

When it is released, the ovum begins a slow journey down a 4-inch-long fallopian tube to the uterus. It is within this tube that one of Patrick's sperm cells will unite with the egg. The fertilized ovum, or zygote, is 1/175th of an inch across—a tiny stage for the drama that is about to unfold.

Developmental psychologists would be pleased to study the development of Patrick and Ling's new child from the time of conception until death. There are several reasons for this. One is that the discovery of early influences and developmental sequences helps psychologists understand adults. Psychologists are also interested in the effects of genetic factors, early interactions with parents and siblings (brothers and sisters), and the school and community on traits such as aggressiveness and intelligence.

Developmental psychologists also seek to learn the causes of developmental abnormalities. For instance, should pregnant women abstain from smoking and drinking? (Yes.) Is it safe for a pregnant woman to take aspirin for a headache or tetracycline to ward off a bacterial invasion? (Perhaps not. Ask your obstetrician.) What factors contribute to child abuse? Developmental psychologists are also concerned with adult development. For example, what conflicts and disillusionments can we expect as we journey through our thirties, forties, and fifties? The information acquired by developmental psychologists can help us make decisions about how we rear our children and lead our own lives.

Developmental psychologists, like other psychologists, see things in different ways. Let us begin by discussing some of the controversies in developmental psychology.

■ CONTROVERSIES IN DEVELOPMENTAL PSYCHOLOGY

• *Does Development Reflect Nature or Nurture?*

What behavior is the result of nature? That is, what aspects of behavior originate in a person's genes and are biologically "programmed" to unfold in the child as long as minimal needs for nutrition and social experience are met?

Truth or Fiction Revisited

It is not true that fertilization takes place in the uterus. Fertilization normally occurs in a fallopian tube.

What behavior is the result of nurture? That is, what aspects of behavior largely reflect environmental influences such as nutrition and learning?

Psychologists seek to understand the influences of nature in our genetic heritage, in the functioning of the nervous system, and in the process of **maturation** (that is, the unfolding of traits, as determined by the genetic code). Psychologists look for the influences of nurture in our nutrition, cultural and family backgrounds, and opportunities for learning, including early mental stimulation and formal education. The American psychologist Arnold Gesell (1880–1961) leaned heavily toward natural explanations of development. He argued that all areas of development are self-regulated by the unfolding of natural plans and processes. John Watson and other behaviorists leaned heavily toward environmental explanations. Today, most researchers would agree that both nature and nurture affect most areas of development (Azar, 1997c).

• *Is Development Continuous or Discontinuous?*

Do developmental changes occur gradually (continuously)? Or do they occur in major leaps (discontinuously) that dramatically alter our bodies and behavior?

Watson and other behaviorists viewed development as a continuous process in which the effects of learning mount gradually, with no major sudden changes. Maturational theorists believe that rapid qualitative changes are ushered in in new stages of development. They point out that the environment, even when enriched, profits us little until we are ready, or mature enough, to develop in a certain direction. For example, newborn babies will not imitate their parents' speech, even when the parents speak clearly and deliberately. Nor does aided practice in "walking" during the first few months after birth significantly accelerate the date at which the child can walk on her or his own.

Stage theorists, such as Sigmund Freud and Jean Piaget, saw development as discontinuous. Both theorists saw biological changes as providing the potential for psychological changes. Freud focused on the ways in which sexual development might provide the basis for personality development. Piaget's research centered on the ways in which maturation of the nervous system permits cognitive advances. (Freud's theory of psychosexual development is discussed in Chapter 12.)

Certain aspects of physical development do occur in stages. For example, from the age of 2 to the onset of **puberty** (the period of development during which reproduction becomes possible), children gradually grow larger. Then the adolescent growth spurt occurs. It is ushered in by hormones and characterized by rapid changes in structure and function (as in the development of the sex organs) as well as in size. Thus a new stage of life has begun. Psychologists disagree more strongly on whether aspects of development such as cognitive development, attachment, and gender typing occur in stages.

Let us now turn to the changes that occur between conception and birth. Although they may be literally "out of sight," the most dramatic biological changes occur within the short span of 9 months.

■ PRENATAL DEVELOPMENT

During the months following conception, the single cell formed by the union of sperm and egg—the zygote—will multiply, becoming two, then four, then eight, and so on. By the time the infant is ready to be born, it will contain trillions of cells. Prenatal development is divided into three periods: the germinal stage (approximately the first 2 weeks), the embryonic stage (which lasts from 2 weeks to about 2 months after conception), and the fetal stage. The infant is referred to as an **embryo** in the second stage and as a **fetus** in the third stage.

MATURATION • (mat-your-RAY-shun). The orderly unfolding of traits, as regulated by the genetic code.
PUBERTY • (PEW-burr-tee *or* POO-burr-tee). The period of physical development during which sexual reproduction first becomes possible.
EMBRYO • (EM-bree-oh). The baby from the third through the eighth weeks following conception, during which time the major organ systems undergo rapid differentiation.
FETUS • (FEE-tuss). The baby from the third month following conception through childbirth, during which time there is maturation of organ systems and dramatic gains in length and weight.

An Exercise Class for Pregnant Women. Years ago pregnant women were not expected to exert themselves. Today, it is recognized that exercise is healthful for pregnant women because it promotes fitness, which is beneficial during childbirth as well as at other times.

THE GERMINAL STAGE The zygote divides repeatedly as it proceeds on its 3- to 4-day journey to the uterus. The ball-like mass of multiplying cells wanders about the uterus for another 3 to 4 days before beginning to implant in the uterine wall. Implantation takes another week or so. The period from conception to implantation is called the **germinal stage,** or the **period of the ovum.**

A few days into the germinal stage, cells are separating into groups according to what they will become. Prior to implantation, the dividing ball of cells is nourished solely by the yolk of the original egg cell and its mass does not increase.

Truth or Fiction Revisited

It is true that your heart started beating when you were only one-fifth of an inch long and weighed a fraction of an ounce. It started about 3 weeks after conception.

THE EMBRYONIC STAGE The embryonic stage lasts from implantation until about the eighth week of development. During this stage, the major body organ systems take form. As you can see from the relatively large heads of embryos and fetuses during prenatal development (see Figure 4.1), the growth of the head precedes that of the lower parts of the body. The growth of the organs—heart, lungs, and so on—also precedes the growth of the extremities. The relatively early maturation of the brain and the organ systems allows them to participate in the nourishment and further development of the embryo. During the fourth week, a primitive heart begins to beat and pump blood—in an organism that is one-fifth of an inch long. The heart will continue to beat without rest every minute of every day for perhaps 80 or 90 years.

By the end of the second month, the head has become rounded and the facial features distinct—all in an embryo that is about 1 inch long and weighs 1/30th of an ounce. During the second month, the nervous system begins to transmit messages. By 5 to 6 weeks, the embryo is only a quarter to half an inch long, yet nondescript sex organs have formed. By about the seventh week, the genetic code (XY or XX) begins to assert itself, causing the sex organs to differentiate. If a Y sex chromosome is present, testes form and begin to produce **androgens** (the male sex hormones), which further masculinize the sex organs. In the absence of these hormones, the embryo develops female sex organs.

GERMINAL STAGE • The first stage of prenatal development during which the dividing mass of cells has not become implanted in the uterine wall.
PERIOD OF THE OVUM • Another term for the *germinal stage.*
ANDROGENS • (AND-row-jennz). Male sex hormones.

As it develops, the embryo is suspended within a protective **amniotic sac** in the mother's uterus. The sac is surrounded by a clear membrane and contains amniotic fluid. The fluid serves as a sort of natural air bag, allowing the child to move or even jerk around without injury. It also helps maintain an even temperature around the child.

The embryo, and later the fetus, exchanges nutrients and wastes with the mother through a pancake-shaped organ called the **placenta.** It is connected to the placenta by the **umbilical cord,** and the placenta is connected to the mother by the system of blood vessels in the uterine wall.

The circulatory systems of the mother and baby do not mix. A membrane in the placenta permits only certain substances to pass through. Oxygen and nutrients are passed from the mother to the embryo. Carbon dioxide and other wastes are passed from the child to the mother, where they are removed by the mother's lungs and kidneys. Unfortunately, a number of other substances can

AMNIOTIC SAC • (am-knee-OTT-tick). A sac within the uterus that contains the embryo or fetus.
PLACENTA • (pluh-SENT-uh). A membrane that permits the exchange of nutrients and waste products between the mother and her developing child but does not allow the maternal and fetal bloodstreams to mix.
UMBILICAL CORD • (um-BILL-lick-al). A tube between the mother and her developing child through which nutrients and waste products are conducted.

FIGURE 4.1
EMBRYOS AND FETUSES AT VARIOUS INTERVALS OF PRENATAL DEVELOPMENT

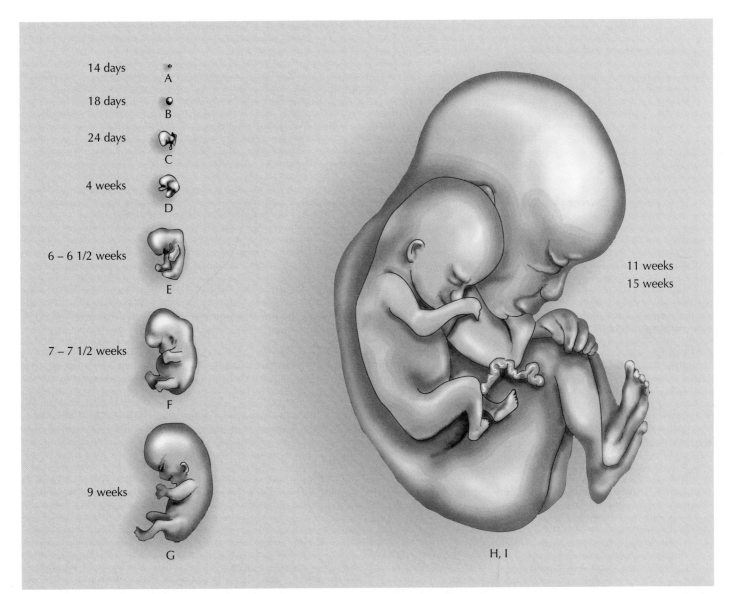

14 days — A
18 days — B
24 days — C
4 weeks — D
6 – 6 1/2 weeks — E
7 – 7 1/2 weeks — F
9 weeks — G
11 weeks / 15 weeks — H, I

pass through the placenta. They include some microscopic disease organisms—such as those that cause syphilis and German measles—and some chemical agents, including acne drugs, aspirin, narcotics, alcohol, and tranquilizers. Because these and other agents may be harmful to the baby, pregnant women are advised to consult their physicians about the advisability of using any drugs, even those that are sold over the counter.

THE FETAL STAGE   The fetal stage lasts from the beginning of the third month until birth. By the end of the third month, the major organ systems and the fingers and toes have been formed. In the middle of the fourth month, the mother usually detects the first fetal movements. By the end of the sixth month, the fetus moves its limbs so vigorously that the mother may complain of being kicked. The fetus opens and shuts its eyes, sucks its thumb, alternates between periods of wakefulness and sleep, and perceives light. It also turns somersaults, which can be clearly perceived by the mother. The umbilical cord is composed so that it will not break or become dangerously wrapped around the fetus, no matter how many acrobatic feats the fetus performs.

During the last 3 months, the organ systems of the fetus continue to mature. The heart and lungs become increasingly capable of sustaining independent life.

psychology and
modern life

AVERTING GENETIC AND CHROMOSOMAL ABNORMALITIES

Genetic counselors obtain information about a couple's medical background to assess the risk that they might pass along genetic defects to their children. Some couples who face a high risk of doing so choose to adopt instead of having their own children. Other couples choose to have an abortion if the fetus is found to have certain abnormalities.

Various procedures are used to learn whether the fetus has these disorders. *Amniocentesis* is usually performed about four months into pregnancy. In this procedure, fluid containing fetal cells is drawn from the amniotic sac (or "bag of waters") with a syringe. The cells are then grown in a culture and examined for the presence of abnormalities. *Chorionic villus sampling (CVS)* is performed several weeks earlier. A narrow tube is used to snip off material from the chorion, a membrane that contains the amniotic sac and fetus, and the material is analyzed. CVS is somewhat riskier than amniocentesis, so most obstetricians prefer to use the latter. These tests are used to detect the presence of Down syndrome, sickle cell anemia, Tay-Sachs disease, spina bifida, muscular dystrophy, Rh incompatibility, and other disorders. They also reveal the gender of the fetus.

Ultrasound bounces high-pitched sound waves off the fetus, revealing a picture of the fetus on a monitor and allowing the obstetrician to detect certain abnormalities. Obstetricians also use ultrasound during amniocentesis to locate the fetus in order to avoid hitting it with the syringe.

Parental blood tests can suggest the presence of problems such as sickle cell anemia, Tay-Sachs disease, and neural tube defects. Still other tests examine fetal DNA and can indicate the presence of Huntington's chorea, cystic fibrosis, and other disorders. ∎

The fetus gains about 5½ pounds and doubles in length. Newborn boys average about 7½ pounds and newborn girls about 7 pounds.

■ PHYSICAL DEVELOPMENT

Physical development includes gains in height and weight; maturation of the nervous system; and development of bones, muscles, and the sex organs.

The most dramatic gains in height and weight occur during prenatal development. Within 9 months a child develops from a nearly microscopic cell to a **neonate** (newborn) about 20 inches long. Its weight increases a billionfold. During infancy, these dramatic gains continue. Babies usually double their birth weight in about 5 months and triple it by their first birthday. Their height increases by about 10 inches in the first year. Children grow another 4 to 6 inches during the second year and gain some 4 to 7 pounds. After that, they gain about 2 to 3 inches a year until they reach the adolescent growth spurt. Weight gains also remain fairly even at about 4 to 6 pounds per year.

• *Reflexes*

Soon after you were born, a doctor or nurse probably pressed her fingers against the palms of your hands. Although you would have had no "idea" what to do in response, most likely you grasped the fingers firmly—so firmly that you could actually have been lifted from your cradle! Grasping at birth is inborn. It is one of the neonate's many **reflexes**—simple, unlearned, stereotypical responses elicited by specific stimuli. Reflexes are essential to survival and do not involve higher brain functions. They occur automatically, without thinking.

Newborn children do not know that it is necessary to eat to survive. Fortunately, they have rooting and sucking reflexes that cause them to eat. They turn their head toward stimuli that prod or stroke the cheek, chin, or corner of the mouth. This is termed **rooting.** They suck objects that touch their lips.

Neonates have numerous other reflexes that aid in survival. They withdraw from painful stimuli. This is known as the withdrawal reflex. They draw up their legs and arch their backs in response to sudden noises, bumps, or loss of support while being held. This is the startle, or Moro, reflex. They grasp objects that press against the palms of their hands (the grasp, or palmar, reflex). They fan their toes when the soles of their feet are stimulated (the Babinski reflex). Pediatricians assess babies' neural functioning by testing these reflexes.

Babies also breathe, sneeze, cough, yawn, and blink reflexively. And it is guaranteed that you will learn about the **sphincter** (anal muscle) reflex if you put on your best clothes and hold an undiapered neonate on your lap for a short while.

• *Perceptual Development*

Newborn children spend about 16 hours a day sleeping and do not have much opportunity to learn about the world. Yet they are capable of perceiving the world reasonably well soon after birth.

By the age of 3 months, infants can discriminate most colors (Banks & Shannon, 1993; Teller & Lindsey, 1993). Within a couple of days, they can follow, or track, a moving light with their eyes (Kellman & von Hofsten, 1992). Neonates are nearsighted but by about the age of 4 months, infants seem able to focus on distant objects about as well as adults can.

NEONATE • A newly born child.
REFLEX • A simple unlearned response to a stimulus.
ROOTING • The turning of an infant's head toward a touch, such as by the mother's nipple.
SPHINCTER • (SFINK-ter). A ringlike muscle that circles a body opening such as the anus. An infant will exhibit the sphincter reflex (have a bowel movement) in response to intestinal pressure.

FIGURE 4.2

MOTOR DEVELOPMENT

At birth, infants appear to be bundles of aimless "nervous energy." They have reflexes but also engage in random movements which are replaced by purposeful activity as they mature. Motor development proceeds in an orderly sequence. Practice prompts sensorimotor coordination, but maturation is essential. The times in the figure are approximate: An infant who is a bit behind may develop with no problems at all, and a precocious infant will not necessarily become a rocket scientist (or gymnast).

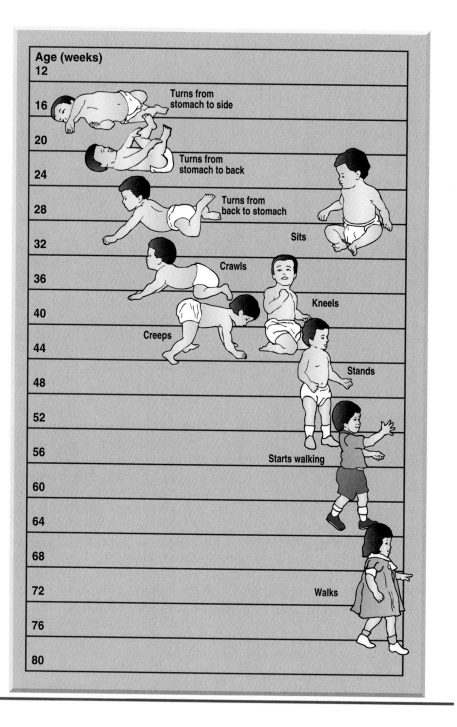

The visual preferences of infants are measured by the amount of time, termed **fixation time,** they spend looking at one stimulus instead of another. In classic research by Robert Fantz (1961), 2-month-old infants preferred visual stimuli that resembled the human face to newsprint, a bull's-eye, and featureless red, white, and yellow disks. Subsequent research suggests that at this age the complexity of facelike patterns may be more important than their content. For example, babies have been shown facelike patterns that differ either in the number of elements they contain or the degree to which they are organized to match the human face. Five- to 10-week-old babies fixate longer on patterns with high numbers of elements. The organization of the elements—that is, the

FIXATION TIME • The amount of time spent looking at a visual stimulus.

degree to which they resemble the face—is less important. By 15 to 20 weeks, the organization of the pattern also matters. At that age babies dwell longer on facelike patterns (e.g., Haaf and others, 1983).

Infants thus seem to have an inborn preference for complex visual stimuli. However, preference for faces as opposed to other equally complex stimuli may not emerge until infants have had experience with people. Nurture as well as nature may influence infants' preferences.

Classic research has shown that infants tend to respond to cues for depth by the time they are able to crawl (at about 6 to 8 months). Most also have the good sense to avoid crawling off ledges and table tops into open space (Campos and others, 1978). Note the setup (Figure 4.3) in the classic "visual cliff" experiment run by Walk and Gibson (1961). An 8-month-old infant crawls freely above the portion of the glass with a checkerboard pattern immediately beneath it, but hesitates to crawl over the portion of the glass beneath which the checkerboard has been dropped a few feet. Since the glass alone would support the infant, this is a "visual cliff," not an actual cliff.

Normal neonates hear well unless their middle ears are clogged with amniotic fluid. In such cases, hearing improves rapidly after the ears are opened up. Most neonates reflexively turn their heads toward unusual sounds, suspending other activities as they do so. This finding, along with findings about visual tracking, suggests that infants are preprogrammed to survey their environments. Speaking or singing softly in a low-pitched tone soothes infants (Papousek and others, 1991). This is why some parents use lullabies to get infants to fall asleep.

Three-day-old babies prefer their mother's voice to those of other women, but they do not show a similar preference for their father's voice (DeCasper & Prescott, 1984; Freeman and others, 1993). By birth, of course, babies have had many months of "experience" in the uterus. For at least 2 or 3 months, babies have been capable of hearing sounds. Because they are predominantly exposed to sounds produced by their mother, learning may contribute to neonatal preferences.

The nasal preferences of babies are similar to those of adults. Newborn infants spit, stick out their tongue, and literally wrinkle their nose at the odor of

FIGURE 4.3
THE CLASSIC VISUAL CLIFF EXPERIMENT
This young explorer has the good sense not to crawl out onto an apparently unsupported surface, even when Mother beckons from the other side. Rats, pups, kittens, and chicks also will not try to walk across to the other side. (So don't bother asking why the chicken crossed the visual cliff.)

Allyn. At the age of 2 the author's daughter Allyn nearly succeeded in preventing the publication of an earlier edition of this book by continually pulling him away from the computer when he was at work. Because of their mutual attachment, separation was painful.

rotten eggs. They smile and make licking motions in response to chocolate, strawberry, vanilla, and honey. The sense of smell, like the sense of hearing, may provide a vehicle for mother–infant recognition. Within the first week, nursing infants prefer to turn to look at their mother's nursing pads (which can be discriminated only by smell) rather than those of strange women (Macfarlane, 1975). By 15 days, nursing infants prefer their mother's underarm odor to those of other women (Porter and others, 1992). Bottle-fed babies do not show this preference.

Shortly after birth, infants can discriminate tastes. They suck liquid solutions of sugar and milk but grimace and refuse to suck salty or bitter solutions.

Newborn babies are sensitive to touch. Many reflexes (including rooting and sucking) are activated by pressure against the skin. Newborns are relatively insensitive to pain, however. This may be adaptive, considering the squeezing that occurs during the birth process. Sensitivity to pain increases within a few days.

The sense of touch is an extremely important avenue of learning and communication for babies. Sensations of skin against skin appear to provide feelings of comfort and security that may contribute to the formation of affectionate bonds between infants and their caregivers.

REFLECTIONS

- Which aspects of your own development seem to be most influenced by nature or nurture? Why?
- How can you use knowledge of prenatal development in your own life?

■ SOCIAL DEVELOPMENT

At the age of 2, my daughter Allyn almost succeeded in preventing the publication of an earlier edition of this book. When I locked myself into my study, she positioned herself outside the door and called, "Daddy, oh Daddy." At other times, she would bang on the door or cry outside. When I would give in (several times a day) and open the door, she would run in and say, "I want you to pick up me" and hold out her arms or climb into my lap. Although we were separate human beings, it was as though she were very much *attached* to me.

Attachment is one of the issues involved in the social development of the child. When we are infants, social relationships are crucial to our very survival. Later in life, they contribute to our feelings of happiness and satisfaction. In this section we discuss many aspects of social development, including Erikson's theory of psychosocial development, attachment, styles of parenting, day care, and child abuse.

• Erik Erikson's Stages of Psychosocial Development

TRUST VERSUS MISTRUST • Erikson's first stage of psychosexual development, during which children do—or do not—come to trust that primary caregivers and the environment will meet their needs.
AUTONOMY • Self-direction.
ATTACHMENT • The enduring affectional tie that binds one person to another.

According to Erik Erikson, we undergo several stages of psychosocial development (see Table 4.1). During his first stage, **trust versus mistrust,** we depend on our primary caregivers (usually our parents) and come to expect that our environments will—or will not—meet our needs. During early childhood and the preschool years, we begin to explore the environment more actively and try new things. At this time, our relationships with our parents and friends can encourage us to develop **autonomy** (self-direction) and initiative, or feelings of

TABLE 4.1 ERIKSON'S STAGES OF PSYCHOSOCIAL DEVELOPMENT

TIME PERIOD	LIFE CRISIS	THE DEVELOPMENTAL TASK
Infancy (0–1)	Trust versus mistrust	Coming to trust the mother and the environment—to associate surroundings with feelings of inner goodness
Early childhood (1–3)	Autonomy versus shame and doubt	Developing the wish to make choices and the self-control to exercise choice
Preschool years (4–5)	Initiative versus guilt	Adding planning and "attacking" to choice, becoming active and on the move
Grammar school years 6–12)	Industry versus in-feriority	Becoming eagerly absorbed in skills, tasks, and productivity; mastering the fundamentals of technology
Adolescence	Identity versus role diffusion	Connecting skills and social roles to formation of career objectives
Young adulthood	Intimacy versus isolation	Committing the self to another; engaging in sexual love
Middle adulthood	Generativity versus stagnation	Needing to be needed; guiding and encouraging the younger generation; being creative
Late adulthood	Integrity versus despair	Accepting the time and place of one's life cycle; achieving wisdom and dignity

Note. From Erikson, 1963, pp. 247–269.

shame and guilt. During the elementary school years, friends and teachers take on more importance, encouraging us to become industrious or to develop feelings of inferiority.

We return to Erikson later in the chapter, in the sections on adolescence and adulthood, and in Chapter 12. We will see that as young adults we tend to form intimate relationships with others. In middle adulthood, other people, including our children, often come to depend on us.

• *Attachment: Ties That Bind*

Mary D. Salter Ainsworth, a psychologist who is renowned for her studies of attachment behavior, defines **attachment** as an emotional tie that is formed between one animal or person and another specific individual. Attachment keeps organisms together and tends to endure over time. It is vital to the survival of the infant (Bowlby, 1988).

The behaviors that define attachment include (1) attempts to maintain contact or nearness and (2) shows of anxiety when separated. Babies and children try to maintain contact with caregivers to whom they are attached. They engage in eye contact, pull and tug at them, ask to be picked up, and may even jump in front of them in such a way that they will be "run over" if they are not picked up!

THE STRANGE SITUATION AND PATTERNS OF ATTACHMENT The ways in which infants behave in strange situations are connected with their bonds of

Attachment. Feelings of attachment bind most parents closely to their children. According to Mary Ainsworth, attachment is an emotional bond between an individual and another specific individual. Secure attachment paves the way for healthy social development.

attachment with their caregivers. Given this fact, Mary Ainsworth and her colleagues (1978) innovated the *strange situation method* as a way of measuring attachment in infants. It involves a series of separations and reunions with a caregiver (usually the mother) and a stranger. Infants are led through episodes involving the mother and a stranger in a laboratory room. For example, the mother carries the infant into the room and puts him or her down. A stranger enters and talks with the mother. The stranger then approaches the infant with a toy and the mother leaves the room. The mother and stranger take turns interacting with the infant in the room, and the infant's behavior is observed in each case.

Using the strange situation, Ainsworth and her colleagues (1978) identified three major types of attachment: secure attachment and two types of insecure attachment:

1. *Secure attachment.* Securely attached infants mildly protest their mother's departure, seek interaction upon reunion, and are readily comforted by her.

2. *Avoidant attachment.* Infants who show avoidant attachment are least distressed by their mother's departure. They play by themselves without fuss and ignore their mothers when they return.

3. *Ambivalent/resistant attachment.* Infants with ambivalent/resistant attachment are the most emotional. They show severe signs of distress when their mother leaves and show ambivalence upon reunion by alternately clinging to and pushing their mother away when she returns.

Attachment is connected with the quality of care that infants receive. The parents of securely attached children are more likely to be affectionate and reliable caregivers (Cox and others, 1992; Isabella, 1993). Securely attached children are happier, more sociable, and more cooperative than insecurely attached children (Belsky and others, 1991; Thompson, 1991a). Securely attached preschoolers have longer attention spans, are less impulsive, and are better at solving problems (Frankel & Bates, 1990; Lederberg & Mobley, 1990). At ages 5 and 6, securely attached children are liked better by their peers and teachers, are more competent, and have fewer behavior problems than insecurely attached children (Lyons-Ruth and others, 1993; Youngblade & Belsky, 1992).

STAGES OF ATTACHMENT Ainsworth also studied phases in the development of attachment by observing Ugandan infants. She noted their efforts to maintain contact with the mother, their protests when separated from her, and their use of her as a base for exploring their environment. At first, the Ugandan infants showed **indiscriminate attachment.** That is, they preferred being held or being with someone to being alone, but they showed no preferences for particular people. Specific attachment to the mother began to develop at about 4 months of age and became intense by about 7 months of age. Fear of strangers, if it developed at all, followed 1 or 2 months later.

From studies such as these, Ainsworth identified three stages of attachment:

1. The **initial-preattachment phase,** which lasts from birth to about 3 months and is characterized by indiscriminate attachment

2. The **attachment-in-the-making phase,** which occurs at about 3 or 4 months and is characterized by preference for familiar figures

3. The **clear-cut-attachment phase,** which occurs at about 6 or 7 months and is characterized by intensified dependence on the primary caregiver

John Bowlby noted that attachment is also characterized by fear of strangers ("stranger anxiety"). But not all children show fear of strangers.

INDISCRIMINATE ATTACHMENT • Showing attachment behaviors toward any person.
INITIAL-PREATTACHMENT PHASE • The first phase in forming bonds of attachment, characterized by indiscriminate attachment.
ATTACHMENT-IN-THE-MAKING PHASE • The second phase in forming bonds of attachment, characterized by preference for familiar figures.
CLEAR-CUT-ATTACHMENT PHASE • The third phase in forming bonds of attachment, characterized by intensified dependence on the primary caregiver.

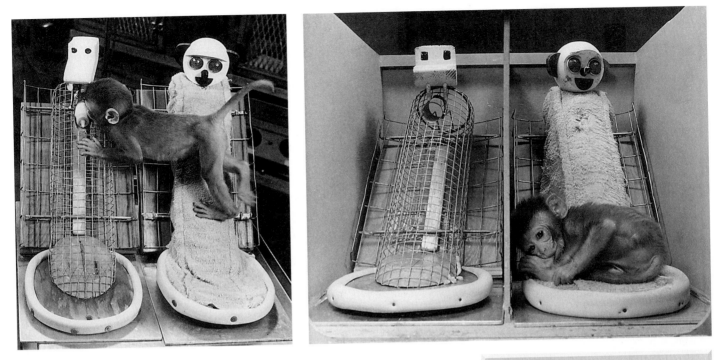

FIGURE 4.4
ATTACHMENT IN INFANT MONKEYS
Although this rhesus monkey infant is fed by the wire "mother," it spends most of its time clinging to the soft, cuddly terrycloth "mother." It knows where to get a meal, but contact comfort is
apparently more important than food in the development of attachment in infant monkeys (and
infant humans?).

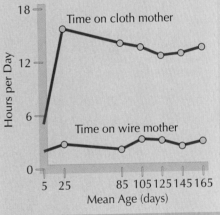

THEORETICAL VIEWS OF ATTACHMENT Early in the century, behaviorists argued that attachment behaviors are learned through experience. Caregivers
feed their infants and tend to their other physiological needs. Thus, infants associate their caregivers with gratification of needs and learn to approach them to
meet their needs. The feelings of gratification associated with the meeting of basic needs generalize into feelings of security when the caregiver is present.

Classic research by psychologist Harry F. Harlow suggests that skin contact
may be more important than learning experiences. Harlow had noted that infant rhesus monkeys reared without mothers or companions became attached
to pieces of cloth in their cages. They maintained contact with them and showed
distress when separated from them. Harlow conducted a series of experiments
to find out why (Harlow, 1959).

In one study, Harlow placed infant rhesus monkeys in cages with two surrogate mothers, as shown in Figure 4.4. One "mother" was made of wire mesh
from which a baby bottle was extended. The other surrogate mother was made
of soft, cuddly terrycloth. The infant monkeys spent most of their time clinging
to the cloth mother, even though "she" did not gratify their need for food. Harlow concluded that monkeys—and perhaps humans—have a primary (unlearned) need for **contact comfort** that is as basic as the need for food.
Gratification of the need for contact comfort, rather than food, might be why infant monkeys (and humans) cling to their mothers.

Harlow and Zimmerman (1959) found that a surrogate mother made of terrycloth could also serve as a comforting base from which an infant monkey
could explore its environment. Toys such as stuffed bears (see Figure 4.5) and
oversized wooden insects were placed in cages with infant rhesus monkeys and

Truth or Fiction Revisited
....
*It is not true that the way to a baby's heart is
through its stomach. (Babies do not necessarily
become attached to the people who feed them.)
Contact comfort may be a stronger wellspring of
attachment. The path to a monkey's heart may
lie through its skin, not its stomach.*

CONTACT COMFORT • A hypothesized primary drive
to seek physical comfort through contact with another.

FIGURE 4.5
SECURITY

With its terrycloth surrogate mother nearby, this infant rhesus monkey apparently feels secure enough to explore the "bear monster" placed in its cage. But infants with wire surrogate mothers or no mothers at all cower in a corner when such "monsters" are introduced.

their surrogate mothers. When the infants were alone or had wire surrogate mothers for companions, they cowered in fear as long as the "bear monster" or "insect monster" was present. But when the terrycloth mothers were present, the infants clung to them for a while and then explored the intruding "monster." With human infants, too, the bonds of mother–infant attachment appear to provide a secure base from which infants feel encouraged to express their curiosity.

Other researchers, such as Konrad Lorenz, note that for many animals, attachment is an instinct—an inborn fixed-action pattern (FAP). Attachment, like other instincts, is theorized to occur in the presence of a specific stimulus and during a **critical period** of life.

Some animals become attached to the first moving object they encounter. The unwritten rule seems to be, "If it moves, it must be mother." It is as if the image of the moving object becomes "imprinted" on the young animal. The formation of an attachment in this manner is therefore called **imprinting**.

Konrad Lorenz (1981) became well known when pictures of his "family" of goslings were made public (see Figure 4.6). How did Lorenz acquire his following? He was present when the goslings hatched and during their critical period, and he allowed them to follow him. The critical period for geese and some other animals is bounded, at the younger end, by the age at which they first walk and, at the older end, by the age at which they develop fear of strangers. The goslings followed Lorenz persistently, ran to him when they were frightened, honked with distress at his departure, and tried to overcome barriers between them. If you substitute crying for honking, it all sounds rather human.

If imprinting occurs with children, the process is not quite the same as that with ducks and geese. The upper limit for waterbirds is the age at which they develop fear of strangers, but not all children develop this fear. When children do develop fear of strangers, they do so at about 6 to 8 months of age—*prior to* independent locomotion, or crawling, which usually occurs 1 or 2 months later. Moreover, the critical period with humans would be quite extended. Despite these differences, Ainsworth and Bowlby (1991) also consider attachment in humans to be instinctive.

• *Parenting Styles: Rearing the Competent Child*

Many children have what psychologist Diana Baumrind terms **instrumental competence.** This means that they can manipulate their environment to achieve

CRITICAL PERIOD • A period of time when a fixed action pattern can be elicited by a releasing stimulus.
IMPRINTING • A process occurring during a critical period in the development of an organism, in which that organism responds to a stimulus in a manner that will afterward be difficult to modify.
INSTRUMENTAL COMPETENCE • Ability to manipulate one's environment to achieve one's goals.

TABLE 4.2 PARENTING STYLES				
		PARENTAL BEHAVIOR		
STYLE OF PARENTING	Restrictiveness	Demands for Mature Behavior	Communication Ability	Warmth and Support
Authoritarian	High (Use of force)	Moderate	Low	Low
Authoritative	High (Use of reasoning)	High	High	High
Permissive	Low (Easygoing)	Low	Low	High

Note. According to Baumrind, the children of authoritative parents are most competent. The children of permissive parents are the least mature.

FIGURE 4.6

IMPRINTING

Quite a following? Konrad Lorenz may not look like Mommy to you, but the goslings in the photo to the left became attached to him because he was the first moving object they perceived and followed. This type of attachment process is referred to as *imprinting.* In the photo to the right, ethologist and aviator Bill Lishman is followed by geese who were imprinted on him.

their goals. Competent children also tend to be energetic and cooperative, self-assertive, self-reliant, mature, achievement-oriented, and curious.

How does competence develop? Baumrind (1973; Lamb & Baumrind, 1978) studied the relationship between parenting styles and the development of competence. She focused on four aspects of parental behavior: strictness; demands for the child to achieve intellectual, emotional, and social maturity; communication ability; and warmth and involvement. The three most important parenting styles she found are the *authoritative, authoritarian,* and *permissive* styles.

1. *Authoritative Parents.* The parents of the most competent children rate high in all four areas of behavior (see Table 4.2). They are strict (restrictive) and demand mature behavior. However, they temper their strictness and demands with willingness to reason with their children, and with love and support. They expect a lot, but they explain why and offer help. Baumrind labeled these parents **authoritative parents** to suggest that they know what they want but are also loving and respectful of their children.

2. *Authoritarian Parents.* **Authoritarian parents** view obedience as a virtue to be pursued for its own sake. They have strict guidelines about what is right and wrong, and they demand that their children adhere to those guidelines. Both authoritative and authoritarian parents are strict. However, authoritative parents explain their demands and are supportive, whereas authoritarian parents rely on force and communicate poorly with their children. They do not respect their children's points of view, and they may be cold and rejecting. When their children ask them why they should behave in a certain way, authoritarian parents often answer, "Because I say so!"

3. *Permissive Parents.* **Permissive parents** are generally easygoing with their children. As a result, the children do pretty much whatever they wish. Permissive parents are warm and supportive, but poor at communicating.

Research evidence shows that warmth is superior to coldness in rearing children (Dix, 1991). Children of warm parents are more likely to be socially and emotionally well-adjusted and to internalize moral standards—that is, to develop a conscience (MacDonald, 1992; Miller and others, 1993).

AUTHORITATIVE PARENTS • Parents who are strict and warm. Authoritative parents demand mature behavior but use reason rather than force in discipline.

AUTHORITARIAN PARENTS • Parents who are rigid in their rules and who demand obedience for the sake of obedience.

PERMISSIVE PARENTS • Parents who impose few, if any, rules and who do not supervise their children closely.

Strictness also appears to pay off, provided that it is tempered by reason and warmth. Children of authoritative parents have greater self-reliance, self-esteem, social competence, and achievement motivation than other children do (Baumrind, 1991b; Dumas & LaFreniere, 1993; Putallaz & Hefflin, 1990). Children of authoritarian parents are often withdrawn or aggressive, and they usually do not do as well in school as children of authoritative parents (Olson and others, 1992; Westerman, 1990). Children of permissive parents seem to be the least mature. They are frequently impulsive, moody, and aggressive. In adolescence, lack of parental monitoring is often linked to delinquency and poor academic performance.

• Day Care

In the 1990s, only about 7% of U.S. families fit the traditional model in which the husband was the breadwinner and the wife was a full-time homemaker (Silverstein, 1991). Most mothers, including more than half of mothers of children younger than 1 year of age, work outside the home (U.S. Bureau of the Census, 1995). As a consequence, millions of American preschoolers are placed in day care. Parents and psychologists are concerned about what happens to children in day care. What, for example, are the effects of day care on cognitive development and social development?

Truth or Fiction Revisited

It is true that children with strict parents are most likely to become competent. This is especially so when the parents also reason with their children and are loving and supportive.

psychology and modern life

BECOMING AN AUTHORITATIVE PARENT

The research shows that an authoritative parenting style is associated with competence in children. On the other hand, authoritarian and permissive parenting styles are associated with a greater risk that children will develop academic, emotional, and social problems.

We can become more authoritative as parents by following four principles:

1. Be reasonably restrictive. Don't allow your children to "run wild." But exert control through reason rather than force.

2. Be willing to demand mature behavior. But temper these demands with knowledge of what your child can do as an individual and at a given stage of development.

3. Communicate with your children. Explain your demands. At an early age, the explanation can be simple: "That hurts!" or "You're breaking things that are important to Mommy and Daddy!" The point is to help your child develop a sense of val-

ues that he or she can use to make his or her own decisions.

4. Be warm. Express feelings of love and caring. Use lots of hugs and kisses. Praise your child's achievements (playing independently for a few minutes at the age of 2 is an achievement).

There are no guarantees, but by following these principles we may decrease our children's risk of developing academic, emotional, and social problems. ■

Day Care. Because most parents in the United States are in the work force, day care is a major influence on the lives of millions of children.

In part, the answer depends on the quality of the day care center. A large-scale study funded by the National Institute on Child Health and Human Development found that children in high-quality day care did as well on cognitive and language tests as children who remained in the home with their mother (Azar, 1997d). Children whose day care providers spent time talking to them and asking them questions achieved the highest scores on tests of cognitive and language ability. A Swedish study found that children in high-quality day care outperformed children who remained in the home on tests of math and language skills (Broberg and others, 1997).

Studies of the effects of day care on parent-child attachment are somewhat mixed. On the one hand, children in full-time day care show less distress when their mothers leave them and are less likely to seek out their mother when they return. Some psychologists suggest that this distancing from the mother could signify insecure attachment (Belsky, 1990). Others suggest, however, that the children are simply adapting to repeated separations from, and reunions with, their mother (Field, 1991; Lamb and others, 1992; Thompson 1991b).

Day care seems to have both positive and negative influences on children's social development. First, the positive: Children in day care are more likely to share their toys and to be independent, self-confident, and outgoing (Clarke-Stewart, 1991; Field, 1991). However, some studies have found that children in day care are less compliant and more aggressive than are other children (Vandell & Corasaniti, 1990). Perhaps some children in day care do not receive the individual attention or resources they need. When placed in a competitive situation, they become more aggressive in an attempt to meet their needs. On the other hand, Clarke-Stewart (1990) interprets the greater noncompliance and aggressiveness of children placed in day care as signs of greater independence rather than social maladjustment.

Truth or Fiction Revisited

It is true that children placed in day care are more aggressive than children cared for in the home. Perhaps they are so because they have become more independent.

• Child Abuse

It is estimated that nearly 1½ million children in the United States are neglected or abused by their parents or other caregivers each year (Wissow, 1995). In a national poll of 1000 parents, 5% admitted to having physically abused their children (Lewin, 1995). One in five (21%) admitted to hitting their children "on the bottom" with a hard object such as a belt, stick, or hairbrush. Most parents (85%) reported that they often shouted, yelled, or screamed at their children. Nearly half (47%) reported spanking or hitting their children on the bottom with their bare hands. And 17% admitted to calling their children "dumb" or "lazy" or a similar name.

Even if these percentages seem high, the fact is that abuse—spouse as well as child abuse—tends to be underreported. Why? Some family members are afraid that reporting abuse will destroy the family unit. Others are reluctant to disclose abuse because they are financially dependent on the abuser or do not trust the authorities (Seppa, 1996).

Why do parents abuse their children? Factors that contribute to child abuse include situational stress, a history of child abuse in at least one of the parents' families of origin, acceptance of violence as a way of coping with stress, failure to become attached to the children, substance abuse, and rigid attitudes toward child rearing (Belsky, 1993; Kaplan, 1991). Unemployment and low socioeconomic status are especially important sources of stress leading to abuse (Lewin, 1995; Trickett and others, 1991).

Children who are abused are quite likely to develop personal and social problems and psychological disorders. They are less likely than other children to venture out to explore the world (Aber & Allen, 1987). They are more likely to have psychological problems such as anxiety, depression, and low self-esteem (Wagner, 1997). They are less likely to be intimate with their peers and more likely to be aggressive (DeAngelis, 1997b; Parker & Herrera, 1996; Rothbart & Ahadi, 1994). As adults, they are more likely to be violent toward their dates and spouses (Malinosky-Rummell & Hansen, 1993).

Child abuse runs in families to some degree (Simons and others, 1991). However, *the majority of children who are abused do* not *abuse their own children as adults* (Kaufman & Zigler, 1989). Why does abuse run in families? There are several hypotheses (Belsky, 1993):

- Parents serve as role models. According to Strauss (1995), "Spanking teaches kids that when someone is doing something you don't like and they won't stop doing it, you hit them."

- Children adopt parents' strict philosophies about discipline. Exposure to violence in their own home leads some children to view abuse as normal. Certainly, people can find justifications for violence—if they are seeking them. ("Spare the rod, spoil the child.")

- Abused children develop hostile personalities. When they have their own children, they are thus liable to continue the pattern of abuse and neglect.

Truth or Fiction Revisited

It is true that child abusers have frequently been abused as children. However, the majority of them do not abuse their own children.

REFLECTIONS

- How would you characterize your own attachment to your parents? How did your feelings of attachment affect your behavior as a child?
- Would you characterize your parents as having been warm or cold, restrictive or permissive? In what ways? How did the parenting style you experienced affect your feelings and behavior?
- Have you or your parents made use of day care services? How did the experience work out? Why?
- Do you know anyone who was abused as a child? What were the effects?

■ COGNITIVE DEVELOPMENT

The developing thought processes of children—that is, their *cognitive development*—is explored in this section. Because cognitive functioning develops over many years, young children have ideas about the world that differ considerably from those of adults. Many of these ideas are charming but illogical.

• Jean Piaget's Cognitive-Developmental Theory

The Swiss philosopher–psychologist Jean Piaget contributed significantly to our understanding of children's cognitive development. He hypothesized that children's cognitive processes develop in an orderly sequence of stages. Although some children may be more advanced than others at particular ages, the developmental sequence is invariant. Piaget (1963) identified four major stages of cognitive development: sensorimotor, preoperational, concrete operational, and formal operational.

Piaget regarded children as natural physicists who seek to learn about and control their world. In the Piagetian view, children who squish their food and laugh enthusiastically are often acting as budding scientists. In addition to enjoying the responses of their parents, they are studying the texture and consistency of their food. (Parents, of course, often wish that their children would practice these experiments in the laboratory, not the dining room.)

Piaget's view differs markedly from the behaviorist view that people merely react to environmental stimuli rather than intending to interpret and act on the world. Piaget saw people as actors, not reactors. He believed that people purposefully form cognitive representations of the world and seek to manipulate it.

ASSIMILATION AND ACCOMMODATION Piaget described human thought, or intelligence, in terms of two basic concepts: assimilation and accommodation. **Assimilation** means responding to a new stimulus through a reflex or existing habit. Infants, for example, usually try to place new objects in their mouth to suck, feel, or explore. Piaget would say that the child is assimilating a new toy to the sucking scheme. A **scheme** is a pattern of action or a mental structure that is involved in acquiring or organizing knowledge.

Accommodation is the creation of new ways of responding to objects or looking at the world. In accommodation, children transform existing schemes—action patterns or ways of organizing knowledge—to incorporate new events. Children (and adults) accommodate to objects and situations that cannot be integrated into existing schemes. (For example, children who study biology learn that whales cannot be assimilated into the "fish" scheme. They accommodate by constructing new schemes, such as "mammals without legs that live in the seas.") The ability to accommodate to novel stimuli advances as a result of maturation and experience.

ASSIMILATION • (as-SIM-me-LAY-shun). According to Piaget, the inclusion of a new event into an existing scheme.
SCHEME • According to Piaget, a hypothetical mental structure that permits the classification and organization of new information.
ACCOMMODATION • (ack-KOM-uh-DAY-shun). According to Piaget, the modification of schemes so that information inconsistent with existing schemes can be integrated or understood.

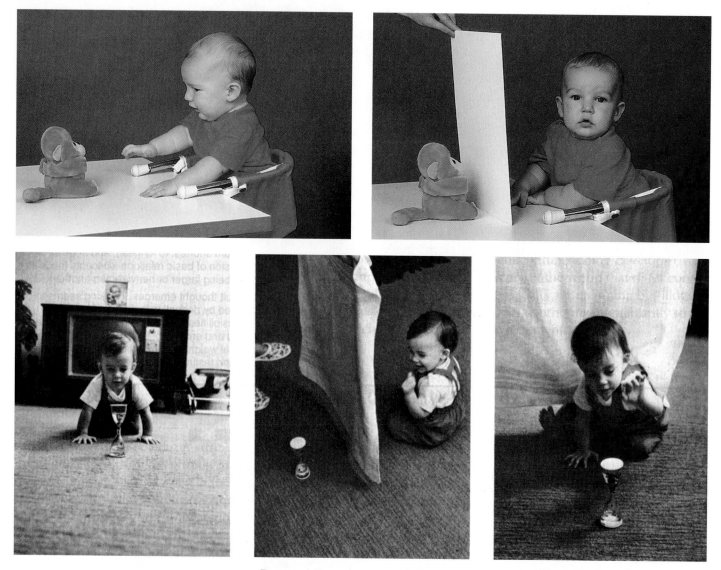

Figure 4.7
Object Permanence

To the infant at the top, who is in the early part of the sensorimotor stage, out of sight is truly out of mind. Once a sheet of paper is placed between the infant and the toy elephant, the infant loses all interest in it. The toy is apparently not yet mentally represented. The photos on the bottom show a child later in the sensorimotor stage. This child does mentally represent objects and pushes through a towel to reach one that has been screened from sight.

Most of the time, newborn children assimilate environmental stimuli according to reflexive schemes, although adjusting the mouth to contain the nipple is a primitive kind of accommodation. Reflexive behavior, to Piaget, is not "true" intelligence. True intelligence involves adapting to the world through a smooth, fluid balancing of the processes of assimilation and accommodation.

Let us now apply these concepts to the stages of cognitive development.

The Sensorimotor Stage The newborn infant is capable of assimilating novel stimuli only to existing reflexes (or ready-made schemes) such as the rooting and sucking reflexes. But by the time an infant reaches the age of 1 month, it will already show purposeful behavior by repeating behavior patterns that are pleasurable, such as sucking its hand. During the first month or so, an infant apparently does not connect stimuli perceived through different senses.

Reflexive turning toward sources of auditory and olfactory stimulation cannot be considered purposeful searching. But within the first few months the infant begins to coordinate vision with grasping so that it looks at what it is holding or touching.

A 3- or 4-month-old infant may be fascinated by its own hands and legs. It may become absorbed in watching itself open and close its fists. The infant becomes increasingly interested in acting on the environment to make interesting results (such as the sound of a rattle) last longer or occur again. Behavior becomes increasingly intentional and purposeful. Between 4 and 8 months of age, the infant explores cause-and-effect relationships such as the thump that can be made by tossing an object or the way kicking can cause a hanging toy to bounce.

Prior to the age of 6 months or so, out of sight is literally out of mind. Objects are not yet represented mentally. For this reason, as you can see in Figure 4.7, a child will make no effort to search for an object that has been removed or placed behind a screen. By the age of 8 to 12 months, however, infants realize that objects removed from sight still exist, and will attempt to find them. In this way, they show what is known as **object permanence,** thereby making it possible to play the game of "peek-a-boo" with their parents.

During the second year of life, children begin to show interest in how things are constructed. It may be for this reason that they persistently touch and finger their parents' faces and their own. Toward the end of the second year, children begin to engage in mental trial and error before they try out overt behaviors. For instance, when they look for an object you have removed, they will no longer begin their search in the last place they saw it. Rather, they may follow you, assuming that you are carrying the object, even though it is not visible. It is as though they are anticipating failure in searching for the object in the place where they last saw it.

Because the first stage of development is dominated by learning to coordinate perception of the self and of the environment with motor (muscular) activity, Piaget termed it the **sensorimotor stage.** This stage comes to a close with the acquisition of the basics of language at about age 2.

THE PREOPERATIONAL STAGE The **preoperational stage** is characterized by the use of words and symbols to represent objects and relationships among them. But be warned—any resemblance between the logic of children between the ages of 2 and 7 and your own logic very often is purely coincidental. Children may use the same words that adults do, but this does not mean that their views of the world are similar to adults'. A major limit on preoperational children's thinking is that it tends to be one-dimensional—to focus on one aspect of a problem or situation at a time.

One consequence of one-dimensional thinking is **egocentrism.** Preoperational children cannot understand that other people do not see things the same way they do. When Allyn was 2½, I asked her to tell me about a trip to the store with her mother. "You tell me," she replied. Upon questioning, it seemed that she did not understand that I could not see the world through her eyes.

To egocentric preoperational children, all the world's a stage that has been erected to meet their needs and amuse them. When asked, "Why does the sun shine?" they may say, "To keep me warm." If asked, "Why is the sky blue?" they may respond, "'Cause blue's my favorite color." Preoperational children also show **animism.** They attribute life and consciousness to physical objects like the sun and the moon. They also show **artificialism.** They believe that environmental events like rain and thunder are human inventions. Asked why the sky is blue, 4-year-olds may answer, "'Cause Mommy painted it." Examples of egocentrism, animism, and artificialism are shown in Table 4.3.

OBJECT PERMANENCE • Recognition that objects removed from sight still exist, as demonstrated in young children by continued pursuit.

SENSORIMOTOR STAGE • The first of Piaget's stages of cognitive development, characterized by coordination of sensory information and motor activity, early exploration of the environment, and lack of language.

PREOPERATIONAL STAGE • The second of Piaget's stages, characterized by illogical use of words and symbols, spotty logic, and egocentrism.

EGOCENTRIC • (ee-go-SENT-trick). According to Piaget, assuming that others view the world as one does oneself.

ANIMISM • The belief that inanimate objects move because of will or spirit.

ARTIFICIALISM • The belief that natural objects have been created by human beings.

TABLE 4.3 EXAMPLES OF PREOPERATIONAL THOUGHT

TYPE OF THOUGHT	SAMPLE QUESTIONS	TYPICAL ANSWERS
Egocentrism	Why does it get dark out? Why does the sun shine? Why is there snow? Why is grass green? What are TV sets for?	So I can go to sleep. To keep me warm. For me to play in. Because that's my favorite color. To watch my favorite shows and cartoons.
Animism (attributing life and consciousness to physical objects)	Why do trees have leaves? Why do stars twinkle? Why does the sun move in the sky? Where do boats go at night?	To keep them warm. Because they're happy and cheerful. To follow children and hear what they say. They sleep like we do.
Artificialism (assuming that environmental events are human inventions)	What makes it rain? Why is the sky blue? What is the wind? What causes thunder? How does a baby get in Mommy's tummy?	Someone emptying a watering can. Somebody painted it. A man blowing. A man grumbling. Just make it first. (How?) You put some eyes on it, put the head on (etc.).

To gain further insight into preoperational thinking, consider these problems:

1. Imagine that you pour water from a tall, thin glass into a low, wide glass. Now, does the low, wide glass contain more, less, or the same amount of water that was in the tall, thin glass? I won't keep you in suspense. If you said the same amount of water (with possible minor exceptions for spillage and evaporation), you were correct. Now that you're on a roll, go on to the next problem.

2. If you flatten a ball of clay into a pancake, do you wind up with more, less, or the same amount of clay? If you said the same amount of clay, you are correct once more.

To arrive at the correct answers to these questions, you must understand the law of **conservation.** This law holds that basic properties of substances such as mass, weight, and volume remain the same—that is, are *conserved*—when you change superficial properties such as their shape or arrangement.

Conservation requires the ability to think about, or **center** on, two aspects of a situation at once, such as height and width. Conserving the mass, weight, or volume of a substance requires the recognition that a change in one dimension can compensate for a change in another. But the preoperational boy in Figure 4.8 focuses on only one dimension at a time. First he is shown two beakers holding orange juice and agrees that they contain the same amount of juice. Then, while he watches, juice from one beaker is poured into a taller, thinner beaker. The boy is surprised by, what he believes, how much more juice goes into the tall beaker. Why? Because when he looks at the beakers he is "overwhelmed" by the fact that one beaker is taller. The preoperational child focuses on the most apparent dimension of the situation—in this case, the greater height of the taller beaker. He does not realize that the increased width of the shorter beakers compensates for the decreased height. By the way, if you ask him whether any juice has been added or taken away in the pouring process, he will readily say no. But if you then repeat the question about which beaker contains *more* juice, he will again point to the taller beaker.

CONSERVATION • According to Piaget, recognition that basic properties of substances such as weight and mass remain the same when superficial features change.

CENTER • According to Piaget, to focus one's attention.

If all this sounds rather illogical, that is because it is illogical—or, to be precise, preoperational.

After you have tried the experiment with juice or water, try the following. Make two rows of five pennies each. In the first row, place the pennies about half an inch apart. In the second row, place the pennies 2 to 3 inches apart. Ask a 4- to 5-year-old child which row has more pennies. What do you think the child will say? Why?

Piaget (1962) found that the moral judgment of preoperational children is also one-dimensional. Five-year-olds are slaves to rules and authority. When you ask them why something should be done in a certain way, they may insist "Because that's the way to do it!" or "Because my Mommy says so!" Right is right and wrong is wrong. Why? "Because!"—that's why.

According to most older children and adults, an act is a crime only when there is criminal intent. Accidents may be hurtful, but the perpetrators are usually seen as blameless. But in the court of the one-dimensional, preoperational child, there is **objective responsibility.** People are sentenced (and harshly!) on the basis of the amount of damage they have done, not their motives or intentions.

To demonstrate objective responsibility, Piaget would tell children stories and ask them which character was naughtier and why. John, for instance, accidentally breaks 15 cups when he opens a door. Henry breaks one cup when he sneaks into a kitchen cabinet to find forbidden jam. The preoperational child usually judges John to be naughtier. Why? Because he broke more cups.

THE CONCRETE-OPERATIONAL STAGE By about age 7, the typical child is entering the stage of **concrete operations.** In this stage, which lasts until about age 12, children show the beginnings of the capacity for adult logic. However, their logical thoughts, or *operations,* generally involve tangible objects rather than abstract ideas. Concrete operational children are capable of **decentration;** they can center on two dimensions of a problem at once. This attainment has implications for moral judgments, conservation, and other intellectual undertakings.

Children now become **subjective** in their moral judgments. When assigning guilt, they center on the motives of wrongdoers as well as on the amount of damage done. Concrete-operational children judge Henry more harshly than John, since John's misdeed was an accident.

Concrete-operational children understand the laws of conservation. The boy in Figure 4.8, now a few years older, would say that the tall beaker still contains the same amount of orange juice. If asked why, he might reply, "Because you can pour it back into the other one." Such an answer also suggests awareness of the concept of **reversibility**—the recognition that many processes can be reversed or undone so that things are restored to their previous condition. Centering simultaneously on the height and the width of the beakers, the boy recognizes that the gain in height compensates for the loss in width.

Concrete-operational children can conserve *number* as well as weight and mass. They recognize that the number of pennies in each of the rows described earlier is the same, even though one row may be spread out to look longer than the other.

Children in this stage are less egocentric. They are able to take on the roles of others and to view the world, and themselves, from other people's perspectives. They recognize that people see things in different ways because of different situations and different sets of values.

During the concrete-operational stage, children's own sets of values begin to emerge and acquire stability. Children come to understand that feelings of love between them and their parents can endure even when someone feels angry or disappointed at a particular moment.

OBJECTIVE RESPONSIBILITY • According to Piaget, the assignment of blame according to the amount of damage done rather than the motives of the actor.
CONCRETE-OPERATIONAL STAGE • Piaget's third stage, characterized by logical thought concerning tangible objects, conservation, and subjective morality.
DECENTRATION • (DEE-sent-TRAY-shun). Simultaneous focusing on more than one dimension of a problem, so that flexible, reversible thought becomes possible.
SUBJECTIVE MORAL JUDGMENT • According to Piaget, moral judgments that are based on the motives of the perpetrator.
REVERSIBILITY • According to Piaget, recognition that processes can be undone, that things can be made as they were.

FIGURE 4.8

CONSERVATION

The boy in these photographs agreed that the amount of orange juice in two identical containers is equal. He then watched as juice from one container was poured into a tall, thin container. In the final photograph, the boy is surprised to see the juice level so high. When asked whether he thinks that the amounts of juice in the two containers are now the same, he says no. Apparently, he is impressed by the height of the new container, and, prior to the development of conservation, he focuses on only one dimension of the situation at a time—in this case, the height of the new container.

THE FORMAL-OPERATIONAL STAGE The stage of **formal operations** is the final stage in Piaget's theory and represents cognitive maturity. Most children enter this stage at puberty, but not all do so, and some people never reach this stage.

Formal-operational children (and adults) think abstractly. They become capable of solving geometric problems about circles and squares without reference to what the circles and squares may represent in the real world. Children in this stage derive rules for behavior from general principles and can focus, or center, on many aspects of a situation at once in arriving at judgments and solving problems.

In a sense, it is during the stage of formal operations that people tend to emerge as theoretical scientists—even though they may see themselves as having little or no interest in science. They become capable of dealing with hypothetical situations. They realize that situations can have different outcomes, and they think ahead, experimenting with different possibilities. Children—adolescents by now—also conduct experiments to determine whether their hypotheses are correct. These experiments are not conducted in the laboratory. Rather, adolescents may try out different tones of voice, ways of carrying themselves, and ways of treating others to see what works best for them.

Children in this stage can reason deductively, or draw conclusions about specific objects or people once they have been classified accurately. Adolescents can be somewhat proud of their new logical abilities. A new sort of egocentrism can develop in which adolescents emotionally press for acceptance of their logic without recognizing the exceptions or practical problems that are often considered by adults. Consider this example: "It is wrong to hurt people. Company A occasionally hurts people" (perhaps through pollution or economic pressures). "Therefore, Company A must be severely punished or shut down." This thinking is logical. By impatiently pressing for immediate major changes or severe penalties, however, one may not fully consider various practical problems such as the thousands of workers who would be laid off if the company were shut down.

FORMAL-OPERATIONAL STAGE • Piaget's fourth stage, characterized by abstract logical thought; deduction from principles.

In Review Piaget's Stages of Cognitive Development

STAGE	APPROXIMATE AGE	DESCRIPTION
Sensorimotor	Birth–2 years	At first, the child lacks language and does not use symbols or mental representations of objects. In time, reflexive responding ends and intentional behavior begins. The child develops the object concept and acquires the basics of language.
Preoperational	2–7 years	The child begins to represent the world mentally, but thought is egocentric. The child does not focus on two aspects of a situation at once and therefore lacks conservation. The child shows animism, artificialism, and immanent justice.
Concrete operational	7–12 years	The child develops conservation concepts, can adopt the viewpoint of others, can classify objects in series, and shows comprehension of basic relational concepts (such as one object being larger or heavier than another).
Formal operational	12 years and above	Mature, adult thought emerges. Thinking seems to be characterized by deductive logic, consideration of various possibilities (mental trial and error), abstract thought, and the formation and testing of hypotheses.

EVALUATION OF PIAGET'S THEORY A number of questions have been raised concerning the accuracy of Piaget's views. Among them are these:

1. *Was Piaget's timing accurate?* Some critics argue that Piaget's methods led him to underestimate children's abilities (Bjorklund, 1995; Meltzoff & Gopnik, 1997). Other researchers using different methods have found, for example, that preschoolers are less egocentric and that children are capable of conservation at earlier ages than Piaget thought.

2. *Does cognitive development occur in stages?* The most damaging criticism of Piaget's theory is that cognitive skills such as egocentrism and conservation appear to develop more continuously than Piaget thought—that is, they may not occur in stages (Bjorklund, 1995; Flavell and others, 1993). Although cognitive developments appear to build on previous cognitive developments, the process may be more gradual than stagelike.

3. *Are developmental sequences invariant?* Here, Piaget's views have fared better. It seems that there is no variation in the sequence in which cognitive developments occur.

In sum, Piaget's theoretical edifice has been rocked, but it has not been reduced to rubble. Psychologist Andrew Meltzoff believes that "Piaget's theories were critical for getting the field of [cognitive development] off the ground, . . . but it's time to move on" (1997, p. 9). There are other approaches to cognitive development—including information-processing approaches, to which we now turn.

• *Information-Processing Approaches to Cognitive Development*

Whereas Piaget viewed children as budding scientists, psychologists who study **information processing** view children (and adults) as akin to computer systems.

INFORMATION PROCESSING • An approach to cognitive development that deals with children's advances in the input, storage, retrieval, manipulation, and output of information.

Children, like computers, obtain information ("input") from their environment, store it, retrieve and manipulate it, and then respond to it overtly ("output") (Harnishfeger & Bjorklund, 1990). One goal of the information-processing approach is to learn how children store, retrieve, and manipulate information—how their "mental programs" develop. Information-processing theorists focus on children's capacity for memory and their use of cognitive strategies, such as the ways in which they focus their attention (Bjorklund, 1995; Case, 1992; Kail & Salthouse, 1994). They assume that neurological developments allow working memory to expand. They note that certain Piagetian tasks require several cognitive strategies instead of one and that young children may fail at them because they cannot simultaneously hold many pieces of information in working memory. Put it this way: Preschoolers can solve problems that contain one or two steps, but older children can retain information from early steps as they carry out later steps.

Reconsider Piaget's story of the cups, the one in which John breaks 15 cups accidentally while Henry breaks one while trying to steal jam. Some aspects of development that Piaget believed to reflect qualitative changes in thought may actually reflect a growing capacity for storage and retrieval of information (Gelman & Baillargeon, 1983).

Most 5-year-olds say that John is naughtier because he broke more cups. Eight-year-olds usually condemn Henry because he was doing something wrong at the time. Piaget explained this age difference in terms of 5-year-olds' tendency to focus on the amount of damage done, rather than on the intentions of the wrongdoer. However, many 5-year-olds say that John is naughtier simply because they can remember that he broke more cups, but not all the other details of the stories. When the stories are repeated carefully, even 5-year-olds often consider the motives of the cup breaker.

DEVELOPMENT OF SELECTIVE ATTENTION A basic strategy for solving problems is simply to attend to their elements. The ability to focus attention and screen out distractions advances steadily through middle childhood. Younger children tend to focus on only one element of a problem at a time—a major reason that they lack the capability for conservation. Older children, in contrast, attend to numerous aspects of a problem at once, and this enables them to conserve number, volume, and so on.

AUTOMATICITY Another factor contributing to children's ability to solve problems is increasing automaticity in applying cognitive strategies (Case, 1992; Kail & Salthouse, 1994). If you ask young children how many objects there are in three sets of two, they may have to count them one by one to arrive at a total of six. But older children, with larger working memories, familiarity with multiplication tables, and more perceptual experience, are likely to arrive at the total automatically. Automaticity in adding, multiplying, and so on allows older children to solve math problems that have several steps. Younger children become lost in individual steps.

METAMEMORY **Metamemory** refers to children's awareness of the functioning of their memory processes. Older children show greater insight into how their memories work (Hashimoto, 1991; Kail, 1990). They are better able to use strategies to remember things. For example, 2- and 3-year-olds do not use rehearsal (repetition) when asked to remember a list of items. Four- and 5-year-olds will usually repeat the list aloud if someone suggests that they do, and they use rehearsal spontaneously by the age of 6 or 7 (Flavell and others, 1993).

METAMEMORY • Knowledge of the functions and processes in one's own memory, as shown by use of cognitive strategies to retain information.

If you were trying to remember a new phone number, you would know to rehearse it several times or to write it down before doing a series of math problems. Ten-year-olds are also aware that new mental activities (the math problems) can interfere with old ones (rehearsing the telephone number), and they usually suggest jotting down the number before trying the problems. Few 5-year-olds see the advantage of jotting down the number before doing the math problems.

Let us now turn our attention to Lawrence Kohlberg's theory of moral development and see how children process information that leads to judgments of right and wrong.

• Lawrence Kohlberg's Theory of Moral Development

Psychologist Lawrence Kohlberg (1981) originated a cognitive-developmental theory of children's moral reasoning. Before we describe Kohlberg's views, read the following tale, which he used in his research, and answer the questions that follow.

In Europe a woman was near death from a special kind of cancer. There was one drug that the doctors thought might save her. It was a form of radium that a druggist in the same town had recently discovered. The drug was expensive to make, but the druggist was charging ten times what the drug cost him to make. He paid $200 for the radium and charged $2,000 for a small dose of the drug. The sick woman's husband, Heinz, went to everyone he knew to borrow the money, but he could only get together about $1,000, which was half of what it cost. He told the druggist that his wife was dying and asked him to sell it cheaper or let him pay later. But the druggist said: "No, I discovered the drug and I'm going to make money from it." So Heinz got desperate and broke into the man's store to steal the drug for his wife. (Kohlberg, 1969)

What do you think? Should Heinz have tried to steal the drug? Was he right or wrong? The answer is more complicated than a simple yes or no. Heinz is caught up in a moral dilemma in which a legal or social rule (in this case, the law forbidding stealing) is pitted against a strong human need (his desire to save his wife). According to Kohlberg's theory, children and adults arrive at yes or no answers for different reasons. These reasons can be classified according to the level of moral development they reflect.

As a stage theorist, Kohlberg argues that the stages of moral reasoning follow a specific sequence. Children progress at different rates, and not all children (or adults) reach the highest stage. But the sequence is always the same: Children must go through stage 1 before they enter stage 2, and so on. According to Kohlberg, there are three levels of moral development and two stages within each level.

THE PRECONVENTIONAL LEVEL The **preconventional level** applies to most children through about the age of 9. Children at this level base their moral

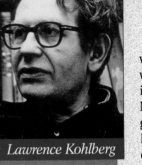
PRECONVENTIONAL LEVEL • According to Kohlberg, a period during which moral judgments are based largely on expectation of rewards or punishments.

judgments on the consequences of behavior. For instance, stage 1 is oriented toward obedience and punishment. Good behavior is obedient and allows one to avoid punishment.

In stage 2, good behavior allows people to satisfy their needs and those of others. (Heinz's wife needs the drug; therefore, stealing the drug—the only way of obtaining it—is not wrong.)

THE CONVENTIONAL LEVEL In the **conventional level** of moral reasoning, right and wrong are judged by conformity to conventional (familial, religious, societal) standards of right and wrong. According to the stage 3, "good-boy orientation," moral behavior is that which meets the needs and expectations of others. Moral behavior is what is "normal"—what the majority does. (Heinz should steal the drug because that is what a "good husband" would do. It is "natural" or "normal" to try to help one's wife. *Or,* Heinz should *not* steal the drug because "good people do not steal.")

In stage 4, moral judgments are based on rules that maintain the social order. Showing respect for authority and doing one's duty are valued highly. (Heinz *must* steal the drug; it would be his fault if he let his wife die. He would pay the druggist later, when he had the money.) Many people do not mature beyond the conventional level.

THE POSTCONVENTIONAL LEVEL At the **postconventional level,** moral reasoning is based on the person's own moral standards. In each instance, moral judgments are derived from personal values, not from conventional standards or authority figures. In the contractual, legalistic orientation characteristic of stage 5, it is recognized that laws stem from agreed-upon procedures and that many laws have great value and should not be violated. But under exceptional circumstances laws cannot bind the individual. (Although it is illegal for Heinz to steal the drug, in this case it is the right thing to do.)

Stage 6 thinking relies on supposed universal ethical principles such as the sanctity of human life, individual dignity, justice, and the Golden Rule ("Do unto others as you would have them do unto you."). Behavior that is consistent with these principles is moral. If a law is unjust or contradicts the rights of the individual, it is wrong to obey it.

People at the postconventional level look to their conscience as the highest moral authority. This point has created confusion. To some it suggests that it is right to break the law when it is convenient. But this interpretation is incorrect. Kohlberg means that people at this level of moral reasoning must do what they believe is right even if this action runs counter to social rules or laws or requires personal sacrifice.

Not all people reach the postconventional level of moral reasoning. Postconventional moral judgments were absent among the 7- to 10-year-olds Kohlberg studied (1969). By age 16, stage 5 reasoning is shown by about 20% and stage 6 reasoning by about 5% of adolescents.

EVALUATION OF KOHLBERG'S THEORY Research suggests that moral reasoning does follow a developmental sequence (Snarey and others, 1985), even though most people do not reach the level of postconventional thought. Postconventional thought, when found, first occurs during adolescence. It also seems that formal operational thinking is a prerequisite for postconventional reasoning, which requires the capacities to understand abstract moral principles and to empathize with the attitudes and emotional responses of other people (Flavell and others, 1993).

CONVENTIONAL LEVEL • According to Kohlberg, a period during which moral judgments largely reflect social conventions. A "law and order" approach to morality.
POSTCONVENTIONAL LEVEL • According to Kohlberg, a period during which moral judgments are derived from moral principles and people look to themselves to set moral standards.

In Review — Kohlberg's Levels and Stages of Moral Development

STAGE OF DEVELOPMENT	EXAMPLES OF MORAL REASONING THAT SUPPORT HEINZ'S STEALING THE DRUG	EXAMPLES OF MORAL REASONING THAT OPPOSE HEINZ'S STEALING THE DRUG
LEVEL I: PRECONVENTIONAL		
STAGE 1: Judgments guided by obedience and the prospect of punishment (the consequences of the behavior)	It isn't wrong to take the drug. After all, Heinz tried to pay the druggist for it, and it's only worth $200, not $2,000.	It's wrong to take the drug because taking things without paying is against the law; Heinz will get caught and go to jail.
STAGE 2: Naively egoistic, instrumental orientation (Things are right when they satisfy people's needs.)	Heinz ought to take the drug because his wife really needs it. He can always pay the druggist back.	Heinz shouldn't take the drug. If he gets caught and winds up in jail, it won't do his wife any good.
LEVEL II: CONVENTIONAL		
STAGE 3: Good-boy orientation (Moral behavior helps others and is socially approved.)	Stealing is a crime, so it's bad, but Heinz should take the drug to save his wife or else people would blame him for letting her die.	Stealing is a crime. Heinz shouldn't just take the drug because his family will be dishonored and they will blame him.
STAGE 4: Law-and-order orientation (Moral behavior means doing one's duty and showing respect for authority.)	Heinz must take the drug to do his duty to save his wife. Eventually, he has to pay the druggist for it, however.	If everybody took the law into his or her own hands, civilization would fall apart, so Heinz shouldn't steal the drug.
LEVEL III: POSTCONVENTIONAL		
STAGE 5: Contractual, legalistic orientation (One must weigh pressing human needs against society's need to maintain social order.)	This thing is complicated because society has a right to maintain law and order, but Heinz has to take the drug to save his wife.	I can see why Heinz feels he has to take the drug, but laws exist for the benefit of society as a whole and can't simply be cast aside.
STAGE 6: Universal ethical principles orientation (People must follow universal ethical principles and their own conscience, even if it means breaking the law.)	This is a case in which the law comes into conflict with the principle of the sanctity of human life. Heinz must take the drug because his wife's life is more important than the law.	If Heinz, in his own conscience, believes that stealing the drug is worse than letting his wife die, he should not take it. People have to make sacrifices to do what they think is right.

Consistent with Kohlberg's theory, children do not appear to skip stages as they progress (Flavell and others, 1993). When children are exposed to adult models who exhibit a lower stage of moral reasoning, they can be induced to follow along (Bandura & McDonald, 1963). Children who are exposed to examples of moral reasoning above and below their own stage generally prefer the higher stage, however (Rest, 1983). The thrust of moral development therefore is from lower to higher, even if children can be sidetracked by social influences.

One of the more controversial notions in the history of research on child development is that men show higher levels of moral development than women. From his psychoanalytic perspective, Freud assumed that men would have stronger "superegos" than females because of the impact of the Oedipus complex and the man's consequent identification with authority figures and social codes. But Freud's views on the Oedipus complex were speculative, and his views on women reflected the ignorance and prejudice of his times. In more recent years, researchers using Heinz's dilemma have also reported gender differences in moral development, as we see in the following section.

Psychology in a World of
DIVERSITY

Are There Gender Differences in Moral Development?

Some studies using Heinz's dilemma have found that boys reason at higher levels of moral development than girls. However, Carol Gilligan (1982; Gilligan and others, 1989) argues that this gender difference is illusory and reflects different patterns of socialization for boys and girls.

Gilligan makes her point through two examples of responses to Heinz's dilemma. Eleven-year-old Jake views the dilemma as a math problem. He sets up an equation showing that life has greater value than property. Heinz is thus obligated to steal the drug. Eleven-year-old Amy vacillates. She notes that stealing the drug and letting Heinz's wife die would both be wrong. Amy searches for alternatives, such as getting a loan, stating that it would profit Heinz's wife little if he went to jail and were no longer around to help her.

According to Gilligan, Amy's reasoning is as sophisticated as Jake's, yet she would be rated as showing a lower level of moral development. Gilligan asserts that Amy, like other girls, has been socialized to focus on the needs of others and forgo simplistic judgments of right and wrong. As a consequence, Amy is more likely to exhibit stage 3 reasoning, which focuses in part on empathy for others. Jake, by contrast, has been socialized to make judgments based purely on logic. To him, clear-cut conclusions are to be derived from a set of premises. Amy was aware of the logical considerations that influenced Jake, but she saw them as one source of information—not as the only source. It is ironic that Amy's empathy, a trait that has "defined the 'goodness' of women," marks Amy "as deficient in moral development" (Gilligan, 1982, p. 18). Prior to his death, Kohlberg had begun to correct the sexism in his scoring system.

REFLECTIONS
- Think of children you know or have known. (You were a child yourself once!) How do their behavior and some of the things they say seem to reflect the stages described by Piaget?
- Can you provide some examples of assimilation and accommodation in your own learning about the various areas of psychology?
- How would you characterize your current level of cognitive development in terms of Piaget's and Kohlberg's theories? Why?

■ ADOLESCENCE

Adolescence is a time of transition from childhood to adulthood. In our society, adolescents often feel that they are "neither fish nor fowl," as the saying goes—neither children nor adults. Although adolescents may be old enough to have children and are as large as their parents, they are often treated quite differently than adults. They may not be eligible for a driver's license until they are 16 or 17.

ADOLESCENCE • The period of life bounded by puberty and the assumption of adult responsibilities.

Adolescents. In our culture adolescents are "neither fish nor fowl." Although they may be old enough to reproduce and may be as large as their parents, they are often treated like children.

They cannot attend R-rated films unless they are accompanied by an adult. They are prevented from working long hours. They are usually required to remain in school through age 16 and may not marry until they reach the "age of consent." Let us consider the physical, social, and personal changes of adolescence.

• *Physical Development*

Adolescence is heralded by puberty, the period during which the body becomes sexually mature. Puberty begins with the appearance of **secondary sex characteristics** such as body hair, deepening of the voice in males, and rounding of the breasts and hips in females. In boys, pituitary hormones stimulate the testes to increase the output of testosterone, which in turn causes enlargement of the penis and testes and the appearance of bodily hair. By the early teens, erections become common, and boys may ejaculate. Ejaculatory ability usually precedes the presence of mature sperm by at least a year. Ejaculation thus is not evidence of reproductive capacity.

In girls, a critical body weight in the neighborhood of 100 pounds is thought to trigger a cascade of hormonal secretions in the brain that cause the ovaries to secrete higher levels of estrogen (Angier, 1997a; Frisch, 1997). Estrogen stimulates the growth of breast tissue and fatty and supportive tissue in the hips and buttocks. Thus the pelvis widens, rounding the hips. Small amounts of androgens produced by the adrenal glands, along with estrogen, spur the growth of pubic and underarm hair. Estrogen and androgens together stimulate the growth of female sex organs. Estrogen production becomes cyclical during puberty and regulates the menstrual cycle. The beginning of menstruation, or **menarche,** usually occurs between the ages of 11 and 14. Girls cannot become pregnant until they begin to ovulate, however, and this may occur as much as two years after menarche.

The stable patterns of growth in height and weight that characterize early and middle childhood come to an abrupt end with the adolescent growth spurt, which lasts for 2 to 3 years. During this time, adolescents grow some 8 to 12 inches. Most boys wind up taller and heavier than most girls.

Truth or Fiction Revisited

It is not usually true that girls are capable of becoming pregnant when they have their first menstrual period. Menarche can precede ovulation by a year or more.

SECONDARY SEX CHARACTERISTICS • Characteristics that distinguish the sexes, such as distribution of body hair and depth of voice, but that are not directly involved in reproduction.

MENARCHE • (men-ARK-key *or* may-NARSH). The beginning of menstruation.

In boys, the weight of the muscle mass increases notably. The width of the shoulders and circumference of the chest also increase. Adolescents may eat enormous quantities of food to fuel their growth spurt. Adults fighting the "battle of the bulge" stare at them in wonder as they wolf down french fries and shakes at the fast-food counter and later go out for pizza.

• *Social and Personality Development*

In the last century, psychologist G. Stanley Hall described adolescence as a time of *Sturm und Drang*—storm and stress. Certainly, many American teenagers abuse drugs, get pregnant, contract sexually transmitted diseases, become involved in violence, fail in school, and even attempt suicide (Garland & Zigler, 1993; Gentry & Eron, 1993; Kazdin, 1993). Each year nearly 1 in 10 adolescent girls becomes pregnant. Nearly 10% of teenage boys and 20% of teenage girls attempt suicide. Alcohol-related incidents are the overall leading cause of death among adolescents.

Hall attributed the conflicts and distress of adolescence to biological changes. Research evidence does suggest that hormonal changes affect the activity levels, mood swings, and aggressive tendencies of many adolescents (Buchanan and others, 1992). Overall, however, it would appear that sociocultural influences have a greater impact than hormones (Buchanan and others, 1992).

Adolescents do try to become more independent from their parents, which often leads to some bickering (Smetana and others, 1991). They usually bicker about issues such as homework, chores, money, appearance, curfews, and dating (Galambos & Almeida, 1992; Smetana and others, 1991). Arguments are common when adolescents want to make their own choices about matters such as clothes and friends (Smetana and others, 1991).

The striving for independence is also characterized by withdrawal from family life, at least relative to prior involvement. In one study, children ranging in age from 9 to 15 carried electronic pagers for a week so that they could report what they were doing and whom they were with when signaled (Larson & Richards, 1991). The amount of time spent with family members decreased dramatically with greater age. The 15-year-olds spent only half as much time with their families as the 9-year-olds. Yet this change does not mean that most adolescents spend their time on the streets. For 15-year-old boys in the study, time with the family tended to be replaced by time spent alone. For older girls, this time was divided between friends and solitude.

Adolescents and parents are often in conflict because adolescents experiment with many things that can be harmful to their health. Yet they often do not perceive such activities to be as risky as their parents see them as being. Lawrence Cohn and his colleagues (1995) found, for example, that parents perceived drinking, smoking, failure to use seat belts, drag racing, and a number of other activities to be riskier than their teenagers saw them as being (see Table 4.4). Various activities were rated according to a scale in which 1 = no harm and 5 = very great harm.

Some distancing from parents is beneficial for adolescents (Galambos, 1992). After all, they do have to form relationships outside the family. But greater independence does not necessarily mean that adolescents become emotionally detached from their parents or fall completely under the influence of their peers. Most adolescents continue to feel love, respect, and loyalty toward their parents (Montemayor & Flannery, 1991). Adolescents who feel close to their parents actually show greater self-reliance and independence than do those who are distant from their parents. Adolescents who retain close ties with their parents also fare better in school and have fewer adjustment problems (Davey, 1993; Papini & Roggman, 1992; Steinberg, 1996).

ACTIVITY	TABLE 4.4 MEAN RATINGS OF PERCEIVED HARMFULNESS OF VARIOUS ACTIVITIES			
	EXPERIMENTAL INVOLVEMENT (DOING FREQUENT INVOLVEMENT ACTIVITY ONCE OR TWICE TO SEE WHAT IT IS LIKE)			
	Teenager	Teenager's Parents	Teenager	Teenager's Parents
Drinking alcohol	2.6	3.5	4.4	4.8
Smoking cigarettes	3.0	3.6	4.4	4.8
Using diet pills	2.8	3.8	4.1	4.7
Not using seat belts	3.0	4.3	4.0	4.8
Getting drunk	3.2	4.2	4.4	4.8
Sniffing glue	3.6	4.6	4.6	4.9
Driving home after drinking a few beers	3.8	4.5	4.6	4.8
Drag racing	3.8	4.6	4.5	4.8
Using steroids	3.8	4.4	4.7	4.9

Note. Adapted from Cohn and others (1995), p. 219.

Despite parent-adolescent conflict over issues of control, parents and adolescents tend to share social, political, religious, and economic views (Paikoff & Collins, 1991). In sum, there are frequent differences between parents and adolescents on issues of personal control. However, there apparently is no "generation gap" on broader matters.

EGO IDENTITY VERSUS ROLE DIFFUSION According to Erik Erikson, the major challenge of adolescence is the creation of an adult identity. Identity is achieved mainly by committing oneself to a particular occupation or a role in life. But identity also extends to sexual, political, and religious beliefs and commitments. (Erikson's theory of psychosocial development is discussed in Chapter 12).

Erikson (1963) theorized that adolescents experience a life crisis of *ego identity versus role diffusion.* **Ego identity** is a firm sense of who one is and what one stands for. It can carry one through difficult times and give meaning to one's achievements. Adolescents who do not develop ego identity may experience **role diffusion.** They spread themselves too thin, running down one blind alley after another and placing themselves at the mercy of leaders who promise to give them the sense of identity that they cannot find for themselves.

REFLECTIONS
- Consider some of the stereotypes of the adolescent as captured in the phrase "storm and stress." Do these stereotypes describe your own experiences as an adolescent? How or how not?
- How did your gender or ethnic group influence the formation of your ego identity?

EGO IDENTITY • Erikson's term for a firm sense of who one is and what one stands for.
ROLE DIFFUSION • Erikson's term for lack of clarity in one's life roles—a function of failure to develop ego identity.

■ ADULT DEVELOPMENT

Development continues throughout a person's lifetime. Many theorists believe that adult concerns and involvements follow observable patterns, so that we can speak of "stages" of adult development. Others argue that there may no longer be a "standard" life cycle with predictable stages or phases (Sheehy, 1995). Age now has an "elastic quality" (Butler, 1998). People are living longer than ever before and are freer than ever to choose their own destiny. Let us consider the adult years according to three broad categories: young adulthood, middle adulthood, and late adulthood.

• *Young Adulthood*

Young, or early, adulthood covers the period between the ages of 20 and 40. According to Erikson (1963), young adulthood is the stage of **intimacy versus isolation.** Erikson saw the establishment of intimate relationships as central to young adulthood. Young adults who have evolved a firm sense of identity during adolescence are ready to "fuse" their identities with those of other people through marriage and abiding friendships.

Erikson warned that we may not be able to commit ourselves to others until we have achieved ego identity—that is, established stable life roles. Achieving ego identity is the central task of adolescence. Lack of personal stability is connected with the high divorce rate for teenage marriages. Erikson also argued that people who do not reach out to develop intimate relationships risk retreating into isolation and loneliness.

Adults in their twenties tend to be fueled by ambition. Journalist Gail Sheehy (1976) labeled this period the **Trying 20s**—a period during which people basically strive to advance their careers. They are concerned about establishing their pathway in life. They are generally responsible for their own support, make their own choices, and are largely free from parental influences.

GENDER DIFFERENCES Most Western men consider separation and individuation to be key goals of personality development during young adulthood (Guisinger & Blatt, 1994). For women, however, the establishment and maintenance of social relationships are also of primary importance (Gilligan and others, 1990, 1991; Jordan and others, 1991). Women, as Gilligan (1982) has pointed out, are likely to undergo a transition from being cared for by others to caring for others. In becoming adults, men are more likely to undergo a transition from being restricted by others to autonomy and perhaps control of other people.

According to Daniel Levinson's in-depth study of 40 men, published in 1978 as *The Seasons of a Man's Life*, men enter the adult world in their early twenties. Upon entry, they are faced with the tasks of exploring adult roles (in terms of careers, intimate relationships, and so on) and establishing stability in the chosen roles. At this time, men also often adopt a **dream**—the drive to "become" someone, to leave their mark on history—which serves as a tentative blueprint for their life.

Although there are differences in the development of women and men, between the ages of 21 and 27 college women also develop in terms of individuation and autonomy (Helson & Moane, 1987). Women, like men, assert increasing control over their own lives. College women, of course, are relatively liberated and career-oriented compared with their less-well-educated peers.

THE THIRTIES Levinson labeled the ages of 28 to 33 the **age-30 transition.** For men and women, the late twenties and early thirties are commonly character-

INTIMACY VERSUS ISOLATION • Erikson's life crisis of young adulthood, which is characterized by the task of developing abiding intimate relationships.
TRYING 20s • Sheehy's term for the third decade of life, when people are frequently occupied with advancement in the career world.
DREAM • In this usage, Levinson's term for the overriding drive of youth to become someone important, to leave one's mark on history.
AGE-30 TRANSITION • Levinson's term for the ages from 28 to 33, which are characterized by reassessment of the goals and values of the 20s.

Establishing Intimate Relationships. According to Erik Erikson, establishing intimate relationships is a central task of young adulthood.

ized by reassessment: "Where is my life going?" "Why am I doing this?" Sheehy (1976) labeled this period the **Catch 30s** because of this tendency toward reassessment. During our thirties, we often find that the lifestyles we adopted during our twenties do not fit as comfortably as we had expected.

One response to the disillusionments of the thirties, according to Sheehy,

> is the tearing up of the life we have spent most of our 20s putting together. It may mean striking out on a secondary road toward a new vision or converting a dream of "running for president" into a more realistic goal. The single person feels a push to find a partner. The woman who was previously content at home with children chafes to venture into the world. The childless couple reconsiders children. And almost everybody who is married . . . feels a discontent. (1976, p. 34)

Many psychologists find that the later thirties are characterized by settling down or planting roots. Many young adults feel a need to make a financial and emotional investment in their home. Their concerns become more focused on promotion or tenure, career advancement, and long-term mortgages.

• *Middle Adulthood*

Middle adulthood spans the years from 40 to 60 or 65. Sheehy (1995) terms the years from 45 onward "second adulthood." Rather than viewing them as years of decline, her interviews suggest that many Americans find that these years present opportunities for new direction and fulfillment.

GENERATIVITY VERSUS STAGNATION Erikson (1963) labeled the life crisis of the middle years **generativity versus stagnation.** Generativity involves doing things that we believe are worthwhile, such as rearing children or producing on the job. Generativity enhances and maintains self-esteem. Generativity also involves helping to shape the new generation. This shaping may involve rearing

CATCH 30s • Sheehy's term for the fourth decade of life, when many people undergo major reassessments of their accomplishments and goals.
GENERATIVITY VERSUS STAGNATION • Erikson's term for the crisis of middle adulthood, characterized by the task of being productive and contributing to younger generations.

our own children or making the world a better place, as through joining church or civic groups.

MIDLIFE TRANSITION According to Levinson, there is a **midlife transition** at about age 40 to 45 that is characterized by a shift in psychological perspective. Previously, we thought of our age in terms of the number of years that have elapsed since birth. Now we begin to think of our age in terms of the number of years we have left to live. Men in their thirties still think of themselves as part of the Pepsi Generation, older brothers to "kids" in their twenties. At about age 40 to 45, however, some marker event—illness, a change of job, the death of a friend or parent, or being beaten at tennis by their son—leads men to realize that they are a full generation older. Suddenly there seems to be more to look back on than forward to. It dawns on men that they'll never be president or chairperson of the board. They'll never play shortstop for the Dodgers. They mourn the passing of their own youth and begin to adjust to the specter of old age and the finality of death.

THE MIDLIFE CRISIS The midlife transition may trigger a crisis—the **midlife crisis.** The middle-level, middle-aged businessperson looking ahead to another 10 to 20 years of grinding out accounts in a Wall Street cubbyhole may encounter severe depression. The housewife with two teenagers, an empty house from 8:00 A.M. to 4:00 P.M., and a 40th birthday on the way may feel that she is coming apart at the seams. Both feel a sense of entrapment and loss of purpose. Some people are propelled into extramarital affairs by the desire to prove to themselves that they are still attractive.

Mid-Life Crisis or "Middlescence"? According to Gail Sheehy, many middle-aged people undergo a second quest for identity (the first occurs during adolescence). They are trying to decide what they will do with their "second adulthoods"—the three to four healthy decades they may have left.

MASTERY Sheehy (1995) is much more optimistic than Levinson. She terms the years from 45 to 65 "the Age of Mastery" because people are frequently at the height of their productive powers during this period. Sheehy believes that the key task for people aged 45 to 55 is to decide what they will do with their "second adulthoods"—the 30 to 40 healthy years that may be left for them once they reach 50. She believes that both men and women can experience great success and joy if they identify meaningful goals and pursue them wholeheartedly.

"MIDDLESCENCE" Yet people need to define themselves and their goals. Sheehy coined the term **middlescence** to describe a period of searching that is in some ways similar to adolescence. Both are times of transition. Middlescence involves a search for a new identity: "Turning backward, going around in circles, feeling lost in a buzz of confusion and unable to make decisions—all this is predictable and, for many people, a necessary precursor to making the passage into midlife" (Sheehy, 1995).

Women may undergo a midlife transition a number of years earlier than men do (e.g., Reinke and others, 1985). Sheehy (1976) writes that women enter midlife about 5 years earlier than men, at about age 35 instead of 40. Once they turn 35, women are usually advised to have their fetuses routinely tested for Down syndrome and other chromosomal disorders. At age 35, women also enter higher risk categories for side effects from birth control pills.

Yet women frequently experience a renewed sense of self in their forties and fifties as they emerge from "middlescence" (Apter, 1995; Sheehy, 1995). Many women in their early forties are already emerging from some of the fears and uncertainties that are first confronting men. For example, Helson and Moane (1987) found that women at age 43 are more likely than women in their early thirties to feel confident; to exert an influence on their community; to feel secure and committed; to feel productive, effective, and powerful; and to extend their interests beyond their family.

MENOPAUSE **Menopause,** or cessation of menstruation, usually occurs during the late forties or early fifties, although there are wide variations in the age at which it occurs. Menopause is the final stage of a broader female experience, the *climacteric,* which is caused by a falling off in the secretion of the hormones estrogen and progesterone. The climacteric begins with irregular periods and ends with menopause.[1] At this time ovulation also draws to an end. There is some loss of breast tissue and of elasticity in the skin. There can also be a loss of bone density that leads to osteoporosis (a condition in which the bones break easily) in late adulthood.

During the climacteric, many women encounter symptoms such as hot flashes (uncomfortable sensations characterized by heat and perspiration) and loss of sleep. However, women are more likely to suffer from depression prior to menopause, when they may feel overwhelmed by the combined demands of the workplace, child rearing, and homemaking (Brody, 1993). In most cases, the mood changes accompanying menopause are relatively mild. According to psychologist Karen Matthews, who has been following a sample of hundreds of women through menopause, some women do encounter problems, but they are in the minority. "The vast majority have no problem at all getting through the menopausal transition" (Matthews, 1994, p. 25).

Menopause does not signal the end of a woman's sexual interests (Brody, 1993). Many women find the separation of sex from reproduction to be sexually liberating. Some of the physical problems that may stem from the falloff in hormone production may be alleviated by hormone replacement therapy (Grodstein and others, 1997). A more important issue may be what menopause means to the individual. Women who equate menopause with loss of femininity are likely to encounter more distress than those who do not (Rathus and others, 1997).

Truth or Fiction Revisited

It is not true that menopause signals the end of a woman's sexual interests. Many women find the separation of sex from reproduction to be sexually liberating.

MANOPAUSE (*MANOPAUSE?*) Men cannot experience menopause, of course. Yet now and then we hear the term *male menopause,* or "manopause." Middle-aged or older men may be loosely alluded to as menopausal. This epithet is doubly offensive: It reinforces the negative, harmful stereotypes of aging people, especially aging women, as crotchety and irritable. Nor is the label consistent with the biology or psychology of aging. Alternate terms are *andropause* (referring to a drop-off in androgens, or male sex hormones) and *viropause* (referring to the end of virility) (Cowley, 1996).

For women, menopause is a time of relatively acute age-related declines in sex hormones and fertility. In men, however, the decline in the production of male sex hormones and fertility is more gradual. Moreover, some viable sperm are produced even in late adulthood. It therefore is not surprising to find a man in his seventies or older fathering a child. On the other hand, many men in their fifties and sixties experience intermittent problems in achieving and maintaining erections (Laumann and others, 1994), which may or may not have to do with hormone production.

Sexual performance is only one part of the story, however. Between the ages of 40 and 70, the typical American male loses 12 to 20 pounds of muscle, about 2 inches in height, and 15% of his bone mass. (Men as well as women are at risk for osteoporosis [Brody, 1996b].) The amount of fat in the body nearly

MIDLIFE TRANSITION • Levinson's term for the ages from 40 to 45, which are characterized by a shift in psychological perspective from viewing ourselves in terms of years lived to viewing ourselves in terms of the years we have left.
MIDLIFE CRISIS • A crisis experienced by many people during the midlife transition when they realize that life may be more than halfway over and reassess their achievements in terms of their dreams.
MIDDLESCENCE • Sheehy's term for a stage of life, from 45 to 55, when people seek new identity and are frequently "lost in a buzz of confusion."
MENOPAUSE • (MEN-no-paws). The cessation of menstruation.

---

[1] There are many other reasons for irregular periods, and women who experience them are advised to discuss them with their doctor.

doubles. The eardrums thicken, as do the lenses of the eyes, resulting in some loss of hearing and vision. There is also loss of endurance as the cardiovascular system and lungs become less capable of responding effectively to exertion.

Some of these changes can be slowed or even reversed. Exercise helps maintain muscle tone and keep the growth of fatty tissue in check. A diet rich in calcium and Vitamin D can help ward off bone loss in men as well as in women. Hormone replacement may also help, but is controversial. Although testosterone replacement appears to boost strength, energy, and the sex drive, it is connected with increased risks of prostate cancer and cardiovascular disease (Cowley, 1996).

Even though sexual interest and performance decline, men can remain sexually active and father children at advanced ages. For both genders, attitudes toward the biological changes of aging—along with general happiness—may affect sexual behavior as much as biological changes do.

THE EMPTY-NEST SYNDROME In earlier decades, psychologists placed great emphasis on a concept referred to as the **empty-nest syndrome.** This concept was applied most often to women. It was assumed that women experience a

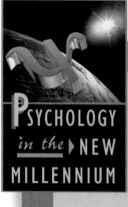

What Biological Clock?

PSYCHOLOGY *in the* NEW MILLENNIUM

As we stand at the edge of the new millennium, we find more and more parents with gray hair at Little League games and PTA meetings—even while most of the other parents are still trying to cope with their acne (Matus, 1996). The trend is clear. Bearing children is no longer defined as an event of young adulthood. Although fertility declines with age (Rathus and others, 1997), fathers have traditionally had children in middle and late adulthood. But today increasing numbers of women in the United States are bearing children in middle age. The birthrate for women aged 40 to 44 doubled between 1974 and 1994 (Clay, 1996a). In 1997, a 63-year-old woman gave birth. The trend to bear children at later ages continues.

MOTHERS IN THEIR FORTIES What kinds of mothers do middle-aged women make? According to Los Angeles psychologist Renee Cohen (1996), they make good ones. These mothers are usually settled in their work and marriage. Their decisions to bear children are well thought out. Because they have usually completed their education, established their career, and traveled, they are less likely to resent children for interfering with their lives.

"By the time older people decide to become parents," notes Cohen (1996, p. 37), "nothing is haphazard. Everything is planned. By having a baby, they're opening a new chapter in their lives."

OLDER FATHERS Older men also tend to be more involved as fathers, whether they are having their first child or parenting a second family (Clay, 1996b). Younger fathers tend to get embroiled in power struggles and physical discipline with their children, but "All of the studies on parenting show that the older the parent, the more nurturing, laid back, flexible, and supportive they are" (Pollack, 1996, p. 37).

Unlike younger men, men who choose fatherhood in their forties are less likely to view themselves as distant breadwinners whose major role in the home is to provide discipline. More mature fathers are more likely to see themselves as "team players" who share parenting with their wives. Moreover, they are likely to have more time and patience for fatherhood because they have already established themselves in their careers. ■

profound sense of loss when their youngest child goes off to college, gets married, or moves out of the home. Research findings paint a more optimistic picture, however. Certainly there can be problems, and these apply to both parents. Perhaps the largest of these is letting go of one's children after so many years of mutual dependence.

Many mothers report increased marital satisfaction and personal changes such as greater mellowness, self-confidence, and stability after their children have left home (Reinke and others, 1985). Middle-aged women show increased dominance and assertiveness, an orientation toward achievement, and greater influence in the worlds of politics and work. It is as if they are cut free from traditional shackles by the knowledge that their childbearing years are behind them.

Family role reversals are not uncommon once the children have left home (Wink & Helson, 1993). Given traditional sociocultural expectations of men and women, men are frequently more competent than their wives in the world outside the family during the early stages of marriage, and their wives are more emotionally dependent. But in the postparental period these differences may decrease or reverse direction, both because of women's enhanced status in the workplace and because of the decreased influence of the mother role.

Now let us consider developments in late adulthood, which begins at the age of 65.

• *Late Adulthood*

> *It's never too late to be what you might have been.*
>
> GEORGE ELIOT

Did you know that an *agequake* is coming? With improved health care and knowledge of the importance of diet and exercise, more Americans than ever before are 65 or older (Abeles, 1997a). In 1900, only 1 American in 30 was over 65, as compared with 1 in 9 in 1970. By 2030, 1 American in 5 will be 65 or older ("Longer, healthier, better," 1997; see Figure 4.9).

The agequake will shake America. It has already influenced the themes of TV shows and movies. Many consumer products are designed to appeal to older

EMPTY-NEST SYNDROME • A sense of depression and loss of purpose felt by some parents when the youngest child leaves home.

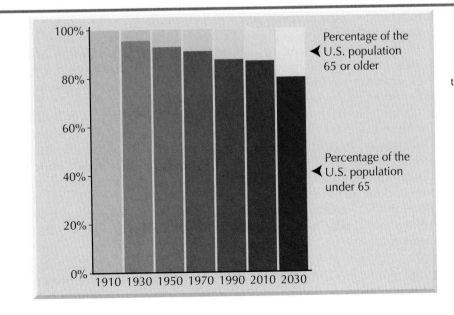

FIGURE **4.9**

LIVING LONGER

As we enter the new millennium, more people in the United States are living to be age 65 or above.

consumers. Leisure communities dot the Sunbelt. Older people today differ from their counterparts of a generation or two ago in that age is becoming less likely to determine their behavior and mental processes (Butler, 1998). However, the prospects are not the same for men and women, or for people from different ethnic backgrounds.

Psychology in a World of
DIVERSITY

Gender, Ethnicity, and Aging

Although Americans in general are living longer, there are gender and ethnic differences in life expectancy. For example, women in our society tend to live longer, but older men tend to live *better* ("Longer, healthier, better," 1997). White Americans from European backgrounds live longer on the average than do Hispanic Americans, African Americans, and Native Americans. Life expectancy for Hispanic Americans falls somewhere between the figures for African Americans and White Americans. The longevity of Asian Americans falls closer to that of White Americans than to that of African Americans. Native Americans have the lowest average longevity of the major racial/ethnic groups in our society (Nevid and others, 1998).

GENDER DIFFERENCES Women in the United States outlive men by six to seven years. Why? For one thing, heart disease, the nation's leading killer, typically develops later in women than in men. Men are also more likely to die because of accidents, cirrhosis of the liver, strokes, suicide, homicide, AIDS, and cancer (excepting cancers of the female sex organs) (Nevid and others, 1998). Many deaths from these causes are the end result of unhealthy habits that are more typical of men, such as excessive drinking and reckless behavior.

Many men are also reluctant to have regular physical exams or to talk to their doctors about their health problems. "In their 20's, [men are] too strong to need a doctor; in their 30's, they're too busy, and in their 40's, too scared" ("Doctors tie male mentality," 1995). Women are much more likely to examine themselves for signs of breast cancer than men are even to recognize the early signs of prostate cancer.

Although women tend to outlive men, their prospects for a happy and healthy old age are dimmer. Men who beat the statistical odds by living beyond their seventies are far less likely than their female counterparts to live alone, suffer from chronic disabling conditions, or be poor.

Older women are more likely than men to live alone largely because they are five times more likely than men to be widowed (Nevid and others, 1998). Older women are also twice as likely to be poor than older men. Several factors account for this difference. Women now age 65 or older were less likely to hold jobs. If they had jobs, they were paid far less than men and received smaller pensions and other retirement benefits. Because more women than men live alone, they more often must shoulder the burdens of supporting a household without being able to draw upon the income of a spouse or other family member.

ETHNICITY Why are there ethnic differences in life expectancy? Socioeconomic differences play a role. Members of ethnic minority groups in our society are more likely to be poor, and poor people tend to eat less nutritious diets, encounter more stress, and have less access to health care. There is a seven-year difference in life expectancy between people in the highest income brackets and those in the lowest. Yet other factors, such as cultural differences in diet and lifestyle, the stress of coping with discrimination, and genetic differences, may also partly account for ethnic group differences in life expectancy.

PHYSICAL DEVELOPMENT Various changes—some of them troublesome— do occur during the later years. Changes in calcium metabolism lead to increased brittleness in the bones and heightened risk of breaks due to accidents such as falls. The skin becomes less elastic and subject to wrinkles and folds.

The senses are also affected. Older people see and hear less acutely. Because of a decline in the sense of smell, they may use more spice to flavor their food. Older people need more time (called **reaction time**) to respond to stimuli. Older drivers, for example, need more time to respond to traffic lights, other vehicles, and changing road conditions. As we grow older, our immune system also functions less effectively, leaving us more vulnerable to disease.

COGNITIVE DEVELOPMENT Although there are some declines in reaction time, intellectual functioning, and memory among older people, they are not as large as many people assume they are (Abeles, 1997b; Butler, 1998). But we understand very little about *why* they occur. Depression and losses of sensory acuity and motivation may contribute to lower cognitive test scores. B. F. Skinner (1983) argued that much of the falloff is due to an "aging environment" rather than an aging person. That is, the behavior of older people often goes unreinforced. Nursing home residents who are rewarded for remembering recent events show improved scores on tests of memory (Langer and others, 1979).

THEORIES OF AGING Although it may be hard to believe that it will happen to us, every person who has walked the Earth so far has aged—which may not be a bad fate, considering the alternative. Why do we age? Various factors, some of which are theoretical, apparently contribute to aging.

The theory of **programmed senescence** sees aging as determined by a biological clock that ticks at a rate governed by instructions in the genes. Just as genes program children to grow and reach sexual maturation, they program people to deteriorate and die. There is evidence to support a role for genes in aging. Longevity runs in families. People whose parents and grandparents lived into their eighties and nineties have a better chance of reaching these ages themselves.

The **wear-and-tear theory** does not suggest that people are programmed to self-destruct. Instead, environmental factors such as pollution, disease, and ultraviolet light are assumed to contribute to wear and tear of the body over time. The body is like a machine whose parts wear out through use. Cells lose the ability to regenerate themselves, and vital organs are worn down by the ravages of time.

Behavior also influences aging. People who exercise regularly seem to live longer. Cigarette smoking, overeating, and stress can contribute to an early death. Fortunately, we can exert control over some of these factors.

PSYCHOSOCIAL VIEWS OF AGING According to Erikson, late adulthood is the stage of **ego integrity versus despair.** The basic challenge is to maintain the belief that life is meaningful and worthwhile in the face of the inevitability of death. Ego integrity derives from wisdom, as well as from the

REACTION TIME • The amount of time required to respond to a stimulus.
PROGRAMMED SENESCENCE • The view that aging is determined by a biological clock that ticks at a rate governed by genes.
WEAR-AND-TEAR THEORY • The view that factors such as pollution, disease, and ultraviolet light contribute to wear and tear on the body, so that the body loses the ability to repair itself.
EGO INTEGRITY VERSUS DESPAIR • Erikson's term for the crisis of late adulthood, characterized by the task of maintaining one's sense of identity despite physical deterioration.

How Long Will You Live?
The Life-Expectancy Scale

The life-expectancy scale is one of several used by physicians and insurance companies to estimate how long people will live. Scales such as these are far from precise—which is a good thing, if you think about it. But they make reasonable "guesstimates" based on our heredity, medical histories, and lifestyles.

Directions: To complete the scale, begin with the age of 72. Then add or subtract years according to the following directions:

RUNNING
TOTAL
PERSONAL FACTS:

____ 1. If you are male, **subtract 3.**

____ 2. If female, **add 4.**

____ 3. If you live in an urban area with a population over 2 million, **subtract 2.**

____ 4. If you live in a town with under 10,000 people or on a farm, **add 2.**

____ 5. If any grandparent lived to 85, **add 2.**

____ 6. If all four grandparents lived to 80, **add 6.**

____ 7. If either parent died of a stroke or heart attack before the age of 50, **subtract 4.**

____ 8. If any parent, brother, or sister under 50 has (or had) cancer or a heart condition, or has had diabetes since childhood, **subtract 3.**

____ 9. Do you earn over $75,000[2] a year? If so, **subtract 2.**

____ 10. If you finished college, **add 1.** If you have a graduate or professional degree, **add 2 more.**

____ 11. If you are 65 or over and still working, **add 3.**

____ 12. If you live with a spouse or friend, **add 5.** If not, **subtract 1** for every ten years alone since age 25.

LIFESTYLE STATUS:

____ 13. If you work behind a desk, **subtract 3.**

____ 14. If your work requires regular, heavy physical labor, **add 3.**

____ 15. If you exercise strenuously (tennis, running, swimming, etc.) five times a week for at least a half-hour, **add 4.** If two or three times a week, **add 2.**

____ 16. Do you sleep more than ten hours each night? **Subtract 4.**

____ 17. Are you intense, aggressive, easily angered? **Subtract 3.**

____ 18. Are you easygoing and relaxed? **Add 3.**

____ 19. Are you happy? **Add 1.** Unhappy? **Subtract 2.**

____ 20. Have you had a speeding ticket in the last year? **Subtract 1.**

____ 21. Do you smoke more than two packs a day? **Subtract 8.** One or two packs? **Subtract 6.** One-half to one? **Subtract 3.**

____ 22. Do you drink the equivalent of $1\frac{1}{2}$ oz. of liquor a day? **Subtract 1.**

____ 23. Are you overweight by 50 lbs. or more? **Subtract 8.** By 30 to 50 lbs? **Subtract 4.** By 10 to 30 lbs? **Subtract 2.**

____ 24. If you are a man over 40 and have annual checkups, **add 2.**

____ 25. If you are a woman and see a gynecologist once a year, **add 2.**

AGE ADJUSTMENT:

____ 26. If you are between 30 and 40, **add 2.**

____ 27. If you are between 40 and 50, **add 3.**

____ 28. If you are between 50 and 70, **add 4.**

____ 29. If you are over 70, **add 5.**

[2] This figure is an inflation-adjusted estimate.

____ YOUR LIFE EXPECTANCY

Note. From Robert F. Allen with Shirley Linde. (1986). *Lifegain.* Human Resources Institute Press, Tempe Wick Road, Morristown, NJ.

acceptance of one's lifespan as occurring at a certain point in the sweep of history and as being limited. We spend most of our lives accumulating objects and relationships. Erikson also argues that adjustment in the later years requires the ability to let go.

Other psychosocial theories of aging include disengagement theory, activity theory, and continuity theory (Berger, 1994).

1. **Disengagement Theory.** Disengagement theory maintains that the individual and society withdraw from each other during the later years. Traditional roles such as those of worker and parent give way to a narrowed social circle and reduced activity.

2. **Activity Theory.** According to this view, life satisfaction is connected with remaining active. Unfortunately, retirement and the narrowing of one's social circle often reduce activity.

3. **Continuity Theory.** Continuity theory maintains that individuals tend to cope with the challenges of late adulthood the same way they coped with earlier challenges. Individual temperament and differences are more important determinants of life satisfaction than one's stage of life.

There is some merit in each of these views. As we see in the following section, "successful aging" is connected with remaining active and involved. On the other hand, biological and social realities may require that older people become more selective in their pursuits.

SUCCESSFUL AGING The later years were once seen mainly as a prelude to dying. Older people were viewed as crotchety and irritable. It was assumed that they reaped little pleasure from life. *No more.* Many stereotypes about aging are becoming less prevalent. Despite the changes that accompany aging, most people in their seventies report being generally satisfied with their lives (Margoshes, 1995). Americans are eating more wisely and exercising at later ages, so that many older people are robust.

Sheehy (1995) coined the term *middlescence* to highlight her finding that people whom she interviewed in their fifties were thinking about what they would do with their *second adulthood*—the 30 to 40 healthy years they had left! Developmental psychologists are using another new term: *successful aging* (Margoshes, 1995). The term is not just meant to put a positive spin on the inevitable. "Successful agers" have a number of characteristics that can inspire all of us to lead more enjoyable and productive lives. There are three components of successful aging:

1. *Reshaping one's life to concentrate on what one finds to be important and meaningful.* Laura Carstensen's (1997) research on people aged 70 and above reveals that successful agers form emotional goals that bring them satisfaction. For example, rather than cast about in multiple directions, they may focus on their family and friends. Successful agers may have less time left than those of us in earlier stages of adulthood, but they tend to spend it more wisely (Garfinkel, 1995).

   Researchers (Baltes, 1997; Schulz & Heckhausen, 1996) use terms such as "selective optimization and compensation" to describe the manner in which successful agers lead their lives. That is, successful agers no longer seek to compete in arenas that are best left to younger people—such as certain kinds of athletic or business activities. Rather, they focus on matters that allow them to maintain a sense of control over their own

"Successful Aging"? The later years were once seen mainly as a prelude to dying. As we approach the new millennium, however, many older people—termed "successful agers"—are seeking new challenges.

DISENGAGEMENT THEORY • The view that the individual and society withdraw from one another during the later years.
ACTIVITY THEORY • The view that life satisfaction is connected with one's level of activity.
CONTINUITY THEORY • The view that people tend to cope with the challenges of late adulthood in the ways that they coped with earlier challenges.

actions. Moreover, they use available resources to make up for losses. If their memory is not quite what it once was, they make notes or other reminders. For example, if their senses are no longer as acute, they use devices such as hearing aids or allow themselves more time to take in information. There are also some ingenious individual strategies. The great pianist Arthur Rubinstein performed into his eighties, even after he had lost much of his pianistic speed. In his later years, he would slow down before playing faster passages in order to enhance the impression of speed during those passages.

2. *A positive outlook.* For example, some older people attribute occasional health problems such as aches and pains to *specific* and *unstable* factors like a cold or jogging too long. Others attribute aches and pains to *global* and *stable* factors such as aging itself. Not surprisingly, those who attribute these problems to specific, unstable factors are more optimistic about surmounting them. They thus have a more positive outlook or attitude. Of particular interest here is research conducted by William Rakowski (1995). Rakowski followed 1,400 people age 70 or older with nonlethal health problems such as aches and pains. He found that those who blamed the problems on aging itself were significantly more likely to die in the near future than those who blamed the problems on specific, unstable factors.

3. *Self-challenge.* Many people look forward to late adulthood as a time when they can rest from life's challenges. But sitting back and allowing the world to pass by is a prescription for vegetating, not for living life to its fullest. Consider an experiment conducted by Curt Sandman and Francis Crinella (1995) with 175 people whose average age was 72. They randomly assigned subjects either to a foster grandparent program with neurologically impaired children or to a control group, and followed both groups for 10 years. The foster grandparents carried out various physical challenges, such as walking a few miles each day, and also engaged in new kinds of social interactions. Those in the control group did not engage in these activities. When they were assessed by the experimenters, the foster grandparents showed improved overall cognitive functioning, including memory functioning, and better sleep patterns. Moreover, the foster grandparents showed superior functioning in these areas compared with people assigned to the control group.

Truth or Fiction Revisited

It is true that older people who blame health problems on aging rather than on specific factors such as a virus are more likely to die in the near future.

ON DEATH AND DYING Death is the last great taboo. Psychiatrist Elisabeth Kübler-Ross commented on our denial of death in her landmark book *On Death and Dying*:

> We use euphemisms, we make the dead look as if they were asleep, we ship the children off to protect them from the anxiety and turmoil around the house if the [person] is fortunate enough to die at home, [and] we don't allow children to visit their dying parents in the hospital. (1969, p. 8)

In her work with terminally ill patients, Kübler-Ross found some common responses to news of impending death. She identified five stages of dying through which many patients pass, and she suggested that older people who suspect that death is approaching may undergo similar stages:

1. *Denial.* In the denial stage, people feel that "It can't be happening to me. The diagnosis must be wrong."

2. *Anger.* Denial usually gives way to anger and resentment toward the young and healthy and, sometimes, toward the medical establishment—"It's unfair. Why me?"

3. *Bargaining.* Next, people may try to bargain with God to postpone their death, promising, for example, to do good deeds if they are given another six months, another year to live.

4. *Depression.* With depression come feelings of loss and hopelessness—grief at the inevitability of leaving loved ones and life itself.

5. *Final acceptance.* Ultimately, an inner peace may come, a quiet acceptance of the inevitable. Such "peace" does not resemble contentment. Instead, it is nearly devoid of feeling.

Psychologist Edwin Shneidman, who has specialized in the concerns of suicidal and dying individuals, acknowledges the presence of feelings such as those identified by Kübler-Ross, but he does not perceive them to be linked in a sequence like the one just described. Instead, he suggests that dying people show a variety of emotional and cognitive responses that tend to be fleeting or relatively stable, to ebb and flow, and to reflect pain and bewilderment. He also points out that the kinds of responses shown by individuals reflect their personality traits and their philosophies of life.

"LYING DOWN TO PLEASANT DREAMS . . ." The American poet William Cullen Bryant is best known for his poem "Thanatopsis," which he composed at the age of 18. "Thanatopsis" expresses Erikson's goal of ego integrity and his optimism that people can maintain a sense of trust throughout life. By meeting the challenges of our adult lives, perhaps we can take our leave with dignity. When our time comes to "join the innumerable caravan"—the billions who have died before us—perhaps we can depart life with integrity.

REFLECTIONS
- Consider middle-aged and older people in your own life. Are their behavior and personalities in any way consistent with the descriptions in this section? How or how not?
- How do you feel about the use of the term *manopause* to describe men who have reached middle age or their later years? Is the term useful or does it merely perpetuate stereotypes? Explain.
- Erikson wrote that one aspect of wisdom is the ability to visualize one's role in the march of history and to accept one's own death. Do you believe that acceptance of death is a sign of wisdom? Why or why not?

1. **Does development reflect nature or nurture?** Development appears to reflect an interaction between nature (genetic factors) and nurture (environmental influences). Maturational theorists focus on the influences of nature, whereas learning theorists focus on environmental influences.

2. **Is development continuous or discontinuous?** Stage theorists like Freud and Piaget view development as discontinuous. According to them, people go through distinct periods of development that differ in quality and follow an orderly sequence. Learning theorists, in contrast, tend to view psychological development as a continuous process.

3. **What are the stages of prenatal development?** These are the germinal, embryonic, and fetal stages. During the germinal stage, the zygote divides as it travels through the fallopian tube and becomes implanted in the uterine wall. The major organ systems are formed during the embryonic stage, and the fetal stage is characterized by maturation and gains in size.

4. **What are the highlights of physical development?** Physical development occurs most rapidly before birth and during the first two years after birth. There is also an adolescent growth spurt during which young people make dramatic gains in height and weight.

5. **What are reflexes?** Reflexes are inborn responses to stimuli that in many cases are essential to infant survival. Examples include breathing, sucking, and swallowing.

6. **How do babies perceive their environment?** Newborn babies can see quite well and show greater interest in complex visual stimuli than in simple ones. Infants are capable of depth perception by the time they can crawl. Newborns can normally hear and show a preference for their mother's voice. Newborns show preferences for pleasant odors and sweet foods.

7. **What are the stages of attachment?** According to Ainsworth, there are three stages of attachment: the initial-preattachment phase, which is characterized by indiscriminate attachment; the attachment-in-the-making phase, which is characterized by preference for familiar figures; and the clear-cut-attachment phase, which is characterized by intensified dependence on the primary caregiver.

8. **What are the major theories of attachment?** Behaviorists have argued that children become attached to their mothers through conditioning, because their mothers feed them and attend to their other needs. Harlow's studies with rhesus monkeys suggest that an innate motive, contact comfort, may be more important than conditioning in the development of at-

tachment. There are critical developmental periods during which animals such as geese and ducks will become imprinted on, or attached to, an object that they follow.

9. **What are the main parenting styles?** These include the authoritative, authoritarian, and permissive styles. The children of authoritative parents are most achievement-oriented and well-adjusted.

10. **How did Jean Piaget view children?** Piaget saw children as budding scientists who actively strive to make sense of the perceptual world. He defined intelligence as involving the processes of assimilation (responding to events according to existing schemes) and accommodation (changing schemes to permit effective responses to new events).

11. **What are the stages of cognitive development, according to Piaget?** Piaget's view of cognitive development includes four stages: sensorimotor (prior to the use of symbols and language); preoperational (characterized by egocentric thought, animism, artificialism, and inability to center on more than one aspect of a situation); concrete operational (characterized by conservation, less egocentrism, reversibility, and subjective moral judgments); and formal operational (characterized by abstract logic).

12. **How do information-processing theorists view cognitive development?** Information-processing theorists view cognitive development in terms of expansion of working memory, growing automaticity in problem solving, development of more sophisticated "mental programs," and increasing knowledge about the functioning of one's own cognitive processes.

13. **How did Kohlberg view moral development?** Kohlberg focused on the processes of moral reasoning. He hypothesized that these processes develop through three "levels," with each level consisting of two stages.

14. **What is adolescence?** Adolescence is a period of life that begins at puberty and ends with assumption of adult responsibilities. Changes that lead to reproductive capacity and secondary sex characteristics are stimulated by increased levels of testosterone in the male and of estrogen and androgens in the female. Adolescents frequently yearn for greater independence from their parents.

15. **What are some of the major events of young adulthood?** Young adulthood is generally characterized by efforts to advance in the business world and the development of intimate ties.

16. **What are some of the major events of middle adulthood?** Middle adulthood is a time of crisis and further reassessment for many, a time when we come to terms with the discrepancies between our achievements and the dreams of our youth. Some

middle-aged adults become depressed when their youngest child leaves home (the so-called "empty-nest syndrome"), but many report increased satisfaction, stability, and self-confidence. However, many people in middle adulthood experience "middle-scence"—during which they redefine themselves and their goals for the 30 to 40 healthy years they expect lie ahead of them.

17. **What are some of the changes that occur during late adulthood?** Older people show less sensory acuity, and their reaction time lengthens. Presumed cognitive deficits sometimes reflect declining motivation or psychological problems such as depression.

18. **What factors are involved in longevity?** Heredity plays a role in longevity. One theory (programmed senescence) suggests that aging and death are determined by our genes. Another theory (wear-and-tear theory) hold that factors such as pollution, disease, and ultraviolet light contribute to wear and tear on the body, so that the body loses the ability to repair itself. Lifestyle factors such as exercise, good nutrition, and not smoking also contribute to longevity.

19. **Are there "stages of dying"?** Kübler-Ross has identified five stages of dying among people who are terminally ill: denial, anger, bargaining, depression, and final acceptance. Other investigators find that psychological reactions to approaching death are more varied than Kübler-Ross suggests, however.

To enhance your understanding of the psychological concepts found in this chapter, please consult the following aids:

STUDY GUIDE

Learning Objectives, p. 63
Exercise, p. 64
Lecture and Textbook Outline, p. 65
Effective Studying Ideas, p. 68

Key Terms and Concepts, p. 69
Chapter Review, p. 70
Chapter Exercises, p. 79
Knowing the Language, p. 80
Do you Know the Material?, p. 82

CORE CONCEPTS SEARCH

Prenatal Development
The Development of Visual Acuity
Social Development
Emotional Development
Personality Development

Object Permanence
Conservation
Formal Operations
Self-Concept and Self-Esteem
Moral Development

World Wide Web

For more information concerning the topics found in this chapter, access psychology links on the World Wide Web through the Harcourt Brace webpage at

www.hbcollege.com

Share your comments and questions with your author at

PsychLinks@aol.com

Sensation is the stimulation of sensory organs by physical energy or chemical substances. Sensation is quite similar from one person to another, but our *perceptions* are based on our cultural experiences as well as on sensation. The cultural experiences of Native American artist Jaune Quick-to-See Smith frequently place her on "the other side." In terms of the color wheel, green is "the other side" of red. *Green Flag* (1995), like much of Smith's work, is about confrontation between Native American culture and the dominant culture in the United States. The words "green" and "money" may refer to the struggle over preservation of the natural environment.

JAUNE QUICK-TO-SEE-SMITH

Chapter 5

Sensation and Perception

TRUTH OR FICTION?

✔ **T F**

☐ ☐ People have five senses.

☐ ☐ On a clear, dark night you could probably see the light from a candle burning 30 miles away.

☐ ☐ If we could see light with slightly longer wavelengths, warm-blooded animals would seem to glow in the dark.

☐ ☐ White sunlight is actually composed of all the colors of the rainbow.

☐ ☐ When we mix blue and yellow light, we attain green light.

☐ ☐ A $500 machine-made violin will produce the same musical notes as a $200,000 Stradivarius.

☐ ☐ Onions and apples have the same taste.

☐ ☐ Many amputees experience pain in limbs that have been removed.

☐ ☐ Rubbing or scratching a sore toe is often an effective way of relieving pain.

☐ ☐ We have a sense that keeps us upright.

☐ ☐ Some people can read other people's minds.

OUTLINE

SENSATION AND PERCEPTION: YOUR TICKET OF ADMISSION TO THE WORLD OUTSIDE
Absolute Threshold: Is It There or Isn't It?
Difference Threshold: Is It the Same or Is It Different?
Signal-Detection Theory: Is It Enough to Be Bright?
Feature Detectors
Sensory Adaptation: Where Did It Go?

VISION: LETTING THE SUN SHINE IN
Light: What Is This Stuff?
The Eye: The Better to See You With
Color Vision: Creating an Inner World of Color
Psychological Dimensions of Color
Theories of Color Vision
Color Blindness

VISUAL PERCEPTION
Perceptual Organization
Perception of Movement
Depth Perception
Problems in Visual Perception
Perceptual Constancies
Visual Illusions

HEARING
Pitch and Loudness
The Ear: The Better to Hear You With
Locating Sounds
Perception of Loudness and Pitch
Deafness
Psychology in a World of Diversity: The Signs of the Times Are Changing

SMELL

TASTE
Psychology in the New Millennium: Will We Use "a Sixth Sense for Sex" in the 21st Century?

THE SKIN SENSES
Touch and Pressure
Psychology in the New Millennium: Sensation, Perception, and Virtual Reality
Temperature
Pain: The Often Unwanted Message
Psychology and Modern Life: Coping With Pain

KINESTHESIS

THE VESTIBULAR SENSE: ON BEING UPRIGHT

EXTRASENSORY PERCEPTION

*F*IVE THOUSAND YEARS AGO IN CHINA, give or take a day or two, an arrow was shot into the air. Where did it land? Ancient records tell us precisely where: in the hand of a fierce warrior and master of the martial arts. As the story was told to me, the warrior had grown so fierce because of a chronic toothache. Incessant pain had ruined his disposition.

One fateful day, our hero watched as invading hordes assembled on surrounding hills. His troops were trembling in the face of the enemy's great numbers, and he raised his arms to boost their morale. A slender wooden shaft lifted into the air from a nearby rise, arced, and then descended—right into the warrior's palm. His troops cringed and muttered among themselves, but our hero said nothing. Although he saw the arrow pass through his palm, he did not scream. He did not run. He did not even complain. He was astounded. His toothache had vanished. In fact, his whole jaw was numb.

Meanwhile the invaders looked on, horrified. They, too, muttered among themselves. What sort of warrior could watch an arrow pierce his hand with such indifference? Even with a smile? If this was the caliber of the local warriors, the invaders would be better off traveling west and looking for a brawl in ancient Sumer or in Egypt. They sounded the retreat and withdrew.

Back in town, our warrior received a hero's welcome. A physician offered to remove the arrow without a fee—a tribute to bravery. But the warrior would have none of it. The arrow had worked wonders for his toothache, and he would brook no meddling. He had already discovered that if the pain threatened to return, he need only twirl the arrow and it would recede once more.

All was not well on the home front, however. His wife was thrilled to find him jovial once more, but the arrow put a crimp in their romance. When he put his arm around her, she was in danger of being stabbed. Finally she gave him an ultimatum: The arrow must go, or she would.

Placed in deep conflict, our warrior consulted a psychologist, who then huddled with the physician and the village elders. After much to-do, they asked the warrior to participate in an experiment. They would remove the arrow and replace it with a pin that the warrior could twirl as needed.

To the warrior's wife's relief, the pin worked. And here, in ancient China, lay the origins of the art of **acupuncture**—the use of needles to relieve pain and treat assorted ills.

I confess that this tale is not entirely accurate. To my knowledge, there were no psychologists in ancient China (their loss). Moreover, the part about the warrior's wife is fictitious. It is claimed, however, that acupuncture as a means of dealing with pain originated in ancient China when a soldier was, in fact, wounded in the hand by an arrow and discovered that a chronic toothache had disappeared. Historians say that the Chinese then set out to map the body by sticking pins into various parts of it to learn how they would influence the perception of pain.

Control of pain is just one of the many issues that interest psychologists who study the closely related concepts of sensation and perception. **Sensation** is the stimulation of sensory receptors and the transmission of sensory information to the central nervous system (the spinal cord or brain). Sensory receptors are located in sensory organs such as the eyes and ears and, as we will see, in the skin and elsewhere in the body. Stimulation of the senses is a mechanical process. It results from sources of energy like light and sound or from the presence of chemicals, as in smell and taste.

Perception is not mechanical. Perception is the process by which sensations are organized and interpreted to form an inner representation of the world. Perception involves more than sensation. It reflects learning and expectations and the ways in which we organize incoming information about the world. It is an active process through which we make sense of sensory stimuli. A human shape and a 12-inch ruler may stimulate paths of equal length among the sensory receptors in our eyes, but whether we interpret the shape to be a foot-long doll or a full-grown person 15 to 20 feet away is a matter of perception.

In this chapter you will see that your personal map of reality—your ticket of admission to a world of changing sights, sounds, and other sources of sensory input—depends largely on the so-called five senses: vision, hearing, smell, taste, and touch. We will see, however, that touch is just one of several "skin senses," which also include pressure, warmth, cold, and pain. There are also senses that alert you to your own body position without your having to watch every step you take. As we explore the nature of each of these senses, we will find that similar sensations may lead to different perceptions in different people—or within the same person in different situations.

Sensory Thresholds. How much stimulation is necessary before a person can detect a stimulus? How bright must the beacon from the lighthouse be to enable you to see it through the fog from several miles offshore?

> ### Truth or Fiction Revisited
>
> *It is not true that people have five senses.* People have more, as we will see in this chapter.

■ SENSATION AND PERCEPTION: YOUR TICKET OF ADMISSION TO THE WORLD OUTSIDE

Before we begin our journey through the senses, let us consider a number of concepts that apply to them all: absolute threshold, difference threshold, signal-detection theory, and sensory adaptation. In doing so, we will learn why we might be able to dim the lights gradually to near darkness without other people becoming aware that we are doing so. We will also learn why we might grow unaware of the savory aromas of delightful dinners.

• *Absolute Threshold: Is It There or Isn't It?*

Gustav Fechner used the term **absolute threshold** to refer to the weakest amount of a stimulus that can be distinguished from no stimulus at all. For example, the amount of physical energy required to activate the visual sensory system is the absolute threshold for light.

Psychophysicists conduct experiments to determine the absolute thresholds of the senses. These involve exposing subjects to stimuli of progressively greater intensity. In the **method of constant stimuli,** researchers present sets of stimuli with magnitudes close to the expected threshold. Subjects say yes if they detect a stimulus and no if they do not. The stimuli are presented repeatedly in random order. An individual's absolute threshold for a stimulus is the lowest magnitude of the stimulus that he or she reports detecting 50% of the time. Weaker stimuli are detected less than 50% of the time and stronger stimuli more than 50% of the time.

ACUPUNCTURE • The ancient Chinese practice of piercing parts of the body with needles to deaden pain and treat illness.

SENSATION • The stimulation of sensory receptors and the transmission of sensory information to the central nervous system.

PERCEPTION • The process by which sensations are organized into an inner representation of the world.

ABSOLUTE THRESHOLD • The minimal amount of energy that can produce a sensation.

PSYCHOPHYSICIST • A person who studies the relationships between physical stimuli (such as light or sound) and their perception.

METHOD OF CONSTANT STIMULI • A psychophysical method for determining thresholds in which the researcher presents stimuli of various magnitudes and asks the person to report detection.

He was interested in parapsychology and reported attending seances in which a bed, a table, and he himself moved in response to strange forces. He was interested in spiritual phenomena and wrote a bereaved friend that death is but a transition to another state of existence, in which one's soul merges with others to join the Supreme Spirit. Under the pen name of "Dr. Mises," he argued (satirically) that angels must have no legs. Insects have six legs, mammals four, and birds, who ascend closest to heaven, only two. Angels, higher yet, must have none.

The son and grandson of German village pastors, Gustav Theodor Fechner (1801-1887), like his father, combined religious faith with a hardheaded scientific outlook. His father scandalously installed a lightning rod on the local church at a time when it was assumed

Gustav T. Fechner

that God would take care of heavenly threats to faithful parishes. His father also went against the fashion and preached without a wig, arguing that Jesus had done the same.

Young Fechner obtained a degree in medicine at the University of Leipzig, but his interests turned to physics and math. He founded the discipline known as *psychophysics,* which deals with the ways in which physical events such as lights and sounds are related to sensation and perception. Some historians believe that psychology as a science began in 1860 with Fechner's publication of *Elements of Psychophysics.*

Many of Fechner's laboratory methods remain in use today. Fechner also devoted his energies to esthetics—attempting to learn why some works of art are more pleasing than others. ■

The relationship between the intensity of a stimulus (a physical event) and its perception (a psychological event) is considered to be **psychophysical.** It bridges psychological and physical events.

Absolute thresholds have been determined for the senses of vision, hearing, taste, smell, and touch. They are approximately as follows:

- For vision, the equivalent of a candle flame viewed from a distance of about 30 miles on a clear, dark night
- For hearing, the equivalent of the ticking of a watch from about 20 feet away in a quiet room
- For taste, the equivalent of about one teaspoon of sugar dissolved in two gallons of water
- For smell, the equivalent of about one drop of perfume diffused throughout a small house (1 part in 500 million)
- For touch, the equivalent of the pressure of the wing of a fly falling on a cheek from a distance of about 0.4 inch

There are individual differences in absolute thresholds. That is, some people are more sensitive to sensory stimuli than others. The same person may also differ somewhat in sensitivity from one day to the next or from one occasion to another.

If the absolute thresholds for the human senses differed significantly, our daily experiences would be unrecognizable. Our ears are particularly sensitive, especially to sounds that are low in **pitch.** If they were any more sensitive, we might hear the collisions among molecules of air. If our eyes were sensitive to light with slightly longer wavelengths, we would perceive infrared light waves. As a result, animals that are warm-blooded and therefore give off heat—including our mates—would literally glow in the dark.

Difference Threshold: Is It the Same or Is It Different?

How much of a difference in intensity between two lights is required before you will detect one as being brighter than the other? The minimum difference in magnitude of two stimuli required to tell them apart is their **difference threshold.** As with the absolute threshold, psychologists have agreed to the criterion of a difference in magnitudes that can be detected 50% of the time.

Psychophysicist Ernst Weber discovered through laboratory research that the threshold for perceiving differences in the intensity of light is about 2% (actually closer to 1/60) of their intensity. This fraction, 1/60, is known as **Weber's constant** for light. A closely related concept is the **just noticeable difference (jnd),** the minimal amount by which a source of energy must be increased or decreased so that a difference in intensity will be perceived. In the case of light, people can perceive a difference in intensity 50% of the time when the bright-

Truth or Fiction Revisited

It is true that on a clear, dark night you could probably see the light from a candle burning 30 miles away. This figure is in keeping with the absolute threshold for light. It is also true that if we could see light with slightly longer wavelengths, warm-blooded animals would seem to glow in the dark.

ness of a light is increased or decreased by $\frac{1}{60}$. Weber's constant for light holds whether we are comparing two quite bright lights or two rather dull lights. However, it becomes inaccurate when we compare extremely bright or extremely dull lights.

Weber's constant for noticing differences in lifted weight is $\frac{1}{53}$. (Round it off to $\frac{1}{50}$.) That means that one would probably have to increase the weight on a 100-pound barbell by about 2 pounds before the lifter would notice the difference. Now think of the 1-pound dumbbells used by many runners. Increasing the weight of each dumbbell by 2 pounds would be readily apparent to almost anyone because the increase would be threefold, not a small fraction. Yet the increase is still "only" 2 pounds. Return to our power lifter. When he is pressing 400 pounds, a 2-pound difference is less likely to be noticeable than when he is pressing 100 pounds. This is because our constant 2 pounds has become a difference of only $\frac{1}{200}$.

People are most sensitive to changes in the pitch (frequency) of sounds. The constant for pitch is $\frac{1}{333}$, meaning that on average, people can tell when a tone rises or falls in pitch by one-third of 1%. (Singers have to be right on pitch. The smallest error makes them sound sharp or flat.) The sense of taste is much less sensitive. On average, people cannot detect differences in saltiness of less than 20%.

• Signal-Detection Theory: Is It Enough to Be Bright?

Does our discussion so far strike you as "inhuman"? We have written about perception of sensory stimuli as if people are simply switched on by certain amounts of stimulation. This is not quite so. People are influenced by psychological factors as well as by external changes. **Signal-detection theory** considers the human aspects of sensation and perception.

The intensity of the signal is just one factor that determines whether people will perceive sensory stimuli (signals) or a difference between signals. Another is the degree to which the signal can be distinguished from background noise. It is easier to hear a friend in a quiet room than in a room in which people are talking loudly and clinking glasses. The sharpness or acuteness of a person's biological sensory system is still another factor. Is sensory capacity fully developed? Is it diminished by advanced age?

Signal-detection theory also considers psychological factors such as motivation, expectations, and learning. For example, the place in which you are reading this book may be abuzz with signals. If you are outside, perhaps a breeze is blowing against your face. Perhaps the shadows of passing clouds darken the scene now and then. If you are inside, perhaps there are the occasional clanks and hums emitted by a heating system. Perhaps the aromas of dinner are hanging in the air, or the voices from a TV set suggest a crowd in another room. Yet you are focusing your attention on this page (I hope). Thus, the other signals recede into the background of your consciousness. One psychological factor in

PSYCHOPHYSICAL • Bridging the gap between the physical and psychological worlds.

PITCH • The highness or lowness of a sound, as determined by the frequency of the sound waves.

DIFFERENCE THRESHOLD • The minimal difference in intensity required between two sources of energy so that they will be perceived as being different.

WEBER'S CONSTANT • The fraction of the intensity by which a source of physical energy must be increased or decreased so that a difference in intensity will be perceived.

JUST NOTICEABLE DIFFERENCE • The minimal amount by which a source of energy must be increased or decreased so that a difference in intensity will be perceived.

SIGNAL-DETECTION THEORY • The view that the perception of sensory stimuli involves the interaction of physical, biological, and psychological factors.

Signal Detection. The detection of signals is determined not only by the physical characteristics of the signals but also by psychological factors such as motivation and attention. The people in this photo are tuned into their newspapers for the moment, and not to each other.

signal detection is the focusing or narrowing of attention to signals that the person deems important.

Consider some examples. One parent may sleep through a baby's crying while the other parent is awakened. This is not necessarily because one parent is innately more sensitive to the sounds of crying (although some men may conveniently assume that mothers are). Instead, it may be because one parent has been assigned the task of caring for the baby through the night and is therefore more motivated to attend to the sounds. Because of training, an artist might notice the use of line or subtle colors that would go undetected by another person looking at the same painting.

The relationship between a physical stimulus and a sensory response is more than mechanical or mathematical. People's ability to detect stimuli such as meaningful blips on a radar screen depends not only on the intensity of the blips themselves but also on their training (learning), motivation (desire to perceive meaningful blips), and psychological states such as fatigue or alertness.

• *Feature Detectors*

Imagine that you are standing by the curb of a busy street as a bus approaches. When neurons in your sensory organs—in this case, your eyes—are stimulated by the approach of the bus, they relay information to the sensory cortex in the brain. Nobel prize winners David Hubel and Torsten Wiesel (1979) discovered that various neurons in the visual cortex fire in response to particular features of the visual input. Many cells, for example, fire in response to lines presented at various angles—vertical, horizontal, and in-between. Other cells fire in response to specific colors. Because they respond to different aspects or features of a scene, these cells are termed **feature detectors.** In the example of the bus, visual feature detectors respond to the bus's edges, depth, contours, textures, shadows, speed, and kinds of motion (up, down, forward, and back). There are also feature detectors for other senses. Auditory feature detectors, for example, respond to the pitch, loudness, and other aspects of the sounds of the bus.

• *Sensory Adaptation: Where Did It Go?*

Our sensory systems are admirably suited to a changing environment. We become more sensitive to stimuli of low magnitude and less sensitive to stimuli that remain the same (such as the background noises outside the window). **Sensory adaptation** refers to these processes of adjustment.

Consider how the visual sense adapts to lower intensities of light. When we first walk into a darkened movie theater, we see little but the images on the screen. As time goes by, however, we become increasingly sensitive to the faces of those around us and to the features of the theater. The process of becoming more sensitive to stimulation is referred to as **sensitization,** or positive adaptation.

But we become less sensitive to constant stimulation. Sources of light appear to grow dimmer as we adapt to them. In fact, if you could keep an image completely stable on the retinas of your eyes—which is virtually impossible to accomplish without a motionless image and stabilizing equipment—the image would fade within a few seconds and be very difficult to see. Similarly, at the beach we soon become less aware of the lapping of the waves. When we live in a city, we become desensitized to traffic sounds except for the occasional backfire or siren. And as you may have noticed from experiences with freshly

FEATURE DETECTORS • Neurons in the sensory cortex that fire in response to specific features of sensory information such as lines or edges of objects.
SENSORY ADAPTATION • The processes by which organisms become more sensitive to stimuli that are low in magnitude and less sensitive to stimuli that are constant or ongoing in magnitude.
SENSITIZATION • The type of sensory adaptation in which we become more sensitive to stimuli that are low in magnitude. Also called *positive adaptation.*

painted rooms, sensitivity to disagreeable odors fades quite rapidly. The process of becoming less sensitive to stimulation is referred to as **desensitization,** or negative adaptation.

REFLECTIONS

- What is the dimmest light you can see? The softest sound you can hear? How do psychophysicists answer such questions?
- Can you think of a personal example of a just noticeable difference? How much weight do you have to gain or lose to notice a difference? How much harder would you have to work to make a noticeable difference in your grades?
- Have you ever been so involved in something that you didn't notice the heat or the cold? Have you gotten so used to sounds like those made by crickets or trains at night that you fall asleep without hearing them? How do these experiences relate to signal-detection theory?

■ VISION: LETTING THE SUN SHINE IN

Our eyes are our "windows on the world." More than half of the cerebral cortex is devoted to visual functions (Basic Behavioral Science Task Force, 1996b). Because vision is our dominant sense, we consider blindness to be the most debilitating type of sensory loss (Moore, 1995). To understand vision, we need to begin with the nature of light.

• Light: What Is This Stuff?

In almost all cultures, light is a symbol of goodness and knowledge. We describe capable people as being "bright" or "brilliant." If we are not being complimentary, we label them as "dull." People who aren't in the know are said to be "in the dark." Just what is this stuff called light?

Visible light is the stuff that triggers visual sensations. It is just one small part of a spectrum of electromagnetic energy (see Figure 5.1) that is described in terms of wavelengths. Wavelengths vary from cosmic rays, which are only a few trillionths of an inch long, to some radio waves, which extend for miles. Radar, microwaves, and X-rays are also forms of electromagnetic energy.

You have probably seen rainbows or light that has been broken down into several colors as it filtered through your windows. Sir Isaac Newton, the British scientist, discovered that sunlight could be broken down into different colors by means of a triangular solid of glass called a *prism* (Figure 5.1). When I took introductory psychology, I was taught that I could remember the colors of the spectrum, from longest to shortest wavelengths, by using the mnemonic device *Roy G. Biv* (red, orange, yellow, green, blue, indigo, violet). I must have been a backward student because I found it easier to recall them in reverse order, using the meaningless acronym *vibgyor*.

The wavelength of visible light determines its color, or **hue.** The wavelength for red is longer than the wavelength for orange, and so on through the rest of the spectrum.

Truth or Fiction Revisited

It is true that white sunlight is actually composed of all the colors of the rainbow.

DESENSITIZATION • The type of sensory adaptation in which we become less sensitive to constant stimuli. Also called *negative adaptation*.

VISIBLE LIGHT • The part of the electromagnetic spectrum that stimulates the eye and produces visual sensations.

HUE • The color of light, as determined by its wavelength.

FIGURE 5.1

THE VISIBLE SPECTRUM

By passing a source of white light, such as sunlight, through a prism, we break it down into the colors of the visible spectrum. The visible spectrum is just a narrow segment of the electromagnetic spectrum. The electromagnetic spectrum also includes radio waves, microwaves, X-rays, cosmic rays, and many others. Different forms of electromagnetic energy have wavelengths which vary from a few trillionths of a meter to thousands of miles. Visible light varies in wavelength from about 400 to 700 *billionths* of a meter. (A meter = 39.37 inches.)

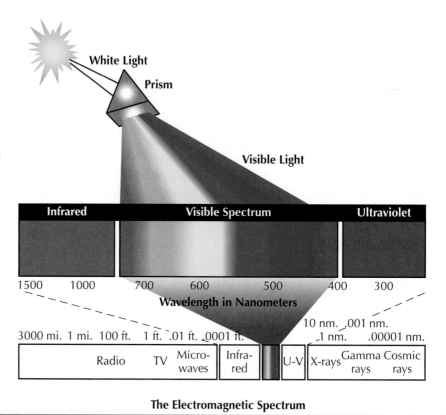

The Electromagnetic Spectrum

• *The Eye: The Better to See You With*

Consider that magnificent invention called the camera, which records visual experiences. In traditional cameras, light enters an opening and is focused onto a sensitive surface, or film. Chemicals on film create a lasting impression of the image that entered the camera.

The eye—our living camera—is no less remarkable. Look at its major parts, as shown in Figure 5.2. As with a film or TV camera, light enters through a narrow opening and is projected onto a sensitive surface. Light first passes through the transparent **cornea,** which covers the front of the eye's surface. (The "white" of the eye, or *sclera,* is composed of a hard protective tissue.) The amount of light that passes through the cornea is determined by the size of the opening of the muscle called the **iris,** which is the colored part of the eye. The opening in the iris is the **pupil.** The size of the pupil adjusts automatically to the amount of light present. You do not have to try purposefully to open your eyes further to see better in low lighting conditions. The more intense the light, the smaller the opening. In a similar fashion, we adjust the amount of light allowed into a camera according to its brightness. Pupil size is also sensitive to emotional response: we can literally be "wide-eyed with fear."

Once light passes through the iris, it encounters the **lens.** The lens adjusts or accommodates to the image by changing its thickness. Changes in thickness permit a clear image of the object to be projected onto the retina. These changes focus the light according to the distance of the object from the viewer. If you hold a finger at arm's length and slowly bring it toward your nose, you will feel tension in the eye as the thickness of the lens accommodates to keep the retinal image in focus. When people squint to bring an object into focus, they are adjusting the thickness of the lens. The lens in a camera does not accommodate to

CORNEA • Transparent tissue forming the outer surface of the eyeball.

IRIS • A muscular membrane whose dilation regulates the amount of light that enters the eye.

PUPIL • The apparently black opening in the center of the iris, through which light enters the eye.

LENS • A transparent body behind the iris that focuses an image on the retina.

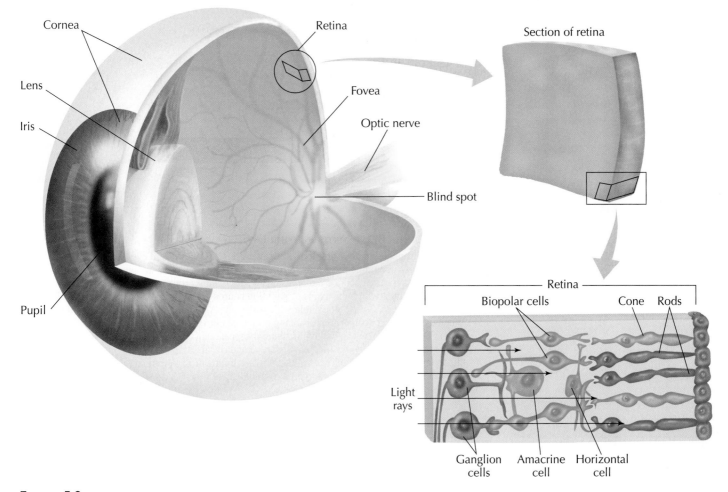

FIGURE 5.2
THE HUMAN EYE
In both the eye and a camera, light enters through a narrow opening and is projected onto a sensitive surface. In the eye, the photosensitive surface is called the retina, and information concerning the changing images on the retina is transmitted to the brain. The retina contains photoreceptors called rods and cones. Rods and cones transmit sensory input back through the bipolar neurons to the ganglion neurons. The axons of the ganglion neurons form the optic nerve, which transmits sensory stimulation through the brain to the visual cortex of the occipital lobe.

the distance of objects. Instead, to focus the light that is projected onto the film, the camera lens is moved farther from the film or closer to it.

The **retina** is like the film or image surface of the camera. However, the retina consists of cells called **photoreceptors** that are sensitive to light (photosensitive). There are two types of photoreceptors, *rods* and *cones*. The retina (see Figure 5.2) contains several layers of cells: the rods and cones, **bipolar cells**, and **ganglion cells**. All of these cells are neurons. Light travels past the ganglion cells and bipolar cells and stimulates the rods and cones. The rods and cones then send neural messages through the bipolar cells to the ganglion cells. The axons of the million or so ganglion cells in our retinae form the **optic nerve**. The optic nerve conducts sensory input to the brain, where it is relayed to the visual area of the occipital lobe. Other neurons in the retina—amacrine cells and horizontal cells—make sideways connections at a level near the receptor cells and at another level near the ganglion cells. As a result of these lateral connections,

RETINA • The area of the inner surface of the eye that contains rods and cones.
PHOTORECEPTORS • Cells that respond to light.
BIPOLAR CELLS • Neurons that conduct neural impulses from rods and cones to ganglion cells.
GANGLION CELLS • Neurons whose axons form the optic nerve.
OPTIC NERVE • The nerve that transmits sensory information from the eye to the brain.

FIGURE 5.3
LOCATING THE BLIND SPOTS IN YOUR EYES

To try a "disappearing act," first look at Drawing 1. Close your right eye. Then move the book back and forth about one foot from your left eye while you stare at the plus sign. You will notice the circle disappear. When the circle disappears it is being projected onto the blind spot of your retina, the point at which the axons of ganglion neurons collect to form the optic nerve. Then close your left eye. Stare at the circle with your right eye and move the book back and forth. When the plus sign disappears, it is being projected onto the blind spot of your right eye. Now look at Drawing 2. You can make this figure disappear and "see" the black line continue through the spot where it was by closing your right eye and staring at the plus sign with your left. When this figure is projected onto your blind spot, your brain "fills in" the line, which is one reason that you're not usually aware that you have blind spots.

FIGURE 5.4
A MUCH ENLARGED PHOTOGRAPH OF RODS AND A CONE

Cones are usually upright fellows. However, the cone at the bottom of this photo has been bent by the photographic process. You have about 125 million rods and 6.5 million cones distributed across the retina of each eye. Only cones provide sensations of color. The fovea of the eye is almost exclusively populated by cones, which are then distributed more sparsely as you work forward toward the lens.

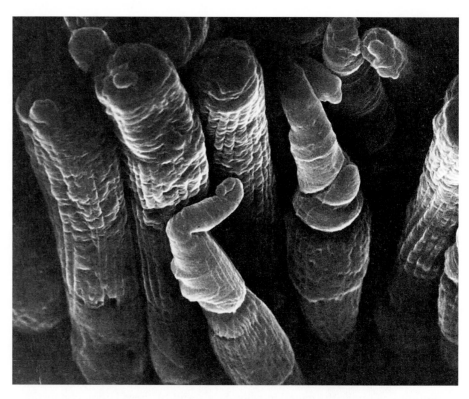

many rods and cones funnel visual information into one bipolar cell, and many bipolar cells funnel information to one ganglion cell. Receptors outnumber ganglion cells by more than 100 to 1.

The **fovea** is the most sensitive area of the retina (see Figure 5.2). Receptors there are more densely packed. The **blind spot,** in contrast, is insensitive to visual stimulation. It is the part of the retina where the axons of the ganglion cells congregate to form the optic nerve (Figure 5.3).

RODS AND CONES **Rods** and **cones** are the photoreceptors in the retina (Figure 5.4). About 125 million rods and 6.5 million cones are distributed across the retina (Solomon and others, 1993). The fovea is composed almost exclusively of cones. Cones become more sparsely distributed as you work forward from the fovea toward the lens. Rods, in contrast, are nearly absent at the fovea but are distributed more densely as you approach the lens.

Rods are sensitive only to the intensity of light. They allow us to see in black and white. Cones provide color vision. In low lighting, it is possible to photograph a clearer image with black-and-white film than with color film. Similarly, rods are more sensitive to light than cones. Therefore, as the illumination grows dim, as during the evening and nighttime hours, objects appear to lose their color well before their outlines fade from view.

LIGHT ADAPTATION Immediately after we enter it, a movie theater may seem too dark to allow us to find seats readily. But as time goes on we begin to see the seats and other people clearly. The process of adjusting to lower lighting conditions is called **dark adaptation.**

Figure 5.5 shows the amount of light needed for detection as a function of the amount of time spent in the dark. The cones and rods adapt at different rates. The cones, which permit perception of color, reach their maximum adaptation to darkness in about 10 minutes. The rods, which allow perception of light and dark only, are more sensitive and continue to adapt to darkness for up to about 45 minutes.

Adaptation to brighter lighting conditions takes place much more rapidly. When you emerge from the theater into the brilliance of the afternoon, you

FOVEA • An area near the center of the retina that is dense with cones and where vision is consequently most acute.
BLIND SPOT • The area of the retina where axons from ganglion cells meet to form the optic nerve.
RODS • Rod-shaped photoreceptors that are sensitive only to the intensity of light.
CONES • Cone-shaped photoreceptors that transmit sensations of color.
DARK ADAPTATION • The process of adjusting to conditions of lower lighting by increasing the sensitivity of rods and cones.

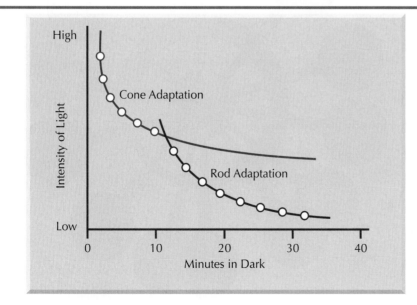

FIGURE 5.5
DARK ADAPTATION
This illustration shows the amount of light necessary for detection as a function of the amount of time spent in the dark. Cones and rods adapt at different rates. Cones, which permit perception of color, reach maximum dark adaptation in about ten minutes. Rods, which permit perception of dark and light only, are more sensitive than cones. Rods continue to adapt for up to about 45 minutes.

may at first be painfully surprised by the featureless blaze around you. The visual experience is not unlike turning the brightness of the TV set to its maximum setting, at which the edges of objects seem to dissolve into light. Within a minute or so of entering the street, however, the brightness of the scene will have dimmed and objects will have regained their edges.

• *Color Vision: Creating an Inner World of Color*

For most of us, the world is a place of brilliant colors—the blue-greens of the ocean, the red-oranges of the setting sun, the deepened greens of June, the glories of rhododendron and hibiscus. Color is a an emotional and aesthetic part of our everyday lives. In this section we explore some of the psychological dimensions of color and then examine theories about how we manage to convert different wavelengths of light into perceptions of color.

• *Psychological Dimensions of Color*

The wavelength of light determines its color, or *hue*. The brightness (or *value*) of a color is its degree of lightness or darkness. The brighter the color, the lighter it is.

If we bend the colors of the spectrum into a circle, we create a color wheel, as shown in Figure 5.6. Yellow is the lightest color on the color wheel. As we work our way around the wheel from yellow to violet-blue, we encounter progressively darker colors.

SATURATION • The degree of purity of a color. **COMPLEMENTARY** • Descriptive of colors of the spectrum that when combined produce white or nearly white light.

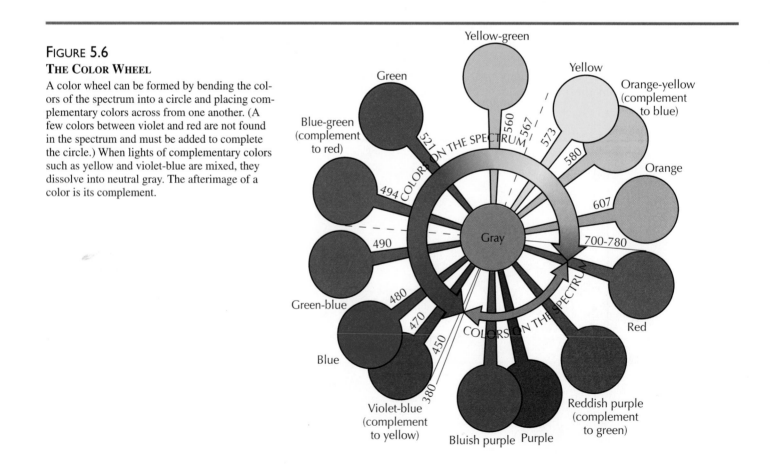

FIGURE 5.6

THE COLOR WHEEL

A color wheel can be formed by bending the colors of the spectrum into a circle and placing complementary colors across from one another. (A few colors between violet and red are not found in the spectrum and must be added to complete the circle.) When lights of complementary colors such as yellow and violet-blue are mixed, they dissolve into neutral gray. The afterimage of a color is its complement.

WARM AND COOL COLORS Psychologically, the colors on the green-blue side of the color wheel are considered to be cool in temperature, while those colors on the yellow-orange-red side are considered to be warm. Perhaps greens and blues suggest the coolness of the ocean and the sky, whereas things that are burning tend to be red or orange. A room decorated in green or blue may seem more appealing on a hot July day than a room decorated in red or orange.

When we look at a painting, warm colors seem to advance toward the viewer, which explains, in part, why the oranges and yellows of Mark Rothko's *Orange and Yellow* (Figure 5.7) seem to pulsate toward the observer. Cool colors seem to recede. Notice how the warm Sunoco sign in Allan d'Arcangelo's *Highway No. 2* (Figure 5.8) leaps out toward the viewer. In contrast, the cool blue sky seems to recede into the distance.

The **saturation** of a color is its purity or *intensity*—that is, how few different wavelengths are included in it. The purest hues are the brightest. The saturation, and also the brightness, decrease when another hue is added or when black, gray, or white is added. Artists produce different *shades* of a given hue by adding black. They produce *tints* by adding white.

COMPLEMENTARY COLORS The colors across from one another on the color wheel are labeled **complementary.** Red-green and blue-yellow are the major complementary pairs. If we mix complementary colors together, they dissolve into gray.

"But wait!" you say. "Blue and yellow cannot be complementary because by mixing pigments of blue and yellow we create green, not gray." True enough, but we have been talking about mixing *lights,* not *pigments.* Light is the source of all color. Pigments reflect and absorb different wavelengths of light selectively. The mixture of lights is an *additive* process. The mixture of pigments is *subtractive.* Figure 5.9 shows mixtures of lights and pigments of various colors.

FIGURE 5.7
ORANGE AND YELLOW
Warm colors such as orange and yellow seem to advance toward the viewer, while cool colors such as blue and green seem to recede. The oranges and yellows of Rothko's painting seem to pulsate toward the observer.

FIGURE 5.8
HIGHWAY 1, NO. 2
The "warm" Sunoco sign in d'Arcangelo's painting leaps out toward the viewer, while the "cool" blue sky recedes into the distance.

FIGURE 5.9

ADDITIVE AND SUBTRACTIVE COLOR MIXTURES PRODUCED BY LIGHTS AND PIGMENTS

Thomas Young discovered that white light and all the colors of the spectrum could be produced by adding combinations of lights of red, green, and violet-blue and varying their intensities (see Part A). Part B shows subtractive color mixtures, which are formed by mixing pigments, not light.

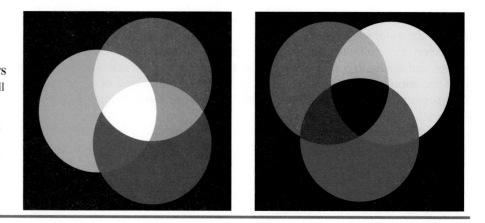

Truth or Fiction Revisited

It is not true that we obtain green light by mixing blue light and yellow light. We obtain a green pigment when we mix blue and yellow pigments.

Pigments gain their colors by absorbing light from certain segments of the spectrum and reflecting the rest. For example, we see most plant life as green because the pigment in chlorophyll absorbs most of the red, blue, and violet wavelengths of light. The remaining green is reflected. A red pigment absorbs most of the spectrum but reflects red. White pigments reflect all colors equally. Black pigments reflect very little light.

PRIMARY, SECONDARY, AND TERTIARY COLORS The pigments of red, blue, and yellow are **primary colors.** Primary colors cannot be produced by mixing pigments of other hues. **Secondary colors** are created by mixing pigments of primary colors. The three secondary colors are orange (derived from mixing red and yellow), green (blue and yellow), and purple (red and blue). **Tertiary colors** are created by mixing pigments of primary and adjoining secondary colors, as in yellow-green and bluish-purple.

In *Sunday Afternoon on the Island of La Grande Jatte* (Figure 5.10), French painter Georges Seurat molded his figures and forms from dabs of pure and complementary colors. Instead of mixing his pigments, he placed points of pure color next to one another. When the painting is viewed from very close, the sensations are of pure color (see detail, Figure 5.10). But from a distance the juxtaposition of pure colors creates the impression of mixtures of color.

AFTERIMAGES Before reading on, why don't you try a brief experiment? Look at the strangely colored American flag in Figure 5.11 for at least half a minute. Then look at a sheet of white or gray paper. What has happened to the flag? If your color vision is working properly, and if you looked at the miscolored flag long enough, you should see a flag composed of the familiar red, white, and blue. The flag you perceive on the white sheet of paper is an **afterimage** of the first. (If you didn't look at the green, black, and yellow flag long enough the first time, try it again. It will work any number of times.)

In afterimages, persistent sensations of color are followed by perception of the complementary color when the first color is removed. The same holds true for black and white. Staring at one will create an afterimage of the other. Stare at d'Arcangelo's *Highway 1, No. 2* (Figure 5.8) for 30 seconds. Then look at a sheet of white paper. You are likely to perceive a black stripe down a white highway, along with a blue Sunoco sign and a yellow sky. The phenomenon of afterimages has contributed to one of the theories of color vision, as we will soon see.

ANALOGOUS COLORS **Analogous** hues lie next to one another on the color wheel, forming families of colors like yellow and orange, orange and red, and

PRIMARY COLORS • Colors that cannot be produced by mixing pigments of other hues.
SECONDARY COLORS • Colors derived by mixing primary colors.
TERTIARY COLORS • Colors derived by mixing primary and adjoining secondary colors.
AFTERIMAGE • The lingering visual impression made by a stimulus that has been removed.
ANALOGOUS • Similar or comparable colors.

FIGURE 5.10

SUNDAY AFTERNOON ON THE ISLAND OF LA GRANDE JATTE

The French painter Seurat molded his figures and forms from dabs of pure and complementary colors. Up close (see the detail), the dabs of pure color are visible. From afar, they create the impression of color mixtures.

green and blue. As we work our way around the wheel, the families intermarry: blue with violet, violet with red, and so on. Works of art that use closely related families of color seem harmonious. For example, Rothko's *Orange and Yellow* (Figure 5.7) draws on the color family containing analogous oranges and yellows.

• *Theories of Color Vision*

Adults with normal color vision can discriminate among hundreds of colors across the visible spectrum. Different colors have different wavelengths. Although we can vary the physical wavelengths of light in a continuous manner from shorter to longer, many changes in color are discontinuous. For example, our perception of a color shifts suddenly from blue to green, even though the

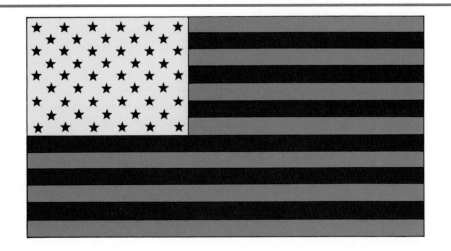

FIGURE 5.11

THREE CHEERS FOR THE . . . GREEN, BLACK, AND YELLOW?

Don't be concerned. We can readily restore Old Glory to its familiar hues. Place a sheet of white paper beneath the book, and stare at the center of the flag for 30 seconds. Then remove the book. The afterimage on the paper beneath will look familiar.

Hermann von Helmholtz

In a sense, he was a bore. Born in Potsdam, Germany, he was frail as a child, went to medical school on a government grant, served in the army to pay back the government, married, had children, and taught and conducted research in universities. On a personal level, he was polite and a bit stiff. He enjoyed classical music and hiking in the mountains. Nevertheless, some say that Hermann von Helmholtz (1821–1894) was the greatest scientist of the nineteenth century. The "von"—a sign of nobility—was added to his name in recognition of his accomplishments.

Helmholtz conducted his research at a time when "vitalists" claimed that life could not be explained in terms of chemical, physical, and biological events. Life, that is, was beyond scientific analysis. In this intellectual environment, Helmholtz conducted research that connected consciousness with the nervous system. He showed, for example, that nerve impulses travel through nerve fibers at measurable speeds (about 90 feet per second in frogs). He refined Thomas Young's theory of color vision by speculating that there are three kinds of color receptors in the retina *(trichromatic theory)* each corresponding to a primary color. In just eight days he invented the *ophthalmoscope,* the instrument that doctors still use (in updated form) to view the living retina. ■

change in wavelength may be smaller than that between two blues.

Our ability to perceive color depends on the eye's transmission of different messages to the brain when lights with different wavelengths stimulate the cones in the retina. In this section we will explore and evaluate two theories of how lights with different wavelengths are perceived as being of different colors: the *trichromatic theory* and the *opponent-process theory.*

THE TRICHROMATIC THEORY **Trichromatic theory** is based on an experiment conducted by the British scientist Thomas Young in the early 1800s. As in Figure 5.9, Young projected three lights of different colors onto a screen so that they partly overlapped. He found that he could create any color from the visible spectrum by simply varying the intensities of the lights. When all three lights fell on the same spot, they created white light, or the appearance of no color at all. The three lights manipulated by Young were red, green, and blue-violet.

The German physiologist Hermann von Helmholtz saw in Young's discovery an explanation of color vision. Von Helmholtz suggested that the eye must have three different types of photoreceptors or cones. Some must be sensitive to red light, some to green, and some to blue. We see other colors when two different types of color receptors are stimulated. The perception of yellow, for example, would result from the simultaneous stimulation of receptors for red and green. The trichromatic theory is also known as the Young-Helmholtz theory.

THE OPPONENT-PROCESS THEORY In 1870, Ewald Hering proposed the **opponent-process theory** of color vision. This theory also holds that there are three types of color receptors, however, they are not sensitive to the simple hues of red, green, and blue. Hering suggested instead that afterimages (such as that of the American flag shown in Figure 5.11) are made possible by three types of color receptors: red-green, blue-yellow, and a type that perceives differences in brightness. A red-green cone could not transmit messages for red and green at the same time. According to Hering, staring at the green, black, and yellow flag for 30 seconds would disturb the balance of neural activity. The afterimage of red, white, and blue would represent the eye's attempt to reestablish a balance.

EVALUATION Research suggests that both theories of color vision are partially correct. For example, it shows that some cones are sensitive to blue, some to green, and some to red parts of the spectrum (Solomon and others, 1993). But studies of the bipolar and ganglion neurons suggest that messages from cones are transmitted to the brain and relayed by the thalamus to the occipital lobe in an opponent-process fashion (DeValois & Jacobs, 1984). Some opponent-process cells that transmit messages to the visual centers in the brain are excited ("turned on") by green light but inhibited ("turned off") by red light. Others can be excited by red light but are inhibited by green light. A second set of

TRICHROMATIC THEORY • The theory that color vision is made possible by three types of cones, some of which respond to red light, some to green, and some to blue. (From the Greek roots *treis,* meaning "three," and *chroma,* meaning "color.")

OPPONENT-PROCESS THEORY • The theory that color vision is made possible by three types of cones, some of which respond to red or green light, some to blue or yellow, and some only to the intensity of light.

opponent-process cells responds in an opposite manner to blue and yellow. A third set responds in an opposite manner to light and dark.

A neural rebound effect apparently helps explain the occurrence of afterimages. That is, a green-sensitive ganglion that had been excited by green light for half a minute or so might switch briefly to inhibitory activity when the light is shut off. The effect would be to perceive red even though no red light is present.

These theoretical updates allow for the afterimage effects with the green, black, and yellow flag and are also consistent with Young's experiments in mixing lights of different colors.

• *Color Blindness*

If you can discriminate among the colors of the visible spectrum, you have normal color vision and are labeled a **trichromat.** This means that you are sensitive to red-green, blue-yellow, and light-dark. People who are totally color blind are called **monochromats** and are sensitive only to lightness and darkness. Total color blindness is quite rare. Fully color blind individuals see the world as trichromats would on a black-and-white TV set or in a black-and-white movie.

Partial color blindness is more common than total color blindness. Partial color blindness is a sex-linked trait that affects mostly males. Partially color blind people are called **dichromats.** Dichromats can discriminate only among two colors—red and green, or blue and yellow—and the colors that are derived from mixing these colors. Figure 5.12 shows the types of tests that are used to diagnose color blindness. (See also Figure 5.13.)

A dichromat might put on one red sock and one green sock, but would not mix red and blue socks. Monochromats might put on socks of any color. They would not notice a difference as long as the socks' colors did not differ in intensity—that is, brightness.

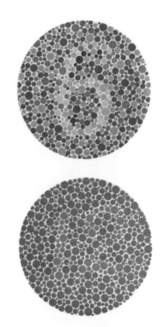

FIGURE 5.12
PLATES FROM A TEST FOR COLOR BLINDNESS

Can you see the numbers in these plates from a test for color blindness? A person with red-green color blindness would not be able to see the 6, and a person with blue-yellow color blindness would probably not discern the 12. (Caution: These reproductions cannot be used for actual testing of color blindness.)

REFLECTIONS
- How do you account for the colors in a rainbow?
- Have you entered a dark theater and gradually seen more and more of your surroundings as time goes on? What processes account for the adjustment?
- How do color blind people know when to stop at a traffic light and when to proceed?

■ VISUAL PERCEPTION

Perception is the process by which we organize or make sense of our sensory impressions. Although visual sensations are caused by electromagnetic energy, visual perception also relies on our knowledge, expectations, and motivations. Whereas sensation may be thought of as a mechanical process, perception is an active process through which we interpret the world around us.

For example, just what do you see in Figure 5.14? Do you see random splotches of ink or a rider on horseback? If you perceive a horse and rider, it is not just because of the visual sensations provided by the drawing. Each of the blobs is meaningless in and of itself, and the pattern they form is also less than clear. Despite the lack of clarity, however, you may still perceive a horse and rider. Why? The answer has something to do with your general knowledge and your desire to fit incoming bits and pieces of information into familiar patterns.

TRICHROMAT • A person with normal color vision.
MONOCHROMAT • A person who is sensitive to black and white only and hence color blind.
DICHROMAT • A person who is sensitive to black-white and either red-green or blue-yellow and hence partially color blind.

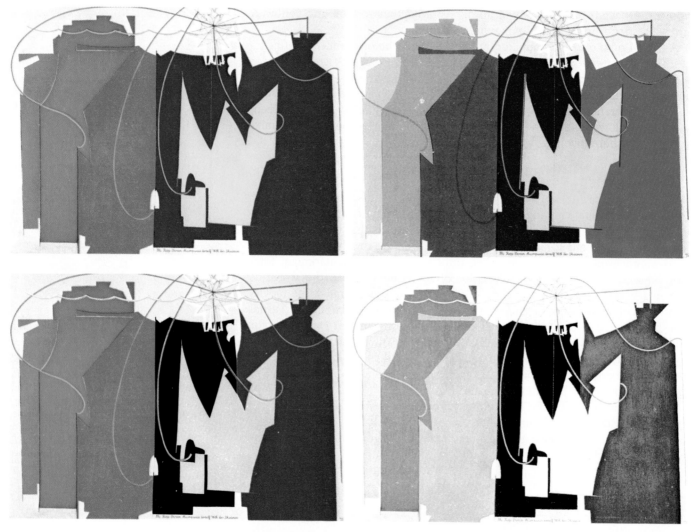

FIGURE 5.13
COLOR BLINDNESS

The painting in the upper left-hand panel—Man Ray's *The Rope Dancer Accompanies Herself with Her Shadows*—appears as it would to a person with normal color vision. If you had red-green color blindness, the picture would appear as it does in the upper right-hand panel. The lower left-hand and lower right-hand panels show how the picture would look to viewers with yellow-blue or total color blindness, respectively. (Museum of Modern Art, New York. Gift of G. David Thompson.)

FIGURE 5.14
CLOSURE

Meaningless splotches of ink or a horse and rider? This figure illustrates the Gestalt principle of closure.

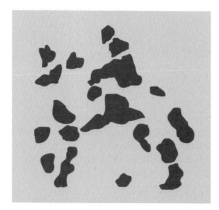

In the case of the horse and rider, your integration of disconnected pieces of information into a meaningful whole also reflects what Gestalt psychologists refer to as the principle of **closure,** or the tendency to perceive a complete or whole figure even when there are gaps in the sensory input. Put another way, in perception the whole can be very much more than the mere sum of the parts. A collection of parts can be meaningless. It is their configuration that matters.

• *Perceptual Organization*

Earlier in the century, Gestalt psychologists noted certain consistencies in the way we integrate bits and pieces of sensory stimulation into meaningful wholes. They attempted to identify the rules that govern these processes. Max Wertheimer, in particular, discovered many such rules. As a group, these rules are referred to as the laws of **perceptual organization.** We will examine several of them, beginning with those concerning figure-ground perception. Then we will consider top-down and bottom-up processing.

FIGURE-GROUND PERCEPTION If you look out your window, you may see people, buildings, cars, and streets, or perhaps grass, trees, birds, and clouds. All these objects tend to be perceived as figures against backgrounds. Cars seen against the background of the street are easier to pick out than cars seen piled on top of each other in a junkyard. Birds seen against the sky are more likely to be perceived than birds seen "in the bush." In short, figures are closer to us than their grounds.

When figure-ground relationships are **ambiguous,** or capable of being interpreted in various ways, our perceptions tend to be unstable, to shift back and forth. As an example, look for a while at Figure 5.15. How many people, objects, and animals can you find? If your eye is drawn back and forth, so that sometimes you are perceiving light figures on a dark background and at other time dark figures on a light background, you are experiencing figure-ground reversals. In other words, a shift is occurring in your perception of what is figure and what is ground, or background. The artist was able to have some fun with us because of our tendency to try to isolate geometric patterns or figures from a background. However, in this case the "background" is as meaningful and detailed as the "figure." Therefore, our perceptions shift back and forth.

THE RUBIN VASE In Figure 5.16 we see a Rubin vase, one of psychologists' favorite illustrations of figure-ground relationships. The figure-ground relationship in part A of the figure is ambiguous. There are no cues that suggest which area must be the figure. For this reason, our perception may shift from seeing the vase as the figure to seeing two profiles as the figure.

CLOSURE • The tendency to perceive a broken figure as being complete or whole.
PERCEPTUAL ORGANIZATION • The tendency to integrate perceptual elements into meaningful patterns.
AMBIGUOUS • Having two or more possible meanings.

FIGURE 5.15
FIGURE AND GROUND
How many animals and demons can you find in this M. C. Escher print? Do we have white figures on a black background or black figures on a white background? Figure ground perception is the tendency to perceive geometric forms against a background.

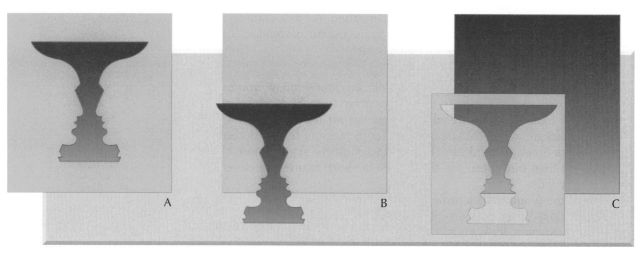

FIGURE 5.16
THE RUBIN VASE

A favorite drawing used by psychologists to demonstrate figure ground perception. Part A is ambiguous, with neither the vase nor the profiles clearly the figure or the ground. In Part B, the vase is the figure; in Part C, the profiles are.

There is no such problem in part B. Since it seems that a white vase has been brought forward against a colored ground, we are more likely to perceive the vase than the profiles. In part C, we are more likely to perceive the profiles than the vase because the profiles are whole and the vase is broken against the background. Of course, if we wish to, we can still perceive the vase in part C, because experience has shown us where it is. Why not have some fun with friends by covering up parts B and C and asking them what they see? (They'll catch on quickly if they can see all three drawings at once.)

THE NECKER CUBE The Necker cube (Figure 5.17) provides another example of how an ambiguous drawing can lead to perceptual shifts.

Hold this page at arm's length and stare at the center of the figure for 30 seconds or so. Try to allow your eye muscles to relax. (The feeling is of your eyes "glazing over.") After a while you will notice a dramatic shift in your perception of these "stacked boxes." What was once a front edge is now a back edge, and vice versa. Again, the dramatic perceptual shift is made possible by the fact that the outline of the drawing permits two interpretations.

OTHER GESTALT RULES FOR ORGANIZATION In addition to the law of closure, Gestalt psychologists have noted that our perceptions are guided by rules or laws of *proximity, similarity, continuity,* and *common fate.*

Without reading further, describe part A of Figure 5.18. Did you say that it consists of six lines or of three groups of two parallel lines? If you said three sets of lines, you were influenced by the **proximity**, or nearness, of some of the lines. There is no other reason for perceiving them in pairs or subgroups: all of the lines are parallel and of equal length.

Now describe part B of the figure. Did you perceive the figure as a 6 × 6 grid, or as 3 columns of *x*'s and 3 columns of *o*'s? According to the law of **similarity**, we perceive similar objects as belonging together. For this reason, you may have been more likely to describe part B in terms of columns than in terms of rows or a grid.

What about part C? Is it a circle with two lines stemming from it, or is it a (broken) line that goes through a circle? If you saw it as a single (broken) line,

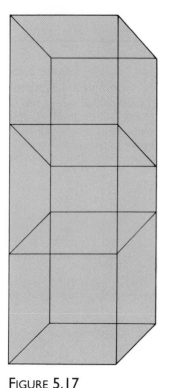

FIGURE 5.17
NECKER CUBES

Ambiguity in the drawing of the cubes makes perceptual shifts possible.

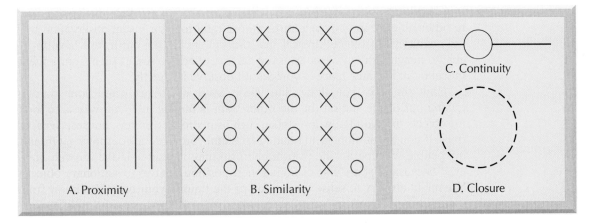

FIGURE 5.18

SOME GESTALT LAWS OF PERCEPTUAL ORGANIZATION

These drawings illustrate the Gestalt laws of proximity, similarity, continuity, and closure.

you were probably organizing your perceptions according to the rule of **conti-nuity.** That is, we perceive a series of points or a broken line as having unity.

According to the law of **common fate,** elements that are seen moving to-gether are perceived as belonging together. A group of people running in the same direction appear unified in purpose. Birds that flock together seem to be of a feather. (Did I get that right?)

Part D of Figure 5.18 provides another example of the law of closure. The arcs tend to be perceived as a circle (or circle with gaps) rather than as just a se-ries of arcs.

TOP-DOWN VERSUS BOTTOM-UP PROCESSING Imagine that you are trying to put together a thousand-piece puzzle—a task that I usually avoid, despite the cajoling of my children. Now imagine that you are trying to accomplish it after someone has walked off with the box that contained the pieces—you know, the box showing the picture formed by the completed puzzle.

When you have the box—when you know what the "big picture" or pattern looks like—cognitive psychologists refer to the task of assembling the pieces as **top-down processing.** The "top" of the visual system refers to the image of the pattern in the brain, and the top-down strategy for putting the puzzle together implies that you use the pattern to guide subordinate perceptual motor tasks such as hunting for particular pieces. Without knowledge of the pattern, the as-sembly process is referred to as **bottom-up processing.** You begin with bits and pieces of information and become aware of the pattern formed by the assem-bled pieces only after you have worked at it for a while.

• *Perception of Movement*

Moving objects—whether they are other people, animals, cars, or boulders plummeting down a hillside—are vital sources of sensory information. Moving objects capture the attention of even newborn infants.

To understand how we perceive movement, recall what it is like to be on a train that has begun to pull out of the station while the train on the adjacent track remains stationary. If your own train does not lurch as it accelerates, you might think at first that the other train is moving. Or you might not be certain whether your train is moving forward or the other train is moving backward.

PROXIMITY • Nearness. The perceptual tendency to group together objects that are near one another.

SIMILARITY • The perceptual tendency to group together objects that are similar in appearance.

CONTINUITY • The tendency to perceive a series of points or lines as having unity.

COMMON FATE • The tendency to perceive elements that move together as belonging together.

TOP-DOWN PROCESSING • The use of contextual information or knowledge of a pattern in order to organize parts of the pattern.

BOTTOM-UP PROCESSING • The organization of the parts of a pattern to recognize, or form an image of, the pattern they compose.

The visual perception of movement is based on change of position relative to other objects. To early scientists, whose only tool for visual observation was the naked eye, it seemed logical that the sun circled the earth. You have to be able to imagine the movement of the earth around the sun as seen from a theoretical point in outer space—you cannot observe it directly.

How, then, do you determine which train is moving when your train is pulling out of the station (or the other train is pulling in)? One way is to look for objects that you know are stable, such as platform columns, houses, signs, or trees. If you are stationary in relation to them, your train is not moving. Observing people walking on the station platform may not provide the answer, however, because they are also changing their position relative to stationary objects. You might also try to sense the motion of the train in your body. You know from experience how to do these things quite well, although it may be difficult to phrase explanations for them.

We have been considering the perception of real movement. Psychologists have also studied several types of apparent movement, or **illusions** of movement. These include the *autokinetic effect, stroboscopic motion,* and the *phi phenomenon.*

THE AUTOKINETIC EFFECT If you were to sit quietly in a dark room and stare at a point of light projected onto the far wall, after a while it might appear that the light had begun to move, even if it actually remained quite still. The tendency to perceive a stationary point of light as moving in a dark room is called the **autokinetic effect.**

Over the years, psychologists have conducted interesting experiments in which they have asked people, for example, what the light is "spelling out." The light has spelled out nothing, of course, and the words perceived by subjects reflect their own cognitive processes, not external sensations.

STROBOSCOPIC MOTION Stroboscopic motion makes motion pictures possible. In **stroboscopic motion,** the illusion of movement is provided by the presentation of a rapid progression of images of stationary objects. So-called motion pictures do not really consist of images that move. Rather, the audience is shown 16 to 22 pictures, or *frames,* per second. Each slightly different from the one before. (See Figure 5.19.) Each frame differs slightly from that preceding it. Showing the frames in rapid succession provides the illusion of movement.

At the rate of at least 16 frames per second, the "motion" in a film seems smooth and natural. With fewer than 16 or so frames per second, the movement looks jumpy and unnatural. That is why slow motion is achieved by filming perhaps 100 or more frames per second. When they are played back at about 22 frames per second, the movement seems slow, yet still smooth and natural.

ILLUSIONS • Sensations that give rise to misperceptions.
AUTOKINETIC EFFECT • The tendency to perceive a stationary point of light in a dark room as moving.
STROBOSCOPIC MOTION • A visual illusion in which the perception of motion is generated by a series of stationary images that are presented in rapid succession.

FIGURE 5.19
STROBOSCOPIC MOTION
In a motion picture, viewing a series of stationary images at the rate of about 16 to 22 frames per second provides an illusion of movement termed *stroboscopic motion.*

THE PHI PHENOMENON Have you seen news headlines spelled out in lights that rapidly wrap around a building? Have you seen an electronic scoreboard in a baseball or football stadium? When the home team scores, some scoreboards suggest explosions of fireworks. What actually happens is that a row of lights is switched on and then off. As the first row is switched off, a second row is switched on, and so on for dozens, perhaps hundreds of rows. When the switching occurs rapidly, the **phi phenomenon** occurs: the on-off process is perceived as movement.

Like stroboscopic motion, the phi phenomenon is an example of apparent motion. Both appear to occur because of the law of continuity. We tend to perceive a series of points as having unity, so each series of lights (points) is perceived as a moving line.

The Phi Phenomenon. The phi phenomenon is an illusion of movement that is produced by lights blinking on and off in sequence, as with this New York Stock Exchange electronic "ticker."

• *Depth Perception*

Think of the problems you might have if you could not judge depth or distance. You might bump into other people, believing them to be farther away than they really are. An outfielder might not be able to judge whether to run toward the infield or the fence to catch a fly ball. You might give your front bumper a workout in stop-and-go traffic. Fortunately, both *monocular and binocular cues* help us perceive the distance of objects.

MONOCULAR CUES Now that you have considered how difficult it would be to navigate through life without depth perception, ponder the problems of the artist who attempts to portray three-dimensional objects on a two-dimensional surface. Artists use **monocular cues**—also termed pictorial cues—to create an illusion of depth. These are cues that can be perceived by one eye. They include perspective, relative size, clearness, interposition, shadows, and texture gradient, and cause certain objects to appear more distant from the viewer than others.

Distant objects stimulate smaller areas on the retina than nearby ones. The amount of sensory input from them is smaller, even though they may be the same size. The distances between far-off objects also appear to be smaller than equivalent distances between nearby objects. For this reason, the phenomenon known as **perspective** occurs. That is, we tend to perceive parallel lines as coming closer together, or converging, as they recede from us. However, as we will see when we discuss *size constancy,* experience teaches us that distant objects that look small will be larger when they are close. In this way, their relative size also becomes a cue to their distance.

The two engravings in Figure 5.20 represent impossible scenes in which the artists use principles of perspective to fool the viewer. In the one on the left, *Waterfall,* note that the water appears to be flowing away from the viewer in a zigzag because the stream gradually becomes narrower (that is, lines that we assume to be parallel are shown to be converging) and the stone sides of the aqueduct appear to be stepping down. However, given that the water arrives at the top of the fall, it must actually be flowing upward somehow. However, the spot from which it falls is no farther from the viewer than the collection point from which it appears to (but does not) begin its flow backward.

According to the principle of relative size, distant objects look smaller than nearby objects of the same size. The paradoxes in the engraving on the right, *False Perspective,* are made possible by the fact that more-distant objects are not necessarily depicted as being smaller than nearby objects. Thus, what at first seems to be background suddenly becomes foreground, and vice versa.

The clearness of an object also suggests its distance from us. Experience shows us that we sense more details of nearby objects. For this reason, artists

PHI PHENOMENON • The perception of movement as a result of sequential presentation of visual stimuli.
MONOCULAR CUES • Stimuli suggestive of depth that can be perceived with only one eye.
PERSPECTIVE • A monocular cue for depth based on the convergence (coming together) of parallel lines as they recede into the distance.

FIGURE 5.20
WHAT IS WRONG WITH THESE PICTURES?

In *Waterfall,* to the left, how does Dutch artist M. C. Escher suggest that fallen water flows back upward, only to fall again? In *False Perspective,* to the right, how does English artist William Hogarth use monocular cues for depth perception to deceive the viewer?

INTERPOSITION • A monocular cue for depth based on the fact that a nearby object obscures a more distant object behind it.

SHADOWING • A monocular cue for depth based on the fact that opaque objects block light and produce shadows.

can suggest that certain objects are closer to the viewer by depicting them in greater detail. Note that the "distant" hill in the Hogarth engraving (Figure 5.20) is given less detail than the nearby plants at the bottom of the picture. Our perceptions are mocked when a man "on" the distant hill in the background is shown conversing with a woman leaning out a window in the middle ground.

How does artist Viktor Vasarely use monocular cues to provide the illusion of a curving surface in his tapestry, *Vega-Tek* (Figure 5.21)?

We also learn that nearby objects can block our view of more-distant objects. Overlapping, or i**nterposition,** is the apparent placing of one object in front of another. Experience encourages us to perceive the partly covered objects as being farther away than the objects that hide parts of them from view (Figure 5.22). In the Hogarth engraving (Figure 5.20), which looks closer: the trees in the background (background?) or the moon sign hanging from the building (or is it buildings?) to the right? How does the artist use interposition to confound the viewer?

Additional information about depth is provided by **shadowing** and is based on the fact that opaque objects block light and produce shadows. Shadows and

FIGURE 5.21
CREATING THE ILLUSION OF THREE DIMENSIONS WITH TWO
How does Op Artist Victor Vasarely use monocular cues for depth perception to make this work look three-dimensional?

highlights give us information about an object's three-dimensional shape and its relationship to the source of light. For example, the left part of Figure 5.23 is perceived as a two-dimensional circle, but the right part tends to be perceived as a three-dimensional sphere because of the highlight on its surface and the shadow underneath. In the "sphere," the highlighted central area is perceived as being closest to us, with the surface receding to the edges.

FIGURE 5.22
THE EFFECTS OF INTERPOSITION
The four circles are all the same size. Which circles seem closer? The complete circles or the circles with chunks bitten out of them?

FIGURE 5.23
SHADOWING AS A CUE FOR DEPTH
Shadowing makes the circle on the right look three-dimensional.

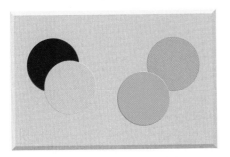

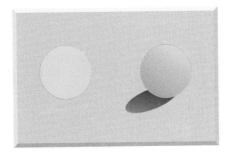

In Review   Cues for Depth Perception

MONOCULAR CUES		
Pictorial Cues*	Perspective	Perceiving parallel lines as coming closer together, or converging, as they recede from us
	Relative Size	Perceiving larger objects as being closer to us
	Clearness	Perceiving objects with greater detail as being closer to us
	Interposition	Perceiving objects that block our view of other objects as being closer to us (also called *overlapping*)
	Shadowing	Perceiving shadows and highlights as giving depth to two-dimensional objects
	Texture Gradient	Perceiving objects with rougher textures as being closer
Motion Cues	Motion Parallax	Perceiving objects that seem to move forward with us as distant and objects that seem to move backward as nearby
BINOCULAR CUES		
Retinal Disparity	Perceiving objects that cast more greatly differing images on the retinas of the eyes as being closer	
Convergence	Perceiving objects for whom focusing requires greater inward movement of the eyes (and therefore greater feelings of tension in the eyes) as being closer	

* These cues are commonly used by artists to create the impression of depth (a third dimension) in two-dimensional works such as drawings and paintings.

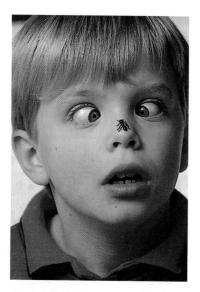

FIGURE 5.24

RETINAL DISPARITY AND CONVERGENCE AS CUES FOR DEPTH

As an object nears your eyes, you begin to see two images of it because of retinal disparity. To maintain perception of a single image, your eyes must converge on the object.

Another monocular cue is **texture gradient.** (A gradient is a progressive change.) Closer objects are perceived as having rougher textures. In the Hogarth engraving (Figure 5.20), the building just behind the large fisherman's head has a rougher texture and therefore seems to be closer than the building with the window from which the woman is leaning. Our surprise is heightened when the moon sign is seen as hanging from both buildings.

MOTION CUES   Motion cues are another kind of monocular cue. If you have ever driven in the country, you have probably noticed that distant objects such as mountains and stars appear to move along with you. Objects at an intermediate distance seem to be stationary, but nearby objects such as roadside markers, rocks, and trees seem to go by quite rapidly. The tendency of objects to seem to move backward or forward as a function of their distance is known as **motion parallax.** We learn to perceive objects that appear to move with us as being at greater distances.

Earlier we noted that nearby objects cause the lens of the eye to accommodate or bend more in order to bring them into focus. The sensations of tension in the eye muscles also provide a monocular cue to depth, especially when we are within about 4 feet of the objects.

BINOCULAR CUES   **Binocular cues,** or cues that involve both eyes, also help us perceive depth. Two binocular cues are *retinal disparity* and *convergence*.

Try an experiment. Hold your index finger at arm's length. Now, gradually bring it closer until it almost touches your nose. If you keep your eyes relaxed as you do so, you will see two fingers. An image of the finger will be projected onto the retina of each eye, and each image will be slightly different because the finger will be seen from different angles. The difference between the projected images is referred to as **retinal disparity** and serves as a binocular cue for depth perception (see Figure 5.24). Note that the closer your finger comes, the farther apart the "two fingers" appear to be. Closer objects have greater retinal disparity.

If we try to maintain a single image of the approaching finger, our eyes must turn inward, or converge on it, giving us a cross-eyed look. **Convergence** is associated with feelings of tension in the eye muscles and provides another binocular cue for depth. The binocular cues of retinal disparity and convergence are strongest when objects are close to us.

• *Problems in Visual Perception*

PROBLEMS IN VISUAL ACUITY **Visual acuity** refers to sharpness of vision, as defined by the ability to discriminate visual details. A familiar means of measuring visual acuity is the Snellen Chart (Figure 5.25). If you were to stand 20 feet from the chart and could discriminate only the *E*, we would say that your vision is 20/200. This means that you can see from a distance of 20 feet what a person with normal vision can discriminate from a distance of 200 feet. In such a case,

TEXTURE GRADIENT • A monocular cue for depth based on the perception that closer objects appear to have rougher (more detailed) surfaces.
MOTION PARALLAX • A monocular cue for depth based on the perception that nearby objects appear to move more rapidly in relation to our own motion.
BINOCULAR CUES • Stimuli suggestive of depth that involve simultaneous perception by both eyes.
RETINAL DISPARITY • A binocular cue for depth based on the difference in the image cast by an object on the retinas of the eyes as the object moves closer or farther away.
CONVERGENCE • A binocular cue for depth based on the inward movement of the eyes as they attempt to focus on an object that is drawing nearer.
VISUAL ACUITY • Sharpness of vision.

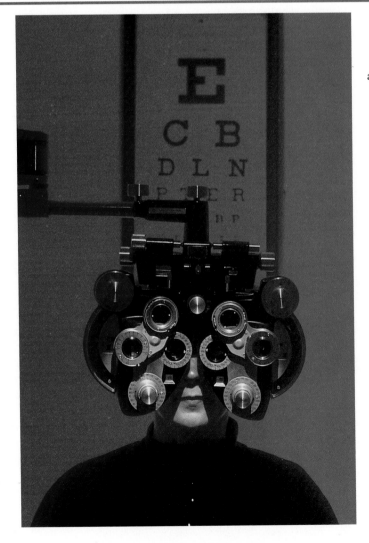

FIGURE 5.25
THE SNELLEN CHART
The Snellen Chart and others like it are used to assess visual acuity. This person is being assessed for corrective lenses to increase his visual acuity.

you would be quite **nearsighted.** This means that you would have to be unusually close to an object to discriminate its details. A person who could read the smallest line on the chart from 20 feet would have 20/15 vision and would be somewhat **farsighted.**

Older people often hold newspapers or books some distance away while reading. As you reach middle age, the lenses of your eyes become relatively brittle, making it more difficult to accommodate to, or focus on, objects. This condition is called **presbyopia** (from the Greek words for "old man" and "eyes") and usually begins in the late 30s to the mid 40s. The lens structure of people with presbyopia differs from that of farsighted young people. Still, the effect of presbyopia is to make it difficult to perceive nearby visual stimuli. People who had normal visual acuity in their youth often require corrective lenses to read in old age. And people who were initially farsighted often have headaches linked to eyestrain during their later years.

• *Perceptual Constancies*

The world is a constantly shifting display of visual sensations. Think of how confusing it would be if we did not perceive a doorway to be the same doorway when seen from 6 feet away as when seen from 4 feet away. As we neared it, we might think that it was larger than the door we were seeking, and become lost. Or consider the problems of the pet owner who recognizes his dog from the side but not from above because its shape is different when seen from above. Fortunately, these problems tend not to occur—at least with familiar objects—because perceptual constancies enable us to recognize objects even when their apparent shape or size differs.

SIZE CONSTANCY We may say that people "look like ants" when viewed from the top of a tall building, but we know that they remain people even if the details of their forms are lost in the distance. We can thus say that we *perceive* people to be the same size, even when viewed from great distances, despite the fact that the images they form on the retina are extremely small.

The image of a dog seen from 20 feet away occupies about the same amount of space on your retina as an inch-long insect crawling on your hand. Yet you do not perceive the dog to be as small as the insect. Through your visual experiences you have acquired **size constancy**—that is, the ability to perceive the same object as being the same size even though the size of its image on your retina varies as a function of its distance. Experience teaches us about perspective. It shows us that the same object seen at a great distance will appear to be much smaller than when it is nearby.

FIGURE 5.26
COLOR CONSTANCY

The orange squares within the blue squares are the same hue, yet the orange within the dark blue square is perceived as purer. Why?

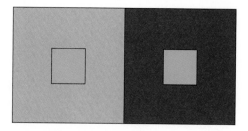

COLOR CONSTANCY We also have **color constancy**—the ability to perceive objects as retaining their color even though lighting conditions may alter their appearance. Your bright orange car may edge toward yellow-gray as the hours wend their way through twilight to nighttime. But when you finally locate the car in the parking lot, you will still think of it as being orange. You expect to find an orange car and still judge it to be "more orange" than the (faded) blue and green cars on either side of it. However, it would be fiercely difficult to find your car in a parking lot filled with yellow and red cars of similar size and shape.

Consider Figure 5.26. The orange squares within the blue squares are the same hue. However, the orange within the dark blue square is perceived as being purer. Why? Again, experience teaches us that the purity of colors fades as the background grows darker. Since the orange squares are equally pure, we assume that the one in the dark background must be more saturated. We would

FIGURE 5.27
SHAPE CONSTANCY
When closed, this door is a rectangle. When open, the retinal image is trapezoidal. But because of shape constancy, we still perceive it as rectangular.

stand ready to perceive the orange squares as being equal in purity if the square within the darker blue field actually had a bit of black mixed in with it.

BRIGHTNESS CONSTANCY Similar to color constancy is **brightness constancy.** The same gray square is perceived as brighter when placed within a black background than when placed within a white background (see Figure 1.3 on p. 13). Again, consider the role of experience. If it were nighttime, we would expect gray to fade to near blackness. The fact that the gray within the black square stimulates the eye with equal intensity suggests that it must be very much brighter than the gray within the white square.

SHAPE CONSTANCY We also perceive objects as maintaining their shape, even if we perceive them from different angles so that the shape of their image on the retina changes dramatically. This ability is called **shape constancy.** You perceive the top of a coffee cup or a glass to be a circle even though it is a circle only when seen from above. When seen from an angle, it is an ellipse. When the cup or glass is seen on edge, its retinal image is the same as that of a straight line. So why do you still describe the rim of the cup or glass as being a circle? Perhaps for two reasons: One is that experience has taught you that the cup will look circular when seen from above. The second is that you may have labeled the cup as circular or round. Experience and labels help make the world a stable place. Can you imagine the chaos that would prevail if we described objects as they appear as they stimulate our sensory organs with each changing moment, rather than according to stable conditions?

In another example, a door is a rectangle only when viewed straight on (Figure 5.27). When we move to the side or open it, the left or right edge comes closer and appears to be larger, changing the retinal image to a trapezoid. Yet we continue to think of doors as being rectangles.

• *Visual Illusions*

The principles of perceptual organization make it possible for our eyes to "play tricks on us." Psychologists, like magicians, enjoy pulling a rabbit out of a hat now and then. Let me demonstrate how the perceptual constancies trick the eye through so-called *visual illusions.*

NEARSIGHTED • Capable of seeing nearby objects with greater acuity than distant objects.
FARSIGHTED • Capable of seeing distant objects with greater acuity than nearby objects.
PRESBYOPIA • A condition characterized by brittleness of the lens.
SIZE CONSTANCY • The tendency to perceive an object as being the same size even as the size of its retinal image changes according to the objects's distance.
COLOR CONSTANCY • The tendency to perceive an object as being the same color even though lighting conditions change its appearance.
BRIGHTNESS CONSTANCY • The tendency to perceive an object as being just as bright even though lighting conditions change its intensity.
SHAPE CONSTANCY • The tendency to perceive an object as being the same shape although the retinal image varies in shape as it rotates.

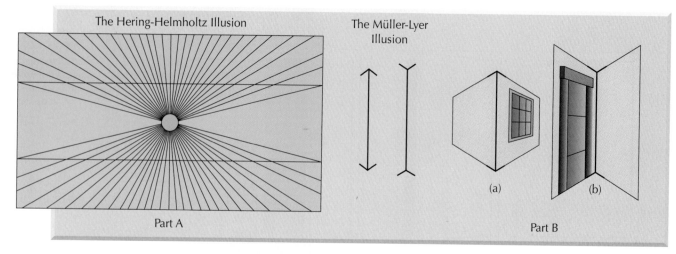

FIGURE 5.28
THE HERING-HELMHOLTZ AND MÜLLER-LYER ILLUSIONS
In the Hering-Helmholtz illusion, are the horizontal lines straight or curved? In the Müller-Lyer illusion, are the vertical lines equal in length?

The Hering-Helmholtz and Müller-Lyer illusions (Figure 5.28, part A) are named after the people who devised them. In the Hering-Helmholtz illusion, the horizontal lines are straight and parallel. However, the radiating lines cause them to appear to be bent outward near the center. The two lines in the Müller-Lyer illusion are the same length, but the line on the left, with its reversed arrowheads, looks longer.

Let us try to explain these illusions. Because of our experience and lifelong use of perceptual cues, we tend to perceive the Hering-Helmholtz drawing as three-dimensional. Because of our tendency to perceive bits of sensory information as figures against grounds, we perceive the white area in the center as being a circle in front of a series of radiating lines, all of which lies in front of a white ground. Next, because of our experience with perspective, we perceive the radiating lines as parallel. We perceive the two horizontal lines as intersecting the "receding" lines, and we know that they would have to appear bent out at the center if they were to be equidistant at all points from the center of the circle.

Experience probably compels us to perceive the vertical lines in the Müller-Lyer illusion as being the corners of a room as seen from inside a house, at left, and from outside a house, at right (see Figure 5.28, part B). In such an example, the reverse arrowheads to the left are lines where the walls meet the ceiling and the floor. We perceive such lines as extending toward us. They push the corner away from us. The arrowheads to the right are lines where exterior walls meet the roof and foundation. We perceive them as receding from us. They push the corner toward us. The vertical line to the left therefore is perceived as being farther away. Since both vertical lines stimulate equal expanses across the retina, the principle of size constancy encourages us to perceive the line to the left as being longer.

Figure 5.29 is known as the Ponzo illusion. In this illusion, the two horizontal lines are the same length. However, do you perceive the top line as being longer? The rule of size constancy may give us some insight into this illusion as well. Perhaps the converging lines again strike us as being parallel lines receding into the distance, like train tracks. If so, we assume from experience that the horizontal line at the top is farther down the track—that is, farther away from us. And again, the rule of size constancy tells us that if two objects appear to be the same size and one is farther away, the farther object must be larger. So we perceive the top line as being larger.

FIGURE 5.29
THE PONZO ILLUSION

The horizontal lines in this drawing are equal in length, but the top line is perceived as being longer. Can you use the principle of size constancy to explain why?

■ HEARING

Consider the advertising slogan for the science fiction film *Alien:* "In space, no one can hear you scream." It's true. Space is an almost perfect vacuum. Hearing requires a medium through which sound can travel, such as air or water.

Sound, or **auditory** stimulation, travels through the air like waves. Sound is caused by changes in air pressure that result from vibrations. These vibrations, in turn, can be created by a tuning fork, your vocal cords, guitar strings, or the slam of a book thrown down on a desk.

Figure 5.30 suggests the way in which a tuning fork creates sound waves. During a vibration back and forth, the right prong of the tuning fork moves to the right. In so doing, it pushes together, or compresses, the molecules of air immediately to the right. Then the prong moves back to the left, and the air molecules to the right expand. By vibrating back and forth, the tuning fork actually sends air waves in many directions. A cycle of compression and expansion is one wave of sound. Sound waves can occur many times in one second. The human ear is sensitive to sound waves that vary in frequency from 20 to 20,000 cycles per second.

• *Pitch and Loudness*

Pitch and loudness are two psychological dimensions of sound. Let's look briefly at each.

I AUDITORY • Having to do with hearing.

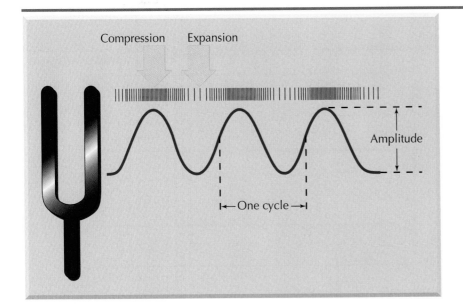

FIGURE **5.30**
CREATION OF SOUND WAVES
The vibration of the prongs of a tuning fork alternately compresses and expands air molecules, sending forth waves of sound.

PITCH The pitch of a sound is determined by its frequency, or the number of cycles per second as expressed in the unit **Hertz (Hz).** One cycle per second is one Hz. The greater the number of cycles per second (Hz), the higher the pitch of the sound. The pitch of women's voices is usually higher than that of men's voices because women's vocal cords are usually shorter and therefore vibrate at a greater frequency. The strings of a violin are shorter than those of a viola or bass viol. They vibrate at greater frequencies, and we perceive them as higher in pitch. Pitch detectors in the brain allow us to tell the difference (Blakeslee, 1995).

LOUDNESS The loudness of a sound is determined by the height, or **amplitude,** of sound waves. The higher the amplitude of the wave, the louder the sound. Figure 5.31 shows records of sound waves that vary in frequency and amplitude. Note that frequency and amplitude are independent dimensions. Both high- and low-pitched sounds can be either high or low in loudness.

The loudness of a sound is usually expressed in **decibels,** abbreviated dB. This unit of measurement is named after the inventor of the telephone, Alexander Graham Bell. Zero dB is equivalent to the threshold of hearing. How loud is that? It's about as loud as the ticking of a watch 20 feet away from you in a very quiet room.

The decibel equivalents of many familiar sounds are shown in Figure 5.32. Twenty dB is equivalent in loudness to a whisper at 5 feet. Thirty dB is roughly the limit of loudness at which your librarian would like to keep your college library. You may suffer hearing damage if you are exposed to sounds of 85 to 90 dB for very long periods.

When musical sounds (also called tones) of different frequencies are played together, we perceive a third tone that results from the difference in their frequencies. If the combination of tones is pleasant, we say that they are in harmony, or **consonant** (from Latin roots meaning "together" and "sound"). Unpleasant combinations of tones are said to be **dissonant** (from "the opposite

HERTZ • A unit expressing the frequency of sound waves. One Hertz, or *1 Hz,* equals one cycle per second.
AMPLITUDE • Height.
DECIBEL • A unit expressing the loudness of a sound. Abbreviated *dB.*
CONSONANT • In harmony.
DISSONANT • Incompatible, not harmonious, discordant.

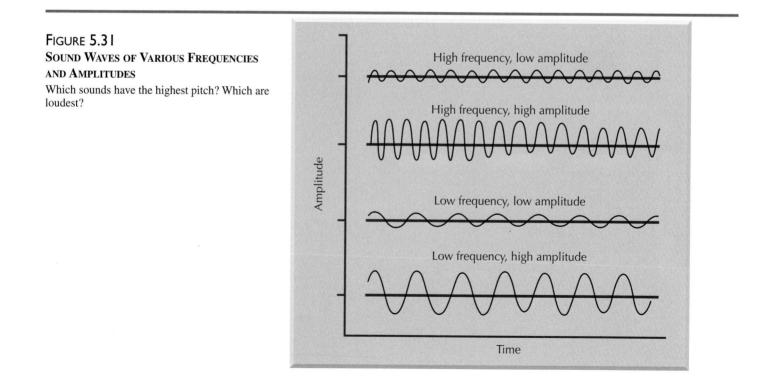

FIGURE 5.31
SOUND WAVES OF VARIOUS FREQUENCIES AND AMPLITUDES
Which sounds have the highest pitch? Which are loudest?

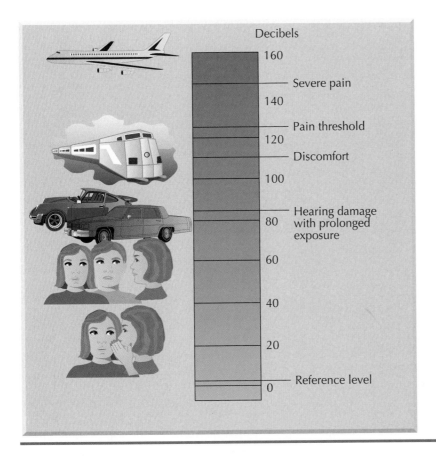

FIGURE **5.32**
DECIBEL RATINGS OF FAMILIAR SOUNDS
Zero dB is the threshold of hearing. You may suffer hearing loss if you incur prolonged exposure to sounds of 85-90 dB.

of" and "sound"). When we say that something "strikes a dissonant chord," we mean that we find it disagreeable.

OVERTONES AND TIMBRE In addition to producing the specified musical note, an instrument like the violin also produces a number of tones that are greater in frequency. These more highly pitched sounds are called **overtones**. Overtones result from vibrations elsewhere in the instrument and contribute to the quality or richness—that is, its **timbre.**

NOISE In terms of the sense of hearing, *noise* is a combination of dissonant sounds.[1] When you place a spiral shell to your ear, you do not hear the roar of the ocean. Rather, you hear nearby noise as reflected from the coils within the shell. **White noise** consists of many different frequencies of sound. Yet, if it is not too loud, the mixture can lull us to sleep.

Now let us turn our attention to the marvelous instrument that senses all these different "vibes": the human ear.

• The Ear: The Better to Hear You With

The human ear is good for lots of things—including catching dust, combing your hair around, hanging jewelry from, and nibbling. It is also admirably suited for sensing sounds. The ear is shaped and structured so as to capture sound waves,

Truth or Fiction Revisited

It is true that a $500 machine-made violin will produce the same musical notes as a $200,000 Stradivarius. The Stradivarius has richer overtones, however, and these give the instrument its greater value.

OVERTONES • Tones of a higher frequency than those played that result from vibrations throughout a musical instrument.
TIMBRE • The quality or richness of a sound.
WHITE NOISE • Discordant sounds of many frequencies, often producing a lulling effect.

[1] Within the broader context of signal-detection theory, *noise* has a different meaning, discussed earlier in the chapter.

vibrate in sympathy with them, and transmit them to centers in the brain. In this way, you not only hear something, you can also figure out what it is. The ear has three parts: the outer ear, middle ear, and inner ear (see Figure 5.33).

THE OUTER EAR The outer ear is shaped to funnel sound waves to the **eardrum,** a thin membrane that vibrates in response to sound waves and thereby transmits them to the middle and inner ears.

THE MIDDLE EAR The middle ear contains the eardrum and three small bones—the hammer, the anvil, and the stirrup—which also transmit sound by vibrating. These bones were given their names (actually the Latin *malleus, incus,* and *stapes* [pronounced STAY-peas], which translate as hammer, anvil, and stirrup) because of their shapes. The middle ear functions as an amplifier: It increases the pressure of the air entering the ear.

The stirrup is attached to another vibrating membrane, the **oval window.** The round window shown in Figure 5.33 balances the pressure in the inner ear. It pushes outward when the oval window pushes in, and it is pulled inward when the oval window vibrates outward.

THE INNER EAR The oval window transmits vibrations into the inner ear, which contains the bony tube called the **cochlea** (from the Greek for "snail"). The cochlea, which is shaped like a snail shell, contains two longitudinal membranes that divide it into three fluid-filled chambers. One of the membranes that lies coiled within the cochlea is called the **basilar membrane.** Vibrations in the fluids within the chambers of the inner ear press against the basilar membrane.

The **organ of Corti,** sometimes referred to as the "command post" of hearing, is attached to the basilar membrane. Thousands of hair cells (receptor cells that project like hair from the organ of Corti) "dance" in response to the vibrations of the basilar membrane (Brownell, 1992). This up-and-down movement generates neural impulses, which are transmitted to the brain via the 31,000 neurons that form the **auditory nerve.** Within the brain, auditory input is projected onto the hearing areas of the temporal lobes of the cerebral cortex.

• *Locating Sounds*

How do you balance the loudness of a stereo set? You sit between the speakers and adjust the volume until the sound seems to be equally loud in each ear. If the sound to the right is louder, the musical instruments will be perceived as being toward the right rather than straight ahead.

There is a resemblance between balancing a stereo set and locating sounds. A sound that is louder in the right ear is perceived as coming from the right. A sound coming from the right also reaches the right ear first. Both loudness and the sequence in which the sounds reach the ears provide directional cues.

But it may not be easy to locate a sound coming from directly in front or in back of you or overhead. Such sounds are equally distant from each ear and equally loud. So what do we do? Simple—usually we turn our head slightly to determine in which ear the sound increases. If you turn your head a few degrees to the right and the loudness increases in your left ear, the sound must be coming from in front of you. Of course, we also use vision and general knowledge in locating the source of sounds. If you hear the roar of jet engines, most of the time you can bet that the airplane is overhead.

EARDRUM • A thin membrane that vibrates in response to sound waves, transmitting the waves to the middle and inner ears.

OVAL WINDOW • A membrane that transmits vibrations from the stirrup of the middle ear to the cochlea within the inner ear.

COCHLEA • The inner ear; the bony tube that contains the basilar membrane and the organ of Corti.

BASILAR MEMBRANE • A membrane that lies coiled within the cochlea.

ORGAN OF CORTI • The receptor for hearing that lies on the basilar membrane in the cochlea.

AUDITORY NERVE • The axon bundle that transmits neural impulses from the organ of Corti to the brain.

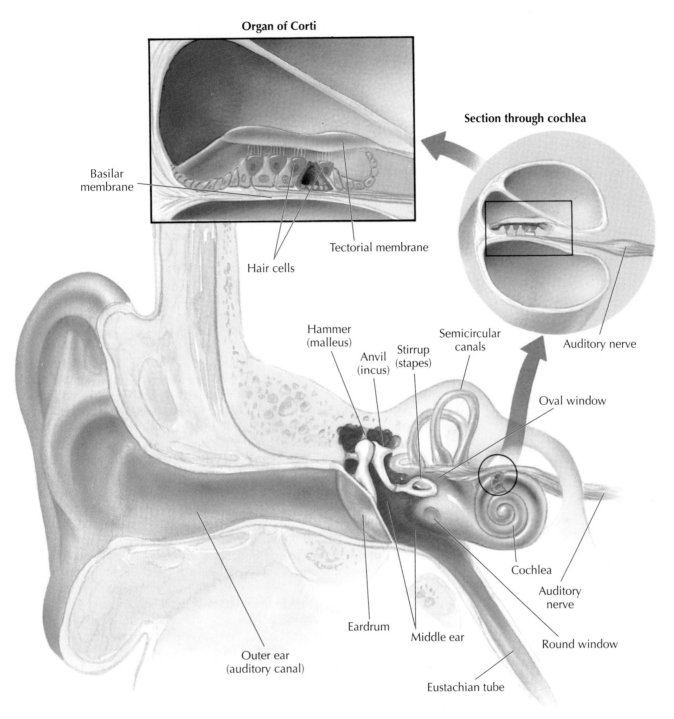

Organ of Corti

Section through cochlea

Basilar membrane

Hair cells

Tectorial membrane

Auditory nerve

Hammer (malleus)

Anvil (incus)

Stirrup (stapes)

Semicircular canals

Oval window

Auditory nerve

Cochlea

Auditory nerve

Round window

Eardrum

Middle ear

Outer ear (auditory canal)

Eustachian tube

FIGURE 5.33

THE HUMAN EAR

The outer ear funnels sound to the eardrum. Inside the eardrum, vibrations of the hammer, anvil, and stirrup transmit sound to the inner ear. Vibrations in the cochlea transmit the sound to the auditory nerve by way of the basilar membrane and the organ of Corti.

• *Perception of Loudness and Pitch*

We know that sounds are heard because they cause vibration in parts of the ear and information about these vibrations is transmitted to the brain. But what determines the loudness and pitch of our perceptions of these sounds?

The loudness and pitch of sounds appear to be related to the number of receptor neurons on the organ of Corti that fire and how often they fire. Psychologists generally agree that sounds are perceived as being louder when more of these sensory neurons fire.

It takes two processes to explain perception of color: trichromatic theory and opponent-process theory. Similarly, it takes at least two processes to explain pitch perception—that is, perception of sound waves with frequencies that vary from 20 to 20,000 cycles per second: *place theory* and *frequency theory.*

Hermann von Helmholtz helped develop the place theory of pitch discrimination as well as the Young-Helmholtz (trichromatic) theory of color vision. **Place theory** holds that the pitch of a sound is sensed according to the place along the basilar membrane that vibrates in response to it. In classic research with guinea pigs and cadavers that led to the award of a Nobel prize, Georg von Békésy (1957) found evidence for place theory: He determined that receptors at different sites along the membrane fire in response to tones of differing frequencies. Receptor neurons appear to be lined up along the basilar membrane like piano keys (Azar, 1996a). The higher the pitch of a sound, the closer the responsive neurons lie to the oval window. However, place theory only appears to apply to sounds that are higher in pitch than 4,000 Hz, and people sense pitches as low as 20 Hz.

Frequency theory accounts for pitches at the lower end of the range. **Frequency theory** notes that pitch perception depends on the stimulation of neural impulses that match the frequency of the sound waves. That is, in response to low pitches—pitches of about 20 to 1,000 cycles per second—hair cells on the basilar membrane fire at the same frequencies as the sound waves. However, neurons cannot fire more than 1,000 times per second. Therefore, frequency theory can only account for perception of pitches between 20 and 1,000 cycles per second. In actuality, frequency theory only appears to account for pitch perception between 20 and a few hundred cycles per second.

I noted that it takes *at least two processes* to explain how people perceive pitch. The *volley principle* is the third, and it accounts for pitch discrimination between a few hundred and 4,000 cycles per second (Matlin & Foley, 1995). In response to sound waves of these frequencies, groups of neurons take turns firing, in the way that one row of soldiers used to fire rifles while another row knelt to reload. Alternating firing—that is, volleying—appears to transmit sensory information about pitches in the intermediate range.

Unfortunately, not everyone perceives sound, and many of us do not perceive sounds of certain frequencies. Let us consider a number of kinds of hearing problems, collectively referred to as deafness.

• *Deafness*

An estimated 28 million Americans have impaired hearing. Two million of them are deaf (Nadol, 1993). They are thus deprived of a key source of information about the world around them. In recent years, however, society has made greater efforts to bring them into the mainstream of sensory experience. People are usually on hand to convert political and other speeches into hand signs (such as those of American Sign Language [ASL]) for hearing-impaired members of the audience. Many television shows are "closed captioned" so that they can be understood by people with hearing problems. Special decoders render the captions visible. Although people are more likely to encounter hearing loss as they age, educators have also grown more aware of the potential language learning problems of hearing-impaired children.

PLACE THEORY • The theory that the pitch of a sound is determined by the section of the basilar membrane that vibrates in response to the sound.
FREQUENCY THEORY • The theory that the pitch of a sound is reflected in the frequency of the neural impulses that are generated in response to the sound.

There are two major types of deafness: conductive deafness and sensorineural deafness.

CONDUCTIVE DEAFNESS **Conductive deafness** occurs because of damage to the structures of the middle ear—either to the eardrum or to the three bones that conduct (and amplify) sound waves from the outer ear to the inner ear (Nadol, 1993). People with conductive hearing loss have high absolute thresholds for detection of sounds at all frequencies. This is the type of hearing impairment that is often found among older people. People with conductive deafness often profit from hearing aids, which provide the amplification that the middle ear does not.

SENSORINEURAL DEAFNESS **Sensorineural deafness** usually stems from damage to the structures of the inner ear, most often the loss of hair cells, which will not regenerate. Sensorineural deafness can also stem from damage to the auditory nerve, for example, because of disease or because of acoustic trauma (prolonged exposure to very loud sounds). In sensorineural deafness, people tend to be more sensitive to some pitches than to others. In so-called Hunter's notch, hearing impairment is limited to particular frequencies—in this case, the frequencies of the sound waves generated by a gun firing. Prolonged exposure to 85 dB can cause hearing loss. People who attend high-volume rock concerts risk damaging their ears, as do workers who run pneumatic drills or drive extremely noisy vehicles. The so-called ringing sensation that often follows exposure to loud sounds probably means that hair cells in the inner ear have been damaged. If you find yourself suddenly exposed to loud sounds, remember that your fingertips serve as good emergency ear protectors.

Experimental cochlear implants, or "artificial ears," contain microphones that sense sounds and electronic equipment that transmits sounds past damaged hair cells to stimulate the auditory nerve directly. Multichannel implants apply the place theory of pitch perception to enable people with impaired hearing to discriminate between high- and low-pitched sounds. Such implants have helped many people with sensorineural deafness. However, they cannot assume the functions of damaged auditory nerves. The following "Psychology in a World of Diversity" section explores how recent changes in American Sign Language—the language of the deaf—have attempted to bring an end to ethnic stereotyping.

Psychology in a World of
DIVERSITY

The Signs of the Times Are Changing

As recently as 1990, a deaf person might make the sign meaning *Japanese person* by twisting the little finger next to the eye (see Figure 5.34). Today many people who use American Sign Language have discarded this sign because it refers to the stereotypical physical feature of slanted eyes. Instead, they are adopting Japanese people's own sign for themselves: They press the thumb and index finger of both hands together and then pull them apart to sculpt the outline of Japan in the air (Senior, 1994).

"In American Sign Language, politically incorrect terms are often a visual representation of the ugly metaphors we have about people," notes psycholinguist

CONDUCTIVE DEAFNESS • The forms of deafness in which there is loss of conduction of sound through the middle ear.
SENSORINEURAL DEAFNESS • The forms of deafness that result from damage to hair cells or the auditory nerve.

FIGURE **5.34**

OLD AND NEW SIGNS FOR JAPAN OR A JAPANESE PERSON IN AMERICAN SIGN LANGUAGE

The old sign for Japanese is now considered offensive because it refers to the stereotypical physical feature of slanted eyes. The new sign outlines the island of Japan.

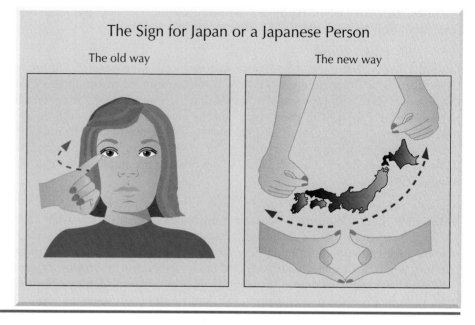

The Sign for Japan or a Japanese Person

The old way | The new way

Elissa Newport (1994). As with the sign for *Japanese,* the signs for *Chinese* and *Korean,* which are made by forming the letters *C* and *K* around the eye, are also changing. There is also a new sign for *African American.* This population group was once indicated by flattening the nose. That sign was replaced by signs for the color black—the index finger either placed by the eyebrow or wiped across the forehead. The current sign for *African American* is still centered on the nose, however, and therefore is being replaced by a sign that outlines Africa (see Figure 5.35).

The old sign for *gay male* was an offensive swish of the wrist. Now it is more widely acceptable to simply spell out words like *homosexual, gay male,* or *lesbian* with the hands.

Politically correct changes in American Sign Language have thus far caught on mainly among highly educated deaf people in urban settings. It is taking

FIGURE **5.35**

OLD AND NEW SIGNS FOR AFRICAN AMERICANS IN AMERICAN SIGN LANGUAGE

The old signs for African Americans were considered offensive because they referred to the shape or location of the nose. The new sign outlines the African continent.

The evolving signs for African American

In the 1950s and '60s the sign, read as "Negro," was made by flattening the nose with one finger.

Later, the hand formed the sign for the letter A, traced a circle in front of the face, and ended with the thumb on the nose.

Today, an open hand held in front of the body outlines the shape of the African continent, usually ending with closed fingers at the bottom of the shape.

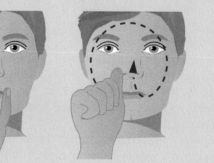

longer for them to catch on in the wider deaf community and to appear in dictionaries of sign language. Nevertheless, the clear trend is for the deaf—who in many ways have been victims of stereotyping themselves—to learn how not to stereotype others through sign language.

REFLECTIONS

- Are you familiar with the violin, viola, cello, and bass fiddle? How do their sounds differ? How do you account for the differences?
- Have you ever been unsure where a sound was coming from? How did you locate the source of the sound?
- Do you know anyone with hearing problems? What is the source of the impairment? How does the person cope with the impairment?

■ SMELL

Smell and taste are the chemical senses. In the cases of vision and hearing, physical energy strikes our sensory receptors. With smell and taste, we sample molecules of the substances being sensed.

You could say that we are underprivileged when it comes to the sense of smell. Dogs, for instance, devote about seven times as much of the cerebral cortex as we do to the sense of smell. Male dogs sniff in order to determine where the boundaries of other dogs' territories leave off and whether female dogs are sexually receptive. Some dogs even make a living sniffing out marijuana in closed packages and suitcases for law enforcement agencies.

Still, smell has an important role in human behavior. It makes a crucial contribution to the flavor of foods, for example (Bartoshuk & Beauchamp, 1994). If you did not have a sense of smell, an onion and an apple would taste the same to you! People's sense of smell may be deficient when we compare them to those of a dog, but we can detect the odor of one one-millionth of a milligram of vanilla in a liter of air.

An **odor** is a sample of the substance being sensed. Odors are detected by sites on receptor neurons in the **olfactory** membrane high in each nostril. Receptor neurons fire when a few molecules of the substance in gaseous form come into contact with them. Their firing transmits information about odors to the brain via the **olfactory nerve**. That is how the substance is smelled.

It is unclear how many basic kinds of odors there are. In any event, olfactory receptors may respond to more than one kind of odor. Mixtures of smell sensations also help produce the broad range of odors that we can perceive (Solomon and others, 1993).

The sense of smell adapts rapidly to odors, even obnoxious ones (Solomon and others, 1993). This might be fortunate if you are in a locker room or an outhouse. It might not be so fortunate if you are exposed to fumes from paints or secondhand smoke, since you may lose awareness of them while danger remains. One odor may also mask another; this is how air fresheners work.

■ TASTE

Your cocker spaniel may jump at the chance to finish off your ice cream cone, but your Siamese cat may turn up her nose at the opportunity. Why? Dogs can perceive the taste quality of sweetness, as can pigs, but cats cannot.

There are four primary taste qualities: sweet, sour, salty, and bitter. The *flavor* of a food involves its taste but is more complex. Although apples and

---

Truth or Fiction Revisited

It is true that onions and apples have the same taste. Their flavors, however, which reflect their odors and other qualities, are very different.

ODOR • The characteristic of a substance that makes it perceptible to the sense of smell.
OLFACTORY • Having to do with the sense of smell.
OLFACTORY NERVE • The nerve that transmits information concerning odors from olfactory receptors to the brain.

onions have the same taste—or the same mix of taste qualities—their flavors differ greatly. After all, you wouldn't chomp into a nice cold onion on a warm day, would you? The flavor of a food depends on its odor, texture, and temperature as well as on its taste. If it were not for odor, heated tenderized shoe leather might pass for steak.

Taste is sensed through **taste cells**—receptor neurons located on **taste buds.** You have about 10,000 taste buds, most of which are located near the edges and back of your tongue. Taste buds tend to specialize a bit. Some, for example, are more responsive to sweetness, whereas others react to several tastes. Other taste receptors are found in the roof, sides, and back of the mouth, even in the throat.

We live in different taste worlds. Those of us with low sensitivity for the sweet taste may require twice the sugar to sweeten our food as others who are more sensitive to sweetness. Those of us who claim to enjoy very bitter foods may actually be taste blind to them. Sensitivities to different tastes apparently have a strong genetic component.

By eating hot foods and scraping your tongue, you regularly kill off many taste cells. But you need not be alarmed at this inadvertent oral aggression. Taste cells are the rabbits of the sense receptors. They reproduce rapidly enough to completely renew themselves about once a week.

TASTE CELLS • Receptor cells that are sensitive to taste.
TASTE BUDS • The sensory organs for taste. They contain taste cells and are located on the tongue.

PSYCHOLOGY *in the* ▶ NEW MILLENNIUM

Will We Use "a Sixth Sense for Sex" in the 21st Century?

For centuries people have searched for a love potion—a magical formula that could make other people fall in love with you or be strongly attracted to you. Some scientists suggest that such potions may already exist in the form of chemical secretions known as *pheromones.*

Pheromones are odorless chemicals that in humans would be detected through a "sixth sense"—the *vomeronasal organ.* This organ, located in the nose, would detect these odorless chemicals and communicate information about them to the hypothalamus, where they might affect sexual response (Blakeslee, 1993).

People may use pheromones in many ways. Infants, for example, may use them to recognize their mothers, and adults might respond to them in seeking a mate. Lower animals use pheromones to stimulate sexual response, organize food gathering, maintain pecking orders, sound alarms, and mark territories (Strom, 1993). Pheromones induce mating behavior in insects. Male rodents show less sexual arousal when their sense of smell is blocked, but the role of pheromones in sexual behavior becomes less vital as one moves upward through the ranks of the animal kingdom.

Only a few years ago, most researchers did not believe that pheromones played a role in human behavior. Today, however, it appears that people do possess vomeronasal organs (Bartoshuk & Beauchamp, 1994), and this field of research has attracted new interest. David Berliner has jumped ahead of the research enterprise by forming companies that plan to commercialize the use of pheromones with people. As the new millennium rolls in, might people be using perfumes and colognes that have a double impact—one on the sense of smell and another on a "sixth sense for sex"? ■

Although older people often complain that their food has little or no "taste," they are more likely to experience a decline in the sense of smell. Because the flavor of a food represents both its tastes and its odors or aromas, older people experience loss in the *flavor* of their food. Since the flavor of food supplies some of the motivation to eat, older people are at risk of becoming malnourished. They are often encouraged to avert malnourishment by adding spices to their food to enhance its flavor.

■ THE SKIN SENSES

The skin discriminates among many kinds of sensations—touch, pressure, warmth, cold, and pain (see Figure 5.36). We have distinct sensory receptors for pressure, temperature, and pain, but some nerve endings may receive more than one type of sensory input.

• *Touch and Pressure*

Sensory receptors located around the roots of hair cells appear to fire when the surface of the skin is touched. You may have noticed that if you are trying to "get the feel of" a fabric or the texture of a friend's hair, you must move your hand over it. Otherwise the sensations quickly fade. If you pass your hand over the skin and then hold it still, again the sensations of touching will fade. This sort of "active touching" involves reception of information concerning not only touch per se but also pressure, temperature, and feedback from the muscles involved in movements of our hands.

Other structures beneath the skin apparently are sensitive to pressure. All in all, there are about half a million receptors for touch and pressure throughout the body. Different parts of the body are more sensitive to touch and pressure than others. Psychophysicists use methods such as the **two-point threshold** to

Sensational? The flavors of foods are determined not only by their taste, but also by their odor, texture, and temperature.

TWO-POINT THRESHOLD • The least distance by which two rods touching the skin must be separated before the person will report that there are two rods, not one, on 50% of occasions.

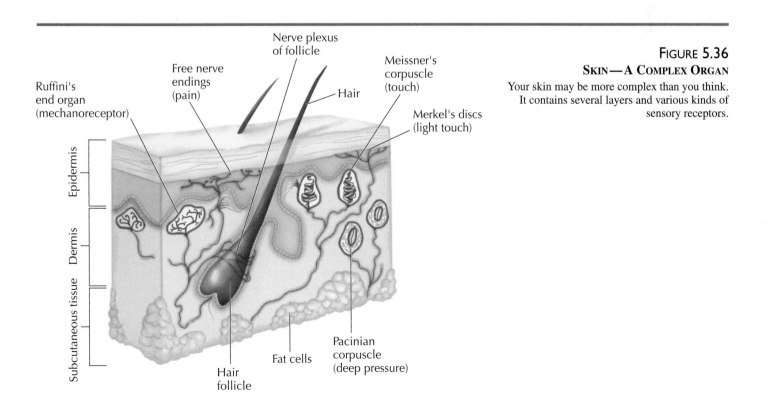

FIGURE 5.36
SKIN—A COMPLEX ORGAN
Your skin may be more complex than you think. It contains several layers and various kinds of sensory receptors.

assess sensitivity to pressure. This method determines the smallest distance by which two rods touching the skin must be separated before the (blindfolded) individual will report that there are two rods rather than one. Using this method, psychophysicists have found that our fingertips, lips, noses, and cheeks are much more sensitive than our shoulders, thighs, and calves. That is, the rods can be closer together and still be perceived as distinct when they touch the lips than when they touch the shoulders. Differential sensitivity occurs for at least two reasons: First, nerve endings are more densely packed in the fingertips and face than in other locations. Second, a greater amount of sensory cortex is devoted to the perception of sensations in the fingertips and face.

The sense of pressure, like the sense of touch, undergoes rapid adaptation. For example, you may have undertaken several minutes of strategic movements to wind up with your hand on the arm or leg of your date, only to discover that adaptation to this delightful source of pressure reduces the sensation you experience.

PSYCHOLOGY in the ▶ NEW MILLENNIUM

Sensation, Perception, and Virtual Reality

"Seeing is believing," or so goes the saying. But can we always believe what we see—or smell or hear or taste or feel? Not necessarily.

As we will see in Chapter 16, psychologists are now using computer-generated images to help people overcome phobias such as fear of heights. When they view the images, people perceive themselves as gradually rising to greater heights, even though they are actually remaining still. Because the images are computer generated rather than real, they are referred to as *virtual reality*. Children also use virtual reality—often in the form of virtual reality goggles or helmets—to feel that they are participating more fully in computer games.

CYBERSEX Consider what some futurists refer to as *cybersex* or *virtual sex*. You don headphones, 3-D glasses, and a light bodysuit with miniature detectors that follow your movements; as well as tiny stimulators for your skin. The detectors and stimulators are connected to computers that record your responses and create the impression of being touched by textures such as virtual satin, virtual wool, or virtual skin. The information superhighway allows you either to interact with another on-line person who is outfitted with similar gear or to be connected with a "canned" program.

What are some of the psychological implications of virtual sex? If we could electronically dress up as movie stars, would our sense of self and our dignity as individuals suffer? If we could at a moment's notice access a satisfying virtual sexual encounter with an appealing person (or program) who was concerned only with meeting our needs, would we become less sensitive to the needs of our real-life romantic partners? Would virtual sex provide additional outlets for people whose needs were not being fully met by others? Or would they become the preferred sexual outlets? If they did become preferred outlets, what would be the implications for the family? For children?

Would a virtual sex interaction be grounds for divorce? What will the new millennium bring? Your guess is as good as mine. ■

• Temperature

The receptors for temperature are neurons located just beneath the skin. When skin temperature increases, the receptors for warmth fire. Decreases in skin temperature cause the receptors for cold to fire. Muscle changes connected with changes in temperature may also play a role in the sensing of temperature (Schiffman, 1990).

Sensations of temperature are relative. When we are at normal body temperature, we might perceive another person's skin as warm. When we are feverish, though, the other person's skin might seem cool. We also adapt to differences in temperature. When we walk out of an air-conditioned house into the July sun, we feel intense heat at first. Then the sensations of heat tend to fade (although we may still be uncomfortable because of high humidity). Similarly, when we first enter a swimming pool, the water may seem cool or cold because it is below our body temperature. Yet after a few moments an 80-degree-Fahrenheit pool may seem quite warm. In fact, we may chide a newcomer for not jumping right in.

• Pain: The Often Unwanted Message

Headaches, backaches, toothaches—these are only a few of the types of pain that most of us encounter from time to time. Some of us also experience bouts of pain caused by arthritis, digestive disorders, cancer, or wounds.

Pain means that something is wrong in the body. It is adaptive in the sense that it motivates us to do something about it. For some of us, however, chronic pain—pain that lasts once injuries or illnesses have cleared—saps our vitality and interferes with the pleasures of everyday life (Karoly & Ruehlman, 1996).

Pain originates at the point of contact, as with a stubbed toe (see Figure 5.37). The pain message to the brain is initiated by the release of chemicals, including prostaglandins, bradykinin, and a chemical called *P* (yes, *P* stands for "pain"). Prostaglandins facilitate transmission of the pain message to the brain and heighten circulation to the injured area, causing the redness and swelling that we call inflammation. Inflammation attracts infection-fighting blood cells to the affected area to protect it against invading bacteria. **Analgesic** drugs such as aspirin and ibuprofen work by inhibiting the production of prostaglandins.

The pain message is relayed from the spinal cord to the thalamus and then projected to the cerebral cortex, making us aware of the location and intensity of the damage.

PHANTOM LIMB PAIN One of the more fascinating phenomena of psychology is the fact that many people experience pain in limbs that are no longer there (Sherman, 1997). About two out of three combat veterans with amputated limbs report feeling pain in missing, or "phantom," limbs (Kimble, 1992). In such cases, the pain occurs in the absence of (present) tissue damage, but the pain itself is real enough. It sometimes involves activation of nerves in the stump of the missing limb, but local anesthesia does not always eliminate the pain. Therefore, the pain must also reflect activation of neural circuits that have stored memories connected with the missing limb (Melzack, 1997).

GATE THEORY Simple remedies like rubbing and scratching an injured toe frequently help relieve pain. Why? One possible answer lies in the *gate theory* of pain originated by Melzack (1980). From this perspective, the nervous system can process only a limited amount of stimulation at a time. Rubbing or

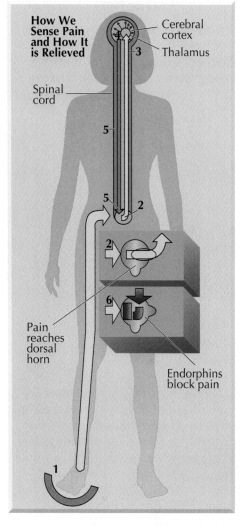

FIGURE 5.37
PERCEPTION OF PAIN
Pain originates at the point of contact, and the pain message to the brain is initiated by the release of prostaglandins, bradykinin, and substance *P.*

Truth or Fiction Revisited

It is true that many amputees experience pain in limbs that have been removed. The pain apparently reflects activation of neural circuits that have stored memories connected with the missing limbs.

ANALGESIC • Giving rise to a state of not feeling pain though fully conscious.

scratching the toe transmits sensations to the brain that, in a sense, compete for the attention of neurons. Many nerves are thus prevented from transmitting pain messages to the brain. The mechanism is analogous to shutting down a "gate" in the spinal cord. It is as a switchboard is being flooded with calls. The flooding prevents any of the calls from getting through.

ACUPUNCTURE Thousands of years ago, the Chinese began mapping the body to learn where pins might be placed to deaden pain elsewhere. The practice of acupuncture was largely unknown in the West, even though Western powers occupied much of China during the 1800s. But in the 1970s *New York Times* columnist James Reston underwent an appendectomy in China, and acupunc-

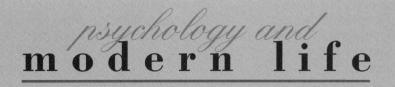

psychology and
modern life

COPING WITH PAIN

Coping with that age-old enemy—pain—has traditionally been a medical issue. The primary treatment has been chemical, as in the use of pain-killing drugs. However, psychology has dramatically expanded our arsenal of weapons for fighting pain (Flor and others, 1992; Ross & Berger, 1996).

ACCURATE INFORMATION One irony of pain management is that giving people accurate and thorough information about their condition often helps them manage pain (Jacox and others, 1994; Ross & Berger, 1996). Most people in pain try *not* to think about why things hurt during the early phases of an illness (Moyers, 1993). Physicians, too, often neglect the human aspects of relating to their patients. That is, they focus on diagnosing and treating the causes of pain, but they often fail to discuss with patients the meaning of the pain and what the patient can expect.

Yet when uncomfortable treatment methods are used, such as cardiac catheterization or chemotherapy for cancer, knowledge of the details of the treatment, including how long it will last and how much pain there will be, can help people cope with the pain (Ludwick-Rosenthal & Neufeld, 1993). Knowledge of medical procedures reduces stress by helping people maintain control over their situation. Some people, on the other hand, do not want information about painful medical procedures. Their attitude is "Do what you have to do and get it over with." It may be most helpful to match the amount of information provided with the amount desired (Ludwick-Rosenthal & Neufeld, 1993).

DISTRACTION AND FANTASY: THE NINTENDO APPROACH TO COPING WITH PAIN? Diverting attention from pain helps many people cope with it (Jensen & Karoly, 1991; Keefe and others, 1992). Psychologists frequently recommend that people use distraction or fantasy as ways of coping with pain.

For example, imagine that you've injured your leg and you're waiting to see the doctor in an emergency room. You can distract yourself by focusing on details of your environment. You can count ceiling tiles or the hairs on the back of a finger. You can describe (or criticize!) the clothes of medical personnel or passers-by. For children, playing video games diminishes the pain and discomfort of the side effects of chemotherapy (Kolko & Rickard-Figueroa, 1985; Redd and others, 1987). While the children are receiving injections of nausea-producing chemicals, they are embroiled in battles on the video screen. Other distraction methods that help children deal with pain include combing one's hair and blowing on a noisemaker (Adler, 1990).

HYPNOSIS In 1842 London physician W. S. Ward amputated a man's leg after using a rather strange anesthetic: hypnosis. According to reports, the man

ture was used as his primary anesthetic. He reported feeling no discomfort. More recently, TV journalist Bill Moyers (1993) reported on current usage of acupuncture in China. For example, one woman underwent brain surgery to remove a tumor after receiving anesthesia that consisted of a mild sedative, a small dose of narcotics, and six needles placed in her forehead, calves, and ankles. The surgery itself and the use of a guiding CAT scan were consistent with contemporary U.S. practices.

Some of the effects of acupuncture may be due to the release of endorphins (Richardson & Vincent, 1986). There is evidence to support this suggestion. The drug *naloxone* is known to block the painkilling effects of morphine. The analgesic effects of acupuncture are also blocked by naloxone (Kimble, 1992).

experienced no discomfort. Several years later, operations were being performed routinely under hypnosis at his infirmary. Today hypnosis is often used to reduce chronic pain (Flor and others, 1992; Patterson & Ptacek, 1997) and as an anesthetic in dentistry, childbirth, and even some forms of surgery.

In using hypnosis to manage pain, the hypnotist usually instructs the person that he or she feels nothing or that the pain is distant and slight. Hypnosis can also aid in the use of distraction and fantasy. For example, the hypnotist can instruct the person to imagine that he or she is relaxing on a warm, exotic shore.

RELAXATION TRAINING AND BIOFEED-BACK When we are in pain, we often tense up. Tensing muscles is uncomfortable in itself, arouses the sympathetic nervous system, and focuses our attention on the pain. Relaxation counteracts these self-defeating behavior patterns (Ross & Berger, 1996). Some

psychological methods of relaxation focus on relaxing muscle groups. Some involve breathing exercises. Others use relaxing imagery: The imagery distracts the person and deepens feelings of relaxation. Biofeedback is also used to help people relax targeted muscle groups. Relaxation training with biofeedback seems to be at least as effective as most medications for chronic pain in the lower back and jaw (Flor & Birbaumer, 1993).

COPING WITH IRRATIONAL BELIEFS Irrational beliefs can heighten pain (Ukestad & Wittrock, 1996). For example, telling oneself that the pain is unbearable and that it will never cease increases discomfort (Keefe and others, 1992). Some people seem to feel obligated to focus on things that distress them. They may be unwilling to allow themselves to be distracted from pain and discomfort. Thus, cognitive methods aimed at changing irrational beliefs hold some promise (Jensen and others, 1994).

OTHER METHODS Pain is a source of stress, and psychologists have uncovered many factors that seem to moderate the effects of stress. One is a sense of commitment. For example, if we are undergoing a painful medical procedure to diagnose or treat an illness, it might help if we recall that we *chose* to participate, rather than see ourselves as helpless victims. Thus, we are in control of the situation, and a sense of control enhances the ability to cope with pain (Jensen & Karoly, 1991).

Supportive social networks help as well. The benefits of having friends visit us—or visiting friends who are unwell—are as consistent with psychological findings as they are with folklore.

And don't forget gate theory. When you feel pain in a toe, squeeze all your toes. When you feel pain in your calf, rub your thighs. People around you may wonder what you're doing, but you're entitled to try to "flood the switchboard" so that some of the pain messages don't get through. ■

Kinesthesis. This young acrobat receives information about the position and movement of the parts of his body through the sense of kinesthesis. Information is fed to his brain from sensory organs in the joints, tendons, and muscles. This allows him to follow his own movements without looking at himself.

Truth or Fiction Revisited

It is true that we have a sense that keeps us upright. The sense — the vestibular sense — keeps us physically upright. It apparently takes more than the vestibular sense to keep us morally upright.

PLACEBO • A bogus treatment that controls for the effect of expectations.
KINESTHESIS • The sense that informs us about the positions and motion of parts of our bodies.
VESTIBULAR SENSE • The sense of equilibrium that informs us about our bodies' positions relative to gravity.
SEMICIRCULAR CANALS • Structures of the inner ear that monitor body movement and position.

Therefore, it may well be that the analgesic effects of acupuncture can be linked to the morphinelike endorphins.

THE PLACEBO EFFECT Interestingly, some scientists have also credited endorphins with the so-called **placebo** effect, in which the expectation of relief sometimes leads to relief from pain and other problems. They speculate that a positive attitude may lead to release of endorphins.

■ KINESTHESIS

Try a brief experiment. Close your eyes, then touch your nose with your finger. If you weren't right on target, I'm sure you came close. But how? You didn't see your hand moving, and you didn't hear your arm swishing through the air.

Kinesthesis is the sense that informs you about the position and motion of parts of the body. The term is derived from the ancient Greek words for "motion" *(kinesis)* and "perception" *(aisthesis)*. In kinesthesis, sensory information is fed back to the brain from sensory organs in the joints, tendons, and muscles. You were able to bring your finger to your nose by employing your kinesthetic sense. When you "make a muscle" in your arm, the sensations of tightness and hardness are also provided by kinesthesis.

Imagine going for a walk without kinesthesis. You would have to watch the forward motion of each leg to be certain that you had raised it high enough to clear the curb. And if you had tried our brief experiment without the kinesthetic sense, you would have had no sensory feedback until you felt the pressure of your finger against your nose (or cheek, or eye, or forehead), and you probably would have missed dozens of times.

Are you in the mood for another experiment? Close your eyes again. Then "make a muscle" in your right arm. Could you sense the muscle without looking at it or feeling it with your left hand? Of course you could. Kinesthesis also provides information about muscle contractions.

■ THE VESTIBULAR SENSE: ON BEING UPRIGHT

Your **vestibular sense** tells you whether you are upright (physically, not morally). Sensory organs located in the **semicircular canals** (Figure 5.33) and elsewhere in the ears monitor your body's motion and position in relation to gravity. They tell you whether you are falling and provide cues to whether your body is changing speed such as when you are in an accelerating airplane or automobile.

REFLECTIONS
• Has food ever seemed to lose its flavor when you had a cold or an allergy attack? Why?
• Why do older people often spice their food heavily?
• How can a drink that is 70 degrees Fahrenheit be either warming or cooling, depending on the weather?
• Has rubbing or scratching a painful area ever reduced the pain? How do you explain the experience?

In Review The Senses

SENSE	WHAT IS SENSED	RECEPTOR ORGANS	NATURE OF SENSORY RECEPTORS
Vision	Visible light (part of the spectrum of electromagnetic energy; different colors have different wavelengths)	The Eyes	Photoreceptors in the retinas (*rods,* which are sensitive to the intensity of light; and *cones,* which are sensitive to color)
Hearing	Changes in air pressure (or in another medium, such as water) that result from vibrations called *sound waves*	The Ears	"Hair cells" in the organ of Corti, which is attached to a membrane (the *basilar membrane*) within the inner ear (the *cochlea*)
Smell	Molecules of the substance	The Nose	Receptor neurons in the olfactory membrane high in each nostril
Taste	Molecules of the substance	The Tongue	Taste cells located on taste buds on the tongue
Touch, Pressure	Pushing or pulling of the body surface	The Skin	Nerve endings in the skin, some of which are located around the hair follicles
Kinesthesis	Muscle contractions	Sensory organs in joints, tendons, and muscles	Receptor cells in joints, tendons, and muscles
Vestibular Sense	Movement and position in relation to gravity	Sensory organs in the ears (e.g., in the *semicicular canals*)	Receptor cells in the ears

■ EXTRASENSORY PERCEPTION

Imagine the wealth you could amass if you had *precognition,* that is, if you were able to perceive future events in advance. Perhaps you would check next month's stock market reports and know what to buy or sell. Or you could bet with confidence on who would win the next Superbowl or World Series.

Or think of the power you would have if you were capable of *psychokinesis,* that is, of mentally manipulating or moving objects. You may have gotten a glimpse of the possibilities in films like *Carrie* and *The Fury.*

Precognition and psychokinesis are two concepts associated with *extrasensory perception* (ESP) or psi communication. ESP by definition refers to the perception of objects or events through means other than sensory organs. Psi communication refers to the transfer of information through an irregular or unusual process—not through the usual senses. Two other theoretical forms of ESP are *telepathy,* or direct transmission of thoughts or ideas from one person to another, and *clairvoyance,* or the perception of objects that do not stimulate the sensory organs. An example of clairvoyance is "seeing" what card will be dealt next, even though it is still in the deck and unseen even by the dealer.

Many psychologists do not believe that ESP is an appropriate area for scientific inquiry. Scientists study natural events, but ESP smacks of the supernatural,

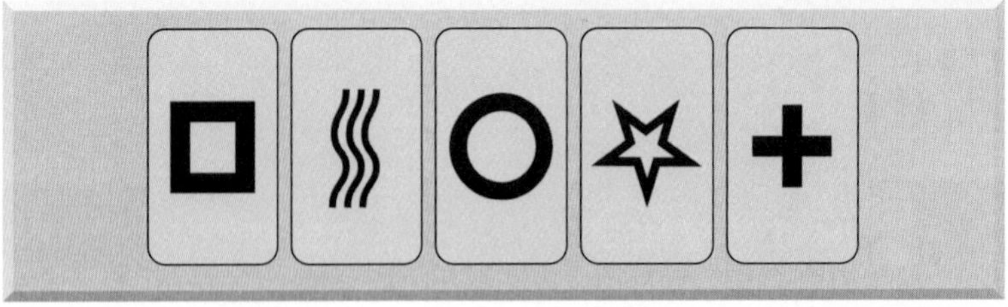

FIGURE 5.38
ZENER CARDS
Zener cards have been used in research on clair-voyance. Subjects are asked to predict which card will be turned up.

even the occult. ESP also has the flavor of a nightclub act in which a blind-folded "clairvoyant" calls out the contents of an audience member's pocket-book. Other psychologists, however, believe that there is nothing wrong with investigating ESP. The issue for them is not whether ESP is sensationalistic but whether its existence can be demonstrated in the laboratory.

Perhaps the best known of the respected ESP researchers was the late Joseph Banks Rhine of Duke University. Rhine studied ESP for several decades, beginning in the late 1920s. In a typical experiment in clairvoyance, Rhine would use a pack of 25 Zener cards, which contained 5 sets of the 5 cards shown in Figure 5.38. Pigeons pecking patterns at random to indicate which one was about to be turned up would select the correct one 20% of the time. Rhine found that some people guessed correctly significantly more often than the 20% chance rate. He concluded that these individuals may have had some degree of ESP.

A preferred contemporary method for studying telepathy is the Ganzfeld procedure. In this method, one subject acts as a "sender" and the other as a "receiver." The sender views randomly selected visual stimuli such as photographs of videotapes, while the receiver, who is in another room and whose eyes and ears are covered, tries to mentally tune in to the sender. After a session, the receiver is shown four visual stimuli and asked to select the one that was transmitted by the sender. A person guessing which stimulus was "transmitted" would be correct 25% of the time (one time in four) by chance alone. An analysis of 28 experiments using the Ganzfeld procedure, however, found that receivers correctly identified the visual stimulus 38% of the time (Honorton, 1985), a percentage highly unlikely to be due to chance. A series of 11 more studies by Honorton and his colleagues using the Ganzfeld procedure obtained comparable results (Bem & Honorton, 1994; Honorton and others, 1990).

Overall, however, there are many reasons for skepticism of ESP. One is the *file-drawer problem.* Just as buyers of supermarket magazines tend to forget "psychics'" predictions when they fail to come true (they "file" them away), ESP researchers are less likely to report research results that show failure (or to get them published!). Therefore, we would expect unusual findings (for example, a subject with a high success rate at psi-communication tasks over a period of several days) to appear in the research literature. In other words, if you flip a coin indefinitely, eventually you will flip 10 heads in a row. The odds against this are high, but if you report your eventual success and do not report the weeks of failure, you give the impression that you have unique coin-flipping ability. (You may even fool yourself.)

Then, too, it has not been easy to replicate experiments in ESP. Hyman (1994) acknowledges that the studies reported by Honorton (Bem & Honorton, 1994; Honorton and others, 1990) are the most tightly controlled studies conducted to date. However, he argues that the studies need to be replicated by other researchers before they are granted credibility. People who have "demonstrated" ESP with one researcher have failed to do so with another researcher or have refused to participate in other studies. Let's make this point a bit more strongly: From all of these studies, *not one person has emerged who can reliably show psi communication from one occasion to another and from one researcher to another.* Science, in other words, has not identified a single indisputable telepath or clairvoyant.

For these and other reasons, most psychologists still do not grant ESP research much credibility. For the time being, most psychologists prefer to study perception that involves sensation. After all, what is life without some sensation?

SUMMARY

1. **What are sensation and perception?** Sensation refers to mechanical processes that involve the stimulation of sensory receptors (neurons) and the transmission of sensory information to the central nervous system. Perception is not mechanical. It is the active organization of sensations into a representation of the outside world, and it reflects learning and expectations.

2. **What are absolute and difference thresholds?** The absolute threshold for a stimulus, such as light, is the lowest intensity at which it can be detected. The minimum difference in intensity that can be discriminated is the difference threshold. Difference thresholds are expressed in Weber's constants.

3. **What is signal-detection theory?** Signal-detection theory explains the ways in which stimulus characteristics and psychological factors—for example, motivation, familiarity with a stimulus, and attention—interact to influence whether a stimulus will be detected.

4. **What is light?** Light is one part of the spectrum of electromagnetic energy.

5. **How does the eye detect light and transmit it to the brain?** The eye senses and transmits visual stimulation to the occipital lobe of the cerebral cortex. After light passes through the cornea, the size of the pupil determines the amount that can pass through the lens. The lens focuses light as it projects onto the retina, which is composed of photoreceptors called *rods* and *cones.* Neurons in the visual cortex of the brain (feature detectors) fire in response to specific features of visual information, such as lines presented at particular angles and colors.

6. **What are rods and cones?** Cones are neurons in the retina that permit perception of color. Rods transmit sensations of light and dark only. Rods are more sensitive than cones to lowered lighting and continue to

adapt to darkness once cones have reached their peak adaptation.

7. **What are the psychological dimensions of color?** These are hue, brightness, and saturation. The wavelength of light determines its color, or hue. The saturation of a color is its purity.

8. **What are the theories of color vision?** There are two theories of color vision. According to the trichromatic theory, there are three types of cones—some sensitive to red, others to blue, and still others to green light. The opponent-process theory proposes three types of color receptors: red-green, blue-yellow, and light-dark. Both theories appear to have some validity.

9. **What is perceptual organization?** Perceptual organization involves recognizing patterns and processing information about relationships between parts and the whole. Gestalt rules of perceptual organization involve figure-ground relationships, proximity, similarity, continuity, common fate, and closure.

10. **How do we perceive movement?** We perceive movement when the light reflected by moving objects moves across the retina and also when objects shift in relation to one another. Distant objects appear to move more slowly than nearby objects, and objects in the middle ground may give the illusion of moving backward.

11. **How do we perceive depth?** Depth perception involves monocular and binocular cues. Monocular cues include perspective, clearness, interposition, shadows, texture gradient, motion parallax, and accommodation. Binocular cues include retinal disparity and convergence.

12. **What are the perceptual constancies?** Through experience we develop a number of perceptual constancies. For example, we learn to assume that objects retain their size, shape, brightness, and color despite

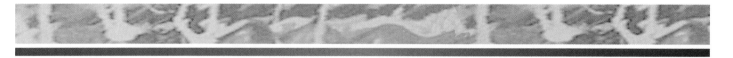

their distance from us, their position, or changes in lighting conditions.

13. **What is sound?** Sound is auditory stimulation, or sound waves. It requires a medium such as air or water to be transmitted. Sound waves alternately compress and expand molecules of the medium, creating vibrations.

14. **What is the range of sounds that can be sensed by the human ear?** The human ear can hear sounds varying in frequency from 20 to 20,000 cycles per second. The greater the frequency, the higher the sound's pitch.

15. **What is meant by the loudness of a sound?** The loudness of a sound corresponds to the amplitude of sound waves as measured in decibels (dB). We can experience hearing loss if we are exposed to protracted sounds of 85–90 dB or more. Noise is a combination of dissonant sounds.

16. **How do we hear sound?** The eardrum, vibrating in sympathy to sound waves, transmits auditory stimuli through the bones of the middle ear to the cochlea of the inner ear. The basilar membrane of the cochlea transmits those stimuli to the organ of Corti. From there, sound travels to the brain via the auditory nerve. Sounds seem louder when more neurons of the organ of Corti fire. Two competing theories account for the perception of pitch: place theory and frequency theory.

17. **How do we detect odors?** We detect odors through the olfactory membrane in each nostril. An odor is a sample of the substance being smelled.

18. **How do we detect tastes?** There are four primary taste qualities: sweet, sour, salty, and bitter. Flavor involves the odor, texture, and temperature of food, as well as its taste. Taste is sensed through taste cells, which are located in taste buds on the tongue.

19. **What are the skin senses?** The skin senses include touch, pressure, warmth, cold, and pain.

20. **How do we detect pain?** Pain originates at the point of contact and is transmitted to the brain by various chemicals, including prostaglandins, bradykinin, and *P*.

21. **What is kinesthesis?** Kinesthesis is the sensation of body position and movement. It relies on sensory organs in the joints, tendons, and muscles. The vestibular sense is housed primarily in the semicircular canals of the ears and tells us whether we are in an upright position.

22. **What is extrasensory perception (ESP)?** ESP, or psi communication, refers to the perception of objects or events through means other than sensory organs. Many psychologists do not believe that ESP is an appropriate area for scientific inquiry. Reliable evidence has not emerged for the existence of ESP.

To enhance your understanding of the psychological concepts found in this chapter, please consult the following aids:

STUDY GUIDE

Learning Objectives, p. 87

Exercises, p. 89

Lecture and Textbook Outline, p. 91

Effective Studying Ideas, p. 95

Key Terms and Concepts, p. 96

Chapter Review, p. 97

Chapter Exercises, p. 105

Knowing the Language, p. 106

Do You Know the Material?, p. 108

CORE CONCEPTS SEARCH

Detection

Discrimination

Receptive Fields

Light

The Eye

Theories of Perception

The Gestalt Approach to Form Perception

Context Effects in Form Perception

Motion Perception

The Perception of Causality

The Perception of Biological Motion

Monocular Depth Cues

Motion Depth Cues

Binocular Depth Cues

Perceptual Constancies in Vision

Lightness Constancy

Visual Illusions

Interpreting 2-D Figures as 3-D

Sound

The Ear

Localizing Sound

Place and Frequency Theory

World Wide Web

For more information concerning the topics found in this chapter, access psychology links on the World Wide Web made through the Harcourt Brace webpage at

www.hbcollege.com

Share your comments and questions with your author at

PsychLinks@aol.com

William James wrote that "The stream of thought flows on." Its contents emerge into consciousness and then submerge into the depths once more. Many of Theodore Waddell's Western landscapes contain elements that seem to flow in and out of consciousness. *Chinook Horses* (1991) suggests something about our consciousness of the United States. The open West, the industrial Midwest, the "Sunbelt," the communications centers on the coasts—how do they influence our awareness of who and where we are?

THEODORE WADDELL

Chapter 6

Consciousness

TRUTH OR FICTION?

✔ **T F**

☐ ☐ We act out our forbidden fantasies in our dreams.

☐ ☐ Many people have insomnia because they try too hard to fall asleep at night.

☐ ☐ It is dangerous to awaken a sleepwalker.

☐ ☐ Alcohol "goes to women's heads" more quickly than to men's.

☐ ☐ Heroin was once used as a cure for addiction to morphine.

☐ ☐ A stimulant is commonly used to treat children who are hyperactive.

☐ ☐ At one time Coca-Cola "added life" through a powerful but now illegal stimulant.

☐ ☐ The number of people who die from smoking-related causes is greater than the number lost to motor vehicle accidents, abuse of alcohol and all other drugs, suicide, homicide, and AIDS combined.

☐ ☐ Some people have managed to control high blood pressure through meditation.

☐ ☐ You can learn to change your heart rate just by thinking about it.

☐ ☐ People can be hypnotized against their will.

OUTLINE

JUST WHAT *IS* CONSCIOUSNESS?
SLEEP AND DREAMS
  The Stages of Sleep
  Functions of Sleep
  Dreams
  Psychology and Modern Life:
    Coping With Insomnia
  Sleep Disorders
ALTERING CONSCIOUSNESS THROUGH
  DRUGS
  Substance Abuse and Dependence
  Causal Factors in Substance Abuse and
    Dependence
DEPRESSANTS
  Alcohol
  Psychology in a World of Diversity:
    Alcoholism, Gender,
    and Ethnicity
  Questionnaire: Why Do You Drink?
  Opiates
  Barbiturates and Methaqualone
STIMULANTS
  Amphetamines
  Cocaine
  Cigarettes (Nicotine)
  Psychology and Modern Life:
    Quitting Smoking
  Psychology in the New Millennium:
    Will We Find That Nicotine Can Be
    (Gasp!) Good for You?
HALLUCINOGENICS
  Marijuana
  LSD and Other Hallucinogenics
MEDITATION
BIOFEEDBACK: GETTING IN TOUCH WITH
  THE UNTOUCHABLE
  Psychology and Modern Life:
    Trying Meditation
HYPNOSIS: ON BEING ENTRANCED
  Changes in Consciousness Brought
    About by Hypnosis
  Theories of Hypnosis

*W*HEN YOU TALK TO YOURSELF, WHO TALKS, and who listens?

This is the type of question posed by philosophers and scientists who study consciousness (Gorman, 1997). Although it might seem that psychologists, who study the brain and mental processes, are also well-equipped to look into consciousness, consciousness has not always been an acceptable topic in psychology (Crick & Koch, 1997). In 1904, for example, William James wrote an article with the intriguing title "Does Consciousness Exist?" James did not think that consciousness was a proper area of study for psychologists because no scientific method could directly observe or measure another person's consciousness.

John Watson, the "father of modern behaviorism," agreed. Watson insisted that only observable, measurable behavior is the province of psychology: "The time seems to have come when psychology must discard all references to consciousness" (1913, p. 163). In 1914 Watson was elected president of the American Psychological Association. This honor further cemented his ideas in the minds of many psychologists.

As we enter the new millennium, however, many psychologists believe that we cannot capture the richness of the human experience without referring to consciousness (Rychlak, 1997). Studies on consciousness have turned from a stream into a flood (Gorman, 1997). Psychologists, neuroscientists, philosophers, physicists, even computer scientists are searching for that elusive marvel. Most assume that consciousness dwells within the brain. And some, like Michael Gazzaniga (1997), even suggest that we look for consciousness in certain sites in the brain. It may be that knowledge about consciousness will blossom forth early in the new millennium. If it does not, perhaps psychologists will speak of the "consciousness craze" at turn of century, and the study of consciousness will again be removed from the, well, consciousness of psychology.

■ JUST WHAT *IS* CONSCIOUSNESS?

Consciousness is one of those mental concepts that cannot be directly seen or touched. Yet it is real enough to most people. Mental concepts such as consciousness acquire scientific status from being tied to behavior (Kimble, 1994). The concept of consciousness has several meanings.

CONSCIOUSNESS AS SENSORY AWARENESS One meaning of consciousness is **sensory awareness** of the environment. The sense of vision enables us to see, or be *conscious* of, the sun gleaming on the snow. The sense of hearing allows us to hear, or be conscious of, a concert.

SENSORY AWARENESS • Knowledge of the environment through perception of sensory stimulation—one definition of consciousness.

CONSCIOUSNESS AS THE SELECTIVE ASPECT OF ATTENTION Sometimes we are not aware of sensory stimulation. We may be unaware, or unconscious, of sensory stimulation when we do not pay attention to it. The world is abuzz with signals, yet you are conscious of, or focusing on, only the words on this page (I hope).

Focusing one's consciousness on a particular stimulus is referred to as **selective attention.** The concept of selective attention is important to self-control. To pay attention in class, you must screen out the pleasant aroma of the cologne or perfume wafting toward you from the person in the next seat. To keep your car on the road, you must pay more attention to driving conditions than to your hunger pangs or your feelings about an argument with a friend. If you are out in the woods at night, attending to rustling sounds in the brush nearby may be crucial to your survival.

Adaptation to our environment involves learning which stimuli must be attended to and which ones can be safely ignored. Selective attention markedly enhances our perceptual abilities (Basic Behavioral Science Task Force, 1996b). This is why we can pick out the speech of a single person across a room at a cocktail party, a phenomenon suitably termed the *cocktail party effect.*

Although we can decide where and when we will focus our attention, various kinds of stimuli also tend to capture attention. Among them are these:

- Sudden changes, as when a cool breeze enters a sweltering room or we receive a particularly high or low grade on an exam
- Novel stimuli, as when a dog enters the classroom or a person shows up with an unusual hairdo
- Intense stimuli, such as bright colors, loud noises, or sharp pain
- Repetitive stimuli, as when the same TV commercial is played a dozen times throughout the course of a football game

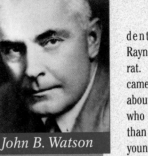
He was the son of a Southern farmer and beat up African Americans in his youth. He taught rats to find their way through a miniature maze that replicated the maze at King Henry VIII's retreat in the London suburbs. He had an affair with a student, which led the president of Johns Hopkins University to demand his resignation as chair of the Psychology Department. He helped make the "coffee break" a custom in the United States. John B. Watson (1878–1958) also popularized behaviorism and became president of the American Psychological Association in 1915.

Watson's aim was to show how most human behavior and emotional reactions—other than a few inborn reflexes—were the result of conditioning. Perhaps his most renowned experiment was with "Little Albert," who was conditioned by Watson and his student, Rosalie Rayner, to fear a rat. Watson became passionate about Rosalie, who was more than 20 years younger than he. He was fired when their affair was discovered and left the academic world for New York, where he worked as a psychologist for the J. Walter Thompson advertising agency. He grew wealthy through successful ad campaigns for products such as Camel cigarettes, Johnson & Johnson Baby Powder, and Maxwell House Coffee—in which he used the idea of the coffee break.

He married Rosalie and the couple had two sons. Rosalie died from dysentery in her thirties and Watson, 58, never married again. He let himself go, dressed carelessly, and put on much weight. A year before he died, the APA awarded him a gold medal for his contributions to psychology. ■

CONSCIOUSNESS AS DIRECT INNER AWARENESS Close your eyes and imagine spilling a can of bright red paint across a black tabletop. Watch it spread across the black, shiny surface and then spill onto the floor. Although this image may be vivid, you did not "see" it literally. Neither your eyes nor any other sensory organs were involved. You were *conscious* of the image through **direct inner awareness.**

We are conscious of—or have direct inner awareness of—thoughts, images, emotions, and memories. We may not be able to measure direct inner awareness scientifically. Nevertheless, many psychologists argue that "It is detectable to anyone that has it" (Miller, 1992, p. 180). These psychological processes are connected with the firings of myriads of neurons—events that we do *not* experience consciously. Yet we are somehow conscious of, or know of, the cognitive parallels of these neural events.

Sigmund Freud, the founder of psychoanalysis, differentiated between the thoughts and feelings that we are conscious, or aware, of and those that are preconscious and unconscious. **Preconscious** material is not currently in awareness but is readily available. For example, if you answer the following questions, you will summon up "preconscious"

SELECTIVE ATTENTION • The focus of one's consciousness on a particular stimulus.

DIRECT INNER AWARENESS • Knowledge of one's own thoughts, feelings, and memories without use of sensory organs—another definition of consciousness.

PRECONSCIOUS • In psychodynamic theory, descriptive of material that is not in awareness but can be brought into awareness by focusing one's attention. (The Latin root *prae-* means "before.")

information: What did you eat for dinner yesterday? About what time did you wake up this morning? What's your phone number? You can make these preconscious bits of information conscious by directing your inner awareness, or attention, to them.

According to Freud, still other mental events are **unconscious.** This means that they are unavailable to awareness under most circumstances. Freud believed that some painful memories and sexual and aggressive impulses are unacceptable to us, so we exclude them from our awareness. In other words, we **repress** them. Repressing these memories and impulses allows us to avoid feelings of anxiety, guilt, or shame.

People can also choose to stop thinking about unacceptable ideas or distractions. Consciously ejecting unwanted mental events from awareness is termed **suppression.** We may, for example, suppress thoughts of a date when we need to study for a test. We may also try to suppress thoughts of a test while we are on a date!

Some bodily processes, such as the firings of neurons, are **nonconscious.** They cannot be experienced through sensory awareness or direct inner awareness. The growing of hair and the carrying of oxygen in the blood are nonconscious. We can see that our hair has grown, but we have no sense receptors that give us sensations of growing. We can feel the need to breathe but do not directly experience the exchange of carbon dioxide and oxygen.

CONSCIOUSNESS AS PERSONAL UNITY: THE SENSE OF SELF As we develop, we differentiate ourselves from that which is not us. We develop a sense of being persons, individuals. There is a totality to our impressions, thoughts, and feelings that makes up our conscious existence—our continuing sense of **self** in a changing world. That self forms intentions and guides its own behavior (Rychlak, 1997). In this usage of the word, consciousness *is* self.

CONSCIOUSNESS AS THE WAKING STATE The word *conscious* also refers to the waking state as opposed, for example, to sleep. From this perspective, sleep, meditation, the hypnotic "trance," and the distorted perceptions that can often accompany the use of consciousness-altering drugs are considered **altered states of consciousness.**

In the remainder of this chapter, we explore various types of altered states of consciousness. They include sleep and dreams, the effects of drugs, meditation, biofeedback, and hypnosis.

UNCONSCIOUS • In psychodynamic theory, descriptive of ideas and feelings that are not available to awareness.
REPRESS • In psychodynamic theory, to eject anxiety-provoking ideas, impulses, or images from awareness, without knowing that one is doing so.
SUPPRESSION • The deliberate, or conscious, placing of certain ideas, impulses, or images out of awareness.
NONCONSCIOUS • Descriptive of bodily processes such as the growing of hair, of which we cannot become conscious. We may "recognize" that our hair is growing but cannot directly experience the biological process.
SELF • The totality of impressions, thoughts, and feelings. The sense of self is another definition of consciousness.
ALTERED STATES OF CONSCIOUSNESS • States other than the normal waking state, including sleep, meditation, the hypnotic trance, and the distorted perceptions produced by use of some drugs.
CIRCADIAN RHYTHM • (sir-KADE-ee-an). Referring to cycles that are connected with the 24-hour period of the earth's rotation. (A scientific term coined from the Latin roots *circa,* meaning "about," and *diem,* meaning "day.")

REFLECTIONS

- Are *you* conscious, or aware, of yourself and the world around you? How do you know whether you are?
- Do you think people have an "unconscious" mind? If so, what do you think happens within it?
- Can a person understand or study the consciousness of another person? Why or why not?

■ SLEEP AND DREAMS

Sleep has always been a fascinating topic. After all, we spend about one third of our adult lives asleep. Most of us complain when we do not sleep at least six hours or so. Some people sleep for an hour or two a night, however, and apparently lead otherwise normal lives (Kimble, 1992).

Our alternating periods of wakefulness and sleep provide an example of an internally generated **circadian rhythm.** A circadian rhythm is a cycle that is connected with the 24-hour period of the earth's rotation. A cycle of wakefulness and sleep is normally 24 hours long. However, when people are removed from cues that signal day or night, a cycle tends to become extended to about 25 hours (Kimble, 1992). Why? We do not know.

Why do we sleep? Why do we dream? Why do some of us have trouble getting to sleep, and what can we do about it? In this section we explore the stages and functions of sleep, dreams, and sleep disorders, including insomnia and sleep terrors.

• *The Stages of Sleep*

A major tool of sleep researchers is the **electroencephalograph,** or **EEG.** The EEG measures the electrical activity of the brain, or brain waves. Figure 6.1 shows EEG patterns that reflect the frequency and strength of brain waves that occur during the waking state, when we are relaxed, and when we are in the various stages of sleep.

Brain waves, like other waves, are cyclical. During the various stages of sleep, the brain emits waves with different frequencies and amplitudes. The printouts in Figure 6.1 show what happens during a period of 15 seconds or so. Brain waves that are high in frequency are associated with wakefulness. The amplitude of brain waves reflects their strength. The strength or energy of brain waves is expressed in volts (an electrical unit).

Figure 6.1 shows five stages of sleep: four stages of **non-rapid-eye-movement (NREM)** sleep, and one stage of **rapid-eye-movement (REM)** sleep. When we close our eyes and begin to relax before going to sleep, our brains emit many **alpha waves.** Alpha waves are low-amplitude brain waves of about 8 to 13 cycles per second.

As we enter stage 1 sleep, our brain waves slow down from the alpha rhythm and enter a pattern of **theta waves.** Theta waves, which have a frequency of about 6 to

ELECTROENCEPHALOGRAPH • An instrument that measures electrical activity of the brain. Abbreviated *EEG*.
NON-RAPID-EYE-MOVEMENT SLEEP • Stages of sleep 1 through 4. Abbreviated *NREM* sleep.
RAPID-EYE-MOVEMENT SLEEP • A stage of sleep characterized by rapid eye movements, which have been linked to dreaming. Abbreviated *REM* sleep.
ALPHA WAVES • Rapid, low-amplitude brain waves that have been linked to feelings of relaxation.
THETA WAVES • Slow brain waves produced during the hypnagogic state.

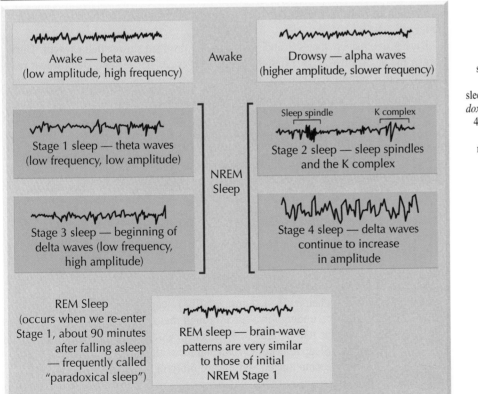

FIGURE 6.1
THE STAGES OF SLEEP

This figure illustrates typical EEG patterns for the stages of sleep. During REM sleep, EEG patterns resemble those of the lightest stage of sleep, stage 1 sleep. For this reason, REM sleep is often termed *paradoxical sleep.* As sleep progresses from stage 1 to stage 4, brain waves become slower and their amplitude increases. Dreams, including normal nightmares, are most vivid during REM sleep. More disturbing sleep terrors tend to occur during deep stage 4 sleep.

FIGURE 6.2

SLEEP CYCLES

This figure illustrates the alternation of REM and non-REM sleep for the typical sleeper. There are about five periods of REM sleep during an 8-hour night. Sleep is deeper earlier in the night, and REM sleep tends to become prolonged toward morning.

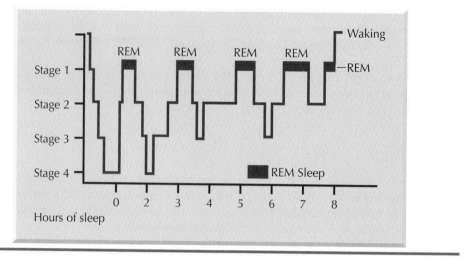

8 cycles per second, are accompanied by slow, rolling eye movements. The transition from alpha waves to theta waves may be accompanied by a **hypnagogic state** during which we may experience brief hallucinatory, dreamlike images that resemble vivid photographs (Winson, 1997). Stage 1 sleep is the lightest stage of sleep. If we are awakened from stage 1 sleep, we may feel that we have not slept at all.

After 30 to 40 minutes of stage 1 sleep, we undergo a rather steep descent into stages 2, 3, and 4 (see Figure 6.2). During stage 2, brain waves are medium in amplitude and have a frequency of about 4 to 7 cycles per second, but these are punctuated by **sleep spindles.** Sleep spindles have a frequency of 12 to 16 cycles per second and represent brief bursts of rapid brain activity. During stage 2, we also experience instances of the so-called **K complex.** This complex occurs in response to external stimuli such as the sound of a book dropped in the room, or to internal stimuli such as muscle tightness in the leg.

During deep sleep stages 3 and 4, our brains produce slower **delta waves.** During stage 3, the delta waves have a frequency of 1 to 3 cycles per second. Delta waves reach relatively great amplitude compared with other brain waves. Stage 4 is the deepest stage of sleep, and the one from which it is most difficult to be awakened. During stage 4 sleep, the delta waves slow to about 0.5 to 2 cycles per second, and their amplitude is greatest.

After perhaps half an hour of deep stage 4 sleep, we begin a relatively rapid journey back upward through the stages until we enter REM sleep (Figure 6.2). REM sleep derives its name from the *rapid eye movements,* observable beneath the closed eyelids, that characterize this stage. During REM sleep we produce relatively rapid, low-amplitude brain waves that resemble those of light stage 1 sleep. REM sleep is also called *paradoxical sleep.* This is because the EEG patterns observed during REM sleep suggest a level of arousal similar to that of the waking state (Figure 6.1). However, it is difficult to awaken a person during REM sleep. When people are awakened during REM sleep, as is the practice in sleep research, about 80% of the time they report that they have been dreaming. (We also dream during NREM sleep, but less frequently. People report dreaming only about 20% of the time when awakened during NREM sleep.)

Each night we tend to undergo five trips through the stages of sleep (see Figure 6.2). These trips include about five periods of REM sleep. Our first journey through stage 4 sleep is usually longest. Sleep tends to become lighter as the night wears on. Our periods of REM sleep tend to become longer, and toward morning our last period of REM sleep may last close to half an hour.

Now that we have some idea of what sleep is like, let us examine the question of *why* we sleep.

HYPNAGOGIC STATE • The drowsy interval between waking and sleeping, characterized by brief, hallucinatory, dreamlike experiences.

SLEEP SPINDLES • Short bursts of rapid brain waves that occur during stage 2 sleep.

K COMPLEX • Bursts of brain activity that occur during stage 2 sleep and reflect external stimulation.

DELTA WAVES • Strong, slow brain waves usually emitted during stage 4 sleep.

• *Functions of Sleep*

Strangely enough, researchers are not at all sure why we sleep (Kimble, 1992). One hypothesis is that sleep helps rejuvenate a tired body. Most of us have had the experience of going without sleep for a night and feeling "wrecked" or "punch drunk" the following day. Perhaps the next evening we went to bed early in order to "catch up on our sleep." What will happen to you if you do not sleep for one night? For several nights?

Compare people who are highly sleep-deprived with people who have been drinking heavily. Their abilities to concentrate and perform may be seriously impaired, but they may be the last ones to recognize their limitations (Adler, 1993b).

Most students can pull successful "all-nighters" (Webb, 1993). They can cram for a test through the night and then perform reasonably well the following day. When we are sleep-deprived for several nights, however, aspects of psychological functioning such as attention, learning, and memory deteriorate notably. Many people sleep late or nap on their days off (Webb, 1993). Perhaps they suffer from mild sleep deprivation during the week and "catch up" on the weekend.

The amount of sleep we need seems to be in part genetically determined (Webb, 1993). People also tend to need more sleep during periods of stress, such as a change of jobs, an increase in work load, or an episode of depression. Sleep seems to help us recover from stress.

DEPRIVATION OF REM SLEEP In some studies, animals or people have been deprived of REM sleep. Under these conditions they learn more slowly and forget what they have learned more rapidly (Adler, 1993b). Rats that are deprived of REM sleep for ten days begin to eat voraciously but die of starvation (Hobson, 1992). REM sleep appears to be essential for brain metabolism and regulation of body temperature (Hobson, 1992).

In people, REM sleep may foster the development of the brain before birth and in infancy (McCarley, 1992). REM sleep may also help maintain neurons in adults by "exercising" them at night (McCarley, 1992). Deprivation of REM sleep is accomplished by monitoring EEG records and eye movements and waking the person during REM sleep. There is too much individual variation to conclude that people who are deprived of REM sleep learn more poorly than they otherwise would. It does seem, though, that such deprivation interferes with memory—that is, retrieval of information that has been learned previously. In any event, people and lower animals that are deprived of REM sleep tend to show *REM-rebound*. They spend more time in REM sleep during subsequent sleep periods. In other words, they catch up.

It is during REM sleep that we tend to dream. Let us now turn our attention to dreams, a mystery about which philosophers, poets, and scientists have theorized for centuries.

• *Dreams*

Just what is the "stuff"[1] of dreams? What are they "made on"? Like memories and fantasies, dreams involve imagery in the absence of external stimulation. Some dreams are so realistic that we feel they must be real. You may have had such a dream the night before a test. You dreamed that you had taken the test and it was all over. (Ah, the disappointment when you woke up and realized that such was not the case!) Other dreams are disorganized and unformed.

Dreams are most vivid during REM sleep. That is when they are most likely to have clear imagery and coherent plots, even if some of the content is fantastic. Plots are

---

[1] The phrase "such stuff as dreams are made on" comes from Shakespeare's *The Tempest.*

Dream Images? In *Winter Night in Vitebsk,* Marc Chagall seems to depict images born in dreams.

vaguer and images more fleeting during NREM sleep. You may dream every time you are in REM sleep. Therefore, if you sleep for eight hours and undergo five sleep cycles, you may have five dreams. Upon waking, you may think that time seemed to expand or contract during your dream, so that during 10 or 15 minutes of actual time, the content of your dream ranged over days or weeks. But dreams actually tend to take place in "real time." Fifteen minutes of events fills about 15 minutes of dreaming. Your dream theater is quite flexible. You can dream in black and white or in full color.

THEORIES OF THE CONTENT OF DREAMS You may recall dreams involving fantastic adventures, but most dreams are simple extensions of the activities and problems of the day (Reiser, 1992). If we are preoccupied with illness or death, sexual or aggressive urges, or moral dilemmas, we are likely to dream about them. The characters in our dreams are more likely to be friends and neighbors than spies, monsters, and princes.

"A dream is a wish your heart makes," goes the song from the Disney film *Cinderella.* Freud theorized that dreams reflect unconscious wishes and urges. He argued that through dreams we can express impulses that we would censor during the day. Moreover, he said that the content of dreams is symbolic of unconscious fantasized objects such as genital organs (see Table 6.1). A key part of Freud's method of psychoanalysis involved interpretation of his clients' dreams. Freud also believed that dreams "protect sleep" by providing imagery that helps keep disturbing, repressed thoughts out of awareness.

The theory that dreams protect sleep has been challenged by the observation that disturbing events of the day tend to be followed by related disturbing dreams—not by protective imagery (Reiser, 1992). Our behavior in dreams is also generally consistent with our waking behavior. Most dreams, then, are unlikely candidates for the expression of repressed urges (even disguised). A person who leads a moral life tends to dream moral dreams.

According to the **activation-synthesis model,** dreams reflect primarily biological, not psychological, activity (Hobson, 1992). According to this view, an abundance of acetyl-

Truth or Fiction Revisited

It is not true that we act out our forbidden fantasies in our dreams. Most dreams are humdrum.

ACTIVATION-SYNTHESIS MODEL • The view that dreams reflect activation of cognitive activity by the reticular activating system and synthesis of this activity into a pattern by the cerebral cortex.

TABLE 6.1   DREAM SYMBOLS IN PSYCHODYNAMIC THEORY

Symbols for the Male Genital Organs

airplanes	fish	neckties	tools	weapons
bullets	hands	poles	trains	
feet	hoses	snakes	trees	
fire	knives	sticks	umbrellas	

Symbols for the Female Genital Organs

bottles	caves	doors	ovens	ships
boxes	chests	hats	pockets	tunnels
cases	closets	jars	pots	

Symbols for Sexual Intercourse

climbing a ladder	entering a room
climbing a staircase	flying in an airplane
crossing a bridge	riding a horse
driving an automobile	riding a roller coaster
riding an elevator	walking into a tunnel or down a hall

Symbols for the Breasts

apples	peaches

Note. Freud theorized that the content of dreams symbolizes urges, wishes, and objects of fantasy that we would censor if we were awake.

The Scream. The Norwegian artist Edvard Munch's well-known painting contains the kind of imagery that we might find in a nightmare.

choline in the brain and a time-triggered mechanism in the pons stimulate a number of responses that lead to dreaming. One is *activation* of the reticular activating system (RAS), which arouses us, but not to the point of waking. During the waking state, firing of these cells in the reticular formation is linked to movement, particularly the semiautomatic movements involved in walking, running, and other physical acts. During REM sleep, however, neurotransmitters generally inhibit motor (muscular) activity, so we don't thrash about as we dream (Blakeslee, 1992a). In this way, we save ourselves (and our bed partners) some wear and tear. The eye muscles are also stimulated, and they show the rapid eye movement associated with dreaming. In addition, the RAS stimulates neural activity in the parts of the cortex involved in vision, hearing, and memory. The cortex then automatically *synthesizes*, or puts together, these sources of stimulation to yield the substance of dreams.

The activation-synthesis model explains why there is a strong tendency to dream about events of the day: The most current neural activity of the cortex would be that which represented the events or concerns of the previous day.

NIGHTMARES   Have you ever dreamed that something heavy was sitting on your chest and watching you as you breathed? Or that you were trying to run away from a terrible threat but couldn't gain your footing or coordinate your leg muscles?

In the Middle Ages, such nightmares were thought to be the work of demons. It was believed that male and female demons could have sexual intercourse with people who were asleep, and that they were a form of retribution. That is, they were sent to make people pay for their sins.

Nightmares, like most pleasant dreams, are generally products of REM sleep. College students who keep dream logs report an average of two nightmares a month (Wood & Bootzin, 1990). Traumatic events can spawn nightmares, as reported in a study of survivors of the San Francisco earthquake of 1989 (Wood and others, 1992). People who suffer frequent nightmares are more likely than other people to also suffer from anxieties, depression, and other kinds of psychological discomfort (Berquier & Ashton, 1992).

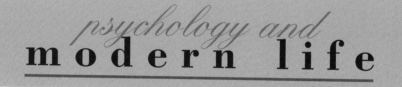

psychology and modern life

COPING WITH INSOMNIA

No question about it: The most common medical method for fighting insomnia in the United States is taking pills (Murtagh & Greenwood, 1995). Sleeping pills may be effective—for a while. They generally work by reducing arousal. At first, lowered arousal may be effective in itself. Focusing on changes in arousal may also distract you from trying to *get* to sleep. Expectations of success may also help.

But there are problems with sleeping pills. First, you attribute your success to the pill and not to yourself. You thus depend on the pill rather than become self-reliant. Second, you develop a tolerance for sleeping pills. With regular use, you come to need higher and higher doses to achieve the same effects. Third, high doses of these chemicals can be dangerous, especially if mixed with alcohol. Both sleeping pills and alcohol depress the activity of the central nervous system, and their effects are additive.

Similarly, people sometimes use tranquilizers and alcohol to help get to sleep. However, these chemical methods have problems similar to, and often more severe than, those posed by sleeping pills.

Psychological methods for coping with insomnia have also been developed. Some methods reduce tension directly, as in the case of muscle relaxation exercises. Psychological methods also divert us from the "task" of trying somehow to *get* to sleep, which, of course, is one of the ways in which we keep ourselves awake. Instead, we need only recline when we are tired and allow sleep to happen.

RELAX! Releasing muscle tension has been shown to reduce the amount of time needed to fall asleep and the incidence of waking up during the night. It increases the number of hours slept and leaves us feeling more rested in the morning (Murtagh & Greenwood, 1995). Biofeedback training (BFT) for insomnia usually focuses on reducing muscle tension in the forehead or in the arms. BFT has also been used to teach peo-

TABLE 6.2	BELIEFS THAT INCREASE TENSION AND ALTERNATIVES	
Beliefs That Increase Tension		**Alternatives**
If I don't get to sleep, I'll feel wrecked tomorrow.		Not necessarily. If I'm tired, I can go to bed early tomorrow night.
It's unhealthy for me not to get more sleep.		Not necessarily. Some people do very well on only a few hours of sleep.
I'll wreck my sleeping schedule for the whole week if I don't get to sleep very soon.		Not at all. If I'm tired, I'll just go to bed a bit earlier. I'll get up about the same time with no problem.
If I don't get to sleep, I won't be able to concentrate on that big test/conference tomorrow.		Possibly, but my fears may be exaggerated. I may just as well relax or get up and do something enjoyable for a while.

• *Sleep Disorders*

There are a number of sleep disorders. Some, like insomnia, are all too familiar. Others, like narcolepsy, seem somewhat exotic. In this section we will discuss insomnia, narcolepsy, apnea, and the deep-sleep disorders—sleep terrors, bed-wetting, and sleepwalking.

INSOMNIA **Insomnia** refers to three types of sleeping problems: difficulty falling asleep (sleep-onset insomnia), difficulty remaining asleep through the night, and early morning awakening. About one third of American adults are affected by insomnia in any given year. Women complain of insomnia more often than men do (Kupfer & Reynolds, 1997).

INSOMNIA • A term for three types of sleeping problems: (1) difficulty falling asleep, (2) difficulty remaining asleep, and (3) waking early. (From the Latin *in-*, meaning "not," and *somnus*, meaning "sleep.")

Insomnia. "You know I can't sleep at night" goes the song from the 1960s by the Mamas and the Papas. Why are women more likely than men to have insomnia? What can people do about insomnia?

ple to produce the kinds of brain waves that are associated with relaxation and sleep.

CHALLENGE EXAGGERATED FEARS You need not be a sleep expert to realize that convincing yourself that the day will be ruined unless you get to sleep *right now* may increase, rather than decrease, bedtime tension. Sleep seems to restore us, especially after physical exertion. However, we often exaggerate the problems that will befall us if we do not sleep (Morin and others, 1993). Table 6.2 shows some beliefs that increase bedtime tension and some alternatives.

DON'T RUMINATE IN BED Don't plan or worry about tomorrow while in bed (Kupfer & Reynolds, 1997). When you lie down for sleep, you may organize your thoughts for the day for a few minutes, but then allow yourself to relax or engage in fantasy. If an important idea comes to you, jot it down on a handy pad so that you won't lose it. If thoughts persist, however, get up and follow them elsewhere. Let your bed be a place for relaxation and sleep—not your second office. A bed—even a waterbed—is not a think tank.

ESTABLISH A REGULAR ROUTINE Sleeping late can encourage sleep-onset insomnia. Set your alarm for the same time each morning and get up, regardless of how many hours you have slept (Morin and oth-

ers, 1993). By rising at a regular time, you'll encourage yourself to go to sleep at a regular time as well.

TRY FANTASY Fantasies or daydreams are almost universal and may occur naturally as we fall asleep. You can allow yourself to "go with" fantasies that occur at bedtime, or purposefully use fantasies to get to sleep. You may be able to ease yourself to sleep by focusing on a sun-drenched beach with waves lapping on the shore or on a walk through a mountain meadow on a summer day. You can construct your own "mind trips" and paint in the details. With mind trips, you conserve fuel and avoid delays at airports. ■

FIGURE 6.3

NARCOLEPSY

In an experiment on narcolepsy, the dog barks, nods, then suddenly falls asleep.

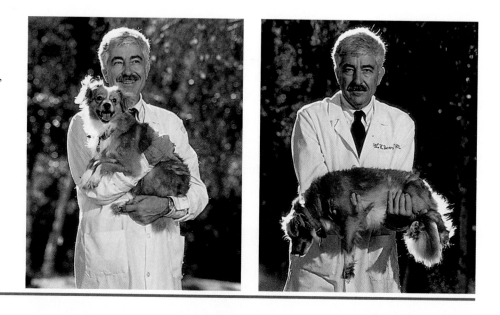

As a group, people who experience insomnia show greater restlessness and muscle tension than those who do not (Lacks & Morin, 1992). People with insomnia are also more likely to worry and report "racing thoughts" at bedtime (White & Nicassio, 1990). Insomnia comes and goes with many people, increasing during periods of stress (Kupfer & Reynolds, 1997) and the premenstrual phase of the menstrual cycle (Manber & Bootzin, 1997).

People with insomnia tend to compound their sleep problems when they try to force themselves to fall asleep (Bootzin and others, 1991). Their concern heightens autonomic activity and muscle tension. You cannot force or will yourself to go to sleep. You can only set the stage for sleep by lying down and relaxing when you are tired. If you focus on sleep too closely, it will elude you. Yet millions of people go to bed each night dreading the possibility of insomnia.

Truth or Fiction Revisited

It is true that many people have insomnia because they try too hard to fall asleep at night. Trying to go to sleep heightens tension and anxiety, both of which counter the feelings of relaxation that help induce sleep.

NARCOLEPSY   **Narcolepsy** is, in a sense, the mirror image of insomnia. A person with narcolepsy falls asleep suddenly and irresistibly. Narcolepsy afflicts as many as 100,000 people in the United States and seems to run in families. The "sleep attack" may last about 15 minutes, after which the person awakens feeling refreshed. Nevertheless, these sleep episodes are dangerous and frightening. They can occur while a person is driving or working with sharp tools. They also may be accompanied by the sudden collapse of muscle groups or even of the entire body (see Figure 6.3)—a condition called *sleep paralysis*. In sleep paralysis, the person cannot move during the transition from the waking state to sleep, and hallucinations (such as of a person or object sitting on the chest) occur.

Although the causes are unknown, narcolepsy is thought to be a disorder of REM-sleep functioning. Stimulants and antidepressant drugs have helped many people with narcolepsy.

APNEA   **Apnea** is a dangerous sleep disorder in which the air passages are obstructed. Those who have it stop breathing periodically, as many as 200 to 400 times through the night (Phillipson, 1993). When obstruction occurs, the sleeper may suddenly sit up, gasp to begin breathing again, then fall back asleep. People with apnea are stimulated nearly, but not quite, to waking by the buildup of carbon dioxide. Apnea afflicts about 4% of men and 2% of women and is strongly associated with obesity and habitual loud snoring

NARCOLEPSY • A sleep disorder characterized by uncontrollable seizures of sleep during the waking state. (From the Greek *narke*, meaning "sleep," and *lepsia*, meaning "an attack.")

APNEA • A temporary cessation of breathing while asleep. (From the Greek *a-*, meaning "without," and *pnoie*, meaning "wind.")

(Young and others, 1993). Apnea is more than just a sleeping problem. It can lead to heart attacks and strokes (Strollo & Rogers, 1996).

Causes of apnea include anatomical deformities that clog the air passageways, such as a thick palate, and problems in the breathing centers in the brain. Apnea is treated by such measures as weight loss, surgery, and *continuous positive airway pressure.* Airway pressure through the nose keeps the airway open during sleep (Strollo & Rogers, 1996).

DEEP-SLEEP DISORDERS: SLEEP TERRORS, BED-WETTING, AND SLEEPWALKING

Sleep terrors, bed-wetting, and sleepwalking all occur during deep (stage 3 or 4) sleep, are more common among children, and may reflect immaturity of the nervous system.

Sleep terrors are similar to, but more severe than, nightmares. They usually occur during deep sleep, whereas nightmares take place during REM sleep. Sleep terrors occur during the first couple of sleep cycles; nightmares are more likely to occur later on. Experiencing a surge in the heart and respiration rates, the dreamer may suddenly sit up, talk incoherently, and move about wildly. The dreamer is never fully awake, returns to sleep, and may recall a brief image such as of someone pressing on his or her chest. In contrast to nightmares, however, in sleep terrors memories of the episode are vivid. Sleep terrors are often decreased by taking a minor tranquilizer at bedtime. The drug reduces the amount of time spent in stage 4 sleep.

Bed-wetting is often seen as a stigma that reflects parental harshness or the child's attempt to punish the parents, but this disorder, too, may stem from immaturity of the nervous system. In most cases it resolves itself before adolescence, often by age eight. Behavior therapy methods that condition children to awaken when they are about to urinate have been helpful. The drug imipramine often helps by increasing bladder capacity. Sometimes all that is needed is reassurance that no one is to blame for bed-wetting and that most children will "outgrow" it.

Perhaps half of all children occasionally talk in their sleep. Nearly 15% walk in their sleep (Mindell, 1993). Sleepwalkers may roam about almost nightly while their parents fret about the accidents that could befall them. Sleepwalkers typically do not remember their excursions, although they may respond to questions while they are up and about. Contrary to myth, there is no evidence that sleepwalkers become violent or highly disturbed if they are awakened. Mild tranquilizers and maturity typically put an end to sleepwalking.

Truth or Fiction Revisited

It is not true that it is dangerous to awaken a sleepwalker. Sleepwalkers may be confused and startled when awakened, but they are not usually violent.

REFLECTIONS
- How much sleep do you need? (How do you know?) Did you ever "pull an all-nighter"? What were the effects?
- What do you dream about? Is the content of your dreams consistent with any of the theories of dreams discussed in the chapter?

■ ALTERING CONSCIOUSNESS THROUGH DRUGS

The world is a supermarket of **psychoactive substances,** or drugs. The United States is flooded with drugs that distort perceptions and change mood—drugs that take you up, let you down, and move you across town. Some people use drugs because their friends do or because their parents tell them not to. Some are seeking pleasure; others are seeking inner truth.

SLEEP TERRORS • Frightening dreamlike experiences that occur during the deepest stage of NREM sleep. Nightmares, in contrast, occur during REM sleep.
PSYCHOACTIVE SUBSTANCES • Drugs that have psychological effects such as stimulation or distortion of perceptions.

TABLE 6.3   TRENDS IN DRUG USE AMONG COLLEGE STUDENTS DURING LIFETIME AND DURING LAST 30 DAYS (IN PERCENTS)

DRUG	USED . . .	1980	1982	1984	1986	1988	1990	1992	1994
Marijuana	Ever?	65.0	60.5	59.0	57.9	51.3	49.1	44.1	42.2
	Last 30 days?	34.0	26.8	23.0	22.3	16.3	14.0	14.6	15.1
Inhalants	Ever?	10.2	10.6	10.4	11.0	12.6	13.9	14.2	12.0
	Last 30 days?	1.5	0.8	0.7	1.1	1.3	1.0	1.1	0.6
Hallucinogens (includes LSD)	Ever?	15.0	15.0	12.9	11.2	10.2	11.2	12.0	10.0
	Last 30 days?	2.7	2.6	1.8	2.2	1.7	1.4	2.3	2.1
Cocaine (includes Crack)	Ever?	22.0	22.4	21.7	23.3	15.8	11.4	7.9	5.0
	Last 30 days?	6.9	7.9	7.6	7.0	4.2	1.2	1.0	0.6
MDMA	Ever?	NA	NA	NA	NA	NA	3.9	2.9	2.1
	Last 30 days?	NA	NA	NA	NA	NA	0.6	0.4	0.2
Heroin	Ever?	0.9	0.5	0.5	0.4	0.3	0.3	0.5	0.1
	Last 30 days?	0.3	0.0	0.0	0.0	0.1	0.0	0.0	0.0
Stimulants (other than Cocaine)	Ever?	NA	30.1	27.8	22.3	17.7	13.2	10.5	9.2
	Last 30 days?	NA	9.9	5.5	3.7	1.8	1.4	1.1	1.5
Barbiturates	Ever?	8.1	8.2	6.4	5.4	3.6	3.8	3.8	3.2
	Last 30 days?	0.9	1.0	0.7	0.6	0.5	0.2	0.7	0.4
Alcohol	Ever?	94.3	95.2	94.2	94.9	94.9	93.1	91.8	88.1
	Last 30 days?	81.8	82.8	79.1	79.7	77.0	74.5	71.4	67.5
Cigarettes	Ever?	NA	NA	NA	NA	NA	NA	NA	NA
	Last 30 days?	25.8	24.4	21.5	22.4	22.6	21.5	23.5	23.5

Note. From Johnston, L. D., O'Malley, P. M., & Bachman, J. G. (1996). National Survey Results on Drug Use From The Monitoring the Future Study, 1975–1994. Volume II. College Students and Young Adults. U.S. Department of Health and Human Services, Public Health Service, National Institutes of Health: National Institute on Drug Abuse. Tables 23 (p. 160) and 25 (p. 162).

Young people often become involved with drugs that impair their ability to learn at school and are connected with reckless behavior (Basen-Engquist and others, 1996). Alcohol is the most popular drug on high school and college campuses (Johnston and others, 1996). More than 40% of college students have tried marijuana, and one in six or seven smokes it regularly (see Table 6.3). Many Americans take **depressants** to get to sleep at night and **stimulants** to get going in the morning. Karl Marx charged that "religion . . . is the opium of the people," but heroin is the real "opium of the people." Cocaine was, until recently, a toy of the well-to-do, but price breaks have brought it into the lockers of high school students. For better or worse, drugs remain a part of American life.

• *Substance Abuse and Dependence*

Where does drug use end and abuse begin? The American Psychiatric Association (1994) defines **substance abuse** as repeated use of a substance despite the fact that it is causing or compounding social, occupational, psychological, or physical problems. If you are missing school or work because you are drunk or "sleeping it off," you are abusing alcohol. The amount you drink is not as crucial as the fact that your pattern of use disrupts your life.

Dependence is more severe than abuse. Dependence has both behavioral and biological aspects (American Psychiatric Association, 1994). Behaviorally, dependence is often

DEPRESSANT • A drug that lowers the rate of activity of the nervous system. (From the Latin *de-*, meaning "down," and *premere*, meaning "to press.")

STIMULANT • A drug that increases activity of the nervous system.

SUBSTANCE ABUSE • Persistent use of a substance even though it is causing or compounding problems in meeting the demands of life.

characterized by loss of control over one's use of the substance. Dependent people may organize their lives around getting and using a substance. Biological or physiological dependence is typified by tolerance, withdrawal symptoms, or both.[2] **Tolerance** is the body's habituation to a substance, so that with regular usage, higher doses are required to achieve similar effects. There are characteristic withdrawal symptoms, or an **abstinence syndrome,** when the level of usage suddenly drops off. The abstinence syndrome for alcohol includes anxiety, tremors, restlessness, weakness, rapid pulse, and high blood pressure.

When doing without a drug, people who are *psychologically* dependent show signs of anxiety (such as shakiness, rapid pulse, and sweating) that may be similar to abstinence syndromes. Because of these signs, they may believe that they are physiologically dependent on a drug when they are actually psychologically dependent. But symptoms of abstinence from some drugs are unmistakably physiological. One is **delirium tremens** ("the DTs"), encountered by some chronic alcoholics when they suddenly lower their intake of alcohol. The DTs are characterized by heavy sweating, restlessness, general disorientation, and terrifying **hallucinations**—often of crawling animals.

• *Causal Factors in Substance Abuse and Dependence*

Substance abuse and dependence usually begin with experimental use (Kessler, 1995; Petraitis and others, 1995). Why do people experiment with drugs? Reasons include curiosity, conformity to peer pressure, parental use, rebelliousness, and escape from boredom or pressure (Chassin and others, 1996; Curran and others, 1997; Swaim and others, 1996). Another reason is self-handicapping. By using alcohol or another drug when faced with a problem, we can blame failure on the alcohol, not on ourselves. Alcohol and other drugs are used as excuses for behaviors such as aggression, sexual forwardness, and forgetfulness.

There are also psychological and biological theories of substance abuse.

PSYCHOLOGICAL VIEWS Psychodynamic explanations of substance abuse propose that drugs help people control or express unconscious needs and impulses. Alcoholism, for example, may reflect the need to remain dependent on an overprotective mother.

Social-cognitive theorists suggest that people commonly try tranquilizing agents such as Valium and alcohol on the basis of a recommendation or observation of others. Cognitive psychologists note that expectancies about the effects of a substance are powerful predictors of its use (Schafer & Brown, 1991; Sher and others, 1996). Use may be reinforced by the drug's positive effects on mood and its reduction of unpleasant sensations such as anxiety, fear, and tension. For people who are physiologically dependent, avoidance of withdrawal symptoms is also reinforcing. Carrying a supply of the substance is reinforcing because one need not worry about doing without it. Some people, for example, will not leave home without taking along some Valium.

Parents who use drugs may increase their children's knowledge of drugs. They also, in effect, show their children when to use them—for example, when they are seeking to reduce tension or to "lubricate" social interactions (Stacy and others, 1991).

BIOLOGICAL VIEWS Certain people may have a genetic predisposition toward physiological dependence on various substances, including alcohol, cocaine, and nicotine (Azar, 1995a, Haney and others, 1994; Pomerleau and others, 1993). For example, the biological children of alcoholics who are reared by adoptive parents seem more likely to

---

[2] The lay term *addiction* is usually used to mean physiological dependence, but here, too, there may be inconsistency. After all, some people speak of being "addicted" to work or to love.

TOLERANCE • Habituation to a drug, with the result that increasingly higher doses of the drug are needed to achieve similar effects.
ABSTINENCE SYNDROME • A characteristic cluster of symptoms that results from sudden decrease in an addictive drug's level of usage. (From the Latin *abstinere,* meaning "to hold back.")
DELIRIUM TREMENS • A condition characterized by sweating, restlessness, disorientation, and hallucinations. The "DTs" occurs in some chronic alcohol users when there is a sudden decrease in usage. (From the Latin *de-,* meaning "from," and *lira,* meaning "line" or "furrow"—suggesting that one's behavior is off the beaten track or norm.)
HALLUCINATIONS • Perceptions in the absence of sensation. (From the Latin *hallucinari,* meaning "to wander mentally.")

Why Does Alcohol Affect Women More Quickly Than Men? Alcohol "goes to women's heads" more quickly, even when we control for body weight.

develop alcohol-related problems than the natural children of the adoptive parents. An inherited tendency toward alcoholism may involve greater sensitivity to alcohol (that is, greater enjoyment of it) and greater tolerance of it (Finn and others, 1997; Newlin & Thomson, 1990). College students with alcoholic parents exhibit better muscular control and visual-motor coordination when they drink than do college students whose parents are not alcoholics. They also feel less intoxicated than their peers when they drink (Pihl and others, 1990).

Let us now consider the effects of frequently used depressants, stimulants, and hallucinogenics on consciousness.

■ DEPRESSANTS

Depressant drugs generally act by slowing the activity of the central nervous system. There are also effects that are specific to each depressant drug. In this section we consider the effects of alcohol, opiates, barbiturates, and methaqualone.

• *Alcohol*

No drug has meant so much to so many as alcohol. Alcohol is our dinnertime relaxant, our bedtime sedative, our cocktail party social facilitator. We use alcohol to celebrate holy days, applaud our accomplishments, and express joyous wishes. The young assert their maturity with alcohol. It is used at least occasionally by eight to nine of every ten high school students (Johnston and others, 1996). Older people use alcohol to stimulate circulation in peripheral areas of the body. Alcohol even kills germs on surface wounds.

Alcohol is the tranquilizer you can buy without prescription. It is the relief from anxiety you can swallow in public without criticism or stigma. A man who takes a Valium tablet may look weak. A man who downs a bottle of beer may be perceived as "macho."

No drug has been so abused as alcohol. Ten million to 20 million Americans are alcoholics. In contrast, 750,000 to 1 million use heroin regularly and about 800,000 use cocaine regularly (O'Brien, 1996). Excessive drinking has been linked to lower productivity, loss of employment, and downward movement in social status. Yet half of all Americans use alcohol. Despite widespread marijuana use, alcohol is the drug of choice among adolescents.

Psychology in a World of
DIVERSITY

Alcoholism, Gender, and Ethnicity

Truth or Fiction Revisited

It is true that alcohol goes to women's heads more quickly than to men's. Women are less likely to metabolize alcohol before it affects psychological functioning.

Men are more likely than women to become alcoholics. A cultural explanation is that tighter social constraints are usually placed on women. A biological explanation is that alcohol hits women harder. If, for example, you have the impression that alcohol "goes to women's heads" more quickly than to men's, you are probably correct. Women seem to be more affected by alcohol because they metabolize very little of it in the stomach. Thus, alcohol reaches women's bloodstream and brain relatively intact. (Women have less of an enzyme that metabolizes alcohol in the stomach than men do [Lieber, 1990].) Women metabolize alcohol mainly in the liver. According to one health professional, for women "drinking alcohol has the same effect as injecting it intravenously" (Lieber, 1990). Strong stuff indeed.

Ethnicity is connected with alcohol abuse. Native Americans and Irish Americans have the highest rates of alcoholism in the United States (Nevid and others, 1997).

Jewish Americans have relatively low rates of alcoholism, a fact for which a cultural explanation is usually offered. Jewish Americans tend to expose children to alcohol (wine) early in life, but they do so within a strong family or religious context. Wine is offered in small quantities, with consequent low blood alcohol levels. Alcohol therefore is not connected with rebellion, aggression, or failure in Jewish culture.

There are also biological explanations for low levels of drinking among some ethnic groups, such as Asian Americans. Asians are more likely than White people to show a "flushing response" to alcohol, as evidenced by rapid heart rate, dizziness, and headaches (Ellickson and others, 1992). Such sensitivity to alcohol may inhibit immoderate drinking among Asian Americans as it may among women.

EFFECTS OF ALCOHOL The effects of alcohol vary with the dose and the duration of use. Low doses of alcohol may be stimulating. Higher doses of alcohol have a sedative effect, which is why alcohol is classified as a depressant. Alcohol relaxes people and deadens minor aches and pains. Alcohol also intoxicates: It impairs cognitive functioning, slurs the speech, and reduces motor coordination. Alcohol is involved in about half of the fatal automobile accidents in the United States.

Alcohol consumption is connected with a drop-off in sexual activity (Leigh, 1993). Yet some drinkers may do things that they would not do if they were sober, such as engage in sexual activity on the first date, or engage in "unprotected" sex (Cooper & Orcutt, 1997; Gordon & Carey, 1996; Leigh & Stall, 1993). Why? Perhaps alcohol impairs the thought processes needed to inhibit impulses (Steele & Josephs, 1990). When drunk, people may be less able to foresee the consequences of their behavior. They may also be less likely to summon up their moral beliefs. Then too, alcohol induces feelings of elation and euphoria that may wash away doubts. Alcohol is also associated with a liberated social role in our culture. Drinkers may place the blame on alcohol ("It's the alcohol, not me"), even though they choose to drink.

As a food, alcohol is fattening. Even so, chronic drinkers may be malnourished. Though it is high in calories, alcohol does not contain nutrients such as vitamins and proteins. Moreover, it can interfere with the body's absorption of vitamins, particularly thiamine, a B vitamin. Thus, chronic drinking can lead to a number of disorders such as **cirrhosis of the liver,** which has been linked to protein deficiency, and **Wernicke-Korsakoff syndrome,** which has been linked to vitamin B deficiency.

Light to moderate drinking may increase levels of high-density lipoprotein (HDL, or "good" cholesterol) and decrease the risk of cardiovascular disorders (Fuchs and others, 1995; Gaziano and others, 1993). However, chronic heavy drinking has been linked to cardiovascular disorders and cancer. In particular, heavy drinking places women at risk for breast cancer (McTiernan, 1997). Drinking by a pregnant woman may harm the embryo.

Adolescent involvement with alcohol has repeatedly been linked to poor school grades and other stressors (Wills and others, 1996). Drinking can, of course, contribute to poor grades and other problems, but people may drink to reduce academic and other stresses.

Regardless of how or why one starts drinking, regular drinking can lead to physiological dependence. Physiological dependence motivates people to drink in order to avoid withdrawal symptoms. Still, even when alcoholics have "dried out"—withdrawn from alcohol—many return to drinking (Schuckit, 1996). Perhaps they still want to use alcohol as a way of coping with stress or as an excuse for failure.

TREATING ALCOHOLISM Alcoholics Anonymous (AA) is the most widely used program to treat alcoholism, yet research suggests that other approaches work as well for most people (Ouimette and others, 1997; "Tailoring treatments," 1997). The National

CIRRHOSIS OF THE LIVER • A disease caused by protein deficiency in which connective fibers replace active liver cells, impeding circulation of the blood. Alcohol does not contain protein; therefore, persons who drink excessively may be prone to this disease. (From the Greek *kirrhos,* meaning "tawny," referring to the yellow-orange color of the diseased liver.)

WERNICKE-KORSAKOFF SYNDROME • A cluster of symptoms associated with chronic alcohol abuse and characterized by confusion, memory impairment, and filling in gaps in memory with false information (confabulation).

WHY DO YOU DRINK?

Do you drink? If so, why? To enhance your pleasure? To cope with your problems? To help you in your social encounters? Half of all Americans use alcohol for a variety of reasons. Perhaps as many as 1 user in 10 is an alcoholic.

To gain insight into your reasons for using alcohol, respond to the following items by circling the *T* if an item is true or mostly true for you, or the *F* if an item is false or mostly false for you. Then turn to the answer key in Appendix B. ■

T F 1. I find it very unpleasant to do without alcohol for some time.

T F 2. Alcohol makes it easier for me to talk to other people.

T F 3. I drink to appear more grown-up and more sophisticated.

T F 4. When I drink, the future looks brighter to me.

T F 5. I like the taste of what I drink.

T F 6. If I go without a drink for some time, I am not bothered or uncomfortable.

T F 7. I feel more relaxed and less tense about things when I drink.

T F 8. I drink so that I will fit in better with the crowd.

T F 9. I worry less about things when I drink.

T F 10. I have a drink when I get together with the family.

T F 11. I have a drink as part of my religious ceremonies.

T F 12. I have a drink when a toothache or some other pain is disturbing me.

T F 13. I feel much more powerful when I have a drink.

T F 14. You really can't blame me for the things I do when I have been drinking.

T F 15. I have a drink before a big test, date, or interview when I'm afraid of how well I'll do.

T F 16. I find I have a drink for the taste alone.

T F 17. I've found a drink in my hand when I can't remember putting it there.

T F 18. I'll have a drink when I feel "blue" or want to take my mind off my cares and worries.

T F 19. I can do better socially and sexually after having a drink or two.

T F 20. Drinking makes me do stupid things.

T F 21. Sometimes when I have a few drinks, I can't get to work.

T F 22. I feel more caring and giving after having a drink or two.

T F 23. I drink because I like the look of a drinker.

T F 24. I like to drink more on festive occasions.

T F 25. When a friend or I have done something well, we're likely to have a drink or two.

T F 26. I have a drink when some problem is nagging away at me.

T F 27. I find drinking pleasurable.

T F 28. I like the "high" of drinking.

T F 29. Sometimes I pour a drink without realizing I still have one that is unfinished.

T F 30. I feel I can better get others to do what I want when I've had a drink or two.

T F 31. Having a drink keeps my mind off my problems at home, at school, or at work.

T F 32. I get a real gnawing hunger for a drink when I haven't had one for a while.

T F 33. A drink or two relaxes me.

T F 34. Things look better when I've had a drink or two.

T F 35. My mood is much better after I've been drinking.

T F 36. I see things more clearly when I've been drinking.

T F 37. A drink or two enhances the pleasure of sex and food.

T F 38. When I'm out of alcohol, I immediately buy more.

T F 39. I would have done much better on some things if it weren't for alcohol.

T F 40. When I have run out of alcohol, I find it almost unbearable until I can get some more.

Institute on Alcohol Abuse and Alcoholism funded an eight-year study in which more than 1,700 problem drinkers were randomly assigned to AA's 12-step program, cognitive-behavioral therapy, or "motivational-enhancement therapy." The cognitive-behavioral treatment taught problem drinkers how to cope with temptations and how to refuse offers of drinks. Motivational enhancement was designed to enhance drinkers' desires to help themselves. The treatments worked equally well for most people with some exceptions. For example, people with psychological problems fared somewhat better with cognitive-behavioral therapy.

Research is also under way on the use of medicines in treating problem drinking. Disulfiram, for example, cannot be mixed with alcohol. People who take disulfiram experience symptoms such as nausea and vomiting if they drink (Schuckit, 1996). Many problem drinkers have lower-than-normal levels of serotonin. Medicines that boost serotonin levels therefore may be helpful for problem drinkers (Azar, 1997b).

The nearby questionnaire may offer some insight into your own reasons for drinking—if you do.

• *Opiates*

Opiates are a group of **narcotics** that are derived from the opium poppy, from which they obtain their name. **Opioids** are similar in chemical structure but are synthesized in a laboratory. The ancient Sumerians gave the opium poppy its name: It means "plant of joy." Opiates include morphine, heroin, codeine, Demerol, and similar drugs whose major medical application is relief from pain.

Morphine was introduced in the United States at about the time of the Civil War and in Europe during the Franco-Prussian War. It was used liberally to deaden pain from wounds. Physiological dependence on morphine therefore became known as the "soldier's disease." There was little stigma attached to dependence before morphine became a legally restricted substance.

Heroin was so named because it made people feel "heroic." It was hailed as the "hero" that would cure physiological dependence on morphine.

Heroin can provide a powerful euphoric "rush." Users of heroin claim that it is so pleasurable it can eradicate any thought of food or sex. Although regular users develop tolerance for heroin, high doses can cause drowsiness, stupor, altered time perception, and impaired judgment.

Heroin is illegal. Because the penalties for possession or sale are high, it is also expensive. For this reason, many physiologically dependent people support their habit through dealing (selling heroin), prostitution, or selling stolen goods.

Methadone is a synthetic opioid. It has been used to treat physiological dependence on heroin in the same way that heroin was once used to treat physiological dependence on morphine. Methadone is slower acting than heroin and does not provide the thrilling rush. Some people must be maintained on methadone for many years before they can be gradually withdrawn from it (O'Brien, 1996). Some must be maintained on methadone indefinitely (Wren, 1997).

Narcotics can have distressing withdrawal syndromes, especially when used in high doses. Such syndromes may begin with flu-like symptoms and progress through tremors, cramps, chills alternating with sweating, rapid pulse, high blood pressure, insomnia, vomiting, and diarrhea. However, these syndromes are variable from one person to another.

Many people who obtain prescriptions for opiates for pain relief neither experience a euphoric rush nor become psychologically dependent on them (Lang & Patt, 1994; Taub, 1993). If they no longer need opiates but have become physiologically dependent on them, they can usually quit with few, if any, side effects by gradually decreasing their dosage (Rosenthal, 1993a).

Truth or Fiction Revisited

It is true that heroin was once used as a cure for addiction to morphine. Today an opioid, methadone, is used to help addicts avert the symptoms caused by withdrawal from heroin.

OPIATES • A group of narcotics derived from the opium poppy that provide a euphoric rush and depress the nervous system.
NARCOTICS • Drugs used to relieve pain and induce sleep. The term is usually reserved for opiates.
OPIOIDS • Chemicals that act on opiate receptors but are not derived from the opium poppy.
MORPHINE • An opioid introduced at about the time of the U.S. Civil War.
HEROIN • An opioid. Heroin, ironically, was used as a "cure" for morphine addiction when first introduced.
METHADONE • An artificial narcotic that is slower acting than, and does not provide the rush of, heroin. Methadone use allows heroin addicts to abstain from heroin without experiencing an abstinence syndrome.

Snorting Cocaine. Cocaine is a powerful stimulant. Health professionals have become concerned about some of its effects, including sudden rises in blood pressure, constriction of blood vessels, and acceleration of heart rate. Several athletes have died from cocaine overdoses.

Truth or Fiction Revisited
....
It is true that a stimulant is commonly used to treat children who are hyperactive. That stimulant is methylphenidate.

BARBITURATE • An addictive depressant used to relieve anxiety or induce sleep.
METHAQUALONE • An addictive depressant. Often called "ludes."
AMPHETAMINES • Stimulants derived from *alpha-methyl-beta-phenyl-ethyl-amine*, a colorless liquid consisting of carbon, hydrogen, and nitrogen.
ATTENTION-DEFICIT/HYPERACTIVITY DISORDER • A disorder that begins in childhood and is characterized by a persistent pattern of lack of attention, with or without hyperactivity and impulsive behavior.
COCAINE • A powerful stimulant.

• *Barbiturates and Methaqualone*

Barbiturates such as amobarbital, phenobarbital, pentobarbital, and secobarbital are depressants with a number of medical uses, including relief of anxiety and tension, deadening of pain, and treatment of epilepsy, high blood pressure, and insomnia. Barbiturates lead rapidly to physiological and psychological dependence.

Methaqualone is a depressant whose effects are similar to those of barbiturates. Methaqualone also leads to physiological dependence and is quite dangerous.

Barbiturates and methaqualone are popular as street drugs because they are relaxing and produce mild euphoria. High doses of barbiturates result in drowsiness, motor impairment, slurred speech, irritability, and poor judgment. A physiologically dependent person who is withdrawn abruptly from barbiturates may experience severe convulsions and die. Because of additive effects, it is dangerous to mix alcohol and other depressants.

■ STIMULANTS

All stimulants increase the activity of the nervous system. Their other effects vary somewhat, and some contribute to feelings of euphoria and self-confidence.

• *Amphetamines*

Amphetamines are a group of stimulants that were first used by soldiers during World War II to help them remain alert through the night. Truck drivers have used them to drive through the night. Amphetamines have become perhaps more widely known through students, who have used them for all-night cram sessions, and through dieters, who use them because they reduce hunger.

Called speed, uppers, bennies (for Benzedrine), and dexies (for Dexedrine), these drugs are often used for the euphoric rush they can produce, especially in high doses. Some people swallow amphetamines in pill form or inject liquid methedrine, the strongest form, into their veins. They may stay awake and "high" for days on end. Such highs must come to an end. People who have been on prolonged highs sometimes "crash," or fall into a deep sleep or depression. Some people commit suicide when crashing.

A related stimulant, methylphenidate (Ritalin), is widely used to treat **attention-deficit/hyperactivity disorder** in children (Wolraich and others, 1990). Ritalin has been shown to increase attention span, decrease aggressive and disruptive behavior, and lead to academic gains (Klorman and others, 1994). Why should Ritalin, a stimulant, calm children? Hyperactivity may be connected with immaturity of the cerebral cortex, and Ritalin may stimulate the cortex to exercise control over more primitive centers in the lower brain.

High doses of amphetamines may cause restlessness, insomnia, loss of appetite, hallucinations, paranoid delusions, and irritability. In the condition known as amphetamine psychosis, there are hallucinations and delusions that mimic the symptoms of paranoid schizophrenia (see Chapter 15).

• *Cocaine*

Do you recall the commercials claiming that "Coke adds life"? Given its caffeine and sugar content, "Coke"—Coca-Cola, that is—should provide quite a lift. But Coca-Cola hasn't been "the real thing" since 1906, when the company discontinued the use of cocaine in its formula. Cocaine is derived from coca leaves—the plant from which the soft drink took its name.

Coca leaves contain **cocaine,** a stimulant that produces euphoria, reduces hunger, deadens pain, and bolsters self-confidence. Cocaine's popularity with college students seems to have peaked in the mid-1980s (Johnston and others, 1996). The majority of high school students now believe that use of cocaine is harmful (Johnston and others, 1996).

Cocaine may be brewed from coca leaves as a "tea," "snorted" in powder form, or injected in liquid form. Repeated snorting constricts blood vessels in the nose, drying the skin and sometimes exposing cartilage and perforating the nasal septum. These problems require cosmetic surgery. The potent cocaine derivatives known as "crack" and "bazooka" are inexpensive because they are unrefined.

Biologically speaking, cocaine stimulates sudden rises in blood pressure, constricts the coronary arteries (which decreases the oxygen supply to the heart), and quickens the heart rate. These events can occasionally cause respiratory and cardiovascular collapse (Moliterno and others, 1994). The sudden deaths of a number of athletes have been caused in this way. Overdoses can lead to restlessness and insomnia, tremors, headaches, nausea, convulsions, hallucinations, and delusions. Use of crack has been connected with strokes (Levine and others, 1990).

Cocaine—also called *snow* and *coke,* like the slang term for the soft drink—has been used as a local anesthetic since the early 1800s. In 1884 it came to the attention of a young Viennese neurologist named Sigmund Freud, who used it to fight his own depression and published an article about it titled "Song of Praise." Freud's early ardor was tempered when he learned that cocaine is habit-forming and can cause hallucinations and delusions. Cocaine causes physiological dependence (Brown & Massaro, 1996).

• *Cigarettes (Nicotine)*

> S*moking: a "custome lothesome to the Eye, hatefull to the Nose, harmefull to the Braine, dangerous to the Lungs."*
>
> KING JAMES I, 1604

Nicotine is the stimulant in cigarettes. Nicotine stimulates discharge of the hormone adrenaline and the release of many neurotransmitters, including dopamine and acetylcholine. Adrenaline creates a burst of autonomic activity that accelerates the heart rate and pours sugar into the blood. Acetylcholine is vital in memory formation, and nicotine appears to enhance memory and attention (Leary, 1997), improve performance on simple, repetitive tasks (Kinnunen and others, 1996; O'Brien, 1996), and enhance mood. Yet it also appears to relax people and reduce stress (O'Brien, 1996).

Some people smoke in order to control their weight (Califano, 1995; Meyers and others, 1997). Nicotine depresses the appetite and raises the metabolic rate (Audrain and others, 1995; Hultquist and others, 1995). People also tend to eat more when they stop smoking (Klesges and others, 1997), a tendency that leads some quitters to return to smoking.

Nicotine is the agent that creates physiological dependence on cigarettes (Kessler, 1995). It may be as addictive as heroin or cocaine (MacKenzie and others, 1994). Regular smokers adjust their smoking to maintain fairly even levels of nicotine in their bloodstream (Drobes & Tiffany, 1997; Shiffman and others, 1997). Symptoms of withdrawal from nicotine include nervousness, drowsiness, loss of energy, headaches, irregular bowel movements, lightheadedness, insomnia, dizziness, cramps, palpitations, tremors, and sweating. Since many of these symptoms resemble those of anxiety, it was once thought that smoking might be a habit rather than an addiction.

THE PERILS OF SMOKING It's no secret. Cigarette packs sold in the United States carry messages such as: "Warning: The Surgeon General Has Determined That Cigarette Smok-

Cigarettes: Smoking Guns? The perils of cigarette smoking are widely known today. One Surgeon General declared that cigarette smoking is the chief preventable cause of death in the United States. The numbers of Americans who die from smoking are comparable to the number of lives that would be lost if two jumbo jets crashed *every day.* If flying were that unsafe, would the government ground all flights? Would the public continue to make airline reservations?

AMERICAN CANCER SOCIETY

ing Is Dangerous to Your Health." Cigarette advertising has been banned on radio and television. Nearly 420,000 Americans die from smoking-related illnesses each year (Rosenblatt, 1994). This is the equivalent of two jumbo jets colliding in midair each day with all passengers lost. It is higher than the number of people who die from motor vehicle accidents, alcohol and drug abuse, suicide, homicide, and AIDS *combined* (Rosenblatt, 1994).

The percentage of American adults who smoke overall declined from 42.2% in 1966 to about 25% in the 1990s, but there have been increases among women, African Americans, and eighth to twelfth graders (Feder, 1997; Gold and others, 1996). The incidence of smoking is connected with gender, age, ethnicity, level of education, and socioeco-

psychology and modern life

QUITTING SMOKING

Is being a quitter a good thing? When it comes to smoking, the answer is yes. More than 40 million Americans have successfully quit smoking (CDC, 1993b). Former smokers have mortality rates similar to those of people who have never smoked (Nevid and others, 1998). So, rather than focusing on the damage already done, people who quit smoking can look forward to a reasonably normal life expectancy.

For those who have decided to quit smoking, the following suggestions may be of help:

- Tell your family and friends that you're quitting—make a public commitment.

- Pick a time to quit when you are likely to be under less stress than usual or away from your usual surroundings. For example, go on a smoke-ending vacation to get away from places and situations in which you're used to smoking.

- Start when you wake up, at which time you've already gone eight hours without nicotine.

- Think of specific things to tell yourself when you feel the urge to smoke: how you'll be stronger, free from fear of cancer, ready for the marathon, and so on.

- Tell yourself that the first few days are the hardest—after that, withdrawal symptoms decrease dramatically.

- Throw out ashtrays and don't allow smokers to visit you at home for a while.

- Don't carry matches or light other people's cigarettes.

- Sit in nonsmokers' sections of restaurants and trains.

- Fill your days with novel activities—with things that won't remind you of smoking.

- Use sugar-free mints, cinnamon sticks, gum (regular or containing nicotine), or nicotine skin patches as substitutes for cigarettes. (Don't light them up.)

- Buy yourself presents with all the cash you're not spending on cigarettes.

- Imagine living a prolonged, non-coughing life. Ah, freedom!

Nicotine gums and skin patches help some people (Cepeda-Benito, 1993; Martin and others, 1997; O'Brien, 1996). Others, however, find it difficult to wean themselves from these nicotine replacement methods. Nicotine gum also appears to help many people avoid gaining weight after they quit smoking (Doherty and others, 1996). A combination of cognitive behavior therapy and nicotine patches looks promising: People experience less discomfort from withdrawal than they do from cognitive behavior therapy alone (Cinciripini and others, 1996).

There is also a high relapse rate for people who quit smoking. Be on guard: We are most likely to relapse—that is, return to drugs such as alcohol and nicotine—when we feel highly anxious, angry, or depressed (Cooney and others, 1997; Kinnunen and others, 1996). If you are tempted, you can reduce the risk of relapse by using almost any of the strategies described here, such as reminding yourself of reasons for quitting, having a mint, or going for a walk. ■

nomic status (see Table 6.4). Better-educated people are less likely to smoke. They are also more likely to quit smoking (Rose and others, 1996).

Every cigarette smoked steals about 7 minutes of a person's life. The carbon monoxide in cigarette smoke impairs the blood's ability to carry oxygen, causing shortness of breath (Gold and others, 1996). It is apparently the **hydrocarbons** ("tars") in cigarette smoke that lead to lung cancer (Stout, 1996). Heavy smokers are about 10 times as likely as nonsmokers to die of lung cancer (Nevid and others, 1998). Cigarette smoking is also linked to death from heart disease, chronic lung and respiratory diseases, and other health problems. Women who smoke show reduced bone density, significantly increasing the risk of fracture of the hip and back (Brody, 1996b; Hopper & Seeman, 1994). Pregnant women who smoke risk miscarriage, premature birth, and birth defects.

Passive smoking is also connected with respiratory illnesses, asthma, and other health problems and accounts for more than 50,000 deaths per year (Nevid and others, 1998). Prolonged exposure to household tobacco smoke during childhood is a risk factor for lung cancer (Janerich and others, 1990). Because of the noxious effects of second-hand smoke, smoking has been banished from many public places such as airplanes, restaurants, and elevators.

Why, then, do people smoke? For many reasons—such as the desire to look sophisticated (though these days smokers may be more likely to be judged foolish than sophisticated), to have something to do with their hands, and—of course—to take in nicotine.

TABLE 6.4 SNAPSHOT, U.S.A.: HUMAN DIVERSITY AND SMOKING		
Factor	*Group*	*Percent Who Smoke*
Gender	Women	23.5
	Men	28.1
Age	18–24	22.9
	25–44	30.4
	45–64	26.9
	65–74	16.5
	75 and above	8.4
Ethnic Group	African American	29.2
	Asian American/Pacific Islander	16.0
	Hispanic American	20.2
	Native American	31.4
	Non-Hispanic White American	25.5
Level of Education	Fewer than 12 years	32.0
	12	30.0
	13–15	23.4
	16 and above	13.6
Socioeconomic Status (SES)	Below poverty level	33.3
	At poverty level or above	24.7

Note. From Office of Smoking and Health, Centers for Disease Control (1993).

HYDROCARBONS • Chemical compounds consisting of hydrogen and carbon.
PASSIVE SMOKING • Inhaling of smoke from the tobacco products and exhalations of other people; also called *second-hand smoking.*

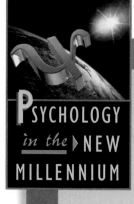
Will We Find That Nicotine Can Be (Gasp!) Good for You?

In the 1950s my father insisted that "pure" foods such as steak, eggs, butter, whole milk, and cheese were good for you but that "spices" were not. Now we know that his "pure foods" are high in harmful fats and cholesterol and that many spices, such as garlic, are good for you. In his movie *Sleeper*, Woody Allen woke up in the new millennium and was informed that research had revealed that cigarettes were actually good for you.

No, cigarettes are *not* good for you. Smoking causes many kinds of cancer and is involved in heart disease and many other health problems, even dental problems (Nevid and others, 1998). Chewing tobacco also causes cancer and other health problems. Nor is there any question that nicotine is addictive. (It is.)

However, nicotine has some positive qualities that are under study and may lead to the development of useful medications in the new millennium. Nicotine turns out to hold potential for the treatment of health problems ranging from Alzheimer's and Parkinson's

diseases to schizophrenia (Grady, 1997a; Leary, 1997). Nicotine binds to receptors (called *nicotinic cholinergic receptors*) on many kinds of cells, particularly in the brain. There it stimulates the release of neurotransmitters, including dopamine and acetylcholine. Deficiencies of these neurotransmitters are implicated in Parkinson's and Alzheimer's diseases. It has been observed that smokers are less likely to develop these diseases (Leary, 1997). Nicotine may also block the formation of the plaque deposits in the nervous system that characterize Alzheimer's disease (Zagorski, 1997).

It has also been observed that people with schizophrenia smoke heavily (Grady, 1997a). People with schizophrenia have difficulty filtering out distractions such as irrelevant sounds, thus impairing their concentration and thought processes. One possible result is hearing voices—"sounds" that are not really there. This may be connected with a defective structure in the brain whose functioning is aided by nicotine. Thus, when people with schizophrenia smoke, they may be seeking relief from interference in their thought processes (Grady, 1997a).

Nobody is suggesting that people take up smoking to alleviate these health problems. The risks of smoking outweigh any potential benefits. However, researchers are developing nicotine-like compounds that are intended to target the symptoms of Parkinson's and Alzheimer's diseases without the problems connected with nicotine (Leary, 1997). ∎

∎ HALLUCINOGENICS

Hallucinogenic drugs are so named because they produce hallucinations—that is, sensations and perceptions in the absence of external stimulation. But hallucinogenic drugs may also have additional effects such as relaxation, euphoria, or, in some cases, panic.

• *Marijuana*

HALLUCINOGENIC • Giving rise to hallucinations.
MARIJUANA • The dried vegetable matter of the *Cannabis sativa* plant. (A Mexican-Spanish word.)
PSYCHEDELIC • Causing hallucinations, delusions, or heightened perceptions.

Marijuana is produced from the *Cannabis sativa* plant, which grows wild in many parts of the world. Marijuana helps some people relax and can elevate their mood. It also sometimes produces mild hallucinations, which is why it is classified as a **psychedelic**, or hallucinogenic, drug. The major psychedelic substance in marijuana is delta-9-tetrahydrocannabinol, or THC. THC is found in the branches and leaves of the plant, but it is highly concentrated in the sticky resin. **Hashish,** or "hash," is derived from the resin. Hashish is more potent than marijuana.

In the 19th century marijuana was used much as aspirin is used today for headaches and minor aches and pains. It could be bought without a prescription in any drugstore. Today marijuana use and possession are illegal in most states. Marijuana also carries a number of health risks. For example, it impairs motor coordination and perceptual functions used in driving and operating machines. It impairs short-term memory and slows learning. Although it causes positive mood changes in many people, there are also disturbing instances of anxiety and confusion and occasional reports of psychotic reactions. Marijuana increases the heart rate to 140–150 beats per minute and, in some people, raises blood pressure. This higher demand on the heart and circulation poses a threat to people with hypertension and cardiovascular disorders.

PSYCHOACTIVE EFFECTS OF MARIJUANA Some people report that marijuana helps them socialize at parties. Moderate to strong intoxication is linked to reports of heightened perceptions and increases in self-insight, creative thinking, and empathy for the feelings of others. Time seems to pass more slowly for people who are strongly intoxicated. A song might seem to last an hour rather than a few minutes. There is increased awareness of bodily sensations such as heartbeat. Marijuana smokers also report that strong intoxication heightens sexual sensations. Visual hallucinations are not uncommon. Strong intoxication may cause smokers to experience disorientation. If the smoker's mood is euphoric, loss of a sense of personal identity may be interpreted as being in harmony with the universe.

Some marijuana smokers have negative experiences. An accelerated heart rate and heightened awareness of bodily sensations leads some smokers to fear that their heart will "run away" with them. Some smokers find disorientation threatening and are afraid that they will not regain their identity. Strong intoxication sometimes causes nausea and vomiting.

People can become psychologically dependent on marijuana, but it is not known to cause physiological dependence. Tolerance of a drug is a sign of physiological dependence. With marijuana, however, regular usage is often associated with the need for *less*, not *more*, to achieve the same effects.

Marijuana has been used to treat health problems, including glaucoma and the nausea experienced by cancer patients undergoing chemotherapy ("More research needed," 1997). However, in most cases other drugs are available for these purposes (Kolata, 1994).

Marijuana's entire story has not yet been told. Whereas certain horror stories about marijuana may have been exaggerated, one cannot assume that smoke that contains 50% more carcinogenic hydrocarbon than tobacco smoke is harmless.

• *LSD and Other Hallucinogenics*

LSD is the abbreviation for lysergic acid diethylamide, a synthetic hallucinogenic drug. Users of "acid" claim that it "expands consciousness" and opens up new worlds to them. Sometimes people believe that they have achieved great insights while using LSD, but when it wears off they often cannot apply or recall these discoveries. As a powerful hallucinogenic, LSD produces vivid and colorful hallucinations.

Some LSD users have **flashbacks**—distorted perceptions or hallucinations that mimic the LSD "trip" but occur days, weeks, or longer after usage. Some researchers have speculated that flashbacks stem from chemical changes in the brain produced by LSD. Others suggest psychological explanations for flashbacks. Matefy (1980) found that

An LSD Trip? This hallucinogenic drug can give rise to a vivid parade of colors and visual distortions. Some users claim to have achieved great insights while "tripping," but typically they have been unable to recall or apply them afterward.

HASHISH • A drug derived from the resin of *Cannabis sativa.* Often called "hash."
LSD • Lysergic acid diethylamide. A hallucinogenic drug.
FLASHBACKS • Distorted perceptions or hallucinations that occur days or weeks after LSD usage but mimic the LSD experience.

In Review   Psychoactive Drugs and Their Effects

DRUG	TYPE	HOW TAKEN	DESIRED EFFECTS	TOLERANCE	ABSTINENCE SYNDROME	SIDE EFFECTS
Alcohol	Depressant	By mouth	Relaxation, euphoria, lowered inhibitions	Yes	Yes	Impaired coordination, poor judgment, hangover
Opiates	Depressants	Injected, smoked, by mouth	Relaxation, euphoria, relief from anxiety and pain	Yes	Yes	Impaired coordination and mental functioning, drowsiness, lethargy
Barbiturates and Methaqualone	Depressants	By mouth, injected	Relaxation, sleep, euphoria, lowered inhibitions	Yes	Yes	Impaired coordination and mental functioning, drowsiness, lethargy
Amphetamines	Stimulants	By mouth, injected	Alertness, euphoria	Yes	?	Restlessness, loss of appetite, psychotic symptoms
Cocaine	Stimulant	By mouth, snorted, injected	Euphoria, self-confidence	Yes	Yes	Restlessness, loss of appetite, convulsions, strokes, psychotic symptoms
Nicotine	Stimulant	By tobacco (smoked, chewed, or sniffed)	Relaxation, stimulation, weight control	Yes	Yes	Cancer, heart disease, lung and respiratory diseases
Marijuana	Hallucinogenic	Smoked, by mouth	Relaxation, perceptual distortions, enhancement of experience	No	No	Impaired coordination, respiratory problems, panic
LSD, Mescaline, PCP	Hallucinogenics	By mouth	Perceptual distortions, vivid hallucinations	Yes	No	Impaired coordination, psychotic symptoms, panic

MESCALINE • A hallucinogenic drug derived from the mescal (peyote) cactus. In religious ceremonies, Mexican Indians chew the buttonlike structures at the tops of the rounded stems of the plant.
PHENCYCLIDINE • Another hallucinogenic drug whose name is an acronym for its chemical structure. Abbreviated *PCP*.
MEDITATION • As a method for coping with stress, a systematic narrowing of attention that slows the metabolism and helps produce feelings of relaxation.
TRANSCENDENTAL MEDITATION • The simplified form of meditation brought to the United States by the Maharishi Mahesh Yogi. Abbreviated *TM*.
MANTRA • A word or sound that is repeated in TM. (A Sanskrit word that has the same origin as the word *mind*.)
RELAXATION RESPONSE • Benson's term for a group of responses that can be brought about by meditation. They involve lowered activity of the sympathetic branch of the autonomic nervous system.

LSD users who have flashbacks can become engrossed in role-playing. Perhaps flashbacks involve enacting the role of being on a trip. This does not mean that people who claim to have flashbacks are lying. They may be more willing to surrender personal control in their quest for psychedelic experience. Users who do not have flashbacks prefer to be more in charge of their thought processes and choose to focus on the demands of daily life.

Other hallucinogenic drugs include **mescaline** (derived from the peyote cactus) and **phencyclidine (PCP)**. Regular use of hallucinogenics may lead to tolerance and psychological dependence. But hallucinogenics are not known to lead to physiological dependence. High doses may induce frightening hallucinations, impaired coordination, poor judgment, mood changes, and paranoid delusions.

■ MEDITATION

There are many kinds of **meditation,** but they share some psychological threads: Through rituals, exercises, and passive observation, the normal relationship between the person and her or his environment is altered. Problem solving, planning, worry, awareness of the events of the day are all suspended (Clay, 1997). In this way consciousness—that is, the normal focus of attention—is altered, and relaxation is induced. The effects of meditation, like those of drugs, appear to reflect bodily changes that are induced by meditation as well as by one's expectations about meditation. Many people believe that spiritual forces are also at work in meditation, but such beliefs cannot be scientifically verified.

Transcendental Meditation, or TM, is a simplified form of Far Eastern meditation that was brought to the United States by the Maharishi Mahesh Yogi in 1959. Hundreds of thousands of Americans practice TM by repeating and concentrating on **mantras**—words or sounds that are claimed to help the person achieve an altered state of consciousness.

TM has a number of spiritual goals, such as expanding consciousness, but there are also more worldly goals, such as reducing anxiety and normalizing blood pressure. In early research, Herbert Benson (1975) found no scientific evidence that TM expands consciousness, despite the claims of many of its practitioners. However, TM lowered the heart and respiration rates and produced what Benson labeled a **relaxation response.** The blood pressure of people with hypertension decreased (Benson and others, 1973). In fact, people who meditated twice daily tended to show more normal blood pressure through the day. Meditators produced more frequent alpha waves—brain waves that are associated with feelings of relaxation.

Other researchers agree that TM lowers a person's level of arousal, but they argue that the same relaxing effects can be achieved in other ways, such as resting quietly (Holmes, 1984). The issue is not whether meditation helps, but whether meditation has special effects as compared with a break from a tense routine.

■ BIOFEEDBACK: GETTING IN TOUCH WITH THE UNTOUCHABLE

In a classic study, Neal E. Miller (1969) trained laboratory rats to increase or decrease their heart rates. His procedure was simple. There is a "pleasure center" in the rat's hypothalamus. A small burst of electricity in this center is strongly reinforcing: Rats will learn to do what they can, such as pressing a lever, to obtain this shock.

Miller implanted electrodes in the rats' pleasure centers. Then some rats were given an electric shock whenever their heart rate happened to increase. Other rats received a shock when their heart rate went lower. In other words, one group of rats was consistently "rewarded" (that is, shocked) when their heart rate showed an increase. The other group was consistently rewarded for a decrease in heart rate. After a single 90-minute training session, the rats learned to alter their heart rates by as much as 20% in the direction for which they had been rewarded.

Meditation. People use many forms of meditation to try to expand their inner awareness and experience inner harmony. The effects of meditation, like those of drugs, reflect both the bodily changes induced by meditation *and* the meditator's expectations.

Biofeedback. Biofeedback is a system that provides, or "feeds back," information about a bodily function to an organism. Through biofeedback training, people have learned to gain voluntary control over a number of functions that are normally automatic, such as heart rate and blood pressure.

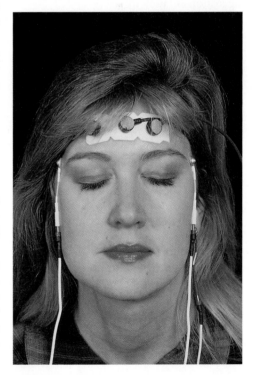

BIOFEEDBACK TRAINING • The systematic feeding back to an organism information about a bodily function so that the organism can gain control of that function. Abbreviated *BFT.*
ELECTROMYOGRAPH • An instrument that measures muscle tension. Abbreviated *EMG.* (From the Greek *mys,* meaning "mouse" and "muscle"—reflecting similarity between the movement of a mouse and the contraction of a muscle.)

Miller's research was an early example of **biofeedback training (BFT).** Biofeedback is a system that provides, or "feeds back," information about a bodily function. Miller used electrical stimulation of the brain to feed back information to rats when they had engaged in a targeted bodily response (in this case, raised or lowered their heart rates). Somehow the rats then used this information to raise or lower their heart rates voluntarily.

Similarly, people have learned to change various bodily functions voluntarily, including heart rate, that were once considered to be beyond their control. However, electrodes are not implanted in people's brains. Rather, people hear a "blip" or observe some other signal that informs them when the targeted response is being displayed.

There are many ways in which BFT helps people combat stress, tension, and anxiety. For example, people can learn to emit alpha waves (and feel somewhat more relaxed) through feedback from an EEG. A blip may increase in frequency whenever alpha waves are being emitted. The psychologist's instructions are simply to "make the blip go faster." An **electromyograph (EMG),** which monitors muscle tension, is commonly used to help people become more aware of muscle tension in the forehead and elsewhere and to learn to lower the tension. Through the use of other instruments, people have learned to lower

psychology and
modern life

TRYING MEDITATION

Do you find meditation intriguing? If you would like to try meditation, these suggestions may help:

1. Begin by meditating once or twice a day for 10 to 20 minutes.

2. In meditation, what you *don't* do is more important than what you *do* do. Adopt a passive, "what happens, happens" attitude.

3. Create a quiet, nondisruptive environment. For example, don't face a light directly.

4. Do not eat for an hour beforehand; avoid caffeine for at least two hours.

5. Assume a comfortable position. Change it as needed. It's okay to scratch or yawn.

6. As a device to aid concentrating, you may focus on your breathing or seat yourself before a calming object such as a plant or burning incense. Benson suggests "perceiving" (rather than mentally saying) the word *one* on every outbreath. This means thinking the word, but "less actively" than usual (good luck). Others suggest thinking or perceiving the word *in* as you are inhaling and *out,* or *ah-h-h,* as you are exhaling.

7. If you are using a mantra, you can prepare for meditation and say the mantra out loud several times. Enjoy it. Then say it more and more softly. Close your eyes and think only the mantra. Allow yourself to perceive, rather

than actively think, the mantra. Again, adopt a passive attitude. Continue to perceive the mantra. It may grow louder or softer, disappear for a while, and then return.

8. If disruptive thoughts enter your mind as you are meditating, you can allow them to "pass through." Don't get wrapped up in trying to squelch them, or you may raise your level of arousal.

9. Allow yourself to drift. (You won't go too far.) What happens, happens.

10. Above all, take what you get. You cannot force the relaxing effects of meditation. You can only set the stage for it and allow it to happen. ■

their heart rate, their blood pressure, and the amount of sweat in the palm of the hand. All of these changes are relaxing. Biofeedback is widely used by sports psychologists to teach athletes how to relax muscle groups that are unessential to the task at hand so that they can control anxiety and tension.

People have also learned to elevate the temperature of a finger. Why bother, you ask? It happens that limbs become subjectively warmer when more blood flows into them. Increasing the temperature of a finger—that is, altering patterns of blood flow in the body—helps some people control migraine headaches, which may be caused by dysfunctional circulatory patterns.

■ HYPNOSIS: ON BEING ENTRANCED

Perhaps you have seen films in which Count Dracula hypnotized resistant victims into a stupor. Then he could give them a bite in the neck with no further nonsense. Perhaps you have watched a fellow student try to place a friend in a "trance" after reading a book on hypnosis. Or perhaps you have seen an audience member hypnotized in a nightclub act. If so, chances are the person acted as if he or she had returned to childhood, imagined that a snake was about to have a nip, or lay rigid between two chairs for a while.

Hypnosis, a term derived from the Greek word for sleep, has only recently become a respectable subject for psychological inquiry. Modern hypnosis seems to have begun with the ideas of Franz Mesmer in the 18th century. Mesmer asserted that everything in the universe was connected by forms of magnetism—which actually may not be far from the mark. He claimed that people, too, could be drawn to one another by "animal magnetism." (No bull's-eye here.) Mesmer used bizarre props to bring people under his "spell." He did manage a respectable cure rate for minor ailments. But skeptics attribute his successes to the placebo effect, not to animal magnetism.

Today hypnotism retains its popularity in nightclubs, but it is also used as an anesthetic in dentistry, childbirth, and even surgery. Some psychologists use hypnosis to teach clients how to reduce anxiety, manage pain, or overcome fears (Crawford & Barabasz, 1993). Research shows that hypnosis is a useful supplement to other forms of therapy, especially in helping obese people lose weight (Kirsch and others, 1995). Police also use hypnosis to prompt the memories of witnesses.

The state of consciousness called the *hypnotic trance* has traditionally been induced by asking people to narrow their attention to a small light, a spot on the wall, an object held by the hypnotist, or the hypnotist's voice. The hypnotist usually suggests that the person's limbs are becoming warm, heavy, and relaxed. People may also be told that they are becoming sleepy or falling asleep. Hypnosis is *not* sleep, however. This is shown by differences between EEG recordings for the hypnotic trance and the stages of sleep. But the word *sleep* is understood by subjects to suggest a hypnotic trance.

It is also possible to induce hypnosis through instructions that direct subjects to remain active and alert (Clkurel & Gruzelier, 1990; Miller and others, 1991). So the effects of hypnosis probably cannot be attributed to relaxation.

People who are readily hypnotized are said to have *hypnotic suggestibility*. Part of "suggestibility" is knowledge of what is expected during the "trance state." Generally speaking, suggestible people have positive attitudes toward hypnosis. They *want* to be

HYPNOSIS • A condition in which people appear to be highly suggestible and behave as though they are in a trance. (From the Greek *hypnos*, meaning "sleep.")

Hypnosis. Hypnotized people become passive and follow the suggestions of the hypnotist. Only recently has hypnosis become a respectable subject for psychological inquiry.

hypnotized. Moreover, they attend closely to the hypnotist's instructions (Crawford and others, 1993). Therefore, it is extremely unlikely that someone could be hypnotized against his or her will.

• *Changes in Consciousness Brought About by Hypnosis*

Hypnotists and people who have been hypnotized report that hypnosis can bring about the following changes in consciousness. As you read them, bear in mind that changes in "consciousness" are inferred from changes in observable behavior and self-reports.

- *Passivity.* When being hypnotized, or in a trance, people await instructions and appear to suspend planning.
- *Narrowed attention.* People focus on the hypnotist's voice or on a spot of light and avoid attending to background noise or intruding thoughts.
- *Pseudomemories and hypermnesia.* People may be instructed to report pseudomemories (false memories) or **hypermnesia.** In police investigations, for example, hypnotists attempt to heighten witnesses' memories by instructing them to focus on details of a crime and then reconstruct the scene. Studies suggest, however, that although people may report recalling more information when they are hypnotized, such information is often incorrect (Weekes and others, 1992).
- *Suggestibility.* People may respond to suggestions that an arm is becoming lighter and will rise or that the eyelids are becoming heavier and must close. They may act as though they cannot unlock hands clasped by the hypnotist or bend an arm "made rigid" by the hypnotist. Hypnotized individuals serving as witnesses may incorporate ideas presented by interviewers into their "memories" and report them as facts (Loftus, 1994).
- *Playing Unusual Roles.* Most people expect to play sleepy, relaxed roles, but they may also be able to play roles calling for increased strength or alertness, such as riding a bicycle with less fatigue than usual. In **age regression,** people may play themselves as infants or children. Research shows that many supposed childhood memories and characteristics are played inaccurately. Nonetheless, some people show excellent recall of such details as hairstyle or speech pattern. A person may speak a language that has been forgotten since childhood.
- *Perceptual Distortions.* Hypnotized people may act as though hypnotically induced hallucinations and delusions are real. In the "thirst hallucination," for example, people act as if they are parched, even if they have just had a drink. People may behave as though they cannot hear loud noises, smell odors, or feel pain (Miller & Bowers, 1993).
- *Posthypnotic Amnesia.* Many people apparently cannot recall events that take place under hypnosis (Bowers & Woody, 1996) or, if so directed, that they were hypnotized at all. However, if they are hypnotized again, they can usually recall what occurred when instructed by the hypnotist to do so.
- *Posthypnotic Suggestion.* People who have been hypnotized may later follow instructions to prearranged cues of which they are supposedly unaware. For instance, during hypnosis a subject may be directed to fall into a deep trance later upon the single command "Sleep!" Smokers frequently seek the help of hypnotists to break their habit, and they may be given the suggestion that upon "waking" they will find cigarette smoke aversive.

• *Theories of Hypnosis*

Hypnotism is no longer explained in terms of animal magnetism, but psychodynamic and learning theorists have offered explanations. According to Freud, the hypnotic trance represents **regression.** Hypnotized adults suspend "ego functioning," or conscious con-

HYPERMNESIA • Greatly enhanced or heightened memory.
AGE REGRESSION • In hypnosis, taking on the role of childhood, commonly accompanied by vivid recollections of one's past.
REGRESSION • Return to a form of behavior characteristic of an earlier stage of development.

trol of their behavior. They permit themselves to return to childish modes of responding that emphasize fantasy and impulse rather than fact and logic.

ROLE THEORY Theodore Sarbin offers a **role theory** view of hypnosis (Sarbin & Coe, 1972). He points out that the changes in behavior that are attributed to the hypnotic trance can be successfully imitated when people are instructed to behave *as though* they were hypnotized. For example, people can lie rigid between two chairs whether they are hypnotized or not. Also, people cannot be hypnotized unless they are familiar with the hypnotic "role"—the behavior that constitutes the trance. Sarbin is not saying that subjects *fake* the hypnotic role. Research evidence suggests that most people who are hypnotized are not faking (Kinnunen and others, 1994). Instead, Sarbin is suggesting that people *allow* themselves to enact this role under the hypnotist's directions.

Research findings that "suggestible" people are motivated to enact the hypnotic role, are good role players, and have vivid and absorbing imaginations seem to support the role theory. The fact that the behaviors shown by hypnotized people can be mimicked by role players means that we need not resort to the concept of the "hypnotic trance"—an unusual and mystifying altered state of awareness—to explain hypnotic events.

DISSOCIATION Runners frequently get through the pain and tedium of long-distance races by *dissociating*—by imagining themselves elsewhere, doing other things. (My students inform me that they manage the pain and tedium of *other* instructors' classes in the same way.) Ernest Hilgard (1994) similarly explains hypnotic phenomena through **neodissociation theory**. This is the view that we can selectively focus our attention on one thing (like hypnotic suggestions) and dissociate ourselves from the things going on around us.

In one experiment related to neodissociation theory, subjects were hypnotized and instructed to submerge their arms in ice water—causing "cold pressor pain" (Miller and others, 1991). Subjects were given suggestions to the effect that they were not in pain, however. Highly hypnotizable people reported dissociative experiences that allowed them to avoid the perception of pain, such as imagining that they were at the beach or that their limbs were floating in air above the icewater.

Though hypnotized people may be focusing on the hypnotist's suggestions and perhaps imagining themselves to be somewhere else, they still tend to perceive their actual surroundings peripherally. In a sense, we do this all the time. We are not fully conscious, or aware, of everything going on about us. Rather, at any given moment we selectively focus on events such as tests, dates, or television shows that seem important or relevant. Yet while taking a test we may be peripherally aware of the color of the wall or the sound of rain.

Role theory and neodissociation theory do not suggest that the phenomena of hypnosis are phony. Instead, they suggest that we do not need to explain these events through an altered state of awareness called a *trance*. Hypnosis may not be special at all. Rather, it is *we* who are special—through our imagination, our role-playing ability, and our capacity to divide our consciousness—concentrating now on one event that we deem important, and concentrating on another event later.

REFLECTIONS

- Agree or disagree, and support your answer: "Through meditation, people have been able to transcend the boundaries of everyday experience."
- Had you heard of hypnosis or hypnotic trance before taking this course? How does the information presented here correspond to what you had heard?
- Agree or disagree, and support your answer: "You can be hypnotized only if you want to be hypnotized."

ROLE THEORY • A theory that explains hypnotic events in terms of the person's ability to act as though he or she were hypnotized. Role theory differs from faking in that subjects cooperate and focus on hypnotic suggestions instead of pretending to be hypnotized.
NEODISSOCIATION THEORY • A theory that explains hypnotic events in terms of the splitting of consciousness.

SUMMARY

1. **What is consciousness?** The term *consciousness* has several meanings, including (1) sensory awareness, (2) direct inner awareness of cognitive processes, (3) personal unity or the sense of self, and (4) the waking state.

2. **What are the stages of sleep?** Electroencephalograph (EEG) records show different stages of sleep, as characterized by different types of brain waves. There are four stages of non-rapid-eye-movement (NREM) sleep and one stage of REM sleep. Stage 1 sleep is the lightest and stage 4 is the deepest.

3. **What are the functions of sleep?** Sleep apparently serves a restorative function, but we do not know exactly how sleep restores us or how much sleep we need.

4. **What are dreams?** Dreams are a form of cognitive activity that occurs mostly while we are sleeping. Most dreaming occurs during REM sleep. The content of most dreams is an extension of the events of the previous day. Nightmares are also dreams that occur during REM sleep.

5. **What are the sleep disorders?** A common sleep disorder is insomnia, which is most often encountered by people who are anxious and tense. Other sleep disorders include narcolepsy, apnea, sleep terrors, bed wetting, and sleepwalking. Sleep terrors usually occur during deep sleep.

6. **What is meant by substance abuse and dependence?** Substance abuse is use that persists even though it impairs one's functioning. Dependence has behavioral and physiological aspects. It may be characterized by organizing one's life around getting and using the substance and by the development of tolerance, withdrawal symptoms, or both.

7. **Why do people abuse drugs?** People usually try drugs out of curiosity, but usage can be reinforced by anxiety reduction, feelings of euphoria, and other positive sensations. People are also motivated to avoid withdrawal symptoms once they become physiologically dependent on a drug. Some people may have genetic predispositions to become physiologically dependent on certain substances.

8. **What are depressants?** The group of substances called depressants act by slowing the activity of the central nervous system.

9. **What are the effects of alcohol?** Alcohol is an intoxicating depressant that can lead to physiological dependence. It provides an excuse for failure or for antisocial behavior, but it has not been shown to induce such behavior directly.

10. **What are the effects of opiates?** The opiates morphine and heroin are depressants that reduce pain, but they are also bought on the street because of the euphoric "rush" they provide. Opiate use can lead to physiological dependence.

11. **What are the effects of barbiturates?** Barbiturates are depressants that are used to treat epilepsy, high blood pressure, anxiety, and insomnia. They lead rapidly to physiological dependence.

12. **What are stimulants?** Stimulants are substances that act by increasing the activity of the nervous system.

13. **What are the effects of amphetamines?** Amphetamines are stimulants that produce feelings of euphoria when taken in high doses. But high doses may also cause restlessness, insomnia, psychotic symptoms, and a "crash" upon withdrawal. Amphetamines and a related stimulant, Ritalin, are commonly used to treat hyperactive children.

14. **What are the effects of cocaine?** As a psychoactive substance, cocaine provides feelings of euphoria and bolsters self-confidence. Cocaine causes sudden rises in blood pressure and constricts blood vessels. Overdoses can lead to restlessness, insomnia, psychotic reactions, and cardiorespiratory collapse.

15. **What are the effects of smoking cigarettes?** Cigarette smoke contains carbon monoxide, hydrocarbons, and the stimulant nicotine. Regular smokers adjust their smoking so as to maintain a consistent level of nicotine in the blood, suggestive of physiological dependence. Cigarette smoking has been linked to death from heart disease and cancer, and to other health problems.

16. **What are hallucinogenics?** Hallucinogenic substances produce hallucinations—sensations and perceptions that occur in the absence of external stimulation.

17. **What are the effects of marijuana?** Marijuana is a hallucinogenic substance whose active ingredients, including THC, often produce relaxation, heightened and distorted perceptions, feelings of empathy, and reports of new insights. Hallucinations may occur. The long-term effects of marijuana use are not fully known, although it appears that marijuana smoke itself is harmful.

18. **What are the effects of LSD?** LSD is a hallucinogenic drug that produces vivid hallucinations.

19. **What is meditation?** In meditation, one focuses "passively" on an object or a mantra in order to alter the normal relationship between oneself and the environment. In this way, consciousness (that is, the normal focuses of attention) is altered, and relaxation is often induced. TM and other forms of meditation appear to reduce high blood pressure as well as produce relaxation.

20. **What is biofeedback?** Biofeedback is a method for increasing consciousness of bodily functions. In biofeedback, the organism is continuously provided with information about a targeted biological response such as heart rate or emission of alpha waves. People and lower animals can learn to control functions such as heart rate and blood pressure through biofeedback training.

21. **What is hypnosis?** Hypnosis is an altered state of consciousness in which the individual may exhibit passivity, narrowed attention, hypermnesia (heightened memory), suggestibility, assumption of unusual roles, perceptual distortions, posthypnotic amnesia, and posthypnotic suggestion.

22. **How do psychologists explain hypnosis?** Current theories of hypnosis deny the existence of a special trance state. Rather, they emphasize people's ability to role-play the "trance" and to divide consciousness as directed by the hypnotist.

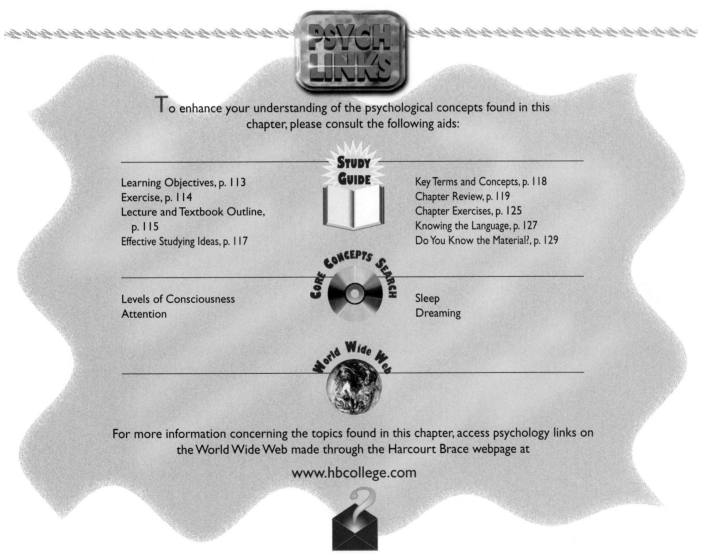

PSYCH LINKS

To enhance your understanding of the psychological concepts found in this chapter, please consult the following aids:

STUDY GUIDE

Learning Objectives, p. 113
Exercise, p. 114
Lecture and Textbook Outline, p. 115
Effective Studying Ideas, p. 117

Key Terms and Concepts, p. 118
Chapter Review, p. 119
Chapter Exercises, p. 125
Knowing the Language, p. 127
Do You Know the Material?, p. 129

CORE CONCEPTS SEARCH

Levels of Consciousness
Attention

Sleep
Dreaming

World Wide Web

For more information concerning the topics found in this chapter, access psychology links on the World Wide Web made through the Harcourt Brace webpage at

www.hbcollege.com

Share your comments and questions with your author at

PsychLinks@aol.com

The mechanisms of learning are similar from one person to another. *What* we learn, however, is a product not only of these mechanisms but of our individual and cultural experiences as well. Part of what artist Roger Shimomura learned about the United States was based on his family's experiences in detention camps during World War II. More than 100,000 Japanese Americans—most of them born in the United States—were confined in these camps, even while other Japanese Americans were fighting for the United States. *Untitled* (1984) combines learned cultural stereotypes of Japan and the United States, which vie for attention in the artist's mind.

ROGER SHIMOMURA

Chapter 7

Learning

TRUTH OR FICTION?

✔ **T F**

☐ ☐ Dogs can be trained to salivate when a bell is sounded.

☐ ☐ One nauseating meal can give rise to a food aversion that persists for years.

☐ ☐ Psychologists helped a young boy overcome his fear of rabbits by having him eat cookies while a rabbit was brought progressively nearer to him.

☐ ☐ During World War II, a psychologist devised a plan for training pigeons to guide missiles to their targets.

☐ ☐ Punishment does not work.

☐ ☐ Rats can be trained to climb a ramp, cross a bridge, climb a ladder, pedal a toy car, and do several other tasks—all in proper sequence.

☐ ☐ Psychologists successfully fashioned a method to teach an emaciated 9-month-old infant to stop throwing up.

☐ ☐ We must make mistakes if we are to learn.

☐ ☐ Despite all the media hoopla, no scientific connection has been established between violence viewed on TV and aggressive behavior in real life.

OUTLINE

CLASSICAL CONDITIONING
Ivan Pavlov Rings a Bell
Stimuli and Responses in Classical
Conditioning
Types of Classical Conditioning
Taste Aversion
Extinction and Spontaneous Recovery
Generalization and Discrimination
Higher-Order Conditioning
Applications of Classical Conditioning

OPERANT CONDITIONING
Edward L. Thorndike and the Law of
Effect
B. F. Skinner and Reinforcement
Types of Reinforcers
Extinction and Spontaneous Recovery
in Operant Conditioning
Reinforcers Versus Rewards and
Punishments
Discriminative Stimuli
Schedules of Reinforcement
Applications of Operant Conditioning
Psychology and Modern Life:
Using Conditioning to Help Children
Overcome Fears
Psychology in the New Millennium:
Virtual Classrooms Draw Cheers,
Fears

COGNITIVE FACTORS IN LEARNING
Contingency Theory: What "Really"
Happens During Classical Con-
ditioning?
Latent Learning: Forming Cognitive
Maps
Observational Learning: Monkey See,
Monkey May Choose to Do
Psychology in a World of Diversity:
Culture, Ethnicity, and Academic
Achievement
Psychology and Modern Life:
Teaching Children *Not* to Imitate
Media Violence

OPERANT CONDITIONING • A simple form of learning in which an organism learns to engage in behavior because it is reinforced.

CLASSICAL CONDITIONING • A simple form of learning in which an organism comes to associate or anticipate events. A neutral stimulus comes to evoke the response usually evoked by another stimulus by being paired repeatedly with the other stimulus. (Cognitive theorists view classical conditioning as the learning of relationships among events so as to allow an organism to represent its environment.) Also referred to as *respondent conditioning* or *Pavlovian conditioning*.

EACHING MY NEW DOG, PHOEBE, TO FETCH was going to be a snap.

I bought a soft yellow ball for her that squeaked when she bit into it. She enjoyed playing with it, and I assumed that she would want to run after it. (Wrong!) I waved it under her nose. She sniffed at it, barked, and wagged her tail excitedly.

Then, as Phoebe watched, I tossed the ball about 20 feet away. "Fetch!" I said as the ball bounced invitingly in the grass.

"People say 'Take it!'" my teenage daughter Allyn said.

Perhaps Allyn was right. Phoebe watched the ball but didn't run after it. Instead she barked at me and snapped softly at my legs.

"Okay," I said (to both of them). I ran after the ball, picked it up, and waved it under Phoebe's nose again. She barked and wagged her tail rapidly like a reed in a brisk wind.

"Take it!" I said and tossed the ball into the air again.

Again Phoebe refused to run after it. She barked and snapped at my legs again. "This is ridiculous," I muttered, and I went to get the ball. As I brought it back to Phoebe, Allyn said, "Don't you see what's happening?"

"What?"

"Phoebe's teaching you to fetch," Allyn laughed.

"Don't you mean to 'Take it'?" I said.

Yes, Phoebe was teaching me to fetch. Somehow she got me to run after the ball. When I brought it back to her, she reinforced my behavior with a show of excitement and (apparent) glee. Phoebe used the method known as operant conditioning. In **operant conditioning,** an organism learns to engage in certain behavior because of the effects of that behavior. Phoebe taught me that fetching the ball would be followed by pleasant events, leading me to repeat the behavior.

Classical conditioning was also at work. **Classical conditioning** leads organisms to anticipate events. On the next day I showed Phoebe the ball. She became excited and barked at the door of the family room, apparently because she had learned to associate the ball with the fun we had had the day before.

Classical and operant conditioning are two forms of learning, which is the subject of this chapter. In lower organisms, much behavior is instinctive, or inborn. Fish are born "knowing" how to swim. Salmon instinctively return to spawn in the stream where they were born after they have spent years roaming the seas. Robins instinctively know how to sing the song of their species and to build nests. Rats instinctively mate and rear their young. Among humans, however, the variety and complexity of behavior patterns are largely products of experience. Experience is essential to learning to walk and acquiring the language of our parents and community. We learn to read, to compute numbers,

How Do We Learn How to Play Chess? Games like chess are learned, but how? Can we explain playing chess as the summation of myriad instances of conditioning, or must we explain it in terms of mental representations and cognitive maps? What developments in the nervous system make us "ready" to learn the right moves? What biological changes register the memories of games played in the past?

and to surf the net. We learn to seek out the foods that are valued in our culture when we are hungry. We get into the habit of starting our day with coffee, tea, or other beverages. We learn which behavior patterns are deemed socially acceptable and which are considered wrong. And, of course, our families and communities use verbal guidance, set examples, and apply rewards and punishments to try to teach us to stick to the straight and narrow.

Sometimes our learning experiences are direct, like Phoebe's reinforcement of my fetching the ball. But we can also learn from the experiences of others. For example, I warn my children against the perils of jumping from high places and running wild in the house. (Occasionally they heed me.) From books and visual media, we learn about the past, about other peoples, and about how to put things together. And we learn as we invent ways of doing things that have never been done before.

Having noted these various ways of learning, let me admit that the very definition of learning stirs controversy in psychology. The term may be defined in different ways.

From the behaviorist perspective, **learning** is a relatively permanent change in behavior that arises from experience. Changes in behavior also arise from maturation and physical changes, but they do not reflect learning. The behaviorist defines learning in terms of the measurable events or changes in behavior by which it is known. From the behaviorist perspective, I learned to fetch the ball because Phoebe reinforced me for doing so.

From the cognitive perspective, learning involves processes by which experience contributes to relatively permanent changes in the way organisms mentally represent their environment. Changes in representation may influence, but do not cause, changes in behavior. From this perspective, learning is *demonstrated* by behavioral change, but it is an internal process. From the cognitive perspective, Phoebe's reinforcement of my fetching of the ball gave me information. It showed me that Phoebe wanted me to repeat the act. But my continued fetching was not mechanical or mandatory. (Or at least I don't think it was.)

LEARNING • (1) According to behaviorists, a relatively permanent change in behavior that results from experience. (2) According to cognitive theorists, the process by which organisms make relatively permanent changes in the way they represent the environment because of experience. These changes influence the organism's behavior but do not fully determine it.

REFLECTIONS
- Are you more in sympathy with the behavioral or the cognitive perspective on learning? Why?

■ CLASSICAL CONDITIONING

Classical conditioning involves some of the ways in which we learn to associate events with other events. Consider: We have a distinct preference for a grade of *A* rather than *F*. We are also (usually) more likely to stop for a red light than for a green light. Why? We are not born with instinctive attitudes toward the letters *A* and *F*. Nor are we born knowing that red means stop and green means go. We learn the meanings of these symbols because they are associated with other events. *A*'s are associated with instructor approval and the likelihood of getting into graduate school. Red lights are associated with avoiding accidents and traffic citations.

• *Ivan Pavlov Rings a Bell*

Lower animals also learn relationships among events, as Ivan Pavlov discovered in research with laboratory dogs. Pavlov was attempting to identify neural receptors in the mouth that triggered a response from the salivary glands. But his efforts were hampered by the dogs' salivating at undesired times, such as when a laboratory assistant inadvertently clanged a food tray.

Because of its biological makeup, a dog will salivate if meat powder is placed on its tongue. Salivation in response to meat powder is a **reflex;** it is not learned. Reflexes are elicited by a certain range of stimuli. A **stimulus** is an environmental condition that evokes a response from an organism, such as meat powder on the tongue or a traffic light's changing from red to green. Reflexes are simple unlearned responses to stimuli. Pavlov discovered that reflexes can also be learned, or *conditioned*, through association. His dogs began salivating in response to clinking food trays because in the past this noise had repeatedly been paired with the arrival of food. The dogs would also salivate when an assistant entered the laboratory. Why? In the past, the assistant had brought food.

REFLEX • A simple unlearned response to a stimulus.
STIMULUS • An environmental condition that elicits a response.
CONDITIONED RESPONSE (CR) • In classical conditioning, a learned response to a conditioned stimulus.

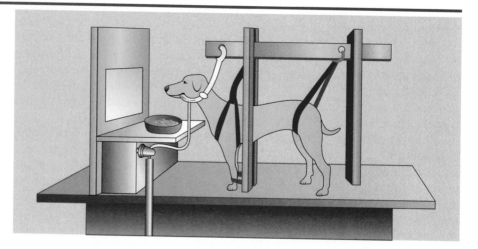

FIGURE 7.1

PAVLOV'S DEMONSTRATION OF CONDITIONED REFLEXES IN LABORATORY DOGS
From behind the two-way mirror at the left, a laboratory assistant rings a bell and then places meat on the dog's tongue. After several pairings, the dog salivates in response to the bell alone. A tube collects saliva and passes it to a vial. The quantity of saliva is taken as a measure of the strength of the animal's response.

When we are faced with novel events, we sometimes have no immediate way of knowing whether they are important. When we are striving for concrete goals, for example, we often ignore the unexpected, even when the unexpected is just as important, or more important, than the goal. So it was that Pavlov at first viewed the uncalled-for canine salivation as an annoyance, a hindrance to his research. But in 1901 he decided that his "problem" was worth looking into. He set about to show that he could train, or condition, his dogs to salivate when he wished and in response to any stimulus he chose.

Pavlov termed these trained salivary responses "conditional reflexes." They were *conditional* upon the repeated pairing of a previously neutral stimulus (such as the clinking of a food tray) and a stimulus (in this case, food) that predictably elicited the target response (in this case, salivation). Today conditional reflexes are more generally referred to as **conditioned responses (CRs).** They are responses to previously neutral stimuli that have been learned, or conditioned.

Pavlov demonstrated conditioned responses by strapping a dog into a harness like the one shown in Figure 7.1. When meat powder was placed on the dog's tongue, the dog salivated. Pavlov repeated the process several times, with one difference. He preceded the meat powder by half a second or so with the sounding of a bell on each occasion. After several pairings of meat powder and bell, Pavlov sounded the bell but did *not* follow the bell with the meat powder. Still the dog salivated. It had learned to salivate in response to the bell.

Why did the dog learn to salivate in response to the bell? Behaviorists and cognitive psychologists explain the learning process in very different ways. Put on your critical thinking cap: Would behaviorists say that after a few

Ivan Pavlov

One severe Russian winter, when he was too poor to heat his home adequately, his butterflies died. At the time, Ivan Pavlov (1849–1936) was studying the life cycle of butterflies. When his wife complained about their lack of money, he insisted that the loss of the butterflies was a greater misfortune. Despite his self-imposed poverty—he had chosen the life of a scholar—he was a generous husband. He bought his wife a pair of shoes for a trip. Yet upon her arrival she discovered that one shoe was missing. She later learned that Ivan had kept it on his desk as a remembrance of her.

Pavlov was the son of an Orthodox priest, and his mother was the daughter of a priest. Pavlov planned to become a priest himself until he read Darwin's *Origin of Species* and Ivan Sechenov's *Reflexes of the Brain.* He decided to devote himself to science and studied under Sechenov at the University of St. Petersburg, thanks to the generosity of the czar.

Pavlov was a dedicated physiologist. He spent much of his professional life studying digestion. He threatened to fire anyone in his lab who used psychological terms to describe conditioned reflexes, which he saw as brain reflexes, not as examples of associative learning. Pavlov eventually obtained professorships at the St. Petersburg Military Academy and the University of St. Petersburg. Although a physiologist, Pavlov believed—as did Watson—that animal and human learning are equivalent processes. ■

Ivan Pavlov. Pavlov, his assistants, and a professional salivator (the dog) in Russia early in the 20th century.

pairings of bell and food a dog "knows" that the bell "means" that food is on its way? Why or why not?

Behaviorists explain the outcome of this process, termed *classical conditioning*, in terms of the publicly observable conditions of learning. They define classical conditioning as a simple form of learning in which one stimulus comes to evoke the response usually evoked by a second stimulus by being paired repeatedly with the second stimulus. In Pavlov's demonstration, the dog learned to salivate in response to the bell *because* the sounding of the bell had been paired with meat powder. That is, in classical conditioning, the organism forms associations between stimuli because the stimuli are **contiguous**. Behaviorists do *not* say that the dog "knew" that food was on the way. They argue that we cannot speak meaningfully about what a dog "knows." We can only outline the conditions under which targeted behaviors will reliably occur. The behaviorists" focus is on *the mechanical acquisition of the conditioned response.*

Cognitive psychologists view classical conditioning as the learning of relationships among events. The relationships allow organisms to mentally represent their environments and make predictions (Holyoak and others, 1989; Rescorla, 1988). In Pavlov's demonstration, the dog salivated in response to the bell because the bell—from the cognitive perspective—became mentally connected with the meat powder. The cognitive focus is on *the information gained by the organism.* Organisms are viewed as seekers of information that generate and test rules about the relationships among events (Weiner, 1991).

CONTIGUOUS • Next to one another.
UNCONDITIONED STIMULUS (US) • A stimulus that elicits a response from an organism prior to conditioning.
UNCONDITIONED RESPONSE (UR) • An unlearned response to an unconditioned stimulus.
ORIENTING REFLEX • An unlearned response in which an organism attends to a stimulus.
CONDITIONED STIMULUS (CS) • A previously neutral stimulus that elicits a conditioned response because it has been paired repeatedly with a stimulus that already elicited that response.

Stimuli and Responses in Classical Conditioning

In the demonstration just described, the meat powder is an unlearned or **unconditioned stimulus (US)**. Salivation in response to the meat powder is an unlearned or **unconditioned response (UR)**. The bell was at first a meaningless or neutral stimulus. It might have produced an **orienting reflex** in the dog because of its distinctness. But it was not yet associated with food. Then, through repeated association with the meat powder, the bell became a learned or **conditioned stimulus (CS)** for the salivation response. Salivation in response to the

FIGURE 7.2

A SCHEMATIC REPRESENTATION OF CLASSICAL CONDITIONING

Prior to conditioning, food elicits salivation. The bell, a neutral stimulus, elicits either no response or an orienting response. During conditioning, the bell is rung just before meat is placed on the dog's tongue. After several repetitions, the bell, now a CS, elicits salivation, the CR.

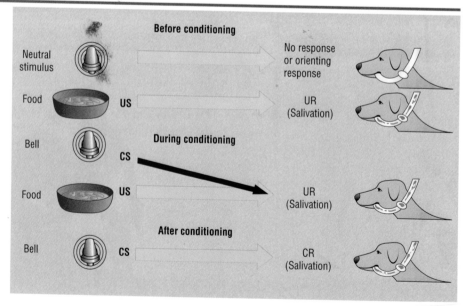

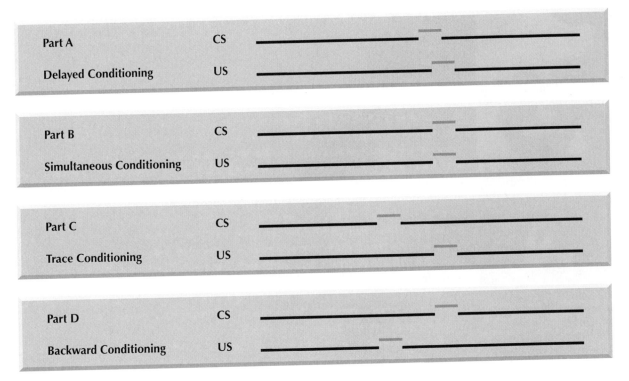

FIGURE 7.3

TYPES OF CLASSICAL CONDITIONING

In delayed conditioning (part A), the CS is presented before the US. In simultaneous conditioning (part B), the CS and US are presented together. In trace conditioning (part C), the CS is presented and removed prior to the US. Thus only the memory trace of the CS remains when the US is presented. In backward conditioning (part D), the US is presented before the CS. Delayed conditioning is most efficient, perhaps because it allows organisms to make predictions about their environments.

bell (or CS) is a learned or conditioned response (CR). A CR is a response similar to a UR, but the response elicited by the CS is by definition a CR, not a UR (see Figure 7.2).

• *Types of Classical Conditioning*

Classical conditioning tends to occur most efficiently when the conditioned stimulus (CS) is presented about 0.5 second before the unconditioned stimulus (US) and is continued until the learner responds to the US. This is an example of **delayed conditioning,** in which the CS (for example, a light) can be presented anywhere from a fraction of a second to several seconds before the US (in this case, meat powder) and is left on until the response (salivation) is shown (see Figure 7.3). Conditioning can also take place via **simultaneous conditioning,** in which a CS such as a light is presented along with a US such as meat powder. In **trace conditioning,** the CS (for example, a light) is presented and then removed (or turned off) prior to presentation of the US (meat powder). Therefore, only the memory trace of the CS (light) remains to be conditioned to the US.

Conditioning occurs most effectively in delayed conditioning, perhaps because it is most adaptive. That is, in delayed conditioning, the occurrence of the CS signals the consequent appearance of the US. As a result, organisms can learn to make predictions about their environment. Predictability is adaptive because it allows the organism to prepare for future events. Learning is inefficient and may not take place at all when the US is presented before the

DELAYED CONDITIONING • A classical conditioning procedure in which the CS is presented before the US and remains in place until the response occurs.

SIMULTANEOUS CONDITIONING • A classical conditioning procedure in which the CS and US are presented at the same time.

TRACE CONDITIONING • A classical conditioning procedure in which the CS is presented and then removed before the US is presented.

Formation of a Taste Aversion? Taste aversions may be acquired as a result of only one association of the US and the CS. Most kinds of classical conditioning require that the US and CS be contiguous, but in a taste aversion the US (nausea) can occur hours after the CS (flavor of food).

Truth or Fiction Revisited

It is true that one nauseating meal can give rise to a food aversion that persists for years.

BACKWARD CONDITIONING • A classical conditioning procedure in which the unconditioned stimulus is presented prior to the conditioned stimulus.
TASTE AVERSION • A kind of classical conditioning in which a previously desirable or neutral food becomes repugnant because it is associated with aversive stimulation.

CS (Hall, 1989), a sequence referred to as **backward conditioning.** Backward conditioning may not permit an organism to make predictions about its environment.

• *Taste Aversion*

When I was a child in The Bronx, my friends and I would go to the movies on Saturday mornings. There would be a serial followed by a feature film, and the price of admission was a quarter. We would also eat candy (I loved Nonpareils and Raisinets) and popcorn. One morning my friends dared me to eat two huge containers of buttered popcorn by myself. I rose to the challenge: Down went an enormous container of buttered popcorn. More slowly—much more slowly—I stuffed down the second container. Predictably, I felt bloated and nauseated. The taste of the butter, corn, and salt lingered in my mouth and nose, and my head spun. It was obvious to me that I would have no more popcorn that day. However, I was surprised that I could not face buttered popcorn again for a year.

Years later I learned that psychologists refer to my response to buttered popcorn as a **taste aversion.** More than forty years have passed, and the odor of buttered popcorn still turns my stomach.

A taste aversion is an example of classical conditioning. Taste aversions are adaptive because they motivate organisms to avoid potentially harmful foods. Although taste aversions are acquired by association, they differ from other kinds of classical conditioning in a couple of ways. First, only one association may be required. I did not have to go back for seconds at the movies to develop my aversion for buttered popcorn! Second, whereas most kinds of classical conditioning require that the US and CS be contiguous, in taste aversion the US (nausea) can occur hours after the CS (flavor of food).

Research on taste aversion also challenges the behaviorist view that organisms learn to associate any stimuli that are contiguous. In reality, not all stimuli are created equal. Instead, it seems that organisms are biologically predisposed to develop aversions that are adaptive in their environmental settings (Garcia and others, 1989). In a classic study, Garcia and Koelling (1966) conditioned two groups of rats. Each group was exposed to the same three-part CS: a taste of sweetened water, a light, and a clicker. Afterward, one group was presented with a US of nausea (induced by poison or radiation), and the other group was presented with a US of electric shock.

After conditioning, the rats who had been nauseated showed an aversion for sweetened water but not to the light or clicker. Although all three stimuli had been presented at the same time, *the rats had acquired only the taste aversion.* After conditioning, the rats that had been shocked avoided both the light and the clicker, *but they did not show a taste aversion to the sweetened water.* For each group of rats, the conditioning that took place was adaptive. In the natural scheme of things, nausea is more likely to stem from poisoned food than from lights or sounds. So, for nauseated rats, acquiring the taste aversion was appropriate. Sharp pain, in contrast, is more likely to stem from natural events involving lights (fire, lightning) and sharp sounds (twigs snapping, things falling). Therefore, it was more appropriate for the shocked animals to develop an aversion to the light and the clicker than to the sweetened water.

This finding fits my experience as well. My nausea led to a taste aversion to buttered popcorn—but not to an aversion to the serials I watched (which, in retrospect, were more deserving of nausea) or the movie theater. I returned every Saturday morning to see what would happen next. Yet, the serial and the theater, as much as the buttered popcorn, had been associated with my nausea. That is, the stimuli had been contiguous.

• *Extinction and Spontaneous Recovery*

Extinction and spontaneous recovery are aspects of conditioning that help organisms adapt by updating their expectations or revising their representations of the changing environment. For example a dog may learn to associate a new scent (CS) with the appearance of a dangerous animal. It can then take evasive action when it catches a whiff of that scent. A child may learn to connect hearing a car pull into the driveway (CS) with the arrival of his or her parents (US). Thus, the child may begin to squeal with delight (CR) when the car is heard.

But times can change. The once dangerous animal may no longer be a threat. (What a puppy perceives to be a threat may lose its fearsomeness once the dog matures.) After moving to a new house, the child's parents may commute by means of public transportation. The sound of a car in a nearby driveway may signal a neighbor's, not a parent's, homecoming. When conditioned stimuli (such as the scent of a dog or the sound of a car) are no longer followed by unconditioned stimuli (a dangerous animal, a parent's homecoming), they lose their ability to elicit conditioned responses. In this way the organism adapts to a changing environment.

EXTINCTION   In classical conditioning, **extinction** is the process by which conditioned stimuli (CSs) lose the ability to elicit conditioned responses (CRs) because the CSs are no longer associated with unconditioned stimuli (USs). From the cognitive perspective, extinction teaches the organism to modify its representation of the environment because the CS no longer serves its predictive function.

In experiments on the extinction of CRs, Pavlov found that repeated presentations of the CS (or bell) without the US (meat powder) led to extinction of the CR (salivation in response to the bell). Figure 7.4 shows that a dog that had

EXTINCTION • An experimental procedure in which stimuli lose their ability to evoke learned responses because the events that had followed the stimuli no longer occur. (The learned responses are said to be *extinguished*.)

FIGURE 7.4

LEARNING AND EXTINCTION CURVES

Actual data from Pavlov (1927) compose the jagged line, and the curved lines are idealized. In the acquisition phase, a dog salivates (shows a CR) in response to a bell (CS) after a few trials in which the bell is paired with meat powder (the US). Afterward, the CR is extinguished in about ten trials during which the CS is not followed by the US. After a rest period, the CR recovers spontaneously. A second series of extinction trials leads to more rapid extinction of the CR.

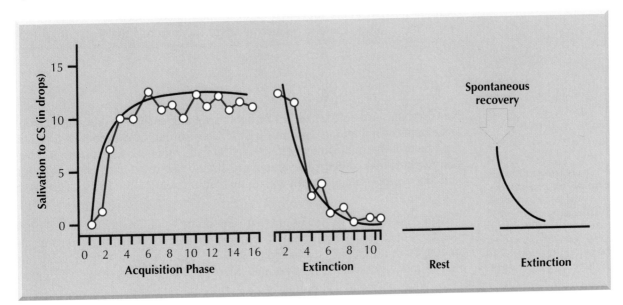

been conditioned began to salivate (show a CR) in response to a bell (CS) after only a couple of pairings—referred to as **acquisition trials**—of the bell with meat powder (the US). Continued pairings of the stimuli led to increased salivation (measured in number of drops of saliva). After seven or eight trials, salivation leveled off at 11 to 12 drops.

In the next series of experiments, salivation in response to the bell (CR) was extinguished through several trials—referred to as **extinction trials**—in which the CS (bell) was presented without the meat powder (US). After about 10 extinction trials, the CR (salivation in response to the bell) was no longer shown.

What would happen if we were to allow a day or two to pass after we had extinguished the CR in a dog and then presented the CS again? Where would you place your bet? Would the dog salivate or not?

If you bet that the dog would again show the CR (salivate in response to the bell), you were correct. Organisms tend to show **spontaneous recovery** of extinguished CRs merely as a function of the passage of time. For this reason, the term *extinction* may be a bit misleading. When a species of animal becomes extinct, all the members of that species that are capable of reproducing have died. The species vanishes. But the experimental extinction of CRs does not lead to the permanent eradication of CRs. Rather, it seems that they *inhibit* the response. The response remains available for future performance under the "right" conditions.

Consider Figure 7.4 again. When spontaneous recovery of the CR does occur, the strength of the response (in this case, the number of drops of saliva) is not as great as it was at the end of the series of acquisition trials. A second set of extinction trials will also extinguish the CR more rapidly than the first series of trials. Although the second time around the CR is weaker at first, pairing the CS with the US once more will build response strength rapidly.

Spontaneous recovery, like extinction, is adaptive. What would happen if the child heard no car in the driveway for several months? It could be that the next time a car entered the driveway, the child would associate the sounds with a parent's homecoming (rather than with the arrival of a neighbor). This expectation could be appropriate. After all, *something* had changed when no car entered the nearby driveway for so long. In the wild, a waterhole may contain water for only a couple of months during the year. But it is useful for animals to associate the waterhole with the thirst drive from time to time so that they will return to it at the appropriate time.

As time passes and the seasons change, things sometimes follow circular paths and arrive where they were before. Spontaneous recovery seems to provide a mechanism whereby organisms adapt to situations that recur from time to time.

• *Generalization and Discrimination*

No two things are quite alike. Traffic lights are hung at slightly different heights, and shades of red and green differ a little. The barking of two dogs differs, and the sound of the same animal differs slightly from one bark to the next. Adaptation requires that we respond similarly to stimuli that are equivalent in function and that we respond differently to stimuli that are not.

GENERALIZATION Pavlov noted that responding to different stimuli as though they are functionally equivalent is adaptive for animals. Rustling sounds in the undergrowth differ, but rabbits and deer do well to flee when they perceive any one of many possible rustling sounds. Sirens differ, but people do well to be-

ACQUISITION TRIAL • In conditioning, a presentation of stimuli such that a new response is learned and strengthened.

EXTINCTION TRIAL • In conditioning, a performance of a learned response in the absence of its predicted consequences so that the learned response becomes inhibited.

SPONTANEOUS RECOVERY • The recurrence of an extinguished response as a function of the passage of time.

Generalization at the Crossroads. Chances are that you have never seen these particular traffic lights in this particular setting. Because of generalization, however, we can safely bet that you would know what to do if you were to drive up to them.

come vigilant or to pull their cars to the side of the road when they hear a siren of any kind.

In a demonstration of **generalization,** Pavlov first conditioned a dog to salivate when a circle was presented. During each acquisition trial, the dog was shown a circle (CS) and then given meat powder (US). After several trials the dog salivated when presented with the circle alone. Pavlov demonstrated that the dog also exhibited the CR (salivation) in response to closed geometric figures such as ellipses, pentagons, and even squares. The more closely the figure resembled a circle, the greater the strength of the response (the more drops of saliva flowed).

DISCRIMINATION Organisms must also learn (1) that many stimuli that are perceived as being similar are functionally different and (2) that they must respond adaptively to each. During the first couple of months of life, babies can discriminate their mother's voice from those of other women. They will often stop crying when they hear their mother but not when they hear a stranger's voice.

Pavlov showed that a dog that was conditioned to salivate in response to circles could be trained *not* to salivate in response to ellipses. The type of conditioning that trains an organism to show a CR in response to a narrow range of stimuli (in this case, circular rather than elliptical geometric figures) is termed **discrimination training.** Pavlov trained the dog by presenting it with circles and ellipses but associating the meat powder (US) with circles only. After a while, the dog no longer showed the CR (salivation) in response to the ellipses. Instead, it showed **discrimination:** It displayed the CR in response to circles only.

Pavlov then discovered that by increasing the difficulty of the discrimination task he could make the dog behave as though it were tormented. After the dog exhibited stimulus discrimination, Pavlov showed it a series of progressively rounder ellipses. Eventually the dog could no longer discriminate the ellipses from circles. The animal then put on an infantile show. It urinated, defecated, barked profusely, and snapped at laboratory personnel.

GENERALIZATION • In conditioning, the tendency for a conditioned response to be evoked by stimuli that are similar to the stimulus to which the response was conditioned.

DISCRIMINATION TRAINING • Teaching an organism to show a learned response in the presence of only one of a series of similar stimuli, accomplished by alternating the stimuli but following only the one stimulus with the unconditioned stimulus.

DISCRIMINATION • In conditioning, the tendency for an organism to distinguish between a conditioned stimulus and similar stimuli that do not forecast an unconditioned stimulus.

"Little Albert"

If you happen across a gentleman nearly 80 years old who cringes at the sight of a fur coat, he may not be concerned about animal rights. Perhaps he is "Little Albert," who was conditioned to fear furry objects before he reached his first birthday.

In 1920 John B. Watson and his future wife, Rosalie Rayner, published a report of their demonstration that emotional reactions can be acquired through classical conditioning. The subject of their demonstration was a lad who has become known as "Little Albert" (a counterpart to Freud's famous case study of "Little Hans"—see Chapter 15). At the age of 11 months, Albert was a phlegmatic fellow. He wasn't given to ready displays of emotion. But he did enjoy playing with a laboratory rat.

Using a method that many psychologists have criticized as unethical, Watson startled Little Albert by clanging steel bars behind his head whenever the infant played with the rat. After repeated pairings, Albert showed fear of the rat even when the clanging was halted. Albert's fear also generalized to objects that were similar in appearance to the rat, such as a rabbit and the fur collar on a woman's coat. Watson has also been criticized for not attempting to *countercondition* Albert's fear. However, a few years later Mary Cover Jones did exactly that with another boy—under Watson's supervision. ■

How do we explain the dog's belligerent behavior? In a classic work written more than half a century ago, titled *Frustration and Aggression*, a group of behaviorally oriented psychologists suggested that frustration induces aggression (Dollard and others, 1939). Why is failure to discriminate circles from ellipses frustrating? For one thing, in such experiments, rewards—such as meat powder—are usually made contingent on correct discrimination. That is, if the dog errs, it forgoes the meat. Cognitive theorists, however, propose that organisms are motivated to construct realistic maps of the world. In doing so they adjust their representations so as to reduce discrepancies and accommodate new information (Rescorla, 1988). In Pavlov's experiment, the dog lost the ability to meaningfully adjust its representation of the environment as the ellipses grew more circular. Thus, it was frustrated.

Daily living requires appropriate generalization and discrimination. No two hotels are alike, but when we travel from one city to another it is adaptive to expect to stay in a hotel. It is encouraging that a green light in Washington has the same meaning as a green light in Paris. But returning home in the evening requires the ability to discriminate between our own home or apartment and those of other people. And if we could not readily tell our spouse from those of other people, we might land in divorce court.

• Higher-Order Conditioning

In **higher-order conditioning,** a previously neutral stimulus comes to serve as a CS after repeatedly being paired with a stimulus that has already become a CS. Pavlov demonstrated higher-order conditioning by first conditioning a dog to salivate (show a CR) in response to a bell (a CS). He then repeatedly paired the shining of a light with the sounding of a bell. After several pairings, shining the light (the higher-order CS) came to elicit the response (salivation) that had been elicited by the bell (the first-order CS).

Consider children who learn that when they hear a car in the driveway their parents are about to arrive. It may be the case that a certain TV cartoon show starts a few minutes before the car enters the driveway. The TV show can begin to elicit the expectation that the parents are coming by repeatedly being paired with the car's entering the driveway. In another example, a boy may burn himself by touching a hot stove. After this experience, the sight of the stove may serve as a CS for eliciting a fear response. And because hearing the word *stove* may evoke a cognitive image of the stove, hearing the word alone may also elicit a fear response.

• Applications of Classical Conditioning

Classical conditioning is a major means by which we learn. It is how stimuli come to serve as signals for other stimuli. It is why, for example, we come to expect that someone will be waiting outside when the doorbell is rung or why we expect a certain friend to appear when we hear a characteristic knock at the door.

HIGHER-ORDER CONDITIONING • (1) According to behaviorists, a classical conditioning procedure in which a previously neutral stimulus comes to elicit the response brought forth by a *conditioned* stimulus by being paired repeatedly with that conditioned stimulus. (2) According to cognitive psychologists, the learning of relationships among events, none of which evokes an unlearned response.

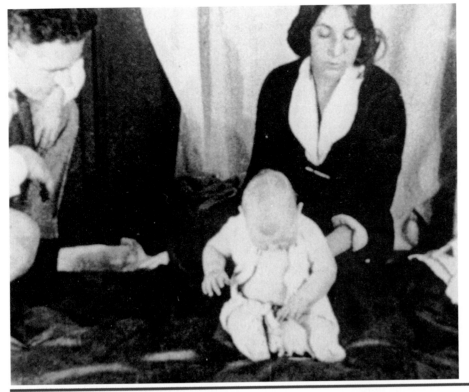

John Watson and Rosalie Rayner with "Little Albert."

THE BELL-AND-PAD TREATMENT FOR BED-WETTING By the age of five or six, children normally awaken in response to the sensation of a full bladder. They inhibit the urge to urinate, which is an automatic or reflexive response to bladder tension, and instead go to the bathroom. But bed wetters tend not to respond to bladder tension while asleep. They remain asleep and frequently wet their beds.

By means of the bell-and-pad method, children are taught to wake up in response to bladder tension. They sleep on a special sheet or pad that has been placed on the bed. When the child starts to urinate, the water content of the urine causes an electrical circuit in the pad to close. The closing of the circuit triggers a bell or buzzer, and the child is awakened. (Similar buzzer circuits have been built into training pants as an aid to toilet training.) In terms of classical conditioning, the bell is a US that wakes the child (waking up is the UR). By means of repeated pairings, a stimulus that precedes the bell becomes associated with the bell and also gains the capacity to awaken the child. What is that stimulus? The sensation of a full bladder. In this way, bladder tension (the CS) gains the capacity to awaken the child *even though the child is asleep during the classical conditioning procedure.*

The bell-and-pad method is a superb example of why behaviorists prefer to explain the effects of classical conditioning in terms of the pairing of stimuli and not in terms of what the learner knows. The behaviorist may argue that we cannot assume that a sleeping child "knows" that wetting the bed will cause the bell to ring. We can only note that by repeatedly pairing bladder tension with the bell, the child eventually *learns* to wake up in response to bladder tension alone. *Learning* is demonstrated by the change in the child's behavior. One can only speculate on what the child *knows* about the learning process.

Can Chocolate Chip Cookies Countercondition Fears? In the 1920s Mary Cover Jones helped a boy overcome his fear of rabbits by having him munch on cookies as the animal was brought closer.

FLOODING AND SYSTEMATIC DESENSITIZATION Two behavior therapy methods for reducing specific fears are based on the classical conditioning principle of extinction (Wolpe & Plaud, 1997). In one, called **flooding**, the client is exposed to the fear-evoking stimulus until the fear response is extinguished (Turner and others, 1994). Little Albert, for example, the subject of the "In Profile" on page 252, might have been placed in close contact with a rat until his fear had become fully extinguished. In extinction, the CS (in this case, the rat) is presented repeatedly in the absence of the US (the clanging of the steel bars) until the CR (fear) is no longer evoked.

Although flooding is usually effective, it is unpleasant. (When you are fearful of rats, being placed in a small room with one is no picnic.) For this reason, behavior therapists frequently prefer to use **systematic desensitization** (see Chapter 16), in which the client is gradually exposed to fear-evoking stimuli under circumstances in which he or she remains relaxed. For example, while feeling relaxed, Little Albert might have been given an opportunity to look at photos of rats or to see live rats from a distance before they were brought closer to him. Systematic desensitization, like flooding, is highly effective. It takes longer but it is not as unpleasant.

COUNTERCONDITIONING Early in the century, John Watson's protégé, Mary Cover Jones, (1924) reasoned that if fears could be conditioned by painful experiences, she could *countercondition* them by substituting pleasant experiences. In **counterconditioning**, a pleasant stimulus is repeatedly paired with a fear-evoking object, thereby counteracting the fear response.

Two-year-old Peter had an intense fear of rabbits. Jones arranged for a rabbit to be gradually brought closer to Peter while he engaged in some of his favorite activities, such as munching on candy and cookies. They did not simply plop the rabbit in Peter's lap, as in flooding. Had she done so, the cookies on the plate, not to mention those already eaten, might have decorated the walls. Instead, she first placed the rabbit in a far corner of the room while Peter munched and crunched. Peter, to be sure, cast a wary eye, but he continued to consume the treat. Gradually the animal was brought closer until eventually, Peter ate treats and touched the rabbit at the same time. Jones theorized that the joy of eating was incompatible with fear and thus counterconditioned it.

Truth or Fiction Revisited

It is true that psychologists helped a young boy overcome fear of rabbits by having him eat cookies while a rabbit was brought progressively nearer to him.

> **REFLECTIONS**
> - Had you heard the expression "That rings a bell"? To what does the expression refer?
> - What is the difference between extinction and forgetting?
> - Do you consider Watson and Rayner's experiment with "Little Albert" ethical? Why or why not?
> - Can you think of examples of classical conditioning in your own life?

FLOODING • A behavioral fear-reduction technique based on principles of classical conditioning. Fear-evoking stimuli (CSs) are presented continuously in the absence of actual harm so that fear responses (CRs) are extinguished.
SYSTEMATIC DESENSITIZATION • A behavioral fear-reduction technique in which a hierarchy of fear-evoking stimuli are presented while the person remains relaxed.
COUNTERCONDITIONING • A fear-reduction technique in which pleasant stimuli are associated with fear-evoking stimuli so that the fear-evoking stimuli lose their aversive qualities.

■ OPERANT CONDITIONING

Through classical conditioning, we learn to associate stimuli so that a simple, usually passive, response made to one stimulus is then made in response to the other. In the case of Little Albert, clanging noises were associated with a rat, so the rat came to elicit the fear response brought forth by the noise. However, classical conditioning is only one kind of learning that occurs in these situations. After Little Albert acquired his fear of the rat, his voluntary behavior changed. He avoided the rat as a way of reducing his fear. Thus, Little Albert engaged in another kind of learning—*operant conditioning*.

After I had acquired my taste aversion, I stayed away from buttered popcorn. My avoidance can also be explained in terms of operant conditioning. In *operant conditioning*, organisms learn to do things—or *not* to do things—because of the consequences of their behavior. I avoided buttered popcorn in order to prevent nausea. But we also seek fluids when we are thirsty, sex when we are aroused, and an ambient temperature of 68 to 70 degrees Fahrenheit when we feel too hot or too cold. *Classical conditioning focuses on how organisms form anticipations about their environments. Operant conditioning focuses on what they do about them.*

We begin this section with the historic work of psychologist Edward L. Thorndike. Then we examine the more recent work of B. F. Skinner.

• *Edward L. Thorndike and the Law of Effect*

In the 1890s stray cats were mysteriously disappearing from the streets and alleyways of Harlem. Many of them, it turned out, were being brought to the quarters of Columbia University doctoral student Edward Thorndike. Thorndike was using the cats as subjects in experiments on the effects of rewards and punishments on learning.

Thorndike placed the cats in so-called puzzle boxes. If the animal managed to pull a dangling string, a latch would be released, allowing it to jump out and reach a bowl of food.

When first placed in a puzzle box, a cat would try to squeeze through any opening and would claw and bite at the confining bars and wire. It would claw at anything it could reach. Through such random behavior, it might take 3 to 4 minutes for the cat to chance upon the response of pulling the string. Pulling the string would open the cage and allow the cat to reach the food. When placed back in the cage, it might again take several minutes for the animal to pull the string. But with repetition, it took progressively less time for the cat to pull the string. After seven or eight repetitions, the cat might pull the string immediately when placed back in the box.

THE LAW OF EFFECT Thorndike explained the cat's learning to pull the string in terms of his **law of effect.** According to this law, a response (such as string pulling) is "stamped in" or strengthened in a particular situation (such as being inside a puzzle box) by a reward (escaping from the box and eating). Rewards, that is, stamp in S-R (stimulus-response) connections. Punishments, in contrast, "stamp out" stimulus-response connections. Organisms would learn *not* to engage in punished responses. Later we shall see that the effects of punishment on learning are not so certain.

• *B. F. Skinner and Reinforcement*

"What did you do in the war, Daddy?" is a question familiar to many who served during America's conflicts. Some stories involve heroism, others involve the unusual. When it comes to unusual war stories, few will top that of Harvard University psychologist Burrhus Frederic Skinner. For one of Skinner's wartime efforts was "Project Pigeon" (Bjork, 1997).

LAW OF EFFECT • Thorndike's principle that responses are "stamped in" by rewards and "stamped out" by punishments.

B. F. Skinner

During his first TV appearance he was asked, "Would you, if you had to choose, burn your children or your books?" He said he would choose to burn his children, since his contribution to the future lay more in his writings than in his genes. B. F. Skinner (1904–1990) delighted in controversy, and his response earned him additional TV appearances.

Skinner was born into a middle-class Pennsylvania family. As a youth he was always building things—scooters, sleds, wagons, rafts, slides, and merry-go-rounds. Later he would build the so-called Skinner box, which improved on Thorndike's puzzle box, as a way of studying operant behavior. He earned an undergraduate degree in English and turned to psychology only after failing to make his mark as a writer in New York's Greenwich Village.

A great popularizer of his own views, Skinner used reinforcement to teach pigeons to play basketball and the piano—sort of. On a visit to his daughter's grammar school class, it occurred to him that similar techniques might work with children. He therefore invented *programmed learning.* Although he had earlier failed at writing, he gathered a cultish following when he published his novel *Walden II,* in which children were socialized from infancy into *wanting* to engage in prosocial behavior.

Skinner and his followers have applied his principles not only to programmed learning but also to behavior modification programs for helping people with disorders ranging from substance abuse to phobias to sexual dysfunctions. He died eight days after receiving an unprecedented Lifetime Contribution to Psychology award from the American Psychological Association. ■

Truth or Fiction Revisited

It is true that during World War II a psychologist devised a plan for training pigeons to guide missiles to their targets. That psychologist was B. F. Skinner, and his plan employed principles of operant conditioning.

REINFORCE • To follow a response with a stimulus that increases the frequency of the response.
OPERANT BEHAVIOR • Voluntary responses that are reinforced.
OPERANT • The same as an operant behavior.

During World War II Skinner proposed that pigeons be trained to guide missiles to their targets. In their training, the pigeons would be **reinforced** with food pellets for pecking at targets projected onto a screen (see Figure 7.5). Once trained, the pigeons would be placed in missiles. Their pecking at similar targets displayed on a screen would correct the missile's flight path, resulting in a "hit" and a sacrificed pigeon. However, plans for building the necessary missile—for some reason called the *Pelican* and not the *Pigeon*—were scrapped. The pigeon equipment was too bulky and, Skinner lamented, his suggestion was not taken seriously. Apparently the Defense Department concluded that Project Pigeon was for the birds.

Project Pigeon may have been scrapped, but the principles of learning that Skinner applied to the project have found wide applications. In operant conditioning, an organism learns to *do* something because of the effects or consequences of that behavior.

This is **operant behavior,** behavior that operates on, or manipulates, the environment. In classical conditioning, involuntary responses such as salivation or eyeblinks are often conditioned. In operant conditioning, *voluntary* responses such as pecking at a target, pressing a lever, or many of the skills required for playing tennis are acquired, or conditioned.

In operant conditioning, organisms engage in operant behaviors, also known simply as **operants,** that result in presumably desirable consequences such as food, a hug, an A on a test, attention, or social approval. Some children learn to conform their behavior to social rules to earn the attention and approval of their parents and teachers. Other children, ironically, may learn to "misbehave," since misbehavior also gets attention from other people. In particular, children may learn to be "bad" when their "good" behavior is routinely ignored.

UNITS OF BEHAVIOR, "SKINNER BOXES," AND CUMULATIVE RECORDERS In his most influential work, *The Behavior of Organisms,* Skinner (1938) made many theoretical and technological innovations. Among them was his focus on discrete behaviors such as lever pressing as the *unit,* or type, of behavior to be studied (Glenn and others, 1992). Other psychologists might focus on how organisms think or "feel." Skinner focused on measurable things that they do. Many psychologists have found these kinds of behavior inconsequential, especially when it comes to explaining and predicting human behavior. But Skinner's supporters point out that focusing on discrete behavior creates the potential for helpful changes. For example, in helping people combat depression, one psychologist might focus on their "feelings." A Skinnerian psychologist would focus on cataloguing (and modifying) the types of things that depressed people actually *do.* Directly modifying depressive behavior might also brighten clients' self-reports about their "feelings of depression."

To study operant behavior efficiently, Skinner devised an animal cage (or "operant chamber") that was dubbed the *Skinner box* by psychologist Clark Hull, whose theory of drive-reductionism is discussed in Chapter 11. (Skinner himself repeatedly requested that his operant chamber *not* be called a Skinner

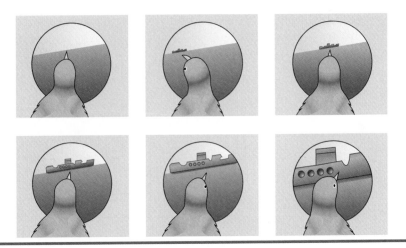

FIGURE 7.5
PROJECT PIGEON
During World War II, B. F. Skinner suggested using operant conditioning to train pigeons to guide missiles to their targets. The pigeons would first be reinforced for pecking targets projected on a screen. Afterward, in combat, pecking the on-screen target would keep the missile on course.

box. History has thus far failed to honor his wishes, however.[1]) Such a box is shown in Figure 7.6. The cage is ideal for laboratory experimentation because experimental conditions (treatments) can be carefully introduced and removed, and the effects on laboratory animals (defined as changes in rates of lever pressing) can be carefully observed. The operant chamber (or Skinner box) is also energy-efficient—in terms of the energy of the experimenter. In contrast to Thorndike's puzzle box, a "correct" response does not allow the animal to escape and have to be recaptured and placed back in the box. According to psychologist John Garcia, Skinner's "great contribution to the study of behavior was the marvelously efficient operant methodology" (1993, p. 1158).

The rat in Figure 7.6 was deprived of food and placed in a Skinner box with a lever at one end. At first it sniffed its way around the cage and engaged in random behavior. When organisms are behaving in a random manner, responses that have favorable consequences tend to occur more frequently. Responses that do not have favorable consequences tend to be performed less frequently.

---

[1] Of course, my using the term *Skinner box* does not exactly help Skinner's cause, either.

FIGURE 7.6
THE EFFECTS OF REINFORCEMENT
One of the celebrities of modern psychology, an albino laboratory rat, earns its keep in a Skinner box. The animal presses a lever because of reinforcement—in the form of food pellets—delivered through the feeder. The habit strength of this operant is the frequency of lever pressing.

FIGURE 7.7
THE CUMULATIVE RECORDER
In the cumulative recorder, paper moves to the left while a pen jerks up to record each targeted response. When the pen reaches the top of the paper, it is automatically reset to the bottom.

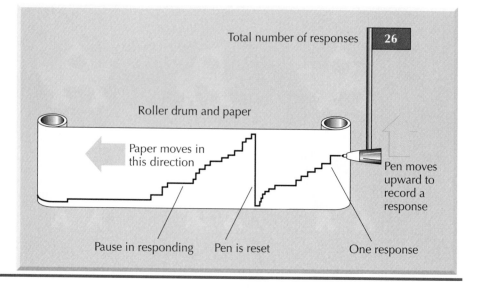

The rat's first pressing of the lever was inadvertent. However, because of this action, a food pellet dropped into the cage. The arrival of the food pellet increased the probability that the rat would press the lever again. The pellet thus is said to have served as a *reinforcement* for lever pressing.

Skinner further mechanized his laboratory procedure by making use of a turning drum, or **cumulative recorder,** a tool that had previously been used by physiologists (see Figure 7.7). The cumulative recorder provides a precise measure of operant behavior. The experimenter need not even be present to record the number of correct responses. In the example used, the lever in the Skinner box is connected to the recorder so that the recording pen moves upward with each correct response. The paper moves continuously to the left at a slow but regular pace. In the sample record shown in Figure 7.7, lever pressings (which record correct responses) were few and far between at first. But after several reinforced responses, lever pressings became fast and furious. When the rat is no longer hungry, the lever pressing will drop off and then stop.

THE FIRST "CORRECT" RESPONSE In operant conditioning, it matters little how the first response that is reinforced comes to be made. The organism can happen on it by chance, as in random learning. The organism can also be physically guided to make the response. You may command your dog to "Sit!" and then press its backside down until it is in a sitting position. Finally you reinforce sitting with food or a pat on the head and a kind word.

Animal trainers use physical guiding or coaxing to bring about the first "correct" response. Can you imagine how long it would take to train your dog if you waited for it to sit or roll over and then seized the opportunity to command it to sit or roll over? Both of you would age significantly in the process.

People, of course, can be verbally guided into desired responses when they are learning tasks such as spelling, adding numbers, or operating a machine. But they need to be informed when they have made the correct response. Knowledge of results often is all the reinforcement people need to learn new skills.

• *Types of Reinforcers*

CUMULATIVE RECORDER • An instrument that records the frequency of an organism's operants (or "correct" responses) as a function of the passage of time.

Any stimulus that increases the probability that responses preceding it will be repeated serves as a reinforcer. Reinforcers include food pellets when an organism has been deprived of food, water when it has been deprived of liquid, the opportunity to mate, and the sound of a bell that has previously been associated with eating.

POSITIVE AND NEGATIVE REINFORCERS Skinner distinguished between positive and negative reinforcers. **Positive reinforcers** increase the probability that an operant will occur when they are applied. Food and approval usually serve as positive reinforcers. **Negative reinforcers** increase the probability that an operant will occur when they are *removed* (see Figure 7.8). People often learn to plan ahead so that they need not fear that things will go wrong. In such cases fear acts as a negative reinforcer, because *removal* of fear increases the probability that the behaviors preceding it (such as planning ahead or fleeing a predator) will be repeated.

Greater reinforcers prompt more rapid learning than do lesser reinforcers. You would probably work much harder for $1,000 than for $10. (If not, get in touch with me—I have some chores that need to be taken care of.) With sufficient reinforcement, operants become *habits*. They have a high probability of recurrence in certain situations.

IMMEDIATE VERSUS DELAYED REINFORCERS Immediate reinforcers are more effective than delayed reinforcers. Therefore, the short-term consequences of behavior often provide more of an incentive than the long-term consequences. Some students socialize when they should be studying because the pleasure of socializing is immediate. Studying may not pay off until the final exam or graduation. (This is why younger students do better with frequent tests.) It is difficult to quit smoking cigarettes because the reinforcement of nicotine is immediate and the health hazards of smoking more distant. Focusing on short-term reinforcement is also connected with careless sexual behavior.

POSITIVE REINFORCER • A reinforcer that when *presented* increases the frequency of an operant.
NEGATIVE REINFORCER • A reinforcer that when *removed* increases the frequency of an operant.

FIGURE 7.8
POSITIVE VERSUS NEGATIVE REINFORCERS

All reinforcers *increase* the frequency of behavior. However, negative reinforcers are aversive stimuli that increase the frequency of behavior when they are *removed*. In these examples, teacher approval functions as a positive reinforcer when students study harder because of it. Teacher *disapproval* functions as a negative reinforcer when its *removal* increases the frequency of studying. Can you think of situations in which teacher approval might function as a negative reinforcer?

Procedure	Behavior	Consequence	Change in behavior
Use of Positive Reinforcement	Behavior (Studying)	Positive reinforcer (Teacher approval) is **presented** when student studies	Frequency of behavior **increases** (Student studies more)
Use of Negative Reinforcement	Behavior (Studying)	Negative reinforcer (Teacher disapproval) is **removed** when student studies	Frequency of behavior **increases** (Student studies more)

PRIMARY AND SECONDARY REINFORCERS We can also distinguish between primary and secondary, or conditioned, reinforcers. **Primary reinforcers** are effective because of an organism's biological makeup. Food, water, adequate warmth (positive reinforcers), and pain (a negative reinforcer) all serve as primary reinforcers. **Secondary reinforcers** acquire their value through being associated with established reinforcers. For this reason they are also termed **conditioned reinforcers.** We may seek money because we have learned that it may be exchanged for primary reinforcers. Money, attention, social approval—all are conditioned reinforcers in our culture. We may be suspicious of, or not "understand," people who are not interested in money or the approval of others. Part of understanding others lies in being able to predict what they will find reinforcing.

• *Extinction and Spontaneous Recovery in Operant Conditioning*

In operant conditioning as in classical conditioning, extinction is a process in which stimuli lose the ability to evoke learned responses because the events that followed the stimuli no longer occur. In classical conditioning, however, the "events" that normally follow and confirm the appropriateness of the learned response (that is, the conditioned response) are the unconditioned stimuli. In Pavlov's experiment, for example, the meat powder was the event that followed and confirmed the appropriateness of salivation. In operant conditioning, in contrast, the ensuing events are reinforcers. Thus, in operant conditioning the extinction of learned responses (that is, operants) results from the repeated performance of operant behavior without reinforcement. After a number of trials, the operant behavior is no longer displayed. If you go for a month without mail, you may stop checking the mailbox.

When some time is allowed to pass after the extinction process, an organism will usually perform the operant again when placed in a situation in which the operant had been reinforced previously. Such spontaneous recovery of learned responses occurs in operant conditioning as well as in classical conditioning. If the operant is reinforced at this time, it quickly regains its former strength. (Finding a few letters in the mailbox one week may again encourage you to check the mailbox daily.) Spontaneous recovery of extinguished operants suggests that they are inhibited or suppressed by the extinction process and not lost permanently.

• *Reinforcers Versus Rewards and Punishments*

Rewards, like reinforcers, are stimuli that increase the frequency of behavior. Rewards are also considered pleasant events. Skinner preferred the concept of reinforcement to that of reward because reinforcement does not suggest trying to "get inside the head" of an organism (whether a human or lower animal) to guess what it would find pleasant or unpleasant. A list of reinforcers is arrived at empirically, by observing what sorts of stimuli will increase the frequency of the behavior. However, it should be noted that some psychologists consider the term *reward* synonymous with positive reinforcement.

Punishments are aversive events that suppress or decrease the frequency of the behavior they follow (see Figure 7.9). Punishment can rapidly suppress undesirable behavior (Rosenfeld, 1995) and may be warranted in "emergencies," such as when a child tries to run into the street.

Despite the fact that punishment works, many learning theorists agree that punishment often fails to achieve the parent's goals (Rosenfeld, 1995). Consider the following reasons for avoiding the use of punishment:

PRIMARY REINFORCER • An unlearned reinforcer.
SECONDARY REINFORCER • A stimulus that gains reinforcement value through association with established reinforcers.
CONDITIONED REINFORCER • Another term for a secondary reinforcer.
REWARD • A pleasant stimulus that increases the frequency of the behavior it follows.
PUNISHMENT • An unpleasant stimulus that suppresses the behavior it follows.

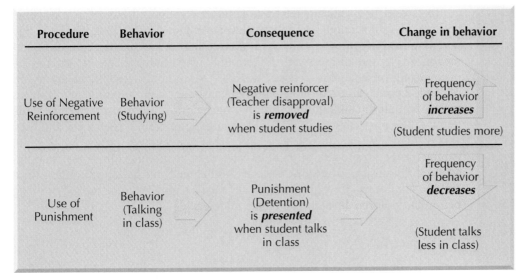

Procedure	Behavior	Consequence	Change in behavior
Use of Negative Reinforcement	Behavior (Studying)	Negative reinforcer (Teacher disapproval) **is removed** when student studies	Frequency of behavior **increases** (Student studies more)
Use of Punishment	Behavior (Talking in class)	Punishment (Detention) **is presented** when student talks in class	Frequency of behavior **decreases** (Student talks less in class)

FIGURE 7.9

NEGATIVE REINFORCERS VERSUS PUNISHMENTS

Negative reinforcers and punishments both tend to be aversive stimuli. However, reinforcers *increase* the frequency of behavior. Punishments *decrease* the frequency of behavior. Negative reinforcers increase the frequency of behavior when they are *removed*. Punishments decrease or suppress the frequency of behavior when they are *applied*. Can you think of situations in which punishing students might have effects other than those desired by the teacher?

1. Punishment does not in itself suggest an alternative acceptable form of behavior.

2. Punishment tends to suppress undesirable behavior only under circumstances in which its delivery is guaranteed. It does not take children long to learn that they can "get away with murder" with one parent or teacher but not with another.

3. Punished organisms may withdraw from the situation. Severely punished children may run away, cut class, or drop out of school.

4. Punishment can create anger and hostility. Adequate punishment will almost always suppress unwanted behavior—but at what cost? The child may express accumulated feelings of hostility against other children.

5. Punishment may generalize too far. A child who is punished severely for bad table manners may stop eating altogether. Overgeneralization is more likely to occur when children do not know exactly why they are being punished and when they have not been shown alternative acceptable behaviors.

6. Punishment may be modeled as a way of solving problems or coping with stress (Strauss, 1994). We will see that one way that children learn is by observing others. Even though children may not immediately perform the behavior they observe, they may perform it later on, even as adults, when their circumstances are similar to those of the **model.**

7. Finally, children learn responses that are punished. Whether or not children choose to perform punished responses, punishment draws their attention to these responses.

It is usually preferable to focus on rewarding children for desirable behavior than on punishing them for unwanted behavior. By ignoring their misbehavior, or by using **time out** from positive reinforcement, we can consistently avoid reinforcing children for misbehavior (Budd, 1993).

Truth or Fiction Revisited

Actually, punishment does work. Strong punishment generally suppresses the behavior it follows. The issues pertaining to punishment concern its limitations and side effects.

MODEL • An organism that engages in a response that is then imitated by another organism.

TIME OUT • Removal of an organism from a situation in which reinforcement is available when unwanted behavior is shown.

A Discriminative Stimulus. You might not think that pigeons are very discriminating, yet they readily learn that pecking will not bring food in the presence of a discriminative stimulus such as a red light.

To reward or positively reinforce children for desired behavior takes time and care. It is not enough simply to never use punishment. First, we must pay attention to children when they are behaving well. If we take their desirable behavior for granted and respond to them only when they misbehave, we may be encouraging misbehavior. Second, we must be certain that children are aware of, and capable of performing, desired behavior. It is harmful and fruitless merely to punish children for unwanted behavior. We must also carefully guide them, either physically or verbally, into making the desired responses, and then reward them. We cannot teach children table manners by waiting for them to exhibit proper responses at random and then reinforcing them for their responses. Try holding a reward of ice cream behind your back and waiting for a child to exhibit proper manners. You will have a slippery dining room floor long before the children develop good table manners.

• *Discriminative Stimuli*

B. F. Skinner might not have been able to get his pigeons into the drivers' seats of missiles during the war, but he had no problem training them to respond to traffic lights. Try the following experiment for yourself.

Find a pigeon. Or sit on a park bench, close your eyes, and one will find you. Place it in a Skinner box with a button on the wall. Drop a food pellet into the cage whenever the pigeon pecks the button. (Soon it will learn to peck the button whenever it has not eaten for a while.) Now place a small green light in the cage. Turn it on and off intermittently throughout the day. Reinforce button pecking with food whenever the green light is on, but not when the light is off. It will not take long for this clever city pigeon to learn that it will gain as much by grooming itself or cooing and flapping around as it will by pecking the button when the light is off.

The green light will have become a **discriminative stimulus.** Discriminative stimuli act as cues. They provide information about when an operant (in this case, pecking a button) will be reinforced (in this case, by a food pellet being dropped into the cage).

Operants that are not reinforced tend to be extinguished. For the pigeon in our experiment, the behavior of pecking the button *when the light is off* is extinguished.

A moment's reflection will suggest many ways in which discriminative stimuli influence our behavior. Wouldn't you rather answer the telephone when it is ringing than when it is not? Do you think it is wise to try to get smoochy when your date is blowing smoke in your face or downing a bottle of antacid tablets? One of the factors involved in social skills is interpreting social discriminative stimuli accurately.

• *Schedules of Reinforcement*

In operant conditioning, some responses are maintained by means of **continuous reinforcement.** You probably become warmer every time you put on heavy clothing. You probably become less thirsty every time you drink water. Yet if you have ever watched people throwing money down the maws of slot machines, you know that behavior can also be maintained by means of **partial reinforcement.**

Some folklore about gambling is based on solid learning theory. You can get a person "hooked" on gambling by fixing the game so as to allow heavy winnings at first. Then you gradually space out the winnings (reinforcements) until gambling is maintained by infrequent winning—or even no winning at all. Par-

DISCRIMINATIVE STIMULUS • In operant conditioning, a stimulus that indicates that reinforcement is available.
CONTINUOUS REINFORCEMENT • A schedule of reinforcement in which every correct response is reinforced.
PARTIAL REINFORCEMENT • One of several reinforcement schedules in which not every correct response is reinforced.

tial reinforcement schedules can maintain behavior for a great deal of time, even though it goes unreinforced. Consider a critical-thinking question: Can you describe how a behaviorist and a cognitive psychologist might each explain the effects of a partial-reinforcement schedule on gamblers?

New operants or behaviors are acquired most rapidly through continuous reinforcement or, in some cases, through "one-trial learning" that meets with great reinforcement. People who cannot control their gambling often had big wins at the racetrack or casino or in the lottery in their late teens or early twenties (Greene, 1982). But once the operant has been acquired, it can be maintained by tapering off to a schedule of partial reinforcement.

There are four basic types of reinforcement schedules. They are determined by changing either the *interval* of time that must elapse between correct responses before reinforcement occurs or the *ratio* of correct responses to reinforcements. If reinforcement of responses is immediate (zero seconds), the reinforcement schedule is continuous. A larger interval of time, such as 1 or 30 seconds, is one kind of partial-reinforcement schedule. A one-to-one (1:1) ratio of correct responses to reinforcements is also a continuous-reinforcement schedule. A higher ratio such as 2:1 or 5:1 creates another kind of partial-reinforcement schedule.

More specifically, the four basic reinforcement schedules are *fixed-interval, variable-interval, fixed-ratio,* and *variable-ratio* schedules.

In a **fixed-interval schedule,** a fixed amount of time—say, one minute—must elapse between the previous and subsequent times when reinforcement for correct responses occurs. In a **variable-interval schedule,** varying amounts of time are allowed to elapse between occurrences of reinforcement. For example, in a 3-minute variable-interval schedule, the mean amount of time that would elapse between reinforcement opportunities would be 3 minutes. However, the intervals might vary from 1 to 5 minutes.

With a fixed-interval schedule, an organism's response rate falls off after each reinforcement and then picks up again as the time when reinforcement will occur approaches. For example, in a 1-minute fixed-interval schedule, a rat will be reinforced with, say, a food pellet for the first operant—for example, the first pressing of a lever—that occurs after a minute has elapsed. After each reinforcement, the rat's rate of lever pressing slows down, but as the end of the 1-minute interval draws near, lever pressing increases in frequency, as suggested in Figure 7.10. It is as if the rat has learned that it must wait a while before reinforcement will be made available. The resultant record on the cumulative recorder shows a series of characteristic upward-moving waves, or scallops, which are referred to as a *fixed-interval scallop.*

Car dealers use fixed-interval reinforcement schedules when they offer incentives for buying up the remainder of the year's line every summer and fall. In a sense, they are suppressing buying at other times, except for consumers whose current cars are in their death throes or those with little self-control. Similarly, you learn to check your e-mail only at a certain time of day if your correspondent writes at that time each day.

Reinforcement is more unpredictable in a variable-interval schedule. Therefore, the response rate is steadier but lower. If the boss calls us in for a weekly report, we will probably work hard to pull things together just before the report is to be given, just as we might cram the night before a weekly quiz. But if we know that the boss might call us in for a report on the progress of a certain project at any time (variable-interval schedule), we are likely to keep things in a state of reasonable readiness at all times. However, our efforts are unlikely to have the intensity they would in a fixed-interval schedule (for example, a weekly report). Similarly, we are less likely to cram for unpredictable "pop quizzes" than we are to study for regularly scheduled quizzes. But we are likely

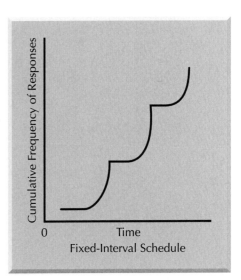

FIGURE 7.10
THE "FIXED-INTERVAL SCALLOP"
Organisms who are reinforced on a fixed-interval schedule tend to slack off responding after each reinforcement. The rate of response picks up as they near the time when reinforcement will become available. The results on the cumulative recorder look like upward-moving waves, or scallops.

FIXED-INTERVAL SCHEDULE • A schedule in which a fixed amount of time must elapse between the previous and subsequent times that reinforcement is available.
VARIABLE-INTERVAL SCHEDULE • A schedule in which a variable amount of time must elapse between the previous and subsequent times that reinforcement is available.

to do at least some studying on a regular basis. If you receive e-mail from your correspondent at irregular intervals, you are likely to check your e-mail regularly, but with somewhat less eagerness.

In a **fixed-ratio schedule,** reinforcement is provided after a fixed number of correct responses have been made. In a **variable-ratio schedule,** reinforcement is provided after a variable number of correct responses have been made. In a 10:1 variable-ratio schedule, the mean number of correct responses that would have to be made before a subsequent correct response would be reinforced is 10, but the ratio of correct responses to reinforcements might be allowed to vary from, say, 1:1 to 20:1 on a random basis.

Fixed- and variable-ratio schedules maintain a high response rate. With a fixed-ratio schedule, it is as if the organism learns that it must make several responses before being reinforced. It then "gets them out of the way" as rapidly as possible. Consider the example of piecework. If a worker must sew five shirts to receive $10, he or she is on a fixed-ratio (5:1) schedule and is likely to sew at a uniformly high rate, although there might be a brief pause after each reinforcement. With a variable-ratio schedule, reinforcement can come at any time. This unpredictability also maintains a high response rate. Slot machines tend to pay off on variable-ratio schedules, and players can be seen popping coins into them and yanking their "arms" with barely a pause. I have seen players who do not even stop to pick up their winnings. Instead, they continue to pop in the coins, whether from their original stack or from the winnings tray.

SHAPING If you are teaching the macarena to people who have never danced, do not wait until they have performed it precisely before telling them they're on the right track. The foxtrot will be back in style before they have learned a thing.

We can teach complex behaviors by **shaping,** or reinforcing progressive steps toward the behavioral goal. At first, for example, it may be wise to smile and say "Good" when a reluctant newcomer gathers the courage to get out on the dance floor, even if your feet are flattened by his initial clumsiness. If you are teaching someone to drive a car with a standard shift, at first generously reinforce the learner simply for shifting gears without stalling.

But as training proceeds, we come to expect more before we are willing to provide reinforcement. We reinforce **successive approximations** of the goal. If you want to train a rat to climb a ladder, first reinforce it with a food pellet when it turns toward the ladder. Then wait until it approaches the ladder before giving it a pellet. Then do not drop a pellet into the cage until the rat touches the ladder. In this way, the rat will reach the top of the ladder more quickly than if you had waited for the target behavior to occur at random.

Learning to drive a new standard-shift automobile to a new job also involves a complex sequence of operant behaviors. At first we actively seek out all the discriminative stimuli or landmarks that give use cues for when to turn—signs, buildings, hills, valleys. We also focus on shifting to a lower gear as we slow down so that the car won't stall. After many repetitions, these responses, or chains of behavior, become "habitual" and we need to pay very little attention to them.

Have you ever driven home from school or work and suddenly realized as you got out of your car that you couldn't recall exactly how you had returned home? Your entire trip may seem "lost." Were you in great danger? How could you allow such a thing to happen? Actually, it may be that your responses to the demands of the route and to driving your car had become so habitual that you did not have to focus on them. As you drove, you were able to think about dinner, a problem at work, or the weekend. But if something unusual had occurred

---

Truth or Fiction Revisited

It is true that rats can be trained to climb a ramp, cross a bridge, climb a ladder, pedal a toy car, and do several other tasks — all in proper sequence. The procedure used to do so is called shaping.

FIXED-RATIO SCHEDULE • A schedule in which reinforcement is provided after a fixed number of correct responses.

VARIABLE-RATIO SCHEDULE • A schedule in which reinforcement is provided after a variable number of correct responses.

SHAPING • A procedure for teaching complex behaviors that at first reinforces approximations of the target behavior.

SUCCESSIVE APPROXIMATIONS • Behaviors that are progressively closer to a target behavior.

Reciting the Pledge. Operant conditioning plays a role in the socialization of children. Parents and teachers usually reward children for expressing attitudes that coincide with their own and punish or ignore them when they express "deviant" attitudes.

on the way, such as hesitation in your engine or a severe rainstorm, you would have devoted as much attention to your driving as was needed to arrive home. Your trip was probably quite safe, after all.

• *Applications of Operant Conditioning*

Operant conditioning, like classical conditioning, is not just an exotic laboratory procedure. We use it every day in our efforts to influence other people. Parents and peers induce children to acquire "gender-appropriate" behavior patterns through rewards and punishments (see Chapter 13). Parents also tend to praise their children for sharing their toys and to punish them for being too aggressive. Peers participate in this **socialization** process by playing with children who are generous and nonaggressive and, often, by avoiding those who are not (Etaugh & Rathus, 1995).

Operant conditioning may also play a role in attitude formation (see Chapter 17). Parents tend to reward their children for expressing attitudes that coincide with their own and to punish or ignore them for expressing attitudes that deviate. Let us now consider some specific applications of operant conditioning.

BIOFEEDBACK TRAINING Biofeedback training (BFT) is based on principles of operant conditioning. As noted in Chapter 6, BFT has enabled people and lower animals to learn to control autonomic responses in order to attain reinforcement. BFT has been an important innovation in the treatment of health-related problems during the past few decades.

Through BFT, organisms can gain control of autonomic functions such as the flow of blood in a finger. They can also learn to improve their control over functions that can be manipulated voluntarily, such as muscle tension. When people receive BFT, reinforcement is given in the form of *information*. Perhaps a sound changes in pitch or frequency of occurrence to signal that they have modified the autonomic function in the desired direction. For example, we can learn to emit alpha waves (and feel somewhat more relaxed) through feedback from an electroencephalograph. Through the use of other instruments, people have

SOCIALIZATION • Guidance of people into socially desirable behavior by means of verbal messages, the systematic use of rewards and punishments, and other methods of teaching.

learned to lower their muscle tension, their heart rates, and even their blood pressure.

BFT is also used with people who have lost neuromuscular control of parts of their body as a result of an accident. A "bleep" sound informs them when they have contracted a muscle or sent an impulse down a neural pathway. By concentrating on changing the bleeps, they also gradually regain voluntary control over the damaged function.

TOKEN ECONOMIES   Behavior therapists apply operant conditioning in mental hospitals to foster desired responses such as social skills and to extinguish unwanted behaviors such as social withdrawal. Techniques like the **token economy** are outlined in Chapter 16. In a token economy, psychologists give hospital residents or prison inmates tokens such as poker chips as reinforcements for desired behavior. The tokens reinforce the desired behavior because they can be exchanged for time watching television, desserts, and other desired commodities.

Principles of operant conditioning have also enabled psychologists and educators to develop many beneficial innovations, such as interventions with young children, behavior modification in the classroom, and programmed learning.

TOKEN ECONOMY • An environmental setting that fosters desired behavior by reinforcing it with tokens (secondary reinforcers) that can be exchanged for other reinforcers.

psychology and
m o d e r n   l i f e

USING CONDITIONING TO HELP CHILDREN OVERCOME FEARS

Imagine that you want to encourage a child to try a new food—perhaps restaurant chicken as opposed to Daddy or Mommy chicken. You may be concerned that forcing the child to eat the new food could lead to hatred of that food. So you may wind up softly urging, "Just take one little bite." In your most encouraging voice, with your broadest smile, and nodding your head, you repeat, "Just one." If the child still refuses, perhaps you say, "Then just smell it!" You may use a little *modeling* too. You may take a bite and say, "Mmmm, this is delicious!" and then encourage the child once more. If the child tries the chicken, you show great approval, including ample hugs and kisses *(reinforcements)*. Another reinforcer, we might hope, would be the taste of the food itself. (If not, find another restaurant.)

The method is *counterconditioning*. In counterconditioning, a pleasing stimulus is paired repeatedly with a fear-evoking object or situation. In this way, it comes to counteract the fear response.

How about encouraging a hesitant child to walk into the surf? Perhaps you cajole the child into putting in one foot at a time to avoid severe anxiety. Then you show approval with each additional step. Once in the water, fear may be further counterconditioned by the fun of splashing around. Counterconditioning is a gradual process that requires some patience.

Some parents, of course, toss a resistant child into the water. This method could be called *flooding* or sink-or-swim. The assumption is that the child will learn that the water is fun and see that hesitating was silly. But the method could backfire; the child could continue to fuss and develop a lasting aversion to swimming. By the way, the cognitive therapist Aaron Beck overcame his own fear of blood by forcing himself to watch surgical operations. ■

USING AVOIDANCE LEARNING TO SAVE A BABY'S LIFE Operant conditioning techniques are sometimes used with children who are too young or distressed to respond to verbal forms of therapy. In one example, reported by Lang and Melamed (1969), a 9-month-old infant vomited regularly within 10 to 15 minutes after eating. Physicians could find no medical basis for the problem, and medical treatments were of no avail. When the case was brought to the attention of Lang and Melamed, the infant weighed only 9 pounds and was in critical condition, being fed by means of a pump.

The psychologists monitored the infant for the first physical indications (local muscle tension) that vomiting was to occur. When the child tensed prior to vomiting, a tone was sounded. The tone was followed by a painful but (presumably) harmless electric shock. After two 1-hour treatment sessions, the infant's muscle tensions ceased in response to the sounding of the tone in the absence of the shock, and vomiting soon ceased altogether. At a 1-year follow-up, the infant was still not vomiting and had gained a reasonable amount of weight.

How do we use principles of conditioning to explain this remarkable procedure? The psychologists first used classical conditioning. Through repeated pairings, the tone (CS) came to elicit the expectation of and electric shock (US). Therefore, the psychologists could use the painful shock sparingly.

Operant conditioning explains the infant's halting of vomiting. The electric shock and the tone (after classical conditioning) were aversive stimuli. The infant soon learned to suppress the behaviors (muscle tensions) that were followed by aversive stimulation. This led to the removal of the aversive stimuli. The aversive stimuli therefore served as negative reinforcers.

This learning occurred at an age long before any sort of verbal intervention could have been understood, and it apparently saved the infant's life. Similar procedures have been used to teach autistic children not to mutilate themselves.

Truth or Fiction Revisited
....
It is true that psychologists successfully fashioned a method to teach an emaciated 9-month-old infant to stop throwing up. They derived the method from principles of conditioning. Conditioning allowed the psychologists to focus on what the child actually did *and not on what the child might know or understand.*

CLASSROOM DISCIPLINE Remember that reinforcers are defined as stimuli that increase the frequency of behavior—not as pleasant events. Ironically, adults frequently reinforce undesirable behavior in children by attending to them, or punishing them, when they misbehave but ignoring them when they behave in desirable ways. Similarly, teachers who raise their voices when children misbehave may be unintentionally conferring hero status on those pupils in the eyes of their peers (Wentzel, 1994). To the teacher's surprise, some children may go out of their way to earn disapproval.

Teacher preparation and in-service programs show teachers how to use behavior modification to reverse these response patterns. Teachers are taught to pay attention to children when they are behaving appropriately and, when possible, to ignore (that is, avoid reinforcing) misbehavior (Abramowitz & O'Leary, 1991). The younger the child, the more powerful the teacher's attention and approval seem to be.

Among older children and adolescents, peer approval is often a more powerful reinforcer than teacher approval. Peer approval may maintain misbehavior, and ignoring misbehavior may only allow peers to become more disruptive. In such cases it may be necessary to separate troublesome children from less disruptive peers.

Teachers also frequently use time out from positive reinforcement to discourage misbehavior. In this method, children are placed in a drab, restrictive environment for a specified period, usually about 10 minutes, when they behave disruptively. While they are isolated, they cannot earn the attention of peers or teachers, and no reinforcers are present.

Praise. Praise from the teacher reinforces desirable behavior in most children. Behavior modification in the classroom applies principles of operant conditioning.

PSYCHOLOGY in the NEW MILLENNIUM

Virtual Classrooms Draw Cheers, Fears

What mental images are conjured up when you reflect on learning? Do you picture children reading and writing at desks in neat rows while a benevolent teacher looks on? Do you envision adults serving apprenticeships in factories or operating rooms? Do you fancy a dynamic teacher dramatizing an obscure point in mathematics or physics? Do you imagine a solitary student studying in the wee hours of the morning? Or does learning evoke the image of students sitting at the feet of a robed philosopher in ancient Greece?

Some of the "robed philosophers" will be electronic in the new millennium. As access to the Internet's World Wide Web has expanded, the spell of computer-assisted or "distance" learning has taken hold of the nation's college campuses.[2] A click of the mouse or a tap of the key unlocks a world of lectures, discussion papers, and even late night rap sessions.

Distance learning, also known as virtual learning or telelearning, revolutionizes the traditional learning environment and relationship between teacher and student through e-mail, the Internet, video and CD-ROM programs. Students can now sit in on lectures being videotaped miles away, and use their computers to download readings, hand in papers, and access their professors 24 hours a day.

The most significant changes on the horizon are the replacement of large, lecture format courses with computerized courses, and the increased use of videoconferencing—teaching live courses in multiple locations via satellite, phone lines, or fiber optics. While most psychologists agree on the merits of distance learning for continuing education or professionals worldwide, many disagree on its uses for teaching on college campuses.

"The challenge for psychology," according to University of Maryland psychologist Robert Brown, "is defining what kinds of material can be transmitted and learned via computer as opposed to those that require face-to-face contact."

A USEFUL ADDITION TO CLASSROOM TEACHING Some see technology as a useful addition to classroom teaching. Others fear that it may isolate students from teachers. They wonder if some students will ever have to set foot on campus—and whether that's good.

Psychology professors need not be so wary, because the technology seeks to enhance, not undermine, traditional teaching, maintains psychologist Sally Johnstone, head of the Western Cooperative for Educational Telecommunications in Boulder, Colorado.

CD-ROM, e-mail, and Internet technologies have great potential for academic psychology once educators determine how best to use them. The Internet can be especially useful for deprived students, whether they are people with disabilities, mothers at home caring for their children, or people in rural areas who can't make it to the university, according to psychologists. Distance learning is often less expensive than traditional instruction because it allows adult learners supporting families to continue working and earning money while they get their degree.

Another advantage of the technologies is their potential to expand communication between students and professors. People who keep to themselves in anonymous undergraduate classes often speak up on e-mail or bulletin board chat groups.

LOSS OF THE HUMAN FACTOR? Some educators are wary of technology's impact on traditional faculty socialization of students, because they foresee a loss of "the human factor" in learning interactions. That is, face-to-face contacts between students and professors are a time-honored element of the learning process. Psychologists will need to explore just how much face-to-face contact is necessary for learning to occur. ∎

---

[2] Adapted from Murray, B. (1996). Virtual classrooms draw cheers, fears. *APA Monitor, 27*(2), pp. 40–41.

PROGRAMMED LEARNING B. F. Skinner developed an educational method called **programmed learning** that is based on operant conditioning. This method assumes that any complex task involving conceptual learning as well as motor skills can be broken down into a number of small steps. These steps can be shaped individually and then combined in sequence to form the correct behavioral chain.

Programmed learning does not punish errors. Instead, correct responses are reinforced. Every child earns "100," but at her or his own pace. Programmed learning also assumes that it is the task of the teacher (or program) to structure the learning experience in such a way that errors will not be made.

REFLECTIONS

- What effects have rewards and punishments had on your behavior over the years?
- A pianist's fingers fly over the keys faster than the player can read notes or even think notes. What kinds of learning are at work in learning to play the piano?
- What role does habit play in your life? Do you have "good habits" and "bad habits"? How did they develop?
- Do you learn from your mistakes? Why or why not? Provide some examples.
- Agree or disagree, and support your answer: "Apparently complex human behavior can be explained as the summation of a series of instances of conditioning."

■ COGNITIVE FACTORS IN LEARNING

Classical and operant conditioning were originally conceived of as relatively simple forms of learning. Much of conditioning's appeal is that it can be said to meet the behaviorist objective of explaining behavior in terms of public, observable events—in this case, laboratory conditions. Building on this theoretical base, some psychologists have suggested that the most complex human behavior involves the summation of a series of instances of conditioning. However, many psychologists believe that the conditioning model is too mechanical to explain all instances of learned behavior, even in laboratory rats (Glover and others, 1990; Hayes, 1989; Weiner, 1991). They turn to cognitive factors to describe and explain additional findings in the psychology of learning.

In addition to concepts such as *association* and *reinforcement*, cognitive psychologists use concepts such as *mental structures, schemas, templates,* and *information processing.* Cognitive psychologists see people as searching for information, weighing evidence, and making decisions. Let us consider some classic research that points to cognitive factors in learning, as opposed to mechanical associations. These cognitive factors are not necessarily limited to humans—although, of course, people are the only species that can talk about them.

• *Contingency Theory: What "Really" Happens During Classical Conditioning?*

Behaviorists and cognitive psychologists interpret the conditioning process in different ways. Behaviorists explain classical conditioning in terms of the pairing of stimuli. Cognitive psychologists explain classical conditioning in terms of

PROGRAMMED LEARNING • A method of learning in which complex tasks are broken down into simple steps, each of which is reinforced. Errors are not reinforced.

the ways in which stimuli provide information that allows organisms to form and revise mental representations of their environment (Basic Behavioral Science Task Force, 1996b).

In classical conditioning experiments with dogs, Robert Rescorla (1967) obtained some results that are difficult to explain without reference to cognitive concepts. Each phase of his work paired a tone (CS) with an electric shock (US), but in different ways. With one group of animals, the shock was consistently presented after the tone. That is, the US followed on the heels of the CS, as in Pavlov's studies. The dogs in this group learned to show a fear response when the tone was presented.

A second group of dogs heard an equal number of tones and received an equal number of electric shocks, but the shock never immediately followed the tone. In other words, the tone and the shock were not paired. Now, from the behaviorist perspective, the dogs should not have learned to associate the tone and the shock, since one did not predict the other. Actually, the dogs learned quite a lot: They learned that they had nothing to fear when the tone was sounded! They showed vigilance and fear when the laboratory was quiet—for apparently the shock could come at any time—but they were calm in the presence of the tone.

The third group of dogs also received equal numbers of tones and shocks, but the stimuli were presented at purely random intervals. Occasionally they were paired, but most often they were not. According to Rescorla, behaviorists might argue that intermittent pairing of the tones and shocks should have brought about some learning. Yet it did not. The animals showed no fear in response to the tone. Rescorla suggests that the animals in this group learned nothing because the tones provided no information about the prospect of being shocked.

Rescorla concluded that contiguity—that is, the co-appearance of two events (the US and the CS)—cannot in itself explain classical conditioning. Instead, learning occurs only when the conditioned stimulus (in this case, the tone) provides information about the unconditioned stimulus (in this case, the shock). According to so-called **contingency theory**, learning occurs because a conditioned stimulus indicates that the unconditioned stimulus is likely to follow.

Behaviorists might counter, of course, that for the second group of dogs the *absence* of the tone became the signal for the shock. Shock may be a powerful enough event that the fear response becomes conditioned to the laboratory environment. For the third group of dogs, the shock was as likely to occur in the presence of the neutral stimulus as in its absence. Therefore, many behaviorists would expect no learning to occur.

• *Latent Learning: Forming Cognitive Maps*

I'm all grown up. I know the whole mall.

THE AUTHOR'S DAUGHTER JORDAN AT AGE 7

Many behaviorists argue that organisms acquire only responses, or operants, for which they are reinforced. E. C. Tolman, however, showed that rats also learn about their environment in the absence of reinforcement.

Tolman trained some rats to run through mazes for standard food goals. Other rats were permitted to explore the same mazes for several days without food goals or other rewards. After the unrewarded rats had been allowed to explore the mazes for 10 days, food rewards were placed in a box at the far end of the maze. The previously unrewarded rats reached the food box as quickly as the rewarded rats after only one or two reinforced trials (Tolman & Honzik, 1930).

CONTINGENCY THEORY • The view that learning occurs when stimuli provide information about the likelihood of the occurrence of other stimuli.

Tolman concluded that rats learned about mazes in which they roamed even when they were unrewarded for doing so. He distinguished between *learning* and *performance*. Rats would acquire a cognitive map of a maze, and even though they would not be motivated to follow an efficient route to the far end, they would learn rapid routes from one end to the other just by roaming about within the maze. Yet this learning might remain hidden, or **latent,** until they were motivated to follow the rapid routes to obtain food goals.

• *Observational Learning: Monkey See, Monkey May Choose to Do*

How many things have you learned from watching other people in real life, in films, and on television? From films and television, you may have gathered vague ideas about how to sky dive, ride a surfboard, climb sheer cliffs, run a pattern to catch a touchdown pass in the Superbowl, and dust for fingerprints, even if you have never tried these activities yourself.

In his studies of social learning, Albert Bandura has conducted experiments (e.g., Bandura and others, 1963) that show that we can acquire operants by observing the behavior of others. We may need some practice to refine the operants, but we can learn them through observation alone. We may also allow these operants or skills to remain latent. For example, we may not imitate aggressive behavior unless we are provoked and believe that we are more likely to be rewarded than punished for it.

Observational learning may account for most human learning. It occurs when, as children, we watch our parents cook, clean, or repair a broken appliance. Observational learning takes place when we watch teachers solve problems on the blackboard or hear them speak in a foreign language. Observational learning is not mechanically acquired through reinforcement. We can learn

LATENT • Hidden or concealed.
OBSERVATIONAL LEARNING • The acquisition of knowledge and skills through the observation of others (who are called *models*) rather than by means of direct experience.

Observational Learning. Much human behavior is acquired by means of observational learning, as in this demonstration of fielding techniques. What kinds of learning in your psychology course are observational?

FIGURE 7.11
CLASSIC RESEARCH ON THE IMITATION OF AGGRESSIVE MODELS
Albert Bandura and his colleagues showed that children frequently imitate aggressive behavior that they observe. In the top row, an adult model strikes a clown doll. The lower rows show a boy and a girl imitating the aggressive behavior.

FIGURE 7.12
WHAT ARE THE CONNECTIONS BETWEEN MEDIA VIOLENCE AND AGGRESSIVE BEHAVIOR?

Does media violence lead to aggression? Does aggressive behavior lead to a preference for viewing violence? Or does a third factor, such as a predisposition toward aggressive behavior, contribute to both? Might such a predisposition be in part genetic?

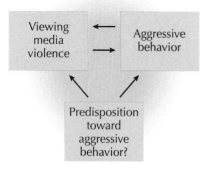

through observation without engaging in overt responses at all. It appears sufficient to pay attention to the behavior of others.

In the terminology of observational learning, a person who engages in a response to be imitated is a *model*. When observers see a model being reinforced for displaying an operant, the observers are said to be *vicariously* reinforced. Display of the operant thus becomes more likely for the observer as well as for the model.

THE EFFECTS OF MEDIA VIOLENCE Much human learning occurs through observation. We learn by observing parents and peers, attending school, reading books, and—in one of the more controversial aspects of modern life—watching media such as television and films (American Psychological Association, 1992b). Nearly all of us have been exposed to television, videotapes, and films in the classroom. Children in day care centers often watch *Sesame Street*. There are filmed and videotaped versions of great works of literature such as Orson Welles' *Macbeth* or Laurence Olivier's *Hamlet*. Nearly every school shows films of laboratory experiments. Sometimes we view "canned lectures" by master teachers.

But what about our viewing *outside* the classroom? Television is one of our major sources of informal observational learning. Children are routinely exposed to scenes of murder, beating, and sexual assault—just by turning on the TV set (Huesmann & Miller, 1994; Wilson, 1997). If a child watches two to four hours of TV a day, she or he will have seen 8,000 murders and another 100,000 acts of violence *by the time she or he has finished elementary school* (Eron, 1993).

Moreover, violence tends to be glamorized on TV. For example, in one cartoon show, superheroes battle villains who are trying to destroy or take over the world. Violence is often shown to have only temporary or minimal effects. (How often has Wily Coyote fallen from a cliff and been pounded into the ground by a boulder, only to bounce back and pursue the Road Runner once more?) In the great majority of violent TV shows, there is no remorse, criticism, or penalty for violent behavior (Cantor, 1997; Wilson, 1997). Few TV programs show harmful long-term consequences of aggressive behavior.

Why all this violence? Simple: Violence sells. But does violence do more than sell? Does media violence *cause* real violence? If so, what can parents and educators do to prevent the fictional from spilling over into the real world?

In study after study, children and adults who view violence in the media later show higher levels of aggressive behavior than people who are not exposed to media violence (DeAngelis, 1993; Liebert and others, 1989). Aggressive video games apparently have similar effects. In one study, 5- to 7-year-olds played one of two video games (Schutte and others, 1988). In one, *Karateka*, villains were destroyed by being hit or kicked. In the other, *Jungle Hunt*, the character swung nonviolently from vine to vine to cross a jungle. Afterward the children were observed in a playroom. Those who had played *Karateka*—both boys and girls—were significantly more likely to hit their playmates and an inflated doll. Most psychologists therefore agree that media violence *contributes* to aggression (Huesmann, 1993; NIMH, 1982).

Consider a number of ways in which depictions of violence make such a contribution:

- *Observational Learning.* Children learn from observation (Bandura, 1986; DeAngelis, 1993). TV violence supplies *models* of aggressive "skills," which children may acquire. In fact, children are more likely to imitate what their parents do than to heed what they say. If adults say that they disapprove of aggression but smash furniture or slap each other when frustrated, children are likely to develop the notion that aggression is the way to handle frustration. Classic experiments show that children tend to imitate the aggressive behavior they see on the media (Bandura and others, 1963) (see Figure 7.11). Media violence also provides viewers with aggressive *scripts*—that is, ideas about how to behave in situations like those they have observed (Huesmann & Miller, 1994).

- *Disinhibition.* Punishment inhibits behavior. Conversely, media violence may disinhibit aggressive behavior, especially when media characters "get away" with violence or are rewarded for it.

- *Increased Arousal.* Media violence and aggressive video games increase viewers' level of arousal. That is, television "works them up." We are more likely to be aggressive under high levels of arousal.

- *Priming of Aggressive Thoughts and Memories.* Media violence "primes" or arouses aggressive ideas and memories (Berkowitz, 1988).

- *Habituation.* We become "habituated to," or used to, repeated stimuli. Repeated exposure to TV violence may decrease viewers' sensitivity to real violence. If children come to perceive violence as the norm, they may become more tolerant of it and place less value on restraining aggressive urges (Eron, 1993; Huesmann, 1993).

Though media violence encourages aggression in viewers, it has its greatest impact on the children who are *already* considered the most aggressive by their teachers (Josephson, 1987). There also seems to be a circular relationship

What Are the Effects of Media Violence?
Preschool children in the United States watch TV an average of four hours a day. Schoolchildren spend more hours at the TV set than in the classroom. Is it any wonder that psychologists, educators, and parents express concern about the effects of media violence?

Truth or Fiction Revisited

Actually, a scientific connection has been established between TV violence and aggression in real life. But does media violence *cause* aggression? What are the possible relationships between media violence and aggression (see Figure 7.12)?

In Review Kinds of Learning

KIND OF LEARNING	WHAT IS LEARNED	HOW IT IS LEARNED
Classical Conditioning	Association of events; anticipations, signs, expectations; automatic responses to new stimuli	A neutral stimulus (CS) is repeatedly paired with a stimulus (US) that elicits a response (UR) until the neutral stimulus produces a response (CR) that anticipates and prepares for the US.
Operant Conditioning	Behavior that operates on, or affects, the environment to produce consequences	A response is rewarded or reinforced so that it occurs with greater frequency in similar situations.
Observational Learning	Expectations (if–then relationships), knowledge, and skills	A person observes the behavior of another person (live or through media such as films, television, or books) and its effects.

between viewing media violence and displaying aggressive behavior (DeAngelis, 1993; Eron, 1982). Yes, TV violence contributes to aggressive behavior, but aggressive children are also more likely to tune in and stay tuned to it.

Aggressive children are frequently rejected by their nonaggressive peers—at least in middle-class culture (Eron, 1982; Patterson, 1993). Aggressive children may watch more television because their peer relationships are less fulfilling and because the high incidence of TV violence tends to confirm their view that aggressive behavior is normal (Eron, 1982). Media violence also interacts with other contributors to violence. For example, parental rejection and use of physical punishment further increase the likelihood of aggression in children (Eron, 1982). A harsh home life may further confirm the TV viewer's vision of the world as a violent place and further encourage reliance on television for companionship.

Psychology in a World of
DIVERSITY

Culture, Ethnicity, and Academic Achievement

Do you know where the Slovak Republic is? In at least one respect—how well children learn in school—the Slovak Republic is more "on the map" than the United States.

Children in the United States chronically fall behind children in Russia, Japan, and England in most academic subjects. According to the Third International Mathematics and Science Study, eighth graders in the United States rank 12th in science when compared with children in 41 selected countries (Murray, 1997a). Math? Children in the United States rank 14th out of the 15. They lag children in Singapore, the Czech and Slovak Republics, Hungary, and several other countries. The Slovak Republic, thus, has more prominence on the math map.

Does it matter that Asian and European children learn more about math and science than children in the United States? Yes, according to Louis Gerstner, Jr.

(1994), the chairperson of IBM. For one thing, U.S. businesses are forced to pick up the slack. They spend billions of dollars a year teaching workers to perform tasks and solve problems using skills that they should have learned in school. Many businesses cannot even upgrade their products or streamline their methods because they cannot teach their employees to do the necessary work. As a result, it costs them more money to produce less competitive products. This trend cannot continue if the United States is to maintain its standard of living.

BEYOND THE CLASSROOM According to APA senior scientist Merry Bullock (1997), "Psychological research on learning can provide important input into curriculum development." However, schools have already poured billions of dollars into reworking their curriculums and training their teachers to do a better job (Tabor, 1996). A survey of 20,000 high school students from a variety of ethnic backgrounds suggests that the fault is more likely to lie with parents and teenagers themselves (Steinberg, 1996).

SERIOUSLY DISCONNECTED According to Steinberg (1996), too many parents have become seriously disconnected from their children's lives. Note some of his findings:

- Half the students said that it would not upset their parents if they brought home grades of C or worse
- 40% of students said that their parents never attended school functions

psychology and
m o d e r n   l i f e

TEACHING CHILDREN *NOT* TO IMITATE MEDIA VIOLENCE

Our children are going to be exposed to media violence—if not in Saturday morning cartoon shows, then in evening dramas and in the news. Or they'll hear about violence from friends, watch other children get into fights, or read about violence in the newspapers. If all those sources of violence were somehow hidden from view, they would learn about violence in *Hamlet, Macbeth,* even the Bible. The notion of preventing children from being exposed to violent models may be impractical.

What, then, should be done? Parents and educators can do many things to tone down the impact of media violence (Huesmann and others, 1983). Children who watch violent shows act less aggressively when they are informed that:

1. The violent behavior they observe in the media does *not* represent the behavior of most people.

2. The apparently aggressive behaviors they watch are not real. They reflect camera tricks, special effects, and stunts.

3. Most people resolve conflicts by nonviolent means.

In observational learning, the emphasis is on the cognitive. If children consider violence inappropriate for them, they will probably not act aggressively even if they have acquired aggressive skills. ■

- One third of the students said that their parents did not know how they were doing in school
- One third said that they spent the day mainly "goofing off" with their friends, and
- Only one third of students said that they had daily conversations with their parents

Steinberg and his co-researchers, Bradford Brown and Sanford Dornbusch (1996), also looked at the situation from the parents' point of view. Many parents say that they would like to be involved in their children's school and leisure activities but are too busy to do so. By the time the children enter high school, many parents admit that they see education as the school's job, not theirs. In fact, half of the parents surveyed admitted that they did not know who their children's friends were or where their children went (and what they did) after school.

Steinberg makes some recommendations. First and foremost, parents need to be more involved with their teenagers. They should:

- Communicate regularly with their teenagers about school and personal matters
- Use consistent discipline (as opposed to being dictatorial or too permissive)
- Regularly attend school functions
- Consult with their children's teachers and follow through on their suggestions

WHAT ABOUT PEERS? The researchers found that some teenagers encourage others to do well in school. However, by and large, peers have a harmful effect on grades. For example, over half the students surveyed said that they did not talk about schoolwork with their friends. In fact, nearly one in five said that he or she did not do as well as possible for fear of earning the disapproval of peers!

ETHNIC BACKGROUND Of many possible factors, including family income and family structure, Steinberg and his colleagues (1996) conclude that ethnic background is most crucial in teenagers' attitudes toward schooling and grades. For example:

- Many White students reported just trying to get by in school
- African and Hispanic American students recognized the value of good grades and college education, but generally did not fear getting poor grades
- Asian American students spent twice as much time doing their homework as students in other ethnic groups and were most fearful of getting poor grades

Sternberg concludes that schools are likely to continue to fight an uphill battle unless parents become more connected with their children's performance and peers become more supportive of students who do well in school.

It would be of little use to discuss how we learn if we were not capable of remembering what we learn from second to second, from day to day, or in many cases for a lifetime. In the next chapter we turn our attention to the subject of memory. And in Chapters 9 and 10 we will see how learning is intertwined with thinking, language, and intelligence.

REFLECTIONS

- What do you think "really" happens during classical conditioning? Why?
- Have you ever studied an atlas, a road map, a cookbook, or a computer manual for the pleasure of doing so? What kind of learning were you engaging in?
- How much violence have you witnessed on television, in films, and on the streets? How has media violence affected your behavior? How has it affected your attitudes toward violence?

SUMMARY

1. **What is learning?** Learning is the process by which experience leads to modified representations of the environment and relatively permanent changes in behavior.

2. **What is classical conditioning?** In classical conditioning as a laboratory procedure, a previously neutral stimulus (the conditioned stimulus, or CS) comes to elicit the response evoked by a second stimulus (the unconditioned stimulus, or US) as a result of repeatedly being paired with the second stimulus.

3. **What kinds of classical conditioning procedures are there?** In the most efficient classical conditioning procedure, the CS is presented about 0.5 second before the US. Other classical conditioning procedures include trace conditioning, simultaneous conditioning, and backward conditioning, in which the US is presented first.

4. **How do extinction and spontaneous recovery occur in classical conditioning?** After a US-CS association has been learned, repeated presentation of the CS (for example, a bell) without the US (meat powder) will extinguish the CR (salivation). But extinguished responses may show spontaneous recovery as a function of the time that has elapsed since the end of the extinction process.

5. **What are generalization and discrimination?** In generalization, organisms show a CR in response to a range of stimuli similar to the CS. In discrimination, organisms learn to show a CR in response to a more limited range of stimuli by pairing only the limited stimulus with the US.

6. **What is the law of effect?** Edward L. Thorndike originated the law of effect, which holds that responses are "stamped in" by rewards and "stamped out" by punishments.

7. **What is operant conditioning?** In operant conditioning, organisms learn to engage in behavior that is reinforced. Initial "correct" responses may be performed at random or as a result of physical or verbal guiding. Reinforced responses occur more frequently.

8. **What kinds of reinforcers are there?** Positive reinforcers increase the probability that operants will occur when they are applied. Negative reinforcers increase the probability that operants will occur when the reinforcers are removed. Primary reinforcers have their value because of the organism's biological makeup. Secondary reinforcers such as money and approval acquire their value through association with established reinforcers.

9. **How do extinction and spontaneous recovery occur in operant conditioning?** In operant conditioning, learned responses are extinguished as a result of repeated performance in the absence of reinforcement. As in classical conditioning, spontaneous recovery occurs as a function of the passage of time.

10. **What are rewards and punishments?** Rewards, like reinforcers, increase the frequency of the rewarded behavior. But rewards differ from reinforcers in that they are pleasant stimuli. Punishments are aversive stimuli that suppress the frequency of the punished behavior.

11. **Why do many learning theorists advise against using punishment in child rearing?** Many learning theorists believe misbehavior should be ignored or recommend using time out from reinforcement. In their view, punishment fails to teach desirable responses, suppresses behavior only when it is guaranteed, creates hostility, can lead to overgeneralization, and serves as a model for aggression.

12. **What is a discriminative stimulus?** A discriminative stimulus indicates when an operant will be reinforced.

13. **What kinds of schedules of reinforcement are there?** Continuous reinforcement leads to the most rapid acquisition of new responses, but operants are maintained most economically through partial reinforcement. There are four basic schedules of reinforcement. In a fixed-interval schedule, a specific amount of time must elapse after a previous correct response before reinforcement again becomes available. In a variable-interval schedule, the amount of time is allowed to vary. In a fixed-ratio schedule, a fixed number of correct responses must be performed before one is reinforced. In a variable-ratio schedule, this number is allowed to vary.

14. **What is shaping?** In shaping, successive approximations of the target response are reinforced.

15. **What is contingency theory?** This is the view that organisms learn associations between stimuli only when stimuli provide new information about each other.

16. **What is latent learning?** In latent learning, as demonstrated by Tolman's classic research with rats, organisms can learn (that is, modify their cognitive map of the environment) in the absence of reinforcement.

17. **What is observational learning?** Bandura has shown that people can learn by observing others without emitting reinforced responses of their own. They may then choose to perform the behaviors they have observed "when the time is ripe"—that is, when they believe that the learned behavior is appropriate or is likely to be rewarded.

To enhance your understanding of the psychological concepts found in this chapter, please consult the following aids:

Learning Objectives, p. 135
Exercise, p. 136
Lecture and Textbook Outline,
    p. 137
Effective Studying Ideas, p. 139

Key Terms and Concepts, p. 140
Chapter Review, p. 141
Chapter Exercises, p. 149
Knowing the Language, p. 150
Do You Know the Material?, p. 154

Preprogrammed Behavior
Classical Conditioning

The Law of Effect
Operant Conditioning

For more information concerning the topics found in this chapter, access psychology links on the World Wide Web made through the Harcourt Brace webpage at

www.hbcollege.com

Share your comments and questions with your author at

PsychLinks@aol.com

Without memory, there is no past. Without memory, experience is meaningless and learning cannot endure. What can you remember about your early childhood? As you will see in this chapter, our memories—even our most vivid ones—are not just snapshots of experiences. Some represent truth, but others are fiction. Amalia Mesa-Bains's *Memories of Childhood #2* (1994) was part of an exhibition of artists' renderings of childhood memories. (By the way, Mesa-Bains has a Ph.D. in clinical psychology from the Wright Institute in Berkeley, California.)

AMALIA MESA-BAINS

Chapter **8**
Memory

✔ **T F**

☐ ☐ Some people have photographic memory.

☐ ☐ It may be easier for you to recall the name of your first-grade teacher than the name of someone you just met at a party.

☐ ☐ All of our experiences are permanently imprinted on the brain so the proper stimulus can cause us to remember them exactly.

☐ ☐ There is no practical limit to the amount of information you can store in your memory.

☐ ☐ Learning must be meaningful if we are to remember it.

☐ ☐ We can remember important episodes that take place during the first two years of life.

☐ ☐ You can use tricks to improve your memory.

OUTLINE

FIVE CHALLENGES TO MEMORY
THREE KINDS OF MEMORY
  Episodic Memory
  Semantic Memory
  Procedural Memory
THREE PROCESSES OF MEMORY
  Encoding
  Storage
  Retrieval
THREE STAGES OF MEMORY
  Sensory Memory
  Short-Term Memory
  Long-Term Memory
THE LEVELS-OF-PROCESSING MODEL OF MEMORY
FORGETTING
  Memory Tasks Used in Measuring
    Forgetting
  Interference Theory
  Repression
  Infantile Amnesia
  Anterograde and Retrograde Amnesia
  Psychology and Modern Life:
    Using Psychology to Improve
    Your Memory
THE BIOLOGY OF MEMORY: FROM ENGRAMS TO ADRENALINE
  Changes at the Neural Level
  Changes at the Structural Level
  Psychology in the New Millennium:
    What Does Research on the Biology
    of Memory Hold in Storage?

*M*Y OLDEST DAUGHTER JILL WAS talking about how she had run into a friend from elementary school and they had had a splendid time recalling the goofy things they did during their school years. Her sister Allyn, age six at the time, was not to be outdone. "I can remember when I was born," she put in.

The family's ears perked up. Being a psychologist, I knew exactly what to say. "You can remember when you were born?" I said.

"Oh, yes," she insisted. "Mommy was there."

So far she could not be faulted. I cheered her on, and she related a remarkably detailed account of how it had been snowing in the wee hours of a bitter December morning when Mommy had to go to the hospital. You see, she said, her memory was so good that she could also summon up what it had been like *before* she was born. She wove a wonderful patchwork quilt, integrating details we had given her with her own recollections of the events surrounding the delivery of her younger sister, Jordan. All in all, she seemed quite satisfied that she had pieced together a faithful portrait of her arrival on the world stage.

Later in the chapter, we will see that children usually cannot recall events that occurred in their first two years, much less those of their first hours. But Allyn's tale dramatized the way we "remember" many of the things that have happened to us. When it comes to long-term memories, truth can take a back seat to drama and embellishment. Very often, our memories are like the bride's apparel—there's something old, something new, something borrowed, and from time to time something blue.

Memory is what this chapter is about. Without memory, there is no past. Without memory, experience is trivial and learning cannot abide. Shortly we will see what psychologists have learned about the ways in which we remember things. First, try to meet the following challenges to your memory.

■ FIVE CHALLENGES TO MEMORY

Before we go any further, let's test your memory. If you want to participate, find four sheets of blank paper and number them 1 through 4. Then follow these directions:

1. Following are 10 letters. Look at them for 15 seconds. Later in the chapter, I will ask you if you can write them on sheet number 1. (No cheating! Don't do it now.)

THUNSTOFAM

2. Look at these nine figures for 30 seconds. Then try to draw them in the proper sequence on sheet number 2. (Yes, right after you've finished looking at them. We'll talk about your drawings later.)

3. Okay, here's another list of letters, 17 this time. Look at the list for 60 seconds and then see whether you can reproduce it on sheet number 3. (I'm being generous this time—a full minute.)

GMC-BSI-BMA-TTC-IAF-BI

4. Which of these pennies is an accurate reproduction of the Lincoln penny you see every day? This time there's nothing to draw on another sheet; just circle or put a checkmark by the penny that you think resembles the ones you throw in the back of the drawer.

5. Examine the following drawings for 1 minute. Then copy the names of the figures on sheet number 4. When you're finished, just keep reading. Soon I'll be asking you to draw those figures.

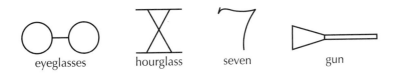

eyeglasses   hourglass   seven   gun

■ THREE KINDS OF MEMORY

Memories contain different kinds of information. Endel Tulving (1985, 1991) classifies memories according to the kind of material they hold. Return to Allyn's "recollection." Of course Allyn could not really remember her own birth. That is, she could not recall the particular event in which she had participated.

• *Episodic Memory*

Memories of the events that happen to a person or take place in his or her presence are referred to as **episodic memories.** Your memories of what you ate for breakfast and of what your professor said in class this afternoon are examples of episodic memory.

What Allyn did recount is more accurately characterized as generalized knowledge than as visions of that important event in her life. From listening to her parents and from her experience with the events of Jordan's birth, she had learned much about what happens during childbirth. She erroneously thought that this knowledge represented her own birth.

EPISODIC MEMORY • Memories of events experienced by a person or that take place in the person's presence.

Procedural Memory. Memories of how to ride a bicycle, how to type, how to turn the lights on and off, and how to drive a car are procedural memories. Procedural memories tend to persist even when we do not use them for many years. Here Jean Piaget, the cognitive-developmental theorist discussed in Chapter 4, demonstrates that we may never forget how to ride a bicycle.

• *Semantic Memory*

General knowledge is referred to as **semantic memory.** *Semantics* concerns meanings. Allyn was reporting her understanding of the meaning of childbirth rather than an episode in her own life. You can "remember" that the United States has 50 states without visiting them and personally adding them up. You "remember" who authored *Hamlet*, although you were not looking over Shakespeare's shoulder as he did so. These, too, are examples of semantic memory.

Your future recollection that there are three kinds of memory is more likely to be semantic than episodic. In other words, you are more likely to "know" that there are three types of memory than to recall the date on which you learned about them, where you were and how you were sitting, and whether you were also thinking about dinner at the time. We tend to use the phrase "I remember. . ." when we are referring to episodic memories, as in "I *remember* the blizzard of 1998." But we are more likely to say "I know. . ." in reference to semantic memories, as in "I *know* about—" (or, "I heard about—") "—the blizzard of 1898." Put it another way: You may *remember* that you wrote your mother, but you *know* that Shakespeare wrote *Hamlet*.

• *Procedural Memory*

The third type of memory is **procedural memory,** also referred to as *skill memory*. Procedural memory means knowing how to do things. You have learned and now "remember" how to ride a bicycle, how to swim or swing a bat, how to type, how to turn on the lights, and how to drive a car. Procedural memories tend to persist even when we have not used them for many years. (Do we ever forget how to ride a bicycle?)

Do you think it would help for a person to have "ESP" (which usually stands for "extrasensory perception") to remember the three types of memory? That is, E = episodic, S = semantic, and P = procedural. As we proceed, we will see that a good deal of information about memory comes in threes. We will also learn more about **mnemonic devices,** or tricks for retaining memories, such as "ESP." By the way, is your use of "ESP" to help remember the kinds of memory an instance of episodic, semantic, or procedural memory?

Before proceeding to the next section, why don't you turn to the piece of paper on which you wrote the names of the four figures—that is, sheet number 4—and draw them from memory as exactly as you can. Hold on to the drawings. We'll talk about them a bit later.

> ### REFLECTIONS
> - You remember that classes have professors, and you remember your professor's name (I hope). Which of these is an episodic memory? Which is a semantic memory? Explain the difference between the two.
> - What procedural memories do you have? Do you remember how to hold a pen or pencil, how to type on a keyboard, how to drive a car? Can you provide other examples?

SEMANTIC MEMORY • General knowledge as opposed to episodic memory.
PROCEDURAL MEMORY • Knowledge of ways of doing things; skill memory.
MNEMONIC DEVICES • Systems for remembering in which items are related to easily recalled sets of symbols such as acronyms, phrases, or jingles.

■ THREE PROCESSES OF MEMORY

Both psychologists and computer scientists speak of processing information. Think of using a computer to write a term paper. Once the system is operating, you begin to enter information. You place information in the computer's memory by typing letters on a keyboard. If you were to do some major surgery on your computer (which I am often tempted to do) and open up its memory, however, you wouldn't find these letters inside it. This is because the computer is programmed to change the letters—that is, the information you have typed—into a form that can be placed in its electronic memory. Similarly, when we perceive information, we must convert it into a form that can be remembered if we are to place it in our memory.

• Encoding

The first stage of information processing is changing information so that we can place it in memory: **encoding.** Information about the outside world reaches our senses in the form of physical and chemical stimuli. When we encode this information, we convert it into psychological formats that can be represented mentally. To do so, we commonly use visual, auditory, and semantic codes.

Let us illustrate the uses of coding by referring to the list of letters you first saw in the section on challenges to memory. Try to write the letters on sheet number 1. Go on, take a minute and then come back.

Okay, now: if you had used a **visual code** to try to remember the list, you would have mentally represented it as a picture. That is, you would have maintained—or attempted to maintain—a mental image of the letters. Some artists and art historians seem to maintain marvelous visual mental representations of works of art. This enables them to quickly recognize whether a work is authentic.

You may also have decided to read the list of letters to yourself—that is, to silently say them in sequence: "t," "h," "u," and so on. By so doing, you would have been using an **acoustic code,** or representing the stimuli as a sequence of sounds. You may also have read the list as a three-syllable word, "thun-sto-fam." This is an acoustic code, but it also involves the "meaning" of the letters, in the sense that you are interpreting the list as a word. This approach has elements of a semantic code.

Semantic codes represent stimuli in terms of their meaning. How can you use a semantic code to help remember the colors blue, yellow, and gray? You may recall from Chapter 5 that blue and yellow are complementary, and when we mix lights of complementary colors we attain gray. Using this relationship among the colors to remember them gives meaning to the grouping and therefore is an example of a semantic code.

Our 10 letters were meaningless in and of themselves. However, they can also serve as an acronym—a term that is made up of the first letters of a phrase—for the familiar phrase "THe UNited STates OF AMerica." This observation lends them meaning.

• Storage

The second memory process is **storage.** Storage means maintaining information over time. If you were given the task of storing the list of letters—that is, told to remember it—how would you attempt to place it in storage? One way would be by **maintenance rehearsal**—by mentally repeating the list, or saying it to yourself. Our awareness of the functioning of our memory, referred to by psychologists as **metamemory,** becomes more sophisticated as we develop.

You could also have condensed the amount of information you were rehearsing by reading the list as a three-syllable word; that is, you could have rehearsed three syllables rather than 10 letters. In either case, repetition would have been the key to memory. (We'll talk about such condensing, or "chunking," very soon.) However, if you had encoded the list semantically, as an acronym for "The United States of America," storage might have been instantaneous and permanent.

ENCODING • Modifying information so that it can be placed in memory. The first stage of information processing.
VISUAL CODE • Mental representation of information as a picture.
ACOUSTIC CODE • Mental representation of information as a sequence of sounds.
SEMANTIC CODE • Mental representation of information according to its meaning.
STORAGE • The maintenance of information over time. The second stage of information processing.
MAINTENANCE REHEARSAL • Mental repetition of information in order to keep it in memory.
METAMEMORY • Self-awareness of the ways in which memory functions, allowing the person to encode, store, and retrieve information effectively.

• *Retrieval*

The third memory process is **retrieval,** or locating stored information and returning it to consciousness. With well-known information such as our names and occupations, retrieval is effortless and, for all practical purposes, immediate. But when we are trying to remember massive quantities of information, or information that is not perfectly understood, retrieval can be tedious and not always successful. It is easiest to retrieve information stored in a computer by using the name of the file. Similarly, retrieval of information from our memories requires knowledge of the proper cues.

If you had encoded THUNSTOFAM as a three-syllable word, your retrieval strategy would involve recollection of the word and rules for decoding. In other words, you would say the "word" *thun-sto-fam* and then decode it by spelling it out. You might err in that "thun" sounds like "thumb" and "sto" could also be spelled "stow." However, using the semantic code, or recognition of the acronym for "The United States of America," could lead to flawless recollection.

I stuck my neck out by predicting that you would immediately and permanently store the list if you recognized it as an acronym. Here, too, there would be recollection (of the name of our country) and rules for decoding. That is, to "remember" the 10 letters, you would have to envision the phrase and read off the first two letters of each word. Since using this semantic code is more complex than simply seeing the entire list (using a visual code), it may take a while to recall (actually, to reconstruct) the list of 10 letters. But by using the phrase, you are likely to remember the list of letters permanently.

Now, what if you were not able to remember the list of 10 letters? What would have gone wrong? In terms of the three processes of memory, it could be that you had (1) not encoded the list in a useful way, (2) not entered the encoded information into storage, or (3) stored the information but lacked the proper cues for remembering it—such as the phrase "The United States of America" or the rule for decoding the phrase.

By now you may have noticed that I have discussed three kinds of memory and three processes of memory, but I have not yet *defined* memory. No apologies—we weren't ready for a definition yet. Now that we have explored some basic concepts, let us give it a try: **Memory** is the processes by which information is encoded, stored, and retrieved.

REFLECTIONS
- Consider this list of letters: THUNSTOFAM. Can you think of two strategies for storing the list? What are the strategies called?
- How do you remember how to spell the words *receive* and *retrieve*?

■ THREE STAGES OF MEMORY

William James (1890) was intrigued by the fact that some memories are unreliable, "going in one ear and out the other," while others could be recalled for a lifetime. He wrote:

> The stream of thought flows on, but most of its elements fall into the bottomless pit of oblivion. Of some, no element survives the instant of their passage. Of others, it is confined to a few moments, hours, or days. Others, again, leave vestiges which are indestructible, and by means of which they may be recalled as long as life endures.

RETRIEVAL • The location of stored information and its return to consciousness. The third stage of information processing.

MEMORY • The processes by which information is encoded, stored, and retrieved.

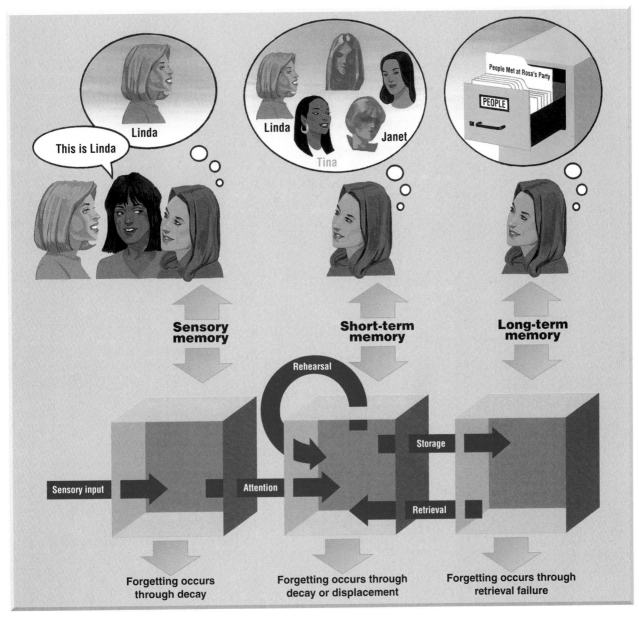

FIGURE 8.1

THREE STAGES OF MEMORY

The Atkinson-Shiffrin model proposes that there are three distinct stages of memory. Sensory information impacts upon the registers of sensory memory, where memory traces are held briefly before decaying. If we attend to the information, much of it is transferred to short-term memory (STM). Information in STM may decay or be displaced if it is not transferred to long-term memory (LTM). We can use rehearsal or elaborative strategies to transfer memories to LTM. If information in LTM is organized poorly, or if we cannot find cues to retrieve it, it may be lost.

Yes, the world is a constant display of sights and sounds and other sources of sensory stimulation, but only some of these things are remembered. James was correct in observing that we remember various "elements" of thought for different lengths of time, and many we do not remember at all. Richard Atkinson and Richard Shiffrin (1968) proposed that there are three stages of memory and that the progress of information through these stages determines whether (and how long) it will be retained (see Figure 8.1). These stages are *sensory memory, short-term memory (STM),* and *long-term memory (LTM).* Let us try to make *sense* of the *short* and the *long* of memory.

• *Sensory Memory*

William James also wrote about the stream of thought, or consciousness:

> Consciousness . . . does not appear to itself chopped up in bits. A "river" or a "stream" are the metaphors by which it is most naturally described. In talking of it hereafter, let us call it the stream of thought, of consciousness, or of subjective life.

When we look at a visual stimulus, our impressions may seem fluid enough. Actually, however, they consist of a series of eye fixations referred to as **saccadic eye movements.** These movements jump from one point to another about four times each second. Yet the visual sensations seem continuous, or streamlike, because of **sensory memory.** Sensory memory is the type or stage of memory that is first encountered by a stimulus. Although it holds impressions briefly, it is long enough so that a series of perceptions seem to be connected.

Let us return to our example of the list of letters: THUNSTOFAM. If the list were flashed on a screen for a fraction of a second, the visual impression, or **memory trace,** of the stimulus would also last for only a fraction of a second afterward. Psychologists speak of the memory trace of the list as being held in a visual **sensory register.**

If the letters had been flashed on a screen for, say, $\frac{1}{10}$ of a second, your ability to remember them on the basis of sensory memory alone would be limited. Your memory would be based on a single eye fixation, and the trace of the image would vanish before a single second had passed. At the turn of the century, psychologist William McDougall (1904) engaged in research in which he showed people one to 12 letters arranged in rows—just long enough to allow a single eye fixation. Under these conditions, people could typically remember only four or five letters. Thus, recollection of THUNSTOFAM, a list of 10 letters arranged in a single row, would probably depend on whether one had encoded it so that it could be processed further.

George Sperling (1960) modified McDougall's experimental method and showed that there is a difference between what people can see and what they can report. McDougall had used a *whole-report procedure,* in which people were asked to report every letter they saw in the array. Sperling used a modified *partial-report procedure,* in which people were asked to report the contents of one of three rows of letters. In a typical procedure, Sperling flashed three rows of letters like the following on a screen for 50 milliseconds ($\frac{1}{20}$ of a second):

A G R E

V L S B

N K B T

Using the whole-report procedure, people could report an average of four letters from the entire display (one out of three). But if immediately after presenting the display Sperling pointed an arrow at a row he wanted viewers to report, they usually reported most of the letters in the row successfully.

If Sperling presented six letters arrayed in two rows, people could usually report either row without error. If people were flashed three rows of four letters each—a total of 12—they reported correctly an average of three of four letters in the designated row, suggesting that about nine of the 12 letters had been perceived.

Sperling found that the amount of time that elapsed before indicating the row to be reported was crucial. If he delayed pointing the arrow for a few fractions of a second after presenting the letters, people were much less successful

SACCADIC EYE MOVEMENT • The rapid jumps made by a person's eyes as they fixate on different points.
SENSORY MEMORY • The type or stage of memory first encountered by a stimulus. Sensory memory holds impressions briefly, but long enough so that series of perceptions are psychologically continuous.
MEMORY TRACE • An assumed change in the nervous system that reflects the impression made by a stimulus. Memory traces are said to be "held" in sensory registers.
SENSORY REGISTER • A system of memory that holds information briefly, but long enough so that it can be processed further. There may be a sensory register for every sense.

in reporting the letters in the target row. If he allowed a full second to elapse, the arrow did not aid recall at all. From these data, Sperling concluded that the memory trace of visual stimuli *decays* within a second in the visual sensory register (see Figure 8.1). With a single eye fixation, people can *see* most of a display of 12 letters clearly, as shown by their ability to immediately read off most of the letters in a designated row. Yet as the fractions of a single second are elapsing, the memory trace of the letters is fading. By the time a second has elapsed, the trace has vanished.

ICONIC MEMORY Psychologists believe that there is a sensory register for each one of our senses. The mental representations of visual stimuli are referred to as **icons**. The sensory register that holds icons is labeled **iconic memory**. Iconic memories are accurate, photographic memories. So those of us who mentally represent visual stimuli have "photographic memories." However, they are very brief. What most of us normally think of as a photographic memory—the ability to retain exact mental representations of visual stimuli over long periods—is referred to as *eidetic imagery*.

EIDETIC IMAGERY A few individuals retain visual stimuli, or icons, for remarkably long periods. About 5% of children can look at a detailed picture, turn away, and several minutes later recall the particulars of the picture with exceptional clarity—as if they were still viewing it. This extraordinary visual memory is referred to as **eidetic imagery** (Haber, 1980). This ability declines with age, however, all but disappearing by adolescence.

Figure 8.2 provides an example of a test of eidetic imagery. Children are asked to look at the first drawing in the series for 20 to 30 seconds, after which it is removed. The children then continue to gaze at a neutral background. Several minutes later the drawing in the center is placed on the backdrop. When asked what they see, many report "a face." A face would be seen only if the children had retained a clear image of the first picture and fused it with the

> ### Truth or Fiction Revisited
>
> It is true that some people have photographic memory. People who can see have what is actually defined as *photographic*, or *iconic*, memory. However, only a few have *eidetic imagery*, which is closer to what laypeople think of as "photographic memory."

ICON • A mental representation of a visual stimulus that is held briefly in sensory memory.
ICONIC MEMORY • The sensory register that briefly holds mental representations of visual stimuli.
EIDETIC IMAGERY • The maintenance of detailed visual memories over several minutes.

FIGURE 8.2

A RESEARCH STRATEGY FOR ASSESSING EIDETIC IMAGERY

Children look at the first drawing for 20 to 30 seconds, after which it is removed. Next, the children look at a neutral background for several minutes. They are then shown the second drawing. When asked what they see, children with the capacity for eidetic imagery report a face. The face is seen only by children who retain the first image and fuse it with the second, thus perceiving the third image.

Echoic Memory. The mental representations of auditory stimuli are called echoes, and the sensory register that holds echoes is referred to as echoic memory. By encoding visual information as echoes and rehearsing the echoes, we commit them to memory.

second so that they are, in effect, perceiving the third picture in Figure 8.2 (Haber, 1980).

Eidetic imagery appears remarkably clear and detailed. It seems to be essentially a perceptual phenomenon in which coding is not a factor. Although eidetic imagery is rare, iconic memory, as we see in the following section, universally transforms visual perceptions into smoothly unfolding impressions of the world.

ICONIC MEMORY AND SACCADIC EYE MOVEMENTS   Saccadic eye movements smooth out the bumps in the visual ride. They occur about four times every second. Iconic memory, however, holds icons for up to a second. As a consequence, the flow of visual information seems smooth and continuous. Your impression that the words you are reading flow across the page, rather than jumping across in spurts, is a product of your iconic memory. Similarly, you may recall from Chapter 5 that motion pictures present 16 to 22 separate frames, or still images, each second. Iconic memory allows you to perceive the imagery in the film as being seamless (Loftus, 1983).

ECHOIC MEMORY   Mental representations of sounds, or auditory stimuli, are called **echoes.** The sensory register that holds echoes is referred to as **echoic memory.**

The memory traces of auditory stimuli (that is, echoes) can last for several seconds, many times longer than the traces of visual stimuli (icons). The difference in the duration of traces is probably based on biological differences between the eye and the ear. This difference is one of the reasons that acoustic codes aid in the retention of information that has been presented visually—or why saying the letters or syllables of THUNSTOFAM makes the list easier to remember.

Yet echoes, like icons, fade with time. If they are to be retained, we must pay attention to them. By selectively attending to certain stimuli, we sort them out from the background noise. For example, in studies on the development of patterns of processing information, young children have been shown photographs of rooms full of toys and then been asked to recall as many of the toys as they can. One such study found that 2-year-old boys are more likely to attend to and remember toys such as cars, puzzles, and trains. Two-year-old girls are more likely to attend to and remember dolls, dishes, and teddy bears (Renninger & Wozniak, 1985). Even by this early age, the things that children attend to frequently fall into stereotypical patterns.

• *Short-Term Memory*

If you focus on a stimulus in the sensory register, you will tend to retain it in **short-term memory**—also referred to as **working memory**—for a minute or so after the trace of the stimulus decays (Baddeley, 1994). As one researcher describes it, "Working memory is the mental glue that links a thought through time from its beginning to its end" (Goldman-Rakic, 1995). When you are given a phone number by the information operator and write it down or immediately dial the number, you are retaining the number in your short-term memory. When you are told the name of someone at a party and then use that name immediately in addressing that person, you are retaining the name in short-term memory. In short-term memory, the image tends to fade significantly after 10 to 12 seconds if it is not repeated or rehearsed. It is possible to focus on maintaining a visual image in the short-term memory, but it is more common to encode visual stimuli as sounds, or auditory stimuli. Then the sounds can be rehearsed, or repeated.

ECHO • A mental representation of an auditory stimulus (sound) that is held briefly in sensory memory.

ECHOIC MEMORY • The sensory register that briefly holds mental representations of auditory stimuli.

SHORT-TERM MEMORY • The type or stage of memory that can hold information for up to a minute or so after the trace of the stimulus decays. Also called *working memory.*

WORKING MEMORY • Same as *short-term memory.*

Most of us know that one way of retaining information in short-term memory—and possibly storing it permanently—is to rehearse it. When an information operator tells me a phone number, I usually rehearse it continuously while I am dialing it or running around frantically searching for a pencil and a scrap of paper. The more times we rehearse information, the more likely we are to remember it. We have the capacity (if not the will or the time) to rehearse information and thereby keep it in short-term memory indefinitely.

ENCODING Let us now return to the task of remembering the first list of letters in the challenges to memory at the beginning of the chapter. If you had coded the letters as the three-syllable word THUN-STO-FAM, you would probably have recalled them by mentally rehearsing (saying to yourself) the three-syllable "word" and then spelling it out from the sounds. A few minutes later, if someone asked whether the letters had been uppercase (THUNSTOFAM) or lowercase (thunstofam), you might not have been able to answer with confidence. You used an acoustic code to help recall the list, and uppercase and lowercase letters sound alike.

Because it can be pronounced, THUNSTOFAM is not too difficult to retain in short-term memory. But what if the list of letters was TBXLFNTSDK? This list of letters cannot be pronounced as it is. You would have to find a complex acronym to code these letters, and do so within a fraction of a second—most likely an impossible task. To aid recall, you would probably choose to try to repeat the letters rapidly—to read each one as many times as possible before the memory trace fades. You might visualize each letter as you say it and try to get back to it (that is, to run through the entire list) before it decays.

Let us assume that you encoded the letters as sounds and then rehearsed the sounds. When asked to report the list, you might mistakenly say T-V-X-L-F-N-T-S-T-K. This would be an understandable error because the incorrect *V* and *T* sounds are similar, respectively, to the correct *B* and *D* sounds.

THE SERIAL-POSITION EFFECT Note that you would also be likely to recall the first and last letters in the series, *T* and *K*, more accurately than the others. Why? The tendency to recall the first and last items in a series more accurately is known as the **serial-position effect.** This effect may occur because we pay more attention to the first and last stimuli in a series. They serve as the visual or auditory boundaries for the other stimuli. It may also be that the first items are likely to be rehearsed more frequently (repeated more times) than other items. The last items are likely to have been rehearsed most recently and hence are most likely to be retained in short-term memory.

According to cognitive psychologists, the tendency to recall the initial items in a list is referred to as the **primacy effect.** Social psychologists have also noted a powerful primacy effect in our formation of impressions of other people. In other words, first impressions tend to last. The tendency to recall the last items in a list is referred to as the **recency effect.** If we are asked to recall the last items in a list soon after we have been shown the list, they may still be in short-term memory. As a result, they can be "read off." Earlier items, in contrast, may have to be retrieved from long-term memory.

CHUNKING: IS SEVEN A MAGIC NUMBER OR DID THE PHONE COMPANY GET LUCKY? Rapidly rehearsing 10 meaningless letters is not an easy task. With TBXLFNTSDK there are 10 discrete elements, or **chunks,** of information that must be kept in short-term memory. When we encode THUNSTOFAM as three syllables, there are only three chunks to swallow at once—a memory task that is much easier on the digestion.

SERIAL-POSITION EFFECT • The tendency to recall more accurately the first and last items in a series.
PRIMACY EFFECT • The tendency to recall the initial items in a series of items.
RECENCY EFFECT • The tendency to recall the last items in a series of items.
CHUNK • A stimulus or group of stimuli that are perceived as a discrete piece of information.

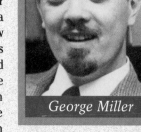

George Miller

George Miller used to have a joke about how to get the kids to bed. He said he would "use psychology" on them. Now, he had written the word *psychology* on a baseball bat, and he would chase them upstairs with it (Sternberg, 1995).

Not true, of course, but Miller's story shows how people can play with their mental representations of objects and words. Miller was part of the cognitive revolution that paralleled the sexual revolution, at least in terms of when it happened—the 1960s and 1970s. Behaviorism was riding high at Harvard University, but Miller was one of those who abandoned rats and mazes and Skinner boxes in order to study higher mental processes, such as memory.

He was not originally in-terested in psychology. He was raised in West Virginia as a Christian Scientist, trained to avoid medical matters. There-fore, when he saw diagrams of the brain and other drawings in a psychology textbook, he was not particularly interested. But as a junior in college he *was* interested in a young woman who was attending psychology seminars at a professor's home. And so he tagged along. The professor was impressed with Miller and a couple of years later gave him a job teaching undergraduate psychology, even though Miller had never taken a course in the subject. But Miller eventually made up for it by earning his doctorate in psychology at Harvard and then teaching psychology there for many years. ■

George Miller wryly noted that the average person is comfortable with digesting about seven integers at a time, the number of integers in a telephone number:

> My problem is that I have been persecuted by an integer [the number *seven*]. For seven years this number has followed me around, has intruded in my most private data, and has assaulted me from the pages of our most public journals. (1956)

It may sound as if Miller was being paranoid, but he was actually talking about research findings. They show that most people have little trouble recalling five chunks of information, as in a zip code. Some can remember nine, which is, for all but a few, an upper limit. So seven chunks, plus or minus one or two, is the "magic" number.

So how, you ask, do we manage to include area codes in our recollections of telephone numbers, hence making them 10 digits long? The truth of the matter is that we usually don't. We tend to recall the area code as a single chunk of information derived from our general knowledge of where a person lives. So we are more likely to remember (or "know") the 10-digit numbers of acquaintances who reside in locales with area codes that we use frequently.

Businesses pay the phone company hefty premiums so that they can attain numbers with two or three zeroes—for example, 592-2000 or 614-3300. These numbers include fewer chunks of information and hence are easier to remember. Customer recollection of business phone numbers increases sales. One financial services company uses the toll-free number CALL-IRA, which reduces the task to two chunks of information that also happen to be meaningfully related (semantically coded) to the nature of the business. Similarly, a clinic that helps people quit smoking arranged for a telephone number that can be reached by dialing the letters NO SMOKE.

Return to the third challenge to memory presented on page 283.
Were you able to remember the six groups of letters? Would your task have been simpler if you had grouped them differently? How about moving the dashes forward by a letter, so that they read GM-CBS-IBM-ATT-CIA-FBI? If we do this, we have the same list of letters, but we also have six chunks of information that can be coded semantically. You may have also been able to generate the list by remembering a rule, such as "big corporations and government agencies."

If we can recall seven or perhaps nine chunks of information, how do children remember the alphabet? The alphabet contains 26 discrete pieces of information. How do children learn to encode the letters of the alphabet, which are visual symbols, as spoken sounds? There is nothing about the shape of an A that suggests its sound. Nor does the visual stimulus *B* sound "B-ish." Children learn to associate letters with their spoken names by **rote.** It is mechanical associative learning that takes time and repetition. If you think that learning the alphabet by rote is a simple task, try learning the Russian alphabet.

If you had recognized THUNSTOFAM as an acronym for the first two letters of each word in the phrase "THe UNited STates OF AMerica," you would also

Rote • Mechanical associative learning that is based on repetition.

Displace • In memory theory, to cause information to be lost from short-term memory by adding new information.

have reduced the number of chunks of information that had to be recalled. You could have considered the phrase to be a single chunk of information. The rule that you must use the first two letters of each word of the phrase would be another chunk.

Reconsider the second challenge to memory on page 283. You were asked to remember nine chunks of visual information. Perhaps you could have used the acoustic codes "L" and "Square" for chunks three and five, but no obvious codes are available for the seven other chunks. Now look at Figure 8.3. If you had recognized that the elements in the challenge could be arranged as the familiar tic-tac-toe grid, remembering the nine elements might have required two chunks of information. The first would have been the mental image of the grid and the second would have been the rule for decoding: each element corresponds to the shape of a section of the grid if read like words on a page (from upper left to lower right). The number sequence one through nine would not in itself present a problem, because you learned this series by rote many years ago and have rehearsed it in countless calculations since then.

INTERFERENCE IN SHORT-TERM MEMORY I mentioned that I often find myself running around looking for a pencil and a scrap of paper to write down a telephone number that has been given to me. If I keep on rehearsing the number while I'm looking, I'm okay. But I have also often cursed myself for failing to keep a pad and pencil by the telephone, and sometimes this has interfered with my recollection of the number. (The moral of the story? Avoid self-reproach.) It has also happened that I have actually looked up a phone number and been about to dial it when someone has asked me for the time or where I said we were going to dinner. Unless I say, "Hold on a minute!" and manage to jot down the number on something, it's back to the phone book. Attending to distracting information, even briefly, prevents me from rehearsing the number, so it falls through the cracks of my short-term memory.

In an experiment with college students, Lloyd and Margaret Peterson (1959) demonstrated how prevention of rehearsal can wreak havoc with short-term memory. They asked students to remember three-letter combinations such as HGB—normally, three easy chunks of information. They then had the students count backward from an arbitrary number, such as 181, by threes (that is, 181, 178, 175, 172, and so on). The students were told to stop counting and to report the letter sequence after the intervals of time shown in Figure 8.4. The percentage of letter combinations that were recalled correctly fell precipitously within seconds. After 18 seconds of interference, counting had dislodged the letter sequences in almost all of these bright young students' memories.

Psychologists say that the appearance of new information in short-term memory **displaces** the old information. Remember: Only a few bits of information can be retained in short-term memory at the same time. Think of short-term memory as a shelf or workbench. Once it is full, some things fall off it when new items are shoved onto it. Here we have another possible explanation for the recency effect: The most recently learned bit of information is least likely to be displaced by additional information.

Displacement occurs at cocktail parties, and I'm not referring to jostling by the crowd. The point is this: When you meet Jennifer or Jonathan at the party, you should have little trouble remembering the name. But then you may meet Tamara or Timothy and, still later, Stephanie or Steven. By that time you may have a hard time dredging up Jennifer or Jonathan's name—unless, of course, you were very, very attracted to one of them. A passionate response would set a person apart and inspire a good deal of selective attention. Recall signal-detection theory from Chapter 5: If you were enamored enough, we may

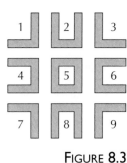

FIGURE 8.3
A FAMILIAR GRID

The nine drawings in the second challenge to memory form this familiar tic-tac-toe grid when the numbers are placed inside them and they are arranged in order. This method for recalling the shapes collapses nine chunks of information into two. One is the tic-tac-toe grid. The second is the rule for decoding the drawings from the grid.

FIGURE 8.4
THE EFFECT OF INTERFERENCE ON SHORT-TERM MEMORY

In this experiment, college students were asked to remember a series of three letters while they counted backward by three's. After just three seconds, retention was cut by half. Ability to recall the words was almost completely lost by 15 seconds.

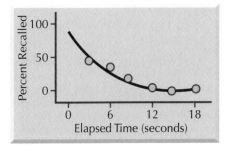

Displacement. Information can be lost to short-term memory through displacement. We may have little trouble remembering the names of the first or second person we meet at a gathering. But as introductions continue, new names may displace the old ones and we may forget the names of people we met only a few minutes earlier.

Truth or Fiction Revisited

It is true that it may be easier for you to recall the name of your first-grade teacher than of someone you just met at a party. Your first-grade teacher's name is stored in long-term memory. However, you may be juggling a new acquaintance's name with many others in short-term memory.

Truth or Fiction Revisited

It is not true that all of our experiences are permanently imprinted on the brain so that proper stimulation can cause us to remember them exactly. We appear to be more likely to store incidents that have a greater impact on us — events that are more laden with personal meaning.

LONG-TERM MEMORY • The type or stage of memory capable of relatively permanent storage.
REPRESSION • In Freud's psychodynamic theory, the ejection of anxiety-evoking ideas from conscious awareness.
SCHEMA • A way of mentally representing the world, such as a belief or an expectation, that can influence perception of persons, objects, and situations.

predict that you would "detect" the person's name (sensory signals) with a vengeance, and all the ensuing names would dissolve into background noise.

• Long-Term Memory

Long-term memory is the third stage of information processing. Think of your long-term memory as a vast storehouse of information containing names, dates, places, what Johnny did to you in second grade, and what Susan said about you when you were 12.

Some psychologists (Freud was one) used to believe that nearly all of our perceptions and ideas are stored permanently. We might not be able to retrieve all of them, but some memories might be "lost" because of lack of proper cues, or they might be kept unconscious by the forces of **repression**. Adherents to this view often pointed to the work of neurosurgeon Wilder Penfield (1969). When parts of their brains were electrically stimulated, many of Penfield's patients reported the appearance of images that had something of the feel of memories.

Today most psychologists view this notion as exaggerated. Memory researcher Elizabeth Loftus, for example, notes that the "memories" stimulated by Penfield's probes lacked detail and were sometimes incorrect (Loftus & Loftus, 1980; Loftus, 1983). Now let us consider some other questions about long-term memory.

HOW ACCURATE ARE LONG-TERM MEMORIES? Elizabeth Loftus notes that memories are distorted by our biases and needs—by the ways in which we conceptualize our worlds. We represent much of our world in the form of **schemas**.

To understand what is meant by the term *schema*, consider the problems of travelers who met up with Procrustes, the legendary highwayman of ancient Greece. Procrustes had a quirk. He was interested not only in travelers' pocketbooks but also in their height. He had a concept—a schema—of how tall people should be, and when people did not fit his schema, they were in trouble.

You see, Procrustes also had a bed, the famous "Procrustean bed." He made his victims lie down in the bed, and if they were too short for it, he stretched them to make them fit. If they were too long for the bed, he practiced surgery on their legs.

Although the myth of Procrustes may sound absurd, it reflects a quirky truth about each of us. We all carry our cognitive Procrustean beds around with us—our unique ways of perceiving the world—and we try to make things and people fit them.

Let me give you an example. Why don't you "retrieve" the fourth sheet of paper you prepared according to the instructions for the challenges to memory. The labels you wrote on the sheet will remind you of the figures. Please take a minute or two to draw them now. Then continue reading.

Now that you made your drawings, turn to Figure 8.5. Are your drawings closer in form to those in Group 1 or to those in Group 2? I wouldn't be surprised if they were more like those in Group 1. After all, they were labeled like the drawings in Group 1. The labels serve as *schemas* for the drawings—ways of organizing your knowledge of them—and these schemas may have influenced your recollections.

Consider another example of the power of schemas in processing information. Loftus and Palmer (1974) showed people a film of a car crash and then asked them to fill out questionnaires that included a question about how fast the cars were going at the time. The language of the question varied in subtle ways, however. Some people were asked to estimate how fast the cars were going when they "hit" each other. Others were asked to estimate the cars' speed when they "smashed into" each other. On average, people who reconstructed the scene on the basis of the cue "hit" estimated a speed of 34 mph. People who watched the same film but reconstructed the scene on the basis of the cue "smashed" estimated a speed of 41 mph! In other words, the use of the word *hit* or *smashed* caused people to organize their knowledge about the crash in different ways. That is, the words served as diverse schemas that fostered the development of very different ways of processing information about the crash.

Subjects in the same study were questioned again a week later: "Did you see any broken glass?" Since there was no broken glass shown in the film, an answer of "yes" would be wrong. Of those who had earlier been encouraged to

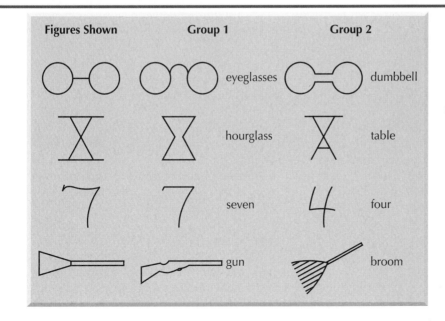

FIGURE 8.5
MEMORY AS RECONSTRUCTIVE
In their classic experiment, Carmichael, Hogan, and Walter (1932) showed people the figures in the left-hand box and made remarks as suggested in the other boxes. For example, the experimenter might say, "This drawing looks like eyeglasses [or a dumbbell]." When people later reconstructed the drawings, they were influenced by the labels.

How Fast Were These Cars Going When They Collided? Our schemas influence our processing of information. When shown pictures such as these, people who were asked how fast the cars were going when they *smashed* into one another offer higher estimates than people who were told that the cars *hit* one another.

process information about the accident in terms of one car "hitting" the other, 14% incorrectly answered yes. But 32% of the subjects who had processed information about the crash in terms of one car "smashing into" the other reported, incorrectly, that they had seen broken glass. Findings such as these have implications for eyewitness testimony.

LONG-TERM MEMORY AND EYEWITNESS TESTIMONY

Jean Piaget, the investigator of children's cognitive development, distinctly remembered an attempt to kidnap him from his baby carriage as he was being wheeled along the Champs Élysées. He recalled the excited throng, the abrasions on the face of the nurse who rescued him, the police officer's white baton, and the flight of the assailant. Although they were graphic, Piaget's memories were false. Years later, the nurse admitted that she had made up the tale.

Legal professionals are concerned about the accuracy of our memories as reflected in eyewitness testimony. Misidentifications of suspects "create a double horror: The wrong person is devastated by this personal tragedy, and the real criminal is still out on the streets" (Loftus, 1993b, p. 550). Is there reason to believe that the statements of eyewitnesses are any more factual than Piaget's?

There is cause for concern. The words chosen by an experimenter—and those chosen by a lawyer interrogating a witness—have been shown to influence the reconstruction of memories (Loftus & Palmer, 1973). For example, as in the experiment described earlier, an attorney for the plaintiff might ask the witness, "How fast was the defendant's car going when it *smashed into* the plaintiff's car?" In such a case, the car might be reported as going faster than if the question had been: "How fast was the defendant's car going when the accident occurred?" Could the attorney for the defendant claim that use of the word *smashed* biased the witness? What about jurors who heard the word *smashed?* Would they be biased toward assuming that the driver had been reckless?

Children tend to be more suggestible witnesses than adults, and preschoolers are more suggestible than older children (Ceci & Bruck, 1993). On the other hand, when questioned properly, even young children may be able to provide accurate and useful testimony (Ceci & Bruck, 1993).

There are cases in which the memories of eyewitnesses have been "refreshed" by hypnosis. Sad to say, hypnosis does more than amplify memories; it can also distort them (Loftus, 1994). One problem is that witnesses may accept and embellish suggestions made by the hypnotist. Another is that hypnotized people may report fantasized occurrences as compellingly as if they were real (Loftus, 1994).

There are also problems in the identification of criminals by eyewitnesses. For one thing, witnesses may pay more attention to the suspect's clothing than to more meaningful characteristics such as facial features, height, and weight. In one experiment, viewers of a videotaped crime incorrectly identified a man as the criminal because he wore the eyeglasses and T-shirt that had been worn by the perpetrator on the tape. The man who had actually committed the crime was identified less often (Sanders, 1984).

Other problems with eyewitness testimony include the following:

- Identification of suspects is less accurate when suspects belong to ethnic or racial groups that differ from that of the witness (Egeth, 1993).

- Identification of suspects is confused when interrogators make misleading suggestions (Loftus, 1997).

- Witnesses are seen as more credible when they claim to be certain in their testimony, but there is little evidence that claims of certainty are accurate (Wells, 1993).

Eyewitness Testimony? How trustworthy is eyewitness testimony? Memories are reconstructive rather than photographic. The wording of questions also influences the content of the memory. Attorneys therefore are sometimes instructed not to phrase questions in such a way that they "lead" the witness.

There are thus many problems with eyewitness testimony. Yet what is the alternative? If we were to prevent witnesses from testifying, how many criminals would go free (Loftus, 1993b)?

HOW MUCH INFORMATION *CAN* BE STORED IN LONG-TERM MEMORY? How many gigabytes of storage are there in your most personal computer—your brain? Unlike a computer, the human ability to store information is practically unlimited (Goldman-Rakic, 1995). New information may replace older information in short-term memory, but there is no evidence that long-term memories are lost by displacement. Long-term memories may endure for a lifetime. Now and then it may seem that we have forgotten, or "lost," a long-term memory such as the names of our elementary or high school classmates. Yet it may be that we cannot find the proper cues to help us retrieve them. If long-term memories are lost, they may be lost in the same way that a misplaced object is lost. It is "lost," but we sense that it is still somewhere in the room. In other words, it is lost but not destroyed.

Truth or Fiction Revisited

It is true that there is no practical limit to the amount of information you can store in your memory. At least, no limit has been discovered to date.

TRANSFERRING INFORMATION FROM SHORT-TERM TO LONG-TERM MEMORY How can you transfer information from short-term to long-term memory? By and large, the more often chunks of information are rehearsed, the more likely they are to be transferred to long-term memory. Repeating information over and over to prevent it from decaying or being displaced is termed *maintenance rehearsal*. But maintenance rehearsal does not give meaning to information by linking it to past learning. Thus it is not considered the best way to permanently store information (Craik & Watkins, 1973).

A more effective method is to make information more meaningful—to purposefully relate new information to things that are already well known (Woloshyn and others, 1994). For example, to better remember the components of levers, physics students might use seesaws, wheelbarrows, and oars as examples (Scruggs & Mastropieri, 1992). The nine chunks of information in our second challenge to memory were made easier to reconstruct once they were associated with the familiar tic-tac-toe grid in Figure 8.3. Relating new material to well-known material is known as **elaborative rehearsal.** For example, have you seen this word before?

FUNTHOSTAM

Say it aloud. Do you know it? If you had used an acoustic code alone to memorize THUNSTOFAM, the list of letters you first saw on page 282, it might not have been easy to recognize FUNTHOSTAM as an incorrect spelling. Let us assume, however, that by now you have encoded THUNSTOFAM semantically as an acronym for "The United States of America." Then you would have been able to scan the spelling of the words in the phrase "The United States of America" to determine that FUNTHOSTAM is an incorrect spelling.

Rote repetition of a meaningless group of syllables, such as *thun-sto-fam*, relies on maintenance rehearsal for permanent storage. The process might be tedious (continued rehearsal) and unreliable. Elaborative rehearsal—tying THUNSTOFAM to the name of a country—might make storage instantaneous and retrieval foolproof.

Language arts teachers encourage students to use new vocabulary words in sentences to help remember them. Each new usage is an instance of elaborative rehearsal. Usage helps build semantic codes that make it easier to retrieve the meanings of words in the future. When I was in high school, teachers of foreign languages told us that learning classical languages "exercises the mind" so that we would understand English better. Not exactly. The mind is not analogous to a muscle that responds to exercise. However, the meanings of many English words are based on foreign ones. A person who recognizes that *retrieve* stems from roots meaning "again" *(re-)* and "find" *(trouver* in French) is less likely to forget that *retrieval* means "finding again" or "bringing back."

Think, too, of all the algebra and geometry problems we were asked to solve in high school. Each problem is an application of a procedure and, perhaps, of certain formulas and theorems. By repeatedly applying the procedures, formulas, and theorems in different contexts, we rehearse them elaboratively. As a consequence, we are more likely to remember them. Knowledge of the ways in which a formula or an equation is used helps us remember the formula. Also, by building one geometry theorem on another, we relate new theorems to ones that we already understand. As a result, we process information about them more deeply and remember them better.

Before proceeding to the next section, let me ask you to cover the preceding paragraph. Now, which of the following words is spelled correctly: *retrieval* or *retreival*? The spellings sound alike, so an acoustic code for reconstructing the correct spelling would fail. Yet a semantic code, such as the spelling rule "*i* before *e* except after *c*," would allow you to reconstruct the correct spelling: retrieval.

FLASHBULB MEMORIES

> *The attention which we lend to an experience is proportional to its vivid or interesting character; and it is a notorious fact that what interests us most vividly at the time is, other things equal, what we remember best. An impression may be so exciting emotionally as almost to leave a scar upon the cerebral tissues.*
>
> WILLIAM JAMES

Do you remember the first time you were in love? Can you remember how the streets and the trees looked transformed? The vibrancy in your step? How generous you felt? How all of life's problems seemed suddenly solved?

ELABORATIVE REHEARSAL • A method for increasing retention of new information by relating it to information that is well known.

Flashbulb Memories. Where were you and what were you doing in 1997 when you learned that Britain's Princess Diana had been killed in an automobile accident? Major events can illuminate everything about them so that we recall everything that was happening at the time.

We tend to remember events that occur under unusual, emotionally arousing circumstances more clearly. Many of us will never forget where we were or what we were doing when we learned that Britain's Princess Diana had died in an automobile accident in 1997. Many of us recall the *Challenger* disaster of 1986, or the day when the Persian Gulf War erupted in 1991, or where they were when they heard that O. J. Simpson was acquitted of murder charges in 1995 (or found liable for wrongful deaths in 1997). We may also remember in detail what we were doing when we learned of a relative's death. These are examples of "flashbulb memories." Flashbulb memories preserve experiences in detail (Brown & Kulik, 1977; Thompson & Cowan, 1986).

Why is the memory etched when the "flashbulb" goes off? One factor is the distinctness of the memory. It is easier to discriminate stimuli that stand out. Such events are striking in themselves. The feelings that are caused by them are also rather special. It is thus relatively easy to pick them out from the storehouse of memories. Major events such as the assassination of a president or the loss of a close relative also tend to have important effects on our lives. We are likely to dwell on them and form networks of associations. That is, we are likely to rehearse them elaboratively. Our rehearsal may include great expectations, or deep fears, for the future.

ORGANIZATION IN LONG-TERM MEMORY The storehouse of long-term memory is usually well organized. Items are not just piled on the floor or thrown into closets. We tend to gather information about rats and cats into a certain section of the storehouse, perhaps the animal or mammal section. We put information about oaks, maples, and eucalyptus into the tree section. Such categorization of stimuli is a basic cognitive function. It allows us to make predictions about specific instances and to store information efficiently (Corter & Gluck, 1992).

We tend to organize information according to a hierarchical structure, as shown in Figure 8.6. A *hierarchy* is an arrangement of items (or chunks of information) into groups or classes according to common or distinct features. As we work our way up the hierarchy shown in Figure 8.6, we find more encompassing, or *superordinate,* classes to which the items below them belong. For

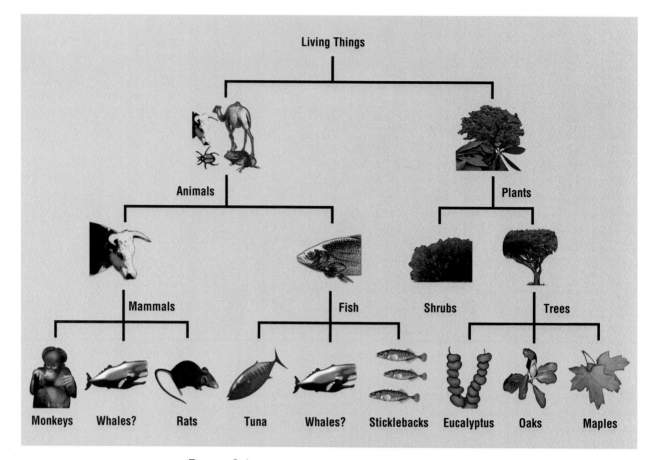

FIGURE 8.6
THE HIERARCHICAL STRUCTURE OF LONG-TERM MEMORY
Where are whales filed in the hierarchical cabinets of your memory? Your classification of whales may influence your answers to these questions: Do whales breathe underwater? Are they warm-blooded? Do they nurse their young?

example, all mammals are animals, but there are many types of animals other than mammals.[1]

When items are correctly organized in long-term memory, you are more likely to recall—or know—accurate information about them (Hasselhorn, 1992; Schneider & Bjorklund, 1992). For instance, do you remember whether whales breathe underwater? If you did not know that whales are mammals (or, in Figure 8.6, *subordinate* to mammals), or if you knew nothing about mammals, a correct answer might depend on some remote instance of rote learning. That is, you might be depending on chancy episodic memory rather than on reliable semantic memory. For example, you might recall some details from a Public Broadcasting System documentary on whales. If you *did* know that whales are mammals, however, you would also know—or remember—that whales do not breathe underwater. How? You would reconstruct information about whales from knowledge about mammals, the group to which whales are subordinate. Similarly, you would know, or remember, that because they are mammals, whales are warm-blooded, nurse their young, and are a good deal more intelligent than, say, tunas and sharks, which are fish. Had you incorrectly

---

[1] A note to biological purists: Figure 8.6 is not intended to represent phyla, classes, orders, and so on accurately. Rather, it shows how an individual's classification scheme might be organized.

classified whales as fish, you might have searched your memory and constructed the incorrect answer that they do breathe underwater.

THE TIP-OF-THE-TONGUE PHENOMENON Have you ever been so close to retrieving information that it seemed to be on "the tip of your tongue"? Yet you still could not quite remember it? This is a frustrating experience, similar to reeling in a fish but having it drop off the line just before it breaks the surface of the water. Psychologists term this experience the **tip-of-the-tongue (TOT) phenomenon,** or the **feeling-of-knowing experience.**

In one classic TOT experiment, Brown and McNeill (1966) defined some rather unusual words for students, such as *sampan,* a small riverboat used in China and Japan. The students were then asked to recall the words they had learned. Some of the students often had the right word "on the tip of their tongue" but reported words with similar meanings such as *junk, barge,* or *houseboat.* Still other students reported words that sounded similar, such as *Saipan, Siam, sarong,* and *sanching.* Why?

To begin with, the words were unfamiliar, so elaborative rehearsal did not take place. The students, that is, did not have an opportunity to relate the words to other things that they knew. Brown and McNeill also suggested that our storage systems are indexed according to cues that include both the sounds and the meanings of words—that is, according to both acoustic and semantic codes. By scanning words that are similar in sound and meaning to the word that is on the tip of the tongue, we sometimes find a useful cue and retrieve the word for which we are searching.

The feeling-of-knowing experience also seems to reflect incomplete or imperfect learning. In such cases, our answers may be "in the ballpark" if not on the mark. In some feeling-of-knowing experiments, people are often asked trivia questions. When they do not recall an answer, they are then asked to guess how likely it is that they will recognize the right answer if it is among a group of possibilities. People turn out to be very accurate in their estimations about whether or not they will recognize the answer. Similarly, Brown and McNeill found that the students in their TOT experiment proved to be very good at estimating the number of syllables in words that they could not recall. The students often correctly guessed the initial sounds of the words. They sometimes recognized words that rhymed with them.

Are the three kinds of memory on the tip of your tongue now? Can you use the acronym *ESP* to recall them?

Sometimes an answer seems to be on the tip of our tongue because our knowledge of the topic is incomplete. We may not know the exact answer, but we know something. (As a matter of fact, if we have good writing skills, we may present our incomplete knowledge so forcefully that we earn a good grade on an essay question on the topic!) At such times, the problem lies not in retrieval but in the original encoding and storage.

CONTEXT-DEPENDENT MEMORY The context in which we acquire information can also play a role in retrieval. I remember walking down the halls of the apartment building where I had lived as a child. I was suddenly assaulted by images of playing under the staircase, of falling against a radiator, of the shrill voice of a former neighbor calling for her child at dinnertime. Have you ever walked the halls of an old school building and been assaulted by memories of faces and names that you would have guessed had been lost forever? Have you ever walked through your old neighborhood and recalled the faces of people or the aromas of cooking that were so real that you actually salivated?

These are examples of **context-dependent memory.** Being in the proper context can dramatically enhance recall (Estes, 1972; Watkins and others, 1976).

TIP-OF-THE-TONGUE (TOT) PHENOMENON • The feeling that information is stored in memory although it cannot be readily retrieved. Also called the *feeling-of-knowing* experience.
FEELING-OF-KNOWING EXPERIENCE • Same as *tip-of-the-tongue phenomenon.*
CONTEXT-DEPENDENT MEMORY • Information that is better retrieved in the context in which it was encoded and stored, or learned.

One fascinating experiment in context-dependent memory included a number of people who were "all wet." Members of a university swimming club were asked to learn lists of words either while they were submerged or while they were literally high and dry (Godden & Baddeley, 1975). Students who learned the list underwater showed superior recall of the list when immersed. Similarly, those who had rehearsed the list ashore showed better retrieval on terra firma.

Other studies have found that students do better on tests when they study in the room where the test is to be given (Smith and others, 1978). When police are interviewing witnesses to crimes, they ask the witnesses to paint the scene verbally as vividly as possible, or they visit the scene of the crime with the witnesses. People who mentally place themselves back in the context in which they encoded and stored information frequently retrieve it more accurately.

STATE-DEPENDENT MEMORY **State-dependent memory** is an extension of context-dependent memory. It sometimes happens that we retrieve information better when we are in a physiological or emotional state that is similar to the one in which we encoded and stored the information. Feeling the rush of love may trigger images of other times when we fell in love. The grip of anger may prompt memories of incidents of frustration and rage.

Gordon Bower (1981) ran experiments in which happy or sad moods were induced by hypnotic suggestion. The subjects then learned lists of words. People who learned a list while in a happy mood showed better recall when a happy state was induced again. But people who had learned the list while in a sad mood showed superior recall when they were saddened again. Bower suggests that in day-to-day life a happy mood influences us to focus on positive events. As a result, we will have better recall of these events in the future. A sad mood, unfortunately, leads us to focus on and recall the negative. Happiness may feed on happiness, but under extreme circumstances sadness can develop into a vicious cycle.

REFLECTIONS

- How do you try to remember names and phone numbers?
- Do you know some people with excellent memories? Some with poor memories? How do you account for the difference?
- Can you remember what to buy at the supermarket without a list? How?
- Are there some things that you feel sure you will never forget? Why?

■ THE LEVELS-OF-PROCESSING MODEL OF MEMORY

Not all psychologists view memory in terms of stages. Fergus Craik and Robert Lockhart (1972) suggest that we do not have a sensory memory, a short-term memory, and a long-term memory per se. Instead, our ability to remember things can be viewed in terms of a single stage or dimension: the *depth* of our processing of information. This view holds that we don't form enduring memories by getting information "into" the mental structure of long-term memory. Rather, memories tend to endure when information is processed *deeply*—when it is attended to, encoded carefully, pondered, and rehearsed elaboratively or related to things that we already know well.

Consider our familiar list of letters, THUNSTOFAM. In an experiment we could ask one group of people to remember the list by repeating it aloud a few

STATE-DEPENDENT MEMORY • Information that is better retrieved in the physiological or emotional state in which it was encoded and stored, or learned.

In Review Three "Threes" of Memory

CONCEPT	WHAT IT MEANS	EXAMPLE
THREE KINDS OF MEMORY		
Episodic Memory	Memories of events experienced by a person	Remembering what you ate for dinner last night
Semantic Memory	General knowledge (as opposed to remembering personal episodes)	Remembering the capital cities of the 50 states
Procedural Memory	Knowledge of ways of doing things; skill memory	Remembering how to hold a pencil or ride a bicycle
THREE PROCESSES OF MEMORY		
Encoding	Modifying information so that it can be placed in memory	Mental representation of the words in this review chart as a sequence of sounds (an acoustic code)
Storage	The maintenance of information over time	Mental repetition (rehearsal) of the information in this chart in order to keep in in memory
Retrieval	The finding of stored information and bringing it into consciousness	Recall of the information in this chart; using a mnemonic device (e.g., Roy G. Biv) to recall the colors of the visible spectrum
THREE STAGES OF MEMORY		
Sensory Memory	The type or stage of memory that is first encountered by a stimulus and briefly holds impressions of it	Continuing to "see" a visual stimulus briefly after it has been removed
Short-Term Memory	The type or stage of memory that can hold the information for up to a minute or so after trace of the stimulus decays (also called *working memory*)	Repeating someone's name in order to remember it, or relating something new to things that are already known
Long-Term Memory	The type or stage of memory that is capable of relatively permanent storage	The "file cabinets" of memory, where you store items like the names of your primary school teachers and your memories of holidays when you were little

times, a letter at a time. Another group could be informed that it is an acronym for "The United States of America." If several months later each group were shown several similar lists of words and asked to select the correct list, which group do you think would be more likely to pick out THUNSTOFAM from the pack? It ought to be the group that had been informed of the acronym, because the information in that group would have been processed more deeply.

Consider why so many people have difficulty selecting the accurate drawing of the Lincoln penny. Is it perhaps because they have processed information about the appearance of a penny rather superficially? If they knew they that were going to be quizzed about the features of a penny, however, wouldn't they process information about its appearance more deeply? That is, wouldn't they study the features and purposefully note whether the profile is facing left or right, what the lettering says, and where the date goes?

Consider a fascinating experiment with three groups of college students, all of whom were asked to study a picture of a living room for one minute (Bransford and others, 1977). The groups' examination of the picture entailed different approaches. Two groups were informed that small *x*'s were imbedded in the picture. The first of these groups was asked to find the *x*'s by scanning the picture horizontally and vertically. The second group was informed that the *x*'s could be found in the edges of the objects in the room and was asked to look for them there. The third group was asked, instead, to think about how it would use the various objects pictured in the room. As a result of the divergent sets of instructions, the first two groups (the *x* hunters) processed information about the objects in the picture superficially. But the third group rehearsed the objects elaboratively—that is, members of this group thought about the objects in terms of their meanings and uses. It should not be surprising that the third group remembered many times more objects than the first two groups.

More recently researchers asked subjects to indicate whether they recognized photos of faces that they had been shown under one of three conditions: being asked to recall the (1) gender or the (2) width of the nose of the person in the photo, or being asked to judge (3) whether the person is honest (Sporer, 1991). It is likely that asking people to judge other people's honesty stimulates deeper processing of the features of the faces (Bloom & Mudd, 1991). That is, subjects look at more facial features, study each in more detail, and attempt to relate what they see to their ideas about human nature.

Note that the levels-of-processing model finds uses for most of the concepts employed by those who think of memory in terms of stages. For example, adherents to this model also speak of the basic memory processes (encoding, storage, and retrieval) and of different kinds of rehearsal. The essential difference is that they view memory as consisting of a single dimension that varies according to depth.

REFLECTIONS

- You can remember the list of letters THUNSTOFAM by repeating it several times or by thinking of the phrase "The United States of America." Would the stage model of memory and the levels-of-processing model of memory agree or disagree on which method would lead to a longer lasting memory? Why?

■ FORGETTING

What do DAL, RIK, BOF, and ZEX have in common? They are all **nonsense syllables**. Nonsense syllables are meaningless sets of two consonants with a vowel sandwiched in between. They were first used by Hermann Ebbinghaus to study memory and forgetting.

Because nonsense syllables are intended to be meaningless, remembering them should depend on simple acoustic coding and maintenance rehearsal rather than on elaborative rehearsal, semantic coding, or other ways of making learning meaningful. Nonsense syllables provide a means of measuring simple memorization ability in studies of the three basic memory tasks of recognition, recall, and relearning. Studying these memory tasks has led to several conclusions about the nature of forgetting.

NONSENSE SYLLABLES • Meaningless sets of two consonants, with a vowel sandwiched in between, that are used to study memory.

• *Memory Tasks Used in Measuring Forgetting*

RECOGNITION There are many ways of measuring **recognition**. In many studies, psychologists ask subjects to read a list of nonsense syllables. The subjects then read a second list of nonsense syllables and indicate whether they recognize any of the syllables as having appeared on the first list. Forgetting is defined as failure to recognize a syllable that has been read before.

In another kind of recognition study, Harry Bahrick and his colleagues (1975) studied high school graduates who had been out of school for various lengths of time. They interspersed photos of the graduates' classmates with four times as many photos of strangers. Recent graduates correctly recognized former classmates 90% of the time. Those who had been out of school for 40 years recognized former classmates 75% of the time. A chance level of recognition would have been only 20% (one photo in five was of an actual classmate). Thus, even older people showed rather solid long-term recognition ability.

Recognition is the easiest type of memory task. This is why multiple-choice tests are easier than fill-in-the-blank or essay tests. We can recognize or identify photos of former classmates more easily than we can recall their names.

RECALL In his own studies of **recall,** another kind of memory task, Ebbinghaus would read lists of nonsense syllables aloud to the beat of a metronome and then see how many he could produce from memory. After reading through a list once, he usually would be able to recall seven syllables—the typical limit for short-term memory.

Psychologists also often use lists of pairs of nonsense syllables, called **paired associates,** to measure recall. A list of paired associates is shown in Figure 8.7. Subjects read through the lists pair by pair. Later they are shown the first member of each pair and asked to recall the second. Recall is more difficult than recognition. In a recognition task, one simply indicates whether an item has been seen before or which of a number of items is paired with a stimulus (as in a multiple-choice test). In a recall task, the person must retrieve a syllable, with another syllable serving as a cue.

Retrieval is made easier if the two syllables can be meaningfully linked—that is, encoded semantically—even if the "meaning" is stretched a bit. Consider the first pair of nonsense syllables in Figure 8.7. The image of a WOMan smoking a CEG-arette may make CEG easier to retrieve when the person is presented with the cue WOM.

It is easier to recall vocabulary words from foreign languages if you can construct a meaningful link between the foreign and English words (Atkinson, 1975). The *peso,* pronounced *pay-so,* is a unit of Mexican money. A link can be

RECOGNITION • In information processing, the easiest memory task, involving identification of objects or events encountered before.
RECALL • Retrieval or reconstruction of learned material.
PAIRED ASSOCIATES • Nonsense syllables presented in pairs in experiments that measure recall.

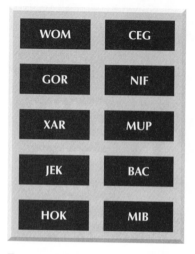

FIGURE 8.7
PAIRED ASSOCIATES

Psychologists often use paired associates to measure recall. Retrieving CEG in response to the cue WOM is made easier by an image of a WOMan smoking a "CEG-arette."

formed by finding a part of the foreign word, such as the *pe-* (pronounced *pay*) in *peso,* and constructing a phrase such as "You pay with money." When you read or hear the word *peso* in the future, you recognize the *pe-* and retrieve the link or phrase. From the phrase, you then reconstruct the translation, "a unit of money."

RELEARNING: IS LEARNING EASIER THE SECOND TIME AROUND? **Relearning** is a third method of measuring retention. Do you remember having to learn all of the state capitals in grade school? What were the capitals of Wyoming and Delaware? Even when we cannot recall or recognize material that had once been learned, such as Cheyenne for Wyoming and Dover for Delaware, we can relearn it more rapidly the second time. Similarly, as we go through our thirties and forties we may forget a good deal of our high school French or geometry. Yet the second time around we could learn what previously took months or years much more rapidly.

To study the efficiency of relearning, Ebbinghaus (1885) devised the **method of savings.** First he recorded the number of repetitions required to learn a list of nonsense syllables or words. Then he recorded the number of repetitions required to relearn the list after a certain amount of time had elapsed. Next he computed the difference between the number of repetitions required to arrive at the **savings.** If a list had to be repeated 20 times before it was learned, and 20 times again after a year had passed, there were no savings. Relearning, that is, was as tedious as the initial learning. However, if the list could be learned with only 10 repetitions after a year had elapsed, half the number of repetitions required for learning had been saved.

Figure 8.8 shows Ebbinghaus's classic curve of forgetting. As you can see, there was no loss of memory as measured by savings immediately after a list had been learned. However, recollection dropped precipitously during the first hour after learning a list. Losses of learning then became more gradual. Retention dropped by half within the first hour. However, it took a month (31 days)

FIGURE 8.8
EBBINGHAUS'S CLASSIC CURVE OF FORGETTING

Recollection of lists of words drops precipitously during the first hour after learning. Losses of learning then becomes more gradual. Retention drops by half within the first hour. However, it takes a month (31 days) for retention to be cut in half again.

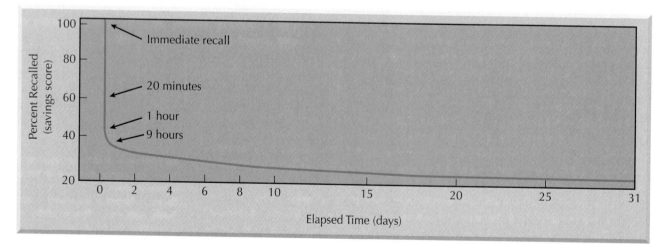

Interference. In retroactive interference, new learning interferes with the retrieval of old learning. In proactive interference, older learning interferes with the capacity to retrieve material learned more recently. For example, high school French vocabulary may "pop in" when you are trying to retrieve words you have learned for a Spanish test in college.

for retention to be cut in half again. In other words, forgetting occurred most rapidly right after material was learned. We continue to forget material as time elapses, but at a relatively slower rate.

Before leaving this section, I have one question for you: What are the capitals of Wyoming and Delaware?

• *Interference Theory*

When we do not attend to, encode, and rehearse sensory input, we may forget it through decay of the trace of the image. Material in short-term memory, like material in sensory memory, can be lost through decay. It can also be lost through displacement, as may happen when we try to remember several new names at a party.

According to **interference theory,** we also forget material in short-term and long-term memory because newly learned material interferes with it. The two basic types of interference are retroactive interference (also called *retroactive inhibition*) and proactive interference (also called *proactive inhibition*).

RETROACTIVE INTERFERENCE In **retroactive interference,** new learning interferes with the retrieval of old learning. For example, a medical student may memorize the names of the bones in the leg through rote repetition. Later he or she may find that learning the names of the bones in the arm makes it more difficult to retrieve the names of the leg bones, especially if the names are similar in sound or in relative location on each limb.

PROACTIVE INTERFERENCE In **proactive interference,** older learning interferes with the capacity to retrieve more recently learned material. High school Spanish may pop in when you are trying to retrieve college French or Italian words. All three are Romance languages, with similar roots and spellings. Previously learned Japanese words probably would not interfere with your ability to

RELEARNING • A measure of retention. Material is usually relearned more quickly than it is learned initially.
METHOD OF SAVINGS • A measure of retention in which the difference between the number of repetitions originally required to learn a list and the number of repetitions required to relearn the list after a certain amount of time has elapsed is calculated.
SAVINGS • The difference between the number of repetitions originally required to learn a list and the number of repetitions required to relearn the list after a certain amount of time has elapsed.
INTERFERENCE THEORY • The view that we may forget stored material because other learning interferes with it.
RETROACTIVE INTERFERENCE • The interference of new learning with the ability to retrieve material learned previously.
PROACTIVE INTERFERENCE • The interference by old learning with the ability to retrieve material learned recently.

retrieve more recently learned French or Italian, because the roots and sounds of Japanese differ considerably from those of the Romance languages.

Consider motor skills. You may learn to drive a standard shift on a car with three forward speeds and a clutch that must be let up slowly after shifting. Later you may learn to drive a car with five forward speeds and a clutch that must be released rapidly. For a while, you may make errors on the five-speed car because of proactive interference. (Old learning interferes with new learning.) If you return to the three-speed car after driving the five-speed car has become natural, you may stall it a few times. This is because of retroactive interference (new learning interfering with the old).

• *Repression*

According to Sigmund Freud, we are motivated to forget painful memories and unacceptable ideas because they produce anxiety, guilt, and shame. (In terms of operant conditioning, anxiety, guilt, and shame serve as negative reinforcers. We learn to behave in ways that lead to the removal of these reinforcers—in this case, we learn to avoid thinking about certain events and ideas.) In Chapter 15 we will see that psychoanalysts believe that repression is at the heart of disorders such as **dissociative amnesia.**

REPRESSION OF MEMORIES OF CHILDHOOD SEXUAL ABUSE? The popular media have recently been filled with stories of people in therapy who have recovered repressed memories of childhood sexual abuse (Pope, 1996). Symptoms such as the following have been presented as evidence of the presence of such memories: poor grades in school, difficulty concentrating, fear of new experiences, problems recollecting parts of childhood, low self-esteem, depression, sexual dysfunctions, and indecision (Hergenhahn, 1997; Loftus & Ketcham, 1994).

Loftus (1993a) does not deny that childhood sexual abuse is a serious problem, but she argues that most such recovered repressed memories are false. Consider that many people enter therapy without such memories but leave therapy with them. Because of the way in which these memories are "acquired," Loftus suspects that some therapists may suggest the presence of such memories to clients (Hergenhahn, 1997). Once more: Loftus is *not* arguing that memories of childhood sexual abuse are false or unimportant. She *is* suggesting that "repressed" memories of abuse that were "recovered" in therapy are suspect.

• *Infantile Amnesia*

When he interviewed people about their early experiences, Freud discovered that they could not recall episodes that had happened prior to the age of three and that their recall was cloudy through the age of five. This phenomenon is referred to as **infantile amnesia.**

Infantile amnesia has nothing to do with the fact that the episodes occurred in the distant past. Middle-aged and older people have vivid memories from the ages of six and 10, yet the events happened many decades ago. But 18-year-olds show steep declines in memory when they try to recall episodes that occurred earlier than the age of six, even though they happened less than 18 years earlier (Wetzler & Sweeney, 1986).

Freud believed that young children have aggressive impulses and perverse lusts toward their parents. He attributed infantile amnesia to repression of these

DISSOCIATIVE AMNESIA • Amnesia thought to stem from psychological conflict or trauma.
INFANTILE AMNESIA • Inability to recall events that occur prior to the age of 2 or 3. Also termed *childhood amnesia.*

impulses (Bauer, 1996). However, the episodes lost to infantile amnesia are not weighted in the direction of such "primitive" impulses.

Infantile amnesia probably reflects the interaction of physiological and cognitive factors. For example, a structure of the limbic system (the **hippocampus**) that is involved in the storage of memories does not become mature until we are about 2-years-old (Squire, 1993, 1996). Also, myelination of brain pathways is incomplete for the first few years, contributing to the inefficiency of information processing and memory formation. There are also cognitive reasons for infantile amnesia:

1. Infants are not particularly interested in remembering the past (Neisser, 1993).
2. Infants, in contrast to older children, tend not to weave episodes together into meaningful stories of their own lives. (Freud also recognized the second possibility [Bauer, 1996].) Information about specific episodes thus tends to be lost.
3. Infants do not make reliable use of language to symbolize or classify events. Their ability to *encode* sensory input—that is, to apply the auditory and semantic codes that facilitate memory formation—is therefore limited.

• *Anterograde and Retrograde Amnesia*

In **anterograde amnesia,** there are memory lapses for the period following a trauma such as a blow to the head, an electric shock, or an operation. In some cases the trauma seems to interfere with all the processes of memory. The ability to pay attention, the encoding of sensory input, and rehearsal are all impaired. A number of investigators have linked certain kinds of brain damage—such as damage to the hippocampus—to amnesia (Corkin and others, 1985; Squire, 1994, 1996).

Consider the classic case of a man with the initials H. M. Parts of the brain are sometimes lesioned to help people with epilepsy. In H. M.'s case, a section of the hippocampus was removed (Milner, 1966). Right after the operation, the man's mental functioning appeared to be normal. As time went on, however, it became quite clear that he had severe problems in processing information. For example, two years after the operation, H. M. believed that he was 27—his age at the time of the operation. When his family moved to a new address, H. M. could not find his new home or remember the new address. He responded with appropriate grief to the death of his uncle, yet he then began to ask about his uncle and why he did not visit. Each time he was informed of his uncle's passing, he grieved as he had when he first heard of it. All in all, it seems that H. M.'s operation prevented him from transferring information from short-term to long-term memory.

In **retrograde amnesia,** the source of trauma prevents people from remembering events that took place before the accident. A football player who is knocked unconscious or a person in an auto accident may be unable to recall events that occurred for several minutes prior to the trauma. The football player may not recall taking to the field. The person in the accident may not recall entering the car. It also sometimes happens that the individual cannot remember events that occurred for several years prior to the traumatic incident.

In one well-known case of retrograde amnesia, a man received a head injury in a motorcycle accident (Baddeley, 1982). When he regained consciousness, he had lost memory for all events that had occurred after the age of 11. In fact, he appeared to believe that he was still 11-years-old. During the next few months

Truth or Fiction Revisited

....

It is not true that we can remember important episodes that take place during the first two years of life. (Really, Allyn, believe me.) Early childhood memories that seem so clear today are probably reconstructed and mostly inaccurate. Or else they may be of events that occurred when we were older than we think we were.

HIPPOCAMPUS • A structure in the limbic system that plays an important role in the formation of new memories.
ANTEROGRADE AMNESIA • Failure to remember events that occur after physical trauma because of the effects of the trauma.
RETROGRADE AMNESIA • Failure to remember events that occur prior to physical trauma because of the effects of the trauma.

USING PSYCHOLOGY TO IMPROVE YOUR MEMORY

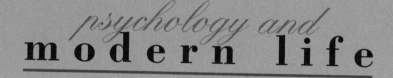

Humans have survived the Ice Age, the Stone Age, the Iron Age, and, a bit more recently, the Industrial Revolution. Now we are trying to cope with the so-called Age of Information, in which there has been an explosion of information. Computers have been developed to process it. Humans, too, process information, and there is more of it to process than ever before. Fortunately, psychologists have helped devise methods for improving your memory. Let us consider some of them.

DRILL AND PRACTICE Repetition (rote maintenance rehearsal) helps transfer information from short-term to long-term memory. Does maintenance rehearsal seem too mechanical for you as a college student? If so, don't forget that this is how you learned the alphabet and how to count! Schoolchildren write spelling words over and over to remember them. Athletes repeat motions so that they will become part of their procedural memory. When you have memorized formulas, during a test you can use your time to think about when to apply them, rather than using up valuable time trying to recall them.

Some students use flash cards to help them remember facts. For example, they might write "The originator of modern behaviorism is _____" on one side of the card and "John Broadus Watson" on the flip side.

In his book *Super Memory*, Douglas Herrmann (1991) recommends the following methods for remembering a person's name:

1. Say the name out loud.
2. Ask the person a question, using her or his name.
3. Use the person's name as many times as you can during your conversation.
4. Write down the name when the conversation has ended.

RELATE NEW INFORMATION TO WHAT IS ALREADY KNOWN Relating new information to what is already known is a form of elaborative rehearsal that helps us to remember it (Willoughby and others, 1994). Herrmann (1991) also suggests that you can better remember the name of a new acquaintance by thinking of a rhyme for it. Now you have done some active thinking about the name, and you also have two tags for the person, not one. If you are trying to retrieve the spelling of the word *retrieve,* do so by retrieving the rule "*i* before *e* except after *c.*" There are exceptions, of course: Remember that "weird" doesn't follow the rule because it's a "weird" word.

We normally expand our knowledge base by relating new items to things already known. Children learn that a cello is like a violin, only bigger. A bass fiddle is also like a violin, but bigger yet. We remember information about whales by relating whales to other mammals. Similarly, we are better able to recall information about porpoises and dolphins if we think of them as small whales (not as bright fish).

The media are filled with stories about people who exhibit psychological disorders of one kind or another. To help remember the disorders discussed in Chapter 15, think of film or TV characters with those disorders. How were the characters' behaviors consistent (or inconsistent) with the descriptions in the text (and those offered by your professor)? You will remember the subject matter better *and* become a good critic of media portrayals of psychological problems if you use this technique.

FORM UNUSUAL, EXAGGERATED ASSOCIATIONS Psychologist Charles L. Brewer uses an interesting method to teach psychology students the fundamentals of shaping:

> In a recent class, Dr. Brewer first danced on his desk, then bleated like a sheep and finally got down on "all fours and oinked like a pig," he said. His antics were in response to a session he teaches on "successive approximation"—shaping behavior into a desired response.
>
> To get students to "shape" him, he told them he would try to figure out what they wanted him to do. If he guessed wrong, they'd "boo and hiss," while if he did what they wanted, they'd applaud him—which is why he eventually acted like a pig. "I'll do anything to get them to learn," he said. (DeAngelis, 1994, p. 40)

It is easier to recall stimuli that stand out from the crowd. We pay more attention to them. Sometimes, therefore,

we are better able to remember information when we create unusual, exaggerated associations.

Assume that you are trying to remember the geography of the cerebral cortex, as shown in Figure 3.9 on page 84. Why not think of what you look like in right profile? (Use your left profile if it is better.) Then imagine a new imaging technique in which we can see through your skull and find four brightly colored lobes in the right hemisphere of your cerebral cortex. Not only that, but there are little people (homunculi) flapping about in the sensory and motor areas (see Figure 3.9 again). In fact, imagine that you're in a crowded line and someone steps on your toe. As a result, the homunculus in the sensory cortex has a throbbing toe. This is communicated to the association areas of the cortex, where you decide that you are annoyed. The language areas of the cortex think up some choice words that are relayed to the throat and mouth of the homunculus in the motor cortex. Then they are sent into your throat and mouth. You also send some messages through the motor cortex that ready your muscles to attack.

Then you see that the perpetrator of the crime is a very attractive and apologetic stranger! What part of the occipital lobe is flashing the wonderful images?

THE METHOD OF LOCI Another way to form unusual associations is the *method of loci* (pronounced LOW-sigh). Select a series of related images such as the parts of your body or the furniture in your home. Then imagine an item from your shopping list, or another list you want to remember, as being attached to each image. Consider this meaty application: Remember your shopping list by imagining meatloaf in your navel and a strip of bacon draped over your nose.

By placing meatloaf or a favorite complete dinner in your navel, rather than a single item such as ground beef, you can combine several items into one chunk of information. At the supermarket, you recall the ingredients for meatloaf and consider whether or not you need each one.

USE MEDIATION The method of mediation also relies on forming associations: You link two items with a third one that ties them together.

What if you are having difficulty remembering that John's wife's name is Tillie? You can mediate between John and Tillie as follows. Reflect that the *john* is a slang term for bathroom. Bathrooms often have ceramic *tiles*. *Tiles*, of course, sounds like *Tillie*. So it goes: John → bathroom tiles → Tillie.

I used a combination of mediation and formation of unusual associations to help me remember foreign vocabulary words in high school. For example, the Spanish word *mujer* (pronounced moo-hair [almost]), means "woman" in English. Women have mo' hair than I do. Woman → mo' hair → mujer. This particular example would no longer work for me because now most men also have more hair than I, but the association was so outlandish that it has stuck with me all this time.

USE MNEMONIC DEVICES Broadly speaking, methods for jogging memory can all be termed *mnemonics*, or systems for remembering information. But so-called "mnemonic devices" usually combine chunks of information into a format such as an acronym, jingle, or phrase. For example, recalling the phrase "Every Good Boy Does Fine" has helped many people remember the musical keys E, G, B, D, F. In Chapter 5, we saw that the acronym *SAME* serves as a mnemonic device for distinguishing between afferent and efferent neurons. In Chapter 6, we noted that most psychology students use the acronym *Roy G. Biv* to remember the colors of the rainbow, even though your "backward" author chose to use the "word" *vibgyor*.

Acronyms have found applications in many disciplines. Consider geography. The acronym *HOMES* stands for the Great Lakes: *H*uron, *O*ntario, *M*ichigan, *E*rie, and *S*uperior. In astronomy, the phrase "Mercury's *v*ery *e*ager *m*other *j*ust *s*erved *u*s *n*ine *p*otatoes" helps students recall the order of the planets Mercury, Venus, Earth, Mars, Jupiter, Saturn, Uranus, Neptune, and Pluto.

What about biology? You can remember that Dromedary camels have one hump while Bactrian camels have two by turning the letters *D* and *B* on their sides.

And how can you math students ever be expected to remember the reciprocal of pi (that is, 1 divided by 3.14)? Simple: Just remember the question "Can I remember the reciprocal?" and count the number of letters in each word. The reciprocal of pi, it turns out, is 0.318310. (Remember the last two digits as 10, not as 1 and 0.)

Finally, how can you remember how to spell *mnemonics*? Easy—be willing to grant "a*MN*esty" to those who cannot. ■

Truth or Fiction Revisited

It is true that you can use tricks to improve your memory. The "tricks" all involve ways of forming associations.

he gradually recovered more knowledge of his past. He moved toward the present year by year, up until the critical motorcycle ride. But he never did recover the events just prior to the accident. The accident had apparently prevented the information that was rapidly unfolding before him from being transferred to long-term memory. In terms of stages of memory, it may be that our perceptions and ideas need to consolidate, or rest undisturbed for a while, if they are to be transferred to long-term memory.

REFLECTIONS

- Consider the memory tasks of recognition, recall, and relearning. What kinds of tasks do most of your tests rely on?
- Can you find an example of retroactive or proactive interference with memory in your own life?
- What are your earliest memories? Are you sure? Why could these memories be distorted?

■ THE BIOLOGY OF MEMORY: FROM ENGRAMS TO ADRENALINE

Psychologists assume that mental processes such as the encoding, storage, and retrieval of information—that is, memory—are accompanied by changes in the brain. Early in the century, many psychologists used the concept of the **engram** in their study of memory. Engrams were viewed as electrical circuits in the brain that corresponded to memory traces—neurological processes that paralleled experiences. Yet biological psychologists such as Karl Lashley (1950) spent many fruitless years searching for such circuits or for the structures of the brain in which they might be housed. Much contemporary research on the biology of memory focuses on the roles of neurons, neurotransmitters, and hormones.

• *Changes at the Neural Level*

Rats who are reared in richly stimulating environments develop more dendrites and synapses in the cerebral cortex than rats reared in relatively impoverished environments (Neisser, 1997). It also has been shown that the level of visual stimulation rats receive is associated with the number of synapses they develop in the visual cortex (Turner & Greenough, 1985). In sum, there is reason to believe that the storage of experience requires that the number of avenues of communication among brain cells be increased.

Thus, changes occur in the visual cortex as a result of visual experience. Changes are also likely to occur in the auditory cortex as a result of heard experiences. Information received through the other senses is just as likely to lead to corresponding changes in the cortical regions that represent them. Experiences that are perceived by several senses are also stored in numerous areas of the brain (Hilts, 1995). The recollection of experiences, as in the production of visual images, apparently involves neural activity in the appropriate regions of the brain (Kosslyn, 1994).

Research with sea snails such as *Aplysia* and *Hermissenda* has offered insight into the events that take place at existing synapses when learning occurs. *Aplysia,* for example, has only about 20,000 neurons compared with humans'

ENGRAM • (1) An assumed electrical circuit in the brain that corresponds to a memory trace. (2) An assumed chemical change in the brain that accompanies learning. (From the Greek *en-*, meaning "in," and *gramma,* meaning "something that is written or recorded.")

billions. As a result, researchers have actually been able to study how experience is reflected at the synapses of specific neurons. When sea snails are conditioned, more of the neurotransmitter serotonin is released at certain synapses. As a consequence, transmission at these synapses becomes more efficient as trials (learning) progress (Kandel & Hawkins, 1992). Many other naturally occurring chemical substances, including adrenaline, acetylcholine, antidiuretic hormone, and even estrogen have also been shown to play roles in memory.

• *Changes at the Structural Level*

Consider the problems that beset H. M. after his operation. Certain parts of the brain such as the hippocampus also appear to be involved in the formation of new memories—or the transfer of information from short-term to long-term memory. The hippocampus does not comprise the "storage bins" for memories themselves, because H. M.'s memories prior to the operation were not destroyed. Rather, it is involved in relaying incoming sensory information to parts of the cortex. Therefore, it appears to be vital to the storage of new information even if old information can be retrieved without it (Squire, 1994, 1996).

Where are the storage bins? Figure 8.9 shows that the brain stores parts of memories in the appropriate areas of the sensory cortex (Moscovitch, 1994). Sights are stored in the visual cortex, sounds in the auditory cortex, and so on (Hilts, 1995). The limbic system is largely responsible for integrating these

---

FIGURE 8.9
WHERE MEMORIES ARE STORED

The brain apparently stores parts of memories in the appropriate areas of the sensory cortex. Memories of sights and sounds are kept in separate bins and pieced back together when we recall an event. An area in the frontal lobe (labeled "Place and Time") apparently stores much information as to the sources of memories.

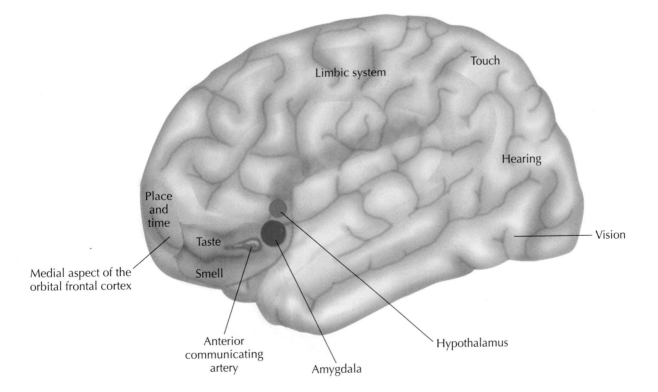

What Does Research on the Biology of Memory Hold in Storage?

As we stand at the edge of the new millennium, research on the biology of memory is in its infancy. But what an exciting area of research it is. What would it mean to you if you could read for an hour, take a pill, and thereby consolidate your learning in long-term memory? You would never have to reread the material; it would be at your fingertips for a lifetime. It would save a bit of study time, would it not?

During the 1950s and 1960s, research groups headed by James McConnell at the University of Michigan believed that they had found the key to the biology of learning in ribonucleic acid (RNA). DNA "remembers" the genetic code from generation to generation. However, it was thought that the related organic compound, RNA, changes with experience as a way of storing personal experiences and knowledge. RNA came to be dubbed "memory molecules." The McConnell group managed to condition flatworms to scrunch up when a light was shone by pairing the light with an electric shock. Then they "taught" this response to other flatworms by feeding them RNA from worms that had been conditioned and then chopped up (Rilling, 1996). At the time, many students joked that the fastest route to knowledge might lie in inviting their professors to dinner—that is, in doing to their professors what the worm researchers had done to their subjects. Unfortunately for this approach—but fortunately for professors—the RNA research could not be replicated by other investigators.

CONTEMPORARY RESEARCH Much contemporary research on the biology of memory focuses on the roles of neurotransmitters and hormones. Consider the following examples:

- Serotonin. This neurotransmitter increases the efficiency of conditioning in sea snails (Kandel & Hawkins, 1992).
- Acetylcholine (ACh). This neurotransmitter is vital in memory formation; low levels of ACh are connected with Alzheimer's disease.
- Adrenaline. This hormone strengthens memory when it is released into the bloodstream following learning (LeDoux, 1994).
- Vasopressin. When people sniff synthetic vasopressin (antidiuretic hormone) in the form of a nasal spray, they show significant improvement in memory (Angier, 1993). Today, excess vasopressin can have serious side effects, but future versions may target specific receptors without causing these effects.

Other research has focused on the potential of substances as diverse as estrogen and nicotine to aid in the formation of memories and to delay the progression of Alzheimer's disease. As with vasopressin, future versions may target specific receptors without causing side effects.

WHY WAIT FOR THE NEW MILLENNIUM? In the new millennium, memory pills may include a combination of these substances. However, you need not wait for the new millennium to commit your coursework to memory. You can rely on methods such as PQ4R:

- *Preview* the material you intend to learn.
- *Question* the material.
- *Read* the material in order to answer your questions. (Make your reading active rather than passive.)
- *Reflect* on the material (using, for example, the Reflections in this text).
- *Recite* answers to your questions.
- *Review* the material on a regular basis.

You can use psychology today to expand your knowledge base and increase your chances of success in the new millennium. ∎

pieces of information when we recall an event. Research with animals and people with brain injuries suggests that an area in the frontal lobe (labeled "Place and Time") stores information about where and when an event occurred (Wheeler and others, 1997). People in whom this part of the frontal lobe is damaged frequently try to fill in the memory gaps by making up stories about when and where certain events took place.

A specific part of the limbic system, the hippocampus, is much involved in the where and when of things. The hippocampus does not become mature until we are about 2-years-old. Immaturity may be connected with infantile amnesia. Adults with hippocampal damage may be able to form new procedural memories, even though they cannot form new episodic ("where and when") memories. For example, they can acquire the skill of reading words backwards even though they cannot recall individual practice sessions (Squire, 1994, 1996).

The thalamus is involved in verbal memories. Part of the thalamus of an Air Force cadet known as N. A. was damaged in a freak fencing accident. After the episode, N. A. could no longer form verbal memories. However, his ability to form visual memories was not impaired (Squire, 1994, 1996).

The encoding, storage, and retrieval of information thus involve biological activity on several levels. As we learn, new synapses are developed, and changes occur at existing synapses. Various parts and structures of the brain are also involved in the formation of different kinds of memories.

REFLECTIONS

- Before reading this section, did you have any thoughts on what happens in the brain when learning occurs and memories are formed? How do they compare to what is shown by the research evidence?
- How do you think substances such as adrenaline and nicotine can affect the functioning of memory?

SUMMARY

1. **What are the three kinds of memory suggested by Tulving?** These are episodic memory (memory for specific events that one has experienced), semantic memory (general knowledge), and procedural memory (skills).

2. **What are the three memory processes?** These are encoding, storage, and retrieval. We commonly use visual, auditory, and semantic codes in the process of encoding.

3. **What are the three stages of memory proposed by the Atkinson-Shiffrin model?** These are sensory, short-term, and long-term memory.

4. **What are sensory registers?** These hold stimuli in sensory memory. Psychologists believe that information perceived through each sense has its own register.

5. **What is the importance of Sperling's research?** Sperling demonstrated that visual stimuli are maintained in sensory memory for only a fraction of a second and that we can see more objects than we can report afterward.

6. **What are icons and echoes?** Icons are mental representations of visual stimuli; echoes are representations of auditory stimuli (sounds).

7. **What is the capacity of short-term memory?** We can hold seven chunks of information (plus or minus two) in short-term, or working, memory.

8. **How do psychologists explain the serial-position effect?** We tend to remember the initial items in a list because they are rehearsed most often (the primacy effect). We tend to remember the final items in a list because they are least likely to have been displaced by new information (the recency effect).

9. **How accurate are long-term memories?** Long-term memories are frequently biased because they are reconstructed according to our schemas—that is, our ways of mentally organizing our experiences.

10. **How is information transferred from short-term to long-term memory?** There are two paths: maintenance rehearsal (rote repetition) and elaborative rehearsal (relating information to things that are already known).

11. **How is knowledge organized in long-term memory?** Knowledge tends to be organized according to a hierarchical structure with superordinate and subordinate concepts. We know things about members of a class when we have information about the class itself.

12. **What are context- and state-dependent memories?** Context dependence refers to the finding that we often retrieve information more efficiently when we are in the same context we were in when we acquired it. State dependence refers to the finding that we often retrieve information better when we are in the same state of consciousness or mood we were in when we first learned it.

13. **What is the levels-of-processing model?** This model views memory in terms of a single dimension—not three stages. It is hypothesized that we encode, store, and retrieve information more efficiently when we have processed it more deeply.

14. **What are nonsense syllables?** These are meaningless syllables that were first used by Ebbinghaus as a way of measuring the functions of memory.

15. **How do psychologists measure retention?** Retention is often tested through three types of memory tasks: recognition, recall, and relearning.

16. **What is interference theory?** According to interference theory, people forget because learning can interfere with retrieval of previously learned material. In retroactive interference, new learning interferes with old learning. In proactive interference, old learning interferes with new learning.

17. **What is repression?** This term refers to Freud's concept of motivated forgetting. Freud suggested that we are motivated to forget threatening or unacceptable material.

18. **What is infantile amnesia?** This term refers to the inability to remember events from the first couple of years of life.

19. **What are anterograde and retrograde amnesia?** In anterograde amnesia, a traumatic event such as damage to the hippocampus prevents the formation of new memories. In retrograde amnesia, shock or other trauma prevents previously known information from being retrieved.

20. **What biological processes are associated with the processes of memory?** These processes include the development of synapses, changes at existing synapses, and changes in various sections of the brain—depending on the type of information that is being processed.

To enhance your understanding of the psychological concepts found in this chapter, please consult the following aids:

Learning Objectives, p. 159
Exercise, p. 160
Lecture and Textbook Outline,
   p. 161
Effective Studying Ideas, p. 163

Chapter Review, p. 164
Chapter Exercises, p. 171
Knowing the Language, p. 172
Do You Know the Material?, p. 175

The Sensory Store
The Short-Term Store
Mental Imagery
Eye-Witness Testimony
Memory Stores or Levels of
   Processing

Tasks Used for Measuring Memory
Mnemonic Devices
Neuropsychology of Memory

For more information concerning the topics found in this chapter, access psychology links on the World Wide Web through the Harcourt Brace webpage at

www.hbcollege.com

Share your comments and questions with your author at

PsychLinks@aol.com

The abilities to think and use language set humans apart from other animals. Jaune Quick-to-See Smith's *Indian Head* (1993) is like the Indian heads that were formerly stamped on U.S. coins. What is it like to be a Native American growing up in a culture that has historically viewed your people as savages? Smith's profile suggests the dignity of the individual human being. And the head, of course, is the seat of thinking and language.

JAUNE QUICK-TO-SEE-SMITH

Chapter 9
Thinking and Language

TRUTH OR FICTION?

✔ **T F**

☐ ☐ Using a "tried and true" formula is the most efficient way to solve a problem.

☐ ☐ Only humans can solve problems by means of insight.

☐ ☐ The best way to solve a frustrating problem is to keep plugging away at it.

☐ ☐ People with great academic ability are also creative.

☐ ☐ If a couple has five sons, the sixth child is likely to be a daughter.

☐ ☐ People change their opinions when they are shown to be wrong.

☐ ☐ The majority of people around the world speak at least two languages.

What Did They
Know—And When?

OUTLINE

CONCEPTS AND PROTOTYPES: BUILDING BLOCKS OF THOUGHT

PROBLEM SOLVING
Approaches to Problem Solving: Getting From Here to There
Factors That Affect Problem Solving

CREATIVITY
Creativity and Academic Ability
Factors That Affect Creativity
Questionnaire:
The Remote Associates Test

REASONING
Types of Reasoning

JUDGMENT AND DECISION MAKING
Heuristics in Decision Making: If It Works, Must It Be Logical?
The Framing Effect: Say That Again?
Psychology in a World of Diversity: Across the Great Divide? Diverse Perspectives on the O.J. Simpson Verdicts
Overconfidence: Is Your Hindsight 20–20?

LANGUAGE
Basic Concepts of Language

LANGUAGE DEVELOPMENT
Development of Vocabulary
Development of Syntax
Development of More Complex Language
Theories of Language Development
Bilingualism
Psychology in a World of Diversity: Ebonics
Psychology and Modern Life: Bilingual Education

LANGUAGE AND THOUGHT
The Linguistic-Relativity Hypothesis

THINKING • Mental activity that is involved in understanding, manipulating, and communicating about information. Thinking entails paying attention to information, mentally representing it, reasoning about it, and making decisions about it.

*A*T THE AGE OF 9, MY DAUGHTER Jordan stumped me with a problem about a bus driver that she had heard in school. Since I firmly believe in exposing students to the kinds of torture I have undergone, see what you can do with her problem:

You're driving a bus that's leaving from Pennsylvania. To start off with, there were 32 people on the bus. At the next bus stop, 11 people got off and 9 people got on. At the next bus stop, 2 people got off and 2 people got on. At the next bus stop, 12 people got on and 16 people got off. At the next bus stop, 5 people got on and 3 people got off. What color are the bus driver's eyes?

Now, I was not about to be fooled when I was listening to this problem. Although it seemed clear that I should be keeping track of how many people were on the bus, I had an inkling that a trick was involved. Therefore, I first instructed myself to remember that the bus was leaving from Pennsylvania. Being clever, I also kept track of the number of stops rather than the number of people getting on and off the bus. When I was finally hit with the question about the bus driver's eyes, I was at a loss. I protested that Jordan had said nothing about the bus driver's eyes, but she insisted that she had given me enough information to answer the question.

One of the requirements of problem solving is paying attention to relevant information (de Jong & Das-Smaal, 1995). To do that, you need some familiarity with the type of problem you are dealing with. I immediately classified the bus driver problem as a trick question and paid attention to information that apparently was superfluous. But I wasn't good enough.

The human ability to solve problems enables us to build skyscrapers, create computers, and scan the interior of the body without surgery. Some people even manage to keep track of their children and balance their checkbooks. Problem solving is one aspect of **thinking**, the mental activity involved in understanding, processing, and communicating information. Thinking entails attending to information, representing it mentally, reasoning about it, and making judgments and decisions about it. The term *thinking* generally refers to conscious, planned attempts to make sense of things. Cognitive psychologists usually do not characterize the less deliberate cognitive activities of daydreaming or the more automatic usages of language as thinking. Yet language is entwined with thought. The uniquely human ability to conceptualize mathematical theorems and philosophical treatises relies on language. Language also allows us to record our thoughts for posterity.

In this chapter we explore thinking and language. We begin with concepts, which provide the building blocks of thought. We then wend our way toward language, which gives human thought a unique richness and beauty.

But before we proceed, I have one question for you: What color were the bus driver's eyes?

■ CONCEPTS AND PROTOTYPES: BUILDING BLOCKS OF THOUGHT

I began the chapter with a problem posed by my daughter Jordan. Let me proceed with a riddle from my own childhood: "What's black and white and read all over?" Since this riddle was spoken, not written, and since it involved the colors black and white, you would probably assume that "read" was spelled "red." Thus, in seeking an answer you might scan your memory for an object that was red although it also somehow managed to be black and white. The answer to the riddle, "newspaper," was usually met with a groan.

The word *newspaper* is a **concept**. *Red, black,* and *white* are also concepts—color concepts. Concepts are mental categories used to class together objects, relations, events, abstractions, or qualities that have common properties. Concepts are crucial to thinking. Concepts can represent objects, events, and activities—and visions of things that never were. Much thinking has to do with categorizing new concepts and manipulating relationships among concepts.

We tend to organize concepts in *hierarchies.* The newspaper category includes objects such as your school paper and the *Los Angeles Times.* Newspapers, college textbooks, novels, and merchandise catalogs can be combined into higher order categories such as *printed matter* or *printed devices that store information.* If you add CD-ROMs and floppy disks, you can create a still higher category, *objects that store information.* Now consider a question that requires categorical thinking: How are a newspaper and a CD-ROM alike? Answers to such questions entail supplying the category that includes both objects. In this case, we can say that both objects store information. That is, their functions are similar, even if their technology is very different.

Here is another question: How are the brain and a CD-ROM alike? Yes, again both can be said to store information. How are the brain and a CD-ROM different? To answer this question, we find a category in which only one of them belongs. For example, only the brain is a living thing. Functionally, moreover, the brain does much more than store information. The CD-ROM is an electronic device. People are not electronic devices. But could we make the case that electricity is involved in human thinking? (Refer to the discussion of neural impulses in Chapter 3).

Prototypes are examples that best match the essential features of categories. In less technical terms, prototypes are good examples. When new stimuli closely match people's prototypes of concepts, they are readily recognized as examples (Sloman, 1996). Which animal seems more birdlike to you, a robin or an ostrich? Why? Which of the following better fits the prototype of a fish, a sea horse or a shark? Both self-love and maternal love may be forms of love, but more people readily agree that maternal love is a kind of love. Apparently maternal love better fits their prototype of love (Fehr & Russell, 1991).

Many lower animals can be said to possess instinctive or inborn prototypes of various concepts. Male robins attack round reddish objects that are similar in appearance to the breasts of other male robins—even when they have been reared in isolation and therefore have never seen another robin. Humans, however, generally acquire prototypes on the basis of experience. Many simple prototypes, such as *dog* and *red,* are taught by means of **exemplars**. We point to a

CONCEPT • A mental category that is used to class together objects, relations, events, abstractions, or qualities that have common properties.
PROTOTYPE • A concept of a category of objects or events that serves as a good example of the category.
EXEMPLAR • A specific example.

A Goat or a Dog? Yes, yes, you know the answer, but little children may at first include goats, horses, and other four-legged animals within the dog concept until they understand the differences among the animals.

dog and say "dog" or "This is a dog" to a child. Dogs represent **positive instances** of the dog concept. **Negative instances**—that is, things that are not dogs—are then shown to the child while we say, "This is *not* a dog." Negative instances of one concept may be positive instances of another. So in teaching a child we may be more likely to say, "This is not a dog—it's a cat" than simply, "This is not a dog."

Children may at first include horses and other four-legged animals within the dog schema or concept until the differences between dogs and horses are pointed out. (To them, the initial category could be more appropriately labeled "fuzzy-wuzzies.") In language development, such overinclusion of instances in a category (reference to horses as dogs) is labeled *overextension*. Children's prototypes become refined after children are shown positive and negative instances and given explanations.

Abstract concepts, such as *bachelor* or *square root,* are typically formed through verbal explanations that involve more basic concepts (Barsalou, 1992). If one points repeatedly to *bachelors* (positive instances) and *not bachelors* (negative instances), a child may eventually learn that bachelors are males or adult males. However, it is doubtful that this show-and-tell method would ever teach them that bachelors are adult human males who are unmarried. The concept *bachelor* is best taught by explanation after the child understands the concepts of maleness and marriage.

REFLECTIONS

- What strategy were you using to try to solve the bus driver problem? Were you misled or not? Why?
- When you were a child, some people were probably introduced to you as Aunt Bea or Uncle Harry. Do you remember when you first understood the concept of aunt or uncle? Can you think of ways of teaching these concepts to small children without using verbal explanations?
- Which concepts in this textbook have you found the easiest and most difficult to understand? Why?

■ PROBLEM SOLVING

Now I would like to share something personal with you. One of the pleasures I derived from my own introductory psychology course lay in showing friends the textbook and getting them involved in the problems in the section on problem solving. First, of course, I struggled with them myself. Now it's your turn. Get some scrap paper, take a breath, and have a go at them. The answers will be discussed in the following pages, but don't peek. *Try* the problems first.

1. Provide the next two letters in the series for each of the following:
   a. ABABABAB??
   b. ABDEBCEF??
   c. OTTFFSSE??

2. Draw straight lines through all the points in part A of Figure 9.1, using only *four* lines. Do not lift your pencil from the paper or retrace your steps. (Answer is given in Figure 9.5.)

3. Move three matches in part B of Figure 9.1 to make four squares of the

POSITIVE INSTANCE • An example of a concept.
NEGATIVE INSTANCE • An idea, event, or object that is *not* an example of a concept. Concept formation is aided by presentation of positive and negative instances.

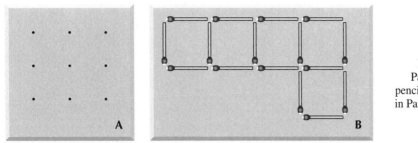

FIGURE 9.1
TWO PROBLEMS
Draw straight lines through all the points in Part A, using only four lines. Do not lift your pencil or retrace your steps. Move three matches in Part B to make four squares equal in size. Use all the matches.

same size. You must use *all* the matches. (The answer is shown in Figure 9.5.)

4. You have three jars—A, B, and C—which hold the amounts of water, in ounces, shown in Table 9.1. For each of the seven problems in Table 9.1, use the jars in any way you wish in order to arrive at the indicated amount of water. Fill or empty any jar as often as you wish. How do you obtain the desired amount of water in each problem? (The solutions are discussed on p. 329.)

• *Approaches to Problem Solving: Getting From Here to There*

What steps did you use to try to solve parts a and b of problem 1? Did you first make sure you understood the problem by rereading the instructions? Or did you dive right in as soon as you saw them on the page? Perhaps the solutions to 1a and 1b came easily, but I'm sure that you studied 1c very carefully.

After you believed that you understood what was required in each problem, you probably tried to discover the structure of the cycles in each series. Series 1a has repeated cycles of two letters: *AB, AB,* and so on. Series 1b may be seen as having four cycles of two consecutive letters: *AB, DE, BC,* and so on.

TABLE 9.1 WATER-JAR PROBLEMS				
	Three Jars Are Present with the Listed Capacity (in Ounces)			
Problem	Jar A	Jar B	Jar C	Goal
1	21	127	3	100
2	14	163	25	99
3	18	43	10	5
4	9	42	6	21
5	20	59	4	31
6	23	49	3	20
7	10	36	7	3

For each problem, how can you use some combination of the three jars given, and a tap, to obtain precisely the amount of water shown?
Source: Adapted from *Rigidity of Behavior* (p. 109), by Abraham S. Luchins and Edith H. Luchins, 1959, Eugene: University of Oregon Press.

Again, did you solve 1a and 1b in a flash of insight, or did you try to find rules that govern each series? In series 1a, the rule is simply to repeat the cycle. Series 1b is more complicated, and different sets of rules can be used to describe it. One correct set of rules is that odd-numbered cycles (*1* and *3*, or *AB* and *BC*) simply repeat the last letter of the previous cycle (in this case *B*) and then advance by one letter in the alphabet. The same rule also applies to even-numbered cycles (*2* and *4*, or *DE* and *EF*).

If you found rules for problems 1a and 1b, you used them to produce the next letters in the series: *AB* in series 1a and *CD* in series 1b. Perhaps you then evaluated the effectiveness of your rules by checking your answers against the solutions in the preceding paragraphs.

UNDERSTANDING THE PROBLEM   Let us begin our discussion of understanding problems by considering a bus driver problem that is very similar to the one Jordan gave me. This one, however, appeared in the psychological literature:

> Suppose you are a bus driver. On the first stop, you pick up 6 men and 2 women. At the second stop, 2 men leave and 1 woman boards the bus. At the third stop, 1 man leaves and 2 women enter the bus. At the fourth stop, 3 men get on and 3 women get off. At the fifth stop, 2 men get off, 3 men get on, 1 woman gets off and 2 women get on. What is the bus driver's name? (Halpern, 1989, p. 392)

Both versions of the bus driver problem demonstrate that a key to understanding a problem is focusing on the right information. If we assume that it is crucial to keep track of the numbers of people getting on and off the bus, we focus on information that turns out to be unessential. In fact, it distracts us from the important information.

When we are faced with a novel problem, how can we know which information is relevant and which is not? Background knowledge helps. If you are given a chemistry problem, it helps if you have taken courses in chemistry. If Jordan gives you a problem, it is helpful to expect the unexpected. (In case you still haven't "gotten it," the critical information you need to solve both bus driver problems is provided in the first sentence.)

Understanding a problem means constructing a logical mental representation of it. The mental representation of the problem can include symbols or concepts, such as algebraic symbols or words. It can include lists, graphs, and visual images (Adeyemo, 1990; Hegarty and others, 1995). Successful understanding of a problem generally requires three features:

1. *The parts or elements of our mental representation of the problem relate to one another in a meaningful way.* If we are trying to solve a problem in geometry, our mental triangles should have angles that total 180 degrees, not 360 degrees.

2. *The elements of our mental representation of the problem correspond to the elements of the problem in the outer world.* If we are neutralizing an acid in order to produce water and a salt, our mental representation of water should be H_2O, not OH. The elements of our mental representations must include the key elements for solving the problem, such as the information in the first sentence of the bus driver problem. We prepare ourselves to solve a problem by familiarizing ourselves with its elements and defining our goals as clearly as possible. Part of understanding algebra and geometry problems is outlining all of the givens.

3. *We have a storehouse of background knowledge that we can apply to the problem.* We have taken the necessary courses to solve problems in

UNDERSTANDING • Constructing a coherent mental representation of a problem.

algebra and chemistry. The architect knows about building materials and styles and applies this knowledge to the design of a particular structure for a particular site. A broad knowledge base may allow us to classify the problem or find analogies. When given a geometry problem involving a triangle, for example, we may think, "Is this problem similar to problems I've solved by using the quadratic equation?"

ALGORITHMS An **algorithm** is a specific procedure for solving a type of problem. An algorithm will invariably lead to the solution—if it is used properly, that is. Mathematical formulas like the Pythagorean theorem are examples of algorithms. They will yield correct answers to problems *as long as the right formula is used.* Finding the right formula to solve a problem may require scanning one's memory for all formulas that contain variables that represent one or more of the elements in the problem. The Pythagorean theorem, for example, concerns triangles with right angles. Therefore, it is appropriate to consider using this formula for problems concerning right angles, but not for others.

Consider anagram problems, in which we try to reorganize groups of letters into words. Some anagram problems require us to use every letter from the pool of letters; others allow us to use only some of the letters. How many words can you make from the pool of letters *DWARG?* If you were to use the **systematic random search** algorithm, you would list every possible letter combination, using from one to all five letters. You could use a dictionary or a spell-checking program to see whether each result is, in fact, a word. Such a method might be time-consuming, but it would work.

HEURISTICS **Heuristics** are rules of thumb that help us simplify and solve problems. In contrast to algorithms, heuristics do not guarantee a correct solution to a problem. They are shortcuts. When they work, they allow for more rapid solutions (Anderson, 1991). A heuristic device for solving the anagram problem would be to look for familiar letter combinations that are found in words and then check the remaining letters for words that include these combinations. In *DWARG,* for example, we can find the familiar combinations *dr* and *gr.* We may then quickly find *draw, drag,* and *grad.* The drawback to this method, however, is that we might miss some words.

One type of heuristic device is the **means-end analysis.** In using this heuristic device, we assess the difference between our current situation and our goals and then do what we can to reduce this discrepancy. Let's say that you are out in your car and have gotten lost. You know that your destination is west of your current location and on the other side of the railroad tracks. A heuristic device would be to drive toward the setting sun (west) and, at the same time, to watch for railroad tracks. If the road comes to an end and you must turn left or right, you can scan in both directions for tracks. If you don't see any, turn right or left, but at the next major intersection turn toward the setting sun. Eventually you may get there. If not, you could use the most boring of algorithms: ask people for directions until you find someone who knows the route.

One strategy for achieving a large goal is to break it up into manageable subgoals. Is your goal to write a term paper on psychological ways of managing stress? Break the goal into subgoals such as making a list of the topics to be included (relaxation, exercise, and so forth), taking notes on research on each topic, creating a first draft in each area, and so on. This approach does not mean that you will have less work to do. However, it provides direction and outlines more readily attainable goals. It makes it easier to get started.

Truth or Fiction Revisited

It is not true that using a "tried and true" formula is the most efficient way to solve a problem. Using a tried and true formula—that is, an algorithm—may be less efficient than using a heuristic device.

ALGORITHM • A systematic procedure for solving a problem that works invariably when it is correctly applied.

SYSTEMATIC RANDOM SEARCH • An algorithm for solving problems in which each possible solution is tested according to a particular set of rules.

HEURISTICS • Rules of thumb that help us simplify and solve problems.

MEANS-END ANALYSIS • A heuristic device in which we try to solve a problem by evaluating the difference between the current situation and the goal.

ANALOGIES An *analogy* is a partial similarity among things that are different in other ways. During the Cold War, some people in the United States believed in the so-called domino theory. Seeing the nations of Southeast Asia as analogous to dominoes, they argued that if one nation were allowed to fall to communism, its neighbor would be likely to follow. In the late 1980s, a sort of reverse domino effect actually occurred as communism collapsed in the nations of Eastern Europe. When communism collapsed in one nation, it became more likely to collapse in neighboring nations as well.

The analogy heuristic applies the solution of an earlier problem to the solution of a new one. We use the analogy heuristic whenever we try to solve a new problem by referring to a previous problem (Halpern and others, 1990). Consider the water jar problems in Table 9.1. Problem 2 is analogous to problem 1. Therefore, the approach to solving problem 1 works with problem 2. (Later we consider what happens when the analogy heuristic fails.)

Let us see whether you can use the analogy heuristic to your advantage in the following number series problem: To solve problems 1a, 1b, and 1c on page 322, you had to figure out the rules that govern the order of the letters. Scan the following series of numbers and find the rule that governs their order:

$$8, 5, 4, 9, 1, 7, 6, 3, 2, 0$$

Hint: The problem is somewhat analogous to problem 1c.[1]

• *Factors That Affect Problem Solving*

The way you approach a problem is central to how effective you are at solving it. Other factors also influence your effectiveness at problem solving. Three of them—your level of expertise, whether you fall prey to a mental set, and whether you develop insight into the problem—reside within you. A couple of characteristics of problems also affect your ability to solve them effectively: the extent to which the elements of the problem are fixed in function, and the way the problem is defined.

EXPERTISE To appreciate the role of expertise in problem solving, unscramble the following anagrams, taken from Novick and Coté (1992). In each case use all of the letters to form an actual English word:

DNSUO

RCWDO

IASYD

How long did it take you to unscramble each anagram? Would a person whose native language is English unscramble each anagram more efficiently than a bilingual person who spoke another language in the home? Why or why not?

Experts solve problems more efficiently and rapidly than novices do. (That is why they are called *experts*.) Although it may be considered "smart" to be able to solve a particular kind of problem, experts do not necessarily exceed novices in general intelligence. In fact, their areas of expertise may be quite limited. For example, the knowledge and skills required to determine whether a Northern

---

[1] The analogous element is that there is a correspondence between these numbers and the first letter in the English word that spells them out (Matlin, 1997).

Renaissance painting is a forgery are quite different from those that are used to find words that rhyme with *elephant* or to determine the area of a parallelogram. Generally speaking, people who are experts at solving a certain kind of problem:

- know the particular area well,
- have a good memory for the elements in the problems,
- form mental images or representations that facilitate problem solving (Clement, 1991),
- relate the problem to other problems that are similar in structure, and
- have efficient methods for problem solving (Hershey and others, 1990).

Jordan. The author's daughter, Jordan, posed the problem, "A farmer had 17 sheep. All but 9 died. How many sheep were left?" What is the answer?

These factors are interrelated. Art historians, for example, acquire a database that permits them to understand the intricacies of paintings. As a result, their memory for paintings—and who painted them—expands vastly.

Novick and Coté (1992) found that among "experts" the solutions to the three anagram problems seemed to "pop out" in under 2 seconds. The experts apparently used more efficient methods than the novices. Experts seemed to use parallel processing. That is, they dealt simultaneously with two or more elements of the problems. In the case of DNSUO, for example, they may have played with the order of the vowels (*UO* or *OU*) at the same time that they tested which consonant (D, N, or S) was likely to precede them, arriving quickly at *sou* and *sound*. Novices were more likely to engage in serial processing—that is, to handle one element of the problem at a time.

MENTAL SETS Jordan hit me with another question: "A farmer had 17 sheep. All but 9 died. How many sheep did he have left?" Being a victim of a mental set, I assumed that this was a subtraction problem and gave the answer 8. She gleefully informed me that she hadn't said "9 died." She had said "*all but 9* died." Therefore, the correct answer was 9. (Get it?) Put it another way: I had not *understood* the problem. My mental representation of the problem did not correspond to the actual elements of the problem.

Return to problem 1, part c, on page 322. To try to solve this problem, did you seek a pattern of letters that involved cycles and the alphabet? If so, it may be because this approach worked in solving parts a and b.

The tendency to respond to a new problem with the same approach that helped solve similar problems is termed a **mental set.** Mental sets usually make our work easier, but they can mislead us when the similarity between problems is illusory, as in part c of problem 1. Here is a clue: Part c is not an alphabet series. Each of the letters in the series *stands for* something. If you can discover what they stand for (that is, if you can discover the rule), you will be able to generate the 9th and 10th letters. (The answer is in Figure 9.5 on p. 332.)

INSIGHT: AHA! To gain insight into the role of insight in problem solving, consider the following problem, which was posed by Janet Metcalfe:

A stranger approached a museum curator and offered him an ancient bronze coin. The coin had an authentic appearance and was marked with the date 544 B.C. The curator had happily made acquisitions from suspicious sources before, but this time he promptly called the police and had the stranger arrested. Why? (1986, p. 624)

MENTAL SET • The tendency to respond to a new problem with an approach that was successfully used with similar problems.

FIGURE 9.2

A DEMONSTRATION OF INSIGHT OR JUST FIDDLING WITH STICKS?

Gestalt psychologist Wolfgang Köhler ran experiments with chimpanzees to highlight the nature of problem solving by insight. This chimp must retrieve a stick outside the cage and attach it to a stick he already has before he can retrieve the distant circular object. While fiddling with two such sticks, Sultan, another chimp, seemed to suddenly recognize that the sticks could be attached. This is an example of problem solving by insight.

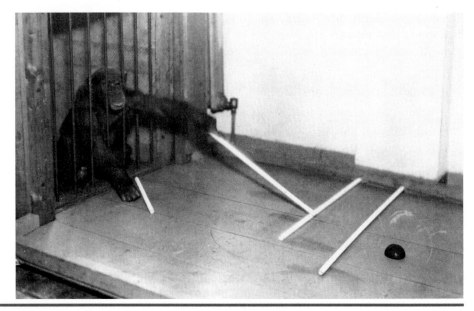

I'm not going to give you the answer to this problem. Instead, I'll give you a guarantee. When you arrive at the solution, it will hit you all at once. You'll think "Aha!" or "Of course!" (or something less polite). It will seem as though the pieces of information in the problem have suddenly been reorganized so that the solution leaps out at you—in a flash.

Problem solving by insight has an important place in the history of psychology (Sternberg & Davidson, 1994). Consider a classic piece of research by the German Gestalt psychologist Wolfgang Köhler, who was stranded in the Canary Islands with some laboratory animals during World War I. Köhler became convinced of the reality of insight when one of his chimpanzees, Sultan, "went bananas." Sultan had learned to use a stick to rake in bananas placed outside his cage. But now Köhler gave Sultan a new problem. He placed the banana beyond the reach of the stick. However, he gave the chimp two bamboo poles that could be fitted together to make a single pole long enough to retrieve the delectable reward. The setup was similar to that shown in Figure 9.2.

As if to make this historic occasion more dramatic, Sultan at first tried to reach the banana with one pole. When he could not do so, he returned to fiddling with the sticks. Köhler left the laboratory after an hour or so of frustration and an assistant was given the task of watching Sultan. But Sultan soon happened to align the two sticks. Then, in what seemed to be a flash of inspiration, he fitted them together and pulled in the elusive banana. Köhler was summoned to the laboratory, but when he arrived the sticks fell apart, as if on cue. Sultan gathered them again, however, fit them firmly together, and actually tested the strength of the fit before retrieving another banana.

Köhler was impressed by Sultan's rapid "perception of relationships" and used the term **insight** to describe it. He noted that such insights are not acquired gradually. Rather, they seem to occur "in a flash" when the elements of a problem are arranged appropriately. Sultan immediately showed that he could string several sticks together to retrieve various objects, not just bananas. It seemed that the chimp understood the principle of joining sticks to reach distant objects.

Bismarck, one of University of Michigan psychologist N. R. F. Maier's rats, provided evidence of insight in laboratory rats (Maier & Schneirla, 1935). Bis-

INSIGHT • In Gestalt psychology, a sudden perception of relationships among elements of the "perceptual field," permitting the solution of a problem.

marck had been trained to climb a ladder to a tabletop where food was placed. On one occasion Maier used a mesh barrier to prevent the rat from reaching his goal. But, as shown in Figure 9.3, a second ladder was provided and was clearly visible to the animal. At first Bismarck sniffed and scratched and made every effort to find a path through the mesh barrier. Then he spent some time washing his face, an activity that apparently signals frustration in rats. Suddenly he jumped into the air, turned, ran down the familiar ladder and around to the new ladder, ran up the new ladder, and claimed his just desserts. It seems that Bismarck suddenly perceived the relationships between the elements of his problem so that the solution occurred by insight. He seems to have had what Gestalt psychologists have termed an "Aha! experience."

INCUBATION Let us return to the problems at the beginning of the section. How did you do with problem 1, part c, and problems 2 and 3? Students tend to fiddle around with them for a while, the way Sultan fiddled with his sticks. The solutions, when they come, appear to arrive in a flash. Students set the stage for the flash of insight by studying the elements in the problems carefully, repeating the rules to themselves, and trying to imagine what a solution might look like. If you tried out solutions that did not meet the goals, you may have become frustrated and thought, "The heck with it! I'll come back to it later." Standing back from the problem may allow for the **incubation** of insight. An incubator warms chicken eggs for a while so that they will hatch. Incubation in problem solving refers to standing back from the problem for a while as some mysterious process within us continues to work on it. Later, the answer may occur to us in a flash of insight. When standing back from the problem is helpful, it may be because it distances us from unprofitable but persistent mental sets (Azar, 1995c).

Have another look at the possible role of incubation in helping us overcome mental sets. Consider the seventh water jar problem. What if we had tried all sorts of solutions involving the three water jars and none had worked? What if we distanced ourselves from this problem for a day or two? Is it not possible that with a little distance we might suddenly recall a 10, a 7, and a 3—three elements of the problem—and realize that we can arrive at the correct answer by using only two water jars? Our solution might seem too easy, and we might check Table 9.1 cautiously to make certain that the numbers are

Truth or Fiction Revisited

It is not true that only humans can solve problems by means of insight. Classic research evidence shows that lower animals, including apes and rats, are also capable of insight (a sudden reorganization of the perceptual field).

Truth or Fiction Revisited

It is not true that the best way to solve a frustrating problem is to keep plugging away at it. It may be better to distance oneself from the problem for a while and allow it to "incubate." Eventually you may solve the problem in what seems to be a flash of insight.

INCUBATION • In problem solving, a hypothetical process that sometimes occurs when we stand back from a frustrating problem for a while and the solution "suddenly" appears.

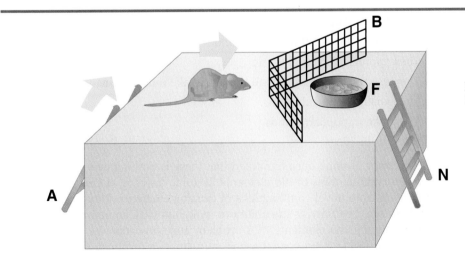

FIGURE 9.3

BISMARCK USES A COGNITIVE MAP TO CLAIM HIS JUST DESSERTS

Bismarck has learned to reach dinner by climbing ladder *A*. But now the food goal *(F)* is blocked by a wire mesh barrier *B*. Bismarck washes his face for a while, but then, in an apparent flash of insight, he runs back down ladder *A* and up new ladder *N* to reach the goal.

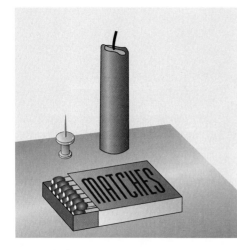

FIGURE 9.4
THE DUNCKER CANDLE PROBLEM
Can you use the objects shown on the table to attach the candle to the wall of the room so that it will burn properly?

there as remembered. Perhaps our incubation period would have done nothing more than release us from the mental set that problem 7 *ought* to be solved by the formula $B - A - 2C$.

FUNCTIONAL FIXEDNESS **Functional fixedness** may also hinder problem solving. For example, first ask yourself what a pair of pliers is. Is it a tool for grasping, a paperweight, or a weapon? A pair of pliers could function as any of these, but your tendency to think of it as a grasping tool is fostered by your experience with it. You have probably used pliers only for grasping things. Functional fixedness is the tendency to think of an object in terms of its name or its familiar function. It can be similar to a mental set in that it makes it difficult to use familiar objects to solve problems in novel ways.

Now that you know what functional fixedness is, let's see if you can overcome it by solving the Duncker candle problem. You enter a room that has the following objects on a table: a candle, a box of matches, and some thumbtacks (see Figure 9.4). Your task is to use the objects on the table to attach the candle to the wall of the room so that it will burn properly. (The answer is shown in Figure 9.5.)

> ### REFLECTIONS
> - How did you go about solving the problems presented at the beginning of the section? Which ones did you get right? Which ones did you get wrong? Why?
> - How can you use subgoals to develop a strategy for doing well in this course? For doing well in an athletic event?
> - Can you think of an example in which you suddenly developed insight into a problem or an academic subject?

■ CREATIVITY

Creativity is the ability to do things that are novel and useful (Sternberg & Lubart, 1996). Creative people can solve problems to which there are no preexisting solutions, no tried and tested formulas. Creative people share several characteristics (Sternberg & Lubart, 1995, 1996):

- They take chances.
- They refuse to accept limitations and try to do the impossible.
- They appreciate art and music.
- They use the materials around them to make unique things.
- They challenge social norms.
- They take unpopular stands.
- They probe ideas.

A professor of mine once remarked that there is nothing new under the sun, only novel combinations of old elements. To him, the core of creativity was the ability to generate novel combinations of existing elements. Many psychologists agree. They see creativity as the ability to make unusual, sometimes remote, associations among the elements of a problem and thus generate new combinations (Boden, 1994). An essential aspect of a creative response is the leap from

FUNCTIONAL FIXEDNESS • The tendency to view an object in terms of its name or familiar usage.
CREATIVITY • The ability to generate novel and useful solutions to problems.

Pablo Picasso at Work. We know that the great artist was creative, but what about his academic ability? Academic ability and creativity often go hand in hand, but academic ability is no guarantee of imagination or of specific talents.

the elements of the problem to the novel solution (Amabile, 1990). A predictable solution is not creative, even if it is difficult to reach.

Creativity demands divergent rather than convergent thinking. In **convergent thinking,** thought is limited to present facts as the problem solver tries to narrow his or her thinking to find the best solution. (You use convergent thinking in trying to arrive at the right answer to a multiple-choice question.) In **divergent thinking,** the problem solver associates more fluently and freely to the various elements of the problem. The problem solver allows "leads" to run a nearly limitless course to determine whether they will eventually combine as needed. (You may use divergent thinking when you are trying to generate ideas to answer an essay question on a test.)

Successful problem solving may require both divergent and convergent thinking. At first divergent thinking generates many possible solutions. Convergent thinking is then used to select the most probable solutions and reject the others.

• *Creativity and Academic Ability*

It might seem that a creative person would also have high academic ability of the sort measured on intelligence tests. However, the relationship between intelligence test scores and creativity is moderate at best (Sternberg & Williams, 1997). Standard intelligence tests and Graduate Record Exams, are not useful in measuring creativity. Intelligence test questions usually require convergent thinking to focus in on the answer. On an intelligence test, an ingenious answer that differs from the designated answer is wrong. Tests of creativity are oriented

CONVERGENT THINKING • A thought process that attempts to narrow in on the single best solution to a problem.
DIVERGENT THINKING • A thought process that attempts to generate multiple solutions to problems.

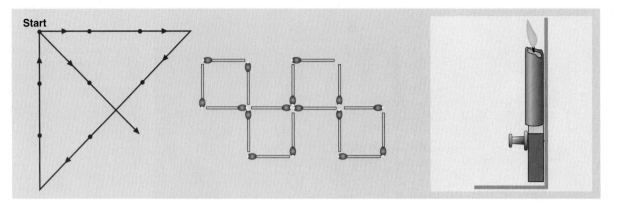

FIGURE 9.5

ANSWERS TO PROBLEMS ON PAGES 322–323 AND 330

For problem 1C, note that each of the letters is the first letter of the numbers one through eight. Therefore, the two missing letters are *NT*, for *n*ine and *t*en. The solutions to problems 2 and 3 are shown in this illustration. To solve the Duncker candle problem, use the thumbtack to pin the match box to the wall. Then set the candle on top of the box. Functional fixedness prevents many people from conceptualizing the match box as anything more than a device to hold matches. Commonly given *wrong* answers include trying to affix the bottom of the candle to the wall with melted wax or trying to tack the candle to the wall.

toward determining how flexible a person's thinking can be. Here, for example, is an item from a test used by Getzels and Jackson (1962) to measure associative ability, a factor in creativity: "Write as many meanings as you can for each of the following words: (a) duck; (b) sack; (c) pitch; (d) fair." Those who write several meanings for each word, rather than only one, are rated as being potentially more creative.

Another measure of creativity might ask people to produce as many words as possible that begin with T and end with N within a minute. Still another item might give people a minute to classify a list of names in as many ways as possible. How many ways can you classify the following group of names?

MARTHA   PAUL   JEFFRY   SALLY   PABLO   JOAN

Truth or Fiction Revisited

It is not necessarily true that people with academic ability are creative. The statement is an overgeneralization. People with high academic ability are more likely to be creative than people with low academic ability, but many bright people are unimaginative.

• *Factors That Affect Creativity*

If there is only a modest connection between creativity and other aspects of intelligence, what other factors contribute to creativity? Some factors reside within the person and some involve the social setting.

PERSONAL FACTORS   Creative people show flexibility, fluency (in generating words and ideas), and originality (Azar, 1995c). They spend time alone, thinking about who they are and exploring new ideas (McIntosh, 1996). Getzels and Jackson (1962) found that creative schoolchildren tend to express, rather than inhibit, their feelings and to be playful and independent. Creative people tend to be independent and nonconformist, but independence and nonconformity by themselves do not make a person creative.

Creative children are often at odds with their teachers because of their independence. Faced with the chore of managing 30 or more pupils, teachers too often label quiet and submissive children as "good" and less inhibited children as "bad."

THE REMOTE ASSOCIATES TEST

One aspect of creativity is the ability to associate freely to all aspects of a problem. Creative people take far-flung ideas and piece them together in novel combinations. Following are items from the Remote Associates Test, which measures the ability to find words that are distantly related to stimulus words. For each set of three words, try to think of a fourth word that is related to all three words. For example, the words *rough, resistance,* and *beer* suggest the word *draft*, as in the phrases *rough draft, draft resistance,* and *draft beer*. The answers are given in Appendix B. ■

1. charming	student	valiant	_____
2. food	catcher	hot	_____
3. hearted	feet	bitter	_____
4. dark	shot	sun	_____
5. Canadian	golf	sandwich	_____
6. tug	gravy	show	_____
7. attorney	self	spending	_____
8. magic	pitch	power	_____
9. arm	coal	peach	_____
10. type	ghost	story	_____

SOCIAL EVALUATION Research evidence shows that concern about evaluation by other people reduces creativity. In one experiment college students were asked to write poems under two very different sets of expectations (Amabile, 1990). Half the students were informed that the experimenter only intended to examine their handwriting—not the aesthetic value of the poetry. The remaining students were informed that judges, who were poets, would supply them with written evaluations of their poetry's content and form. The students who expected to be evaluated according to the form and content of their work turned in significantly less creative poems.

The literature is mixed as to whether people are more creative when they are rewarded for being creative. It has been argued that rewards reduce inner interest in problem solving and thereby undermine creativity. Yet the research shows that rewarding people for being creative on one task can actually enhance creativity on other tasks (Eisenberger & Cameron, 1996).

BRAINSTORMING **Brainstorming** is a group process that is intended to encourage creativity. The group leader stimulates group members to generate a great number of ideas—even wild ideas. In order to avoid inhibiting group members, judgment is suspended until a great many ideas are on the table.

Psychologists have become somewhat skeptical of the brainstorming concept, however (Matlin, 1997). For one thing, research evidence suggests that people working alone are often more creative than people working in groups. (Consider the cliché, "A camel is a horse made by a committee.") Moreover, the ideas produced by brainstorming are often lower in quality than those produced by people working alone.

BRAINSTORMING • A group process that encourages creativity by stimulating a large number of ideas and suspending judgment until the process is completed.

■ REASONING

We are not finished yet. I have more puzzles to solve, more weighty things to consider. Ponder this proposition:

> If A are B, and some B are C, then some A are C.

Is it true or false? What say you?

I confess that upon first seeing this proposition, I believed that it was true. It seemed that we were logically progressing to higher-order categories at each step along the way (see Figure 9.6, Part A). For example, if apples (A) are fruit (B), and fruit (B) are food (C), then apples (A) are food (C). But I was bamboozled by the "some." My example with the apples omitted the word. Consider another example of this proposition, one that uses "some": If *some* circles (A) are shapes (B), and *some* shapes (B) are squares (C), then *some* circles (A) are squares (C). Not so! By using the qualifying term "some," we can move both up, to a higher-order category (from circles to shapes), and back down, to a lower-order category (from shapes to squares) (see Figure 9.6, Part B).

• *Types of Reasoning*

We have just been toying with an example of reasoning. **Reasoning** is the transformation of information in order to reach conclusions. Let us consider two kinds of reasoning: deductive and inductive.

Deductive reasoning is a form of reasoning in which the conclusion must be true if the premises are true. Consider this classic three-sentence argument:

1. All persons are mortal.
2. Socrates is a person.
3. Therefore, Socrates is mortal.

Sentences 1 and 2 in this argument are called the *premises*. Premises provide the assumptions or basic information that allow people to draw conclusions. Sentence 3 is the conclusion. In this example, sentence 1 makes a statement about a category (persons). Sentence 2 assigns an individual (Socrates) to the category (persons). Sentence 3 concludes that what is true of the category (persons) is true for the member of the category (Socrates). The conclusion, sentence 3, is said to be *deduced* from the premises. The conclusion about Socrates is true if the premises are true.

In **inductive reasoning,** we reason from individual cases or particular facts to a general conclusion. Consider this transformation of the previous example:

1. Socrates is a person.
2. Socrates is mortal.
3. Therefore, persons are mortal.

FIGURE 9.6

WHEN ARE A ALSO C?

In Part A of this figure, A (apples) are also C (food) because food represents a higher-order category that contains all apples. In Part B, however, C (squares) is not higher order than A (circles). Therefore, C does not contain A. B (shapes), however, is higher order than both A and C and contains both.

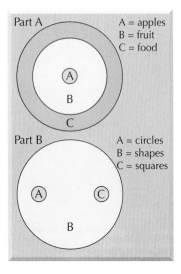

Part A
A = apples
B = fruit
C = food

Part B
A = circles
B = shapes
C = squares

The conclusion happens to be correct, but it is illogical. The fact that one person is mortal does not guarantee that all people are mortal.

Inductive reasoning, then, does not permit us to draw absolute conclusions (Sloman, 1996). Yet inductive reasoning is used all the time. We conclude that a certain type of food will or will not make us feel sick because of our experiences on earlier occasions. ("Buttered popcorn made me nauseous. This is buttered popcorn. Therefore, this will make me nauseous.") We assume that a cheerful smile and "Hello!" will break the ice with a new acquaintance because it has worked before. Although none of these conclusions is as logical as a deductive conclusion, inductive conclusions are correct often enough so that we can get on with our daily lives with some degree of confidence.

Inductive reasoning is also used in psychological research. We select samples that we believe represent certain populations. We then conduct research with those samples. We assume that the conclusions we reach with a research sample will apply to the whole population. However, we cannot be absolutely certain that our samples are representative. Even if they are, there may be a few cases in the population that are so unusual that we cannot generalize our findings to them. Nevertheless, we are correct in our conclusions often enough that our research efforts are largely successful.

> ## REFLECTIONS
> * Do you recognize the following kind of argument?
>
>   1. John says that too much money is spent on education.
>   2. John is a (pick one: teacher, father, man, doctor, minister, congressional representative, talk show host).
>   3. Therefore, too much money is spent on education.
>   What sort of appeal is being used in this argument? Is the argument logical? Is the conclusion correct? Can you think of examples of similar kinds of arguments from your own experience?

■ JUDGMENT AND DECISION MAKING

Decisions, decisions. Should you go have breakfast before classes begin or catch a few extra winks? Should you get married or remain single? (Should you get divorced or remain married?) Should you take a job or go on for advanced training when you complete your college program? If you opt for the job, cash will soon be jingling in your pockets. Yet later you may wonder if you have enough education to reach your full potential. By furthering your education, you may have to delay independence and gratification, but you may find a more fulfilling position later on. Ah, decisions, decisions.

Other kinds of decisions are judgments about the nature of the world. We make judgments about which route to school or work will be the least crowded. We make judgments about where it will be safe and convenient to live. We make judgments about what political candidates to vote for and which brand of ice cream to buy.

You might like to think that people are so rational that they carefully weigh all the pros and cons when they make judgments or decisions. Or you might think that they insist on finding and examining all the relevant information. Actually, people make most of their decisions on the basis of limited information.

REASONING • The transforming of information to reach conclusions.
DEDUCTIVE REASONING • A form of reasoning about arguments in which conclusions are deduced from premises. The conclusions are true if the premises are true.
INDUCTIVE REASONING • A form of reasoning in which we reason from individual cases or particular facts to a general conclusion.

They take shortcuts. They use heuristic devices—rules of thumb—in their judgments and decision making, just as they do in problem solving. For example, they may let a financial advisor select stocks for them rather than research the companies themselves. Or they may see a doctor recommended by a friend rather than examine the doctor's credentials. In this section we consider heuristic devices and two other factors in judgments and decision making: the framing effect and overconfidence.

• *Heuristics in Decision Making: If It Works, Must It Be Logical?*

Let us begin by asking you to imagine that you flip a coin six times. In the following three possible outcomes, H stands for head and T for tail. Circle the sequence that is most likely:

H H H H H H

H H H T T T

T H H T H T

Did you select T H H T H T as the most likely sequence of events? Most people do (Matlin, 1997). Why? There are two reasons. First, people recognize that the sequence of six heads in a row is unlikely. (The probability of achieving it is $\frac{1}{2} \times \frac{1}{2} \times \frac{1}{2} \times \frac{1}{2} \times \frac{1}{2} \times \frac{1}{2}$, or $\frac{1}{64}$.) Three heads and three tails are more likely than six heads (or six tails). Second, people recognize that the sequence of heads and tails ought to appear random. T H H T H T has a random look to it, whereas H H H T T T does not.

People tend to select T H H T H T because of the **representativeness heuristic**. According to this decision-making heuristic, people make judgments about events (samples) according to the populations of events that they appear to represent (Kosonen & Winne, 1995). In this case, the sample of events is six coin tosses. The "population" is an infinite number of random coin tosses. But guess what? *Each* of the sequences is equally likely (or unlikely). If the question had been whether six heads or three heads and three tails had been more likely, the correct answer would have been three and three. If the question had been whether heads and tails would be more likely to be consecutive or in random order, the correct answer would have been random order.

But each of the three sequences shown is a specific sequence. What is the probability of attaining the specific sequence T H H T H T? The probability that the first coin toss will result in a tail is $\frac{1}{2}$. The probability that the second will result in a head is $\frac{1}{2}$, and so on. Thus, the probability of attaining the exact sequence T H H T H T is identical to that of achieving any other specific sequence: $\frac{1}{2} \times \frac{1}{2} \times \frac{1}{2} \times \frac{1}{2} \times \frac{1}{2} \times \frac{1}{2} = \frac{1}{64}$. (Don't just sit there. Try this out on a friend.)

Or consider this question: If a couple has five children, all of whom are boys, is their sixth child more likely to be a boy or a girl? Use of the representativeness heuristic would lead one to imagine that the couple is due for a girl. That is, five boys and one girl is closer to the assumed random distribution that accounts for roughly equal numbers of boys and girls in the world. But people with some knowledge of reproductive biology might predict that another boy is actually more likely, since five boys in a row may be too many to be a random biological event. On the other hand, if the couple's conception of a boy or girl were truly random, what would be the probability of conceiving another boy? Answer: $\frac{1}{2}$.

Truth or Fiction Revisited

It is not true that if a couple has five sons, the sixth child is likely to be a daughter.

REPRESENTATIVENESS HEURISTIC • A decision-making heuristic in which people make judgments about samples according to the populations they appear to represent.

Another heuristic device used in decision making is the **availability heuristic.** According to this heuristic, our estimates of frequency or probability are based on how easy it is to find examples of relevant events. Let me ask you whether there are more art majors or sociology majors at your college. Unless you are familiar with the enrollment statistics, you will probably answer on the basis of the numbers of art majors and sociology majors that you personally know.

Events that are more recent or well publicized tend to be more available to us. Diseases such as emphysema and diabetes cause many times more deaths than accidents, but accidents are more likely to be reported in the media. Therefore, most people tend to exaggerate the number of deaths due to accidents but to underestimate the numbers of deaths due to emphysema and diabetes. Similarly, the media tend to focus on murder and other acts of violence, leading people to overestimate the incidence of aggression in our society.

The **anchoring and adjustment heuristic** suggests that there can be a good deal of inertia in our judgments. In forming opinions or making estimates, we have an initial view, or presumption. This is the anchor. As we receive additional information, we make adjustments, sometimes grudgingly. That is, if you grow up believing that one religion or one political party is the "right" one, that belief serves as a cognitive anchor. When inconsistencies show up in your religion or political party, you may adjust your views of them, but perhaps not very willingly.

Let us illustrate further by means of a math problem. Write each of the following multiplication problems on a separate piece of paper:

A. $8 \times 7 \times 6 \times 5 \times 4 \times 3 \times 2 \times 1$

B. $1 \times 2 \times 3 \times 4 \times 5 \times 6 \times 7 \times 8$

Show problem A to a few friends. Give them each 5 seconds to estimate the answer. Show problem B to some other friends and give them 5 seconds to estimate the answer.

The answers to the multiplication problems are the same, since the order of the quantities being multiplied does not change the outcome. However, when Tversky and Kahneman (1982) showed these problems to high school students, the average estimate given by students who were shown version A was significantly higher than that given by students who were shown version B. Students who saw 8 in the first position offered an average estimate of 2,250. Students who saw 1 in the first position gave an average estimate of 512. That is, the estimate was larger when 8 served as the anchor. By the way, what is the correct answer to the multiplication problems? Can you use the anchoring and adjustment heuristic to explain why both groups of students were so far off in their estimates?

• *The Framing Effect: Say That Again?*

If you were on a low-fat diet, would you be more likely to choose an ice cream that is 97% fat free or one whose fat content makes up 10% of its calorie content? On one shopping excursion I was impressed with an ice cream package's claims that the product was 97% fat free. Yet when I read the label closely, I noticed that a 4-ounce serving had 160 calories, 27 of which were contributed by fat. Fat, then, accounted for $^{27}/_{160}$, or about 17%, of the ice cream's calorie content. But fat accounted only for 3% of the ice cream's *weight*. The packagers of

AVAILABILITY HEURISTIC • A decision-making heuristic in which our estimates of frequency or probability of events are based on how easy it is to find examples.
ANCHORING AND ADJUSTMENT HEURISTIC • A decision-making heuristic in which a presumption or first estimate serves as a cognitive anchor. As we receive additional information, we make adjustments, but tend to remain in the proximity of the anchor.

the ice cream knew all about the *framing effect*. They understood that labeling the ice cream as "97% fat free" would make it sound more healthful than "Only 17% of calories from fat."

The **framing effect** refers to the way in which wording, or the context in which information is presented, can influence decision making. Political groups are as aware as advertisers of the role of the framing effect. For example, proponents of legalized abortion refer to themselves as "pro-choice," while opponents refer to themselves as "pro-life." Thus each group frames itself in a way that is positive ("pro" something) and refers to a value (freedom, life) with which it would be difficult to argue.

Because early detection of cancer enhances the likelihood of survival, health professionals encourage people to obtain regular screening for cancer. Their arguments can be framed to emphasize the benefits of obtaining screening or the costs of failing to do so (Rothman & Salovey, 1997). In an experiment run by psychologist Sara Banks and her colleagues (1995), one group of women was informed that using mammography to screen for breast cancer could save their lives. Another group was informed that *failure* to detect breast cancer early could cost them their lives. Women who were warned of the costs of failure to use mammography were more likely to obtain a mammogram during the next year.

Parents are also aware of the framing effect. My 3-year-old, Taylor, was invited to a play date at Abigail's house. I asked Taylor, "Would you like to play with Abigail at her house?" The question met with a resounding no. I thought things over and reframed the question: "Would you like to play at Abigail's house and have a real fun time? She has lots of toys and games, and I'll pick you up real soon." This time Taylor's decision was yes.

Consider the following two questions to gain insight into the role of the framing effect in surveys:

1. Do you agree or disagree that women should have the same opportunities as men to seek fulfillment in the workplace?
2. Do you agree or disagree that women who have difficulty finding good day care for very young children should remain with them in the home rather than work outside the home?

Try them out on your friends and see which one meets with greater agreement. Can you account for the difference?

The following diversity feature applies psychological knowledge of judgment and decision making to African Americans' and White people's opinions about the trials of O. J. Simpson.

Psychology in a World of
DIVERSITY

Across the Great Divide? Diverse Perspectives on the O.J. Simpson Verdicts

From 1994 through 1997, Americans were held spellbound by the trials of sports celebrity O. J. Simpson, who was charged with the murders (and then the wrongful deaths) of Nicole Brown Simpson and Ronald Goldman. In October of 1995, a jury with a majority of African Americans acquitted Simpson of

FRAMING EFFECT • The influence of wording, or the context in which information is presented, on decision making.

Across the Great Divide. White and African American college students react to the jury's verdict in the O. J. Simpson murder trial.

murder. In February of 1997, a jury with a majority of White Americans found Simpson liable for their deaths.

Polls found that most African Americans were pleased with the first verdict and displeased with the second (Cose, 1997). They found that most White Americans were displeased with the first and pleased with the second. Table 9.2 reports the results of a national telephone survey of 760 adults concerning the 1995 verdict.

HEURISTICS IN DECISION MAKING How do we account for the racial difference in opinions about the verdicts? People use heuristic devices to arrive at judgments and decisions. Consider the *representativeness heuristic*. To many White observers, the first Simpson case represented a more or less standard case of spouse abuse and murder. To many African American observers, the most important aspect of the case was that officers in the Los Angeles Police Department had proved themselves to be racist.

TABLE 9.2 RESULTS OF *NEWSWEEK* POLL ON ATTITUDES TOWARD THE VERDICT IN THE O. J. SIMPSON MURDER CASE		
	Race	
	African American	White
Percent agreeing with the verdict of not guilty	85%	32%
Percent saying they thought the verdict was fair and impartial	80%	50%

Note: From Mark Whitaker, "Whites v. Blacks," *Newsweek,* October 16, 1995, pp. 28–35.

What about the *availability heuristic?* Many White observers were skeptical of the first verdict because of Simpson's financial ability to assemble a "dream team" of attorneys. Many African American observers, on the other hand, had suffered discrimination at the hands of police.

And what about the *anchoring and adjustment* statistic? Most White observers began with faith in the police and the criminal justice system. Most African American observers began with lack of faith in both.

FRAMING EFFECTS Interviews of jurors after the first verdict also suggested the presence of *framing effects.* That is, some jurors who voted to acquit said that they believed Simpson might actually have committed the murders. However, they had been asked to find him guilty or not guilty on the basis of the evidence presented. Some of that evidence had been gathered by a police officer who was revealed to be a racist.

Simpson attorney Johnnie Cochran also contributed to the framing effect in the first trial. He asked the jury to use the verdict to send a message concerning racism and its tolerance in the Los Angeles Police Department, not just Simpson's guilt or innocence.

White and African American observers may agree on one thing: Their reactions to the Simpson verdicts reflect the use of heuristics and framing effects in judgment and decision making.

• *Overconfidence: Is Your Hindsight 20–20?*

Whether our decisions are correct or incorrect, most of us tend to be overconfident in them (Gigerenzer and others, 1991; Lundeberg and others, 1994). Overconfidence applies to judgments as wide-ranging as whether one will be infected by the virus that causes AIDS (Goldman & Harlow, 1993), predicting the outcome of elections (Hawkins & Hastie, 1990), asserting that one's answers to test items are correct (Lundeberg and others, 1994), and selecting stocks. Many people refuse to alter their judgments even in the face of statistical evidence that shows them to be flawed. (Have you ever known someone to maintain unrealistic confidence in a candidate who was far behind in the polls?)

We also tend to view our situations with 20–20 hindsight. When we are proven wrong, we frequently find a way to show that we "knew it all along." We also become overconfident that we would have known the actual outcome if we had had access to the information that became available after the event (Hawkins & Hastie, 1990). For example, if we had known that a key player would pull a hamstring muscle, we would have predicted a different outcome for the football game. If we had known that it would be blustery on Election Day, we would have predicted a smaller voter turnout and a different outcome.

There are a number of reasons for overconfidence, even when our judgments are erroneous. Here are some of them:

- We tend to be unaware of how flimsy our assumptions may be.
- We tend to focus on examples that confirm our judgments and to ignore those that do not.
- Our working memories have limited space, and we tend not to recall information that runs counter to our judgments.
- We work to bring about the events we believe in, so they sometimes become self-fulfilling prophecies.
- Even when people are told that they tend to be overconfident in their decisions, they usually fail to make use of this information (Gigerenzer and others, 1991).

Truth or Fiction Revisited

....

It is not necessarily true that people change their opinions when they are shown to be wrong. In some cases they may, but the statement is too general to be true.

REFLECTIONS

- How did you answer the "Truth or Fiction?" item, "If a couple has five sons, the sixth child is likely to be a daughter"? Why?
- Do you imagine that you could ever give up or greatly change your political or religious beliefs? Why or why not?
- Have you ever used the framing effect to try to persuade someone to believe or do something? How?
- Have you ever known people who have refused to change their minds even though they were shown to be wrong? How do you explain their reluctance to change?

■ LANGUAGE

When I was in high school, I was taught that humans differ from other creatures that run, swim, or fly because only we can use tools and language. Then I learned that lower animals also use tools. Otters use rocks to open clam shells. Chimpanzees toss rocks as weapons and use sticks to dig out grubs for food.

In recent years our exclusive claim to language has also been questioned because apes have been taught to use symbols to communicate. (*Symbols* such as words stand for or represent other objects, events, or ideas.) Some communicate by making signs with their hands. Others use plastic symbols or press keys on a computer keyboard (Johnson, 1995). (See Figure 9.7.)

Language is the communication of thoughts and feelings by means of symbols that are arranged according to rules of grammar. Language makes it possible for one person to communicate knowledge to another and for one generation to communicate to another. It creates a vehicle for recording experiences. It allows us to put ourselves in the shoes of other people, to learn more than we could ever learn from direct experience. Language also provides many of the basic units of thought.

Language is one of our great strengths. Other species may be stronger, run faster, smell more keenly, even live longer, but only humans have produced

LANGUAGE • The communication of information by means of symbols arranged according to rules of grammar.

FIGURE 9.7
AN APE USES SIGNS TO COMMUNICATE
Apes at Emory University's Yerkes Primate Center have been taught to express concepts by pressing keys on a computer-controlled keyboard.

literature, music, mathematics, and science. Language ability has made all this possible.

Many species have systems of communication. Birds warn other birds of predators. Through particular types of chirps and shrieks, they communicate that they have taken possession of a certain tree or bush. The "dances" of bees inform other bees of the location of a food source or a predator. Vervet monkeys make sounds that signal the distance and species of predators. But these are all inborn communication patterns. Swamp sparrows that have been reared in isolation, for example, produce songs that are very similar to those produced by birds that have been reared naturally in the wild (Brody, 1991). True language is distinguished from the communication systems of lower animals by properties such as semanticity, infinite creativity, and displacement (Ratner & Gleason, 1993).

Semanticity refers to the fact that the sounds (or signs) of a language have meaning. Words serve as symbols for actions, objects, relational concepts (*over, in, more,* and so on), and other ideas. The communications systems of the birds and the bees lack semanticity. Specific sounds and—in the case of bees—specific waggles do *not* serve as symbols.

Infinite creativity refers to the capacity to combine words into original sentences. An "original" sentence is *not* one that has never been spoken before. Rather, it is a sentence that is produced by the individual instead of imitated. To produce original sentences, children must have a basic understanding of *syntax,* or the structure of grammar. Two-year-old children string signs (words) together in novel combinations.

Displacement is the capacity to communicate information about events and objects in another time or place.[2] Language makes possible the efficient transmission of complex knowledge from one person to another and from one generation to another. Displacement permits parents to warn children about the mistakes they made as children. Displacement allows children to tell their parents what they did in school.

• *Basic Concepts of Language*

The basic concepts of language include *phonology* (sounds[3]), *morphology* (units of meaning), *syntax* (word order), and *semantics* (the meanings of words and groups of words).

PHONOLOGY **Phonology** is the study of the basic sounds in a language. There are 26 letters in the English alphabet but a greater number of **phonemes,** or basic sounds. These include the *t* and *p* in *tip,* which a psycholinguist would designate as the /t/ and /p/ phonemes. The *o* in *go* and the *o* in *gone* are different phonemes. They are spelled with the same letter, but they sound different. English speakers who learn French may be confused because /o/, as in the word *go,* has various spellings in French, including *o, au, eau,* even *eaux.*

MORPHOLOGY **Morphemes** are the smallest units of meaning in a language. A morpheme consists of one or more phonemes in a certain order. Some mor-

SEMANTICITY MEANING • The quality of language in which words are used as symbols for objects, events, or ideas.
INFINITE CREATIVITY • The capacity to combine words into original sentences.
DISPLACEMENT • The quality of language that permits one to communicate information about objects and events in another time and place.
PHONOLOGY • (foe-NOLL-oh-gee). The study of the basic sounds in a language.
PHONEME • (FOE-neem). A basic sound in a language.
MORPHEME • (MORE-feem). The smallest unit of meaning in a language.

---

[2] The word *displacement* has a different meaning in Sigmund Freud's psychodynamic theory, as we will see in Chapter 12.

[3] American Sign Language and Signed English, which are languages used by people whose hearing is impaired, are exceptions.

phemes, such as *dog* and *cat,* function as words, but others must be used in combination. The words *dogs* and *cats* each consist of two morphemes. Adding /z/ to *dog* makes the word plural. Adding /s/ to *cat* serves the same function.

An *ed* morpheme at the end of a regular verb places it in the past tense, as with *add* and *added* and *subtract* and *subtracted.* A *ly* morpheme at the end of an adjective often makes the word an adverb, as with *strong* and *strongly* and *weak* and *weakly.*

Morphemes such as *s* and *ed* tacked onto the ends of nouns and verbs are referred to as grammatical "markers," or **inflections.** Inflections change the form of words to indicate grammatical relationships such as number (singular or plural) and tense (for example, present or past). Languages have grammatical rules for the formation of plurals, tenses, and other inflections.

SYNTAX

> since feeling is first
> who pays any attention
> to the syntax of things
> will never wholly kiss you . . .
>
> E. E. CUMMINGS

The lines from a poem by e. e. cummings are intriguing because their syntax permits various interpretations. Syntax deals with the ways words are strung together, or ordered, to create phrases and sentences. The rules for word order are the *grammar* of a language.

In English, statements usually follow the pattern *subject, verb,* and *object of the verb.* Note this example:

The young boy (subject) → has brought (verb) → the book (object).

The sentence would be confusing if it were written "The young boy *has* the book *brought*." But this is how the words would be ordered in German. German syntax differs from that of English. In German, a past participle *(brought)* is placed at the end of the sentence, whereas the helping verb *(has)* follows the subject. Although the syntax of German differs from that of English, children reared in German-speaking homes[4] acquire German syntax readily.

SEMANTICS **Semantics** is the study of meaning. It involves the relationship between language and the objects or events that language depicts. Words that sound (and are spelled) alike can have different meanings, depending on their usage. Compare these sentences:

A rock sank the boat.

Don't rock the boat.

In the first sentence, *rock* is a noun and is the subject of the verb *sank.* The sentence probably means that the hull of a boat was ripped open by an underwater rock, causing the boat to sink. In the second sentence, *rock* is a verb. The second sentence is usually used as a figure of speech in which a person is being warned not to change things—not to "make waves" or "upset the apple cart."

---

[4] No, homes do not speak German or any other language. This is an example of idiomatic English. Idioms like these are readily acquired by children.

INFLECTIONS • Grammatical markers that change the forms of words to indicate grammatical relationships such as number and tense.
SEMANTICS • The study of the meanings of a language—the relationships between language and objects and events.

Crying. Crying is a prelinguistic vocalization that parents find aversive in their infants. Most parents therefore try to soothe or placate the infant so that it will stop crying.

Compare these sentences:

The chicken is ready for dinner.

The lion is ready for dinner.

The shark is ready for dinner.

The first sentence probably means that a chicken has been cooked and is ready to be eaten. The second sentence probably means that a lion is hungry or about to devour its prey. Our interpretation of the phrase "is ready for dinner" reflects our knowledge about chickens and lions. Whether we expect a shark to be eaten or to do some eating might reflect our seafood preferences or how recently we saw the movie *Jaws*.

REFLECTIONS

- Can you think of some English idioms or phrases that might be difficult to understand for immigrants learning English? Why?
- Have you ever known someone to claim that a pet could "speak" or understand English or another language? *Did* the pet really "speak"? *Did* the pet "understand" language? What do you think?

■ LANGUAGE DEVELOPMENT

Children appear to develop language in an invariant sequence of steps. We begin with the **prelinguistic** vocalizations of crying, cooing, and babbling.

As parents are well aware, newborn children have an unlearned but highly effective form of verbal expression: crying and more crying. Crying is accomplished by blowing air through the vocal tract. There are no distinct, well-formed sounds.

Crying is about the only sound that babies make during the first month. During the second month they also begin **cooing**. Babies use their tongues when they coo. For this reason, coos are more articulated than cries. Coos are often vowel-like and may resemble extended "oohs" and "ahs." Cooing appears to be linked to feelings of pleasure or positive excitement. Babies do not coo when they are hungry, tired, or in pain. Parents soon learn that different cries and coos can indicate different things: hunger, gas pains, or pleasure at being held or rocked. By about 8 months, cooing decreases markedly.

Cries and coos are innate, but they can be modified by experience. When parents reinforce cooing by talking to their babies, smiling at them, and imitating them, the rate of cooing increases. Early parent-child "conversations," in which parents respond to coos and then pause as the baby coos, may foster early infant awareness of turn-taking as a way of relating verbally to other people. However, this is not the same as using language. True language has *semanticity*. Sounds (or signs, in the case of sign language) are symbols. Cries and coos do not represent objects or events and therefore are prelinguistic.

By about the fifth or sixth month, children have begun to babble. **Babbling** is the first vocalizing that sounds like human speech. Children babble phonemes that occur in several languages, including the throaty German *ch*, the clicks of certain African languages, and rolling *r*'s. In babbling, babies frequently combine consonants and vowels, as in "ba," "ga," and, sometimes, the much valued "dada." "Dada" at first is purely coincidental (sorry, you Dads), despite the family's jubilation over its appearance.

PRELINGUISTIC • Prior to the development of language.
COOING • Prelinguistic, articulated, vowel-like sounds that appear to reflect feelings of positive excitement.
BABBLING • The child's first vocalizations that have the sounds of speech.

Babbling, like crying and cooing, appears to be inborn. Children from cultures whose languages sound very different all seem to babble the same sounds, including many that they could not have heard (Gleason & Ratner, 1993). As time progresses, however, their babbling takes on more of the sounds of the language spoken in their home environment.

Children seem to single out the types of phonemes used in the home within a few months. By the age of 9 or 10 months they repeat these phonemes regularly and foreign phonemes begin to drop out. Thus, there is an overall reduction in the variety of phonemes that infants produce.

Babbling, like crying and cooing, is a prelinguistic event. Yet infants usually understand much of what others are saying well before they utter their first words. Comprehension precedes the production of language, and infants demonstrate comprehension through their actions and gestures.

• *Development of Vocabulary*

Ah, that long-awaited first word! What a thrill! What a milestone! Children tend to utter their first word at about 1 year of age, but many parents miss it, often because it is not pronounced clearly or because pronunciation varies from one usage to the next. *Ball* may be pronounced "ba," "bee," or even "pah." The majority of an infant's early words are names of things (Nelson and others, 1993).

The growth of vocabulary is slow at first. It may take children 3 to 4 months to achieve a 10-word vocabulary after they have spoken their first word (Nelson, 1973). By about 18 months, children are producing nearly two dozen words. Many words, such as *no, cookie, mama, hi,* and *eat,* are quite familiar. Others, like *allgone* and *bye-bye,* may not be found in the dictionary, but they function as words. Reading to children increases their vocabulary, so parents would do well to stock up on story books (Arnold and others, 1994; Robbins & Ehri, 1994).

Children try to talk about more objects than they have words for. As a result they often extend use of a word to refer to other things and actions for which they do not yet have words. This phenomenon is termed **overextension.** At some point, for example, many children refer to horses as *doggies.* At age 6, my daughter Allyn counted by tens as follows: sixty, seventy, eighty, ninety, *tenty.*

• *Development of Syntax*

Children's first utterances are single words, but those words are sometimes used to express complex meanings. Such utterances are called **holophrases.** For example, *mama* may be used by the child to signify meanings as varied as "There goes Mama," "Come here, Mama," and "You are my Mama." Similarly, *poo-cat* can signify "There is a pussycat," "That stuffed animal looks just like my pussycat," or "I want you to give me my pussycat right now!" Most children readily teach their parents what they intend by augmenting their holophrases with gestures, intonations, and reinforcers. That is, they act delighted when parents do as requested and howl when they do not.

Toward the end of the second year, children begin to speak in two-word sentences. These sentences are termed *telegraphic speech* because they resemble telegrams. Telegrams use the principles of syntax to cut out all the "unnecessary" words. "Home Tuesday" might stand for "I expect to be home on Tuesday." Similarly, only essential words are used in children's telegraphic speech—in particular, nouns, verbs, and some modifiers. When a child says "That ball," the words *is* and *a* are implied. Two-word utterances seem to appear at about the same time in the development of all languages (Slobin, 1983).

OVEREXTENSION • Overgeneralizing the use of words to objects and situations to which they do not apply—a normal characteristic of the speech of young children.
HOLOPHRASE • A single word used to express complex meanings.

Also, the sequence of emergence of the types of two-word utterances (for example, first, agent-action; then action-object, location, and possession) is the same in languages as diverse as English, Luo (an African tongue), German, Russian, and Turkish (Slobin, 1983).

Two-word utterances, although brief, show understanding of syntax. The child will say, "Sit chair" to tell a parent to sit in a chair, not "Chair sit." The child will say, "My shoe," not "Shoe my," to show possession. "Mommy go" means Mommy is leaving. "Go Mommy" expresses the wish for Mommy to go away. (For this reason, "Go Mommy" is not heard often.)

• *Development of More Complex Language*

Between the ages of 2 and 3, children's sentence structure usually expands to include the missing words in telegraphic speech. Children usually add articles *(a, an, the)*, conjunctions *(and, but, or)*, possessive and demonstrative adjectives *(your, her, that)*, pronouns *(she, him, one)*, and prepositions *(in, on, over, around, under,* and *through)* to their utterances. Their grasp of syntax is shown in linguistic oddities such as *your one* instead of simply *yours,* and *his one* instead of *his.*

Usually between the ages of 2 and 3 children begin to combine phrases and clauses into complex sentences. An early example of a complex sentence is "You goed and Mommy goed, too." A more advanced example is "What will we do when we get there?"

One of the more intriguing language developments is **overregularization.** To understand children's use of overregularization, consider the formation of the past tense and of plurals in English. We add *d* or *ed* phonemes to regular verbs and *s* or *z* phonemes to regular nouns. Thus, *walk* becomes *walked* and *look* becomes *looked. Pussycat* becomes *pussycats* and *doggy* becomes *doggies.* There are also irregular verbs and nouns. For example, *see* becomes *saw, sit* becomes *sat,* and *go* becomes *went. Sheep* remains *sheep* (plural) and *child* becomes *children.*

At first children learn a small number of these irregular verbs by imitating their parents. Two-year-olds tend to form them correctly—at first (Kuczaj, 1982)! Then they become aware of the syntactic rules for forming the past tense and plurals. As a result, they tend to make charming errors (Pinker, 1994a). Some 3- to 5-year-olds, for example, are more likely to say "I seed it" than "I saw it" and to say "Mommy sitted down" than "Mommy sat down." They are likely to talk about the "gooses" and "sheeps" they "seed" on the farm and about all the "childs" they ran into at the playground. This tendency to regularize the irregular is what is meant by overregularization.

Some parents recognize that at one point their children were forming the past tense of irregular verbs correctly and that they later began to make errors. The thing to remember is that overregularization reflects knowledge of grammar, not faulty language development. In another year or two, *mouses* will be boringly transformed into *mice,* and Mommy will no longer have *sitted* down. Parents might as well enjoy overregularization while they can.

As language ability develops beyond the third year, children show increasing facility in their use of pronouns (such as *it* and *she*) and prepositions (such as *in, before,* or *on*), which represent physical or temporal relationships among objects and events. Children's first questions are telegraphic and characterized by a rising pitch (which signifies a question mark) at the end. "More milky?" for example, can be translated into "May I have more milk?" or "Would you like more milk?" or "Is there more milk?"—depending on the context.

OVERREGULARIZATION • The application of regular grammatical rules for forming inflections (e.g., past tense and plurals) to irregular verbs and nouns.

Jn Review Milestones in Language Development

APPROXIMATE AGE	DEVELOPMENT	COMMENTS
Birth	Crying	Prelinguistic expression of discomfort, fear
2nd month	Cooing	Prelinguistic extended "oohs" and "ahs" that may be used to express pleasure
5 or 6 months	Babbling appears	Prelinguistic, but comes to sound more and more like the phonemes of the language spoken in the home environment
1 year	First word appears	Frequently missed by parents because of inconsistent or incorrect pronunciation
18 months	Utters some 2 dozen words	Vocabulary growth is slow at first; single words may be used to express complex meanings *(holophrases)*
2 years	Telegraphic two-word utterances appear	Sequence of development of types of two-word (telegraphic) utterances is the same in diverse languages; form of two-word utterances shows understanding of syntax (grammar)
2–3 years	Missing words added to telegraphic speech	Articles, conjunctions, possessive and demonstrative adjectives, and prepositions are used
3–5 years	Overregularization	Knowledge of syntax leads children to overregularize irregular plurals and verbs
6 years	Vocabulary of 10,000 words	Much individual variation

It is usually during the third year that the *wh* questions appear. Consistent with the child's general cognitive development, certain *wh* questions (*what, who,* and *where*) appear earlier than others (*why, when, which,* and *how*) (Bloom and others, 1982). *Why* is usually too philosophical for the 2-year-old, and *how* is too involved. Two-year-olds are also likely to be now-oriented, so *when* is of less than immediate concern. By the fourth year, however, most children are asking *why, when,* and *how* questions—frequently when their parents are trying to do something else.

By the fourth year, children are also taking turns talking and engaging in lengthy conversations. By the age of 6, their vocabularies have expanded to 10,000 words, give or take a few thousand. By age 7 to 9, most children realize that words can have more than one meaning, and they are entertained by riddles and jokes that require semantic sophistication ("What's black and white, but read all over?"). Between the elementary school and high school years, vocabulary continues to grow rapidly. There are also subtle advances in articulation and the capacity to use complex syntax.

• *Theories of Language Development*

Since all normal humans talk but no house pets or house plants do, no matter how pampered, heredity must be involved in language. But since a child growing up in Japan speaks Japanese whereas the same child brought up in California would speak English, the environment is also crucial. Thus, there is no question about whether heredity or environment is involved in language, or even whether one or the other is "more important." Instead, . . . our best hope [might be] finding out how they interact.

STEVEN PINKER

Countless billions of children have acquired the languages spoken by their parents and passed them down, with minor changes, from generation to generation. Theories of language development are concerned with *how* they manage to do so. In language development, as in many other areas of psychology, we study the interactions between the influences of heredity (nature) and the environment (nurture). Let us see how these broad views are expressed in learning and nativist theories of language development.

LEARNING THEORIES Learning theorists claim that language develops according to laws of learning and is similar to other kinds of learned behavior (Gleason & Ratner, 1993). They usually refer to the concepts of imitation and reinforcement. From a social-cognitive perspective, parents serve as *models*. Children learn language, at least in part, through observation and imitation. It seems likely that many words, especially nouns and verbs (including irregular verbs), are learned by imitation.

At first children accurately repeat the irregular verb forms they observe. This repetition can probably be explained in terms of modeling, but modeling does not explain all the events involved in learning. Children later begin to overregularize irregular verb forms *because of* their knowledge of rules of syntax, not through imitation. Nor does imitative learning explain how children come to utter phrases and sentences that they have *not* observed. Parents, for example, are unlikely to model utterances such as "bye-bye sock" and "allgone Daddy," but children do say them.

Sometimes children steadfastly avoid imitating language forms suggested by adults, even when the adults are insistent. Note the following exchange between 2-year-old Ben and a (very frustrated) adult:

> BEN: I like these candy. I like they.
> ADULT: You like them?
> BEN: Yes. I like they.
> ADULT: Say *them.*
> BEN: Them.
> ADULT: Say "I like *them.*"
> BEN: I like them.
> ADULT: Good.
> BEN: I'm good. These candy good too.
> ADULT: Are they good?
> BEN: Yes. I like they. You like they? (Kuczaj, 1982, p. 48)

In *Verbal Behavior,* B. F. Skinner outlined his view of the role of reinforcement in language development: "A child acquires verbal behavior when relatively unpatterned vocalizations, selectively reinforced, assume forms which produce appropriate consequences in a given verbal community" (Skinner, 1957, p. 31). Skinner allowed that prelinguistic vocalizations such as cooing and babbling are inborn. But parents reinforce children for babbling that approximates real words such as *da*, which in English resembles *dog* or *daddy.* Children do in fact increase their babbling when it results in adults smiling at them, stroking them, and talking back to them.

As the first year progresses, children babble the sounds of their native tongue with increasing frequency, while "foreign" sounds drop out. The behaviorist explains this pattern of changing frequencies in terms of reinforcement (of the sounds of the adults' language) and extinction (of foreign sounds). An alternate (nonbehavioral) explanation is that children actively attend to the sounds in their linguistic environment and are intrinsically motivated to utter them.

From Skinner's (1957) perspective, children acquire vocabulary through shaping. That is, parents require children's utterances to come progressively closer to actual words before they are reinforced. Skinner views multiword utterances as complex stimulus-response chains that are also taught through shaping. As children's utterances become longer, parents foster correct word order by uttering sentences to their children and reinforcing imitation. As with Ben, when children make grammatical errors, parents recast their utterances correctly. They then reinforce the children for repeating them.

But recall Ben's refusal to be shaped into using correct syntax. If the reinforcement explanation were sufficient, parental reinforcement would facilitate children's learning of phonetics, syntax, and semantics. We do not have evidence that this occurs. For one thing, parents are more likely to reinforce their children for the accuracy, or "truth value," of their utterances than for their grammatical correctness. Parents, in other words, generally accept the syntax of their children's vocal efforts. The child who points down and says, "The grass is purple" is not likely to be reinforced, despite his use of correct syntax. But the enthusiastic child who shows her parents an empty plate and blurts out "I eated it all up!" is likely to be reinforced, despite her overregularization of *to eat*.

Learning theory also cannot account for the invariant sequence of language development and the spurts in children's language acquisition. Even the types of two-word utterances emerge in a consistent pattern in diverse cultures. Although timing differs from one child to another, the types of questions used, passive versus active sentences, and so on, all emerge in the same order.

NATIVIST THEORY The nativist theory of language development holds that innate or inborn factors cause children to attend to and acquire language in certain ways. From this perspective, children bring a certain neurological "prewiring" to language learning ((Pinker, 1994a).

According to **psycholinguistic theory,** language acquisition involves the interaction of environmental influences—such as exposure to parental speech and reinforcement—and an inborn tendency to acquire language. Noam Chomsky (1980, 1991) refers to the inborn tendency as a **language acquisition device (LAD).** Evidence for an LAD is found in the universality of human language abilities and in the invariant sequence of language development.

The LAD prepares the nervous system to learn grammar. On the surface, languages differ a great deal. However, the LAD serves children all over the world because languages share what Chomsky refers to as a "universal

PSYCHOLINGUISTIC THEORY • The view that language learning involves an interaction between environmental factors and an inborn tendency to acquire language.
LANGUAGE ACQUISITION DEVICE • In psycholinguistic theory, neural "prewiring" that facilitates the child's learning of grammar. Abbreviated LAD.

grammar"—an underlying set of rules for turning ideas into sentences (Pinker, 1990, 1994a). Consider an analogy with computers: According to psycholinguistic theory, the universal grammar that resides in the LAD is the same as a computer's basic operating system. The particular language that a child learns to use is the same as a word-processing program.

Lenneberg (1967) proposes that there is a **sensitive period** for learning language that begins at about 18 to 24 months and lasts until puberty. This period reflects neural maturation. During the sensitive period, the brain is flexible and language learning is relatively easy. Evidence for a sensitive period is found in recovery from certain kinds of brain injuries. Injuries to the dominant hemi-

SENSITIVE PERIOD • In linguistic theory, the period from about 18 months to puberty when the brain is thought to be particularly capable of learning language because of plasticity.

psychology and
modern life

BILINGUAL EDUCATION

Many U.S. children who speak a different language in the home experience difficulty when learning English in school. Early in the century the educational approach to teaching English to non-English-speaking children was simple: sink or swim. Children were taught in English from the outset. They had to catch on as best they could. Most children swam. Some sank.

A more formal term for the sink-or-swim method is *total immersion*. Total immersion has a checkered history. There are many successes but there are also more failures than most educators are willing to tolerate. For this reason, bilingual education has been adopted in many school systems.

Bilingual education legislation requires that non-English-speaking children be given the chance to study in their own language to smooth their transition into life in the United States. The official purpose of federal bilingual programs is to help children who speak foreign languages use their native tongue to learn English rapidly, then switch to a regular school program. Yet the degree of emphasis on English differs from one program to another.

So-called transitional programs shoot students into regular English-speaking classrooms as quickly as possible. In a second technique, called the *maintenance method*, rapid mastery of English is still the goal. But students continue to study their own culture and language. A third approach, which has been tried in areas with large Hispanic populations, such as New York, Florida, Northern Virginia, and Southern California, is *two-way immersion*. These programs encourage native-born U.S. children to achieve fluency in a foreign language at the same time immigrant children are learning English (Cavaliere, 1996). In this method, all students study half a day in Spanish and half a day in English (Sleek, 1994).

Critics of bilingual education contend that it is often more political than educational. For example, children with Spanish surnames may be segregated in separate classes long after they have shown that they can handle lessons in English. These critics recognize the benefits of cultural pluralism but believe that the key to success in the United States is the ability to communicate in English.

It appears that bilingual education is most successful if the following criteria are met:

- The bilingual program focuses specifically on teaching English and does not just teach other subjects in English, even at a low level.

- The child's parents understand and support the goals and methods of the program.

- Teachers, parents, and other members of the community have mutual respect for one another and for each others' language (Cavaliere, 1996). ■

sphere can impair or destroy the ability to speak. But children whose brain is injured before puberty frequently recover a good deal of their speaking ability.

• *Bilingualism*

Most people throughout the world speak two or more languages. Most countries have minority populations whose languages differ from the national tongue. Nearly all Europeans are taught English and the languages of neighboring nations. Consider the Netherlands. Dutch is the native tongue, but all children are also taught French, German, and English and are expected to become fluent in each of them.

For more than 30 million people in the United States, English is a second language (Barringer, 1993b). Spanish, French, Chinese, Russian, or Arabic is spoken in the home and, perhaps, the neighborhood.

Early in the century it was widely believed that children reared in bilingual homes were retarded in their cognitive and language development. The theory was that cognitive capacity is limited, so people who store two linguistic systems are crowding their mental abilities (Lambert, 1990). However, the U.S. Bureau of the Census reports that more than 75% of Americans who first spoke another language in the home also speak English "well" or "very well" (Barringer, 1993b). Moreover, a careful analysis of older studies in bilingualism shows that the bilingual children observed often lived in families with low socioeconomic status and little education. Yet these bilingual children were compared to middle-class monolingual children. In addition, achievement and intelligence tests were conducted in the monolingual child's language, which was the second language of the bilingual child (Reynolds, 1991). Lack of education and inadequate testing methods, rather than bilingualism per se, accounted for the apparent differences in achievement and intelligence.

Today most linguists consider it advantageous for children to be bilingual. For one thing, knowledge of more than one language expands children's awareness of different cultures and broadens their perspectives (Cavaliere, 1996). For example, bilingual children are more likely to understand that the symbols used in language are arbitrary. Monolingual children are more likely to think erro-

Truth or Fiction Revisited

It is true that the majority of people around the world speak at least two languages. Bilingualism thus is the normal state of affairs, not merely an issue of concern to immigrants.

Bilingualism. Throughout the world most people speak two or more languages, and most countries have minority populations whose languages differ from that of the dominant population.

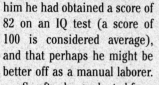

Robert Williams

He wasn't supposed to become a psychologist. He wasn't even supposed to go to college. His guidance counselor told him he had obtained a score of 82 on an IQ test (a score of 100 is considered average), and that perhaps he might be better off as a manual laborer.

So after he graduated from high school Robert Williams obtained work as a waiter in his hometown of Little Rock, Arkansas. But when he helped a friend solve an algebra problem, the friend encouraged him to go back to school. Williams followed the advice, enrolling in a local junior college and eventually receiving his doctorate in clinical psychology from St. Louis's Washington University.

Williams' own experience with intelligence tests led him to wonder whether they are culturally biased. He hypothesized that African American children would fare better on them if they were sensitive to African American culture. To demonstrate his point, Williams devised the *BITCH*—the Black Intelligence Test of Cultural Homogeneity. One question asked children to select a synonym for *blood* from the following choices: (a) a vampire, (b) a dependent individual, (c) an injured person, (d) a brother of color. The correct choice is *d*, and African American students proved to be more "intelligent" than White students, according to the *BITCH*.

Williams is now retired, but he has remained an active voice in the Ebonics debate and on the issue of cultural bias in intelligence testing. ∎

neously that the word *dog* is somehow intertwined with the nature of the beast. Bilingual children therefore have somewhat more cognitive flexibility. Second, learning a second language does not crowd children's available "cognitive space." Instead, learning a second language has been shown to increase children's expertise in their first (native) language. Research evidence reveals that learning French enhances knowledge of the structure of English among Canadian children whose native language is English (Lambert and others, 1991).

Psychology in a World of
DIVERSITY

Ebonics

The term *Ebonics* is derived from the words *ebony* and *phonics*. It was coined by the African American psychologist Robert Williams (Burnette, 1997). Ebonics was previously called Black English or Black Dialect (Pinker, 1994a). Williams explains that a group of African American scholars convened "to name our language, which had always been named by White scholars in the past" (Burnette, 1997, p. 12).

According to linguists, Ebonics is rooted in the remnants of the West African dialects used by slaves. It reflects attempts by the slaves, who were denied formal education, to imitate the speech of the dominant White culture. Some observers believe that Ebonics uses verbs haphazardly, downgrading standard English. As a result, some school systems react to the concept of Ebonics with contempt—which is hurtful to the child who speaks Ebonics. Other observers say that Ebonics has different grammatical rules than standard English, but that the rules are consistent and allow for complex thought (Pinker, 1994a). In 1996 the Oakland, California, school board recognized Ebonics as the primary language of African American students, just as Spanish had been recognized as the primary language of Hispanic American students. "I was honored," said Williams. "And truthfully, I was shocked. It was like the truth that had been covered up in the ground for so long just exploded one day" (Burnette, 1997, p. 12).

"TO BE OR NOT TO BE": USE OF VERBS IN EBONICS There are differences between Ebonics and standard English in the use of verbs. For example, the Ebonics usage "She-ah touch us" corresponds to the standard English "She will touch us." The Ebonics "He be gone" is the equivalent of the standard English "He has been gone for a long while." "He gone" is the same as "He is not here right now" in standard English.

Consider the rules in Ebonics that govern the use of the verb *to be*. In standard English, *be* is part of the infinitive form of the verb and is used to form the future tense, as in "I'll be angry tomorrow." Thus, "I *be* angry" is incorrect. But in Ebonics *be* refers to a continuing state of being. The Ebonics sentence "I be angry" is the same as the standard English "I have been angry for a while" and is grammatically correct.

Ebonics leaves out *to be* in cases in which standard English would use a contraction. For example, the standard "She's the one I'm talking about" could be "*She* the one *I* talking about" in Ebonics. Ebonics also often drops *ed* from the past tense and lacks the possessive *'s*.

"NOT TO BE OR NOT TO BE NOTHING": NEGATION IN EBONICS   Consider the sentence "I don't want no trouble," which is, of course, commendable. Middle-class White children would be corrected for using double negation (do*n't* along with *no*) and would be encouraged to say "I don't want *any* trouble." Yet double negation is acceptable in Ebonics (Pinker, 1994a). Nevertheless, many teachers who use standard English have demeaned African American children who speak this way.

Some African American children are bicultural and bilingual. They function competently within the dominant culture in the United States and among groups of people from their own ethnic background. They use standard English in a conference with their teacher or in a job interview, but switch to Ebonics among their friends. Other children cannot switch back and forth. The decision by the Oakland school board was intended in part to help children maintain their self-esteem and stay in school.

REFLECTIONS

- Can you recall any of your own experiences when learning the language spoken in your home? Do you recall any "cute" errors you made in choice of words or in pronunciation (such as *soupcase* or *sparegrass*)?
- Did you grow up speaking a language other than English in the home? If so, what special opportunities and problems were connected with the experience?
- Should children who do not speak English in the home be taught in their native language in U.S. schools? Why or why not?

■ LANGUAGE AND THOUGHT

Theories of language development are of little importance to a 20-month-old boy who has just polished off a plate of chocolate chip cookies and exclaimed (or signed) "All gone!" In the previous section we were concerned with how the child comes to say or sign "All gone" when he has finished his cookies. Now let us bring the chapter full circle by returning to matters of thinking: What does the child's use of "All gone" suggest about his thought processes? In other words, would the boy have *known* that there were no cookies left if he did not have a word he could use to express this idea? (Modern theorists of language would answer yes [Larson, 1990; Miller, 1990; Pinker, 1990].) Do you always think in words? (Modern theorists would say no [Larson, 1990; Miller, 1990; Pinker, 1990].) Can you think *without* using language? (Yes.) Would you be able to solve problems without using words or sentences? (That depends on the problem.)

Jean Piaget believed that language reflects knowledge of the world but that much knowledge can be acquired without language. For example, it is possible to understand the concepts of roundness or redness even when we do not know

Inuit Eskimos in an Igloo. The Inuit of Alaska and the Canadian Northwestern Territories have many more words for snow than most of us. They spend most of their lives in snow, and the subtle differences among various kinds of snow are meaningful to them.

or use the words *round* or *red*. But is it possible for English speakers to share the thoughts experienced by people who speak other languages? This question brings us to the linguistic-relativity hypothesis.

• *The Linguistic-Relativity Hypothesis*

Language may not be needed for all thought. However, according to the **linguistic-relativity hypothesis** proposed by Benjamin Whorf (1956), language structures the way we perceive the world. That is, the categories and relationships we use to understand the world are derived from our language. Therefore, speakers of various languages conceptualize the world in different ways.

According to the linguistic-relativity hypothesis, most English speakers' ability to think about snow may be rather limited compared to that of the Inuit (Eskimos). We have only a few words for snow. The Inuit have many words. They differ according to whether the snow is hard-packed, falling, melting, covered by ice, and so on. When we think about snow, we have fewer words to choose from and have to search for descriptive adjectives. The Inuit, however, can readily find a single word that describes a complex weather condition. It might therefore be easier for them to think about this variety of snow in relation to other aspects of their world. Similarly, the Hanunoo people of the Philippines use 92 words for rice, depending on whether the rice is husked or unhusked and on how it is prepared. And while we have one word for camel, Arabs have more than 250.

In English, we have hundreds of words to describe different colors, but people who speak Shona use only three words for colors. People who speak Bassa use only two words for colors; these correspond to light and dark. The Hopi Indians had two words for flying objects, one for birds and an all-inclusive word for anything else that might be found traveling through the air.

Does this mean that the Hopi were limited in their ability to think about bumblebees and airplanes? Are English speakers limited in their ability to think about skiing conditions? Are people who speak Shona and Bassa "color-blind" for practical purposes? Probably not. People who use only a few words to dis-

LINGUISTIC-RELATIVITY HYPOTHESIS • The view that language structures the way in which we view the world.

tinguish among colors seem to perceive the same color variations as people with dozens of words. For example, the Dani of New Guinea, like the Bassa, have just two words for colors: one which refers to yellows and reds, and one which refers to greens and blues. Still, performance on matching and memory tasks shows that the Dani can discriminate the many colors of the spectrum when they are motivated to do so. English-speaking skiers who are concerned about different skiing conditions have developed a comprehensive vocabulary about snow, including the terms *powder, slush, ice, hard-packed,* and *corn snow,* that allows them to communicate and think about snow with the facility of the Inuit. When a need to expand a language's vocabulary arises, the speakers of that language apparently have little difficulty meeting the need.

Modern cognitive scientists generally do not accept the linguistic-relativity hypothesis (Pinker, 1990). For one thing, adults use images and abstract logical propositions, as well as words, as units of thought (Larson, 1990; Miller, 1990). Infants, moreover, display considerable intelligence before they have learned to speak. Another criticism is that a language's vocabulary suggests the range of concepts that the speakers of the language have traditionally found important, not their cognitive limits. For example, a person who was magically lifted from the 19th century and placed inside an airplane probably would not think that she or he was flying inside a bird or a large insect, even if his or her language lacked a word for airplane.

We noted that infants display considerable intelligence before they can speak. Yet knowledge of the meaning of words is one of the key measures of general intelligence. The concept of intelligence is explored in Chapter 10. We will see how intelligence is intertwined with other aspects of cognition, including memory, problem solving, reasoning, decision making, and language.

Before leaving this chapter, however, I have a final problem for you:

> You're driving a bus that's leaving from Pennsylvania. To start off with, there were 32 people on the bus. At the next bus stop, 11 people got off and 9 people got on. At the next bus stop, 2 people got off and 2 people got on. At the next bus stop, 12 people got on and 16 people got off. At the next bus stop, 5 people got on and 3 people got off. How many people are now on the bus?

REFLECTIONS

- How sophisticated is your thinking about information processing? For example, do you know what the terms *megabyte, RAM, DVD, zip drive,* and *PCMCIA card* mean? Does your knowledge of these terms affect your ability to think about computers? Why or why not?
- Does understanding of such terms as *alliteration, trochaic foot,* and *blank verse* enhance your ability to appreciate poetry? Why or why not?

SUMMARY

1. **What is thinking?** Thinking is cognitive activity that is involved in understanding, processing, and communicating information. It refers to conscious, planned attempts to make sense of the world.

2. **What are concepts?** Concepts are mental categories that group together objects, events, or ideas with common properties. We tend to organize concepts in hierarchies.

3. **What are prototypes?** Prototypes are good examples of particular concepts.

4. **How do people approach problem solving?** People first attempt to understand the problem. Then they use various strategies for attacking the problem, including algorithms, heuristic devices, and analogies.

5. **What are algorithms, heuristic devices, and analogies?** Algorithms are specific procedures for solving problems (such as formulas) that will invariably work as long as they are applied correctly. Heuristics are rules of thumb that help us simplify and solve problems. Heuristics are less reliable than algorithms, but when they are effective, they allow us to solve problems more rapidly. One commonly used heuristic device is means-end analysis, in which we assess the difference between our current situation and our goals and do what we can to reduce the discrepancy. The analogy heuristic applies the solution of an earlier problem to the solution of a new, similar problem.

6. **What are some factors that affect problem solving?** Five key factors are one's level of expertise, whether one falls prey to a mental set, whether one develops insight into a problem, functional fixedness, and the definition of the problem.

7. **What is creativity?** Creativity is the ability to make unusual and sometimes remote associations to or among the elements of a problem in order to generate new combinations.

8. **What factors appear to account for creativity?** There is only a moderate relationship between creativity and academic ability. Creative people show traits such as flexibility, fluency, and independence. The pressure of social evaluation appears to reduce creativity, and the effects of brainstorming in fostering creativity are debatable.

9. **What kinds of reasoning are there?** In deductive reasoning, one reaches conclusions about premises that are true so long as the premises are true. In inductive reasoning, we reason from individual cases or particular facts to a general conclusion that is not necessarily true.

10. **How do people make decisions?** People sometimes make decisions by carefully weighing the pluses and minuses. However, people who are making decisions frequently use rules of thumb or heuristics, which are shortcuts that are correct (or correct enough) most of the time. According to the representativeness heuristic, people make judgments about events according to the populations of events that they appear to represent. According to the availability heuristic, people's estimates of frequency or probability are based on how easy it is to find examples of relevant events. According to the anchoring and adjustment heuristic, we adjust our initial estimates as we receive additional information—but we often do so unwillingly.

11. **What are some factors that affect decision making?** Our decisions are influenced by the framing effect and by overconfidence.

12. **What is language?** Language is the communication of thoughts and feelings through symbols that are arranged according to rules of grammar. Language has the properties of semanticity, infinite creativity, and displacement.

13. **What are the basic concepts of language?** The basic concepts of language include phonology, morphology, syntax, and semantics.

14. **What are prelinguistic vocalizations?** Crying, cooing, and babbling are prelinguistic; that is, they occur before the infant can use language.

15. **What is telegraphic speech?** Children's early utterances are telegraphic; that is, they eliminate unessential words. Two-word telegraphic utterances appear toward the end of the second year.

16. **How do psychologists explain language development?** The two main theories are learning theories and nativist theories. Learning theories focus on the roles of reinforcement and imitation. Nativist theories assume that innate factors cause children to attend to and perceive language in certain ways.

17. **What are some of the relationships between thought and language?** Thought is possible without language, but language facilitates thought. According to the linguistic-relativity hypothesis, language structures the ways in which we perceive the world. However, most modern cognitive scientists do not support this hypothesis.

To enhance your understanding of the psychological concepts found in this chapter, please consult the following aids:

STUDY GUIDE

Learning Objectives, p. 181
Exercise, p. 182
Lecture and Textbook Outline,
   p. 184
Effective Studying Ideas, p. 186

Key Terms and Concepts, p. 187
Chapter Review, p. 188
Chapter Exercises, p. 196
Knowing the Language, p. 197
Do you Know the Material?, p. 200

CORE CONCEPTS SEARCH

Well-Structured Problems
Ill-Structured Problems
Blocks to Problem Solving
Creativity
Reasoning
The Prisoner's Dilemma
Judgment Heuristics and Fallacies

Ape Communication
Bee Communication
The Phonemic Level
Prototypes
Syntax
Pragmatics

World Wide Web

For more information concerning the topics found in this chapter, access psychology links on the World Wide Web through the Harcourt Brace webpage at

www.hbcollege.com

Share your comments and questions with your author at

PsychLinks@aol.com

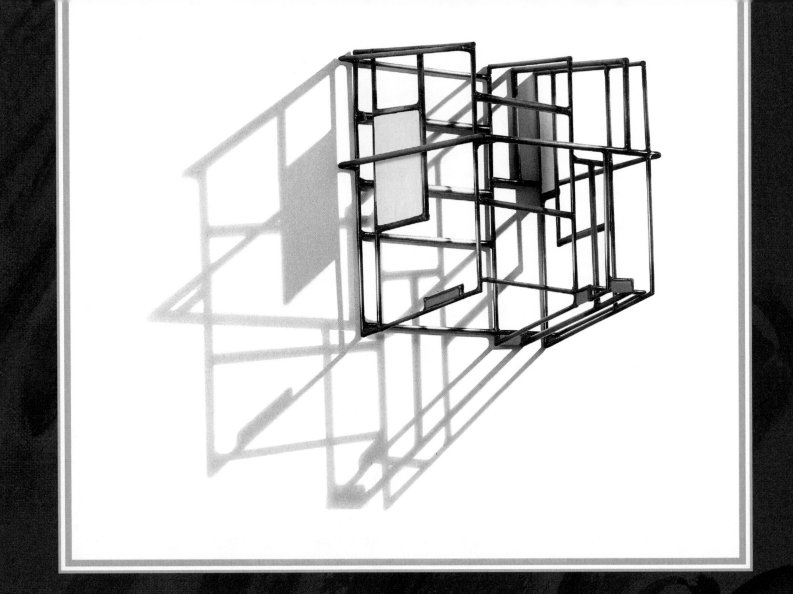

Human intelligence is characterized by the ability to think abstractly and to create shapes and designs that were never found in nature. Helene Brandt's *Mondrian Variations, Construction No. 3B with Four Red Squares and Two Planes* (1996) is an abstraction of an abstraction. Mondrian created two-dimensional paintings with abstract lines and colors. Brandt's three-dimensional sculpture literally adds another dimension to Mondrian's work. How is intelligence related to special talents such as artistic ability? *Is* artistic ability a particular kind of intelligence?

HELENE BRANDT

Chapter 10

Intelligence

TRUTH OR FICTION?

✔ **T F**

☐ ☐ The terms *intelligence* and *IQ* mean the same thing.

☐ ☐ "Street smarts" are a kind of intelligence.

☐ ☐ Two children can answer exactly the same items on an intelligence test correctly, yet one child can be above average and the other below average in IQ.

☐ ☐ Early users of IQ tests administered them in English to immigrants who did not understand the language.

☐ ☐ Head Start programs have raised children's IQs.

OUTLINE

THEORIES OF INTELLIGENCE
Factor Theories
Gardner's Theory of Multiple Intelligences
Sternberg's Triarchic Theory
The Theory of Emotional Intelligence
Psychology in the New Millennium:
Artificial Intelligence

THE MEASUREMENT OF INTELLIGENCE
Individual Intelligence Tests
Group Tests
Psychology in a World of Diversity:
Socioeconomic and Ethnic Differences
in Intelligence

EXTREMES OF INTELLIGENCE
Mental Retardation
Giftedness
Psychology and Modern Life:
Facilitating Development of the
Gifted Child

**THE TESTING CONTROVERSY: JUST
WHAT DO INTELLIGENCE TESTS
MEASURE?**
Is It Possible to Develop Culture-Free
Intelligence Tests?

**DETERMINANTS OF INTELLIGENCE:
WHERE DOES INTELLIGENCE COME
FROM?**
Genetic Influences on Intelligence
Environmental Influences on Intelligence
Psychology in the New Millennium:
Will Music Provide Children With
the Sweet Sounds of Success?
Psychology and Modern Life:
Enhancing Intellectual Functioning
Ethnicity and Intelligence: A Concluding
Note

INTELLIGENCE • A complex and controversial concept. According to David Wechsler (1975), the "capacity . . . to understand the world [and] resourcefulness to cope with its challenges."

*W*HAT FORM OF LIFE IS SO ADAPTIVE THAT it can survive in desert temperatures of 120 degrees Fahrenheit or Arctic climes of −40 degrees Fahrenheit? What form of life can run, walk, climb, swim, live underwater for months on end, and fly to the moon and back?

I won't keep you in suspense any longer. We are that form of life. Yet our unclad bodies do not allow us to adapt to these extremes of temperature. Brute strength does not allow us to live underwater or travel to the moon. Rather, it is our **intelligence** that permits us to adapt to these conditions and to challenge our physical limitations. Our ability to think about abstractions like space and time sets us apart from all other species (Campbell, 1994).

The term *intelligence* is familiar enough. At an early age, we gain impressions of how intelligent we are compared to other people. We associate intelligence with academic success, advancement on the job, and appropriate social behavior. Psychologists view intelligence as a trait—an aspect of personality that may explain, at least in part, why people do (or fail to do) things that are adaptive and inventive.

Even though it's a familiar concept, intelligence cannot be seen, touched, or measured by any physical means. However, the concept of intelligence is tied to predictors, such as scores on intelligence tests, school performance, and occupational status (Brody, 1997; Wagner, 1997). Still, the concept of intelligence is subject to various interpretations. In this chapter we discuss different ways of looking at intelligence. We see how intelligence is measured and discuss group differences in intelligence. Finally, we examine the determinants of intelligence: heredity and the environment.

■ THEORIES OF INTELLIGENCE

Let us distinguish between intelligence and achievement. *Achievement* refers to knowledge and skills that are gained from experience (Ackerman & Heggestad, 1997). It involves specific content such as English, history, or math. The relationship between achievement and experience seems obvious: We are not surprised to find that a student who has taken Spanish, but not French, does better on a Spanish achievement test than on a French achievement test.

The meaning of *intelligence* is more difficult to pin down. Most psychologists agree that intelligence somehow provides the cognitive basis for academic achievement. Intelligence has to do with understanding complex ideas, adapting effectively to the environment, learning from experience, reasoning, and solving problems (Neisser and others, 1996; Sternberg, 1997b). However, psychologists disagree about the nature and origins of intelligence.

• *Factor Theories*

Many investigators have viewed intelligence as consisting of one or more mental abilities, or *factors*. Alfred Binet, the French psychologist who developed modern intelligence-testing methods about 100 years ago, believed that intelligence consists of several related factors. Other investigators have argued that intelligence consists of from one to hundreds of factors.

In 1904, British psychologist Charles Spearman suggested that the behaviors we consider intelligent have a common underlying factor. He labeled this factor **g**, for "general intelligence" or broad reasoning and problem-solving abilities. Spearman supported his view by noting that people rarely score very high in one area (such as knowledge of the meaning of words) and very low in another (such as the ability to compute numbers). People who excel in one area are also likely to excel in others. But he also noted that even the most capable people are relatively superior in some areas—such as music or business or poetry. For this reason, he suggested that specific, or **s**, factors account for specific abilities.

To test his views, Spearman developed **factor analysis.** Factor analysis is a statistical technique that allows researchers to determine which items on tests seem to be measuring the same things. In his research on relationships among scores on tests of verbal, mathematical, and spatial reasoning, Spearman repeatedly found evidence supporting the existence of *s* factors. The evidence for *g* was more limited.

The U.S. psychologist Louis Thurstone (1938) used factor analysis with various tests of specific abilities and also found only limited evidence for the existence of *g*. Thurstone concluded that Spearman had oversimplified the concept of intelligence. Thurstone's data suggested the presence of nine specific factors, which he labeled **primary mental abilities** (see Table 10.1). Thurstone suggested, for example, that we might have high word fluency, enabling us to rapidly develop lists of words that rhyme but not enabling us to solve math problems efficiently (Thurstone & Thurstone, 1963).

This view seems to make sense. Most of us know people who are good at math but poor in English, and vice versa. Still there seems to be some sort of linkage between specific mental abilities. The data still show that a person with excellent reasoning ability is likely to have a larger-than-average vocabulary and better-than-average numerical ability. Few, if any, people exceed 99% of the

Going for a "Walk." Human intelligence permits us to live underwater for months on end or to fly to the moon and back. We are weaker than many other organisms, but intelligence enables us to adapt to the environment, to create new environments, even to go for leisurely "spacewalks." Who can say what wonders human intelligence will devise in the new millennium?

g • Spearman's symbol for general intelligence, which he believed underlay more specific abilities.

s • Spearman's symbol for specific factors, or s factors, which he believed accounted for individual abilities.

FACTOR ANALYSIS • A statistical technique that allows researchers to determine the relationships among large number of items such as test items.

PRIMARY MENTAL ABILITIES • According to Thurstone, the basic abilities that make up intelligence.

TABLE 10.1 PRIMARY MENTAL ABILITIES, ACCORDING TO THURSTONE	
Ability	*Description*
Visual and spatial abilities	Visualizing forms and spatial relationships
Perceptual speed	Grasping perceptual details rapidly, perceiving similarities and differences between stimuli
Numerical ability	Computing numbers
Verbal meaning	Knowing the meanings of words
Memory	Recalling information (words, sentences, etc.)
Word fluency	Thinking of words quickly (rhyming, doing crossword puzzles, etc.)
Deductive reasoning	Deriving examples from general rules
Inductive reasoning	Deriving general rules from examples

population in one mental ability but are exceeded by 80% or 90% of the population in others.

Over the years, psychologist J. P. Guilford (1988) expanded the numbers of factors found in intellectual functioning to hundreds. The problem with this approach seems to be that the more factors we generate, the more overlap we find among them. For example, several of his "factors" deal with solving math problems and computing numbers.

• *Gardner's Theory of Multiple Intelligences*

Howard Gardner (1983) proposes the existence of seven kinds of intelligence. He refers to each of them as "an intelligence" because they can be so different from

FIGURE 10.1

GARDNER'S THEORY OF MULTIPLE INTELLIGENCES

According to Gardner, there are seven *intelligences,* not one, and each is based in a different area of the brain. Two of these involve language ability and logic, which are familiar aspects of intelligence. But Gardner also refers to bodily talents, musical ability, spatial-relations skills, and two kinds of personal intelligence—sensitivity to one's own feelings (intrapersonal sensitivity) and sensitivity to the feelings of others (interpersonal sensitivity) as *intelligences.* Gardner's critics question whether such special talents are truly "intelligences" or specific talents.

one another (see Figure 10.1). He also believes that each kind of intelligence has its neurological base in a different area of the brain. Two of these "intelligences" are familiar ones: language ability and logical-mathematical ability. However, Gardner also refers to bodily-kinesthetic talents (of the sort shown by dancers, mimes, and athletes), musical talent, spatial-relations skills, and two kinds of personal intelligence: awareness of one's own inner feelings and sensitivity to other people's feelings. According to Gardner, one can compose symphonies or advance mathematical theory yet be average in, say, language and personal skills. (Are not some academic "geniuses" foolish in their personal lives?)

Critics of Gardner's view grant that people do function more intelligently in some aspects of life than in others. They also concur that many people have special talents, such as bodily-kinesthetic talents, even if their overall intelligence is quite average. However, they question whether such special talents are "intelligences" per se or whether we should continue to think of them as specific talents (Neisser and others, 1996). Language skills, reasoning ability, and ability to solve math problems seem to be more closely related than musical or gymnastic talent to what most people mean by intelligence. If people have no musical ability, do we really think of them as being *unintelligent?*

• *Sternberg's Triarchic Theory*

Yale University psychologist Robert Sternberg (1985, 1997a) views intelligence in terms of information processing. He focuses on how information "flows" through us and is modified as we adapt to our environments. Sternberg's analysis led him to construct a three-pronged, or *triarchic,* model of intelligence (see Figure 10.2). The types are *componential, experiential,* and *contextual.*

COMPONENTIAL INTELLIGENCE Componential intelligence is what we generally think of as academic ability. It enables us to solve problems and to acquire new knowledge. Problem-solving skills include encoding information, combining and comparing pieces of information, and generating a solution. Consider Sternberg's analogy problem:

Washington is to *one* as *Lincoln* is to (a) 5, (b) 10, (c) 15, (d) 50?

To solve the analogy, we must first correctly *encode* the elements—*Washington, one,* and *Lincoln*—by identifying them and comparing them to other information. We must first encode *Washington* and *Lincoln* as the names of presidents[1] and then try to combine *Washington* and *one* in a meaningful manner. Two possibilities quickly come to mind. Washington was the first president, and his picture is on the $1 bill. We can then generate two possible solutions and try them out. First, was Lincoln the fifth, tenth, fifteenth, or fiftieth president? Second, on what bill is Lincoln's picture found? (Do you need to consult a history book or peek into your wallet at this point?)

Sternberg illustrates academic intelligence through the example of a Yale graduate student. Let's call her Ashley. Ashley scored high on standardized tests such as the Graduate Record Exam and had a nearly perfect undergraduate record. But the Graduate Record Exam does not always predict success (Sternberg & Williams, 1997). Ashley did well her first year of graduate school but then dropped in academic standing because of difficulty in generating ideas for research.

EXPERIENTIAL INTELLIGENCE Experiential intelligence is closest in meaning to creativity. It is defined by the abilities to cope with novel situations and to

---

[1] There are other possibilities. Both are the names of memorials and cities, for example.

Componential Intelligence
(Academic Ability)
Abilities to solve problems,
compare and contrast, judge,
evaluate, and criticize

Experiential Intelligence
(Creativity and Insight)
Abilities to invent, discover,
suppose, or theorize

Practical Intelligence
("Street Smarts")
Abilities to adapt to the demands
of one's environment, apply
knowledge in practical situations

FIGURE 10.2

According to Robert Sternberg, there are three types of intelligence: componential (academic ability), experiential (creativity), and contextual ("street smarts").

profit from experience. The ability to relate novel situations quickly to familiar situations (that is, to perceive similarities and differences) fosters adaptation. Moreover, as a result of experience, we also become able to solve problems more rapidly.

"Beth," another of Sternberg's students, had obtained excellent letters of recommendation from undergraduate instructors who found her highly creative. However, her undergraduate average and her standardized test scores were low compared to those of other students applying to Yale. Nevertheless, Sternberg found Beth an inventive colleague at Yale. Because of her imagination, she surpassed Ashley in performance.

CONTEXTUAL INTELLIGENCE Contextual intelligence is closest in meaning to practical intelligence, or "street smarts." Practical intelligence enables people to adapt to the demands of their environment. For example, keeping a job by adapting one's behavior to the employer's requirements is adaptive. But if the employer is making unreasonable demands, reshaping the environment (by changing the employer's attitudes) or selecting an alternate environment (by finding a more suitable job) is also adaptive (Sternberg, 1997b).

A third graduate student of Sternberg's—"Cheryl"—had the greatest practical intelligence of the three. Cheryl's test scores and letters of recommendation fell between those of Ashley and Beth. Cheryl did average-quality graduate work but landed the best job of the three upon graduation—apparently because of her practical intelligence.

Truth or Fiction Revisited

According to Sternberg, "street smarts" are a type of intelligence — practical intelligence.

● *The Theory of Emotional Intelligence*

In recent years, psychologists Peter Salovey and John Mayer developed the theory of emotional intelligence, which was popularized by *The New York Times* writer Daniel Goleman (1995c). In essence, the theory holds that social and emotional skills are a form of intelligence, just as academic skills are. "Emotional intelligence" bears more than a little resemblance to two of Gardner's "intelligences"—intrapersonal skills and interpersonal skills.

The theory suggests that self-awareness and social awareness are best learned during the "window" of childhood. Failure to develop emotional intelligence is connected with childhood depression and aggression. Moreover, childhood experiences may even mold the brain's emotional responses to life's challenges. Therefore, it is useful for schools to teach skills related to emotional intelligence as well as academic ability. "I can foresee a day," wrote Goleman (1995c), "when education will routinely include [teaching] essential human competencies such as self-awareness, self-control and empathy, and the arts of listening, resolving conflicts and cooperation."

No one argues that self-awareness, self-control, empathy, and cooperation are unimportant. But critics of the theory of emotional intelligence argue that schools may not have the time (or the competence) to teach these skills, and that emotional intelligence may not really be a kind of intelligence at all.

Should emotional intelligence be taught in the schools? Some psychologists believe that "emotional literacy" is as important as literacy (in reading). However, psychologist Robert McCall (1997) echoes the views of other psychologists when he says that "There are so many hours in a day, and one of the characteristics of American schools is we've saddled them with teaching driver's education, sex education, drug education and other skills, to the point that we don't spend as much time on academics as other countries do. There may be consequences for that."

Is emotional intelligence a form of intelligence? Psychologist Ulric Neisser (1997b) says that "The skills that Goleman describes . . . are certainly important for determining life outcomes, but nothing is to be gained by calling them forms of intelligence."

There are thus many views of intelligence—what intelligence is and how many types or kinds of intelligence there may be. We do not yet have the final word on the nature of intelligence, but I would like to share with you David Wechsler's definition of intelligence. Wechsler is the originator of the most widely used series of contemporary intelligence tests, and he defined intelligence as the "capacity of an individual to understand the world [and the] resourcefulness to cope with its challenges" (1975, p. 139). To Wechsler, intelligence involves accurate representation of the world and effective problem solving (adapting to one's environment, profiting from experience, selecting the appropriate formulas and strategies, and so on). His definition leaves open the kinds of resourcefulness—academic, practical, emotional—that are to be considered intelligent.

REFLECTIONS

- How would you have defined *intelligence* before you began reading this chapter? How do psychologists' definitions of intelligence agree with or differ from yours?
- From your own experiences, what seem to be the relationships between general intelligence and special talents such as musical or artistic ability? Do you know people who are "good at everything"? Do you know people who seem to be extremely talented in some areas but not in others? In what areas are they talented?

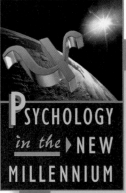

Artificial Intelligence

Saying that Deep Blue (an IBM computer) doesn't really think is like saying an airplane doesn't really fly because it doesn't flap its wings.

DREW MCDERMOTT

Science has brought us a number of artificial objects—artificial sweeteners, designer drugs, and artificial limbs, to name a few. But the new millennium promises to bring major developments in the realm of artificial intelligence. Artificial intelligence, or A.I., is the duplication of human intellectual functioning in computers.

The concept of A.I. has a long history both in science fiction and in actual practice. Think of HAL, the computer in the film *2001.* Not only could HAL coordinate all the monitors and controls of a spaceship but it could also engage in such human activities as committing murder, lying with a straight . . . monitor, and striving to save its own . . . memory chips. The robot C3PO in *Star Wars* not only mimicked human intelligence but also displayed remarkably human anxieties and self-doubts. What about the *Terminator* films? The programming in the artificial combination of flesh and metal portrayed by Arnold Schwarzenegger presented him with options that enabled him to size up any situation and efficiently curse, kill, or utter notable Arnoldisms like "I'll be back."

So much for Hollywood. The idea that human intelligence could be copied in computer form originated in the 1950s. It was predicted that machines with A.I. would "one day" be able to understand spoken language, decipher bad handwriting, search their memories for relevant information, reason, solve problems, make decisions, write books, and explain themselves out loud.

At the time, these predictions were visionary. No longer. "One day" is today. Within certain limits, today's computers are very, very good at encoding storing, retrieving, and manipulating information to solve problems and make decisions.

In some ways, A.I. goes beyond human intelligence. "Deep Blue," the IBM computer that beat grandmaster Garry Kasparov in a 1997 chess match, examined 200 million possible chess moves *each second* (McDermott, 1997). A.I. can solve problems that would take people years to solve, if they could solve them at all. Given clear direction and the right formulas, computers can carry out complex intellectual functions in a flash. "Who," asks University of Illinois professor Patrick Hayes (1993), "can keep track of 10,000 topics like a computer?"

In other ways, A.I. remains less than human. Today's computers do not have the insights, intuitions, and creativity found in people. Their ability to produce original written material is sluggish. (So I still have a job.) The sparks of brilliance we find in computational ability turn into dense wood when we ask today's computers to write prose or compose music. (I hope my computer's not reading this.) Despite our increasing ability to pack huge amounts of memory into tiny chips, the possibility of a HAL—a computer with original thoughts and goals—still seems like science fiction.

The ultimate goal of A.I., notes Hayes, is the creation of a computer that has a human mind. Yet some observers suggest that this goal is unnecessary. They believe that computer science will continue to evolve by improving on the things that computers already do better than people. Freedman (1994) describes projects involving antlike robots, hybrids of computer chips and neurons, even programs that mutate and mate to produce better programs.

Whether or not scientists continue trying to make computers think more like people, we will apparently continue to create computers that have bits and pieces of humanlike intelligence. But what exactly makes our minds human is likely to elude us for the foreseeable future. That thought doesn't bother me a byte. ∎

■ THE MEASUREMENT OF INTELLIGENCE

Although there are disagreements about the nature of intelligence, thousands of intelligence tests are administered by psychologists and educators every day. In this section we examine some of the most widely used intelligence tests.

• Individual Intelligence Tests

Many of the concepts of psychology have their origins in common sense (Kimble, 1994). The commonsense notion that academic achievement depends on children's intelligence led Alfred Binet and Theodore Simon to invent measures of intelligence.

THE STANFORD-BINET INTELLIGENCE TEST   Early in this century, the French public school system was looking for a test that could identify children who were unlikely to benefit from regular classroom instruction (Daniel, 1997). If these children were identified, they could be given special attention. The first version of such a test, the Binet-Simon scale, came into use in 1905. Since that time it has undergone much revision and refinement. The current version is the Stanford-Binet Intelligence Scale (SBIS).

Despite his view that many factors are involved in intellectual functioning, Binet constructed a test that would yield a single overall score so that it could be easily used by the school system. He also assumed that intelligence increases with age, so older children should get more items right than younger children. Binet therefore included a series of age-graded questions, as in Table 10.2, arranged in order of difficulty.

The Binet-Simon scale yielded a score called a **mental age,** or MA. The MA shows the intellectual level at which a child is functioning. For example, a child with an MA of 6 is functioning intellectually like the average 6-year-old. In taking the test, children earned "months" of credit for each correct answer. Their MA was determined by adding up the years and months of credit they attained.

Louis Terman adapted the Binet-Simon scale for use with children in the United States. The first version of the *Stanford*-Binet Intelligence Scale (SBIS)[2] was published in 1916. The SBIS included more items than the original test and was used with children aged 2 to 16. The SBIS also yielded an **intelligence quotient (IQ)** rather than an MA. As a result, American educators developed interest in learning the IQs of their pupils. The SBIS is used today with children from the age of 2 upward and with adults.

[2] The test is so named because Terman carried out his work at Stanford University.

MENTAL AGE • The accumulated months of credit that a person earns on the Stanford-Binet Intelligence Scale. Abbreviated *MA.*

INTELLIGENCE QUOTIENT (IQ) • (1) Originally, a ratio obtained by dividing a child's score (or mental age) on an intelligence test by his or her chronological age. (2) Generally, a score on an intelligence test.

TABLE 10.2		ITEMS SIMILAR TO THOSE ON THE STANFORD-BINET INTELLIGENCE SCALE
Level (Years)	**Item**	
2	1.	Children show knowledge of basic vocabulary words by identifying parts of a doll, such as the mouth, ears, and hair.
	2.	Children show counting and spatial skills along with visual-motor coordination by building a tower of four blocks to match a model.
4	1.	Children show word fluency and categorical thinking by filling in the missing words when they are asked questions such as: "Father is a man; mother is a _____?" "Hamburgers are hot; ice cream is_____?"
	2.	Children show comprehension by answering correctly when they are asked questions such as: "Why do people have automobiles?" "Why do people have medicine?"
9	1.	Children can point out verbal absurdities, as in this question: "In an old cemetery, scientists unearthed a skull which they think was that of George Washington when he was only five years of age. What is silly about that?"
	2.	Children display fluency with words, as shown by answering these questions: "Can you tell me a number that rhymes with snore?" "Can you tell me a color that rhymes with glue?"
Adult	1.	Adults show knowledge of the meanings of words and conceptual thinking by correctly explaining the differences between word pairs like "sickness and misery," "house and home," and "integrity and prestige."
	2.	Adults show spatial skills by correctly answering questions like: "If a car turned to the right to head north, in what direction was it heading before it turned?"

Truth or Fiction Revisited

The terms intelligence *and* IQ *do not mean the same thing. Intelligence is a hypothetical concept on whose meanings psychologists do not agree. An* IQ *is a score on an intelligence test. Can you see any danger in using the terms as if they meant the same thing?*

Truth or Fiction Revisited

It is true that two children can answer exactly the same items on an intelligence test correctly, yet one can be above average and the other below average in IQ. This is because the ages of the children may differ. The more intelligent child would be the younger of the two.

The IQ reflects the relationship between a child's mental age and his or her actual or chronological age (CA). Use of this ratio reflects the fact that the same MA score has different implications for children of different ages. That is, an MA of 8 is an above average score for a 6-year-old but below average for a 10-year-old. In 1912 the German psychologist Wilhelm Stern suggested the IQ as a way to deal with this problem. Stern computed IQ using the formula

$$IQ = \frac{\text{Mental Age (MA)}}{\text{Chronological Age (CA)}} \times 100$$

According to this formula, a child with an MA of 6 and a CA of 6 would have an IQ of 100. Children who can handle intellectual problems as well as older children do will have IQs above 100. For instance, an 8-year-old who does as well on the SBIS as the average 10-year-old will attain an IQ of 125. Children who do not answer as many items correctly as other children of the same age will attain MAs lower than their CAs. Thus, their IQ scores will be below 100.

Today, IQ scores on the SBIS are derived by seeing how much children's and adults' performances deviate from those of other people of the same age.

People who answer more items correctly than the average for people of the same age attain IQ scores above 100. People who answer fewer items correctly than the average for their age attain scores below 100.

THE WECHSLER SCALES The SBIS is the "classic" individual intelligence test. However, today the Wechsler scales are more widely used (Watkins and others, 1995).

David Wechsler developed a series of scales for use with children and adults. The Wechsler scales group test questions into a number of separate subtests such as those shown in Table 10.3. Each subtest measures a different type of intellectual task. For this reason, the test shows how well a person does on one type of task (such as defining words) as compared with another (such as using blocks to construct geometric designs). In this way, the Wechsler scales highlight children's relative strengths and weaknesses, as well as measure overall intellectual functioning.

As you can see in the table, Wechsler described some of his scales as measuring *verbal* tasks and others as assessing *performance* tasks. In general, verbal subtests require knowledge of verbal concepts, whereas performance subtests require familiarity with spatial-relations concepts. (Figure 10.3 shows items similar to those found on the performance scales of the Wechsler tests.) But it is not that easy to distinguish between the two groupings. For example, associating to the name of the object being pieced together in subtest 11—a sign of word fluency and general knowledge as well as of spatial-relations ability—helps the person construct it more rapidly. In any event, Wechsler's scales permit the computation of verbal and performance IQs. It is not unusual for nontechnically oriented college students to attain higher verbal than performance IQs.

Taking the Wechsler. The Wechsler intelligence scales consist of verbal and performance subtests such as the one shown in this photograph.

TABLE 10.3 SUBTESTS FROM THE WECHSLER ADULT INTELLIGENCE SCALE	
Verbal Subtests	**Performance Subtests**
1. *Information:* "What is the capital of the United States?" "Who was Shakespeare?"	7. *Digit Symbol:* Learning and drawing meaningless figures that are associated with numbers.
2. *Comprehension:* "Why do we have ZIP codes?" "What does 'A stitch in time saves 9' mean?"	8. *Picture completion:* Pointing to the missing part of a picture.
3. *Arithmetic:* "If 3 candy bars cost 25 cents, how much will 18 candy bars cost?"	9. *Block Design:* Copying pictures of geometric designs using multicolored blocks.
4. *Similarities:* "How are good and bad alike?" "How are peanut butter and jelly alike?"	10. *Picture Arrangement:* Arranging cartoon picures in sequence so that they tell a meaningful story.
5. *Digit Span:* Repeating a series of numbers forwards and backwards.	11. *Object Assembly:* Putting pieces of a puzzle together so that they form a meaningful object.
6. *Vocabulary:* "What does *canal* mean?"	

Note: Items for verbal subtests 1, 2, 3, 4, and 6 are similar, but not identical, to actual test items on the Wechsler Adult Intelligence Scale.

FIGURE 10.3

PERFORMANCE ITEMS OF AN INTELLIGENCE TEST

These tasks resemble those in the performance subtests of the Wechsler Adult Intelligence Scale.

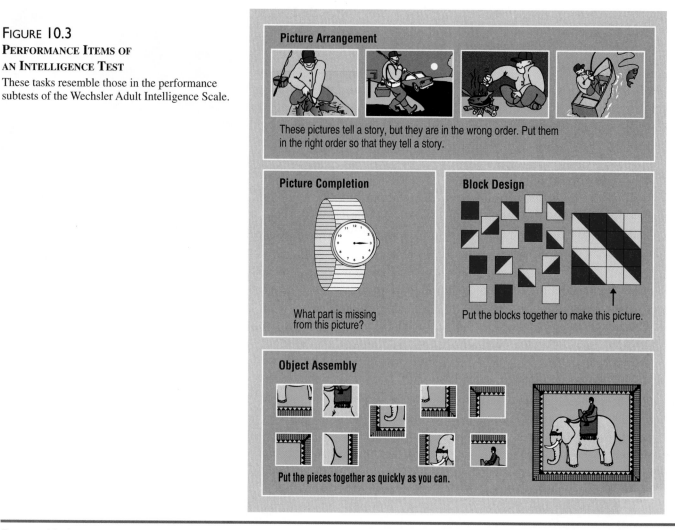

FIGURE 10.4

APPROXIMATE DISTRIBUTION OF IQ SCORES

Wechsler defined the deviation IQ so that 50% of scores fall within the broad average range of 90–110. This bell-shaped curve is referred to as a *normal curve* by psychologists. It describes the distribution of many traits, including height.

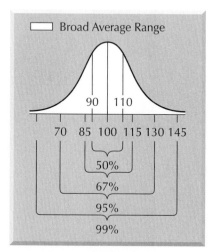

Wechsler also introduced the concept of the deviation IQ. Instead of using mental and chronological ages to compute an IQ, he based IQ scores on how a person's answers compare with (or deviate from) those attained by people in the same age group. The average test result at any age level is defined as an IQ score of 100. Wechsler then distributed IQ scores so that the middle 50% of them would fall within the "broad average range" of 90 to 110.

As you can see in Figure 10.4, most IQ scores cluster around the average. Only 4% of the population have IQ scores of above 130 or below 70. Table 10.4 indicates the labels that Wechsler assigned to various IQ scores and the approximate percentages of the population who attain IQ scores at those levels.

• *Group Tests*

The SBIS and Wechsler scales are administered to one person at a time. This one-to-one ratio is considered optimal. It allows the examiner to facilitate performance (within the limits of the standardized directions) and to observe the test taker closely. Examiners thus are alerted to factors that impair performance, such as language difficulties, illness, or a noisy or poorly lit room. But large institutions with few trained examiners, such as the public schools and

TABLE 10.4	VARIATIONS IN IQ SCORES	
Range of Scores	**Percent of Population**	**Brief Description**
130 and above	2	Very superior
120–129	7	Superior
110–119	16	Above average
100–109	25	High average
90–99	25	Low average
80–89	16	Slow learner
70–79	7	Borderline
Below 70	2	Intellectually deficient

armed forces, require tests that can be administered simultaneously to large groups of people.

Group tests for children, first developed during World War I, were administered to 4 million children by 1921, a couple of years after the war had ended. At first these tests were heralded as remarkable instruments because they helped school administrators place children. However, as the years passed, group tests came under increasing attack, because many administrators relied on them exclusively and did not seek other sources of information about children's abilities and achievements.

At their best, intelligence tests provide just one source of information about individual children. Numbers alone, and especially IQ scores, cannot adequately reflect children's special abilities and talents.

REFLECTIONS

- Have you ever taken an intelligence test? Was it an individual test or a group test? What was the experience like? Were you told your score? Do you believe that the test assessed your abilities fairly? Why or why not?
- What types of items ought to be included on intelligence tests? Do the tests discussed in this chapter appear to include the types of things that you consider important?

Psychology in a World of
DIVERSITY

Socioeconomic and Ethnic Differences in Intelligence

There is a body of research suggestive of differences in intelligence between socioeconomic and ethnic groups (Suzuki & Valencia, 1997). Lower-class U.S. children obtain IQ scores some 10 to 15 points lower than those obtained by middle- and upper-class children. African American children tend to obtain

Who's Smart? Asian children and Asian American children frequently outperform American children on tests of cognitive skills. Sue and Okazaki suggest that Asian Americans place great value on education because they have been discriminated against in careers that do not require advanced education.

IQ scores some 15 points lower than those obtained by their White agemates (Neisser and others, 1996). Hispanic American and Native American children also tend to score below the norms for White children (Neisser and others, 1996).

Several studies of IQ have confused the factors of social class and ethnicity because disproportionate numbers of African Americans, Hispanic Americans, and Native Americans are found among the lower socioeconomic classes (Neisser and others, 1996). When we limit our observations to particular ethnic groups, however, we still find an effect for social class. That is, middle-class Whites outscore lower-class Whites. Middle-class African Americans, Hispanic Americans, and Native Americans also outscore lower-class members of their own ethnic groups.

Research has also suggested that there may be cognitive differences between Asians and White people. Asian Americans, for example, frequently outscore White Americans on the math portion of the Scholastic Aptitude Test. Students in China (Taiwan) and Japan also outscore Americans on standardized achievement tests in math and science (Stevenson and others, 1986). In the United States, moreover, people of Asian Indian, Korean, Japanese, Filipino, and Chinese descent are more likely to graduate from high school and complete four years of college than White Americans, African Americans, and Hispanic Americans (Sue & Okazaki, 1990). Asian Americans are vastly overrepresented in competitive colleges and universities. They make up only about 3% of the U.S. population but account for 12% of the undergraduates at MIT and 24% and 33%, respectively, at the University of California campuses at Berkeley and Irvine (*Chronicle of Higher Education,* 1992).

These ethnic differences appear to reflect cultural attitudes toward education rather than differences in intelligence, per se (Neisser and others, 1996). That is, the Asian children may be more motivated to work hard in school. Research shows that Chinese and Japanese students and their mothers tend to attribute academic successes to hard work. American mothers, in contrast, are more likely to attribute their children's academic successes to "natural" ability (Basic Behavioral Science Task Force, 1996c).

Sue and Okazaki (1990) agree. They note that the achievements of Asian students reflect different values in the home, the school, or the culture at large. They argue that Asian Americans have been discriminated against in careers that do not require advanced education. They therefore place relatively greater emphasis on education. Looking to other environmental factors, Steinberg and his colleagues (1992a) claim that parental encouragement and supervision in combination with peer support for academic achievement partially explain the superior performances of White and Asian Americans as compared with African and Hispanic Americans. Even so, one-third of a sample of 20,000 high school students of all ethnic backgrounds reported that their parents had no idea how well they were doing in school (Steinberg, 1996). One in three admitted to spending their days basically "goofing off with friends" (Steinberg, 1996).

REFLECTIONS

- Lower-class children in the United States obtain IQ scores some 10 to 15 points lower than those obtained by middle- and upper-class children. Explain this finding from a genetic point of view. Then explain it from an environmental point of view. (Later in the chapter we will explore how genetic and environmental factors contribute to intellectual functioning.)
- Agree or disagree, and support your answer: "Studies of IQ have confused the factors of social class and ethnicity."
- What is your ethnic background? Are there stereotypes about how people from your background perform on intelligence tests? Do these stereotypes affect you? If so, how?

■ EXTREMES OF INTELLIGENCE

The average IQ score in the United States is very close to 100. About 50% of U.S. children obtain IQ scores in the broad average range from 90 to 110. Nearly 95% obtain scores between 70 and 130. But what about the other 5%? Children who obtain IQ scores below 70 are generally labeled as intellectually deficient or mentally retarded. Children who obtain scores of 130 or above are usually labeled as gifted. Both of these labels create certain expectations. Both can place heavy burdens on children and their parents.

• *Mental Retardation*

According to the American Association on Mental Retardation, mental retardation "refers to substantial limitations in present functioning [as] characterized by significantly sub-average intellectual functioning [including an IQ score of no more than 70 to 75], existing concurrently with related limitations in two or more of the following applicable adaptive skill areas: communication, self-care, home living, social skills, community use, self-direction, health and safety, functional academics, leisure and work" (Michaelson,

TABLE 10.5 ITEMS FROM THE VINELAND ADAPTIVE BEHAVIOR SCALES

Age Level	Item
1 year, 8 months	Removes front-opening coat, sweater, or shirt without assistance.
1 year, 10 months	Says at least 50 recognizable words.
3 years, 7 months	Tells popular story, fairy tale, lengthy joke, or plot of television program.
4 years, 9 months	Ties shoelaces into a bow without assistance.
5 years, 2 months	Keeps secrets or confidences for more than one day.
7 years, 7 months	Watches television or listens to radio for information about a particular area of interest.
8 years, 8 months	Uses the telephone for all kinds of calls without assistance.
10 years, 2 months	Responds to hints or indirect cues in conversation.
12 years, 2 months	Looks after own health.

Note: Adapted from *Vineland Adaptive Behavior Scales,* by S. S. Sparrow, D. A. Ballo, and D. V. Cicchetti, 1984, Circle Pines, MN: American Guidance Service.

1993). Mental retardation is typically assessed through a combination of children's IQ scores and behavioral observations. A number of scales have been developed to assess adaptive behavior. Items from the Vineland Adaptive Behavior Scales are shown in Table 10.5.

Table 10.6 describes several levels of retardation. Most of the children who are retarded (about 80%) are mildly retarded. They are capable of adjusting to the demands of educational institutions and, eventually, to society at large. Mildly retarded children are also likely to be taught in regular classrooms, as opposed to being placed in special needs classes. This approach is intended to give mildly retarded children the best possible education and encourage socialization with children at all intellectual levels. Unfortunately, some mildly retarded children are overwhelmed by regular classrooms and avoided by their classmates.

Children with Down syndrome are most likely to fall within the moderately retarded range. As suggested in Table 10.6, moderately retarded children can learn to speak; to dress, feed, and clean themselves; and eventually to engage in work under supportive conditions, as in sheltered workshops. However, they usually do not learn how to read or compute numbers. Severely and profoundly retarded children may not acquire speech and self-help skills and are likely to remain highly dependent on others throughout their lives.

CAUSES OF RETARDATION Some of the causes of mental retardation are biological. Retardation, for example, can stem from chromosomal abnormalities such as Down syndrome, from genetic disorders such as phenylketonuria, or from brain damage. Brain damage may have many origins, including accidents during childhood and problems during pregnancy. Maternal alcohol abuse, malnutrition, or diseases during pregnancy can all lead to retardation in the infant.

TABLE 10.6	LEVELS OF RETARDATION, TYPICAL RANGES OF IQ SCORES, AND TYPES OF ADAPTIVE BEHAVIORS		
Approximate IQ Score Range	*Preschool Age (0–5) Maturation and Development*	*School Age (6–21) Training and Education*	*Adult (21 and Over) Social and Vocational Adequacy*
Mild (50–70)	Often not noticed as retarded by casual observer but is slower than most children to walk, feed self, and talk	Can acquire practical skills and useful reading and arithmetic to a 3rd to 6th grade level with special education. Can be guided toward social conformity.	Can usually achieve social and vocational skills adequate to self-maintenance; may need occasional guidance and support when under unusual social or economic stress.
Moderate (35–49)	Noticeable delays in motor development, especially in speech; responds to training in various self-help activities.	Can learn simple communication, elementary health and safety habits, and simple manual skills; does not progress in functional reading or arithmetic.	Can perform simple tasks under sheltered conditions; participates in simple recreation; travels alone in familiar places; usually incapable of self-maintenance.
Severe (20–34)	Marked delay in motor development; little or no communication skill; may respond to training in elementary self-help—e.g., self-feeding.	Usually walks, barring specific disability; has some understanding of speech and some response; can profit from systematic habit training.	Can conform to daily routines and repetitive activities; needs continuing direction and supervision in protective environment.
Profound (Below 20)	Gross retardation; minimal capacity for functioning in sensorimotor areas; needs nursing care.	Obvious delays in all areas of development; shows basic emotional responses; may respond to skillful training in use of legs, hands, and jaws; needs close supervision.	May walk, need nursing care, have primitive speech; will usually benefit from regular physical activity; incapable of self-maintenance.

• *Giftedness*

Giftedness involves more than excellence in the tasks provided by standard intelligence tests. Most educators include children who have outstanding abilities, are capable of high performance in a specific academic area such as language arts or mathematics, or who show creativity or leadership, distinction in the visual or performing arts, or talent in physical activities such as gymnastics and dancing. This view of giftedness exceeds the realm of intellectual ability alone and is consistent with Gardner's view that there are multiple intelligences, not just one.

THE TERMAN STUDIES OF GENIUS Much of our knowledge of the progress of children who are gifted in overall intellectual functioning stems from Louis Terman's classic longitudinal studies of genius (Janos, 1987). In 1921, Terman began to track the progress of some 1,500 California schoolchildren who had attained IQ scores of 135 or above. The average score was 150, which places these children in a very superior group.

As adults, the group was extremely successful, compared with the general population, in terms of level of education (nearly 10% had earned doctoral degrees), socioeconomic status, and creativity (the group had published more than 90 books and many more shorter pieces). Boys were much more likely than girls to climb the corporate ladder or distinguish themselves in science, literature, or the arts. But we must keep in mind that the Terman study began in the 1920s, when it was generally agreed that a woman's place was in the home. As a result, more than two-thirds of the girls became full-time homemakers or office workers (Lips, 1993). Some of the women later expressed regret that they had not fulfilled their potential. But both the women and men in the study were well-adjusted, with rates of psychological disorders and suicide below the national average.

> ## REFLECTIONS
>
> - Do you know a person who is mentally retarded? What is known about the causes of the retardation? Does the person have social and other adjustment problems? What kind of educational or training experiences is he or she receiving? Do they seem to be appropriate? Why or why not?
> - Do you know a person who is gifted? Does this person also have special talents, as in math, music, or art? Does the giftedness seem to be connected with social advantages or social problems? In what ways? What kinds of educational experiences is this person receiving? Do they seem to be appropriate? Why or why not?

psychology and modern life

FACILITATING DEVELOPMENT OF THE GIFTED CHILD

Two to 3 percent of our children are gifted. How can we help them achieve their full potentials? In a number of ways:

- Give them books, CD-ROMs, and other learning devices. Research shows that the parents of gifted children spend more time reading to them, playing with them, and taking them on stimulating outings than do the parents of other children (Fowler and others, 1993). Responsive, sensitive parenting—and not pushing—appears to facilitate development of the gifted child (Robinson, 1992).

- Enrich the school curriculum. Educational programs for gifted students typically involve enriching

or accelerating the curriculum. Enrichment may include after school activities in language, art, and music (Winner, 1997). Acceleration may involve covering all of the normal curriculum but in a shorter period of time (Mills, 1992).

- Consider skipping a grade. Many gifted children accelerate their curriculum by skipping grades. Unless children are "ready" to be advanced socially as well as intellectually, skipping may cause them to experience social and emotional problems (Southern & Jones, 1991). But most studies find that skipping grades can be beneficial to the social and emotional development of gifted chil-

dren, as well as to their academic progress (Benbow, 1991; Robinson, 1992). The task here is to pay attention to *the whole child*—not just her or his intellectual ability.

In case you have not noticed, this "Psychology and Modern Life" features contains some advice that is suitable for all children. Nearly all children—not just gifted children—can profit from books (reading books or having books read to them) and stimulating outings. Nearly all children can profit from facilitating the development of their special talents—or ordinary abilities. Even physically and mentally challenged children profit from participating in programs such as Special Olympics, which encourage them to be all that they can be. ■

THE TESTING CONTROVERSY: JUST WHAT DO INTELLIGENCE TESTS MEASURE?

It is no secret that during the 1920s intelligence tests were used to prevent many Europeans and others from immigrating to the United States. For example, testing pioneer H. H. Goddard assessed 178 newly arrived immigrants at Ellis Island and claimed that the great majority of Jews, Hungarians, Italians, and Russians were "feeble-minded." Apparently it was of little concern to Goddard that these immigrants, by and large, did not understand English—the language in which the tests were administered!

It is now recognized that intelligence tests cannot be considered valid when they are used with people who do not understand the language. But what of cultural differences? Are the tests valid when used with ethnic minority groups or people who are poorly educated? A survey of psychologists and educational specialists by Mark Snyderman and Stanley Rothman (1987, 1990) found that most consider intelligence tests somewhat biased against African Americans and members of the lower classes. Elementary and secondary schools may also place too much emphasis on them in making educational placements.

Intelligence tests measure traits that are required in developed, "high-tech" societies. The vocabulary and arithmetic subtests on the Wechsler scales, for example, reflect achievements in language skills and computational ability. The broad achievements measured by these tests reflect intelligence, but they also reflect familiarity with the cultural concepts required to answer test questions correctly. In particular, the tests seem to reflect middle-class White culture in the United States (Garcia, 1981).

• Is It Possible to Develop Culture-Free Intelligence Tests?

If scoring well on intelligence tests requires a certain type of cultural experience, the tests are said to have a **cultural bias.** Children reared in African American neighborhoods could be at a disadvantage, not because of differences in intelligence but because of cultural differences (Helms, 1992) and economic deprivation. For this reason, some psychologists, including Raymond B. Cattell (1949) and Florence Goodenough (1954), have tried to construct **culture-free** intelligence tests.

Cattell's Culture-Fair Intelligence Test evaluates reasoning ability through the child's ability to comprehend the rules that govern a progression of geometric designs, as shown in Figure 10.5. Goodenough's Draw-A-Person test is based on the premise that children from all cultural backgrounds have had the opportunity to observe people and note the relationships between the parts and the whole. Her instructions simply require children to draw a picture of a man or a woman.

FIGURE 10.5

SAMPLE ITEMS FROM CATTELL'S CULTURE-FAIR INTELLIGENCE TEST

Culture-fair tests attempt to exclude items that discriminate on the basis of cultural background.

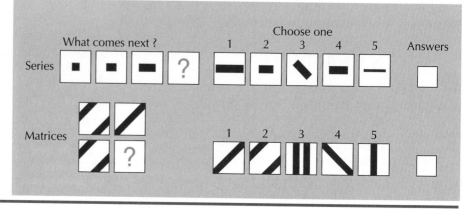

> ## REFLECTIONS
> * Consider your own ethnic group and the shared experiences of members of that group. Could you write an "intelligence test" that would give members of your ethnic group an advantage over other test takers? What types of items might you include?

■ DETERMINANTS OF INTELLIGENCE: WHERE DOES INTELLIGENCE COME FROM?

When I was in graduate school, a professor remarked that many people think of intelligence as "a knob in the head. Some people have a bigger knob and some people have a smaller one." That is, many people see intelligence as a fixed commodity. From this perspective, some people have more intelligence, some people less, and nothing much can be done about it.

In recent years this view of intelligence—as a sort of knob in the head—has been expressed most forcefully by psychologist Richard Herrnstein and political theorist Charles Murray (1994) in their book *The Bell Curve*. The book made the following assertions:

1. Intelligence tests are valid indicators of intelligence (that is, *IQ* is an accurate measure of intelligence).

2. A person's intelligence is mainly due to heredity.

3. People with less intelligence (smaller "knobs in the head") are having more children than people with more intelligence ("bigger knobs"), so that the overall intelligence of the population of the United States is declining.

4. The United States is becoming divided in two, with a large lower class of people with low intelligence and a smaller class of wealthier people who are higher in intelligence.

5. Education can do little to affect intelligence (the size of the "knob").

The Bell Curve poured oil onto the fires of controversy over social class, race, and intelligence, even though Murray (1995) asserts that the book had nothing to do with race. Because of Murray's reasonable speaking style, his apparent scientific approach, and his claim that the book is not intended to justify or maintain the status quo of White economic supremacy, Murray has been referred to as "the most dangerous conservative in America" (Upstream, 1997). Of course it is true that poorer people tend to be lower in IQ than wealthier people are. It is also true that African Americans are poorer than the average American, and that the IQ scores of African Americans are lower, on the average, than those of the average American.

As pointed out by Herrnstein and Murray's critics, however, intelligence is *not* a knob in the head. Nor is intelligence mainly heritable. They argue that IQ is affected by early learning experiences, academic and vocational motivation, and formal education (Kamin, 1995; Steele, 1994).

Let us now discuss the roles of heredity and environmental influences on intelligence more fully. If different ethnic groups tend to score differently on intelligence tests, psychologists—like educators and other people involved in public life—want to know why. We will see that this is one debate that can make use of key empirical findings. Psychologists can point with pride to a rich mine of contemporary research on the roles of nature (genetic influences) and nurture (environmental influences) in the development of intelligence.

• *Genetic Influences on Intelligence*

Research on genetic influences on human intelligence employs several basic strategies. These include kinship studies, twin studies, and adoptee studies (Neisser and others, 1996).

KINSHIP STUDIES We can examine the IQ scores of closely and distantly related people who have been reared together or apart. If heredity is involved in human intelligence, closely related people ought to have more similar IQs than distantly related or unrelated people, even when they are reared separately.

Figure 10.6 is a composite of the results of more than 100 studies of IQ and heredity in human beings (Bouchard and others, 1990). The IQ scores of identical

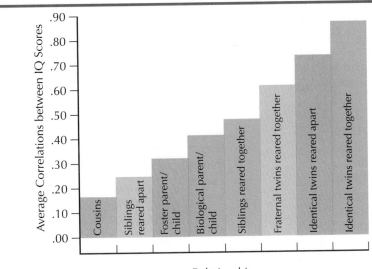

FIGURE 10.6

FINDINGS OF STUDIES OF THE RELATIONSHIP BETWEEN IQ SCORES AND HEREDITY

The data are a composite of studies summarized in *Science* magazine (Bouchard and others, 1990). By and large, correlations are greater between pairs of people who are more closely related. Yet people who are reared together also have more similar IQ scores than people who are reared apart. Such findings suggest that both genetic and environmental factors contribute to IQ scores.

(monozygotic or MZ) twins are more alike than scores for any other pairs, even when the twins have been reared apart. There are moderate correlations between the IQ scores of fraternal (dizygotic or DZ) twins, between those of siblings, and between those of parents and their children. Correlations between the scores of children and their foster parents and between those of cousins are weak.

TWIN STUDIES The results of large-scale twin studies are consistent with the data in Figure 10.6. For instance, a study of 500 pairs of MZ and DZ twins in Louisville, Kentucky (Wilson, 1983), found that the correlations in intelligence between MZ twins were about the same as that for MZ twins in Figure 10.6. The correlations in intelligence between DZ twin pairs was the same as that between other siblings. Research at the University of Minnesota with sets of twins who were reared together and others who were reunited in adulthood has obtained essentially similar results (Bouchard and others, 1990). In the MacArthur Longitudinal Twin Study, Robert Emde (1993) and his colleagues examined the intellectual abilities of 200 primarily White, healthy 14-month-old pairs of twins. They found that identical (MZ) twins were more similar than fraternal (DZ) twins in spatial memory, ability to categorize things, and word comprehension. Emde and his colleagues concluded that genes tend to account for about 40% to 50% of differences in children's cognitive skills (Adler, 1993a).

All in all, studies generally suggest that the **heritability** of intelligence is between 40% and 60% (Bouchard and others, 1990; Neisser and others, 1996). In other words, about half of the variations (the technical term is *variance*) in IQ scores can be accounted for by heredity. This is *not* the same as saying that you inherited about half of your intelligence. The implication of such a statement would be that you "got" the other half of your intelligence somewhere else. It means, rather, that about half of the difference between your IQ score and the IQ scores of other people can be explained in terms of genetic factors.

Even this view of the heritability of intelligence may be too broad to be highly accurate. Research also suggests that the heritability of verbal ability is greater than the heritability of factors such as spatial-relations ability and the ability to recall a list of numbers (Thompson and others, 1991).

Note, too, that genetic pairs (such as MZ twins) who were reared together show higher correlations in their IQ scores than similar genetic pairs (such as other MZ twins) who were reared apart. This finding holds for MZ twins, siblings, parents and their children, and unrelated people. Being reared together is therefore related with similarities in IQ. *For this reason, the same group of studies that are used to demonstrate a role for the heritability of IQ scores also suggests that the environment plays a role in the determination of IQ scores.*

ADOPTEE STUDIES Another strategy for exploring genetic influences on intelligence is to compare the correlations between the IQ scores of adopted children and those of their biological and adoptive parents (Coon and others, 1990). When children are separated from their biological parents at an early age, one can argue that strong relationships between their IQs and those of their natural parents reflect genetic influences. Strong relationships between the childrens' IQs and those of their adoptive parents might reflect environmental influences.

Several studies with 1- and 2-year-old children in Colorado (Baker and others, 1983), Texas (Horn, 1983), and Minnesota (Scarr & Weinberg, 1983) have

HERITABILITY • The degree to which the variations in a trait from one person to another can be attributed to, or explained by, genetic factors.

found a stronger relationship between the IQ scores of adopted children and those of their biological parents than between the children's scores and those of their adoptive parents. The Scarr and Weinberg report concerns African American children reared by White adoptive parents. We will return to its findings in the section on environmental influences on intelligence.

In sum, genetic factors may account for about half of the variation in intelligence test scores among individuals. Environmental factors also affect scores on intelligence tests.

• Environmental Influences on Intelligence

Studies of environmental influences also employ a variety of research strategies. These include manipulation of the testing situation, observation of the role of the home environment, and evaluation of the effects of educational programs.

THE TESTING SITUATION One approach focuses on the situational factors that determine IQ scores. Remember that an IQ is a score on a test. Thus, in some cases the testing situation itself can explain part of the social class difference in IQ. In one study the experimenters (Zigler and others, 1982) simply made children as comfortable as possible during the test. Rather than being cold and impartial, the examiner was warm and friendly. Care was also taken to see that the children understood the directions. One result was that the children's test anxiety was markedly reduced. Another was that their IQ scores were 6 points higher than those for a control group of children who were treated in a more indifferent manner. Disadvantaged children made relatively greater gains from the modified testing procedure. The argument of *The Bell Curve* that intelligence tests are valid indicators of intelligence begins to fall apart with the nature of the testing situation. *By doing nothing more than make testing conditions more optimal for* all *children, we may narrow the IQ gap between White and African American children.*

Stereotype vulnerability also affects test scores. Psychologist Claude Steele (1996, 1997) suggests that African American students carry an extra burden in performing scholastic tasks: They believe that they risk confirming their group's negative stereotype by doing poorly on such tasks. This concern creates performance anxiety. Performance anxiety distracts them from the tasks, and as a result they perform more poorly than White students in the same situation.

In an experiment designed to test this view, Steele and Aronson (1995) gave two groups of African American and White Stanford undergraduates the most difficult verbal skills test questions from the Graduate Record Exam. One group was told that the researchers were attempting to learn about the "psychological factors involved in solving verbal problems." The other group was told that the

STEREOTYPE VULNERABILITY • The tendency to focus on a conventional, negative belief about one's group, such that the individual risks behaving in a way that confirms that belief.

items were "a genuine test of your verbal abilities and limitations." African American students who were given the first message performed as well as White students. African American students who were given the second message—that proof of their abilities was on the line—performed significantly more poorly than the White students. Apparently the second message triggered their stereotype vulnerability, which led them to self-destruct on the test. Steele's findings are further evidence of the limits of the validity of intelligence tests as valid indicators of intelligence.

HOME ENVIRONMENT AND STYLES OF PARENTING The home environment and styles of parenting also appear to have an effect on IQ scores (Coon and others, 1990; Olson and others, 1992; Steinberg and others, 1992b; Suzuki & Valencia, 1997). Children of mothers who are emotionally

PSYCHOLOGY in the ▶ NEW MILLENNIUM

Will Music Provide Children With the Sweet Sounds of Success?

We can expect that technological innovations will overleap themselves in the new millennium. Parents will undoubtedly be concerned about what they can do to help their children grasp the new technologies. Whatever environmental factors are found to enhance children's intellectual functioning may well be music to parents' ears. But it may also turn out that music will be spatial reasoning to children's ears.

Research in the 1990s suggests that listening to and studying music may enhance one aspect of intellectual functioning—spatial reasoning. In October 1993 the research team of Frances Rauscher, Gordon Shaw, and Katherine Ky—all of the University of California at Irvine—published an intriguing article in *Nature* on the effects of listening to the music of Mozart. According to

that study, listening to 10 minutes of Mozart's Piano Sonata K 448 on a number of occasions enhanced college students' scores on spatial reasoning tasks of the kind found on intelligence tests.

At the 1994 meeting of the American Psychological Association, the research team of Rauscher, Shaw, Linda Levine, Ky, and Eric Wright reported the results of a follow-up study with preschoolers in a paper titled "Music and spatial task performance: A causal relationship." They recruited 19 preschool children aged from 3 years to 4 years 9 months and gave them 8 months of music lessons, including singing and use of a keyboard. After the lessons the children's scores on an object assembly task significantly exceeded those of 15 preschoolers who did not receive the musical training.

How might listening to music or training in music affect spatial reasoning? The neural pathways involved in processing music apparently overlap those involved in a number of other cognitive functions—such as spatial reasoning (Blakeslee, 1995). Musical training thus develops the neural firing patterns used in spatial reasoning, which may eventually help children solve geometry problems, design skyscrapers, navigate ships, perhaps even fit suitcases into the trunk of a car.

Note the implications for Gardner's theory of multiple intelligences. If the Rauscher team's research withstands the tests of time and replication, it may be that

and verbally responsive, provide appropriate play materials, are involved with their children, and provide varied daily experiences during the early years obtain higher IQ scores later on (Bradley and others, 1989; Gottfried and others, 1994). Organization and safety in the home have also been linked to higher IQs at later ages and to higher achievement test scores during the first grade (Bradley and others, 1989).

Dozens of other studies support the view that children's early environment is linked to IQ scores and academic achievement. For example, McGowan and Johnson (1984) found that good parent-child relationships and maternal encouragement of independence were both positively linked to Mexican American children's IQ scores by the age of three. A number of studies have also found that high levels of maternal restrictiveness and punishment of children at 24 months are linked to *lower* IQ scores later on.

The Sweet Sounds of Success?
Research suggests that training in music improves children's spatial reasoning ability. Do musical activities and spatial reasoning use the same neural pathways?

musical talent and spatial skills represent one kind of intelligence and not two.

The researchers caution that their findings should be considered preliminary. It is not known, for example, whether the training effects endure or whether they will extend to older children, whose cerebral cortex is more mature.

But perhaps the findings are enticing enough to encourage school administrators to maintain music programs, which are often among the first to go when school districts tighten the purse strings. Music, after all, may contribute to the sweet sounds of success. ∎

Head Start. Preschoolers who are placed in Head Start programs have shown dramatic improvements in readiness for elementary school and in IQ scores.

Truth or Fiction Revisited
....
It is true that Head Start programs have raised children's IQs.

EDUCATION Government-funded efforts to provide preschoolers with enriched early environments have also led to intellectual gains. Head Start programs, for example, enhance the IQ scores, achievement test scores, and academic skills of disadvantaged children (Barnett & Escobar, 1990; Hauser-Cram and others, 1991; Zigler, 1995) by exposing them to materials and activities that middle-class children take for granted. These include letters and words, numbers, books, exercises in drawing, pegs and pegboards, puzzles, toy animals, and dolls.

There is solid research evidence that preschool intervention programs can have major long-term effects on children. During the elementary and high school years, graduates of preschool programs are less likely to be left back or placed in classes for slow learners. They are more likely to graduate from high school, go on to college, and earn higher incomes. Early childhood intervention also decreases the likelihood of juvenile delinquency, unemployment, and welfare recipiency (Schweinhart & Weikart, 1993; Zigler and others, 1992).

Schooling at later ages also contributes to intelligence test scores. When children of about the same age start school a year apart because of admissions standards related to their date of birth, children who have been in school longer obtain higher IQ scores (Neisser and others, 1996). Moreover, IQ test scores tend to decrease during the summer vacation (Neisser and others, 1996).

All these findings—on intelligence and the home environment and educational experiences—contradict *The Bell Curve's* argument that little or nothing can be done to enhance intellectual functioning in children.

ADOPTEE STUDIES The Minnesota adoption studies reported by Scarr and Weinberg suggest a genetic influence on intelligence. But the same studies (Scarr & Weinberg, 1976, 1977) also suggest a role for environmental influences. African American children who were adopted during their first year by White parents with above average income and education obtained IQ scores some 15 to 25 points higher than those obtained by African American children reared by their natural parents (Scarr & Weinberg, 1976). There are two cautions regarding these findings. One is that the adoptees' average IQ score, about 106, remained below those of their adoptive parents' natural children—117 (Scarr & Weinberg, 1977). The second is that follow-up studies of the adopted children at the age of 17 found that the mean IQ score of the adopted African American children had decreased by 9 points, to 97 (Weinberg and others, 1992). The meaning of the change remains to be unraveled (Neisser, 1997a).

ENVIRONMENTAL INFLUENCES ON ADULT INTELLECTUAL FUNCTIONING

So far we have focused on the intellectual development of children. However, psychologists are also concerned with intellectual functioning among adults. They have found that older people decline somewhat in general intellectual ability as measured by scores on intelligence tests (Baltes, 1997). The drop-off is most acute in processing speed (Schaie, 1994; Schaie & Willis, 1991). Speed is involved in timed items such as those included in the performance scales of the Wechsler Adult Intelligence Scale. On the other hand, intellectual functioning tends to endure—and may even continue to grow—in areas involving knowledge and information about the world and human affairs (Baltes, 1997).

Certainly the biological changes associated with aging are involved in the decline in intellectual ability (Abeles, 1997b). For example, many older people show losses in sensory sharpness that affect their intellectual functioning. Moreover, people who retain good physical health tend to have higher levels of intellectual functioning in their later years (Schaie, 1994). It is unclear, however, whether good health is a causal factor in intelligence or whether a health-conscious lifestyle has cognitive as well as physical benefits (Gruber-Baldini, 1991).

The Seattle Longitudinal Study has been tracking intellectual changes among adults for nearly four decades. It has identified several environmental factors that affect intellectual functioning among older people (Schaie, 1993, 1994). Among them are the following:

1. *Socioeconomic status.* People with high SES tend to maintain intellectual functioning more adequately than people with low SES. High SES is also connected with above-average income and levels of education, a history of stimulating occupational pursuits, and maintenance of intact families.

2. *Stimulating activities.* People who maintain their level of intellectual functioning also tend to attend cultural events, travel, participate in professional organizations, and read extensively.

3. *Marriage to a spouse with a high level of intellectual functioning.* The spouse whose level of intellectual functioning is lower at the beginning of a marriage tends to narrow the gap as time goes by. Perhaps that partner is continually challenged by the other.

4. *Openness to new experience.*

Yes, Head Start programs have enhanced the intellectual development of children. It also turns out that training in reasoning and visual-spatial skills improves the cognitive functioning of older people (Schaie, 1994).

All in all, intellectual functioning at any age appears to reflect the interaction of a complex web of genetic, physical, personal, and sociocultural factors, as suggested by Figure 10.7. The views of *The Bell Curve*—that intelligence is largely heritable and that little can be done to affect intellectual functioning—are contradicted by evidence that clearly supports a more balanced view.

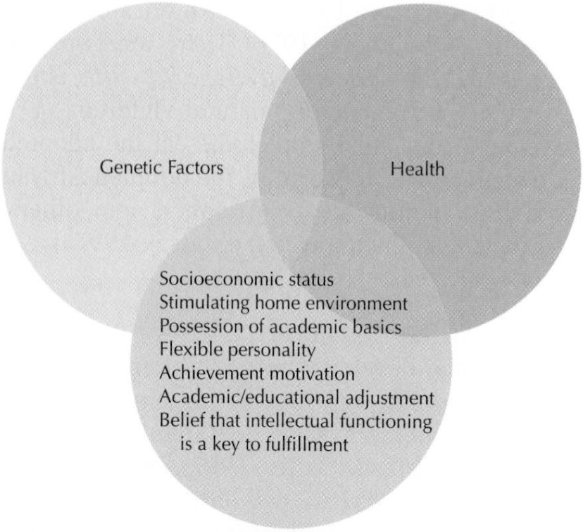

FIGURE 10.7

THE COMPLEX WEB OF FACTORS THAT APPEARS TO AFFECT INTELLECTUAL FUNCTIONING IN CHILDREN AND ADULTS

Intellectual functioning appears to be influenced by the interaction of genetic factors, health, personality, and sociocultural factors.

Genetic Factors

Health

Socioeconomic status
Stimulating home environment
Possession of academic basics
Flexible personality
Achievement motivation
Academic/educational adjustment
Belief that intellectual functioning
is a key to fulfillment

psychology and
modern life

ENHANCING INTELLECTUAL FUNCTIONING

Does enhancing intellectual functioning sound like an impossible dream? Only if you believe that intelligence is a fixed commodity—a sort of "knob in the head." Actually, intelligence—or intellectual functioning—changes with age, experiences in the home, education, and many other factors. Research suggests that there are many things you can do to enhance your children's intellectual functioning—*and your own.*

- Be emotionally and verbally responsive to your children. Provide appropriate play materials. Get involved in their play. Provide a variety of experiences.

- Provide a safe, organized home for your children.

- Encourage your children to be in-dependent, to try to solve their own problems, to do as much of their schoolwork on their own as they can. Note that restrictiveness and punishment are linked to *lower* IQ scores.

- Make sure your children know the basics. Expose them to materials and activities that include letters and words, numbers, books, exercises in drawing, pegs and pegboards, puzzles, toy animals, and dolls.

- Consider giving them training in music. Not only will music broaden their intellectual horizons but it may also enhance their spatial relations skills.

And what about you? It is not too late to enhance your own intellectual functioning, even if you are a grandparent.

- Engage in stimulating activities. Attend cultural events. Travel. Participate in professional organizations. Read widely.

- Choose intellectually challenging companions.

- Remain (or become) flexible. Be open to new experiences. Try new things. Be willing to consider evidence and change your opinions, even on political issues.

None of these measures are guarantees, of course. But regardless of how they affect intelligence, they will certainly lead to a more stimulating life—both for your children and for you. ■

• *Ethnicity and Intelligence: A Concluding Note*

Many psychologists believe that heredity and environment interact to influence intelligence. Forty-five percent of Snyderman and Rothman's (1987, 1990) sample of 1,020 psychologists and educational specialists believe that differences in IQ between African Americans and White people are a "product of both genetic and environmental variation, compared to only 15% who feel the difference is entirely due to environmental variation [see Figure 10.8]. Twenty-four percent of experts do not believe there are sufficient data to support any reasonable opinion, [and 1%] indicate a belief in an entirely genetic determination" (1987, p. 141).

Diana Baumrind (1993) and Jacquelyne Jackson (1993) of the Institute of Human Development at the University of California argue that belief in the predominance of genetic factors can undermine parental and educational efforts to enhance children's intellectual development. Such a view can be particularly harmful to African American children. Parents are most effective when they *believe* that their efforts will improve their children's functioning. Since parents cannot change their children's genetic codes, it is better for parents to assume that good parenting can make a difference.

Perhaps we need not be so concerned with whether we can sort out exactly how much of a person's IQ is due to heredity and how much is due to environmental influences. A majority of psychologists and educators believe that IQ reflects the complex interaction of heredity, early childhood experiences, sociocultural factors and expectations, and even the atmosphere in which intelligence tests are conducted. Psychology has traditionally supported the dignity of the individual. It might be more appropriate for us to try to identify children *of all ethnic groups* whose environments place them at risk for failure and do what we can to enrich their environments. As Richard Rose of Indiana University has noted,

> We inherit dispositions, not destinies. Life outcomes are consequences of lifetimes of behavior choices. . . . We actively seek opportunities to develop and display our dispositional characteristics. . . . Lives are not simple consequences of genetic [factors]. (Rose, 1995, p. 648)

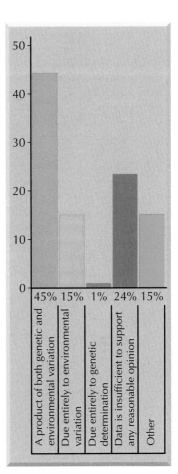

FIGURE 10.8

BELIEFS OF PSYCHOLOGISTS AND EDUCATIONAL SPECIALISTS CONCERNING REASONS FOR RACIAL DIFFERENCES IN IQ

The largest group of psychologists and educational specialists views racial differences in IQ as reflecting the interaction of genetic and environmental factors. (Source: Snyderman and Rothman [1987, 1990]).

REFLECTIONS
- Do members of your family seem to be similar in overall intellectual functioning? Does one or more family members stand out from the others in intelligence? If so, in what ways?
- What kinds of family or educational experiences seem to have affected your own intellectual development? Would you say that your background was deprived or enriched? In what ways?

SUMMARY

1. **What is intelligence?** Achievement is what a person has learned. Intelligence is presumed to underlie achievement and has been defined by Wechsler as the "capacity . . . to understand the world . . . and . . . resourcefulness to cope with its challenges."

2. **What is artificial intelligence?** Artificial intelligence refers to the replication of human intellectual functioning that is built into computers.

3. **What are Spearman and Thurstone's theories of intelligence?** Spearman and Thurstone believed that intelligence is composed of a number of factors. Spearman believed that a common factor, *g*, underlies all intelligent behavior but that people also have specific abilities, or *s* factors. Thurstone suggested that there are several primary mental abilities, including word fluency and numerical ability.

4. **What is Gardner's theory of multiple intelligences?** Gardner believes that people have several intelligences, not one, and that each is based in a different area of the brain. Two such "intelligences" are language ability and logical-mathematical ability, but Gardner also includes bodily-kinesthetic intelligence and others.

5. **What is Sternberg's triarchic theory of intelligence?** Sternberg's triarchic theory proposes that there are three kinds of intelligence: componential (academic ability), experiential (creativity), and contextual ("street smarts").

6. **What is the theory of emotional intelligence?** This theory holds that social and emotional skills are a form of intelligence that helps children avert depression and violence. The theory suggests that emotional skills are best learned during the "window" of childhood.

7. **What is the IQ?** Intelligence tests yield scores called intelligence quotients, or IQs. The Stanford-Binet Intelligence Scale, originated by Alfred Binet, derives the IQ score by dividing a child's mental age score by his or her chronological age and then multiplying by 100. The Wechsler scales use deviation IQs, which are derived by comparing a person's performance with that of his or her age-mates.

8. **What kinds of items are included in intelligence tests?** The Wechsler scales contain verbal and performance subtests that measure general information, comprehension, similarities (conceptual thinking), vocabulary, mathematics, block design (copying designs), and object assembly (piecing puzzles together).

9. **What is the nature of the controversy over cultural bias in intelligence tests?** It turns out that intelligence test scores reflect cultural factors as well as general learning ability. Cultural factors include familiarity with testing, socioeconomic status, familiarity with the mainstream culture, motivation, and academic adjustment.

10. **How do IQ scores of people in various socioeconomic and ethnic groups differ?** Lower-class U.S. children obtain IQ scores some 10 to 15 points lower than those of middle- and upper-class children. African American children tend to obtain IQ scores some 15–20 points lower than those of their White agemates. Asians and Asian Americans usually obtain higher IQ scores than White British or U.S. citizens.

11. **Where does intelligence come from?** The largest number of psychologists believe that intelligence reflects the interaction of genetic and environmental influences.

To enhance your understanding of the psychological concepts found in this chapter, please consult the following aids:

STUDY GUIDE

Learning Objectives, p. 205
Exercise, p. 206
Lecture and Textbook Outline,
    p. 207
Effective Studying Ideas, p. 209

Key Terms and Concepts, p. 210
Chapter Review, p. 210
Knowing the Language, p. 216
Do You Know the Material?, p. 217

CORE CONCEPTS SEARCH

Defining Intelligence
The Stanford-Binet
The Wechsler Scales Aptitude Tests

Extremes of Intelligence
Culture-Relevant Intelligence Tests

World Wide Web

For more information concerning the topics found in this chapter, access psychology links on the World Wide Web through the Harcourt Brace webpage at

www.hbcollege.com

Share your comments and questions with your author at

PsychLinks@aol.com

The psychology of motivation is concerned with the *whys* of behavior. Why do we eat? Why do we dance, strive to get ahead, seek the company of others, or try new things? Miriam Schapiro's *Master of Ceremonies* (1985) suggests the joy that we can derive from some kinds of activity. Joy is an emotion that adds color to life. An emotion can be a response to a situation, as fear is a response to a threat. An emotion can motivate behavior, as anger can flare into aggression. An emotion can also be a goal in itself, as when we try to experience joy or find love.

MIRIAM SCHAPIRO

Chapter 11

Motivation and Emotion

TRUTH OR FICTION?

✓ **T F**

☐ ☐ One American adult in three is obese.

☐ ☐ Americans overeat by an amount great enough to feed the entire nation of Germany.

☐ ☐ Getting away from it all by going on a vacation from all sensory input for a few hours is relaxing.

☐ ☐ We appreciate things more when we have to work for them.

☐ ☐ Efficient, skillful employees are evaluated more highly than hardworking employees who must struggle to get the job done.

☐ ☐ Misery loves company.

☐ ☐ You may be able to fool a lie detector by wiggling your toes.

☐ ☐ Smiling can produce pleasant feelings.

OUTLINE

COMING TO TERMS WITH MOTIVATION

THEORIES OF MOTIVATION: THE *WHYS* OF BEHAVIOR

Instinct Theory: "Doing What Comes Naturally"

Drive-Reductionism and Homeostasis: "Steady, Steady . . . "

Humanistic Theory: "I've Got to Be Me"

Cognitive Theory: "I Think, Therefore I Am *Consistent*"

Psychology in a World of Diversity: Sociocultural Perspectives on Motivation

Evaluation of Theories of Motivation

HUNGER: DO YOU GO BY "TUMMY-TIME"?

Obesity—A Serious and Pervasive Problem

Psychology and Modern Life: Controlling Your Weight

STIMULUS MOTIVES

Sensory Stimulation and Activity

Questionnaire: The Sensation-Seeking Scale

Exploration and Manipulation

COGNITIVE-DISSONANCE THEORY: MAKING THINGS FIT

Effort Justification: "If I Did It, It Must Be Important"?

THE THREE A'S OF MOTIVATION: ACHIEVEMENT, AFFILIATION, AND AGGRESSION

Achievement

Affiliation: "People Who Need People"

Aggression: Some Facts of Life and Death

Psychology and Modern Life: Enhancing Productivity and Job Satisfaction

EMOTION: ADDING COLOR TO LIFE

Arousal, Emotions, and Lie Detection

How Many Emotions Are There? Where Do They Come From?

The Expression of Emotions

The Facial-Feedback Hypothesis

Theories of Emotion: *Is Feeling First?*

COGNITIVE-DISSONANCE THEORY • The view that we are motivated to make our cognitions or beliefs consistent.

HE SEEKERS WERE QUITE A GROUP. THEIR brave leader, Marian Keech, dutifully recorded the messages that she believed were sent to her by the Guardians from outer space. One particular message was somewhat disturbing. It specified that the world would come to an end on December 21. A great flood would engulf Lake City, the home of Ms. Keech and many of her faithful followers.

Another message brought good news, however. Ms. Keech received word that the Seekers would be rescued from the flood. Ms. Keech reported that she received messages through "automatic writing." The messengers would communicate through her: She would write down their words, supposedly without awareness. This bit of writing was perfectly clear: The Seekers would be saved by flying saucers at the stroke of midnight on the 21st.

In their classic observational study, Leon Festinger and his colleagues (1956) described how they managed to be present in Ms. Keech's household at the fateful hour by pretending to belong to the group. Their purpose was to observe the behavior of the Seekers during and following the prophecy's failure. The cognitive theory of motivation that Festinger was working on—**cognitive-dissonance theory**—suggested that there would be a discrepancy or conflict between two key cognitions: (1) Ms. Keech is a prophet, and (2) Ms. Keech is wrong.

How might such a conflict be resolved? One way would be for the Seekers to lose faith in Ms. Keech. But the researchers argued that according to cognitive-dissonance theory, the Seekers might be motivated to resolve the conflict by going out to spread the word and find additional converts. Otherwise the group would be painfully embarrassed.

Let us return to the momentous night. Many members of the group had quit their jobs and gone on spending sprees before the anticipated end. Now they were all gathered together. As midnight approached they fidgeted, awaiting the flying saucers. Midnight came, but no saucers. Anxious glances were exchanged. Silence. Coughs. A few minutes passed, tortuously slowly. Watches were checked, more glances exchanged. At 4:00 A.M. a bitter and frantic Ms. Keech complained that she sensed that members of the group were doubting her. At 4:45 A.M., however, she seemed suddenly relieved. Still another message was arriving, and Ms. Keech was spelling it out through automatic writing! The Seekers, it turned out, had managed to save the world through their faith. The universal powers had decided to let the world travel on along its sinful way for a while longer. Why? Because of the faith of the Seekers, there was hope!

You guessed it. The faith of most of those present was renewed. They called wire services and newspapers to spread the word. All but three psychologists from the University of Minnesota. They went home, weary but enlightened, and wrote a book entitled *When Prophecy Fails,* which serves as one of the key documents of cognitive-motivational theory.

What about Mr. Keech? He was a tolerant sort. He slept through it all.

The psychology of motivation is concerned with the *whys* of behavior. Why do we eat? Why do some of us strive to get ahead? Why do some of us ride motorcycles at breakneck speeds? Why do we try new things? Why were the Seekers in a state of acute discomfort?

■ COMING TO TERMS WITH MOTIVATION

Let us begin our journey into the *whys* of behavior with some definitions. **Motives** are hypothetical states within an organism that activate behavior and propel the organism toward goals. Why do we say "hypothetical states"? Because motives are not seen and measured directly. Like many other psychological concepts, they are inferred from behavior (Kimble, 1994). Psychologists assume that motives give rise to behavior. These may take the form of *needs, drives,* and *incentives.*

Psychologists speak of physiological and psychological **needs.** We must meet physiological needs to survive. Examples include the needs for oxygen, food, drink, pain avoidance, proper temperature, and elimination of waste products. Some physiological needs, such as hunger and thirst, are states of physical deprivation. When we have not eaten or drunk for a while, we develop needs for food and water. The body also has needs for oxygen, vitamins, minerals, and so on.

Examples of psychological needs are the needs for achievement, power, self-esteem, social approval, and belonging. Psychological needs differ from physiological needs in two ways. First, psychological needs are not necessarily based on states of deprivation. A person with a need for achievement may already have a history of successful achievements. Second, psychological needs may be acquired through experience, or learned. By contrast, physiological needs reside in the physical makeup of the organism. Because our biological makeups are similar, we all share similar physiological needs. However, we are influenced by our sociocultural milieu, and our needs may be expressed in diverse ways. All people need food, for example, but some prefer a vegetarian diet whereas others prefer meat. Because learning enters into psychological needs, these needs can differ markedly from one person to the next.

Needs give rise to **drives.** Depletion of food gives rise to the hunger drive, and depletion of liquids gives rise to the thirst drive. **Physiological drives** are the psychological counterparts of physiological needs. When we have gone without food and water, our body may *need* these substances. However, our *experience* of the drives of hunger and thirst is psychological. Drives arouse us to action. Our drive levels tend to be greater the longer we have been deprived. Thus, we are usually more highly aroused by the hunger drive when we have not eaten for several hours than when we have not eaten for, say, 5 minutes.

Psychological needs for approval, achievement, and belonging also give rise to drives. We can be driven to get ahead in the business world just as surely as we can be driven to eat. The drives for achievement and power consume the daily lives of many people.

An **incentive** is an object, person, or situation that is perceived as being capable of satisfying a need or as desirable for its own sake. Money, food, a sexually attractive person, social approval, and attention can all act as incentives that motivate behavior.

In the following section, we explore theories of motivation. We ask: Just what is so motivating about motives?

MOTIVE • A hypothetical state within an organism that propels the organism toward a goal. (From the Latin *movere*, meaning "to move.")

NEED • A state of deprivation.

DRIVE • A condition of arousal in an organism that is associated with a need.

PHYSIOLOGICAL DRIVES • Unlearned drives with a biological basis, such as hunger, thirst, and avoidance of pain.

INCENTIVE • An object, person, or situation perceived as being capable of satisfying a need.

■ THEORIES OF MOTIVATION: THE *WHYS* OF BEHAVIOR

Although psychologists agree that it is important to understand why humans and lower animals do things, they do not agree about the precise nature of motivation. Let us consider a number of theoretical perspectives on motivation.

• *Instinct Theory: "Doing What Comes Naturally"*

Animals are "prewired"—that is, born with preprogrammed tendencies—to respond to certain situations in certain ways. Birds that are reared in isolation from other birds build nests during the mating season even though they have never observed another bird building a nest (or, for that matter, seen a nest). Siamese fighting fish that are reared in isolation assume stereotypical threatening stances and attack other males when they are introduced into their tank.

These behaviors are found in particular species (they are *species-specific*). They do not rely on learning. Such behaviors are called **instincts** or **fixed-action patterns (FAPs)**. Spiders spin webs. Bees "dance" to communicate the location of food to other bees. All of this activity is inborn. It is genetically transmitted from generation to generation.

FAPs occur in response to stimuli called **releasers.** For example, male members of many species are sexually aroused by **pheromones** secreted by females. Pheromones thus release the FAP of sexual response.

The question arises as to whether humans have instincts. Around the turn of the century, psychologists William James (1890) and William McDougall (1908) argued that humans have instincts that foster self-survival and social behavior. James asserted that we have social instincts such as love, sympathy, and modesty. McDougall compiled 12 "basic" instincts, including hunger, sex, and self-assertion. Other psychologists have made longer lists.

Sigmund Freud also used the term *instincts* to refer to physiological needs in humans. He believed that the instincts of sex and aggression give rise to *psychic energy,* which is perceived as a feeling of tension. Tension motivates us to restore ourselves to a calmer, resting state. The behavior patterns we use to reduce the tension—for example, using a weapon or a push when acting aggressively—are largely learned.

• *Drive-Reductionism and Homeostasis: "Steady, Steady . . . "*

Freud's psychodynamic views coincide reasonably well with those of a group of learning theorists who presented a **drive-reduction theory** of learning. According to this theory, as set forth by psychologist Clark Hull in the 1930s, **primary drives** such as hunger, thirst, and pain trigger arousal (tension) and activate behavior. We learn responses that reduce the drives. Through association, we also learn **acquired drives.** We may acquire a drive for money because money enables us to obtain food, drink, and homes, which protect us from predators and extremes of temperature. We might acquire drives for social approval and affilia-

INSTINCT • An inherited disposition to activate specific behavior patterns that are designed to reach certain goals.
FIXED-ACTION PATTERN • An instinct; abbreviated *FAP*.
RELEASER • In ethology, a stimulus that elicits a FAP.
PHEROMONES • Chemical secretions that are detected by other members of the same species and stimulate stereotypical behaviors.
DRIVE-REDUCTION THEORY • The view that organisms learn to engage in behaviors that have the effect of reducing drives.
PRIMARY DRIVES • Unlearned, or physiological, drives.
ACQUIRED DRIVES • Drives that are acquired through experience, or learned.

A Fixed-Action Pattern. In the presence of another male, Siamese fighting fish assume threatening stances in which they extend their fins and gills and circle each other. If neither male retreats, there will be a conflict.

tion because other people, and their good will, help us reduce primary drives, especially when we are infants. In all cases, reduction of tension is the goal.

Primary drives like hunger are triggered when we are in a state of deprivation. Sensations of hunger motivate us to act in ways that will restore the bodily balance. This tendency to maintain a steady state is called **homeostasis.** Homeostasis works much like a thermostat. When the temperature in a room drops below the set point, the heating system is triggered. The heat stays on until the set point is reached. Similarly, most animals eat until they are no longer hungry. (The fact many people eat "recreationally"—for example, when they are presented with an appealing dessert—suggests that there is more to eating than drive reduction.)

• *Humanistic Theory: "I've Got to Be Me"*

Humanistic psychologists, particularly Abraham Maslow, note that the instinct and drive-reduction theories of motivation are defensive. They suggest that human behavior is rather mechanical and is aimed toward survival and reduction of tension. As a humanist, Maslow believed that people are also motivated by the conscious desire for personal growth. Humanists note that people will tolerate pain, hunger, and many other sources of tension to obtain personal fulfillment.

Maslow believed that we are separated from lower animals by our capacity for **self-actualization,** or self-initiated striving to become whatever we believe we are capable of being. Maslow considered self-actualization to be as important a need in humans as hunger. It is that need that impels people to strive to become concert pianists or chief executive officers or best-selling authors.

Maslow (1970) organized human needs into a hierarchy, from physiological needs such as hunger and thirst, through self-actualization (see Figure 11.1). He believed that we naturally strive to travel up through this hierarchy. Maslow's hierarchy consists of the following sets of needs:

1. *Physiological needs:* hunger, thirst, elimination, warmth, fatigue, pain avoidance, sexual release.
2. *Safety needs:* protection from the environment through housing and clothing; security from crime and financial hardship.

HOMEOSTASIS • (HOME-me-oh-STAY-sis). The tendency of the body to maintain a steady state.
SELF-ACTUALIZATION • According to Maslow and other humanistic psychologists, self-initiated striving to become what one is capable of being. The motive for reaching one's full potential, for expressing one's unique capabilities.

FIGURE 11.1

MASLOW'S HIERARCHY OF NEEDS
Maslow believed that we progress toward higher psychological needs once basic survival needs have been met. Where do you fit in this picture?

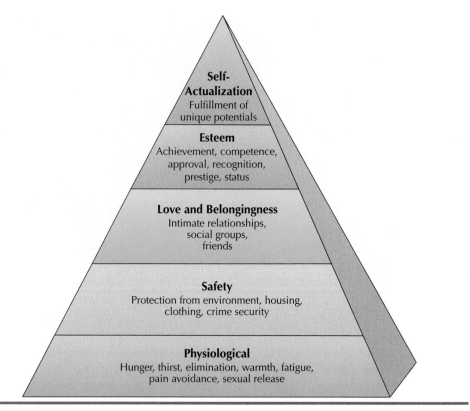

3. *Love and belongingness needs:* love and acceptance through intimate relationships, social groups, and friends. Maslow believed that in a generally well-fed society such as ours, much frustration stems from failure to meet needs at this level.

4. *Esteem needs:* achievement, competence, approval, recognition, prestige, status.

5. *Self-actualization:* fulfillment of our unique potentials. For many individuals, self-actualization involves needs for cognitive understanding (novelty, exploration, knowledge) and aesthetic needs (music, art, poetry, beauty, order).

• *Cognitive Theory: "I Think, Therefore I Am* Consistent"

The Brain, within it's groove
Runs evenly—and true—

EMILY DICKINSON

"I think, therefore I am," said the French philosopher René Descartes. If he had been a cognitive psychologist, he might have said, "I think, therefore I am *consistent.*"

Cognitive theorists note that people represent their worlds mentally (Rescorla, 1988). Jean Piaget and George Kelly (1955) hypothesized that people are born scientists who strive to understand the world so that they can predict and control events. In order to predict and control events, one must represent the world accurately. This means that people are also motivated to eliminate inconsistences in their worldviews.

For example, Sandra Bem (1993) argues that children try to create consistency between their own gender and their society's "gender schema"—their society's expectations as to what behaviors are appropriate for males and females. As soon as they know whether they are male or female, children imitate the behavior of adults of the same gender (see Chapter 13). Leon Festinger (1957) believed that people are generally motivated to hold consistent beliefs and to justify their behavior. That is why we are more likely to appreciate things that we must work to obtain. (We discuss Festinger's theory in greater depth later in the chapter.)

Psychology in a World of
DIVERSITY

Sociocultural Perspectives on Motivation

Sociocultural theory pervades other viewpoints. For example, primary drives may be inborn, but sociocultural experiences affect the *behavior* that satisfies those drives. Eating meat or fish, drinking coffee or tea, kissing lips or rubbing noses are all influenced by sociocultural factors. The stimuli that stoke the sex drive are influenced by the person's cultural experiences. Women's breasts have become eroticized in Western culture and usually must be covered from public view. In some preliterate societies, however, the breasts are considered to be of interest only to nursing children, and women usually go bare-breasted. Among the Abkhasian people of Asia, men regard the female armpit as highly arousing. A woman's armpits, therefore, may be seen only by her husband.

The experiences of anthropologist Margaret Mead (1935) on the South Pacific island of New Guinea showed how the sociocultural milieu influences motives such as aggressiveness and nurturance. Among the Mundugumor, a tribe of headhunters and cannibals, both women and men were warlike and aggressive. The women felt that motherhood sidetracked them from more important activities, such as butchering inhabitants of neighboring villages. In contrast, both women and men of the Arapesh tribe were gentle and nurturant of children. Then there were the Tchambuli. In that tribe the women earned a living while the men spent most of their time nurturing the children, primping, and gossiping.

• Evaluation of Theories of Motivation

There are thus various perspectives on motivation. Let us evaluate them to see which one or ones seem to be most logical and most consistent with the research evidence.

There is no question that many animals are born with preprogrammed tendencies to respond to certain situations in certain ways. Yet instinct theory has been criticized for yielding circular explanations of behavior with humans. For example, if we say that mothers care for their children because of a maternal instinct, and then we take maternal care as evidence of the instinct, we have come full circle. But we have explained nothing. As another example, consider William James's notion that sympathy is an instinct. Many people are cruel and cold-hearted; are we to assume that they possess less of this "instinct"? Such an explanation would also be circular.

Then, too, there is the question as to how important instincts are to human beings. Some behaviors, including reflexes and the development of attachment in infants, may be considered instinctive (Ainsworth & Bowlby, 1991). However, there is so much variation in human behavior that most of it would appear to be learned or planned by the individual.

Drive-reduction theory appears to apply in physiological drives such as hunger and thirst. However, we often eat when we are not hungry! Drive reduction also runs aground when we consider evidence showing that we often act in ways that *increase*, rather than decrease, the tensions acting on us. When we are hungry, for example, we may take the time to prepare a gourmet meal instead of a snack, even though the snack would satisfy the hunger drive sooner. We drive fast cars, ride roller coasters, and sky dive for sport—all activities that heighten rather than decrease arousal.

People and many lower animals also seek novel stimulation. We may be willing to try a new dish ("just a taste") even when we feel full. We often seek novel ways of doing things—shunning the tried and the true—because of the stimulation provided by novelty. Yet the familiar tried-and-true ways would reduce tension more reliably. In view of examples like these, some psychologists have theorized the existence of *stimulus motives* that outweigh the motivation to reduce drives. (We will discuss stimulus motives later in the chapter.)

Critics of Maslow's theory argue that there is too much individual variation for the hierarchy of motives to apply to everyone. Some people whose physiological, safety, and love needs are met show little interest in achievement and recognition. Some artists, musicians, and writers devote themselves fully to their art, even if they have to live in a garret to do so. However, people do appear to seek distant, self-actualizing goals, even while exposing themselves to great danger. This behavior is certainly more consistent with a humanistic than a drive-reductionist explanation of human behavior.

Some psychologists criticize cognitive theory for its reliance on unobservable concepts such as mental representations rather than observable behavior. However, cognitive psychologists tie their concepts to observable behavior, whenever possible. It also appears to be difficult to explain the child's active efforts to experiment with and understand other people and the world without resorting to cognitive concepts (Meltzoff, 1997).

It seems that each of the theories of motivation has something to offer. Each would appear to apply to certain aspects of behavior. As the chapter progresses, we will describe research that lends some support to each of these theories. It remains to be seen whether one grand theory of motivation will emerge that includes all the others.

Let us first describe research on the hunger drive. Hunger is based on physiological needs, and drive reduction would appear to explain some—though not all—eating behavior. Because physiological drives such as hunger are unlearned, they are also referred to as *primary drives.*

REFLECTIONS

- Do you believe that humans have instincts? What kinds of instincts? What evidence is there for your belief?
- What needs in Maslow's hierarchy are you attempting to meet by attending college?
- How have the ways in which you try to meet your needs been affected by sociocultural factors?

■ HUNGER: DO YOU GO BY "TUMMY-TIME"?

I go by tummy-time and I want my dinner.

SIR WINSTON CHURCHILL

We need food to survive, but to many of us food means more than survival. Food is a symbol of family togetherness and caring. We associate food with the nurturance of the parent-child relationship, with visits home during holidays. Friends and relatives offer us food when we enter their homes, and saying no may be viewed as a personal rejection. Bacon and eggs, coffee with cream and sugar, meat and mashed potatoes—all seem to be part of sharing American values and agricultural abundance. What bodily mechanisms regulate the hunger drive? What psychological processes are at work?

In considering the bodily mechanisms that regulate hunger, let us begin with the mouth. This is an appropriate choice since we are discussing eating. Chewing and swallowing provide some sensations of **satiety,** or satisfaction with the amount eaten. If they did not, we might eat for a long time after we had taken in enough food. It takes the digestive tract time to metabolize food and provide signals of satiety to the brain by way of the bloodstream.

In classic "sham feeding" experiments with dogs, researchers implanted a tube in the animals' throats so that any food that was swallowed fell out of the dog's body. Even though no food arrived at the stomach, the animals stopped feeding after a brief period (Janowitz & Grossman, 1949). However, they resumed feeding sooner than animals whose food did reach the stomach.

Let us proceed to the stomach, too, as we seek further regulatory factors in hunger. An empty stomach will lead to stomach contractions, which we call *hunger pangs.* These pangs are not as influential as was formerly thought. People and animals whose stomachs have been removed still regulate food intake so as to maintain their normal weight. This finding led to the discovery of many other mechanisms that regulate hunger, including the hypothalamus, blood sugar level, and even receptors in the liver. When we are deprived of food, the level of sugar in the blood drops. The drop in blood sugar is communicated to the hypothalamus (see Chapter 3) and apparently indicates that we have been burning energy and need to replenish it by eating.

EXPERIMENTS WITH THE HYPOTHALAMUS: THE SEARCH FOR "START EATING" AND "STOP EATING" CENTERS IN THE BRAIN If you were just reviving from a surgical operation, fighting your way through the fog of the anesthesia, food would probably be the last thing on your mind. But when a researcher uses a probe to destroy the **ventromedial nucleus (VMN)** of a rat's hypothalamus, the rat will grope toward food as soon as its eyes open. Then it will eat vast quantities of Purina Rat Chow or whatever else it can find.

The VMN seems to be a "stop-eating center" in the rat's brain. If the VMN is electrically stimulated—that is, "switched on"—the rat will stop eating until the current is turned off. When the VMN is destroyed, the rat becomes **hyperphagic.** It will continue to eat until it has about doubled its normal weight (see Figure 11.2). Then it will level off its eating rate and maintain the higher weight. It is as if the set point of the stop-eating center has been raised to a higher level (Keesey, 1986). Hyperphagic rats are also more finicky. They will eat more fats or sweet-tasting food, but if their food is salty or bitter they will actually eat less (Kimble, 1992).

The **lateral hypothalamus** may be a "start-eating center." If you electrically stimulate the lateral hypothalamus, the rat will start to eat (Miller, 1995). If you destroy the lateral hypothalamus, the rat may stop eating altogether—that is,

Hunger. How do *you* feel while waiting for someone to carve the meat? Hunger is a physiological drive that motivates us to eat. Why do we feel hungry? Why do we feel satiated? Why do many people continue to eat when they have already supplied their bodies with the needed nutrients?

SATIETY • (SAY-she-uh-tee *or* sat-TIE-uh-tee). The state of being satisfied; fullness.
VENTROMEDIAL NUCLEUS • A central area on the underside of the hypothalamus that appears to function as a stop-eating center.
HYPERPHAGIC • Characterized by excessive eating.
LATERAL HYPOTHALAMUS • An area at the side of the hypothalamus that appears to function as a start-eating center.

FIGURE 11.2
A Hyperphagic Rat
This rodent winner of the basketball look-alike
contest went on a binge after it received a lesion
in the ventromedial nucleus (VMN) of the hypothalamus. It is as if the lesion pushed the "set
point" for body weight up several notches; the
rat's weight is now about five times normal. But
now it eats only enough to maintain its pleasantly
plump stature, so you need not be concerned that
it will eventually burst. If the lesion had been
made in the lateral hypothalamus, the animal
might have become the "Twiggy" of the rat
world.

Truth or Fiction Revisited

....

*It is true that one adult American in three
is obese.*

Truth or Fiction Revisited

....

*Yes, Americans do overeat by an amount great
enough to feed the entire nation of Germany.
The excess calories would feed another 80
million people!*

become **aphagic.** If you force-feed an aphagic rat for a while, however, it will
begin to eat on its own and level off at a relatively low body weight. You have
lowered the rat's set point. It is like turning down the thermostat from, say, 70
degrees to 40 degrees Fahrenheit.

Although many areas of the body work in concert to regulate the hunger
drive, this is only part of the story. In human beings, the hunger drive is more
complex. Psychological as well as physiological factors play an important role.
How many times have you been made hungry by the sight or aroma of food?
How many times have you eaten not because you were hungry but because you
were at a relative's home or in a cafeteria? The next section further explores
psychological factors that affect eating.

• *Obesity—A Serious and Pervasive Problem*

> *There is no sincerer love than the love of food.*
>
> GEORGE BERNARD SHAW

> *The two biggest sellers in any bookstore are the cookbooks and
> the diet books. The cookbooks tell you how to prepare the
> food and the diet books tell you how not to eat any of it.*
>
> ANDY ROONEY

Consider some facts about obesity:

- The prevalence of obesity in the United States has increased by 25% in
the last decade (Brownell, 1997).
- One American adult in three is now obese (Meyer, 1997).
- Nearly half of African American women are obese, possibly because they
have lower metabolic rates than White women do (Brody, 1997a).
- Americans eat more than a total of 800 billion calories of food each day
(200 billion calories more than they need to maintain their weights). The
extra calories could feed a nation of 80 million people.
- Compared with other women, overweight women are less likely to get
married, have lower incomes, and complete fewer years of school (Gortmaker and others, 1993).
- Within a few years, most dieters regain most of the weight they have lost,
even when they have used diet pills "successfully" (Rosenbaum and others, 1997).
- About 300,000 Americans die each year because of excess weight
(Brownell, 1997).

American culture idealizes slender heroes and heroines. For those who
"more than measure up" to TV and film idols, food may have replaced sex as
the central source of guilt. Obese people encounter more than their fair share
of illnesses, including heart disease, diabetes, gout, respiratory problems, even
certain kinds of cancer (Nevid and others, 1998). Obesity is also connected
with psychological, social, and economic problems (Fitzgibbon and others,
1993; Stunkard & Sørensen, 1993). If obesity is connected with health problems and unhappiness with the image in the mirror, why do so many people
overeat? Psychological research has contributed to our understanding of obesity and what can be done about it.

HEREDITY Obesity runs in families. It was once assumed that obese parents
encouraged their children to be overweight by serving fattening foods and setting poor examples. However, a study of Scandinavian adoptees by Stunkard
and his colleagues (1990) found that children bear a closer resemblance in

APHAGIC • Characterized by undereating. |

weight to their biological parents than to their adoptive parents. Heredity, then, plays a role in obesity (Friedman & Brownell, 1995).

FAT CELLS The efforts of obese people to maintain a slender profile may also be sabotaged by microscopic units of life within their own bodies: fat cells. No, fat cells are not overweight cells. They are adipose tissue, or cells that store fat. Hunger might be related to the amount of fat stored in these cells. As time passes after a meal, the blood sugar level drops. Fat is then drawn from these cells to provide further nourishment. At some point, referred to as the *set point*, fat deficiency in these cells is communicated to the hypothalamus, triggering the hunger drive.

People with more adipose tissue than others feel food-deprived earlier, even though they may be equal in weight. This might occur because more signals are being sent to the brain. Obese and *formerly* obese people tend to have more adipose tissue than people of normal weight. Thus, many people who have lost weight complain that they are always hungry when they try to maintain normal weight levels.

Fatty tissue also metabolizes (burns) food more slowly than muscle does. For this reason, a person with a high fat-to-muscle ratio will metabolize food more slowly than a person of the same weight with a lower fat-to-muscle ratio. That is, two people who are identical in weight will metabolize food at different rates, depending on the distribution of muscle and fat in their bodies. Obese people therefore are doubly handicapped in their efforts to lose weight—not only by their extra weight but by the fact that much of their body is composed of adipose tissue.

In a sense, the normal distribution of fat cells could be considered "sexist." The average man is 40% muscle and 15% fat. The average woman is 23% muscle and 25% fat. Therefore, if a man and a woman with typical distributions of muscle and fat are of equal weight, the woman—who has more fat cells—will have to eat less to maintain that weight.

DIETING AND METABOLISM People on diets and those who have lost substantial amounts of weight burn fewer calories. That is, their metabolic rates slow down (Schwartz & Seeley, 1997; Wadden and others, 1997). This appears to be a built-in mechanism that helps preserve life in times of famine. However, it also make it more difficult for dieters to continue to lose weight. The pounds seem to come off more and more reluctantly.

PSYCHOLOGICAL FACTORS Psychological factors, such as observational learning, stress, and emotional states also play a role in obesity (Greeno & Wing, 1994). Our children are exposed to an average of 10,000 food commercials a year. More than 9 of 10 of these commercials are for fast foods (like McDonald's fries), sugared cereals, candy, and soft drinks (Brownell, 1997). Situations also play a role. Family celebrations, watching TV, arguments, and tension at work can all lead to overeating or going off a diet (Drapkin and others, 1995). Dieting efforts may be also impeded by negative emotions like depression and anxiety (Cools and others, 1992).

REFLECTIONS

- How do you feel about your own weight and body shape? Why?
- How many dieters do you know? How successful are they? What methods, if any, seem to work for them?
- Agree or disagree, and support your answer: "People who are overweight simply eat too much."

psychology and
modern life

CONTROLLING YOUR WEIGHT

Do you need to shed a few pounds? Perhaps, but psychologists warn that not everyone should be trying to slim down. Women in the United States today are under social pressure to conform to an unnaturally slender female ideal (Brownell & Rodin, 1994). As a result, they tend to set unrealistic weight loss goals (Foster and others, 1997). Moreover, many attempts to lose weight are ineffective. On the other hand, for many obese people, especially those who are severely obese, shedding excess pounds lowers the risks of health problems such as diabetes and heart disease.

Research on motivation and on methods of therapy has enhanced our knowledge of healthful ways to lose weight. Sound weight control programs do not involve fad diets such as fasting, eliminating carbohydrates, or eating excessive amounts of one particular food. Instead, they involve changes in lifestyle that include improving nutritional knowledge, decreasing calorie intake, exercising, and modifying eating behavior (Kumanyika, 1996; Nevid and others, 1998; see Table 11.1).

Most people in the United States eat too much fat and not enough fruits and vegetables (Kumanyika, 1996). Eating foods that are low in saturated fats and cholesterol not only is good for the heart but also can contribute to weight loss. Because dietary fat is converted into bodily fat more efficiently than carbohydrates are, a low-fat diet also leads to weight loss. Nutritional knowledge leads to suggestions for tak-

ing in fewer calories, which results in lower weight. Taking in fewer calories doesn't just mean eating smaller portions. It means switching to some lower-calorie foods—relying more on fresh, unsweetened fruits and vegetables (eating apples rather than apple pie), lean meats, fish and poultry, and skim milk and cheese. It means cutting down on—or eliminating—butter, margarine, oils, and sugar.

The same foods that help control weight also tend to be high in vitamins and fiber and low in fats. Such foods therefore may also reduce the risk of developing heart disease, cancer, and a number of other illnesses.

Dieting plus exercise is more effective than dieting alone for shedding

pounds and keeping them off. When we restrict our intake of calories, our metabolic rate compensates by slowing down (Wadden and others, 1997). Exercise burns calories and builds muscle tissue, which metabolizes more calories than fatty tissue does.

Cognitive and behavioral methods have also provided many strategies for losing weight. Among them are the following:

- *Establish calorie-intake goals and keep track of whether you are meeting them.* Get a book that shows how many calories are found in foods. Keep a diary of your calorie intake.

- *Substitute low-calorie foods for*

TABLE 11.1 DIETARY RECOMMENDATIONS OF THE AMERICAN ACADEMY OF SCIENCES
Reduce your total fat intake to 30% or less of your total calorie intake.
Reduce your intake of saturated fats to less than 10% of your total calorie intake.
Reduce your cholesterol intake to less than 300 mg per day.
Eat 5 or more servings of vegetables and fruits each day.
Increase your intake of starches and other complex carbohydrates by eating 6 or more servings of breads, cereals, and legumes each day.
Keep your intake of protein to moderate levels.
Limit your total intake of sodium (salt) to 2400 mg or less per day.
Maintain adequate intake of calcium.

Note: From Popkin, B. M., Siega-Riz, A. M., & Haines, P. S. (1996). A comparison of dietary trends among racial and socioeconomic groups in the United States. *New England Journal of Medicine,* 335, pp. 716–720.

A Sampler of Dietary Methods. At any given time nearly half of the adult American population is on a diet. Dieting has become the "normal" pattern of eating for women. Dozens of diets vie for attention on bookstore shelves. How can we know which ones contain truth and which ones contain fiction?

high-calorie foods. Fill your stomach with celery rather than cheesecake and enchiladas. Eat preplanned low-calorie snacks instead of bingeing on a jar of peanuts or a container of ice cream.

- *Take a 5-minute break between helpings.* Ask yourself whether you're still hungry. If not, stop eating.

- *Avoid temptations that have sidetracked you in the past.* Shop at the mall with the Alfalfa Sprout Café, not the Cheese Cake Factory. Plan your meal before entering a restaurant. (Avoid ogling that tempting full-color menu.) Attend to your own plate, not to the sumptuous dish at the next table. (Your salad probably looks greener to them, anyhow.) Shop from a list. Walk briskly through the supermarket, preferably after dinner when you're no longer hungry. Don't be sidetracked by pretty packages (fattening things may come in them). Don't linger in the kitchen. Study, watch TV, or write letters elsewhere. Don't

bring fattening foods into the house. Prepare only enough food to keep within your calorie goals.

- *Exercise to burn more calories and increase your metabolic rate.* Reach for your mate, not your plate (to coin a phrase). Take a brisk walk instead of eating an unplanned snack. Build exercise routines by adding a few minutes each week.

- *Reward yourself for meeting calorie goals (but not with food).* Imagine how great you'll look in that new swimsuit next summer. Do not go to the latest movie unless you have met your weekly calorie goal. When you meet your weekly calorie goal, put cash in the bank toward a vacation or a new camera.

- *Use imagery to help yourself lose weight.* Tempted by a fattening dish? Imagine that it's rotten, that you would be nauseated by it and have a sick taste in your mouth for the rest of the day.

- *Mentally walk through solutions to problem situations.* Consider

what you will do when cake is handed out at the office party. Rehearse your next visit to relatives who tell you how painfully thin you look and try to stuff you with food (Drapkin and others, 1995). Imagine how you'll politely (but firmly) refuse seconds and thirds, despite their objections.

- *Above all, if you slip from your plan for a day, don't blow things out of proportion.* Dieters are often tempted to binge, especially when they rigidly see themselves either as perfect successes or as complete failures or when they experience powerful emotions—either positive or negative (Cools and others, 1992). Consider the weekly or monthly trend, not just a single day. Credit yourself for the long-term trend. If you do binge, resume dieting the next day.

Losing weight—and keeping it off—is not easy, but it can be done. Making a personal commitment to losing weight and a workable plan for doing so are two of the keys. ■

Sensation Seeking? Is patriotism the sole motive of people who pilot aircraft such as the Lockheed A-117 Stealth fighter? Might they also be seeking to raise their arousal to more stimulating levels?

■ STIMULUS MOTIVES

One day when my daughter Taylor was 5 months old, I was batting her feet. (Why not?) She was sitting back in her mother's lap, and I repeatedly batted her feet up toward her middle with the palms of my hands. After a while, she began to laugh. When I stopped, she pushed a foot toward me, churned her arms back and forth, and blew bubbles as forcefully as she could. So I batted her feet again. She laughed and pushed them toward me again. This went on for a while, and it dawned on me that Taylor was doing what she could to make the stimulation last.

Physical needs give rise to drives like hunger and thirst. In such cases, organisms are motivated to *reduce* the tension or stimulation that impinges on them. But in the case of **stimulus motives,** organisms seek to *increase* stimulation, as Taylor did when she sought to have me bat her feet. Stimulus motives include sensory stimulation, activity, exploration, and manipulation of the environment.

Some stimulus motives provide a clear evolutionary advantage. Humans and lower animals that are motivated to learn about and manipulate their environment are more likely to survive. Learning about the environment increases awareness of resources and of potential dangers, and manipulation permits one to change the environment in beneficial ways. Exploring the environment helps animals locate sources of food and places to hide from predators. Learning and manipulation thus increase the animal's chances of survival until sexual maturity and of transmitting whatever genetic codes may underlie these motives to future generations.

• *Sensory Stimulation and Activity*

STIMULUS MOTIVES • Motives to increase the stimulation impinging upon an organism.
SENSORY DEPRIVATION • A research method for systematically decreasing the amount of stimulation that impinges upon sensory receptors.

When I was a teenager during the 1950s, I was unaware that some lucky students at McGill University in Montreal were being paid $20 a day (which, with inflation, would be well above $100 today) for doing absolutely nothing. Would you like to "work" by doing nothing for $100 a day? Don't answer too quickly. According to the results of classic research on **sensory deprivation,** you might not like it at all.

THE SENSATION-SEEKING SCALE

Some people seek higher levels of stimulation and activity than others. John is a couch potato, content to sit by the TV set all evening. Marsha doesn't feel right unless she's out on the tennis court or jogging. Cliff isn't content unless he has ridden his motorcycle over back trails at breakneck speeds, and Janet feels exuberant when she's catching the big wave or free-fall diving from an airplane.

What about you? Are you content to read or watch television all day? Or must you catch the big wave or bounce the bike across the dunes of the Mojave Desert? Sensation-seeking scales measure the level of stimulation or arousal a person will seek.

Marvin Zuckerman and his colleagues have identified four factors that are involved in sensation seeking: (1) seeking thrill and adventure, (2) disinhibition (that is, tendency to express impulses), (3) seeking experience, and (4) susceptibility to boredom. People who are high in sensation seeking are also less tolerant of sensory deprivation. They are more likely to use drugs and become involved in sexual experiences, to be drunk in public, and to volunteer for high-risk activities and unusual experiments (Pihl & Peterson, 1992; Stacy, 1997).

A shortened version of one of Zuckerman's scales follows. To gain insight into your own sensation-seeking tendencies, circle the choice, A or B, that best describes you. Then compare your answers to those in the answer key in Appendix B. ■

____ 1. A. I would like a job that requires a lot of traveling.
       B. I would prefer a job in one location.

____ 2. A. I am invigorated by a brisk, cold day.
       B. I can't wait to get indoors on a cold day.

____ 3. A. I get bored seeing the same old faces.
       B. I like the comfortable familiarity of everyday friends.

____ 4. A. I would prefer living in an ideal society in which everyone is safe, secure, and happy.
       B. I would have preferred living in the unsettled days of our history.

____ 5. A. I sometimes like to do things that are a little frightening.
       B. A sensible person avoids activities that are dangerous.

____ 6. A. I would not like to be hypnotized.
       B. I would like to have the experience of being hypnotized.

____ 7. A. The most important goal in life is to live it to the fullest and experience as much as possible.
       B. The most important goal in life is to find peace and happiness.

____ 8. A. I would like to try parachute jumping.
       B. I would never want to try jumping out of a plane, with or without a parachute.

____ 9. A. I enter cold water gradually, giving myself time to get used to it.
       B. I like to dive or jump right into the ocean or a cold pool.

____ 10. A. When I go on a vacation, I prefer the change of camping out.
        B. When I go on a vacation, I prefer the comfort of a good room and bed.

____ 11. A. I prefer people who are emotionally expressive even if they are a bit unstable.
        B. I prefer people who are calm and even tempered.

____ 12. A. A good painting should shock or jolt the senses.
        B. A good painting should give one a feeling of peace and security.

____ 13. A. People who ride motorcycles must have some kind of unconscious need to hurt themselves.
        B. I would like to drive or ride a motorcycle.

Student volunteers were placed in quiet cubicles and blindfolded (Bexton and others, 1954). Their arms were bandaged, and they could hear nothing but the dull, continuous hum of air conditioning. With nothing to do, many of the students slept for a while. After a few hours of sensory-deprived wakefulness, most felt bored and irritable. As time went on, many of them grew more uncomfortable, and some reported hallucinations of images of dots and geometric shapes.

Many students quit the experiment during the first day despite the financial incentive. Many of those who remained for a few days found it difficult to concentrate on simple problems for a few days afterward. For many, the experimental conditions did not provide a relaxing vacation. Instead, they produced boredom and disorientation.

• *Exploration and Manipulation*

Have you ever brought a dog or cat into a new home? At first, it may show excitement. New kittens are also known to hide under a couch or bed for a few hours. But then they will begin to explore every corner of their new environment. When placed in novel environments, many animals appear to possess an innate motive to engage in exploratory behavior.

Once they are familiar with their environment, both lower animals and humans appear to be motivated to seek novel stimulation. For example, when they have not been deprived of food for a great deal of time, rats will often explore unfamiliar arms of mazes rather than head straight for the section of the maze in which they have learned to expect food. Animals who have just copulated and thereby reduced their sex drives will often show renewed interest in sexual behavior when presented with a novel sex partner. Monkeys will learn how to

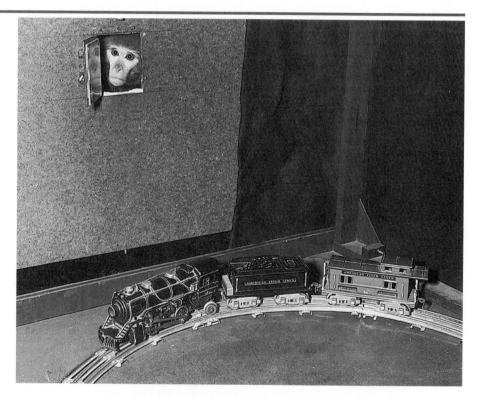

FIGURE 11.3
THE ALLURE OF NOVEL STIMULATION
People and many lower animals are motivated to explore the environment and to seek novel stimulation. This monkey has learned to unlock a door for the privilege of viewing a model train.

manipulate gadgets for the incentive of being able to observe novel stimulation through a window (see Figure 11.3). Children will spend hour after hour manipulating the controls of video games for the pleasure of zapping video monsters.

The question has arisen of whether people and animals seek to explore and manipulate their environment *because* these activities help them reduce primary drives such as hunger and thirst or whether they engage in these activities for their own sake. Many psychologists believe that such stimulating activities are reinforcing in and of themselves. Monkeys do seem to get a kick out of "monkeying around" with gadgets (see Figure 11.4). They learn how to manipulate hooks and eyes and other mechanical devices without any external incentive whatsoever (Harlow and others, 1950). Young children prolong their play with "busy boxes"—boxes filled with objects that honk, squeak, rattle, and buzz. They seem to find discovery of the cause-and-effect relationships in these gadgets pleasurable even though they are not rewarded with food, ice cream, or even hugs from their parents.

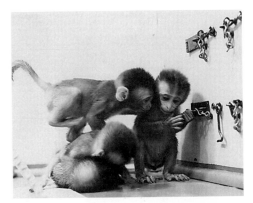

FIGURE 11.4
MONKEYING AROUND
Is there such a thing as a manipulation drive? These young rhesus monkeys appear to monkey around with gadgets just for the fun of it. No external incentives are needed. Children similarly enjoy manipulating gadgets that honk, squeak, rattle, and buzz, even though the resultant honks and squeaks do not satisfy physiological drives such as hunger or thirst.

REFLECTIONS
- Can you think of times when you were tired but "got a second wind" when you started to do something new or intriguing? Why do you think this happened?
- Do you find it relaxing to lie on the beach and "do nothing"? For how long? Or do you find it difficult to lie on the beach and do nothing? Why?

COGNITIVE-DISSONANCE THEORY: MAKING THINGS FIT

Do I contradict myself?
Very well then I contradict myself,
(I am large, I contain multitudes.)

WALT WHITMAN, *SONG OF MYSELF*

Most of us are unlike Walt Whitman, according to cognitive-dissonance theory (Festinger, 1957; Festinger & Carlsmith, 1959). Whitman may not have minded contradicting himself, but most people do not like their attitudes (cognitions) to be inconsistent. Cognitive theorists propose that organisms are motivated to create realistic mental maps of the world. Organisms adjust their representations of the world, as needed, to make things fit (Rescorla, 1988). Awareness that two cognitions are dissonant, or that our attitudes are incompatible with our behavior, is unpleasant and motivates us to reduce the discrepancy.

Effort Justification: "If I Did It, It Must Be Important"?

In the first and still one of the best-known studies on cognitive dissonance, one group of subjects received $1 for telling someone else that a boring task

Leon Festinger

Stanley Schachter

For seven weeks, Festinger and two colleagues, Henry Riecken and Stanley Schachter, were undercover agents pretending to be true followers of Marian Keech, the leader of the Seekers. When Ms. Keech asked for their names, Schachter—with what Hunt (1993) calls an "irrepressible sense of humor"—said "Leon Festinger." Stunned, Festinger took the name of Stanley Schachter. The twosome had to maintain each others' names throughout their relationship with Ms. Keech and the Seekers.

Hunt characterizes Festinger as "a peppery fellow, . . . a lover of cribbage and chess, both of which he played with fierce competitiveness. Festinger had the tough, brash, aggressive spirit so often found in men who grew up between the world wars on the tempestuous Lower East Side of New York" (p. 406). He describes Schachter as a "bluff, craggy-faced man with a zany sense of humor and . . . a taste for daring and deceptive experimentation" (p. 497).

Festinger is best known for his research on cognitive dissonance. We will see more of Schachter's "daring and deceptive experimentation" later in the chapter, where we discuss the role of cognitive appraisal in emotional states. ■

was interesting (Festinger & Carlsmith, 1959). Members of a second group received $20 to describe the chore positively. Both groups were paid to engage in **attitude-discrepant behavior**—that is, behavior that ran counter to their cognitions. After "selling" the job to others, the subjects were asked to rate their own liking for it. Ironically, those who were paid *less* rated the task as more interesting. Why?

According to learning theory, this result would be confusing. After all, shouldn't we learn to like that which is highly rewarding? But cognitive-dissonance theory would predict this "less-leads-to-more effect" for the following reason: The cognitions "I was paid very little" and "I told someone that this assignment was interesting" are dissonant. People tend to engage in **effort justification.** They tend to explain their behavior to themselves in such a way that unpleasant undertakings seem worth it. Subjects who were paid only $1 may have justified their lie by concluding that they may not have been lying in the first place. Similarly, we appreciate things more when they are more difficult to obtain.

Consider another situation. Cognitive dissonance would be created if we believed that our preferred candidate was unlikely to win the next presidential election. One cognition would be that our candidate would be better for the country or would "save" it from harmful forces. A second, dissonant, cognition would be that our candidate does not have a chance of winning. Research shows that in presidential elections from 1952 to 1980, four out of five people reduced such dissonance by expressing the belief that their candidate would win (Granberg & Brent, 1983). They often clung to their prediction despite lopsided polls to the contrary.

Truth or Fiction Revisited

It is true that we appreciate things more when we have to work for them. This is an example of the principle of effort justification.

REFLECTIONS

- Have you ever changed your opinion of someone when you learned that she or he liked something that you disliked? What happened? Why?
- Were you subjected to rough hazing upon joining a sorority, fraternity, or club? Did the experience affect your feelings about being a member of the group? How? Can you connect your experience to the concept of *effort justification?*

■ THE THREE A'S OF MOTIVATION: ACHIEVEMENT, AFFILIATION, AND AGGRESSION

Let us consider some of the powerful motives that bind us together or tear us asunder: achievement, affiliation, and aggression. The Harvard psychologist

Henry Murray (1938) hypothesized that each of these "A's" reflects a psychological need. He also referred to them as *social motives*, which he believed differ from primary motives such as hunger in that they are acquired through social learning. However, contemporary researchers believe that hereditary predispositions may also play a role in these behavior patterns.

• *Achievement*

Many students persist in studying despite being surrounded by distractions. Many people strive relentlessly to get ahead, to "make it," to earn large sums of money, to invent, to accomplish the impossible. These people are said to have strong achievement motivation.

Psychologist David McClelland (1958) helped pioneer the assessment of achievement motivation through evaluation of fantasies. One method involves the **Thematic Apperception Test (TAT)**, which was developed by Henry Murray. The TAT contains cards with pictures and drawings that are subject to various interpretations (see Chapter 12). Individuals are shown one or more TAT cards and asked to construct stories about the pictured theme: to indicate what led up to it, what the characters are thinking and feeling, and what is likely to happen.

One TAT card is similar to that in Figure 11.5. The meaning of the card is ambiguous—unclear. Is the girl thinking about the book, or is she wishing she were out with friends? Consider two stories that could be told about this card:

Story 1: "She's upset that she's got to read the book because she's behind in assignments and doesn't particularly like to work. She'd much rather be out somewhere with her friends, and she may very well sneak out and do that."

Story 2: "She's thinking, 'Someday I'll be a great scholar. I'll write books like this, and everybody will be proud of me.' She reads all the time."

The second story suggests the presence of more achievement motivation than the first. Classic studies find that people with high achievement motivation earn higher grades than people with comparable learning ability but lower achievement motivation. They are more likely to earn high salaries and be promoted than less motivated people with similar opportunities. They perform better at math problems and at unscrambling anagrams, such as decoding RSTA into STAR, TARS, ARTS, or RATS.[1]

McClelland (1965) found that 83% of college graduates with high achievement motivation found jobs in occupations characterized by risk, decision making, and the chance for great success, such as business management, sales, or businesses of their own making. Most (70%) of the graduates who chose

[1] Laboratory rats, of course.

| **THEMATIC APPERCEPTION TEST** • A test devised by Henry Murray to measure needs through fantasy production.

FIGURE 11.5

TAPPING FANTASIES IN PERSONALITY RESEARCH

This picture is similar to a Thematic Apperception Test card that is used to measure the need for achievement. What is happening in this picture? What is the person thinking and feeling? What is going to happen? Your answers to these questions reflect your own needs as well as the content of the picture itself.

nonentrepreneurial positions showed low achievement motivation. People with high achievement motivation seem to prefer challenges and are willing to take moderate risks to achieve their goals.

WHAT FLAVOR IS YOUR ACHIEVEMENT MOTIVATION? Do you want to do well in this course? If you do, why? Carol Dweck (1997) finds that achievement motivation can be driven by different forces. Are you motivated mainly by performance goals? That is, is your grade in the course of most importance? If it is, it may be in part because your motives concern tangible rewards such as getting into graduate school, getting a good job, reaping approval from parents or your instructor, or avoiding criticism. Or are you motivated mainly by learning goals? Is your central motive the enhancing of your knowledge and skills—your ability to understand and master the subject matter? Performance goals are usually met through extrinsic rewards—for example, a good income and prestige. Learning goals usually lead to intrinsic rewards, such as satisfaction with oneself. Many of us strive to meet both performance and learning goals in many subjects, as well as in other areas of life.

DEVELOPMENT OF ACHIEVEMENT MOTIVATION Parents with strong achievement motivation tend to encourage their children to think and act independently from an early age. They help their children develop learning goals by praising them for their efforts to learn, and encouraging persistence, enjoyment, and independence (Dweck, 1997; Ginsburg & Bronstein, 1993; Gottfried and others, 1994). They expose their children to new, stimulating experiences. Parents of children who develop performance goals are more likely to reward their children with toys or money for getting good grades and to respond to poor grades with anger and removal of privileges. Parents of children with strong achievement motivation also show warmth and praise their children profusely for their accomplishments. Children of such parents frequently set high standards for themselves, associate their achievements with self-worth, and attribute their achievements to their own efforts rather than to chance or to the intervention of others.

Achievement motivation resides within the individual. However, as noted in "Psychology and Modern Life," psychologists have done much to enhance achievement motivation—and productivity—on the job.

• Affiliation: "People Who Need People"

The motive for **affiliation** prompts us to make friends, join groups, and prefer to do things with others rather than alone. Affiliation motivation is part of the social glue that holds families and other groups together. In this sense, it is certainly a positive trait. Yet some people have such a strong need to affiliate that they find it painful to make their own decisions or to be alone. Research by Stanley Schachter suggests that a very high need to affiliate may indicate anxiety, such as when people "huddle together" in fear of some outside force.

In a classic experiment on the effects of anxiety on affiliation, Schachter (1959) manipulated subjects' anxiety levels by leading them to believe that they would receive either painful electric shocks (the high-anxiety condition) or mild electric shocks (the low-anxiety condition). Subjects were then asked to wait while the shock apparatus was supposedly being set up. They could choose to wait alone or in a room with others. The majority (63%) of those who expected a painful shock chose to wait in a room with other people. Only one third (33%) of those who expected a mild shock chose to wait with others.

Why did subjects in Schachter's study wish to affiliate only with people who shared their misery? Schachter explained their choice with his **theory of social comparison**. This theory holds that in an ambiguous situation—that is, a situation in which we are not certain about what we should do or how we should feel—we will affiliate with people with whom we can compare feelings and behaviors. Schachter's anxious recruits could compare their reactions with those of other "victims," but not with people who had no reason to feel anxious. Anxious subjects may also have resented uninvolved people for "getting away free."

• Aggression: Some Facts of Life and Death

Consider the following facts:

- After the end of the Cold War and the demise of the Soviet Union, you might have expected the world to become more peaceful. Yet civil wars and other conflicts rage on every continent.
- In the United States, violence has replaced communicable diseases as the leading cause of death among young people. Homicide has become the second leading cause of death among 15- to 24-year-olds (Lore & Schultz, 1993). (Accidents are the leading cause.)
- Aggression is not limited to foreign battlefields or dark streets and alleyways. Each year more than a million U.S. children are brought to the attention of authorities as victims of child abuse. "My sense is that something is deeply wrong with the core unit of our civilization, the

Truth or Fiction Revisited

Schachter found that misery does love company — but only company of a special sort. Highly anxious subjects were placed in two social conditions. In the first, they could choose either to wait alone or with others who would also receive painful shocks. Sixty percent of these people chose to affiliate — that is, to wait with others. In the second condition, highly anxious subjects could choose to wait alone or with people they believed were not involved with the study. In this second condition, no one chose to affiliate.

AFFILIATION • Association or connection with a group.
THEORY OF SOCIAL COMPARISON • The view that people look to others for cues about how to behave when they are in confusing or unfamiliar situations.

family," notes former APA president Ronald Fox (1996). "It's no longer a safe haven for many Americans."

- The video games *Mortal Kombat* and *Night Trap* are best-sellers among U.S. children. In *Mortal Kombat,* the player can decapitate the loser. In *Night Trap,* the player attempts to prevent a gang of vampires from capturing scantily clad sorority sisters. If the player fails, the vampires drain the women's blood from their necks.

Why do people treat each other like this? Let us consider some theories of aggression.

psychology and
modern life

ENHANCING PRODUCTIVITY AND JOB SATISFACTION

Achievement motivation, productivity, and job satisfaction go hand in hand. Enhancing workers' satisfaction on the job motivates them to be more productive (Katzell & Thompson, 1990). That is why businesses and organizations employ industrial/organizational (I/O) psychologists to help them enhance worker satisfaction.

Many I/O psychologists apply behavioral principles to train workers in a step-by-step fashion, to modify problem behaviors at work, and to make sure workers are rewarded for targeted behaviors. When required behaviors are made clear and the rewards (raises, bonuses, promotions, time off) for completing tasks are spelled out, workers' morale rises and complaints about favoritism decrease.

Consider some of the functions of I/O psychologists in recruitment, training, and evaluation.

RECRUITMENT AND PLACEMENT Worker motivation is enhanced right at the beginning when the right person for the job is hired. When the company's needs

mesh with the worker's, both profit. Unfortunately, people sometimes get hired for reasons that are irrelevant to their potential to perform well in the job. Sometimes people are hired because they are physically attractive (Mack & Rainey, 1990). On other occasions relatives or friends of friends are chosen. By and large, however, businesses seek employees who can do the job and are likely to be reasonably satisfied with it. Employees who are satisfied with their jobs are less likely to be absent or quit. I/O psychologists facilitate recruitment procedures by analyzing jobs, specifying the skills and personal attributes that are needed, and constructing tests and interviews to determine whether candidates have those skills and attributes. These procedures can enhance job satisfaction and productivity.

Psychologists help improve methods of selecting, training, and evaluating managers for sensitive positions (Hogan and others, 1994). As we reach the new millennium, only 15% of new workers will be White males, as com-

pared with more than 40% during the 1980s. As the workforce becomes more diverse—including more minority and female employees—we should be increasing the numbers of minority group members and women in management (Hogan and others, 1994). This can be accomplished with the assistance of psychologists who develop appropriate testing and selection procedures.

TRAINING AND INSTRUCTION I/O psychologists are versed in principles of learning, and worker training and instruction is the most common way of enhancing productivity (Katzell & Thompson, 1990). Training gives workers the appropriate skills, knowledge, and attitudes. Equipping them to solve problems on the job also reduces the stress they will encounter and enhances their feelings of self-worth. Why do psychologists address workers' attitudes? Consider just one example: A factory worker might resist wearing protective devices, even when taught how to do so, if he has the attitude that safety devices are for sissies.

THE BIOLOGICAL PERSPECTIVE Numerous biological structures and chemicals appear to be involved in aggression. One is the hypothalamus. In response to certain releasers, many lower animals show instinctive aggressive reactions. The hypothalamus appears to be involved in this inborn reaction pattern: Electrical stimulation of part of the hypothalamus triggers stereotypical aggressive behaviors in many lower animals. However, in humans, whose brains are more complex, other brain structures apparently moderate possible aggressive instincts.

The sociobiological view is that aggression is natural. Sociobiology views much social behavior, including aggressive behavior, as influenced by genetic

APPRAISAL OF WORKERS' PERFORMANCE Workers are more highly motivated when they receive individualized guidance and reinforcers are based on accurate appraisals of their performance. Criticism of workers' performance is necessary if workers are to improve, but it is important that criticism be delivered in a constructive way (Weisinger, 1990; see Table 11.2). Destructive criticism saps workers' motivation and belief in their ability to perform. Constructive criticism helps workers feel that they are being shown how to improve their performance (Baron, 1990).

In an ideal world, appraisal of workers' performances would be based solely on how well they do their jobs. But cognitive biases play a role in worker appraisal. Sometimes managers focus on the *worker* rather than on the performance. A supervisor is more likely to appraise the work of a subordinate positively who is also a friend (Fiske, 1993). There is also a tendency—called the *halo effect*—to rate workers according to general impressions (for example, liking or disliking).

Another bias in appraisal is the tendency to evaluate workers according to how much effort they put into their work. Many managers evaluate "hard workers" more positively than other workers, even if they accomplish less (Dugan, 1989; Tsui & O'Reilly, 1989). Hard work is not necessarily good work, however. (Should students who work harder than you do be given higher grades on tests, even when you get the answers right and they make errors?) ■

TABLE 11.2	CRITICISM: THE GOOD, THE BAD, AND THE UGLY
Constructive Criticism (Good)	**Destructive Criticism (Bad and Ugly)**
Specific: The supervisor is specific about what the employee is doing wrong. For example, she or he says "This is what you did that caused the problem, and this is why it caused the problem."	**Vague:** The supervisor makes a blanket condemnation, such as, "That was an awful thing to do," or "That was a lousy job." No specifics are given.
Supportive: The supervisor gives the employee the feeling that the criticism is meant to help him or her perform better on the job.	**Condemnatory of the employee:** The supervisor attributes the problem to an unchangeable cause such as the employee's personality.
Helpful in problem solving: The supervisor helps employees improve things or solve their problems on the job.	**Threatening:** The supervisor attacks the employee, as by saying, "If you do this again, you'll be docked," or "Next time, you're fired."
Timely: The supervisor offers the criticism as soon as possible after the problem occurs.	**Pessimistic:** The supervisor seems doubtful that the employee will be able to improve.

Truth or Fiction Revisited

It is not true that efficient, skillful employees are evaluated more highly than hard-working employees who must struggle to get the job done. Supervisors often focus on employees' efforts, sometime more so than on their performance.

factors (Hergenhahn, 1997). Consider the theory of evolution. Darwin held that many more individuals are produced than can find food and survive into adulthood. Therefore, a struggle for survival ensues. Individuals who possess characteristics that give them an advantage in the struggle for existence are more likely to survive and contribute their genes to the next generation. In many species, those characteristics include aggressiveness. Because aggressive individuals are more likely to survive and reproduce, whatever genes are linked to aggressive behavior are more likely to be transmitted to new generations.

Intelligence, of course, is another key to human survival. The capacity to outwit other species may be more important to human survival than aggressiveness.

THE PSYCHODYNAMIC PERSPECTIVE Sigmund Freud believed that aggressive impulses are inevitable reactions to the frustrations of daily life. Children (and adults) normally desire to vent aggressive impulses on other people, including parents, because even the most attentive parents cannot gratify all of their demands immediately. Yet children also fear punishment and loss of love, so they repress most aggressive impulses and store them in the unconscious recesses of the mind. The Freudian perspective, in a sense, sees humans as "steam engines." By holding in steam rather than venting it, we set the stage for future explosions. Pent-up aggressive impulses demand an outlet. They may be expressed toward parents in roundabout ways, such as destroying furniture; later in life they may be expressed toward strangers.

According to psychodynamic theory, the best way to prevent harmful aggression may be to encourage less harmful aggression. In the steam engine analogy, verbal aggression (through wit, sarcasm, or expression of negative feelings) may vent some of the aggressive steam in a person's unconscious mind. So might cheering on a football team or attending a prize fight. Psychoanalysts refer to the venting of aggressive impulses as **catharsis**. Catharsis thus is viewed as a safety valve. But research findings on the usefulness of catharsis are mixed. Some studies suggest that catharsis leads to pleasant reductions in tension and reduced likelihood of future aggression (e.g., Doob & Wood, 1972). Other studies, however, suggest that letting some steam escape actually encourages more aggression later on (e.g., Geen and others, 1975).

THE COGNITIVE PERSPECTIVE Cognitive psychologists assert that our behavior is influenced by our values, by how we interpret situations, and by choice. From the cognitive perspective, for example, people who believe that aggression is necessary and justified—as during wartime—are likely to act aggressively. People who believe that a particular war or act of aggression is unjust, or who oppose aggression regardless of the circumstances, are less likely to behave aggressively (Feshbach, 1994).

One cognitive theory suggests that frustrating and painful events trigger unpleasant feelings (Rule and others, 1987). These feelings, in turn, prompt aggression. Aggression is *not* automatic, however. Cognitive factors intervene (Berkowitz, 1994). People *decide* whether they will strike out or not on the basis of factors such as their previous experiences with aggression and their interpretation of the other person's motives.

Researchers find that many aggressive people distort other people's motives. For example, they assume that other people wish them harm when they actually do not (Akhtar & Bradley, 1991; Crick & Dodge, 1994; Dodge and others, 1990).

CATHARSIS • In psychodynamic theory, the purging of strong emotions or the relieving of tensions. (A Greek word meaning "purification.")

Cognitive therapists note that we are more likely to respond aggressively to a provocation when we magnify the importance of the insult or otherwise stir up feelings of anger (e.g., Lochman, 1992; Lochman & Dodge, 1994). How do you respond when someone bumps into you? If you view it as an intentional insult to your honor, you may respond with aggression. If you view it as an accident, or as a social problem in need of a solution, you are less likely to act aggressively.

LEARNING PERSPECTIVES From the behavioral perspective, learning is acquired through reinforcement. Organisms that are reinforced for aggressive behavior are more likely to behave aggressively in similar situations. Environmental consequences make it more likely that strong, agile organisms will be reinforced for aggressive behavior.

From the social-cognitive perspective, aggressive skills are mainly acquired by observation. Social-cognitive theorists do, however, believe that consciousness and choice may play a role. In this view, we are not likely to act aggressively unless we believe that aggression is appropriate under the circumstances.

THE SOCIOCULTURAL PERSPECTIVE The sociocultural perspective focuses on ways in which ethnicity and gender may be related to aggression. Note the following facts:

- African American men aged 15 to 34 are about 9 times as likely as non-Hispanic White Americans to be victims of homicide (Tomes, 1993).
- Hispanic American men are about 5 times as likely to be homicide victims (Tomes, 1993).
- Each year in the United States about 30 women per 1,000 are victims of violence at the hands of their male partners (Tomes, 1993).
- Perhaps half the women in the United States have been subjected to severe physical, sexual, or psychological abuse (Walker, 1993).

Sociocultural theorists note that U.S. culture—like the culture of the Mundugumor—has a way of breeding violence. For example, in Thailand and Jamaica aggression in children is discouraged and politeness and deference are encouraged (Tharp, 1991). In the United States, by contrast, competitiveness and independence are encouraged. Perhaps as a result of this cultural difference, children in the United States are more likely to be argumentative, disobedient, and belligerent (Tharp, 1991).

REFLECTIONS

- Do you want to do well in this course? How hard will you strive to do well? How would you rate you own level of achievement motivation? When you consider your own experiences in life, where does the achievement motivation (or lack of it) seem to come from?
- Do you feel a strong need to make friends, join groups, and do things with other people? Why or why not?
- What were your beliefs about aggressiveness before you began this course? Has the information in this chapter affected your views? How?

■ EMOTION: ADDING COLOR TO LIFE

Emotions color our lives. We are green with envy, red with anger, blue with sorrow. Poets paint a thoughtful mood as a "brown study." Positive emotions such as love and desire can fill our days with pleasure. Negative emotions such as fear, depression, and anger can fill us with dread and make each day a chore.

An emotion can be a response to a situation, in the way that fear is a response to a threat. An emotion can motivate behavior, as anger can motivate us to act aggressively. An emotion can also be a goal in itself. We may behave in ways that will lead us to experience joy or feelings of love.

Emotions are feeling states with cognitive, physiological, and behavioral components (Carlson & Hatfield, 1992). Strong emotions arouse the autonomic nervous system (LeDoux, 1997). The greater the arousal, the more intense the emotion. *Fear,* which usually occurs in response to a threat, involves cognitions that one is in danger, arousal of the sympathetic nervous system (rapid heartbeat and breathing, sweating, muscle tension), and tendencies to avoid or escape from the situation (see Table 11.3). As a response to a social provocation, *anger* involves cognitions that the provocateur should be paid back, arousal of both the sympathetic and parasympathetic nervous systems, and tendencies to attack. *Depression* usually involves cognitions of helplessness and hopelessness, parasympathetic arousal, and tendencies toward inactivity—or, sometimes—self-destruction. *Joy, grief, jealousy, disgust, embarrassment, liking*—all have cognitive, physiological, and behavioral components.

• *Arousal, Emotions, and Lie Detection*

The connection between autonomic arousal and emotions has led to the development of many kinds of lie detectors. Such instruments detect something, but do they detect specific emotional responses that signify lies? Let us take a closer look at the problem of lying.

Lying—for better or worse—is an integral part of life (Saxe, 1991a). Political leaders lie to get elected. Some students lie about why they have not completed assignments (Saxe, 1991a). ('Fess up!) The great majority of people lie to their lovers—most often about other relationships (Saxe, 1991a). (Is it really true that you never kissed anyone else before?) People also lie about their qualifications to obtain jobs, and of course, some people lie in denying guilt for

EMOTION • A state of feeling that has cognitive, physiological, and behavioral components.

TABLE 11.3	COMPONENTS OF EMOTIONS		
Emotion	*Cognitive*	*Physiological*	*Behavioral*
Fear	Belief that one is in danger	Sympathetic arousal	Avoidance tendencies
Anger	Frustration or belief that one is being mistreated	Sympathetic and parasympathetic arousal	Attack tendencies
Depression	Thoughts of helplessness, hopelessness, worthlessness	Parasympathetic arousal	Inactivity, possible self-destructive tendencies

crimes. Although we are unlikely to subject political leaders, students, and lovers to lie detector tests, such tests are frequently used in hiring and in police investigations.

Facial expressions often offer clues to deceit, but some people can lie with a straight face—or a smile. As Shakespeare pointed out in *Hamlet,* "One may smile, and smile, and be a villain." The use of devices to detect lies has a long, if not laudable, history:

> The Bedouins of Arabia . . . until quite recently required conflicting witnesses to lick a hot iron; the one whose tongue was burned was thought to be lying. The Chinese, it is said, had a similar method for detecting lying: Suspects were forced to chew rice powder and spit it out; if the powder was dry, the suspect was guilty. A variation of this test was used during the Inquisition. The suspect had to swallow a "trial slice" of bread and cheese; if it stuck to the suspect's palate or throat he or she was not telling the truth. (Kleinmuntz & Szucko, 1984, pp. 766–767)

These methods may sound primitive, even bizarre, but they are broadly consistent with modern psychological knowledge. Anxiety about being caught in a lie is linked to arousal of the sympathetic division of the autonomic nervous system. One sign of sympathetic arousal is lack of saliva, or dryness in the mouth. The emotions of fear and guilt are also linked to sympathetic arousal and, hence, to dryness in the mouth.

Modern lie detectors, or polygraphs (see Figure 11.6), monitor indicators of sympathetic arousal while a witness or suspect is being examined. These indicators include heart rate, blood pressure, respiration rate, and electrodermal response (sweating). Questions have been raised about the validity of assessing truth or fiction in this way, however.

The American Polygraph Association claims that use of the polygraph is 85% to 95% accurate. Critics find polygraph testing to be less accurate and claim that it is sensitive to more than lies (Bashore & Rapp, 1993; Furedy, 1990; Saxe, 1991b; Steinbrook, 1992). Studies have found that factors such as tense muscles, drugs, and previous experience with polygraph tests can significantly reduce the accuracy rate (Steinbrook, 1992). In one experiment, people were able to reduce the accuracy of polygraph-based judgments to about 50% by biting their tongue (to produce pain) or by pressing their toes against the floor (to tense muscles) while being interviewed (Honts and others, 1985).

In a review of the literature on this subject, the government Office of Technology Assessment (OTA) found that there was little valid research on the use of the polygraph in preemployment screening, "dragnet" investigations (attempts to distinguish a guilty person from other suspects), or determining who should be given access to classified information (U.S. Congress, 1983). The OTA also looked into studies involving investigations of specific indictments. The studies' conclusions varied widely. In 28 studies that were judged to have employed adequate methodology, accurate detections of guilt ranged from 35% to 100%. Accurate judgments of innocence ranged from 12.5% to 94%.

In sum, no identifiable pattern of autonomic arousal pinpoints lying (Bashore & Rapp, 1993; Saxe, 1991b; Steinbrook, 1992). Because of validity problems, results of polygraph examinations are no longer admitted as evidence in many courts. Polygraph interviews are still often conducted in criminal investigations and job interviews, but this practice is also being questioned.

Truth or Fiction Revisited

It is true that you may be able to fool a lie detector by wiggling your toes. This creates patterns of autonomic arousal that may be misread in interpreting the polygraph.

FIGURE 11.6
WHAT DO "LIE DETECTORS" DETECT?

The polygraph monitors heart rate, blood pressure, respiration rate, and sweat in the palms of the hands. Is the polygraph sensitive to lying only? Is it foolproof? Because of the controversy surrounding these questions, many courts no longer admit polygraph evidence.

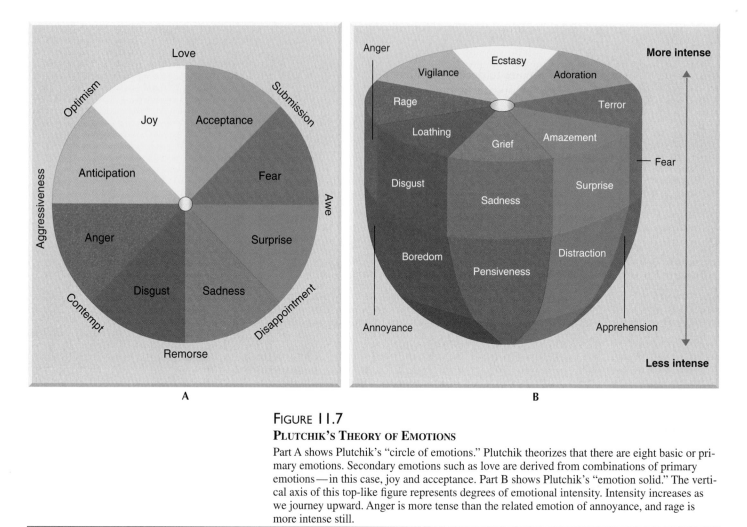

FIGURE 11.7

PLUTCHIK'S THEORY OF EMOTIONS

Part A shows Plutchik's "circle of emotions." Plutchik theorizes that there are eight basic or primary emotions. Secondary emotions such as love are derived from combinations of primary emotions—in this case, joy and acceptance. Part B shows Plutchik's "emotion solid." The vertical axis of this top-like figure represents degrees of emotional intensity. Intensity increases as we journey upward. Anger is more tense than the related emotion of annoyance, and rage is more intense still.

• *How Many Emotions Are There? Where Do They Come From?*

The ancient Chinese believed that there are four basic or instinctive emotions—happiness, anger, sorrow, and fear. They arise, respectively, in the heart, liver, lungs, and kidneys (Carlson & Hatfield, 1992). (No, there is no evidence for this view.) The behaviorist psychologist John B. Watson (1924) believed that there are three basic or inborn emotions: fear, rage, and love. Others, such as Paul Ekman (1980) and Robert Plutchik (1984), have argued for somewhat larger numbers of basic emotions (see Figure 11.7). The question remains unresolved (Fischer and others, 1990).

In 1932 Katherine Bridges proposed that people are born with a single basic emotion—diffuse excitement—and that other emotions differentiate over time. More recently Carroll Izard (1984, 1990) argued that all emotions are present at birth. However, they are not *displayed* all at once. Instead, they emerge in response to the child's developing needs and maturational sequences. In keeping with Izard's view, researchers have found that infants appear to show a number of different emotions at ages earlier than those suggested by Bridges. In one study of the emotions shown by babies during their first 3 months, 99% of the mothers interviewed reported that their babies showed the emotion of interest. Ninety-five percent of the mothers reported joy; 84%, anger; 74%, surprise; and 58%, fear (Johnson and others, 1982).

• *The Expression of Emotions*

Joy and sadness are found in all cultures, but how can we tell when other people are happy or despondent? It turns out that the expression of many emotions may be universal (Rinn, 1991). Smiling is apparently a universal sign of friendliness and approval. Baring the teeth, as noted by Charles Darwin (1872) in the last century, may be a universal sign of anger. As the originator of the theory of evolution, Darwin believed that the universal recognition of facial expressions would have survival value. For example, in the absence of language, facial expressions could signal the approach of enemies (or friends).

Most investigators (e.g., Brown, 1991; Buss, 1992; Ekman, 1994; Izard, 1994) concur that certain facial expressions suggest the same emotions in all people. Moreover, people in diverse cultures recognize the emotions manifested by certain facial expressions. In a classic study, Paul Ekman (1980) took photographs of people exhibiting anger, disgust, fear, happiness, sadness, and surprise. (Some of the photos are shown in Figure 11.8.) He then asked people around the world to indicate what emotions were being depicted. Those queried ranged from European college students to members of the Fore, a tribe that dwells in the New Guinea highlands. All groups, including the Fore, who had almost no contact with Western culture, agreed on the emotions being portrayed. The Fore also displayed familiar facial expressions when asked how they would respond if they were the characters in stories that called for basic emotional responses. More recently, Ekman and his colleagues (1987) obtained similar results in a study of 10 cultures. In that study, subjects were allowed to identify more than one emotion in facial expressions. The subjects generally agreed on which two emotions were being shown and which emotion was more intense.

FIGURE 11.8

PHOTOGRAPHS USED IN RESEARCH BY PAUL EKMAN

Ekman's research suggests that the expression of several basic emotions such as happiness, anger, surprise, and fear is universally recognized.

 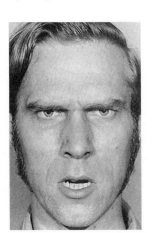  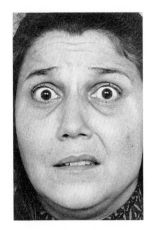

The Facial-Feedback Hypothesis

We generally recognize that facial expressions reflect emotional states. In fact, various emotional states give rise to certain patterns of electrical activity in the facial muscles and in the brain (Cacioppo and others, 1988; Ekman and others, 1990). The **facial-feedback hypothesis** argues, however, that the causal relationship between emotions and facial expressions can also work in the opposite direction:

> The free expression by outward signs of an emotion intensifies it. On the other hand, the repression, as far as possible, of all outward signs softens our emotions. (Darwin, 1872, p. 22)

Does this mean that smiling can give rise to feelings of good will? Can frowning produce anger?

Psychological research has yielded some interesting findings concerning the facial-feedback hypothesis (Ekman, 1993b). Inducing people to smile, for example, leads them to report more positive feelings (Basic Behavioral Science Task Force, 1996c) and to rate cartoons as more humorous. When induced to frown, they rate cartoons as more aggressive. When they exhibit pain through facial expressions, they rate electric shocks as more painful.

What are the possible links between facial feedback and emotion? One link is arousal. Intense contraction of facial muscles such as those used in signifying fear heightens arousal, which, in turn, boosts emotional response. Kinesthetic feedback of the contraction of facial muscles may also induce feeling states. Ekman (1993b) has found that the so-called Duchenne smile, which is characterized by "crow's feet wrinkles around the eyes and a subtle drop in the eye cover fold so that the skin above the eye moves down slightly toward the eyeball," can induce pleasant feelings.

You may have heard the British expression "Keep a stiff upper lip" as a recommendation for handling stress. It might be that a "stiff" lip suppresses emotional response—as long as the lip is relaxed rather than quivering with fear or tension. But when the lip is stiffened through strong muscle tension, facial feedback may heighten emotional response. In the following section we see that the facial-feedback hypothesis is related to the James-Lange theory of emotion.

Theories of Emotion: Is Feeling First?

In Chapter 9, I asked you to consider the syntax of the following lines from an e. e. cummings poem:

> since feeling is first
> who pays any attention
> to the syntax of things
> will never wholly kiss you . . .

Now let us address the subject matter of the poem—not the kiss, but the question. *Does* feeling, in fact, come first?

Emotions have physiological, situational, and cognitive components, but psychologists disagree about how these components interact to produce feeling states and actions. Some psychologists argue that physiological arousal ("feeling" in the cummings poem) is a more basic component of emotional response than cognition and that the type of arousal we experience strongly influences our cognitive appraisal and our labeling of the emotion (e.g., Izard, 1984). For these psychologists, "feeling is first." Other psychologists argue that cognitive

---

Truth or Fiction Revisited

It is true that smiling can produce pleasant feelings. Research has shown that the Duchenne smile can indeed give rise to pleasant feelings.

FACIAL-FEEDBACK HYPOTHESIS • The view that stereotypical facial expressions can contribute to stereotypical emotions.

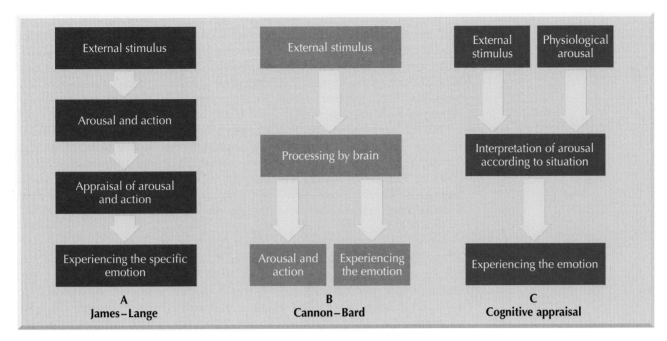

FIGURE 11.9
WHAT THEORIES OF EMOTION ARE THERE?

Several theories of emotion have been advanced, each of which proposes a different role for the components of emotional response. According to the James-Lange theory (part A), events trigger specific arousal patterns and actions. Emotions result from our appraisal of our body responses. According to the Cannon-Bard theory (part B), events are first processed by the brain. Body patterns of arousal, action, and our emotional responses are then triggered simultaneously. According to the theory of cognitive appraisal (part C), events and arousal are appraised by the individual. The emotional response stems from the person's appraisal of the situation and his or her level of arousal.

appraisal and physiological arousal are so strongly intertwined that cognitive processes may determine the emotional response.

The "commonsense theory" of emotions is that something happens (a situation) that is cognitively appraised (interpreted) by the person, and the feeling state (a combination of arousal and thoughts) follows. For example, you meet someone new, appraise that person as being delightful, and feelings of attraction follow. Or you flunk a test, recognize that you're in trouble, and feel down in the dumps.

However, both historic and contemporary theories of how the components of emotions interact are at variance with this commonsense view. Let us consider a number of theories and see if we can arrive at some useful conclusions.

THE JAMES-LANGE THEORY At the turn of the century, William James suggested that our emotions follow, rather than cause, our behavioral responses to events. At about the same time this view was also proposed by the Danish physiologist Karl G. Lange. It is therefore termed the James-Lange theory of emotion.

According to James and Lange, certain external stimuli instinctively trigger specific patterns of arousal and action, such as fighting or fleeing (see Figure 11.9, part A). We then become angry *because* we are acting aggressively or become afraid *because* we are running away. Emotions are simply the cognitive representations (or by-products) of automatic physiological and behavioral responses.

Walter Cannon (1927) criticized the James-Lange assertion that each emotion has distinct physiological correlates. He argued that the physiological arousal associated with emotion A is not as distinct from the arousal associated with emotion B as the theory asserts. We should also note that the James-Lange view downplays the importance of human cognition; it denies the roles of cognitive appraisal, personal values, and personal choice in our behavioral and emotional responses to events.

On the other hand, the James-Lange theory is consistent with the facial-feedback hypothesis. That is, smiling apparently can induce pleasant feelings, "even though we don't know if the effect is strong enough to override sadness" (Ekman, 1993b). The theory also suggests that we may be able to change our feelings by changing our behavior. Changing one's behavior to change one's feelings is one aspect of behavior therapy, which is discussed in Chapter 16.

THE CANNON-BARD THEORY Walter Cannon (1927) was not content to criticize the James-Lange theory. Along with Philip Bard (1934), he suggested that an event might *simultaneously* trigger bodily responses (arousal and action) and the experience of an emotion. As shown in Figure 11.9 (part B), when an event is perceived (processed by the brain), the brain stimulates autonomic and muscular activity (arousal and action) *and* cognitive activity (experience of the emotion). Thus, according to the Cannon-Bard theory emotions *accompany* bodily responses. They are not *produced by* bodily changes, as in the James-Lange theory.

The central criticism of the Cannon-Bard theory focuses on whether bodily responses (arousal and action) and emotions are actually stimulated simultaneously. For example, pain or the perception of danger may trigger arousal before we begin to feel distress or fear. Also, many of us have had the experience of having a "narrow escape" and becoming aroused and shaky afterward, when we have had time to consider the damage that might have occurred. What is needed is a theory that allows for an ongoing interaction of external events, physiological changes (such as autonomic arousal and muscular activity), and cognitive activities.

THE THEORY OF COGNITIVE APPRAISAL Recent theoretical approaches to emotion have stressed cognitive factors. Among those who argue that thinking comes first are Gordon Bower, Richard Lazarus, Stanley Schachter, and Robert Zajonc.

Stanley Schachter asserts that emotions are associated with similar patterns of bodily arousal that may be weaker or stronger, depending on the level of arousal. The label we give to an emotion depends largely on our cognitive appraisal of the situation. Cognitive appraisal is based on many factors, including our perception of external events and the ways in which other people seem to respond to those events (see Figure 11.9, part C). Given the presence of other people, we engage in social comparison to arrive at an appropriate response.

In a classic experiment, Schachter and Singer (1962) showed that arousal can be labeled quite differently, depending on the situation. The investigators told subjects in the study that they wanted to determine the effects of a vitamin on vision. Half of the subjects received an injection of adrenaline, a hormone that increases autonomic arousal (see Chapter 3). A control group received an injection of an inactive solution. Those who had been given adrenaline then received one of three "cognitive manipulations," as shown in Table 11.4. Group 1 was told nothing about possible emotional effects of the "vitamin." Group 2

TABLE 11.4	INJECTED SUBSTANCES AND COGNITIVE MANIPULATIONS IN THE SCHACHTER-SINGER STUDY	
Group	*Substance*	*Cognitive Manipulation*
1	Adrenaline	No information given about effects
2	Adrenaline	Misinformation given: itching, numbness, etc.
3	Adrenaline	Accurate information: physiological arousal
4	(Inactive)	None

Note: From Schachter & Singer (1962).

was deliberately misinformed; members of this group were led to expect itching, numbness, or other irrelevant symptoms. Group 3 was informed accurately about the increased arousal they would experience.

After receiving injections and cognitive manipulations, the subjects were asked to wait in pairs while the experimental apparatus was being set up. The subjects did not know that the person with whom they were waiting was a confederate of the experimenter. The confederate's purpose was to exhibit a response that the subject would believe was caused by the injection.

Some of those who took part in the experiment waited with a confederate who acted in a happy-go-lucky manner. He flew paper airplanes about the room and tossed paper balls into a wastebasket. Other subjects waited with a confederate who acted angry. He complained about the experiment, tore up a questionnaire, and left the waiting room in a huff. As the confederates worked for their Oscar awards, the real subjects were observed through a one-way mirror.

The people in groups 1 and 2 were likely to imitate the behavior of the confederate. Those who were exposed to the happy-go-lucky confederate acted jovial and content. Those who were exposed to the angry confederate imitated that person's complaining, aggressive behavior. But those in groups 3 and 4 were less influenced by the confederate's behavior.

Schachter and Singer concluded that subjects in groups 1 and 2 were in an ambiguous situation. Members of these groups felt arousal from the adrenaline injection but had no basis for attributing it to any specific event or emotion. Social comparison with a confederate led them to attribute their arousal either to happiness or to anger. Members of group 3 expected arousal from the injection, with no particular emotional consequences. These subjects did not imitate the confederate's display of happiness or anger because they were not in an ambiguous situation. Members of group 4 had no physiological arousal for which they needed an attribution, except perhaps for some arousal induced by observing the confederate. They also did not imitate the behavior of the confederate.

Now, happiness and anger are quite different emotions. Happiness is a positive emotion, whereas anger, for most of us, is a negative emotion. Yet Schachter and Singer suggest that any physiological differences between these two emotions are so slight that opposing cognitive appraisals of the same situation can lead one person to label arousal as happiness and another person to label it as anger. The Schachter-Singer view could not be further removed from the James-Lange theory, which holds that each emotion is associated with specific and readily recognized body sensations.

The truth, it happens, may lie somewhere in between.

In science, it must be possible to replicate experiments and attain identical or similar results; otherwise a theory cannot be considered valid. The Schachter

In Review   Theories of Emotion

THEORY	DESCRIPTION	COMMENTS
Commonsense Theory	Something happens that is interpreted (cognitively appraised) by the person, and the emotion follows.	Compare to Albert Ellis's A → B → C approach to explaining emotions such as anxiety and depression (in Chapter 14).
The James-Lange Theory	Emotions follow, rather than cause, our behavioral responses to events. Certain stimuli trigger specific instinctive patterns of arousal and action.	Research does not show that each emotion has distinct biological correlates.
The Cannon-Bard Theory	Events simultaneously trigger bodily responses (arousal and action) and the experience of an emotion. Emotions *accompany* bodily responses but are not *produced by* them.	Research does not show that bodily responses (arousal and action) and emotions are stimulated simultaneously.
Theory of Cognitive Appraisal	The label we give to an emotion depends largely on our cognitive appraisal of the situation. Emotions are associated with similar patterns of bodily arousal. When we are uncertain about what we feel, we engage in social comparison to arrive at an appropriate emotional response.	Research suggests that the patterns of arousal associated with different emotions are more specific than suggested by Schachter and Singer.

and Singer study has been replicated, but with *different* results (Ekman, 1993a). For instance, a number of studies found that subjects were less likely to imitate the behavior of the confederate and were likely to perceive unexplained arousal in negative terms, attributing it to nervousness, anger, even jealousy (Zimbardo and others, 1993).

EVALUATION   What can we make of all this? Research by Paul Ekman and his colleagues (1983) suggests that the patterns of arousal connected with various emotions are more specific than suggested by Schachter and Singer—although less so than suggested by James and Lange. Research with the PET scan suggests that different emotions, such as happiness and sadness, involve different structures within the brain (Goleman, 1995a). Moreover, lack of control over our emotions and lack of understanding of what is happening to us are disturbing experiences (Zimbardo and others, 1993). Thus, our cognitive appraisals of situations apparently do affect our emotional responses, even if not quite in the way envisioned by Schachter.

In sum, various components of an experience—cognitive, physiological, and behavioral—contribute to our emotional responses. Humans are thinking beings who gather information from all three sources in determining their behavioral responses and labeling their emotional responses. The fact that none of the theories we have discussed applies to all people in all situations is comforting. Apparently our emotions are not quite as easily understood or manipulated as some theorists have suggested.

REFLECTIONS

- Do you know people who are highly emotional? What behavior leads you to infer that they are emotional?
- Have you ever tried to tell whether someone was lying to you? What clues did you seek? Can you "keep a straight face" when you lie?
- Have you had experiences that seem to support one of the theories of emotion presented in the chapter? What were they? Which theory do they seem to support?

SUMMARY

1. **What are motives, needs, drives, and incentives?** A motive is a state within an organism that activates and directs behavior toward a goal. A physiological need is a state of deprivation. Needs give rise to drives, which are psychological in nature and arouse us to action. An incentive is an object, person, or situation that is perceived as being capable of satisfying a need.

2. **What are some psychological theories of motivation?** According to instinct theory, organisms are born with preprogrammed tendencies to behave in certain ways in certain situations. According to drive-reduction theory, we are motivated to engage in behavior that reduces drives. Humanistic psychologists argue that behavior can be growth-oriented; people are motivated to strive consciously for self-fulfillment. Maslow hypothesized that people have a hierarchy of needs, including an innate need for self-actualization. According to cognitive theory, people are motivated to understand and predict events and to make their cognitions harmonious with one another.

3. **What are physiological drives?** Physiological, or primary, drives are unlearned and generally function according to a homeostatic principle—the tendency to maintain a steady state.

4. **What factors give rise to the hunger drive?** Hunger is regulated by several internal mechanisms, including stomach contractions, blood sugar level, receptors in the mouth and liver, and the responses of the hypothalamus. The ventromedial hypothalamus functions as a stop-eating center. Lesions in this area lead to hyperphagia in rats, causing the animals to grow to several times their normal body weight, but their weight eventually levels off. The lateral hypothalamus has a start-eating center. External stimuli such as the aroma of food can also trigger hunger.

5. **What are stimulus motives?** Stimulus motives, like physiological motives, are innate, but they involve motives to increase rather than decrease stimulation. Sensory-deprivation studies show that lack of stimulation is aversive. People and many lower animals have needs for stimulation and activity, exploration and manipulation. Sensation seekers may seek thrills, act on impulses, and be easily bored.

6. **Do people seek cognitive consistency?** Cognitive-dissonance theory hypothesizes that people dislike situations in which their attitudes and behavior are inconsistent. Such situations apparently induce cognitive dissonance, which people can reduce by changing their attitudes. People also engage in effort justification; that is, they tend to justify attitude-discrepant behavior to themselves by concluding that their attitudes may be different than they thought they were.

7. **What is achievement motivation?** Achievement motivation is the need to accomplish things. People with high achievement motivation attain higher grades and earn more money than people of comparable ability with lower achievement motivation.

8. **What is the need for affiliation?** This is the need to be with other people. It prompts us to join groups and make friends. Anxiety tends to increase our need for affiliation, especially with people who share our predicament.

9. **Why are people aggressive?** Various theories account for aggression in different ways. Sociobiological

theory views aggression as instinctive and linked to evolution. Psychodynamic theory views aggression as stemming from inevitable frustrations. Learning theories view aggression as stemming from experience and reinforcement. Cognitive perspectives predict that people are aggressive when they see aggression as appropriate for them.

10. **What is an emotion?** An emotion is a state of feeling with cognitive, physiological, and behavioral components. Emotions motivate behavior and also serve as goals.

11. **Are emotions expressed in the same way in different cultures?** According to Ekman, there are several basic emotions whose expression is recognized in cultures around the world.

12. **What is the facial-feedback hypothesis?** This is the view that intense facial expressions can heighten emotional response. Evidence for this hypothesis is mixed.

13. **What is the James-Lange theory of the activation of emotions?** According to the James-Lange theory, emotions are associated with specific patterns of arousal and action that are triggered by certain external events. The emotion follows the behavioral response.

14. **What is the Cannon-Bard theory of the activation of emotions?** The Cannon-Bard theory proposes that processing of events by the brain gives rise simultaneously to feelings and bodily responses. According to this view, feelings accompany bodily responses.

15. **What is the cognitive-appraisal theory of the activation of emotions?** According to Schachter and Singer's theory of cognitive appraisal, emotions are associated with similar patterns of arousal, but the level of arousal can differ. The emotion a person will experience in response to an external stimulus reflects that person's appraisal of the stimulus—that is, the meaning of the stimulus to him or her.

16. **Does research evidence support any of these theories?** Research seems to suggest that although patterns of arousal are more specific than suggested by the theory of cognitive appraisal, cognitive appraisal does play an important role in determining our responses to events.

To enhance your understanding of the psychological concepts found in this chapter, please consult the following aids:

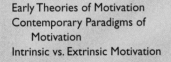

Learning Objectives, p. 223
Exercise, p. 224
Lecture and Textbook Outline,
    p. 225
Effective Studying Ideas, p. 227

Key Terms and Concepts, p. 228
Chapter Review, p. 228
Chapter Exercises, p. 236
Knowing the Language, p. 237
Do You Know the Material?, p. 240

Early Theories of Motivation
Contemporary Paradigms of
    Motivation
Intrinsic vs. Extrinsic Motivation

Hunger
Some Major Emotions
The Facial Expression of Emotion

For more information concerning the topics found in this chapter, access psychology links on the World Wide Web through the Harcourt Brace webpage at

www.hbcollege.com

Share your comments and questions with your author at

PsychLinks@aol.com

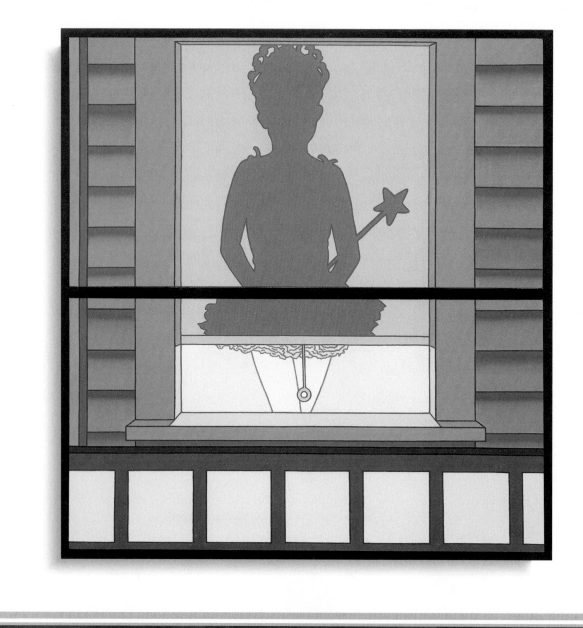

Much of personality is about identity. Who are *you*? How did you get to be who you are? Who is the little girl in Roger Shimomura's *The Princess Next Door* (1995)? One answer is that she is an American girl who aspires, like so many other American girls, to be a ballerina. Yet there is much more to her. If the shade were raised, we would see that this princess is Japanese American. The shade hides the features that reveal the girl's ethnic background; we see only the ballet costume that makes her one with other American girls. What do you think the artist is suggesting about personality development?

ROGER SHIMOMURA

Chapter 12

Personality

TRUTH OR FICTION?

✔ **T F**

☐ ☐ According to Sigmund Freud, the human mind is like a vast submerged iceberg. Only its tip rises above the surface into conscious awareness.

☐ ☐ According to Freud, biting one's fingernails or smoking cigarettes as an adult is a sign of conflict experienced during very early childhood.

☐ ☐ We are more likely to persist at difficult tasks when we believe we will succeed.

☐ ☐ We can build our self-esteem by becoming good at something.

☐ ☐ Psychologists can determine whether a person has told the truth on a personality test.

☐ ☐ There is a psychological test made up of inkblots, one of which looks like a bat.

OUTLINE

INTRODUCTION TO PERSONALITY:
"WHY ARE THEY SAD AND GLAD AND BAD?"

THE PSYCHODYNAMIC PERSPECTIVE
Sigmund Freud's Theory of Psychosexual Development
Other Psychodynamic Theorists
Evaluation of the Psychodynamic Perspective
Psychology in a World of Diversity:
Individuality Versus Relatedness

THE TRAIT PERSPECTIVE
From Hippocrates to the Present
Hans Eysenck
The Five-Factor Model
Psychology in the New Millennium:
Beyond Wellness: Using Biological Treatments to Improve Personality
Evaluation of the Trait Perspective

THE LEARNING PERSPECTIVE
Behaviorism
Social-Cognitive Theory
Questionnaire: Will You Be a Hit or a Miss? The Expectancy for Success Scale
Evaluation of the Learning Perspective

THE HUMANISTIC-EXISTENTIAL PERSPECTIVE
Questionnaire: Do You Strive to Be All That You Can Be?
Abraham Maslow and the Challenge of Self-Actualization
Carl Rogers' Self Theory
Psychology and Modern Life:
Enhancing Self-Esteem
Evaluation of the Humanistic-Existential Perspective

THE SOCIOCULTURAL PERSPECTIVE
Individualism Versus Collectivism
Sociocultural Factors and the Self
Acculturation and Self-Esteem
Evaluation of the Sociocultural Perspective

MEASUREMENT OF PERSONALITY
Objective Tests
Psychology and Modern Life:
Using Psychological Tests to Find a Career That Fits
Projective Tests

PERSONALITY • The distinct patterns of behavior, thoughts, and feelings that characterize a person's adaptation to life.
PSYCHODYNAMIC THEORY • Sigmund Freud's perspective, which emphasizes the importance of unconscious motives and conflicts as forces that determine behavior. *Dynamic* refers to the concept of (psychological) forces being in motion.

WAS READING DR. SEUSS'S *ONE FISH, Two Fish, Red Fish, Blue Fish* to my daughter Taylor when she was 2-years-old. The sneaky author had set up a trap for fathers. A part of the book reads that "Some [fish] are sad. And some are glad. And some are very, very bad. Why are they sad and glad and bad? I do not know. Go ask your dad."

Thanks, Dr. Seuss.

For many months I had just recited this section and then moved on. One day, however, Taylor's cognitive development had apparently flowered, and she would not let me get away with glossing over this. Why indeed, she wanted to know, were some fish sad whereas others were glad and bad. I paused and then, being a typical American dad, I gave the answer I'm sure has been given by thousands of other fathers:

"Uh, some fish are sad and others are glad or bad because of, uh, the interaction of nature and nurture—I mean, you know, heredity and environmental factors."

At which Taylor laughed and replied, "Not!"

■ INTRODUCTION TO PERSONALITY: "WHY ARE THEY SAD AND GLAD AND BAD?"

I'm still not certain whether Taylor thought my words came out silly or that my psychological theorizing was simplistic or off base. When applied to people—that is, why are people sad or glad or bad—this is the kind of question that is of interest to psychologists who study personality.

People do not necessarily agree on what the word *personality* means. Many equate personality with liveliness, as in "She's got a lot of personality." Others characterize a person's personality as consisting of his or her most striking traits, as in a "shy personality" or a "happy-go-lucky personality." Psychologists define **personality** as the reasonably stable patterns of emotions, motives, and behavior that distinguish one person from another.

Psychologists also seek to explain how personality develops—that is, why some (people) are sad or glad or bad—and to predict how people with certain personality traits will respond to life's demands. In this chapter we explore five perspectives on personality: the psychodynamic, trait, learning, humanistic-existential, and sociocultural perspectives. Then we discuss personality tests—the methods used to measure whether people are sad, glad, bad, and lots of other things.

■ THE PSYCHODYNAMIC PERSPECTIVE

There are several **psychodynamic theories** of personality, each of which owes its origin to the thinking of Sigmund Freud. These theories have a number of features in common. Each teaches that personality is characterized by a dynamic struggle. Drives such as sex, aggression, and the need for superiority come into conflict with laws, social rules, and moral codes. At some point laws and social rules become internalized—that is, we make them part of ourselves. After that the dynamic struggle becomes a clash between opposing *inner* forces. At any given moment our behavior, thoughts, and emotions represent the outcome of these inner contests.

• Sigmund Freud's Theory of Psychosexual Development

Sigmund Freud was trained as a physician. Early in his practice he was astounded to find that some people apparently experience loss of feeling in a hand or paralysis of the legs in the absence of any medical disorder. These odd symptoms often disappear once the person has recalled and discussed stressful events and feelings of guilt or anxiety that seem to be related to the symptoms. For a long time, these events and feelings have lain hidden beneath the surface of awareness. Even so, they have the capacity to influence behavior.

From this sort of clinical evidence, Freud concluded that the human mind is like an iceberg. Only the tip of an iceberg rises above the surface of the water; the great mass of it is hidden in the depths (see Figure 12.1). Freud came to believe that people, similarly, are aware of only a small portion of the ideas and impulses that dwell within their minds. He argued that a much greater portion of the mind—our deepest images, thoughts, fears, and urges—remains beneath the surface of conscious awareness, where little light illumines them.

Freud labeled the region that pokes through into the light of awareness the **conscious** part of the mind. He called the regions below the surface the *preconscious* and the *unconscious*. The **preconscious** mind contains elements of experience that are out of awareness but can be made conscious simply by focusing on them. The **unconscious** mind is shrouded in mystery. It contains biological instincts such as sex and aggression. Some unconscious urges cannot be experienced consciously because mental images and words could not portray them in all their color and fury. Other unconscious urges may be kept below the surface through repression.

Repression is the automatic ejection of anxiety-evoking ideas from awareness. Research evidence suggests that many people repress bad childhood experiences (Myers & Brewin, 1994). Perhaps "something shocking happens, and the mind pushes it into some inaccessible corner of the unconscious" (Loftus, 1993a). Repression may also protect us from perceiving morally unacceptable impulses.

In the unconscious mind, primitive drives seek expression, while internalized values try to keep them in check. The resulting conflict can arouse emotional outbursts and psychological problems.

To explore the unconscious mind, Freud engaged in a form of mental detective work called **psychoanalysis.** For this reason, his theory of personality is also

CONSCIOUS • Self-aware.

PRECONSCIOUS • Capable of being brought into awareness by the focusing of attention.

UNCONSCIOUS • In psychodynamic theory, not available to awareness by simple focusing of attention.

REPRESSION • A defense mechanism that protects the person from anxiety by ejecting anxiety-evoking ideas and impulses from awareness.

PSYCHOANALYSIS • In this usage, Freud's method of exploring human personality.

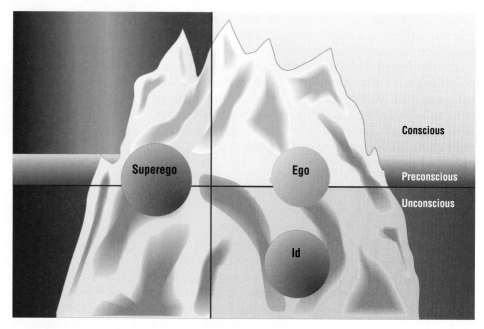

FIGURE 12.1
THE HUMAN ICEBERG ACCORDING TO FREUD

According to psychodynamic theory, only the tip of human personality rises above the surface of the mind into conscious awareness. Material in the preconscious can become conscious if we direct our attention to it. Unconscious material tends to remain shrouded in mystery.

Truth or Fiction Revisited

According to Freud, it is true that the human mind is like a vast submerged iceberg. Only the top rises above the surface into conscious awareness. Most personality theorists place more emphasis on conscious thought than Freud did.

SELF-INSIGHT • Accurate awareness of one's motives and feelings.

RESISTANCE • A blocking of thoughts whose awareness could cause anxiety.

PSYCHIC STRUCTURE • In psychodynamic theory, a hypothesized mental structure that helps explain different aspects of behavior.

ID • The psychic structure, present at birth, that represents physiological drives and is fully unconscious.

PLEASURE PRINCIPLE • The governing principle of the id—the seeking of immediate gratification of instinctive needs.

EGO • The second psychic structure to develop, characterized by self-awareness, planning, and delay of gratification.

referred to as *psychoanalytic theory.* In psychoanalysis, people are prodded to talk about anything that pops into their mind while they remain comfortable and relaxed. They may gain **self-insight** by pursuing some of the thoughts that pop into awareness. But they are also motivated to evade threatening subjects. The same repression that ejects unacceptable thoughts from awareness prompts **resistance,** or the desire to avoid thinking about or discussing those thoughts. Repression and resistance can make psychoanalysis a tedious process that lasts for years, or even decades.

THE STRUCTURE OF PERSONALITY When is a structure not a structure? When it is a mental or **psychic structure.** Freud used this term to describe the clashing forces of personality. They cannot be seen or measured directly, but their presence is suggested by behavior, expressed thoughts, and emotions. Freud hypothesized the existence of three psychic structures: the id, the ego, and the superego.

The **id** is present at birth. It represents physiological drives and is entirely unconscious. Freud described the id as "a chaos, a cauldron of seething excitations" (1964, p. 73). The conscious mind might find it inconsistent to love and hate the same person, but Freud believed that conflicting emotions could dwell side by side in the id. In the id, one can feel hatred for one's mother for failing to gratify immediately all of one's needs, while also feeling love for her.

The id follows what Freud termed the **pleasure principle.** It demands instant gratification of instincts without consideration of law, social custom, or the needs of others.

The **ego** begins to develop during the first year of life, largely because a child's demands for gratification cannot all be met immediately. The ego stands for reason and good sense, for rational ways of coping with frustration. It curbs the appetites of the id and makes plans that are compatible with social convention. Thus, a person can find gratification yet avoid social disapproval. The id lets you know that you are hungry, but it is the ego that decides to microwave some enchiladas.

The ego is guided by the **reality principle.** It takes into account what is practical along with what is urged by the id. The ego also provides the person's conscious sense of self.

Although most of the ego is conscious, some of its business is carried out unconsciously. For instance, the ego also acts as a censor that screens the impulses of the id. When the ego senses that improper impulses are rising into awareness, it may use psychological defenses to prevent them from surfacing. Repression is one such psychological defense, or **defense mechanism.** Several defense mechanisms are described in Table 12.1.

TABLE 12.1 DEFENSE MECHANISMS		
Defense Mechanism	*Definition*	*Examples*
Repression	Ejection of anxiety-evoking ideas from awareness.	A student forgets that a difficult term paper is due. A person in therapy forgets an appointment when anxiety-evoking material is to be discussed.
Regression	The return, under stress, to a form of behavior characteristic of an earlier stage of development.	An adolescent cries when forbidden to use the family car. An adult becomes highly dependent on his parents after the breakup of his marriage.
Rationalization	The use of self-deceiving justifications for unacceptable behavior.	A student blames her cheating on her teacher's leaving the room during a test. A man explains his cheating on his income tax by saying "Everyone does it."
Displacement	The transfer of ideas and impulses from threatening or unsuitable objects to less threatening objects.	A worker picks a fight with her spouse after being sharply criticized by her supervisor.
Projection	The thrusting of one's own unacceptable impulses onto others so that others are assumed to have those impulses.	A hostile person perceives the world as a dangerous place. A sexually frustrated person interprets innocent gestures as sexual advances.
Reaction formation	Assumption of behavior in opposition to one's genuine impulses in order to keep those impulses repressed.	A person who is angry with a relative behaves in a "sickly sweet" manner toward that relative. A sadistic individual becomes a physician.
Denial	Refusal to accept the true nature of a threat.	Belief that one will not contract cancer or heart disease even though one smokes heavily. "It can't happen to me."
Sublimation	The channeling of primitive impulses into positive, constructive efforts.	A person paints nudes for the sake of "beauty" and "art." A hostile person becomes a tennis star.

REALITY PRINCIPLE • Consideration of what is practical and possible in gratifying needs; the governing principle of the ego.
DEFENSE MECHANISM • In psychodynamic theory, an unconscious function of the ego that protects it from anxiety-evoking material by preventing accurate recognition of this material.

The Oral Stage? According to Sigmund Freud, during the first year the child is in the oral stage of development. If it fits, into the mouth it goes. What, according to Freud, are the effects of insufficient or excessive gratification during the oral stage? Is there evidence to support his views?

SUPEREGO • The third psychic structure, which functions as a moral guardian and sets forth high standards for behavior.

IDENTIFICATION • In psychodynamic theory, the unconscious assumption of the behavior of another person.

MORAL PRINCIPLE • The governing principle of the superego, which sets moral standards and enforces adherence to them.

EROS • In psychodynamic theory, the basic instinct to preserve and perpetuate life.

LIBIDO • (1) In psychodynamic theory, the energy of Eros; the sexual instinct. (2) Generally, sexual interest or drive.

EROGENOUS ZONE • An area of the body that is sensitive to sexual sensations.

PSYCHOSEXUAL DEVELOPMENT • In psychodynamic theory, the process by which libidinal energy is expressed through different erogenous zones during different stages of development.

ORAL STAGE • The first stage of psychosexual development, during which gratification is hypothesized to be attained primarily through oral activities.

FIXATION • In psychodynamic theory, arrested development. Attachment to objects of an earlier stage.

ANAL STAGE • The second stage of psychosexual development, when gratification is attained through anal activities.

The **superego** develops throughout early childhood, usually incorporating the moral standards and values of parents and important members of the community through **identification**. The superego functions according to the **moral principle**. The superego holds forth shining examples of an ideal self and also acts like the conscience, an internal moral guardian. Throughout life, the superego monitors the intentions of the ego and hands out judgments of right and wrong. It floods the ego with feelings of guilt and shame when the verdict is negative.

The ego does not have an easy time of it. It stands between the id and the superego, striving to satisfy the demands of the id and the moral sense of the superego. From the Freudian perspective, a healthy personality has found ways to gratify most of the id's demands without seriously offending the superego. Most of the id's remaining demands are contained or repressed. If the ego is not a good problem solver or if the superego is too stern, the ego will have a hard time of it.

STAGES OF PSYCHOSEXUAL DEVELOPMENT Freud stirred controversy by arguing that sexual impulses are a central factor in personality development, even among children. Freud believed that sexual feelings are closely linked to children's basic ways of relating to the world, such as sucking on their mother's breasts and moving their bowels.

Freud believed that a major instinct, which he termed **eros,** is aimed at preserving and perpetuating life. Eros is fueled by psychological, or psychic, energy, which Freud labeled **libido**. Libidinal energy involves sexual impulses, so Freud considered it to be *psychosexual.* As the child develops, libidinal energy is expressed through sexual feelings in different parts of the body, or **erogenous zones**. To Freud, human development involves the transfer of libidinal energy from one erogenous zone to another. He hypothesized five periods of **psychosexual development**: oral, anal, phallic, latency, and genital.

During the first year of life a child experiences much of its world through the mouth. If it fits, into the mouth it goes. (Anyone who knows a small child will be familiar with this tendency.) This is the **oral stage**. Freud argued that oral activities such as sucking and biting give the child sexual gratification as well as nourishment.

Freud believed that children encounter conflict during each stage of psychosexual development. During the oral stage, conflict centers on the nature and extent of oral gratification. Early weaning (cessation of breast feeding) could lead to frustration. Excessive gratification, on the other hand, could lead an infant to expect that it will routinely be given anything it wants. Insufficient or excessive gratification in any stage could lead to **fixation** in that stage and to the development of traits that are characteristic of that stage. Oral traits include dependency, gullibility, and excessive optimism or pessimism (depending on the child's experiences with gratification).

Freud theorized that adults with an *oral fixation* could experience exaggerated desires for "oral activities," such as smoking, overeating, alcohol abuse, and nail biting. Like the infant whose very survival depends on the mercy of an adult, adults with oral fixations may be disposed toward clinging, dependent relationships.

During the **anal stage** sexual gratification is attained through contraction and relaxation of the muscles that control elimination of waste products from the body. Elimination, which was controlled reflexively during most of the first year of life, comes under voluntary muscular control, even if such control is not reliable at first. The anal stage is said to begin in the second year of life.

During the anal stage children learn to delay the gratification that comes from eliminating as soon as they feel the urge. The general issue of self-control may become a source of conflict between parent and child. *Anal fixations* may stem from this conflict and lead to two sets of traits in adulthood. So-called *anal-retentive* traits involve excessive use of self-control. They include perfectionism, a strong need for order, and exaggerated neatness and cleanliness. *Anal-expulsive* traits, on the other hand, "let it all hang out." They include carelessness, messiness, even sadism.

Children enter the **phallic stage** during the third year of life. During this stage the major erogenous zone is the phallic region (the penis in boys, and the **clitoris** in girls). Parent-child conflict is likely to develop over masturbation, to which parents may respond with threats or punishment. During the phallic stage children may develop strong sexual attachments to the parent of the other gender and begin to view the parent of the same gender as a rival for the other parent's affections. Thus boys may want to marry Mommy and girls may want to marry Daddy.

Children have difficulty dealing with feelings of lust and jealousy. Home life would be tense indeed if they were aware of them. These feelings, therefore, remain unconscious, but their influence is felt through fantasies about marriage with the parent of the other gender and hostility toward the parent of the same gender. In boys, this conflict is labeled the **Oedipus complex,** after the legendary Greek king who unwittingly killed his father and married his mother. Similar feelings in girls give rise to the **Electra complex.** According to Greek legend, Electra was the daughter of the king Agamemnon. She longed for him after his death and sought revenge against his slayers—her mother and her mother's lover.

The Oedipus and Electra complexes are resolved by about the ages of five or six. Children then repress their hostilities toward the parent of the same gender and begin to identify with her or him. Identification leads them to play the social and gender roles of that parent and to internalize his or her values. Sexual feelings toward the parent of the other gender are repressed for a number of years. When the feelings emerge again during adolescence, they are **displaced,** or transferred, to socially appropriate members of the other gender.

Freud believed that by the age of five or six, children have been in conflict with their parents over sexual feelings for several years. The pressures of the Oedipus and Electra complexes cause them to repress all sexual urges. In so doing, they enter a period of **latency** during which their sexual feelings remain unconscious. During the latency phase it is not uncommon for children to prefer playmates of their own gender.

Freud believed that we enter the final stage of psychosexual development, the **genital stage,** at puberty. Adolescent males again experience sexual urges toward their mother and adolescent females experience such urges toward their father. However, the **incest taboo** causes them to repress these impulses and displace them onto other adults or adolescents of the other gender. Boys still might seek girls "just like the girl that married dear old Dad." Girls still might be attracted to men who resemble their fathers.

People in the genital stage prefer, by definition, to find sexual gratification through intercourse with a member of the other gender. In Freud's view, oral or anal stimulation, masturbation, and sexual activity with people of the same gender all represent *pregenital* fixations and immature forms of sexual conduct. They are not consistent with the life instinct, eros.

• *Other Psychodynamic Theorists*

Several personality theorists are among Freud's intellectual heirs. Their theories, like his, include dynamic movement of psychological forces, conflict, and

PHALLIC STAGE • The third stage of psychosexual development, characterized by a shift of libido to the phallic region. (From the Greek *phallos,* referring to an image of the penis. However, Freud used the term *phallic* to refer both to boys and girls.)

CLITORIS • An external female sex organ that is highly sensitive to sexual stimulation.

OEDIPUS COMPLEX • A conflict of the phallic stage in which the boy wishes to possess his mother sexually and perceives his father as a rival in love.

ELECTRA COMPLEX • A conflict of the phallic stage in which the girl longs for her father and resents her mother.

DISPLACED • Transferred.

LATENCY • A phase of psychosexual development characterized by repression of sexual impulses.

GENITAL STAGE • The mature stage of psychosexual development, characterized by preferred expression of libido through intercourse with an adult of the other gender.

INCEST TABOO • The cultural prohibition against marrying or having sexual relations with a close blood relative.

She was drummed out of the New York Psychoanalytic Institute because she took issue with the way in which psychoanalytic theory portrayed women. Early in the century, psychoanalytic theory taught that a woman's place was in the home. Women who sought to compete with men in the business world were assumed to be suffering from unconscious penis envy. Psychoanalytic theory taught that little girls feel inferior to boys when they learn that boys have a penis and they do not. Karen Horney (1885–1952) argued that little girls do *not* feel inferior to boys, and that these views were founded on Western cultural prejudice, not scientific evidence.

Karen Horney

Horney was born in Germany and emigrated to the United States before the outbreak of World War II. Trained in psychoanalysis, she agreed with Freud that childhood experiences are important factors in the development of adult personality. Like other neoanalysts, however, she asserted that unconscious sexual and aggressive impulses are less important than social relationships in children's development. She also believed that genuine and consistent love can alleviate the effects of even the most traumatic childhood. ∎

ANALYTICAL PSYCHOLOGY • Jung's psychodynamic theory, which emphasizes the collective unconscious and archetypes.

COLLECTIVE UNCONSCIOUS • Jung's hypothesized store of vague racial memories.

ARCHETYPES • Basic, primitive images or concepts hypothesized by Jung to reside in the collective unconscious.

INFERIORITY COMPLEX • Feelings of inferiority hypothesized by Adler to serve as a central motivating force.

DRIVE FOR SUPERIORITY • Adler's term for the desire to compensate for feelings of inferiority.

CREATIVE SELF • According to Adler, the self-aware aspect of personality that strives to achieve its full potential.

INDIVIDUAL PSYCHOLOGY • Adler's psychodynamic theory, which emphasizes feelings of inferiority and the creative self.

defensive responses to anxiety that involve repression and cognitive distortion of reality. In other respects, however, their theories differ considerably.

CARL JUNG Carl Jung (1875–1961) was a Swiss psychiatrist who had been a member of Freud's inner circle. He fell into disfavor with Freud when he developed his own psychodynamic theory—**analytical psychology.** In contrast to Freud (for whom, he said, "the brain is viewed as an appendage of the genital organs"), Jung downplayed the importance of the sexual instinct. He saw it as just one of several important instincts.

Jung, like Freud, was intrigued by unconscious processes. He believed that we not only have a *personal* unconscious that contains repressed memories and impulses but also an inherited **collective unconscious.** The collective unconscious contains primitive images, or **archetypes,** that reflect the history of our species. Examples of archetypes are the all-powerful God, the young hero, the fertile and nurturing mother, the wise old man, the hostile brother—even fairy godmothers, wicked witches, and themes of rebirth or resurrection. Archetypes themselves remain unconscious, but Jung declared that they influence our thoughts and emotions and cause us to respond to cultural themes in stories and films.

ALFRED ADLER Alfred Adler (1870–1937), another follower of Freud, also felt that Freud had placed too much emphasis on sexual impulses. Adler believed that people are basically motivated by an **inferiority complex.** In some people, feelings of inferiority may be based on physical problems and the need to compensate for them. Adler believed, however, that all of us encounter some feelings of inferiority because of our small size as children, and that these feelings give rise to a **drive for superiority.** For instance, the English poet Lord Byron, who had a crippled leg, became a champion swimmer. As a child Adler was crippled by rickets and suffered from pneumonia, and it may be that his theory developed in part from his own childhood striving to overcome repeated bouts of illness.

Adler believed that self-awareness plays a major role in the formation of personality. He spoke of a **creative self,** a self-aware aspect of personality that strives to overcome obstacles and develop the individual's potential. Because each person's potential is unique, Adler's views have been termed **individual psychology.**

ERIK ERIKSON Erik Erikson (1902–1994) also believed that Freud had placed undue emphasis on sexual instincts. He asserted that social relationships are more crucial determinants of personality than sexual urges. To Erikson, the nature of the mother-infant relationship is more important than the details of the feeding process or the sexual feelings that might be stirred by contact with the mother. Erikson also argued that to a large extent we are the conscious architects of our own personalities. His view grants more powers to the ego than Freud did. In Erikson's theory, it is possible for us to make real choices. In Freud's theory, we may think that we are making choices but may actually be merely rationalizing the compromises forced upon us by internal conflicts.

Erikson, like Freud, is known for devising a comprehensive theory of personality development. But whereas Freud proposed stages of psycho*sexual* development, Erikson proposed stages of psycho*social* development. Rather than label stages for various erogenous zones, Erikson labeled them for the traits that might be developed during them (see Table 4.1). Each stage is named according to its possible outcomes. For example, the first stage of **psychosocial development** is labeled the stage of trust versus mistrust because of its two possible outcomes: (1) A warm, loving relationship with the mother (and others) during infancy might lead to a sense of basic trust in people and the world. (2) On the other hand, a cold, ungratifying relationship might generate a pervasive sense of mistrust. Erikson believed that most people would wind up with some blend of trust and mistrust—hopefully more trust than mistrust. A basic sense of mistrust could interfere with the formation of relationships unless it was recognized and challenged.

For Erikson, the goal of adolescence is the attainment of **ego identity,** not genital sexuality. The focus is on who we see ourselves as being and what we stand for, not on sexual interests.

• *Evaluation of the Psychodynamic Perspective*

Psychodynamic theories have tremendous appeal. They involve many concepts and explain many varieties of human behavior and traits.

Although today concepts such as "the id" and "libido" strike many psychologists as unscientific, Freud fought for the idea that human personality and behavior are subject to scientific analysis. He developed his theories at a time when many people still viewed psychological problems as signs of possession by the devil or evil spirits, as they had during the Middle Ages. Freud argued that psychological disorders stem from problems within the individual—not evil spirits. His thinking contributed to the development of compassion for people with psychological disorders and methods for helping them.

Psychodynamic theory has also focused attention on the far-reaching effects of childhood events. Freud and other psychodynamic theorists are to be credited for suggesting that personality and behavior *develop* and that it is important for parents to be aware of the emotional needs of their children.

Freud has helped us recognize that sexual and aggressive urges are commonplace and that there is a difference between acknowledging these urges and acting on them. As W. Bertram Wolfe put it, "Freud found sex an outcast in the outhouse, and left it in the living room an honored guest."

Freud also noted that people have defensive ways of looking at the world. His list of defense mechanisms has become part of everyday speech. Whether or not we attribute these cognitive distortions to unconscious ego functioning, our

PSYCHOSOCIAL DEVELOPMENT • Erikson's theory of personality and development, which emphasizes social relationships and eight stages of growth.
EGO IDENTITY • A firm sense of who one is and what one stands for.

thinking may be distorted by our efforts to avert anxiety and guilt. If these concepts no longer strike us as innovative, it is largely because of Freud's influence. Psychodynamic theorists also developed many methods of therapy, which we describe in Chapter 16.

A number of critics note that "psychic structures" such as the id, ego, and superego are too vague to measure scientifically (Hergenhahn, 1997). Nor can they be used to predict behavior with precision. They are little more than useful fictions—poetic ways to express inner conflict. Freud's critics thus have the right to use other descriptive terms.

Nor have the stages of psychosexual development escaped criticism. Children begin to masturbate as early as the first year, not in the phallic stage. As parents know from discovering their children play "doctor," the latency stage is not as sexually latent as Freud believed. Much of Freud's thinking about the Oedipus and Electra complexes remains little more than speculation. The evidence for some of Erikson's developmental views seems somewhat sturdier. For example, people who fail to develop ego identity in adolescence seem to encounter problems developing intimate relationships later on.

Freud's method of gathering evidence from clinical sessions is also suspect (Hergenhahn, 1997). In subtle ways, therapists may influence clients to produce memories and feelings they expect to find. Therapists may also fail to separate what they are told from their own interpretations. Also, Freud and many other psychodynamic theorists restricted their evidence gathering to case studies with individuals who sought help for psychological problems. Their clients were also mostly White and from the middle and upper classes. People who seek therapy are likely to have more problems than the general population.

In the following section on diversity, we see that many theories of personality—including many psychodynamic theories—have been accused of being biased against women.

Psychology in a World of
DIVERSITY

Individuality Versus Relatedness

Most Western theories of personality and human development have been accused of having a "phallocentric" and individualist bias (Jordan and others, 1991). This criticism applies to the views of Freud, Erikson, Piaget, and Kohlberg, among others. Each of these uses the yardsticks of male development as the norms. Each neglects important aspects of personality development, such as the relatedness of the individual to other people (Guisinger & Blatt, 1994). In Western culture, the male view is that the self is supreme and distinct from other people. Moreover, separation and individuation are presented as the highest goal of personality development. Yet social critics (e.g., Gilligan and others, 1991; Jordan and others, 1991) consider a crucial aspect of a woman's sense of self to be her relatedness—her establishment and maintenance of social relationships.

Guisinger and Blatt (1994) suggest that the male tendency toward individualism might arise from the different developmental tasks faced by boys and girls. For example, when a boy recognizes that he and his mother are not of the same gender, he must set himself apart from her. This process of differentiation may cause boys to feel greater concern about being separate and distinct from other people. For girls, of course, such differentiation from the mother is unnecessary.

Gender stereotypes and cultural expectations also enter the picture in early childhood. True, in our society the great majority of women are in the workforce. Yet girls are still taught from an early age that they will have the primary responsibilities for homemaking and child rearing. Today women and men share child-rearing chores more than they did in the past. However, research shows that women are still more likely than men to supply the emotional glue that holds the family together (Bianchi & Spain, 1997).

Guisinger and Blatt (1994) suggest that women's and men's personality development may frustrate both genders. Women's relational development is both an undervalued strength and a source of vulnerability for women. Women are often at risk of losing themselves in their relationships and failing to develop an adequate sense of self. Although men may be more involved as fathers today than they were in the past, young daughters may still have to struggle to engage relatively distant fathers. As adults, when they attempt to engage other men in relationships, they may feel that the men care less about them than they care about the men.

Men tend to underemphasize interpersonal relatedness. Although their needs to be strong individuals may prevent them from acknowledging or getting in touch with their feelings, they may suffer from feelings of alienation and grief over their loss of relatedness to others, including other men (Bly, 1990; Keen, 1991). Consider the title of Robert Bly's popular book, *Iron John*. Iron Johns are less likely than women to reveal intimate information about themselves (Dindia & Allen, 1992). They are less likely than women to have intimate friends, even though they may be part of a large sporting crowd. Iron Johns who do many things "with the guys" may still feel that they have no one to talk to. Moreover, just as women may struggle to engage distant men, men are likely to have problems in their relationships with women.

Is This "Iron John"? The masculine gender role stereotype is characterized by separation and individuation. Do theories of personality present this stereotype as the highest goal of personality development? Women are more likely than men to emphasize interpersonal relatedness as a key goal of personality development. Although their need to be stoic may prevent men from getting in touch with their feelings, they may experience alienation and grief over lack of relatedness to other people.

REFLECTIONS
- Do you believe that you are aware of all of your feelings? Why or why not? Would Freud agree with you?
- Agree or disagree, and support your answer: "People are basically antisocial. Their primitive impulses must be suppressed if they are to function productively in social settings."
- If you were fixated in a stage of psychosocial development, which stage would it be? Why?

■ THE TRAIT PERSPECTIVE

> In most of us by the age of thirty, the character has set like plaster, and will never soften again.
>
> WILLIAM JAMES

The notion of **traits** is very familiar. If I asked you to describe yourself, you would probably do so in terms of traits such as bright, sophisticated, and witty. (That is you, is it not?) We also describe other people in terms of traits.

Traits are reasonably stable elements of personality that are inferred from behavior. If you describe a friend as "shy," it may be because you have observed social anxiety or withdrawal in that person's encounters with others. Traits are assumed to account for consistent behavior in diverse situations. You probably expect your "shy" friend to be quiet and retiring in most social

TRAIT • A relatively stable aspect of personality that is inferred from behavior and assumed to give rise to consistent behavior.

A Creative Artist. Faith Ringgold works on a quilt. What traits are shown by creative artists? How do psychologists measure traits?

confrontations—"all across the board," as the saying goes. The concept of traits is also found in other approaches to personality. Recall that Freud linked the development of certain traits to children's experiences in each stage of psychosexual development.

• *From Hippocrates to the Present*

The trait approach dates back to the Greek physician Hippocrates (ca. 460–377 B.C.) And could be even older (Maher & Maher, 1994). It has generally been assumed that traits are embedded in people's bodies, but *how?* Hippocrates believed that traits were embedded in bodily fluids, which gave rise to certain types of personalities. In his view, an individual's personality depended on the balance of four basic fluids, or "humors," in the body. Yellow bile was associated with a choleric (quick-tempered) disposition; blood with a sanguine (warm, cheerful) one; phlegm with a phlegmatic (sluggish, calm, cool) disposition; and black bile with a melancholic (gloomy, pensive) temperament. Disease was believed to reflect an imbalance among the humors. Methods such as bloodletting and vomiting were recommended to restore the balance (Maher & Maher, 1994). Although Hippocrates' theory was pure speculation, the terms *choleric, sanguine,* and so on are still used in descriptions of personality.

More enduring trait theories assume that traits are heritable and are embedded in the nervous system. They rely on the mathematical technique of factor analysis in attempting to determine basic human traits.

Sir Francis Galton was among the first scientists to suggest that many of the world's languages use single words to describe fundamental differences in personality. More than 50 years ago, Gordon Allport and a colleague (Allport & Oddbert, 1936) catalogued some 18,000 human traits from a search through word lists like dictionaries. Some were physical traits such as *short, black,* and *brunette.* Others were behavioral traits such as *shy* and *emotional.* Still others were moral traits such as *honest.* This exhaustive list has served as the basis for personality research by many other psychologists. Other psychologists have used factor analysis to reduce this universe of traits to smaller lists of traits that show common features.

• *Hans Eysenck*

British psychologist Hans J. Eysenck ((Eysenck & Eysenck, 1985) has focused much of his research on the relationships between two important traits: **introversion-extraversion** and emotional stability-instability. (Emotional *in*stability is also known as **neuroticism**). Carl Jung was first to distinguish between introverts and extraverts. Eysenck added the dimension of emotional stability-instability to introversion-extraversion. He has catalogued various personality traits according to where they are situated along these dimensions or factors (see Figure 12.2). For instance, an anxious person would be high in both introversion and neuroticism—that is, preoccupied with his or her own thoughts and emotionally unstable.

Eysenck notes that his scheme is reminiscent of that suggested by Hippocrates. According to Eysenck's dimensions, the choleric type would be extraverted and unstable; the sanguine type, extraverted and stable; the phlegmatic type, introverted and stable; and the melancholic type, introverted and unstable.

INTROVERSION • A trait characterized by intense imagination and the tendency to inhibit impulses.
EXTRAVERSION • A trait characterized by tendencies to be socially outgoing and to express feelings and impulses freely.
NEUROTICISM • Eysenck's term for emotional instability.

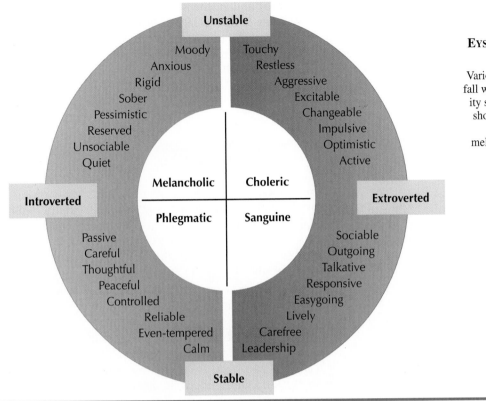

FIGURE 12.2

EYSENCK'S PERSONALITY DIMENSIONS AND HIPPOCRATES' PERSONALITY TYPES

Various personality traits shown in the outer ring fall within the two major dimensions of personality suggested by Hans Eysenck. The inner circle shows how Hippocrates' four major personality types—choleric, sanguine, phlegmatic, and melancholic—fit within Eysenck's dimensions.

• *The Five-Factor Model*

Recent research suggests that there may be five basic personality factors (Mc-Crae, 1996). These include the two found by Eysenck—extraversion and neuroticism—along with conscientiousness, agreeableness, and openness to new experience (see Table 12.2). Many personality theorists, especially Louis Thurstone, Raymond Cattell, Donald Fiske, Robert McCrae, and Paul T. Costa, Jr. have played a role in the development of the five-factor model. The five-factor model has found applications in areas such as personnel selection

TABLE 12.2	THE FIVE-FACTOR MODEL	
Factor	*Name*	*Traits*
I	Extraversion	Contrasts talkativeness, assertiveness, and activity with silence, passivity, and reserve
II	Agreeableness	Contrasts kindness, trust, and warmth with hostility, selfishness and distrust
III	Conscientiousness	Contrasts organization, thoroughness, and reliability with carelessness, negligence, and unreliability
IV	Neuroticism	Contrasts traits such as nervousness, moodiness, and sensitivity to negative stimuli with coping ability
V	Openness to Experience	Contrasts imagination, curiosity, and creativity with shallowness and lack of perceptiveness

and classification (Azar, 1995b) and in the study of psychological disorders (Clark and others, 1994; Widiger & Costa, 1994). Moreover, cross-cultural research has found that these five factors appear to define the personality structure of American, German, Portuguese, Hebrew, Chinese, Korean, and Japanese people (McCrae & Costa, 1997).

PSYCHOLOGY *in the* ▶ NEW MILLENNIUM

Beyond Wellness: Using Biological Treatments to Improve Personality

Biological therapies for psychological disorders may date from prehistoric times. They hark back at least to ancient times, when the Greeks and Romans used mineral water containing lithium to treat people with bipolar disorder. Only in the 20th century, however, have we gained insights into how biological therapies affect biochemical processes. This knowledge raises the possibility that biological treatments may soon be used to improve people's personalities.

One drug that some see as enhancing personality is the antidepressant Prozac (Newman, 1994). In *Listening to Prozac,* psychiatrist Peter D. Kramer (1993) writes that Prozac not only lifted depression in a number of his patients but also transformed their personalities. Kramer claimed that Prozac could give introverted people the social skills of a good salesperson. Prozac could allow inhibited people to be impetuous. Kramer argues that Prozac not only leads to predictable improvements such as reduced sluggishness (that is, reversal of the depressive symptom of psychomotor retardation) but also improves memory functioning, enhances social poise, increases resilience, allows people to shrug off insults, and heightens mental agility and thoughtfulness.

Kramer's critics, such as Daniel X. Freedman (1993), a former editor of the journal *Archives of General Psychiatry,* argue that Prozac's effects are much more limited. Freedman allows that Kramer's *Listening to Prozac* demonstrates how drugs and psychotherapy provide helpful treatment for depression and other psychological problems when used together. He points out, however, that the number of users of Prozac "who experience startling personality changes is rather small. Indeed, it will be news to the millions of [people] who take it for depression [and other psychological problems] that this drug can cause dramatic changes in temperament" (p. 6).

Regardless of the effects—or limitations—of Prozac, many biological therapies, including drugs with psychological effects, are in the research pipeline (Newman, 1994). One or more of them may foster remarkable changes in personality. If that is so, what questions are raised for society to ponder?

The value of psychological and biological approaches in alleviating psychological disorders would appear to be unquestioned. But who will decide what is an ideal personality? If drugs that can eliminate shyness are available, will outgoing mothers use them on timid children? Will people who are naturally reserved, and who might prefer to remain diffident, feel pressured to join the ranks of "drug-engineered personalities" (Freedman, 1993, p. 6)? In ousting shyness, do we also eradicate introversion and introspection? Do we risk creating a society of smiling, outgoing risk takers?

If chemicals are available to make us well-adjusted, do we risk forgoing the creativity of people with "tortured" personalities such as Vincent Van Gogh, Sylvia Plath, and Edgar Allan Poe? Would a person with antisocial personality disorder obtain a chemical conscience?

If the new millennium brings ways of transforming personality in specified directions, we will face many ethical and practical issues concerning what it means to be human. Will psychologists argue that "perfecting" the individual actually destroys the dignity of the individual? If so, why? ■

Psychologists still disagree on the number of basic personality factors (Block, 1995). Zuckerman (1992), for example, questions the ways in which researchers determine which personality factors are basic and which are not.

• Evaluation of the Trait Perspective

Trait theories, like psychodynamic theories, have both strengths and weaknesses. Trait theorists have focused much attention on the development of personality tests. They have also given rise to theories about the fit between personality and certain kinds of jobs (Holland, 1996). The qualities that suit a person for various kinds of work can be expressed in terms of abilities, personality traits, and interests (Azar, 1995b). By using interviews and tests to learn about an individual's abilities and traits, testing and counseling centers can make valuable suggestions about that person's chances of success and fulfillment in various kinds of jobs.

One limitation of trait theory is that it is descriptive, not explanatory. It focuses on describing traits rather than on tracing their origins or finding out how they may be modified. Moreover, the "explanations" provided by trait theory are often criticized as being **circular.** That is, they restate what is observed and do not explain it. Saying that John failed to ask Marsha on a date *because* of shyness is an example of a circular explanation: We have merely restated John's (shy) behavior as a trait (shyness).

> ## REFLECTIONS
> - What traits do you mention when you describe yourself? Why?
> - How would you describe yourself in terms of extraversion, agreeableness, conscientiousness, neuroticism, and openness to experience? Why?

■ THE LEARNING PERSPECTIVE

The learning perspective has also contributed to our understanding of personality. In this section we will focus on two learning approaches: behaviorism and social-cognitive theory.

• Behaviorism

In 1924, at Johns Hopkins University John B. Watson raised the battle cry of the behaviorist movement:

> Give me a dozen healthy infants, well-formed, and my own specified world to bring them up in and I'll guarantee to take any one at random and train him to become any type of specialist I might suggest—doctor, lawyer, merchant-chief and, yes, even beggar-man and thief, regardless of his talents, penchants, tendencies, abilities, vocations, and the race of his ancestors. (p. 82)

Watson thus proclaimed that situational variables or environmental influences—not internal, individual variables—are the key shapers of human preferences and behaviors. In contrast to the psychoanalysts and structuralists of his day, Watson argued that unseen, undetectable mental structures must be rejected in favor of that which can be seen and measured. In the 1930s Watson's

CIRCULAR • Descriptive of an explanation that restates its own concepts instead of offering additional information.

battle cry was taken up by B. F. Skinner, who agreed that psychologists should avoid trying to see into the "black box" of the organism and instead emphasized the effects that reinforcements have on behavior.

The views of Watson and Skinner largely ignored the notions of personal freedom, choice, and self-direction. Most of us assume that our wants originate within us. But Skinner suggested that environmental influences such as parental approval and social custom shape us into *wanting* certain things and *not wanting* others.

In his novel *Walden Two*, Skinner (1948) described a Utopian society in which people are happy and content because they are allowed to do as they please. However, from early childhood, they have been trained or conditioned to be cooperative. Because of their reinforcement histories, they *want* to behave in decent, kind, and unselfish ways. They see themselves as free because society makes no effort to force them to behave in particular ways.

Some object to behaviorist notions because they play down the importance of consciousness and choice. Others argue that humans are not blindly ruled by pleasure and pain. In some circumstances people have rebelled against the so-called necessity of survival by choosing pain and hardship over pleasure, or death over life. Many people have sacrificed their own lives to save those of others.

The behaviorist defense might be that the apparent choice of pain or death is forced on altruistic individuals just as conformity to social custom is forced on others. The altruist is also shaped by external influences, even if those influences differ from those that affect many other people.

• *Social-Cognitive Theory*

Social-cognitive theory[1] is a contemporary view of learning developed by Albert Bandura (1986, 1991) and other psychologists (e.g., Mischel & Shoda, 1995). It focuses on the importance of learning by observation and on the cognitive processes that underlie individual differences. Social-cognitive theorists see people as influencing their environment just as their environment influences them. Bandura terms this mutual pattern of influence **reciprocal determinism.** Social-cognitive theorists agree with behaviorists and other empirical psychologists that discussions of human nature should be tied to observable experiences and behaviors. They assert, however, that variables within people—which they call **person variables**—must also be considered if we are to understand them.

One goal of psychological theories is the prediction of behavior. We cannot predict behavior from situational variables alone. Whether a person will behave in a certain way also depends on the person's **expectancies** about the outcomes of that behavior and the perceived or **subjective values** of those outcomes.

To social-cognitive theorists, people are not simply at the mercy of the environment. Instead, they are self-aware and purposefully engage in learning. They seek to learn about their environment and to alter it in order to make reinforcers available.

OBSERVATIONAL LEARNING   Observational learning (also termed **modeling** or *cognitive learning*) refers to acquiring knowledge by observing others. For operant conditioning to occur, an organism (1) must engage in a response, and

SOCIAL-COGNITIVE THEORY • A cognitively oriented learning theory in which observational learning and person variables such as values and expectancies play major roles in individual differences.
RECIPROCAL DETERMINISM • Bandura's term for the social-cognitive view that people influence their environment just as their environment influences them.
PERSON VARIABLES • Factors within the person, such as expectancies and competencies, that influence behavior.
EXPECTANCIES • Personal predictions about the outcomes of potential behaviors.
SUBJECTIVE VALUE • The desirability of an object or event.
MODEL • In social-cognitive theory, an organism that exhibits behaviors that others will imitate or acquire through observational learning.
COMPETENCIES • Knowledge and skills.

---

[1] The name of this theory is in flux. It was formerly referred to as social-learning theory. Today it is also sometimes referred to as *cognitive social theory* (Miller and others, 1996).

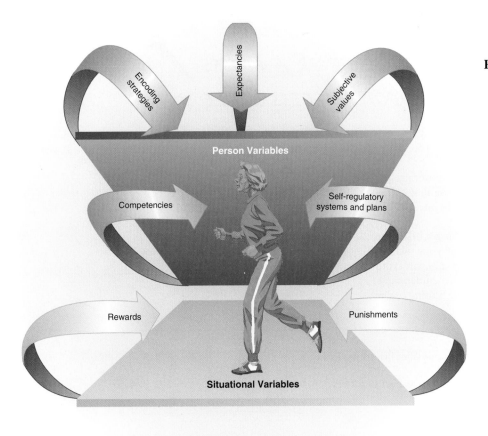

FIGURE 12.3
**PERSON VARIABLES AND SITUATIONAL VARI-
ABLES IN SOCIAL-COGNITIVE THEORY**
According to social-cognitive theory, person
variables and situational variables interact to
influence behavior.

(2) that response must be reinforced. But observational learning occurs even
when the learner does not perform the observed behavior. Therefore, direct reinforcement is not required either. Observing others extends to reading about
them or seeing what they do and what happens to them in books, TV, radio, and
film.

Our expectations stem from our observations of what happens to ourselves
and other people. For example, teachers are more likely to call on males and
more accepting of "calling out" in class by males than by females (Sadker &
Sadker, 1994). As a result, many males expect to be rewarded for calling out.
Females, however, may learn that they will be reprimanded for behaving in
what some might term an "unladylike" manner.

Social-cognitive theorists believe that behavior reflects person variables and
situational variables. Person variables include competencies, encoding strategies, expectancies, emotions, and self-regulatory systems and plans (Mischel &
Shoda, 1995; see Figure 12.3).

COMPETENCIES: WHAT CAN YOU DO? **Competencies** include knowledge
of rules that guide conduct, concepts about ourselves and other people, and
skills. Our ability to use information to make plans depends on our competencies. Knowledge of the physical world and of cultural codes of conduct are important competencies. So are academic skills such as reading and writing,
athletic skills such as swimming and tossing a football, social skills such as
knowing how to ask someone out on a date, and many others.

**How Do Competencies Contribute to Perfor-
mance?** What factors contribute to this girl's performance on the balance beam? Individual differences in competencies stem from variations in
genetic endowment, nutrition, and learning opportunities.

WILL YOU BE A HIT OR A MISS?
THE EXPECTANCY FOR SUCCESS SCALE

Life is filled with opportunities and obstacles. What happens when you are faced with a difficult challenge? Do you rise to meet it, or do you back off?

Social-cognitive theorists note that our self-efficacy expectancies influence our behavior. When we believe that we are capable of succeeding through our own efforts, we marshal our resources and apply ourselves.

The following scale, created by Fibel and Hale (1978) can give you insight as to whether you believe that your own efforts are likely to meet with success. You can compare your own expectancies for success with those of other undergraduates taking psychology courses by turning to the scoring key in Appendix B. ■

Directions: Indicate the degree to which each item applies to you by circling the appropriate number, according to this key:

1 = highly improbable

2 = improbable

3 = equally improbable and probable, not sure

4 = probable

5 = highly probable

IN THE FUTURE I EXPECT THAT I WILL:

1. Find that people don't seem to understand what I'm trying to say 1 2 3 4 5

2. Be discouraged about my ability to gain the respect of others 1 2 3 4 5

3. Be a good parent 1 2 3 4 5

4. Be unable to accomplish my goals 1 2 3 4 5

5. Have a stressful marital relationship 1 2 3 4 5

6. Deal poorly with emergency situations 1 2 3 4 5

7. Find my efforts to change situations I don't like are ineffective 1 2 3 4 5

8. Not be very good at learning new skills 1 2 3 4 5

9. Carry through my responsibilities successfully 1 2 3 4 5

10. Discover that the good in life outweighs the bad 1 2 3 4 5

Individual differences in competencies reflect genetic variation, learning opportunities, and other environmental factors. People do not perform well at given tasks unless they have the competencies needed to do so.

ENCODING STRATEGIES: HOW DO YOU SEE IT? Different people **encode** (symbolize or represent) the same stimuli in different ways. Their encoding strategies are an important factor in their behavior. One person might encode a tennis game as a chance to bat the ball back and forth and have some fun. Another person might encode the game as a demand to perfect his or her serve. One person might encode a date that doesn't work out as a sign of her or his

ENCODE • Interpret; transform.

446

11. Handle unexpected problems successfully		1 2 3 4 5
12. Get the promotions I deserve		1 2 3 4 5
13. Succeed in the projects I undertake		1 2 3 4 5
14. Not make any significant contributions to society		1 2 3 4 5
15. Discover that my life is not getting much better		1 2 3 4 5
16. Be listened to when I speak		1 2 3 4 5
17. Discover that my plans don't work out too well		1 2 3 4 5
18. Find that no matter how hard I try, things just don't turn out the way I would like		1 2 3 4 5
19. Handle myself well in whatever situation I'm in		1 2 3 4 5
20. Be able to solve my own problems		1 2 3 4 5
21. Succeed at most things I try		1 2 3 4 5
22. Be successful in my endeavors in the long run		1 2 3 4 5
23. Be very successful working out my personal life		1 2 3 4 5
24. Experience many failures in my life		1 2 3 4 5
25. Make a good first impression on people I meet for the first time		1 2 3 4 5
26. Attain the career goals I have set for myself		1 2 3 4 5
27. Have difficulty dealing with my superiors		1 2 3 4 5
28. Have problems working with others		1 2 3 4 5
29. Be a good judge of what it takes to get ahead		1 2 3 4 5
30. Achieve recognition in my profession		1 2 3 4 5

Note: Reprinted with permission from Fibel and Hale, 1978, p. 931.

social incompetence. Another person might encode the date as reflecting the fact that people are not always "made for each other."

Some people make themselves miserable by encoding events in self-defeating ways (see Chapter 15). A linebacker may encode an average day on the field as a failure because he didn't make any sacks. Cognitive therapists foster adjustment by challenging people to view life in more optimistic ways.

EXPECTANCIES: WHAT WILL HAPPEN? There are various kinds of expectancies. Some are predictions about what will follow various stimuli or signs. For example, some people predict other people's behavior on the basis of signs such as "tight lips" or "shifty eyes" (Ross & Nisbett, 1991). Other expectancies involve what will happen if we engage in certain behaviors. **Self-efficacy expectations** are beliefs that we can accomplish certain things, such as speaking before a group or doing a backflip into a swimming pool or solving math problems (Pajares & Miller, 1994).

Competencies influence expectancies. Expectancies, in turn, influence motivation to perform. People with positive self-efficacy expectations are more likely to try difficult tasks than people who do not believe that they can master those tasks. One way that psychotherapy helps people is by changing their self-efficacy expectations from "I can't" to "I can" (Bandura, 1986). As a result, people are motivated to try new things.

EMOTIONS: HOW DOES IT FEEL? Because of our different learning histories, similar situations can arouse different feelings in us—anxiety, depression, fear, hopelessness, and anger. What frightens one person may entice another. What bores one person may excite another. From the social-cognitive perspective, in contrast to the behaviorist perspective, we are not controlled by stimuli. Instead, stimuli arouse feelings in us, and feelings influence our behavior. Hearing Chopin may make one person weep and another person switch to a rock 'n' roll station.

SELF-REGULATORY SYSTEMS AND PLANS: HOW CAN YOU ACHIEVE IT? We tend to regulate our own behavior, even in the absence of observers and external constraints. We set our own goals and standards. We make plans to achieve them. We congratulate or criticize ourselves, depending on whether or not we achieve them (Bandura, 1991).

Self-regulation helps us influence our environments. We can select the situations to which we expose ourselves and the arenas in which we will compete. Depending on our expectancies, we may choose to enter the academic or athletic worlds. We may choose marriage or the single life. And when we cannot readily select our environment, we can to some degree select our responses within an environment—even an aversive one. For example, if we are undergoing an uncomfortable medical procedure, we may try to reduce the stress by focusing on something else—an inner fantasy or something in the environment such as the cracks in the tiles on the ceiling. This is one of the techniques used in prepared or "natural" childbirth.

• Evaluation of the Learning Perspective

Learning theorists have made monumental contributions to the scientific understanding of behavior, but they have left some psychologists dissatisfied.

Psychodynamic theorists and trait theorists propose the existence of psychological structures that cannot be seen and measured directly. Learning theorists—particularly behaviorists—have dramatized the importance of referring to publicly observable variables, or behaviors, if psychology is to be accepted as a science.

Similarly, psychodynamic theorists and trait theorists focus on internal variables such as unconscious conflict and traits to explain and predict behavior. Learning theorists emphasize the importance of environmental conditions, or situational variables, as determinants of behavior. They have also elaborated on the conditions that foster learning—even automatic kinds of learning. They have shown that we can learn to do things because of reinforcements and that many behavior patterns are acquired by observing others.

SELF-EFFICACY EXPECTATIONS • Beliefs to the effect that one can handle a task.

On the other hand, behaviorism is limited in its ability to explain personality. Behaviorism does not describe, explain, or even suggest the richness of inner human experience. We experience thoughts and feelings and browse through our complex inner maps of the world, but behaviorism does not deal with these. To be fair, however, the "limitations" of behaviorism are self-imposed. Personality theorists have traditionally dealt with thoughts, feelings, and behavior, whereas behaviorism, which insists on studying only that which is observable and measurable, deals with behavior alone.

Critics of social-cognitive theory cannot accuse its supporters of denying the importance of cognitive activity and feelings. But they often contend that social-cognitive theory has not come up with satisfying statements about the development of traits or accounted for self-awareness. Also, social-cognitive theory—like its intellectual forebear, behaviorism—may not pay enough attention to genetic variation in explaining individual differences in behavior. Learning theories have done very little to account for the development of traits or personality types.

REFLECTIONS

- Given cultural and social conditioning, is true freedom possible? To behaviorists, even *telling ourselves* that we have free will is determined by the environment. Is free will an illusion? What is the evidence for your belief?
- Which theorists believe that people are "ruled" by pleasure and pain? Do you share this belief? Why or why not?
- Social-cognitive theorists suggest that our self-efficacy expectations are connected with how hard we work at things. Do examples from your own life support this view?

■ THE HUMANISTIC-EXISTENTIAL PERSPECTIVE

You are unique, and if that is not fulfilled, then something has been lost.

MARTHA GRAHAM

Humanists and existentialists dwell on the meaning of life. Self-awareness is the hub of the humanistic-existential search for meaning.

The term **humanism** has a long history and many meanings. It became a third force in American psychology in the 1950s and 1960s, partly in response to the predominant psychodynamic and behavioral models. Humanism also represented a reaction to the "rat race" spawned by industrialization and automation. Humanists felt that work on assembly lines produced "alienation" from inner sources of meaning. The humanistic views of Abraham Maslow and Carl Rogers emerged from these concerns.

Existentialism in part reflects the horrors of mass destruction of human life through war and genocide, frequent events in the 20th century. The term *existentialism* implies that our existence, or being, in the world is more central to human nature than theories or abstractions about human nature.

The European existentialist philosophers Jean-Paul Sartre and Martin Heidegger saw human life as trivial in the grand scheme of things. But psychiatrists

HUMANISM • The view that people are capable of free choice, self-fulfillment, and ethical behavior.
EXISTENTIALISM • The view that people are completely free and responsible for their own behavior.

DO YOU STRIVE TO BE
ALL THAT YOU CAN BE?

Are you a self-actualizer? Do you strive to be all that you can be? Maslow attributed the following eight characteristics to the self-actualizing individual. How many of them describe you? Why not check them and undertake some self-evaluation? ■

YES	NO		
____	____	1.	*Do you fully experience life in the present—the here and now?* (Self-actualizers do not focus excessively on the lost past or wish their lives away as they stride toward distant goals.)
____	____	2.	*Do you make growth choices rather than fear choices?* (Self-actualizers take reasonable risks to develop their unique potentials. They do not bask in the dull life of the status quo. They do not "settle.")
____	____	3.	*Do you seek to acquire self-knowledge?* (Self-actualizers look inward. They search for values, talents, and meaningfulness. It might be enlightening to take an interest inventory—a test frequently used to help make career decisions—at your college testing and counseling center.)
____	____	4.	*Do you strive toward honesty in interpersonal relationships?* (Self-actualizers strip away the social facades and games that stand in the way of self-disclosure and the formation of intimate relationships.)
____	____	5.	*Do you behave self-assertively and express your own ideas and feelings, even at the risk of occasional social disapproval?* (Self-actualizers do not bottle up their feelings for the sake of avoiding social disapproval.)
____	____	6.	*Do you strive toward new goals? Do you strive to be the best that you can be in a chosen life role?* (Self-actualizers do not live by the memory of past accomplishments. Nor do they present second-rate efforts.)
____	____	7.	*Do you seek meaningful and rewarding life activities?* Do you experience moments of actualization that humanistic psychologists call *peak experiences*? (Peak experiences are brief moments of rapture filled with personal meaning. Examples might include completing a work of art, falling in love, redesigning a machine tool, suddenly solving a complex problem in math or physics, or having a baby. Note that we differ as individuals; one person's peak experience might bore another person silly.)
____	____	8.	*Do you remain open to new experiences?* (Self-actualizers do not hold themselves back for fear that novel experiences might shake their views of the world, or of right and wrong. Self-actualizers are willing to revise their expectations, values, and opinions.)

like Viktor Frankl, Ludwig Binswanger, and Medard Boss argued that seeing human existence as meaningless could give rise to withdrawal and apathy—even suicide. Psychological salvation therefore requires giving personal meaning to things and making personal choices. Yes, there is pain in life, and yes, sooner or later life comes to an end, but people can see the world for what it is and make real, genuine choices.

Freud argued that defense mechanisms prevent us from seeing the world as it is. Therefore, the concept of free choice is meaningless. Behaviorists view freedom as an illusion determined by social forces. Social-cognitive theorists also speak of external or situational forces that influence us. To existentialists, we are really and painfully free to do what we choose with our lives.

• Abraham Maslow and the Challenge of Self-Actualization

Humanists see Freud as preoccupied with the "basement" of the human condition. Freud wrote that people are basically motivated to gratify biological drives. The humanistic psychologist Abraham Maslow argued that people also have a need for **self-actualization**—to become all that they can be. Because people are unique, they must follow unique paths to self-actualization. Self-actualization requires taking risks. People who adhere to the "tried and true" may find their lives degenerating into monotony and predictability. (Maslow's theoretical *hierarchy of needs* is discussed in Chapter 11.)

• Carl Rogers' Self Theory

Carl Rogers (1902–1987) wrote that people shape themselves through free choice and action. But what is your *self?*

Rogers defined the *self* as the center of experience. Your self is your ongoing sense of who and what you are, your sense of how and why you react to the environment and how you choose to act on the environment. Your choices are made on the basis of your values, and your values are also part of your self.

THE SELF-CONCEPT AND FRAMES OF REFERENCE Our self-concepts consist of our impressions of ourselves and our evaluations of our adequacy. It may be helpful to think of us as rating ourselves according to various scales or dimensions such as good-bad, intelligent-unintelligent, strong-weak, and tall-short.

Rogers believed that we all have unique ways of looking at ourselves and the world—that is, unique **frames of reference.** It may be that we each use a different set of dimensions in defining ourselves and that we judge ourselves according to different sets of values. To one person, achievement-failure may be the most important dimension. To another person, the most important dimension may be decency-indecency. A third person may not even think in terms of decency.

SELF-ESTEEM AND POSITIVE REGARD Rogers assumed that we all develop a need for self-regard, or self-esteem, as we develop and become aware of ourselves. At first, self-esteem reflects the esteem in which others hold us. Parents help children develop self-esteem when they show them **unconditional positive regard**—that is, when they accept them as having intrinsic merit regardless of their behavior at the moment. But when parents show children **conditional positive regard**—that is, when they accept them only when they behave in a desired manner—children may develop **conditions of worth.** That is, they may come to think that they have merit only if they behave as their parents wish them to behave.

Because each individual is thought to have a unique potential, children who develop conditions of worth must be somewhat disappointed in themselves. We

SELF-ACTUALIZATION • In humanistic theory, the innate tendency to strive to realize one's potential.
FRAME OF REFERENCE • One's unique patterning of perceptions and attitudes according to which one evaluates events.
UNCONDITIONAL POSITIVE REGARD • A persistent expression of esteem for the value of a person, but not necessarily an unqualified acceptance of all of the person's behaviors.
CONDITIONAL POSITIVE REGARD • Judgment of another person's value on the basis of the acceptability of that person's behaviors.
CONDITIONS OF WORTH • Standards by which the value of a person is judged.

cannot fully live up to the wishes of others and remain true to ourselves. This does not mean that the expression of the self inevitably leads to conflict. Rogers was optimistic about human nature. He believed that we hurt others or act in antisocial ways only when we are frustrated in our efforts to develop our potential. But when parents and others are loving and tolerant of our differentness, we, too, are loving—even if some of our preferences, abilities, and values differ from those of our parents.

psychology and
modern life

ENHANCING SELF-ESTEEM

N*o one can make you feel inferior without your consent.*

ELEANOR ROOSEVELT

According to humanistic-existential theory, self-esteem is central to our sense of well-being. Self-esteem helps us develop our potential as unique individuals. It may originate in childhood and reflect the esteem others have for us. Nevertheless, there are many things you can do—here and now—to raise your own self-esteem.

IMPROVE YOURSELF For example, are you miserable because of excess dependence on another person? Perhaps you can enhance your social skills or your vocational skills in an effort to become more independent. Are you too heavy? Perhaps you can follow some of the suggestions for losing weight, presented in Chapter 11.

Truth or Fiction Revisited

It is true that we can build our self-esteem by becoming good at something. Competence boosts self-esteem.

CHALLENGE THE REALISM OF YOUR IDEAL SELF Our internal list of "oughts" and "shoulds" can create perfectionistic standards. We constantly fall short of these standards and experience frustration. Challenge your perfectionistic demands on yourself and, when appropriate, revise them. It may be harmful to abolish worthy and realistic goals, even if we do have trouble measuring up now and then. However, some of our goals or values may not stand up to scrutiny. It is useful to consider them objectively.

SUBSTITUTE REALISTIC GOALS FOR UN-ATTAINABLE GOALS Perhaps we will never be as artistic, as tall, or as graceful as we would like to be. We can work to enhance our drawing skills, but if it becomes clear that we will not become Michelangelos, perhaps we can enjoy our scribblings for what they are and also find satisfaction elsewhere. We cannot make ourselves taller (except by wearing elevator shoes or high heels), but we can take off five pounds and cut our time for running the mile by a few seconds. We can also learn to whip up a great fettuccine Alfredo.

BUILD SELF-EFFICACY EXPECTATIONS Our self-efficacy expectations define the degree to which we believe that our efforts will bring about a positive outcome. They affect our willingness to take on challenges and persist in efforts to meet them. We can build self-efficacy expectations by selecting tasks that are consistent with our interests and abilities and then working at those tasks. Psychologists have devised many tests to help people focus in on their interests and abilities. They are probably available at your college testing and counseling center. But we can also build self-efficacy expectations by working at athletics or hobbies or charitable causes.

Realistic self-assessment, realistic goals, and a reasonable schedule for improvement are the keys to building self-efficacy expectations. Chances are that you will not be able to run a four-minute mile, but after a few months of reasonably taxing workouts under the advice of a skilled trainer, you might be able to put a few seven- or eight-minute miles back to back. (You might even enjoy them.) ■

However, children in some families learn that it is bad to have ideas of their own, especially about sexual, political, or religious matters. When they perceive their parents' disapproval, they may come to see themselves as rebels and label their feelings as selfish, wrong, or evil. If they wish to retain a consistent self-concept and self-esteem, they may have to deny many of their feelings or disown aspects of themselves. In this way the self-concept becomes distorted. According to Rogers, anxiety often stems from recognition that people have feelings and desires that are inconsistent with their distorted self-concept. Since anxiety is unpleasant, people may deny the existence of their genuine feelings and desires.

According to Rogers, the path to self-actualization requires getting in touch with our genuine feelings, accepting them, and acting on them. This is the goal of Rogers's method of psychotherapy, *client-centered therapy,* which we discuss in Chapter 16.

Rogers also believed that we have mental images of what we are capable of becoming. These are termed **self-ideals.** We are motivated to reduce the discrepancy between our self-concepts and our self-ideals.

Unique. According to humanistic psychologists like Carl Rogers, each of us views the world from a unique frame of reference. What matters to one person may mean little to another.

• *Evaluation of the Humanistic-Existential Perspective*

Humanistic-existential theories have tremendous appeal for college students because of their focus on the importance of personal experience. We tend to treasure our conscious experiences (our "selves") and those of the people we care about. For lower organisms, to be alive is to move, to process food, to exchange oxygen and carbon dioxide, and to reproduce. But for human beings, an essential aspect of life is conscious experience—the sense of oneself as progressing through space and time. Humanistic-existential theorists emphasize the central role of consciousness in our daily lives.

Psychodynamic theories see individuals largely as victims of their childhood. Learning theories, to some degree, see people as "victims of circumstances"—or at least as victims of situational variables. But humanistic-existential theorists see humans as free to make choices. Psychodynamic theorists and learning theorists wonder whether our sense of freedom is merely an illusion. Humanistic-existential theorists, in contrast, begin by assuming personal freedom.

Ironically, the primary strength of the humanistic-existential approaches—their focus on conscious experience—is also their main weakness. Conscious experience is private and subjective. Therefore, the validity of formulating theories in terms of consciousness has been questioned. On the other hand, some psychologists (e.g., Bevan & Kessel, 1994) believe that the science of psychology can afford to loosen its methods somewhat if this will help it address the richness of human experience.

Self-actualization, like trait theory, yields circular explanations for behavior. When we see someone engaging in what seems to be positive striving, we gain little insight by attributing this behavior to a self-actualizing force. We have done nothing to account for the origins of the force. And when we observe someone who is not engaging in growth-oriented striving, it seems arbitrary to "explain" this outcome by suggesting that the self-actualizing tendency has been blocked or frustrated.

Humanistic-existential theories, like learning theories, have little to say about the development of traits and personality types. They assume that we are all unique, but they do not predict the sorts of traits, abilities, and interests we will develop.

SELF-IDEAL • A mental image of what we believe we ought to be.

■ THE SOCIOCULTURAL PERSPECTIVE

Thirteen-year-old Hannah brought her lunch tray to the table in the cafeteria. Her mother, Julie, eyed with horror the french fries, the plate of mashed potatoes in gravy, the bag of potato chips, and the large paper cup brimming with soda. "You can't eat that!" she said. "It's garbage!"

"Oh come on, Mom! Chill, okay?" Hannah rejoined before taking her tray to sit with some friends rather than with us.

I spend Saturdays with my children at the Manhattan School of Music. Not only do they study voice and piano. They—and I—have widened our cultural perspective by relating to families and students from all parts of the world.

Julie and Hannah are Korean Americans. Flustered, Julie shook her head and said, "I've now been in the United States longer than I was in Korea, and I still can't get used to the way children act here." Barbara, a Polish American parent, chimed in. "I never would have spoken to my parents the way Thomas speaks to me. I would have been . . . whipped or beaten."

"I try to tell Hannah she is part of the family," Julie continued. "She should think of other people. When she talks that way, it's embarrassing."

"Over here children are not part of the family," said Ken, an African American parent. "They are either part of their own crowd or they are 'individuals.'"

"Being an individual does not mean you have to talk back to your mother," Julie said. "What do you think, Spencer? You're the psychologist."

I think I made some unhelpful comments about the ketchup on the french fries having antioxidants and some slightly helpful comments about what is typical of teenagers in the United States. But I'm not sure, because I was thinking deeply about Hannah at the time. Not about her lunch, but about the formation of her personality and the influences on her behavior.

It occurred to me that in a multicultural society, personality cannot be understood without reference to the **sociocultural perspective.** Moreover, as we head toward the new millennium, trends in immigration are making the population an even richer mix. Different cultural groups within the United States have different attitudes, beliefs, norms, self-definitions, and values (Basic Behavioral Science Task Force, 1996c; Triandis, 1996).

Back to Hannah. Perhaps there were some unconscious psychodynamic influences operating on her. Her traits included exceptional academic ability and musical talent, which were at least partly determined by her heredity. Clearly, she was consciously striving to become a great violinist. But one could not fully understand her personality without also considering the sociocultural influences acting on her.

Here was a youngster who was strongly influenced by her peers—she was completely at home with blue jeans and french fries. She was also a daughter in an Asian American immigrant group that views education as the key to success in our culture (Gibson & Ogbu, 1991; Ogbu, 1993). Belonging to this ethnic

SOCIOCULTURAL PERSPECTIVE • The view that focuses on the roles of ethnicity, gender, culture, and socioeconomic status in personality formation, behavior, and mental processes.

group had certainly contributed to her ambition. But being a Korean American had not prevented her from becoming an outspoken American teenager. (Would she have been outspoken if she had been reared in Korea? I wondered. Of course, this question cannot be answered with certainty.) Predictably, her outspoken behavior had struck her mother as brazen and inappropriate (Lopez & Hernandez, 1986). Julie was deeply offended by behavior that I consider acceptable in my own children. She reeled off the things that were "wrong" with Hannah from her Korean American perspective. I listed some things that were very right with Hannah and encouraged Julie to worry less.

Let us consider how sociocultural factors can affect one's sense of self.

• *Individualism Versus Collectivism*

In a sense, Julie's complaint was that Hannah saw herself as an individual and an artist to a greater extent than as a family member and a Korean girl. Crosscultural research reveals that people in the United States and many northern European nations tend to be individualistic. **Individualists** tend to define themselves in terms of their personal identities and to give priority to their personal goals (Triandis, 1995). When asked to complete the statement "I am . . . ," they are likely to respond in terms of their personality traits ("I am outgoing," "I am artistic") or their occupations ("I am a nurse," "I am a systems analyst") (Triandis, 1990). In contrast, many people from cultures in Africa, Asia, and Central and South America tend to be collectivistic (Basic Behavioral Science Task Force, 1996c). **Collectivists** tend to define themselves in terms of the groups to which they belong and to give priority to the group's goals (Triandis, 1995). They feel complete in terms of their relationships with others (Markus & Kitayama, 1991; see Figure 12.4). They are more likely than individualists to conform to group norms and judgments (Bond & Smith, 1996; Okazaki, 1997). When asked to complete the statement "I am . . . ," they are more likely to respond in terms of their families, gender, or nation ("I am a father," "I am a Buddhist," "I am a Japanese") (Triandis, 1990, 1994).

The seeds of individualism and collectivism are found in the culture in which a person grows up. The capitalist system fosters individualism to some degree. It assumes that individuals are entitled to amass personal fortunes and that the process of doing so creates jobs and wealth for large numbers of people. The individualist perspective is found in the self-reliant heroes and antiheroes of Western literature and mass media—from Homer's Odysseus to Clint Eastwood's gritty cowboys and Walt Disney's Pocahontas. The traditional writings of the East have exalted people who resisted personal temptations in order to do their duty and promote the welfare of the group.

INDIVIDUALIST • A person who defines herself or himself in terms of personal traits and gives priority to her or his own goals.
COLLECTIVIST • A person who defines herself or himself in terms of relationships to other people and groups and gives priority to group goals.

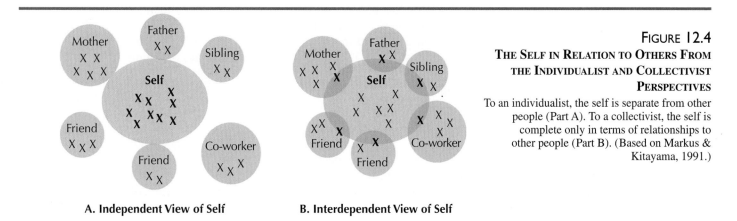

A. Independent View of Self   B. Interdependent View of Self

FIGURE 12.4
THE SELF IN RELATION TO OTHERS FROM THE INDIVIDUALIST AND COLLECTIVIST PERSPECTIVES
To an individualist, the self is separate from other people (Part A). To a collectivist, the self is complete only in terms of relationships to other people (Part B). (Based on Markus & Kitayama, 1991.)

This Hispanic American Woman Is Highly Acculturated to Life in the United States. Some immigrants are completely assimilated by the dominant culture and abandon the language and customs of their country of origin. Others retain the language and customs of their country of origin and never become comfortable with those of their new country. Still others become bicultural. They become fluent in both languages and blend the customs and values of both cultures.

• Sociocultural Factors and the Self

Sociocultural factors also affect self-concept and self-esteem. Carl Rogers noted that our self-concepts tend to reflect how other people see us. Thus, members of the dominant culture in the United States are likely to have a positive sense of self. They share in the expectations of personal achievement and respect that are accorded to those who ascend to power. Similarly, members of ethnic groups that have been subjected to discrimination and poverty may have poorer self-concepts and lower self-esteem than members of the dominant culture (Greene, 1993, 1994; Lewis-Fernández & Kleinman, 1994).

Despite the persistence of racial prejudices, a survey by the American Association of University Women (1992) found that African American girls are likely to be happier with their appearance than White girls are. Sixty-five percent of African American elementary schoolgirls said that they were happy with the way they were, compared with 55% of White girls. By high school age, 58% of African American girls remained happy with the way they were, compared with a surprisingly low 22% of White girls. Why the discrepancy? It appears that the parents of African American girls teach them that there is nothing wrong with them if they do not match the ideals of the dominant culture. The world mistreats them because of prejudice, not because of who they are as individuals or what they do (Williams, 1992). The White girls are more likely to blame themselves for not attaining the unreachable ideal.

• Acculturation and Self-Esteem

Should Hindu women who emigrate to the United States surrender the sari in favor of California Casuals? Should Russian immigrants try to teach their children English at home? Should African American children be acquainted with the music and art of African peoples or those of Europe? How do these activities, which are examples of **acculturation,** affect the psychological well-being of immigrants and their families?

Self-esteem is connected with patterns of acculturation among immigrants. Those patterns take various forms. Some immigrants are completely assimilated by the dominant culture. They lose the language and customs of their country of origin and become like the dominant culture in the new host country. Others maintain separation. They retain the language and customs of their country of origin and never become comfortable with those of the new country. Still others become bicultural. They remain fluent in the language of their country of origin while learning that of their new country, and they blend the customs and values of both cultures.

Research evidence suggests that people who identify with the bicultural pattern have the highest self-esteem (Phinney and others, 1992). For example, Mexican Americans who are more proficient in English are less likely to be anxious and depressed than less proficient Mexican Americans (Salgado de Snyder and others, 1990). The ability to adapt to the ways of the new society, combined with a supportive cultural tradition and a sense of ethnic identity, apparently helps people adjust.

• Evaluation of the Sociocultural Perspective

The sociocultural perspective provides valuable insights into the roles of ethnicity, gender, culture, and socioeconomic status in personality formation. When we ignore sociocultural factors, we deal only with the core of the human being—the potentials that allow the person to adapt to external forces. Sociocul-

ACCULTURATION • The process of adaptation in which immigrants and native groups identify with a new, dominant culture by learning about that culture and making behavioral and attitudinal changes.

In Review   Perspectives on Personality

PERSPECTIVE	FOCUS	KEY POINTS
Psychodynamic	Unconscious conflict, in which drives such as sex, aggression, and the need for superiority come into conflict with laws, social rules, and moral codes	Freud hypothesized three structures of personality (id, ego, superego) and five stages of psychosexual development (oral, anal, phallic, latency, genital).
Trait	Use of mathematical techniques to catalogue and organize basic human personality traits	Hippocrates hypothesized the existence of four basic traits, which were, in effect, updated by Eysenck. Contemporary researchers find five (the five-factor model).
Learning	Factors that determine behavior	Behaviorists see personality as plastic and determined by external, situational variables. Social-cognitive theorists also look for variables within the person—person variables such as competencies, encoding strategies, expectancies, emotions, and self-regulatory systems—that affect behavior.
Humanistic-Existential	The experiences of being human and developing one's unique potential within an often hostile environment	People have inborn drives to become what they are capable of being. Unconditional positive regard leads to self-esteem, which facilitates individual growth and development.
Sociocultural	The roles of ethnicity, gender, culture, and socioeconomic status in personality formation	Development differs in individualistic and collectivist societies. Discrimination, poverty, and acculturation affect the self-concept and self-esteem.

tural factors are external forces that are internalized. They run through us deeply, touching many aspects of our cognitions, motives, emotions, and behavior. Without reference to sociocultural factors, we may be able to understand generalities about behavior and cognitive processes. However, we will not be able to understand how individuals think, behave, and feel about themselves within a given cultural setting. The sociocultural perspective enhances our sensitivity to cultural differences and expectations and allows us to appreciate the richness of human behavior and mental processes.

REFLECTIONS

- When you were a child, were you given conflicting messages about the importance of competing and sharing? Do you think the experiences in your own home were more oriented toward individualism or collectivism? How so?
- How have sociocultural factors affected your self-concept?
- For how many generations have the families of your parents lived in the United States? What acculturation problems did your forebears experience? If you do not have specific information about their experiences, what do you imagine they might have been like? Why?

■ MEASUREMENT OF PERSONALITY

Methods of personality assessment take a sample of behavior to predict future behavior. Standardized interviews are often used. Many psychologists even use computers to conduct routine interviews (Bloom, 1992). Some measures of personality are **behavior-rating scales,** which assess behavior in settings such as classrooms or mental hospitals. With behavior-rating scales, trained observers usually check off each occurrence of a specific behavior within a certain time frame—say, 15 minutes. However, standardized objective and projective tests are used more frequently, and we will focus on them in this section.

Measures of personality are used to make important decisions, such as whether a person is suited for a certain type of work, a particular class in school, or a drug to reduce agitation (Saccuzzo, 1994). As part of their admissions process, graduate schools often ask professors to rate prospective students on scales that assess traits such as intelligence, emotional stability, and cooperation. Students may take tests to measure their **aptitudes** and interests to gain insight into whether they are suited for certain occupations. It is assumed that students who share the aptitudes and interests of people who function well in certain positions are also likely to function well in those positions.

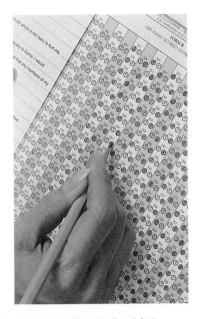

Is this Test Taker Telling the Truth? How can psychologists determine whether or not people answer test items honestly? What are the validity scales of the MMPI?

• *Objective Tests*

Objective tests present respondents with a **standardized** group of test items in the form of a questionnaire. Respondents are limited to a specific range of answers. One test might ask respondents to indicate whether items are true or false for them. (I have included questionnaires of this sort in several chapters of this book.) Another might ask respondents to select the preferred activity from groups of three.

Some tests have a **forced-choice format,** in which respondents are asked to indicate which of two statements is more true for them or which of several activities they prefer. The respondents are not given the option of answering "none of the above." Forced-choice formats are frequently used in interest inventories, which help predict whether the person would function well in a certain occupation. The following item is similar to those found in occupational interest inventories:

I would rather

a. be a forest ranger.

b. work in a busy office.

c. play a musical instrument.

The Minnesota Multiphasic Personality Inventory (MMPI) contains hundreds of items presented in a true-false format. The MMPI is designed to be used by clinical and counseling psychologists to help diagnose psychological disorders (see Chapter 15). Accurate measurement of an individual's problems should point to appropriate treatment. The MMPI is the most widely used psychological test in clinical work (Helmes & Reddon, 1993; Watkins and others, 1995). It is also the most widely used instrument for personality measurement in psychological research.

Psychologists can score tests by hand, send them to computerized scoring services, or have them scored by on-site computers. Computers generate reports by interpreting the test record according to certain rules or by comparing it with records in memory.

BEHAVIOR-RATING SCALE • A systematic means for recording the frequency with which target behaviors occur.
APTITUDE • A natural ability or talent.
OBJECTIVE TESTS • Tests whose items must be answered in a specified, limited manner. Tests whose items have concrete answers that are considered correct.
STANDARDIZED TEST • A test that is given to a large number of respondents so that data concerning the typical responses can be accumulated and analyzed.
FORCED-CHOICE FORMAT • A method of presenting test questions that requires a respondent to select one of a number of possible answers.

TABLE 12.3	MINNESOTA MULTIPHASIC PERSONALITY INVENTORY (MMPI) SCALES	
Scale	*Abbreviation*	*Possible Interpretations*
VALIDITY SCALES		
Question	?	Corresponds to number of items left unanswered
Lie	L	Lies or is highly conventional
Frequency	F	Exaggerates complaints or answers items haphazardly; may have bizarre ideas
Correction	K	Denies problems
CLINICAL SCALES		
Hypochondriasis	Hs	Has bodily concerns and complaints
Depression	D	Is depressed; has feelings of guilt and helplessness
Hysteria	Hy	Reacts to stress by developing physical symptoms; lacks insight
Psychopathic deviate	Pd	Is immoral, in conflict with the law; has stormy relationships
Masculinity/Femininity	Mf	High scores suggest interests and behavior considered stereotypical of the other gender
Paranoia	Pa	Is suspicious and resentful; highly cynical about human nature
Psychasthenia	Pt	Is anxious, worried, high-strung
Schizophrenia	Sc	Is confused, disorganized, disoriented; has bizarre ideas
Hypomania	Ma	Is energetic, restless, active, easily bored
Social introversion	Si	Is introverted, timid, shy; lacks self-confidence

The MMPI is usually scored for the 4 **validity scales** and 10 **clinical scales** described in Table 12.3. The validity scales suggest whether answers actually represent the person's thoughts, emotions, and behaviors. However, they cannot guarantee that deception will be disclosed.

The validity scales in Table 12.3 assess different **response sets,** or biases, in answering the questions. People with high L scores, for example, may be attempting to present themselves as excessively moral and well-behaved individuals. People with high F scores may be trying to seem bizarre or are answering haphazardly. Many personality measures have some kind of validity scale. The clinical scales of the MMPI assess the problems shown in Table 12.3, as well as stereotypical masculine or feminine interests and introversion.

The MMPI scales were constructed *empirically*—that is, on the basis of actual clinical data rather than on the basis of psychological theory. A test-item bank of several hundred items was derived from questions that are often asked in clinical interviews. Here are some examples of the kinds of items that were used:

My father was a good man.	T F
I am very seldom troubled by headaches.	T F

Truth or Fiction Revisited

Psychologists cannot necessarily determine whether a person has told the truth on a personality test. However, validity scales allow them to make educated guesses.

VALIDITY SCALES • Groups of test items that indicate whether a person's responses accurately reflect that individual's traits.
CLINICAL SCALES • Groups of test items that measure the presence of various abnormal behavior patterns.
RESPONSE SET • A tendency to answer test items according to a bias—for instance, to make oneself seem perfect or bizarre.

USING PSYCHOLOGICAL TESTS TO FIND A CAREER THAT FITS

At social gatherings, *"What* do you do?"* is asked more frequently than *"How* do you do?"* Psychologists use psychological tests to help people predict whether or not they are likely to adjust to various occupations by matching their key traits to a particular type of job. Several kinds of tests are used for this purpose.

PERSONNEL TESTS Industrial/organizational psychologists attempt to match performances on personnel tests with specific job requirements. Personnel tests include tests of intellectual abilities, spatial and mechanical abilities, perceptual accuracy, motor abilities, and personality and interests.

Tests of mechanical comprehension are appropriate for many factory workers, construction workers, and of course, mechanics. They include items such as indicating which of two pairs of shears would cut metal better. Spatial relations ability is needed in any job that requires the ability to visualize objects in three dimensions. Examples include drafting, clothing design, and architecture. Tests of perceptual accuracy are useful for clerical positions, such as bank tellers and secretaries. Some items on these tests ask respondents to compare columns of letters, words, or numbers and indicate which ones do or do not match. Tests of motor abilities are useful for jobs that require strength, coordination, rapid reaction time, or dexterity. Moving furniture, driving certain kinds of equipment, and sewing all require some motor skills.

The relationships between personality and performance in a job are less

clear. It seems logical that one might wish to hire a candidate for a sales position who has a strong need to persuade others. Many businesses have used personality tests to measure candidates' general "stability." However, such use has sometimes been criticized as an invasion of privacy.

INTEREST INVENTORIES Psychologists have devised interest inventories that predict psychological adjustment in various occupations. Although interest in an occupation does not guarantee ability to excel in that occupation, there are many types of jobs in a broad occupational area. Tests may reveal that a candidate is better suited for one type than for another. Consider medicine. There are medical technicians (X-ray technicians, blood analysts, and so on), nurses, physical therapists, physicians, and other occupations within this broad field. Assessment of interests and aptitudes can help a person zero in on one of them.

HOLLAND'S TYPES Psychologist John Holland has developed a theory in which six traits (realistic, investigative, and so on) are matched to particular occupations. To obtain insight into what might be a match for you, let's attend a job fair.

Directions: Figure 12.5 shows the people at a job fair in a college gymnasium. When the fair got under way, students and prospective employers began to chat. As time elapsed, they found mutual interests and collected in different parts of the gym according to those interests.

Now *you* enter the room. Groups have already formed. As you decide which group to join, you overhear

snatches of conversation that indicate the types of people in various groups. Now consider the types of people in the six groups by reading the descriptions in Figure 12.5:

Which group would you most like to join? Write the letter that signifies the group (R, I, A, S, E, or C) here: ____

What is your second choice? After you had met and chatted with the folks in the first group, with whom else might you like to chat? Write the letter here: ____

Now, which group looks most boring to you? With which group do you have nothing in common? Which group would you most like to avoid? Write the letter signifying the group that should have stayed at home here: ____

Where, then, did you fit in at the fair? What might it mean for your vocational adjustment? Holland has predicted how well people will enjoy a certain kind of work by matching six traits—realistic, investigative, artistic, social, enterprising, and conventional—to the job. Each of the groups in Figure 12.5 represents one of these traits:

1. *Realistic.* Realistic people tend to be concrete in their thinking, mechanically oriented, and interested in jobs that involve motor activity. Examples include farming; unskilled labor, such as attending gas stations; and skilled trades, such as construction and electrical work.

2. *Investigative.* Investigative people tend to be creative, intro-

C
These people have clerical or numerical skills. They like to work with data, to carry out other people's directions, or to carry things out in detail.

E
These people like to work with people. They like to lead and influence others for economic or organizational gains.

R
These people have mechanical or athletic abilities. They like to work with machines and tools, to be outdoors, or to work with animals or plants.

I
These people like to learn new things. They enjoy investigating and solving problems and advancing knowledge.

S
This group enjoys working with people. They like to help others, including the sick. They enjoy informing and enlightening people.

A
This group is highly imaginative and creative. They enjoy working in unstructured situations. They are artistic and innovative.

FIGURE 12.5
TRAITS AND CAREERS

Picture yourself at a job fair like that pictured here. In such fairs, students and prospective employers begin to chat. As time elapses, they find mutual interests and collect into groups accordingly. Consider the types of people in the six groups by reading the descriptions for each. Which group would you most like to join? What does your choice suggest about your coping style? If you wanted to learn more about your coping style, what resources would be available to you?

verted, and abstract in their thinking. They are frequently well adjusted in research and college and university teaching.

3. *Artistic.* Artistic individuals tend to be creative, emotional, interested in subjective feelings, and intuitive. They tend to gravitate toward the visual and performing arts.

4. *Social.* Socially oriented people tend to be extraverted and socially concerned. They frequently show high verbal ability and strong needs for affiliating with others. They are often well-suited to jobs such as social work, counseling, and teaching children.

5. *Enterprising.* Enterprising individuals tend to be adventurous and impulsive, domineering, and extraverted. They gravitate toward leadership and planning roles in industry, government, and social organizations. The successful real estate developer or tycoon is usually enterprising.

6. *Conventional.* Conventional people tend to enjoy routines. They show high self-control, a need for order, and a desire for social approval. They are not particularly imaginative. Jobs that suit them include banking, accounting, and clerical work.

Many occupations call for combinations of these traits. A copywriter in an advertising agency might be both artistic and enterprising. Clinical and counseling psychologists tend to be investigative, artistic, and socially oriented. Military personnel and beauticians tend to be realistic and conventional. (But military leaders who plan major operations and form governments are also enterprising; and individuals who create new hair styles and fashions are also artistic.)

Holland has created the Vocational Preference Inventory in order to assess these traits. These styles are also measured by some interest inventories. Check with your college testing and counseling center if you would like to learn more about your vocational preferences. ■

Hermann Rorschach

The Swiss psychiatrist Hermann Rorschach (1884–1922) might very well have been the proverbial frustrated artist. His father, Ulrich, was a painter whose work was undistinguished. Ulrich supported his family by teaching at the elementary and secondary levels. Nevertheless, Hermann grew up in a picturesque village on the Rhine. There were hills, an old fort, and an assortment of relics, monuments, and cultural activities—even a museum. During his last two years in the equivalent of high school, Hermann was given the nickname "Klex" by his fraternity brothers. The proper spelling of the word in German is *Klecks,* and it translates as "inkblot" in English. Even

then, Hermann was likely pre-occupied with the child's game of *klecksographie*—dropping ink onto paper and arranging and folding the paper to cause the ink to take on an appealing shape.

Later, through extensive testing of patients at a sanitarium, Rorschach narrowed down an assortment of many dozens of inkblots to 15. These 15, he believed, would tell him and other professionals what they needed to know about the personalities of the people they sought to help. Why are there only 10 Rorschach inkblots today? There was not enough money to print all 15 of the plates in Rorschach's research report. ■

Truth or Fiction Revisited

It is true that there is a psychological test made up of inkblots, one of which looks like a bat. This is the Rorschach inkblot test.

My hands and feet are usually warm enough.	T	F
I have never done anything dangerous for the thrill of it.	T	F
I work under a great deal of tension.	T	F

The items were administered to people with previously identified symptoms, such as depressive or schizophrenic symptoms. Items that successfully set these people apart were included on scales named for these conditions.

• *Projective Tests*

You may have heard that there is a personality test that asks people what a drawing or inkblot looks like and that people commonly answer "a bat." There are a number of such tests, the best known of which is the Rorschach inkblot test, named after its originator, Hermann Rorschach.

THE RORSCHACH INKBLOT TEST The Rorschach test is a **projective test.** In projective techniques there are no clear, specified answers. People are shown ambiguous stimuli such as inkblots or vague drawings and may be asked to say what these stimuli look like to them or to tell stories about them. There is no one correct response. It is assumed that people *project* their own personalities into their responses. The meanings they attribute to these stimuli are assumed to reflect their personalities as well as the drawings or blots themselves.

The facts of the matter are slightly different. Yes, there is no single "correct" response to the Rorschach inkblots shown in Figure 12.6. However, some responses are not in keeping with the features of the blots. Figure 12.6 could be a bat or a flying insect, the pointed face of an animal, the face of a jack o'lantern, or many other things. But responses like "an ice cream cone," "diseased lungs," or "a metal leaf in flames" are not suggested by the features of the blot and may indicate personality problems.

The Rorschach inkblot test contains ten cards. Five are in black and white and shades of gray. Five use a variety of colors. People are given the cards, one by one, and are asked what they look like or what they could be. A response that reflects the shape of the blot is considered to be a sign of adequate **reality testing.** A response that richly integrates several features of the blot is considered a sign of high intellectual functioning. The Rorschach test is thought to provide insight into a person's intelligence, interests, cultural background, degree of introversion or extraversion, level of anxiety, reality testing, and many other variables.

THE THEMATIC APPERCEPTION TEST The Thematic Apperception Test (TAT) was developed in the 1930s by Henry Murray and Christiana Morgan. It consists of drawings, like the one shown in Figure 11.5 (see p. 410), that are open to a variety of interpretations. Individuals are given the cards one at a time and asked to make up stories about them.

PROJECTIVE TEST • A psychological test that presents ambiguous stimuli onto which the test taker projects his or her own personality in making a response.
REALITY TESTING • The capacity to perceive one's environment and oneself according to accurate sensory impressions.

FIGURE 12.6
RORSCHACH INKBLOTS
The Rorschach is the most widely used projective personality test. What do these look like to you? What could they be?

The TAT is widely used in research on motivation and in clinical practice (Watkins and others, 1995). The notion is that we are likely to project our own needs into our responses to ambiguous situations, even if we are unaware of them or reluctant to talk about them. The TAT is also widely used to assess attitudes toward other people, especially parents, lovers, and spouses.

REFLECTIONS
- Have you ever taken psychological tests? For what purposes? What were your feelings about the test at the time? Did the test seem valid to you? Why or why not?
- Do you believe that psychological tests should be used as the sole means for making decisions about people's personalities or assessing psychological problems? Why or why not?

SUMMARY

1. **What is the "personality"?** Personality comprises the reasonably stable patterns of behavior, including thoughts and emotions, that distinguish one person from another. These behavior patterns characterize a person's ways of adapting to the demands of his or her life.

2. **What is the role of conflict in Freud's psychodynamic theory?** Psychodynamic theory assumes that we are driven largely by unconscious motives. Conflict is inevitable as basic instincts of hunger, sex, and aggression come up against social pressures to follow laws, rules, and moral codes. At first this conflict is external, but as we develop, it is internalized.

3. **What are the psychic structures in psychodynamic theory?** The unconscious id is present at birth. The id represents psychological drives and operates according to the pleasure principle, seeking instant gratification. The ego is the sense of self or "I." It develops through experience and operates according to the reality principle. It takes into account what is practical and possible in gratifying the impulses of the id. Defense mechanisms protect the ego from anxiety by repressing unacceptable ideas or distorting reality. The superego is the moral sense, a partly conscious psychic structure that develops largely through identification with others.

4. **What are Freud's stages of psychosexual development?** People undergo psychosexual development as psychosexual energy, or libido, is transferred from one erogenous zone to another during childhood.

There are five stages of development: oral, anal, phallic, latency, and genital.

5. **What is Carl Jung's theory?** Jung's psychodynamic theory, called analytical psychology, features a collective unconscious and numerous archetypes, both of which reflect the history of our species.

6. **What is Alfred Adler's theory?** Adler's psychodynamic theory, called individual psychology, features the inferiority complex and the compensating drive for superiority.

7. **What is Erik Erikson's theory?** Erikson's psychodynamic theory of psychosocial development highlights the importance of early social relationships rather than the gratification of childhood sexual impulses. Erikson extended Freud's five developmental stages to eight, including stages that occur in adulthood.

8. **What are traits?** Traits are personality elements that are inferred from behavior and that account for behavioral consistency. Trait theory adopts a descriptive approach to personality.

9. **What are Gordon Allport's views?** Allport saw traits as embedded in the nervous system and as steering an individual's behavior.

10. **What are Hans Eysenck's views?** Eysenck theorized that there are two broad, independent personality dimensions (introversion-extraversion and emotional stability-instability) and described personalities according to combinations of these dimensions.

11. **What is the five-factor model?** Mathematical analyses that seek common factors in multiple personality traits often arrive at a list of five factors: extraversion, agreeableness, conscientiousness, emotional stability, and openness to experience.

12. **How do behaviorists view personality?** Behaviorists emphasize the situational determinants of behavior. John B. Watson, the father of modern behaviorism, rejected notions of mind and personality altogether. Watson and B. F. Skinner opposed the idea of personal freedom and argued that environmental contingencies can shape people into wanting to do the things that society and the physical environment require of them.

13. **How do social-cognitive theorists view personality?** Social-cognitive theory, in contrast to behaviorism, has a cognitive orientation and focuses on learning by observation. To predict behavior, social-cognitive theorists consider situational variables (rewards and punishments) and person variables (competencies, encoding strategies, expectancies, emotions, and self-regulatory systems and plans).

14. **What is Carl Rogers' self theory?** Self theory begins by assuming the existence of the self. According to Rogers, the self is an organized and consistent way in which a person perceives his or her "I" in relation to others. The self will attempt to actualize (develop its unique potential) when the person receives unconditional positive re-gard. Conditions of worth may lead to a distorted self-concept, disowning of parts of the self, and anxiety.

15. **What is the sociocultural perspective?** This is the view that focuses on the roles of ethnicity, gender, culture, and socioeconomic status in personality formation, behavior, and mental processes. Sociocultural theorists are interested in issues such as individualism versus collectivism and the effects of sociocultural factors on the sense of self.

16. **What are objective tests?** Objective tests present test takers with a standardized set of test items to which they must respond to in specific, limited ways (as in multiple-choice or true-false tests). A forced-choice format asks respondents to indicate which of two or more statements is true for them or which of several activities they prefer.

17. **What is the Minnesota Multiphasic Personality Inventory (MMPI)?** The MMPI is the most widely used psychological test in clinical settings. It is an objective personality test that uses a true-false format to assess abnormal behavior. It contains validity scales as well as clinical scales.

18. **What are projective tests?** Projective tests present ambiguous stimuli and allow the test taker to give a broad range of response.

19. **What is the Rorschach inkblot test?** The foremost projective technique is the Rorschach, in which test takers are asked to report what inkblots look like or could be. The Rorschach test is thought to provide insight into a person's reality testing, intelligence, and many other variables.

20. **What is the Thematic Apperception Test?** The TAT consists of ambiguous drawings, which test takers are asked to interpret. It is widely used in research on social motives as well as in clinical practice.

To enhance your understanding of the psychological concepts found in this chapter, please consult the following aids:

STUDY GUIDE

Learning Objectives, p. 245
Exercise, p. 246
Lecture and Textbook Outline,
　p. 247
Effective Studying Ideas, p. 250

Key Terms and Concepts, p. 251
Chapter Review, p. 252
Chapter Exercises, p. 258
Knowing the Language, p. 259
Do You Know the Material?, p. 261

CORE CONCEPTS SEARCH

The Psychodynamic Paradigm
The Trait-Based Paradigm
The Cognitive-Behavioral Paradigm

Humanistic Paradigms
Measuring Personality

World Wide Web

For more information concerning the topics found in this chapter, access to psychology links on the World Wide Web can be made through the Harcourt Brace webpage at

www.hbcollege.com

Share your comments and questions with your author at

PsychLinks@aol.com

What are the differences between men and women? How do these differences develop? Hung Liu's *Blue Boy* (1993) portrays a man assuming a female identity for the Chinese stage. Much of Liu's work focuses on issues of identity and exploitation, especially the exploitation of women. Only men were permitted to be actors in many traditional cultures—not only that of China but also those of ancient Greece and Elizabethan England. (Yes, Juliet was originally portrayed by a male actor.) Why was the stage forbidden to women for so many centuries?

HUNG LIU

Chapter 13

Gender and Sexuality

TRUTH OR FICTION?

✔ T F

- ☐ ☐ While Christmas Eve is a time of religious devotion in most Western nations, it has become a time of sexual devotion in Japan.

- ☐ ☐ Men behave more aggressively than women do.

- ☐ ☐ Beauty is in the eye of the beholder.

- ☐ ☐ People are perceived as being more attractive when they are smiling.

- ☐ ☐ Children's preferences for gender-typed toys and activities remain flexible until the resolution of the Oedipus or Electra complex at the age of five or six.

- ☐ ☐ Most Americans believe that some women like to be talked into sex.

- ☐ ☐ Women say no when they mean yes.

- ☐ ☐ People who truly love each other enjoy the sexual aspects of their relationships.

- ☐ ☐ Only gay males and substance abusers are at serious risk for contracting AIDS.

OUTLINE

GENDER POLARIZATION: GENDER STEREOTYPES AND THEIR COSTS
Psychology in a World of Diversity:
Machismo/Marianismo Stereotypes
and Hispanic Culture
Costs of Gender Polarization

PSYCHOLOGICAL GENDER DIFFERENCES: VIVE LA DIFFÉRENCE OR VIVE LA SIMILARITÉ?
Cognitive Abilities
Social Behavior

GENDER-TYPING: ON BECOMING A WOMAN OR A MAN
Biological Influences
Psychological Influences

ATTRACTION: ON LIKING, LOVING, AND RELATIONSHIPS
Factors Contributing to Attraction
Love: Doing What Happens . . . Culturally?
Questionnaire: The Love Scale
Sexual Orientation
Psychology in a World of Diversity:
Ethnicity and Sexual Orientation:
A Matter of Belonging
Psychology in the New Millennium:
The Gay Global Village

SEXUAL COERCION
Rape
Questionnaire: Cultural Myths That Create a Climate That Supports Rape
Psychology and Modern Life:
Preventing Rape
Psychology and Modern Life:
Resisting Sexual Harassment
Sexual Harassment

SEXUAL RESPONSE
The Sexual Response Cycle
Sexual Dysfunctions and Sex Therapy

AIDS AND OTHER SEXUALLY TRANSMITTED DISEASES
AIDS
Psychology and Modern Life:
Preventing STDs

Truth or Fiction Revisited

It is true that Christmas Eve has become a time of sexual devotion in Japan, even while it is a time of religious devotion in most Western nations. There is a good deal of social pressure on single people to have a date that includes an overnight stay.

OFF THE MISTY COAST OF IRELAND LIES THE small island of Inis Beag. From the air it is a green jewel, warm and inviting. At ground level, things are somewhat different.

For example, the residents of Inis Beag do not believe that women experience orgasm. The woman who chances to find pleasure in sex is considered deviant. Premarital sex is all but unknown. Women engage in sexual relations to conceive children and to appease their husbands' carnal cravings. They need not worry about being called on for frequent performances, however, since the men of Inis Beag believe, erroneously, that sex saps their strength. Sex on Inis Beag is carried out in the dark—both literally and figuratively—and with nightclothes on. The man lies on top in the so-called missionary position. In accordance with local concepts of masculinity, he ejaculates as fast as he can. Then he rolls over and falls asleep.

If Inis Beag does not sound like your cup of tea, you may find the atmosphere of Mangaia more congenial. Mangaia is a Polynesian pearl of an island, lifting lazily from the blue waters of the Pacific. It is on the other side of the world from Inis Beag—in more ways than one.

From an early age, Mangaian children are encouraged to get in touch with their sexuality through masturbation. Mangaian adolescents are expected to engage in sexual intercourse. They may be found on secluded beaches or beneath the swaying fronds of palms, diligently practicing techniques learned from village elders.

Mangaian women are expected to reach orgasm several times before their partners do. Young men want their partners to reach orgasm, and they compete to see who is more effective at bringing young women to multiple orgasms.

On the island of Inis Beag, a woman who has an orgasm is considered deviant. On Mangaia, multiple orgasms are the norm (Rathus and others, 1997). If we take a quick tour of the world of sexual diversity, we also find that

- Nearly every society has an incest taboo, but some societies believe that a brother and sister who eat at the same table are engaging in a mildly sexual act. The practice is therefore forbidden.

- What is considered sexually arousing varies enormously among different cultures. Women's breasts and armpits stimulate a sexual response in some cultures, but not in others.

- Kissing is a nearly universal form of petting in the United States but is unpopular in Japan and unknown among some cultures in Africa and South America. Upon seeing European visitors kissing, a member of an African tribe remarked, "Look at them—they eat each other's saliva and dirt."

- Sexual exclusiveness in marriage is valued highly in most parts of the United States, but among the people of Alaska's Aleutian Islands it is considered good manners for a man to offer his wife to a houseguest.

- The United States has its romantic Valentine's Day, but Japan has eroticized another day—Christmas Eve. (You read that right: Christmas Eve.) Christmas Eve may be a time of religious devotion in many Western nations, but it has become a time of sexual devotion in Japan. On Christmas Eve every single person must have a date that includes an overnight visit (Reid, 1990). During the weeks prior to Christmas, the media brim with reports on hotels for overnight stays, the correct attire, and breakfast ideas for the morning after. Where do Tokyo singles like to go before their overnighter? Tokyo Disneyland.

The residents of Inis Beag and Mangaia have similar anatomical features but vastly different attitudes toward sex. Their sociocultural settings influence their patterns of sexual behavior and the pleasure they gain—or do not gain—from sex. Sex may be a natural function, but few natural functions have been influenced so strongly by religious and moral beliefs, cultural tradition, folklore, and superstition.

This chapter is about gender and sexuality. We begin by exploring gender polarization—the behaviors that make up the stereotypes of "masculinity" and "femininity." We then examine *actual* psychological differences between males and females and consider the development of these differences. Next we turn our attention to attraction, love, and relationships. We ask why some people are attracted to people of their own gender while most are attracted to people of the other gender. We discuss important issues in sexual coercion, including rape and sexual harassment. We examine sexual response and see that women and men are probably more alike in their sexual response than you may have thought. We consider sexual dysfunctions and their treatment. Finally, we discuss AIDS and other sexually transmitted diseases (STDs). Although AIDS captures most of the headlines, other STDs can be quite serious and are more widespread.

■ GENDER POLARIZATION: GENDER STEREOTYPES AND THEIR COSTS

"Why Can't a Woman Be More Like a Man?" You may recognize this song title from the musical *My Fair Lady.* In the song, Henry Higgins laments that women are emotional and fickle whereas men are logical and dependable.

The excitable woman is a **stereotype.** Stereotypes are fixed, conventional ideas about a group of people that can give rise to prejudice and discrimination. The logical man is a **gender** stereotype. Higgins's stereotypes reflect cultural beliefs. Cultural beliefs about men and women involve clusters of stereotypes called **gender roles.** Gender roles define the ways in which men and women are expected to behave.

STEREOTYPE • A fixed, conventional idea about a group.
GENDER • The state of being male or female.
GENDER ROLE • A cluster of behaviors that characterizes traditional female or male behaviors within a cultural setting.

TABLE 13.1	GENDER-ROLE STEREOTYPES AROUND THE WORLD		
Stereotypes of Males		**Stereotypes of Females**	
Active	Opinionated	Affectionate	Nervous
Adventurous	Pleasure-seeking	Appreciative	Patient
Aggressive	Precise	Cautious	Pleasant
Arrogant	Quick	Changeable	Prudish
Autocratic	Rational	Charming	Self-pitying
Capable	Realistic	Complaining	Sensitive
Coarse	Reckless	Complicated	Sentimental
Conceited	Resourceful	Confused	Sexy
Confident	Rigid	Dependent	Shy
Courageous	Robust	Dreamy	Softhearted
Cruel	Sharp-witted	Emotional	Sophisticated
Determined	Show-off	Excitable	Submissive
Disorderly	Steady	Fault-finding	Suggestible
Enterprising	Stern	Fearful	Superstitious
Hardheaded	Stingy	Fickle	Talkative
Individualistic	Stolid	Foolish	Timid
Inventive	Tough	Forgiving	Touchy
Loud	Unscrupulous	Frivolous	Unambitious
Obnoxious		Fussy	Understanding
		Gentle	Unstable
		Imaginative	Warm
		Kind	Weak
		Mild	Worrying
		Modest	

Source of data: Williams & Best, 1994, p. 193, Table 1. Psychologists John Williams and Deborah Best (1994) found that people in 30 nations around the world tended to agree on the nature of masculine and feminine gender role stereotypes. Men are largely seen as more adventurous and hardheaded than women. Women are generally seen as more emotional and dependent.

Sandra Lipsitz Bem (1993) writes that three beliefs about women and men have prevailed throughout the history of Western culture:

1. Women and men have basically different psychological and sexual natures.
2. Men are the superior, dominant gender.
3. Gender differences and male superiority are "natural."

These beliefs have tended to polarize our views of women and men. It is thought that gender differences in power and psychological traits are natural, but what does "natural" mean? Throughout most of history, people viewed naturalness in terms of religion, or God's scheme of things (Bem, 1993). For the past century or so, naturalness has been seen in biological, evolutionary terms—at least by most scientists. But these views ignore cultural influences.

What are perceived as the "natural" gender roles? In our society, people tend to see the feminine gender role as warm, emotional, dependent, gentle, helpful, mild, patient, submissive, and interested in the arts (Bem, 1993). The typical masculine gender role is perceived as independent, competitive, tough, protective, logical, and competent at business, math, and science. Women are typically expected to care for the kids and cook the meals. Cross-cultural studies confirm that these gender role stereotypes are widespread (see Table 13.1). For example, in their survey of 30 countries, John Williams and Deborah Best (1994) found that men are more likely to be judged to be active, adventurous, aggressive, arrogant, and autocratic (and we have only gotten through the *a*'s.) Women are more likely to be seen as fearful, fickle, foolish, frivolous, and fussy (and these are only a handful of *f*'s.)

Gender polarization in the United States is linked to the traditional view of men as breadwinners and women as homemakers (Eagly & Steffen, 1984; Hoffman & Hurst, 1990). Despite the persistence of this stereotype in the United States, 6 of every 10 new jobs are held by women (National Institute of Occupational Safety and Health, 1990). Stereotypes also affect the opportunities open to men and women in Hispanic communities, as can be seen in the following discussion of *machismo* and *marianismo*.

Psychology in a World of
DIVERSITY

Machismo/Marianismo Stereotypes and Hispanic Culture[1]

Machismo is a Hispanic American cultural stereotype that defines masculinity in terms of an idealized view of manliness. To be macho is to be strong, virile, and dominant. Each Hispanic culture puts its own particular cultural stamp on the meaning of machismo, however. In the Spanish-speaking cultures of the Caribbean and Central America, the macho code encourages men to restrain their feelings and maintain an emotional distance. In my travels in Argentina and some other Latin American countries, however, I have observed that men who are sensitive and emotionally expressive are not perceived as compromising their macho code.

In counterpoint to the macho ideal among Hispanic peoples is the cultural idealization of femininity embodied in the concept of **marianismo.** The marianismo stereotype, which derives its name from the Virgin Mary, refers to the ideal of the virtuous woman as one who "suffers in silence," submerging her needs and desires to those of her husband and children. With the marianismo stereotype, the image of a woman's role as a martyr is raised to the level of a cultural ideal. According to this cultural stereotype, a woman is expected to demonstrate

---

[1] This diversity feature was written by Rafael Art. Javier, Ph.D. Javier is a clinical professor of psychology and Director of the Center for Psychological Services and Clinical Studies at St. John's University in Jamaica, New York.

MACHISMO • The Hispanic cultural stereotype of the male as strong, virile, and dominant.
MARIANISMO • The Hispanic cultural stereotype of the virtuous woman as one who "suffers in silence," submerging her needs and desires to those of her husband and children.

her love for her husband by waiting patiently at home and having dinner prepared for him at any time of day or night he happens to come home, to have his slippers ready for him, and so on. The feminine ideal involves self-sacrifice and providing joy, even in the face of pain. Strongly influenced by the patriarchal Spanish tradition, the marianismo stereotype has historically been used to maintain women in a subordinate position in relation to men.

Acculturation has challenged this traditional machismo/marianismo division of marital roles among Hispanic couples in the United States. I have seen in my own work treating Hispanic American couples in therapy that marriages are under increasing strain from the conflict between traditional and modern expectations about marital roles. Hispanic American women have been entering the workforce in increasing numbers, usually in domestic or child care positions. Yet, they are still expected to assume responsibility for tending their own children, keeping the house, and serving their husbands' needs when they return home. In many cases, a reversal of traditional roles occurs in which the wife works and supports the family, while the husband remains at home because he is unable to find or maintain employment.

It is often the Hispanic American husband who has the greater difficulty accepting a more flexible distribution of roles within the marriage and giving up a rigid set of expectations tied to traditional machismo/marianismo gender expectations. Although some couples manage to reshape their expectations and marital roles in the face of changing conditions, many relationships buckle under the strain and end in divorce. While I do not expect either the machismo or marianismo stereotype to disappear entirely, I would not be surprised to find a greater flexibility in gender role expectations as a product of continued acculturation.

• *Costs of Gender Polarization*

Gender polarization can be costly in terms of education, activities, careers, psychological well-being, and interpersonal relationships. Let us take a closer look at each of these areas.

EDUCATION Polarization has historically worked to the disadvantage of women. In past centuries, girls were considered unable to learn. Even the great Swiss-French philosopher Jean-Jacques Rousseau, who was in the forefront of a movement toward a more open approach to education, believed that girls are basically irrational and naturally disposed to child rearing and homemaking—certainly not to commerce, science, and industry, pursuits for which education is required.

Intelligence tests show that boys and girls are about equal in overall learning ability. Nevertheless, girls are expected to excel in language arts, and boys in math and science. Such expectations dissuade girls from taking advanced courses in the "male domain." Boys take more math courses in high school than girls do (AAUW, 1992). Math courses open doors for them in fields such as natural science, engineering, and economics. There are several reasons why boys are more likely than girls to feel at home with math (AAUW, 1992):

1. Fathers are more likely than mothers to help children with math homework.

2. Advanced math courses are more likely to be taught by men.

3. Teachers often show higher expectations for boys in math courses.

4. Math teachers spend more time working with boys than with girls.

ACCULTURATION • The merging of cultures that occurs when immigrant groups become assimilated into the mainstream culture.

Given these experiences, we should not be surprised that by junior high, boys view themselves as more competent in math than girls do, even when they receive the same grades (AAUW, 1992). Boys are more likely to have positive feelings about math. Girls are more likely to have math anxiety. Even girls who excel in math and science are less likely than boys to choose courses or careers in these fields (AAUW, 1992).

If women are to find their places in professions related to math, science, and engineering, we may need to provide more female role models in these professions. As we enter the new millennium, such models will help shatter the stereotype that these are men's fields. We also need to encourage girls to take more courses in math and science.

CAREERS

> I *have yet to hear a man ask for advice on how to combine marriage and a career.*
>
> GLORIA STEINEM

Women are less likely than men to enter higher-paying careers in math, science, and engineering. They account for perhaps 1 in 6 of the nation's scientists and engineers. Although women are awarded more than half of the bachelor's degrees in the United States, they receive fewer than one third of the degrees in science and engineering. Why? It is partly because math, science, and engineering are perceived as being inconsistent with the feminine gender role. Many little girls are dissuaded from thinking about professions such as engineering and architecture because they are given dolls, rather than trucks and blocks, as toys. Many boys are likewise deterred from entering child care and nursing professions because others scorn them when they play with dolls.

There are also inequalities in the workplace that are based on gender polarization. For example, women's wages average only about 72% of men's (Bianchi & Spain, 1997). Women physicians and college professors earn less than men in the same positions (Honan, 1996; "Study finds smaller pay gap," 1996). Women are less likely than men to be promoted into high-level managerial positions (Kilborn, 1995; Rosenberg and others, 1993). Once in managerial positions, women often feel pressured to be "tougher" than men in order to seem just as tough. They feel pressured to be careful about their appearance because coworkers pay more attention to what they wear, how they style their hair, and so forth. If they don't look crisp and tailored every day, others may think they are not in command. But if they dress up too much, they may be denounced as fashion plates rather than serious workers! Female managers who are deliberate and take time making decisions may be seen as "wishy-washy." What happens when female managers change their minds? They run the risk of being labeled fickle and indecisive rather than flexible.

Women in the workplace are also often expected to make the coffee or clean up after the conference lunch, along with the jobs they were hired to do. Women who work also usually have the responsibility of being the major caretaker for children in the home (Bianchi & Spain, 1997). Yet in the 1990s women's wages averaged 72% of men's, compared to 59% in 1970 (Bianchi & Spain, 1997). Wives share about equally with their husbands in supporting their families. Nearly half of them say they provide at least half of their family's income: not just vacation money—half of the mortgage, half of the clothing, half of the medical bills, half of the new Nikes and mountain bikes (Lewin, 1995).

A Female Architectural Engineer. Women remain underrepresented in many kinds of careers. Although women have made marked gains in medicine and law, their numbers remain relatively low in math and engineering. Why?

PSYCHOLOGICAL WELL-BEING AND RELATIONSHIPS Gender polarization also interferes with psychological well-being and relationships. Women who adhere to the traditional feminine gender role are likely to believe that women, like children, should be seen and not heard. They therefore are unlikely to assert themselves to make their needs and wants known. They are likely to feel frustrated as a result.

Men who accept the traditional masculine gender role are less likely to feel comfortable performing the activities involved in caring for children, such as bathing them, dressing them, and feeding them (Bem, 1993). Such men are less likely to ask for help—including medical help—when they need it ("Doctors tie male mentality," 1995). They are also less likely to be sympathetic and tender or express feelings of love in their marital relationships (Coleman & Ganong, 1985).

> **REFLECTIONS**
> - Do you believe that some kinds of work are women's work and others are men's work? Why or why not?
> - Have you ever received special treatment from a teacher or a school on the basis of your gender? If so, describe the incident. How did you feel about it then? How do you feel about it now?
> - Gender polarization has affected the quality of life of millions of women and men. Have you been guilty of gender polarization? What will you do to change your views?

■ PSYCHOLOGICAL GENDER DIFFERENCES: VIVE LA DIFFÉRENCE OR VIVE LA SIMILARITÉ?

The French have an expression "Vive la différence," which means "Long live the difference" (between men and women). Yet modern life has challenged our concepts of what it means to be a woman or a man. The anatomical differences between women and men are obvious and are connected with the biological aspects of reproduction. Biologists therefore have a relatively easy time of it describing and interpreting the gender differences they study. The task of psychology

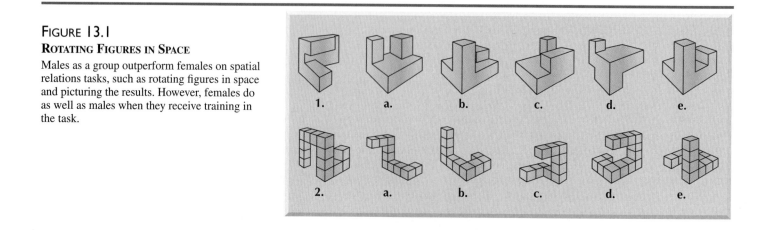

FIGURE 13.1
ROTATING FIGURES IN SPACE
Males as a group outperform females on spatial relations tasks, such as rotating figures in space and picturing the results. However, females do as well as males when they receive training in the task.

is more complex and is wrapped up with sociocultural and political issues (Eagly, 1995; Marecek, 1995). Psychological gender differences are not as obvious as biological gender differences. In fact, in many ways women and men are more similar than different.

To put it another way: to reproduce, women and men have to be biologically different. Throughout history, it has also been assumed that women and men must be psychologically different in order to fulfill different roles in the family and society (Bem, 1993). But what are the psychological differences between women and men? Key studies on this question span three decades.

• *Cognitive Abilities*

It was once believed that males were more intelligent than females because of their greater knowledge of world affairs and their skill in science and industry. We now know that greater male knowledge and skill did not reflect differences in intelligence. Rather, it reflected the systematic exclusion of females from world affairs, science, and industry. Assessments of intelligence do not show overall gender differences in cognitive abilities. However, reviews of the research suggest that girls are somewhat superior to boys in verbal abilities, such as verbal fluency, ability to generate words that are similar in meaning to other words, spelling, knowledge of foreign languages, and pronunciation (Halpern, 1997). Males, on the other hand, seem to be somewhat superior in visual-spatial abilities. Differences in mathematical ability are more complex (Neisser and others, 1996).

Girls seem to acquire language somewhat faster than boys do (Hyde & Linn, 1988). Also, in the United States far more boys than girls have reading problems, ranging from reading below grade level to severe disabilities (Halpern, 1997; Neisser and others, 1996). On the other hand, at least the males headed for college seem to catch up in verbal skills.

Males apparently excel in visual-spatial abilities of the sort used in math, science, and even reading a map (Voyer and others, 1995). Tests of spatial ability assess skills such as mentally rotating figures in space (see Figure 13.1) and finding figures embedded within larger designs (see Figure 13.2).

In math, differences at all ages are small and seem to be narrowing (Hyde and others, 1990). Females excel in computational ability in elementary school, however. Males excel in mathematical problem solving in high school and college (Hyde and others, 1990). Boys outperform girls on the math part of the Scholastic Aptitude Test (Byrnes & Takahira, 1993). According to Byrnes and Takahira (1993), boys' superiority in math does not reflect gender per se. Instead, boys do as well as they do because of greater experience in solving math problems.

In any event, psychologists note three factors that should caution us not to attach too much importance to apparent gender differences in cognition:

1. In most cases, the differences are small (Hyde & Plant, 1995). In addition, differences in verbal, mathematical, and spatial abilities are getting smaller (Hyde and others, 1990; Voyer and others, 1995).

2. These gender differences are *group* differences. There is greater variation in these skills between individuals *within* the groups than between males and females (Maccoby, 1990). That is, there may be a greater difference in, say, verbal skills between two women than between a woman and a man. Millions of females outdistance the "average" male in math and spatial abilities. Men have produced their Shakespeares. Women have produced their Madame Curies.

FIGURE 13.2

ITEMS FROM AN EMBEDDED-FIGURES TEST

3. Some differences may largely reflect sociocultural influences. In our culture spatial and math abilities are stereotyped as masculine. Women who are given just a few hours of training in spatial skills—for example, rotating geometric figures or studying floor plans—perform at least as well as men on tests of these skills (Baenninger & Elenteny, 1997; Lawton & Morrin, 1997).

• *Social Behavior*

There are many other psychological differences between males and females. For example, women exceed men in extraversion, anxiety, trust, and nurturance (Feingold, 1994). Men exceed women in assertiveness and tough-mindedness. In the arena of social behavior, women seem more likely than men to cooperate with other people and hold groups, such as families, together (Bjorklund & Kipp, 1996).

Despite the stereotype of women as gossips and chatterboxes, research in communication styles suggests that in many situations men spend more time talking than women do. Men are more likely to introduce new topics and to interrupt (Hall, 1984). Women, on the other hand, seem more willing to reveal their feelings and personal experiences (Dindia & Allen, 1992).

Women interact at closer distances than men do. They also seek to keep more space between themselves and strangers of the other gender than men do (Rüstemli, 1986). Men are made more uncomfortable by strangers who sit across from them, whereas women are more likely to feel "invaded" by strangers who sit next to them. In libraries, men tend to pile books protectively in front of them. Women place books and coats in adjacent seats to discourage others from taking them.

There are also gender differences in three major areas of social behavior (Archer, 1996): sex and relationships, mate selection, and aggression.

SEX AND RELATIONSHIPS Men are more interested than women in casual sex and in having more than one sex partner (Leitenberg & Henning, 1995). In our society there are constraints on unbridled sexual behavior, so most men are not promiscuous (Archer, 1996). Women are more likely to want to combine sex with a romantic relationship.

GENDER DIFFERENCES IN MATE SELECTION

> Oh yo' daddy's rich,
> an' you' ma is good lookin'
> So hush, little baby, don' yo' cry.

"SUMMERTIME," FROM *PORGY AND BESS*

Studies of mate selection find that women place more emphasis than men on traits such as professional status, consideration, dependability, kindness, and fondness for children. Men place relatively greater emphasis on physical allure, cooking ability (can't they turn on the microwave themselves?), even thriftiness (Buss, 1994; Feingold, 1992a).

Susan Sprecher and her colleagues (1994) surveyed more than 13,000 people in the United States. They asked how willing they would be to marry someone who was older, younger, of a different religion, unlikely to hold a steady job, not good-looking, and so on. Each item was answered by checking off a

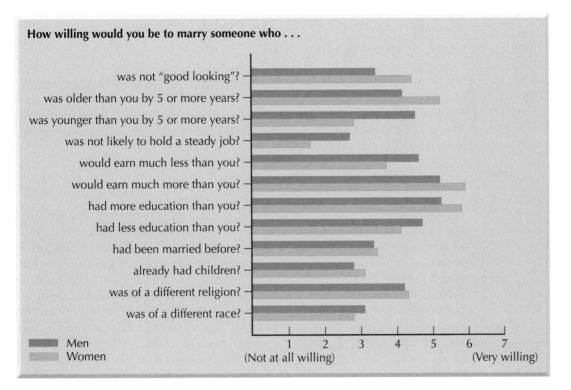

How willing would you be to marry someone who . . .

- was not "good looking"?
- was older than you by 5 or more years?
- was younger than you by 5 or more years?
- was not likely to hold a steady job?
- would earn much less than you?
- would earn much more than you?
- had more education than you?
- had less education than you?
- had been married before?
- already had children?
- was of a different religion?
- was of a different race?

■ Men
■ Women

1 2 3 4 5 6 7
(Not at all willing)   (Very willing)

FIGURE 13.3

GENDER DIFFERENCES IN MATE PREFERENCES

Susan Sprecher and her colleagues found that men are more willing than women to marry someone who is several years younger and less well-educated. Women, on the other hand, are more willing than men to marry someone who is not good-looking and who earns more money than they do.

7-point scale in which 1 meant "not at all" and 7 meant "very willing." Women were more willing than men to marry someone who was not good-looking (see Figure 13.3). On the other hand, they were less willing to marry someone who was unlikely to hold a steady job.

AGGRESSION In most cultures, it is the males who march off to war and battle for glory (and sneaker ads in TV commercials). Psychological studies of aggression find that male children and adults behave more aggressively than females do (Archer, 1996).

In a classic review of 72 studies concerning gender differences in aggression, Ann Frodi and her colleagues (1977) found that females are more likely to act aggressively under some circumstances than others:

1. Females are more likely to feel anxious or guilty about aggression. Such feelings inhibit aggressive behavior.
2. Females behave as aggressively as males when they have the means to do so and believe that aggression is justified.
3. Females are more likely to empathize with the victim—to put themselves in the victim's place. Empathy encourages helping behavior, not aggression.
4. Gender differences in aggression decrease when the victim is anonymous. Anonymity may prevent females from empathizing with their victims.

Truth or Fiction Revisited

It is true that men behave more aggressively than women do — at least in most cultures. The issue is whether this gender difference is inborn or reflects sociocultural factors.

■ GENDER-TYPING: ON BECOMING A WOMAN OR A MAN

There are thus a number of psychological gender differences. They include minor differences in cognitive functioning and differences in personality and social behavior. The process by which these differences develop is termed **gender-typing.** In this section we explore several possible sources of gender-typing, both biological and psychological.

• *Biological Influences*

BRAIN ORGANIZATION A number of studies suggest that we can speak of "left brain" versus "right brain" functions. Some psychological activities, such as language, seem to be controlled largely by the left side of the brain. Other psychological activities, such as spatial relations and aesthetic and emotional responses, seem to be controlled largely by the right side. Brain-imaging research suggests that the brain hemispheres are more specialized in males than in females (Shaywitz and others, 1995). For example, men with damage to the left hemisphere are more likely to experience difficulties in verbal functioning than women with similar damage. Men with damage to the right hemisphere are more likely to have problems with spatial relations than women with similar injuries.

Gender differences in brain organization might, in part, explain why women exceed men in verbal skills that require some spatial organization, such as reading, spelling, and crisp articulation of speech. Men, however, might be superior at more specialized spatial relations tasks such as interpreting road maps and visualizing objects in space.

SEX HORMONES Sex hormones are responsible for the prenatal differentiation of sex organs. Prenatal sex hormones may also "masculinize" or "feminize" the brain by creating predispositions that are consistent with some gender role stereotypes (Collaer & Hines, 1995; Crews, 1994). Yet John Money (1987) argues that social learning plays a stronger role in the development of **gender identity,** personality traits, and preferences. Money claims that social learning is powerful enough to counteract many prenatal predispositions.

Some evidence for the possible role of hormonal influences have been obtained from animal studies (Collaer & Hines, 1995; Crews, 1994). For example, male rats are generally superior to females in maze-learning ability, a task that requires spatial skills. Female rats that are exposed to androgens in the uterus or soon after birth learn maze routes as rapidly as males, however. They also roam over larger distances and mark larger territories than most females do (Vandenbergh, 1993).

Men are more aggressive than women, and aggression in lower animals has been connected with the male sex hormone testosterone (Collaer & Hines, 1995). However, cognitive psychologists argue that boys (and girls) can choose whether or not to act aggressively, regardless of the levels of hormones in their bloodstreams.

• *Psychological Influences*

PSYCHODYNAMIC THEORY Sigmund Freud explained the acquisition of gender roles in terms of *identification.* He believed that gender identity remains flexible until the Oedipus and Electra complexes are resolved at about the age

GENDER-TYPING • The process by which people acquire a sense of being female or male and acquire the traits considered typical of females or males within a cultural setting.
GENDER IDENTITY • One's psychological sense of being female or male.

Acquiring Gender Roles. How do people develop gender roles? What contributions are made by biological and psychological factors? Social-cognitive theory focuses on imitation of the behavior of adults of the same gender and reinforcement by parents and peers.

of five or six. Appropriate gender-typing requires that boys identify with their fathers and give up the wish to possess their mothers. Girls have to give up the wish to have a penis and identify with their mothers.

Boys and girls develop stereotypical preferences for toys and activities much earlier than might be predicted by psychodynamic theory, however. Even within their first year, boys are more explorative and independent. Girls are relatively more quiet, dependent, and restrained (Etaugh & Rathus, 1995). By 18 to 36 months, girls are more likely to prefer soft toys and dolls and to dance. Boys of this age are more likely to prefer blocks and toy cars, trucks and airplanes.

Let us consider the ways in which cognitive theories account for gender-typing.

SOCIAL-COGNITIVE THEORY Social-cognitive theorists explain gender-typing in terms of observational learning, identification, and socialization.

Children learn much of what is considered masculine or feminine by **observational learning,** as suggested by a classic experiment conducted by David Perry and Kay Bussey (1979). In this study, children learned how behaviors are gender-typed by observing the *relative frequencies* with which men and women performed them. The adult role models expressed arbitrary preferences for one item from each of 16 pairs of items—pairs such as oranges versus apples and toy cows versus toy horses—while 8-and 9-year-old boys and girls watched them. The children were then asked to show their own preferences. Boys selected an average of 14 of 16 items that agreed with the "preferences" of the

Truth or Fiction Revisited

It is not true that children's preferences for gender-typed toys and activities remain flexible until the resolution of the Oedipus or Electra complexes at the age of 5 or 6. Children's preferences for gender-typed toys and activities become rather fixed by the age of three.

OBSERVATIONAL LEARNING • The acquisition of knowledge and skills through the observation of others (who are called *models*) rather than by means of direct experience.

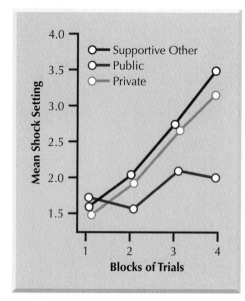

Figure 13.4
Mean Shock Settings Selected by Women in Retaliation Against Male Opponents

Women in the Richardson study chose higher shock levels for their opponents when they were alone or when another person (a "supportive other") urged them on.

men. Girls selected an average of only 3 of 16 items that agreed with the choices of the men. In other words, boys and girls learned gender-typed preferences even though those preferences were completely arbitrary.

Social-cognitive theorists view **identification** as a continuous learning process in which children are influenced by rewards and punishments to imitate adults of the same gender—particularly the parent of the same gender. In identification, as opposed to imitation, children do not simply imitate a certain behavior pattern. They also try to become similar to the model.

Socialization also plays a role. Parents and other adults—even other children—inform children about how they are expected to behave. They reward children for behavior they consider appropriate for their gender. They punish (or fail tonforce) children for behavior they consider inappropriate. Girls, for example, are given dolls while they are still sleeping in their cribs. They are encouraged to use the dolls to rehearse caretaking behaviors in preparation for traditional feminine adult roles.

Concerning gender and aggression, Maccoby and Jacklin (1974) note that aggression is more actively discouraged in girls through punishment, withdrawal of affection, or being told that "girls don't act that way." If girls retaliate when they are insulted or attacked, they usually experience social disapproval. They therefore learn to feel anxious about the possibility of acting aggressively. Boys, on the other hand, are usually encouraged to strike back (Frodi and others, 1977).

Classic experiments point up the importance of social learning in female aggressiveness. In one study, for example, college women competed with men to see who could respond to a stimulus more quickly (Richardson and others, 1979). There were four blocks of trials, with six trials in each block. The subjects could not see their opponents. The loser of each trial received an electric shock whose intensity was set by the opponent on the same sort of fearsome-looking console that was used in the Milgram experiments on obedience to authority (see Figure 2.1, p. 35). Women competed under one of three experimental conditions: public, private, or with a supportive other. In the public condition, another woman observed the subject silently. In the private condition, there was no observer. In the supportive-other condition, another woman urged the subject to retaliate strongly when her opponent selected high shock levels. As shown in Figure 13.4, women in the private and supportive-other conditions selected increasingly higher levels of shock in retaliation. Presumably, the women assumed that an observer, though silent, would frown on aggressive behavior. This assumption is likely to reflect the women's own early socialization experiences. Women who were not observed or who were urged on by another person apparently felt free to violate the gender norm of nonaggressiveness when their situations called for aggressive responses.

Social-cognitive theory outlines ways in which rewards, punishments, and modeling foster "gender-appropriate" behavior. Gender-schema theory suggests that we tend to assume gender-appropriate behavior patterns by blending our self-concept with cultural expectations.

Gender-Schema Theory You have probably heard the expression, "looking at the world through rose-colored glasses." According to Sandra Bem (1993), the originator of **gender-schema theory**, people look at the social world through "the lenses of gender." Bem argues that our culture polarizes females and males by organizing social life around mutually exclusive gender roles. Children come to accept the polarizing scripts without realizing it. Unless parents or unusual events encourage them to challenge the validity of gender polarization, children attempt to construct identities that are consistent with the "proper" script. Most children reject behavior—in others and in themselves—

Identification • The process of becoming broadly like another person.
Socialization • The guiding of behavior through instruction and rewards and punishments.
Gender-schema theory • The view that gender identity plus knowledge of the distribution of behavior patterns into feminine and masculine roles motivate and guide the gender-typing of the child.

In Review — Influences on Gender-Typing

	BIOLOGICAL INFLUENCES
Brain Organization	The brain hemispheres are apparently more specialized in males than in females. As a result, women may exceed men in verbal skills that require some spatial organization, such as reading and spelling, while men may excel at more specialized spatial-relations tasks such as visualizing objects in space.
Sex Hormones	Prenatal sex hormones may "masculinize" or "feminize" the brain by creating predispositions that are consistent with gender role stereotypes, such as the greater aggressiveness of males.
	PSYCHOLOGICAL INFLUENCES
Psychodynamic Theory	Freud connected gender-typing with resolution of the Oedipus and Electra complexes. However, research shows that gender-typing occurs prior to the age at which these complexes would be resolved.
Social-Cognitive Theory	Social-cognitive theorists explain gender-typing in terms of observational learning, identification (as a broad form of imitation), and socialization. Research supports a role for social learning in aggressive behavior.
Gender-Schema Theory	Children come to look at the social world through "the lenses of gender." Our culture polarizes females and males by organizing social life around mutually exclusive gender roles. Children come to accept these without realizing it and attempt to construct identities that are consistent with the "proper" script.

that deviates from it. Children's self-esteem soon becomes wrapped up in the ways in which they measure up to the gender schema. For example, boys soon learn to hold a high opinion of themselves if they excel in sports.

Once children understand the labels *boy* and *girl*, they have a basis for blending their self-concepts with the gender schema of their culture. No external pressure is required. Children who have developed a sense of being male or being female, which usually occurs by the age of 3, actively seek information about their gender schema. As in social-cognitive theory, children seek to learn through observation what is considered appropriate for them.

There is evidence that the polarized female-male scripts serve as cognitive anchors within our culture (Bowes & Goodnow, 1996). Researchers in one study showed 5- and 6-year-old boys and girls pictures of actors engaged in "gender-consistent" or "gender-inconsistent" activities. The gender-consistent pictures showed boys playing with trains or sawing wood. Girls were shown cooking and cleaning. Gender-inconsistent pictures showed actors of the other gender engaged in these gender-typed activities. Each child was shown a randomized set of pictures that included only one picture of each activity. One week later, the children were asked who had engaged in the activity, a male or a female. Both boys and girls gave wrong answers more often when the picture they had seen showed gender-*inconsistent* activity. In other words, they distorted what they had seen to conform to the gender schema.

In sum, brain organization and sex hormones may contribute to gender-typed behavior and play a role in verbal ability, math skills, and aggression. Yet the effects of social learning may counteract the biological influences. Social-cognitive theory outlines the environmental factors that influence children to engage in "gender-appropriate" behavior. Gender-schema theory focuses on how children blend their self-identities with the gender schema of their culture.

■ ATTRACTION: ON LIKING, LOVING, AND RELATIONSHIPS

Sexual interactions usually take place within relationships. Feelings of attraction can lead to liking and perhaps to love, and to a more lasting relationship. In this section we see that **attraction** to another person is influenced by factors such as physical appearance and attitudes. We will see that most people are heterosexual; that is, they are sexually attracted to people of the other gender. However, some people are homosexual; that is, they are sexually attracted to people of their own gender.

• *Factors Contributing to Attraction*

Among the factors contributing to attraction are physical appearance, similarity, and reciprocity.

ATTRACTION • In social psychology, an attitude of liking or disliking (negative attraction).

PHYSICAL APPEARANCE: HOW IMPORTANT IS LOOKING GOOD? Physical appearance is a key factor in attraction and in the consideration of partners

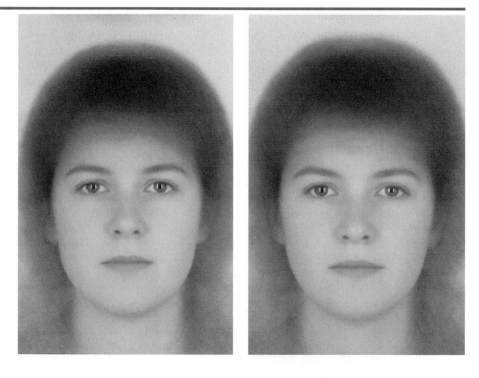

FIGURE 13.5

WHAT FEATURES CONTRIBUTE TO FACIAL ATTRACTIVENESS?

In both England and Japan, features such as large eyes, high cheekbones, and narrow jaws contribute to perceptions of the attractiveness of women. Part A shows a composite of the faces of 15 women rated as the most attractive of a group of 60. Part B is a composite in which the features of these 15 women are exaggerated—that is, developed further in the direction that separates them from the average of the entire 60.

"Looking Good." Naomi Campbell, Claudia Schiffer, and Christie Turlington are among those who set the standards for beauty in contemporary American culture. How important is physical attractiveness?

for dates and marriage. What determines physical allure? Are our standards subjective—that is, "in the eye of the beholder"? Or is there general agreement on what is appealing?

Some aspects of beauty appear to be cross-cultural. For example, a study of people in England and Japan found that both British and Japanese men consider women with large eyes, high cheekbones, and narrow jaws to be most attractive (Perret, 1994). In his research, Perret created computer composites of the faces of 60 women and, as shown in Part A of Figure 13.5, of the 15 women who were rated the most attractive. He then used computer enhancement to exaggerate the differences between the composite of the 60 and the composite of the 15 most attractive women. He arrived at the image shown in Part B of Figure 13.5. Part B, which shows higher cheekbones and a narrower jaw than Part A, was rated as the most attractive image. Similar results were found for the image of a Japanese woman. Works of art suggest that the ancient Greeks and Egyptians favored similar facial features.

In our society, tallness is an asset for men, but tall women are viewed less positively (Sheppard & Strathman, 1989). College women prefer their dates to be about 6 inches taller than they are. College men tend to favor women who are about 4½ inches shorter than they are (Gillis & Avis, 1980).

Although preferences for facial features may transcend time and culture, preferences for body weight and shape may be more culturally determined. For example, plumpness has been valued in many cultures. Grandmothers who worry that their granddaughters are starving themselves often come from cultures in which stoutness is acceptable or desirable. In contemporary Western society, both genders find slenderness appealing (Franzoi & Herzog, 1987). Women generally favor men with a V-taper—broad shoulders and a narrow waist.

Although both genders perceive overweight people as unappealing, there are fascinating gender differences in perceptions of desirable body shapes. College

Truth or Fiction Revisited

It is not true that beauty is in the eye of the beholder, despite the familiarity of the adage. It appears that some aspects of physical appeal may be innate or inborn. There are also cultural standards for beauty that influence people who are reared in that culture.

FIGURE 13.6
CAN YOU EVER BE TOO THIN?
Research suggests that most college women believe that they are heavier than they ought to be. However, men actually prefer women to be a bit heavier than women assume the men would like them to be.

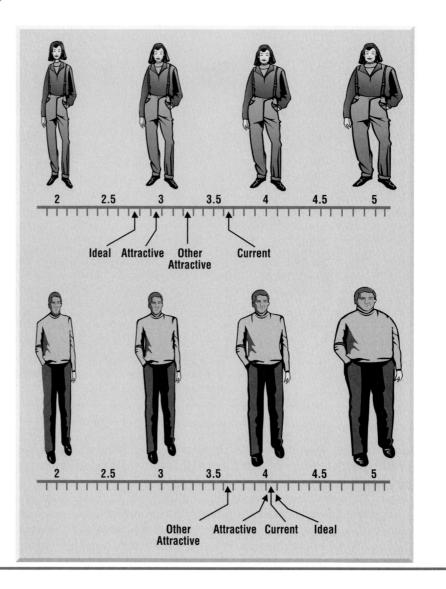

---

men tend to consider their current physique similar to the ideal male build and to the one that women find most appealing (Fallon & Rozin, 1985). College women, in contrast, generally see themselves as markedly heavier than the figure that is most appealing to men and heavier still than the ideal (see Figure 13.6). Both mothers and fathers of college students see themselves as heavier than their ideal weight (Rozin & Fallon, 1988). Both genders err in their estimates of the other gender's preferences, however. Men of both generations actually prefer women to be heavier than the women presume. Both college women and their mothers prefer men who are slimmer than the men presume.

"PRETTY IS AS PRETTY DOES?"
Both men and women are perceived as more attractive when they are smiling (Reis and others, 1990). There is thus ample reason to, as the song goes, "put on a happy face" when you are meeting people or looking for a date.

Other aspects of behavior also affect interpersonal attraction. Women who are shown videotapes of prospective dates prefer men who act outgoing and self-assertive (Riggio & Woll, 1984). College men who exhibit dominance (defined as control over a social interaction with a professor) in a videotape are

---

Truth or Fiction Revisited

It is true that people are perceived as being more attractive when they are smiling. Does this research finding provide a reason to "put on a happy face" early in the development of social relationships?

MATCHING HYPOTHESIS • The view that people tend to choose persons similar to themselves in attractiveness and attitudes in the formation of interpersonal relationships.
RECIPROCITY • In interpersonal attraction, the tendency to return feelings and attitudes that are expressed about us.

rated as more attractive by women (Sadalla and others, 1987). However, college men respond negatively to women who show self-assertion and social dominance (Riggio & Woll, 1984; Sadalla and others, 1987). Despite the liberating trends of recent years, the cultural stereotype of the ideal woman still includes modesty. I am *not* suggesting that self-assertive women should take a back seat in order to make themselves more appealing to traditional men. Assertive women might find nothing but conflict in their interactions with such men in any case.

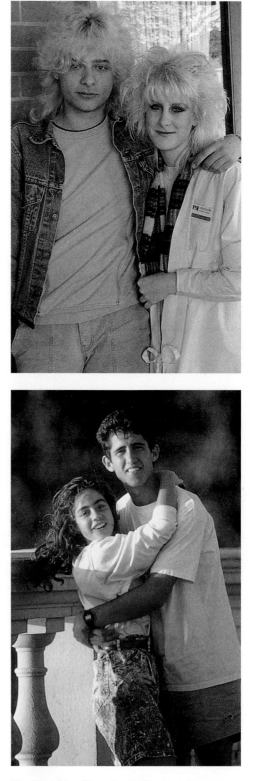

THE MATCHING HYPOTHESIS: DO "OPPOSITES ATTRACT" OR DO "BIRDS OF A FEATHER FLOCK TOGETHER"? Although we may rate highly attractive people as most desirable, most of us are not left to blend in with the wallpaper. According to the **matching hypothesis,** we tend to date people who are similar to ourselves in physical attractiveness rather than the local Will Smith or Sandra Bullock look-alike. One motive for asking out "matches" seems to be fear of rejection by more attractive people (Bernstein and others, 1983).

The quest for similarity extends beyond physical attractiveness. Our marital and sex partners tend to be similar to us in race/ethnicity, age, level of education, and religion. Consider some findings of the National Health and Social Life Survey (Michael and others, 1994, pp. 45–47):

- Nearly 94% of single White men have White women as their sex partners; 2% are partnered with Hispanic American women, 2% with Asian American women, and less than 1% with African American women.

- About 82% of African American men have African American women as their sex partners; nearly 8% are partnered with White women and almost 5% with Hispanic American women.

- About 83% of the women and men in the study chose partners within five years of their own age and of the same or a similar religion.

- Of nearly 2,000 women in the study, not one with a graduate college degree had a partner who had not finished high school.

Why do most people have partners from the same background as their own? One reason is that marriages are made in the neighborhood and not in heaven (Michael and others, 1994). We tend to live among people who are similar to us in background, and we therefore come into contact with them more often than with people from other backgrounds. Another reason is that we are drawn to people whose attitudes are similar to ours. People from a similar background are more likely to have similar attitudes. Similarity in attitudes and tastes is a key contributor to attraction, friendships, and love relationships (Cappella & Palmer, 1990; Griffin & Sparks, 1990; Laumann and others, 1994).

RECIPROCITY: IF YOU LIKE ME, YOU MUST HAVE EXCELLENT JUDGMENT Has anyone told you how good-looking, brilliant, and mature you are? That your taste is refined? That all in all, you are really something special? If so, have you been impressed by his or her fine judgment?

Reciprocity is a powerful determinant of attraction (Condon & Crano, 1988). We tend to return feelings of admiration. We tend to be more open, warm, and helpful when we are interacting with strangers who seem to like us (Curtis & Miller, 1986).

Feelings of attraction are influenced by factors such as physical appearance and similarity. Let us explore what we mean when we say that feelings of attraction have blossomed into love.

The Matching Hypothesis. Do opposites attract, or do we tend to pair off with people who look and think the way we do? As suggested by these photographs, similarity often runs at least skin-deep.

• *Love: Doing What Happens . . . Culturally?*

Love—the ideal for which we make great sacrifice. Love—the sentiment that launched a thousand ships in Homer's epic poem *The Iliad*. Through the millennia, poets have sought to capture love in words. Dante, the Italian poet who shed some light on the Dark Ages, wrote of "the love that moves the sun and the other stars." The Scottish poet Robert Burns wrote that his love was like "a red, red rose." Love is beautiful and elusive. Passion and romantic love are also lusty, surging with sexual desire.

THE LOVE TRIANGLE No, this love triangle does not refer to two men wooing the same woman. It refers to Robert Sternberg's **triangular model of love.** Sternberg (1988) believes that love can include combinations of three components: intimacy, passion, and decision/commitment (see Figure 13.7).

Intimacy refers to a couple's closeness, to their mutual concern and sharing of feelings and resources. Passion means romance and sexual feelings. Decision/commitment refers to deciding that one is in love and, in the long term, making a commitment to enhance and maintain the relationship. Passion is

TRIANGULAR MODEL OF LOVE • Sternberg's view that love involves combinations of three components: intimacy, passion, and decision/commitment.

FIGURE 13.7
THE TRIANGULAR MODEL OF LOVE
According to this model, love has three components: intimacy, passion, and decision/commitment. The ideal of consummate love consists of romantic love plus commitment.

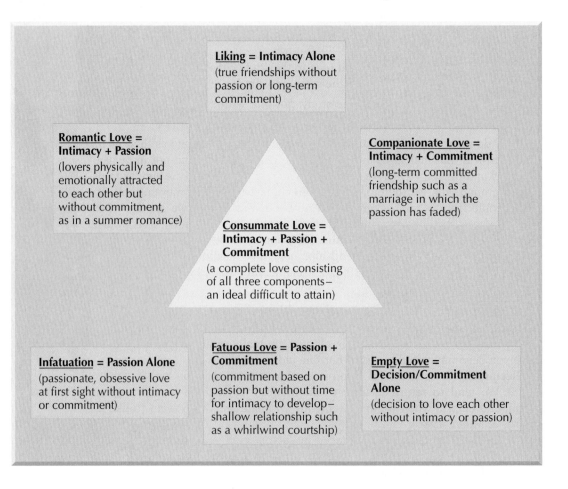

Liking = Intimacy Alone
(true friendships without passion or long-term commitment)

Romantic Love = Intimacy + Passion
(lovers physically and emotionally attracted to each other but without commitment, as in a summer romance)

Companionate Love = Intimacy + Commitment
(long-term committed friendship such as a marriage in which the passion has faded)

Consummate Love = Intimacy + Passion + Commitment
(a complete love consisting of all three components—an ideal difficult to attain)

Infatuation = Passion Alone
(passionate, obsessive love at first sight without intimacy or commitment)

Fatuous Love = Passion + Commitment
(commitment based on passion but without time for intimacy to develop—shallow relationship such as a whirlwind courtship)

Empty Love = Decision/Commitment Alone
(decision to love each other without intimacy or passion)

THE LOVE SCALE

Are you in love?

The Love Scale was developed at Northeastern University in Boston. To compare your own score with those of Northeastern University students, think of your dating partner or partners and fill out the scale with each of them in mind. Then compare your scores to those in Appendix B.

Directions: Circle the number that best shows how true or false the items are for you according to this key:

7 = definitely true
6 = rather true
5 = somewhat true
4 = not sure, or equally true and false
3 = somewhat false
2 = rather false
1 = definitely false ■

---

1. I look forward to being with _____ a great deal.
   definitely false   1   2   3   4   5   6   7   definitely true

2. I find _____ to be sexually exciting.
   definitely false   1   2   3   4   5   6   7   definitely true

3. _____ has fewer faults than most people.
   definitely false   1   2   3   4   5   6   7   definitely true

4. I would do anything I could for _____.
   definitely false   1   2   3   4   5   6   7   definitely true

5. _____ is very attractive to me.
   definitely false   1   2   3   4   5   6   7   definitely true

6. I like to share my feelings with _____.
   definitely false   1   2   3   4   5   6   7   definitely true

7. Doing things is more fun when _____ and I do them together.
   definitely false   1   2   3   4   5   6   7   definitely true

8. I like to have _____ all to myself.
   definitely false   1   2   3   4   5   6   7   definitely true

9. I would feel horrible if anything bad happened to _____.
   definitely false   1   2   3   4   5   6   7   definitely true

10. I think about _____ very often.
    definitely false   1   2   3   4   5   6   7   definitely true

11. It is very important that _____ cares for me.
    definitely false   1   2   3   4   5   6   7   definitely true

12. I am most content when I am with _____.
    definitely false   1   2   3   4   5   6   7   definitely true

13. It is difficult for me to stay away from _____ for very long.
    definitely false   1   2   3   4   5   6   7   definitely true

14. I care about _____ a great deal.
    definitely false   1   2   3   4   5   6   7   definitely true

Total Score for Love Scale: _____.

most crucial in short-term relationships. Intimacy and commitment are relatively more important in enduring relationships. The ideal form of love, which combines all three, is **consummate love.** Consummate love, in this model, is romantic love plus commitment.

Romantic love is characterized by passion and intimacy. Passion involves fascination (preoccupation with the loved one); sexual craving; and the desire for exclusiveness (a special relationship with the loved one). Intimacy involves caring—championing the interests of the loved one, even if it entails sacrificing one's own. People who are dating, or who expect to be dating each other, are cognitively biased toward evaluating each other positively (Fiske, 1993). They tend to pay attention to information that confirms their romantic interests. In less technical terms, romantic lovers often idealize each another. They magnify each other's positive features and overlook their flaws.

To experience romantic love, in contrast to attachment or sexual arousal, one must be exposed to a culture that idealizes the concept. In Western culture, romantic love blossoms in fairy tales about Sleeping Beauty, Cinderella, Snow White, and all their princes charming. It matures with romantic novels, television tales and films, and the personal accounts of friends and relatives about dates and romances.

REFLECTIONS

- Agree or disagree, and support your answer: "Beauty is in the eye of the beholder."
- What do men you know look for in a date? What do women you know seek? Are their desires similar or dissimilar? How?
- Agree or disagree, and support your answer: "Opposites attract."

• *Sexual Orientation*

Sexual orientation refers to the organization or direction of one's erotic interests. **Heterosexual** people are sexually attracted to people of the other gender and interested in forming romantic relationships with them. **Homosexual** people are sexually attracted to people of their own gender and interested in forming romantic relationships with them. Homosexual males are also referred to as **gay males** and homosexual females as **lesbians. Bisexual** people are sexually attracted to, and interested in forming romantic relationships with, both women and men.

The concept of *sexual orientation* is not to be confused with *sexual activity.* For example, engaging in sexual activity with people of one's own gender does not necessarily mean that one has a homosexual orientation. Sexual activity between males sometimes reflects limited sexual opportunities. Adolescent males may manually stimulate one another while fantasizing about girls. Men in prisons may similarly turn to each other as sexual outlets. Young Sambian men in New Guinea engage in sexual practices exclusively with older males, since it is believed that they must drink "men's milk" to achieve the fierce manhood of the headhunter (Money, 1987). Once they reach marrying age, however, their sexual activities are limited to female partners.

Surveys in the United States, Britain, France, and Denmark find that about 3% of men identify themselves as gay (Hamer and others, 1993; Janus & Janus, 1993; Laumann and others, 1994). About 2% of the U.S. women surveyed say

CONSUMMATE LOVE • The ideal form of love within Sternberg's model, which combines passion, intimacy, and commitment.

ROMANTIC LOVE • An intense, positive emotion that involves sexual attraction, feelings of caring, and the belief that one is in love.

SEXUAL ORIENTATION • The directionality of one's erotic interests—that is, whether one is sexually attracted to, and interested in forming romantic relationships with, people of the other or the same gender.

HETEROSEXUAL • Referring to people who are sexually aroused by, and interested in forming romantic relationships with, people of the other gender.

HOMOSEXUAL • Referring to people who are sexually aroused by, and interested in forming romantic relationships with, people of the same gender. (Derived from the Greek *homos,* meaning "same," not from the Latin *homo,* meaning "man.")

GAY MALE • A male homosexual.

LESBIAN • A female homosexual.

BISEXUAL • A person who is sexually aroused by, and interested in forming romantic relationships with, people of either gender.

L'Abandon (Les Deux Amies). This painting by Henri de Toulouse-Lautrec is of lesbian lovers.

that they have a lesbian sexual orientation (Janus & Janus, 1993; Laumann and others, 1994). The following section discusses the experiences of homosexual people from various ethnic groups.

Psychology in a World of
DIVERSITY

Ethnicity and Sexual Orientation: A Matter of Belonging

Societal prejudices make it difficult for many young people to come to terms with an emerging homosexual orientation (Rathus and others, 1997). You might assume that members of ethnic minority groups in the United States, who themselves have been subjected to prejudice and discrimination, would be more tolerant of a homosexual orientation. However, according to psychologist Beverly Greene (1994) of St. John's University, you might be wrong.

Greene (1994) notes that it is difficult to generalize about ethnic groups in the United States. For example, African Americans may find their cultural origins in the tribes of West Africa, but they have also been influenced by Christianity and the local subcultures of North American towns and cities. Native Americans represent hundreds of tribal groups, languages, and cultures. By and large, homosexuality is rejected by ethnic minority groups in the United States. Lesbians and gay males are pressured to keep their sexual orientation a secret or to move to communities where they can express it without condemnation.

HISPANIC AMERICANS In traditional Hispanic American culture, the family is the primary social unit. Men are expected to support and defend the family, and women are expected to be submissive, respectful, and deferential (Morales, 1992). Because women are expected to remain virgins until marriage, men sometimes engage in sexual behavior with other men without considering themselves gay (Greene, 1994). Also, Hispanic American culture frequently denies the sexuality of women. Thus, lesbians are doubly condemned—because of their sexual orientation and because their independence from men threatens the tradition of male dominance (Trujillo, 1991).

ASIAN AMERICANS Asian American cultures emphasize respect for one's elders, obedience to one's parents, and distinct masculine and feminine gender roles (Chan, 1992). The topic of sex is generally taboo within the family. Asian Americans, like Hispanic Americans, tend to assume that sex is unimportant to women. Women are also considered to be less important than men. Open admission of a homosexual orientation is seen as a rejection of one's traditional cultural roles and a threat to the continuity of the family line (Chan, 1992).

AFRICAN AMERICANS Because many African American men have had difficulty finding jobs, gender roles among African Americans have been more flexible than those found among most other ethnic minority groups and among White Americans (Greene, 1994). Nevertheless, the African American community appears to reject gay men and lesbians strongly, pressuring them to remain secretive about their sexual orientation (Gomez & Smith, 1990; Poussaint, 1990). One factor that influences African Americans to be hostile toward lesbians and gay men is allegiance to Christian beliefs and Biblical scripture (Greene, 1994).

NATIVE AMERICANS Prior to the European conquest of the Americas, sex was seen as a natural part of life. Native American individuals who incorporated both traditional feminine and masculine styles were generally accepted, even

PSYCHOLOGY *in the* ▶ NEW MILLENNIUM

The Gay Global Village

The gay community has been active online for quite some time. An *Out* magazine survey shows that gay men and lesbians are more likely than the general population to use personal computers, modems, and on-line services. In an average month in the 1990s, 40,000 gay people spent more than 100,000 hours online with America Online's Gay and Lesbian Community Forum.

Planet Out, the electronic media company, seeks to become the "gay global village" of cyberspace. It has received the endorsement of virtually all the leading gay organizations. The Human Rights Campaign Fund, the National Gay and Lesbian Task Force, Parents and Friends of Lesbians and Gays, the Gay and Lesbian Victory Fund, Digital Queers, and the Gay and Lesbian Alliance Against Defamation all provide information on the service.

Planet Out is also a meeting place for millions of gay men, lesbians, bisexuals, and others who may be reluctant to associate with one another in public. A creative director of Netscape and the former head of design at Apple Computer said that chatting electronically with gay men and lesbians on America Online had given him the courage to discuss his homosexual orientation openly. "It's something that would have been unthinkable for me even a year or two ago," he said. "If I had relied on more traditional ways of meeting people, like going to bars, or going to meetings of various organizations, or picking up gay publications, it never would have happened" (Lewis, 1995).■

admired. The influence of colonists' religions led to greater rejection of lesbians and gay men and pressure on them to move from reservations to large cities (Greene, 1994). Native American lesbians and gay men thus often feel doubly removed from their families.

If any generalization is possible, it may be that lesbians and gay men find a greater sense of belonging in the gay community than in their ethnic communities.

ORIGINS OF SEXUAL ORIENTATION There are psychological and biological theories of sexual orientation, as well as theories that combine elements of both.

Psychodynamic theory ties sexual orientation to identification with male or female figures. Identification, in turn, is related to resolution of the Oedipus and Electra complexes. In men, faulty resolution of the Oedipus complex would stem from a "classic pattern" of child rearing in which there is a "close binding" mother and a "detached hostile" father. Boys reared in such a home environment would identify with their mother and not with their father. Psychodynamic theory has been criticized, however, because many gay males have had excellent relationships with both parents (Isay, 1990). Also, the childhoods of many heterosexuals fit the "classic pattern."

From a learning theory point of view, early reinforcement of sexual behavior (for example, by orgasm achieved through interaction with people of one's own gender) can influence one's sexual orientation. But most people are aware of their sexual orientation before they have sexual contacts (Bell and others, 1981).

Biopsychologists note that there is evidence of familial patterns in sexual orientation (Pillard, 1990; Pillard & Weinrich, 1986). In one study, 22% of the brothers of 51 primarily gay men were either gay or bisexual themselves. This is about four times the percentage found in the general population (Pillard & Weinrich, 1986). A study published in *Science* reported that genes connected with sexual orientation may be found on the X sex chromosome and be transmitted from mother to child (Hamer and others, 1993). Moreover, according to research by Bailey and Pillard (1991), identical (MZ) twins have a higher agreement rate for a gay male sexual orientation than do fraternal (DZ) twins: 52% for MZ twins versus 22% for DZ twins. Although genetic factors may partly determine sexual orientation, psychologist John Money, who has specialized in research on sexual behavior, concludes that sexual orientation is "not under the direct governance of chromosomes and genes" (1987, p. 384).

Sex hormones may play a role in sexual orientation. These hormones promote biological sexual differentiation and regulate the menstrual cycle. They also have organizing and activating effects on sexual behavior. They predispose lower animals toward masculine or feminine mating patterns—a directional or **organizing effect** (Crews, 1994). They also affect the sex drive and promote sexual response; these are **activating effects.**

Sexual behavior among many lower animals is almost completely governed by hormones (Crews, 1994). In many species, if the sex organs and brains of fetuses are exposed to large doses of **testosterone** in the uterus (which occurs naturally when they share the uterus with many brothers, or artificially as a result of hormone injections), they become masculine in structure (Crews, 1994). Prenatal testosterone organizes the brains of females in the masculine direction, predisposing them toward masculine behaviors in adulthood. Testosterone in adulthood then apparently activates the masculine behavior patterns.

ORGANIZING EFFECT • The directional effect of sex hormones—for example, along stereotypically masculine or feminine lines.
ACTIVATING EFFECT • The arousal-producing effects of sex hormones that increase the likelihood of sexual behavior.
TESTOSTERONE • A male sex hormone that promotes development of male sexual characteristics and that has activating effects on sexual arousal.

Because sex hormones predispose lower animals toward masculine or feminine mating patterns, some have asked whether gay males and lesbians might differ from heterosexuals in levels of sex hormones. However, a gay male or lesbian sexual orientation has not been reliably linked to current (adult) levels of male or female sex hormones (Friedman & Downey, 1994). What about the effects of sex hormones on the developing fetus? As just noted, we know that prenatal sex hormones can masculinize or feminize the brains of laboratory animals.

Lee Ellis (1990; Ellis & Ames, 1987) theorizes that sexual orientation is hormonally determined prior to birth and is affected by genetic factors, synthetic hormones (such as **androgens**), and maternal stress. Why maternal stress? Stress causes the release of hormones such as **adrenaline** and **cortisol,** which can affect the prenatal development of the brain. Perhaps the brains of some gay males have been feminized and the brains of some lesbians masculinized prior to birth (Collaer & Hines, 1995; Friedman & Downey, 1994).

In sum, the determinants of sexual orientation are mysterious and complex. Research suggests that they may involve prenatal hormone levels—which can be affected by factors such as heredity, drugs, and maternal stress—and postnatal socialization. However, the precise interaction among these influences is not yet understood.

■ SEXUAL COERCION

Sexual coercion includes rape and other forms of sexual pressure. It also includes *any* sexual activity between an adult and a child. Even when children cooperate, sexual relations with children are coercive because the child is below the legal age of consent. In this section we focus on rape and sexual harassment.

• *Rape*

From 14% to 25% of women in the United States have been raped (Koss, 1993). Parents regularly encourage their daughters to be wary of strangers and strange places—places where they could fall prey to rapists. Certainly the threat of rape from strangers is real enough. Yet four out of five rapes are committed by acquaintances (Schafran, 1995).

Date rape is a pressing concern on college campuses, where thousands of women have been victimized and there is much controversy over what exactly constitutes rape. Nine percent of one sample of 6,159 college women reported that they had given in to sexual intercourse as a result of threats or physical force (Koss and others, 1987). Consider one woman's account:

> I first met him at a party. He was really good looking and he had a great smile. I wanted to meet him but I wasn't sure how. I didn't want to appear too forward. Then he came over and introduced himself. We talked and found we had a lot in common. I really liked him. When he asked me over to his place for a drink, I thought it would be OK. He was such a good listener, and I wanted him to ask me out again.
>
> When we got to his room, the only place to sit was on the bed. I didn't want him to get the wrong idea, but what else could I do? We talked for awhile and then he made his move. I was so startled. He started by kissing. I really liked him so the kissing was nice. But then he pushed me down on the bed. I tried to get up and I told him to stop. He

ANDROGENS • Male sex hormones.
ADRENALINE • A hormone produced by the adrenal glands that generally arouses people and heightens their emotional responsiveness.
CORTISOL • A hormone produced by the adrenal glands that increases resistance to stress.

CULTURAL MYTHS THAT CREATE A CLIMATE THAT SUPPORTS RAPE

The following statements are based on a questionnaire by Martha Burt (1980). Read each statement and indicate whether you believe it to be true or false by circling the T or the F. Then turn to the key in Appendix B to learn about the implications of your answers. ■

T   F   1. A woman who goes to the home or apartment of a man on their first date implies that she is willing to have sex.

T   F   2. Any female can get raped.

T   F   3. One reason why women falsely report a rape is because they need to call attention to themselves.

T   F   4. Any healthy woman can successfully resist a rapist if she really wants to.

T   F   5. When women go around braless or wearing short skirts and tight tops, they are just asking for trouble.

T   F   6. In the majority of rapes, the victim is promiscuous or has a bad reputation.

T   F   7. If a girl engages in necking or petting and she lets things get out of hand, it is her own fault if her partner forces sex on her.

T   F   8. Women who get raped while hitchhiking get what they deserve.

T   F   9. A woman who is stuck-up and thinks she is too good to talk to guys on the street deserves to be taught a lesson.

T   F   10. Many women have an unconscious wish to be raped and may then unconsciously set up a situation in which they are likely to be attacked.

T   F   11. If a woman gets drunk at a party and has intercourse with a man she's just met there, she should be considered "fair game" to other males at the party who want to have sex with her too, whether she wants to or not.

T   F   12. Many women who report a rape are lying because they are angry and want to get back at the man they accuse.

T   F   13. Many, if not most, rapes are merely invented by women who discovered they were pregnant and wanted to protect their reputation.

---

was so much bigger and stronger. I got scared and I started to cry. I froze and he raped me.

It took only a couple of minutes and it was terrible, he was so rough. When it was over he kept asking me what was wrong, like he didn't know. He had just forced himself on me and he thought that was OK. He drove me home and said he wanted to see me again. I'm so afraid to see

Kristine, Amy, and Karen. These college women are among the thousands who have been raped by their dates. The great majority of rapes are committed by dates or acquaintances, not by strangers.

him. I never thought it would happen to me. (Rathus & Fichner-Rathus, 1997)

If we add to these statistics instances in which women are subjected to forced kissing and petting, the numbers grow even more alarming. At a major university, 40% of 201 male students surveyed admitted to using force to unfasten a woman's clothing, and 13% reported that they had forced a woman to engage in sexual intercourse (Rapaport & Burkhart, 1984). Forty-four percent of the college women in the Koss study (Koss and others, 1987) reported that they had "given in to sex play" because of a "man's continual arguments and pressure."

WHY DO MEN RAPE WOMEN? Why do men force women into sexual activity? Sex is not the only reason. Many social scientists argue that rape is often a man's way of expressing social dominance over, or anger toward, women (Hall & Barongan, 1997). With some rapists, violence appears to enhance sexual arousal. They therefore seek to combine sex and aggression (Barbaree & Marshall, 1991).

Many social critics contend that American culture socializes men—including the nice young man next door—into becoming rapists (Powell, 1996). This occurs because males are often reinforced for aggressive and competitive behavior (Hall & Barongan, 1997). The date rapist could be said to be asserting culturally expected dominance over women.

College men frequently perceive a date's protests as part of an adversarial sex game. One male undergraduate said "Hell, no" when asked whether a date had consented to sex. He added, ". . . but she didn't say no, so she must have wanted it, too. . . . It's the way it works" (Celis, 1991). Consider the comments of the man who victimized the woman whose story appeared earlier in the section:

PREVENTING RAPE

Don't accept rides from strange men—and remember that all men are strange.

ROBIN MORGAN

The aftermath of rape can include physical harm, anxiety, depression, sexual dysfunction, sexually transmitted disease, and/or pregnancy (Kimerling & Calhoun, 1994; Koss, 1993). From a sociocultural perspective, prevention of rape involves publicly examining and challenging the widely held cultural attitudes and ideals that contribute to rape. The traditions of male dominance and rewards for male aggressiveness take a daily toll on women. One thing we can do is encourage colleges and universities to require students to attend lectures and seminars on rape. The point is for men to learn that "No" means "No," despite the widespread belief that some women like to be talked into sex. We can also encourage community and national leaders to pay more attention to the problem.

On a personal level, there are things that women can do to protect themselves. *The New Our Bodies, Ourselves* (Boston Women's Health Book Collective, 1992) includes the following suggestions for preventing rape by strangers:

- Establish signals and arrangements with other women in an apartment building or neighborhood.
- List only first initials in the telephone directory or on the mailbox.
- Use dead-bolt locks.
- Keep windows locked and obtain iron grids for first-floor windows.

- Keep entrances and doorways brightly lit.
- Have keys ready for the front door or the car.
- Do not walk alone in the dark.
- Avoid deserted areas.
- Never allow a strange man into your apartment or home without checking his credentials.
- Drive with the car windows up and the door locked.
- Check the rear seat of the car before entering.
- Avoid living in an unsafe building.
- Do not pick up hitchhikers (including women).
- Do not talk to strange men in the street.
- Shout "Fire!" not "Rape!" People crowd around fires but avoid scenes of violence.

Powell (1996) adds the following suggestions for avoiding date rape:

- Communicate your sexual limits to your date. Tell your partner how far you would like to go so that he will know what the limits are. For example, if your partner starts fondling you in ways that make you uncomfortable, you might say, "I'd prefer if you didn't touch me there. I really like you, but I prefer not getting so intimate at this point in our relationship."
- Meet new dates in public places, and avoid driving with a stranger or a group of people you've just met. When meeting a new date, drive in your own car and meet your date at a public place. Don't

drive with strangers or offer rides to strangers or groups of people. In some cases of date rape, the group disappears just prior to the assault.
- State your refusal in definitive terms. Be firm in refusing a sexual overture. Look your partner straight in the eye. The more definite you are, the less likely your partner will be to misinterpret your wishes.
- Become aware of your fears. Take notice of any fears of displeasing your partner that might stifle your assertiveness. If your partner is truly respectful of you, you need not fear an angry or demeaning response. But if your partner is not respectful, it is best to become aware of it early and end the relationship right away.
- Pay attention to your "vibes." Trust your gut-level feelings. Many victims of acquaintance rape said afterward that they had had a strange feeling about the man but failed to pay attention to it.
- Be especially cautious if you are in a new environment, such as college or a foreign country. You may be especially vulnerable to exploitation when you are becoming acquainted with a new environment, different people, and different customs.
- If you have broken off a relationship with someone you don't really like or feel good about, don't let him into your place. Many so-called date rapes are committed by ex-lovers and ex-boyfriends. ■

496   CHAPTER 13   *Gender and Sexuality*

I first met her at a party. She looked really hot, wearing a sexy dress that showed off her great body. We started talking right away. I knew that she liked me by the way she kept smiling and touching my arm while she was speaking. She seemed pretty relaxed so I asked her back to my place for a drink. . . . When she said yes, I knew that I was going to be lucky!

When we got to my place, we sat on the bed kissing. At first, everything was great. Then, when I started to lay her down on the bed, she started twisting and saying she didn't want to. Most women don't like to appear too easy, so I knew that she was just going through the motions. When she stopped struggling, I knew that she would have to throw in some tears before we did it.

She was still very upset afterwards, and I just don't understand it! If she didn't want to have sex, why did she come back to the room with me? You could tell by the way she dressed and acted that she was no virgin, so why she had to put up such a big struggle I don't know. (Rathus & Fichner-Rathus, 1997)

psychology and modern life

RESISTING SEXUAL HARASSMENT

What can you do if you are sexually harassed on campus or in the workplace? Here are some suggestions:

1. Behave in a professional manner. Harassment often can be stopped cold if you respond to the harasser in a curt, businesslike manner.

2. Discourage harassment and promote the kind of social behavior you want. Speak up. If your supervisor or professor asks you to come to the office after hours, say that you would rather talk during office hours. Stick to business. If the harasser does not take this suggestion, be more direct: "Mr. Smith, I'd like to keep our relationship purely business, okay?"

3. Don't get into a situation in which you are alone with someone who might harass you. Have a co-worker around when you consult your supervisor. Or see your professor before or after class, when other people are around.

4. Keep a record of incidents to document them in case you decide to lodge an official complaint.

5. Put the harasser on direct notice that you recognize the harassment for what it is and that you want it to stop.

6. Confide about harassment to reliable friends, school counselors or advisers, union representatives, or parents or relatives. Harassment is stressful, and social support helps us cope with stress. Other people may also have helpful advice.

7. Many places of business and campuses have offices where complaints about sexual harassment are filed and acted on. Check with the dean of students or the president's office.

8. See a lawyer. Sexual harassment is illegal, and you can stop it. ■

MYTHS ABOUT RAPE In the United States there are numerous myths about rape—myths that tend to blame the victim, not the aggressor. For example, a majority of Americans aged 50 and above believe that the woman is partly responsible for being raped if she dresses provocatively (Gibbs, 1991). As a result, they are unlikely to be sympathetic if such a woman complains of being raped. A majority of Americans believe that some women like to be talked into sex.

Other myths include the notions that "women say no when they mean yes," "all women like a man who is pushy and forceful," and "rapists are crazed by sexual desire" (Powell, 1996, p. 139). Still another myth is that deep down inside, women *want* to be raped. All these myths deny the impact of the assault and transfer blame onto the victim. They contribute to a social climate that is too often lenient toward rapists and unsympathetic toward victims.

If you want to learn whether you harbor some of the more common myths about rape, complete the nearby questionnaire on cultural myths that create a climate that supports rape.

• *Sexual Harassment*

Sexual harassment is frequent on college campuses, in the business world, and in the military (Seppa, 1997b). It is sometimes difficult to draw the line between sexual persuasion and attempted rape. It can be even *more* difficult to distinguish between a legitimate (if unwelcome) sexual invitation and sexual harassment (Barchoff, 1997). People accused of sexual harassment often claim that the charges are exaggerated. They say that the victim "overreacted" to normal male-female interaction. Or "She took me too seriously." However, sexual harassment *is* a serious problem, and most harassers know very well what they are doing (Powell, 1996).

Where does "normal male-female interaction" end and sexual harassment begin? Sexual harassment involves deliberate or repeated unwanted comments, gestures, or physical contact of a sexual nature (Powell, 1996). Consider some examples:

- Verbal abuse,
- Unwelcome sexual overtures or advances,
- Pressure to engage in sexual activity,
- Remarks about a person's body, clothing, or sexual activities,
- Leering at, or ogling, someone,
- Telling unwanted dirty jokes in mixed company,
- Unnecessarily touching, patting, or pinching,
- Whistles and catcalls,
- Brushing up against someone,
- Demands for sex that are accompanied by threats, such as being fired from a job or not getting a promotion.

Your college may publish guidelines about sexual harassment. Check with the dean of students or the president's office.

College students are sexually harassed by other students and sometimes by professors. Professors are sometimes harassed by students. Most often the victims of sexual harassment are women. Some cases are so serious that women switch majors or schools to avoid it. Ironically, as with rape, society often blames the victim of sexual harassment for being provocative or for not saying no firmly enough (Powell, 1996).

Sexual Harassment. Is this behavior acceptable in the workplace? Many women have switched jobs or colleges because of sexual harassment.

Truth or Fiction Revisited

It is true that most Americans believe that some women like to be talked into sex. A majority of Americans — including a majority of American women — share this belief. Does this encourage men to pressure their dates into sex?

Truth or Fiction Revisited

It is not true that women say no when they mean yes. Myths such as this foster a social climate that encourages rape.

SEXUAL HARASSMENT • Deliberate or repeated verbal comments, gestures, or physical contact of a sexual nature that is unwanted by the recipient.

REFLECTIONS

- What sociocultural factors affect your sexual attitudes and behavior? Are your attitudes and behavior similar to or different from those of most of your classmates? Why or why not?
- What stimuli arouse you sexually? Why do you think they arouse you?
- What attitudes toward gay males and lesbians were expressed in your home and neighborhood? Have these attitudes affected your own beliefs? How? Has the information in this chapter changed your beliefs about gay males and lesbians? If so, how?

■ SEXUAL RESPONSE

Although we may be culturally attuned to focus on gender differences rather than similarities, William Masters and Virginia Johnson (1966) found that the biological responses of males and females to sexual stimulation are quite similar. They use the term *sexual response cycle* to describe the changes that occur in the body as men and women become sexually aroused. In this section we first outline the phases of the sexual response cycle. Then we consider some of the things that can go wrong with the cycle. These are known as *sexual dysfunctions.*

FIGURE 13.8

LEVELS OF SEXUAL AROUSAL DURING THE PHASES OF THE SEXUAL RESPONSE CYCLE

Masters and Johnson divide the sexual response cycle into four phases: excitement, plateau, orgasm, and resolution. During the resolution phase, the level of sexual arousal returns to the prearoused state. For men there is a refractory period following orgasm. As shown by the broken line, however, men can become rearoused to orgasm once the refractory period is past and their levels of sexual arousal have returned to pre-plateau levels. Pattern A for women shows a typical response cycle, with the broken line suggesting multiple orgasms. Pattern B shows the cycle of a woman who reaches the plateau phase but for whom arousal is "resolved" without reaching the orgasmic phase. Pattern C shows the possibility of orgasm in a highly aroused woman who passes quickly through the plateau phase.

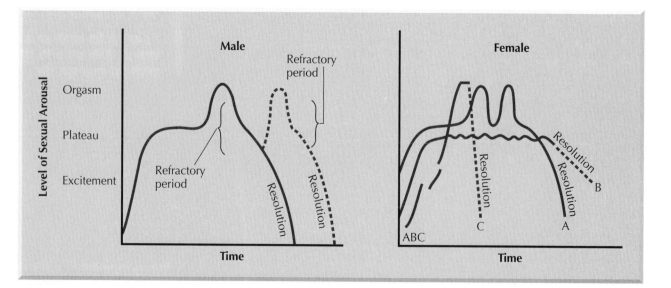

• *The Sexual Response Cycle*

Masters and Johnson divide the **sexual response cycle** into four phases: *excitement*, *plateau*, *orgasm*, and *resolution*. Figure 13.8 suggests the levels of sexual arousal associated with each phase.

The sexual response cycle is characterized by vasocongestion and myotonia. **Vasocongestion** is the swelling of the genital tissues with blood. It causes erection of the penis and swelling of the area surrounding the vaginal opening. The testes, the nipples, and even the earlobes swell as blood vessels dilate in these areas.

Myotonia is muscle tension. It causes facial grimaces, spasms in the hands and feet, and then the spasms of orgasm. In this section we will explore these and other bodily changes that make up the sexual response cycle.

EXCITEMENT PHASE Vasocongestion during the **excitement phase** can cause erection in young men as soon as 3 to 8 seconds after sexual stimulation begins. The scrotal skin also thickens, becoming less baggy. The testes increase in size and become elevated.

In the female, excitement is characterized by vaginal lubrication, which may start 10 to 30 seconds after sexual stimulation begins. Vasocongestion swells the **clitoris** and flattens and spreads the vaginal lips. The inner part of the vagina expands. The breasts enlarge, and blood vessels near the surface become more prominent.

In the excitement phase the skin may take on a rosy *sex flush*. This is more pronounced in women. The nipples may become erect in both men and women. Heart rate and blood pressure also increase.

PLATEAU PHASE The level of sexual arousal remains somewhat stable during the **plateau phase** of the cycle. Because of vasocongestion, men show some increase in the circumference of the head of the penis, which also takes on a purplish hue. The testes are elevated into position for **ejaculation** and may reach one and a half times their unaroused size.

In women, vasocongestion swells the outer part of the vagina, contracting the vaginal opening in preparation for grasping the penis. The inner part of the vagina expands further. The clitoris withdraws beneath the clitoral hood and shortens.

Breathing becomes rapid, like panting. Heart rate may increase to 100 to 160 beats per minute. Blood pressure continues to rise.

ORGASMIC PHASE The orgasmic phase in the male consists of two stages of muscular contractions. In the first stage, **seminal fluid** collects at the base of the penis. The internal sphincter of the urinary bladder prevents urine from mixing with semen. In the second stage, muscle contractions propel the ejaculate out of the body. Sensations of pleasure tend to be related to the strength of the contractions and the amount of seminal fluid present. The first 3 to 4 contractions are generally most intense and occur at 0.8-second intervals (5 contractions every 4 seconds). Another two to four contractions occur at a somewhat slower pace. Rates and patterns can vary from one man to another.

Orgasm in the female is manifested by 3 to 15 contractions of the pelvic muscles that surround the vaginal barrel. The contractions first occur at 0.8-second intervals. As in the male, they produce release of sexual tension. Weaker and slower contractions follow.

SEXUAL RESPONSE CYCLE • Masters and Johnson's model of sexual response, which consists of four stages or phases.

VASOCONGESTION • Engorgement of blood vessels with blood, which swells the genitals and breasts during sexual arousal.

MYOTONIA • Muscle tension.

EXCITEMENT PHASE • The first phase of the sexual response cycle, which is characterized by muscle tension, increases in the heart rate, and erection in the male and vaginal lubrication in the female.

CLITORIS • The female sex organ that is most sensitive to sexual sensation; a smooth, round knob of tissue that resembles a button and is situated above the urethral opening.

PLATEAU PHASE • The second phase of the sexual response cycle, which is characterized by increases in vasocongestion, muscle tension, heart rate, and blood pressure in preparation for orgasm.

EJACULATION • The process of propelling seminal fluid (semen) from the penis.

SEMINAL FLUID • The fluid produced by the prostate and other glands that carries and nourishes sperm. Also called *semen.*

ORGASM • The height or climax of sexual excitement, involving involuntary muscle contractions, release of sexual tensions, and, usually, subjective feelings of pleasure.

Blood pressure and heart rate reach a peak, with the heart beating up to 180 times per minute. Respiration may increase to 40 breaths per minute.

RESOLUTION PHASE After orgasm the body returns to its unaroused state. This is called the **resolution phase.** After ejaculation, blood is released from engorged areas, so that the erection disappears. The testes return to their normal size.

In women orgasm also triggers the release of blood from engorged areas. The nipples return to their normal size. The clitoris and vaginal barrel gradually shrink to their unaroused sizes. Blood pressure, heart rate, and breathing also return to their levels before arousal. Both partners may feel relaxed and satisfied.

Unlike women, men enter a **refractory period** during which they cannot experience another orgasm or ejaculate. The refractory period of adolescent males may last only minutes, whereas that of men age 50 and above may last from several minutes to a day. Women do not undergo a refractory period and therefore can become quickly rearoused to the point of repeated (multiple) orgasm if they desire and receive continued sexual stimulation.

• *Sexual Dysfunctions and Sex Therapy*

Sexual dysfunctions are persistent problems in becoming sexually aroused or reaching orgasm. Many people will be troubled by a sexual dysfunction at one time or another. Let's take a look at the main types of sexual dysfunctions and their causes.

TYPES OF SEXUAL DYSFUNCTIONS The sexual dysfunctions include hypoactive sexual desire disorder, female sexual arousal disorder, male erectile disorder, orgasmic disorder, premature ejaculation, dyspareunia, and vaginismus.

In **hypoactive sexual desire disorder,** a person lacks interest in sexual activity and frequently reports a lack of sexual fantasies. This diagnosis exists because it is assumed that sexual fantasies and interests are normal responses that may be blocked by anxiety or other factors.

In women, sexual arousal is characterized by lubrication of the vaginal walls, which facilitates entry by the penis. Sexual arousal in men is characterized by erection. Almost all women sometimes have difficulty becoming or remaining lubricated. Almost all men have occasional difficulty attaining or maintaining an erection through intercourse. When these events are persistent or recurrent, they are considered dysfunctions (**female sexual arousal disorder** and **male erectile disorder**).

In **orgasmic disorder,** the man or woman, though sexually excited, takes a long time to reach orgasm or does not reach it at all. Orgasmic disorder is more common among women than among men. In **premature ejaculation,** the male ejaculates after minimal sexual stimulation, too soon to permit his partner or himself to enjoy sexual relations fully. Other dysfunctions include **dyspareunia** (painful sexual activity) and **vaginismus** (involuntary contraction of the muscles surrounding the vaginal opening, which makes entry painful and/or difficult).

CAUSES OF SEXUAL DYSFUNCTIONS Some sexual dysfunctions reflect biological problems. Lack of desire, for example, can be due to diabetes or to diseases of the heart and lungs. Fatigue can reduce sexual desire and inhibit orgasm. Depressants such as alcohol, narcotics, and tranquilizers can also impair

RESOLUTION PHASE • The fourth phase of the sexual response cycle, during which the body gradually returns to its prearoused state.
REFRACTORY PERIOD • In the sexual response cycle, a period of time following orgasm during which an individual is not responsive to sexual stimulation.
SEXUAL DYSFUNCTION • A persistent or recurrent problem in becoming sexually aroused or reaching orgasm.
HYPOACTIVE SEXUAL DESIRE DISORDER • A sexual dysfunction in which people lack sexual desire.
FEMALE SEXUAL AROUSAL DISORDER • A sexual dysfunction in which females fail to become adequately sexually aroused to engage in sexual intercourse.
MALE ERECTILE DISORDER • A sexual dysfunction in which males fail to obtain erections that are adequate for sexual intercourse.
ORGASMIC DISORDER • A sexual dysfunction in which people have persistent or recurrent problems in reaching orgasm.
PREMATURE EJACULATION • Ejaculation that occurs before the couple are satisfied with the length of sexual relations.
DYSPAREUNIA • A sexual dysfunction characterized by persistent or recurrent pain during sexual intercourse. (From roots meaning "badly paired.")
VAGINISMUS • A sexual dysfunction characterized by involuntary contraction of the muscles surrounding the vagina, preventing entry by the penis or making entry painful.

sexual response. Physical factors sometimes interact with psychological factors. For instance, dyspareunia can heighten anxiety, and extremes of anxiety can dampen sexual arousal.

Physically or psychologically painful sexual experiences, such as rape, can block future sexual response (Koss, 1993). Moreover, a sexual relationship is usually no better than other aspects of a relationship or marriage. Couples who have difficulty communicating are at a disadvantage in expressing their sexual desires.

Cognitive psychologists point out that irrational beliefs and attitudes can contribute to sexual dysfunctions. If we believe that we need a lover's approval at all times, we may view a disappointing sexual episode as a catastrophe. If we demand that every sexual encounter be perfect, we set ourselves up for failure.

In most cases of sexual dysfunction, the physical and psychological factors we have outlined lead to yet another psychological factor—**performance anxiety,** or fear of not being able to perform sexually. People with performance anxiety may focus on past failures and expectations of another disaster rather than enjoying present erotic sensations and fantasies. Performance anxiety can make it difficult for a man to attain erection, yet also spur him to ejaculate prematurely. It can prevent a woman from becoming adequately lubricated and can contribute to vaginismus.

Truth or Fiction Revisited

It is not necessarily true that people who truly love each other enjoy the sexual aspects of their relationships. The statement is too broad to be true. Sexual dysfunctions can occur even in a loving relationship.

SEX THERAPY **Sex therapy** is a collection of techniques that help people overcome sexual dysfunctions. It is largely indebted to the pioneering work of Masters and Johnson, although other therapists have also developed important techniques. It generally focuses on reducing performance anxiety, changing self-defeating attitudes and expectations, teaching sexual skills, enhancing sexual knowledge, and improving sexual communication. Readers who are interested in learning more about sex therapy are advised to consult a human sexuality textbook, contact their state's psychological association, or ask their professors or college counseling centers for referral.

REFLECTIONS
- Consider your sociocultural background once more. Are women from this background traditionally expected to derive as much pleasure from sex as men are? Why or why not?
- Do sexual dysfunctions seem to be things that could happen to you? Why or why not?
- How can a negative sexual experience lead to a sexual dysfunction? Can you give an example?

■ AIDS AND OTHER SEXUALLY TRANSMITTED DISEASES

Sexual relationships can be sources of pleasure and personal fulfillment. They also carry some risks. One of the risks is that of contracting **AIDS** or other sexually transmitted diseases (STDs). According to Theresa Crenshaw, president of the American Association of Sex Educators, Counselors and Therapists, "You're not just sleeping with one person, you're sleeping with everyone *they* ever slept with."

PERFORMANCE ANXIETY • Anxiety concerning one's ability to perform, especially when performance may be evaluated by other people.
SEX THERAPY • A collective term for short-term cognitive-behavioral models for treatment of sexual dysfunctions.
AIDS • The acronym for acquired immunodeficiency syndrome, a condition caused by the human immunodeficiency virus (HIV) and characterized by destruction of the immune system so that the body is stripped of its ability to fend off life-threatening diseases.

TABLE 13.2 CAUSES, METHODS OF TRANSMISSION, SYMPTOMS, DIAGNOSIS, AND TREATMENT OF SEXUALLY TRANSMITTED DISEASES (STDs)

STD and Cause	Methods of Transmission	Symptoms	Diagnosis	Treatment
Acquired immune deficiency syndrome (AIDS): *Human immunodeficiency virus (HIV)*	HIV is transmitted by sexual intercourse, direct infusion of contaminated blood, or from mother to child during childbirth, or breast-feeding	Infected people may not have any symptoms; they may develop mild flu-like symptoms which disappear for many years prior to the development of "full-blown" AIDS. Full-blown AIDS is symptomized by fever, weight loss, fatigue, diarrhea, and opportunistic in infections such as Kaposi's sarcoma, pneumonia (PCP), and invasive cancer of the cervix.	Blood, saliva, and urine tests can detect HIV *antibodies* in the bloodstream. The Western blot blood test may be used to confirm positive results.	There is no safe, effective vaccine for HIV. Combinations of antiviral drugs, including AZT and protease inhibitors, may reduce the amount of HIV in the bloodstream, in some cases to levels that are undetectable. Although new treatments offer hope, it remains wisest to assume that AIDS is a lethal condition.
Bacterial Vaginosis: *Gardnerella vaginalis* - bacterium and others	Can arise by overgrowth of organisms in vagina, allergic reactions, etc.; transmitted by sexual contact	In women, thin, foul-smelling vaginal discharge. Irritation of genitals and mild pain during urination. In men, inflammation of penile foreskin and glans, urethritis, and cystitis. May be asymptomatic in both genders	Culture and examination of bacterium.	Oral treatment with metronidazole (brand name: Flagyl)
Candidiasis (moniliasis, thrush, "yeast infection"): *Candida albicans*—a yeast-like fungus	Can arise by overgrowth of fungus in vagina; transmitted by sexual contact, or by sharing a washcloth with an infected person	In women, vulval itching; white, cheesy, foul-smelling discharge; soreness or swelling of vaginal and vulval tissues. In men, itching and burning on urination, or a reddening of the penis.	Diagnosis usually made on basis of symptoms.	Vaginal suppositories, creams, or tablets containing miconazole, clotrimazole, or teraconazole; modification of use of other medicines and chemical agents; keeping infected area dry.
Chlamydia and **Nongonococcal urethritis (NGU):** *Chlamydia trachomatous* bacterium; NGU in men may also be caused by *Ureaplasma urealycticum* bacterium and other pathogens	Transmitted by vaginal, oral, or anal sexual activity; to the eye by touching one's eyes after touching the genitals of an infected partner, or by passing through the birth canal of an infected mother	In women, frequent and painful urination, lower abdominal pain and inflammation, and vaginal discharge (but most women are symptom-free). In men, symptoms are similar to but milder than those of gonorrhea—burning or painful urination, slight penile discharge (some men are also asymptomatic). Sore throat may indicate infection from oral-genital contact.	The Abbott Testpack analyzes a cervical smear in women.	Antibiotics

TABLE 13.2 *cont'd*

STD and Cause	Methods of Transmission	Symptoms	Diagnosis	Treatment
Genital herpes: *Herpes simplex virus-type 2 (H.S.V.–2)*	Almost always by means of vaginal, oral, or anal sexual activity; most contagious during active outbreaks of the disease	Painful, reddish bumps around the genitals, thigh, or buttocks; in women, may also be in the vagina or on the cervix. Bumps become blisters or sores that fill with pus and break, shedding viral particles. Other possible symptoms: burning urination, fever, aches and pains, swollen glands; in women, vaginal discharge.	Clinical inspection of sores; culture and examination of fluid drawn from the base of a genital sore.	The antiviral drug acyclovir (brand name: Zovirax) may provide relief and prompt healing over, but is not a cure.
Genital warts: (venereal warts): *Human papilloma virus (H.P.V.)*	Transmission is by sexual and other forms of contact, as with infected towels or clothing. Women are especially vulnerable, particularly women who have multiple sex partners.	Appearance of painless warts, often resembling cauliflowers, on the penis, foreskin, scrotum, or internal urethra in men, and on the vulva, labia, wall of the vagina, or cervix in women. May occur around the anus and in the rectum.	Clinical inspection. (Because H.P.V. is connected with cervical cancer, regular Pap tests are also advised)	Methods of removal include cryotherapy (freezing), podophyllin, burning, and surgical removal (by a physician!)
Gonorrhea "clap," "drip"): Gonococcus bacterium (*Neisseria gonorrhoeae*)	Transmitted by vaginal, oral, or anal sexual activity, or from mother to newborn during delivery	In men, yellowish, thick penile discharge, burning urination. In women, increased vaginal discharge, burning urination, irregular menstrual bleeding (most women show no early symptoms).	Clinical inspection, culture of sample discharge.	Antibiotics
Pubic lice ("crabs"): *Pthirus pubis* (an insect)	Transmission is by sexual contact, or by contact with an infested towel, sheet, or toilet seat	Intense itching in pubic area and other hairy regions to which lice can attach.	Clinical examination.	Lindane (brand name: Kwell)—a prescription drug; over-the-counter medications containing pyrethrins or piperonal butoxide (brand names: NIX, A200, RID, Triple X)
Syphilis: *Treponema pallidum*	Transmitted by vaginal, oral, or anal sexual activity; or by touching an infectious chancre	In primary stage, a hard, round painless chancre or sore appears at site of infection within 2 to 4 weeks. May progress through secondary, latent, and tertiary stages, if left untreated.	Primary-stage syphilis is diagnosed by clinical examination; or fluid from a chancre is examined in a test. Secondary stage syphilis is diagnosed by blood test (the VDRL).	Antibiotics
Trichomoniasis ("trich"): *Trichomonas vaginalis*—a protozoan (one-celled animal)	Almost always transmitted sexually	In women, foamy, yellowish, odorous, vaginal discharge; itching or burning sensation in vulva. Many women are asymptomatic. In men, usually asymptomatic, but mild urethritis is possible.	Microscopic examination of a smear of vaginal secretions; or of culture of the sample (latter method preferred).	Metronidazole (Flagyl)

Although media attention usually focuses on AIDS, a survey of more than 16,000 students at 19 universities found that only 30 were infected with **HIV** (the virus that causes AIDS). That's two (0.2%) of every thousand blood samples tested (Gayle and others, 1990). Since AIDS is fatal, this finding is cause for concern. Other sexually transmitted diseases (STDs) are more widespread, however. *Chlamydia trachomatous* (the bacterium that causes **chlamydia**) was found in 1 sample in 10, or 10% of the college population. *Human papilloma virus (HPV)* (the organism that causes **genital warts**) is estimated to be present in one-third of college women and 8% of men aged 15 to 49 (Cannistra & Niloff, 1996).

Most college students appear to be reasonably well-informed about HIV transmission and AIDS (Wulfert & Wan, 1993). Yet many are unaware that chlamydia can go undetected for years. Moreover, if it is not treated, it can cause pelvic inflammation and infertility. Many, perhaps most, students are also ignorant of HPV, which is linked to cervical cancer (Cannistra & Niloff, 1996). Yet as many as 1 million new cases of HPV infection occur each year in the United States—more than **syphilis, genital herpes,** and AIDS combined. Fewer than 2 million Americans are thought to be infected with HIV. However, about 56 million are infected with other STD-causing viruses, such as those causing genital warts, herpes, and **hepatitis** (Barringer, 1993a).

Women experience the effects of STDs disproportionately. They are more likely to develop infertility if an STD spreads through the reproductive system. Each year an estimated 100,000 to 150,000 U.S. women become **infertile** (unable to get pregnant) because of STDs (Barringer, 1993a). Overall, STDs are believed to account for 15% to 30% of cases of infertility among U.S. women. In addition to their biological effects, STDs take an emotional toll and can strain relationships to the breaking point.

In the rest of this section we focus on AIDS, but there are many other STDs that you should be aware of. Information about these STDs is presented in Table 13.2. Readers who want more information are advised to talk to their professor or doctor, consult human sexuality or health textbooks, or visit their college counseling and health center.

• *AIDS*

AIDS is a fatal condition in which the person's immune system is so weakened that he or she falls prey to **opportunistic diseases.** It is caused by the human immunodeficiency virus (HIV).

HIV is transmitted by infected blood, semen, vaginal and cervical secretions, and breast milk (Meier, 1997; Royce and others, 1997). The first three fluids may enter the body through vaginal, anal, or oral sex with an infected partner. Other means of infection include sharing a hypodermic needle with an infected person (as is common among people who inject illicit drugs) and transfusion with contaminated blood. There need be no concern about closed-mouth kissing. Note, too, that saliva does not transmit HIV (AIDS Hotline, 1997). *However,* transmission through deep kissing is theoretically possible if blood in an infected person's mouth (e.g., from toothbrushing or gum disease) enters cuts (again, as from toothbrushing or gum disease) in the other person's mouth ("Man transmits HIV," 1997). HIV may also be transmitted from mother to fetus during pregnancy or from mother to child through childbirth or breast-feeding. There is no evidence that public toilets, insect bites, holding or hugging an infected person, or living or attending school with one can transmit the virus.

HIV • The acronym for the human immunodeficiency virus, a sexually transmitted virus that destroys white blood cells in the immune system and causes AIDS.

CHLAMYDIA • A sexually transmitted disease caused by the *Chlamydia trachomatous* bacterium. Many infected people have no symptoms, but they may experience painful urination and a discharge from the vagina or penis.

GENITAL WARTS • A sexually transmitted disease caused by the *human papilloma virus* and possibly involved in cancers of the genital organs.

SYPHILIS • An STD that is caused by the *Treponema pallidum* bacterium, which may progress through several stages of development—from a chancre to a skin rash to eventually damaging the cardiovascular or central nervous systems.

GENITAL HERPES • A sexually transmitted disease caused by the *Herpes simplex* virus type 2 and characterized by painful shallow sores and blisters on the genitals.

HEPATITIS • An inflammation of the liver that can be caused by sexually transmitted viral infections.

INFERTILE • Incapable of conceiving a child (becoming pregnant).

OPPORTUNISTIC DISEASES • Diseases that develop within people whose immune systems are impaired by conditions such as AIDS.

"Dying in America at the End of the Millennium." This is a lyric from the Broadway musical *Rent*, which portrays young people with AIDS. They become infected with HIV by means of needle sharing (when injecting heroin), male-female sex, and male-male sex.

HIV kills white blood cells called *CD4 lymphocytes*[2] (or, more simply, *CD4 cells*) that are found in the immune system. CD4 cells recognize viruses and "instruct" other white blood cells—called *B lymphocytes*—to make antibodies, which combat disease. (See Chapter 14.) Eventually, however, CD4 cells are depleted and the body is left vulnerable to opportunistic diseases.

AIDS is characterized by fatigue, fever, unexplained weight loss, swollen lymph nodes, diarrhea, and, in many cases, impairment of learning and memory. Among the opportunistic infections that may take hold are Kaposi's sarcoma, a cancer of the blood cells that occurs in many gay males who contract AIDS; PCP (pneumocystis carinii pneumonia), a kind of pneumonia that is characterized by coughing and shortness of breath; and, in women, invasive cancer of the cervix.

People in the United States have been most likely to become infected with HIV by engaging in male-male sexual activity or injecting ("shooting up") illicit drugs (Centers for Disease Control and Prevention, 1997). Other people at particular risk include sex partners of people who inject drugs, babies born to women who inject drugs or whose sex partners inject drugs, prostitutes and men who visit them, and sex partners of men who visit infected prostitutes. People today are unlikely to be infected by means of blood transfusions because blood supplies are routinely screened for HIV (Schreiber and others, 1996).

One *psychological* risk factor for HIV infection is that people tend to underestimate their risk of infection (Seppa, 1997a). This finding is as true for college students (Goldman & Harlow, 1993) as it is for inner city residents (Hobfoll and others, 1993). Because AIDS has often been characterized as transmitted by anal intercourse (a practice that is fairly common among gay males) and the sharing of contaminated needles, many heterosexual Americans who do not abuse drugs dismiss the threat of AIDS. Yet male-female sexual intercourse accounts for the majority of cases in the world today (Royce and others, 1997). Thus, although gays and drug abusers have been hit hardest by the epidemic, HIV cuts across all boundaries of gender, sexual orientation, ethnicity, and socioeconomic status.

Truth or Fiction Revisited

It is not true that only gay males and substance abusers are at serious risk for contracting AIDS. We all need to be aware of the risk factors and take appropriate precautions.

---

[2] Also called T_4 cells or *helper T cells.*

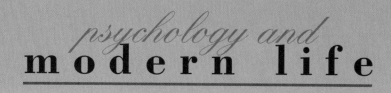

PREVENTING STDS

What can *you* do to prevent the transmission of HIV and other STD-causing organisms? A number of things.

1. *Refuse to deny the prevalence and harmful nature of STDs.* Many people try to put AIDS and other STDs out of their minds. They "wing it" when it comes to sex. The first and most important aspect of prevention is psychological: Do not ignore STDs or assume that they are unlikely to affect you.

2. *Remain abstinent.* One way to curb the sexual transmission of HIV and other organisms that cause STDs is sexual abstinence. Of course, most people who remain abstinent do so while they are looking for Mr. or Ms. Right. Thus, they eventually face the risk of contracting STDs through sexual intercourse. Moreover, students want to know just what "abstinence" means. Does it mean avoiding sexual intercourse (yes) or any form of sexual activity with another person (not necessarily)? Kissing, hugging, and petting to orgasm (without coming into contact with semen or vaginal secretions) are generally considered safe in terms of HIV transmission. However, kissing can transmit oral herpes (as shown by

cold sores) and some bacterial STDs.

3. *Engage in a monogamous relationship with someone who is not infected.* Sexual activity within a monogamous relationship with an uninfected person is safe. The question here is how certain you can be that *your partner* is uninfected and monogamous.

Readers who do not abstain from sexual relationships or limit themselves to a monogamous relationship can do some things to make sex safer—if not perfectly safe:

4. *Be selective.* Engage in sexual activity only with people you know well. Consider whether they are likely to have engaged in the kinds of behaviors that transmit HIV or other STDs.

5. *Inspect your partner's genitals.* People who have STDs often have a variety of symptoms. Examining your partner's genitals for blisters, discharges, chancres, rashes, warts, lice, and unpleasant odors during foreplay may reveal signs of such diseases.

6. *Wash your own genitals before and after contact.* Washing beforehand helps protect your partner. Washing promptly afterward with soap and water helps remove germs.

7. *Use spermicides.* Many spermicides kill HIV and organisms that cause some other STDs as well as sperm. Check with a pharmacist.

8. *Use condoms. Latex* condoms (but not condoms made from animal membrane) protect the woman from having HIV-infected semen enter the vagina and the man from contact with HIV-infected vaginal (or other) body fluids. Condoms also prevent transmission of bacterial STDs.

9. *If you fear that you have been exposed to HIV or another disease-causing organism, talk to your doctor about it.* Early treatment is usually more effective than later treatment. It may even prevent infection (Zuger, 1997a).

10. *When in doubt, stop.* If you are not sure that sex is safe, stop and think things over or seek expert advice.

If you think about it, the last item is rather good general advice. When in doubt, why not stop and think, regardless of whether the doubt is about your sex partner, your college major, or a financial investment? In sex as in most areas of life, pausing when in doubt can pay off in many, many ways. ∎

DIAGNOSIS AND TREATMENT OF HIV INFECTION AND AIDS Infection by HIV is generally diagnosed by means of blood, saliva, or urine tests. For many years researchers were frustrated in their efforts to develop effective vaccines and treatments for HIV infection and AIDS. There is still no safe, effective vaccine, but recent developments in drug therapy have raised hopes about treatment.

AZT and similar antiviral drugs—ddI, ddC—inhibit reproduction of HIV by targeting the enzyme called *reverse transcriptase*. A newer generation of drugs, *protease inhibitors*, targets the *protease* enzyme (Corey & Holmes, 1996). A "cocktail" of antiviral drugs such as AZT, 3TC, and protease inhibitors has become the more or less standard treatment and has reduced HIV to below detectable levels in many infected people (Altman, 1997). Many doctors treat people who fear that they have been exposed to HIV with antiviral drugs to reduce the likelihood of infection (Katz & Gerberding, 1997). *If you fear that you have been exposed to HIV, talk to your doctor about it immediately.*

Current drug therapy has given rise to the hope that AIDS will become "increasingly manageable, a chronic disease as opposed to a terminal illness" (Chesney, 1996). However, the new treatment is expensive, and many people who could benefit from it cannot afford it. In addition, some people with AIDS do not respond to the drug cocktail, and HIV levels bounce back in many cases (Haney, 1997). *Therefore, the most effective way of dealing with AIDS is prevention.*

For the latest information on AIDS, call the National AIDS Hotline at 1-800-342-AIDS. If you want to receive information in Spanish, call 1-800-344-SIDA.

SUMMARY

1. **What are gender stereotypes?** Cultures have broad expectations of men and women that are termed *gender roles*. In our culture the stereotypical female is gentle, dependent, kind, helpful, patient, and submissive. The stereotypical male is tough, competitive, gentlemanly, and protective.

2. **What are some psychological gender differences?** Boys have historically been seen as excelling in math and spatial relations skills, whereas girls have been viewed as excelling in language skills. Gender differences in these areas are small, however, and cultural expectations play a role in them. Males are also more aggressive than females, but the question is *why?*

3. **What is gender-typing?** Gender-typing is the process of acquiring stereotypical gender roles.

4. **What are some biological views of gender-typing?** Biological views of gender-typing focus on the role of genetics and prenatal influences in predisposing men and women to gender-linked behavior patterns. Testosterone in the brains of male fetuses spurs greater growth of the right hemisphere of the brain, which may be connected with the ability to manage spatial relations tasks.

5. **What are some psychological views of gender-typing?** Psychologists have attempted to explain gender typing in terms of psychodynamic, social-cognitive, and gender-schema theories. Freud explained gender-typing in terms of identification with the parent of the same gender through resolution of the Oedipus complex. Social-cognitive theorists explain the development of gender-typed behavior in terms of processes such as observational learning, identification, and socialization. Gender-schema theory proposes that children develop a gender schema as a means of organizing their perceptions of the world. Once children acquire a gender schema, they begin to judge themselves according to traits that are considered relevant to their gender. In doing so they blend their developing self-concept with the prominent gender schema of their culture.

6. **What is interpersonal attraction?** In social psychology, attraction is an attitude of liking (positive attraction) or disliking (negative attraction).

7. **What factors contribute to attraction?** In our culture, slenderness is considered attractive in both men and women, and tallness is valued in men. We are more attracted to good-looking people. Similarity in attitudes and reciprocity in feelings of admiration also enhance attraction.

8. **What is the matching hypothesis?** According to the matching hypothesis, we tend to seek dates and mates at our own level of attractiveness, largely because of fear of rejection.

9. **What is love?** Sternberg's theory suggests that love has three components: intimacy, passion, and commitment. Different kinds of love combine these components in different ways. Romantic love is characterized by the combination of passion and intimacy.

10. **How do psychologists explain gay male and lesbian sexual orientations?** Psychoanalytic theory connects sexual orientation with unconscious castration anxiety and improper resolution of the Oedipus complex. Learning theorists focus on the role of reinforcement of early patterns of sexual behavior. Evidence of a genetic contribution to sexual orientation is accumulating. Research has failed to connect sexual orientation with differences in current (adult) levels of sex hormones. But prenatal sex hormones may play a role in determining sexual orientation in humans.

11. **Why do men rape women?** Social attitudes such as gender role stereotyping, seeing sex as adversarial, and acceptance of violence in interpersonal relationships help create a climate that encourages rape.

12. **What is sexual harassment?** Sexual harassment consists of gestures, verbal comments, or physical contact of a sexual nature that is unwelcome to the recipient.

13. **What are the phases of the sexual response cycle?** The sexual response cycle includes the excitement, plateau, orgasm, and resolution phases.

14. **What are sexual dysfunctions?** Sexual dysfunctions are persistent or recurrent problems in becoming sexually aroused or reaching orgasm. They include hypoactive sexual desire disorder, female sexual arousal disorder, male erectile disorder, orgasmic disorder, premature ejaculation, dyspareunia, and vaginismus.

15. **What are the causes of sexual dysfunctions?** Sexual dysfunctions may be caused by physical problems, negative attitudes toward sex, lack of sexual knowledge and skills, problems in the relationship, and performance anxiety.

16. **What is AIDS?** AIDS is a sexually transmitted disease that is caused by the human immunodeficiency virus (HIV). It attacks the body's immune system and thus makes the body vulnerable to opportunistic diseases that are normally held in check. HIV is a blood-borne virus that is also found in semen, vaginal secretions, and breast milk.

To enhance your understanding of the psychological concepts found in this chapter, please consult the following aids:

Learning Objectives, p. 267
Exercise, p. 268
Lecture and Textbook Outline, p. 269
Key Terms and Concepts, p. 272

Chapter Review, p. 273
Chapter Exercises, p. 280
Knowing the Language, p. 281
Do You Know The Material?, p. 282

Gender Comparisons and Intelligence
The Triangular Theory of Love
Measuring Loving and Liking

Sexual Orientations
Sexual Coercion
Sexual Motivation
STDs

For more information concerning the topics found in this chapter, access psychology links on the World Wide Web through the Harcourt Brace webpage at

www.hbcollege.com

Share your comments and questions with your author at

PsychLinks@aol.com

Budding, growth, vitality, potential—these all signify health and are captured in Beverly Buchanan's *Flowers in a Vase* (1985). Health psychologists study how behavior and mental processes, such as attitudes, are related to health. They also guide people toward more healthful behavior patterns, such as managing stress, exercising, quitting smoking, and eating a more nutritious diet.

BEVERLY BUCHANAN

Chapter 14
Stress and Health

TRUTH OR FICTION?

✔ **T F**

☐ ☐ Since variety is the spice of life, the more change the better.

☐ ☐ A sense of humor can moderate the impact of stress.

☐ ☐ At any given moment, countless microscopic warriors within our bodies are carrying out search-and-destroy missions against foreign agents.

☐ ☐ People who exercise regularly live two years longer, on the average, than their sedentary counterparts.

☐ ☐ Poor people in the United States eat less than more affluent people.

☐ ☐ Women can do nothing to affect the risk of contracting breast cancer.

OUTLINE

HEALTH PSYCHOLOGY
STRESS: PRESSES, PUSHES, AND PULLS
Sources of Stress: Don't Hassle Me?
Questionnaire: The Social Readjustment
  Rating Scale
Psychological Moderators of Stress
Questionnaire: Are You Type A or
  Type B?
Psychology and Modern Life: Alleviating
  the Type A Behavior Pattern
The General Adaptation Syndrome
Questionnaire: The Locus of Control
  Scale
Effects of Stress on the Immune System
Psychology and Modern Life: Coping
  With Stress
**A MULTIFACTORIAL APPROACH TO
  HEALTH AND ILLNESS**
"An Opportunity to Keep Those Nasty
  Genes From Expressing Themselves"
Psychology in a World of Diversity:
  Human Diversity and Health: Nations
    Within the Nation
Headaches
Coronary Heart Disease
Cancer
Psychology in the New Millennium:
  Health Psychology in the 21st
    Century
Psychology and Modern Life: Reducing
  the Risk of Breast Cancer

$\mathscr{S}$IRENS. AMBULANCES. STRETCHERS. THE emergency room at Dallas's public Parkland Memorial Hospital is a busy place. Sirens wail endlessly as ambulances pull up to the doors and discharge people who need prompt attention. Because of the volume of patients, beds line the halls, and people who do not require immediate care cram the waiting room. Many hours may pass before they are seen by a doctor. It is not unusual for people who are not considered to be in danger to wait 10 to 12 hours.

All this may sound rather foreboding, but good things are happening at Parkland as well. One of them is the attention physicians are devoting to patients' psychological needs as well as to their physical needs. For example, influenced both by his own clinical experience and by Native American wisdom about the healing process, Dr. Ron Anderson teaches his medical students that caring about patients is not an outdated ideal. Rather, it is a powerful weapon against disease.

TV journalist Bill Moyers describes Anderson on his medical rounds with students:

> I listen as he stops at the bedside of an elderly woman suffering from chronic asthma. He asks the usual questions: "How did you sleep last night?" "Is the breathing getting any easier?" His next questions surprise the medical students: "Is your son still looking for work?" "Is he still drinking?" "Tell us what happened right before the asthma attack." He explains to his puzzled students. "We know that anxiety aggravates many illnesses, especially chronic conditions like asthma. So we have to find out what may be causing her episodes of stress and help her find some way of coping with it. Otherwise she will land in here again, and next time we might not be able to save her. We cannot just prescribe medication and walk away. That is medical neglect. We have to take the time to get to know her, how she lives, her values, what her social supports are. If we don't know that her son is her sole support and that he's out of work, we will be much less effective in dealing with her asthma." (Moyers, 1993, p. 2)

■ HEALTH PSYCHOLOGY

Note some key concepts from the slice of hospital life reported by Moyers: "Anxiety aggravates many illnesses." "We have to find out what may be causing . . . stress and . . . find some way of coping with it." "We cannot just prescribe medication and walk away." "We have to take the time to get to know [patients], how [they] live, [their] values, what [their] social supports are."

Anderson and Moyers have given us a fine introduction to the field of health psychology. **Health psychology** studies the relationships between psychological

HEALTH PSYCHOLOGY • The field of psychology that studies the relationships between psychological factors (e.g., attitudes, beliefs, situational influences, and behavior patterns) and the prevention and treatment of physical illness.

A Daily Hassle. Daily hassles are notable daily conditions and experiences that are threatening or harmful to a person's well-being. The hassles shown in this photograph center on commuting. What are some of the daily hassles in your life?

factors and the prevention and treatment of physical illness (Taylor, 1990). The case of the woman with asthma is a useful springboard for discussion because health psychologists study the ways in which

- psychological factors such as stress, behavior patterns, and attitudes can lead to or aggravate illness
- people can cope with stress
- stress and **pathogens** (disease-causing organisms such as bacteria and viruses) interact to influence the immune system
- people decide whether or not to seek health care
- psychological forms of intervention such as health education (for example, concerning nutrition, smoking, and exercise) and behavior modification can contribute to physical health

In this chapter we consider a number of issues in health psychology: sources of stress, factors that moderate the impact of stress, and the body's response to stress.

■ STRESS: PRESSES, PUSHES, AND PULLS

> *Americans will put up with anything provided it doesn't block traffic.*
>
> DAN RATHER

In physics, stress is defined as a pressure or force exerted on a body. Tons of rock pressing on the earth, one car smashing into another, a rubber band stretching—all are types of physical stress. Psychological forces, or stresses, also press, push, or pull. We may feel "crushed" by the weight of a big decision, "smashed" by adversity, or "stretched" to the point of snapping.

In psychology, **stress** is the demand made on an organism to adapt, cope, or adjust. Some stress is healthful and necessary to keep us alert and occupied. Stress researcher Hans Selye (1980) referred to such healthful stress as **eustress.**

PATHOGEN • A microscopic organism (e.g., bacterium or virus) that can cause disease.
STRESS • The demand that is made on an organism to adapt.
EUSTRESS • (YOU-stress). Stress that is healthful.

But intense or prolonged stress can overtax our adjustive capacity, affect our moods, impair our ability to experience pleasure, and harm the body (Berenbaum & Connelly, 1993; Cohen and others, 1993; Repetti, 1993).

• *Sources of Stress: Don't Hassle Me?*

DAILY HASSLES Which straw will break the camel's back? The last straw, according to the saying. Similarly, stresses can pile up until we can no longer cope with them. Some of these stresses are **daily hassles**—regularly occurring conditions and experiences that can threaten or harm our well-being. Others are life changes. Lazarus and his colleagues (1985) analyzed a scale that measures daily hassles and their opposites—termed **uplifts**—and found that hassles could be grouped as follows:

1. *Household hassles:* preparing meals, shopping, and home maintenance
2. *Health hassles:* physical illness, concern about medical treatment, and side effects of medication
3. *Time-pressure hassles:* having too many things to do, too many responsibilities, and not enough time
4. *Inner concern hassles:* being lonely and fearful of confrontation
5. *Environmental hassles:* crime, neighborhood deterioration, and traffic noise
6. *Financial responsibility hassles:* concern about owing money such as mortgage payments and loan installments
7. *Work hassles:* job dissatisfaction, not liking one's duties at work, and problems with coworkers
8. *Future security hassles:* concerns about job security, taxes, property investments, stock market swings, and retirement

These hassles are linked to psychological variables such as nervousness, worrying, inability to get started, feelings of sadness, and feelings of loneliness. For example, 83% of people in the United States will be victimized by a violent

DAILY HASSLES • Notable daily conditions and experiences that are threatening or harmful to a person's well-being.
UPLIFTS • Notable pleasant daily conditions and experiences.

TABLE 14.1 STUDENTS' REASONS FOR SEEKING COUNSELING	
Reason	*Percent Reporting Reason*
Stress, anxiety, nervousness	51
Romantic relationships	47
Low self-esteem, self-confidence	42
Depression	41
Family relationships	37
Academic problems, grades	29
Transition to the career world	25
Loneliness	25
Financial problems	24

Note: From Murray, B. (1996). College youth haunted by increased pressures. *APA Monitor,* 26(4), p. 47.

Life Changes. Life changes differ from daily hassles in that they tend to be more episodic. Also, life changes can be positive as well as negative. What is the relationship between life changes and illness? Is the relationship causal?

crime at some time, and victimization is connected with problems such as anxiety, physical complaints, hostility, and depression (Norris & Kaniasty, 1994).

Stress is the number one reason that college students seek help at college counseling centers (Gallagher, 1996). Various kinds of hassles are shown in Table 14.1.

LIFE CHANGES You might think that marrying Mr. or Ms. Right, finding a good job, and moving to a better neighborhood all in the same year would propel you into a state of bliss. It might. But too much of a good thing may also make you ill. All of these events, coming one after another, may also lead to headaches, high blood pressure, and other symptoms. As pleasant as they may be, they entail life changes. Life changes require adjustment and thus are a source of stress.

Life changes differ from daily hassles in two key ways:

1. Many life changes are positive and desirable. Hassles, by definition, are negative.
2. Hassles occur regularly. Life changes occur at irregular intervals.

Holmes and Rahe (1967) constructed a scale to measure the impact of life changes by assigning an arbitrary weight of 50 "life change units" to one major change: marriage. Using marriage as the baseline, they asked subjects to assign units to other life changes, using marriage as the baseline. Most events were rated as less stressful than marriage. A few were more stressful, such as the death of a spouse (100 units) and divorce (73 units). Changes in work hours and residence (20 units each) were included, regardless of whether they were negative or positive. Positive life changes such as an outstanding personal achievement (28 units) and going on vacation (13 units) also made the list.

HASSLES, LIFE CHANGES, AND HEALTH PROBLEMS Hassles and life changes—especially negative life changes—affect us psychologically. They can cause us to worry and affect our moods. But stressors such as hassles and life

THE SOCIAL READJUSTMENT RATING SCALE

Life changes can be a source of stress. How much stress have you experienced in the past year as a result of life changes? To compare your stress to that experienced by other college students, complete this questionnaire.

Directions: Indicate how many times (frequency) you have experienced the following events during the past 12 months (do not enter a number larger than five). Then multiply the frequency by the number of life change units (value) associated with each event. Write the product in the column on the right (total). Then add up the points and check the key in Appendix B. ∎

EVENT	VALUE	FREQUENCY	TOTAL
1. Death of a spouse, lover, or child	94	___	___
2. Death of a parent or sibling	88	___	___
3. Beginning formal higher education	84	___	___
4. Death of a close friend	83	___	___
5. Miscarriage or stillbirth of pregnancy of self, spouse, or lover	83	___	___
6. Jail sentence	82	___	___
7. Divorce or marital separation	82	___	___
8. Unwanted pregnancy of self, spouse, or lover	80	___	___
9. Abortion of unwanted pregnancy of self, spouse, or lover	80	___	___
10. Detention in jail or other institution	79	___	___
11. Change in dating activity	79	___	___
12. Death of a close relative	79	___	___
13. Change in marital situation other than divorce or separation	78	___	___
14. Separation from significant other whom you like very much	77	___	___
15. Change in health status or behavior of spouse or lover	77	___	___
16. Academic failure	77	___	___
17. Major violation of the law and subsequent arrest	76	___	___
18. Marrying or living with lover against parents' wishes	75	___	___
19. Change in love relationship or important friendship	74	___	___
20. Change in health status or behavior of a parent or sibling	73	___	___
21. Change in feelings of loneliness, insecurity, anxiety, boredom	73	___	___
22. Change in marital status of parents	73	___	___
23. Acquiring a visible deformity	72	___	___
24. Change in ability to communicate with a significant other whom you like very much	71	___	___
25. Hospitalization of a parent or sibling	70	___	___
26. Reconciliation of marital or love relationship	68	___	___
27. Release from jail or other institution	68	___	___
28. Graduation from college	68	___	___
29. Major personal injury or illness	68	___	___
30. Wanted pregnancy of self, spouse, or lover	67	___	___
31. Change in number or type of arguments with spouse or lover	67	___	___
32 Marrying or living with lover with parents' approval	66	___	___
33. Gaining a new family member through birth or adoption	65	___	___
34. Preparing for an important exam or writing a major paper	65	___	___
35. Major financial difficulties	65	___	___
36. Change in the health status or behavior of a close relative or close friend	65	___	___
37. Change in academic status	64	___	___
38. Change in amount and nature of interpersonal conflicts	63	___	___
39. Change in relationship with members of your immediate family	62	___	___
40. Change in own personality	62	___	___
41. Hospitalization of yourself or a close relative	61	___	___
42. Change in course of study, major field, vocational goals, or work status	60	___	___
43. Change in own financial status	59	___	___
44. Change in status of divorced or widowed parent	59	___	___
45. Change in number or type of arguments between parents	59	___	___

EVENT	VALUE	FREQUENCY	TOTAL
46. Change in acceptance by peers, identification with peers, or social pressure by peers	58	____	____
47. Change in general outlook on life	57	____	____
48. Beginning or ceasing service in the armed forces	57	____	____
49. Change in attitudes toward friends	56	____	____
50. Change in living arrangements, conditions, or environment	55	____	____
51. Change in frequency or nature of sexual experiences	55	____	____
52. Change in parents' financial status	55	____	____
53. Change in amount or nature of pressure from parents	55	____	____
54. Change in degree of interest in college or attitudes toward education	55	____	____
55. Change in the number of personal or social relationships you've formed or dissolved	55	____	____
56. Change in relationship with siblings	54	____	____
57. Change in mobility or reliability of transportation	54	____	____
58. Academic success	54	____	____
59. Change to a new college or university	54	____	____
60. Changes in feelings of self-reliance, independence, or amount of self-discipline	53	____	____
61. Change in number or type of arguments with roommate	52	____	____
62. Spouse or lover beginning or ceasing work outside the home	52	____	____
63. Change in frequency of use of amounts of drugs other than alcohol, tobacco, or marijuana	51	____	____
64. Change in sexual morality, beliefs, or attitudes	50	____	____
65. Change in responsibility at work	50	____	____
66. Change in amount or nature of social activities	50	____	____
67. Change in dependencies on parents	50	____	____
68. Change from academic work to practical fieldwork experience or internship	50	____	____
69. Change in amount of material possessions and concomitant responsibilities	50	____	____
70. Change in routine at college or work	49	____	____
71. Change in amount of leisure time	49	____	____
72. Change in amount of in-law trouble	49	____	____
73. Outstanding personal achievement	49	____	____
74. Change in family structure other than parental divorce or separation	48	____	____
75. Change in attitude toward drugs	48	____	____
76. Change in amount and nature of competition with same gender	48	____	____
77. Improvement of own health	47	____	____
78. Change in responsibilities at home	47	____	____
79. Change in study habits	46	____	____
80. Change in number or type of arguments or close conflicts with close relatives	46	____	____
81. Change in sleeping habits	46	____	____
82. Change in frequency of use or amounts of alcohol	45	____	____
83. Change in social status	45	____	____
84. Change in frequency of use or amounts of tobacco	45	____	____
85. Change in awareness of activities in external world	45	____	____
86. Change in religious affiliation	44	____	____
87. Change in type of gratifying activities	43	____	____
88. Change in amount or nature of physical activities	43	____	____
89. Change in address or residence	43	____	____
90. Change in amount or nature of recreational activities	43	____	____
91. Change in frequency of use or amounts of marijuana	43	____	____
92. Change in social demands or responsibilities due to your age	43	____	____
93. Court appearance for legal violation	40	____	____
94. Change in weight or eating habits	39	____	____
95. Change in religious activities	37	____	____
96. Change in political views or affiliations	34	____	____
97. Change in driving pattern or conditions	33	____	____
98. Minor violation of the law	31	____	____
99. Vacation or travel	30	____	____
100. Change in number of family get-togethers	30	____	____

Source: *Self-assessment and behavior change manual* (pp. 43–47), by Peggy Blake, Robert Fry, & Michael Pesjack, 1984, New York: Random House. Reprinted by permission of Random House, Inc.

FIGURE 14.1

WHAT ARE THE RELATIONSHIPS AMONG DAILY HASSLES, LIFE CHANGES, AND PHYSICAL ILLNESS?
There are positive correlations between daily hassles and life events, on the one hand, and illness on the other. It may seem logical that hassles and life changes cause illness, but research into the issue is correlational and not experimental. The results are therefore subject to rival interpretations. One is that people who are predisposed toward medical or psychological problems encounter or generate more hassles and amass more life change units.

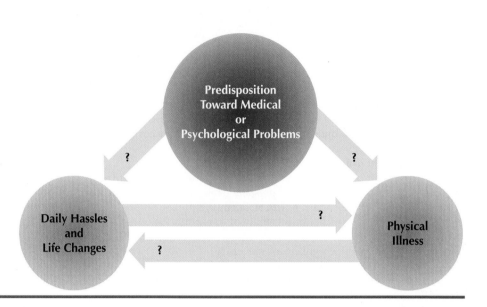

Truth or Fiction Revisited

Although variety may be the spice of life, psychologists have not found that "the more change the better." Changes, even changes for the better, are sources of stress that require adjustment.

changes also predict health problems such as heart disease and cancer and even athletic injuries (Smith and others, 1990; Stewart and others, 1994). Holmes and Rahe found that people who "earned" 300 or more life change units within a year, according to their scale, were at greater risk for health problems. Eight of 10 developed health problems, compared with only 1 of 3 people whose totals of life change units for the year were below 150.

Moreover, people who remain married to the same person live longer than people who experience marital breakups and remarry (Tucker and others, 1996). Apparently the life changes of divorce and remarriage—or the instability associated with them—can be harmful to health.

EVALUATION Although the links between daily hassles, life changes, and illness seem to have been supported by a good deal of research, a careful evaluation reveals a number of limitations:

1. *Correlational Evidence.* The links that have been uncovered between hassles, life changes, and illness are correlational rather than experimental. It may seem logical that the hassles and life changes caused the disorders, but these variables were not manipulated experimentally. Other explanations of the data are possible (Figure 14.1). One possible explanation is that people who are predisposed toward medical or psychological problems encounter more hassles and amass more life change units. For example, undiagnosed medical disorders may contribute to sexual problems, arguments with spouses or in-laws, changes in living conditions and personal habits, and changes in sleeping habits. People may also make certain changes in their lives that lead to physical and psychological disorders (Simons and others, 1993).

2. *Positive Versus Negative Life Changes.* Other aspects of the research on the relationship between life changes and illness have also been challenged. For instance, positive life changes may be less disturbing than hassles and negative life changes, even though the number of life change units assigned to them is high (Lefcourt and others, 1981).

3. *Personality Differences.* People with different kinds of personalities respond to life stresses in different ways (Vaillant, 1994). For example, people who are easygoing or psychologically hardy are less likely to become ill under the impact of stress.

4. *Cognitive Appraisal.* The stress of an event reflects the meaning of the event to the individual (Whitehead, 1994). Pregnancy, for example, can be a positive or negative life change, depending on whether one wants and is prepared to have a child. We appraise the hassles, traumatic experiences, and life changes that we encounter (Creamer and others, 1992; Kiecolt-Glaser, 1993). In responding to them, we take into account their perceived danger, our values and goals, our beliefs in our coping ability, our social support, and so on. The same event will be less taxing to someone with greater coping ability and support than to someone who lacks these advantages.

Despite these methodological flaws, hassles and life changes require adjustment. It seems wise to be aware of hassles and life changes and how they may affect us.

CONFLICT Have you ever felt "damned if you do and damned if you don't"? Regretted that you couldn't do two things, or be in two places, at the same time? In psychology this is termed **conflict.** It is the feeling of being pulled in two or more directions by opposing motives. Conflict is frustrating and stressful. Psychologists often classify conflicts into four types: approach-approach, avoidance-avoidance, approach-avoidance, and multiple approach–avoidance.

Approach-approach conflict (Figure 14.2, Part A) is the least stressful type. Here, each of two goals is desirable, and both are within reach. You may not be able to decide between pizza or tacos, Tom or Dick, or a trip to Nassau or Hawaii. Such conflicts are usually resolved by making a decision. People who experience this type of conflict may vacillate until they make a decision.

Avoidance-avoidance conflict (Figure 14.2, Part B) is more stressful because you are motivated to avoid each of two negative goals. However, avoiding one of them requires approaching the other. You may be fearful of visiting the dentist but also afraid that your teeth will decay if you do not make an appointment and go. You may not want to contribute to the Association for the Advancement of Lost Causes, but you fear that your friends will consider you cheap or uncommitted if you do not. Each goal in an avoidance-avoidance conflict is negative. When an avoidance-avoidance conflict is highly stressful and no resolution is in sight, some people withdraw from the conflict by focusing on other matters or doing nothing. Highly conflicted people have been known to refuse to get up in the morning and start the day.

When the same goal produces both approach and avoidance motives, we have an **approach-avoidance conflict** (Figure 14.2, Part C). People and things have their pluses and minuses, their good points and their bad points. Cream cheese pie may be delicious, but oh, the calories! Goals that produce mixed motives may seem more attractive from a distance but undesirable from up close. Many couples repeatedly break up and then reunite. When they are apart and lonely, they may recall each other fondly and swear that they could make the relationship work if they got together again. But after they spend time together again, they may find themselves thinking, "How could I ever have believed that this so-and-so would change?"

The most complex form of conflict is the **multiple approach–avoidance conflict,** in which each of several alternative courses of action has both promising and distressing aspects. An example with two goals is shown in Figure 14.2, Part D. This sort of conflict might arise on the eve of an examination, when you are faced with the choice of studying or, say, going to a film. Each alternative has both positive and negative aspects: "Studying's a bore, but I won't have to worry about flunking. I'd love to see the movie, but I'd just be worrying about how I'll do tomorrow."

CONFLICT • Being torn in different directions by opposing motives. Feelings produced by being in conflict.
APPROACH-APPROACH CONFLICT • A type of conflict in which the goals that produce opposing motives are positive and within reach.
AVOIDANCE-AVOIDANCE CONFLICT • A type of conflict in which the goals are negative, but avoidance of one requires approaching the other.
APPROACH-AVOIDANCE CONFLICT • A type of conflict in which the same goal produces approach and avoidance motives.
MULTIPLE APPROACH–AVOIDANCE CONFLICT • A type of conflict in which each of a number of goals produces approach and avoidance motives.

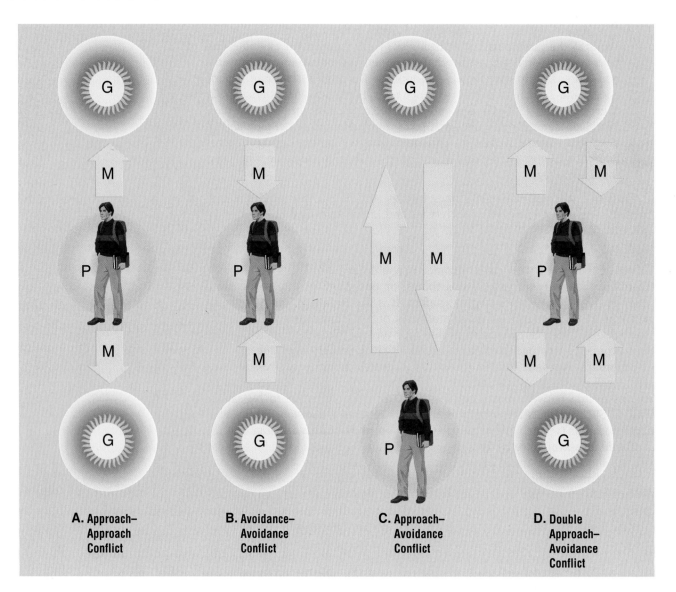

**A. Approach–
Approach
Conflict**

**B. Avoidance–
Avoidance
Conflict**

**C. Approach–
Avoidance
Conflict**

**D. Double
Approach–
Avoidance
Conflict**

FIGURE 14.2
MODELS FOR CONFLICT

Part A shows an approach-approach conflict, in which a person (P) has motives (M) to reach two goals (G) that are desirable, but approach of one requires exclusion of the other. Part B shows an avoidance-avoidance conflict in which both goals are negative, but avoiding one requires approaching the other. Part C shows an approach-avoidance conflict, in which the same goal has desirable and undesirable properties. Part D shows a double approach–avoidance conflict, which is the simplest kind of *multiple* approach–avoidance conflict. In a multiple approach–avoidance conflict, two or more goals have mixed properties.

All forms of conflict entail motives that aim in opposite directions. When one motive is much stronger than the other—such as when you feel "starved" and are only slightly concerned about your weight—it will probably not be too stressful to act in accordance with the powerful motive—in this case, to eat. When each conflicting motive is powerful, however, you may experience high levels of stress and confusion about the proper course of action. At such times you are faced with the need to make a decision. Yet decision making can also be stressful, especially when there is no clear correct choice.

IRRATIONAL BELIEFS: TEN DOORWAYS TO DISTRESS Psychologist Albert Ellis (1977, 1993) notes that our beliefs about events, as well as the events themselves, can be stressors. Consider a case in which a person is fired from a job and is anxious and depressed about it. It may seem logical that losing the job is responsible for the misery, but Ellis points out how the individual's beliefs about the loss compound his or her misery.

Let us examine this situation according to Ellis's A → B → C approach: Losing the job is an *activating event* (A). The eventual outcome, or *consequence* (C), is misery. Between the activating event (A) and the consequence (C), however, lie *beliefs* (B), such as: "This job was the most important thing in my life," "What a no-good failure I am," "My family will starve," "I'll never find a job as good," "There's nothing I can do about it." Beliefs such as these compound misery, foster helplessness, and divert us from planning and deciding what to do next. The belief that "There's nothing I can do about it" fosters helplessness. The belief that "I am a no-good failure" internalizes the blame and may be an exaggeration. The belief that "My family will starve" may also be an exaggeration.

We can diagram the situation like this:

Activating events → Beliefs → Consequences

or A → B → C

Anxieties about the future and depression over a loss are normal and to be expected. However, the beliefs of the person who lost the job tend to **catastrophize** the extent of the loss and contribute to anxiety and depression. By heightening the individual's emotional reaction to the loss and fostering feelings of helplessness, these beliefs also impair coping ability. They lower the person's self-efficacy expectations.

TABLE 14.2 IRRATIONAL BELIEFS
Irrational Belief 1: You must have sincere love and approval almost all the time from the people who are important to you.
Irrational Belief 2: You must prove yourself to be thoroughly competent, adequate, and achieving at something important.
Irrational Belief 3: Things must go the way you want them to go. Life is awful when you don't get your first choice in everything.
Irrational Belief 4: Other people must treat everyone fairly and justly. When people act unfairly or unethically, they are rotten.
Irrational Belief 5: When there is danger or fear in your world, you must be preoccupied with and upset by it.
Irrational Belief 6: People and things should turn out better than they do. It's awful and horrible when you don't find quick solutions to life's hassles.
Irrational Belief 7: Your emotional misery stems from external pressures that you have little or no ability to control. Unless these external pressures change, you must remain miserable.
Irrational Belief 8: It is easier to evade life's responsibilities and problems than to face them and undertake more rewarding forms of self-discipline.
Irrational Belief 9: Your past influenced you immensely and must therefore continue to determine your feelings and behavior today.
Irrational Belief 10: You can achieve happiness by inertia and inaction, or by just enjoying yourself from day to day.

CATASTROPHIZE • (kuh-TASS-trow-fize). To interpret negative events as being disastrous; to "blow out of proportion."
TYPE A BEHAVIOR • Behavior characterized by a sense of time urgency, competitiveness, and hostility.

Ellis proposes that many of us carry with us the irrational beliefs shown in Table 14.2. They are our personal doorways to distress. In fact, they can give rise to problems in themselves. When problems assault us from other sources, these beliefs can magnify their effect. How many of these beliefs do you harbor? Are you sure?

Ellis finds it understandable that we would want the approval of others but irrational to believe that we cannot survive without it. It would be nice to be competent in everything we do, but it's unreasonable to *expect* it. Sure, it would be nice to be able to serve and volley like a tennis pro, but most of us haven't the time or natural ability to perfect the game. Demanding perfection prevents us from going out on the court on weekends and batting the ball back and forth just for fun. Belief number 5 is a prescription for perpetual emotional upheaval. Beliefs numbers 7 and 9 lead to feelings of helplessness and demoralization. Sure, Ellis might say, childhood experiences can explain the origins of irrational beliefs, but it is our own cognitive appraisal—here and now—that causes us to be miserable.

Research findings support the connections between irrational beliefs (for example, excessive dependence on social approval and perfectionism) and feelings of anxiety and depression (Blatt, 1995). Perfectionists are also more likely than other people to commit suicide when they are depressed (Pilkonis, 1996). Later in the chapter we will see that combating irrational beliefs may reduce stress.

TYPE A BEHAVIOR Some people create stress for themselves through the **Type A behavior** pattern. Type A people are highly driven, competitive, impatient, and aggressive (Thoresen & Powell, 1992). They feel rushed and under pressure all the time and keep one eye constantly on the clock. They are not only prompt for appointments but often early. They eat, walk, and talk rapidly and become restless when others work slowly. They attempt to dominate group discussions. Type A people find it difficult to give up control or share power. They are often reluctant to delegate authority in the workplace, and because of this they increase their own workloads. Type A people criticize themselves mercilessly when they fail at a task (Moser & Dyck, 1989). They even seek out negative information about themselves in order to improve themselves (Cooney & Zeichner, 1985).

Type A people find it difficult just to go out on the tennis court and bat the ball back and forth. They watch their form, perfect their strokes, and demand continual self-improvement. They hold to the irrational belief that they must be perfectly competent and achieving in everything they undertake.

Type B people, in contrast, relax more readily and focus more on the quality of life. They are less ambitious and less impatient, and they pace themselves. Type A people earn higher grades and more money than Type B's of equal intelligence. Type A people also seek greater challenges than Type B's (Ortega & Pipal, 1984).

Are you a Type A person? The nearby questionnaire should afford you some insight into the matter.

• *Psychological Moderators of Stress*

There is no one-to-one relationship between the amount of stress we undergo and the physical illnesses or psychological distress we experience. Physical factors account for some of the variability in our responses: Some people inherit predispositions toward specific disorders. Psychological factors also play a role, however (Holahan & Moos, 1990). They can influence, or *moderate,* the effects of stress. In this section we discuss several psychological moderators of stress:

Type A Behavior. The Type A behavior pattern is characterized by a sense of time urgency, competitiveness, and hostility.

self-efficacy expectations, psychological hardiness, a sense of humor, predictability, and social support.

SELF-EFFICACY EXPECTATIONS: "THE LITTLE ENGINE THAT COULD"

Our **self-efficacy expectations** affect our ability to withstand stress (Basic Behavioral Science Task Force, 1996a). For example, when we are faced with fear-inducing objects, high self-efficacy expectations are accompanied by relatively *lower* levels of adrenaline and noradrenaline in the bloodstream (Bandura and others, 1985). Adrenaline is secreted when we are under stress. It arouses the body in several ways, such as accelerating the heart rate and releasing glucose from the liver. As a result, we may have "butterflies in the stomach" and feel nervous. Excessive arousal can impair our ability to manage stress by boosting our motivation beyond optimal levels and by distracting us from the tasks at hand. People with higher self-efficacy expectations thus have biological as well as psychological reasons for remaining calmer.

People who are self-confident are less prone to be disturbed by adverse events (Benight and others, 1997; Holahan & Moos, 1991). People with higher self-efficacy expectations are more likely to lose weight or quit smoking and less likely to relapse afterward (DiClemente and others, 1991). They are better able to function in spite of pain (Lackner and others, 1996).

People are more likely to comply with medical advice when they believe that it will work. Women, for example, are more likely to engage in breast self-examination when they believe that they will really be able to detect abnormal growths (Miller and others, 1996). People with diabetes are more likely to use insulin when they believe that it will help control their blood sugar level (Brownlee-Duffeck and others, 1987). People are more likely to try to quit smoking when they believe that they can do so successfully (Mischel & Shoda, 1995).

PSYCHOLOGICAL HARDINESS

Psychological hardiness also helps people resist stress. Our understanding of this phenomenon is derived largely from the

SELF-EFFICACY EXPECTATIONS • Our beliefs that we can bring about desired changes through our own efforts.
PSYCHOLOGICAL HARDINESS • A cluster of traits that buffer stress and are characterized by commitment, challenge, and control.

Are You Type A or Type B?

Complete the questionnaire by placing a check mark under Yes if the behavior pattern described is typical of you and under No if it is not. Try to work rapidly and leave no items blank.

Then read the section on Type A behavior and turn to the scoring key in Appendix B. ▪

DO YOU: **YES NO**

1. Strongly accent key words in your everyday speech? ____ ____

2. Eat and walk quickly? ____ ____

3. Believe that children should be taught to be competitive? ____ ____

4. Feel restless when watching a slow worker? ____ ____

5. Hurry other people to get on with what they're trying to say? ____ ____

6. Find it highly aggravating to be stuck in traffic or waiting for a seat at a restaurant? ____ ____

7. Continue to think about your own problems and business even when listening to someone else? ____ ____

8. Try to eat and shave, or drive and jot down notes at the same time? ____ ____

9. Catch up on your work while on vacations? ____ ____

10. Bring conversations around to topics of concern to you? ____ ____

11. Feel guilty when you spend time just relaxing? ____ ____

12. Find that you're so wrapped up in your work that you no longer notice office decorations or the scenery when you commute? ____ ____

13. Find yourself concerned with getting more *things* rather than developing your creativity and social concerns? ____ ____

14. Try to schedule more and more activities into less time? ____ ____

15. Always appear for appointments on time? ____ ____

16. Clench or pound your fists or use other gestures to emphasize your views? ____ ____

17. Credit your accomplishments to your ability to work rapidly? ____ ____

18. Feel that things must be done *now* and quickly? ____ ____

19. Constantly try to find more efficient ways to get things done? ____ ____

20. Insist on winning at games rather than just having fun? ____ ____

21. Interrupt others often? ____ ____

22. Feel irritated when others are late? ____ ____

23. Leave the table immediately after eating? ____ ____

24. Feel rushed? ____ ____

25. Feel dissatisfied with your current level of performance? ____ ____

pioneering work of Suzanne Kobasa and her colleagues (1994). They studied business executives who seemed able to resist illness despite stress. In one phase of the research, executives completed a battery of psychological tests. Kobasa (1990) found that the psychologically hardy executives had three important characteristics:

1. They were high in *commitment.* They tended to involve themselves in, rather than feel alienated from, whatever they were doing or encountering.

2. They were high in *challenge.* They believed that change, rather than stability, is normal in life. They appraised change as an interesting incentive to personal growth, not as a threat to security.

3. They were high in perceived *control* over their lives. They felt and behaved as though they were influential, rather than helpless, in facing the various rewards and punishments of life. Psychologically hardy people tend to have what Julian B. Rotter (1990) terms an internal **locus of control.**

Hardy people are more resistant to stress because they *choose* to face it (Kobasa, 1990). They also interpret stress as making life more interesting. For example, they see a conference with a supervisor as an opportunity to persuade the supervisor rather than as a risk to their positions.

A sense of control is essential to psychological hardiness. You may wish to complete the nearby questionnaire to see whether you feel that you are in charge of your own life.

SENSE OF HUMOR: "A MERRY HEART DOETH GOOD LIKE A MEDICINE" The idea that humor lightens the burdens of life and helps people cope with stress has been with us for millennia (Lefcourt & Martin, 1986). Consider the biblical maxim "A merry heart doeth good like a medicine" (Proverbs 17:22).

In *Anatomy of an Illness,* Norman Cousins (1979) reported his bout with a painful collagen illness that is similar to arthritis. He found that ten minutes of belly laughter of the sort he experienced while watching Marx Brothers movies relieved much of his pain. Laughter allowed him to sleep. It may also have reduced the inflammation he suffered. This is consistent with some findings that emotional responses such as happiness and anger may have beneficial effects on the immune system (Kemeny, 1993).

Research has also shown that humor can moderate the effects of stress. In one study, students completed a checklist of negative life events and a measure of mood disturbance (Martin & Lefcourt, 1983). The measure of mood disturbance also yielded a stress score. The students also rated their sense of humor. Behavioral assessments were made of their ability to produce humor under stress. Overall, there was a significant relationship between negative life events and stress scores: High accumulations of negative life events predicted higher levels of stress. However, students who had a greater sense of humor and produced humor in difficult situations were less affected by negative life events than other students. In other studies, Lefcourt (1997) found that watching humorous videotapes raised the level of immunoglobin A (a measure of the functioning of the immune system) in students' saliva.

PREDICTABILITY The ability to predict a stressor apparently moderates its impact. Predictability allows us to brace ourselves for the inevitable and, in many cases, plan ways of coping with it. There is also a relationship between the

Self-Efficacy Expectations and Performance. Outstanding athletes like figure skater Michelle Kwan tend to have high self-efficacy expectations. That is, they believe in themselves. These expectations moderate the amount of stress that affects us.

Truth or Fiction Revisited

It is true that a sense of humor can moderate the impact of stress. In an experiment run by Martin and Lefcourt, humor was shown to serve as a buffer against stress.

LOCUS OF CONTROL • The place (locus) to which an individual attributes control over the receiving of reinforcers— either inside or outside the self.

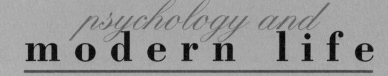

ALLEVIATING THE TYPE A BEHAVIOR PATTERN

Type A behavior is identified by a sense of time urgency, hostility, and hard-driving, self-destructive behavior patterns. Meyer Friedman (one of the originators of the Type A concept) and Diane Ulmer (1984) reported on some of the results of the San Francisco Recurrent Coronary Prevention Project. The project was designed to help Type A people who had heart attacks modify their behavior in order to avert future attacks. After three years, subjects who were placed in a treatment group in which they learned to reduce Type A behavior patterns had only one-third as many recurrent heart attacks as subjects who were placed in a control group.

The three broad guidelines were alleviating the sense of time urgency, hostility, and self-destructive tendencies. Subjects were also counseled to give up smoking, eat a low-fat diet, and establish a peaceful environment. The buffering effects of a sense of humor were noted, too.

ALLEVIATING YOUR SENSE OF TIME URGENCY Stop driving yourself—get out and walk. Too often we jump out of bed to the sound of an abrasive alarm, hop into a shower, fight crowds of commuters, and arrive at class or work with no time to spare. Then we become involved in our hectic day. For Type A people, the day begins urgently and never lets up.

The first step in coping with a sense of time urgency is confronting and replacing the beliefs that support it. Friedman and Ulmer (1984) note that Type A individuals tend to harbor the following beliefs:

1. "My sense of time urgency has helped me gain social and economic success" (p. 179). *According to Friedman and Ulmer, the idea that impatience and irritation contribute to success is absurd.*

2. "I can't do anything about it" (p. 182). The belief that we cannot change ourselves is self-defeating and irrational, as noted by Albert Ellis. *Even in late adulthood old habits can be discarded and new habits can be acquired.*

Friedman and Ulmer (1984) also use exercises to help combat the sense of time urgency. Here is a sample:

1. Engage in more social activities with family and friends.

2. Spend a few minutes each day recalling events from the distant past. Check old photos of family and friends.

3. Read books—literature, drama, politics, biographies, science, nature, science fiction (not books on business or on climbing the corporate ladder!).

4. Visit museums and art galleries for their aesthetic value—not to speculate about the prices of paintings.

5. Go to the movies, the ballet, and the theater.

6. Write letters to family and friends.

7. Take a course in art or begin violin or piano lessons.

8. Remind yourself each day that life is by nature unfinished and you do not need (and should not want) to have all your projects finished by a given date.

9. Ask a family member what he or she did that day and actually listen to the answer.

Psychologist Richard Suinn (1982, 1995) adds the following suggestions for alleviating the sense of time urgency:

10. Get a nice-sounding alarm clock!

11. Move about slowly as you wake up. Stretch.

12. Drive more slowly.

13. Don't wolf down lunch. Make it an occasion to rest or chat with friends.

14. Don't tumble words out. Speak more slowly. Interrupt less frequently.

15. Get up earlier to sit and relax, watch the morning news with a cup of tea, or meditate. This may mean going to bed earlier.

16. Leave home earlier and take a more scenic route to work or school. Avoid rush hour traffic.

Coping With the Type A Sense of Time Urgency. The San Francisco Recurrent Coronary Prevention Project has helped Type A heart attack victims modify their behavior so as to avert future attacks. Type A individuals are taught to alleviate their sense of time urgency and their hostility.

17. Don't carpool with last-minute rushers. Drive with a group that leaves earlier, or use public transportation.

18. Have a snack or relax at school or work before the "day" begins.

19. Don't do two things at once. Avoid scheduling too many classes or appointments back to back.

20. Use breaks to read, exercise, or meditate.

21. Space chores. Why try to have the car repaired, work, shop, and drive a friend to the airport all in one day?

22. Allow unessential work to go undone until the next day.

23. Set aside some time for yourself: for music, a hot bath, exercise, relaxation. (If your life will not permit this, get a new life.)

ALLEVIATING HOSTILITY Friedman and Ulmer (1984) note that hostility, like time urgency, is supported by a number of irrational beliefs. It is up to us to recognize our irrational beliefs and replace them with new beliefs. Irrational beliefs that support hostility include the following:

1. "I need a certain amount of hostility to get ahead in the world" (p. 222). *Becoming readily irritated, aggravated, and angered does not contribute to getting ahead.*

2. "I can't do anything about my hostility" (p. 222). *Is any comment necessary here?*

3. "Other people tend to be ignorant and inept" (p. 223). *Surely some of them are, but the world is what it is.* Ellis points out that we just expose ourselves to irritation by demanding that other people be what they are not.

4. "I don't believe I can ever feel at ease with doubt and uncertainty" (p. 225). *There are ambiguities in life. Certain things are unpredictable. Becoming irritated doesn't make things less uncertain.*

5. "Giving and receiving love is a sign of weakness" (p. 228). *This belief is rugged individualism carried to the extreme. It can isolate us from social support.*

Friedman and Ulmer (1984) offer other suggestions as well:

1. Tell your spouse and children that you love them.

2. Make some new friends.

3. Let friends know that you stand ready to help them.

4. Get a pet. (And take care of it!)

5. Don't talk to another person about subjects on which you know that the two of you hold divergent opinions.

6. When other people do things that fall short of your expectations, consider situational factors such as level of education or cultural background that might affect their behavior. Don't assume that they intend to get you upset.

7. Look for the beauty and joy in things.

8. Stop cursing so much.

9. Express appreciation for the help and encouragement of others.

10. Play to lose, at least some of the time. (Ouch?)

11. Say a cheerful "Good morning."

12. Look at your face in the mirror at various times during the day. Search for signs of irritation and anger and ask yourself if you need to look like that. ■

Social Support. Simply doing things together, even shopping, is a simple way of giving and receiving social support.

desire to assume control over one's situation and the usefulness of information about impending stressors (Lazarus & Folkman, 1984). Predictability is of greater benefit to "internals"—that is, to people who wish to exercise control over their situations—than to "externals." People who want information about medical procedures and what they will experience cope better with pain when they undergo those procedures (Ludwick-Rosenthal & Neufeld, 1993).

SOCIAL SUPPORT Social support also seems to act as a buffer against the effects of stress (Burman & Margolin, 1992; Uchino and others, 1996).

Sources of social support include the following:

1. *Emotional concern*—listening to people's problems and expressing feelings of sympathy, caring, understanding, and reassurance.
2. *Instrumental aid*—the material supports and services that facilitate adaptive behavior. For example, after a disaster the government may arrange for low-interest loans so that survivors can rebuild. Relief organizations may provide foodstuffs, medicines, and temporary living quarters.
3. *Information*—guidance and advice that enhances people's ability to cope.
4. *Appraisal*—feedback from others about how one is doing. This kind of support involves helping people interpret, or "make sense of," what has happened to them.
5. *Socializing*—simple conversation, recreation, even going shopping with another person. Socializing has beneficial effects, even when it is not oriented specifically toward solving problems.

Research supports the value of social support. Introverts, people who lack social skills, and people who live by themselves seem more prone to developing

GENERAL ADAPTATION SYNDROME • Selye's term for a hypothesized three-stage response to stress. Abbreviated *GAS*.

ALARM REACTION • The first stage of the GAS, which is triggered by the impact of a stressor and characterized by sympathetic activity.

FIGHT-OR-FLIGHT REACTION • An innate adaptive response to the perception of danger.

infectious diseases such as colds under stress (Cohen & Williamson, 1991; Gilbert, 1997). Social support helps people cope with the stresses of cancer and other health problems (Azar, 1996b; Wilcox and others, 1994). People find caring for persons with Alzheimer's disease less stressful when they have social support (Haley and others, 1996). People who have buddies who help them start exercising or quit drinking or smoking are more likely to succeed (Gruder and others, 1993; Nides and others, 1995). Social support helped children cope with the stresses of Hurricane Andrew (Vernberg and others, 1996). It appears to protect people from feelings of depression and to aid in recovery from depression (Holahan and others, 1995; Lewinsohn and others, 1994b). It has been found to help women cope with the aftermath of rape (Valenteiner and others, 1996). Stress is also less likely to lead to high blood pressure or alcohol abuse in people who have social support (Linden and others, 1993).

• *The General Adaptation Syndrome*

How can stress make us ill? Hans Selye suggested that under stress the body is like a clock with an alarm system that does not shut off until its energy has been depleted.

Selye (1976) observed that the body's response to different stressors shows certain similarities whether the stressor is a bacterial invasion, perceived danger, or a major life change. For this reason, he labeled this response the **general adaptation syndrome (GAS)**. The GAS consists of three stages: an alarm reaction, a resistance stage, and an exhaustion stage.

THE ALARM REACTION The **alarm reaction** is triggered by perception of a stressor. This reaction mobilizes or arouses the body in preparation for defense. Early in the century, physiologist Walter Cannon termed this alarm system the **fight-or-flight reaction.** The alarm reaction involves a number of body changes

Are Their Alarm Systems Going Off as They Take Out a Loan? The alarm reaction of the general adaptation syndrome can be triggered by daily hassles and life changes—such as taking out a large loan—as well as by physical threats. When the stressor persists, diseases of adaptation may develop.

THE LOCUS OF CONTROL SCALE

Psychologically hardy people tend to have an internal locus of control. They believe that they are in control of their own lives. In contrast, people with an external locus of control tend to see their fate as being out of their hands.

Are you "internal" or "external"? To learn more about your perception of your locus of control, respond to this questionnaire, which was developed by Nowicki and Strickland (1973). Place a check mark in either the Yes or the No column for each question. When you are finished, turn to the answer key in Appendix B. ■

		YES	NO
1.	Do you believe that most problems will solve themselves if you just don't fool with them?		
2.	Do you believe that you can stop yourself from catching a cold?		
3.	Are some people just born lucky?		
4.	Most of the time, do you feel that getting good grades meant a great deal to you?		
5.	Are you often blamed for things that just aren't your fault?		
6.	Do you believe that if somebody studies hard enough he or she can pass any subject?		
7.	Do you feel that most of the time it doesn't pay to try hard because things never turn out right anyway?		
8.	Do you feel that if things start out well in the morning, it's going to be a good day no matter what you do?		
9.	Do you feel that most of the time parents listen to what their children have to say?		
10.	Do you believe that wishing can make good things happen?		
11.	When you get punished, does it usually seem it's for no good reason at all?		
12.	Most of the time, do you find it hard to change a friend's opinion?		
13.	Do you think cheering more than luck helps a team win?		
14.	Did you feel that it was nearly impossible to change your parents' minds about anything?		
15.	Do you believe that parents should allow children to make most of their own decisions?		
16.	Do you feel that when you do something wrong there's very little you can do to make it right?		
17.	Do you believe that most people are just born good at sports?		
18.	Are most other people your age stronger than you are?		
19.	Do you feel that one of the best ways to handle most problems is just not to think about them?		
20.	Do you feel that you have a lot of choice in deciding who your friends are?		
21.	If you find a four-leaf clover, do you believe that it might bring you good luck?		
22.	Did you often feel that whether or not you did your homework had much to do with what kind of grades you got?		
23.	Do you feel that when a person your age is angry with you, there's little you can do to stop him or her?		
24.	Have you ever had a good luck charm?		
25.	Do you believe that whether or not people like you depends on how you act?		
26.	Did your parents usually help you if you if you asked them to?		
27.	Have you ever felt that when people were angry with you, it was usually for no reason at all?		
28.	Most of the time, do you feel that you can change what might happen tomorrow by what you did today?		
29.	Do you believe that when bad things are going to happen they are just going to happen no matter what you try to do to stop them?		
30.	Do you think that people can get their own way if they just keep trying?		
31.	Most of the time, do you find it useless to try to get your own way at home?		
32.	Do you feel that when good things happen, they happen because of hard work?		
33.	Do you feel that when somebody your age wants to be your enemy there's little you can do to change matters?		
34.	Do you feel that it's easy to get friends to do what you want them to do?		
35.	Do you usually feel that you have little to say about what you get to eat at home?		
36.	Do you feel that when someone doesn't like you, there's little you can do about it?		
37.	Did you usually feel it was almost useless to try in school, because most other children were just plain smarter than you were?		
38.	Are you the kind of person who believes that planning ahead makes things turn out better?		
39.	Most of the time, do you feel that you have little to say about what your family decides to do?		
40.	Do you think it's better to be smart than to be lucky?		

that are initiated by the brain and further regulated by the endocrine system and the sympathetic division of the autonomic nervous system (ANS) (Gallucci and others, 1993). Let us consider the roles of these systems.

Stress has a domino effect on the endocrine system (Figure 14.3). The hypothalamus secretes corticotrophin-releasing hormone (CRH). CRH causes the pituitary gland to secrete adrenocorticotrophic hormone (ACTH). ACTH then causes the adrenal cortex to secrete cortisol and other corticosteroids (steroidal hormones produced by the adrenal cortex). Corticosteroids help protect the body by combating allergic reactions (such as difficulty breathing) and producing inflammation. Inflammation increases circulation to parts of the body that are injured. It ferries in hordes of white blood cells to fend off invading pathogens.

Two other hormones that play a major role in the alarm reaction are secreted by the adrenal medulla. The sympathetic division of the ANS activates the adrenal medulla, causing it to release a mixture of adrenaline and noradrenaline. This mixture arouses the body by accelerating the heart rate and causing the liver to release glucose (sugar). This provides the energy that fuels the fight-or-flight reaction, which activates the body so that it is prepared to fight or flee from a predator.

The fight-or-flight reaction stems from a period in human prehistory when many stressors were life-threatening. It was triggered by the sight of a predator at the edge of a thicket or by a sudden rustling in the undergrowth. Today it may be aroused when you are caught in stop-and-go traffic or learn that your mortgage payments are going to increase. Once the threat is removed, the body returns to a lower state of arousal. Many of the bodily changes that occur in the alarm reaction are outlined in Table 14.3.

FIGURE 14.3

STRESS AND THE ENDOCRINE SYSTEM

Stress has a domino effect on the endocrine system, leading to the release of corticosteroids and a mixture of adrenaline and noradrenaline. Corticosteroids combat allergic reactions (such as difficulty in breathing) and cause inflammation. Adrenaline and noradrenaline arouse the body to cope by accelerating the heart rate and providing energy for the fight-or-flight reaction.

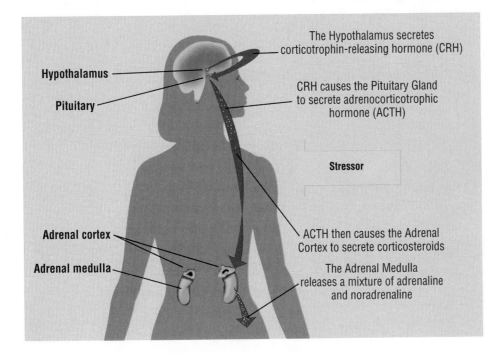

TABLE 14.3 COMPONENTS OF THE ALARM REACTION	
Corticosteroids are secreted	Muscles tense
Adrenaline is secreted	Blood shifts from internal organs to the skeletal musculature
Noradrenaline is secreted	Digestion is inhibited
Respiration rate increases	Sugar is released from the liver
Heart rate increases	Blood coagulability increases
Blood pressure increases	

The alarm reaction is triggered by various types of stressors. It is defined by the release of corticosteroids and adrenaline and by activity of the sympathetic branch of the autonomic nervous system. It prepares the body to fight or flee from a source of danger.

THE RESISTANCE STAGE If the alarm reaction mobilizes the body and the stressor is not removed, we enter the adaptation or **resistance stage** of the GAS. Levels of endocrine and sympathetic activity are lower than in the alarm reaction but still higher than normal. In this stage the body attempts to restore lost energy and repair bodily damage.

THE EXHAUSTION STAGE If the stressor is still not dealt with adequately, we may enter the **exhaustion stage** of the GAS. Individual capacities for resisting stress vary, but anyone will eventually become exhausted when stress continues indefinitely. The muscles become fatigued. The body is depleted of the resources required for combating stress. With exhaustion, the parasympathetic division of the ANS may predominate. As a result, our heartbeat and respiration rate slow down and many aspects of sympathetic activity are reversed. It might sound as if we would profit from the respite, but remember that we are still under stress—possibly an external threat. Continued stress in the exhaustion stage may lead to what Selye terms "diseases of adaptation." These are connected with constriction of blood vessels and alternation of the heart rhythm, and can range from allergies and hives to ulcers and coronary heart disease—and, ultimately, death.

Let us now consider the effects of stress on the body's immune system. Our discussion will pave the way for understanding the links between various psychological factors and physical illnesses.

• *Effects of Stress on the Immune System*

Research shows that stress suppresses the **immune system** (Coe, 1993; Delahanty and others, 1996; O'Leary, 1990). Psychological factors such as feelings of control and social support moderate these effects (Gilbert, 1997).

RESISTANCE STAGE • The second stage of the GAS, characterized by prolonged sympathetic activity in an effort to restore lost energy and repair damage. Also called the *adaptation stage*.
EXHAUSTION STAGE • The third stage of the GAS, characterized by weakened resistance and possible deterioration.
IMMUNE SYSTEM • (im-YOON). The system of the body that recognizes and destroys foreign agents (antigens) that invade the body.
LEUKOCYTES • (LOO-coe-sites). White blood cells. (Derived from the Greek words *leukos,* meaning "white," and *kytos,* literally meaning "a hollow" but used to refer to cells.)

THE IMMUNE SYSTEM Given the complexity of the human body and the fast pace of scientific change, we often feel that we are dependent on trained professionals to cope with illness. Yet we actually do most of this coping by ourselves, by means of the immune system.

The immune system has several functions that combat disease. One of these is the production of white blood cells, which engulf and kill pathogens such as bacteria, fungi, and viruses as well as worn-out body cells and even cancerous cells. The technical term for white blood cells is **leukocytes** (Figure 14.4). Leukocytes carry on microscopic warfare. They engage in search-and-destroy missions in which they "recognize" and eradicate foreign agents and unhealthy cells.

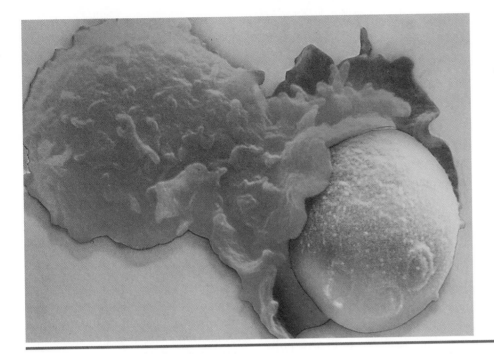

FIGURE 14.4

MICROSCOPIC WARFARE

The immune system helps us to combat disease. It produces white blood cells (leukocytes), such as that shown here, which routinely engulf and kill pathogens like bacteria and viruses.

Leukocytes recognize foreign substances by their shapes. These substances are also termed **antigens** because the body reacts to them by generating specialized proteins, or **antibodies.** Antibodies attach themselves to the foreign substances, deactivating them and marking them for destruction. The immune system "remembers" how to battle antigens by maintaining their antibodies in the bloodstream, often for years.[1]

Inflammation is another function of the immune system. When injury occurs, blood vessels in the area first contract (to stem bleeding) and then dilate. Dilation increases the flow of blood to the damaged area, causing the redness and warmth that characterize inflammation. The increased blood supply also floods the region with white blood cells to combat invading microscopic life forms such as bacteria, which otherwise might use the local damage as a port of entry into the body.

STRESS AND THE IMMUNE SYSTEM Psychologists, biologists, and medical researchers have combined their efforts in a field of study that addresses the relationships among psychological factors, the nervous system, the endocrine system, the immune system, and disease. This field is called **psychoneuroimmunology.** One of its major concerns is the effect of stress on the immune system.

One of the reasons that stress eventually exhausts us is that it stimulates the production of steroids. Steroids suppress the functioning of the immune system. Suppression has negligible effects when steroids are secreted intermittently. However, persistent secretion of steroids decreases inflammation and interferes with the formation of antibodies. As a consequence, we become more vulnerable to various illnesses, including the common cold (Cohen and others, 1993).

Truth or Fiction Revisited

It is true that countless microscopic warriors within our bodies are carrying out search-and-destroy missions against foreign agents at any given moment. The warriors are the white blood cells of the immune system.

ANTIGEN • (ANT-tee-jenn *or* ANT-eye-jenn). A substance that stimulates the body to mount an immune system response to it. (The contraction for *antibody generator.*)
ANTIBODIES • Substances formed by white blood cells that recognize and destroy antigens.
INFLAMMATION • (IN-flam-MAY-shun). Increased blood flow to an injured area of the body, resulting in redness, warmth, and an increased supply of white blood cells.
PSYCHONEUROIMMUNOLOGY • (sigh-coe-new-row-im-you-NOLL-oh-gee). The field that studies the relationships between psychological factors (e.g., attitudes and overt behavior patterns) and the functioning of the immune system.

[1] Vaccination is the introduction of a weakened form of an antigen (usually a bacteria or a virus) into the body to stimulate the production of antibodies. Antibodies can confer immunity for many years, in some cases for a lifetime. Smallpox has been eradicated by means of vaccination.

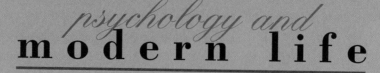
COPING WITH STRESS

What do these things have in common: (1) telling yourself that you can live with another person's disappointment, (2) taking a deep breath and telling yourself to relax, (3) taking the scenic route to work, and (4) jogging for half an hour? These are all methods suggested by psychologists to help people cope with the stresses of modern life.

Stress takes many forms and can harm our psychological well-being and physical health. Here we will highlight ways of coping with stress: controlling irrational thoughts, lowering arousal, modifying the Type A behavior pattern, and exercising.

CONTROLLING IRRATIONAL THOUGHTS
People often feel pressure from their own thoughts. Consider the following experiences:

1. You have difficulty with the first item on a test and become convinced that you will flunk.

2. You want to express your genuine feelings but think that if you do so you might make another person angry or upset.

3. You haven't been able to get to sleep for 15 minutes and assume that you will lie awake all night and feel "wrecked" in the morning.

4. You're not sure what decision to make, so you try to put the problem out of your mind by going out, playing cards, or watching TV.

5. You decide not to play tennis because your form isn't perfect

and you're in less than perfect condition.

If you have had these or similar experiences, it may be because you harbor some of the irrational beliefs identified by Albert Ellis (see pages 521–522). These beliefs may make you overly concerned about the approval of others (item 2 in the preceding list) or perfectionistic (item 5). They may lead you to think that you can solve problems by pretending that they do not exist (item 4) or that a minor setback will invariably lead to greater problems (items 1 and 3).

How, then, do we change irrational thoughts? The answer is deceptively simple: We just change them. However, this may require work. Moreover, before we can change our thoughts we must become aware of them.

THREE STEPS FOR CONTROLLING IRRATIONAL THOUGHTS
Meichenbaum and Jaremko (1983) suggest a three-step procedure for controlling the irrational or catastrophizing thoughts that often accompany feelings of anxiety, conflict, or tension:

1. Develop awareness of these thoughts through careful self-

TABLE 14.4 CONTROLLING IRRATIONAL BELIEFS AND THOUGHTS

Irrational Thoughts	*Incompatible (Coping) Thoughts*
"Oh my God, I'm going to completely lose control!"	"This is painful and upsetting, but I don't have to go to pieces over it."
"This will never end."	"This will end even if it's hard to see the end right now."
"It'll be awful if Mom gives me that look again."	"It's more pleasant when Mom's happy with me, but I can live with it if she isn't."
"How can I go out there? I'll look like a fool."	"So you're not perfect. That doesn't mean that you're going to look stupid. And so what if someone thinks you look stupid? You can live with that, too. Just stop worrying and have some fun."
"My heart's going to leap out of my chest! How much can I stand?"	"Easy—hearts don't leap out of chests. Stop and think! Distract yourself. Breathe slowly, in and out."
"What can I do? There's nothing I can do!"	"Easy—stop and think. Just because you can't think of a solution right now doesn't mean there's nothing you can do. Take it a minute at a time. Breathe easy."

Do irrational beliefs or catastrophizing thoughts compound the stress you experience? Cognitive psychologists suggest that you can cope with stress by becoming aware of your self-defeating beliefs and thoughts and replacing them with rational, calming beliefs and thoughts.

examination. Study the examples at the beginning of this section or in Table 14.4 to see if they apply to you. (Also carefully read Ellis's list of irrational beliefs on pages 521–522 and ask yourself whether any of them governs your behavior.) When you encounter anxiety or frustration, pay close attention to your thoughts. Are they guiding you toward a solution, or are they compounding your problems?

2. Prepare thoughts that are incompatible with the irrational or catastrophizing thoughts and practice saying them firmly to yourself. (If nobody is nearby, why not say them firmly aloud?)

3. Reward yourself with a mental pat on the back for making effective changes in your beliefs and thought patterns.

LOWERING AROUSAL Stress tends to trigger intense activity in the sympathetic branch of the autonomic nervous system—in other words, arousal. Arousal is a sign that something may be wrong. It is a message telling us to survey the situation and take appropriate action. But once we are aware that a stressor is acting upon us and have developed a plan to cope with it, it is no longer helpful to have blood pounding fiercely through our arteries. Psychologists and other scientists have developed many methods for teaching people to reduce arousal. These include meditation, biofeedback (both discussed in Chapter 6), and progressive relaxation.

Meditation seems to focus on the cognitive components of a stress reaction. Biofeedback can be directed at various physiological functions, such as heart rate and muscle tension. Progressive relaxation focuses on reducing muscle tension. All three methods reduce arousal, enhance self-efficacy expectations, and promote an internal locus of control.

PROGRESSIVE RELAXATION In progressive relaxation, people purposefully tense a particular muscle group before relaxing it. This sequence allows them to develop awareness of their muscle tensions and also to differentiate between feelings of tension and relaxation.

Progressive relaxation lowers the arousal produced by the alarm reaction. It has been found to be useful for stress-related illnesses ranging from headaches (Blanchard and others, 1990a) to hypertension (Agras and others, 1983). You can experience muscle relaxation in the arms by doing the following exercise:

Settle down in a reclining chair, dim the lights, and loosen any tight clothing. Use the instructions given below. They can be memorized (slight variations from the text are all right), recorded and played back, or read aloud by a friend. For instructions about relaxation of the entire body, consult a psychologist or other helping professional who is familiar with the technique.

Settle back as comfortably as you can. Let yourself relax to the best of your ability. . . . Now, as you relax like that, clench your right fist, just clench your fist tighter and tighter, and study the tension as you do so. Keep it clenched and feel the tension in your right fist, hand, forearm . . . and now relax. Let the fingers of your right hand become loose, and observe the contrast in your feelings. . . . Now, let yourself go and try to become more relaxed all over. . . . Once more, clench your right fist really tight . . . hold it, and notice the tension again. . . . Now let go, relax; your fingers straighten out, and you notice the difference once more. . . . Now repeat that with your left fist. Clench your left fist while the rest of your body relaxes; clench that fist tighter and feel the tension . . . and now relax. Again enjoy the contrast. . . . Repeat that once more, clench the left fist, tight and tense. . . . Now do the opposite of tension—relax and feel the difference. Continue relaxing like that for a while. . . . Clench both fists tighter and together, both fists tense, forearms tense, study the sensations . . . and relax; straighten out your fingers and feel that relaxation. Continue relaxing your hands and forearms more and more. . . . Now bend your elbows and tense your biceps, tense them harder and study the tension feelings . . . all right, straighten out your arms, let them relax and feel that difference again. Let the relaxation develop. . . . Once more, tense your biceps; hold the tension and observe it carefully. . . . Straighten the arms and relax; relax to the best of your ability. . . . Each time, pay close attention to your feelings when you tense up and when you relax. Now straighten your arms, straighten them so that you feel most tension in the triceps muscles along the back of your arms; stretch your arms and feel that tension. . . . And

(continued)

now relax. Get your arms back into a comfortable position. Let the relaxation proceed on its own. The arms should feel comfortably heavy as you allow them to relax. . . . Straighten the arms once more so that you feel the tension in the triceps muscles; straighten them. Feel that tension . . . and relax. Now let's concentrate on pure relaxation in the arms without any tension. Get your arms comfortable and let them relax further and further. Continue relaxing your arms even further. Even when your arms seem fully relaxed, try to go that extra bit further; try to achieve deeper and deeper levels of relaxation. (Wolpe & Lazarus, 1966, p. 177)

Together, reducing arousal and controlling irrational thoughts lessen the impact of the stressor. These methods give you a chance to develop a plan for effective action. When effective action is not possible, controlling your thoughts and your level of arousal can enhance your capacity to tolerate discomfort.

EXERCISING: RUN FOR YOUR LIFE?

> I *like long walks, especially when they are taken by people who annoy me.*
>
> FRED ALLEN

Exercise, particularly aerobic exercise, not only fosters physical health but can also enhance our psychological well-being and help in coping with stress (Hays, 1995). *Aerobic exercise* refers to exercise that requires a sustained increase in consumption of oxygen. Aerobic exercise promotes cardiovascular fitness. Aerobic exercises include, but are not limited to, running and jogging, running in place, walking (at more than a leisurely pace), aerobic dancing, jumping rope, swimming, bicycle riding, basketball, racquetball, and cross-country skiing.

Anaerobic exercises, in contrast, involve short bursts of muscle activity. Examples of anaerobic exercises are weight training, calisthenics (which usually allow rest periods between exercises), and sports such as baseball, in which there are infrequent bursts of strenuous activity. Anaerobic exercises can strengthen muscles and improve flexibility.

PHYSIOLOGICAL BENEFITS OF EXERCISE

The major physiological effect of exercise is greater fitness. Fitness includes muscle strength; muscle endurance; suppleness or flexibility; cardiorespiratory, or aerobic, fitness; and a higher ratio of muscle to fat (usually due to both building muscle and reducing fat). Cardiovascular fitness, or "condition," means that the body can use more oxygen during vigorous activity and pump more blood with each heartbeat. Because conditioned athletes' hearts pump more blood with each beat, they usually have a slower pulse rate—that is, fewer heartbeats per minute. However, during aerobic exercise they may double or triple their resting heart rate for minutes at a time.

Sustained physical activity does more than promote fitness. It also reduces the risk of heart attacks (Castelli, 1994; Curfman, 1993a). In one research program, Paffenbarger and his colleagues (1986, 1993) have been tracking some 17,000 Harvard University alumni by means of university records and questionnaires. They have correlated the incidence of heart attacks in this group with their levels of physical activity. As shown in Figure 14.5, the incidence of heart attacks declines as physical activity rises to a level at which about 2,000 calories are used per week—the equivalent of jogging about 20 miles a week. Inactive alumni have the highest risk of heart attacks. Alumni who burn at least 2,000 calories a week through exercise live 2 years longer, on the average, than their less active counterparts.

Truth or Fiction Revisited

It is true that people who exercise regularly live 2 years longer, on the average, than their sedentary counterparts.

Of course, there is an important limitation to Paffenbarger's research: It is correlational, not experimental. It is possible that people who are in better health *choose* to engage in higher levels of physical activity. If such is the case, then their lower incidence of heart attacks and their lower mortality rates would be attributable to their initial superior health, not to their physical activity.

Aerobic exercise raises blood levels of high-density lipoproteins (HDL, or "good cholesterol") (Castelli, 1994; Curfman, 1993b). HDL lowers the amount of low-density lipoproteins (LDL, or "bad cholesterol") in the blood. This is another way in which exercise may reduce the risk of heart attacks.

PSYCHOLOGICAL BENEFITS OF EXERCISE

Psychologists are keenly interested in

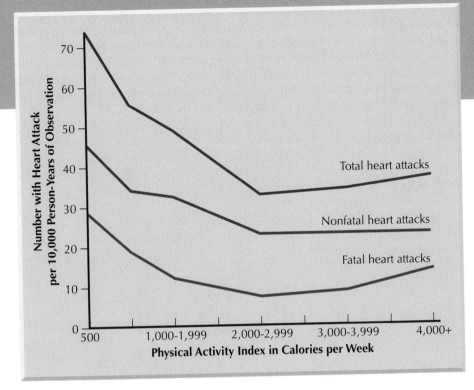

FIGURE 14.5

HEART ATTACKS AND PHYSICAL ACTIVITY

Paffenbarger and his colleagues have correlated the incidence of heart attacks with level of physical activity among 17,000 Harvard alumni. The incidence of heart attacks declines as the activity level rises to burning about 2,000 calories a week by means of physical activity. Above 2,000 calories a week, however, the incidence of heart attacks begins to climb gradually again, although not steeply.

the effects of exercise on psychological variables. Articles have appeared on exercise as "therapy"—for example, "running therapy."

Consider depression. Depression is characterized by inactivity and feelings of helplessness. Exercise is, in a sense, the opposite of inactivity. Exercise might also help alleviate feelings of helplessness. In one experiment, McCann and Holmes (1984) randomly assigned mildly depressed college women to aerobic exercise, progressive relaxation, and a no-treatment control group. The relaxation group showed some improvement, but aerobic exercise dramatically reduced students' depression. Other experiments also find that exercise alleviates feelings of depression, at least among mildly and moderately depressed individuals (Buffone, 1984; Greist, 1984; Norvell & Belles, 1993). Exercise has also been shown to decrease anxiety and hostility and to boost self-esteem (Norvell & Belles, 1993).

GETTING STARTED How about you? Are you thinking of climbing onto the exercise bandwagon? If so, consider these suggestions:

1. Unless you have engaged in sustained and vigorous exercise recently, seek the advice of a medical expert. If you smoke, have a family history of heart disease, are overweight, or are over 40, get a stress test.

2. Consider joining a beginner's aerobics class. Group leaders are not usually experts in physiology, but at least they "know the steps." You'll also be among other beginners and derive the benefits of social support.

3. Get the proper equipment to facilitate performance and avert injury.

4. Read up on the activity you are considering. Books, magazines, and newspaper articles will give you ideas as to how to get started and how fast to progress.

5. Try to select activities that you can sustain for a lifetime. Don't worry about building yourself up rapidly. Enjoy yourself. Your strength and endurance will progress on their own. If you do not enjoy what you're doing, you're not likely to stick to it.

6. If you feel severe pain, don't try to exercise "through" it. Soreness is to be expected for beginners (and for old-timers now and then). In that sense, soreness, at least when it is intermittent, is normal. But sharp pain is abnormal and a sign that something is wrong.

7. Have fun! ∎

In one study, dental students showed lower immune system functioning, as measured by lower levels of antibodies in their saliva, during stressful periods of the school year than immediately following vacations (Jemmott and others, 1983). In contrast, social support buffers the effects of stress and enhances the functioning of the immune system (Gilbert, 1997; Uchino and others, 1996). In the Jemmott study, students who had many friends showed less suppression of immune system functioning than students with few friends.

Other studies have shown that the stress of exams depresses the immune system's response to the Epstein-Barr virus, which causes fatigue and other problems (Glaser and others, 1991, 1993). Here too, students who were lonely showed greater suppression of the immune system than students who had more social support. A study of older people found that a combination of relaxation training, which decreases sympathetic nervous system activity, and training in coping skills *improves* the functioning of the immune system (Glaser and others, 1991). Moreover, psychological methods that reduce stress and anxiety in cancer patients may prolong their survival by boosting the functioning of their immune system (Azar, 1996c).

REFLECTIONS

- What kinds of life changes and daily hassles are you experiencing? Do you find these events stressful? How do you know?
- What kinds of conflict, if any, are you involved in? What are you doing to resolve them?
- Are you a Type A person? Explain your answer.
- Agree or disagree, and support your answer: "It is better not to know about bad things that are going to happen."

■ A MULTIFACTORIAL APPROACH TO HEALTH AND ILLNESS

Why do people become ill? Why do some people develop cancer? Why do others have heart attacks? Why do still others seem to be immune to these illnesses? Why do some of us seem to come down with everything that is going around, while others ride out the roughest winters without a sniffle? There is no single, simple answer to these questions. The likelihood of contracting an illness—be it a case of the flu or a kind of cancer—can reflect the interaction of many factors (Coie and others, 1993; Stokols, 1992).

- *"An Opportunity to Keep Those Nasty Genes From Expressing Themselves"*

Biological factors such as pathogens, inoculations, injuries, age, gender, and a family history of disease may strike us as the most obvious causes of illness. Genetics, in particular, tempts some people to assume that there is little they can do about their health. But genes only create *predispositions* toward illness. As Jane Brody (1995b) notes, predispositions "need a conducive environment in which to express themselves. A bad family medical history should not be considered a portent of doom. Rather, it should be welcomed as an opportunity to keep those nasty genes from expressing themselves."

As shown in Table 14.5, psychological, social, technological, and natural environmental factors also play key roles in health and illness. Many health prob-

					Natural Environmental
Biological	**Personality**	**Behavioral**	**Sociocultural**	**Technological**	**Natural Environmental**
Family history of illness	Seeking (or avoiding) information about health risks and stressors	Diet (intake of calories, fats, fiber, vitamins, etc.)	Socioeconomic status	Adequacy of available health care	Natural disasters (earthquakes, floods, hurricanes, drought, extremes of temperature, tornados)
Exposure to infectious organisms (e.g., bacteria and viruses)	Self-efficacy expectations	Consumption of alcohol	Availability and use of social support vs. peer rejection or isolation	Vehicular safety	Radon
Functioning of the immune system	Psychological hardiness	Cigarette smoking	Family circumstances: social class, family size, conflict, disorganization	Architectural features (e.g., injury-resistant design, nontoxic construction materials, aesthetic design, air quality, noise insulation)	
Inoculations	Psychological conflict (approach-approach, avoidance-avoidance, approach-avoidance)	Level of physical activity	Social climate in the workplace, sexual harassment	Aesthetics of residential, workplace, and communal architecture and landscape architecture	
Medication history	Optimism or pessimism	Sleep patterns	Prejudice and discrimination	Water quality	
Congenital disabilities, birth complications	Attributional style (how one explains one's failures and health problems to oneself)	Safety practices (e.g., using seat belts; careful driving; practice of sexual abstinence, monogamy, or "safer sex"; adequate prenatal care)	Major life changes of a social nature, such as divorce or death of a spouse	Solid waste treatment and sanitation	
Physiological conditions (e.g., hypertension serum cholesterol level)	Health locus of control (belief that one is or is not in charge of one's own health)	Having or not having regular medical and dental checkups	Health-related cultural and religious beliefs and practices	Pollution	
Reactivity of the cardiovascular system to stress (e.g., "hot reactor")	Introversion/extraversion	Compliance with medical and dental advice	Major economic life changes, such as taking out a large mortgage or losing one's job	Radiation	
Pain and discomfort	Coronary-prone (Type A) personality	Interpersonal/social skills	Health promotion in the workplace or community	Global warming	
Age	Tendencies to express or hold in feelings of anger and frustration		Health-related legislation	Ozone depletion	
Gender	Depression/anxiety		Availability of health insurance		
Ethnicity (e.g., genetic vulnerability to Tay-Sachs disease or sickle cell disease)	Hostility/suspiciousness		Availability of transportation to health care facilities		

Note: This table incorporates elements from Coie and others (1993), Mischel & Shoda (1995), and Stokols (1992).

lems are affected by psychological factors, such as attitudes and behavior (Ader, 1993; Mischel & Shoda, 1995). As shown in Table 14.6, nearly 1 million deaths each year in the United States are preventable (National Center for Health Statistics, 1996). Stopping smoking, eating right, exercising, and controlling alcohol use would prevent nearly 80% of these. Psychological states such as anxiety and depression can impair the functioning of the immune system, rendering us more vulnerable to physical disorders (Esterling and others, 1993; Herbert & Cohen, 1993; Kemeny and others, 1994).

In this section we first focus on some of the sociocultural factors that are connected with health and illness, as reflected in human diversity. Then we discuss a number of health problems, including headaches, heart disease, and cancer. In each case we consider the interplay of biological, psychological, social, technological, and environmental factors. Although these are medical problems, we also explore ways in which psychologists have contributed to their treatment.

TABLE 14.6 ANNUAL PREVENTABLE DEATHS IN THE UNITED STATES

- Elimination of tobacco use could prevent 400,000 deaths each year from cancer, heart and lung diseases, and stroke.
- Improved diet and exercise could prevent 300,000 deaths from conditions like heart disease, stroke, diabetes, and cancer.
- Control of underage and excess drinking of alcohol could prevent 100,000 deaths from motor vehicle accidents, falls, drownings, and other alcohol-related injuries.
- Immunizations for infectious diseases could prevent up to 100,000 deaths.
- Safer sex or sexual abstinence could prevent 30,000 deaths from sexually transmitted diseases (STDs).

Other measures for preventing needless deaths include improved worker training and safety to prevent accidents in the workplace, wider screening for breast and cervical cancer, and control of high blood pressure and elevated blood cholesterol levels.

Psychology in a World of
DIVERSITY

Human Diversity and Health: Nations Within the Nation

Today we know more about the connections between behavior and health than ever before. The United States also has the resources to provide the most advanced health care in the world. But not all American take advantage of contemporary knowledge. Nor do all profit equally from the health care system. Health psychologists note, therefore, that from the perspective of health and health care we are many nations and not just one. Many factors influence whether people engage in good health practices or let themselves go. Many factors affect whether they act to prevent illness or succumb to it. As noted in Table 14.5, such factors include ethnicity, gender, level of education, and socioeconomic status.

ETHNICITY AND HEALTH The life expectancy of African Americans is seven years shorter than that of White Americans (Flack and others, 1995). It is unclear whether this difference is connected with ethnicity per se or with factors such as income (Angell, 1993) and level of education (Guralnik and others, 1993).

Because of lower socioeconomic status, African Americans have less access to health care than White Americans do (Flack and others, 1995; Penn and others, 1995). They are also more likely to live in unhealthful neighborhoods, eat high-fat diets, and smoke (Pappas and others, 1993).

African Americans also experience different treatment by medical practitioners. Even when they have the same medical conditions as White people, African Americans are less likely to receive treatments such as coronary artery bypass surgery, hip and knee replacements, kidney transplants, mammography, and flu shots (Geiger, 1996). Why? Various explanations have been offered, including cultural differences, patient preferences, and lack of information about health care. Another possible explanation, of course, is racism (Geiger, 1996).

Disproportionate numbers of deaths from AIDS occur within ethnic minority groups in the United States, predominantly among African Americans and

Hispanic Americans (Centers for Disease Control and Prevention, 1997). Only 12% of the U.S. population is African American, but African American men account for 31% of people with AIDS. African American women account for 55% of women with AIDS. Only 9% of the population is Hispanic American, but Hispanic American men account for 17% of the men with AIDS. Hispanic American women account for 20% of women with AIDS.

African Americans are five to seven times more likely than European Americans to have hypertension (Leary, 1991). However, African Americans are also more likely to suffer from hypertension than Black Africans are. Many health professionals thus infer that environmental factors found among many African Americans—such as stress, diet, and smoking—contribute to high blood pressure in people who are genetically vulnerable to it (Betancourt & López, 1993; Leary, 1991).

African Americans are more likely than White Americans to have heart attacks and to die from them (Becker and others, 1993). Early diagnosis and treatment might help decrease the racial gap (Ayanian, 1993). African Americans with heart disease are less likely than White Americans to obtain procedures such as bypass surgery, even when it appears that they would benefit equally from the procedure (Peterson and others, 1997).

African Americans are also more likely than White Americans to contract most forms of cancer. Possibly because of genetic factors, the incidence of lung cancer is significantly higher among African Americans than White Americans (Blakeslee, 1994; "Smoke Rises," 1993). Once they contract cancer, African Americans are more likely than White Americans to die from it (Andersen, 1992; Bal, 1992). The results for African Americans are connected with their lower socioeconomic status (Baquet and others, 1991).

Also consider some cultural differences in health. Death rates from cancer are higher in such nations as the Netherlands, Denmark, England, Canada, and—yes—the United States, where average rates of daily fat intake are high (Cohen, 1987). Death rates from cancer are much lower in such nations as Thailand, the Philippines, and Japan, where average daily fat intake is much lower. Don't assume that the difference is racial just because Thailand, the Philippines, and Japan are Asian nations! The diets of Japanese Americans are similar in fat content to those of other Americans—and so are their rates of death from cancer.

There are health care "overusers" and "underusers" among cultural groups. For example, Hispanic Americans visit physicians less often than African Americans and non-Hispanic White Americans do because of lack of health insurance, difficulty speaking English, misgivings about medical technology, and—for illegal aliens—fear of deportation (Ziv & Lo, 1995).

GENDER AND HEALTH   Also consider a few gender differences. Men are more likely than women to have coronary heart disease. Women are apparently "protected" by high levels of estrogen until menopause (Brody, 1993). After menopause, women are dramatically more likely to incur heart disease (although this can be counteracted by estrogen replacement therapy). Women are less likely than men to exercise (Cimons, 1996).

The gender of the physician can also make a difference. According to a study of more than 90,000 women, women whose internists or family practitioners are women are more likely to have screening for cancer (mammograms and Pap smears) than women whose internists or family practitioners are men (Lurie and others, 1993). It is unclear from this study, however, whether female physicians are more likely than their male counterparts to encourage women to seek preventive care, or whether women who choose female physicians are also more likely to seek preventive care. Other research shows that female physicians are more likely than male physicians to conduct breast examinations properly (Hall and others, 1990).

Men's life expectancy is seven years shorter, on the average, than women's. A survey of 1,500 physicians suggests that this difference is due, at least in part, to women's greater willingness to seek health care ("Doctors tie male mentality," 1995). Men often let symptoms go until a problem that could have been prevented or readily treated becomes serious or life-threatening.

HEALTH AND SOCIOECONOMIC STATUS: THE RICH GET RICHER AND THE POOR GET . . . SICKER? **Socioeconomic status (SES)** and health are intimately connected. Generally speaking, people with higher SES enjoy better health and lead longer lives (Leary, 1995). The question is *why*.

Consider three possibilities (Adler and others, 1994). One is that there is no causal connection between health and SES. Perhaps both SES and health reflect genetic factors. For example, "good genes" might lead both to good health and to high social standing. Second, poor health might lead to socioeconomic "drift" (that is, loss of social standing). Third, SES might affect biological functions that, in turn, influence health.

How might SES influence health? SES is defined in part in terms of education. That is, people who attain low levels of education are also likely to have low SES. Less well educated people are more likely to smoke (Winkleby and others, 1991), and smoking has been linked to many physical illnesses. People with lower SES are also less likely to exercise and more likely to be obese—both of which, again, are linked to poor health outcomes (Ford and others, 1991).

Anorexia and bulimia nervosa are uncommon among poor people, but obesity is most prevalent among the poor. The incidence of obesity is also greater in cultures that associate obesity with happiness and health—as is true of some Haitian and Puerto Rican groups. People living in poor urban neighborhoods are more likely to be obese because junk food is heavily promoted in those neighborhoods and many residents tend to eat as a way of coping with stress (Johnson and others, 1995; Myers and others, 1995).

Let us also not forget that poorer people also have less access to health care (Leary, 1995). The problem is compounded by the fact that people with low SES are less likely to be educated about the benefits of regular health checkups and early medical intervention when symptoms arise.

• *Headaches*

Headaches are among the most common stress-related physical ailments. Nearly 20% of people in the United States suffer from severe headaches.

MUSCLE TENSION HEADACHE The single most frequent kind of headache is the muscle tension headache. During the first two stages of the GAS we are likely to contract muscles in the shoulders, neck, forehead, and scalp. Persistent stress can lead to persistent contraction of these muscles, giving rise to muscle tension headaches. Psychological factors, such as the tendency to catastrophize negative events—that is, blow them out of proportion—can bring on a tension headache (Ukestad & Wittrock, 1996). Tension headaches usually come on gradually. They are most often characterized by dull, steady pain on both sides of the head and feelings of tightness or pressure.

MIGRAINE HEADACHE Most other headaches, including severe **migraine headaches,** are vascular in nature. That is, they stem from changes in the blood

---

Truth or Fiction Revisited

It is not true that poor people in the United States eat less than more affluent people. Obesity is actually most prevalent among the lowest socioeconomic groups. (This is not to deny the fact that some poor people in the United States cannot afford food.)

SOCIOECONOMIC STATUS • One's social and financial level, as indicated by measures such as income, level of education, and occupational status. Abbreviated *SES.*

MIGRAINE HEADACHES • (MY-grain). Throbbing headaches that are connected with changes in the supply of blood to the head.

supply to the head (Welch, 1993). There is often a warning "aura" that may include vision problems and perception of unusual odors. The attacks themselves are often accompanied by sensitivity to light, loss of appetite, nausea, vomiting, sensory and motor disturbances such as loss of balance, and changes in mood. The so-called common migraine headache is identified by sudden onset and throbbing on one side of the head. The so-called classic migraine is characterized by sensory and motor disturbances that precede the pain.

The origins of migraine headaches are not clearly understood. It is believed, however, that they can be induced by barometric pressure; pollen; certain drugs; monosodium glutamate (MSG), a chemical which is often used to enhance flavor; chocolate; aged cheese; beer, champagne, and red wine; and the hormonal changes connected with menstruation (Brody, 1992a). Type A behavior may also contribute to migraine headaches. In one study, 53% of people who had migraine headaches showed the Type A behavior pattern, compared with 23% of people who had muscle tension headaches (Rappaport and others, 1988).

Regardless of the source of the headache, we can unwittingly propel ourselves into a vicious cycle. Headache pain is a stressor that can lead us to increase, rather than relax, muscle tension in the neck, shoulders, scalp, and face.

TREATMENT Aspirin and ibuprofen are frequently used to decrease pain, including headache pain. They inhibit the production of the prostaglandins that help initiate transmission of pain messages to the brain. Drugs that affect the blood flow in the brain help many people with migraine (Welch, 1993). Behavioral methods can also help. Progressive relaxation focuses on decreasing muscle tension and has been shown to be highly effective in relieving muscle tension headaches (Blanchard, 1992a; Blanchard and others, 1990a, 1991). Biofeedback training that alters the flow of blood to the head has helped many people with migraine headaches (Blanchard and others, 1990b; Gauthier and others, 1994). People who are sensitive to MSG or red wine can request meals without MSG and switch to white wine.

When we encounter stress, why do some of us develop ulcers, others develop coronary heart disease, and still others suffer no physical problems? In the following sections we see that there may be an interaction between stress and certain biological and psychological differences between individuals.

• Coronary Heart Disease

Coronary heart disease (CHD) is the leading cause of death in the United States, most often from heart attacks (National Center for Health Statistics, 1996). Consider the risk factors for CHD:

1. *Family History.* People with a family history of CHD are more likely to develop the disease themselves (Marenberg and others, 1994).

2. *Physiological Conditions.* Obesity, high **serum cholesterol** levels (Keil and others, 1993; Rossouw and others, 1990; Stampfer and others, 1991), and **hypertension** are risk factors for CHD.

   About one American in five has hypertension, or abnormally high blood pressure (Leary, 1991). When high blood pressure has no identifiable cause, it is referred to as *essential hypertension.* This condition appears to have a genetic component (Caulfield and others, 1994). However, blood pressure also rises when we inhibit the expression of strong feelings or are angry or on guard against threats (Jorgensen and others, 1996; Suls and others, 1995). When we are under stress, we may believe that we can

SERUM CHOLESTEROL • (SEE-rum coe-LESS-ter-all). Cholesterol found in the blood.
HYPERTENSION • (HIGH-purr-TEN-shun). High blood pressure.

feel our blood pressure "pounding through the roof," but this notion is usually false. Most people cannot recognize hypertension. Therefore it is important to have blood pressure checked regularly.

3. *Patterns of Consumption.* Patterns include heavy drinking, smoking, overeating, and eating food that is high in cholesterol, like saturated fats (Castelli, 1994; Jeffery, 1991).

4. *Type A Behavior.* Most studies suggest that there is at least a modest relationship between Type A behavior and CHD (Thoresen & Powell, 1992). It also seems that alleviating Type A behavior patterns may reduce the risk of *recurrent* heart attacks (Friedman & Ulmer, 1984).

5. *Hostility and Holding in Feelings of Anger* (Miller and others, 1996; Powch & Houston, 1996).

6. *Job Strain.* Overtime work, assembly line labor, and exposure to conflicting demands can all contribute to CHD. High-strain work, which makes heavy demands on workers but gives them little personal control, puts workers at the highest risk (Karasek and others, 1982; Krantz and others, 1988). As shown in Figure 14.6, the work of waiters and waitresses may best fit this description.

7. *Chronic Fatigue and Chronic Emotional Strain.*

8. *Sudden Stressors.* For example, after the Los Angeles earthquake in 1994 there was an increased incidence of death from heart attacks in people with heart disease (Leor and others, 1996).

9. *A Physically Inactive Lifestyle* (Dubbert, 1992; Lakka and others, 1994).

REDUCING CHD THROUGH BEHAVIOR MODIFICATION   Once CHD has been diagnosed, a number of medical treatments, including surgery and medication, are available. However, people who have not had CHD (as well as those who have) can profit from behavior modification techniques designed to reduce the risk factors. These methods include:

1. *Stopping Smoking.* (See Chapter 6.)

2. *Weight Control.* (See Chapter 11.)

3. *Reducing Hypertension.* There is medication for reducing hypertension, but behavioral changes such as the following often do the trick: relaxation training (Agras and others, 1983), meditation (Benson and others, 1973), aerobic exercise (Danforth and others, 1990), eating more fruits and vegetables and less fat (Appel and others, 1997), and eating less salt.

4. *Lowering Low-Density Lipoprotein (Harmful) Serum Cholesterol.* Major methods involve exercise, medication, and cutting down on foods that are high in cholesterol and saturated fats (Castelli, 1994; Shepherd and others, 1995).

5. *Modifying Type A Behavior.* See the Psychology and Modern Life feature, "Alleviating the Type A Behavior Pattern."

6. *Exercise.* Sustained physical activity protects people from CHD (Castelli, 1994; Curfman, 1993b). If you haven't exercised for a while, check with your physician about getting started.

● *Cancer*

Cancer is the number one killer of women in the United States, and the number two killer of men (Andersen, 1996). Cancer is characterized by the development of abnormal, or mutant, cells that may take root anywhere in the body:

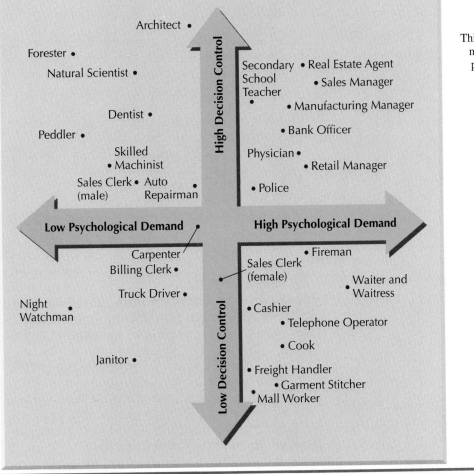

FIGURE 14.6
THE JOB-STRAIN MODEL
This model highlights the psychological demands made by various occupations and the amount of personal (decision) control they allow. Occupations characterized by high demand and low decision control place workers at greatest risk for heart disease.

in the blood, bones, digestive tract, lungs, and genital organs. If their spread is not controlled early, the cancerous cells may *metastasize*—that is, establish colonies elsewhere in the body. It appears that our bodies develop cancerous cells frequently. However, these are normally destroyed by the immune system. People whose immune system is damaged by physical or psychological factors are more likely to develop tumors (Azar, 1996b).

RISK FACTORS As with many other disorders, people can inherit a disposition toward cancer (Croyle and others, 1997; Lerman and others, 1997; Vernon and others, 1997). Carcinogenic genes may remove the brakes from cell division, allowing cells to multiply wildly. Or they may allow mutations to accumulate unchecked. However, many behavior patterns markedly heighten the risk for cancer. These include smoking, drinking alcohol (especially in women), eating animal fats, and sunbathing (which may cause skin cancer due to exposure to ultraviolet light). Agents in cigarette smoke, such as benzopyrene, may damage a gene that would otherwise block the development of many tumors, including lung cancer ("Damaged gene," 1996). Prolonged psychological conditions such as depression or stress may also heighten the risk of cancer (Azar, 1996b).

STRESS AND CANCER Researchers have uncovered links between stress and cancer (Azar, 1996b). For example, a study by Jacob and Charles (1980)

HEALTH PSYCHOLOGY IN THE 21ST CENTURY

During the 1980s, coronary-prone behavior received the lion's share of attention from researchers in health psychology. Although some observers questioned this emphasis, it now seems that it was extremely valuable. For example, the focus on coronary-prone behavior led to vastly increased understanding of the roles of stressors, cognitive appraisal, and personality factors (especially hostility) in CHD.

In the 1990s, AIDS became the focus of research in health psychology, and again some researchers wondered whether too much attention was being paid to this illness. Margaret A. Chesney (1993) argues that this focus is appropriate because AIDS has such a devastating effect on the lives of so many people. Moreover, the AIDS epidemic has pointed health psychology toward five trends that are likely to become even more prominent in the 21st century:

- *Early identification of people at risk for disease.* The experience of the AIDS epidemic is showing that health psychology needs to encourage early identification of people who are at risk for health problems. Risk for many disorders, such as cancer, is defined largely in terms of family history and patterns of consumption such as poor diet, smoking, and drinking alcohol. In the case of AIDS, however, risk is defined more in terms of behavior and mental processes—factors that place people at risk of being infected with the AIDS virus (HIV). Sociocultural considerations are also connected with risk. In the United States, for example, non-Hispanic White men are most likely to be infected with HIV through engaging in sex with male partners. African American men are equally likely to be infected through sex with other men and by injecting ("shooting up") drugs (Centers for Disease Control and Prevention, 1997). Throughout the world, however, sex between men and women is the most common way in which the virus is transmitted (Weniger & Brown, 1996).

- *Rising expectations for programs that encourage people to change high-risk behavior.* Health psychology needs to learn more about the planning and execution of programs that foster healthful behavioral changes. For example, most people in the United States have become generally aware of the threat and modes of transmission of HIV. Yet knowledge of danger alone apparently does not lead to necessary changes in sexual practices and injection of drugs (Klepinger and others, 1993; Rotheram-Borus and others, 1991). (Nor does knowledge of danger alone stop people from smoking or drinking to excess.)

- *Growing numbers of people who are coping with chronic diseases.* Health psychologists are developing more effective ways to help people cope with chronic diseases. Today more than 31 million Americans are age 65 or older. That number will increase to about 60 million by 2020. Almost four out of five people age 65 or older have at least one chronic condition such as heart disease, hypertension, arthritis, or declining cognitive functioning (Chesney, 1993). In addition to younger people who are at risk for serious illnesses like AIDS, the increasing numbers of older people will profit from better coping strategies that are being devised and tested today.

- *A shift toward inclusion of community and public health perspectives.* Psychology promotes the dignity of the individual, and health psychology has traditionally focused on the health of the individual. However, the AIDS epidemic has spurred health psychologists to also consider community and public health perspectives. Health psychologists, for example, are working with community psychologists to explore more effective ways of changing norms and values in the community at large. They are studying barriers to behavioral change among groups that are likely to engage in high-risk behavior.

- *The need to address health problems on a global scale.* There is increasing awareness that health psychology must address health problems on a global scale. Since chronic illnesses such as cancer and heart disease know no boundaries, it appears that the international perspective is here to stay. ∎

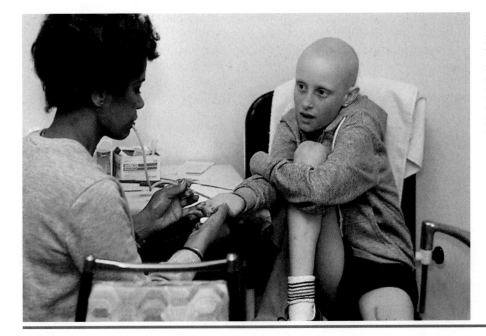

How Have Health Psychologists Helped This Youngster Cope With Cancer? Cancer is a medical disorder, but psychologists have contributed to the treatment of people with cancer. For example, psychologists help people with cancer remain in charge of their lives, combat feelings of hopelessness, manage stress, and cope with the side effects of chemotherapy.

revealed that a significant percentage of children with cancer had encountered severe life changes within a year of the diagnosis. These often involved the death of a loved one or the loss of a close relationship.

Experimental research that could not be conducted with humans has been carried out using rats and other animals. In one type of study, animals are injected with cancerous cells or with viruses that cause cancer and then exposed to various conditions. In this way researchers can determine which conditions influence the likelihood that the animals' immune systems will be able to fend off the disease. Such experiments suggest that once cancer has developed, stress can influence its course. In one study, for example, rats were implanted with small numbers of cancer cells so that their own immune systems would have a chance to combat them (Visintainer and others, 1982). Some of the rats were then exposed to inescapable shocks. Others were exposed to escapable shocks or to no shock. The rats that were exposed to the most stressful condition—the inescapable shock—were half as likely as the other rats to reject the cancer and twice as likely to die from it.

PSYCHOLOGICAL FACTORS IN THE TREATMENT OF CANCER People with cancer not only must cope with the biological aspects of their illnesses. They may also face a host of psychological problems. These include feelings of anxiety and depression about treatment methods and the eventual outcome, changes in body image after the removal of a breast or testicle, feelings of vulnerability, and family problems (Azar, 1996b). For example, some families criticize members with cancer for feeling sorry for themselves or not fighting the disease hard enough (Andersen and others, 1994; Rosenthal, 1993b). Psychological stress due to cancer can impair the immune system, setting the stage for more health problems, such as respiratory tract infections (Andersen and others, 1994).

There are also psychological treatments for the nausea that often accompanies chemotherapy. People undergoing chemotherapy who also obtain relaxation training and guided imagery techniques experience significantly less nausea and vomiting than patients who do not use these methods (Azar, 1996d). Studies with preteenagers and teenagers find that playing video games also reduces the discomfort of chemotherapy (Kolko & Rickard-Figueroa, 1985;

Redd and others, 1987). The children focus on battling computer-generated monsters rather than the effects of the drugs.

Of course, cancer is a medical disorder. However, health psychologists have improved the methods used to treat people with cancer. For example, a crisis like cancer can lead people to feel that life has spun out of control (Merluzzi & Martinez Sanchez, 1997). Control is a factor in psychological hardiness. A sense of loss of control can heighten stress and impair the immune system. Health psychology therefore stresses the value of encouraging people with cancer to remain in charge of their lives (Jacox and others, 1994).

Cancer requires medical treatment, and in many cases, there are few treatment options. However, people with cancer can still choose how they will deal

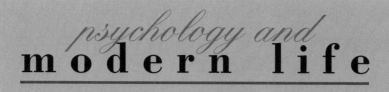

psychology and

modern life

REDUCING THE RISK OF BREAST CANCER

Why should we discuss reducing the risk of breast cancer in a psychology textbook? Because psychology is the study of behavior and mental processes, and your behavior and mental processes—especially your commitment to leading a healthier lifestyle—affect your risk of contracting breast cancer. Sure, there are factors you can do little or nothing about. These include early menarche, beginning menopause at a late age, having a mother or sister with breast cancer, and inheriting a gene that accounts for familial breast cancer (McTiernan, 1997). But then there are factors you can do a great deal about, including exercise, diet, alcohol, body weight, and smoking.

- *Exercise.* A Norwegian study followed 25,000 women for an average of 14 years (Thune and others, 1997). It was found that women who exercised about 4 hours per week reduced their risk of contracting breast cancer by 37%. Estrogen is connected with the incidence of breast

cancer, and exercise may help protect women from the disease by decreasing their estrogen production.

- *Diet.* A low-fat, high-fiber diet may reduce the risk of breast cancer by nearly 50% (Brody, 1997b). A diet high in fruits and vegetables also lowers the level of circulating estrogens. It is advisable to consume few saturated fats (found in meat and dairy products) and polyunsaturated fats (found in margarines and most vegetable oils), but mono-unsaturated fats like olive oil and canola oil may actually be protective.

- *Alcohol.* Drinking alcohol increases the risk of breast cancer. If you do drink, limit consumption to the equivalent of a glass of wine a day, which may protect against heart disease.

- *Body weight.* Abdominal fat produces estrogen, and women who put on extra pounds appear to increase their risk of breast cancer (McTiernan, 1997). Exercising and following the

dietary suggestions made above will also help women remain lean.

- *Smoking.* Carcinogens in cigarette smoke are factors in breast cancer as well as lung cancer. If you don't smoke, don't start. If you do smoke, cut down or quit. (See methods for doing so in Chapter 6.)

> ### Truth or Fiction Revisited
> ....
> *It is not true that women can do nothing to affect the risk of contracting breast cancer. Exercise, diet, drinking alcohol, and smoking all affect the risk of contracting breast cancer.*

In case you haven't noticed, these recommendations are useful for men as well as women. Following them will not only reduce the risk of breast cancer, but also the risk of heart disease, stroke, high blood pressure, diabetes, arthritis, osteoporosis, and other types of cancer—including lung cancer and colorectal cancer (Nevid and others, 1998). Go for it. ■

with the disease. A 10-year follow-up of women with breast cancer found a significantly higher survival rate for women who responded to their diagnosis with anger and a "fighting spirit" rather than with stoic acceptance (Pettingale and others, 1985). Desire to fight the illness is a key component of treatment. Emotional states like hostility, anxiety, even horror are all associated with increased rates of survival in people with breast cancer. Social support also apparently increases the survival rate (Sleek, 1995b).

Psychologists are teaching coping skills to people with cancer in order to relieve psychological distress as well as pain. Psychological methods such as relaxation training, meditation, biofeedback training, and exercise can all be of help (Lang & Patt, 1994). Coping skills are beneficial in themselves and help people with cancer regain a sense of control.

Yet another psychological application is helping people undergoing chemotherapy keep up their strength by eating. The problem is that chemotherapy often causes nausea. Nausea then becomes associated with foods eaten earlier in the day, causing taste aversions (Azar, 1996d). So people with cancer, who may already be losing weight because of their illness, may find that taste aversions aggravate the problems caused by lack of appetite. To combat these conditions, Bernstein (1996) recommends eating unusual ("scapegoat") foods prior to chemotherapy. If taste aversions develop, they are associated with the unusual food rather than with the patient's normal diet.

In sum, cancer is frightening, and in many cases, there may be little that can be done about its eventual outcome. However, we are not helpless in the face of cancer. We can take measures like the following:

1. Limit exposure to behavioral risk factors for cancer.

2. Modify diet by reducing intake of fats and increasing intake of fruits and vegetables (Mevkens, 1990). Tomatoes, broccoli, cauliflower, and cabbage appear to be especially helpful (Angier, 1994a; Brody, 1997a). (Yes, Grandma was right about veggies.)

3. Have regular medical checkups so that cancer will be detected early. Cancer is most treatable in the early stages.

4. Regulate exposure to stress.

5. If we are struck by cancer, we can fight it energetically rather than become passive victims.

We conclude this chapter with good news for readers of this book: *Better educated* people—that means *you*—are more likely to modify health-impairing behavior and reap the benefits of change (Angell, 1993; Guralnik and others, 1993; Pappas and others, 1993).

REFLECTIONS

- Agree or disagree, and support your answer: "Health is basically a matter of heredity or luck. People cannot really do much to improve their health or stave off illness."
- Consider your sociocultural background: What health problems are more common, or less common, among people of your background than among the U.S. population in general? Why do you think these problems are more common or less common among people of your background?
- Agree or disagree, and support your answer: "Some people can 'refuse' to become ill."

SUMMARY

1. **What is health psychology?** Health psychology studies the relationships between psychological factors and the prevention and treatment of physical illness.

2. **What is stress?** Stress is the demand made on an organism to adjust. Whereas some stress is desirable to keep us alert and occupied, too much stress can tax our adjustive capacities and contribute to physical illness.

3. **What are some sources of stress?** Sources of stress include daily hassles, life changes, conflict, irrational beliefs, and Type A behavior. Type A behavior is characterized by aggressiveness, time urgency, and competitiveness.

4. **What psychological factors moderate the impact of stress?** These include positive self-efficacy expectations, psychological hardiness, a sense of humor, predictability of stressors, and social support. Self-efficacy expectations encourage us to persist in difficult tasks and to endure discomfort. Psychological hardiness is characterized by commitment, challenge, and control.

5. **What is the general adaptation syndrome (GAS)?** The GAS is a body response that is triggered by the perception of a stressor. It consists of three stages: alarm, resistance, and exhaustion.

6. **What is the role of the endocrine system in the body's response to stress?** The hypothalamus and pituitary glands secrete hormones that stimulate the adrenal cortex to release corticosteroids. Corticosteroids help resist stress by fighting inflammation and allergic reactions. Adrenaline and noradrenaline are secreted by the adrenal medulla. Adrenaline arouses the body by activating the sympathetic nervous system.

7. **What is the role of the autonomic nervous system (ANS) in the body's response to stress?** The sympathetic division of the ANS is highly active during the alarm and resistance stages of the GAS. This activity is characterized by rapid heartbeat and respiration rate, release of stores of sugar, muscle tension, and other responses that deplete the body's supply of energy. The parasympathetic division of the ANS predominates during the exhaustion stage of the GAS. Its activity is characterized by responses such as digestive processes that help restore the body's reserves of energy.

8. **What are the functions of the immune system?** One function of the immune system is to engulf and kill pathogens, worn-out body cells, and cancerous cells. Another is to "remember" pathogens and combat them in the future. A third function is to facilitate inflammation, which increases the number of white blood cells brought to a damaged area.

9. **What are the effects of stress on the immune system?** By stimulating the release of corticosteroids, stress depresses the functioning of the immune system. (For example, steroids counter inflammation.)

10. **What kinds of headaches are there, and how are they related to stress?** The most common kinds are muscle tension headaches and migraine headaches. Stress causes headache pain by stimulating muscle tension.

11. **What are the risk factors for coronary heart disease?** They include family history; physiological conditions such as hypertension and high levels of serum cholesterol; behavior patterns such as heavy drinking, smoking, eating fatty foods, and Type A behavior; work overload; chronic tension and fatigue; and physical inactivity.

12. **What are the risk factors for cancer?** Risk factors for cancer include family history, smoking, drinking alcohol, eating animal fats, sunbathing, and stress.

13. **What behavioral measures contribute to the prevention and treatment of cancer?** The following measures can be helpful: controlling exposure to behavioral risk factors for cancer, having regular medical checkups, regulating exposure to stress, and vigorously fighting cancer if it develops.

To enhance your understanding of the psychological concepts found in this chapter, please consult the following aids:

Learning Objectives, p. 287
Exercise, p. 288
Lecture and Textbook Outline,
   p. 289
Effective Studying Ideas, p. 291

Key Terms and Concepts, p. 292
Chapter Review, p. 292
Knowing the Language, p. 299
Do You Know the Material?, p. 301

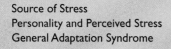

Source of Stress
Personality and Perceived Stress
General Adaptation Syndrome

Enhancing Health Through Lifestyle
Cancer

For more information concerning the topics found in this chapter, access psychology links on the World Wide Web through the Harcourt Brace webpage at

www.hbcollege.com

Share your comments and questions with your author at

PsychLinks@aol.com

Some psychological disorders are characterized by faulty perception of the outside world. In *Henriette's Yard* (1995), Beverly Buchanan recreates the South Carolina shacks of her impoverished childhood. The structures are askew and the colors overblown, as if emotions were ruling the intellect. Although some of Buchanan's work seems suggestive of psychological disorder, there is much—as Shakespeare might have put it—"method" in its "madness." What do you think she may be saying about the lives of the people who dwell in these shacks?

BEVERLY BUCHANAN

Chapter 15

Psychological Disorders

TRUTH OR FICTION?

✔ **T F**

☐ ☐ A man shot the president of the United States in front of millions of television witnesses, yet was found not guilty by a court of law.

☐ ☐ In the Middle Ages, innocent people were drowned to prove that they were not possessed by the Devil.

☐ ☐ It is abnormal to feel anxious.

☐ ☐ Some people have more than one identity, and the different identities may have varying allergies and eyeglass prescriptions.

☐ ☐ Wearing clean clothes and breathing clean air can alleviate feelings of depression.

☐ ☐ People who threaten suicide are only seeking attention.

☐ ☐ You can never be too rich or too thin.

☐ ☐ Some college women control their weight by going on cycles of binge eating and self-induced vomiting.

OUTLINE

WHAT ARE PSYCHOLOGICAL DIS-
ORDERS?
CLASSIFYING PSYCHOLOGICAL DIS-
ORDERS
Psychology in the New Millennium: Will
Your Problems Be Diagnosed by
Computer?
ANXIETY DISORDERS
Types of Anxiety Disorders
Theoretical Views
DISSOCIATIVE DISORDERS
Types of Dissociative Disorders
Theoretical Views
SOMATOFORM DISORDERS
MOOD DISORDERS
Types of Mood Disorders
Theoretical Views
Psychology in a World of Diversity:
The Case of Women and Depression
Psychology and Modern Life: Alleviating
Depression (Getting Out of the
Dumps)
Suicide
Psychology and Modern Life: Suicide
Prevention
SCHIZOPHRENIA
Types of Schizophrenia
Theoretical Views
PERSONALITY DISORDERS
Types of Personality Disorders
Theoretical Views
EATING DISORDERS
Types of Eating Disorders
Psychology in the New Millennium:
Will We Be Competing With
"Cyberbabes" and "Cyberhunks" in
the New Millennium?
Psychology in a World of Diversity:
Eating Disorders: Why the Gender
Gap?
Theoretical Views

Truth or Fiction Revisited
....
*It is true that a man shot the president of the
United States in front of millions of television
witnesses and was found not guilty by a court of
law. His name is John Hinckley, and he was
found not guilty by reason of insanity.*

*D*URING ONE LONG FALL SEMESTER, THE
Ohio State campus lived in terror. Four college women were abducted, forced to
cash checks or obtain money from automatic teller machines, and then raped. A
mysterious phone call led to the arrest of a 23-year-old drifter, William, who
had been dismissed from the Navy.

William was not the boy next door.

Psychologists and psychiatrists who interviewed William concluded that 10
personalities—8 male and 2 female—resided within him (Scott, 1994). His
personality had been "fractured" as a result of an abusive childhood. His various personalities displayed distinct facial expressions, speech patterns, and
memories. They even performed differently on psychological tests.

Arthur, the most rational personality, spoke with a British accent. Danny
and Christopher were quiet adolescents. Christine was a 3-year-old girl. It was
Tommy, a 16-year-old, who had enlisted in the Navy. Allen was 18 and smoked.
Adelena, a 19-year-old lesbian personality, had committed the rapes. Who had
made the mysterious phone call? Probably David, 9, an anxious child.

The defense claimed that William's behavior was caused by a psychological
disorder termed **dissociative identity disorder** (also referred to as **multiple personality disorder**). Several distinct identities or personalities dwelled within
him. Some of them were aware of the others. Some believed that they were
unique. Billy, the core identity, had learned to sleep as a child in order to avoid
his father's abuse. A psychiatrist asserted that Billy had also been "asleep," or in
a "psychological coma," during the abductions. Billy should therefore be found
not guilty by reason of **insanity.**

William was found not guilty. He was committed to a psychiatric institution
and released six years later.

In 1982, John Hinckley was also found not guilty of the assassination attempt on President Reagan's life. Expert witnesses testified that he should be
diagnosed with **schizophrenia.** Hinckley, too, was committed to a psychiatric institution.

Dissociative identity disorder and schizophrenia are two **psychological disorders.** If William and Hinckley had lived in Salem, Massachusetts, in 1692, just
200 years after Columbus set foot in the New World, they might have been
hanged or burned as witches. At that time, most people assumed that psychological disorders were caused by possession by the Devil. A score of people
were executed in Salem that year for allegedly practicing the arts of Satan.

Throughout human history people have attributed unusual behavior and
psychological disorders to demons. The ancient Greeks believed that the gods
punished humans by causing confusion and madness. An exception was the
physician Hippocrates, who made the radical suggestion that psychological

disorders are caused by an abnormality of the brain. The notion that biology could affect thoughts, feelings, and behavior was to lie dormant for about 2,000 years.

During the Middle Ages in Europe, as well as during the early period of European colonization of Massachusetts, it was generally believed that psychological disorders were signs of possession by the Devil. Possession could stem from retribution, in which God caused the Devil to possess a person's soul as punishment for committing certain kinds of sins. Agitation and confusion were ascribed to such retribution. Possession was also believed to result from deals with the Devil, in which people traded their souls for earthly gains. Such individuals were called witches. Witches were held responsible for unfortunate events ranging from a neighbor's infertility to a poor harvest. In Europe, as many as 500,000 accused witches were killed during the next two centuries (Hergenhahn, 1997). The goings on at Salem were trivial by comparison.

A document authorized by Pope Innocent VIII, *The Hammer of Witches*, proposed ingenious "diagnostic" tests to identify those who were possessed. The water-float test was based on the principle that pure metals sink to the bottom during smelting. Impurities float to the surface. Suspects were thus placed in deep water. Those who sank to the bottom and drowned were judged to be pure. Those who managed to keep their heads above water were assumed to be "impure" and in league with the Devil. Then they were in real trouble. This ordeal is the origin of the phrase, "Damned if you do and damned if you don't."

Few people in the United States today would argue that unusual or unacceptable behavior is caused by demons. Still, we continue to use phrases that are suggestive of demonology. How many times have you heard the expressions "Something got into me" or "The Devil made me do it"?

Let us now define what is meant by a psychological disorder.

WHAT ARE PSYCHOLOGICAL DISORDERS?

Psychology is the study of behavior and mental processes. Psychological disorders are behaviors or mental processes that are connected with various kinds of distress or disability. However, they are not predictable responses to specific events.

For example, some psychological disorders are characterized by anxiety, but many people are anxious now and then without being considered disordered. It is appropriate to be anxious before an important date or on the eve of a midterm exam. When, then, are feelings like anxiety deemed to be abnormal or signs of a psychological disorder? For one thing, anxiety may suggest a disorder when it is not appropriate to the situation. It is inappropriate to be anxious when entering an elevator or looking out of a fourth-story window. The magnitude of the problem may also suggest disorder. Some anxiety is usual before a job interview. However, feeling that your heart is pounding so intensely that it might leap out of your chest—and then avoiding the interview—are not usual.

Behavior or mental processes are suggestive of psychological disorders when they meet some combination of the following criteria:

1. *They are unusual.* Although people with psychological disorders are a minority, uncommon behavior or mental processes are not abnormal in themselves. Only one person holds the record for running or swimming the fastest mile. That person is different from you and me but is not abnormal. Only a few people qualify as geniuses in mathematics, but mathematical genius is not a sign of a psychological disorder.

Exorcism. This medieval woodcut represents the practice of exorcism, in which a demon is expelled from a person who has been "possessed."

Truth or Fiction Revisited

It is true that innocent people were drowned in the Middle Ages to prove that they were not possessed by the Devil. This method was based on a water-float test designed to determine whether metals are pure.

Truth or Fiction Revisited

It may not be abnormal to feel anxious. It is normal to feel anxious when one is in a stressful or fearful situation.

DISSOCIATIVE IDENTITY DISORDER • A disorder in which a person appears to have two or more distinct identities or personalities that may alternately emerge. (A term first used in DSM-IV.)
MULTIPLE PERSONALITY DISORDER • The previous DSM term for *dissociative identity disorder.*
INSANITY • A legal term descriptive of a person judged to be incapable of recognizing right from wrong or of conforming his or her behavior to the law.
SCHIZOPHRENIA • (skit-so-FREE-knee-uh). A psychotic disorder characterized by loss of control of thought processes and inappropriate emotional responses.
PSYCHOLOGICAL DISORDERS • Patterns of behavior or mental processes that are connected with emotional distress or significant impairment in functioning.

The Hammer of Witches

In 1484 Pope Innocent VIII authorized the persecution of witches. Two Dominican priests, Heinrich Kramer and James Sprenger, were named to act as inquisitors. To guide their work, Kramer and Sprenger wrote *The Hammer of Witches (Malleus Maleficarum)*. Over the next two centuries, this document was translated into many languages and went through 30 editions. It was found on the bench of nearly every judge in central Europe, Catholic and Protestant alike.

The *Hammer* "proved" the existence of witches, who were mainly women. It described—in detail—how witches engaged in sexual relations with male demons (*incubi*) and suggested ways of eliciting confessions through the use of hot irons and boiling water.

The *Hammer* was devastating on the subject of women:

"Since women are feebler both in mind and body, it is not surprising that they are more likely to come under the spell of witchcraft. . . . And it should be noted that there was a defect in the formation of the first woman, since she was formed from a bent rib, that is, a rib of the breast, which is bent as it were in a contrary direction to a man. And since through this defect she is an imperfect animal, she always deceives. . . . Therefore, a wicked woman is by her nature quicker to waver in her faith, and consequently quicker to forsake the faith, which is the root of witchcraft. . . . In conclusion: All witchcraft comes from carnal lust, which is insatiable in women." ■

Rarity or statistical deviance may not be sufficient for behavior or mental processes to be labeled abnormal, but it helps. Most people do not see or hear things that are not there, and "seeing things" and "hearing things" are considered abnormal. We must also consider the situation. Although many of us feel "panicked" when we realize that a term paper or report is due the next day, most of us do not have panic attacks "out of the blue." Unpredictable panic attacks thus are suggestive of psychological disorder.

2. *They suggest faulty perception or interpretation of reality.* Our society considers it normal to be inspired by religious beliefs but abnormal to believe that God is literally speaking to you. "Hearing voices" and "seeing things" are considered **hallucinations.** Similarly, **ideas of persecution,** such as believing that the Mafia or the FBI are "out to get you," are considered signs of disorder. (Unless, of course, they *are* out to get you.)

3. *They suggest severe personal distress.* Anxiety, exaggerated fears, and other psychological states cause personal distress, and severe personal distress may be considered abnormal. Anxiety may also be an appropriate response to a situation, however, as in the case of a threat.

4. *They are self-defeating.* Behavior or mental processes that cause misery rather than happiness and fulfillment may suggest psychological disorder. Chronic drinking that impairs work and family life and cigarette smoking that impairs health may therefore be deemed abnormal.

5. *They are dangerous.* Behavior or mental processes that are hazardous to the self or others may be considered suggestive of psychological disorders. People who threaten or attempt suicide may be considered abnormal, as may people who threaten or attack others. Yet criminal behavior or aggressive behavior in sports need not imply a psychological disorder.

6. *The individual's behavior is socially unacceptable.* We must consider the cultural context of a behavior pattern in judging whether or not it is normal. In the United States, it is deemed normal for males to be aggressive in sports and in combat. In other situations warmth and tenderness are valued. Many people in the United States admire women who are self-assertive, yet Hispanic American, Asian American, and "traditional" non-Hispanic White American groups may consider outspoken women to be disrespectful.

■ CLASSIFYING PSYCHOLOGICAL DISORDERS

Toss some people, apes, seaweed, fish, and sponges into a room—preferably a well ventilated one. Stir slightly. What do you have? It depends on how you classify this hodgepodge of organisms.

HALLUCINATION • (hal-LOOSE-sin-nay-shun). A perception in the absence of sensory stimulation that is confused with reality.
IDEAS OF PERSECUTION • Erroneous beliefs that one is being victimized or persecuted.

Hallucinations. Hallucinations are a feature of schizophrenia. They are perceptions that occur in the absence of external stimulation, as in "hearing voices" or "seeing things." Hallucinations cannot be distinguished from real perceptions. Are the cats in this Sandy Skoglund photograph real or hallucinatory?

Classify them as plants versus animals and you lump the people, chimpanzees, fish, and, yes, sponges together. Classify them as stuff that carries on its business on land or underwater, and we throw in our lot with the chimps and none of the others. How about those that swim and those that don't? Then the chimps, the fish, and some of us are grouped together.

Classification is at the heart of science (Barlow, 1991). Without classifying psychological disorders, investigators would not be able to communicate with each other and scientific progress would come to a standstill. The most widely used classification scheme for psychological disorders[1] is the *Diagnostic and Statistical Manual* (DSM) of the American Psychiatric Association. Psychologists are studying the possibility of creating alternatives to the DSM (Follette, 1996).

The current edition of the DSM—DSM-IV—uses a "multiaxial" system of assessment. It provides information about a person's overall functioning, not just a diagnosis. The axes are shown in Table 15.1. People may receive Axis I or Axis II diagnoses or a combination of the two.

Axis III, general medical conditions, lists physical disorders or problems that may affect people's functioning or their response to psychotherapy or drug treatment. Axis IV, psychosocial and environmental problems, includes difficulties that may affect the diagnosis, treatment, or outcome of a psychological disorder. Axis V, global assessment of functioning, allows the clinician to rate the client's current level of functioning and her or his highest level of functioning prior to the onset of the psychological disorder. The purpose is to help determine what kinds of psychological functioning are to be restored through therapy.

---

[1] The American Psychiatric Association refers to psychological disorders as *mental disorders*.

Will Your Problems Be Diagnosed by Computer?

Imagine yourself seated in a comfortable chair in a room with a computer as we enter the new millennium. The computer has powerful voice-recognition software and asks for your name. Not wanting to offend, you pronounce your name carefully. The computer says "Thank you" and prints your name on the screen. "Did I get it right?" the computer asks self-effacingly. "Yes," you respond. In the same way, you provide your address, telephone number, and PIN (personal identification number). The computer then says, "I'm now going to ask you some questions so that I can learn more about you. Whatever you tell me will be shared only with a psychologist who is bound by professional ethics to keep it confidential. May I begin?" Without thinking, you nod your head yes. "Do I take that for a yes?" the computer asks. You realize that you hadn't spoken aloud and that the computer's body language–recognition software picked up your head nod and is seeking confirmation. "Yes," you say again. "Let's get on with it."

This scenario presupposes that you have decided to seek help for some personal problems. The helping professional asked if you would have a dialogue with her computer as a way of learning more about your problems. Living in a world of computers, you assumed that the interaction would be worthwhile. So here you are.

Sound farfetched? Actually, primitive computers have been interviewing clients for more than 20 years. One current system is named CASPER, which stands for Computerized Assessment System for Psychotherapy Evaluation and Research. A CASPER interview covers a wide range of topics, such as age, income, family relations, social activities, sexual behavior, life satisfaction, and health problems. Questions and response options, such as the following, are shown on the screen:

> "About how many days in the past month did you have difficulty falling asleep, staying asleep, or waking too early (include sleep disturbed by bad dreams)?"

> "During the past month, how have you been getting along with your spouse/partner? (1) Very satisfactory; (2) Mostly satisfactory; (3) Sometimes satisfactory, sometimes unsatisfactory; (4) Mostly unsatisfactory; (5) Very unsatisfactory." (Farrell and others, 1987, p. 692)

The client presses a numeric keypad to respond. CASPER is a branching program that follows up on problems suggested by responses to earlier questions. If the client reports difficulty sleeping, CASPER delves into whether sleep has become a key problem—"something causing you great personal distress or interfering with your daily functioning" (Farrell and others, 1987, p. 693). If the client responds yes, the computer will investigate still more deeply. The program allows clients to add or drop complaints. That is, clients can change their minds.

Most clients respond favorably to a CASPER interview (Bloom, 1992; Farrell and others, 1987). It also appears that clients are willing to report a greater number of problems to CASPER than to a live clinician. Perhaps the computer helps identify problems that the client would be unwilling to report otherwise. Or perhaps the computer seems more willing to take the time needed to record complaints.

Computer diagnostic programs offer some advantages over traditional human interviewers (Farrell and others, 1987):

1. Computers can be programmed to ask specific sets of questions in a definite order. Clinicians sometimes omit important questions or allow the interview to veer off course into less critical issues.

2. Clients may be less disconcerted about reporting personal matters to a computer because computers do not respond emotionally or judgmentally.

3. Use of the computer for diagnosis frees clinicians to spend more time in providing direct clinical services.

As such programs become capable of handling vastly increased amounts of information, they are also likely to become more accurate at diagnosis and more capable of identifying unusual problems. They may also connect the client's complaints to similar cases in the literature, indicating what treatment has been most effective in the past. On the other hand, computerized interviews may not be for everyone. Research shows that younger, better-educated people who are experienced with computers react more favorably to computerized assessment (Spinhoven and others, 1993). ■

TABLE 15.1	**THE MULTIAXIAL CLASSIFICATION SYSTEM OF DSM-IV**	
Axis	**Type of Information**	**Description**
Axis I	Clinical Syndromes	Psychological disorders that impair functioning and are stressful to the individual (a wide range of diagnostic classes, such as substance-related disorders, anxiety disorders, mood disorders, schizophrenia, somatoform disorders, and dissociative disorders).
Axis II	Personality Disorders	Deeply ingrained, maladaptive ways of perceiving others and behaviors that are stressful to the individual or to persons who relate to that individual.
Axis III	General Medical Conditions	Chronic and acute illnesses, injuries, allergies, and so on, that affect functioning and treatment, such as cardiovascular disorders, athletic injuries, and allergies to certain medications.
Axis IV	Psychosocial and Environmental Problems	Stressors that occurred during the past year that may have contributed to the development of a new mental disorder or the recurrence of a prior disorder, or that may have exacerbated an existing disorder.
Axis V	Global Assessment of Functioning	Overall judgment of current functioning and the highest level of functioning in the past year according to psychological, social, and occupational criteria.

The DSM-IV groups disorders on the basis of observable features or symptoms. However, early editions of the DSM, which was first published in 1952, grouped many disorders on the basis of assumptions about their causes. Because Freud's psychodynamic theory was widely accepted at the time, one major diagnostic category contained so-called neuroses.[2] From the psychodynamic perspective, all neuroses—no matter how differently people with various neuroses might behave—were caused by unconscious neurotic conflict. Each neurosis was thought to reflect a way of coping with the unconscious fear that primitive impulses might break loose. As a result, sleepwalking was included as a neurosis (psychoanalysts assumed that sleepwalking reduced this unconscious fear by permitting the partial expression of impulses during the night). Now that the focus is on observable behaviors, sleepwalking is classified as a sleep disorder, not as a neurosis. I mention all this because the words *neurosis* and *neurotic* are still frequently used. Without some explanation, it might seem strange that they have been largely abandoned by professionals.

Some professionals, such as psychiatrist Thomas Szasz, believe that the categories described in the DSM are really "problems in living" rather than "disorders." At least, they are not disorders in the sense that high blood pressure, cancer, and the flu are disorders. Szasz argues that labeling people with problems in living as being "sick" degrades them and encourages them to evade their personal and social responsibilities. Since sick people are encouraged to obey doctors' orders, Szasz (1984) also contends that labeling people as "sick" accords too much power to health professionals. Instead, he believes, troubled people need to be encouraged to take greater responsibility for solving their own problems.

---

[2] The neuroses included what are today referred to as anxiety disorders, dissociative disorders, somatoform disorders, mild depression, and some other disorders, such as sleepwalking.

> ### REFLECTIONS
> - Do any of your friends or family members have psychological disorders? Do their behaviors or mental processes correspond to the criteria discussed in this section?
> - Do you believe that people who try to commit suicide are insane? Why or why not?
> - Had you heard of the term neurotic before reading this chapter? What had you imagined it to mean? What does it really mean?

■ ANXIETY DISORDERS

Anxiety is characterized by subjective and physical features (Zinbarg & Barlow, 1996). Subjective features include worrying, fear of the worst things happening, fear of losing control, nervousness, and inability to relax. Physical features reflect arousal of the sympathetic branch of the autonomic nervous system. They include trembling, sweating, a pounding or racing heart, elevated blood pressure (a flushed face), and faintness. Anxiety is an appropriate response to a real threat. It can be abnormal, however, when it is excessive or when it "comes out of the blue"—that is, when events do not seem to warrant it.

• *Types of Anxiety Disorders*

The anxiety disorders include phobias, panic disorder, generalized anxiety, obsessive-compulsive disorder, and stress disorders.

PHOBIAS   There are several types of phobias, including specific phobias, social phobia, and agoraphobia. **Specific phobias** are excessive, irrational fears of specific objects or situations such as snakes or heights. **Social phobias** are persistent fears of scrutiny by others or of doing something that will be humiliating or embarrassing. Fear of public speaking is a common social phobia.

One specific phobia is fear of elevators. Some people will not enter elevators despite the hardships they incur as a result (such as walking up six flights of steps). Yes, the cable *could* break. The ventilation *could* fail. One *could* be stuck in midair waiting for repairs. These problems are uncommon, however, and it does not make sense for most people to walk up and down several flights of stairs to elude them. Similarly, some people with a specific phobia for hypodermic needles will not have injections, even to treat profound illness. Injections can be painful, but most people with a phobia for needles would gladly suffer an even more painful pinch if it would help them fight illness. Other specific phobias include **claustrophobia** (fear of tight or enclosed places), **acrophobia** (fear of heights), and fear of mice, snakes, and other creepy-crawlies. Fears of animals and imaginary creatures are common among children.

Phobias can seriously disrupt a person's life. The person may know that the phobia is irrational yet still experience acute anxiety and avoid the phobic article or circumstance.

Agoraphobia is among the most widespread phobias among adults. Agoraphobia is derived from the Greek words meaning "fear of the marketplace," or fear of being out in open, busy areas. Persons with agoraphobia fear being in places from which it might be difficult to escape or in which help might not be available if they get upset. In practice, people who receive this diagnosis often refuse to venture out of their homes, especially by themselves. They find it difficult to hold a job or to maintain an ordinary social life.

SPECIFIC PHOBIA • Persistent fear of a specific object or situation.

SOCIAL PHOBIA • An irrational, excessive fear of public scrutiny.

CLAUSTROPHOBIA • (claws-troe-FOE-bee-uh). Fear of tight, small places.

ACROPHOBIA • (ack-row-FOE-bee-uh). Fear of high places.

AGORAPHOBIA • (ag-or-uh-FOE-bee-uh). Fear of open, crowded places.

PANIC DISORDER • The recurrent experiencing of attacks of extreme anxiety in the absence of external stimuli that usually elicit anxiety.

GENERALIZED ANXIETY DISORDER • Feelings of dread and foreboding and sympathetic arousal of at least 6 months' duration.

OBSESSION • A recurring thought or image that seems beyond control.

COMPULSION • An apparently irresistible urge to repeat an act or engage in ritualistic behavior such as hand washing.

POSTTRAUMATIC STRESS DISORDER • A disorder that follows a distressing event outside the range of normal human experience and that is characterized by features such as intense fear, avoidance of stimuli associated with the event, and reliving of the event. Abbreviated *PTSD*.

PANIC DISORDER

> My *heart would start pounding so hard I was sure I was having a heart attack. I used to go to the emergency room. Sometimes I felt dizzy, like I was going to pass out. I was sure I was about to die.*
>
> KIM WEINER

Panic disorder is an abrupt attack of acute anxiety that is not triggered by a specific object or situation. People with panic disorder have strong physical symptoms such as shortness of breath, heavy sweating, tremors, and pounding of the heart. Like Kim Weiner (1992), they are particularly aware of cardiac sensations (Schmidt and others, 1997). It is not unusual for them to think they are having a heart attack (Clark and others, 1997). Many fear suffocation (McNally & Eke, 1996). People with the disorder may also experience choking sensations; nausea; numbness or tingling; flushes or chills; and fear of going crazy or losing control. Panic attacks may last minutes or hours. Afterwards, the person usually feels drained.

Many people panic now and then. The diagnosis of panic disorder is reserved for those who undergo a series of attacks or live in fear of attacks.

Panic attacks seem to come from nowhere. Thus, some people who have had them stay home for fear of having an attack in public. They are diagnosed as having panic disorder with agoraphobia.

Panic Disorder. This man was overcome by feelings of panic as he was walking to his car. The physical aspects of panic attacks tend to be stronger than those of other kinds of anxiety. They include shortness of breath, dizziness, and pounding of the heart.

GENERALIZED ANXIETY DISORDER The central feature of **generalized anxiety disorder** is persistent anxiety. As with panic disorder, the anxiety cannot be attributed to a phobic object, situation, or activity. Rather, it seems to be free floating. Features of this disorder may include motor tension (shakiness, inability to relax, furrowed brow, fidgeting); autonomic overarousal (sweating, dry mouth, racing heart, light-headedness, frequent urinating, diarrhea); feelings of dread and foreboding; and excessive vigilance, as shown by irritability, insomnia, and a tendency to be easily distracted.

OBSESSIVE-COMPULSIVE DISORDER **Obsessions** are recurrent, anxiety-provoking thoughts or images that seem irrational and beyond control. They are so compelling and recurrent that they disrupt daily life. They may include doubts about whether one has locked the doors and shut the windows, or images such as one mother's repeated fantasy that her children had been run over on the way home from school. One woman became obsessed with the idea that she had contaminated her hands with Sani-Flush and that the chemicals were spreading to everything she touched. A 16-year-old boy found "numbers in his head" when he was about to study or take a test.

Compulsions are thoughts or behaviors that tend to reduce the anxiety connected with obsessions. They are seemingly irresistible urges to engage in specific acts, often repeatedly, such as elaborate washing after using the bathroom. The impulse is recurrent and forceful, interfering with daily life. The woman who felt contaminated by Sani-Flush spent 3 to 4 hours at the sink each day and complained, "My hands look like lobster claws."

POSTTRAUMATIC STRESS DISORDER Fires, stabbings, shootings, suicides, medical emergencies, accidents, bombs, and hazardous material explosions—these are just some of the traumatic experiences firefighters confront on a fairly regular basis. Because of such experiences, one study found that the prevalence of **posttraumatic stress disorder (PTSD)** among firefighters is 16.5%. This rate is 1% higher than the rate among Vietnam veterans and far above that for the general population, which is 1% to 3% (DeAngelis, 1995a).

A Traumatic Experience. Traumatic experiences like the destruction of one's home can lead to posttraumatic stress disorder (PTSD). PTSD is characterized by intrusive memories of the experience, recurrent dreams about it, and the sudden feeling that it is, in fact, recurring (as in "flashbacks").

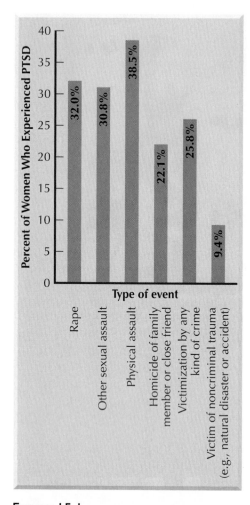

FIGURE 15.1

POSTTRAUMATIC STRESS DISORDER AMONG FEMALE VICTIMS OF CRIME AND AMONG OTHER WOMEN

According to Resnick and her colleagues (1993), about one woman in four (25.8%) who was victimized by crime could be diagnosed with PTSD at some point following the crime. By contrast, fewer than one woman in ten (9.4%) who was not victimized by crime experienced PTSD.

ACUTE STRESS DISORDER • A disorder, like PTSD, that is characterized by feelings of anxiety and helplessness and caused by a traumatic event. Unlike PTSD, acute stress disorder occurs within a month of the event and lasts from 2 days to 4 weeks. (A category first included in DSM-IV.)

PTSD is characterized by a rapid heart rate (Blanchard and others, 1996) and feelings of anxiety and helplessness that are caused by a traumatic experience. Such experiences may include a threat or assault, destruction of one's community, or witnessing a death. PTSD may occur months or years after the event. It frequently occurs among combat veterans, people whose homes and communities have been swept away by natural disasters or who have been subjected to toxic hazards, and survivors of childhood sexual abuse (Baum & Fleming, 1993; Rodriguez and others, 1997). A study of victims of Hurricane Andrew, which devastated South Florida in 1992, found that one man in four and about one woman in three (36%) had developed PTSD (Ironson, 1993). A national study of more than 4,000 women found that about one woman in four who had been victimized by crime experienced PTSD (Resnick and others, 1993; see Figure 15.1).

The traumatic event is revisited in the form of intrusive memories, recurrent dreams, and flashbacks—the sudden feeling that the event is recurring. People with PTSD typically try to avoid thoughts and activities connected to the traumatic event. They may also have sleep problems, irritable outbursts, difficulty concentrating, extreme vigilance, and an intensified "startle" response.

ACUTE STRESS DISORDER **Acute stress disorder,** like PTSD, is characterized by feelings of anxiety and helplessness that are caused by a traumatic event. However, PTSD can occur 6 months or more after the traumatic event and tends to persist. Acute stress disorder occurs within a month of the event and lasts from 2 days to 4 weeks. Women who have been raped, for example, experience acute distress that tends to peak in severity about 3 weeks after the assault (Davidson & Foa, 1991; Rothbaum and others, 1992).

• *Theoretical Views*

According to the psychodynamic perspective, phobias symbolize conflicts originating in childhood. Psychodynamic theory explains generalized anxiety as persistent difficulty in repressing primitive impulses. Obsessions are explained as leakage of unconscious impulses, and compulsions are seen as acts that allow people to keep such impulses partly repressed.

Some learning theorists consider phobias to be conditioned fears that were acquired in early childhood. Therefore, their origins are beyond memory. Avoidance of feared stimuli is reinforced by the reduction of anxiety.

Social-cognitive theorists note that observational learning plays a role in the acquisition of fears (Basic Behavioral Science Task Force, 1996b). If parents squirm, grimace, and shudder at the sight of mice, blood, or dirt on the kitchen floor, children might assume that these stimuli are awful and imitate their parents' behavior. Cognitive theorists suggest that anxiety is maintained by thinking that one is in a terrible situation and helpless to change it. People with anxiety disorders may be cognitively biased toward paying more attention to threats than other people do (Foa and others, 1996; Mineka, 1991). Psychoanalysts and learning theorists generally agree that compulsive behavior reduces anxiety.

Cognitive theorists note that people's appraisals of the magnitude of threats help determine whether they are traumatic and can lead to PTSD (Creamer and others, 1992). People with panic attacks tend to misinterpret bodily cues and to view them as threats (Meichenbaum, 1993). Obsessions and compulsions may serve to divert attention from more frightening issues, such as "What am I going to do with my life?" When anxieties are acquired at a young age, we may later interpret them as enduring traits and label ourselves as "people who fear _____" (you fill it in). We then live up to the labels. We also entertain thoughts that heighten and perpetuate anxiety such as "I've got to get out of here," or "My heart is going to leap out of my chest." Such ideas intensify physical signs of anxiety, disrupt planning, make stimuli seem worse than they really are, motivate avoidance, and decrease self-efficacy expectations. The belief that we will not be able to handle a threat heightens anxiety. The belief that we are in control reduces anxiety (Bandura and others, 1985).

Biological factors play a role in anxiety disorders. Genetic factors are implicated in most psychological disorders, including anxiety disorders (Carey & DiLalla, 1994). For one thing, anxiety disorders tend to run in families (Michels & Marzuk, 1993b). Twin studies also find a higher **concordance** rate for anxiety disorders among identical twins than among fraternal twins (Torgersen, 1983). Studies of adoptees who are anxious similarly show that the biological parent places the child at risk for anxiety and related traits (Pedersen and others, 1988).

Susan Mineka (1991) suggests that humans (and nonhuman primates) are genetically predisposed to respond with fear to stimuli that may have once posed a threat to their ancestors. Evolutionary forces would have favored the survival of individuals who were predisposed toward acquiring fears of large animals, spiders, snakes, heights, entrapment, sharp objects, and strangers.

Perhaps a predisposition toward anxiety—in the form of a highly reactive autonomic nervous system—can be inherited. What might make a nervous system "highly reactive"? In the case of panic disorder, faulty regulation of levels of serotonin and norepinephrine may be involved. In other anxiety disorders, receptor sites in the brain may not be sensitive enough to **gamma-aminobutyric acid (GABA),** an inhibitory neurotransmitter that may help calm anxiety reactions. The **benzodiazepines,** a class of drugs that reduce anxiety, may work by increasing the sensitivity of receptor sites to GABA. However, it is unlikely that GABA levels fully explain anxiety disorders (Michels & Marzuk, 1993a).

In many cases anxiety disorders may reflect the interaction of biological and psychological factors. In panic disorder, biological imbalances may initially trigger attacks. However, subsequent fear of attacks—and of the bodily cues that signal their onset—may heighten discomfort and give one the idea there is nothing one can do about them (McNally, 1990; Meichenbaum, 1993). Feelings of helplessness increase fear. People with panic disorder therefore can be helped by psychological methods that provide ways of reducing physical discomfort—including regular breathing—and show them that there are, after all, things they can do to cope with attacks (Klosko and others, 1990).

IN PROFILE

Little Hans

Do you want to talk about conflict? Do you want to talk about drama? Do you want to talk about raw, unnerving fear? Well, forget about aliens from outer space. Forget about income taxes and things that go bump in the night. For there, in turn of the century Vienna, that flourishing European capital of the arts, horses were biting people in the streets. Or so thought one petrified 5-year-old boy by the name of Hans.

In 1908 Hans's distraught father wrote to Sigmund Freud for advice. Freud psychoanalyzed Hans's fear of horses *by mail.* He went on to write one of his most famous case studies, "Analysis of a Phobia in a 5-Year-Old Boy." Freud concluded that the horses were symbols that represented Hans's father. Being bitten symbolized being castrated. In other words, Hans unconsciously feared that his father would castrate him. Why? Because Hans was his father's rival in a contest for the affection of his mother. Hans, that is, was in the throes of the Oedipus complex.

Freud's analysis has been criticized on many grounds. Historically speaking, however, the case of Little Hans laid much of the groundwork for the psychoanalytic belief that phobic objects symbolize unconscious conflicts that date from early childhood. ■

REFLECTIONS
- Have you ever felt anxious? Did your anxiety strike you as normal under the circumstances? Why or why not?
- Do you know anyone with a phobia? Does the phobia seriously interfere with his or her life? How?
- Do you ever find yourself "in a panic"? What is the difference between "being in a panic" and having a panic disorder?
- Do you know anyone who is obsessive-compulsive? Describe his or her behavior.

CONCORDANCE • (con-CORD-ants). Agreement.
GAMMA-AMINOBUTYRIC ACID (GABA) • (a-me-no-byoo-TIE-rick). An inhibitory neurotransmitter that is implicated in anxiety reactions.
BENZODIAZEPINES • (ben-zoe-die-AZZ-uh-peans). A class of drugs that reduce anxiety; minor tranquilizers.

■ DISSOCIATIVE DISORDERS

In the **dissociative disorders** there is a separation of mental processes such as thoughts, emotions, identity, memory, or consciousness—the processes that make the person feel whole (Spiegel & Cardeña, 1991). In this section we will describe several types of dissociative disorders.

•*Types of Dissociative Disorders*

The DSM lists several dissociative disorders. Among them are dissociative amnesia, dissociative fugue, dissociative identity disorder, and depersonalization.

DISSOCIATIVE AMNESIA In **dissociative amnesia** the person is suddenly unable to recall important personal information. The loss of memory cannot be attributed to organic problems such as a blow to the head or alcoholic intoxication. It is thus a psychological dissociative disorder and not an organic one. In the most common example, the person cannot recall events for a number of hours after a stressful incident, as in warfare or in the case of an uninjured survivor of an accident. In generalized amnesia, people forget their entire lives. Amnesia may last for hours or years.

People sometimes claim that they cannot recall engaging in socially unacceptable behavior, promising to do something, and the like. Claiming to have a psychological problem such as amnesia in order to escape responsibility is known as **malingering**. Using current research methods we cannot always distinguish malingerers from people with dissociative disorders.

DISSOCIATIVE FUGUE In **dissociative fugue,** the person abruptly leaves his or her home or place of work and travels to another place, having lost all memory of his or her past life. While at the new location the person either does not think about the past or reports a past filled with invented memories. The new personality is often more outgoing and less inhibited than the "real" identity. Following recovery, the events that occurred during the fugue are not recalled.

DISSOCIATIVE IDENTITY DISORDER Dissociative identity disorder (formerly termed *multiple personality disorder*) is the name given to William's disorder, described at the beginning of the chapter. In this disorder, two or more identities or personalities, each with distinct traits and memories, "occupy" the same person. Each identity may or may not be aware of the others. Different identities might even have different eyeglass prescriptions (Braun, 1988).

Braun reports cases in which assorted identities showed different allergic responses. In one person, an identity named Timmy was not sensitive to orange juice. But when other identities gained control over him and drank orange juice, he would break out with hives. Hives would also erupt if another identity emerged while the juice was being digested. If Timmy reappeared when the allergic reaction was present, the itching of the hives would cease and the blisters would start to subside. In other cases reported by Braun, different identities within a person might show various responses to the same medicine. Or one identity might exhibit color blindness while others had intact color vision.

A few celebrated cases of this disorder have been portrayed in the popular media. One of them became the subject of the film *The Three Faces of Eve*. A timid housewife named Eve White harbored two other identities. One was Eve Black, a sexually aggressive, antisocial personality. The third was Jane, an emerging identity who was able to accept the existence of her primitive impulses yet

Truth or Fiction Revisited

It is true that some people have more than one identity, and the identities may have different allergies and eyeglass prescriptions.

DISSOCIATIVE DISORDERS • (diss-SO-she-uh-tivv). Disorders in which there are sudden, temporary changes in consciousness or self-identity.
DISSOCIATIVE AMNESIA • (am-KNEE-she-uh). A dissociative disorder marked by loss of memory or self-identity; skills and general knowledge are usually retained. Previously termed *psychogenic amnesia.*
MALINGERING • Pretending to be ill to escape duty or work.
DISSOCIATIVE FUGUE • (FYOOG). A dissociative disorder in which one experiences amnesia and then flees to a new location. Previously termed *psychogenic fugue.*

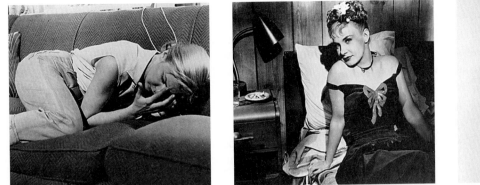

Dissociative Identity Disorder. In the film *The Three Faces of Eve,* Joanne Woodward played three personalities in the same woman: the shy, inhibited Eve White (lying on couch); the flirtatious, promiscuous Eve Black (in dark dress); and a third personality (Jane) who could accept her sexual and aggressive impulses and still maintain her sense of identity.

engage in socially appropriate behavior. Finally the three faces merged into one—Jane. Ironically, later on, Jane (Chris Sizemore in real life) reportedly split into 22 identities. Another well-publicized case is that of Sybil, a woman with 16 identities who was portrayed by Sally Field in the film *Sybil.*

DEPERSONALIZATION DISORDER **Depersonalization disorder** is characterized by persistent or recurrent feelings that one is detached from one's own body, as if one is observing one's thought processes from the outside. For this reason, it is sometimes referred to as an "out-of-body experience." One may also feel as though he or she is functioning on automatic pilot or as if in a dream.

The case of Richie illustrates a transient episode of depersonalization:

We went to Orlando with the children after school let out. I had also been driving myself hard, and it was time to let go. We spent three days "doing" Disneyworld, and it got to the point where we were all wearing shirts with mice and ducks on them and singing Disney songs like "Yo ho, yo ho, a pirate's life for me." On the third day I began to feel unreal and ill at ease while we were watching these middle-American Ivory-soap teenagers singing and dancing in front of Cinderella's Castle. The day was finally cooling down, but I broke into a sweat. I became shaky and dizzy and sat down on the cement next to the 4-year-old's stroller without giving [my wife] an explanation. There were strollers and kids and [adults'] legs all around me, and for some strange reason I became fixated on the pieces of popcorn strewn on the ground. All of a sudden it was like the people around me were all silly mechanical creatures, like the dolls in the "It's a Small World" [exhibit] or the animals on the "Jungle Cruise." Things sort of seemed to slow down, the way they do when you've smoked marijuana, and there was this invisible wall of cotton between me and everyone else.

Then the concert was over and my wife was like "What's the matter?" and did I want to stay for the Electrical Parade and the fireworks or was I sick? Now I was beginning to wonder if I was going crazy and I said I was sick, that my wife would have to take me by the hand and drive us back to the [motel]. Somehow we got back to the monorail and turned in the strollers. I waited in the herd [of people] at the station like a dead person, my eyes glazed over, looking out over kids with Mickey Mouse ears and Mickey Mouse balloons. The mechanical voice on the monorail almost did me in and I got really shaky.

DEPERSONALIZATION DISORDER • A dissociative disorder in which one experiences persistent or recurrent feelings that one is not real or is detached from one's own experiences or body.

I refused to go back to the Magic Kingdom. I went with the family to Sea World, and on another day I dropped [my wife] and the kids off at the Magic Kingdom and picked them up that night. My wife thought I was goldbricking or something, and we had a helluva fight about it, but we had a life to get back to and my sanity had to come first.

• *Theoretical Views*

According to psychodynamic theory, people with dissociative disorders use massive repression to prevent them from recognizing improper impulses or remembering ugly events (Vaillant, 1994). In dissociative amnesia and fugue, the person forgets a profoundly disturbing event or impulse. In dissociative identity disorder, the person expresses unacceptable impulses through alternate identities. In depersonalization, the person stands outside—removed from the turmoil within.

According to learning theorists, people with dissociative disorders have learned *not to think* about bad memories or disturbing impulses in order to avoid feelings of anxiety, guilt, and shame. Technically speaking, *not thinking about these matters* is reinforced[3] by *removal* of the aversive stimulus of anxiety, guilt, or shame.

Both psychodynamic and learning theories suggest that dissociative disorders help people keep disturbing memories or ideas out of mind. Of what could such memories be? Research suggests that many—perhaps most—cases involve memories of sexual or physical abuse during childhood, usually by a relative or caretaker (Coons, 1994; Weaver & Clum, 1995). Surveys find that the great majority of people who are diagnosed with dissociative identity disorder report sexual abuse in childhood (Putnam and others, 1986; Ross and others, 1990). Many report both physical and sexual abuse. In a survey of people with dissociative amnesia, the great majority also reported physical or sexual abuse in childhood (Coons and others, 1989).

Perhaps all of us are capable of dividing our awareness so that we become unaware, at least temporarily, of events that we usually focus more attention on. The dissociative disorders raise fascinating questions about the nature of human self-identity and memory (Kihlstrom and others, 1994). Perhaps it is no surprise that attention can be divided. Perhaps the surprising thing is that human consciousness normally integrates an often chaotic set of experiences into a meaningful whole.

REFLECTIONS
- Have you known someone who claimed "amnesia" for a particular event? Was the term used correctly? Why or why not?
- Have you ever felt removed from the world—as though the things around you could not be really happening? Can you relate the feelings to depersonalization?
- Have you seen a film or a TV show in which a character was supposed to have dissociative identity disorder (perhaps it was called "multiple personality")? Was the person's behavior consistent with the description in this section? What were the supposed origins of the disorder?

---

[3] This is an example of negative reinforcement, because the frequency of behavior—in this case, the frequency of diverting attention from a certain topic—is increased by *removal* of a stimulus—in this case, by removal of feelings of anxiety, guilt, or shame.

■ SOMATOFORM DISORDERS

People with **somatoform disorders** complain of physical problems such as paralysis, pain, or a persistent belief that they have a serious disease. Yet no evidence of a physical abnormality can be found. In this section we discuss two somatoform disorders: conversion disorder and hypochondriasis.

Conversion disorder is characterized by a major change in, or loss of, physical functioning, although there are no medical findings to explain the loss of functioning. The behaviors are not intentionally produced. That is, the person is not faking. Conversion disorder is so named because it appears to "convert" a source of stress into a physical difficulty.

If you lost the ability to see at night, or if your legs became paralyzed, you would understandably show concern. But some people with conversion disorder show indifference to their symptoms, a remarkable feature referred to as **la belle indifférence.**

During World War II, some bomber pilots developed night blindness. They could not carry out their nighttime missions, although no damage to the optic nerves was found. In rare cases, women with large families have been reported to become paralyzed in the legs, again with no medical findings. More recently, a Cambodian woman who had witnessed atrocities became blind as a result.

Another more common type of somatoform disorder is **hypochondriasis.** People with this insist that they are suffering from a serious physical illness, even though no medical evidence of illness can be found. They become preoccupied with minor physical sensations and continue to believe that they are ill despite the reassurance of physicians that they are healthy. They may run from doctor to doctor, seeking the one who will find the causes of the sensations. Fear of illness may disrupt their work or home life.

Consistent with psychodynamic theory, early versions of the DSM labeled what are now referred to as somatoform disorders as "hysterical neuroses." "Hysterical" derives from the word *hystera,* the Greek word for uterus or womb. Like many other Greeks, Hippocrates believed that hysteria was a sort of female trouble that was caused by a wandering uterus. It was erroneously thought that the uterus could roam through the body—that it was not anchored in place! As the uterus meandered, it could cause pains and odd sensations almost anywhere. The Greeks also believed that pregnancy anchored the uterus and ended hysterical complaints. What do you think Greek physicians prescribed to end monthly aches and pains? Good guess.

Even in the earlier years of the 20th century, it was suggested that strange sensations and medically unfounded complaints were largely the province of women. Moreover, viewing the problem as a neurosis suggested that it stemmed from unconscious childhood conflicts. The psychodynamic view of conversion disorders is that the symptoms protect the individual from feelings of guilt or shame, or from another source of stress. Conversion disorders, like dissociative disorders, often seem to serve a purpose. For example, the "blindness" of the World War II pilots may have enabled them to avoid feelings of fear of being literally shot down or of guilt for killing civilians.

REFLECTIONS

- What kinds of problems do you think are involved in trying to determine whether someone has a medical problem or a conversion disorder?
- Have you heard the term *hypochondriac* used sarcastically or as an insult? How so?

SOMATOFORM DISORDERS • (so-MAT-oh-form). Disorders in which people complain of physical (somatic) problems even though no physical abnormality can be found.
CONVERSION DISORDER • A disorder in which anxiety or unconscious conflicts are "converted" into physical symptoms that often have the effect of helping the person cope with anxiety or conflict.
LA BELLE INDIFFÉRENCE • (lah bell an-DEEF-fay-rants). A French term descriptive of the lack of concern sometimes shown by people with conversion disorders.
HYPOCHONDRIASIS • (high-poe-con-DRY-uh-sis). Persistent belief that one has a medical disorder despite lack of medical findings.

■ MOOD DISORDERS

Mood disorders are characterized by disturbance in expressed emotions. The disruption generally involves sadness or elation. Most instances of sadness are normal, or "run-of-the-mill." If you have failed an important test, if you have lost money in an unsuccessful business investment, or if your closest friend becomes ill, it is understandable and fitting for you to be sad about it. It would be odd, in fact, if you were *not* affected by adversity.

• *Types of Mood Disorders*

In this section we discuss two mood disorders: major depression and bipolar disorder.

MAJOR DEPRESSION Depression is the "common cold" of psychological problems, affecting upwards of 10% of adults at any given time (Alloy and others, 1990). People with run-of-the-mill depression may feel sad, blue, or "down in the dumps." They may complain of lack of energy, loss of self-esteem, difficulty concentrating, loss of interest in activities and other people, pessimism, crying, and thoughts of suicide.

These feelings are more intense in people with **major depression.** People with this disorder may also show poor appetite, serious weight loss, and agitation or **psychomotor retardation.** They may be unable to concentrate and make decisions. They may say that they "don't care" anymore and in some cases attempt suicide. They may also display faulty perception of reality—so-called psychotic behaviors. These include delusions of unworthiness, guilt for imagined wrongdoings, even the notion that one is rotting from disease. There may also be delusions, as of the Devil administering deserved punishment, or hallucinations, as of strange bodily sensations.

BIPOLAR DISORDER In **bipolar disorder,** formerly known as manic-depressive disorder, the person undergoes wide mood swings, from ecstatic elation to deep depression. These cycles seem to be unrelated to external events. In the elated, or **manic** phase, the person may show excessive excitement or silliness, carrying jokes too far. The manic person may be argumentative. He or she may show poor judgment, destroying property, making huge contributions to charity, or giving away expensive possessions. People may avoid manic individuals, finding them abrasive. Manic people often speak rapidly ("pressured speech") and jump from topic to topic, showing **rapid flight of ideas.** It is hard to get a word in edgewise. The manic individual may also be unable to sit still or may sleep restlessly.

Depression is the other side of the coin. People with bipolar depression often sleep more than usual and are lethargic. People with major (or unipolar) depression are more likely to have insomnia and agitation. Those with bipolar depression also exhibit social withdrawal and irritability.

Some people with bipolar disorder attempt suicide when the mood shifts from the elated phase toward depression. They will do almost anything to escape the depths of depression that lie ahead.

You may have heard the expression, "There is a thin line between genius and madness." It may sound as if the "madness" in question should be schizophrenia because there are flights of fancy in that disorder as well as among geniuses. Yet researchers have found links between creative genius and the mood disorders of depression and bipolar disorder (Jamison, 1997). Many artists have

MAJOR DEPRESSION • A severe depressive disorder in which the person may show loss of appetite, psychomotor behaviors, and impaired reality testing.

PSYCHOMOTOR RETARDATION • Slowness in motor activity and (apparently) in thought.

BIPOLAR DISORDER • A disorder in which the mood alternates between two extreme poles (elation and depression). Also referred to as *manic-depression.*

MANIC • Elated, showing excessive excitement.

RAPID FLIGHT OF IDEAS • Rapid speech and topic changes, characteristic of manic behavior.

peered into the depths of their own despair and found inspiration, but an alarming number of writers—including Virginia Woolf, Sylvia Plath, and Ernest Hemingway—have taken their own lives. As noted by Kay Redfield Jamison (1997), artists are 18 times more likely to commit suicide than the general population. They are 8 to 10 times more likely to be depressed, and 10 to 20 times as likely to have bipolar disorder. Many writers, painters, and composers were also at their most productive during manic periods, including the poet Alfred, Lord Tennyson and the composer Robert Schumann. As of today, we can only speculate about the meaning of the connection between creativity and mood disorders, but let us note two interesting pieces of information. First, the medicines that are used to treat mood disorders tend to limit the individual's emotional and perceptual range, which is a reason why many people stop taking them. Second, artistic creativity and emotional response are both considered right-brain functions.

• *Theoretical Views*

Depression may be a reaction to losses and unpleasant events. Problems such as marital discord, physical discomfort, incompetence, and failure or pressure at work all contribute to feelings of depression. We tend to be more depressed by things we bring upon ourselves, such as academic problems, financial problems, unwanted pregnancy, conflict with the law, arguments, and fights (Simons and others, 1993). However, some people recover from depression less readily than others. People who remain depressed have lower self-esteem (Andrews & Brown, 1993), are less likely to be able to solve social problems (Marx and others, 1992), and have less social support.

Psychology in a World of
DIVERSITY

The Case of Women and Depression

Women are about two times more likely to be diagnosed with depression than men (Culbertson, 1997; Leutwyler, 1997). Some therapists, like many laypeople, assume that biological gender differences largely explain why women are more likely to become depressed. How often do we hear degrading remarks such as "It must be that time of the month" when a woman expresses feelings of anger or irritation?

Hormonal changes during the menstrual cycle and childbirth may contribute to depression in women (McGrath and others, 1990). However, a panel convened by the American Psychological Association attributed most of the difference to the greater stresses placed on women (McGrath and others, 1990). Women are more likely to experience physical and sexual abuse, poverty, single parenthood, and sexism. Women are also more likely than men to help other people who are under stress. Supporting other people heaps additional caregiving burdens on themselves (Shumaker & Hill, 1991). One panel member, Bonnie Strickland, expressed surprise that even more women are not depressed, given that they are often treated as second-class citizens.

Belle (1990) argues that social inequality creates many of the problems that lead people to seek therapy. This is particularly true among members of oppressed groups, such as women (Brown, 1992). Women—especially single mothers—have lower socioeconomic status than men, and depression and other psychological disorders are more common among poor people (Hobfoll and others, 1995). Even capable, hard-working women are likely to become depressed when they see how society limits their opportunities (Rothbart & Ahadi, 1994).

A part of "therapy" for women, then, is to modify the overwhelming demands that are placed on women today (Comas-Diaz, 1994). The pain may lie in the individual, but the cause often lies in society.

PSYCHODYNAMIC VIEWS Psychoanalysts suggest various explanations for depression. In one, people who are at risk for depression are overly concerned about hurting other people's feelings or losing their approval. As a result, they hold in feelings of anger rather than expressing them. Anger is turned inward and experienced as misery and self-hatred. From the psychodynamic perspective, bipolar disorder may be seen as alternating states in which the personality is first dominated by the superego and then by the ego. In the depressive phase of the disorder, the superego dominates, producing exaggerated ideas of wrongdoing and associated feelings of guilt and worthlessness. After a while the ego asserts supremacy, producing the elation and self-confidence often seen in the manic phase. Later, in response to the excessive display of ego, feelings of guilt return and plunge the person into depression once again.

LEARNING VIEWS Many people with depressive disorders have an external locus of control. That is, they do not believe that they can control events so as to achieve desired outcomes (Weisz and others, 1993).

Research has also found links between depression and **learned helplessness.** In classic research, psychologist Martin Seligman taught dogs that they were helpless to escape an electric shock. The dogs were prevented from leaving a cage in which they received repeated shocks. Later, a barrier to a safe compartment was removed, offering the animals a way out. When they were shocked again, however, the dogs made no effort to escape. They had apparently learned that they were helpless. Seligman's dogs were also, in a sense, reinforced for doing nothing. That is, the shock *eventually* stopped when the dogs were showing helpless behavior—inactivity and withdrawal. "Reinforcement" might have increased the likelihood of repeating the "successful behavior"—that is, doing nothing—in a similar situation. This helpless behavior resembles that of people who are depressed.

COGNITIVE FACTORS The concept of learned helplessness bridges the learning and cognitive approaches in that it is an attitude, a general expectation. Other cognitive factors also contribute to depression. For example, perfectionists set themselves up for depression by making irrational demands on themselves. They are likely to fall short of their (unrealistic) expectations and to feel depressed as a result (Blatt and others, 1995; Hewitt and others, 1996).

People who ruminate about feelings of depression are more likely to prolong them (Just & Alloy, 1997). Women are more likely than men to ruminate about feelings of depression (Nolen-Hoeksema and others, 1993). Men seem more likely to try to fight off negative feelings by distracting themselves. Men are also more likely to distract themselves by turning to alcohol (Nolen-Hoeksema, 1991). They thus expose themselves and their families to further problems.

Seligman (1996) suggests that when things go wrong we may think of the causes of failure as either *internal* or *external, stable* or *unstable, global* or *specific.* These various **attributional styles** can be illustrated using the example of

LEARNED HELPLESSNESS • A model for the acquisition of depressive behavior, based on findings that organisms in aversive situations learn to show inactivity when their operants go unreinforced.
ATTRIBUTIONAL STYLE • (at-rib-BYOO-shun-al). One's tendency to attribute one's behavior to internal or external factors, stable or unstable factors, and so on.

Why Did He Miss That Tackle? This football player is compounding his feelings of depression by attributing his shortcomings on the field to factors that he cannot change. For example, he tells himself that he missed the tackle out of stupidity and lack of athletic ability. He ignores the facts that his coaching was poor and his teammates failed to support him.

having a date that does not work out. An internal attribution involves self-blame, as in "I really loused it up." An external attribution places the blame elsewhere (as in "Some couples just don't take to each other," or, "She was the wrong sign for me"). A stable attribution ("It's my personality") suggests a problem that cannot be changed. An unstable attribution ("It was because I had a head cold") suggests a temporary condition. A global attribution of failure ("I have no idea what to do when I'm with other people") suggests that the problem is quite large. A specific attribution ("I have problems making small talk at the beginning of a relationship") chops the problem down to a manageable size.

Research has shown that people who are depressed are more likely to attribute the causes of their failures to internal, stable, and global factors—factors that they are relatively powerless to change (Kinderman & Bentall, 1997; Simons and others, 1995). Such attributions can give rise to feelings of hopelessness.

BIOLOGICAL FACTORS Researchers are also searching for biological factors in mood disorders. Depression, for example, is often associated with the trait of **neuroticism,** which is heritable (Clark and others, 1994). Anxiety is also connected with neuroticism, and mood and anxiety disorders are frequently found in the same person (Clark and others, 1994).

Genetic factors appear to be involved in bipolar disorder. Mood swings tend to run in families (Rose, 1995; Wachtel, 1994). There is also a higher concordance rate for bipolar disorder among identical twins than among fraternal twins (Goodwin & Jamison, 1990).

Other researchers focus on the actions of the neurotransmitters serotonin and noradrenaline (Cooper and others, 1991; Michels & Marzuk, 1993b). A deficiency in serotonin may create a general disposition toward mood disorders. Serotonin deficiency *combined with* noradrenaline deficiency may be linked with depression. People with severe depression often respond to antidepressant drugs that heighten the action of noradrenaline and serotonin. Moreover, the metal lithium, which is a major chemical treatment for bipolar disorder, seems to flatten out manic-depressive cycles by moderating levels of noradrenaline.

NEUROTICISM • A personality trait characterized largely by persistent anxiety.

ALLEVIATING DEPRESSION (GETTING OUT OF THE DUMPS)

Be *not afraid of life. Believe that life is worth living and your belief will help create the fact.*

WILLIAM JAMES

Depression is characterized by inactivity, feelings of sadness, and cognitive distortions. If you suspect that your feelings may fit the picture of a major depressive episode or bipolar disorder, why not talk things over with your instructor or visit the college counseling or health center? However, there are also many things we can do on our own to cope with milder feelings of depression. Among them are the following:

- Engaging in pleasant events
- Thinking rationally
- Exercising
- Asserting ourselves

PLEASANT EVENTS There is a relationship between our moods and what we do. Losses, failures, and tension can trigger feelings of depression. Pleasant events can generate feelings of happiness and joy. You may be able to use pleasant events to lift your mood purposefully by taking the following steps:

1. Check off items in Table 15.2 that appeal to you.
2. Engage in at least three pleasant events each day.
3. Record your activities in a diary. Add other activities and events that strike you as pleasant, even if they are unplanned.
4. Toward the end of each day, rate your response to each activity, using a scale like this one:

   + 3 Wonderful

   + 2 Very nice

   + 1 Somewhat nice

     0 No particular response

   − 1 Somewhat disappointing

   − 2 Rather disappointing

   − 3 The pits

5. After a week or so, check the items in the diary that received positive ratings.
6. Repeat successful activities and experiment with new ones.

RATIONAL THINKING

Public opinion is a weak tyrant compared with our own private opinion. What a man thinks of himself, that it is which determines . . . his fate.

HENRY DAVID THOREAU, *WALDEN*

Depressed people tend to blame themselves for failures and problems, even when they are not at fault. They *internalize* blame and see their problems as *stable* and *global*—as all but impossible to change. Depressed people also make cognitive errors such as *catastrophizing* their problems and *minimizing* their accomplishments.

Column 1 in Table 15.3 illustrates a number of irrational, depressing thoughts. How many of them have you had? Column 2 indicates the type of cog-

TABLE 15.2	A CATALOG OF PLEASANT EVENTS	
1. Being in the country	10. Being at the beach	19. Reading stories, novels, poems, plays, magazines, newspapers
2. Wearing expensive or formal clothes	11. Doing art work (painting, sculpture, drawing, moviemaking, etc.)	20. Going to a bar, tavern, club
3. Making contributions to religious, charitable, or political groups	12. Rock climbing or mountaineering	21. Going to lectures or talks
4. Talking about sports	13. Reading the Scriptures	22. Creating or arranging songs or music
5. Meeting someone new	14. Playing golf	23. Boating
6. Going to a rock concert	15. Rearranging or redecorating your room or house	24. Restoring antiques, refinishing furniture
7. Playing baseball, softball, football, or basketball	16. Going naked	25. Watching television or listening to the radio
8. Planning trips or vacations	17. Going to a sports event	26. Camping
9. Buying things for yourself	18. Going to the races	

Source: Adapted from D. J. MacPhillamy & P. M. Lewinsohn, *Pleasant Events Schedule, Form III-S*, University of Oregon, Mimeograph, 1971.

nitive error being made (such as internalizing or catastrophizing), and column 3 shows examples of more rational, less depressing alternatives.

You can pinpoint irrational, depressing thoughts by identifying the kinds of thoughts you have when you feel low. Look for the fleeting thoughts that can trigger mood changes. It helps to jot them down. Then challenge their accuracy. Do you characterize difficult situations as impossible and hopeless? Do you expect too much from yourself and minimize your achievements? Do you internalize more than your fair share of blame?

You can use Table 15.3 to classify your cognitive errors and construct rational alternatives. Write these next to each irrational thought. Review them from time to time. When you are alone, you can read the irrational thought aloud. Then follow it by saying to yourself firmly, "No, that's irrational!" Then read the rational alternative aloud twice, *emphatically*.

After you have thought or read aloud the rational alternative, think or say things like, "That makes more sense! That's a more accurate view of things! I feel better now that I have things in perspective."

EXERCISE Exercise not only fosters physical health. It can enhance psychological well-being and help us cope with depression (Hays, 1995; Slaven & Lee, 1997). Depression is characterized by inactivity and feelings of helplessness. Exercise, in a sense, is the opposite of inactivity. Experiments suggest that exercise alleviates feelings of depression, at least among mildly and moderately depressed people (Buffone, 1984; Greist, 1984; Norvell & Belles, 1993).

ASSERTIVE BEHAVIOR Since we humans are social creatures, social interactions are important to us. Nonassertive behavior patterns are linked to feelings of depression. Learning to express our feelings and relate to others has been shown to alleviate feelings of depression (Hersen

and others, 1984). Assertive behavior permits more effective interactions with family members, friends, coworkers, and strangers. In this way we remove sources of frustration and expand our social support. Expressions of positive feelings—saying you love someone or simply say-

ing "Good morning" cheerfully—help reduce feelings of hostility and pave the way toward further social involvement.

Perhaps these strategies will work for you. If they do not, why not talk things over with your professor or visit the college health or counseling center? ■

TABLE 15.3	IRRATIONAL, DEPRESSING THOUGHTS AND RATIONAL ALTERNATIVES	
Irrational Thought	*Type of Cognitive Error*	*Rational Alternative*
"There's nothing I can do"	Catastrophizing, minimizing, stabilizing	"I can't think of anything to do right now, but if I work at it, I may."
"I'm no good."	Internalizing, globalizing, stabilizing	"I did something I regret, but that doesn't make me evil or worthless as a person."
"This is absolutely awful."	Catastrophizing	"This is pretty bad, but it's not the end of the world."
"I just don't have the brains for college."	Stabilizing, globalizing	"I guess I really need to go back over the basics in that course."
"I just can't believe I did something so disgusting!"	Catastrophizing	"That was a bad experience. Well, I won't be likely to try that again soon."
"I can't imagine ever feeling right."	Stabilizing, catastrophizing	"This is painful, but if I try to work it through step by step, I'll probably eventually see my way out of it."
"It's all my fault."	Internalizing	"I'm not blameless, but I wasn't the only one involved. It may have been my idea, but he/she went into it with his/her eyes open."
"I can't do anything right."	Globalizing, stabilizing, catastrophizing, minimizing	"I sure screwed this up, but I've done a lot of things well, and I'll do other things well in the future."
"I hurt everybody who gets close to me."	Internalizing, globalizing, stabilizing	"I'm not totally blameless, but I'm not responsible for the whole world. Others make their own decisions, and they have to live with the results, too."
"If people knew the real me, they would have it in for me."	Globalizing, minimizing (the positive in yourself)	"I'm not perfect, but nobody's perfect. I have positive as well as negative features, and I am entitled to self-interests."

Many of us create or compound feelings of depression because of cognitive errors such as those in this table. Have you had any of these thoughts? Will you challenge them if they occur again?

Relationships between mood disorders and biological factors are complex and under intense study. Even if people are biologically predisposed toward depression, self-efficacy expectations and attitudes—particularly attitudes about whether one can change things for the better—may also play a role.

• *Suicide*

They called themselves Heaven's Gate. Yet according to The *New York Times,* the only gate involved was a "Gateway to Madness" (1997).

In 1997, 39 members of Heaven's Gate committed suicide as the Hale-Bopp Comet—which they took as a sign that the gate to heaven was open—approached our planet. By now the comet, a ball of ice with a lustrous tail, has spun back far into the reaches of space. The Heaven's Gaters are buried within the Earth.

The Heaven's Gaters were persuaded that they were leaving their bodies, their "physical containers," behind. They were about to enter the "Level Above Human." Yet most suicides are connected with depression (Beck and others, 1990; Lewinsohn and others, 1994a, 1994b), which is why we discuss suicide in the section on mood disorders.

Consider some facts about suicide:

• Suicide is more common among college students than among people of the same age who do not attend college. Each year about 10,000 college students attempt suicide.

• Three times as many women as men attempt suicide, but about four times as many men succeed in killing themselves (see Figure 15.2; Rich and others, 1988).

• Among people who attempt suicide, men prefer to use guns or hang themselves, while women prefer to use sleeping pills. Males, that is, tend to use quicker and more lethal means (Gelman, 1994).

FIGURE 15.2

SUICIDE RATES ACCORDING TO GENDER AND ETHNICITY

Men are more likely than women to commit suicide. Women, however, make more suicide attempts. How can we account for this discrepancy? White people are also more likely to commit suicide than African Americans.

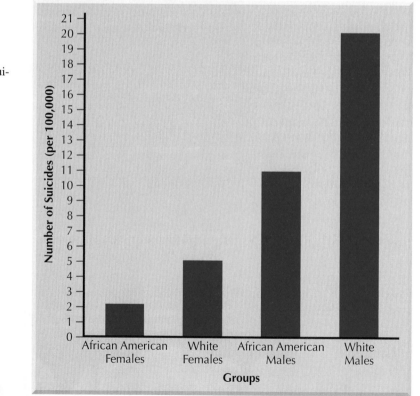

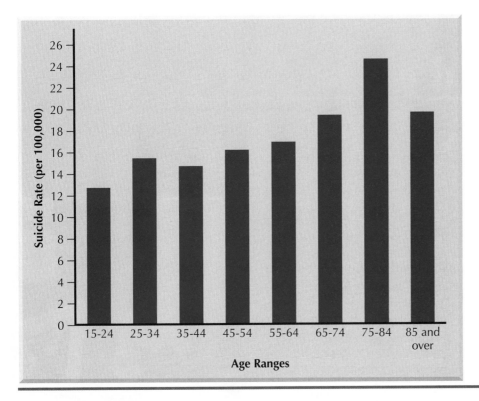

FIGURE 15.3
SUICIDE RATES ACCORDING TO AGE
Older people (aged 65 and above) are more likely to commit suicide than the young and the middle-aged, yet suicide is the second leading cause of death among college students.

- Although African Americans are more likely than White Americans to live in poverty and experience the effects of discrimination, the suicide rate is about twice as high among White Americans (Figure 15.2).

- One in four Native American teenagers has attempted suicide—a rate four times higher than that for other U.S. teenagers (Resnick and others, 1992). Among Zuni adolescents of New Mexico, the rate of completed suicides is more than twice the national rate (Howard-Pitney and others, 1992).

- Teenage suicides loom large in the media spotlight, but older people are actually much more likely to commit suicide (Richman, 1993; Figure 15.3). The suicide rate among older people is nearly twice the national rate.

All in all, about 30,000 people each year take their lives in the United States (Michels & Marzuk, 1993a). Most suicides are linked to feelings of depression and hopelessness. Other factors in suicide include anxiety, drug abuse, problems in school or at work, and social problems (Howard-Pitney and others, 1992; Sommers-Flanagan & Sommers-Flanagan, 1995). Exposure to other people who are committing suicide can increase the risk that an adolescent will attempt suicide (CDC, 1995). Copycat suicides contribute to a so-called "cluster effect" among adolescents.

Suicide attempts are more common after stressful events, especially events that entail loss of social support—as in the loss of a spouse, friend, or relative. People under stress who consider suicide have been found to be less capable of solving problems—particularly interpersonal problems—than nonsuicidal people (Rotheram-Borus and others, 1990; Sadowski & Kelley, 1993; Schotte and others, 1990). Suicidal people thus are less likely to find other ways out of a stressful situation.

Perfectionists are more likely than other people to commit suicide when they are depressed. One possible reason is that perfectionists look upon even small successes as failures (Pilkonis, 1996). Perfectionists are also likely to

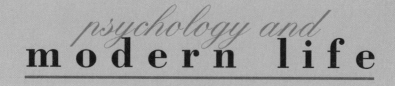

psychology and
m o d e r n   l i f e

SUICIDE PREVENTION

Imagine that you are having a heart-to-heart talk with Jamie, who is one of your best friends. Things haven't been going well. Jamie's grandmother died a month ago, and they were very close. Jamie's coursework has been suffering, and things have also been going downhill with the person Jamie has been seeing. But you are not prepared when Jamie looks you straight in the eye and says, "I've been thinking about this for days, and I've decided that the only way out is to kill myself."

If someone tells you that he or she is considering suicide, you may become frightened and flustered or feel that an enormous burden has been placed on you. You are right: It has. In such a case your objective should be to encourage the person to consult a health care provider, or to consult one yourself, as soon as possible. But if the person refuses to talk to anyone else and you feel that you can't break free for a consultation, there are a number of things you can do:

1. Keep talking. Edwin Shneidman, cofounder of the Los Angeles Suicide Prevention Center, suggests asking questions such as "What's going on?" "Where do you hurt?" "What would you like to see happen?" (1985, p. 11). Questions like these may encourage the person to express frustrated psychological needs and provide some relief. They

also give you time to assess the danger and think.

2. Be empathetic. Show that you understand how upset the person is. Do *not* say, "Don't be silly."

3. Suggest that something other than suicide might solve the problem, even if it is not evident at the time. Many suicidal people see only two solutions—either death or a magical resolution of their problems. Therapists try to "remove the mental blinders" from suicidal people.

4. Ask how the person intends to commit suicide. People with concrete plans and a weapon are at greater risk. Ask if you might hold on to the weapon for a while. Sometimes the answer is yes.

5. Suggest that the person go *with you* to obtain professional help *now*. The emergency room of a general hospital, the campus counseling center or infirmary, or the campus or local police station will do. Some campuses have hot lines you can call. Some cities have suicide prevention centers with hot lines that people can use anonymously.

6. Extract a promise that the person will not commit suicide before seeing you again. Arrange a specific time and place to meet. Get professional help as soon as you are apart.

A Suicide-Prevention Hotline. At suicide-prevention centers, staff members stand by hot-lines around the clock. If you know someone who is threatening to commit suicide, consult a professional as soon as possible.

7. Do *not* tell people threatening suicide that they're silly or crazy. Do *not* insist on contact with specific people, such as parents or a spouse. Conflict with these people may have led to the suicidal thinking in the first place.

Above all, remember that your main goal is to talk to a helping professional. Don't go it alone for one moment more than you have to. ■

believe that key people in their lives—their families or their employers—are making demands that they cannot meet (Hewitt and others, 1996).

Suicide, like so many other psychological problems, tends to run in families. Nearly one in four people who attempt suicide reports that a family member has committed suicide (Sorensen & Rutter, 1991). Psychological disorders among family members may also be a factor (Wagner, 1997). The causal connections are unclear, however. Do people who attempt suicide inherit disorders that can lead to suicide? Does the family environment subject family members to feelings of hopelessness? Does the suicide of a family member give a person the idea of committing suicide or create the impression that he or she is somehow fated to commit suicide? What do you think?

MYTHS ABOUT SUICIDE Some people believe that individuals who threaten suicide are only seeking attention. Those who are serious just "do it." Actually, most people who commit suicide give warnings about their intentions (Brody, 1992b).

Some believe that those who fail at suicide attempts are only seeking attention. But many people who commit suicide have made prior attempts (Lewinsohn and others, 1994a). Contrary to widespread belief, discussing suicide with a person who is depressed does not prompt the person to attempt suicide (CDC, 1995). Extracting a promise not to commit suicide before calling or visiting a helping professional seems to prevent some suicides.

Some believe that only "insane" people (meaning people who are out of touch with reality) would take their own lives. However, suicidal thinking is not necessarily a sign of psychosis, neurosis, or personality disorder. Instead, contemplation of suicide can reflect a narrowing of the range of options that people believe are available to them (Rotheram-Borus and others, 1990; Schotte and others, 1990).

Truth or Fiction Revisited

It is not true that people who threaten suicide are only seeking attention.

REFLECTIONS
- Would you find it easy or difficult to admit to feeling depressed? Why?
- Do you ever feel depressed? Under what circumstances? When you fall short of your goals, do you tend to criticize yourself or blame other people or the situation?
- Did you ever feel that there was nothing you could do to improve your situation or solve a personal problem? How did that feeling affect your mood?
- Agree or disagree, and support your answer: "It is abnormal to consider committing suicide."

■ SCHIZOPHRENIA

Joyce was 19. Her husband Ron brought her into the emergency room because she had slit her wrists. When she was interviewed, her attention wandered. She seemed distracted by things in the air, or something she might be hearing. It was as if she had an invisible earphone.

She explained that she had cut her wrists because the "hellsmen" had told her to. Then she seemed frightened. Later she said that the hellsmen had warned her not to reveal their existence. She had been afraid that they would punish her for talking about them.

Ron and Joyce had been married for about one year. At first they had been together in a small apartment in town. But Joyce did not want to be near other people and had convinced him to rent a bungalow in the

Paranoid Schizophrenia. People with paranoid schizophrenia have systematized delusions, often involving the idea that they are being persecuted or are on a special mission. Although they cannot be argued out of their delusions, their cognitive functioning is relatively intact compared to that of disorganized and catatonic schizophrenics.

country. There she would make fantastic drawings of goblins and monsters during the days. Now and then she would become agitated and act as if invisible things were giving her instructions.

"I'm bad," Joyce would mutter. "I'm bad." She would begin to jumble her words. Ron would then try to convince her to go to the hospital, but she would refuse. Then the wrist cutting would begin. Ron thought he had made the cottage safe by removing knives and blades. But Joyce would always find something.

Then Joyce would be brought to the hospital, have stitches put in, be kept under observation for a while, and medicated. She would explain that she cut herself because the hellsmen had told her that she was bad and must die. After a few days she would deny hearing the hellsmen, and she would insist on leaving the hospital.

Ron would take her home. The pattern continued.

When the emergency room staff examined Joyce's wrists and heard that she believed she had been following the orders of "hellsmen," they suspected that she could be diagnosed with schizophrenia. Schizophrenia touches every aspect of a person's life. It is characterized by disturbances in thought and language, perception and attention, motor activity, and mood, and by withdrawal and absorption in daydreams or fantasy.

Schizophrenia has been referred to as the worst disorder affecting human beings (Carpenter & Buchanan, 1994). It afflicts nearly 1% of the population worldwide. Its onset occurs relatively early in life, and its adverse effects tend to endure. It has been estimated that one third to one half of the homeless people in the United States have schizophrenia (Bachrach, 1992).

People with schizophrenia have problems in memory, attention, and communication (Docherty and others, 1996). Their thinking becomes unraveled. Unless we are allowing our thoughts to wander, our thinking is normally tightly knit. We start at a certain point, and thoughts that come to mind (the associations) tend to be logically connected. But people with schizophrenia often think illogically. Their speech may be jumbled. They may combine parts of words into new words or make meaningless rhymes. They may jump from topic to topic, conveying little useful information. They usually do not recognize that their thoughts and behavior are abnormal.

Many people with schizophrenia have **delusions**—for example, delusions of grandeur, persecution, or reference. In the case of delusions of grandeur, a person may believe that he is a famous historical figure such as Jesus, or a person on a special mission. He may have grand, illogical plans for saving the world. Delusions tend to be unshakable even in the face of evidence that they are not true. People with delusions of persecution may believe that they are sought by the Mafia, CIA, FBI, or some other group. A woman with delusions of reference said that news stories contained coded information about her. A man with such delusions complained that neighbors had "bugged" his walls with "radios." Other people with schizophrenia have had delusions that they have committed unpardonable sins, that they were rotting away from disease, or that they or the world did not exist.

The perceptions of people with schizophrenia often include hallucinations—imagery in the absence of external stimulation that the person cannot distinguish from reality. In Shakespeare's *Macbeth*, for example, after killing King Duncan, Macbeth apparently experiences a hallucination:

Is this a dagger which I see before me,
The handle toward my hand? Come, let me clutch thee:
I have thee not, and yet I see thee still.
Art thou not, fatal vision, sensible

DELUSIONS • False, persistent beliefs that are unsubstantiated by sensory or objective evidence.

To feeling as to sight? or art thou but
A dagger of the mind, a false creation,
Proceeding from the heat-oppressed brain?

Joyce apparently hallucinated the voices of "hellsmen." Other people who experience hallucinations may see colors or even obscene words spelled out in midair. Auditory hallucinations are the most common type.

In individuals with schizophrenia, motor activity may become wild or become so slow that the person is said to be in a **stupor.** There may be strange gestures and facial expressions. The person's emotional responses may be flat or blunted, or inappropriate—as in giggling upon hearing bad news. People with schizophrenia have problems understanding other people's feelings (Penn and others, 1997), tend to withdraw from social contacts, and become wrapped up in their own thoughts and fantasies.

• *Types of Schizophrenia*

There are three major types of schizophrenia: paranoid, disorganized, and catatonic.

PARANOID TYPE People with **paranoid schizophrenia** have systematized delusions and, frequently, related auditory hallucinations. They usually have delusions of grandeur and persecution, but they may also have delusions of jealousy, in which they believe that a spouse or lover has been unfaithful. They may show agitation, confusion, and fear, and may experience vivid hallucinations that are consistent with their delusions. People with paranoid schizophrenia often construct a complex or systematized delusions involving themes of wrongdoing or persecution.

DISORGANIZED TYPE People with **disorganized schizophrenia** show incoherence, loosening of associations, disorganized behavior, disorganized delusions, fragmentary delusions or hallucinations, and flat or highly inappropriate emotional responses. Extreme social impairment is common. People with this type of schizophrenia may also exhibit silliness and giddiness of mood, giggling, and nonsensical speech. They may neglect their appearance and personal hygiene and lose control of their bladder and bowels.

CATATONIC TYPE People with **catatonic schizophrenia** show striking impairment in motor activity. It is characterized by a slowing of activity into a stupor that may suddenly change into an agitated phase. Catatonic individuals may maintain unusual, even difficult postures for hours, even as their limbs grow swollen or stiff. A striking feature of this condition is **waxy flexibility,** in which the person maintains positions into which he or she has been manipulated by others. Catatonic individuals may also show **mutism,** but afterward they usually report that they heard what others were saying at the time.

• *Theoretical Views*

Psychologists have investigated various factors that may contribute to schizophrenia. They include psychological and biological factors.

Catatonic schizophrenia. People with catatonic schizophrenia show striking motor impairment and may hold unusual positions for hours.

STUPOR • (STEW-pour). A condition in which the senses and thought are dulled.
PARANOID SCHIZOPHRENIA • A type of schizophrenia characterized primarily by delusions—commonly of persecution—and by vivid hallucinations.
DISORGANIZED SCHIZOPHRENIA • A type of schizophrenia characterized by disorganized delusions and vivid hallucinations.
CATATONIC SCHIZOPHRENIA • A type of schizophrenia characterized by striking impairment in motor activity.
WAXY FLEXIBILITY • A feature of catatonic schizophrenia in which persons maintain postures into which they are placed.
MUTISM • (MU-tizm). Refusal to talk.

PSYCHODYNAMIC VIEWS According to the psychodynamic perspective, schizophrenia occurs because the ego is overwhelmed by sexual or aggressive impulses from the id. The impulses threaten the ego and cause intense inner conflict. Under this threat, the person regresses to an early phase of the oral stage in which the infant has not yet learned that it and the world are separate. Fantasies become confused with reality, giving rise to hallucinations and delusions. Yet critics point out that schizophrenic behavior is not the same as infantile behavior.

LEARNING VIEWS Learning theorists explain schizophrenia in terms of conditioning and observational learning. From this perspective, people engage in schizophrenic behavior when it is more likely to be reinforced than normal behavior. This may occur when a person is reared in a socially unrewarding or punitive situation. Inner fantasies then become more reinforcing than social realities.

Patients in a psychiatric hospital may learn what is "expected" by observing others. Hospital staff may reinforce schizophrenic behavior by paying more attention to patients who behave bizarrely. This view is consistent with folklore that the child who disrupts the class attracts more attention from the teacher than the "good" child.

Critics note that many people are reared in socially punitive settings but apparently are immune to the extinction of socially appropriate behavior. Others develop schizophrenic behavior without having had opportunities to observe other people with schizophrenia.

SOCIOCULTURAL VIEWS Many investigators have considered whether and how social and cultural factors such as poverty, discrimination, and overcrowding contribute to schizophrenia—especially among people who are genetically vulnerable to the disorder. A classic study in New Haven, Connecticut, showed that the rate of schizophrenia was twice as high in the lowest socioeconomic class as in the next-higher class on the socioeconomic ladder (Hollingshead & Redlich, 1958). Some sociocultural theorists therefore suggest that treatment of schizophrenia requires reforming society so as to alleviate poverty and other social ills, rather than trying to change people whose behavior is deviant.

Critics of this view suggest that low socioeconomic status may be a result, rather than a cause, of schizophrenia. People with schizophrenia may drift toward low social status because they lack the social skills and cognitive abilities to function at higher social class levels. Thus, they may wind up in poor neighborhoods in disproportionately high numbers.

Evidence for the hypothesis that people with schizophrenia drift downward to lower socioeconomic status is mixed (Nevid and others, 1997). Many people with schizophrenia do drift downward occupationally in comparison with their fathers' occupations. Many others, however, were reared in families in which the father came from the lowest socioeconomic class. Because the stresses of poverty may play a role in the development of schizophrenia, many researchers are interested in the possible interactions between psychosocial stressors and biological factors (Carpenter & Buchanan, 1994).

BIOLOGICAL RISK FACTORS Research evidence suggests that there are three biological risk factors for schizophrenia: heredity, complications during pregnancy and birth, and birth during winter (Carpenter & Buchanan, 1994; Goleman, 1996a).

Schizophrenia, like many other psychological disorders, runs in families (Grove and others, 1991). People with schizophrenia constitute about 1% of the population. However, children with one parent who has been diagnosed as schizophrenic have about a 10% chance of being diagnosed as schizophrenic themselves. Children with two such parents have about a 35–40% chance of doing so (Gottesman, 1991; Straube & Oades, 1992). Twin studies also find about a 40–50% concordance rate for the diagnosis among pairs of identical (MZ) twins, whose genetic codes are the same, compared with about a 10% rate among pairs of fraternal (DZ) twins (Gottesman, 1991; Straube & Oades, 1992). Moreover, adoptee studies find that the biological parent typically places the child at greater risk for schizophrenia than the adoptive parent—even though the child has been reared by the adoptive parent (Gottesman, 1991; Carpenter & Buchanan, 1994). Sharing genes with relatives who have schizophrenia apparently places a person at risk of developing the disorder.

There seems to be strong evidence for a genetic role in schizophrenia. However, heredity cannot be the sole factor. If it were, we would expect a 100% concordance rate between identical twins, as opposed to the 40–50% rate found by researchers (Carpenter & Buchanan, 1994). It also turns out that many people with schizophrenia have undergone complications during pregnancy and birth (Goleman, 1996a). For example, the mothers of many people with schizophrenia had influenza during the sixth or seventh month of pregnancy (C. E. Barr and others, 1990). Maternal starvation has also been implicated (Susser & Lin, 1992). Individuals with schizophrenia are also somewhat more likely to have been born during winter than would be predicted by chance (Carpenter & Buchanan, 1994). Considered together, these three biological risk factors suggest that schizophrenia involves atypical development of the central nervous system. Problems in the nervous system may involve neurotransmitters as well as the development of brain structures, and research on these problems has led to the dopamine theory of schizophrenia.

THE DOPAMINE THEORY OF SCHIZOPHRENIA Much research has been conducted on the chemistry of schizophrenia. Numerous chemical substances have been suspected of playing a role. Much recent research has focused on

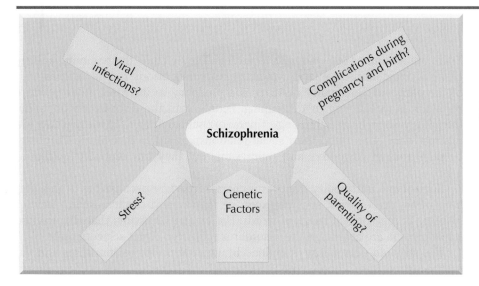

FIGURE 15.4
A MULTIFACTORIAL MODEL OF SCHIZOPHRENIA
According to the multifactorial model of schizophrenia, people with a genetic vulnerability to the disorder experience increased risk for schizophrenia when they encounter problems such as viral infections, birth complications, stress, and poor parenting. People without the genetic vulnerability would not develop schizophrenia despite such problems.

the neurotransmitter dopamine (Carpenter & Buchanan, 1994). According to the dopamine theory of schizophrenia, people with schizophrenia use more dopamine than other people do, although they may not *produce* more of it. Why? They may have more dopamine receptors in the brain than other people, or their dopamine receptors may be hyperactive (Davis and others, 1991). Post-mortem studies of the brains of people with schizophrenia have yielded evidence that is consistent with both possibilities.

Many researchers agree that dopamine plays a role in schizophrenia but argue that other neurotransmitters are also involved (Maas and others, 1993; van Kammen and others, 1990). Supportive evidence is found in the fact that drugs that act on dopamine alone are not always effective in the treatment of schizophrenia (Carpenter & Buchanan, 1994).

Because so many psychological and biological factors have been implicated in schizophrenia, most investigators today favor a *multifactorial* model. According to this model, genetic factors create a predisposition toward schizophrenia (see Figure 15.4). Genetic vulnerability to the disorder interacts with other factors, such as complications during pregnancy and birth, stress, and quality of parenting, to cause the disorder to develop (Michels & Marzuk, 1993a; Venables, 1996).

REFLECTIONS

- Have you ever heard the expression "split personality"? Does the expression seem to apply more to dissociative identity disorder or to schizophrenia? Why?
- Can you imagine what it might be like to have schizophrenia? Why might it be frightening not to be able to distinguish between reality and hallucinations?

■ PERSONALITY DISORDERS

Personality disorders, like personality traits, are characterized by enduring patterns of behavior. Personality disorders, however, are inflexible and maladaptive. They impair personal or social functioning and are a source of distress to the individual or to other people (Widiger & Costa, 1994).

• *Types of Personality Disorders*

There are a number of personality disorders. They include the paranoid, schizotypal, schizoid, antisocial, and avoidant personality disorders. The defining trait of the **paranoid personality disorder** is a tendency to interpret other people's behavior as threatening or demeaning. People with the disorder do not show the grossly disorganized thinking of paranoid schizophrenia. However, they are mistrustful of others, and their social relationships suffer as a result. They may be suspicious of coworkers and supervisors, but they can generally hold onto a job.

Schizotypal personality disorder is characterized by peculiarities of thought, perception, or behavior, such as excessive fantasy and suspiciousness, feelings of being unreal, or odd usage of words. The bizarre behaviors that characterize schizophrenia are absent, so this disorder is schizo*typal,* not schizophrenic.

The **schizoid personality** is defined by indifference to relationships and flat emotional response. People with this disorder are "loners." They do not develop warm, tender feelings for others. They have few friends and rarely get married.

PERSONALITY DISORDERS • Enduring patterns of maladaptive behavior that are sources of distress to the individual or others.

PARANOID PERSONALITY DISORDER • A disorder characterized by persistent suspiciousness, but not involving the disorganization of paranoid schizophrenia.

SCHIZOTYPAL PERSONALITY DISORDER • A disorder characterized by oddities of thought and behavior, but not involving bizarre psychotic behaviors.

SCHIZOID PERSONALITY DISORDER • A disorder characterized by social withdrawal.

Some people with schizoid personality disorder do very well on the job provided that continuous social interaction is not required. They do not have hallucinations or delusions.

People with **antisocial personality disorder** persistently violate the rights of others and are often in conflict with the law (see Table 15.4). They often show a superficial charm and are at least average in intelligence. Striking features are their lack of guilt or anxiety about their misdeeds and their failure to learn from punishment or to form meaningful bonds with other people (Widiger and others, 1996). Though they are often heavily punished by their parents and rejected by peers, they continue in their impulsive, careless styles of life (Patterson, 1993; White and others, 1994). Many people with antisocial personality disorder are also alcoholic (Sher & Trull, 1994). Women are more likely than men to have anxiety and depressive disorders. Men are more likely to have antisocial personality disorder (Sutker, 1994).

People with **avoidant personality disorder** are generally unwilling to enter a relationship without some assurance of acceptance because they fear rejection and criticism. As a result, they may have few close relationships outside their immediate families. Unlike people with schizoid personality disorder, however, they have some interest in, and feelings of warmth toward, other people.

• *Theoretical Views*

Many of the theoretical explanations of personality disorders are derived from the psychodynamic model. Traditional Freudian theory focuses on Oedipal problems as the source of many psychological disorders, including personality disorders. Faulty resolution of the Oedipus complex might lead to antisocial personality disorder, since the moral conscience, or superego, is believed to depend on proper resolution of the Oedipus complex. Research evidence supports the theory that lack of guilt, a frequent characteristic of people with antisocial personality disorder, is more likely to develop among children who are rejected and punished by their parents rather than given warmth and affection (Baumeister and others, 1994; Zahn-Waxler & Kochanska, 1990). Psychodynamic theory proposed that men were more likely than women to experience feelings of guilt because men were subjected to the throes of the Oedipus complex. However, empirical research shows that *women* are actually more likely to

A Person With an Antisocial Personality. Some people with antisocial personalities fit the stereotype of the amoral, violent career criminal. Gary Gilmore was executed after being convicted of two murders. As a child, Gilmore showed conduct problems at home and in school. He began a violent career in adolescence. He never held a steady job or maintained a committed relationship. Though he was intentionally cruel, he never showed guilt or remorse for his misdeeds.

TABLE 15.4 CHARACTERISTICS OF PEOPLE DIAGNOSED WITH ANTISOCIAL PERSONALITY DISORDER	
Key Characteristics	**Other Common Characteristics**
History of delinquency and truancy	Lack of loyalty or formation of enduring relationships
Persistent violation of the rights of others	
Impulsiveness	Failure to maintain good job performance over the years
Poor self-control	Failure to develop or adhere to a life plan
Lack of remorse for misdeeds	Sexual promiscuity
Lack of empathy	Substance abuse
Deceitfulness and manipulativeness	Inability to tolerate boredom
Irresponsibility	Low tolerance for frustration
Glibness; superficial charm	Irritability
Exaggerated sense of self-worth	

Sources: Harris and others, 1994; White and others, 1994; Widiger and others, 1996.

ANTISOCIAL PERSONALITY DISORDER • The diagnosis given a person who is in frequent conflict with society, yet who is undeterred by punishment and experiences little or no guilt and anxiety.
AVOIDANT PERSONALITY DISORDER • A personality disorder in which the person is generally unwilling to enter relationships without assurance of acceptance because of fears of rejection and criticism.

feel guilty about moral transgressions (Baumeister and others, 1994; Tangney, 1990). Men are more likely to fear being caught.

Learning theorists suggest that childhood experiences can contribute to maladaptive ways of relating to others in adulthood—that is, can lead to personality disorders. Cognitive psychologists find that antisocial adolescents encode social information in ways that bolster their misdeeds. For example, they tend to interpret other people's behavior as threatening, even when it is not (Crick & Dodge, 1994; Dodge and others, 1990; Lochman, 1992). Cognitive therapists have encouraged some antisocial adolescents to view social provocations as problems to be solved rather than as threats to their "manhood," with some favorable initial results (Lochman, 1992).

From a trait theory perspective, many personality disorders seem to be extreme variations of normal personality traits. Referring to the five-factor model of personality, people with schizoid personalities tend to be highly introverted (Widiger & Costa, 1994). People with avoidant personalities tend to be both introverted and emotionally unstable (neurotic) (Widiger & Costa, 1994).

Genetic factors are apparently involved in some personality disorders (Rutter, 1997). For example, antisocial personality disorder tends to run in families. Adoptee studies reveal higher incidences of antisocial behavior among the biological parents than among the adoptive relatives of individuals with the disorder (DiLalla & Gottesman, 1991). Yet genetic influences seem to be moderate at most. The family environment also contributes to antisocial behavior (Plomin and others, 1997).

Genetic factors in antisocial personality disorder may influence the level of arousal of the nervous system. Consider that antisocial personality disorder is characterized by deficiency in self-control (Sher & Trull, 1994). People with the disorder are unlikely to show guilt for their misdeeds or to be deterred by punishment. Low levels of guilt and anxiety may reflect lower-than-normal levels of arousal, which, in turn, may be partially genetically based (Lykken, 1982).

Why are people with antisocial personality disorder undeterred by punishment? Experiments show that people with antisocial personality disorder do not learn as rapidly as other people who are equal in intelligence when the payoff is ability to stop a threatened electric shock. But when their levels of arousal are increased by injections of adrenaline, they learn to avoid punishment as rapidly as others (Chesno & Kilmann, 1975; Schachter & Latané, 1964). Other research finds that people with antisocial personality disorder are not as shocked by unpleasant slides that include mutilated people and snakes as other people are (Patrick and others, 1993). All in all, people with antisocial personality disorder may practically live without fear.

Genetic factors such as a lower-than-normal level of arousal would not by itself cause the development of an antisocial personality (Rutter, 1997). Perhaps a person must also be reared under conditions that do not foster the self-concept of a law-abiding citizen. Punishment for deviant behavior would then be unlikely to induce feelings of guilt and shame. Such an individual might well be "undeterred" by punishment.

REFLECTIONS

- Agree or disagree, and support your answer: "All criminals have antisocial personality disorder."
- Do you know anyone whom you believe to have "a bad personality"? How does the term "bad personality" differ from the diagnosis of personality disorder?

■ EATING DISORDERS

Most of us either deprive ourselves or consume vast quantities of food now and then. This is normal. The **eating disorders** listed in the DSM are characterized by persistent, gross disturbances in eating patterns.

• *Types of Eating Disorders*

In this section we will discuss the major types of eating disorders and some proposed explanations for them. These include anorexia nervosa and bulimia nervosa.

ANOREXIA NERVOSA There is a saying that you can never be too rich or too thin. Excess money may be pleasant enough, but, as in the case of Karen, one can certainly be too thin.

> Karen was the 22-year-old daughter of a renowned English professor. She had begun her college career full of promise at the age of 17. But two years ago, after "social problems" occurred, she had returned to live at home and taken progressively lighter course loads at a local college. Karen had never been overweight, but about a year ago her mother noticed that she seemed to be gradually "turning into a skeleton."
>
> Karen spent hours every day shopping at the supermarket, butcher, and bakeries; and in conjuring up gourmet treats for her parents and younger siblings. Arguments over her lifestyle and eating habits had divided the family into two camps. The camp led by her father called for patience. That headed by her mother demanded confrontation. Her mother feared that Karen's father would "protect her right into her grave" and wanted Karen placed in residential treatment "for her own good." The parents finally compromised on an outpatient evaluation.
>
> At an even 5 feet, Karen looked like a prepubescent 11-year-old. Her nose and cheekbones protruded crisply, like those of an elegant young fashion model. Her lips were full, but the redness of the lipstick was unnatural, as if too much paint had been dabbed on a corpse for the funeral. Karen weighed only 78 pounds, but she had dressed in a stylish silk blouse, scarf, and baggy pants so that not one inch of her body was revealed. More striking than her mouth was the redness of her rouged cheeks. It was unclear whether she had used too much makeup or whether minimal makeup had caused the stark contrast between the parts of her face that were covered and those that were not.
>
> Karen vehemently denied that she had a problem. Her figure was "just about where I want it to be" and she engaged in aerobic exercise daily. A deal was struck in which outpatient treatment would be tried as long as Karen lost no more weight and showed steady gains back to at least 90 pounds. Treatment included a day hospital with group therapy and two meals a day. But word came back that Karen was artfully toying with her food—cutting it up, sort of licking it, and moving it about her plate—rather than eating it. After three weeks Karen had lost another pound. At that point her parents were able to persuade her to enter a residential treatment program where her eating could be carefully monitored.

Karen was diagnosed with **anorexia nervosa,** a life-threatening disorder characterized by refusal to maintain a healthful body weight, intense fear of

EATING DISORDERS • Psychological disorders that are characterized by distortion of the body image and gross disturbances in eating patterns.
ANOREXIA NERVOSA • A life-threatening eating disorder characterized by refusal to maintain a healthful body weight, intense fear of being overweight, a distorted body image, and, in females, lack of menstruation (amenorrhea.)

being overweight, a distorted body image, and, in women, lack of menstruation (amenorrhea). People with anorexia usually weigh less than 85% of what would be considered a healthy weight.

By and large, eating disorders afflict women during adolescence and young adulthood (Heatherton and others, 1997). Nearly 1 in 200 school-aged girls has trouble gaining or maintaining weight. The incidences of anorexia nervosa and bulimia nervosa have increased markedly in recent years. Women with anorexia

PSYCHOLOGY in the NEW MILLENNIUM

Will We Be Competing with "Cyberbabes" and "Cyberhunks" in the New Millennium?

At the turn of the millennium, many American women find themselves competing against the ideal of the tall, slender, "buffed up" woman (Williams, 1992). That image has sent millions of women, young and older, to their mirrors, searching out that extra ounce of fat. It has given rise to an epidemic of eating disorders, as women starve themselves or upchuck their food to control their weight. Men, too, have been feeling the pressure to slim down—and buff up. Many dancers, wrestlers, and male models have also developed eating disorders (DeAngelis, 1997a; Gilbert, 1996b).

It is difficult enough for people to compete against the flesh-and-blood supermodels they see in the media. But what of the *virtual* models that will be assaulting us from every medium imaginable—and some that may be

not so imaginable? Consider Lara Croft, the 29-year-old epitome of female perfection. She's tall (5 ft. 9 in.), slim (110 lbs.), and well-muscled. (Unreal?) You won't find her sitting in your class. It's not that she's opposed to education, it's that she's *unreal* in more ways than one. Lara's not a flesh-and-blood "babe"—she's what her devotees call a "cyberbabe," and you'll find her on videogames and in ads. Ads, ads, and more ads.

Her name is Lara Croft, and she seems to be everywhere (Barboza, 1998[1]). Her image is popping up in magazines, on television and computer screens, even on pinup posters like the one in the [January 1998] issue of *PC Games* magazine, which shows her reclining in a bikini, a handgun resting suggestively on her hip.

And she's not even real. Lara is a digitized female image from one of the hottest-selling video games of [1998], *Tomb Raider 2,* which is published by Eidos Interactive, based in London. But that has not stopped Lara—whose tanned, voluptuous cyberframe is the equivalent of 34-24-34—from becoming a popular female icon. She is a far cry from Betty Boop, and she is no Barbie doll. She is more like a female Indiana Jones, but pumped up, vertically and horizontally.

Her fans say she is gritty, sexy, sassy, smart and, well, virtually real. And that's exactly what her British creators were hoping for. "It's really a strange phenomenon because people talk about her as if she's a real person," said Cindy Church, a spokeswoman for Eidos. "A lot of people who play video games fantasize about her." Unsure of just how to portray the silicon icon, Church went

[1]Reprinted with permission from David Barboza (1998, January 19) "Video World Is Smitten by a Gun-Toting, Tomb-Raiding Sex Symbol," *The New York Times*, p. D3.

greatly outnumber men with the disorder, as noted in the following "Psychology in a World of Diversity" feature.

Women with anorexia may lose 25% or more of their body weight in a year. Severe weight loss stops ovulation (Frisch, 1997). Their overall health declines.

In the typical pattern, a girl notices some weight gain after menarche and decides that it must come off. However, dieting—and, often, exercise—continue at a fever pitch. They persist even after the girl reaches an average weight,

Lara Croft. Will people be competing with cyberbabes like Lara and cyberhunks as well as real people in the new millennium?

on, "She's not overly sexual," then paused. "OK, she is physically sexual, but she has a personality behind her."

Because of those attributes, Eidos executives are being flooded with gifts and presents for the silicon princess. There are flowers, Christmas gifts, even vows from young boys and men. "People all over the world have sent in their pictures," said Tricia Gray at the Eidos office in San Francisco. "She's had dozens of marriage proposals and all these cheesy letters."

Indeed, in Britain, only the bubbly Spice Girls are said to be more popular. And in the United States, her Indiana Jones-like video exploits are being sold in large quantities to game players who are well into their 30s.

Lara's first game, *Tomb Raider,* was released in November 1996 and sold about 3.5 million copies worldwide. *Tomb Raider 2,* which came out [in November 1997], has sold several million, according to Eidos. As a result, just about every game and computer magazine wants to reprint Lara's sexy image. There are even entire

World Wide Web sites devoted to her and sites created by individuals who even take the liberty of posing the digital Lara in the nude.

"The most obvious reason Lara Croft is so popular is that 99.5 percent of the gaming population is young men," says Steve Klett, editor of *PC Games* magazine, which has Lara gracing its cover this month. "And it doesn't hurt that she's so outrageously proportioned."

Indeed, the craze surrounding Lara (there is also an online newspaper dedicated to chronicling her life) might be yet another sign that technological advances in human imagery are creating lifelike portraits that further blur the line between reality and fantasy. Devoted fans, who see a three-dimensional image and hear a real British voice projecting out of their computer speakers, have dubbed Lara a "cyberbabe" and the "silicon chick."

And to bolster such realism, Lara has her own biography and a rebellious past. Born into an aristocratic family in Wimbledon, England, Lara Croft—whose given age is 29—grew up in a world of private tutors, boarding schools and a Swiss finishing school. But on a skiing trip to the Himalayas, her plane crashed. Lara, who was the sole survivor, soon realized that she could not stand the "suffocating atmosphere of the upper-class British society" and preferred a new adventurous life. Thus she began searching for ancient artifacts and fighting villains and a zoo of animals, like tigers and wolves.

But her creators say that Lara's future is not about slaying dragons but winning eyeballs. "The digital Lara is going to sign a modeling contract with a big agency," Church boasts. "She'll become a supermodel, like Naomi Campbell and Linda Evangelista."

Even her creators think she's real. ∎

Truth or Fiction Revisited

The statement that "You can never be too rich or too thin" is false. I won't pass judgment on whether or not you can be too rich. You can clearly be too thin, however. About 4% of women with anorexia die from related problems such as weakness or imbalances in body chemistry (Herzog and others, 1988).

and even after family members and others have told her that she is losing too much. Girls with anorexia almost always adamantly deny that they are wasting away. They may point to their fierce exercise regimens as proof. Their body image is distorted (Williamson and others, 1993). Penner and his colleagues (1991) studied women who averaged 31% below their ideal body weight according to Metropolitan Life Insurance Company charts. The women, ironically, overestimated the size of parts of their bodies by 31%! Other people perceive women with anorexia as "skin and bones." The women themselves frequently sit before the mirror and see themselves as heavy.

Many people with anorexia become obsessed with food. They engross themselves in cookbooks, take on the family shopping chores, and prepare elaborate dinners—for others.

Psychology in a World of
DIVERSITY

Eating Disorders: Why the Gender Gap?

The typical person with anorexia or bulimia is a young White female of higher socioeconomic status. Yet anorexia is becoming more prevalent among males, other ethnic groups, and older people (DeAngelis, 1997a; Gilbert, 1996).

Women with eating disorders vastly outnumber men with these disorders. Theorists account for the gender gap in different ways. Because anorexia is connected with amenorrhea, some psychodynamic theorists suggest that anorexia represents an effort by the girl to revert to a prepubescent stage. Anorexia allows the girl to avoid growing up, separating from her family, and taking on adult responsibilities. Because of the loss of fatty deposits, her breasts and hips flatten. In her fantasies, perhaps, a woman with anorexia remains a child, sexually undifferentiated.

Cognitive-behavioral approaches suggest that weight loss has strong reinforcement value because it provides feelings of personal perfectibility (Vitousek & Manke, 1994). Yet "perfection" is an impossible goal for most people. Fashion models, who represent the female ideal, are 9% taller and 16% slimmer than the average woman (Williams, 1992). Sixteen percent! For most women, that is at least 16 pounds!

Consider the sociocultural aspects of eating disorders: As the cultural ideal grows slimmer, women with average or heavier-than-average figures come under more pressure to control their weight. Agras and Kirkley (1986) documented interest in losing weight by counting the numbers of diet articles printed in three women's magazines: *Ladies' Home Journal, Good Housekeeping,* and *Harper's Bazaar*—since 1900. Diet articles were absent until the 1930s. During the 1930s and 1940s, only about one such article appeared in every 10 issues. During the 1950s and 1960s, the number of diet articles jumped to about one in every other issue. During the 1980s, however, the number mushroomed to about 1.3 articles per issue. This means that in recent years there has been an average of *more than one* diet article per issue!

Many men with eating disorders are involved in sports or occupations that require them to remain within certain weight ranges, such as dancing, wrestling, and modeling (Gilbert, 1996). (Women ballet dancers are also at special risk of developing eating disorders [Dunning, 1997].) Men are more likely than women to control their weight through intense exercise. Men, like women, are under social pressure to conform to an ideal body image—one that builds their upper bodies and trims their abdomens (DeAngelis, 1997a).

BULIMIA NERVOSA The case of Nicole is a vivid account of a young woman who was diagnosed with bulimia nervosa:

> Nicole awakens in her cold dark room and already wishes it was time to go back to bed. She dreads the thought of going through this day, which will be like so many others in her recent past. She asks herself the question every morning, "Will I be able to make it through the day without being totally obsessed by thoughts of food, or will I blow it again and spend the day [binge eating]"? She tells herself that today she will begin a new life, today she will start to live like a normal human being. However, she is not at all convinced that the choice is hers. (Boskind-White & White, 1983, p. 29)

It turns out that this day Nicole begins by eating eggs and toast. Then she binges on cookies; doughnuts; bagels smothered with butter, cream cheese, and jelly; granola; candy bars; and bowls of cereal and milk—all within 45 minutes. When she cannot take in any more food, she turns her attention to purging. She goes to the bathroom, ties back her hair, turns on the shower to mask any noise she will make, drinks a glass of water, and makes herself vomit. Afterward she vows, "Starting tomorrow, I'm going to change." But she knows that tomorrow she will probably do the same thing.

Bulimia nervosa is characterized by recurrent cycles of binge eating followed by dramatic measures to purge the food. Binge eating frequently follows food deprivation—for example, severe dieting (Lowe and others, 1996; Polivy and others, 1994). Purging includes self-induced vomiting, fasting or strict dieting, use of laxatives, and vigorous exercise. People with bulimia are often perfectionistic about body shape and weight (Joiner and others, 1997). Like anorexia, bulimia afflicts many more women than men.

• Theoretical Views

Numerous explanations of anorexia nervosa and bulimia nervosa have been proposed. Some psychoanalysts suggest that anorexia represents an unconscious effort by the girl to cope with sexual fears, particularly the prospect of pregnancy. Others suggest that adolescents may use refusal to eat as a weapon against their parents. One study compared mothers of adolescents with eating disorders with mothers of adolescents without such problems. Mothers of adolescents with eating disorders were relatively more likely to be unhappy with their family's functioning, to have problems with eating and dieting themselves, to think that their daughters should lose weight, and to consider their daughter to be unattractive (Pike & Rodin, 1991). The researchers speculate that some adolescents develop eating disorders as a way of coping with feelings of loneliness and alienation that they experience in the home. Could binge eating symbolize the effort to gain parental nurturance and comfort (Humphrey, 1986)? Is purging a symbolic ridding oneself of negative feelings toward the family?

Other psychologists connect eating disorders with extreme fear of gaining weight because of cultural idealization of the slender female. This ideal may

On a Binge. Bulimia nervosa is characterized by recurrent cycles of binge eating and purging. Why do more women than men have eating disorders?

Truth or Fiction Revisited

It is true that some college women control their weight by going on cycles of binge eating followed by self-induced vomiting. Many other women do so as well. People who behave in this way are diagnosed with bulimia nervosa.

BULIMIA NERVOSA • An eating disorder characterized by recurrent cycles of binge eating followed by dramatic measures to purge the food.

In Review   Psychological Disorders

CLASS OF DISORDERS	DESCRIPTION	MAJOR SUBTYPES
Anxiety Disorders	Generally characterized by worrying, fear of the worst happening, fear of losing control, nervousness, and inability to relax	Phobic, panic, generalized anxiety, obsessive-compulsive, and stress disorders
Dissociative Disorders	Generally characterized by separation of mental processes such as thoughts, emotions, identity, memory, or consciousness	Dissociative amnesia, dissociative fugue, dissociative identity disorder, and depersonalization
Somatoform Disorders	Generally characterized by complaints of physical problems such as paralysis or pain, or the persistent belief that one has a serious disease in the absence of medical findings	Conversion disorder and hypochondriasis
Mood Disorders	Generally characterized by disturbance in expressed emotions	Major depression and bipolar disorder
Schizophrenia	Generally characterized by disturbances in language and thought (e.g., delusions, loose associations), attention and perception (e.g., hallucinations), motor activity, and mood, and by withdrawal and absorption in daydreams or fantasy	Paranoid, disorganized, and catatonic schizophrenia
Personality Disorders	Generally characterized by inflexible and maladaptive patterns of behavior that impair personal or social functioning and are a source of distress to oneself or others	Paranoid, schizotypal, schizoid, antisocial, and avoidant personality disorders
Eating Disorders	Generally characterized by persistent, gross disturbances in eating patterns	Anorexia nervosa and bulimia nervosa

contribute to the distortion of a woman's body image and to excess efforts to match the ideal.

REFLECTIONS
- Are you happy with your body shape? Do you feel pressure to be thinner than you are? Why or why not?
- Consider your sociocultural background. Are women from this background traditionally expected to be well-rounded in shape, or are they expected to be slender? What attitudes are connected with weight and body shape?

Although the causes of many psychological disorders remain in dispute, a variety of methods of therapy have been devised to deal with them. Those are the focus of Chapter 16.

SUMMARY

1. **What are psychological disorders?** Psychological disorders are characterized by unusual behavior, socially unacceptable behavior, faulty perception of reality, personal distress, dangerous behavior, or self-defeating behavior.

2. **How are psychological disorders classified?** The most commonly used system for classifying psychological disorders is the Diagnostic and Statistical Manual (DSM-IV) of the American Psychiatric Association. The DSM-IV is a "multiaxial" system with five axes. The axes assess clinical syndromes, personality disorders, general medical conditions, psychosocial and environmental problems, and global assessment of functioning.

3. **What are anxiety disorders?** Anxiety disorders are characterized by motor tension, feelings of dread, and overarousal of the sympathetic branch of the autonomic nervous system. These disorders include irrational, excessive fears, or phobias; panic disorder, which is characterized by sudden attacks in which people typically fear that they may be losing control or going crazy; generalized anxiety; obsessive-compulsive disorders, in which people are troubled by intrusive thoughts or impulses to repeat some activity; and stress disorders, in which a stressful event is followed by persistent fears and intrusive thoughts about the event.

4. **How do psychologists explain anxiety disorders?** Psychoanalysts tend to view anxiety disorders as representing difficulty in repressing primitive impulses. Many learning theorists view phobias as conditioned fears. Cognitive theorists focus on ways in which people interpret threats. Some people may also be genetically predisposed to acquire certain kinds of fears. Anxiety disorders tend to run in families, and some psychologists suggest that biochemical factors that create a predisposition toward anxiety disorders may be inherited.

5. **What are dissociative disorders?** Dissociative disorders are characterized by sudden, temporary changes in consciousness or self-identity. They include dissociative amnesia, or "motivated forgetting"; dissociative fugue, which involves forgetting plus fleeing and adopting a new identity; dissociative identity disorder (multiple personality), in which a person behaves as if more than one personality occupies his or her body; and depersonalization, which is characterized by feelings that one is not real or that one is standing outside oneself.

6. **What are somatoform disorders?** People with somatoform disorders exhibit or complain of physical problems, although no medical evidence of such problems can be found. The somatoform disorders include conversion disorder and hypochondria.

7. **What are mood disorders?** Mood disorders involve disturbances in expressed emotions. Major depression is characterized by persistent feelings of sadness, loss of interest, feelings of worthlessness or guilt, inability to concentrate, and physical symptoms that may include disturbances in regulation of eating and sleeping. Feelings of unworthiness and guilt may be so excessive that they are considered delusional. Bipolar disorder is characterized by dramatic swings in mood between elation and depression.

8. **How do psychologists explain mood disorders?** Research emphasizes possible roles for learned helplessness, attributional styles, and neurotransmitters in depression. People who are depressed are more likely than other people to make internal, stable, and global attributions for failures. It might be that a deficiency in serotonin creates a predisposition toward mood disorders. A concurrent *deficiency* of noradrenaline might contribute to depression. A concurrent *excess* of noradrenaline might contribute to manic behavior.

9. **What is schizophrenia?** Schizophrenia is characterized by disturbances in thought and language, such as loosening of associations and delusions; in perception and attention, as found in hallucinations; in motor activity, as shown by a stupor or by excited behavior; and in mood, as in flat or inappropriate emotional responses. It is also characterized by withdrawal and absorption in daydreams or fantasy.

10. **How do psychologists explain schizophrenia?** There is a tendency for schizophrenia to run in families, suggesting that genetic factors may play a role. According to the dopamine theory, people with schizophrenia may utilize more dopamine than people without the disorder because of a greater-than-normal number of dopamine receptors in the brain. People with schizophrenia may also be relatively more sensitive to dopamine. Multifactorial approaches view schizophrenia in terms of the interaction of psychological and biological factors.

11. **What are personality disorders?** Personality disorders are inflexible, maladaptive behavior patterns that impair personal or social functioning and are a source of distress to the individual or others. The defining trait of paranoid personality disorder is suspiciousness. People with schizotypal personality disorders show oddities of thought, perception, and behavior. Social withdrawal is the major characteristic of schizoid personality disorder. People with antisocial personality disorders persistently violate the rights of others and are in conflict with the law. They show little or no guilt or shame over their misdeeds and are largely undeterred by punishment.

12. **How do psychologists explain antisocial personality disorder?** Research suggests that antisocial personality disorder may develop from some combination of inconsistent discipline, an antisocial father, cynical processing of social information, and lower-than-normal levels of arousal, which would help explain why people with this disorder are undeterred by punishment.

13. **What are the eating disorders?** The eating disorders include anorexia nervosa and bulimia nervosa. Anorexia is characterized by refusal to eat and extreme thinness. Bulimia is characterized by cycles of binge eating and purging. Women are more likely than men to develop these disorders.

14. **How do psychologists explain eating disorders?** Although there are psychodynamic explanations of the eating disorders, most psychologists look to cultural idealization of the very slender female as a major contributor.

To enhance your understanding of the psychological concepts found in this chapter, please consult the following aids:

STUDY GUIDE

Learning Objectives, p. 307
Exercise, p. 308
Lecture and Textbook Outline, p. 309
Effective Studying Ideas, p. 312

Key Terms and Concepts, p. 313
Chapter Review, p. 313
Chapter Exercises, p. 321
Knowing the Language, p. 322
Do You Know the Material?, p. 324

CORE CONCEPTS SEARCH

Diagnosing Abnormal Behavior
Childhood Disorders
Anxiety Disorders
Dissociative Disorders

Mood Disorders
The Schizophrenic Disorders
Causes of Schizophrenia
Personality Disorders

WORLD WIDE WEB

For more information concerning the topics found in this chapter, access psychology links on the World Wide Web made through the Harcourt Brace webpage at

www.hbcollege.com

Share your comments and questions with your author at

PsychLinks@aol.com

Methods of therapy are intended to help people create order and unity in their lives, to help them achieve inner peace. Paul Brach's *Ahola #5* (1991) possesses warmth, serenity, wholeness. It has a mantra-like quality; you fix your eyes on it and it has a calming effect. Methods of therapy are intended to help people find calmness and wholeness. For example, some methods of therapy teach people to accept disparate aspects of themselves as valuable parts of the whole person.

PAUL BRACH

Chapter 16

Methods of Therapy

✓ **T F**

☐ ☐ Residents of London used to visit the local insane asylum for a fun night out on the town.

☐ ☐ To be effective, psychotherapy must continue for months, perhaps years.

☐ ☐ Some psychotherapists interpret clients' dreams.

☐ ☐ Other psychotherapists encourage their clients to take the lead in therapy sessions.

☐ ☐ Still other psychotherapists tell their clients precisely what to do.

☐ ☐ Lying in a reclining chair and fantasizing can be an effective way of confronting fears.

☐ ☐ Smoking cigarettes can be an effective method for helping people . . . stop smoking cigarettes.

☐ ☐ You might be able to put an end to bad habits merely by keeping a record of where and when you engage in those habits.

☐ ☐ The originator of a surgical technique designed to reduce violence learned that it was not always successful . . . when one of his patients shot him.

OUTLINE

WHAT IS THERAPY? THE SEARCH FOR A "SWEET OBLIVIOUS ANTIDOTE"
The History of Therapies
PSYCHODYNAMIC THERAPIES
Traditional Psychoanalysis: "Where Id Was, There Shall Ego Be"
Modern Psychodynamic Approaches
HUMANISTIC-EXISTENTIAL THERAPIES
Client-Centered Therapy: Removing Roadblocks to Self-Actualization
Gestalt Therapy: Getting It Together
BEHAVIOR THERAPY: ADJUSTMENT IS WHAT YOU DO
Fear-Reduction Methods
Psychology in the New Millennium: Getting High (and Keeping Cool) With Virtual Reality
Aversive Conditioning
Operant Conditioning Procedures
Questionnaire: The Rathus Assertiveness Schedule
Psychology and Modern Life: Becoming More Assertive
Self-Control Methods
COGNITIVE THERAPIES
Cognitive Therapy: Correcting Cognitive Errors
Rational Emotive Behavior Therapy: Overcoming "Musts" and "Shoulds"
GROUP THERAPIES
Encounter Groups
Couple Therapy
Family Therapy
DOES PSYCHOTHERAPY WORK?
Problems in Conducting Research on Psychotherapy
Analyses of Therapy Effectiveness
Psychology in a World of Diversity: Psychotherapy and Human Diversity
BIOLOGICAL THERAPIES
Drug Therapy
Psychology in the New Millennium: Looking Ahead From the "Decade of the Brain"
Electroconvulsive Therapy
Psychosurgery
Does Biological Therapy Work?

*J*ASMINE, A 19-YEAR-OLD COLLEGE SOPHOmore, has been crying almost without letup for several days. She feels that her life is falling apart. Her college aspirations are in a shambles. She has brought shame upon her family. Thoughts of suicide have crossed her mind. She can barely drag herself out of bed in the morning. She is avoiding her friends. She can pinpoint some sources of stress in her life: a couple of poor grades, an argument with a boyfriend, friction with roommates. Still, her misery seemed to descend on her out of nowhere.

Jasmine is depressed—so depressed that her family and friends have finally prevailed upon her to seek professional help. Had she broken her leg, her treatment by a qualified professional would have followed a fairly standard course. Yet treatment of psychological problems and disorders like depression may be approached from very different perspectives. Depending on whom Jasmine sees, she may be

- Lying on a couch talking about anything that pops into her awareness and exploring the hidden meanings of a recurrent dream.
- Sitting face to face with a gentle, accepting therapist who places the major responsibility for what happens in therapy on Jasmine's shoulders.
- Listening to a frank, straightforward therapist assert that her problems stem from self-defeating attitudes and perfectionistic beliefs.
- Taking antidepressant medication.
- Participating in some combination of these approaches.

These methods, though different, all represent methods of therapy. In this chapter we explore various methods of psychotherapy and biological therapy.

■ WHAT IS THERAPY? THE SEARCH FOR A "SWEET OBLIVIOUS ANTIDOTE"[1]

There are many kinds of psychotherapy, but they all have certain things in common. **Psychotherapy** is a systematic interaction between a therapist and a client that applies psychological principles to affect the client's thoughts, feelings, or behavior in order to help the client overcome psychological disorders, adjust to problems in living, or develop as an individual.

Quite a mouthful? True. But note the essentials:

1. *Systematic Interaction.* Psychotherapy is a systematic interaction between a client and a therapist. The therapist's theoretical point of view

PSYCHOTHERAPY • A systematic interaction between a therapist and a client that brings psychological principles to bear on influencing the client's thoughts, feelings, or behavior to help that client overcome abnormal behavior or adjust to problems in living.

---
[1]The phrase is from Shakespeare's *Macbeth,* as seen in the following pages.

St. Mary's of Bethlehem. This famous London institution is the source of the term *bedlam*.

interacts with the client's to determine how the therapist and client relate to each other.

2. *Psychological Principles.* Psychotherapy is based on psychological theory and research in areas such as personality, learning, motivation, and emotion.

3. *Thoughts, Feelings, and Behavior.* Psychotherapy influences clients' thoughts, feelings, and behavior. It can be aimed at any or all of these aspects of human psychology.

4. *Psychological Disorders, Adjustment Problems, and Personal Growth.* Psychotherapy is often used with people who have psychological disorders. Other people seek help in adjusting to problems such as shyness, weight problems, or loss of a spouse. Still other clients want to learn more about themselves and to reach their full potential as individuals, parents, or creative artists.

• *The History of Therapies*

Ancient and medieval "treatments" of psychological disorders often reflected demonological thinking. As such, they tended to involve cruel practices such as exorcism and death by hanging or burning. Some people who could not meet the demands of everyday life were tossed into prisons. Others begged in the streets, stole food, or became prostitutes. A few found their way to monasteries or other retreats that offered a kind word and some support. Generally speaking, they died early.

ASYLUMS **Asylums** originated in European monasteries. They were the first institutions meant primarily for people with psychological disorders. But their function was warehousing, not treatment. Their inmate populations mushroomed until the stresses created by noise, overcrowding, and disease actually aggravated the problems they were meant to ease. Inmates were frequently chained and beaten.

ASYLUM • (uh-SIGH-lum). An institution for the care of the mentally ill.

Philippe Pinel

He almost singlehandedly turned the treatment of people with psychological disorders topsy-turvy. The Frenchman Philippe Pinel (1745–1826) was born into a family of physicians and received his own degree in medicine from the University of Toulouse. Concerned about the greed and callousness of his fellow doctors, he moved to Paris to treat the poor. He became interested in psychological disorders when a friend developed one and there was no treatment for him. At this time, people with severe psychological disorders were warehoused and abused in asylums. They were typically chained, sometimes whirled in chairs, and bloodletting was also in vogue. Pinel would write in his *A Treatise on Insanity* (1801) that the blood of patients was spilled so lavishly that one might wonder who was the real "madman"—the patient or his physician. Pinel argued for the humane treatment of people with such disorders and had his chance to make a dif-

ference when he was appointed director of La Bicêtre.

Pinel first unchained an English soldier who had once crushed the head of a guard with his chains. Once freed of his shackles, the man was unviolent, and two years later he was discharged. Pinel unchained more and more patients and improved their diets. He put patients with similar kinds of problems together. He promoted the use of occupational therapy. Pinel was also the first to take careful case histories of patients and maintain a record of cure rates. Pinel soon amassed a solid record of success and in 1795 was appointed director of La Salpêtrière hospital, which was Europe's largest asylum and housed 8,000 women. (Almost a century later, La Salpêtrière would be directed by Jean Martin Charcot, who influenced Alfred Binet and Sigmund Freud.) Pinel's influence was soon felt throughout Europe and in the United States. ■

The word *bedlam* derives from St. Mary's of *Bethlehem*, the London asylum that opened its gates in 1547. Here unfortunate people with psychological disorders were chained, whipped, and allowed to lie in their own waste. And here the ladies and gentlemen of the British upper class might stroll on a lazy afternoon to be amused by the inmates' antics. The price of admission was one penny.

Humanitarian reform movements began in the 18th century. In Paris, the physician Philippe Pinel unchained the patients at La Bicêtre. Rather than running amok, most patients profited from kindness and freedom. Many could eventually reenter society. Later movements to reform institutions were led by the Quaker William Tuke in England and by Dorothea Dix in America.

MENTAL HOSPITALS In the United States mental hospitals gradually replaced asylums. In the mid-1950s more than a million people resided in state, county, Veterans Administration, or private facilities. The mental hospital's function is treatment, not warehousing. Still, because of high patient populations and understaffing, many patients received little attention. Even today, with somewhat improved conditions, one psychiatrist may be responsible for the welfare of several hundred residents on a weekend when other staff members are absent.

THE COMMUNITY MENTAL HEALTH MOVEMENT Since the 1960s, efforts have been made to maintain people with serious psychological disorders in their communities. Community mental health centers attempt to maintain new patients as outpatients and to serve patients who have been released from mental hospitals. Today most people with chronic psychological disorders live in the community, not the hospital.

Critics note that many people who had resided in hospitals for decades were suddenly discharged to "home" communities that seemed foreign and forbidding to them. Many do not receive adequate follow-up care. Many join the ranks of the homeless (Carling, 1990; Levine & Rog, 1990).

Truth or Fiction Revisited

It is true that residents of London used to visit the insane asylum for amusement.

REFLECTIONS

- Have people you know said they have undergone "therapy"? What kind of therapy? What are your attitudes toward people who seek professional help for psychological problems? Why?
- Had you heard of insane asylums or mental hospitals? What pictures were conjured up in your mind? How did your impressions match the information in this chapter?

The Unchaining of the Patients at La Bicêtre.
Philippe Pinel sparked the humanitarian reform movement by unchaining the patients at this asylum in Paris.

■ PSYCHODYNAMIC THERAPIES

Psychodynamic therapies are based on the thinking of Sigmund Freud, the founder of psychodynamic theory. They assume that psychological problems reflect early childhood experiences and internal conflicts. According to Freud, these conflicts involve the shifting of psychic, or libidinal, energy among the three psychic structures—the id, ego, and superego. These shifts of psychic energy determine our behavior. When primitive urges threaten to break through from the id or when the superego floods us with excessive guilt, defenses are established and distress is created. Freud's psychodynamic therapy method—psychoanalysis—aims to modify the flow of energy among these structures, largely to bulwark the ego against the torrents of energy loosed by the id and the superego. With impulses and feelings of guilt and shame placed under greater control, clients are freer to develop adaptive behavior.

- *Traditional Psychoanalysis: "Where Id Was, There Shall Ego Be"*

> Canst thou not minister to a mind diseas'd,
> Pluck out from the memory a rooted sorrow,
> Raze out the written troubles of the brain,
> And with some sweet oblivious antidote
> Cleanse the stuff'd bosom of that perilous stuff
> Which weighs upon the heart?
>
> Shakespeare, *Macbeth*

In this passage, Macbeth asks a physician to minister to Lady Macbeth after she has gone mad. In the play, her madness is caused partly by events—namely, her role in murders designed to seat her husband on the throne of Scotland. There are also hints of mysterious, deeply rooted problems, such as conflicts about infertility.

A View of Freud's Consulting Room. Sigmund Freud would sit in a chair by the head of the couch while a client free-associated. The basic rule of free association is that no thought is censored.

If Lady Macbeth's physician had been a traditional psychoanalyst, he might have asked her to lie on a couch in a slightly darkened room. He would have sat behind her and encouraged her to talk about anything that came to mind, no matter how trivial, no matter how personal. To avoid interfering with her self-exploration, he might have said little or nothing for session after session. That would have been par for the course. A traditional **psychoanalysis** can extend for months or even years.

Psychoanalysis is the clinical method devised by Freud for plucking "from the memory a rooted sorrow," for razing "out the written troubles of the brain." It aims to provide *insight* into the conflicts that are presumed to lie at the roots of a person's problems. Insight means many things, including knowledge of the experiences that lead to conflicts and maladaptive behavior, recognition of unconscious feelings and conflicts, and conscious evaluation of one's thoughts, feelings, and behavior.

Psychoanalysis also aims to help the client express feelings and urges that have been repressed. By so doing, Freud believed that the client spilled forth the psychic energy that had been repressed by conflicts and guilt. He called this spilling forth **catharsis.** Catharsis would provide relief by alleviating some of the forces assaulting the ego.

Freud was also fond of saying, "Where id was, there shall ego be." In part, he meant that psychoanalysis could shed light on the inner workings of the mind. He also sought to replace impulsive and defensive behavior with coping behavior. In this way, for example, a man with a phobia for knives might discover that he had been repressing the urge to harm someone who had taken advantage of him. He might also find ways to confront the person verbally.

FREE ASSOCIATION Early in his career as a therapist, Freud found that hypnosis allowed his clients to focus on repressed conflicts and talk about them. The relaxed "trance state" provided by hypnosis seemed to allow clients to "break through" to topics of which they would otherwise be unaware. Freud also found, however, that many clients denied the accuracy of this material once they were out of the trance. Other clients found them to be premature and painful. Freud therefore turned to **free association,** a more gradual method of breaking through the walls of defense that block a client's insight into unconscious processes.

PSYCHOANALYSIS • Freud's method of psychotherapy.
CATHARSIS • (CUH-**THAR**-SIS). In psychoanalysis, the expression of repressed feelings and impulses to allow the release of the psychic energy associated with them.
FREE ASSOCIATION • In psychoanalysis, the uncensored uttering of all thoughts that come to mind.

In free association, the client is made comfortable—for example, lying on a couch—and is asked to talk about any topic that comes to mind. No thought is to be censored—that is the basic rule. Psychoanalysts ask their clients to wander "freely" from topic to topic, but they do not believe that the process occurring *within* the client is fully free. Repressed impulses clamor for release.

The ego persists in trying to repress unacceptable impulses and threatening conflicts. As a result, clients might show **resistance** to recalling and discussing threatening ideas. A client about to entertain such thoughts might claim that "my mind is blank." The client might accuse the analyst of being demanding or inconsiderate. He or she might "forget" the next appointment when threatening material is about to surface.

The therapist observes the dynamic struggle between the compulsion to utter certain thoughts and the client's resistance to uttering them. Through discreet remarks, the analyst subtly tips the balance in favor of utterance. A gradual process of self-discovery and self-insight ensues. Now and then the analyst offers an **interpretation** of an utterance, showing how it suggests resistance or deep-seated feelings and conflicts.

DREAM ANALYSIS

Sometimes a cigar is just a cigar.

SIGMUND FREUD, ON DREAM ANALYSIS

Freud often asked clients to jot down their dreams upon waking so that they could be discussed in therapy. Freud considered dreams the "royal road to the unconscious." He believed that the content of dreams is determined by unconscious processes as well as by the events of the day. Unconscious impulses tend to be expressed in dreams as a form of **wish fulfillment.**

But unacceptable sexual and aggressive impulses are likely to be displaced onto objects and situations that reflect the client's era and culture. These objects become symbols of the unconscious wishes. For example, long, narrow dream objects might be **phallic symbols,** but whether the symbol takes the form of a spear, rifle, stick shift, or spacecraft partially reflects the dreamer's cultural background.

In psychodynamic theory, the perceived content of a dream is referred to as its shown or **manifest content.** Its presumed hidden or symbolic content is its **latent content.** Suppose a man dreams that he is flying. Flying is the manifest content of the dream. Freud usually interpreted flying as being symbolic of erection, so issues concerning sexual potency might make up the latent content of such a dream.

• Modern Psychodynamic Approaches

Some psychoanalysts adhere faithfully to Freud's techniques. In recent years, however, briefer, less intense forms of psychodynamic therapy have been devised. They make treatment available to clients who do not have the time or money for long-term therapy. Many of these therapists also believe that prolonged therapy is not needed or justifiable in terms of the ratio of cost to benefits.

Some modern psychodynamic therapies continue to focus on revealing unconscious material and breaking through psychological defenses. Nevertheless, they differ from traditional psychoanalysis in several ways. One is that the client and therapist usually sit face to face (the client does not lie on a couch). The therapist is usually directive. That is, modern therapists often suggest helpful behavior instead of focusing on insight alone. Finally, there is usually more focus on the ego as the "executive" of personality, and less emphasis on the id.

Truth or Fiction Revisited

It is true that some psychotherapists interpret clients' dreams. Psychoanalysis is a case in point.

Truth or Fiction Revisited

It is not true that psychotherapy must continue for months, perhaps years, to be effective. There are many effective brief forms of psychotherapy.

RESISTANCE • The tendency to block the free expression of impulses and primitive ideas—a reflection of the defense mechanism of repression.
INTERPRETATION • An explanation of a client's utterance according to psychoanalytic theory.
WISH FULFILLMENT • A primitive method used by the id to attempt to gratify basic instincts.
PHALLIC SYMBOL • A sign that represents the penis.
MANIFEST CONTENT • In psychodynamic theory, the reported content of dreams.
LATENT CONTENT • In psychodynamic theory, the symbolized or underlying content of dreams.

Client-Centered Therapy. By showing the qualities of unconditional positive regard, empathic understanding, genuineness, and congruence, client-centered therapists create an atmosphere in which clients can explore their feelings.

For this reason, many modern psychodynamic therapists are considered **ego analysts.**

Many of Freud's followers, the "second generation" of psychoanalysts—from Jung and Adler to Horney and Erikson—believed that Freud had placed too much emphasis on sexual and aggressive impulses and underestimated the role of the ego. For example, Freud aimed to establish conditions under which clients could spill forth psychic energy and eventually shore up the ego. Erikson, in contrast, spoke to clients directly about their values and concerns, encouraging them to develop desired traits and behavior patterns. Even Freud's daughter, the psychoanalyst Anna Freud (1895-1982), was more concerned with the ego than with unconscious forces and conflicts.

REFLECTIONS

- Did you have a mental picture of psychoanalysis before reading this section? What was it like? Did it differ from what you have just read?
- Does it make you feel good to talk with someone about your problems? Why or why not?

■ HUMANISTIC-EXISTENTIAL THERAPIES

Psychodynamic therapies focus on internal conflicts and unconscious processes. Humanistic-existential therapies focus on the quality of the client's subjective, conscious experience. Traditional psychoanalysis focuses on early childhood experiences. Humanistic-existential therapies usually focus on what clients are experiencing "here and now."

These differences, however, are mainly a matter of emphasis. The past has a way of influencing current thoughts, feelings, and behavior. Carl Rogers, the originator of client-centered therapy, believed that childhood experiences gave rise to the conditions of worth that troubled his clients here and now. He and Fritz Perls, the originator of Gestalt therapy, recognized that early incorporation of other people's values often leads clients to "disown" parts of their own personalities.

• Client-Centered Therapy: Removing Roadblocks to Self-Actualization

Truth or Fiction Revisited

It is true that some psychotherapists encourage their clients to take the lead in the therapy session. Client-centered therapists are an example.

EGO ANALYST • A psychodynamically oriented therapist who focuses on the conscious, coping behavior of the ego instead of the hypothesized, unconscious functioning of the id.
CLIENT-CENTERED THERAPY • Carl Rogers' method of psychotherapy which emphasizes the creation of a warm, therapeutic atmosphere that frees clients to engage in self-exploration and self-expression.

Client-centered therapy was originated by Rogers (1951). Rogers believed that we are free to make choices and control our destinies, despite the burdens of the past. He also believed that we have natural tendencies toward health, growth, and fulfillment. Psychological problems arise from roadblocks placed in the path of self-actualization. If, when we are young, other people only approve of us when we are doing what they want us to do, we may learn to disown the parts of ourselves to which they object. We may learn to be seen but not heard—not even by ourselves. As a result, we may experience stress and discomfort and the feeling that we—or the world—are not real.

Client-centered therapy aims to provide insight into the parts of us that we have disowned so that we can feel whole. It creates a warm, therapeutic atmosphere that encourages self-exploration and self-expression. The therapist's acceptance of the client is thought to foster self-acceptance and self-esteem. Self-acceptance frees the client to make choices that develop his or her unique potential.

Client-centered therapy is nondirective. The client takes the lead, stating and exploring problems.

An effective client-centered therapist has several qualities:

- **Unconditional positive regard:** respect for clients as human beings with unique values and goals.
- **Empathic understanding:** recognition of the client's experiences and feelings. Therapists view the world through the client's **frame of reference** by setting aside their own values and listening closely.
- **Genuineness:** Openness and honesty in responding to the client. Client-centered therapists must be able to tolerate differentness, because they believe that every client is different in important ways.

Client-centered therapy is practiced widely in college and university counseling centers, not just to help students experiencing, say, anxieties or depression but also to help them make decisions. Many college students have not yet made career choices or wonder whether they should become involved with particular people or in sexual activity. Client-centered therapists do not tell clients what to do. Instead, they help clients arrive at their own decisions.

• Gestalt Therapy: Getting It Together

Gestalt therapy was originated by Fritz Perls (1893–1970). Like client-centered therapy, it aims to help individuals integrate conflicting parts of their personality. Perls used the term *Gestalt* to signify his interest in giving the conflicting parts of the personality an integrated form or shape. He aimed to have his clients become aware of inner conflict, accept the reality of conflict rather than deny it or keep it repressed, and make productive choices despite misgivings and fears.

Although Perls' ideas about conflicting personality elements owe much to psychodynamic theory, his form of therapy, unlike psychoanalysis, focuses on the here and now. In Gestalt therapy, clients perform exercises to heighten their awareness of their current feelings and behavior, rather than exploring the past. Perls also believed, along with Rogers, that people are free to make choices and to direct their personal growth. Unlike client-centered therapy, however, Gestalt therapy is highly directive. The therapist leads the client through planned experiences.

One Gestalt technique that increases awareness of internal conflict is the **dialogue.** The client undertakes verbal confrontations between opposing wishes and ideas. An example of these clashing personality elements is "top dog" and "underdog." One's top dog might conservatively suggest, "Don't take chances. Stick with what you have or you might lose it all." One's frustrated underdog might then rise up and assert, "You never try anything. How will you ever get out of this rut if you don't take on new challenges?" Heightened awareness of the elements of conflict can clear the path toward resolution, perhaps through a compromise of some kind.

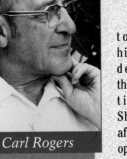
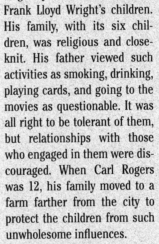
UNCONDITIONAL POSITIVE REGARD • Acceptance of the value of another person, although not necessarily acceptance of everything the person does.
EMPATHIC UNDERSTANDING • **(em-PATH-ick).** Ability to perceive a client's feelings from the client's frame of reference. A quality of the good client-centered therapist.
FRAME OF REFERENCE • One's unique patterning of perceptions and attitudes, according to which one evaluates events.
GENUINENESS • Recognition and open expression of the therapist's own feelings.
GESTALT THERAPY • Fritz Perls' form of psychotherapy, which attempts to integrate conflicting parts of the personality through directive methods designed to help clients perceive their whole selves.
DIALOGUE • A Gestalt therapy technique in which clients verbalize confrontations between conflicting parts of their personality.

Body language also provides insight into conflicting feelings. Clients might be instructed to attend to the ways in which they furrow their eyebrows and tense their facial muscles when they express certain ideas. In this way, they often find that their body language asserts feelings that they have been denying in their spoken statements. To increase clients' understanding of opposing points of view, Gestalt therapists might encourage them to argue in favor of ideas opposed to their own.

Psychodynamic theory views dreams as the "royal road to the unconscious." Perls saw the content of dreams as representing disowned parts of the personality. Perls would often ask clients to role-play the elements of their dreams in order to get in touch with these parts of their personality.

REFLECTIONS
* Have you experienced unconditional positive regard or conditional positive regard in your home life? How do you think your experiences have shaped your self-esteem?
* Do you feel that parts of your personality pull you in different directions? If so, how?

■ BEHAVIOR THERAPY: ADJUSTMENT IS WHAT YOU DO

Behavior therapy—also called *behavior modification*—applies principles of learning to directly promote desired behavioral changes (Wolpe & Plaud, 1997). Behavior therapists rely heavily on principles of conditioning and observational learning. They help clients discontinue self-defeating behavior patterns such as overeating, smoking, and phobic avoidance of harmless stimuli. They also help clients acquire adaptive behavior patterns such as the social skills required to start social relationships or say no to insistent salespeople.

Behavior therapists may help clients gain "insight" into maladaptive behavior in the sense of fostering awareness of the circumstances in which it occurs. They do not foster insight in the psychoanalytic sense of unearthing the childhood origins of problems and the symbolic meanings of maladaptive behavior. Behavior therapists, like other therapists, may also build warm, therapeutic relationships with clients, but they see the efficacy of behavior therapy as deriving from specific, learning-based procedures (Wolpe, 1990). They insist that their methods be established by experimentation and that therapeutic outcomes be assessed in terms of observable, measurable behavior. In this section we consider some frequently used behavior therapy techniques.

• *Fear-Reduction Methods*

Behavior therapists use many methods for reducing fears. These include flooding (see Chapter 7), systematic desensitization, and modeling.

SYSTEMATIC DESENSITIZATION   Adam has a phobia for receiving injections. His behavior therapist treats him as he reclines in a comfortable padded chair. In a state of deep muscle relaxation, Adam observes slides projected on a screen. A slide of a nurse holding a needle has just been shown three times, 30

BEHAVIOR THERAPY • Systematic application of the principles of learning to the direct modification of a client's problem behaviors.

Overcoming a Phobia. One way behavior thera-pists help clients overcome phobias is by having them gradually approach the feared object or situ-ation while they remain relaxed.

seconds at a time. Each time Adam has shown no anxiety. So now a slightly more discomforting slide is shown: one of the nurse aiming the needle toward someone's bare arm. After 15 seconds, our armchair adventurer notices twinges of discomfort and raises a finger as a signal (speaking might disturb his relax-ation). The projector operator turns off the light, and Adam spends 2 minutes imagining his "safe scene"—lying on a beach beneath the tropical sun. Then the slide is shown again. This time Adam views it for 30 seconds before feeling anxiety.

Adam is undergoing **systematic desensitization,** a method for reducing pho-bic responses originated by psychiatrist Joseph Wolpe (1990). Systematic desen-sitization is a gradual process in which the client learns to handle increasingly disturbing stimuli while anxiety to each one is being counterconditioned. About 10 to 20 stimuli are arranged in a sequence, or **hierarchy,** according to their ca-pacity to elicit anxiety. In imagination or by being shown photos, the client travels gradually up through this hierarchy, approaching the target behavior. In Adam's case, the target behavior was the ability to receive an injection without undue anxiety.

Wolpe developed systematic desensitization on the assumption that anxi-ety responses, like other behaviors, are learned or conditioned. He reasoned that they can be unlearned by means of counterconditioning or extinction. In counterconditioning, a response that is incompatible with anxiety is made to appear under conditions that usually elicit anxiety. Muscle relaxation is in-compatible with anxiety. For this reason, Adam's therapist is teaching him to relax in the presence of (usually) anxiety-evoking slides of needles. (Muscle relaxation is usually achieved by means of *progressive relaxation,* which we described in Chapter 14 as a method for lowering the arousal created by anxi-ety reactions.)

Remaining in the presence of phobic imagery, rather than running away from it, is also likely to enhance self-efficacy expectations (Galassi, 1988). Self-efficacy expectations are negatively correlated with levels of adrenaline in the bloodstream (Bandura and others, 1985). Raising clients' self-efficacy expecta-tions thus may help lower their adrenaline levels and reduce their feelings of nervousness.

Truth or Fiction Revisited

It is true that lying in a reclining chair and fantasizing can be an effective way of confronting fears. This is what happens in the method of systematic desensitization.

SYSTEMATIC DESENSITIZATION • Wolpe's method for reducing fears by associating a hierarchy of images of fear-evoking stimuli with deep muscle relaxation.
HIERARCHY • An arrangement of stimuli according to the amount of fear they evoke.

MODELING **Modeling** relies on observational learning. In this method clients observe, and then imitate, people who approach and cope with the objects or situations that the clients fear. Bandura and his colleagues (1969) found that modeling worked as well as systematic desensitization—and more rapidly—in reducing fear of snakes. Like systematic desensitization,

PSYCHOLOGY *in the* ▶ NEW MILLENNIUM

Getting High (and Keeping Cool) With Virtual Reality

Chris Klock peered down from a dizzying height. He was 40 floors above the ground in a tiny glass-walled atrium in the Atlanta Marriott Marquis. Or so it seemed. In weekly sessions lasting 45 minutes each, he was going higher and higher in the elevator until his fear at each level faded, allowing him to move on. In addition to looking down into the hotel's cavernous atrium, the Georgia Institute of Technology junior was also looking out from small balconies at various heights and scrambling across a narrow bridge high above a rapid river. Or so it seemed.

The reality was quite different from the apparent reality, or virtual reality. The elevator, balconies, and bridge were all displays in a virtual reality setup designed to help people with acrophobia.

In "exposure therapy" for phobias, psychologists accompany clients into feared situations. For example, they help them get on airplanes that are standing still in the airport, or onto high balconies. Then they help them remain in the situation until the anxiety fades. The client feels less anxious on subsequent exposures and can accept greater challenges, such as actually flying or standing on a higher balcony. Through repetition in progressively more frightening situations, clients eventually overcome their fears.

The virtual reality treatment used by Chris Klock was created by psychologist Barbara O. Rothbaum of Emory University and computer scientist Larry F. Hodges of Georgia Tech. The balcony scene was a cartoonlike rendering of the view from a balcony. Klock was in the lab room, wearing a virtual reality headset and standing by the rail. As he moved, it seemed that he was getting closer to or farther away from the edge of the balcony.

AN IDEAL PSYCHOLOGICAL TOOL Virtual reality is an ideal psychological tool. It provides an environment that psychologists can control precisely (Russo, 1996). Although he knew it wasn't real, Klock felt as though he were on the edge of the ledge. "Even though it looks like animated reality," he said, "all the depth and movement cues are realistic, so it feels real."

Klock recalled his initial experience with fear of heights. He was 10-years-old and was climbing the stairs to the top of the Statue of Liberty. Halfway up there was a view of the surrounding harbor. "It just terrified me," Klock reported. "I turned around and walked right down the steps."

Klock is one of 12 people with acrophobia who were successfully treated by Rothbaum (1995) with the virtual reality apparatus. Other researchers are trying virtual reality to treat other phobias, such as agoraphobia and speech anxiety. Virtual reality technology is expanding into other areas. There is even virtual reality group therapy. One "group" for men with erectile problems meets with simulated faces in an Internet "chat room." (The men in the group meet several times a week by signing on simultaneously. They each have virtual reality goggles and gloves so that they seem to be in the same room.) Someday clients and their therapists may share virtual worlds peopled by significant figures in the clients' lives, such as their parents.

"I think virtual reality is a potentially great advance for psychotherapy, especially for treating phobias," notes psychologist David Barlow (1995), director of the Phobia and Anxiety Disorders Clinic at the University at Albany. "You can have people experience scary situations through the virtual reality goggles that can be very difficult to arrange for in real life." ∎

modeling is likely to increase self-efficacy expectations in coping with feared stimuli.

• *Aversive Conditioning*

Aversive conditioning is one of the more controversial procedures in behavior therapy. In this method painful or aversive stimuli are paired with unwanted impulses, such as desire for a cigarette or desire to engage in antisocial behavior, in order to make the impulse less appealing. For example, to help people control alcohol intake, tastes of different alcoholic beverages can be paired with drug-induced nausea and vomiting or with electric shock.

Aversive conditioning has been used with problems as diverse as cigarette smoking, sexual abuse (Rice and others, 1991), and retarded children's self-injurious behavior. **Rapid smoking** is an aversive-conditioning method designed to help smokers quit. In this method, the would-be quitter inhales every 6 seconds. In another method the hose of a hair dryer is hooked up to a chamber containing several lit cigarettes. Smoke is blown into the quitter's face as he or she also smokes a cigarette. A third method uses branching pipes so that the smoker draws in smoke from several cigarettes at the same time. In all of these methods overexposure causes once-desirable cigarette smoke to become aversive. The quitter becomes motivated to avoid, rather than seek, cigarettes. Many reports have shown a quit rate of 60% or higher at 6-month follow-ups. Yet interest in these methods for quitting smoking has waned because of side effects such as raising blood pressure and the availability of nicotine-replacement techniques.

In one study of aversive conditioning in the treatment of alcoholism, 63% of the 685 people treated remained abstinent for one year afterward, and about a third remained abstinent for at least three years (Wiens & Menustik, 1983). It may seem ironic that punitive aversive stimulation is sometimes used to stop children from punishing themselves, but people sometimes hurt themselves in order to obtain sympathy and attention. If self-injury leads to more pain than anticipated and no sympathy, it might be discontinued.

• *Operant Conditioning Procedures*

We usually prefer to relate to people who smile at us rather than ignore us and to take courses in which we do well rather than fail. We tend to repeat behavior that is reinforced. Behavior that is not reinforced tends to become extinguished. Behavior therapists have used these principles of operant conditioning with psychotic patients as well as with clients with milder problems.

The staff at one mental hospital was at a loss about how to encourage withdrawn schizophrenic patients to eat regularly. Ayllon and Haughton (1962) observed that staff members were making the problem worse by coaxing patients into the dining room and even feeding them. Staff attention apparently reinforced the patients' lack of cooperation. Some rules were changed. Patients who did not arrive at the dining hall within 30 minutes after serving were locked out. Staff could not interact with patients at mealtime. With uncooperative behavior no longer reinforced, patients quickly changed their eating habits. Then patients were required to pay one penny to enter the dining hall. Pennies were earned by interacting with other patients and showing other socially appropriate behaviors. These target behaviors also became more frequent.

THE TOKEN ECONOMY Many psychiatric wards and hospitals now use **token economies** in which patients must use tokens such as poker chips to purchase

Aversive Conditioning. In aversive conditioning, unwanted behaviors take on a noxious quality as a result of being repeatedly paired with aversive stimuli. Overexposure is making cigarette smoke aversive to this smoker.

Truth or Fiction Revisited

It is true that smoking cigarettes can be an effective treatment for helping people stop smoking cigarettes. The trick is to inhale enough smoke so that it is aversive rather than enjoyable.

MODELING • A behavior therapy technique in which a client observes and imitates a person who approaches and copes with feared objects or situations.

AVERSIVE CONDITIONING • A behavior therapy technique in which undesired responses are inhibited by pairing repugnant or offensive stimuli with them.

RAPID SMOKING • An aversive conditioning method for quitting smoking in which the smoker inhales every 6 seconds, thus rendering once-desirable cigarette smoke aversive.

THE RATHUS ASSERTIVENESS SCHEDULE

How assertive are you? Do you stick up for your rights, or do you allow other people to walk all over you? Do you say what you feel or what you think other people want you to say? Do you initiate relationships with attractive people, or do you shy away from them?

One way to gain insight into how assertive you are is to take the following self-report test of assertive behavior. Once you have finished, turn to Appendix B to find out how to calculate and interpret your score. ∎

Directions: Indicate how well each item describes you by using this code:

> 3 = very much like me
> 2 = rather like me
> 1 = slightly like me
> −1 = slightly unlike me
> −2 = rather unlike me
> −3 = very much unlike me

_____ 1. Most people seem to be more aggressive and assertive than I am.*

_____ 2. I have hesitated to make or accept dates because of "shyness."*

_____ 3. When the food served at a restaurant is not done to my satisfaction, I complain about it to the waiter or waitress.

_____ 4. I am careful to avoid hurting other people's feelings, even when I feel that I have been injured.*

_____ 5. If a salesperson has gone to considerable trouble to show me merchandise that is not quite suitable, I have a difficult time saying "No."*

_____ 6. When I am asked to do something, I insist upon knowing why.

_____ 7. There are times when I look for a good, vigorous argument.

_____ 8. I strive to get ahead as well as most people in my position.

_____ 9. To be honest, people often take advantage of me.*

_____ 10. I enjoy starting conversations with new acquaintances and strangers.

_____ 11. I often don't know what to say to people I find attractive.*

_____ 12. I will hesitate to make phone calls to business establishments and institutions.*

_____ 13. I would rather apply for a job or for admission to a college by writing letters than by going through with personal interviews.*

_____ 14. I find it embarrassing to return merchandise.*

_____ 15. If a close and respected relative were annoying me, I would smother my feelings rather than express my annoyance.*

_____ 16. I have avoided asking questions for fear of sounding stupid.*

_____ 17. During an argument, I am sometimes afraid that I will get so upset that I will shake all over.*

_____ 18. If a famed and respected lecturer makes a comment which I think is incorrect, I will have the audience hear my point of view as well.

_____ 19. I avoid arguing over prices with clerks and salespeople.*

_____ 20. When I have done something important or worthwhile, I manage to let others know about it.

_____ 21. I am open and frank about my feelings.

_____ 22. If someone has been spreading false and bad stories about me, I see him or her as soon as possible and "have a talk" about it.

_____ 23. I often have a hard time saying "No."*

_____ 24. I tend to bottle up my emotions rather than make a scene.*

_____ 25. I complain about poor service in a restaurant and elsewhere.

_____ 26. When I am given a compliment, I sometimes just don't know what to say.*

_____ 27. If a couple near me in a theater or at a lecture were conversing rather loudly, I would ask them to be quiet or to take their conversation elsewhere.

_____ 28. Anyone attempting to push ahead of me in a line is in for a good battle.

_____ 29. I am quick to express an opinion.

_____ 30. There are times when I just can't say anything.*

*Reprinted from Rathus, 1973, pp. 398–406.

TV viewing time, extra visits to the canteen, or a private room (Nevid and others, 1997). The tokens are reinforcements for productive activities such as making beds, brushing teeth, and socializing. Token economies have not eliminated all features of schizophrenia. However, they have enhanced patient activity and cooperation. Tokens have also been used to modify the behavior of children with conduct disorders. In one program, for example, children received tokens for helpful behaviors such as volunteering and lost tokens for behaviors such as arguing and failing to pay attention (Schneider & Byrne, 1987).

SUCCESSIVE APPROXIMATIONS The operant conditioning method of **successive approximations** is often used to help clients build good habits. Let us use a (not uncommon!) example: You wish to study three hours each evening but can only concentrate for half an hour. Rather than attempting to increase your study time all at once, you could do so gradually by adding, say, five minutes each evening. After every hour or so of studying, you could reinforce yourself with five minutes of people-watching in a busy section of the library.

SOCIAL SKILLS TRAINING In social skills training, behavior therapists decrease social anxiety and build social skills through operant-conditioning procedures that employ **self-monitoring,** coaching, modeling, role-playing, **behavior rehearsal,** and **feedback.** Social skills training has been used to help formerly hospitalized mental patients maintain jobs and apartments in the community. For example, a worker can rehearse politely asking a supervisor for assistance or asking a landlord to fix the plumbing in an apartment.

Social skills training is effective in groups. Group members can role-play important people—such as parents, spouses, or potential dates—in the lives of other members.

ASSERTIVENESS TRAINING Are you a person who can't say no? Do other people walk all over you? Brush off those footprints and get some assertiveness training! Assertiveness training is a kind of social skills training that helps clients demand their rights and express their genuine feelings. It helps decrease social anxiety, but it has also been used to optimize the functioning of individuals without problems.

Assertive behavior can be contrasted with both *nonassertive* (submissive) behavior and *aggressive* behavior. Assertive people express their genuine feelings, stick up for their legitimate rights, and refuse unreasonable requests. But they do not insult, threaten, or belittle. Assertive people also do not shy away from meeting people and building relationships, and they express positive feelings such as liking and love. The Rathus Assertiveness Schedule will give you some insight into how assertive you are. The Psychology and Modern Life section may help you become a more assertive person.

BIOFEEDBACK TRAINING Through **biofeedback training (BFT),** therapists help clients become more aware of, and gain control over, various bodily functions (see Chapters 6 and 7). Therapists attach clients to devices that measure bodily functions such as heart rate. "Bleeps" or other electronic signals are used to indicate (and thereby reinforce) changes in the desired direction—for example, a slower heart rate. (Knowledge of results is a powerful reinforcer.) One device, the electromyograph (EMG), monitors muscle tension. It has been used to augment control over muscle tension in the forehead and elsewhere, thereby alleviating anxiety, stress, and headaches.

BFT also helps clients voluntarily regulate functions that were once thought to be beyond conscious control, such as heart rate and blood pressure. Hypertensive

TOKEN ECONOMY • A controlled environment in which people are reinforced for desired behaviors with tokens (such as poker chips) that may be exchanged for privileges.

SUCCESSIVE APPROXIMATIONS • In operant conditioning, a series of behaviors that gradually become more similar to a target behavior.

SELF-MONITORING • Keeping a record of one's own behavior to identify problems and record successes.

BEHAVIOR REHEARSAL • Practice.

FEEDBACK • In assertiveness training, information about the effectiveness of a response.

BIOFEEDBACK TRAINING • The systematic feeding back to an organism of information about a bodily function so that the organism can gain control of that function. Abbreviated *BFT.*

clients use a blood pressure cuff and electronic signals to gain control over their blood pressure. The electroencephalograph (EEG) monitors brain waves and can be used to teach people how to produce alpha waves, which are associated with relaxation. Some people have overcome insomnia by learning to produce the kinds of brain waves associated with sleep.

psychology and
modern life

BECOMING MORE ASSERTIVE

Assertive people express their genuine feelings and beliefs. They stand up for their rights and communicate who they are as individuals. But assertiveness is not the same as aggressiveness. Assertive people are not bossy or hostile. They don't have a chip on their shoulder or put other people down. Assertive people express their positive feelings as well as their grievances.

The following guidelines may help you become more assertive:

• *Confront irrational beliefs that turn you into a doormat.* Do you believe that it is your duty to make everyone else happy all the time? Stop thinking that the world will end if someone doesn't like you. You cannot expect that everyone will approve of you all the time.

• *Make eye contact with other people.* Look people in the eye when you talk to them. (Don't stare; make it a friendly or assertive look, not an aggressive look.) Practice by looking at yourself in the mirror, or ask a trusted friend for feedback.

• *Start the day with a cheerful "Good morning."* Greet people in the morning—in the elevator, in

the office, at the store. Don't pass them by. Don't slink into a corner of the elevator. Make small talk with strangers at the store or on the train or bus.

• *Start sentences with, "I feel" or "I think that."* Talk about how you *feel*, not just what you *think*. This will help you become more accustomed to expressing your feelings.

• *Join social organizations on and off campus.* Select organizations whose goals are consistent with your own. You will meet new people and work with them to achieve common goals. (You may even find dates this way.)

• *Accentuate the positive.* Share positive as well as negative feelings with other people. When people do something that pleases you, say so. Tell them that you appreciate what they did. When you feel bubbly, bubble!

• *Don't apologize for yourself.* Don't start conversations by saying things like, "I'm sorry. I know I really shouldn't bother you with this, but . . . " You have a right to express your feelings.

Becoming More Assertive. Sometimes what you do is what you are. You can become more assertive by greeting people cheerfully, making eye contact, and talking about your feelings.

• *Practice, practice, practice.* Give yourself ample opportunity to practice assertive behavior. Above all, remember that we all stumble now and then. Don't berate yourself when you do. Pick yourself up and go at it again. ■

• *Self-Control Methods*

Do mysterious forces sometimes seem to be at work in your life? Forces that delight in wreaking havoc on New Year's resolutions and other efforts to put an end to your bad habits? Just when you go on a diet, that juicy pizza stares at you from the TV set. Just when you resolve to balance your budget, that sweater goes on sale. Behavior therapists have developed a number of self-control techniques to help people cope with such temptations.

FUNCTIONAL ANALYSIS OF BEHAVIOR Behavior therapists usually begin with a **functional analysis** of the problem behavior. In this way, they help determine the stimuli that trigger the behavior and the reinforcers that maintain it. You can use a diary to jot down each instance of a problem behavior. Note the time of day, location, your activity at the time (including your thoughts and feelings), and reactions (yours and others). Functional analysis serves a number of purposes. It makes you more aware of the environmental context of your behavior and can increase your motivation to change.

Brian used functional analysis to master his nail biting. Table 16.1 shows a few items from his notebook. He discovered that boredom and humdrum activities seemed to serve as triggers for nail biting. He began to watch out for feelings of boredom as signs to practice self-control. He also made some changes in his life so that he would feel bored less often.

There are numerous self-control strategies aimed at the stimuli that trigger behavior, the behaviors themselves, and reinforcers. Table 16.2 looks briefly at some of these strategies.

> **Truth or Fiction Revisited**
>
> It is true that you might be able to put an end to bad habits merely by keeping a record of where and when you engage in them. The record may help motivate you, make you more aware of the problems, and suggest strategies for behavior change.

> **Truth or Fiction Revisited**
>
> It is true that some psychotherapists tell their clients precisely what to do. That is, they outline behavioral prescriptions for their clients. Behavior therapists, Gestalt therapists, and some cognitive therapists are examples.

REFLECTIONS

- Does behavior therapy strike you as "behavioral"? Do some methods seem more behavioral than others? Explain your answers.
- Can you relate the methods discussed in this section to principles of conditioning and observational learning? As an example, how about the methods used in fear reduction?
- Consider some of your own concerns. Do you think they can be dealt with by means of behavior therapy? Why or why not?

TABLE 16.1	**EXCERPTS FROM BRIAN'S DIARY OF NAIL BITING FOR APRIL 14**			
Incident	*Time*	*Location*	*Activity (Thoughts, Feelings)*	*Reactions*
1	7:45 A.M.	Freeway	Driving to work, bored, not thinking	Finger bleeds, pain
2	10:30 A.M.	Office	Writing report	Self-disgust
3	2:25 P.M.	Conference	Listening to dull financial report	Embarrassment
4	6:40 P.M.	Living room	Watching evening news	Self-disgust

A functional analysis of problem behavior like nail biting increases awareness of the environmental context in which it occurs, spurs motivation to change, and, in highly motivated people, might lead to significant behavioral change.

FUNCTIONAL ANALYSIS • A systematic study of behavior in which one identifies the stimuli that trigger problem behavior and the reinforcers that maintain it.

TABLE 16.2 BEHAVIORAL STRATEGIES FOR SELF-CONTROL

Strategy	*Description*
STRATEGIES AIMED AT STIMULI THAT TRIGGER BEHAVIOR	
Restriction of the stimulus field	Gradually exclude the problem behavior from more environments. For example, at first make smoking off limits in the car, then in the office.
Avoidance of powerful stimuli that trigger habits	Avoid obvious sources of temptation. People who go window-shopping often wind up buying more than windows. If eating at The Pizza Glutton tempts you to forget your diet, eat at home or at The Celery Stalk instead.
Stimulus control	Place yourself in an environment in which desirable behavior is likely to occur. Maybe it's difficult to lift your mood directly at times, but you can place yourself in the audience of an uplifting concert or film. It might be difficult to force yourself to study, but how about rewarding yourself for spending time in the library?
STRATEGIES AIMED AT BEHAVIOR	
Response prevention	Make unwanted behavior difficult or impossible. Impulse buying is curbed when you shred your credit cards, leave your checkbook home, and carry only a couple of dollars with you. You can't reach for the strawberry cream cheese pie in your refrigerator if you didn't buy it at the supermarket.
Competing responses	Engage in behaviors that are incompatible with the bad habit. It is difficult to drink a glass of water and a fattening milk shake simultaneously. Grasping something firmly is a useful competing response for nail biting or scratching.
Chain breaking	Interfere with unwanted habitual behavior by complicating the process of engaging in it. Break the chain of reaching for a readily available cigarette and placing it in your mouth by wrapping the pack in aluminum foil and placing it on the top shelf of a closet. Rewrap the pack after taking one cigarette. Put your cigarette in the ashtray between puffs, or put your fork down between mouthfuls of dessert. Ask yourself if you really want more.
Successive approximations	Gradually approach targets through a series of relatively painless steps. Increase studying by only 5 minutes a day. Decrease smoking by pausing for a minute when the cigarette is smoked halfway, or by putting it out a minute before you would wind up eating the filter. Decrease your daily intake of food by 50 to 100 calories every couple of days, or cut out one type of fattening food every few days.
STRATEGIES AIMED AT REINFORCEMENTS	
Reinforcement of desired behavior	Why give yourself something for nothing? Make pleasant activities such as going to films, walking on the beach, or reading a new novel contingent upon meeting reasonable daily behavioral goals. Each day you remain within your calorie limit, put one dollar away toward that camera or vacation trip you've been dreaming of.
Response cost	Heighten awareness of the long-term reasons for dieting or cutting down on smoking by punishing yourself for not meeting a daily goal or for engaging in a bad habit. For example, if you bite your nails or inhale that cheesecake, make out a check to a cause you oppose and mail it at once.
"Grandma's method"	How did Grandma persuade children to eat their vegetables? Simple: no veggies, no dessert. In this method, desired behaviors such as studying and brushing your teeth can be increased by insisting that those behaviors be done before you engage in a pleasant or frequently occurring activity. For example, don't watch television unless you have studied first. Don't leave the apartment until you've brushed your teeth. You can also place reminders about new attitudes you're trying to acquire on little cards and read them regularly. For example, in quitting smoking, you might write "Every day it becomes a little easier" on one card and "Your lungs will turn pink again" on another. Place these cards and others in your wallet, and read them each time you leave the house.
Covert sensitization	Create imaginary horror stories about problem behavior. Psychologists have successfully reduced overeating and smoking by having clients imagine that they become acutely nauseated at the thought of fattening foods or that a cigarette is made from vomit. Some horror stories are not so "imaginary." Deliberately focusing on heart strain and diseased lungs every time you overeat or smoke, rather than ignoring these long-term consequences, might also promote self-control.
Covert reinforcement	Create rewarding imagery for desired behavior. When you have achieved a behavioral goal, fantasize about how wonderful you are. Imagine friends and family members patting you on the back.

■ COGNITIVE THERAPIES

There is nothing either good or bad, but thinking makes it so.

SHAKESPEARE, HAMLET

In this line from *Hamlet,* Shakespeare did not mean to suggest that injuries and misfortunes are painless or easy to manage. Rather, he meant that our appraisals of unfortunate events can heighten our discomfort and impair our coping ability. In so doing, Shakespeare was providing a kind of motto for **cognitive therapists.**

Cognitive therapists focus on the beliefs, attitudes, and automatic types of thinking that create and compound their clients' problems (Beck, 1993; Ellis, 1993). Cognitive therapists, like psychodynamic and humanistic-existential therapists, aim to foster self-insight, but they aim to heighten insight into *current cognitions* as well as those of the past. Cognitive therapists also aim to directly *change* maladaptive cognitions in order to reduce negative feelings, provide insight, and help the client solve problems.

You may have noticed that many behavior therapists incorporate cognitive procedures in their methods (Jacobson and others, 1996; Meichenbaum, 1993). For example, techniques such as systematic desensitization, covert sensitization, and covert reinforcement ask clients to focus on visual imagery. Behavioral methods for treating bulimia nervosa focus on clients' irrational attitudes toward their weight and body shape as well as foster healthful eating habits (Wilson & Fairburn, 1993).

Let us look at the approaches and methods of some major cognitive therapists.

• *Cognitive Therapy: Correcting Cognitive Errors*

Cognitive therapy is the name of an approach to therapy as well as psychiatrist Aaron Beck's specific methods. Beck (1991, 1993) focuses on clients' cognitive distortions. He questions people in a way that encourages them to see the irrationality of their ways of thinking. For example, depressed people tend to minimize their accomplishments and to assume that the worst will happen. Both distortions heighten feelings of depression. Beck notes that cognitive distortions can be fleeting and automatic, difficult to detect. His therapy methods help clients pin down such distortions and challenge them.

Beck notes the pervasive influence of cognitive errors that contribute to clients' miseries. For example:

1. Clients may *selectively perceive* the world as a harmful place and ignore evidence to the contrary.
2. Clients may *overgeneralize* on the basis of a few examples. For example, they may perceive themselves as worthless because they were laid off at work, or as unattractive because they were refused a date.
3. Clients may *magnify,* or blow out of proportion, the importance of negative events. As noted in the discussion of Ellis's views, clients may catastrophize failing a test by assuming they will flunk out of college, or catastrophize losing a job by believing that they will never find another one and that serious harm will befall their family as a result.
4. Clients may engage in *absolutist thinking,* or looking at the world in black and white rather than in shades of gray. In doing so, a rejection on a date takes on the meaning of a lifetime of loneliness; an uncomfortable illness takes on life-threatening proportions.

COGNITIVE THERAPY • A form of therapy that focuses on how clients' cognitions (expectations, attitudes, beliefs, etc.) lead to distress and may be modified to relieve distress and promote adaptive behavior.

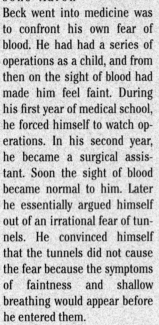

Aaron Beck

He used cognitive and behavioral techniques on himself before he became a psychiatrist. One of the reasons Aaron Beck went into medicine was to confront his own fear of blood. He had had a series of operations as a child, and from then on the sight of blood had made him feel faint. During his first year of medical school, he forced himself to watch operations. In his second year, he became a surgical assistant. Soon the sight of blood became normal to him. Later he essentially argued himself out of an irrational fear of tunnels. He convinced himself that the tunnels did not cause the fear because the symptoms of faintness and shallow breathing would appear before he entered them.

As a psychiatrist, Beck, like Albert Ellis, first practiced psychoanalysis. However, he could not find scientific evidence for psychoanalytic beliefs. Psychoanalytic theory explained depression as anger turned inward, so that it is transformed into a need to suffer. Beck's own clinical experiences led him to believe that it is more likely that depressed people experience cognitive distortions such as the *cognitive triad*. That is, they expect the worst of themselves ("I'm no good"), the world at large ("This is an awful place"), and their future ("Nothing good will ever happen"). Beck's cognitive therapy, like Ellis', is active. Beck encourages clients to challenge beliefs that are not supported by evidence. He currently teaches health professionals his form of therapy at the University of Pennsylvania. ■

The concept of pinpointing and modifying errors may become more clear from the following excerpt from a case in which a 53-year-old engineer obtained cognitive therapy for severe depression. The engineer had left his job and become inactive. As reported by Beck and his colleagues, the first goal of treatment was to foster physical activity—even things like raking leaves and preparing dinner—because activity is incompatible with depression. Then:

[The engineer's] cognitive distortions were identified by comparing his assessment of each activity with that of his wife. Alternative ways of interpreting his experiences were then considered.

In comparing his wife's résumé of his past experiences, he became aware that he had (a) undervalued his past by failing to mention many previous accomplishments, (2) regarded himself as far more responsible for his "failures" than she did, and (3) concluded that he was worthless since he had not succeeded in attaining certain goals in the past. When the two accounts were contrasted, he could discern many of his cognitive distortions. In subsequent sessions, his wife continued to serve as an "objectifier."

In midtherapy, [he] compiled a list of new attitudes that he had acquired since initiating therapy. These included:

1. "I am starting at a lower level of functioning at my job, but it will improve if I persist."
2. "I know that once I get going in the morning, everything will run all right for the rest of the day."
3. "I can't achieve everything at once."
4. "I have my periods of ups and downs, but in the long run I feel better."
5. "My expectations from my job and life should be scaled down to a realistic level."
6. "Giving in to avoidance [e.g., staying away from work and social interactions] never helps and only leads to further avoidance."

He was instructed to reread this list daily for several weeks even though he already knew the content. (Rush and others, 1975)

The engineer gradually became less depressed and returned to work and an active social life. Along the way, he learned to combat inappropriate self-blame for problems, perfectionistic expectations, magnification of failures, and overgeneralization from failures.

Becoming aware of cognitive errors and modifying catastrophizing thoughts helps us cope with stress. Internal, stable, and global attributions of failure lead to depression and feelings of helplessness. Cognitive therapists also alert clients to cognitive errors such as these so that the clients can change their attitudes and pave the way for more effective overt behavior.

Many theorists consider cognitive therapy to be a collection of techniques that are part of the overall approach known as behavior therapy, which is discussed in the following section. Some members of this group use the term "cognitive *behavioral* therapy." Others argue that the term *behavior therapy* is broad enough to include cognitive techniques. Many cognitive therapists and behavior therapists differ in focus, however. Behavior therapists deal with client cognitions in order to change *overt* behavior. Cognitive therapists also see the value of tying treatment outcomes to observable behavior, but they tend to assert that cognitive change is a key goal in itself.

• Rational Emotive Behavior Therapy: Overcoming "Musts" and "Shoulds"

Albert Ellis (1977, 1993), the founder of **rational emotive behavior therapy (REBT),** points out that our beliefs about events, as well as the events themselves, shape our responses to them. Moreover, many of us harbor a number of irrational beliefs that can give rise to problems or magnify their impact. Two of the most important ones are the belief that we must have the love and approval of people who are important to us and the belief that we must prove ourselves to be thoroughly competent, adequate, and achieving.

Ellis's methods are active and directive. He does not sit back like the traditional psychoanalyst and occasionally offer an interpretation. Instead, he urges clients to seek out their irrational beliefs, which can be hard to pinpoint. He then shows them how those beliefs lead to misery and challenges them to change them. According to Ellis, we need less misery and less blaming in our lives, and more action.

Ellis also straddles behavioral and cognitive therapies. He originally dubbed his method of therapy *rational-emotive therapy*, because his focus was on the cognitive—irrational beliefs and how to change them. However, Ellis has also always promoted behavioral changes to cement cognitive changes and provide "a fuller experience of life" (Albert Ellis Institute, 1997, p. 2). In keeping with his broad philosophy, he recently changed the name of rational-emotive therapy to rational emotive *behavior* therapy.

REFLECTIONS
- Do you ever magnify the importance of negative events? If so, does this belief ever give rise to feelings of frustration, anxiety, or depression?
- Do you believe that you must have the love and approval of people who are important to you? If so, does this belief ever give rise to feelings of frustration, anxiety, or depression?
- Do you believe that you must prove yourself to be thoroughly competent, adequate, and achieving? If so, does this belief ever give rise to feelings of frustration, anxiety, or depression?

■ GROUP THERAPIES

When a psychotherapist has several clients with similar problems—anxiety, depression, adjustment to divorce, lack of social skills—it often makes sense to treat them in a group rather than in individual sessions. The methods and characteristics of the group reflect the needs of the members and the theoretical orientation of the leader. In group psychoanalysis, clients might interpret one

RATIONAL EMOTIVE BEHAVIOR THERAPY • (REBT) Albert Ellis' form of therapy which encourages clients to challenge and correct irrational expectations and maladaptive behaviors.

In Review — Methods of Therapy

TYPE OF THERAPY	GOALS	METHODS	COMMENTS
Psychodynamic Therapies	To strengthen the ego; to provide self-insight into unconscious conflict	Traditional psychoanalysis is lengthy and nondirective and involves methods such as free association and dream analysis.	Most effective with verbal, "upscale" clients. Modern ego analytic approaches are briefer and more directive.
Humanistic-Existential Therapies	To help clients get in touch with parts of themselves that they have "disowned" and actualize their unique desires and abilities	Client-centered therapy is nondirective; it provides an atmosphere in which clients can engage in self-exploration without fear. Gestalt therapy is highly directive.	Client-centered therapy is practiced widely in college and university counseling centers to help students make academic and personal decisions.
Behavior Therapy	To use principles of learning to help clients engage in adaptive behavior and discontinue maladaptive behavior	Behavior therapy is directive and uses fear-reduction methods (including systematic desensitization), aversive conditioning (to help clients discontinue bad habits), operant conditioning procedures (e.g., social skills training), and self-control methods (beginning with functional analysis of behavior).	Behavior therapists have developed treatments for problems (e.g., smoking, phobias, sexual dysfunctions) for which there previously were no effective treatment methods.
Cognitive Therapies	To make clients aware of the beliefs, attitudes, and automatic types of thinking that create and compound their problems, and help them correct these kinds of thinking so as to reduce negative feelings and solve problems	Beck's cognitive therapy helps people recognize and correct cognitive errors such as selective perception, overgeneralization, magnification of negative events, and absolutist thinking. Rational emotive behavior therapists show clients how irrational beliefs, make them miserable.	Many theorists consider cognitive therapy to be part of behavior therapy and may label it "cognitive *behavioral* therapy." In fact, Ellis recently changed the name of his approach to therapy from rational-emotive therapy to rational-emotive *behavior* therapy.

another's dreams. In a client-centered group, they might provide an accepting atmosphere for self-exploration. Members of behavior therapy groups might be jointly desensitized to anxiety-evoking stimuli or might practice social skills together.

Group therapy has the following advantages:

1. It is economical (Sleek, 1995a). It allows the therapist to work with several clients at once.

2. Compared with one-to-one therapy, group therapy provides more information and life experience for clients to draw upon.

3. Appropriate behavior receives group support. Clients usually appreciate an outpouring of peer approval.

Group Therapy. Group therapy has a number of advantages over individual therapy for many clients. It is economical, provides a fund of experience for clients to draw upon, elicits group support, and provides an opportunity to relate to other people. On the other hand, some clients do need individual attention.

4. When we run into troubles, it is easy to imagine that we are different from other people or inferior to them. Affiliating with people with similar problems is reassuring.

5. Group members who show improvement provide hope for other members.

6. Many individuals seek therapy because of problems in relating to other people. People who seek therapy for other reasons also may be socially inhibited. Members of groups have the opportunity to practice social skills in a relatively nonthreatening atmosphere. In a group consisting of men and women of different ages, group members can role-play one another's employers, employees, spouses, parents, children, and friends. Members can role-play asking one another out on dates, saying no (or yes), and so on.

But group therapy is not for everyone. Some clients fare better with individual treatment. Many prefer not to disclose their problems to a group. They may be overly shy or want individual attention. It is the responsibility of the therapist to insist that group disclosures be kept confidential, to establish a supportive atmosphere, and to ensure that group members obtain the attention they need.

Many types of therapy can be conducted either individually or in groups. Encounter groups, couple therapy, and family therapy are conducted only in groups.

• *Encounter Groups*

Encounter groups are not appropriate for treating serious psychological problems. Rather, they are intended to promote personal growth by heightening awareness of one's own needs and feelings and those of others. This goal is sought through intense confrontations, or encounters, between strangers. Like ships in the night, group members come together out of the darkness, touch one

ENCOUNTER GROUP • A type of group that aims to foster self-awareness by focusing on how group members relate to each other in a setting that encourages open expression of feelings.

another briefly, then sink back into the shadows of one another's lives. But something is gained from the passing.

Encounter groups stress interactions between group members in the here and now. Discussion of the past may be outlawed. Interpretation is out. However, expression of genuine feelings toward others is encouraged. When group members think that a person's social mask is phony, they may descend en masse to rip it off.

Encounter groups can be damaging when they urge overly rapid disclosure of intimate matters or when several members attack one member. Responsible leaders do not tolerate these abuses and try to keep the group moving in a growth-enhancing direction.

• Couple Therapy

Couple therapy helps couples enhance their relationship by improving their communication skills and helping them manage conflict (Markman and others, 1993). There are often power imbalances in relationships, and couple therapy helps individuals find "full membership" in the couple. Correcting power imbalances increases happiness and can decrease the incidence of domestic violence. Ironically, in situations of domestic violence, the partner with *less* power in the relationship is usually the violent one. Violence sometimes appears to be a way of compensating for inability to share power in other aspects of the relationship (Babcock and others, 1993).

Today, the main approach to couple therapy is cognitive-behavioral (Jacobson & Addis, 1993; Markman and others, 1993). It teaches couples communications skills (such as how to listen to one another and how to express feelings), ways of handling feelings like depression and anger, and ways of solving problems.

• Family Therapy

In **family therapy,** one or more families constitute the group. Family therapy may be undertaken from various theoretical viewpoints. One is the "systems approach," in which family interaction is studied and modified to enhance the growth of individual family members and of the family unit as a whole (Annunziata & Jacobson-Kram, 1995; Mikesell and others, 1995).

Family members with low self-esteem often cannot tolerate different attitudes and behaviors in other family members. Faulty communication within the family also creates problems. In addition, it is not uncommon for the family to present an "identified patient"—that is, the family member who has *the* problem and is *causing* all the trouble. Yet family therapists usually assume that the identified patient is a scapegoat for other problems within and among family members. It is a sort of myth: Change the bad apple—or identified patient— and the barrel—or family—will be functional once more.

The family therapist—who is often a specialist in this field—attempts to teach the family to communicate more effectively and encourage growth and, eventually, autonomy in each family member.

FAMILY THERAPY • A form of therapy in which the family unit is treated as the client.

REFLECTIONS
- If you went for therapy, do you think that you would prefer being treated on an individual basis or in a group? Why?
- Could a couple or a family you know of benefit from couple or family therapy? If so, in what way?

■ DOES PSYCHOTHERAPY WORK?

Many of us know people who swear by their therapists, but the evidence is often shaky—for example, "I was a wreck before, but now . . . ," or "I feel so much better now." Anecdotes like these are encouraging, but we do not know what would have happened to these people had they not sought help. Many people feel better about their problems as time goes on, with or without therapy. Sometimes, happily, problems seem to go away by themselves. Sometimes people find solutions on their own. Then, too, we hear some stories about how therapy was useless and about people who hop fruitlessly from one therapist to another.

• *Problems in Conducting Research on Psychotherapy*

Before we report on research dealing with the effectiveness of therapy, let us review some of the problems of this kind of research (see Figure 16.1). As noted by Hans Strupp, "The problem of evaluating outcomes from psychotherapy continues to bedevil the field" (1996, p. 1017).

PROBLEMS IN RUNNING EXPERIMENTS ON PSYCHOTHERAPY The ideal method for evaluating a treatment—such as a method of therapy—is the experiment (Shadish & Ragsdale, 1996). However, experiments on therapy methods are difficult to arrange and control. The outcomes can be difficult to define and measure.

Consider psychoanalysis. In well-run experiments, people are assigned at random to experimental and control groups. A true experiment on psychoanalysis would require randomly assigning people seeking therapy to psychoanalysis and to a control group or other kinds of therapy for comparison (Luborsky and others, 1993). But a person may have to remain in traditional psychoanalysis for years to attain beneficial results. Could we create control treatments that last as long? Moreover, some people seek psychoanalysis per se, not psychotherapy in general. Would it be ethical to assign them at random to other treatments or to a no-treatment control group? Clearly not.

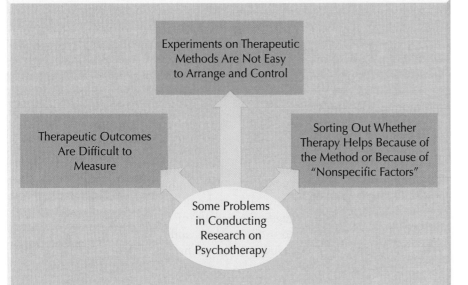

FIGURE 16.1

PROBLEMS IN CONDUCTING RESEARCH ON PSYCHOTHERAPY

Numerous problems make it difficult to conduct research in psychotherapy. For example, experiments on therapy methods are difficult to arrange and control. It is hard to measure the outcomes of therapy, many of which are subjective. It may also be difficult to sort out the effects of the therapy method from those of nonspecific factors, such as instilling a sense of hope.

In an ideal experiment, subjects and researchers are "blind" with regard to the treatment the subjects receive. Blind research designs allow researchers to control for subjects' expectations. In an ideal experiment on therapy, individuals would be blind as to the type of therapy they are obtaining—or as to whether they are obtaining a placebo (Carroll and others, 1994). However, it is difficult to mask the type of therapy clients are obtaining (Seligman, 1995). Even if we could conceal it from clients, could we hide it from therapists?

PROBLEMS IN MEASURING OUTCOMES OF THERAPY Consider the problems we run into when measuring outcomes of therapy (Azar, 1994b). Behavior therapists define their goals in behavioral terms—such as a formerly phobic individual being able to obtain an injection or look out of a 20th-story window. Therefore, behavior therapists do not encounter many problems in this area. But what about the client-centered therapist who fosters insight and self-actualization? We cannot directly measure these qualities. We must assess what clients say and do and make inferences about them.

ARE CLINICAL JUDGMENTS VALID? Because of problems like these, many clinicians believe that important clinical questions cannot be answered through research (Newman & Howard, 1991). For them, clinical judgment is the basis for evaluating the effectiveness of therapy. Unfortunately, therapists have a stake in believing that their clients profit from treatment. They are not unbiased judges, even when they try to be.

DOES THERAPY HELP BECAUSE OF THE METHOD OR BECAUSE OF "NONSPECIFIC FACTORS"? Sorting out the benefits of therapy per se from other aspects of the therapy situation is a staggering task. These other aspects are termed *nonspecific factors*. They refer to features that are found in most therapies, such as the the client's relationship with the therapist. Most therapists, regardless of theoretical outlook, show warmth and empathy, encourage exploration, and instill hope (Blatt and others, 1996; Burns & Nolen-Hoeksema, 1992). The benefits of therapy thus could stem largely from these behaviors. If so, the method itself might have little more value than a "sugar pill" has in combating physical ailments.

WHAT IS THE EXPERIMENTAL TREATMENT IN PSYCHOTHERAPY OUTCOME STUDIES? We may also ask, what exactly is the experimental "treatment" being evaluated? Various therapists may say that they are practicing psychoanalysis, but they differ both as individuals and in their training. It is therefore difficult to specify just what is happening in the therapeutic session (Luborsky and others, 1993).

• Analyses of Therapy Effectiveness

Despite these evaluation problems, research on the effectiveness of therapy has been encouraging (Barlow, 1996; Shadish and others, 1997; VandenBos, 1996). This research has relied heavily on a technique termed **meta-analysis.** Meta-analysis combines and averages the results of individual studies. Generally speaking, the studies included in the analysis address similar issues in a similar way. Moreover, the analysts judge them to have been conducted in a valid manner.

META-ANALYSIS • A method for combining and averaging the results of individual research studies.

In their classic early use of meta-analysis, Mary Lee Smith and Gene Glass (1977) analyzed the results of dozens of outcome studies of various types of therapies. They concluded that people who obtained psychodynamic therapy showed greater well-being, on the average, than 70% to 75% of those who did not obtain treatment. Similarly, nearly 75% of the clients who obtained client-centered therapy were better off than people who did not obtain treatment. Psychodynamic and client-centered therapies appear to be most effective with well educated, verbal, strongly motivated clients who report problems with anxiety, depression (of light to moderate proportions), and interpersonal relationships. Neither form of therapy appears to be effective with people with psychotic disorders such as major depression, bipolar disorder, and schizophrenia. Smith and Glass (1977) found that people who obtained Gestalt therapy showed greater well-being than about 60% of those who did not obtain treatment. The effectiveness of psychoanalysis and client-centered therapy thus was reasonably comparable. Gestalt therapy fell behind.

Smith and Glass (1977) did not include cognitive therapies in their meta-analysis because at the time of their study many cognitive approaches were relatively new. Because behavior therapists also incorporate many cognitive techniques, it can be difficult to sort out which aspects—cognitive or otherwise—of behavioral treatments are most effective. However, many meta-analyses of cognitive-behavioral therapy have been conducted since the early work of Smith and Glass. Their results are encouraging (Lipsey & Wilson, 1993).

A number of studies of cognitive therapy per se have also been conducted. For example, they show that modifying irrational beliefs of the type described by Albert Ellis helps people with problems such as anxiety and depression (Engels and others, 1993; Haaga & Davison, 1993). Modifying self-defeating beliefs of the sort outlined by Aaron Beck also frequently alleviates anxiety and depression (Robins & Hayes, 1993; Whisman and others, 1991). Cognitive therapy may be helpful with people with severe depression, who had been thought responsive only to biological therapies (Jacobson & Hollon, 1996; Simons and others, 1995). Cognitive therapy has also helped people with personality disorders (Beck & Freeman, 1990).

Behavioral and cognitive therapies have also provided strategies for treating anxiety disorders, social skills deficits, and problems in self-control (DeRubeis & Curtis-Christoph, 1998). These two kinds of therapies—which are often integrated as *cognitive behavioral therapy*—have also provided empirically supported methods for helping couples and families in distress (Baucom and others, 1998) and for modifying behaviors related to health problems such as headaches (Blanchard, 1992), smoking, chronic pain, and bulimia nervosa (Compas and others, 1998). Cognitive behavioral therapists have also innovated treatments for sexual problems for which there previously were no effective treatments (Rathus and others, 1997). Cognitive therapy has helped many people with schizophrenia (who are also using drug therapy) modify their delusional beliefs (Chadwick & Lowe, 1990). Behavior therapy has helped to coordinate the care of institutionalized patients, including people with schizophrenia and mental retardation (Spreat & Behar, 1994). However, there is little evidence that psychological therapy alone is effective in treating the quirks of thought exhibited in people who have severe psychotic disorders (Wolpe, 1990).

Thus, it is not enough to ask which type of therapy is most effective. We must ask which type is most effective for a particular problem and a particular patient. What are its advantages? Its limitations? Clients may successfully use systematic desensitization to overcome stagefright, as measured by ability to speak to a group of people. If clients also want to know *why* they have stagefright, however, behavior therapy alone will not provide the answer.

Psychology in a World of
DIVERSITY

Psychotherapy and Human Diversity

The United States, they are a-changing. Most of the "prescriptions" for psychotherapy discussed in this chapter were originated by, and intended for use with, European Americans (Hall, 1997)—and especially for male heterosexuals. Yet people from ethnic minority groups are less likely than European Americans to seek therapy (Penn and others, 1995). Reasons for their lower participation rate include:

- Unawareness that therapy would help
- Lack of information about the availability of professional services, or inability to pay for them (DeAngelis, 1995b)
- Distrust of professionals, particularly White professionals and (for women) male professionals (Basic Behavioral Science Task Force, 1996c)
- Language barriers (American Psychological Association, 1993)
- Reluctance to open up about personal matters to strangers—especially strangers who are not members of one's own ethnic group (LaFramboise, 1994)
- Cultural inclinations toward other approaches to problem solving, such as religious approaches and psychic healers (LaFramboise, 1994)
- Negative experiences with professionals and authority figures

Women and gay males and lesbians have also sometimes found therapy to be insensitive to their particular needs. Let us consider ways in which psychotherapy can be of more use to people from ethnic minority groups, women, and gay males and lesbians.

PSYCHOTHERAPY AND ETHNIC MINORITY GROUPS Clinicians need to be sensitive to the cultural heritage, language, and values of the people they see in therapy (American Psychological Association, 1993; Comas-Diaz, 1994). Let us consider some of the issues involved in conducting psychotherapy with African Americans, Asian Americans, Hispanic Americans, and Native Americans.

In addition to addressing the psychological problems of African American clients, therapists often need to help them cope with the effects of prejudice and discrimination. Beverly Greene (1993) notes that some African Americans develop low self-esteem because they internalize negative stereotypes.

African Americans often are reluctant to seek psychological help because of cultural assumptions that people should manage their own problems and because of mistrust of the therapy process. They tend to assume that people are supposed to solve their own problems. Signs of emotional weakness such as tension, anxiety and depression are stigmatized (Boyd-Franklin, 1995; Greene, 1993).

Many African Americans are also suspicious of their therapists—especially when the therapist is a non-Hispanic White American. They may withhold personal information because of the society's history of racial discrimination (Boyd-Franklin, 1995; Greene, 1993).

Asian Americans tend to stigmatize people with psychological disorders. As a result, they may deny problems and refuse to seek help for them (Sue,

1991). Asian Americans, especially recent immigrants, also may not understand or believe in Western approaches to psychotherapy. For example, Western psychotherapy typically encourages people to express their feelings openly. This mode of behavior may conflict with the Asian tradition of restrain in public. Many Asians prefer to receive concrete advice rather than Western-style encouragement to develop their own solutions (Isomura and others, 1987).

Because of a cultural tendency to turn away from painful thoughts, many Asians experience and express psychological complaints as physical symptoms (Zane & Sue, 1991). Rather than thinking of themselves as being anxious, they may focus on physical features of anxiety such as a pounding heart and heavy sweating. Rather than thinking of themselves as depressed, they may focus on fatigue and low energy levels.

Many Hispanic Americans adhere to a patriarchal (male-dominated) family structure and strong kinship ties. Many Hispanic Americans also share the values described in the following passage:

> One's identity is in part determined by one's role in the family. The male, or *macho,* is the head of the family, the provider, the protector of the family honor, and the final decision maker. The woman's role *(marianismo)* is to care for the family and the children. Obviously, these roles are changing, with women entering the work force and achieving greater educational opportunities. Cultural values of *respeto* (respect), *confianza* (trust), *dignidad* (dignity), and *personalismo* (personalism) are highly esteemed and are important factors in working with many [Hispanic-Americans]. (De La Cancela & Guzman, 1991, p. 60)

Therapists need to be aware of potential conflicts between the traditional Hispanic American value of interdependency in the family and the typical non-Hispanic White American belief in independence and self-reliance (De la Cancela & Guzman, 1991). Measures like the following may help bridge the gaps between psychotherapists and Hispanic American clients:

1. Interacting with clients in the language requested by them or, if this is not possible, referring them to professionals who can do so.

2. Using methods that are consistent with the client's values and levels of *acculturation,* as suggested by fluency in English and level of education.

3. Developing therapy methods that incorporate clients' cultural values. Malgady and his colleagues (1990), for example, use *cuento therapy* with Puerto Ricans. *Cuento therapy* modifies Hispanic

folktales, or *cuentos,* such that the characters serve as models for adaptive behavior.

Many psychological disorders experienced by Native Americans involve the disruption of their traditional culture caused by European colonization (LaFramboise, 1994). Native Americans have also been denied full access to key institutions in Western culture (LaFramboise, 1994). Loss of cultural identity and social disorganization have set the stage for problems such as alcoholism, substance abuse, and depression. Theresa LaFramboise (1994) argues that if psychologists are to help Native Americans cope with psychological disorders, they must do so in a way that is sensitive to their culture, customs, and values. Efforts to prevent such disorders should focus on strengthening Native American cultural identity, pride, and cohesion. They should help Native Americans regain a sense of mastery over their world. When cultural and language differences create so great a gulf between Native Americans and the dominant culture, perhaps only trained Native Americans will be able to provide effective counseling.

Some therapists use ceremonies that reflect clients' cultural or religious traditions (Edwards, 1995). Purification and cleansing rites are therapeutic for many Native Americans (Lefley, 1990). Such rites are commonly sought by Native Americans who believe that their problems are caused by failure to placate malevolent spirits or perform required rituals (Lefley, 1990).

FEMINIST PSYCHOTHERAPY Feminist psychotherapy is not a particular method of therapy. It is an approach to therapy that is rooted in feminist political theory and philosophy. Feminism challenges the validity of stereotypical gender role stereotypes and the traditional of male dominance (Greene, 1993).

Feminist therapy developed as a response to male dominance of health professions and institutions. It suggested that the mental health establishment often worked to maintain inequality between men and women by trying to help women "adjust" to traditional gender roles when they wished to challenge these roles in their own lives. Feminist therapists note that many women experience depression and other psychological problems as a result of being treated as second-class citizens, and they argue that society rather than the individual woman must change if these psychological problems are to be alleviated.

PSYCHOTHERAPY AND SEXUAL ORIENTATION The American Psychiatric Association (1994) does not consider a gay male or a lesbian sexual orientation to be a psychological disorder. The association did list homosexuality as a mental disorder until 1973, however, and there have been many efforts to "help" gay males and lesbians change their sexual orientation. For example, William Masters and Virginia Johnson (1979) adapted methods they had innovated for the treatment of sexual dysfunctions and reported that the majority of gays seen in therapy "reversed" their sexual orientations. However, most of these individuals were bisexuals and not exclusively gay. More than half were married, and, they all were motivated to change their sexual behavior.

Many critics argue that it is unprofessional to try to help people change their sexual orientations (e.g., Isay, 1990). They note that the great majority of gay males and lesbians are satisfied with their sexual orientations and only seek therapy because of conflicts that arise from social pressure and prejudice. They believe that the purpose of therapy for gay males and lesbians should be to help relieve conflicts caused by prejudice so that they will find life as gay people to be more gratifying.

In sum, psychotherapy is most effective when therapists attend to and respect people's sociocultural as well as individual differences. Although it is the individual who experiences psychological anguish, the fault often lies in the cultural setting and not the individual.

An Arsenal of Chemical Therapies. Many drugs have been developed to combat psychological disorders. They include antianxiety drugs, antipsychotic drugs, antidepressants, and lithium.

> ### REFLECTIONS
> - Agree or disagree, and support your answer: "Psychotherapy is just common sense."
> - Justin swears that he feels much better because of psychoanalysis. Deborah swears by her experience with Gestalt therapy. Are these endorsements acceptable as scientific evidence? Why or why not?
> - Agree or disagree, and support your answer: "It has never been shown that psychotherapy does any good."
> - Agree or disagree, and support your answer: "The effects of traditional psychoanalysis cannot be determined by the experimental method."

■ BIOLOGICAL THERAPIES

In the 1950s Fats Domino popularized the song "My Blue Heaven." Fats was singing about the sky and happiness. Today "blue heavens" is one of the street names for the 10-milligram dose of the antianxiety drug Valium. Clinicians prescribe Valium and other drugs for people with various psychological disorders. In this section, we discuss three biological, or medical, approaches to treating people with psychological disorders: drug therapy, such as use of Valium; electroconvulsive therapy; and psychosurgery.

• *Drug Therapy*

ANTIANXIETY DRUGS Most antianxiety drugs (also called *minor tranquilizers*) belong to the chemical class known as *benzodiazepines.* Valium (diazepam) is a benzodiazepine. Other benzodiazepines include chlordiazepoxide (for example, Librium), oxazepam (Serax), and alprazolam (Xanax). Antianxiety drugs are usually prescribed for outpatients who complain of generalized anxiety or panic attacks, although many people also use them as sleeping pills (Lydiard and others, 1996). Valium and other antianxiety drugs depress the activity of the central nervous system (CNS). The CNS, in turn, decreases sympathetic activity, reducing the heart rate, respiration rate, and feelings of nervousness and tension.

Many people come to tolerate antianxiety drugs very quickly. When tolerance occurs, dosages must be increased for the drug to remain effective.

Sedation (feelings of being tired or drowsy) is the most common side effect of antianxiety drugs. Problems associated with withdrawal from these drugs include **rebound anxiety.** That is, some people who have been using these drugs regularly report that their anxiety becomes worse than before once they discontinue them. Antianxiety drugs can induce physical dependence, as evidenced by withdrawal symptoms such as tremulousness, sweating, insomnia, and rapid heartbeat.

ANTIPSYCHOTIC DRUGS People with schizophrenia are often given antipsychotic drugs (also called *major tranquilizers*). In most cases these drugs reduce

REBOUND ANXIETY • Strong anxiety that can attend the suspension of usage of a tranquilizer.

agitation, delusions, and hallucinations (Kane, 1996). Many antipsychotic drugs, including phenothiazines (for example, Thorazine) and clozapine (Clozaril) are thought to act by blocking dopamine receptors in the brain (Kane, 1996). Research along these lines supports the dopamine theory of schizophrenia discussed in Chapter 15.

ANTIDEPRESSANTS People with major depression often take so-called **antidepressant** drugs. These drugs are also helpful for some people with eating disorders, panic disorder, obsessive-compulsive disorder, and social phobia (Abramowitz, 1997; Lydiard and others, 1996; Thase & Kupfer, 1996). Problems in the regulation of noradrenaline and serotonin may be involved in eating and panic disorders as well as in depression. Antidepressants are believed to work by increasing levels of one or both of these neurotransmitters, which can affect both depression and eating disorders. However, cognitive-behavior therapy addresses irrational attitudes concerning weight and body shape, fosters

ANTIDEPRESSANT • (ANT-EYE-DEE-**PRESS-ANT**). Acting to relieve depression.

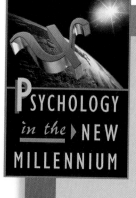

Looking Ahead From the "Decade of the Brain"

The National Institute of Mental Health has labeled the 1990s the "Decade of the Brain" (Goleman, 1996b) and encouraged researchers to push back the frontiers of knowledge about the brain. One of the expected payoffs will be a new generation of "designer drugs." Today's miracle drugs, such as Prozac for depression and Xanax for anxiety, may be little more than chemical dinosaurs in the new millennium.

Current research has shown that there are many different kinds of receptors for neurotransmitters. It is now known, for example, that there are at least 15 different kinds of receptors for serotonin, a neurotransmitter implicated in mood disorders, eating disorders, sexual response, and other aspects of behavior and mental activity (Goleman, 1996b). There are at least five kinds of receptors for dopamine, a neurotransmitter involved in schizophrenia.

One of the problems with the current generation of psychiatric drugs is that they affect all of the receptors for the neurotransmitter they target, rather than the one or two they ought to be targeting. Consider the case of depression and serotonin. Only one or a few of serotonin's receptors are likely to be involved in depression. Current antidepressant drugs therefore cause unwanted side effects, such as digestive and sexual problems.

AND WHAT ABOUT SUBSTANCE ABUSE? Research is also underway concerning chemical methods of treating substance abuse. For example, drugs such as naltrexone help block the pleasant effects of opiates (O'Brien, 1996). More is being learned about cocaine's effects on neurotransmitters such as dopamine, norepinephrine, and serotonin—information which may eventually be connected with more effective treatments for cocaine dependence (O'Brien, 1996). Similarly, marijuana receptors in the brain have been identified, which may lead to treatments for dependence on marijuana (O'Brien, 1996).

Once we know exactly how each kind of receptor is involved in psychological disorders, we may be able to increase the potency of drug therapies and reduce side effects. The ultimate goal, of course, would be to prevent psychological disorders altogether. Dare we dream that we will reach this goal sometime in the new millennium? ■

normal eating habits, and helps people resist the urges to binge and purge. This form of therapy therefore apparently is more effective with people with bulimia than antidepressants (Wilson & Fairburn, 1993).

There are various kinds of antidepressant drugs. Each increases the concentration of noradrenaline or serotonin in the brain. **Monoamine oxidase (MAO) inhibitors** such as Nardil and Parnate block the activity of an enzyme that breaks down noradrenaline and serotonin. **Tricyclic antidepressants** such as Tofranil and Elavil prevent the reuptake of noradrenaline and serotonin by the axon terminals of the transmitting neurons. Selective **serotonin-uptake inhibitors** such as Prozac and Zoloft also block the reuptake of serotonin by presynaptic neurons. As a result, the neurotransmitters remain in the synaptic cleft longer, influencing receiving neurons.

Typically, antidepressant drugs must build up to a therapeutic level over several weeks. Because overdoses of antidepressants can be lethal, some people enter a hospital during the buildup period to prevent suicide attempts. There are also side effects, such as a racing heart and weight gain (Sleek, 1996).

LITHIUM The ancient Greeks and Romans were among the first people to use the metal lithium as a psychoactive drug. They prescribed mineral water for people with bipolar disorder. They had no inkling as to why this treatment sometimes helped, but it might have been because mineral water contains lithium. A salt of the metal lithium (lithium carbonate), in tablet form, flattens out cycles of manic behavior and depression in most people. It is not known precisely how lithium works, although it is clear that it affects the functioning of the neurotransmitters dopamine, acetylcholine, serotonin, and norepinephrine (Price & Heninger, 1994).

It might be necessary for people with bipolar disorder to use lithium indefinitely, just as a person with diabetes must continue to use insulin to control the illness. Lithium also has been shown to have side effects such as hand tremors, memory impairment, and excessive thirst and urination (Price & Heninger, 1994). Memory impairment is reported as the main reason why people discontinue lithium.

• *Electroconvulsive Therapy*

Electroconvulsive therapy (ECT) was introduced by the Italian psychiatrist Ugo Cerletti in 1939 for use with people with psychological disorders. Cerletti had noted that some slaughterhouses used electric shock to render animals unconscious. The shocks also produced convulsions. Along with other European researchers of the period, Cerletti erroneously believed that convulsions were incompatible with schizophrenia and other major psychological disorders.

ECT was originally used for a variety of psychological disorders. Because of the advent of antipsychotic drugs, however, it is now used mainly for people with major depression who do not respond to antidepressants (Thase & Kupfer, 1996).

People typically obtain one ECT treatment three times a week for up to 10 sessions. Electrodes are attached to the temples and an electrical current strong enough to produce a convulsion is induced. The shock causes unconsciousness, so the patient does not recall it. Nevertheless, patients are given a **sedative** so that they are asleep during the treatment.

ECT is controversial for many reasons. First, many professionals are distressed by the thought of passing an electric shock through a patient's head and producing convulsions. Second, there are side effects, including memory problems (Coleman, 1990). Third, nobody knows *why* ECT works.

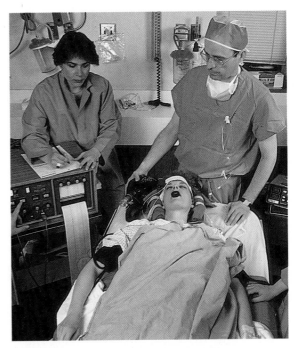

Electroconvulsive Therapy. In ECT, electrodes are placed on each side of the patient's head and a current is passed between them, inducing a seizure. ECT is used mainly in cases of major depression when antidepressant drugs and psychotherapy fail.

MONOAMINE OXIDASE INHIBITORS • (MON-OH-AH-MEAN OX-SEE-DASE). Antidepressant drugs that work by blocking the action of an enzyme that breaks down noradrenaline and serotonin. Abbreviated *MAO inhibitors*.
TRICYCLIC ANTIDEPRESSANTS • (TRY-SIGH-CLICK). Antidepressant drugs that work by preventing the reuptake of noradrenaline and serotonin by transmitting neurons.
SEROTONIN-UPTAKE INHIBITORS • Antidepressant drugs that work by blocking the reuptake of serotonin by presynaptic neurons.
ELECTROCONVULSIVE THERAPY • Treatment of disorders like major depression by passing an electric current (that causes a convulsion) through the head. Abbreviated *ECT*.
SEDATIVE • A drug that relieves nervousness or agitation, or puts one to sleep.

• *Psychosurgery*

Psychosurgery is more controversial than ETC. The best-known modern technique, **prefrontal lobotomy,** has been used with people with severe disorders. In this method, a picklike instrument is used to sever the nerve pathways that link the prefrontal lobes of the brain to the thalamus. This method was pioneered by the Portuguese neurologist Antonio Egas Moniz and was brought to the United States in the 1930s. As pointed out by Valenstein (1986), the theoretical rationale for the operation was vague and misguided. Moreover, Moniz's reports of success were exaggerated. Nevertheless, by 1950 prefrontal lobotomies were performed on more than a thousand people in an effort to reduce violence and agitation. Anecdotal evidence of the method's unreliable outcomes is found in an ironic footnote to history: One of Dr. Moniz's "failures" shot him, leaving a bullet lodged in his spine and paralyzing his legs.

Prefrontal lobotomy also has a host of side effects, including hyperactivity and distractibility, impaired learning ability, overeating, apathy and withdrawal, epileptic-type seizures, reduced creativity, and, now and then, death. Because of these side effects, and because of the advent of antipsychotic drugs, this method has been largely discontinued in the United States.

• *Does Biological Therapy Work?*

There is little question that drug therapy has helped many people with severe psychological disorders. For example, antipsychotic drugs largely account for the reduced need for the use of restraint and supervision (padded cells, straitjackets, hospitalization, and so on) with people diagnosed with schizophrenia. Antipsychotic drugs have allowed hundreds of thousands of former mental hospital residents to lead largely normal lives in the community, hold jobs, and maintain family lives. Most of the problems related to these drugs concern their side effects.

On the other hand, many comparisons of psychotherapy (in the form of cognitive therapy) and drug therapy for depression suggest that cognitive therapy may be more effective than antidepressants (Antonuccio, 1995; Muñoz and others, 1994). For one thing, cognitive therapy provides coping skills that reduce the risk of recurrence of depression once treatment ends (Hollon and others, 1991). Perhaps antidepressant medication is most appropriate for people who fail to respond to psychotherapy.

Many psychologists and psychiatrists are comfortable with the short-term use of antianxiety drugs in helping clients manage periods of unusual anxiety or tension. However, many people use antianxiety drugs routinely to dull the arousal stemming from anxiety-producing lifestyles or interpersonal problems. Rather than make the often painful decisions required to confront their problems and change their lives, they prefer to take a pill.

Despite the controversies surrounding ECT, it helps many people who do not respond to antidepressant drugs (Thase & Kupfer, 1996). Moreover, depressed people who undergo ECT have a lower mortality rate following treatment than those who do not (Martin and others, 1985). This finding is partly attributable to a lower suicide rate.

In sum, drug therapy and perhaps ECT seem to be effective for some disorders that do not respond to psychotherapy alone. Yet common sense and research evidence suggest that psychotherapy is preferable for problems such as anxiety, mild depression, and interpersonal conflict. No chemical can show a person how to change an idea or solve an interpersonal problem.

Truth or Fiction Revisited

It is true that the originator of a surgical technique intended to reduce violence learned that it was not always successful . . . when one of his patients shot him. That technique is prefrontal lobotomy.

PSYCHOSURGERY • Surgery intended to promote psychological changes or to relieve disordered behavior.
PREFRONTAL LOBOTOMY • The severing or destruction of a section of the frontal lobe of the brain.

REFLECTIONS

- Agree or disagree, and support your answer: "Drugs cause more problems than they solve when they are used to treat people with psychological disorders."
- Agree or disagree, and support your answer: "Biological treatments only provide a sort of Band-Aid therapy for psychological disorders. They don't get at the heart of the problems."

SUMMARY

1. **What is psychotherapy?** Psychotherapy is a systematic interaction between a therapist and a client that uses psychological principles to help the client overcome psychological disorders or adjust to problems in living. Behavior therapy is a kind of therapy that relies on psychological learning principles (for example, conditioning and observational learning) to help clients develop adaptive behavior patterns and discontinue maladaptive ones.

2. **What are the goals of traditional psychoanalysis?** The goals are to provide self-insight, encourage the spilling forth (catharsis) of psychic energy, and replace defensive behavior with coping behavior.

3. **What are the methods of traditional psychoanalysis?** The methods include free association and dream analysis.

4. **How do modern psychodynamic approaches differ from traditional psychoanalysis?** Modern approaches are briefer and more directive, and the therapist and client usually sit face to face.

5. **What are the goals and traits of the client-centered therapist?** The client-centered therapist uses nondirective methods to help clients overcome obstacles to self-actualization. The therapist shows unconditional positive regard, empathic understanding, and genuineness.

6. **What are some behavior therapy fear reduction methods?** These include flooding, systematic desensitization, and modeling. Systematic desensitization counterconditions fears by gradually exposing clients to a hierarchy of fear-evoking stimuli while they remain deeply relaxed.

7. **What is aversive conditioning?** This is a behavior-therapy method for discouraging undesirable behaviors by repeatedly pairing their goals (for example, alcohol, cigarette smoke, deviant sex objects) with aversive stimuli so that the goals become aversive rather than tempting.

8. **What are operant-conditioning procedures in behavior therapy?** These are behavior therapy methods that foster adaptive behavior through principles of reinforcement. Examples include token economies, successive approximation, social skills training, and biofeedback training.

9. **What are behavioral self-control methods?** These are behavior therapy methods for adopting desirable behavior patterns and breaking bad habits. They focus on modifying the antecedents (stimuli that act as triggers) and consequences (reinforcers) of behavior and on modifying the behavior itself.

10. **What are the goals and methods of cognitive therapies?** Cognitive therapies aim to give clients insight into irrational beliefs and cognitive distortions and replace these cognitive errors with rational beliefs and accurate perceptions. Beck notes that clients may become depressed because they minimize accomplishments, catastrophize failures, and are generally pessimistic. Ellis notes that clients often show one or more of his 10 irrational beliefs, including excessive needs for approval and perfectionism.

11. **What are the advantages of group therapy?** Group therapy is more economical than individual therapy. Moreover, group members benefit from the social support and experiences of other members.

12. **Does psychotherapy work?** Apparently it does. Statistical analyses show that people who obtain most forms of psychotherapy fare better than people who do not. Psychodynamic and client-centered approaches are particularly helpful with highly verbal and motivated individuals. Cognitive and behavior

therapies are probably most effective. Behavior therapy also helps in the treatment of people with mental retardation and severe psychological problems.

13. **What are the uses of drug therapy?** Antipsychotic drugs help many people with schizophrenia by blocking the action of dopamine receptors. Antidepressants often help people with severe depression, apparently by raising the levels of noradrenaline and serotonin available to the brain. Lithium often helps people with bipolar disorder, apparently by moderating levels of noradrenaline. The use of antianxiety drugs for daily tensions and anxieties is not recommended because people who use them rapidly build tolerance for the drugs. Also, these drugs do not solve personal or social problems, and people at-

tribute their resultant calmness to the drug and not to self-efficacy.

14. **What is electroconvulsive therapy (ECT)?** In ECT an electrical current is passed through the temples, inducing a seizure and frequently relieving severe depression. ECT is controversial because of side effects such as loss of memory and because nobody knows why it works.

15. **What is psychosurgery?** Psychosurgery is an extremely controversial method for alleviating severe agitation by severing nerve pathways in the brain. The best-known psychosurgery technique, prefrontal lobotomy, has been largely discontinued because of side effects.

Chap 13. Social Psychology

social psy - how we think about influence and relate to one another

Attribution Theory → explaination (Internal traits) (Extend
→ Fundamental Attribution Error -
tend to over estimate internal traits route
→ Self-serving Bias - put yourself in the most favorble
light (for our success due to our personality (failures are usually the external sit.)

acting becuz its their personality

happens because situation

Attitudes and Actions (behaviors)
→ Attitudes - felling, Ideas, and beliefs that affect how
we approach and react to other people, objects, and events
→ Central route persuasion (Infinti ad) - going directly through
the rational mind, Influence attit. w/ evidence & logic {Ex: Handwritten = you give all evidence} better not

ex: show picture →
acting writing note
& hope it convinces them?

→ Peripheral route persuasion (subaru ad) - changing attit.
by going around the rational mind & appealing to fears or desires too.
goes to head
→ role (Zimbardo Standford prision study) (In society)

Culture Influences
→ Culture - behaviors, Ideas, traditions, shared by large group of people (Pass down generation to generation)
→ Norms - rules; rules for what is accepted & expected (Ex: In class

Ex: I don't like football so I won't watch?

Ex: likely the people they want to help once they help then can change attit.}

Zimbardo movie

Culture We need to raise my hand and call professor by title)
→ Foot-In-the-door Phenomenon - the tendency to be more
likely to agree to a large request after agreeing to a small one
→ Cognitive dissonance - when attit. & behavior dont match
theirs theres tension {Ex: attit. Im a giving person
but when someone needs money I don't give} but you
have to change & match

Conformity (Soloman Asch); Confederate → actor playing a role for experiment

→ adjust behavior to match groups

A 1^1 2^1 3^1 always 2 but last one says 3; once {follow class?} everyone picks wrong 33%

↳ Normative Social Influence – when you go along with wrong awnser because to ignore embarrassment

↳ Info social influence -- when you dont know anwser you go along with group because you think they are right

Obt obedience (Stanley milgram) – doing something because youve been told to do it (script fist first on and off get it wrong) 65% shocked the high never knew you told them to follow orders and 2/3 went to end

To enhance your understanding of the psychological concepts found in this chapter, please consult the following aids:

Learning Objectives, p. 329
Exercise, p. 330
Lecture and Textbook Outline,
  p. 331
Effective Studying Ideas, p. 333

Key Terms and Concepts, p. 334
Chapter Review, p. 335
Chapter Exercises, p. 344
Knowing the Language, p. 345
Do You Know The Material?, p. 348

History of Therapy
Approaches to Therapy
Psychoanalysis
Humanistic Therapies
Cognitive Therapies

Behavior Therapies
Alternatives to Individual
  Psychotherapy
Biological Therapies

For more information concerning the topics found in this chapter, access psychology links on the World Wide Web through the Harcourt Brace webpage at

www.hbcollege.com

Share your comments and questions with your author at

PsychLinks@aol.com

Social psychologists study the nature and causes of people's behavior and thoughts in social situations. What are the thoughts of the *Sports Captains* (1996) in the sculpture of that name by Richard Cleaver? Why have they come together? The coaches seated here are from South Africa in the early 20th century. The clay figures represent people with huge differences in their worldview who are joined in a sports-related goal—to have their team win.

RICHARD CLEAVER

Chapter 17
Social Psychology

633

OUTLINE

ATTITUDES

The A–B Problem: Do We Do as We Think?

Origins of Attitudes

Changing Attitudes Through Persuasion
Prejudice

Psychology and Modern Life: Combating Prejudice

SOCIAL PERCEPTION

Primacy and Recency Effects: The Importance of First Impressions

Attribution Theory: You're Free, but I'm Caught in the Middle?

Psychology and Modern Life: Making a Good First Impression

Body Language

Psychology in the New Millennium: Can Psychologists Usher in an Age of Peace?

SOCIAL INFLUENCE

Obedience to Authority: Does Might Make Right?

Conformity: Do Many Make Right?

Psychology in a World of Diversity: Muslim Women Face Pressure to Conform

GROUP BEHAVIOR

Social Facilitation: Monkey See, Monkey Do Faster?

Group Decision Making

Polarization and the "Risky Shift"

Groupthink

Mob Behavior and Deindividuation

Altruism and the Bystander Effect: Some Watch While Others Die

ENVIRONMENTAL PSYCHOLOGY: THE BIG PICTURE

Noise: Of Muzak, Rock 'n' Roll, and Low-Flying Aircraft

Temperature: Getting Hot Under the Collar

Of Aromas and Air Pollution: Facilitating, Fussing, and Fuming

Crowding and Personal Space: "Don't Burst My Bubble, Please"

ANDY AND STRETCH. A NEW TECHNIQUE for controlling weight gains? No, these are the names of a couple who have just met at a camera club. Candy and Stretch stand above the crowd—literally. Candy, an attractive woman in her early thirties, is almost 6 feet tall. Stretch is more plain looking, but wholesome, in his late thirties, and 6 feet 5 inches tall.

Stretch has been in the group for some time. Candy is a new member. Let's listen in on them as they make conversation during a coffee break.[1] As you will see, there are some differences between what they say and what they are thinking:

THEY SAY	THEY THINK
Stretch: Well, you're certainly a welcome addition to our group.	(Can't I ever say something clever?)
Candy: Thank you. It certainly is friendly and interesting.	(He's cute.)
Stretch: My friends call me Stretch. It's left over from my basketball days. Silly, but I'm used to it.	(It's safer than saying my name is David Stein.)
Candy: My name is Candy.	(At least my nickname is. He doesn't have to hear Hortense O'Brien.)
Stretch: What kind of camera is that?	(Why couldn't a girl named Candy be Jewish? It's only a nickname, isn't it?)
Candy: Just this old German one of my uncle's. I borrowed it from the office.	(He could be Irish. And that camera looks expensive.)
Stretch: May I? (He takes her camera, brushing her hand and then tingling with the touch.) Fine lens. You work for your uncle?	(Now I've done it. Brought up work.)
Candy: Ever since college. It's more than being just a secretary. I get into sales, too.	(So okay, what if I only went for a year. If he asks what I sell, I'll tell him anything except underwear.)

---

[1] From *Pairing*, by G. R. Bach and R. M. Deutsch, 1970, New York: Peter H. Wyden.

Stretch: Sales? That's funny. I'm in sales, too, but mainly as an executive. I run our department. I started using cameras on trips. Last time I was in the Bahamas. I took—

(Is there a nice way to say used cars? I'd better change the subject.)

(Great legs! And the way her hips move . . .)

Candy: Oh! Do you go to the Bahamas, too? I love those islands.

(So I went just once, and it was for the brassiere manufacturers' convention. At least we're off the subject of jobs.)

Stretch:

(She's probably been around. Well, at least we're off the subject of jobs.)

I did a little underwater work there last summer. Fantastic colors. So rich in life.

(And lonelier than hell.)

Candy:

(Look at that build. He must swim like a fish. I should learn.)

I wish I'd had time when I was there. I love the water.

(Well, I do. At the beach, anyway, where I can wade in and not go too deep.)

So begins a relationship. Candy and Stretch have a drink and talk, sharing their likes and dislikes. Amazingly, they seem to agree on everything—from cars to clothing to politics. The attraction is very strong, and neither is willing to risk turning the other off by disagreeing. They scrupulously avoid one topic: religion. Their religious differences become apparent when they exchange last names. But that doesn't mean they have to talk about it.

They also put off introductions to their parents. The O'Briens and the Steins are narrow-minded about religion. If the truth be known, so are Candy and Stretch.

What happens in this tangled web of deception? After some deliberation, and not without misgivings, they decide to get married. Do they live happily ever after? We can't say. "Ever after" isn't here yet.

We do not have all the answers, but we have some questions. Candy and Stretch pretended to share each other's attitudes. What are *attitudes?* Why didn't Candy and Stretch introduce each other to their parents? Did they fear that their parents would want them to *conform* to their own standards? Would their parents try to *persuade* them to limit dating to people of their own religions? Would they *obey?*

Attitudes, conformity, persuasion, obedience—these topics are the province of **social psychology.** Candy and Stretch went to dinner at a restaurant where they served fine wine and soft music swelled in the background. The ways in which their behavior was influenced by this environment are also part of social psychology. Social psychologists study the nature and causes of behavior and mental processes in social situations. The social psychological topics we discuss in this chapter include attitudes, social perception, social influence, group behavior, and environmental psychology.

■ ATTITUDES

How do you feel about abortion, Japanese cars, and the Republican party? The only connection I draw among these items is that people have *attitudes* toward

SOCIAL PSYCHOLOGY • The field of psychology that studies the nature and causes of people's thoughts and behavior in social situations.

them. They each give rise to cognitive evaluations (such as approval or disapproval), feelings (liking, disliking, or something stronger), and behavioral tendencies (such as approach or avoidance). Although I asked you how you "feel," attitudes are not just feelings or emotions. Many psychologists view thinking—or judgment—as primary. Feelings and behavior follow (Eagly & Chaiken, 1993).

Attitudes are behavioral and cognitive tendencies that are expressed by evaluating particular people, places, or things with favor or disfavor (Eagly & Chaiken, 1993). Attitudes are learned, and they affect behavior (Shavitt, 1990; Snyder & DeBono, 1989). They can foster love or hate. They can give rise to helping behavior or to mass destruction. They can lead to social conflict or to the resolution of conflicts. Attitudes can change, but not easily. Most people do not change their religion or political affiliation without serious reflection or coercion.

• *The A–B Problem: Do We Do as We Think?*

Our definition of attitude implies that our behavior is consistent with our cognitions—that is, with our beliefs and feelings. When we are free to do as we wish, it often is. But, as indicated by the term **A–B problem,** the links between attitudes (A) and behaviors (B) tend to be weak to moderate (Eagly & Chaiken, 1993). For example, research reveals that attitudes toward health-related behaviors such as use of alcohol, smoking, and drunken driving are not consistent predictors of these behaviors (Stacy and others, 1994).

A number of factors influence the likelihood that we can predict behavior from attitudes:

1. *Specificity.* We can better predict specific behavior from specific attitudes than from global attitudes. For example, we can better predict church attendance by knowing people's attitudes toward church attendance than by knowing whether they are Christian. Similarly, a study of female juvenile delinquents found that those who were prostitutes made weaker judgments against prostitution than other delinquents did (Bartek and others, 1993).

2. *Strength of attitudes.* Strong attitudes are more likely to determine behavior than weak attitudes (Fazio, 1990). A person who believes that the nation's destiny depends on Republicans taking control of Congress is more likely to vote than a person who leans toward the Republican party but does not believe that the outcome of elections makes much difference.

3. *Vested interest.* People are more likely to act on their attitudes when they have a vested interest in the outcome (Johnson & Eagly, 1989). People are more likely to vote for (or against) unionization of their workplace, for example, when they believe that their job security depends on the outcome.

4. *Accessibility.* People are more likely to express their attitudes when they are accessible—that is, when they are brought to mind (Fazio, 1990; Krosnick, 1989). This is why politicians attempt to "get out the vote" by means of media blitzes just prior to an election. It does them little good to have supporters who forget them on election day. Attitudes with a strong emotional impact are more accessible (Wu & Shaffer, 1987), which is one reason that politicians strive to get their supporters "worked up" over the issues.

ATTITUDE • An enduring mental representation of a person, place, or thing that evokes an emotional response and related behavior.

A–B PROBLEM • The issue of how well we can predict behavior on the basis of attitudes.

Candy and Stretch avoided discussing matters on which they differed. One motive might have been to avoid heightening the *accessibility* of their clashing attitudes. By keeping them under the table, they might be less likely to act on them and go their separate ways.

• Origins of Attitudes

You were not born a Republican or a Democrat. You were not born a Catholic or a Muslim—although your parents may have practiced one of these religions when you came along. Political, religious, and other attitudes are learned. In this section we describe some of the processes that result in the learning of attitudes.

Conditioning may play a role in the acquisition of attitudes. Experiments have shown that attitudes toward national groups can be influenced by associating them with positive words (such as *gift* or *happy*) or negative words (such as *ugly* or *failure*) (Lohr & Staats, 1973). Parents often reward children for saying and doing things that agree with their own attitudes. Patriotism is encouraged by showing approval to children when they sing the national anthem or wave the flag.

Attitudes formed through direct experience may be stronger and easier to recall, but we also acquire attitudes by observing others. The approval or disapproval of peers leads adolescents to prefer short or long hair, baggy jeans, or preppy sweaters. Television shows us that body odor, bad breath, and the frizzies are dreaded diseases—and, perhaps, that people who use harsh toilet paper are somehow un-American.

COGNITIVE APPRAISAL Despite what we have said, the learning of attitudes is not so mechanical. Now and then we evaluate information and attitudes on the basis of evidence. We may revise **stereotypes** on the basis of new information (Weber & Crocker, 1983). For example, we may believe that a car is more reliable than we had thought if a survey by *Consumer Reports* finds that it has an excellent repair record. Still, our initial attitudes act as cognitive anchors. We often judge new ideas in terms of how much they deviate from our existing attitudes. Accepting larger deviations requires more information processing—in other words, more intellectual work (Quattrone, 1982). For this reason, perhaps, great deviations—such as changes from liberal to conservative attitudes, or vice versa—are apt to be resisted.

• Changing Attitudes Through Persuasion

> Let advertisers spend the same amount of money improving their product that they do on advertising and they wouldn't have to advertise it.
>
> WILL ROGERS

Rogers's social comment sounds on the mark, but he was probably wrong. It does little good to have a wonderful product if its existence remains a secret.

The **elaboration likelihood model** describes the ways in which people respond to persuasive messages (Petty and others, 1994). Consider two routes to persuading others to change attitudes. The first, or central, route inspires thoughtful consideration of arguments and evidence (Eagly & Chaiken, 1993). The second, or peripheral, route associates objects with positive or negative

STEREOTYPE • A fixed, conventional idea about a group.
ELABORATION LIKELIHOOD MODEL • The view that persuasive messages are evaluated (elaborated) on the basis of central and peripheral cues.

cues. When politicians avow that, "This bill is supported by Jesse Jackson (or Jesse Helms)," they are seeking predictable, knee-jerk reactions, not careful consideration of a bill's merits. Other cues are rewards (such as a smile or a hug), punishments (such as parental disapproval), and such factors as the trustworthiness and attractiveness of the communicator.

Advertisements, which are a form of persuasive communication, also rely on central and peripheral routes. Some ads focus on the quality of the product (central route). Others attempt to associate the product with appealing images (peripheral route). Ads for Total cereal, which highlight its nutritional benefits, provide information about the quality of the product. So, too, did the "Pepsi Challenge" taste test ads, which claimed that Pepsi tastes better than Coca-Cola. Marlboro cigarette ads that focus on the masculine, rugged image of the "Marlboro man"[2] offer no information about the product itself. Nor do Virginia Slims cigarette ads, which show "sophisticated, contemporary" women smoking.

In this section we look at one central factor in persuasion—the nature of the message—and three peripheral factors: the messenger, the context of the message, and the audience. We also examine the foot-in-the-door technique.

THE PERSUASIVE MESSAGE: SAY WHAT? SAY HOW? SAY HOW OFTEN?

How do we respond when TV commercials are repeated until we have memorized every dimple on the actors' faces? Research suggests that familiarity breeds content, not contempt.

You might not be crazy about *zebulons* and *afworbu's* at first, but Robert Zajonc (1968) found that people began to react favorably toward these bogus foreign words on the basis of repeated exposure. In fact, repeated exposure to people and things as diverse as the following enhances their appeal:

- political candidates (who are seen in repeated TV commercials) (Grush, 1980)
- photographs of African Americans (Hamm and others, 1975)
- photographs of college students (Moreland & Zajonc, 1982)
- abstract art (Heingartner & Hall, 1974)
- classical music (Smith & Dorfman, 1975)

The more complex the stimuli, the more likely it is that frequent exposure will have favorable effects (Smith & Dorfman, 1975). The 100th playing of a Bach fugue may be less tiresome than the 100th performance of a pop tune.

When trying to persuade someone, is it helpful or self-defeating to alert them to the arguments presented by the opposition? In two-sided arguments, the communicator recounts the arguments of the opposition in order to refute them. Theologians and politicians sometimes expose their followers to the arguments of the opposition and then refute each one. By doing so, they create a kind of psychological immunity to them in their followers. Two-sided product claims, in which advertisers admit their product's weak points in addition to highlighting its strengths, are the most believable (Bridgwater, 1982). For example, one motel chain admits that it does not offer a swimming pool or room service, but points out that the customer therefore saves money.

It would be nice to think that people are too sophisticated to be persuaded by a **fear appeal**. However, women who are warned of the dire risk they run if they fail to be screened for breast cancer are more likely to obtain mammograms

Truth or Fiction Revisited

It is not true that airing a TV commercial repeatedly hurts sales. Repeated exposure frequently leads to liking and acceptance.

FEAR APPEAL • A type of persuasive communication that influences behavior on the basis of arousing fear instead of rational analysis of the issues.

---

[2] The rugged actor in the original TV commercials died of lung cancer. Apparently cigarettes were more rugged than he was.

Would You Buy This Product? Advertisers use a combination of central and peripheral cues to sell their products. What factors contribute to the persuasiveness of messages? To the persuasiveness of communicators? Why is Michael Jordan considered an MVE ("most valuable endorser")?

than women who are informed of the *benefits* of mammography (Banks and others, 1995). Interestingly, although sun tanning has been shown to increase the likelihood of skin cancer, warnings against sun tanning were shown to be more effective when students were warned of risks to their *appearance* (premature aging, wrinkling, and scarring of the skin) than when the warning dealt with the risk to their health (Jones & Leary, 1994). That is, students who were informed of tanning's cosmetic effects were more likely to say that they would protect themselves from the sun than were students who were informed about the risk of cancer. Fear appeals are most effective when the audience believes that the risks are serious and that it can change (Eagly & Chaiken, 1993).

Audiences also tend to believe arguments that appear to run counter to the vested interests of the communicator (Eagly & Chaiken, 1993). If the president of Chrysler or General Motors said that Toyotas and Hondas were superior, you can bet that we would prick up our ears.

THE PERSUASIVE COMMUNICATOR: WHOM DO YOU TRUST? Would you buy a used car from a person who had been convicted of larceny? Would you leaf through fashion magazines featuring homely models? Probably not. Research shows that persuasive communicators are characterized by expertise, trustworthiness, attractiveness, or similarity to their audiences (Mackie and others, 1990; Wilder, 1990). Because of the adoration of their fans, sports superstars such as Michael Jordan are also persuasive as endorsers of products (Goldman, 1993). Fans may consider Jordan to be an MVP, or Most Valuable Player. To advertisers, however, Jordan is an MVE, or Most Valuable Endorser (Goldman, 1993).

TV news anchors enjoy high prestige. One study (Mullen and others, 1987) found that before the 1984 presidential election, Peter Jennings of ABC News had shown significantly more favorable facial expressions when reporting on Ronald Reagan than when reporting on Walter Mondale. Tom Brokaw of NBC and Dan Rather of CBS had not shown favoritism. The researchers also found that viewers of ABC News voted for Reagan in greater proportions than viewers of NBC or CBS News. It is tempting to conclude that Jennings subtly persuaded viewers to vote for Reagan—and maybe this did happen in a number of cases.

But viewers do not simply absorb, spongelike, whatever the tube feeds them. Instead, they show **selective avoidance** and **selective exposure** (Sweeney & Gruber, 1984). They often switch channels when the news coverage runs counter to their own attitudes. They also seek communicators whose outlook coincides with their own. Thus, it may simply be that Reaganites favored Jennings over Brokaw and Rather.

THE CONTEXT OF THE MESSAGE: "GET 'EM IN A GOOD MOOD" You are too shrewd to let someone persuade you by buttering you up, but perhaps someone you know would be influenced by a sip of wine, a bite of cheese, and a sincere compliment. Aspects of the immediate environment, such as music, increase the likelihood of persuasion. When we are in a good mood, we apparently are less likely to evaluate the situation carefully (Mackie & Worth, 1989; Schwarz and others, 1991).

It is also counterproductive to call your dates fools when they differ with you—even though their ideas are bound to be foolish if they do not agree with yours. Agreement and praise are more effective ways to encourage others to embrace your views. Appear sincere, or else your compliments will look manipulative. (It seems unfair to let out this information.)

THE PERSUADED AUDIENCE: ARE YOU A PERSON WHO CAN'T SAY NO? Why do some people have sales resistance? Why do others enrich the lives of every door-to-door salesperson? It may be that people with high self-esteem and low social anxiety are more likely to resist social pressure (Santee & Maslach, 1982).

A classic study by Schwartz and Gottman (1976) reveals the cognitive nature of the social anxiety that can make it difficult for some people to refuse requests. The researchers found that people who comply with unreasonable requests are more apt to report thoughts like the following:

- "I was worried about what the other person would think of me if I refused."
- "It is better to help others than to be self-centered."
- "The other person might be hurt or insulted if I refused."

People who refuse unreasonable requests reported thoughts like these:

- "It doesn't matter what the other person thinks of me."
- "I am perfectly free to say no."
- "This request is unreasonable."

THE FOOT-IN-THE-DOOR TECHNIQUE You might suppose that contributing money to door-to-door solicitors for charity will get you off the hook. Perhaps they'll take the cash and leave you alone for a while. Actually, the opposite is true. The next time they mount a campaign, they may call on you to go door to door on their behalf! Organizations compile lists of people they can rely on. Because they have gotten their "foot in the door," this is known as the **foot-in-the-door technique.**

Consider a classic experiment by Freedman and Fraser (1966). Groups of women received phone calls from a consumer group requesting that they let a six-person crew come to their home to catalog their household products. The job could take hours. Only 22% of one group acceded to this irksome request. But 53% of another group of women assented to a visit from this wrecking crew. Why was the second group more compliant? They had been phoned a few days earlier and had agreed to answer a few questions about the soap products

SELECTIVE AVOIDANCE • Diverting one's attention from information that is inconsistent with one's attitudes.
SELECTIVE EXPOSURE • Deliberately seeking and attending to information that is consistent with one's attitudes.
FOOT-IN-THE-DOOR TECHNIQUE • A method for inducing compliance in which a small request is followed by a larger request.

they used. Thus they had been primed for the second request: The caller had gotten a foot in the door.

Research suggests that people who accede to small requests become more amenable to larger ones because they come to see themselves as the kind of people who help in this way (Eisenberg and others, 1987). Regardless of how the foot-in-the-door technique works, if you want to say no, it may be easier to do so (and stick to your guns) the first time a request is made. Later may be too late.

• *Prejudice*

People have condemned billions of other people. Without ever meeting them. Without ever learning their names. In this section, we discuss some of the reasons for this. We will be dealing with a particularly troubling kind of attitude: prejudice.

Prejudice is an attitude toward a group that leads people to evaluate members of that group negatively. On a cognitive level, it is linked to expectations that members of the target group will behave poorly, say, in the workplace, or engage in criminal behavior. On an emotional level, prejudice is associated with negative feelings such as dislike or hatred. In behavioral terms, it is connected with avoidance, aggression, and discrimination.

> **Truth or Fiction Revisited**
> ....
> *It is true that people have condemned others without meeting them or learning their names. Such are the effects of prejudice.*

DISCRIMINATION One form of negative behavior that results from prejudice is **discrimination.** Many groups in the United States have experienced discrimination—women, gay males and lesbians, older people, and ethnic groups such as African Americans, Asian Americans, Hispanic Americans, Irish Americans, Jewish Americans, and Native Americans. Discrimination takes many forms, including denial of access to jobs, housing, and the voting booth.

STEREOTYPES Are Jewish Americans shrewd and ambitious? Are African Americans superstitious and musical? Are gay men and lesbians unfit for military service? Such ideas are *stereotypes*—prejudices about certain groups that lead people to view members of those groups in a biased fashion.

> **PREJUDICE** • The unfounded belief that a person or group—on the basis of assumed racial, ethnic, sexual, or other features—will possess negative characteristics or perform inadequately.
> **DISCRIMINATION** • The denial of privileges to a person or a group on the basis of prejudice.

Stereotyping. How well is this child doing? Research shows that our expectations about a child's performance on a test are linked to our awareness of that child's socioeconomic background.

There are also cultural stereotypes about physically attractive people. By and large, we rate what is beautiful as good. We expect attractive people to be poised, sociable, popular, intelligent, mentally healthy, fulfilled, persuasive, and successful in their jobs and marriages (Eagly and others, 1991; Feingold, 1992b). Research shows that attractiveness is positively correlated with popularity, social skills, and sexual experience (Feingold, 1992b).

Attractive people are also more likely to be judged innocent of crimes in mock jury experiments and observational studies (Mazzella & Feingold, 1994). When they are found guilty, they are given less severe sentences. Perhaps we assume that attractive people have less need to resort to deviant behavior to

psychology and modern life

COMBATING PREJUDICE

Prejudice has been with us throughout history, and it is unlikely that a miracle cure is at hand. Yet there is much that we can do to combat it. Here are some suggestions:

1. *Encourage intergroup contact and cooperation.* Prejudice encourages us to avoid other groups, which is unfortunate because intergroup contact is one way of breaking down prejudices (Baron & Byrne, 1997). Intergroup contact reveals that members of religious and racial groups have varying values, abilities, interests, and personalities. Intergroup contact is especially effective when people are striving to meet common goals. Playing on the same team, working together on a joint educational project or the yearbook are examples.

   A classic experiment by Muzafer Sherif and his colleagues (1961/1988) showed how feelings of prejudice can be created and reduced. They randomly divided 11-year-old male campers at Oklahoma's Robbers Cave State Park into two groups, who labeled themselves the Eagles and the Rattlers. After being kept apart for a week, the Eagles and Rattlers met in competitive games. A bitter rivalry quickly erupted, in which the Eagles burned the Rattlers' flag and the Rattlers retaliated by trashing the Eagles' cabin. Eating and watching movies together were not enough to overcome the feelings of hostility felt by the groups. The Eagles and the Rattlers became friends only after they had worked together to achieve common goals, such as repairing the camp's water supply and fixing a truck that was carrying food to the camp (both of which had been sabotaged by the experimenters).

2. *Attack discriminatory behavior.* It is sometimes easier to change people's behavior than to alter their feelings. Yet cognitive dissonance theory suggests that when we change people's behavior, their feelings may follow along. It is illegal to deny access to an education and jobs on the basis of gender, religion, race, or disability. Seek legal remedies if you have been discriminated against. Have you been denied access to living accommodations or a job because of prejudice? Talk about it to your academic advisor, the college equal opportunity office, or the dean of students.

3. *Hold discussion forums.* Many campuses conduct workshops and discussion groups on gender,

achieve their goals. Even when they have erred, perhaps they will be more likely to change their evil ways.

SOURCES OF PREJUDICE The sources of prejudice are many and varied. Here are some of them:

1. *Dissimilarity.* We are apt to like people who share our attitudes. In forming impressions of others, we are influenced by attitudinal similarity and dissimilarity (Duckitt, 1992). People of different religions and races often have different backgrounds, however, giving rise to dissimilar attitudes.

Intergroup Contact. Intergroup contact can reduce feelings of prejudice when people work together toward common goals.

race, and diversity. Talk to your dean of students about holding such workshops.

4. *Examine your own beliefs.* Prejudice isn't "out there." Prejudice dwells within us. It is easy to focus on the prejudices of others, but what about our own? It is first necessary personally to decide that feelings of prejudice are wrong (Devine & Zuwerink, 1994; Hilton & von Hippel, 1996). Have you examined your own attitudes and rejected any feelings of prejudice?

Even if we do not personally harbor feelings of racial or religious enmity, are we doing anything to counter such feelings in others? Do we confront people who make prejudiced remarks? Do we belong to organizations that deny access to members of other racial and religious groups? Do we strike up conversations with people from other groups or avoid them? College is meant to be a broadening experience, and we deny ourselves much of the education we could be receiving when we limit our encounters to people who share our own backgrounds. ■

Even when people of different races share important values, they may assume that they do not.

2. *Social conflict.* There is a lengthy history of social and economic conflict between people of different races and religions. For example, for many decades Southern White people and African Americans have competed for jobs, giving rise to negative attitudes, even lynchings (Hepworth & West, 1988).

3. *Social learning.* Children acquire some attitudes from other people, especially their parents. Children tend to imitate their parents, and parents reinforce their children for doing so (Duckitt, 1992). In this way prejudices can be transmitted from generation to generation.

4. *Information processing.* One cognitive view is that prejudices act as cognitive filters through which we perceive the social world. Prejudice is a way of processing social information. It is easier to attend to, and remember, instances of behavior that are consistent with our prejudices than it is to reconstruct our mental categories (Devine, 1989; Fiske, 1993). If you believe that Jewish Americans are stingy, it is easier to recall a Jewish American's negotiation of a price than a Jewish American's charitable donation. If you believe that Californians are airheads, it may be easier to recall TV images of surfing than of scientific conferences at Caltech and Berkeley.

5. *Social Categorization.* A second cognitive perspective focuses on the tendency to divide our social world into "us" and "them." People usually view those who belong to their own groups—the "in-group"—more favorably than those who do not—the "out-group" (Duckitt, 1992; Linville and others, 1989; Schaller & Maas, 1989). Moreover, there is a tendency to assume that members of the out-group are more similar in their attitudes and behavior than members of our own groups (Judd & Park, 1988). Our isolation from the out-group makes it easier to maintain our stereotypes.

6. *Victimization by Prejudice.* Ironically, people who have been victims of prejudice sometimes attempt to gain a sense of pride by asserting superiority over other socioeconomic or ethnic groups (Van Brunt, 1994). For example, *some* Irish immigrants who had been subjected to prejudice and discrimination by British Americans then discriminated against Polish and Italian Americans. *Some* Polish and Italian Americans then discriminated against African Americans. *Some* African Americans then discriminated against recent waves of Hispanic Americans and Asian Americans. In many cases, of course, experiencing discrimination leads people to *combat* prejudice and discrimination.

Truth or Fiction Revisited

It is true that victimization by prejudice can lead people to be become prejudiced themselves.

REFLECTIONS

- Agree or disagree, and support your answer: "People vote with their conscience."
- What are your political attitudes? Liberal? Conservative? Middle of the road? How did you develop these attitudes? (Are you sure?)
- Are you entertained by radio or TV commercials? Which ones? Why? Did these commercials ever convince you to buy a product? Which one? Was the commercial accurate?
- What stereotypes of other ethnic groups can you identify in yourself? How did they develop? Has taking this course affected your stereotypes? If so, how?

In Review — Sources of Prejudice

Dissimilarity	People prefer to affiliate with people who have similar attitudes. People of different religions and races often have different backgrounds, which may give rise to *dissimilar* attitudes. People also tend to *assume* that people of different races have different attitudes, even when they do not.
Social conflict	Social and economic conflict give rise to feelings of prejudice. People of different races and religions often compete for jobs, giving rise to feelings of prejudice.
Social learning	Children acquire some attitudes by observing other people, especially their parents. Parents often reinforce their children for behaving in ways that express their attitudes, including prejudices.
Information processing	Prejudices serve as cognitive schemes or anchors, filters through which people perceive the social world. It is easier to remember instances of behavior that are consistent with prejudices than those that might force people to reconstruct their mental categories.
Social categorization	People tend to divide their social world into "us" and "them." People usually view people who belong to their own groups—the "in-group"—more favorably than those who do not—the "out-group."
Victimization by prejudice	People who have been victims of prejudice sometimes attempt to rebuild a sense of pride by asserting superiority over other groups of people.

■ SOCIAL PERCEPTION

In this section, we explore some factors that contribute to **social perception.** These include the primacy and recency effects, attribution theory, and body language.

• *Primacy and Recency Effects: The Importance of First Impressions*

Why do you wear a suit to a job interview? Why do defense attorneys make sure that their clients dress neatly and get their hair cut before they are seen by the jury? Because first impressions are important and reasonably accurate (Gleitman and others, 1997).

When I was a teenager, a young man was accepted or rejected by his date's parents the first time they were introduced. If he was considerate and made small talk, her parents would allow the couple to stay out past curfew—perhaps even to watch submarine races at the beach during the early morning hours. If he was boorish or uncommunicative, he was seen as a cad forever after. Her parents would object to him, no matter how hard he worked to gain their favor.

First impressions often make or break us. This phenomenon is known as the **primacy effect.** We infer traits from behavior. If we act considerately at first, we are labeled considerate. The trait of consideration is used to explain and predict our future behavior. If, after being labeled considerate, one keeps a date out past curfew, this lapse is likely to be seen as an exception to a rule—excused by circumstances or external causes. If one is first seen as inconsiderate, however, several months of considerate behavior may be perceived as a cynical effort to "make up for it."

SOCIAL PERCEPTION • A subfield of social psychology that studies the ways in which we form and modify impressions of others.
PRIMACY EFFECT • The tendency to evaluate others in terms of first impressions.

First Impressions. Why is it important to make a good first impression? What are some ways of doing so?

Truth or Fiction Revisited

It is true that you may never get a second chance, if you don't make a good first impression. People interpret future events in the light of first impressions.

Subjects in a classic experiment on the primacy effect read different stories about "Jim" (Luchins, 1957). The stories consisted of one or two paragraphs. The one-paragraph stories portrayed Jim as either friendly or unfriendly. These paragraphs were also used in the two-paragraph stories, but in this case the paragraphs were read in the reverse order. Of those reading only the "friendly" paragraph, 95% rated Jim as friendly. Of those who read just the "unfriendly" paragraph, 3% rated him as friendly. Seventy-eight percent of those who read two-paragraph stories in the "friendly-unfriendly" order labeled Jim as friendly. When they read the paragraphs in the reverse order, only 18% rated Jim as friendly.

How can we encourage people to pay more attention to impressions occurring after the first encounter? Abraham Luchins accomplished this by allowing time to elapse between the presentations of the two paragraphs. In this way, fading memories allowed more recent information to take precedence. This is known as the **recency effect.** Luchins found a second way to counter first impressions: He simply asked subjects to avoid making snap judgments and to weigh all the evidence.

• *Attribution Theory: You're Free, but I'm Caught in the Middle?*

At the age of three, one of my daughters believed that a friend's son was a boy because he *wanted* to be a boy. Since she was three at the time, this error in my daughter's **attribution** of the boy's gender is understandable. Adults tend to make somewhat similar attribution errors, however. While they do not believe that people's preferences have much to do with their gender, they do tend to exaggerate the role of choice in their behavior.

An assumption about why people do things is an attribution (Jones, 1990). The process by which we makes inferences about the motives and traits of others through observation of their behavior is the **attribution process.** In this section we focus on attribution theory, or the processes by which people draw conclusions about the factors that influence one another's behavior. Attribution theory is important because attributions lead us to perceive others either as purposeful actors or as victims of circumstances.

RECENCY EFFECT • The tendency to evaluate others in terms of the most recent impression.
ATTRIBUTION • A belief concerning why people behave in a certain way.
ATTRIBUTION PROCESS • The process by which people draw inferences about the motives and traits of others.

DISPOSITIONAL AND SITUATIONAL ATTRIBUTIONS Social psychologists describe two types of attributions. **Dispositional attributions** ascribe a person's behavior to internal factors such as personality traits and free will. **Situational attributions** attribute a person's actions to external factors such as social influence or socialization.

THE FUNDAMENTAL ATTRIBUTION ERROR In cultures that view the self as independent, such as ours, people tend to attribute other people's behavior primarily to internal factors such as personality, attitudes, and free will (Basic Behavioral Science Task Force, 1996c). This bias in the attribution process is known as the **fundamental attribution error.** In such individualistic societies, people tend to focus on the behavior of others rather than on the circumstances surrounding their behavior. For example, if a teenager gets into trouble with the law, individualistic societies are more likely to blame the teenager than the social environment in which the teenager lives.

One reason for the fundamental attribution error is that we tend to infer traits from behavior. But in cultures that stress interdependence, such as Asian cultures, people are more likely to attribute other people's behavior to that person's social roles and obligations (Basic Behavioral Science Task Force, 1996c).

THE ACTOR-OBSERVER EFFECT When we see people (including ourselves) doing things that we do not like, we tend to see the others as willful actors but to see ourselves as victims of circumstances (Baron & Byrne, 1997). The tendency to attribute other people's behavior to dispositional factors and our own behavior to situational influences is called the **actor-observer effect.**

Consider an example. Parents and children often argue about the children's choice of friends or dates. When they do, the parents tend to infer traits from behavior and to see the children as stubborn and resistant. The children also infer traits from behavior. Thus they may see their parents as bossy and controlling. Parents and children alike attribute the others' behavior to internal causes. That is, both make dispositional attributions about other people's behavior.

How do the parents and children perceive themselves? The parents probably see themselves as being forced into combat by their children's foolishness. If they become insistent, it is in response to the children's stubbornness. The children probably see themselves as responding to peer pressures and, perhaps, to sexual urges that may have come from within but seem like a source of outside pressure. The parents and the children both tend to see their own behavior as motivated by external forces. That is, they make situational attributions for their own behavior.

The actor-observer effect extends to our perceptions of both the in-group (an extension of ourselves) and the out-group. Consider conflicts between nations, for example. Both sides may engage in brutal acts of violence. Each side usually considers the other to be calculating, inflexible, and—not infrequently—sinister. Each side also typically views its own people as victims of circumstances and its own violent actions as justified or dictated by the situation. After all, we may look at the other side as being in the wrong, but can we expect them to agree with us?[3]

The Actor-Observer Effect. Who is at fault here? When parents and teenagers argue about the teenagers' choices of friends or dates, the parents tend to perceive the teenagers as stubborn and independent. But the children may perceive their parents as bossy and controlling. Parents and children alike make dispositional attributions for each other's behavior. But the parents and teenagers both tend to see their own behavior as motivated by situational factors. Teenagers often see themselves as caught between peer pressures and parental restrictiveness. Parents, on the other hand, tend to see themselves as forced to act out of love of their impetuous children and fear for what might happen to them.

> ▌ *Truth or Fiction Revisited*
> ....
> *It is true that we take others to task for their misdeeds but tend to see ourselves as victims of circumstances when our conduct falls short of our ideals. This bias in the attribution process is referred to as the actor-observer effect.*

DISPOSITIONAL ATTRIBUTION • An assumption that a person's behavior is determined by internal causes such as personal attitudes or goals.
SITUATIONAL ATTRIBUTION • An assumption that a person's behavior is determined by external circumstances such as the social pressure found in a situation.
FUNDAMENTAL ATTRIBUTION ERROR • The tendency to assume that others act predominantly on the basis of their dispositions, even when there is evidence suggesting the importance of their situations.
ACTOR-OBSERVER EFFECT • The tendency to attribute our own behavior to situational factors but to attribute the behavior of others to dispositional factors.

---

[3] I am not suggesting that all nations are equally blameless (or blameworthy) for their brutality toward other nations. I am pointing out that there is a tendency for the people of a nation to perceive themselves as being driven to undesirable behavior. Yet they are also likely to perceive other nations' negative behavior as willful.

MAKING A GOOD FIRST IMPRESSION

The first impressions you make on others, and the first impressions others make on you, are important to your relationships. You can manage first impressions in a number of ways:

1. Be aware of the impression you make on others. When you meet people for the first time, remember that they are forming impressions of you. Once formed, these impressions are resistant to change.

2. When you apply for a job, your "first impression"—your vita or résumé—may reach your prospective employer before you walk through the door. Make it neat, and present some of your more important accomplishments at the beginning.

3. Why not plan and rehearse your first few remarks on a date or a job interview? Imagine the situation and, in the case of an interview, questions that you are likely to be asked. If you have some relatively smooth statements prepared, along with a nice smile, you are more likely to be considered socially competent, and competence is respected.

4. Smile. You're more attractive when you smile.

5. Dress well for job interviews, col-lege interviews, first dates, important meetings—even when you go to the doctor's office. The appropriate dress for making a good impression on a first date might differ from what you would wear to a job interview. In each case ask yourself, "What type of dress is expected for this occasion? How can I make a positive first impression?"

6. When you answer essay questions, attend to your penmanship. It is the first thing your instructor notices when looking at your paper. Present relevant knowledge in the first sentence or paragraph of the answer, or restate the question by writing something like, "In this essay I will show how . . ."

7. In class, make eye contact with your instructor. Look interested. That way, if you do poorly on a couple of quizzes your instructor may think of you as a "basically good student who made a couple of errors," rather than as "a poor student who is revealing her or his shortcomings." (Don't tell your instructor about this paragraph. Maybe he or she won't notice it.)

8. The first time you talk to your instructor outside of class, be reasonable and sound interested in the subject.

9. When you pass someone in a race, put on a burst of speed. The other person may think that trying to catch you will be futile.

10. Ask yourself if you are being fair to other people in your life. If your date's parents are a bit cold toward you on the evening of your first date, maybe it's because they don't know you and are concerned about their child's welfare. If you show them that you are treating their child decently, they may come around. Don't assume that they're permanent prunefaces.

11. Before you eliminate people from your life on the basis of first impressions, ask yourself, "Is the first impression the 'real person' or just one instance of that person's behavior?" Give people a second chance and you may find that they have something to offer. After all, would you want to be held accountable for everything you've ever said and done? Haven't you changed for the better as time has gone on? Haven't you become more sophisticated and knowledgeable? (You're reading this book, aren't you?) ■

THE SELF-SERVING BIAS There is also a **self-serving bias** in the attribution process. We are likely to ascribe our successes to internal, dispositional factors but our failures to external, situational influences (Baumgardner and others, 1986). When we have done well on a test or impressed a date, we are likely to credit our intelligence and charm. But when we fail, we are likely to blame bad luck, an unfair test, or our date's bad mood.

It seems that we extend the self-serving bias to others in our perceptions of why we win or lose when we gamble. If we win a bet on a football game, we tend to attribute our success to the greater ability of the winning team—a dispositional factor (Gilovich, 1983). But when we lose the bet, we tend to ascribe the outcome to a fluke such as an error by a referee.

There are exceptions to the self-serving bias. For example, depressed people are more likely than other people to ascribe their failures to internal factors, even when external forces are mostly to blame.

Another interesting attribution bias is a gender difference in attributions for friendly behavior. Men are more likely than women to interpret a woman's friendliness toward a man as flirting (Abbey, 1987). Perhaps traditional differences in gender roles still lead men to expect that a "decent" woman will be passive.

FACTORS CONTRIBUTING TO THE ATTRIBUTION PROCESS Our attribution of behavior to internal or external causes can apparently be influenced by three factors: *consensus, consistency,* and *distinctiveness* (Kelley & Michela, 1980). When few people act in a certain way—that is, when **consensus** is low—we are likely to attribute behavior to dispositional (internal) factors. Consistency refers to the degree to which the same person acts in the same way on other occasions. Highly consistent behavior can often be attributed to dispositional factors. Distinctiveness is the extent to which the person responds differently in different situations. If the person acts similarly in different situations, distinctiveness is low. We therefore are likely to attribute his or her behavior to dispositional factors.

Let us apply the criteria of consensus, consistency, and distinctiveness to the behavior of a customer in a restaurant. She takes one bite of her blueberry cheesecake and calls the waiter. She tells him that her food is inedible; she demands that it be replaced. The question is whether she complained as a result of internal causes (for example, because she is hard to please) or external causes (that is, because the food really is bad). Under the following circumstances, we are likely to attribute her behavior to internal, dispositional causes: (1) No one else at the table is complaining, so consensus is low. (2) She has returned her food on other occasions, so consistency is high. (3) She complains in other restaurants also, so distinctiveness is low (see Table 17.1).

Under the following circumstances, however, we are likely to attribute the customer's behavior to external, situational causes: (1) Everyone else at the

TABLE 17.1 FACTORS LEADING TO INTERNAL OR EXTERNAL ATTRIBUTIONS OF BEHAVIOR

	Internal Attribution	*External Attribution*
Consensus	Low: Few people behave this way.	High: Most people behave this way.
Consistency	High: The person behaves this way frequently.	Low: The person does not behave this way frequently.
Distinctiveness	Low: The person behaves this way in many situations.	High: The person behaves this way in few situations.

SELF-SERVING BIAS • The tendency to view one's successes as stemming from internal factors and one's failures as stemming from external factors.
CONSENSUS • General agreement.

table is also complaining, so consensus is high. (2) She does not usually return food, so consistency is low. (3) She usually does not complain at restaurants, so distinctiveness is high. Given these conditions, we are likely to believe that the blueberry cheesecake really is awful and that the customer is justified in her response.

• *Body Language*

Body language is important in social perception. Nonverbal behavior can express our feelings. It can regulate social interactions (Patterson, 1991). People

PSYCHOLOGY *in the* ▶ **NEW MILLENNIUM**

Can Psychologists Usher in an Age of Peace?

One of the most pressing human issues concerns conflict and warfare. It would be nice to think that technological advances would somehow minimize human brutality. However, the fact is that technological innovations have been repeatedly used by warlords and governments as more efficient ways of maiming and killing.

Fortunately, psychologists have not given in to the view that we are helpless to prevent people from harming others (Kelman, 1997). Many psychologists are focusing on "zealous nationalism and what motivates some groups to start war [while others] are able to live in peace" (Meade, 1994, p. 15).

Many topics discussed in this book relate to war and peace. Chapter 11 explores the origins of aggression and ways in which psychologists try to deal with it (see, e.g., Crick & Dodge, 1994; Lochman & Dodge, 1994). This chapter and Chapter 2 discuss the tendency to obey authority figures even when they demand that people act in harmful or brutal ways. Although we have outlined the forces that act on individuals in the presence of authority figures, can we hope that readers of this book will act to prevent authority figures from committing crimes against humanity in the new millennium? (That answer lies in your hands, not mine.) Knowledge of

ways of battling prejudice can also be of help. For example, Israelis and Palestinians worked in small groups for many years before arriving at their peace treaty. The group experiences broke down stereotypes about the out-group, helped individuals form coalitions across the lines of conflict, and formed the cores of new relationships (Kelman, 1997).

Let us also consider how psychologists might use what they know about attributional processes to heighten the chances of peace.

CAN ATTRIBUTION THEORY BE USED TO MEDIATE INTERNATIONAL CONFLICTS? Biases in the attribution process interfere with people's ability to understand other nation's motives for their behavior. As a result, they may unfairly blame citizens of those nations, and conflict may result.

Psychologists conduct individual and group therapy. Can they also mediate international conflicts? Research on attribution process suggests the following possibilities:

• *Helping Nations Avoid Jumping to the Conclusion That Other Nations Are Always to Blame for Their Behavior.* Nations, like people, tend to attribute too much of other nations' behavior to dispositional factors. That is, they make the fundamental attribution error. The fact is that nations are influenced by situational variables as well as by dispositional variables. These include financial hardship, short-sighted leaders, conflict among ethnic groups, unwise alliances, the promise of reward, and the threat of punishment.

When one nation is offended by another nation's behavior, leaders might try to imagine the internal

even use body language to deceive other people as to how they feel (DePaulo, 1992). For example, they may smile when they are really angry and planning revenge.

At an early age we learn that the way people carry themselves provides cues to how they feel and are likely to behave (Saarni, 1990). You may have noticed that when people are "uptight" they may also be rigid and straight-backed. People who are relaxed are more likely to "hang loose." Factors such as eye contact, posture, and the distance between two people provide cues to the individuals' moods and their feelings toward their companions. When people face us and lean toward us, we may assume that they like us or are interested in

and external pressures that are influencing the other nation and its leaders. Empathy might foster understanding and encourage more suitable behavior.

- *Helping Nations Avoid Jumping to the Conclusion That They Are Never to Blame for Their Own Behavior.* Psychologists have also learned that nations, like people, tend to be highly aware of the situational forces that are influencing their behavior. They may focus on situational factors to the point that they ignore dispositional factors—for example, the role by their leaders' decisions. A nation may see itself as leaning toward war because of a shortage of natural resources and pressure from an ally. However, its leaders make decisions on the basis of numerous factors in addition to these. Recognizing the importance of decision making can help place the blame for bad decisions where it belongs—on specific leaders rather than entire nations.

  Do you ever say to yourself, "How can I be expected to relax and be a nice guy when I'm going to this pressure cooker of a college?" or "How can I let such an insult go unpunished?" Situational and dispositional variables affect nations' behavior as well as our own. When nations focus on the situational variables, they may lose sight of their own causal role in aggressive behavior.

- *Helping a Nation Recognize That Other Nations May Tend to Blame It for Things That Are Not Its Fault.* Partly because of its wealth, partly because of its history, and partly because it is a big target, the United States is frequently blamed for problems that are not of its making. Other people may attribute too much of our nation's behavior to dispositional

factors. When in conflict, it is useful for a nation to explain the forces that it perceives to be acting upon it. In this way it can give other nations the information that will help them empathize with its situation.

- *Helping a Nation Recognize That Other Nations Often See Themselves as Forced to Act as They Do.* We tend to see ourselves as victims of circumstances, compelled by situations. Consider the United States' involvement in Vietnam in the 1960s and 1970s. The nation perceived itself as coming to the aid of its South Vietnamese allies, who valued democracy and sought U.S. protection against invaders from the north. But many North Vietnamese perceived themselves as attempting to unify their country and resist the influence of a superpower from the other side of the world.

  It is helpful to try to perceive events from the perspective of one's adversary. It helps to realize that other people can feel that they are forced to behave as they do, just as we can. Then we can begin to focus on the forces that compel us all—not just on our own sense of injury.

Can psychologists help make the new millennium an age of peace? Can they succeed where national leaders, philosophers, kings and queens, and great historic figures have failed? Perhaps they can. Perhaps not. But there are two compelling reasons why psychologists will try to help. One is that psychology brings a unique perspective to the problems of nations as well as those of individuals. Another is that even if psychologists fail, the greater crime would be to not try to help. ■

what we are saying. If we overhear a conversation between a couple and observe that the woman is leaning toward the man but the man is sitting back and toying with his hair, we are likely to infer that he is not interested in what she is saying.

TOUCHING: PUT THE ARM ON PEOPLE (LITERALLY) Touching also communicates. Women are more likely than men to touch other people when they are interacting with them (Stier & Hall, 1984). In one "touching"experiment, Kleinke (1977) showed that appeals for help can be more effective when the distressed person makes physical contact with people who are asked for aid. A woman obtained more coins for phone calls when she touched the arm of the person she was asking for money. In another experiment, waitresses obtained higher tips when they touched patrons on the hand or the shoulder while making change (Crusco & Wetzel, 1984).

In these experiments, the touching was noncontroversial. It was usually gentle, brief, and done in familiar settings. However, when touching suggests greater intimacy than is desired, it can be seen as negative. A study in a nursing home found that responses to being touched depended on factors such as the status of the staff member, the type of touch, and the part of the body that was touched (Hollinger & Buschmann, 1993). Touching was considered positive when it was appropriate to the situation and did not appear to be condescending. It was seen as negative when it was controlling, unnecessary, or overly intimate.

Body language can also be used to establish and maintain territorial control (Brown & Altman, 1981), as anyone knows who has had to step aside because a football player was walking down the hall. Werner and her colleagues (1981) found that players in a game arcade used touching as a way of signaling others to keep their distance. Solo players engaged in more touching than did groups, perhaps because they were surrounded by strangers.

FIGURE 17.1

DIAGRAM OF AN EXPERIMENT IN HARD STARING AND AVOIDANCE

In the Greenbaum and Rosenfeld study, the confederate of the experimenter stared at some drivers and not at others. Recipients of the stares drove across the intersection more rapidly once the light turned green. Why?

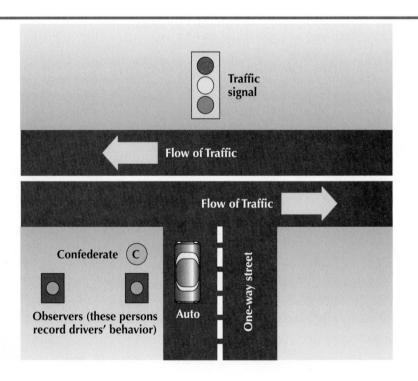

GAZING AND STARING: THE EYES HAVE IT We usually feel that we can learn much from eye contact. When other people "look us squarely in the eye," we may assume that they are being assertive or open with us. Avoidance of eye contact may suggest deception or depression. Gazing is interpreted as a sign of liking or friendliness (Kleinke, 1986). In one penetrating study, men and women were asked to gaze into each other's eyes for two minutes (Kellerman and others, 1989). After doing so, they reported having passionate feelings toward one another. (Watch out!)

Of course, a gaze is not the same thing as a persistent hard stare. A hard stare is interpreted as a provocation or a sign of anger. Adolescent males sometimes engage in staring contests as an assertion of dominance. The male who looks away first loses the contest. In a classic series of field experiments, Phoebe Ellsworth and her colleagues (1972) subjected drivers stopped at red lights to hard stares by riders of motor scooters (see Figure 17.1). When the light changed, people who were stared at crossed the intersection more rapidly than people who were not. People who are stared at exhibit higher levels of physiological arousal than people who are not (Strom & Buck, 1979).

REFLECTIONS
- Think of an instance in which you tried to make a good first impression on someone. How did you do it?
- Did you ever try to excuse your behavior by making a situational attribution? Do you make the fundamental attribution error of attributing too much of other people's behavior to choice? Give examples.
- How do you feel when strangers touch you? Why? How do you feel when a physician or nurse touches you during a physical examination? Why?

■ SOCIAL INFLUENCE

Most people would be reluctant to wear blue jeans to a funeral, walk naked on city streets, or, for that matter, wear clothes at a nudist colony. This is because other people and groups can exert enormous pressure on us to behave according to their norms. **Social influence** is the area of social psychology that studies the ways in which people alter the thoughts, feelings, and behavior of others. We already learned how attitudes can be changed through persuasion. In this section we describe a couple of classic experiments that demonstrate how people influence others to engage in destructive obedience or conform to social norms.

• Obedience to Authority: Does Might Make Right?

Throughout history soldiers have followed orders—even when it comes to slaughtering innocent civilians. The Turkish slaughter of Armenians, the Nazi slaughter of Jews, the Serbian slaughter of Bosnian Muslims, the mutual slaughter of Hutus and Tutsis in Rwanda—these are all examples of the tragedies that can arise from simply following orders. We may say that we are horrified by such crimes and that we can't imagine why people engage in them. But how many of us would refuse to follow orders issued by authority figures?

SOCIAL INFLUENCE • The area of social psychology that studies the ways in which people influence the thoughts, feelings, and behavior of others.

THE MILGRAM STUDIES Stanley Milgram also wondered how many people would resist immoral requests made by authority figures. To find out, he ran the series of experiments described at the beginning of Chapter 2. People responded to newspapers ads seeking subjects for an experiment on "the effects of punishment on learning." The experiment required a "teacher" and a "learner." The newspaper recruit was assigned the role of teacher—supposedly by chance.

Figures 2.1 and 2.2 show the bogus shock apparatus employed in the experiment, and the layout of the laboratory. "Teachers" were given the task of administering shock to learners when they made errors. The level of shock was to increase with each consecutive error. Despite the professed purpose of the research, Milgram's sole aim was to determine how many people would deliver high levels of apparently painful electric shock to "learners."

In various phases of Milgram's research, nearly half or the majority of the subjects complied throughout the series, believing that they were delivering 450-volt, XXX-rated shocks. These findings held for men from the New Haven community and for male students at Yale, and for women.

Many people obey the commands of others even when they are required to perform immoral tasks. But *why?* Why did Germans "just follow orders" during the Holocaust? Why did "teachers" obey the experimenter in Milgram's study? We do not have all the answers, but we can offer a number of hypotheses:

1. *Socialization.* Despite the expressed American ideal of independence, we are socialized from early childhood to obey authority figures such as parents and teachers. Obedience to immoral demands may be the ugly sibling of socially desirable respect for authority figures (Blass, 1991).

2. *Lack of social comparison.* In Milgram's experimental settings, experimenters displayed command of the situation. Teachers (subjects), however, were on the experimenter's ground and very much on their own. Being on their own, they did not have the opportunity to compare their ideas and feelings with those of other people in the same situation. They therefore were less likely to have a clear impression of what to do.

3. *Perception of legitimate authority.* One phase of Milgram's research took place within the hallowed halls of Yale University. Subjects might have been overpowered by the reputation and authority of the setting. An experimenter at Yale might have appeared to be a highly legitimate authority figure—as might a government official or a high-ranking officer in the military. Yet further research showed that the university setting contributed to compliance but was not fully responsible for it. The percentage of individuals who complied with the experimenter's demands dropped from 65% to 48% when Milgram (1974) replicated the study in a dingy storefront in a nearby town. At first glance, this finding might seem encouraging. But the main point of the Milgram studies is that most people are willing to engage in morally reprehensible acts at the behest of a legitimate-looking authority figure. Hitler and his henchmen were authority figures in Nazi Germany. "Science" and Yale University legitimized the authority of the experimenters in the Milgram studies.

4. *The foot-in-the-door technique.* The foot-in-the-door technique might also have contributed to the obedience of the teachers (Gilbert, 1981). Once they had begun to deliver shocks to learners, they might have found it progressively more difficult to extricate themselves from the situation. Soldiers, similarly, are first taught to obey orders unquestioningly in

In Review — Possible Reasons for "Following Orders" in the Milgram Studies

Socialization	People are socialized from early childhood to obey authority figures such as parents and teachers.
Lack of social comparison	Being on their own, subjects ("teachers") did not have the opportunity to compare their feelings with those of other people in the same situation.
Perception of legitimate authority	When Milgram's research took place at Yale University, subjects may have been influenced by the reputation and authority of the setting. An experimenter at Yale may have appeared to be a legitimate authority figure.
The foot-in-the-door technique	Once they had begun to deliver shocks to learners, subjects may have found it progressively more difficult to pull out of the situation.
Inaccessibility of values	People are more likely to act in accordance with their attitudes when their attitudes are readily available, or accessible. Most people believe that it is wrong to harm innocent people, but strong emotions interfere with clear thinking. As the subjects in the Milgram experiments became more upset, their attitudes may have become less accessible.
Buffers	Buffers may have decreased the effect of the "learners'" pain on the subjects (the "teachers"). For example, the learners were in another room.

unimportant matters such as dress and drill. By the time they are ordered to risk their lives, they have been saluting smartly and following commands without question for a long time.

5. *Inaccessibility of values.* People are more likely to act in accordance with their attitudes when their attitudes are readily available, or accessible. Most people believe that it is wrong to harm innocent people. But strong emotions interfere with clear thinking. As the teachers in the Milgram experiments became more aroused, their attitudes might thus have become less "accessible." As a result, it might have become progressively more difficult for them to behave according to these attitudes.

6. *Buffers.* Several buffers decreased the effect of the learners' pain on the teachers. For example, the "learners" (who were actually confederates of the experimenter) were in another room. When they were in the same room with the teachers—that is, when the teachers had full view of their victims—the compliance rate dropped from 65% to 40% (Miller, 1986). Moreover, when the teacher held the learner's hand on the shock plate, the compliance rate dropped to 30%. In modern warfare, opposing military forces may be separated by great distances. They may be little more than a blip on a radar screen. It is one thing to press a button to launch a missile or aim a piece of artillery at a distant troop carrier or a faraway mountain ridge. It is quite another to hold a weapon to a victim's throat.

Thus there are many possible explanations for obedience. Milgram's research has alerted us to a real danger—the tendency of many, if not most, people to obey the orders of an authority figure even when they run counter to moral values. It has happened before. Unless we remain alert, it will happen again.

Conformity. In the military, individuals are taught to conform until the group functions in machine-like fashion. What pressures to conform do you experience? Do you surrender to them? Why or why not?

• Conformity: Do Many Make Right?

We are said to **conform** when we change our behavior in order to adhere to social norms. **Social norms** are widely accepted expectations concerning social behavior. Explicit social norms require us to whisper in libraries and to slow down when driving past a school. One unspoken or implicit social norm causes us to face the front of an elevator. Another implicit norm causes us to be "fashionably late" for social gatherings.

The tendency to conform to social norms is often a good thing. Many norms have evolved because they promote comfort and survival. Group pressure can also promote maladaptive behavior, as when people engage in risky behavior because "everyone is doing it."

Let us look at a classic experiment on conformity conducted by Solomon Asch in the early 1950s. We will then examine factors that promote conformity.

SEVEN LINE JUDGES CAN'T BE WRONG: THE ASCH STUDY Can you believe what you see with your own eyes? Seeing is believing, isn't it? Not if you were a subject in Asch's (1952) study.

You entered a laboratory room with seven other subjects, supposedly taking part in an experiment on visual discrimination. At the front of the room stood a man holding cards with lines drawn on them.

The eight of you were seated in a series. You were given the seventh seat, a minor fact at the time. The man explained the task. There was a single line on the card on the left. Three lines were drawn on the card at the right (Figure 17.2). One line was the same length as the line on the other card. You and the other subjects were to call out, one at a time, which of the three lines—1, 2, or 3—was the same length as the one on the card on the left. Simple.

The subjects to your right spoke out in order: "3," "3," "3," "3," "3," "3." Now it was your turn. Line 3 was clearly the same length as the line on the first card, so you said "3." The fellow after you then chimed in: "3." That's all there was to it. Then two other cards were set up at the front of the room. This time

CONFORM • To changes one's attitudes or overt behavior to adhere to social norms.

SOCIAL NORMS • Explicit and implicit rules that reflect social expectations and influence the ways people behave in social situations.

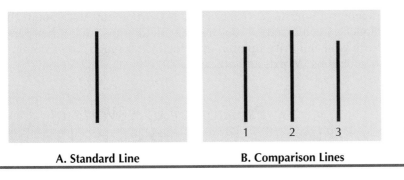

FIGURE 17.2
CARDS USED IN THE ASCH STUDY ON CONFORMITY
Which line on card B — 1, 2, or 3 — is the same length as the line on card A? Line 2, right? But would you say "2" if you were a member of a group and six people answering ahead of you all said "3"? Are you sure?

A. Standard Line   **B. Comparison Lines**

line 2 was clearly the same length as the line on the first card. The answers were "2," "2," "2," "2," "2," "2." Again it was your turn. You said "2," and perhaps your mind began to wander. Your stomach was gurgling a bit. The fellow after you said "2."

Another pair of cards was held up. Line 3 was clearly the correct answer. The six people on your right spoke in turn: "1," "1 . . ." Wait a second! ". . . 1," "1." You forgot about dinner and studied the lines briefly. No, line 1 was too short by a good half inch. But the next two subjects said "1" and suddenly it was your turn. Your hands had become sweaty and there was a lump in your throat. You wanted to say "3," but was it right? There was really no time, and you had already paused noticeably. You said "1," and so did the last fellow.

Now your attention was riveted on the task. Much of the time you agreed with the other seven judges, but sometimes you did not. And for some reason beyond your understanding, they were in perfect agreement even when they were wrong—assuming that you could trust your eyes. The experiment was becoming an uncomfortable experience, and you began to doubt your judgment.

The discomfort in the Asch study was caused by the pressure to conform. Actually, the other seven recruits were confederates of the experimenter. They prearranged a number of incorrect responses. The sole purpose of the study was to see whether you would conform to the erroneous group judgments.

How many people in Asch's study caved in? How many went along with the crowd rather than give what they thought to be the right answer? Seventy-five percent. *Three out of four agreed with the majority's wrong answer at least once.*

Truth or Fiction Revisited
....
Research evidence reveals that *seeing is not necessarily believing* — at least when most people seem to see things differently than we do.

FACTORS THAT INFLUENCE CONFORMITY Several factors increase the tendency to conform. They include the following:

- belonging to a collectivist rather than an individualistic society (Bond & Smith, 1996),

- the desire to be liked by other members of the group (but valuing being right over being liked *decreases* the tendency to conform),

- low self-esteem,

- social shyness (Santee & Maslach, 1982),

- lack of familiarity with the task.

Other factors in conformity include group size and social support. The likelihood of conformity, even to incorrect group judgments, increases rapidly as group size grows to five members, then rises more slowly to about eight members (Tanford & Penrod, 1984). At about that point the maximum chance of conformity is reached. Yet finding just one other person who supports your minority opinion apparently is enough to encourage you to stick to your guns (Morris and others, 1977).

Muslim Women in the United States. Traditional Muslim women often complain of being treated as oddities in the United States. Because of their need to support one another and tackle practical problems, Muslim women across the nation are organizing groups to explore ways of getting people to accept them in malls, on school boards, and in investment banks.

Psychology in a World of DIVERSITY

Muslim Women Face Pressure to Conform

"People look at me and they're like, 'She wants to work here?'" complained 19-year-old Maha Alkateeb. After a frustrating job search at the mall, she pulled off her hejab, the black scarf with which many Muslim women cover their hair, and allowed her long, dark hair to cascade out.

Wanda Khan, 37, suffered a similar setback in Charlotte, North Carolina. She was denied a teaching job because of her hejab. "I know that I am more than qualified," she said, "but a school official told me that there is a school policy against wearing hats. I told him it was a religious thing, and that I couldn't remove it, and that I would take it up with the school board."

Muslim women find that they are usually treated as oddities in the United States. Maha's mother, Sharifa, explained that most people in the United States think of Muslim women as wearing huge sheets. In the common stereotype, the Muslim woman has three children trailing behind her, and she herself is "trailing behind her husband who just finished beating her."

SUPPORT GROUPS Because of the need to support one another and address practical problems, Muslim women across the nation are organizing neighborhood groups and national associations. Some groups debate the merits of wearing a veil. (There is nothing in the Islamic religion that requires the hejab per se, but wearing one is a traditional way for Muslim women to meet Islamic mandates for modesty.) Many groups explore ways of getting people to accept them in malls, PTAs, and investment banks. They convene to discuss ways of tackling school boards that do not excuse their children for Muslim holidays and businesses that deny jobs to Muslims.

"Muslim women here are starting to mobilize because they feel demonized," noted Yvonne Haddad, a professor at the University of Massachusetts. The act of organizing brings Muslim women out from behind their husbands and fathers, who have traditionally been the first to try to decode the cultural values and language of a new host nation. "When it looks like things are falling apart, the women step up," Professor Haddad said. "They used to defer to men, but when they see things aren't getting done, they organize themselves."

Muslim women in the United States are also likely to organize and assert themselves because of the freedoms and mobility they lacked in their countries of origin. For some, the issue seems to be how to continue to embrace Islam and at the same time adopt appealing values of the dominant U.S. culture, such as those concerning women's independence, self-assertiveness, and advancement in the workplace.

SKIPPING THE PROM Maha Alkhateeb is one of a number of young Muslim American women who find that Islamic religious obligations tend to further muddle an already stressful adolescence. Stringent Islamic practices, such as praying five times a day and fasting from dawn to sunset during Ramadan, can be burdensome for Muslims living in a generally secular society like the United States. Many Americans consider such overt and frequent religious displays to be oddities. Fasting during the month of Ramadan made Maha's gym class arduous. Her clothing drew scorn from classmates, and her values led her to skip the prom. She explains about the prom: "At the time of the prom, I was sad, but just about everyone I knew had sex that night, which I think was immoral. Now, I like saying that I didn't go. I didn't go there just because it was a cool thing to do."

Mayada el-Zoghbi, a 24-year-old Egyptian who grew up spending time in Minnesota and Egypt, is now a graduate student at Columbia University. In keeping with Islamic tradition, Mayada fasts during Ramadan and abstains from alcohol. On the other hand, she prays "occasionally," not the traditional five times per day. Moreover, she goes out dancing and on dates—practices that are frowned upon by traditional Muslims. Dorm life, she notes, makes it difficult to pray as often as her family would expect her to. "Asking me why I don't feel comfortable praying in front of other people here in the United States is like asking me why I don't wear shorts in Cairo," she explains. "I just can't."

REFLECTIONS

- Why do you think that most participants in the Milgram studies obeyed orders?
- It has been shown that people who value being right more than being liked by others are less likely to conform to group pressure. Which is more important to you?
- Can you think of some instances in which you have conformed to social pressure? (Would you wear blue jeans if everyone else wore slacks or skirts?)
- Have the pressures placed on you by your own sociocultural group ever come into conflict with the values and customs of the larger society? If so, how?

■ GROUP BEHAVIOR

Gail Maeder, thin as a sapling, grew up in Sag Harbor, Long Island. She went to Suffolk Community College. She loved animals, especially cats. She did not like to use paper towels because she equated that with killing trees. And she would have turned 27 [in August 1997] if she had not joined what her parents called "the UFO cult." (Bearak, 1997, p. A1)

Gail had joined the Heaven's Gate group. To be human is to belong to groups. Groups have much to offer us. They help us satisfy the needs for affection, attention, and belonging. They empower us to do things we could not manage by ourselves.

But Gail had joined the wrong group. Cults, like Gail's, often provide instant friendship, group identity, security, and structure (Zimbardo, 1997). But groups can also pressure us into taking life, or surrendering our own lives, because other members of the group are doing so. Thirty-nine Heaven's Gaters

Social Facilitation. Runners tend to move faster when they are members of a group. Does the presence of other people raise our level of arousal or produce "evaluation apprehension"?

committed suicide in 1997, apparently in the belief that they would ascend to a higher level of being. Bunch after bunch of them went to their deaths in a frighteningly orderly manner. They departed life in a way they might never have permitted if they had been acting as individuals.

This section considers ways in which people behave differently as group members than they would as individuals. We begin with social facilitation.

Social Facilitation: Monkey See, Monkey Do Faster?

One effect of groups on individual behavior is **social facilitation,** or the effects on performance that result from the presence of others. Bicycle riders and runners tend to move faster when they are members of a group. This effect is not limited to people. Dogs and cats eat more rapidly around others. Even roaches—yes, roaches—run more rapidly when other roaches are present (Zajonc, 1980).

According to Robert Zajonc (1980), the presence of other people increases our levels of arousal, or motivation. At high levels of arousal, our performance of simple tasks is facilitated. Our performance of complex responses may be impaired, however. For this reason, a well rehearsed speech may be delivered more masterfully before a larger audience. An offhand speech or a question-and-answer session may be hampered by a large audience.

Social facilitation may be influenced by **evaluation apprehension** as well as arousal (Bray & Sugarman, 1980; Sanna & Shotland, 1990). Our performance before a group is affected not only by the presence of others but also by concern that they are evaluating us. When giving a speech, we may "lose our thread" if we are distracted by the audience and focus too much on its apparent reaction (Seta, 1982). If we believe that we have begun to flounder, evaluation apprehension may skyrocket. As a result, our performance may falter even more.

The presence of others can also impair performance—not when we are acting *before* a group but when we are anonymous members *of* a group (Harkins,

SOCIAL FACILITATION • The process by which a person's performance is increased when other members of a group engage in similar behavior.
EVALUATION APPREHENSION • Concern that others are evaluating our behavior.

1987; Shepperd, 1993). Workers, for example, may "goof off" or engage in *social loafing* on humdrum jobs when they believe they will not be found out and held accountable. Under these conditions there is no evaluation apprehension. There may also be **diffusion of responsibility** in groups. Each person may feel less obligation to help because others are present. Group members may also reduce their efforts if an apparently capable member makes no contribution but "rides free" on the efforts of others.

How would you perform in a tug of war? Would the presence of other people pulling motivate you to pull harder? Or would the fact that no one can tell how hard you are pulling encourage you to "loaf"?

• Group Decision Making

Organizations use groups such as committees or juries to make decisions in the belief that group decisions are more accurate than individual decisions (Gigone & Hastie, 1997). How are group decisions made? Social psychologists have discovered a number of "rules," or **social decision schemes,** that govern much of group decision making (Davis and others, 1984; Stasser and others, 1989). Here are some examples:

1. *The majority-wins scheme.* In this commonly used scheme, the group arrives at the decision that was initially supported by the majority. This scheme appears to guide decision making most often when there is no single objectively correct decision. An example would be a decision about which car models to build when their popularity has not been tested in the court of public opinion.

2. *The truth-wins scheme.* In this scheme, as more information is provided and opinions are discussed, the group comes to recognize that one approach is objectively correct (Gigone & Hastie, 1997). For example, a group deciding whether to use SAT scores in admitting students to college would profit from information about whether the scores do predict college success.

3. *The two-thirds majority scheme.* Juries tend to convict defendants when two-thirds of the jury initially favors conviction.

4. *The first-shift rule.* In this scheme, the group tends to adopt the decision that reflects the first shift in opinion expressed by any group member. If a car-manufacturing group is divided on whether to produce a convertible, it may opt to do so after one member of the group who initially was opposed to the idea changes her mind. Similarly, if a jury is deadlocked, the members may eventually follow the lead of the first juror to switch his position.

• Polarization and the "Risky Shift"

We might think that a group decision would be more conservative than an individual decision. After all, shouldn't there be an effort to compromise, to "split the difference"? We might also expect that a few mature individuals would be able to balance the opinions of daredevils. Groups do not generally seem to work in these ways, however.

Consider the **polarization** effect. As an individual, you might recommend that your company risk an investment of $500,000 to develop or market a new product. Other company executives, polled individually, might risk similar amounts. If you were gathered together to make a group decision, however, you

DIFFUSION OF RESPONSIBILITY • The spreading or sharing of responsibility for a decision or behavior within a group.
SOCIAL DECISION SCHEMES • Rules for predicting the final outcome of group decision making on the basis of the members' initial positions.
POLARIZATION • In social psychology, taking an extreme position or attitude on an issue.

would probably recommend either an amount well above this figure or nothing at all (Burnstein, 1983). This group effect is called *polarization,* or the taking of an extreme position. If you had to gamble on which way the decision would go, however, you would do better to place your money on movement toward the higher sum—that is, to bet on a **risky shift.** Why?

One possibility is that one member of the group may reveal information that the others were not aware of. This information may clearly point in one direction or the other. With doubts removed, the group becomes polarized. It moves decisively in the appropriate direction. It is also possible that social facilitation occurs in the group setting and that the resulting greater motivation prompts more extreme decisions.

Why, however, do groups tend to take *greater* risks than those their members would take as individuals? One answer is diffusion of responsibility (Burnstein, 1983). If the venture flops, the blame will not be placed on you alone. Remember the self-serving bias: You can always say (and think) that the failure was the result of a group decision. You thus protect your self-esteem (Larrick, 1993). If the venture pays off, however, you can attribute the outcome to your cool analysis and boast of your influence on the group.

• *Groupthink*

Groupthink is a problem that sometimes arises in group decision making (Janis, 1982). In **groupthink,** group members tend to be more influenced by group cohesiveness and a dynamic leader than by the realities of the situation. Group problem solving may degenerate into groupthink when a group senses an external threat. Groupthink is usually fueled by a dynamic group leader and occurs under the perception of external threat. The threat heightens the cohesiveness of the group and is a source of stress. Group members under stress tend not to consider all their options carefully (Keinan, 1987). Flawed decisions are frequently made as a result.

Groupthink has been connected with fiascos such as the Bay of Pigs invasion of Cuba, the Watergate scandal, the Iran-Contra affair, and NASA's decision to launch the *Challenger* space shuttle despite engineers' warnings about the dangers created by very cold weather (Aldag & Fuller, 1993). Irving Janis notes five characteristics of groupthink that contribute to such flawed group decisions:

1. *Feelings of invulnerability.* Each decision-making group might have believed that it was beyond the reach of critics or the law—in some cases, because the groups consisted of powerful people who were close to the president of the United States.

2. *The group's belief in its rightness.* These groups apparently believed in the rightness of what they were doing. In some cases, they were carrying out the president's wishes. In the case of the *Challenger* launch, NASA had a track record of successful launches. Members of the Heaven's Gaters, who committed suicide with the arrival of the Hale-Bopp comet in 1997, held a religious belief that they were ascending to a "Level Above Human" ("Gateway to Madness," 1997).

3. *Discrediting of information contrary to the group's decision.* The government group involved in the Iran-Contra affair knowingly broke the law. Its members apparently discredited the law by (1) deciding that it was inconsistent with the best interests of the United States and (2) enlisting private citizens to do the dirty work so that the government was not directly involved.

Truth or Fiction Revisited

It is not true that group decisions tend to represent conservative compromises among the opinions of the group's members. Group decisions tend to be riskier than the average decision that would be made by each member of the group acting as an individual — probably because of diffusion of responsibility.

RISKY SHIFT • The tendency to make riskier decisions as a member of a group than as an individual acting independently.

GROUPTHINK • A process in which group members are influenced by cohesiveness and a dynamic leader to ignore external realities as they make decisions.

4. *Pressures on group members to conform.* Group cohesiveness pressures group members to conform. In committing suicide, members of Heaven's Gate were conforming to each other's behavior.

5. *Stereotyping of members of the out-group.* Members of the group that broke the law in the Iran-Contra affair reportedly stereotyped people who would oppose them as "communist sympathizers" and "knee-jerk liberals."

Groupthink can be averted if group leaders encourage members to remain skeptical about options and to feel free to ask probing questions and disagree with one another.

• Mob Behavior and Deindividuation

The Frenchman Gustave Le Bon (1895/1960) branded mobs and crowds as irrational, as resembling a "beast with many heads." Mob actions such as race riots and lynchings sometimes seem to operate on a psychology of their own. Do mobs bring out the beast in us? How is it that mild-mannered people will commit mayhem when they are part of a mob? In seeking an answer, let us examine a lynching.

THE LYNCHING OF ARTHUR STEVENS In their classic volume *Social Learning and Imitation*, Neal Miller and John Dollard (1941) vividly described a lynching that occurred in the South in the 1930s. Arthur Stevens, an African American, was accused of murdering his lover, a White woman, when she wanted to break up with him. Stevens was arrested, and he confessed to the crime. Fearing violence, the sheriff moved Stevens to a town 200 miles away during the night. But his location was discovered. On the next day a mob of a hundred people stormed the jail and returned Stevens to the scene of the crime.

Outrage spread from one member of the mob to another like a plague bacillus. Laborers, professionals, women, adolescents, and law enforcement officers alike were infected. Stevens was tortured and murdered. His corpse was dragged through the streets. The mob then went on a rampage, chasing and assaulting other African Americans. The riot ended only when troops were sent in to restore law and order.

DEINDIVIDUATION When people act as individuals, fear of consequences and self-evaluation tend to prevent them from engaging in antisocial behavior. But in a mob, they may experience **deindividuation,** a state of reduced self-awareness and lowered concern for social evaluation. Many factors lead to deindividuation. These include anonymity, diffusion of responsibility, arousal due to noise and crowding, and a focus on emerging group norms rather than on one's own values (Baron & Byrne, 1997). Under these

DEINDIVIDUATION • The process by which group members may discontinue self-evaluation and adopt group norms and attitudes.

An Angry Mob Is Contained by Police. Gustave Le Bon branded mobs as irrational, like a "beast with many heads."

circumstances crowd members behave more aggressively than they would as individuals.

Police know that mob actions are best averted early by dispersing small groups that could gather into a crowd. On an individual level, perhaps we can resist deindividuation by instructing ourselves to stop and think whenever we begin to feel highly aroused in a group. If we dissociate ourselves from such groups when they are forming, we are more likely to remain critical and avoid behavior that we might later regret.

• *Altruism and the Bystander Effect: Some Watch While Others Die*

People throughout the nation were shocked by the murder of 28-year-old Kitty Genovese in New York City. Murder was not unheard of in the Big Apple, but Kitty had screamed for help as her killer stalked her for more than half an hour and stabbed her in three separate attacks (Rosenthal, 1994). Thirty-eight neighbors heard the commotion. Twice the assault was interrupted by their voices and bedroom lights. Each time the attacker returned. Yet nobody came to the victim's aid. No one even called the police. Why? Some witnesses said matter-of-factly that they did not want to get involved. One said that he was tired. Still others said "I don't know." As a nation, are we a callous bunch who would rather watch than help when others are in trouble?

Truth or Fiction Revisited

It is true that nearly 40 people stood by and did nothing while a woman was being stabbed to death. Their failure to come to her aid has been termed the bystander effect.

THE HELPER: WHO HELPS? Many factors affect helping behavior:

1. Empathic observers are more likely to help. Most psychologists focus on the roles of a helper's mood and personality traits. By and large, we are more likely to help others when we are in a good mood (Baron & Byrne, 1997; George, 1991). Perhaps good moods impart a sense of personal power (Cunningham and others, 1990). People who are empathic are also more likely to help people in need (Darley, 1993). Empathic people feel

the distress of others, feel concern for them, and can imagine what it must be like to be in need. Women are more likely than men to be empathic, and thus more likely to help people in need (Trobst and others, 1994).

2. Bystanders may not help unless they believe that an emergency exists (Baron & Byrne, 1997). Perhaps some people who heard Kitty Genovese's calls for help were not certain as to what was happening. (But remember that others admitted they did not want to get involved.)

3. Observers must assume the responsibility to act (Baron & Byrne, 1997). It may seem logical that a group of people would be more likely to have come to the aid of Kitty Genovese than a lone person. After all, a group could more effectively have overpowered her attacker. Yet research by Darley and Latané (1968) suggests that a lone person may have been more likely to try to help her.

   In their classic experiment, male subjects were performing meaningless tasks in cubicles when they heard a (convincing) recording of a person apparently having an epileptic seizure. When the men thought that four other persons were immediately available, only 31% tried to help the victim. When they thought that no one else was available, however, 85% of them tried to help. As in other areas of group behavior, it seems that *diffusion of responsibility* inhibits helping behavior in groups or crowds. When we are in a group, we are often willing to let George (or Georgette) do it. When George isn't around, we are more willing to help others ourselves. (Perhaps some who heard Kitty Genovese thought, "Why should I get involved? Other people can hear her too.")

4. Observers must know what to do (Baron & Byrne, 1997). We hear of cases in which people impulsively jump into the water to save a drowning child and then drown themselves. Most of the time, however, people do not try to help unless they know what to do. For example, nurses are more likely than people without medical training to try to help accident victims (Cramer and others, 1988). Observers who are not sure that they can take charge of the situation may stay on the sidelines for fear of making a social blunder and being ridiculed. Or they may fear getting hurt themselves. (Perhaps some who heard Kitty Genovese thought, "If I try to intervene, I may get killed or make an idiot of myself.")

5. Observers are more likely to help people they know (Rutkowski and others, 1983). Aren't we also more likely to give to charity when asked directly by a coworker or supervisor in the socially exposed situation of the office as compared with a letter received in the privacy of our own homes?

   Some theorists (e.g., Guisinger & Blatt, 1994) suggest that **altruism** is a natural aspect of human nature. Self-sacrifice sometimes helps close relatives or others who are similar to us to survive. Ironically, self-sacrifice is selfish from a genetic or sociobiological point of view. It helps us

I ALTRUISM • Unselfish concern for the welfare of others.

Office Design. Environmental psychologists study how aspects of the physical environment influence behavior, including work. They therefore consider issues such as the best colors for office walls and what kinds of music facilitate work.

perpetuate a genetic code similar to our own. This view suggests that we are more likely to be altruistic with our relatives rather than strangers, however. The Kitty Genoveses of the world may remain out of luck unless they are surrounded by kinfolk or friends.

6. Observers are more likely to help people who are similar to themselves. Similarity also seems to promote helping behavior. Poorly dressed people are more likely to succeed in requests for a dime with poorly dressed strangers. Well dressed people are more likely to get money from well dressed strangers (Hensley, 1981).

THE VICTIM: WHO IS HELPED? Although women are more likely than men to help people in need, it is traditional for men to help women, particularly in the South. Women were more likely than men to receive help, especially from men, when they dropped coins in Atlanta (a southern city) than in Seattle or Columbus (northern cities) (Latané & Dabbs, 1975). Why? The researchers suggest that traditional gender roles persist more strongly in the South.

Women are also more likely than men to be helped when their cars have broken down on the highway or they are hitchhiking. Is this gallantry or are there sexual overtones to some of this "altruism"? There may be, because attractive and unaccompanied women are most likely to be helped by men (Benson and others, 1976; Snyder and others, 1974).

REFLECTIONS

- Families, classes, religious groups, political parties, nations, circles of friends, bowling teams, sailing clubs, conversation groups, therapy groups—how many groups do you belong to? How does belonging to groups influence your behavior?
- When you are given a group assignment, do you work harder or less hard than you would alone? Why?
- Have you ever done something as a member of a group that you would not have done if you had been acting on your own? Why?
- Altruism and the bystander effect highlight the fact that we are members of a vast, interdependent social fabric. The next time you see a stranger in need, what will you do? Are you sure?

■ ENVIRONMENTAL PSYCHOLOGY: THE BIG PICTURE

What do you think of when you hear the phrase "the environment?" Vast tracks of wilderness? Deep, rolling oceans? Or do you picture shore birds draped in oil as a result of an oil spill? Do you think of billowing summer storm clouds and refreshing rain, or do you conjure up visions of crowded sidewalks and acid rain? All this—the beauty and the horror—is the province of environmental psychology.

Social psychologists study the nature and causes of behavior and mental processes in *social* situations. **Environmental psychologists** study the ways in which humans and the *physical environment* influence each other. However, crowds are part of the physical environment, as are temperature and noise pollution. They all affect our behavior, feelings, and ability to meet our needs. We

ENVIRONMENTAL PSYCHOLOGY • The field of psychology that studies the ways in which people and the environment influence one another.

also affect the environment. We have pushed back forests and driven many species to extinction. In recent years, our impact has mushroomed. So have the controversies over the greenhouse effect, the loss of much of the ozone layer, and acid rain. Many people have an aesthetic interest in the environment and appreciate the few areas of wilderness that remain. Protecting the environment also ultimately means protecting ourselves, however—for it is within the environment that we will either flourish or fade away. In this section we consider some findings of environmental psychologists concerning the effects of atmospheric conditions, noise, heat, and crowding.

• *Noise: Of Muzak, Rock 'n' Roll, and Low-Flying Aircraft*

Environmental psychologists apply their knowledge about sensation and perception to design environments that induce positive emotional responses and improve performance. They may suggest soundproofing certain environments or using pleasant background sounds such as music or recordings of water in natural environments (rain, the beach, brooks, and so on). Noise can be aversive, however—especially loud noise (Staples, 1996). How do you react when a fingernail is scraped along a blackboard or an airplane roars overhead?

Noise Levels. Listeners at a rock concert may enjoy high noise levels (up to 140 dB). Less desirable noises of only 80 dB, however, can decrease feelings of attraction and helping behavior and contribute to aggressive behavior.

A unit known as the decibel (dB) is used to measure the loudness of noise. The hearing threshold is defined as zero dB. The noise level in your school library is probably about 30 to 40 dB. Noise on a freeway is about 70 dB. One hundred forty dB is painfully loud, and 150 dB can rupture your eardrums. After 8 hours of exposure to 110 to 120 dB, your hearing may be damaged (rock groups play at this level). High noise levels are stressful and can lead to illnesses such as hypertension, neurological and intestinal disorders, and ulcers (Cohen and others, 1986; Staples, 1996).

High noise levels also impair daily functioning. They can lead to forgetfulness, perceptual errors, even dropping things. Children who are exposed to louder traffic noise on the lower floors of apartment buildings or to loud noise from low-flying airplanes at school may experience stress, hearing loss, and impairments in learning and memory.

Couples may enjoy high noise levels at the disco, but grating noises of 80 dB seem to decrease feelings of attraction. They cause people to stand farther apart. Loud noise also reduces helping behavior. People are less likely to help pick up a dropped package when the background noise of a construction crew is at 92 dB than when it's at 72 dB (Staples, 1996). They're even less willing to make change for a quarter.

If you and your date have had a fight and are then exposed to a tire blowout, look out. Angry people are more likely to behave aggressively when exposed to a sudden noise of 95 dB than when exposed to one of 55 dB (Donnerstein & Wilson, 1976).

• *Temperature: Getting Hot Under the Collar*

Environmental psychologists study the ways in which temperature can facilitate or impair behavior and mental processes. When a car's engine is too hot, there may be great demands on the vehicle's circulatory system. The water may overheat and the radiator pop its cap. Extreme heat can also make great demands on our bodies' circulatory systems, leading to dehydration, heat exhaustion, and heat stroke.

When it is too cold, the body attempts to generate and retain heat. Metabolism increases. We shiver. Blood vessels in the skin constrict, decreasing the flow of blood to the periphery of the body and thereby preventing loss of warmth through the skin.

Despite their obvious differences, both hot and cold temperatures are aversive events with some similar consequences, the first of which is increased arousal. Moderate shifts in temperature appear to be mildly arousing. They thus may facilitate learning and performance and increase feelings of attraction. Extreme temperatures, however, cause performance and activity levels to deteriorate.

Environmental psychologists point out that small changes in arousal tend to get our attention, motivate us, and facilitate the performance of tasks. Great increments in arousal, such as those caused by major deviations from ideal temperatures, are aversive and hinder the performance of complex tasks. We try to cope with uncomfortable temperatures by wearing warmer or cooler clothing, using air conditioning, or traveling to a more comfortable climate. Extreme temperatures can sap our ability to cope.

Heat apparently makes some people hot under the collar. That is, high temperatures are connected with aggression. The frequency of honking at traffic lights in Phoenix increases with the temperature (Kenrick & MacFarlane, 1986). In Houston, murders and rapes are most likely to occur when the temperature is in the nineties Fahrenheit (Anderson & DeNeve, 1992). In Raleigh, North Carolina, the incidence of rape and aggravated assault rises with the average monthly temperature (Cohn, 1990; Simpson & Perry, 1990).

Some psychologists (e.g., Anderson & DeNeve, 1992) suggest that the probability of aggressive behavior continues to increase as the temperature soars. Others (e.g., Bell, 1992) argue that once temperatures become extremely aversive, people tend to avoid aggressive behavior so that they will not be doubly struck by hot temper and hot temperature. The evidence does not absolutely support either view. The issue remains . . . well, heated.

• *Of Aromas and Air Pollution: Facilitating, Fussing, and Fuming*

Environmental psychologists study the effects of odors ranging from perfumes to auto exhaust, industrial smog, cigarette smoke, fireplaces, even burning leaves. For example, the lead in auto exhaust may impair children's intellectual functioning in the same way that eating lead paint does.

Carbon monoxide, a colorless, odorless gas found in cigarette smoke and auto fumes, decreases the oxygen-carrying capacity of the blood. Carbon monoxide impairs learning ability and perception of the passage of time. It may also contribute to highway accidents. Residents of Los Angeles, New York, and other cities are accustomed to warnings to stay indoors or remain inactive in order to reduce air consumption when atmospheric inversions allow smog to accumulate. In December 1952, high amounts of smog collected in London, causing nearly 4,000 deaths (Schenker, 1993). High levels of air pollution have also been connected with higher mortality rates in U.S. cities (Dockery and others, 1993).

People tend to become psychologically accustomed to air pollution. For example, newcomers to polluted regions like Southern California are more concerned about the air quality than long-term residents (Evans and others, 1982). Acceptance of pollution backfires when illness results.

Unpleasant smelling pollutants, like other forms of aversive stimulation, decrease feelings of attraction and heighten aggression (Baron & Byrne, 1997).

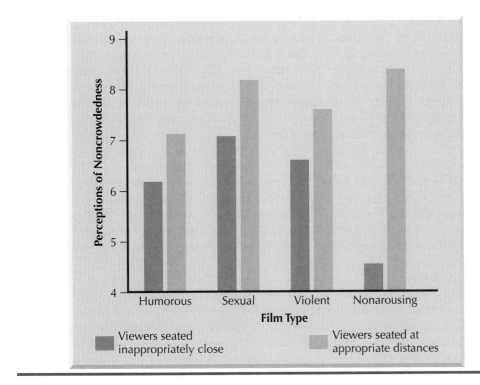

FIGURE 17.3
**TYPE OF FILM AND APPRAISAL OF HIGH-
DENSITY SEATING**
In a study by Worchel and Brown, viewers seated
uncomfortably closely or at comfortable distances watched four kinds of films. Of the individuals seated too closely, those who could
attribute their arousal to the film were less likely
to experience crowding than those who could not.

• Crowding and Personal Space: "Don't Burst My Bubble, Please"

Psychologists distinguish between "density" and "crowding." *Density* refers to
the number of people in an area. *Crowding* suggests an aversive high-density
social situation.

Not all instances of density are equal. Whether we feel crowded depends on
who is thrown in with us and on our interpretation of the situation (Baron &
Byrne, 1997). Environmental psychologists apply principles of information processing and social psychology in explaining why this is so.

A fascinating experiment illustrates the importance of cognitive factors—in
this case, attributions for arousal—in transforming high density into crowding.
Worchel and Brown (1984) showed films to small groups of people who were
either spaced comfortably apart or uncomfortably close. There were four different films. Three were arousing (either humorous, sexual, or violent), and one
was unarousing.

As shown in Figure 17.3, viewers who were seated closer together generally
felt more crowded than those who were seated farther apart. Those who were
seated at appropriate distances from one another uniformly rated the seating
arrangements as uncrowded. Among those who were seated inappropriately
close together, viewers of the unarousing film felt most crowded. Viewers of the
arousing films felt less crowded. Why? The researchers suggest that viewers who
were packed in could attribute their arousal to the content of the films. But
viewers of the unarousing film could not. Thus, they were likely to attribute
their arousal to the seating arrangements.

PSYCHOLOGICAL MODERATORS OF THE IMPACT OF HIGH DENSITY A
sense of control enhances psychological hardiness. Examples from everyday life
suggest that a sense of control over the situation—of being able to choose—
also helps us cope with the stress of being packed in. When we are at a concert,

disco, or sports event, we may encounter higher density than we do in a frustrating ticket line. But we may be having a wonderful time. Why? Because we have *chosen* to be at the concert and are focusing on our good time (unless a tall or noisy person is sitting in front of us). We feel that we are in control.

We tend to moderate the effects of high density in subway cars and other vehicles by ignoring our fellow passengers and daydreaming, reading newspapers and books, or finding humor in the situation. Some people catch a snooze and wake up just before their stop.

SOME EFFECTS OF CITY LIFE Big city dwellers are more likely to experience stimulus overload and to fear crime than suburbanites and rural folk. Overwhelming crowd stimulation, bright lights, shop windows, and so on cause them to narrow their perceptions to a particular face, destination, or job. The pace of life increases—pedestrians walk faster in bigger cities (Sadalla and others, 1990).

City dwellers are less willing to shake hands with, make eye contact with, or help strangers (Milgram, 1977; Newman & McCauley, 1977). People who move to the city from more rural areas adjust by becoming more deliberate in their daily activities. They plan ahead to take safety precautions, and they increase their alertness to potential dangers.

Farming, anyone?

PERSONAL SPACE One adverse effect of crowding is the invasion of one's **personal space**. Personal space is an invisible boundary, a sort of bubble, that surrounds you. You are likely to become anxious and perhaps angry when others invade your space. This may happen when someone sits down across from or next to you in an otherwise empty cafeteria or stands too close to you in an elevator. Personal space appears to serve both protective and communicative functions.

People sit and stand closer to people who are similar to themselves in race, age, or socioeconomic status. Dating couples come closer together as the attraction between them increases.

North Americans and Northern Europeans apparently maintain a greater distance between themselves and others than Southern Europeans, Asians, and Middle Easterners do (Baron & Byrne, 1997). Puerto Ricans tend to interact more closely than Americans of Northern European extraction. Puerto Ricans reared in New York City require more personal space when interacting with others of the same gender than do Puerto Ricans reared in Puerto Rico (Pagan & Aiello, 1982).

People in some cultures apparently learn to cope with high density and also share their ways of coping with others (Gillis and others, 1986). Asians in crowded cities such as Tokyo and Hong Kong interact more harmoniously than North Americans and Britishers, who dwell in less dense cities. The Japanese are used to being packed sardinelike into subway cars by white-gloved pushers employed by the transit system. Imagine the rebellion that would occur if such treatment were attempted in American subways! It has been suggested that Asians are accustomed to adapting to their environment, whereas Westerners are more prone to try to change it.

Southern Europeans apparently occupy a middle ground between Asians, on the one hand, and Northern Europeans, on the other. They are more outgoing and comfortable with interpersonal propinquity than Northern Europeans but not as tolerant of crowding as Asians.

PERSONAL SPACE • A psychological boundary that surrounds a person and serves protective functions.

As you complete this text, I hope that you will have decided to allow psychology to enter your personal psychological space. A professor of mine once remarked that the true measure of the success of a course is whether the student decides to take additional courses in the field. The choice is yours. *Enjoy.*

REFLECTIONS

- As you read this book, crises loom concerning disposal of toxic wastes, industrial and vehicular emissions, population growth, devastation of the rain forest, pollution, and other environmental issues. You dwell on planet Earth. It is your home. How can you become better informed? How can you encourage people to be kinder to the environment?
- How do loud noises and extremes of temperature affect your behavior? Can you think of some examples?
- Agree or disagree, and support your answer: "Crowding people together is aversive."

SUMMARY

1. **What do social psychologists do?** Social psychologists study the factors that influence our thoughts, feelings, and behaviors in social situations.

2. **What are attitudes?** Attitudes are enduring mental representations of people, places, and things that elicit emotional reactions and influence behavior.

3. **What is the elaboration likelihood model for understanding persuasive messages?** According to this model, persuasion occurs through both central and peripheral routes. Change occurs through the central route by means of consideration of arguments and evidence. Peripheral routes involve associating the objects of attitudes with positive or negative cues, such as attractive or unattractive communicators.

4. **What factors affect the persuasiveness of messages?** Repeated messages generally "sell" better than messages delivered only once. People tend to show greater response to fear appeals than to purely factual presentations. This is especially so when the appeals offer concrete advice for avoiding negative outcomes. Persuasive communicators tend to show expertise, trustworthiness, attractiveness, or similarity to the audience.

5. **What is the foot-in-the-door technique?** In this technique, people are asked to accede to larger requests after they have acceded to smaller ones.

6. **What is the importance of first impressions?** First impressions can last (the primacy effect) because we tend to label or describe people in terms of the behavior we see initially.

7. **What is the attribution process?** Inference of the motives and traits of others through observation of their behavior is referred to as the attribution process. In dispositional attributions, we attribute people's behavior to internal factors such as their personality traits and decisions. In situational attributions, we attribute people's behavior to their circumstances or external forces.

8. **What are some biases in the attribution process?** According to the actor-observer effect, we tend to attribute the behavior of others to internal, dispositional factors. However, we tend to attribute our own behavior to external, situational factors. The so-called fundamental attribution error is the tendency to attribute too much of other people's behavior to dispositional factors.

9. **What can we infer from body language?** People who feel positively toward one another position themselves closer together and are more likely to touch. Gazing into another's eyes can be a sign of love, but a hard stare is an aversive challenge.

10. **Will people obey authority figures who order them to engage in improper behavior?** Many people in the Milgram studies on obedience complied with the demands of authority figures even when the demands seemed immoral. Factors contributing to obedience include socialization, lack of social comparison, perception of legitimate authority figures, the foot-in-the-door technique, inaccessibility of values, and buffers between perpetrator and victim.

11. **What factors contribute to conformity?** Personal factors such as low self-esteem, high self-consciousness, and shyness contribute to conformity. Group size is also a factor.

12. **What is social facilitation?** Social facilitation refers to the effects on performance that result from the presence of other people. The presence of others may facilitate performance for reasons such as increased arousal and evaluation apprehension. However, when we are anonymous group members, task performance may fall off. This phenomenon is termed *social loafing.*

13. **How do group decisions differ from individual decisions?** Group decisions tend to be more polarized and riskier than individual decisions, largely because groups diffuse responsibility. Group decisions may be highly productive when group members are knowledgeable, there is an explicit procedure for arriving at decisions, and there is a process of give and take.

14. **How do groups make decisions?** Social psychologists have identified several decision-making schemes, including the majority-wins scheme, the truth-wins scheme, the two-thirds majority scheme, and the first-shift rule.

15. **What is groupthink?** Groupthink is an unrealistic kind of decision making that is fueled by the perception of external threats to the group or to those whom the group wishes to protect. It is facilitated by feelings of invulnerability, the group's belief in its rightness, discrediting of information that contradicts the group's decision, conformity, and stereotyping of members of the out-group.

16. **How do social psychologists explain mob behavior?** Highly emotional crowds may induce attitude-discrepant behavior through the process of deindividuation, which is a state of reduced self-awareness and lowered concern for social evaluation.

17. **What is the bystander effect?** According to the bystander effect, we are unlikely to aid people in distress when we are members of crowds. Crowds tend to diffuse responsibility.

18. **What is environmental psychology?** Environmental psychologists study the ways in which humans and the physical environment influence each other. They investigate how factors such as noise, temperature, pollution, and population density affect human behavior and mental processes.

To enhance your understanding of the psychological concepts found in this chapter, please consult the following aids:

Learning Objectives, p. 353
Exercises, p. 354
Lecture and Textbook Outline,
    p. 355
Effective Studying Ideas, p. 358

Key Terms and Concepts, p. 359
Chapter Review, p. 359
Chapter Exercises, p. 368
Knowing the Language. p. 369
Do You Know the Material?, p. 372

Attitudes and Behavior
Conformity, Compliance, and
    Obedience
Defining Stereotypes, Prejudice, and
    Discrimination
Attributions

Impression Formation
The Mere Exposure Effect
Nonverbal Communication
Deindividuation
Prosocial Behavior

For more information concerning the topics found in this chapter, access psychology links on the World Wide Web through the Harcourt Brace webpage at

www.hbcollege.com

Share your comments and questions with your author at

PsychLinks@aol.com

Appendix A

Statistics

Imagine that some visitors from outer space arrive outside Madison Square Garden in New York City. Their goal this dark and numbing winter evening is to learn all they can about the inhabitants of planet Earth. They are drawn inside the Garden by lights, shouts, and warmth. The spotlighting inside rivets their attention to a wood-floored arena where the New York Apples are hosting the California Quakes in a briskly contested basketball game.

Our visitors use their sophisticated instruments to take some measurements of the players. Some surprising statistics are sent back to the planet of their origin: It appears that (1) 100% of Earthlings are male, and (2) the height of Earthlings ranges from 6 feet 1 inch to 7 feet 2 inches.

Statistics is the name given the science concerned with obtaining and organizing numerical measurements or information. Our imagined visitors have sent home some statistics about the sex and size of human beings that are at once accurate and misleading. Although they accurately measured the basketball players, their small **sample** of Earth's **population** was quite distorted. Fortunately for us Earthlings, about half of us are female. And the **range** of heights observed by the aliens, of 6 feet 1 to 7 feet 2, is both restricted and too high. People vary in height by more than 1 foot and 1 inch. And our **average** height is not between 6 feet 1 inch and 7 feet 2 inches but a number of inches below.

Psychologists, like our imagined visitors, are vitally concerned with measuring human as well as animal characteristics and traits—not just physical characteristics like sex and height but also psychological traits like intelligence, aggressiveness, anxiety, or self-assertiveness. By observing the central tendencies (averages) and variations in measurements from person to person, psychologists can state that some person is average or above average in intelligence or that another person is less assertive than, say, 60% of the population.

But psychologists, unlike our aliens, are careful in their attempts to select a sample that accurately represents the entire population. Professional basketball players do not represent the human species. They are taller, stronger, and more agile than the rest of us, and they make more shaving cream commercials.

In this appendix, we shall survey some of the statistical methods used by psychologists to draw conclusions about the measurements they take in research activities. First, we shall discuss *descriptive statistics* and learn what types of statements we can make about the heights of basketball players and some other human traits. Then, we shall discuss the *normal curve* and learn why basketball players are abnormal—at least in terms of height. We shall explore *correlation coefficients* and provide you with some less-than-shocking news: More intelligent people attain higher grades than less intelligent people. Finally, we shall have a brief look at *inferential statistics* and see why we can be bold enough to say that the difference in height between basketball players and other people is not just a chance accident, or fluke. Basketball players are in fact statistically significantly taller than the general population.

STATISTICS • Numerical facts assembled in such a manner that they provide significant information about measures or scores. (From the Latin word *status*, meaning "standing" or "position.")
SAMPLE • Part of a population.
POPULATION • A complete group from which a sample is selected.
RANGE • A measure of variability; the distance between extreme measures or scores.
AVERAGE • Central tendency of a group of measures, expressed as mean, median, and mode.

■ DESCRIPTIVE STATISTICS

Being told that someone is a "10" is not very descriptive unless you know something about how possible scores are distributed and how frequently one finds a 10. Fortunately—for 10s, if not for the rest of us—one is usually informed that someone is a 10 on a scale of 1 to 10 and that 10 is the positive end of the scale. If this is not sufficient, one will also be told that 10s are few and far between—rather unusual statistical events.

This business of a scale from 1 to 10 is not very scientific, to be sure, but it does suggest something about **descriptive statistics.** We can use descriptive statistics to clarify our understanding of a distribution of scores such as heights, test grades, IQs, or increases or decreases in measures of sexual arousal following the drinking of alcohol. For example, descriptive statistics can help us to determine measures of central tendency, or averages, and to determine how much variability there is in the scores. Being a 10 loses some of its charm if the average score is an 11. Being a 10 is more remarkable in a distribution whose scores range from 1 to 10 than in one that ranges from 9 to 10.

Let us now examine some of the concerns of descriptive statistics: the frequency distribution, measures of central tendency (types of averages), and measures of variability.

• *The Frequency Distribution*

A **frequency distribution** takes scores or items of raw data, puts them into order as from lowest to highest, and groups them according to class intervals. Table A.1 shows the rosters for a recent California Quakes—New York Apples basketball game. The members of each team are listed according to the numbers on their uniforms. Table A.2 shows a frequency distribution of the heights of the players of both teams combined, with a class interval of 1 inch.

TABLE A.I	ROSTERS OF QUAKES VERSUS APPLES AT NEW YORK			
California			*New York*	
2 Callahan	6' 7"		3 Roosevelt	6' 1"
5 Daly	6' 11"		12 Chaffee	6' 5"
6 Chico	6' 2"		13 Baldwin	6' 9"
12 Capistrano	6' 3"		25 Delmar	6' 6"
21 Brentwood	6' 5"		27 Merrick	6' 8"
25 Van Nuys	6' 3"		28 Hewlett	6' 6"
31 Clemente	6' 9"		33 Hollis	6' 9"
32 Whittier	6' 8"		42 Bedford	6' 5"
41 Fernando	7' 2"		43 Coram	6' 2"
43 Watts	6' 9"		45 Hampton	6' 10"
53 Huntington	6' 6"		53 Ardsley	6' 10"

A glance at the rosters for a recent California Quakes–New York Apples basketball game shows you that the heights of the team members, combined, ranged from 6 feet 1 inch to 7 feet 2 inches. Are the heights of the team members representative of those of the general male population?

DESCRIPTIVE STATISTICS • The branch of statistics that is concerned with providing information about a distribution of scores.
FREQUENCY DISTRIBUTION • An ordered set of data that indicates how frequently scores appear.

TABLE A.2	FREQUENCY DISTRIBUTION OF HEIGHTS OF BASKETBALL PLAYERS, WITH A ONE-INCH CLASS INTERVAL
Class Interval	**Number of Players in Class**
6′ 1″–6′ 1.9″	1
6′ 2″–6′ 2.9″	2
6′ 3″–6′ 3.9″	2
6′ 4″–6′ 4.9″	0
6′ 5″–6′ 5.9″	3
6′ 6″–6′ 6.9″	3
6′ 7″–6′ 7.9″	1
6′ 8″–6′ 8.9″	2
6′ 9″–6′ 9.9″	4
6′ 10″–6′ 10.9″	2
6′ 11″–6′ 11.9″	1
7′ 0″–7′ 0.9″	0
7′ 1″–7′ 1.9″	0
7′ 2″–7′ 2.9″	1

It would also be possible to use 3-inch class intervals, as in Table A.3. In determining how large a class interval should be, a researcher attempts to collapse that data into a small enough number of classes to ensure that they will appear meaningful at a glance. But the researcher also attempts to maintain a large enough number of categories to ensure that important differences are not obscured.

Table A.3 obscures the fact that no players are 6 feet 4 inches tall. If the researcher believes that this information is extremely important, a class interval of 1 inch may be maintained.

Figure A.1 shows two methods for representing the information in Table A.3 with graphs. Both in frequency **histograms** and frequency **polygons,** the class intervals are typically drawn along the horizontal line, or X-axis, and the number of scores (persons, cases, or events) in each class is drawn along the vertical line, or Y-axis. In a histogram, the number of scores in each class interval is rep-

TABLE A.3	FREQUENCY DISTRIBUTION OF HEIGHTS OF BASKETBALL PLAYERS, WITH A THREE-INCH CLASS INTERVAL
Class Interval	**Number of Players in Class**
6′ 1″–6′ 3.9″	5
6′ 4″–6′ 6.9″	6
6′ 7″–6′ 9.9″	7
6′ 10″–7′ 0.9″	3
7′ 1″–7′ 3.9″	1

HISTOGRAM • A graphic representation of a frequency distribution that uses rectangular solids. (From the Greek *historia*, meaning "narrative," and gramma, meaning "writing" or "drawing.")
POLYGON • A closed figure. (From the Greek *polys*, meaning "many," and gonia, meaning "angle.")

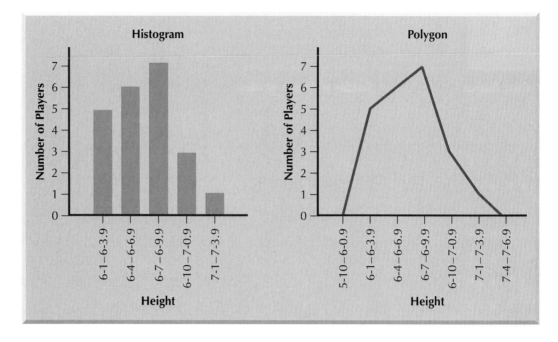

FIGURE A.1
TWO GRAPHICAL REPRESENTATIONS OF THE DATA IN TABLE A.3

resented by a rectangular solid so that the graph resembles a series of steps. In a polygon, the number of scores in each class interval is plotted as a point, and the points are then connected to form a many-sided geometric figure. Note that class intervals were added at both ends of the horizontal axis of the frequency polygon so that the lines could be brought down to the axis to close the geometric figure.

• *Measures of Central Tendency*

> *Never try to walk across a river just because it has an average depth of four feet.*
>
> MARTIN FRIEDMAN

There are three types of measures of central tendency, or averages: *mean, median,* and *mode.* Each tells us something about the way in which the scores in a distribution may be summarized by a typical or representative number.

The **mean** is what most people think of as "the average." The mean is obtained by adding up all the scores in a distribution and then dividing this sum by the number of scores. In the case of our basketball players, it would be advisable first to convert all heights into one unit, such as inches (6'1" becomes 73", and so on). If we add all the heights in inches, then divide by the number of players, or 22, we obtain a mean height of 78.73", or 6'6.73".

The **median** is the score of the middle case in a frequency distribution. It is the score beneath which 50% of the cases fall. In a distribution with an even number of cases, such as the distribution of the heights of the 22 basketball players in Table A.2, the median is determined by finding the mean of the two middle cases. Listing these 22 cases in ascending order, we find that the 11th case is 6'6" and the 12th case is 6'7". Thus the median is (6'6" + 6'7")/2, or 6'6 1/2".

MEAN • A type of average calculated by dividing the sum of scores by the number of scores. (From the Latin *medius,* meaning "middle.")

MEDIAN • The score beneath which 50% of the class fall. (From the Latin *medius,* meaning "middle.")

In the case of the heights of the basketball players, the mean and the median are similar, and either serves as a useful indicator of the central tendency of the data. But suppose we are attempting to determine the average savings of 30 families living on a suburban block. Let us assume that 29 of the 30 families have savings between $8,000 and $12,000, adding up to $294,000. But the 30th family has savings of $1,400,000! The mean savings for a family on this block would thus be $56,467. A mean can be greatly distorted by one or two extreme scores, and for such distributions the median is a better indicator of the central tendency. The median savings on our hypothetical block would lie between $8,000 and $12,000 and so would be more representative of the central tendency of savings. Studies of the incomes of American families usually report median rather than mean incomes just to avoid the distortions that would result from treating incomes of the small numbers of multimillionaires in the same way as other incomes.

The **mode** is simply the most frequently occurring score in a distribution. The mode of the data in Table A.1 is 6′9″ because this height occurs most often. The median class interval for the data in Table A.3 is 6′6 1/2″ to 6′9 1/2″. In these cases, the mode is somewhat higher than the mean or median height.

In some cases, the mode is a more appropriate description of a distribution than the mean or median. Figure A.2 shows a **bimodal** distribution, or a distribution with two modes. In this hypothetical distribution of the test scores, the mode at the left indicates the most common class interval for students who did not study, and the mode at the right indicates the most frequent class interval for students who did. The mean and median test scores would probably lie within the 55–59 class interval, yet use of that interval as a measure of central tendency would not provide very meaningful information about the distribution of scores. It might suggest that the test was too hard, not that a number of students chose not to study. One would be better able to visualize the distribution of scores if it were reported as a bimodal distribution. Even in similar cases in which the modes are not exactly equal, it might be more appropriate to describe a distribution as being bimodal or even multimodal.

• *Measures of Variability*

Measures of variability of a distribution inform us about the spread of scores, or about the typical distances of scores from the average score. Measures of variability include the *range* of scores and the *standard deviation.*

The **range** of scores in a distribution is defined as the difference between the highest score and the lowest score, and it is obtained by subtracting the lowest score from the highest score. The range of heights in Table A.2 is 7′2″ minus 6′1″, or 1′1″. It is important to know the range of temperatures if we move to a

MODE • The most frequently occurring number or score in a distribution. (From the Latin *modus,* meaning "measure.")
BIMODAL • Having two modes.
RANGE • The difference between the highest and the lowest scores in a distribution.

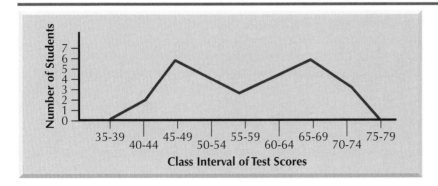

FIGURE A.2
A BIMODAL DISTRIBUTION
This hypothetical distribution represents students' scores on a test. The mode at the left represents the central tendency of students who did not study, and the mode at the right represents the mode of students who did study.

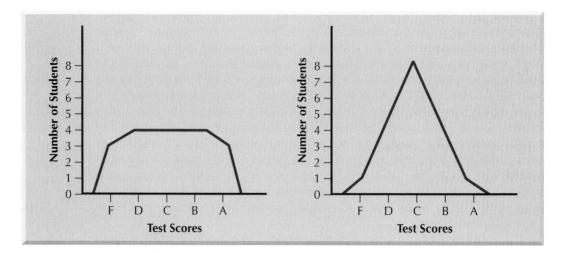

FIGURE A.3

HYPOTHETICAL DISTRIBUTIONS OF STUDENT TEST SCORES

Each distribution has the same number of scores, the same mean, and even the same range, but the standard deviation is greater for the distribution on the left because the scores tend to be farther from the mean.

new climate so that we may anticipate the weather and dress appropriately. A teacher must have some understanding of the range of abilities or skills in a class to teach effectively.

The range is an imperfect measure of variability because of the manner in which it is influenced by extreme scores. In our earlier discussion of the savings of 30 families on a suburban block, the range of savings is $1,400,000 to $8,000, or $1,392,000. This tells us little about the typical variability of savings accounts, which lie within a restricted range of $8,000 to $12,000. The **standard deviation** is a statistic that indicates how scores are distributed about a mean of a distribution.

The standard deviation considers every score in a distribution, not just the extreme scores. Thus, the standard deviation for the distribution on the right in Figure A.3 would be smaller than that of the distribution on the left. Note that each distribution has the same number of scores, the same mean, and the same range of scores. But the standard deviation for the distribution on the right is smaller than that of the distribution on the left, because the scores tend to cluster more closely about the mean.

The standard deviation (S.D.) is calculated by the formula

$$S.D. = \sqrt{\frac{\text{Sum of } d^2}{N}}$$

where d equals the deviation of each score from the mean of the distribution, and N equals the number of scores in the distribution.

Let us find the mean and standard deviation of the IQ scores listed in column 1 of Table A.4. To obtain the mean, we add all the scores, attain 1,500, and then divide by the number of scores (15) to obtain a mean of 100. We obtain the deviation score *(d)* for each IQ score by subtracting the score from 100. The *d* for an IQ of 85 equals 100 minus 85, or 15, and so on. Then we square each *d* and add these squares. The S.D. equals the square root of the sum of squares (1,426) divided by the number of scores (15), or 9.75.

As an additional exercise, we can show that the S.D. of the test scores on the left (in Figure A.3) is greater than that for the scores on the right by assigning the grades points according to a 4.0 system. Let A = 4, B = 3, C = 2, D = 1, and

STANDARD DEVIATION • A measure of the variability of a distribution, attained by the formula

$$\sqrt{\frac{\text{Sum of } d^2}{N}}$$

TABLE A.4	HYPOTHETICAL SCORES ATTAINED FROM AN IQ TESTING	
IQ Score	*d (Deviation Score)*	*d² (Deviation Score Squared)*
85	15	225
87	13	169
89	11	121
90	10	100
93	7	49
97	3	9
97	3	9
100	0	0
101	−1	1
104	−4	16
105	−5	25
110	−10	100
112	−12	144
113	−13	169
117	−17	289

Sum of IQ scores = 1,500   Sum of d^2 scores = 1,426

$$\text{Mean} = \frac{\text{Sum of scores}}{\text{Number of scores}} = \frac{1,500}{15} = 100$$

$$\text{Standard Deviation (S.D.)} = \sqrt{\frac{\text{Sum of } d^2}{\text{Number of scores}}} = \sqrt{\frac{1,426}{15}} = \sqrt{95.07} = 9.75$$

F = 0. The S.D. for each distribution of test scores is computed in Table A.5. The greater S.D. for the distribution on the left indicates that the scores in that distribution are more variable, or tend to be farther from the mean.

■ THE NORMAL CURVE

Many human traits and characteristics such as height and intelligence seem to be distributed in a pattern known as a normal distribution. In a **normal distribution,** the mean, median, and mode all fall at the same data point or score. Scores cluster most heavily about the mean, fall off rapidly in either direction at first (as shown in Figure A.4), and then taper off more gradually.

The curve in Figure A.4 is bell shaped. This type of distribution is also called a **normal curve.** It is hypothesized to reflect the distribution of variables in which different scores are determined by chance variation. Height is thought to be largely determined by chance combinations of genetic material. A distribution of the heights of a random sample of the population approximates normal distributions for men and women, with the mean of the distribution for men a few inches higher than the mean for women.

Test developers traditionally assumed that intelligence was also randomly or normally distributed among the population. For that reason, they constructed

NORMAL DISTRIBUTION • A symmetrical distribution in which approximately 68% of cases lie within a standard deviation of the mean.
NORMAL CURVE • Graphic presentation of a normal distribution, showing a bell shape.

| TABLE A.5 | COMPUTATION OF STANDARD DEVIATIONS FOR TEST-SCORE DISTRIBUTIONS IN FIGURE A.3 |

Distribution at Left			*Distribution at Right*		
GRADE	d	d^2	**GRADE**	d	d^2
A (4)	2	4	A (4)	2	4
A (4)	2	4	B (3)	1	1
A (4)	2	4	B (3)	1	1
B (3)	1	1	B (3)	1	1
B (3)	1	1	B (3)	1	1
B (3)	1	1	C (2)	0	0
B (3)	1	1	C (2)	0	0
C (2)	0	0	C (2)	0	0
C (2)	0	0	C (2)	0	0
C (2)	0	0	C (2)	0	0
C (2)	0	0	C (2)	0	0
D (1)	−1	1	C (2)	0	0
D (1)	−1	1	C (2)	0	0
D (1)	−1	1	D (1)	−1	1
D (1)	−1	1	D (1)	−1	1
F (0)	−2	4	D (1)	−1	1
F (0)	−2	4	D (1)	−1	1
F (0)	−2	4	F (0)	−2	4

Sum of grades = 36
Mean grade = 36/18 = 2
Sum of d^2 = 32

S.D. = $\sqrt{32/18}$ = 1.33

Sum of grades = 36
Mean grade = 36/18 = 2
Sum of d^2 = 16

S.D. = $\sqrt{16/18}$ = 0.94

intelligence tests so that scores would be distributed as close to "normal" as possible. In actuality, IQ scores are also influenced by environmental factors and chromosomal abnormalities, so the resultant curves are not perfectly normal. Most IQ tests have means defined as scores of 100 points, and the Wechsler scales are constructed to have standard deviations of 15 points, as shown in Figure A.4. This means that 50% of the Wechsler scores fall between 90 and 100 (the "broad average" range), about 68% (or two of three) fall between 85 and 115, and more than 95% fall between 70 and 130—that is, within two S.D.s of the mean.

The Scholastic Assessment Tests (SATs) were constructed so that the mean scores would be 500 points, and an S.D. would be 100 points. Thus, a score of 600 would equal or excel that of some 84 to 85% of the test takers. Because of the complex interaction of variables determining SAT scores, the distribution of SAT scores is not exactly normal either. The normal curve is an idealized curve.

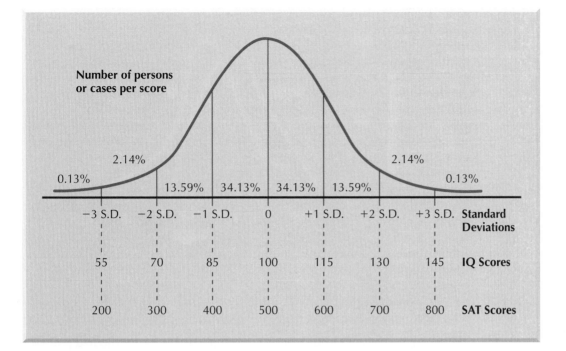

FIGURE A.4
A BELL-SHAPED OR NORMAL CURVE
In a normal curve, approximately 68 percent of the cases lie within a standard deviation (S.D.) from the mean, and the mean, median, and mode all lie at the same score. IQ tests and Scholastic Assessment Tests have been constructed so that distributions of scores approximate the normal curve.

■ THE CORRELATION COEFFICIENT

What is the relationship between intelligence and educational achievement? Between cigarette smoking and lung cancer in human beings? Between introversion and frequency of dating among college students? We cannot run experiments to determine whether the relationships between these variables are causal, because we cannot manipulate the independent variable. For example, we cannot randomly assign a group of people to cigarette smoking and another group to nonsmoking. People must be permitted to make their own choices, and so it is possible that the same factors that lead people to choose to smoke may also lead to lung cancer. However, the **correlation coefficient** may be used to show that there is a relationship between smoking and cancer.

The correlation coefficient is a statistic that describes the relationship between two variables. It varies from +1.00 to −1.00; therefore, a correlation coefficient of +1.00 is called a perfect positive correlation, a coefficient of −1.00 is a perfect negative correlation, and a coefficient of 0.00 shows no correlation between variables. The meanings of various correlation coefficients are discussed further in Chapter 2.

■ INFERENTIAL STATISTICS

In a study reported in Chapter 10, children enrolled in a Head Start program earned a mean IQ score of 99, whereas children similar in background who were not enrolled in Head Start earned a mean IQ score of 93. Is this difference

CORRELATION COEFFICIENT • A number between −1.00 and +1.00 that indicates the degree of relationship between two variables.

FIGURE A.5

DISTRIBUTION OF HEIGHTS FOR RANDOM SAMPLES OF MEN AND WOMEN

Inferential statistics permit us to apply our findings to the populations sampled.

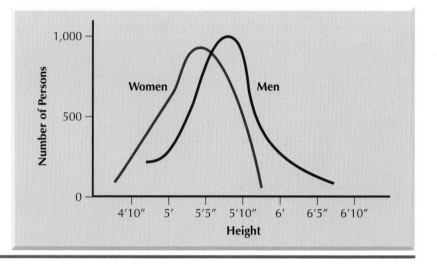

of six points in IQ significant, or does it represent chance fluctuation of scores? In a study reported in Chapter 10, people who believed they had drunk alcohol chose higher levels of electric shock to be applied to persons who had provoked them than did people who believed they had not drunk alcohol. Did the difference in level of shock chosen reflect an actual difference between the two groups, or could it have been a chance fluctuation? Inferential statistics help us make decisions about whether differences found between such groups reflect real differences or just fluctuations.

Figure A.5 shows the distribution of heights of 1,000 men and 1,000 women selected at random. The mean height for men is greater than the mean height for women. Can we draw the conclusion, or **infer,** that this difference in heights represents the general population of men and women? Or must we avoid such an inference and summarize our results by stating only that the sample of 1,000 men in the study had a higher mean height than that of the sample of 1,000 women in the study?

If we could not draw inferences about populations from studies of samples, our research findings would be very limited indeed—limited only to the specific individuals studied. However, the branch of statistics known as **inferential statistics** uses mathematical techniques in such a way that we can draw conclusions about populations from which samples have been drawn.

• *Statistically Significant Differences*

In determining whether differences in measures taken of research samples may be applied to the populations from which they were drawn, psychologists use mathematical techniques that indicate whether differences are statistically significant. Was the difference in IQ scores for children attending and those not attending Head Start significant? Did it represent only the children participating in the study, or can it be applied to all children represented by the sample? Is the difference between the height of men and the height of women in Figure A.5 statistically significant? Can we apply our findings to all men and women?

Psychologists use formulas involving the means and standard deviations of sample groups to determine whether group differences are statistically significant. As you can see in Figure A.6, the farther apart the group means are, the more likely it is that the difference between them is statistically significant. This

INFER • To draw a conclusion, to conclude. (From the Latin *in,* meaning "in," and *ferre,* meaning "to bear.")
INFERENTIAL STATISTICS • The branch of statistics concerned with the confidence with which conclusions drawn about samples may be extended to the populations from which they were drawn.

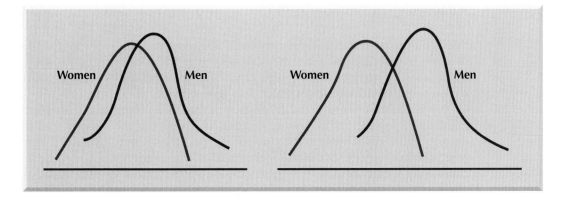

FIGURE A.6

Psychologists use group means and standard deviations to determine whether the difference between group means is statistically significant. The difference between the means of the groups on the right is greater and thus more likely to be statistically significant.

makes a good deal of common sense. After all, if you were told that your neighbor's car had gotten one-tenth of a mile more per gallon of gasoline than your car had last year, you might assume that this was a chance difference. But if the difference was farther apart, say 14 miles per gallon, you might readily believe that this difference reflected an actual difference in driving habits or efficiency of the automobiles.

As you can see in Figure A.7, the smaller the standard deviations (a measure of variability) of the two groups, the more likely it is that the difference of the means is statistically significant. As an extreme example, if all women sampled were exactly 5'5" tall, and all men sampled were exactly 5'10", we would be highly likely to assume that the difference of 5 inches in group means is statistically significant. But if the heights of women varied from 2' to 14', and the heights of men varied from 2'1" to 14'3", we might be more likely to assume that the 5-inch difference in group means could be attributed to chance fluctuation.

FIGURE A.7

The variability of the groups on the left is smaller than the variability of the groups on the right. Thus, it is more likely that the difference between the means of the groups on the left is statistically significant.

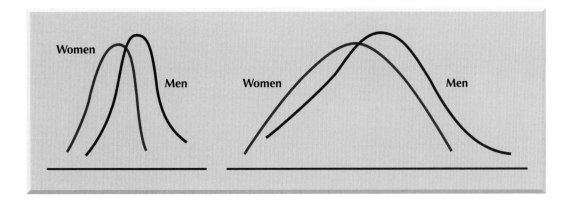

• Samples and Populations

Inferential statistics are mathematical tools that psychologists apply to samples of scores to determine whether they can generalize their findings to populations of scores. Thus, they must be quite certain that the samples involved actually represent the populations from which they were drawn.

Psychologists often use the techniques of random sampling and stratified sampling of populations to draw representative samples. If the samples studied do not accurately represent their intended populations, it matters very little how sophisticated the statistical techniques of the psychologist may be. We could use a variety of statistical techniques on the heights of the New York Apples and California Quakes, but none would tell us much about the height of the general population.

ANSWER KEYS FOR QUESTIONNAIRES

SCORING KEY FOR THE "WHY DO YOU DRINK?" QUESTIONNAIRE (CHAPTER 6, P. 224)

Why do you drink? Score your questionnaire by seeing how many items you answered for each of the reasons for drinking shown in Table B.1. Consider the key as *suggestive* only. For example, if you answered several items in the manner indicated on the *addiction* factor, it may be

wise to examine seriously what your drinking means to you. But do not interpret a few test item scores as binding evidence of addiction.

TABLE B.1: REASONS FOR DRINKING

Addiction	Social Reward
1. T	3. T
6. F	8. T
32. T	23. T
38. T	
40. T	**Celebration**
	10. T
Anxiety/	24. T
Tension Reduction	25. T
7. T	
9. T	**Religion**
12. T	11. T
15. T	
18. T	**Social Power**
26. T	2. T
31. T	13. T
33. T	19. T
	30. T
Pleasure/Taste	Scapegoating (using alcohol
2. T	as an excuse for failure or
5. T	social misconduct)
16. T	14. T
27. T	15. T
28. T	20. T
35. T	21. T
37. T	39. T
Transforming Agent	**Habit**
2. T	17. T
4. T	29. T
19. T	
22. T	
28. T	
30. T	
34. T	
36. T	

SCORING KEY FOR THE "REMOTE ASSOCIATES TEST" (CHAPTER 9, P. 333)

1. Prince	5. Club	8. Black
2. Dog	6. Boat	9. Pit
3. Cold	7. Defense	10. Writer
4. Glasses		

SCORING KEY FOR "ARE YOU A SENSATION SEEKER?" (CHAPTER 11, P. 405)

Since this is a shortened version of a questionnaire, no norms are available. However, answers in agreement with the following key point in the direction of sensation seeking:

1. A	6. B	10. A
2. A	7. A	11. A
3. A	8. A	12. A
4. B	9. B	13. B
5. A		

SCORING KEY FOR THE EXPECTANCY-FOR-SUCCESS SCALE (CHAPTER 12, P. 446)

In order to calculate your total score for the expectancy-for-success scale, first reverse the scores for the following items: 1, 2, 4, 6, 7, 8, 14, 15, 17, 18, 24, 27, and 28. That is, change a 1 to a 5; a 2 to a 4; leave a 3 alone; change a 4 to a 2; and a 5 to a 1. Then add the scores.

The range of total scores can vary from 30 to 150. The higher your score, the greater your expectancy for success in the future—and, according to social-learning theory, the more motivated you will be to apply yourself in facing difficult challenges.

Fibel and Hale administered their test to undergraduates taking psychology courses and found that women's scores ranged from 65 to 143 and men's from 81 to 138. The average score for each gender was 112 (112.32 for women and 112.15 for men).

TABLE B.2: LOVE-SCALE SCORES OF NORTHEASTERN UNIVERSITY STUDENTS		
Condition	*N**	**Mean Scores**
Absolutely in love	56	89
Probably in love	45	80
Not sure	36	77
Probably not in love	40	68
Definitely not in love	43	59

*N = Number of students

NORMS FOR THE LOVE SCALE (CHAPTER 13, P. 487)

The Love Scale was validated with a sample of 220 undergraduates, aged 19–24 (mean age = 21), from Northeastern University. Students were asked to indicate whether they were "absolutely in love," "probably in love," "not sure," "probably not in love," or "definitely not in love" with a person they were dating. Then they answered the items on the Love Scale with the same person in mind.

Table B.2 shows the mean score for each category. Mean scores for men and women in each of the five categories did not differ, so they were lumped together. If your Love-Scale score for your date is 84, it may be that your feelings lie somewhere in between those of Northeastern University students who claimed that they were "probably in love" and "absolutely in love."

Be warned: A number of students broke into arguments after taking the Love Scale—their "love" for one another differed by a few points! Please do not take the scale so seriously. Such scales are fun, but they will not hold up in court as grounds for divorce. Rely on your feelings, not on your scores.

ANSWER KEY FOR "CULTURAL MYTHS THAT CREATE A CLIMATE THAT SUPPORTS RAPE" QUESTIONNAIRE (CHAPTER 13, P. 493)

Actually, each item, with the exception of number 2, represents a cultural myth that supports rape. These myths tend to view sex as an adversarial game, stereotype women as flirtatious and deceitful, and blame the victim.

TABLE B.3: LIFE-CHANGE SCORES AND AMOUNT OF STRESS	
Final Score	**Amount of Stress**
From 0 to 1500	Minor stress
1501–3500	Mild stress
3501–5500	Moderate stress
5501 and above	Major stress

ANSWER KEY FOR SOCIAL READJUSTMENT RATING SCALE (CHAPTER 14, P. 516)

Add all the scores in the "Total" column to arrive at your final score.

FINAL SCORE _____

INTERPRETATION

As shown in Table B.3, your final score is indicative of the amount of stress you have experienced during the past 12 months.

Research has shown that the probability of encountering physical illness within the *following* year is related to the amount of stress experiences during the *past* year. That is, college students who experienced minor stress have a 28 percent chance of becoming ill; mild stress, a 45 percent chance; moderate stress, a 70 percent chance; and major stress, an 82 percent chance. Moreover, the seriousness of the illness also increases with the amount of stress.

It should be recognized that these percentages reflect previous research with college students. Do not assume that if you have encountered a great deal of stress you are "doomed" to illness. Also keep in mind that a number of psychological factors moderate the impact of stress, as described in this chapter. For example, psychologically hardy college students would theoretically withstand the same amount of stress that could enhance the risk of illness for nonhardy individuals.

ANSWER KEY FOR THE "ARE YOU TYPE A OR B?" QUESTIONNAIRE (CHAPTER 14, P. 524)

Type A people are ambitious, hard driving, and chronically discontent with their current achievements. Type Bs, by contrast, are more relaxed, more involved with the quality of life.

Yeses suggest the Type A behavior pattern, which is marked by a sense of time urgency and constant struggle. In appraising your "type," you need not be overly concerned with the precise number of "yes" answers; we have no normative data for you. But as Freidman and Rosenman (1974, p. 85) note, you should have little trouble spotting yourself as "hard core" or "moderately afflicted"—that is, if you are honest with yourself.

ANSWER KEY FOR THE "LOCUS OF CONTROL SCALE" (CHAPTER 14, P. 530)

Place a check mark in the blank space in the scoring key, below, each time your answer agrees with the answer in the key. The number of checkmarks is your total score.

SCORING KEY:

1. Yes ____	11. Yes ____	21. Yes ____	31. Yes ____
2. No ____	12. Yes ____	22. No ____	32. No ____
3. Yes ____	13. No ____	23. Yes ____	33. Yes ____
4. No ____	14. Yes ____	24. Yes ____	34. No ____
5. Yes ____	15. No ____	25. No ____	35. Yes ____
6. No ____	16. Yes ____	26. No ____	36. Yes ____
7. Yes ____	17. Yes ____	27. Yes ____	37. Yes ____
8. Yes ____	18. Yes ____	28. No ____	38. No ____
9. No ____	19. Yes ____	29. Yes ____	39. Yes ____
10. Yes ____	20. No ____	30. No ____	40. No ____

TOTAL SCORE ____

INTERPRETING YOUR SCORE

LOW SCORERS (0–8). About one respondent in three earns a score of from 0 to 8. Such respondents tend to have an internal locus of control. They see themselves as responsible for the reinforcements they attain (and fail to attain) in life.

AVERAGE SCORERS (9–16). Most respondents earn from 9 to 16 points. Average scorers may see themselves as partially in control of their lives. Perhaps they see themselves as in control at work, but not in their social lives—or vice versa.

HIGH SCORERS (17–40). About 15 percent of respondents attain scores of 17 or above. High scorers tend largely to see life as a game of chance, and success as a matter of luck or the generosity of others.

SCORING KEY FOR THE RATHUS ASSERTIVENESS SCHEDULE (CHAPTER 16, P. 608)

Tabulate your score as follows: For those items followed by an asterisk (*), change the signs (plus to minus; minus to plus). For example, if the response to an asterisked item was 2, place a minus sign (−) before the two. If the response to an asterisked item was −3, change the minus sign to a plus sign (+) by adding a vertical stroke. Then add up the scores of the 30 items.

Scores on the assertiveness schedule can vary from +90 to −90. Table B.4 will show you how your score compares to those of 764 college women and 637 men from 35 campuses across the United States. For example, if you are a woman and your score was 26, it exceeded that of 80 percent of the women in the sample. A score of 15 for a male exceeds that of 55–60 percent of the men in the sample.

TABLE B.4: PERCENTILES FOR SCORES ON THE RAS

Women's Scores	Percentile	Men's Scores
55	99	65
48	97	54
45	95	48
37	90	40
31	85	33
26	80	30
23	75	26
19	70	24
17	65	19
14	60	17
11	55	15
8	50	11
6	45	8
2	40	6
−1	35	3
−4	30	1
−8	25	−3
−13	20	−7
−17	15	−11
−24	10	−15
−34	5	−24
−39	3	−30
−48	1	−41

Source: Nevid, J. S., & Rathus, S. A. (1978). Multivariate and normative data pertaining to the RAS with the college population. *Behavior Therapy, 9,* 675.

A

A–B problem The issue of how well we can predict behavior on the basis of attitudes.

Abreaction In psychodynamic theory, the expression of previously repressed feelings and impulses to allow the psychic energy associated with them to spill forth.

Absolute refractory period A phase following a neuron's firing during which an action potential cannot be triggered.

Absolute threshold The minimal amount of energy that can produce a sensation.

Abstinence syndrome A characteristic cluster of symptoms that results from sudden decrease in the level of usage of a drug on which one is physiologically dependent.

Accommodation According to Piaget, the modification of existing concepts or schemas so that new information can be integrated or understood.

Acculturation The process of adaptation in which immigrants and native groups identify with a new, dominant culture by learning about that culture and making behavioral and attitudinal changes.

Acetylcholine A neurotransmitter that is involved in muscle contractions. Abbreviated *ACh.*

Achievement Accomplishment; that which is attained by one's efforts and presumed to be made possible by one's abilities.

Acoustic code Mental representation of information as a sequence of sounds.

Acquired drives Drives that are acquired through experience, or learned.

Acquired immunodeficiency syndrome A fatal, sexually transmitted disease that is caused by the human immunodeficiency virus (HIV). HIV destroys cells of the immune system, leaving the body vulnerable to opportunistic diseases. Abbreviated *AIDS.*

Acquisition trial In conditioning, a presentation of stimuli such that a new response is learned and strengthened.

Acrophobia Fear of high places.

Action potential The firing of a neuron (more technically, the electrical impulse that provides the basis for the conduction of a neural impulse along an axon of a neuron).

Activating effects The arousal-producing effects of sex hormones that increase the likelihood of dominant sexual responses.

Activation-synthesis model The view that dreams reflect activation by the reticular activating system and synthesis of activated cognitions by the cerebral cortex.

Active coping A response to stress that manipulates the environment or changes the response patterns of the individual to remove the stressor permanently or to render it harmless.

Actor-observer effect In attribution theory, the tendency to attribute our own behavior to situational factors but to attribute the behavior of others to dispositional factors.

Acupuncture The practice, originated in ancient China, of piercing parts of the body with needles to deaden pain and treat illness.

Adaptation stage See *resistance stage.*

ADH Abbreviation of antidiuretic hormone.

Adipose tissue Tissue that contains fat.

Adjustment The process of responding to stress.

Adolescence The stage of development between childhood and adulthood that is bounded by the advent of puberty and the capacity to assume adult responsibilities.

Adrenal cortex The outer part of the adrenal gland, which produces steroids.

Adrenaline A hormone produced by the adrenal medulla that stimulates the sympathetic division of the autonomic nervous system. Also called *epinephrine.*

Adrenal medulla The inner part of the adrenal gland, which produces adrenaline.

Adrenocorticotrophic hormone A pituitary hormone that regulates the adrenal cortex. Abbreviated *ACTH.*

Aerobic exercise Exercise that requires sustained increase in oxygen consumption.

Affective disorders Disorders characterized primarily by prolonged disturbances of mood or emotional response. (Now referred to as *mood disorders.*)

Afferent neuron A neuron that transmits messages from sensory receptors to the spinal cord and brain. Also called *sensory neuron.*

Affiliation motive The social motive to be with others and to cooperate.

Afterimage The lingering impression made by a stimulus that has been removed.

Age regression In hypnosis, taking on the role of childhood, frequently accompanied by vivid recollections of the early years.

Agoraphobia Fear of open, crowded places.

AIDS Acronym for *Acquired Immunodeficiency Syndrome.* A disorder of the immune system caused by the human immunodeficiency virus (HIV) and characterized by suppression of the immune response, leaving the body prey to opportunistic diseases.

Alarm reaction The first stage of the general adaptation syndrome, which is triggered by the impact of a stressor and characterized by heightened sympathetic activity.

Alcoholism Drinking that persistently impairs personal, social, or physical well-being.

Algorithm A specific procedure such as a formula for solving a problem that will work invariably if it is applied correctly.

All-or-none principle The principle that a neuron fires an impulse of the same strength whenever its action potential has been triggered.

Alpha waves Rapid, low-amplitude brain waves that have been linked to feelings of relaxation.

Altered states of consciousness States other than the normal waking state, including sleep, meditation, the hypnotic trance, and the distorted perceptions that can be caused by use of certain drugs.

Alternate-form reliability The consistency of a test as determined by correlating scores attained on one form of the test with scores attained on another form. The Scholastic Aptitude Tests and Graduate Record Exams, for example, have many forms.

Altruism Selflessness; unselfish concern for the welfare of others.

Alzheimer's disease A progressive disease that is associated with degeneration of hippocampal cells that produce acetylcholine. It is symptomized by the inability to form new memories and the loss of other cognitive functions.

Amenorrhea Absence of menstruation.

American Sign Language The communication of meaning through the use of symbols that are formed by moving the hands and arms and associated gestures. Abbreviated *ASL.*

Amniocentesis A method for tapping amniotic fluid and examining fetal chromosomes that have been sloughed off, making it possible to determine the presence of genetic abnormalities and the sex of the fetus.

Amniotic fluid Fluid within the amniotic sac, formed largely from the fetus's urine, that protects the fetus from jarring or injury.

Amniotic sac A sac within the uterus that contains the embryo or fetus.

Amotivational syndrome Loss of ambition or motivation to achieve.

Amphetamines Stimulants such as Dexedrine and Benzedrine that are derived from *a*lpha- *m*ethyl-beta-*ph*enyl-*e*thyl-*a*mine. Abuse can trigger symptoms that mimic schizophrenia.

Amplitude Height. The extreme range of a variable quantity.

Amygdala A part of the limbic system that apparently facilitates stereotypical aggressive responses.

Anabolic steroids Steroids, the chief of which is testosterone, that promote the growth of muscle tissue by creating protein and other substances. Anabolic steroids also foster feelings of invincibility. See also *corticosteroids.*

Anaerobic exercise Exercise that does not require sustained increase in oxygen consumption, such as weight lifting.

Anal expulsive A Freudian personality type characterized by unregulated self-expression such as messiness.

Anal fixation In psychodynamic theory, attachment to objects and behaviors characteristic of the anal stage.

Analgesia (1) A conscious state in which pain is reduced or terminated. (2) A method for inducing such a state.

Analogous hues Colors that lie next to one another on the color wheel, forming families of harmonious colors such as yellow and orange, and green and blue.

Anal retentive A Freudian personality type characterized by self-control such as excessive neatness and punctuality.

Anal stage In psychodynamic theory, the second stage of psychosexual development, in which gratification is obtained through anal activities like eliminating wastes.

Analytical psychology Jung's psychodynamic theory which emphasizes archetypes, a collective unconscious, and a unifying force of personality called the Self.

Anchoring and adjustment heuristic A decision-making heuristic in which a presumption or first estimate serves as a cognitive anchor. As we receive additional information, we make adjustments, but tend to remain in the proximity of the anchor.

Androgen Male sex hormone.

Angiotensin A kidney hormone that signals the hypothalamus of depletion of body fluids.

Animism The belief, characteristic of preoperational thought, that inanimate objects move because of will or spirit.

Anorexia nervosa An eating disorder characterized by maintenance of an abnormally low body weight, intense fear of weight gain, a distorted body image, and, in females, amenorrhea.

Anosmia Lack of sensitivity to a specific odor.

ANS Abbreviation for *autonomic nervous system.*

Antecedent An event or thing that occurs before another. (An *antecedent* of behavior is not necessarily a *cause* of behavior.)

Anterograde amnesia Failure to remember events that occur after physical trauma because of the effects of the trauma.

Antibodies Substances formed by white blood cells that recognize and destroy antigens.

Antidepressant drug A drug that acts to relieve depression.

Antidiuretic hormone A pituitary hormone that conserves body fluids by increasing the reabsorption of urine. Abbreviated *ADH.*

Antigen A substance that stimulates the body to mount an immune system response to it. (The contraction for *anti*body *gen*erator.)

Antisocial personality disorder The diagnosis given a person who is in frequent conflict with society yet is undeterred by punishment and experiences little or no guilt and anxiety. Also referred to as *psychopathy* or *sociopathy.*

Anvil A bone of the middle ear.

Anxiety A psychological state characterized by tension and apprehension, foreboding and dread.

Aphagic Characterized by undereating.

Aphasia Impaired ability to comprehend speech or to express oneself through speech.

Apnea A life-threatening sleep disorder that is characterized by temporary discontinuation of breathing during sleep.

Applied research Research conducted in an effort to find solutions to particular problems.

Approach-approach conflict Conflict involving two positive but mutually exclusive goals.

Approach-avoidance conflict Conflict involving a goal with positive and negative features.

Aptitude A natural ability or talent.

Archetypes In Jung's personality theory, primitive images or concepts that reside in the collective unconscious.

Arousal (1) A general level of activity or preparedness for activity in an organism. (2) A general level of motivation in an organism.

Arteriosclerosis A disease characterized by thickening and hardening of the arteries.

Artificialism The belief, characteristic of preoperational thought, that natural objects have been created by human beings.

Assertiveness training A form of social skills training including techniques such as coaching, modeling, feedback, and behavior rehearsal that teaches clients to express their feelings and seek fair treatment.

Assimilation According to Piaget, the inclusion of a new event into an existing concept or schema.

Association areas Parts of the cerebral cortex involved in learning, thought, memory, and language.

Astigmatism A visual disorder in which vertical and horizontal contours cannot be focused on simultaneously.

Astrology A pseudoscience that is based on the notion that the positions of the sun, the moon, and the stars affect human affairs and that one can foretell the future by studying the positions of these bodies.

Asylum (1) An early institution for the care of the mentally ill. (2) A safe place, or refuge.

Attachment The enduring affectional tie that binds one person to another.

Attachment-in-the-making phase According to Ainsworth, the second phase in forming bonds of attachment, characterized by preference for familiar figures.

Attention-deficit/hyperactivity disorder A disorder that begins in childhood and is characterized by a persistent pattern of lack of attention, with or without hyperactivity and impulsive behavior. Abbreviated *ADHD*.

Attitude An enduring mental representation of people, places, or things that evokes feelings and influences behavior.

Attitude-discrepant behavior Behavior that is inconsistent with an attitude and may have the effect of modifying an attitude.

Attraction A force that draws bodies or people together. In social psychology, an attitude of liking (positive attraction) or disliking (negative attraction).

Attribution A belief about why people behave in a certain way.

Attributional style One's tendency to attribute one's behavior to internal or external factors, stable or unstable factors, and so on.

Attribution process The process by which people draw conclusions about the motives and traits of others.

Auditory Having to do with hearing.

Auditory nerve The axon bundle that transmits neural impulses from the organ of Corti to the brain.

Authoritarianism Belief in the importance of unquestioning obedience to authority.

Autism (1) Self-absorption. Absorption in daydreaming and fantasy. (2) A childhood disorder marked by problems such as failure to relate to others, lack of speech, and intolerance of change.

Autokinetic effect The tendency to perceive a stationary point of light in a dark room as moving.

Autonomic nervous system The division of the peripheral nervous system that regulates glands and involuntary activities like heartbeat, respiration, digestion, and dilation of the pupils. Abbreviated *ANS*. Also see *sympathetic* and *parasympathetic* branches of the ANS.

Autonomy Self-direction. The motive to be free, unrestrained, and independent.

Autonomy versus shame and doubt Erikson's second stage of psychosocial development, during which the child develops (or does not develop) the wish to make choices and the capacity to exercise self-control.

Availability heuristic A decision-making heuristic in which our estimates of frequency or probability of events are based on how easy it is to find examples.

Average The central tendency of a group of measures, expressed as *mean, median,* or *mode.*

Aversive conditioning A behavior therapy technique in which a previously desirable or neutral stimulus is made obnoxious by being paired repeatedly with a repugnant or offensive stimulus.

Avoidance-avoidance conflict Conflict involving two negative goals in which avoidance of one requires approaching the other.

Avoidance learning An operant conditioning procedure in which an organism learns to exhibit an operant that permits it to avoid an aversive stimulus.

Axon A long, thin part of a neuron that transmits impulses to other neurons from branching structures called *terminals.*

B

B lymphocytes The white blood cells of the immune system that produce antibodies.

Babbling The child's first verbalizations that have the sound of speech.

Babinski reflex An infant's fanning of the toes in response to stimulation of the sole of the foot.

Backward conditioning A classical conditioning procedure in which the unconditioned stimulus is presented prior to the conditioned stimulus.

Barbiturate An addictive depressant used to relieve anxiety or induce sleep.

Bargaining The third stage in Kübler-Ross's theory of dying, in which the terminally ill try to bargain with God to postpone death, usually by offering to do good deeds in exchange for time.

Barnum effect The tendency to believe in the accuracy of a generalized personality report or prediction about oneself.

Basal ganglia Ganglia located in the brain between the thalamus and the cerebrum that are involved in motor coordination.

Basic anxiety Horney's term for enduring feelings of insecurity that stem from harsh or indifferent parental treatment.

Basic hostility Horney's term for enduring feelings of anger that accompany basic anxiety but that are directed toward nonfamily members in adulthood.

Basilar membrane A membrane to which the organ of Corti is attached. The basilar membrane lies coiled within the cochlea.

Behavior The observable or measurable actions of people and lower animals.

Behavioral competencies Skills.

Behavior genetics The study of the genetic transmission of structures and traits that give rise to behavior.

Behaviorism The school of psychology that defines psychology as the study of observable behavior and investigates the relationships between stimuli and responses.

Behaviorist A psychologist who believes that psychology should address observable behavior and the relationships between stimuli and responses.

Behavior modification Use of principles of learning to change behavior in desired directions.

Behavior-outcome relations A kind of expectancy in social-cognitive theory: predictions as to the outcomes (reinforcement contingencies) of one's behavior.

Behavior rating scale A systematic means of recording the frequency with which target behaviors occur. (An alternative to self-report methods of personality testing.)

Behavior rehearsal Practice.

Behavior therapy Use of the principles of learning in the direct modification of problem behavior.

Benzodiazepines A class of drugs that reduce anxiety. Minor tranquilizers.

Binocular cues Stimuli that suggest depth by means of simultaneous perception by both eyes. Examples: retinal disparity and convergence.

Biofeedback training The systematic feeding back to an organism information about a body function so that the organism can gain control of that function. Abbreviated *BFT*.

Biological psychologist A psychologist who studies the relationships between biological processes and behavior.

Bipolar cells Neurons that conduct neural impulses from rods and cones to ganglion cells.

Bipolar disorder A disorder in which the mood inappropriately alternates between extremes of elation and depression. Formerly called *manic-depression*.

Blind In experimental terminology, unaware of whether one has obtained a treatment.

Blind spot The area of the retina where axons from ganglion cells meet to form the optic nerve. It is insensitive to light.

Blocking In conditioning, the phenomenon whereby a new stimulus fails to gain the capacity to signal an unconditioned stimulus (US) when the new stimulus is paired repeatedly with a stimulus that already effectively foretells the US.

Bottom-up processing The organization of the parts of a pattern to recognize, or form an image of, the pattern they compose.

Brainstorming A group process that encourages creativity by stimulating a large number of ideas and suspending judgment until the process is completed.

Brightness constancy The tendency to perceive an object as being just as bright even though lighting conditions change the intensity with which it impacts on the eye.

Broca's aphasia A speech disorder caused by damage to Broca's area of the brain. It is characterized by slow, laborious speech and by difficulty articulating words and forming grammatical sentences.

Bulimia nervosa An eating disorder characterized by recurrent episodes of binge eating followed by purging and by persistent overconcern with body shape and weight.

C

Cannon-Bard theory The theory of emotion that holds that events are processed by the brain and that the brain induces patterns of activity and autonomic arousal *and* cognitive activity—that is, the experiencing of the appropriate emotion.

Carcinogen An agent that gives rise to cancerous changes.

Cardinal trait Allport's term for pervasive traits that steer practically all of a person's behavior.

Cardiovascular disorders Diseases of the cardiovascular system, including heart disease, hypertension, and arteriosclerosis.

Case study A carefully drawn biography that may be obtained through interviews, questionnaires, psychological tests, and, sometimes, historical records.

Catastrophize To exaggerate or magnify the noxious properties of negative events; to "blow out of proportion."

Catatonic schizophrenia A subtype of schizophrenia characterized by striking impairment in motor activity.

Catch 30s Sheehy's term for the fourth decade of life, which is frequently characterized by major reassessment of one's accomplishments and goals.

Catecholamines A number of chemical substances produced from an amino acid that are important as neurotransmitters (dopamine and noradrenaline) and as hormones (adrenaline and noradrenaline).

Catharsis In psychodynamic theory, the purging of strong emotions or the relieving of tensions. Also called *abreaction*.

CD4 cells The white blood cells of the immune system that recognize invading pathogens and are attacked by the human immunodeficiency virus (HIV). Also called *T helper cells* or *T_4 cells*.

Cellular-aging theory The view that aging occurs because body cells lose the capacity to reproduce and maintain themselves.

Center According to Piaget, to focus one's attention.

Central fissure The valley in the cerebral cortex that separates the frontal and parietal lobes.

Central nervous system The brain and spinal cord.

Central traits Characteristics that are outstanding and noticeable but not necessarily all-pervasive.

Cephalocaudal Proceeding from top to bottom.

Cerebellum A part of the hindbrain involved in muscle coordination and balance.

Cerebral cortex The wrinkled surface area of the cerebrum, often called "gray matter" because of the appearance afforded by the many cell bodies.

Cerebrum The large mass of the forebrain, which consists of two hemispheres.

Chain breaking A behavior therapy self-control technique in which one disrupts problematic behavior by complicating its execution.

Chemotherapy The use of drugs to treat medical problems or abnormal behavior.

Childhood amnesia Inability to recall events that occurred before the age of 3. Also termed *infantile amnesia*.

Chorionic villus sampling The detection of genetic abnormalities by sampling the membrane that envelopes the amniotic sac and the fetus within. Abbreviated *CVS*.

Chromosomes Genetic structures consisting of genes that are found in the nuclei of the body's cells.

Chronological age A person's actual age—as contrasted with *mental age*.

Chunk A stimulus or group of stimuli that are perceived or encoded as a discrete piece of information.

Circadian rhythm Referring to cycles that are connected with the 24-hour period of the earth's rotation. (A scientific term coined from the Latin roots *circa*, meaning "about," and *dies*, meaning "day.")

Circular explanation   An explanation that merely repeats its own concepts instead of offering additional information.

Cirrhosis of the liver   A health problem caused by protein deficiency in which connective fibers replace active liver cells, impairing circulation of the blood. Alcohol does not contain protein; therefore, people who drink excessively may be prone to acquiring this disease.

Clairvoyance   The terms means ability to perceive things in the absence of sensory stimulation. However, most psychologists do not believe that this ability exists. (A French word meaning "clear-sightedness.")

Classical conditioning   A simple form of learning in which an organism comes to associate or anticipate events. A neutral stimulus comes to evoke the response usually evoked by another stimulus by being paired repeatedly with the other stimulus. (Cognitive theorists view classical conditioning as the learning of relationships among events so as to allow an organism to represent its environment.) Also referred to as *respondent conditioning* or *Pavlovian conditioning.*

Claustrophobia   Fear of tight, small places.

Clear-cut attachment phase   According to Ainsworth, the third phase in forming bonds of attachment, which is characterized by intensified dependence on the primary caregiver.

Client-centered therapy   See *person-centered therapy.*

Clinical scales   Groups of test items that measure the presence of various abnormal behavior patterns, as on the Minnesota Multiphasic Personality Inventory.

Closure   The tendency to perceive a broken figure as being complete or whole.

Cocaine   A powerful stimulant derived from coca leaves that is usually snorted, brewed, or injected.

Cochlea   The inner ear; the bony tube that contains the basilar membrane and the organ of Corti.

Cognitive   Having to do with mental processes such as sensation and perception, memory, intelligence, language, thought, and problem solving.

Cognitive-dissonance theory   The view that we are motivated to make our cognitions or beliefs consistent.

Cognitive map   A mental representation or picture of the elements in a learning situation, such as a maze.

Cognitive therapy   A form of psychotherapy that focuses on how clients' cognitions (expectations, attitudes, beliefs, etc.) lead to distress and may be modified to relieve distress and promote adaptive behavior.

Collective unconscious   Jung's hypothesized store of vague racial memories and archetypes.

Collectivist   A person who defines herself or himself in terms of relationships to other people and groups and gives priority to group goals.

Color constancy   The tendency to perceive an object as being the same color even as lighting conditions change its appearance.

Common fate   The tendency to perceive elements that move together as belonging together.

Community psychology   A field of psychology, related to clinical psychology, that focuses on the prevention of psychological problems and the maintenance of distressed persons in the community.

Companionate love   A type of love characterized by intimacy, respect, trust, and commitment.

Competencies   Within social-cognitive theory, knowledge and skills.

Competing response   In behavior therapy, a response that is incompatible with an unwanted response.

Complementary   (1) In sensation and perception, descriptive of colors of the spectrum that, when combined, produce white or nearly white light. (2) In transactional analysis, descriptive of a transaction in which the ego states of two people interact harmoniously.

Componential level   According to Sternberg, the level of intelligence that consists of metacomponents, performance components, and knowledge-acquisition components.

Compulsion   An apparently irresistible urge to repeat an act or engage in ritualistic behavior, such as hand-washing.

Computerized axial tomography   Formation of a computer-generated image of the anatomical details of the brain by passing a narrow X-ray beam through the head and measuring from different angles the amount of radiation that passes through. Abbreviated *CAT scan.*

Concept   A mental category that is used to class together objects, relations, events, abstractions, or qualities that have common properties.

Concordance   Agreement.

Concrete operational stage   Piaget's third stage of cognitive development, characterized by logical thought processes concerning tangible objects, conservation, reversibility, and subjective morality.

Conditional positive regard   In Rogers's self theory, judgment of another person's basic value as a human being on the basis of the acceptability of that person's behaviors.

Conditional reasoning   A form of reasoning about arguments that is used to reach conclusions about if-then relationships.

Conditioned reinforcer   Another term for *secondary reinforcer.*

Conditioned response   In classical conditioning, a learned response to a previously neutral stimulus. A response to a conditioned stimulus. Abbreviated *CR.*

Conditioned stimulus   A previously neutral stimulus that elicits a conditioned response because it has been paired repeatedly with a stimulus that had already elicited that response. Abbreviated *CS.*

Conditioning   A simple form of learning in which responses become associated with stimuli. See *classical conditioning* and *operant conditioning.*

Conditions of worth   Standards by which the value of a person, or the self, is judged.

Conductive deafness   The forms of deafness in which there is loss of conduction of sound through the middle ear.

Cone   A cone-shaped photoreceptor in the eye that transmits sensations of color.

Confederate   In experimental terminology, a person who pretends to be a participant in a study but who is in league with the experimenter.

Confidential Secret, not to be disclosed.

Conflict (1) Being torn in different directions by opposing motives. (2) Feelings produced by being in conflict.

Conformity Behavior that is in accordance with group norms and expectations.

Congruence In Rogers's self-theory, a fit between one's self-concept and one's behaviors, thoughts, and feelings. A quality shown by the person-centered therapist.

Conscious Aware, in the normal waking state.

Consciousness A complex and controversial concept in psychology. Consciousness has several meanings in addition to the normal waking state; see *sensory awareness, direct inner awareness,* and *self.*

Consensus General agreement.

Conservation According to Piaget, recognition that certain properties of substances remain constant even though their appearance may change. For example, the weight and mass of a ball of clay remain constant (are conserved) even if the ball is flattened into a pancake.

Consolidation The fixing of information in long-term memory.

Consonant In harmony.

Construe Interpret.

Consultation The provision of professional advice or services.

Consumer psychology The field of psychology that studies the nature, causes, and modification of consumer behavior and mental processes.

Consummate love In Sternberg's triangular model, the kind of love characterized by passion, intimacy, and commitment.

Contact comfort (1) The pleasure attained from physical contact with another. (2) A hypothesized primary drive to seek physical comfort through physical contact with another.

Context-dependent memory Information that is better retrieved in the context in which it was encoded and stored, or learned.

Contextual level According to Sternberg, those aspects of intelligent behavior that permit people to adapt to their environment.

Contiguous Next to one another.

Contingency theory (1) In conditioning, the view that learning occurs when stimuli provide information about the likelihood of the occurrence of other stimuli. (2) In industrial/organizational psychology, a theory that holds that organizational structure should depend on factors such as goals, workers' characteristics, and the overall economic or political environment.

Continuity As a rule of perceptual organization, the tendency to perceive a series of stimuli as having unity.

Continuous reinforcement A schedule of reinforcement in which every correct response is reinforced. See *partial reinforcement.*

Control group A groups of participants in an experiment who do not receive the experimental treatment but for whom all other conditions are comparable with those of individuals in the experimental group.

Conventional level According to Kohlberg, a period of moral development during which moral judgments largely reflect social conventions. A "law and order" approach to morality.

Convergence A binocular cue for depth based on the inward movement of the eyes as they attempt to focus on an object that is drawing nearer.

Convergent thinking A thought process that attempts to narrow in on the single best solution to a problem.

Conversion disorder A disorder in which anxiety or unconscious conflicts are "converted" into physical symptoms that often have the effect of helping the person cope with the anxiety or conflicts.

Cooing Prelinguistic, articulated, vowel-like sounds that appear to reflect feelings of positive excitement.

Cornea Transparent tissue that forms the outer surface of the eyeball.

Corpus callosum A thick bundle of fibers that connects the two hemispheres of the cerebrum.

Correlational research A method of scientific investigation that studies the relationships between variables. Correlational research can imply but cannot show cause and effect, because no experimental treatment is introduced.

Correlation coefficient A number ranging from +1.00 to −1.00 that expresses the strength and direction (positive or negative) of the relationship between two variables.

Corticosteroids Steroids produced by the adrenal cortex that regulate carbohydrate metabolism and increase resistance to stress by fighting inflammation and allergic reactions. Also called *cortical steroids.*

Cortisol A hormone (steroid) produced by the adrenal cortex that helps the body cope with stress by counteracting inflammation and allergic reactions.

Counterconditioning A behavior therapy technique that involves the repeated pairing of a stimulus that elicits a problematic response (such as fear) with a stimulus that elicits an antagonistic response (such as relaxation instructions) so that the first stimulus loses the capacity to evoke the problematic response. See also *systematic desensitization* and *aversive conditioning.*

Countertransference In psychoanalysis, the generalization to the client of feelings toward another person in the analyst's life.

Covert reinforcement A behavior therapy self-control technique in which one creates pleasant imagery to reward desired behavior.

Covert sensitization A behavior therapy self-control technique in which one creates aversive imagery and associates it with undesired behavior.

CR Conditioned response.

Creative self According to Adler, the self-aware aspect of personality that strives to achieve its full potential.

Creativity The ability to generate novel solutions to problems. A trait characterized by originality, ingenuity, and flexibility.

Cretinism A condition caused by thyroid deficiency in childhood and characterized by mental retardation and stunted growth.

Criteria Plural of *criterion.*

Criterion A standard; a means for making a judgment.

Critical period A period in an organism's development during which it is capable of certain types of learning.

CS Conditioned stimulus.

Cultural bias A factor hypothesized to be present in intelligence tests that provides an advantage for test takers from certain cultural or ethnic backgrounds but that does not reflect actual intelligence.

Culture-free Describing a test in which there are no cultural biases. On such a test, test takers from different cultural backgrounds would have an equal opportunity to earn scores that reflect their true abilities.

Cumulative incidence The occurrence of an event or act by a given time or age.

Cumulative recorder An instrument used in operant conditioning laboratory procedures to record automatically the frequency of targeted responses.

D

Daily hassles Notable daily conditions and experiences that are threatening or harmful to a person's well-being.

Dark adaptation The process of adjusting to conditions of lower lighting by increasing the sensitivity of rods and cones.

Decibel A unit expressing the loudness of a sound. Abbreviated *dB*.

Deductive reasoning A form of reasoning about arguments in which conclusions are deduced from premises. The conclusions are true if the premises are true.

Deep structure The underlying meaning of a sentence as determined by interpretation of the meanings of the words.

Defense mechanisms In psychodynamic theory, unconscious functions of the ego that protect it from anxiety-evoking material by preventing accurate recognition of this material.

Defensive coping A response to stress that reduces the stressor's immediate effect but frequently at some cost to the individual. Defensive coping may involve self-deception and does not change the environment or the person's response patterns to remove or modify the effects of the stressor permanently. Contrast with *active coping*.

Deindividuation The process by which group members may discontinue self-evaluation and adopt group norms and attitudes.

Delayed conditioning A classical conditioning procedure in which the CS is presented several seconds before the US and remains in place until the response occurs.

Delirium tremens A condition characterized by sweating, restlessness, disorientation, and hallucinations that occurs in some chronic users of alcohol when there is a sudden decrease in the level of drinking. Abbreviated *DTs*.

Delta-9-tetrahydrocannabinol The major active ingredient in marijuana. Abbreviated *THC*.

Delta waves Strong, slow brain waves usually emitted during stage 4 sleep.

Delusions False, persistent beliefs that are unsubstantiated by sensory or objective evidence.

Delusions of grandeur Erroneous beliefs that one is a grand person, like Jesus or a secret agent on a special mission.

Delusions of persecution Erroneous beliefs that one is being threatened or persecuted.

Dendrites Rootlike structures attached to the cell body of a neuron that receive impulses from other cells.

Denial (1) A defense mechanism in which threatening events are misperceived to be harmless. (2) The first stage in Kübler-Ross's theory of dying.

Dependent variable A measure of an assumed effect of an independent variable. An outcome measure in a scientific study.

Depersonalization disorder A dissociative disorder characterized by persistent or recurrent feelings that one is not real or is detached from one's own experiences or body.

Depolarization The reduction of the resting potential of a cell membrane from about −70 millivolts toward zero.

Depressant A drug that lowers the nervous system's rate of activity.

Depression (1) A negative emotion frequently characterized by sadness, feelings of helplessness, and a sense of loss. (2) The fourth stage in Kübler-Ross's theory of dying.

Descriptive statistics The branch of statistics that is concerned with providing descriptive information about a distribution of scores.

Desensitization The type of sensory adaptation in which we become less sensitive to constant stimuli. Also called *negative adaptation*.

Determinant A factor that defines or sets limits.

Deviation IQ A score on an intelligence test that is derived by determining how far an individual's score deviates from the norm. On the Wechsler scales, the mean IQ score is defined as 100, and approximately two of three scores fall between 85 and 115.

Diabetes A disorder caused by inadequate secretion or utilization of insulin and characterized by excess sugar in the blood.

Diagnosis A decision or opinion about the nature of a diseased condition.

Dialogue A Gestalt therapy technique in which people verbalize confrontations between conflicting parts of their personality.

Dichromat A person who is sensitive to the intensity of light and to red and green or blue and yellow and who thus is partially color-blind.

Difference threshold The minimal difference in intensity that is required between two sources of energy so that they will be perceived as being different.

Differentiation The modification of tissues and organs in structure, function, or both during the course of development.

Diffusion of responsibility The spreading or sharing of responsibility for a decision or behavior among the members of a group.

Direct coping See *active coping*.

Direct inner awareness One of the definitions of consciousness: knowledge of one's own thoughts, feelings, and memories, without use of sensory organs.

Discrimination (1) In conditioning, the tendency for an organism to distinguish between a conditioned stimulus and similar stimuli that do not forecast an unconditioned stimulus. (2) In social psychology, the denial of privileges to a person or a group on the basis of prejudice.

Discrimination training Teaching an organism to show a conditioned response to only one of a series of similar stimuli by pairing that stimulus with the unconditioned stimulus and presenting similar stimuli in the absence of the unconditioned stimulus.

Discriminative stimulus In operant conditioning, a stimulus that indicates that reinforcement is available.

Disinhibit In social-cognitive theory, to trigger a response that is usually inhibited, generally as a consequence of observing a model engage in the behavior without negative consequences.

Disorganized schizophrenia A subtype of schizophrenia characterized by disorganized delusions and vivid hallucinations. Formerly *hebephrenic schizophrenia.*

Disorientation Gross confusion. Loss of awareness of time, place, and the identity of people.

Displacement (1) In information processing, the causing of chunks of information to be lost from short-term memory by adding too many new items. (2) In psychodynamic theory, a defense mechanism that involves the transference of feelings or impulses from threatening or unacceptable objects onto unthreatening or acceptable objects. (3) As a property of language, the ability to communicate information about events in other times and places.

Dispositional attribution An assumption that a person's behavior is determined by internal causes such as personal attitudes or goals. Contrast with *situational attribution.*

Dissociative amnesia A dissociative disorder marked by loss of episodic memory or self-identity. Skills and general knowledge are usually retained. Formerly termed *psychogenic amnesia.*

Dissociative disorder A disorder in which there is a sudden, temporary change in consciousness or self-identity, such as dissociative amnesia, dissociative fugue, dissociative identity disorder, or depersonalization disorder.

Dissociative fugue A dissociative disorder in which one experiences amnesia, then flees to a new location. Formerly termed *psychogenic fugue.*

Dissociative identity disorder A dissociative disorder in which a person has two or more distinct identities or personalities. Formerly termed *multiple personality disorder.*

Dissonant Incompatible, discordant.

Divergent thinking A thought process that attempts to generate multiple solutions to problems. Free and fluent associations to the elements of a problem.

Dizygotic twins Twins who develop from separate zygotes. Fraternal twins. Abbreviated *DZ twins.* Contrast with *monozygotic twins.*

DNA Deoxyribonucleic acid. The substance that carries the genetic code and makes up genes and chromosomes.

Dominant trait In genetics, a trait that is expressed. See *recessive trait.*

Dopamine A neurotransmitter that is involved in Parkinson's disease and theorized to play a role in schizophrenia.

Double approach–avoidance conflict Conflict involving two goals, each of which has positive and negative aspects.

Double-blind study A study in which neither the participants nor the persons measuring results know who has obtained the treatment.

Down syndrome A chromosomal abnormality caused by an extra chromosome in the 21st pair ("trisomy 21") and characterized by slanted eyelids and mental retardation.

Dream A form of cognitive activity—usually a sequence of images or thoughts—that occurs during sleep. Dreams may be vague and loosely plotted or vivid and intricate.

Drive A condition of arousal within an organism that is associated with a need.

Drive for superiority Adler's term for the desire to compensate for feelings of inferiority.

Drive-reduction theory The view that organisms are motivated to learn to engage in behaviors that have the effect of reducing drives.

DSM The *Diagnostic and Statistical Manual of the Mental Disorders,* a publication of the American Psychiatric Association. A frequently used compendium of psychological disorders.

Duplicity theory A combination of the place and frequency theories of pitch discrimination.

Dyslexia A severe reading disorder characterized by problems such as letter reversals, reading as if one were seeing words reflected in a mirror, slow reading, and reduced comprehension.

Dyspareunia Persistent or recurrent pain during or after sexual intercourse.

E

Eardrum A thin membrane that vibrates in response to sound waves, transmitting them from the outer ear to the middle and inner ears.

Eating disorders Psychological disorders that are characterized by distortion of the body image and gross disturbances in eating patterns. See *anorexia nervosa* and *bulimia nervosa.*

Echo A mental representation of an auditory stimulus that is held briefly in sensory memory.

Echoic memory The sensory register that briefly holds mental representations of auditory stimuli.

Eclectic Selecting from various systems or theories.

ECT Acronym for *electroconvulsive therapy.*

Educational psychology The field of psychology that studies the nature, causes, and enhancement of teaching and learning.

Efferent neuron A neuron that transmits messages from the brain or spinal cord to muscles or glands. Also called *motor neuron.*

Effort justification In cognitive-dissonance theory, the tendency to seek justification (acceptable reasons) for strenuous efforts.

Ego In psychodynamic theory, the second psychic structure to develop. The ego is governed by the reality principle and its functioning is characterized by self-awareness, planning, and capacity to tolerate frustration and delay gratification.

Ego analyst A psychodynamically oriented therapist who focuses on the conscious, coping behavior of the ego instead of the hypothesized unconscious functioning of the id.

Egocentric According to Piaget, assuming that others view the world as oneself does. Unable or unwilling to view the world as through the eyes of others.

Ego identity Erikson's term for the sense of who one is and what one stands for.

Ego identity versus role diffusion Erikson's fifth stage of psychosocial development, which challenges the adolescent to connect skills and social roles to career objectives.

Ego integrity Erikson's term for a firm sense of identity during the later years, characterized by the wisdom to accept the fact that life is limited and the ability to let go.

Ego integrity versus despair Erikson's eighth stage of psychosocial development, which challenges persons to accept the limits of their own life cycles during the later years.

Eidetic imagery The maintenance of detailed visual memories over several minutes.

Elaboration likelihood model The view that persuasive messages are evaluated (elaborated) on the basis of central and peripheral cues.

Elaborative rehearsal A method for increasing retention of new information by relating it to information that is well known.

Electra complex In psychodynamic theory, a conflict of the phallic stage in which the girl longs for her father and resents her mother.

Electroconvulsive therapy Treatment of disorders like major depression by passing an electric current through the head, causing a convulsion. Abbreviated *ECT.*

Electroencephalograph An instrument that measures electrical activity of the brain (brain waves). Abbreviated *EEG.*

Electromyograph An instrument that measures muscle tension. Abbreviated *EMG.*

Elicit To bring forth, evoke.

Embryo The developing organism from the third through the eighth weeks following conception, during which time the major organ systems undergo rapid differentiation.

Embryonic period The period of prenatal development between the period of the ovum and fetal development, approximately from the third through the eighth weeks following conception.

Emetic Causing vomiting.

Emotion A state of feeling that has cognitive, physiological, and behavioral components.

Emotional appeal A type of persuasive communication that influences behavior on the basis of feelings that are aroused instead of rational analysis of the issues.

Empathic understanding Ability to perceive a client's feelings from the client's frame of reference. A quality of a good person-centered therapist.

Empathy Ability to understand and share another person's feelings.

Empirical Experimental. Emphasizing or based on observation and measurement, in contrast to theory and deduction.

Empty-nest syndrome A sense of depression and loss of purpose that is experienced by some parents when the youngest child leaves home.

Encoding Modifying information so that it can be placed in memory. The first stage of information processing.

Encounter group A structured group process that aims to foster self-awareness by focusing on how group members relate to each other in a setting that encourages frank expression of feelings.

Endocrine system The body's system of ductless glands that secrete hormones and release them directly into the bloodstream.

Endorphins Neurotransmitters that are composed of amino acids and are functionally similar to morphine.

Engram (1) An assumed electrical circuit in the brain that corresponds to a memory trace. (2) An assumed chemical change in the brain that accompanies learning.

Enuresis Lack of bladder control at an age by which control is normally attained.

Environmental psychology The field of psychology that studies the ways in which people and the physical environment influence one another.

Epilepsy Temporary disturbances of brain functions that involve sudden neural discharges.

Epinephrine A hormone produced by the adrenal medulla that stimulates the sympathetic division of the ANS. Also called *adrenaline.*

Episodic memory Memories of specific events experienced by a person.

Equilibrium Another term for the *vestibular sense.*

Erogenous zone An area of the body that is sensitive to sexual sensations.

Eros In psychodynamic theory, the basic life instinct, which aims toward the preservation and perpetuation of life.

Estrogen A generic term for several female sex hormones that promote growth of female sexual characteristics and regulate the menstrual cycle.

Estrus The periodic sexual excitement of many female mammals, during which they are capable of conceiving and are receptive to sexual advances by males.

Ethical Moral; referring to one's system of deriving standards for determining what is moral.

Ethologist A scientist who studies behavior patterns that are characteristic of various species.

Euphoria Feelings of extreme well-being, elation.

Eustress Stress that is healthful.

Evaluation apprehension Concern that others are evaluating our behavior.

Excitatory synapse A synapse that influences receiving neurons in the direction of firing by increasing depolarization of their cell membranes.

Excitement phase The first phase of the sexual response cycle, characterized by erection in the man and by vaginal lubrication and clitoral swelling in the woman.

Exhaustion stage The third stage of the general adaptation syndrome, characterized by parasympathetic activity, weakened resistance, and possible deterioration.

Existentialism The view that people are completely free and responsible for their own behavior.

Expectancies A person variable in social-cognitive theory. Personal predictions about outcomes—"if-then" statements.

Experiential level According to Sternberg, those aspects of intelligence that permit people to cope with novel situations and process information automatically.

Experiment A scientific method that seeks to discover cause-and-effect relationships by introducing independent variables and observing their effects on dependent variables.

Experimental group A group of participants who obtain a treatment in an experiment.

Expressive vocabulary The sum total of the words that one can use in the production of language.

"Externals" People who have an external locus of control—who perceive the ability to attain reinforcements as largely outside themselves.

Extinction In the psychology of learning, an experimental procedure in which stimuli lose their ability to evoke learned responses because the events that had followed the stimuli no longer occur. (The learned responses are said to be *extinguished.*)

Extinction trial In conditioning, a performance of a learned response in the absence of its predicted consequences so that the learned response becomes inhibited.

Extrasensory perception Perception of external objects and events in the absence of sensation. Abbreviated *ESP*. A controversial area of investigation. (*Not* to be confused with hallucinations, which typify certain psychological disorders and are defined as confusion of fantasies with reality.)

Extroversion A source trait in which one's attention is directed to persons and things outside the self, often associated with a sociable, outgoing approach to others and the free expression of feelings and impulses. Opposite of *introversion*.

F

Facial-feedback hypothesis The view that stereotypical facial expressions can contribute to the experiencing of stereotypical emotions.

Factor A cluster of related items such as those found on an intelligence test.

Factor analysis A statistical technique that allows researchers to determine the relationships among large number of items such as test items.

Fallopian tube A tube that conducts ova from an ovary to the uterus.

Family therapy A form of therapy in which the family unit is treated as the client.

Farsighted Capable of seeing distant objects with greater acuity than nearby objects.

Fat cells Cells that store fats. Also called *adipose tissue*.

Fear A negative emotion characterized by perception of a threat, sympathetic nervous system activity, and avoidance tendencies.

Feature detectors Neurons in the visual cortex that fire in response to specific features of visual information, such as lines or edges presented at particular angles.

Feedback Information about one's own behavior.

Feeling-of-knowing experience See *tip-of-the-tongue phenomenon*.

Female sexual arousal disorder A sexual dysfunction characterized by difficulty in becoming sexually aroused, as defined by vaginal lubrication, or sustaining arousal long enough to engage in satisfying sexual relations.

Feminists People (of both genders) who seek social change and legislation to reverse discrimination against women and to otherwise advance the concerns of women.

Fetus The developing organism from the third month following conception through childbirth, during which time there are maturation of organ systems and dramatic gains in length and weight.

Fight-or-flight reaction Cannon's term for a hypothesized innate adaptive response to the perception of danger.

File-drawer problem In research, the tendency to file away (and forget) negative results, such that positive results tend to achieve greater visibility or impact than they may deserve.

Final acceptance The fifth stage in Kübler-Ross's theory of dying, which is characterized by lack of feeling.

Fissure Valley—referring to the valleys in the wrinkled surface of the cerebral cortex.

Fixation In psychodynamic theory, arrested development. Attachment to objects of an earlier stage.

Fixation time The amount of time spent looking at a visual stimulus. A measure of interest in infants.

Fixed-action pattern An instinct; abbreviated *FAP*.

Fixed-interval schedule A partial reinforcement schedule in which a fixed amount of time must elapse between the previous and subsequent times that reinforcement is made available.

Fixed-ratio schedule A partial reinforcement schedule in which reinforcement is made available after a fixed number of correct responses.

Flashbacks Distorted perceptions or hallucinations that occur days or weeks after usage of a hallucinogenic drug (usually LSD) but that mimic the effects of the drug.

Flashbulb memories Memories that are preserved in great detail because they reflect intense emotional experiences.

Flat affect Monotonous, dull emotional response.

Flooding A behavioral fear-reduction technique that is based on principles of classical conditioning. Fear-evoking stimuli (CSs) are presented continuously in the absence of actual harm so that fear responses (CRs) are extinguished.

Foot-in-the-door technique A method of persuasion in which compliance with a large request is encouraged by first asking the recipient of the request to comply with a smaller request.

Forced-choice format A method of presenting test questions that requires a respondent to select one of a number of possible answers.

Forensic psychology The field that applies psychological knowledge within the criminal justice system.

Formal-operational stage Piaget's fourth stage of cognitive development, characterized by abstract logical and theoretical thought and deduction from principles.

Fovea A rodless area near the center of the retina where vision is most acute.

Frame of reference In self theory, one's unique patterning of perceptions and attitudes, according to which one evaluates events.

Framing effect The influence of wording, or the context in which information is presented, on decision making.

Free association In psychoanalysis, the uncensored uttering of all thoughts that come to mind.

Free-floating anxiety Chronic, persistent anxiety. Anxiety that is not tied to particular events.

Frequency distribution An ordered set of data that indicates how frequently scores appear.

Frequency theory The theory that the pitch of a sound is reflected in the frequency of the neural impulses that are generated in response.

Frontal lobe The lobe of the cerebral cortex that is involved with movement and that lies to the front of the central fissure.

Frustration (1) The thwarting of a motive. (2) The emotion produced by the thwarting of a motive.

Functional analysis A systematic study of behavior in which one identifies the stimuli that trigger it (antecedents) and the reinforcers that maintain it (consequences).

Functional fixedness The tendency to view an object in terms of its name or familiar usage; an impediment to creative problem solving.

Functionalism The school of psychology, founded by William James, that emphasizes the uses or functions of the mind.

Fundamental attribution error A bias in social perception characterized by the tendency to assume that others act predominantly on the basis of their dispositions, even when there is evidence suggesting the importance of their situations.

G

g Spearman's symbol for general intelligence, a general factor that he hypothesized underlay more specific abilities.

Galvanic skin response A sign of sympathetic arousal detected by the amount of sweat in the hand. The greater the amount of sweat, the more electricity is conducted across the skin, suggesting greater sympathetic arousal. Abbreviated *GSR*.

Ganglia Plural of *ganglion*. A group of neural cell bodies found elsewhere in the body other than the brain or spinal cord.

Ganglion See *ganglia*.

Ganglion cells Neurons whose axons form the optic fiber.

Ganzfeld procedure In ESP research, a method for studying telepathy in which a "sender" tries to mentally transmit information to a "receiver" whose eyes and ears are covered. (*Ganzfeld* is German for "whole field.")

GAS Abbreviation for general adaptation syndrome.

Gay male A male who is sexually aroused by and interested in forming romantic relationships with other males.

Gender The state of being female or male.

Gender constancy The concept that one's gender remains the same, despite superficial changes in appearance or behavior.

Gender identity One's psychological sense of being female or male.

Gender polarization The tendency in Western culture to view women and men as opposites in terms of personality and appropriate behavior patterns.

Gender role A complex cluster of behaviors that characterizes traditional female or male behaviors.

Gender-schema theory The view that gender identity plus knowledge of the distribution of behavior patterns into feminine and masculine roles motivates and guides the gender-typing of the child.

Gender stability The concept that one's gender is a permanent feature.

Gender-typing The process by which people acquire a sense of being female or male and acquire the traits considered typical of females or males within a given cultural setting.

Gene The basic building block of heredity, which consists of deoxyribonucleic acid (DNA).

General adaptation syndrome Selye's term for a theoretical three-stage response to stress. Abbreviated *GAS*.

General anesthetics Methods that control pain by putting a person to sleep.

Generalization (1) The process of going from the particular to the general. (2) In conditioning, the tendency for a conditioned response to be evoked by stimuli that are similar to the stimulus to which the response was conditioned.

Generalized anxiety disorder Feelings of dread and foreboding and sympathetic arousal of at least six months' duration.

Generativity versus stagnation Erikson's seventh stage of psychosocial development; the middle years during which persons find (or fail to find) fulfillment in expressing creativity and in guiding and encouraging the younger generation.

Genetic counseling Advice or counseling that concerns the probability that a couple's offspring will have genetic abnormalities.

Genetics The branch of biology that studies heredity.

Genital stage In psychodynamic theory, the fifth and mature stage of psychosexual development, characterized by preferred expression of libido through intercourse with an adult of the opposite gender.

Genuineness Recognition and open expression of one's feelings. A quality of the good person-centered therapist.

Germinal stage The first stage of prenatal development during which the dividing mass of cells has not become implanted in the uterine wall.

Gestalt psychology The school of psychology that emphasizes the tendency to organize perceptions into wholes, to integrate separate stimuli into meaningful patterns.

Gestalt therapy Fritz Perls's form of psychotherapy which attempts to integrate conflicting parts of the personality through directive methods designed to help clients perceive their whole selves.

Glaucoma An eye disease characterized by increased fluid pressure within the eye. A cause of blindness.

Glial cells Cells that nourish and insulate neurons, direct their growth, and remove waste products from the nervous system.

Grasp reflex An infant reflex in which an object placed on the palms or soles is grasped. Also called *palmar* or *plantar reflex*.

Gray matter In the spinal cord, the neurons and neural segments that are involved in spinal reflexes. They are gray in appearance. Also see *white matter*.

Groupthink A process in which group members, as they make decisions, are influenced by cohesiveness and a dynamic leader to ignore external realities.

Growth hormone A pituitary hormone that regulates growth.

Growth hormone releasing factor A hormone produced by the hypothalamus that causes the pituitary to secrete growth hormone.

GSR Abbreviation for *galvanic skin response*.

H

Habit A response to a stimulus that becomes automatic with repetition.

Habituate To become accustomed to a stimulus, as determined by no longer showing a response to the stimulus.

Hallucination A sensory experience in the absence of sensory stimulation that is confused with reality.

Hallucinogenic Giving rise to hallucinations.

Halo effect The tendency for one's general impression of a person to influence one's perception of aspects of, or performances by, that person.

Hammer A bone of the middle ear.

Hashish A psychedelic drug derived from the resin of *Cannabis sativa*. Often called "hash."

Hassle A source of annoyance or aggravation.

Health psychology The field of psychology that studies the relationships between psychological factors (e.g., attitudes, beliefs, situational influences, and overt behavior patterns) and the prevention and treatment of physical illness.

Hebephrenic schizophrenia See *disorganized schizophrenia.*

Heredity The transmission of traits from one generation to another through genes.

Heroin A powerful opioid that provides a euphoric "rush" and feelings of well-being.

Hertz A unit expressing the frequency of sound waves. One Hertz, or *1 Hz*, equals one cycle per second.

Heterosexual A person who is sexually aroused by, and interested in forming romantic relationships with, people of the other gender.

Heuristic device A rule of thumb that helps us simplify and solve problems.

Higher-order conditioning (1) According to cognitive psychologists, the learning of relations among events, none of which evokes an unlearned response. (2) According to behaviorists, a classical-conditioning procedure in which a previously neutral stimulus comes to elicit the response brought forth by a *conditioned* stimulus by being paired repeatedly with that conditioned stimulus.

Hippocampus A part of the limbic system of the brain that plays an important role in the formation of new memories.

Histogram A graphic representation of a frequency distribution that uses rectangular solids.

HIV See *Human immunodeficiency virus.*

Holocaust The name given the Nazi murder of millions of Jews during World War II.

Holophrase A single word used to express complex meanings.

Homeostasis The tendency of the body to maintain a steady state, such as body temperature or level of sugar in the blood.

Homosexuality See *sexual orientation, gay male, lesbian.*

Homunculus Latin for "little man." A homunculus within the brain was once thought to govern human behavior.

Hormone A substance secreted by an endocrine gland that promotes development of body structures or regulates bodily functions.

Horoscope A forecast based on astrological (pseudoscientific) principles. (From Greek roots referring to observation *[skopos]* of the hour *[hora]* during which one was born.)

Hot reactors People who respond to stress with accelerated heart rate and constriction of blood vessels in peripheral areas of the body.

Hue The color of light, as determined by its wavelength.

Human factors The field that studies the efficiency and safety of person-machine systems and work environments.

Human immunodeficiency virus The virus that gives rise to acquired immune deficiency syndrome (AIDS) by destroying cells of the immune system and leaving the body prey to opportunistic diseases. Abbreviated *HIV*. Sometimes referred to as "the AIDS virus."

Humanism The philosophy (and school of psychology) that asserts that people are conscious, self-aware, and capable of free choice, self-fulfillment, and ethical behavior.

Humanistic psychology The school of psychology that assumes the existence of the self and emphasizes the importance of consciousness, self-awareness, and the freedom to make choices.

Hyperactivity A disorder found most frequently in young boys, characterized by restlessness and short attention span. It is thought to reflect immaturity of the nervous system.

Hyperglycemia A disorder caused by excess sugar in the blood that can lead to coma and death.

Hypermnesia Greatly enhanced memory.

Hyperphagic Characterized by excessive eating.

Hypertension High blood pressure.

Hyperthyroidism A condition caused by excess thyroxin and characterized by excitability, weight loss, and insomnia.

Hypnagogic state The drowsy interval between waking and sleeping, characterized by brief, hallucinatory, dreamlike experiences.

Hypnosis A condition in which people appear to be highly suggestible and behave as though they are in a trance.

Hypoactive sexual desire disorder Persistent or recurrent lack of sexual fantasies and of interest in sexual activity.

Hypochondriasis Persistent belief that one has a medical disorder despite the lack of medical findings.

Hypoglycemia A metabolic disorder that is characterized by shakiness, dizziness, and lack of energy. It is caused by a low level of sugar in the blood.

Hypothalamus A bundle of nuclei below the thalamus involved in the regulation of body temperature, motivation, and emotion.

Hypothesis An assumption about behavior that is tested through research.

Hypothesis testing In concept formation, an active process in which we try to ferret out the meanings of concepts by testing our assumptions.

Hypothyroidism A condition caused by a deficiency of thyroxin and characterized by sluggish behavior and a low metabolic rate.

Hysterical disorder, conversion type Former term for *conversion disorder.*

I

Icon A mental representation of a visual stimulus that is held briefly in sensory memory.

Iconic memory The sensory register that briefly holds mental representations of visual stimuli.

Id In psychodynamic theory, the psychic structure that is present at birth and that is governed by the pleasure principle. The id represents physiological drives and is fully unconscious.

Ideas of persecution Erroneous beliefs (delusions) that one is being victimized or persecuted.

Identification (1) In psychodynamic theory, unconscious incorporation of the personality of another person. (2) In social-cognitive theory, a broad, continuous process of imitation during which children strive to become like role models.

Identity crisis According to Erikson, a period of inner conflict during which one examines his or her values and makes decisions about life roles.

Identity diffusion See *role diffusion.*

Ill-defined problem A problem in which the original state, the goal, or the rules are less than clear.

Illusions Sensations that give rise to misperceptions.

Immune system The system of the body that recognizes and destroys foreign agents (antigens) that invade the body.

Imprinting A process that occurs during a critical period in an organism's development, in which that organism forms an attachment that will afterward be difficult to modify.

Incentive An object, person, or situation perceived as being capable of satisfying a need.

Incest taboo The cultural prohibition against marrying or having sexual relations with a close blood relative.

Incidence The extent to which an event occurs.

Incubation In problem solving, a hypothetical process that sometimes occurs when we stand back from a frustrating problem for a while and the solution suddenly appears.

Incus A bone of the middle ear. Latin for "anvil."

Independent variable A condition in a scientific study that is manipulated so that its effects may be observed.

Indiscriminate attachment The showing of attachment behaviors toward any person.

Individualist A person who defines herself or himself in terms of personal traits and gives priority to her or his own goals.

Individual psychology Adler's psychodynamic theory which emphasizes feelings of inferiority and the creative self.

Individuation The process by which one separates from others and gains control over one's own behavior.

Inductive reasoning A form of reasoning in which we reason from individual cases or particular facts to a general conclusion.

Industrial psychology The field of psychology that studies the relationships between people and work.

Industry versus inferiority Erikson's fourth stage of psychosocial development in which the child is challenged to master the fundamentals of technology during the primary school years.

Infant A very young organism, a baby.

Infantile autism A developmental disorder of childhood, characterized by extreme aloneness, communication problems, preservation of sameness, and ritualistic behavior.

Infer Draw a conclusion.

Inference Conclusion.

Inferential statistics The branch of statistics concerned with the confidence with which conclusions drawn about samples may be extended to the populations from which they were drawn.

Inferiority complex Feelings of inferiority hypothesized by Adler to serve as a central source of motivation.

Inflammation Increased blood flow to an injured area of the body, resulting in redness, warmth, and increased supply of white blood cells.

Inflections Grammatical markers that change the forms of words to indicate grammatical relationships such as number and tense.

Information processing The processes by which information is encoded, stored, and retrieved.

Informed consent Agreement to participate in research after receiving information about the purposes of the study and the nature of the treatments.

Inhibited orgasm Persistent or recurrent delay in, or absence of, orgasm in a sexually excited person who has been engaging in sexually stimulating activity.

Inhibited sexual desire Lack of interest in sexual activity, usually accompanied by absence of sexual fantasies.

Inhibited sexual excitement Persistent lack of sexual response during sexual activity.

Inhibitory synapse A synapse that influences receiving neurons in the direction of not firing by encouraging changes in their membrane permeability in the direction of the resting potential.

Initial-preattachment phase According to Ainsworth, the first phase in forming bonds of attachment, which is characterized by indiscriminate attachment.

Initiative versus guilt Erikson's third stage of psychosocial development, during which the child is challenged to add planning and "attacking" to the exercise of choice.

Innate Existing at birth. Unlearned, natural.

Innate fixed-action pattern An instinct.

Inner ear The cochlea.

Insanity A legal term descriptive of a person judged to be incapable of recognizing right from wrong or of conforming his or her behavior to the law.

Insecure attachment A negative type of attachment, in which children show indifference or ambivalence toward attachment figures.

Insight (1) In Gestalt psychology, the sudden perception of relationships among elements of the perceptual field, allowing the sudden solution of a problem. (2) In psychotherapy, awareness of one's genuine motives and feelings.

Insomnia A term for three types of sleeping problems: (1) difficulty falling asleep (sleep-onset insomnia); (2) difficulty remaining asleep; and (3) waking early.

Instinct An inherited disposition to activate specific behavior patterns that are designed to reach certain goals. Also termed *fixed action pattern.*

Instinctive Inborn, natural, unlearned.

Instrumental conditioning Another term for *operant conditioning,* reflecting the fact that in operant conditioning, the learned behavior is instrumental in achieving certain effects.

Instrumental learning See *instrumental conditioning.*

Insulin A pancreatic hormone that stimulates the metabolism of sugar.

Intellectualization A defense mechanism in which threatening events are viewed with emotional detachment.

Intelligence A complex and controversial concept: (1) Learning ability, as contrasted with achievement. (2) Defined by David Wechsler as the "capacity . . . to understand the world [and the] resourcefulness to cope with its challenges."

Intelligence quotient (1) Originally, a ratio obtained by dividing a child's mental age on an intelligence test by his or her chronological age. (2) Generally, a score on an intelligence test. Abbreviated *IQ.*

Interactionism An approach to understanding behavior that emphasizes specification of the relationships among the various determinants of behavior instead of seeking the first cause of behavior.

Interference theory The view that we may forget stored material because other learning interferes with it.

"Internals" People who have an internal locus of control—who perceive the ability to attain reinforcements as being largely within themselves.

Interneuron A neuron that transmits a neural impulse from a sensory neuron to a motor neuron, or to another associative neuron. Also termed *associative neuron*.

Interpersonal attraction See *attraction*.

Interposition A monocular cue for depth based on the fact that closer objects obscure vision of objects behind them.

Interpretation In psychoanalysis, an analyst's explanation of a client's utterance according to psychodynamic theory.

Intimacy versus isolation Erikson's sixth stage of psychosocial development; the young adult years during which persons are challenged to commit themselves to intimate relationships with others.

Intonation The use of pitches of varying levels to help communicate meaning.

Intoxication Drunkenness.

Intrapsychic Referring to the psychodynamic movement of psychic energy among the psychic structures hypothesized by Sigmund Freud.

Introjection In psychodynamic theory, the bringing within oneself of the personality of another individual.

Introspection An objective approach to describing one's mental content.

Introversion A trait characterized by intense imagination and the tendency to inhibit impulses. Opposite of *extraversion*.

Intuitive The direct learning or knowing of something without conscious use of reason.

Involuntary Automatic, not consciously controlled—referring to functions like heartbeat and dilation of the pupils.

IQ Intelligence quotient. A score on an intelligence test.

Iris A muscular membrane whose dilation regulates the amount of light that enters the eye.

J

James-Lange theory The theory that certain external stimuli trigger stereotypical patterns of activity and autonomic arousal. Emotions are the cognitive representations of this behavior and arousal.

Just noticeable difference The minimal amount by which a source of energy must be increased or decreased so that a difference in intensity will be perceived. Abbreviated *jnd*.

K

Kinesthesis The sense that provides information about the position and motion of parts of the body.

Knobs Swellings at the ends of axon terminals. Also referred to as *bulbs* or *buttons*.

Korsakoff syndrome See *Wernicke-Korsakoff syndrome*.

L

La belle indifférence A French term descriptive of the lack of concern shown by some persons with conversion disorder.

LAD Acronym for *language acquisition device*.

Language The communication of information through symbols that are arranged according to rules of grammar.

Language acquisition device In psycholinguistic theory, neural "prewiring" that is theorized to facilitate the child's learning of grammar. Abbreviated *LAD*.

Larynx The structure in the throat that contains the vocal cords.

Latency stage In psychodynamic theory, the fourth stage of psychosexual development during which sexual impulses are repressed.

Latent content In psychodynamic theory, the symbolized or underlying content of dreams.

Latent learning Learning that is not exhibited at the time of learning but is shown when adequate reinforcement is introduced.

Lateral fissure The valley in the cerebral cortex that separates the temporal lobe from the frontal and parietal lobes.

Lateral hypothalamus An area at the side of the hypothalamus that appears to function as a start-eating center.

Law of effect Thorndike's principle that responses are "stamped in" by rewards and "stamped out" by punishments.

Learned helplessness A model for the acquisition of depressive behavior, based on findings that organisms in aversive situations learn to show inactivity when their operants are not reinforced.

Learning (1) According to cognitive theorists, the process by which organisms make relatively permanent changes in the way they represent the environment because of experience. These changes influence the organism's behavior. (2) According to behaviorists, a relatively permanent change in behavior that results from experience.

Lens A transparent body between the iris and the vitreous humor of the eye that focuses an image onto the retina.

Lesbian A female who is sexually aroused by, and interested in forming romantic relationships with, other females.

Lesion An injury that results in impaired behavior or loss of a function.

Leukocytes The white blood cells of the immune system.

Libido (1) In psychodynamic theory, the energy of Eros, the sexual instinct. (2) Generally, sexual interest or drive.

Lie detector See *polygraph*.

Life-change units Numbers assigned to various life events that indicate the degree of stress they cause.

Light Electromagnetic energy of various wavelengths. The part of the spectrum of energy that stimulates the eye and produces visual sensations.

Limbic system A group of brain structures that form a fringe along the inner edge of the cerebrum. These structures are involved in memory and motivation.

Linguistic relativity hypothesis The view that language structures the way in which we perceive the world. As a consequence, our thoughts would be limited by the concepts available in our languages.

Linguists Scientists who study the structure, functions, and origins of language.

Locus of control The place (locus) to which an individual attributes control over the receiving of reinforcements—either inside or outside the self.

Long-term memory The type or stage of memory capable of relatively permanent storage.

Love A strong, positive emotion with many meanings. See, for example, *romantic love* and *attachment.*

LSD Lysergic acid diethylamide. A hallucinogenic drug.

Lysergic acid diethylamide A hallucinogenic drug. Abbreviated *LSD.*

M

Magnetic resonance imaging Formation of a computer-generated image of the anatomical details of the brain by measuring the signals that these structures emit when the head is placed in a strong magnetic field. Abbreviated *MRI.*

Maintenance rehearsal Mental repetition of information in order to keep it in memory.

Major depression A severe mood disorder in which the person may show loss of appetite, psychomotor symptoms, and impaired reality testing.

Major tranquilizer A drug that decreases severe anxiety or agitation in psychotic patients or in violent individuals.

Male erectile disorder A sexual dysfunction characterized by difficulty in becoming sexually aroused, as defined by achieving erection, or in sustaining arousal long enough to engage in satisfying sexual relations.

Malingering Pretending to be ill to escape duty or work.

Malleus A bone of the middle ear. Latin for "hammer."

Mania A state characterized by elation and restlessness. (A Greek word meaning "madness.")

Manic-depression Former term for *bipolar disorder.*

Manifest content In the psychodynamic theory of dreams, the reported or perceived content of dreams.

Mantra A word or sound that is repeated in transcendental meditation as a means of narrowing consciousness and inducing relaxation.

Marijuana The dried vegetable matter of the *Cannabis sativa* plant. A mild hallucinogenic drug that is most frequently taken in by smoking.

Masochism The attainment of gratification, frequently sexual, through the receiving of pain or humiliation.

Masturbation Self-stimulation of the sexual organs.

Matching hypothesis The view that people tend to choose persons similar to themselves in attractiveness and attitudes in the formation of interpersonal relationships.

Maturation Changes that result from heredity and minimal nutrition but that do not appear to require learning or exercise. A gradual, orderly unfolding or developing of new structures or behaviors as a result of heredity.

Mean A type of average calculated by dividing the sum of scores by the number of scores.

Means-end analysis A heuristic device in which we try to solve a problem by evaluating the difference between the current situation and the goal.

Median A type of average defined as the score beneath which 50% of the cases fall.

Mediation In information processing, a method of improving memory by linking two items with a third that ties them together.

Medical model The view that abnormal behavior is symptomatic of underlying illness.

Meditation A systematic narrowing of attention that slows the metabolism and helps produce feelings of relaxation.

Medulla An oblong-shaped area of the hindbrain involved in heartbeat and respiration.

Meiosis A process of reduction division in which sperm and ova are formed, each of which contains 23 chromosomes.

Memory The processes by which information is encoded, stored, and retrieved.

Memory trace An assumed change in the nervous system that reflects the impression made by a stimulus. Memory traces are said to be "held" in sensory registers.

Menarche The onset of menstruation.

Menopause The cessation of menstruation.

Menstrual synchrony The convergence of the menstrual cycles of women who spend time in close quarters.

Menstruation The monthly shedding of the uterine lining by nonpregnant women.

Mental age The accumulated months of credit that a test taker earns on the Stanford-Binet Intelligence Scale.

Mental set (1) Readiness to respond to a situation in a set manner. (2) In problem-solving, a tendency to respond to a new problem with an approach that was successful with similar problems.

Mescaline A hallucinogenic drug derived from the mescal (peyote) cactus. In religious ceremonies, Mexican Indians chew the buttonlike structures at the tops of the rounded stems of the plant.

Metabolism In organisms, a continuous process that converts food into energy.

Metacognition Awareness and control of one's cognitive abilities, as shown by the intentional use of cognitive strategies in solving problems.

Metamemory Self-awareness of the ways in which memory functions, as shown by use of cognitive strategies to foster the effective encoding, storing, and retrieval of information.

Methadone An artificial narcotic that is slower acting than, and does not provide the rush of, heroin. Methadone allows heroin addicts to abstain from heroin without experiencing an abstinence syndrome.

Methaqualone An addictive depressant often referred to as "ludes."

Method of constant stimuli A psychophysical method for determining thresholds in which the researcher presents stimuli of various magnitudes and asks the subject to report detection.

Method of loci A method of retaining information in which chunks of new material are related to a series of well-established or well-known images.

Method of savings A measure of retention in which the difference between the number of repetitions originally required to learn a list and the number of repetitions required to relearn the list after a certain amount of time has elapsed is calculated.

Middle ear The central part of the ear that contains three small bones, the "hammer," "anvil," and "stirrup."

Midlife crisis According to theorists of adult development, a crisis experienced by many people at about age 40 when they realize that life may be halfway over and they feel trapped in meaningless life roles.

Migraine headache A throbbing headache, usually occurring on one side of the head, that stems from change in the blood supply to the head. It is often accompanied by nausea and impaired vision.

Mind That part of consciousness that is involved in perception and awareness.

Minor tranquilizer A drug that relieves feelings of anxiety and tension.

Mitosis The process of cell division by which the identical genetic code is carried into new cells in the body.

Mnemonics A system for remembering in which items are related to easily recalled sets of symbols such as acronyms, phrases, or jingles.

Mode A type of average defined as the most frequently occurring score in a distribution.

Model In social-cognitive theory: (1) As a noun, an organism that engages in a response that is imitated by another organism. (2) As a verb, to engage in behavior patterns that are imitated by others.

Monoamine oxidase inhibitors Antidepressant drugs that work by blocking the action of an enzyme that breaks down norepinephrine and serotonin. Abbreviated *MAO inhibitors*.

Monochromat A person who is sensitive to the intensity of light only and thus color-blind.

Monocular cues Stimuli that suggest depth and that can be perceived with only one eye, such as perspective and interposition.

Monozygotic twins Twins who develop from the same zygote, thus carrying the same genetic instructions. Identical twins. Abbreviated *MZ twins*. See *dizygotic twins*.

Moral principle In psychodynamic theory, the governing principle of the superego, which sets moral standards and enforces adherence to them.

Moro reflex An infant reflex characterized by arching of the back and drawing up of the legs in response to a sudden, startling stimulus. Also called the *startle reflex*.

Morpheme The smallest unit of meaning in a language.

Morphine A narcotic derived from opium that reduces pain and produces feelings of well-being.

Morphology The study of the units of meaning in a language.

Motion parallax A monocular cue for depth based on the perception that nearby objects appear to move more rapidly in relation to our own motion.

Motive A hypothetical state within an organism that propels the organism toward a goal.

Motor cortex The section of cerebral cortex that lies in the frontal lobe, just across the central fissure from the sensory cortex. Neural impulses in the motor cortex are linked to muscular responses.

Multiple approach–avoidance conflict A type of conflict in which a number of goals each produces approach and avoidance motives.

Multiple personality disorder The earlier term for *dissociative identity disorder:* A dissociative disorder in which a person has two or more distinct identities or personalities.

Mutation Sudden variations in the genetic code that usually occur as a result of environmental influences.

Mutism Refusal to talk.

Myelination The process by which the axons of neurons become coated with a fatty, insulating substance.

Myelin sheath A fatty substance that encases and insulates axons, permitting more rapid transmission of neural impulses.

N

Narcolepsy A sleep disorder characterized by uncontrollable seizures of sleep during the waking state.

Narcotics Drugs used to relieve pain and induce sleep. The term is usually reserved for opioids.

Naturalistic observation A method of scientific investigation in which organisms are observed carefully and unobtrusively in their natural environments.

Nature In behavior genetics, inherited influences on behavior, as contrasted with *nurture*.

Nearsightedness Inability to see distant objects with the acuity with which a person with normal vision can see distant objects.

Need A state of deprivation.

Need for achievement The need to master, to accomplish difficult things.

Need for affiliation The need for affiliation; the need to be associated with groups.

Negative correlation A relationship between two variables in which one variable increases as the other variable decreases.

Negative feedback Descriptive of a system in which information that a quantity (e.g., of a hormone) has reached a set point suspends action of the agency (e.g., a gland) that gives rise to that quantity.

Negative instance In concept formation, events that are *not* examples of a concept.

Negative reinforcer A reinforcer that increases the frequency of operant behavior when it is removed. Pain, anxiety, and disapproval usually, but not always, function as negative reinforcers. See *positive reinforcer*.

Neodissociation theory A theory that explains hypnotic events in terms of an ability to divide our awareness so that we can focus on hypnotic instructions and, at the same time, perceive outside sources of stimulation.

Neo-Freudians Theorists in the psychodynamic tradition who usually place less emphasis than Freud did on the importance of sexual impulses and unconscious determinants of behavior. Instead, they place more emphasis than Freud did on conscious motives and rational decision making.

Neonate A newborn child.

Nerve A bundle of axons from many neurons.

Neural impulse The electrochemical discharge (or "firing") of a neuron.

Neuron A nerve cell.

Neurosis One of a number of psychological disorders characterized chiefly by anxiety, feelings of dread and foreboding, and avoidance behavior. Neuroses are theorized to stem from unconscious conflict. (Contemporary systems of classifying psychological disorders focus more on observable behavior and therefore deemphasize this concept.)

Neuroticism   A trait in which a person is given to emotional instability, anxiety, feelings of foreboding, inhibition of impulses, and avoidance behavior.

Neurotransmitter   A chemical substance that is involved in the transmission of neural impulses from one neuron to another.

Nicotine   A stimulant found in tobacco smoke.

Nightmare   A frightening dream that usually occurs during rapid-eye-movement (REM) sleep.

Night terrors   See *sleep terrors.*

Node of Ranvier   A noninsulated segment of an otherwise myelinated axon.

Noise   (1) In signal-detection theory, any unwanted signal that interferes with perception of the desired signal. (2) More generally, a combination of dissonant sounds.

Nonconscious   Descriptive of bodily processes, such as the growing of hair, of which we cannot become conscious. We may know that our hair is growing, but we cannot directly experience the biological process.

Non-rapid-eye-movement sleep   Stages 1 through 4 of sleep, which are not characterized by rapid eye movements. Abbreviated *NREM sleep.*

Nonsense syllables   Meaningless sets of two consonants, with a vowel sandwiched in between, that are used to study memory.

Norepinephrine   A neurotransmitter whose action is similar to that of the hormone *epinephrine* and which may play a role in depression.

Normal curve   A graphic presentation of a normal distribution, showing a bell shape.

Normal distribution   A symmetrical distribution in which approximately two thirds of the cases lie within a standard deviation of the mean. A distribution that represents chance deviations of a variable.

Normative data   Information concerning the behavior of a population.

Novel stimulation   (1) New or different stimulation. (2) A hypothesized primary drive to experience new or different stimulation.

Noxious   Harmful, injurious.

Nuclei   Plural of *nucleus.* A group of neural cell bodies found in the brain or spinal cord.

Nurturance   The quality of nourishing, rearing, and fostering the development of children, animals, or plants.

Nurture   In behavior genetics, environmental influences on behavior, including factors such as nutrition, culture, socioeconomic status, and learning. Contrast with *nature.*

O

Objective   Of known or perceived objects rather than existing only in the mind; real.

Objective morality   According to Piaget, objective moral judgments assign guilt according to the amount of damage done rather than the motives of the actor.

Objective tests   Tests whose items must be answered in a specified, limited manner. Tests that have concrete answers that are considered to be correct.

Object permanence   Recognition that objects removed from sight still exist, as demonstrated in young children by continued pursuit.

Observational learning   In social-cognitive theory, the acquisition of expectations and skills by observing the behavior of others. As opposed to operant conditioning, skill acquisition by means of observational learning occurs without the emission and reinforcement of a response.

Obsession   A recurring thought or image that seems to be beyond control.

Occipital lobe   The lobe of the cerebral cortex that is involved in vision. It lies below and behind the parietal lobe and behind the temporal lobe.

Odor   The characteristic of a substance that makes it perceptible to the sense of smell. An odor is a sample of the molecules of the substance being sensed.

Oedipus complex   In psychodynamic theory, a conflict of the phallic stage in which the boy wishes to possess his mother sexually and perceives his father as a rival in love.

Olfactory   Having to do with the sense of smell.

Olfactory membrane   A membrane high in each nostril that contains receptor neurons for the sense of smell.

Olfactory nerve   The nerve that transmits information about odors from olfactory receptors to the brain.

Opaque   (1) Not permitting the passage of light. (2) In psychoanalysis, descriptive of the analyst, who is expected to hide her or his own feelings from the client.

Operant behavior   Voluntary responses that are reinforced.

Operant conditioning   A simple form of learning in which an organism learns to engage in behavior because it is reinforced.

Operational definition   A definition of a variable in terms of the methods used to create or measure the variable.

Opioid   An addictive drug derived from the opium poppy, or similar in chemical structure, that provides a euphoric rush and depresses the nervous system.

Opponent-process theory   (1) In sensation and perception, the theory that color vision is made possible by three types of cones, some of which respond to red or green light, some to blue or yellow light, and some to the intensity of light only. (2) In motivation and emotion, the view that our emotions trigger opposing emotions.

Optic nerve   The nerve that transmits sensory information from the eye to the brain.

Optimal arousal   A level of arousal at which an organism has the greatest feelings of well-being or functions most efficiently.

Oral fixation   In psychodynamic theory, attachment to objects and behaviors characteristic of the oral stage.

Oral stage   The first stage in Freud's theory of psychosexual development, during which gratification is obtained primarily through oral activities like sucking and biting.

Organizational psychology   The field of psychology that studies the structure and functions of organizations.

Organizing effects The directional effects of sex hormones—for example, along stereotypical masculine or feminine lines.

Organ of Corti The receptor for hearing, which lies on the basilar membrane in the cochlea. Called the command post of hearing, it contains the receptor cells that transmit auditory information to the auditory nerve.

Orgasm The height or climax of sexual excitement, involving involuntary muscle contractions, release of sexual tensions, and, usually, intense subjective feelings of pleasure.

Orienting reflex An unlearned response in which an organism attends to a stimulus.

Osmoreceptors Receptors in the hypothalamus that are sensitive to depletion of fluid in the body.

Osteoporosis A condition caused by calcium deficiency and characterized by brittleness of the bones.

Outer ear The funnel-shaped outer part of the ear that transmits sound waves to the eardrum.

Oval window A membrane that transmits vibrations from the stirrup of the middle ear to the inner ear.

Ovaries The female reproductive organs located in the abdominal cavity. The ovaries produce egg cells (ova) and the hormones estrogen and progesterone.

Overextension Overgeneralizing the use of words into situations in which they do not apply (characteristic of the speech of young children).

Overregularization The formation of plurals and past tenses of irregular nouns and verbs according to rules of grammar that apply to regular nouns and verbs (characteristic of the speech of young children).

Overtones Tones higher in frequency than those played on an instrument. Overtones result from vibrations throughout the instrument.

Ovulation The releasing of an egg cell (ovum) from an ovary.

Oxytocin A pituitary hormone that stimulates labor (childbirth).

P

Paired associates Nonsense syllables presented in pairs in experiments that measure recall. After viewing pairs, participants are shown one member of each pair and asked to recall the other.

Palmar reflex See *grasp reflex.*

Pancreas A gland behind the stomach whose secretions, including insulin, influence the level of sugar in the blood.

Panic disorder The recurrent experiencing of attacks of extreme anxiety in the absence of external stimuli that usually elicit anxiety.

Paradoxical sleep Another term for the period of sleep during which rapid eye movements occur. The term *paradoxical* reflects the fact that brain waves found during REM sleep suggest a level of arousal similar to that shown during the waking state.

Paranoia A rare psychotic disorder in which a person shows a persistent delusional system but not the confusion of the paranoid schizophrenic.

Paranoid personality disorder A disorder characterized by persistent suspiciousness but not the disorganization of paranoid schizophrenia.

Paranoid schizophrenia A subtype of schizophrenia characterized primarily by delusions—commonly of persecution—and by vivid hallucinations.

Paraphilia A disorder in which the person shows sexual arousal in response to unusual or bizarre objects or situations.

Parasympathetic nervous system The branch of the autonomic nervous system that is most active during processes such as digestion and relaxation that restore the body's reserves of energy. See *sympathetic division.*

Parietal lobe The lobe of the cerebral cortex that lies behind the central fissure and that is involved in body senses.

Partial reinforcement One of several types of reinforcement schedules in which correct responses receive intermittent reinforcement, as opposed to *continuous reinforcement.*

Participant modeling A behavior therapy technique in which a client observes and imitates a person who approaches and copes with feared objects or situations.

Passionate love See *romantic love.*

Pathogen An organism such as a bacterium or virus that can cause disease.

Pathological gambler A person who gambles habitually despite consistent losses. A compulsive gambler.

PCP Phencyclidine; a hallucinogenic drug.

Peak experience In humanistic theory, a brief moment of rapture that stems from the realization that one is on the path toward self-actualization.

Pelvic inflammatory disease Inflammation of the woman's abdominal region that is caused by pathogens such as the gonorrhea bacterium and characterized by fever, local pain, and, frequently, fertility problems. Abbreviated *PID.*

Penis envy In psychodynamic theory, jealousy of the male sexual organ attributed to girls in the phallic stage.

Perceived self-efficacy In social-cognitive theory, a person's belief that she or he can achieve goals through her or his own efforts.

Perception The process by which sensations are organized into an inner representation of the world—a psychological process through which we interpret sensory information.

Perceptual organization The tendency to integrate perceptual elements into meaningful patterns.

Performance anxiety Fear concerning whether or not one will be able to perform adequately.

Period of the ovum The period following conception before the developing ovum (now fertilized) has become securely implanted in the uterine wall. Another term for the *germinal stage.*

Peripheral nervous system The part of the nervous system consisting of the somatic nervous system and the autonomic nervous system.

Permeability The degree to which a membrane allows a substance to pass through it.

Personality The distinct patterns of behaviors, including thoughts and feelings, that characterize a person's adaptation to the demands of life.

Personality disorder An enduring pattern of maladaptive behavior that is a source of distress to the individual or to others.

Personality structure One's total pattern of traits.

Personal space A psychological boundary that surrounds a person and permits that person to maintain a protective distance from others.

Person-centered therapy Carl Rogers's method of psychotherapy, which emphasizes the creation of a warm, therapeutic atmosphere that frees clients to engage in self-expression and self-exploration. Also referred to as *client-centered therapy*.

Person variables In social-cognitive theory, determinants of behavior that lie within the person, including competencies, encoding strategies, expectancies, subjective values, and self-regulatory systems and plans.

Perspective A monocular cue for depth based on the convergence (coming together) of parallel lines as they recede into the distance.

Phallic stage In psychodynamic theory, the third stage of psychosexual development, characterized by shifting of libido to the phallic region and by the Oedipus and Electra complexes.

Phallic symbol In psychodynamic theory, an object that represents the penis.

Phencyclidine A hallucinogenic drug whose name is an acronym for its chemical structure. Abbreviated *PCP*.

Phenomenological Having to do with subjective, conscious experience.

Phenothiazines Drugs that act as major tranquilizers and that are effective in treating many cases of schizophrenic disorders.

Phenylketonuria A genetic abnormality transmitted by a recessive gene, in which one is unable to metabolize phenylpyruvic acid, leading to mental retardation. Abbreviated *PKU*.

Pheromones Chemical secretions detected by the sense of smell that stimulate stereotypical behaviors in other members of the same species.

Phi phenomenon The perception of movement as a result of sequential presentation of visual stimuli, as with lights going on and off in a row on a theater marquee.

Phobic disorder Excessive, irrational fear. Fear that is out of proportion to the actual danger and that interferes with one's life. Formerly called *phobic neurosis*.

Phoneme A basic sound in a language.

Phonology The study of the basic sounds in a language.

Photographic memory See *iconic memory*.

Photoreceptors Cells that respond to light. See *rod* and *cone*.

Phrenology An unscientific method of analyzing personality by measurement of the shapes and protuberances of the skull.

Physiological Having to do with the biological functions and vital processes of organisms.

Physiological dependence Addiction to a drug, which occurs when regular usage renders the presence of the drug within the body the normal state.

Physiological drives Unlearned drives with a biological basis, such as hunger, thirst, and avoidance of pain. Also called *primary drives*.

Physiological psychologist See *biological psychologist*.

Pitch The highness or lowness of a sound, as determined by the frequency of the sound waves.

Pituitary gland The body's master gland, located in the brain, that secretes growth hormone, prolactin, antidiuretic hormone, and other hormones.

Placebo A bogus treatment that controls for the effects of expectations. A so-called sugar pill.

Placenta A membrane that permits the exchange of nutrients and waste products between the mother and the fetus but that does not allow the maternal and fetal bloodstreams to mix.

Place theory The theory that the pitch of a sound is determined by the section of the basilar membrane that vibrates in response to it.

Plantar reflex See *grasp reflex*.

Plateau phase An advanced state of sexual arousal that precedes orgasm.

Pleasure principle In psychodynamic theory, the principle that governs the id; the demanding of immediate gratification of instinctive needs.

Polarization (1) In physiological psychology, the readying of a neuron for firing by creating an internal negative charge in relation to the body fluid outside the cell membrane. (2) In social psychology, the taking of an extreme position or attitude on an issue.

Polygenic Determined by more than one gene.

Polygraph An instrument that is theorized to be sensitive to whether or not an individual is telling lies by assessing four measures of arousal: heart rate, blood pressure, respiration rate, and galvanic skin response (GSR). Also called a *lie detector*.

Pons A structure of the hindbrain involved in respiration.

Population A complete group of organisms or events.

Positive correlation A relationship between variables in which one variable increases as the other variable also increases.

Positive instance In concept formation, an example of a concept.

Positive reinforcer A reinforcer that increases the frequency of operant behavior when it is presented. Food and approval are usually, but not always, positive reinforcers. See *negative reinforcer*.

Positron-emission tomography Formation of a computer-generated image of the neural activity of parts of the brain by tracing the amount of glucose used by the various parts. Abbreviated *PET scan*.

Postconventional level According to Kohlberg, a period of moral development during which moral judgments are derived from moral principles and people look to themselves to set moral standards.

Posthypnotic amnesia Inability to recall material presented while hypnotized, following the suggestion of the hypnotist.

Post-traumatic stress disorder A disorder that follows a distressing event outside the range of normal human experience. It is characterized by symptoms such as intense fear, avoidance of stimuli associated with the event, and reliving of the event.

Pragmatics The practical aspects of communication. Adaptation of language to fit the social context.

Precognition The term means ability to foresee the future; however, most psychologists do not believe that this ability exists. (From the Latin *prae-*, meaning "before," and *cognitio*, meaning "knowledge.")

Preconscious In psychodynamic theory, descriptive of material of which one is not currently aware but which can be brought into awareness by focusing one's attention. Also see *unconscious*.

Preconventional level According to Kohlberg, a period of moral development during which moral judgments are based largely on expectation of rewards and punishments.

Prefrontal lobotomy A form of psychosurgery in which a section of the frontal lobe of the brain is severed or destroyed.

Pregenital In psychodynamic theory, characteristic of stages less mature than the genital stage.

Prejudice The unfounded belief that a person or group—on the basis of assumed racial, ethnic, sexual, or other features—will possess negative characteristics or perform inadequately.

Prelinguistic Prior to the development of language.

Premature ejaculation Ejaculation that occurs before the couple are satisfied with the length of sexual relations.

Premenstrual syndrome A cluster of symptoms—which may include tension, irritability, depression, and fatigue—that some women experience before menstruating.

Premise A statement or assertion that serves as the basis for an argument.

Prenatal Prior to birth.

Preoperational stage The second of Piaget's stages of cognitive development, characterized by illogical use of words and symbols, egocentrism, animism, artificialism, and objective moral judgments.

Presbyopia Brittleness of the lens, a condition that impairs visual acuity for nearby objects.

Primacy effect (1) In information processing, the tendency to recall the initial items in a series of items. (2) In social psychology, the tendency to evaluate others in terms of first impressions.

Primary colors Colors that we cannot produce by mixing other hues; colors from which other colors are derived.

Primary drives Unlearned drives; physiological drives.

Primary mental abilities According to Thurstone, the basic abilities that compose human intelligence.

Primary narcissism In psychodynamic theory, the type of autism that describes the newborn child who has not learned that he or she is separate from the rest of the world.

Primary reinforcer A stimulus that has reinforcement value without learning. Examples: food, water, warmth, and pain. See *secondary reinforcer.*

Primary sex characteristics Physical traits that distinguish the sexes and that are directly involved in reproduction.

Primate A member of an order of mammals including monkeys, apes, and human beings.

Prism A transparent triangular solid that breaks down visible light into the colors of the spectrum.

Proactive interference Interference from previously learned material in one's ability to retrieve or recall recently learned material. See *retroactive interference.*

Proband The family member first studied or tested.

Procedural memory Knowledge of ways of doing things; skill memory.

Productivity A property of language; the ability to combine words into unlimited, novel sentences.

Progesterone A sex hormone that promotes growth of the sexual organs and helps maintain pregnancy.

Prognosis A prediction of the probable course of a disease.

Programmed learning A method of learning, based on operant conditioning principles, in which complex tasks are broken down into simple steps. The proper performance of each step is reinforced. Incorrect responses go unreinforced but are not punished.

Progressive relaxation Jacobson's method for reducing muscle tension, which involves alternate tensing and relaxing of muscle groups throughout the body.

Projection In psychodynamic theory, a defense mechanism in which unacceptable ideas and impulses are cast out or attributed to others.

Projective test A psychological test that presents questions for which there is no single correct response. A test that presents ambiguous stimuli into which the test taker projects his or her own personality in making a response.

Prolactin A pituitary hormone that regulates production of milk and, in lower animals, maternal behavior.

Propinquity Nearness.

Prosocial Behavior that is characterized by helping others and making a contribution to society.

Prototype A concept of a category of objects or events that serves as a good example of the category.

Proximity Nearness. The perceptual tendency to group together objects that are near one another.

Proximodistal Proceeding from near to far.

***Psi* communication** The terms means the transfer of information through an irregular or unusual process—not the usual senses. However, most psychologists do not believe that psi communication exists.

Psychedelic Causing hallucinations or delusions or heightening perceptions.

Psychiatrist A physician who specializes in the application of medical treatments to psychological disorders.

Psychic structure In psychodynamic theory, a hypothesized mental structure that helps explain various aspects of behavior. See *id, ego,* and *superego.*

Psychoactive Describing drugs that give rise to psychological effects.

Psychoanalysis The school of psychology, founded by Sigmund Freud, that emphasizes the importance of unconscious motives and conflicts as determinants of human behavior. Also the name of Freud's methods of psychotherapy and clinical investigation.

Psychodynamic Descriptive of Freud's view that various forces move within the personality, frequently clashing, and that the outcome of these clashes determines behavior.

Psychogenic amnesia The earlier term for *dissociative amnesia:* A dissociative disorder marked by loss of episodic memory or self-identity. Skills and general knowledge are usually retained.

Psychogenic fugue The earlier term for *dissociative fugue:* A dissociative disorder in which one experiences amnesia, then flees to a new location.

Psychokinesis The term means ability to manipulate objects by thought processes. However, most psychologists do not believe that this ability exists.

Psycholinguist A psychologist who studies how we perceive and acquire language.

Psycholinguistic theory The view that language learning involves an interaction between environmental influences and an inborn tendency to acquire language. The emphasis is on the innate tendency.

Psychological dependence   Repeated use of a substance as a way of dealing with stress.

Psychological disorders   Patterns of behavior or mental processes that are connected with distress or disability, and are not expected responses to particular events.

Psychological hardiness   A cluster of traits that buffer stress and that are characterized by commitment, challenge, and control.

Psychology   The science that studies behavior and mental processes.

Psychomotor retardation   Slowness in motor activity and, apparently, in thought.

Psychoneuroimmunology   The field that studies the relationships between psychological factors (e.g., attitudes and overt behavior patterns) and the functioning of the immune system.

Psychopath   Another term for a person who shows an antisocial personality disorder.

Psychophysics   The study of the relationships between physical stimuli, such as light and sound, and their perception.

Psychophysiological   Having to do with physical illnesses that are believed to have psychological origins or to be stress-related. Also termed *psychosomatic.*

Psychosexual development   In psychodynamic theory, the process by which libidinal energy is expressed through different erogenous zones during different stages of development.

Psychosexual trauma   A distressing sexual experience that may have lingering psychological effects.

Psychosis   A major psychological disorder in which a person shows impaired reality testing and has difficulty meeting the demands of everyday life.

Psychosocial development   Erikson's theory of personality and development, which emphasizes the importance of social relationships and conscious choice throughout eight stages of development, including three stages of adult development.

Psychosomatic   Having to do with physical illnesses that are believed to have psychological origins or to be stress-related. Also termed *psychophysiological.*

Psychosurgery   Biological treatments in which specific areas or structures of the brain are destroyed to promote psychological changes or to relieve disordered behavior.

Psychotherapy   A systematic interaction between a therapist and a client that brings psychological principles to bear on influencing the client's thoughts, feelings, or behaviors to help that client overcome psychological disorders or adjust to problems in living.

Puberty   The period of early adolescence during which hormones spur rapid physical development.

Punishment   An unpleasant stimulus that suppresses the frequency of the behavior it follows.

Pupil   The apparently black opening in the center of the iris, through which light enters the eye.

Pupillary reflex   The automatic adjusting of the irises to permit more or less light to enter the eye.

Pure research   Research conducted without concern for immediate applications.

R

Random sample   A sample drawn in such a manner that every member of a population has an equal chance of being selected.

Range   A measure of variability; the distance between extreme measures or scores in a distribution.

Rapid-eye-movement sleep   A stage of sleep characterized by rapid eye movements that have been linked to dreaming. Abbreviated *REM sleep.* See also *paradoxical sleep.*

Rapid flight of ideas   Rapid speech and topic changes, characteristic of manic behavior.

Rapid smoking   A type of aversive conditioning in which cigarettes are inhaled every few seconds, making the smoke aversive.

Rational-emotive therapy   Albert Ellis's form of cognitive psychotherapy, which focuses on how irrational expectations create negative feelings and maladaptive behavior, and which encourages clients to challenge and correct these expectations.

Rationalization   In psychodynamic theory, a defense mechanism in which an individual engages in self-deception, finding justifications for unacceptable ideas, impulses, or behaviors.

Reaction formation   In psychodynamic theory, a defense mechanism in which unacceptable impulses and ideas are kept unconscious through the exaggerated expression of opposing ideas and impulses.

Reaction time   The amount of time required to respond to a stimulus.

Readiness   In developmental psychology, referring to a stage in the maturation of an organism when it is capable of engaging in a certain response.

Reality principle   In psychodynamic theory, the principle that guides ego functioning; consideration of what is practical and possible in gratifying needs.

Reality testing   The capacity to form an accurate mental representation of the world, including socially appropriate behavior, reasonably accurate knowledge of the motives of others, undistorted sensory impressions, and self-insight.

Reasoning   The transforming of information to reach conclusions.

Rebound anxiety   Strong anxiety that can attend the suspension of usage of a tranquilizer.

Recall   Retrieval or reconstruction of learned material.

Recency effect   (1) In information processing, the tendency to recall the last items in a series of items. (2) In social psychology, the tendency to evaluate others in terms of the most recent impression.

Receptive vocabulary   The extent of one's knowledge of the meanings of words that are communicated to one by others.

Receptor site   A location on a receiving neuron that is tailored to receive a neurotransmitter.

Recessive trait   In genetics, a trait that is not expressed when the gene or genes involved have been paired with *dominant* genes. However, recessive traits are transmitted to future generations and expressed if paired with other recessive genes. See *dominant trait.*

Reciprocity   (1) Mutual action. Treating others as one is treated. (2) In interpersonal attraction, the tendency to return feelings and attitudes that are expressed about us.

Recognition In information processing, a relatively easy memory task in which one identifies objects or events as having been encountered previously.

Reconstructive memories Memories that are based on the piecing together of memory fragments with general knowledge and expectations rather than a precise picture of the past.

Reflex A simple, unlearned response to a stimulus.

Refractory period (1) In discussion of the nervous system, a period following firing during which a neuron's action potential cannot be triggered. (2) In human sexuality, a period following orgasm when a male is insensitive to further sexual stimulation.

Regression In psychodynamic theory, return to a form of behavior characteristic of an earlier stage of development. As a defense mechanism, regression to less mature behavior is a means of coping with stress.

Reinforcement A stimulus that follows a response and increases the frequency of that response. See *positive* and *negative, primary* and *secondary* reinforcers.

Relative refractory period A phase following the absolute refractory period during which a neuron will fire in response to stronger-than-usual messages from other neurons.

Relaxation response Benson's term for a cluster of responses brought about by meditation that lower the activity of the sympathetic division of the autonomic nervous system.

Relearning A measure of retention. Material is usually relearned more quickly than it is learned initially.

Releaser In ethology, a stimulus that elicits an instinctive response.

Reliability In psychological measurement, consistency. Also see *validity.*

Replication The repetition or duplication of scientific studies in order to double-check their results.

Representativeness heuristic A decision-making heuristic in which people make judgments about events (samples) according to the populations they appear to represent.

Repression In psychodynamic theory, the ejection of anxiety-provoking ideas, impulses, or images from awareness, without the awareness that one is doing so. A defense mechanism.

Resistance During psychoanalysis, a blocking of thoughts, the awareness of which could cause anxiety. The client may miss sessions or verbally abuse the analyst as threatening material is about to be unearthed.

Resistance stage The second stage of the general adaptation syndrome, characterized by prolonged sympathetic activity in an effort to restore lost energy and repair damage. Also called the *adaptation stage.*

Response A movement or other observable reaction to a stimulus.

Response cost A behavior therapy self-control technique in which one uses self-punishment for practicing a bad habit or failing to meet a goal.

Response prevention A behavior therapy self-control technique in which one makes unwanted behaviors difficult or impossible.

Response set A tendency to answer test items according to a bias—for example, with the intention of making oneself appear perfect or bizarre.

Resting potential The electrical potential across the neural membrane when it is not responding to other neurons.

Restriction of the stimulus field A behavior therapy self-control technique in which a problem behavior is gradually restricted from more environments.

Reticular activating system A part of the brain involved in attention, sleep, and arousal. Abbreviated *RAS.*

Retina The area of the inner surface of the eye that contains rods and cones.

Retinal disparity A binocular cue for depth based on the difference of the image cast by an object on the retinas of the eyes as the object moves closer or farther away.

Retrieval The location of stored information and its return to consciousness. The third stage of information processing.

Retroactive interference The interference by new learning in one's ability to retrieve material learned previously. See *proactive interference.*

Retrograde amnesia Failure to remember events that occur prior to physical trauma because of the effects of the trauma.

Reversibility According to Piaget, recognition that processes can be undone, leaving things as they were before. Reversibility is a factor in conservation of the properties of substances. See *conservation* and *concrete operational stage.*

Reward A pleasant stimulus that increases the frequency of the behavior it follows.

Risky shift The tendency to make riskier decisions as a member of a group than as an individual acting independently.

Rod A rod-shaped photoreceptor in the eye that is sensitive to the intensity of light. Rods permit "black and white" vision.

Role diffusion According to Erikson, a state of confusion, insecurity, and susceptibility to the suggestions of others; the probable outcome if ego identity is not established during adolescence.

Role theory A theory that explains hypnotic events in terms of the person's ability to act *as though* he or she were hypnotized. Role theory differs from faking in that people cooperate and focus on hypnotic suggestions instead of cynically pretending to be hypnotized.

Romantic love An intense, positive emotion that involves arousal, a cultural setting that idealizes love, feelings of caring, and the belief that one is in love. Also called *passionate love.* Within Sternberg's triangular model, the kind of love that is characterized by passion and intimacy.

Rooting (1) A reflex in which an infant turns its head toward a touch, such as by the mother's nipple. (2) In adult development, the process of establishing a home, which frequently occurs in the second half of the thirties.

Rorschach Inkblot Test A projective personality test that presents test takers the task of interpreting inkblots.

Rote Mechanical associative learning that is based on repetition.

"Roy G. Biv" A mnemonic device for remembering the colors of the visible spectrum.

S

s Spearman's symbol for specific or "s" factors, which he believed account for individual abilities.

Saccadic eye movement   The rapid jumps made by a reader's eyes as they fixate on different points in the text.

Sadism   The attainment of gratification, frequently sexual, from inflicting pain on, or humiliating, others.

"SAME"   The mnemonic device for remembering that *sensory* neurons are called *a*fferent neurons and that *motor* neurons are termed *e*fferent neurons.

Sample   Part of a population.

Satiety   The state of being satisfied; fullness.

Saturation   The degree of purity of a color, as measured by its freedom from mixture with white or black.

Savings   The difference between the number of repetitions originally required to learn a list and the number of repetitions required to relearn the list after a certain amount of time has elapsed.

Scatter diagram   A graphic presentation formed by plotting the points defined by the intersections of two variables.

Schachter-Singer theory   The theory of emotion that holds that emotions have generally similar patterns of bodily arousal, and that the label we give to an emotion depends on our level of arousal and our cognitive appraisal of our situation.

Schema   A way of mentally representing the world, such as a belief or an expectation, that can influence perception of persons, objects, and situations.

Schizoid personality disorder   A disorder characterized by social withdrawal.

Schizophrenia   A psychotic disorder of at least six months' duration in which thought processes and reality testing are impaired and emotions are not appropriate to one's situation. Also see *schizophreniform disorder, brief reactive psychosis,* and *schizotypal personality disorder.*

Schizophreniform disorder   A disorder whose symptoms resemble schizophrenia but that is relatively brief (two weeks to less than six months in duration).

Schizotypal personality disorder   A disorder characterized by oddities of thought and behavior but not involving bizarre psychotic symptoms. Formerly called *simple schizophrenia.*

Scientific method   A method for obtaining scientific evidence in which a hypothesis is formed and tested.

Secondary colors   Colors derived by mixing primary colors.

Secondary reinforcer   A stimulus that gains reinforcement value through association with other, established reinforcers. Money and social approval are secondary reinforcers. Also called *conditioned reinforcer.* See *primary reinforcer.*

Secondary sex characteristics   Physical traits that differentiate the genders, such as the depth of the voice, but that are not directly involved in reproduction.

Secondary traits   Allport's term for traits that appear in a limited number of situations and govern a limited number of responses.

Secure attachment   A type of attachment characterized by positive feelings toward attachment figures and feelings of security.

Sedative   A drug that soothes or quiets restlessness or agitation.

Selective attention   The focus of consciousness on a particular stimulus.

Selective avoidance   Diverting one's attention from information that is inconsistent with one's attitudes.

Selective exposure   The deliberate seeking of, and attending to, information that is consistent with one's attitudes.

Self   The totality of one's impressions, thoughts, and feelings. The center of consciousness that organizes sensory impressions and governs one's perceptions of the world.

Self-actualization   According to Maslow and other humanistic psychologists, self-initiated striving to become what one is capable of being. The motive for reaching one's full potential, for expressing one's unique capabilities.

Self-efficacy expectations   A kind of expectancy in social-cognitive theory: Beliefs that one can bring about desired changes through one's own efforts.

Self-esteem   One's evaluation of, and the placement of value on, oneself.

Self-fulfilling prophecy   An expectation that is confirmed because of the behavior of those who hold the expectation.

Self-ideal   A mental image of what we believe we ought to be.

Self-insight   In psychodynamic theory, accurate awareness of one's own motives and feelings.

Self-monitoring   A behavior therapy technique in which one keeps a record of his or her behavior in order to identify problems and record successes.

Self-serving bias   The tendency to view one's successes as stemming from internal factors and one's failures as stemming from external factors.

Self theory   The name of Carl Rogers's theory of personality, which emphasizes the importance of self-awareness, choice, and self-actualization.

Semantic code   Mental representation of information according to its meaning.

Semanticity   Meaning. The property of language in which words are used as symbols for objects, events, or ideas.

Semantic memory   General knowledge, as opposed to episodic memory.

Semantics   The study of the relationships between language and objects or events. The study of the meaning of language.

Semicircular canals   Structures of the inner ear that monitor body movement and position.

Sensation   The stimulation of sensory receptors and the transmission of sensory information to the central nervous system.

Sensitive period   In linguistic theory, the period from about 18 months to puberty when the brain is thought to be particularly capable of learning language because of plasticity.

Sensitization   The type of sensory adaptation in which we become more sensitive to stimuli that are low in magnitude. Also called *positive adaptation.*

Sensorimotor stage   The first of Piaget's stages of cognitive development, characterized by coordination of sensory information and motor activity, early exploration of the environment, and lack of language.

Sensorineural deafness   The forms of deafness that result from damage to hair cells or the auditory nerve.

Sensory adaptation   The processes by which organisms become more sensitive to stimuli that are low in magnitude and less sensitive to stimuli that are constant or ongoing in magnitude.

Sensory awareness One of the definitions of consciousness: Knowledge of the environment through perception of sensory stimulation.

Sensory cortex The section of the cerebral cortex that lies in the parietal lobe, just behind the central fissure. Sensory stimulation is projected in this section of cortex.

Sensory deprivation (1) In general, insufficient sensory stimulation. (2) A research method for systematically decreasing the stimuli that impinge on sensory receptors.

Sensory memory The type or stage of memory first encountered by a stimulus. Sensory memory holds impressions briefly, but long enough so that series of perceptions are psychologically continuous.

Sensory register A system of memory that holds information briefly, but long enough so that it can be processed further. There may be a sensory register for every sense.

Septum A part of the limbic system that apparently restrains stereotypically aggressive responses.

Serial position effect The tendency to recall more accurately the first and last items in a series.

Serotonin A neurotransmitter which is involved in mood, sleeping and waking, and eating.

Serotonin reuptake inhibitor An antidepressant medication that works by inhibiting the reuptake of serotonin in the synaptic cleft.

Serum cholesterol A fatty substance (cholesterol) in the blood (serum) that has been linked to heart disease.

Set point A value that the body attempts to maintain. For example, the body tries to maintain a certain weight by adjusting the metabolism.

Sex chromosomes The 23rd pair of chromosomes, which determine whether a child will be male or female.

Sex flush A reddish hue on body surfaces that is caused by vasocongestion during sexual excitement.

Sexism The prejudgment that a person, on the basis of his or her gender, will possess negative traits or perform inadequately.

Sex norms Social rules or conventions that govern the ways in which males and females interact.

Sex role See *gender role.*

Sex therapy A number of cognitive and behavioral methods that seek to reverse sexual dysfunctions by reducing performance anxiety, reversing defeatist expectations, and fostering sexual competencies.

Sex-typing See *gender-typing.*

Sexual apathy Lack of interest in sexual activity.

Sexual dysfunctions Persistent or recurrent problems in achieving or maintaining sexual arousal or in reaching orgasm.

Sexual orientation The directionality of one's erotic and romantic interests—that is, toward people of the other gender, people of the same gender, or in the case of bisexuality, people of both genders. See *heterosexual, gay male, lesbian.*

Sexual response cycle A four-phase process that describes response to sexual stimulation in males and females.

Shadowing A monocular cue for depth based on the fact that opaque objects block light and produce shadows.

Shape constancy The tendency to perceive an object as being the same shape even though its retinal image changes in shape as the object rotates.

Shaping In operant conditioning, a procedure for teaching complex behaviors that at first reinforces approximations of these behaviors.

Short-term memory The type or stage of memory that can hold information for up to a minute or so after the trace of the stimulus decays. Also called *working memory.*

Siblings Brothers and sisters.

Signal-detection theory In psychophysics, the view that the perception of sensory stimuli is influenced by the interaction of physical, biological, and psychological factors.

Similarity As a rule of perceptual organization, the tendency to group together objects that are similar in appearance.

Simple phobia Persistent fear of a specific object or situation.

Simultaneous conditioning A classical conditioning procedure in which the CS and US are presented at the same time, and the CS remains in place until the response occurs.

Situational attribution An assumption that a person's behavior is determined by external circumstances, such as social pressure. Contrast with *dispositional attribution.*

Situational variables In social-cognitive theory, external determinants of behavior, such as rewards and punishments.

Size constancy The tendency to perceive an object as being the same size even as the size of its retinal image changes according to its distance.

Skewed distribution A slanted distribution, drawn out toward the low or high scores.

Sleep-onset insomnia Difficulty falling asleep.

Sleep spindles Short bursts of rapid brain waves that occur during stage 2 sleep.

Sleep terrors Frightening, dreamlike experiences that usually occur during deep stage 4 sleep.

Social-cognitive theory A cognitively oriented learning theory in which observational learning and person variables such as values and expectancies play major roles in individual differences. Also termed *cognitive social-learning theory* or *social-learning theory.*

Social-comparison theory The view that people look to others for cues about how to behave in confusing situations.

Social decision schemes Rules for predicting the final outcome of group decision making on the basis of the initial positions of the members.

Social facilitation The process by which a person's performance is increased when other members of a group engage in similar behavior.

Social influence The area of social psychology that studies the ways in which people influence the thoughts, feelings, and behavior of others.

Socialization Guidance of people—and children in particular—into socially desirable behavior by means of verbal messages, the systematic use of rewards and punishments, and other methods of teaching.

Social-learning theory See *social-cognitive theory.*

Social loafing The process by which a person's performance is decreased as a function of being a member of a group.

Social motives Learned or acquired motives such as the needs for achievement and affiliation.

Social norms Explicit and implicit rules that reflect social expectations and influence the ways people behave in social situations.

Social perception A subfield of social psychology that studies the ways in which we form and modify impressions of others.

Social phobias Irrational fears that involve themes of public scrutiny.

Social psychology The field of psychology that studies the nature and causes of people's thoughts, feelings, and behavior in social situations.

Sociobiology A biological theory of social behavior that assumes that the underlying purpose of behavior is to ensure the transmission of an organism's genes from generation to generation.

Sociocultural perspective The perspective in psychology that focuses on the roles of ethnicity, gender, culture, and socioeconomic status in personality formation, behavior, and mental processes.

Sociopath Another term for a person who shows an antisocial personality disorder.

Soma Cell body.

Somatic nervous system The division of the peripheral nervous system that connects the central nervous system (brain and spinal cord) with sensory receptors, muscles, and the surface of the body.

Somatoform disorders Disorders in which people complain of physical (somatic) problems although no physical abnormality can be found. See *conversion disorder* and *hypochondriasis*.

Spectrograph An instrument that converts sounds to graphs or pictures according to their acoustic qualities.

Sphincter A ringlike muscle that circles a body opening such as the anus. An infant will exhibit the sphincter reflex (have a bowel movement) in response to intestinal pressure.

Spinal cord A column of nerves within the spine that transmits messages from the sensory receptors to the brain and from the brain to muscles and glands throughout the body.

Spinal reflex A simple, unlearned response to a stimulus that may involve only two neurons.

Split-brain operation An operation in which the corpus callosum is severed, usually in an effort to control epileptic seizures.

Split-half reliability A method for determining the internal consistency of a test (an index of reliability) by correlating scores attained on half the items with scores attained on the other half of the items.

Spontaneous recovery Generally, the recurrence of an extinguished response as a function of the passage of time. In classical conditioning, the eliciting of a conditioned response by a conditioned stimulus after some time has elapsed following the extinction of the conditioned response. In operant conditioning, the performance of an operant in the presence of discriminative stimuli after some time has elapsed following the extinction of the operant.

Sports psychology The field of psychology that studies the nature, causes, and modification of the behavior and mental processes of people involved in sports.

Stage In developmental psychology, a distinct period of life that is qualitatively different from other stages. Stages follow one another in an orderly sequence.

Standard deviation A measure of the variability of a distribution, obtained by taking the square root of the sum of difference scores squared divided by the number of scores.

Standardization The process of setting standards for a psychological test, accomplished by determining how a population performs on it. Standardization permits psychologists to interpret individual scores as deviations from a norm.

Standardized tests Tests for which norms are based on the performance of a range of individuals.

Stapes A bone of the middle ear. Latin for "stirrup."

Startle reflex See *Moro reflex*.

State-dependent memory Information that is better retrieved in the physiological or emotional state in which it was encoded (stored) or learned.

Statistically significant difference As indicated by inferential statistics, a difference between two groups that is so large that it is not probable that it results from chance fluctuation.

Statistics Numerical facts assembled in such a manner that they provide useful information about measures or scores.

Stereotype A fixed, conventional idea about a group.

Steroids A family of hormones that includes testosterone, estrogen, progesterone, and corticosteroids.

Stimulant A drug that increases the activity of the nervous system.

Stimuli Plural of *stimulus*.

Stimulus (1) A feature in the environment that is detected by an organism or that leads to a change in behavior (a response). (2) A form of physical energy, such as light or sound that impinges on the sensory receptors.

Stimulus control A behavior therapy self-control technique in which one places oneself in an environment in which desired responses are likely to occur.

Stimulus discrimination The eliciting of a conditioned response by only one of a series of similar stimuli.

Stimulus generalization The eliciting of a conditioned response by stimuli that are similar to the conditioned stimulus.

Stimulus motives Motives to increase the stimulation impinging on an organism.

Stimulus-outcome relations A kind of expectancy in social-cognitive theory: Predictions as to what events will follow certain stimuli or signs.

Stirrup A bone of the middle ear.

Storage The maintenance of information over time. The second stage of information processing.

Strabismus A visual disorder in which the eyes point in different directions and thus do not focus simultaneously on the same point.

Stratified sample A sample drawn in such a way that known subgroups within a population are represented in proportion to their numbers in the population.

Stress The demand made on an organism to adjust or adapt.

Stressor An event or stimulus that acts as a source of stress.

Stroboscopic motion A visual illusion in which the perception of motion is generated by presentation of a series of stationary images in rapid succession.

Structuralism The school of psychology, founded by Wilhelm Wundt, that argues that the mind consists of three basic elements—sensations, feelings, and images—that combine to form experience.

Structure-of-intellect model Guilford's three-dimensional model of intelligence, which focuses on the operations, contents, and products of intellectual functioning.

Stupor A condition in which the senses and thought processes are dulled.

Subject A participant in a scientific study. Many psychologists consider this term dehumanizing and no longer use it in reference to human participants.

Subjective Of the mind; personal; determined by thoughts and feelings rather than by external objects.

Subjective morality According to Piaget, subjective moral judgments assign guilt according to the motives of the actor. See *objective morality.*

Subjective value The desirability of an object or event.

Sublimation In psychodynamic theory, a defense mechanism in which primitive impulses—usually sexual or aggressive—are channeled into positive, constructive activities.

Subordinate Descriptive of a lower (included) class or category in a hierarchy; contained by another class; opposite of *superordinate.*

Substance abuse Persistent use of a substance despite the fact that it is disrupting one's life.

Substance dependence A term whose definition is in flux: Substance dependence is characterized by loss of control over use of a substance, but some professionals consider *physiological* dependence, as typified by tolerance, withdrawal, or both, is essential to the definition.

Successive approximations In operant conditioning, a series of behaviors that gradually become more similar to a target behavior.

Superego In psychodynamic theory, the psychic structure that is governed by the moral principle, sets forth high standards for behavior, and floods the ego with feelings of guilt and shame when it falls short.

Superordinate Descriptive of a higher (including) class or category in a hierarchy, containing another class; opposite of *subordinate.*

Suppression The deliberate, or conscious, placing of certain ideas, impulses, or images out of awareness. Contrast with *repression.*

Surface structure The superficial construction of a sentence as defined by the placement of words.

Survey A method of scientific investigation in which large samples of people answer questions.

Symbol Something that stands for or represents another thing.

Sympathetic nervous system The branch of the autonomic nervous system that is most active when the person is engaged in behavior or experiencing feeling states that spend the body's reserves of energy, such as fleeing or experiencing fear or anxiety.

Synapse A junction between neurons, consisting of a terminal knob of a transmitting neuron, the space between the neurons (synaptic cleft), and a dendrite or soma of a receiving neuron.

Synaptic cleft The space between neurons, across which messages are transmitted by means of neurotransmitters.

Syndrome A cluster of symptoms characteristic of a disorder.

Syntax The rules in a language for placing words in proper order to form meaningful sentences.

Syphilis A sexually transmitted disease.

Systematic desensitization A behavior therapy fear-reduction technique in which a hierarchy of fear-evoking stimuli are presented while the person remains in a state of deep muscle relaxation.

Systematic random search An algorithm for solving problems in which each possible solution is tested according to a particular set of rules.

T

TA Abbreviation for *transactional analysis.*

Tactile Of the sense of touch.

Target behavior Goal.

Task analysis The breaking down of a job or behavior pattern into its component parts.

Taste aversion A kind of classical conditioning in which a previously desirable or neutral food comes to be perceived as repugnant because it is associated with aversive stimulation.

Taste buds The sensory organs for taste. They contain taste cells and are located on the tongue.

Taste cells Receptor cells that are sensitive to taste.

TAT Thematic Apperception Test.

Telegraphic speech Speech in which only the essential words are used, as in a telegram.

Telepathy The term refers to the direct transference of thought from one person to another. However, most psychologists do not believe that telepathy exists.

Temporal lobe The lobe of the cerebral cortex that is involved in hearing. It lies below the lateral fissure, near the temples.

Terminal A small branching structure found at the tip of an axon.

Territory In sociobiology, the particular area acquired and defended by an animal, or pair of animals, for purposes of feeding and breeding.

Tertiary colors Colors derived by mixing primary and adjoining secondary colors.

Tertiary prevention In community psychology, the treatment of ripened psychological problems. (See *primary* and *secondary prevention.*)

Testes The male reproductive organs that produce sperm and the hormone testosterone.

Testosterone A male sex hormone (steroid) that is produced by the testes and promotes growth of male sexual characteristics and sperm.

Test-retest reliability A method for determining the reliability of a test by comparing (correlating) test takers' scores on separate occasions.

Texture gradient A monocular cue for depth based on the perception that nearby objects appear to have rougher or more detailed surfaces.

Thalamus An area near the center of the brain that is involved in the relay of sensory information to the cortex and in the functions of sleep and attention.

THC Delta-9-tetrahydrocannabinol. The major active ingredient in marijuana.

Thematic Apperception Test (TAT) A projective test devised by Henry Murray to measure needs through the production of fantasy.

Theory A formulation of relationships underlying observed events. A theory involves assumptions and logically derived explanations and predictions.

Theory of social comparison The view that people look to others for cues about how to behave when they are in confusing or unfamiliar situations.

Theta waves Slow brain waves produced during the hypnagogic state.

Thinking Mental activity that is involved in understanding, manipulating, and communicating about information. Thinking entails paying attention to information, mentally representing it, reasoning about it, and making decisions about it.

Threshold The point at which a stimulus is just strong enough to produce a response.

Thyroxin The thyroid hormone that increases the metabolic rate.

Timbre The quality or richness of a sound. The quality that distinguishes the sounds of one musical instrument from those of another.

Time out In operant conditioning, a method for decreasing the frequency of undesired behaviors by removing an organism from a situation in which reinforcement is available as a consequence of showing the undesired behavior.

Tip-of-the-tongue phenomenon The feeling that information is stored in memory although it cannot be readily retrieved. Also called the *feeling-of-knowing experience.*

TM Transcendental meditation.

Token economy A controlled environment in which people are reinforced for desired behaviors with tokens (such as poker chips) that may be exchanged for privileges.

Tolerance Habituation to a drug, with the result that increasingly higher doses of the drug are required to achieve similar effects.

Tolerance for frustration Ability to delay gratification, to maintain self-control when a motive is thwarted.

Top-down processing The use of contextual information or knowledge of a pattern to organize parts of the pattern.

Total immersion A method of teaching a second language in which all instruction is carried out in the second language.

Trace conditioning A classical conditioning procedure in which the CS is presented and then removed before the US is presented.

Trait A distinguishing quality or characteristic of personality that is inferred from behavior and assumed to account for consistency in behavior.

Tranquilizers Drugs used to reduce anxiety and tension. See *minor* and *major* tranquilizer.

Transactional analysis A form of psychotherapy that deals with how people interact and how their interactions reinforce attitudes, expectations, and "life positions." Abbreviated *TA.*

Transcendental meditation The simplified form of meditation brought to the United States by the Maharishi Mahesh Yogi in which one focuses on a repeated mantra. Abbreviated *TM.*

Transference In psychoanalysis, the generalization to the analyst of feelings toward another person in the client's life.

Treatment In experiments, a condition obtained by participants and whose effects are observed by the researchers.

Trial In conditioning, a presentation of the stimuli.

Trial and error In operant conditioning, refers to behavior that occurs prior to learning what behavior is reinforced. The implication is that in a novel situation, the organism happens upon the first correct (reinforced) response by chance.

Triangular model Sternberg's model of love, which refers to combinations of passion, intimacy, and decision/commitment.

Triarchic Governed by three (referring to Sternberg's triarchic theory of intelligence).

Trichromat A person with normal color vision.

Trichromatic theory The theory that color vision is made possible by three types of cones, some of which respond to red light, some to green, and some to blue.

Tricyclic antidepressants Antidepressant drugs that work by preventing the reuptake of norepinephrine and serotonin by transmitting neurons.

Trust versus mistrust The first of Erikson's stages of psychosocial development, during which the child comes to (or not to) develop a basic sense of trust in others.

Trying 20s Sheehy's term for the third decade of life, which is frequently characterized by preoccupation with advancement in the career world.

Two-point threshold The least distance by which two rods touching the skin must be separated before an individual will report that there are two rods, not one, on 50% of occasions.

Type In personality theory, a group of traits that cluster in a meaningful way.

Type A behavior Behavior characterized by a sense of time urgency, competitiveness, and hostility.

U

Umbilical cord A tube between the mother and her fetus through which nutrients and waste products are conducted.

Unconditional positive regard In self theory, a consistent expression of esteem for the basic value of a person, but not necessarily an unqualified endorsement of all that person's behaviors. A quality shown by the person-centered therapist.

Unconditioned response An unlearned response. A response to an unconditioned stimulus. Abbreviated *UR.*

Unconditioned stimulus A stimulus that elicits a response from an organism without learning. Abbreviated *US.*

Unconscious In psychodynamic theory, descriptive of ideas and feelings that are not available to awareness, in many instances because of the *defense mechanism* of *repression.*

Unobtrusive Not interfering.

Uplifts Notable pleasant daily conditions and experiences.

UR Unconditioned response.

US Unconditioned stimulus.

Uterus The hollow organ within women in which the embryo and fetus develop.

V

Vaccination   Purposeful infection with a small amount of an antigen, or weakened antigen, so that in the future the immune system will recognize and efficiently destroy the antigen.

Vaginismus   Persistent or recurrent spasm of the muscles surrounding the outer part of the vaginal barrel, making entry difficult or impossible.

Validity   The degree to which a test or instrument measures or predicts what it is supposed to measure or predict. Also see *reliability.*

Validity scale   A group of test items that suggests whether or not the results of a test are valid—whether a person's test responses accurately reflect his or her traits.

Variable   A condition that is measured or controlled in a scientific study. A variable can be altered in a measurable manner.

Variable-interval schedule   A partial reinforcement schedule in which a variable amount of time must elapse between the previous and subsequent times that reinforcement is available.

Variable-ratio schedule   A partial reinforcement schedule in which reinforcement is provided after a variable number of correct responses.

Vasopressin   Another term for *antidiuretic hormone.*

Ventromedial nucleus   A central area on the underside of the hypothalamus that appears to function as a stop-eating center. Abbreviated *VMN.*

Vestibular sense   The sense that provides information about the position of the body relative to gravity. Also referred to as the sense of *equilibrium.*

Visible light   The band of electromagnetic energy that produces visual sensations.

Visual accommodation   Automatic adjustment of the thickness of the lens in order to focus on objects.

Visual acuity   Keenness or sharpness of vision.

Visual capture   The tendency of vision to dominate the other senses.

Visual code   Mental representation of information as a picture.

Volley principle   A modification of the *frequency theory* of pitch perception. The hypothesis that groups of neurons may be able to achieve the effect of firing at very high frequencies by "taking turns" firing—that is, by firing in volleys.

Volt   A unit of electrical potential.

W

Waxy flexibility   A symptom of catatonic schizophrenia in which the person maintains a posture or position into which he or she is placed.

Weaning   Accustoming the child not to suck the mother's breast or a baby bottle.

Weber's constant   The fraction of the intensity by which a source of physical energy must be increased or decreased so that a difference in intensity will be perceived.

Well-defined problem   A problem in which the original state, the goal, and the rules for reaching the goal are clearly spelled out.

Wernicke-Korsakoff syndrome   An alcohol-related disorder that is characterized by loss of memory and that is thought to reflect nutritional deficiency.

Wernicke's aphasia   An aphasia caused by damage to Wernicke's area of the brain. It is characterized by difficulty comprehending the meaning of spoken language and by the production of language that is grammatically correct but confused or meaningless in content.

White matter   In the spinal cord, axon bundles that carry messages from and to the brain.

White noise   Discordant sounds of many frequencies, which often produce a lulling effect.

Wish fulfillment   In psychodynamic theory, a primitive method used by the id—such as in fantasy and dreams—to attempt to gratify basic impulses.

Working memory   See *short-term memory.*

Y

Yerkes-Dodson law   The principle that a high level of arousal increases performance on a relatively simple task, whereas a low level of arousal increases performance on a relatively complex task.

Z

Zygote   A fertilized egg cell or ovum.

AAUW (1992). *How schools shortchange women: The A.A.U.W. report.* Washington, DC: American Association of University Women Educational Foundation.

Abbey, A. (1987). Misperceptions of friendly behavior as sexual interest. *Psychology of Women Quarterly, 11,* 173–194.

Abeles, N. (1997a). Psychology and the aging revolution. *APA Monitor, 28*(4), 2.

Abeles, N. (1997b). Memory problems in later life. *APA Monitor, 28*(6), 2.

Aber, J. L., & Allen, J. P. (1987). Effects of maltreatment of young children on young children's socioemotional development. *Developmental Psychology, 23,* 406–414.

Abramowitz, A. J., & O'Leary, S. G. (1991). Behavioral interventions for the classroom. *School Psychology Review, 20,* 220–234.

Abramowitz, J. S. (1997). Effectiveness of psychological and pharmacological treatments for obsessive-compulsive disorder. *Journal of Consulting and Clinical Psychology, 65,* 44–52.

Ackerman, P. L., & Heggestad, E. D. (1997). Intelligence, personality, and interests. *Psychological Bulletin, 121,* 219–245.

Ader, D. N., & Johnson, S. B. (1994). Sample description, reporting, and analysis of sex in psychological research. *American Psychologist, 49,* 216–218.

Ader, R. (1993). Conditioned responses. In B. Moyers (Ed.), *Healing and the mind.* New York: Doubleday.

Adeyemo, S. A. (1990). Thinking imagery and problem-solving. *Psychological Studies, 35,* 179–190.

Adler, N. E., and others (1994). Socioeconomic status and health. *American Psychologist, 49,* 15–24.

Adler, T. (1990). Distraction, relaxation can help "shut off" pain. *APA Monitor, 21*(9), 11.

Adler, T. (1993a). Shy, bold temperament? It's mostly in the genes. *APA Monitor, 24*(1), 7, 8.

Adler, T. (1993b). Sleep loss impairs attention—and more. *APA Monitor, 24*(9), 22–23.

Agras, W. S., & Kirkley, B. G. (1986). Bulimia: Theories of etiology. In K. D. Brownell & J. P. Foreyt (Eds.), *Handbook of eating disorders.* New York: Basic Books.

Agras, W. S., Southam, M. A., & Taylor, C. B. (1983). Long-term persistence of relaxation-induced blood pressure lowering during the working day. *Journal of Consulting and Clinical Psychology, 51,* 792–794.

AIDS hotline. (1997). Personal communications.

Ainsworth, M. D. S., Blehar, M. C., Waters, E., & Wall, S. (1978). *Patterns of attachment: A psychological study of the strange situation.* Hillsdale, NJ: Erlbaum.

Ainsworth, M. D. S., & Bowlby, J. (1991). An ethological approach to personality development. *American Psychologist, 46,* 333–341.

Akhtar, N., & Bradley, E. J. (1991). Social information processing deficits of aggressive children. *Clinical Psychology Review, 11,* 621–644.

Albert Ellis Institute. (1997). Albert Ellis Institute for Rational Emotive Behavior Therapy Brochure, September '97–March '98. New York: Author.

Aldag, R. J., & Fuller, S. R. (1993). Beyond fiasco: A reappraisal of the groupthink phenomenon and a new model of group decision processes. *Psychological Bulletin, 113,* 533–552.

Allen, L. (1993, August). Integrating a sociocultural perspective into the psychology curriculum. G. Stanley Hall lecture presented to the American Psychological Association, Toronto, Canada.

Allison, K. W., Crawford, I., Echemendia, R., Robinson, L. V., & Knepp, D. (1994). Human diversity and professional competence. *American Psychologist, 49,* 792–796.

Alloy, L. B., Abramson, L. Y., & Dykman, B. M. (1990). Depressive realism and nondepressive optimistic illusions. In R. E. Ingram (Ed.), *Contemporary psychological approaches to depression.* New York: Plenum.

Allport, G. W., & Oddbert, H. S. (1936). Trait names: A psycholexical study. *Psychological Monographs, 47,* 2–11.

Altman, L. K. (1997, January 19). With AIDS advance, more disappointment. *The New York Times,* pp. A1, A14.

Amabile, T. M. (1990). Within you, without you: The social psychology of creativity, and beyond. In M. A. Runco & R. S. Albert (Eds.), *Theories of creativity.* Newbury Park, NY: Sage.

American Association of University Women. (1992). *How schools shortchange women: The A.A.U.W. report.* Washington, DC: A.A.U.W. Educational Foundation.

American Psychiatric Association (1994). *Diagnostic and statistical manual of the mental disorders* (4th ed.). Washington, DC: Author.

American Psychological Association (1992a). *Big world, small screen: The role of television in American society.* Washington, DC: Author.

American Psychological Association (1992b). Ethical principles of psychologists and code of conduct. *American Psychologist, 47,* 1597–1611.

American Psychological Association (1992c). *Guidelines for ethical conduct in the care and use of animals.* Washington, DC: Author.

American Psychological Association. (1993). Guidelines for providers of psychological services to ethnic, linguistic, and culturally diverse populations. *American Psychologist, 48,* 45–48.

American Psychological Association. (1994). *Publication manual of the American Psychological Association* (4th ed.). Washington, DC: Author.

American Psychological Association (1996, 1997). Personal communications.

Andersen, B. L. (1992). Psychological interventions for cancer patients to enhance the quality of life. *Journal of Consulting and Clinical Psychology, 60,* 552–568.

Andersen, B. L. (1996). Psychological and behavioral studies in cancer prevention and control. *Health Psychology, 15,* 411–412.

Andersen, B. L., Kiecolt-Glaser, J. K., & Glaser, R. (1994). A biobehavioral model of cancer stress and disease course. *American Psychologist, 49,* 389–404.

Anderson, C. A., & DeNeve, K. M. (1992). Temperature, aggression, and the negative affect escape model. *Psychological Bulletin, 111,* 347–351.

Anderson, J. R. (1991). Is human cognition adaptive? *Behavioral and Brain Sciences, 14,* 471–517.

Andrews, B., & Brown, G. W. (1993). Self-esteem and vulnerability to depression. *Journal of Abnormal Psychology, 102,* 565–572.

Angell, M. (1993). Privilege and health—What is the connection? *New England Journal of Medicine, 329,* 126–127.

Angier, N. (1993, August 13). Scientists detect a genetic key to Alzheimer's. *The New York Times,* pp. A1, A12.

Angier, N. (1994a). Benefits of broccoli confirmed as chemical blocks tumors. *The New York Times,* p. C11.

Angier, N. (1994b). Factor in female sexuality. *The New York Times,* p. C13.

Angier, N. (1995, May 14). Why science loses women in the ranks. *The New York Times,* p. E5.

Angier, N. (1996, January 2). Variant gene tied to a love of new thrills. *The New York Times,* pp. A1, B11.

Angier, N. (1997a). Chemical tied to fat control could help trigger puberty. *The New York Times,* pp. C1, C3.

Annunziata, J., & Jacobson-Kram, P. (1995). *Solving your problems together.* Washington, DC: American Psychological Association.

Antonuccio, D. (1995). Psychotherapy for depression: No stronger medicine. *American Psychologist, 50,* 452–454.

Appel, L. J., and others. (1997). A clinical trial of the effects of dietary patterns on blood pressure. *New England Journal of Medicine, 336,* 1117–1124.

Apter, T. (1995). *Secret paths.* New York: W. W. Norton.

Archer, J. (1996). Sex differences in social behavior. *American Psychologist, 51,* 909–917.

Archer, S. L. (1991). Gender differences in identity development. In R. M. Lerner, A. C. Peterson, & J. Brooks-Gunn (Eds.), *Encyclopedia of Adolescence, I.* New York: Garland.

Arnold, D. H., Lonigan, C. J., Whitehurst, G. J., &

Epstein, J. N. (1994). Accelerating language development through picture book reading. *Journal of Educational Psychology, 86,* 235–243.

Asch, S. E. (1952). *Social psychology.* Englewood Cliffs, NJ: Prentice-Hall.

Atkinson, R. C. (1975). Mnemotechnics in second-language learning. *American Psychologist, 30,* 821–828.

Atkinson, R. C., & Shiffrin, R. M. (1968). Human memory: A proposed system and its control processes. In K. Spence (Ed.), *The psychology of learning and motivation* Vol. 2. New York: Academic Press.

Audrain, J. E., Klesges, R. C., & Klesges, L. M. (1995). Relationship between obesity status and the metabolic effects of smoking in women. *Health Psychology, 14,* 116–123.

Ayanian, J. Z. (1993). Heart disease in Black and White. *New England Journal of Medicine, 329,* 656–658.

Ayllon, T., & Haughton, E. (1962). Control of the behavior of schizophrenic patients by food. *Journal of the Experimental Analysis of Behavior, 5,* 343–352.

Azar, B. (1994a). Women are barraged by media on "the change." *APA Monitor, 25*(5), 24–25.

Azar, B. (1994b). Outcomes measurement is debated by profession. *APA Monitor, 25*(5), 29.

Azar, B. (1994c). Computers create global research lab. *APA Monitor, 25*(8), 1–16.

Azar, B. (1994d). Research made easier by computer networks. *APA Monitor, 25*(8), 16.

Azar, B. (1995a). Several genetic traits linked to alcoholism. *APA Monitor, 26*(5), 21–22.

Azar, B. (1995b). Which traits predict job performance? *APA Monitor, 26*(7), 30–31.

Azar, B. (1995c). Breaking through barriers to creativity. *APA Monitor, 26*(8), 1, 20.

Azar, B. (1996a). Musical studies provide clues to brain functions. *APA Monitor, 27*(4), 1, 24.

Azar, B. (1996b). Scientists examine cancer patients' fears. *APA Monitor, 27*(8), 32.

Azar, B. (1996c). Studies investigate the link between stress and immunity. *APA Monitor, 27*(8), 32.

Azar, B. (1996d). Research could help patients cope with chemotherapy. *APA Monitor, 27*(8), 33.

Azar, B. (1997a). Poor recall mars research and treatment. *APA Monitor, 28*(1), 1, 29.

Azar, B. (1997b). Environment is key to serotonin levels. *APA Monitor, 28*(4), 26, 29.

Azar, B. (1997c). Nature, nurture: Not mutually exclusive. *APA Monitor, 28*(5), 1, 28.

Azar, B. (1997d). It may cause anxiety, but day care can benefit kids. *APA Monitor, 28*(6), 13.

Babcock, J. C., Waltz, J., Jacobson, N. S., & Gottman, J. M. (1993). Power and violence: The relation between communication patterns, power discrepancies, and domestic violence. *Journal of Consulting and Clinical Psychology, 61,* 40–50.

Bachrach, L. L. (1992). What we know about homelessness among mentally ill persons. In H. R. Lamb, L. L. Bachrach, & F. I. Kass (Eds.), *Treating the homeless mentally ill.* Washington, DC: American Psychiatric Press.

Baddeley, A. (1982). Your memory: A user's guide. New York: Macmillan.

Baddeley, A. (1994). Working memory. In D. L. Schacter & E. Tulving (Eds.), *Memory systems 1994.* Cambridge, MA: The MIT Press, a Bradford Book.

Baenninger, M. A., & Elenteny, K. (1997). Cited in Azar, B. (1997). Environment can mitigate differences in spatial ability. *APA Monitor, 28*(6), 28.

Bagatell, C. J., & Bremner, W. J. (1996). Drug therapy: Androgens in men—Uses and abuses. *New England Journal of Medicine, 334,* 707–714.

Bahrick, H. P., Bahrick, P. O., & Wittlinger, R. P. (1975). Fifty years of memory for names and faces. *Journal of Experimental Psychology: General, 104,* 54–75.

Bailey, J. M., & Pillard, R. C. (1991). A genetic study of male sexual orientation. *Archives of General Psychiatry, 48,* 1089–1096.

Baker, L. A., DeFries, J. C., & Fulker, D. W. (1983). Longitudinal stability of cognitive ability in the Colorado adoption project. *Child Development, 54,* 290–297.

Bal, D. G. (1992). Cancer in African Americans. *Ca-A Cancer Journal for Clinicians, 42,* 5–6.

Baltes, P. B. (1997). On the incomplete architecture of human ontogeny: Selection, optimization, and compensation as foundation of developmental theory. *American Psychologist, 52,* 366–380.

Bandura, A. (1986). *Social foundations of thought and action: A social-cognitive theory.* Englewood Cliffs, NJ: Prentice-Hall.

Bandura, A. (1991). Human agency. *The American Psychologist, 46,* 157–162.

Bandura, A., Blanchard, E. B., & Ritter, B. (1969). The relative efficacy of desensitization and modeling approaches for inducing behavioral, affective, and cognitive changes. *Journal of Personality and Social Psychology, 13,* 173–199.

Bandura, A., & McDonald, F. J. (1963). Influence of social reinforcement and the behavior of models in shaping children's moral judgments. *Journal of Abnormal and Social Psychology, 67,* 274–281.

Bandura, A., Ross, S. A., & Ross, D. (1963). Imitation of film-mediated aggressive models. *Journal of Abnormal and Social Psychology, 66,* 3–11.

Bandura, A., Taylor, C. B., Williams, S. L., Medford, I. N., & Barchas, J. D. (1985). Catecholamine secretion as a function of perceived coping self-efficacy. *Journal of Consulting and Clinical Psychology, 53,* 406–414.

Banks, M. S., & Shannon, E. (1993). Spatial and chromatic visual efficiency in human neonates. In C. E. Granrud (Ed.), *Visual perception and cognition in infancy.* Hillsdale, NJ: Erlbaum.

Banks, S. M., and others. (1995). The effects of message framing on mammography utilization. *Health Psychology, 14,* 178–184.

Baquet, C. R., Horm, J. W., Gibbs, T., & Greenwald, P. (1991). Socioeconomic factors and cancer incidence among Blacks and Whites. *Journal of the National Cancer Institute, 83,* 551–557.

Barbaree, H. E., & Marshall, W. L. (1991). The role of male sexual arousal in rape. *Journal of Consulting and Clinical Psychology, 59,* 621–631.

Barchoff, H. (1997, January 26). Sexual harassment, in uncertain terms. *The New York Times,* p. F15.

Bard, P. (1934). The neurohumoral basis of emotional reactions. In C. A. Murchison (Ed.), *Handbook of general experimental psychology.* Worcester, MA: Clark University Press.

Barlow, D. H. (1991). Introduction to the special issue on diagnoses, definitions, and *DSM-IV*. *Journal of Abnormal Psychology, 100,* 243–244.

Barlow, D. H. (1995). Cited in Goleman, D. (1995, June 21). "Virtual reality" conquers fear of heights. *The New York Times,* p. C11.

Barlow, D. H. (1996). Health care policy, psychotherapy research, and the future of psychotherapy. *American Psychologist, 51,* 1050–1058.

Barnett, W. S., & Escobar, C. M. (1990). Economic costs and benefits of early intervention. In S. J. Meisels & J. P. Shonkoff (Eds.), *Handbook of early childhood intervention,* New York: Cambridge University Press.

Baron, R. A. (1990). Countering the effects of destructive criticism. *Journal of Applied Psychology, 75,* 235–245.

Baron, R. A., & Byrne, D. (1997). *Social psychology* (8th ed.). Boston: Allyn & Bacon.

Barr, C. E., Mednick, S. A., & Munk-Jorgensen, P. (1990). Exposure to influenza epidemics during gestation and adult schizophrenia. *Archives of General Psychiatry, 47,* 869–874.

Barringer, F. (1993a, April 1). Viral sexual diseases are found in 1 of 5 in U.S. *The New York Times,* pp. A1, B9.

Barringer, F. (1993b, April 15). Sex survey of American men finds 1% are gay. *The New York Times,* pp. A1, A18.

Barringer, F. (1993c, April 28). For 32 million Americans, English is a second language. *The New York Times,* p. A18.

Barsalou, L. W. (1992). *Cognitive psychology.* Hillsdale, NJ: Erlbaum.

Bartek, S. E., Krebs, D. L., & Taylor, M. C. (1993). Coping, defending, and the relations between moral judgment and moral behavior in prostitutes and other female juvenile delinquents. *Journal of Abnormal Psychology, 102,* 66–73.

Bartoshuk, L. M., & Beauchamp, G. K. (1994). Chemical senses. *Annual Review of Psychology, 45,* 419–449.

Basen-Engquist, K., Edmundson, E. W., & Parcel, G. S. (1996). Structure of health risk behavior among high school students. *Journal of Consulting and Clinical Psychology, 64,* 764–775.

Bashore, T. R., & Rapp, P. E. (1993). Are there alternatives to traditional polygraph procedures? *Psychological Bulletin, 113,* 3–22.

Basic Behavioral Science Task Force of the National Advisory Mental Health Council. (1996a). Basic behavioral science research for mental health: Vulnerability and resilience. *American Psychologist, 51,* 22–28.

Basic Behavioral Science Task Force of the National Advisory Mental Health Council. (1996b). Basic behavioral science research for mental health: Perception, attention, learning, and memory. *American Psychologist, 51,* 133–142.

Basic Behavioral Science Task Force of the National Advisory Mental Health Council. (1996c). Basic behavioral science research for mental health: Sociocultural and environmental practices. *American Psychologist, 51,* 722–731.

Baucom, D. H., Shoham, V., Mueser, K. T., Daiuto, A. D., & Stickle, T. R. (1998). Empirically supported couple and family interventions for marital distress and adult mental health problems. *Journal of Consulting and Clinical Psychology, 66,* 53–88.

Bauer, P. J. (1996). What do infants recall of their lives? Memory for specific events by one- to two-year-olds. *American Psychologist, 51,* 29–41.

Baum, A., & Fleming, I. (1993). Implications of psychological research on stress and technological accidents. *American Psychologist, 48,* 665–672.

Baum, A., Friedman, A. L., & Zakowski, S. G. (1997). Stress and genetic testing for disease risk. *Health Psychology, 16,* 8–19.

Baumeister, R. F., Stillwell, A. M., & Heatherton, T. F. (1994). Guilt. *Psychological Bulletin, 115,* 243–267.

Baumgardner, A. H., Heppner, P. P., & Arkin, R. M. (1986). Role of causal attribution in personal problem solving. *Journal of Personality and Social Psychology, 50,* 636–643.

Baumrind, D. (1973). The development of instrumental competence through socialization. In A. D. Pick (Ed.), *Minnesota Symposia on Child Development, Vol. 7.* Minneapolis: University of Minnesota Press.

Baumrind, D. (1991a). The influence of parenting style on adolescent competence and substance abuse. *Journal of Early Adolescence, 11,* 56–95.

Baumrind, D. (1991b). Parenting styles and adolescent development. In J. Brooks-Gunn, R. Lerner, & A. C. Petersen (Eds.), *Encyclopedia of Adolescence, II.* New York: Garland.

Baumrind, D. (1993). The average expectable environment is not good enough. *Child Development, 64,* 1299–1317.

Bearak, B. (1997, March 29). Time of puzzled heartbreak binds relatives. *The New York Times,* p. A1.

Beck, A. T. (1991). Cognitive therapy: A 30-year retrospective. *American Psychologist, 46,* 368–375.

Beck, A. T. (1993). Cognitive therapy: Past, present, and future. *Journal of Consulting and Clinical Psychology, 61,* 194–198.

Beck, A. T., Brown, G., Berchick, R. J., Stewart, B. L., & Steer, R. A. (1990). Relationship between hopelessness and ultimate suicide. *American Journal of Psychiatry, 147,* 190–195.

Beck, A. T., & Freeman, A. (1990). *Cognitive therapy of personality disorders.* New York: Guilford.

Becker, L. B., and others. (1993). Racial differences in the incidence of cardiac arrest and subsequent survival. *New England Journal of Medicine, 329,* 600–606.

A behavior transplant. (1997, March 11). *The New York Times,* p. C3.

Bell, A. P., Weinberg, M. S., & Hammersmith, S. K. (1981). *Sexual preference: Its development in men and women.* Bloomington, IN: University of Indiana Press.

Bell, P. A. (1992). In defense of the negative affect escape model of heat and aggression. *Psychological Bulletin, 111,* 342–346.

Belle, D. (1990). Poverty and women's mental health. *American Psychologist, 45,* 385–389.

Belsky, J. (1990). Developmental risks associated with infant day care. I. S. Cherazi (Ed.), *Psychosocial issues in day care* (pp. 37–68). New York: American Psychiatric Press.

Belsky, J. (1993). Etiology of child maltreatment. *Psychological Bulletin, 114,* 413–434.

Belsky, J., Fish, M., & Isabella, R. (1991). Continuity and discontinuity in infant negative and positive emotionality: Family attachments and attachment consequences. *Developmental Psychology, 27,* 421–431.

Bem, D. J., & Honorton, C. (1994). Does Psi exist? Replicable evidence for an anomalous process of information transfer. *Psychological Bulletin, 115,* 4–18.

Bem, S. L. (1993). *The lenses of gender.* New Haven: Yale University Press.

Benbow, C. P. (1991). Meeting the needs of gifted students through use of acceleration. In M. C. Wang, M. C. Reynolds, & H. J. Walberg (Eds.), *Handbook of special education: Research and practice.* Oxford, England: Pergamon.

Benight, C. C., and others. (1997). Coping self-efficacy buffers psychological and physiological disturbances in HIV-infected men following a natural disaster. *Health Psychology, 16,* 248–255.

Benson, H. (1975). *The relaxation response.* New York: Morrow.

Benson, H., Manzetta, B. R., & Rosner, B. (1973). Decreased systolic blood pressure in hypertensive subjects who practiced meditation. *Journal of Clinical Investigation, 52,* 8.

Benson, P. L., Karabenick, S. A., & Lerner, R. M. (1976). Pretty pleases: The effects of physical attractiveness, race, and sex on receiving help. *Journal of Experimental Social Psychology, 12,* 409–415.

Berenbaum, H., & Connelly, J. (1993). The effect of stress on hedonic capacity. *Journal of Abnormal Psychology, 102,* 474–481.

Berger, K. S. (1994). *The developing person through the life span* (3rd ed.). New York: Worth Publishers.

Berke, R. L. (1997, June 15). Suddenly, the new politics of morality. *The New York Times,* p. E3.

Berkowitz, L. (1988). Frustrations, appraisals, and aversively stimulated aggression. *Aggressive Behavior, 14,* 3–11.

Berkowitz, L. (1994). Is something missing? Some observations prompted by the cognitive-neoassociationist view of anger and emotional aggression. In L. R. Huesmann (Ed.), *Aggressive behavior: Current perspectives.* New York: Plenum.

Bernal, M. E., & Castro, F. G. (1994). Are clinical psychologists prepared for service and research with ethnic minorities? *American Psychologist, 49,* 797–805.

Bernstein, I. (1996). Cited in Azar, B. (1996). Research could help patients cope with chemotherapy. *APA Monitor, 27*(8), 33.

Bernstein, W. M., Stephenson, B. O., Snyder, M. L., & Wicklund, R. A. (1983). Causal ambiguity and heterosexual affiliation. *Journal of Experimental Social Psychology, 19,* 78–92.

Berquier, A., & Ashton, R. (1992). Characteristics of the frequent nightmare sufferer. *Journal of Abnormal Psychology, 101,* 246–250.

Betancourt, H., & López, S. R. (1993). The study of culture, ethnicity, and race in American psychology. *American Psychologist, 48,* 629–637.

Bettencourt, B. A., & Miller, N. (1996). Gender differences in aggression as a function of provocation. *Psychological Bulletin, 119,* 422–447.

Bevan, W., & Kessel, F. (1994). Plain truths and home cooking. *American Psychologist, 49,* 505–509.

Bexton, W. H., Heron, W., & Scott, T. H. (1954). Effects of decreased variation in the sensory environment. *Canadian Journal of Psychology, 8,* 70–76.

Bianchi, S. M., & Spain, D. (1997). *Women, work and family in America.* Population Reference Bureau.

Bjork, D. W. (1997). *B. F. Skinner: A life.* Washington, DC: American Psychological Association.

Bjorklund, D. F. (1995). *Children's thinking* (2nd. ed). Pacific Grove, CA: Brooks/Cole.

Bjorklund, D. F., & Kipp, K. (1996). Parental investment theory and gender differences in the evolution of inhibition mechanisms. *Psychological Bulletin, 120,* 163–188.

Blakeslee, S. (1992a, January 7). Scientists unraveling chemistry of dreams. *The New York Times,* pp. C1, C10.

Blakeslee, S. (1992b, January 22). An epidemic of genital warts raises concern but not alarm. *The New York Times,* p. C12.

Blakeslee, S. (1993, September 7). Human nose may hold an additional organ for a real sixth sense. *The New York Times,* p. C3.

Blakeslee, S. (1994, April 13). Black smokers' higher risk of cancer may be genetic. *The New York Times,* p. C14.

Blakeslee, S. (1995, May 16). The mystery of music. *The New York Times,* pp. C1, C10.

Blanchard, E. B. (1992). Psychological treatment of benign headache disorders. *Journal of Consulting and Clinical Psychology, 60,* 537–551.

Blanchard, E. B., and others (1990a). Placebo-controlled evaluation of abbreviated progressive muscle relaxation and of relaxation combined with cognitive therapy in the treatment of tension headache. *Journal of Consulting and Clinical Psychology, 58,* 210–215.

Blanchard, E. B., and others (1990b). A controlled evaluation of thermal biofeedback and thermal feedback combined with cognitive therapy in the treatment of vascular headache. *Journal of Consulting and Clinical Psychology, 58,* 216–224.

Blanchard, E. B., and others (1991). The role of regular home practice in the relaxation treatment of tension headache. *Journal of Consulting and Clinical Psychology, 59,* 467–470.

Blass, T. (1991). Understanding behavior in the Milgram obedience experiment: The roles of personality, situations, and their interactions. *Journal of Personality and Social Psychology, 60,* 398–413.

Blatt, S. J. (1995). The destructiveness of perfectionism: Implications for the treatment of depression. *American Psychologist, 50,* 1003–1020.

Blatt, S. J., Quinlan, D. M., Pilkonis, P. A., & Shea, M. T. (1995). Impact of perfectionism and need for approval on the brief treatment of depression. *Journal of Consulting and Clinical Psychology, 63,* 125–132.

Blatt, S. J., Zuroff, D. C., Quinlan, D. M., & Pilkonis, P. A. (1996). Interpersonal factors in brief treatment of depression. *Journal of Consulting and Clinical Psychology, 64,* 162–171.

Block, J. (1995). A contrarian view of the five-factor approach to personality description. *Psychological Bulletin, 117,* 187–215.

Bloom, B. L. (1992). Computer assisted psychological intervention. *Clinical Psychology Review, 12,* 169–197.

Bloom, L., Merkin, S., & Wootten, J. (1982). Wh-questions: Linguistic factors that contribute to the sequence of acquisition. *Child Development, 53,* 1084–1092.

Bloom, L., & Mudd, S. A. (1991). Depth of processing approach to face recognition. *Journal of Experimental Psychology: Learning, Memory, and Cognition, 17,* 556–565.

Blum, D. (1997). *Sex on the brain: The biological differences between men and women.* New York: Viking.

Bly, R. (1990). *Iron John.* Reading, MA: Addison-Wesley.

Boden, M. A. (1994). What is creativity? In M. A. Boden (Ed.), *Dimensions of creativity.* Cambridge, MA: The MIT Press, a Bradford Book.

Bogen, J. E. (1969). The other side of the brain II: An appositional mind. *Bulletin of the Los Angeles Neurological Society, 34,* 135–162.

Bond, R., & Smith, P. B. (1996). Culture and conformity. *Psychological Bulletin, 119,* 111–137.

Boneau, C. A. (1992). Observations on psychology's past and future. *American Psychologist, 47,* 1586–1596.

Bootzin, R. R., Epstein, D., & Wood, J. N. (1991). Stimulus control instructions. In P. Hauri (Ed.), *Case studies in insomnia.* New York: Plenum.

Borgida, E., & Campbell, B. (1982). Belief relevance and attitude-behavior consistency. *Journal of Personality and Social Psychology, 42,* 239–247.

Boskind-White, M., & White, W. C. (1983). *Bulimarexia: The binge/purge cycle.* New York: W. W. Norton.

Boston Women's Health Book Collective. (1992). *The new our bodies, ourselves.* New York: Simon & Schuster.

Bouchard, T. J., Jr., Lykken, D. T., McGue, M., Segal, N. L., & Tellegen, A. (1990). Sources of human psychological differences: The Minnesota study of twins reared apart. *Science, 250,* 223–228.

Bower, G. H. (1981). Mood and memory. *American Psychologist, 36,* 129–148.

Bowers, K. S., & Woody, E. Z. (1996). Hypnotic amnesia and the paradox of intentional forgetting. *Journal of Abnormal Psychology, 105,* 381–390.

Bowes, J. M., & Goodnow, J. J. (1996). Work for home, school, or labor force. *Psychological Bulletin, 119,* 300–321.

Bowlby, J. (1988). *A secure base.* New York: Basic Books.

Boyatzis, R. E. (1974). The effect of alcohol consumption on the aggressive behavior of men. *Quarterly Journal for the Study of Alcohol, 35,* 959–972.

Boyd-Franklin, N. (1995). A multisystems model for treatment interventions with inner-city African American families. Master lecture delivered to the meeting of the American Psychological Association, New York, August 12.

Bradley, R. H., and others (1989). Home environment and cognitive development in the first 3 years of life. *Developmental Psychology, 25,* 217–235.

Bransford, J. D., Nitsch, K. E., & Franks, J. J. (1977). Schooling and the facilitation of knowing. In R. C. Anderson, R. J. Spiro, & W. E. Montague (Eds.), *Schooling and the acquisition of knowledge.* Hillsdale, NJ: Erlbaum.

Braun, B. G. (1988). *Treatment of multiple personality disorder.* Washington, DC: American Psychiatric Press.

Bray, R. M., & Sugarman, R. (1980). Social facilitation among interaction groups: Evidence for the evaluation-apprehension hypothesis. *Personality and Social Psychology Bulletin, 6,* 137–142.

Brewin, C. R., Andrews, B., & Gotlib, I. H. (1993). Psychopathology and early experience. *Psychological Bulletin, 113,* 82–98.

Bridges, K. (1932). Emotional development in early infancy. *Child Development, 3,* 324–341.

Bridgwater, C. A. (1982). What candor can do. *Psychology Today, 16*(5), 16.

Broberg, A., Hwang, P., Wessels, H., & Lamb, M.

(1997). Cited in Azar, B. (1997). It may cause anxiety, but day care can benefit kids. *APA Monitor, 28*(6), 13.

Brody, J. E. (1991, April 9). Not just music, bird song is a means of courtship and defense. *The New York Times,* pp. C1, C9.

Brody, J. E. (1992a, January 8). Migraines and the estrogen connection. *The New York Times,* p. C12.

Brody, J. E. (1992b, June 17). Psychotherapists warn parents not to dismiss their children's statements about suicide. *The New York Times,* p. B8.

Brody, J. E. (1993, December 1). Liberated at last from the myths about menopause. *The New York Times,* p. C15.

Brody, J. E. (1995a, August 30). Hormone replacement therapy for men. *The New York Times,* p. C8.

Brody, J. E. (1995b). Cited in DeAngelis, T. (1995), Eat well, keep fit, and let go of stress. *APA Monitor, 26*(10), 20.

Brody, J. E. (1996a, August 28). PMS need not be the worry it was just decades ago. *The New York Times,* p. C9.

Brody, J. E. (1996b, September 4). Osteoporosis can threaten men as well as women. *The New York Times,* p. C9.

Brody, J. E. (1997a, March 26). Race and weight. *The New York Times,* p. C8.

Brody, J. E. (1997b, May 7). What is a woman to do to avoid breast cancer? Plenty, new studies suggest. *The New York Times,* p. C12.

Brody, N. (1997). Intelligence, schooling, and society. *American Psychologist, 52,* 1046–1050.

Brown, B. B., & Altman, J. (1981). Territoriality and residential crime. In P. A. Brantingham & P. L. Brantingham (Eds.), *Urban crime and environmental criminology.* Beverly Hills, CA: Sage.

Brown, D. E. (1991). *Human universals.* Philadelphia: Temple University Press.

Brown, J. D., & Rogers, R. J. (1991). Self-serving attributions. *Personality and Social Psychology Bulletin, 17,* 501–506.

Brown, L. S. (1992). A feminist critique of the personality disorders. In L. Brown & M. Balou (Eds.), *Personality and psychopathology: Feminist reappraisals.* New York: Guilford.

Brown, M., & Massaro, S. (1996). New brain studies yield insights into cocaine binging and addiction. *Journal of Addictive Diseases, 15*(4).

Brown, R., & Kulik, J. (1977). Flashbulb memories. *Cognition, 5,* 73–99.

Brown, R., & McNeill, D. (1966). The tip-of-the-tongue phenomenon. *Journal of Verbal Learning and Verbal Behavior, 5,* 325–337.

Browne, A. (1993). Violence against women by male partners. *American Psychologist, 48,* 1077–1087.

Browne, M. W. (1995, June 6). Scientists deplore flight from reason. *The New York Times,* pp. C1, C7.

Brownell, K. D. (1997). We must be more militant about food. *APA Monitor, 28*(3), 48.

Brownell, K. D., & Rodin, J. (1994). The dieting

maelstrom. *American Psychologist, 49,* 781–791.

Brownell, W. E. (1992). Cited in Browne, M. W. (1992, June 9). Ear's own sounds may underlie its precision. *The New York Times,* pp. C1, C8.

Brownlee-Duffeck, M., and others (1987). The role of health beliefs in the regimen adherence and metabolic control of adolescents and adults with diabetes mellitus. *Journal of Consulting and Clinical Psychology, 55,* 139–144.

Buchanan, C. M., Eccles, J. S., & Becker, J. B. (1992). Are adolescents the victims of raging hormones? Evidence for activational effects of hormones on moods and behavior at adolescence. *Psychological Bulletin, 111,* 62–107.

Budd, L. S. (1993). *Living with the active alert child.* St. Paul, MN: Parenting Press.

Buffone, G. W. (1984). Running and depression. In M. L. Sachs & G. W. Buffone (Eds.), *Running as therapy: An integrated approach.* Lincoln: University of Nebraska Press.

Bullock, M. (1997). Cited in Murray, B. (1997). America still lags behind in mathematics test scores. *APA Monitor, 28*(1), 44.

Burman, B., & Margolin, G. (1992). Analysis of the association between marital relationships and health problems. *Psychological Bulletin, 112,* 39–63.

Burnette, E. (1997). "Father of Ebonics" continues his crusade. *APA Monitor, 28*(4), 12.

Burns, D. D., & Nolen-Hoeksema, S. (1992). Therapeutic empathy and recovery from depression in cognitive-behavioral therapy. *Journal of Consulting and Clinical Psychology, 60,* 441–449.

Burnstein, E. (1983). Persuasion as argument processing. In M. Brandstatter, J. H. Davis, & G. Stocker-Kreichgauer (Eds.), *Group decision processes.* London: Academic Press.

Burt, M. R. (1980). Cultural myths and supports for rape. *Journal of Personality and Social Psychology, 38,* 217–230.

Buss, D. M. (1992). Is there a universal human nature? *Contemporary Psychology, 37,* 1262–1263.

Buss, D. M. (1994). *The evolution of desire.* New York: Basic Books.

Buss, D. M. (1995). Psychological sex differences. *American Psychologist, 50,* 164–168.

Butler, R. (1998). Cited in CD-ROM that accompanies Nevid, J. S., Rathus, S. A., & Rubenstein, H. (1998). *Health in the new millennium.* New York: Worth Publishers.

Byrnes, J., & Takahira, S. (1993). Explaining gender differences on SAT–math items. *Developmental Psychology, 29,* 805–810.

Cacioppo, J. T., Martzke, J. S, Petty, R. E., & Tassinary, L. G. (1988). Specific forms of facial EMG response index emotions during an interview. *Journal of Personality and Social Psychology, 54,* 552–604.

Califano, J. A. (1995). The wrong way to stay slim. *New England Journal of Medicine, 333,* 1214–1216.

Campbell, J. (1994). *Past, space, and self.* Cambridge, MA: The MIT Press, A Bradford Book.

Campos, J. J., Hiatt, S., Ramsey, D., Henderson, C., & Svejda, M. (1978). The emergence of fear on the visual cliff. In M. Lewis & L. Rosenblum (Eds.), *The origins of affect.* New York: Plenum.

Cannistra, S. A., & Niloff, J. M. (1996). Cancer of the uterine cervix. *New England Journal of Medicine, 334,* 1030–1038.

Cannon, W. B. (1927). The James-Lange theory of emotions: A critical examination and an alternative theory. *American Journal of Psychology, 39,* 106–124.

Cantor, J. (1997). Cited in Seppa, N. (1997). Children's TV remains steeped in violence. *APA Monitor, 28*(6), 36.

Cappella, J. N., & Palmer, M. T. (1990). Attitude similarity, relational history, and attraction. *Communication Monographs, 5,* 161–183.

Carey, G., & DiLalla, D. L. (1994). Personality and psychopathology: Genetic perspectives. *Journal of Abnormal Psychology, 103,* 32–43.

Carling, P. J. (1990). Major mental illness, housing, and supports. *American Psychologist, 45,* 969–975.

Carlson, J. G., & Hatfield, E. (1992). *Psychology of emotion.* Fort Worth: Harcourt Brace Jovanovich.

Carmichael, L. L., Hogan, H. P., & Walter, A. A. (1932). An experimental study of the effect of language on the reproduction of visually perceived form. *Journal of Experimental Psychology, 15,* 73–86.

Carpenter, W. T., Jr., & Buchanan, R. W. (1994). Schizophrenia. *New England Journal of Medicine, 330,* 681–690.

Carroll, K. M., Rounsaville, B. J., & Nich, C. (1994). Blind man's bluff: Effectiveness and significance of psychotherapy and pharmacotherapy blinding procedures in a clinical trial. *Journal of Consulting and Clinical Psychology, 62,* 276–280.

Carstensen, L. (1997, August 17). The evolution of social goals across the life span. Paper presented to the American Psychological Association, Chicago.

Case, R. (1992). *The mind's staircase.* Hillsdale, NJ: Erlbaum.

Castelli, W. (1994). Cited in Brody, J. E. (1994, February 8). Scientist at work—William Castelli. *The New York Times,* pp. C1, C10.

Cattell, R. B. (1949). The *culture-free intelligence test.* Champaign, IL: Institute for Personality and Ability Testing.

Cattell, R. B. (1965). *The scientific analysis of personality.* Baltimore: Penguin Books.

Caulfield, M., and others (1994). Linkage of the angiotensinogen gene to essential hypertension. *New England Journal of Medicine, 330,* 1629–1633.

Cavaliere, F. (1996). Bilingual schools face big political challenges. *APA Monitor, 27*(2), 36.

Ceci, S. J., & Bruck, M. (1993). Suggestibility of the child witness. *Psychological Bulletin, 113,* 403–439.

Celis, W. (1991, January 2). Students trying to draw line between sex and an assault. *The New York Times,* pp. 1, B8.

Centers for Disease Control (1995). *Suicide surveillance: 1980–1990.* Washington, DC: USDHHS.

Centers for Disease Control and Prevention. (1997). *HIV/AIDS surveillance report: U.S. HIV and AIDS cases reported through December 1996, 8*(2).

Cepeda-Benito, A. (1993). Meta-analytical review of the efficacy of nicotine chewing gum in smoking treatment programs. *Journal of Consulting and Clinical Psychology, 61,* 822–830.

Chadwick, P. D. J., & Lowe, C. F. (1990). Measurement and modification of delusional beliefs. *Journal of Consulting and Clinical Psychology, 58,* 225–232.

Chan, C. (1992). Cultural considerations in counseling Asian American lesbians and gay men. In S. Dworkin & F. Gutierrez (Eds.), *Counseling gay men and lesbians.* Alexandria, VA: American Association for Counseling and Development.

Chassin, L., Curran, P. J., Hussong, A. M., & Colder, C. R. (1996). The relation of parent alcoholism to adolescent substance use. *Journal of Abnormal Psychology, 105,* 70–80.

Chesney, M. A. (1993). Health psychology in the 21st century: Acquired immunodeficiency syndrome as a harbinger of things to come. *Health Psychology 12,* 259–268.

Chesney, M. A. (1996). Cited in Freiberg, P. (1996). New drugs give hope to AIDS patients. *APA Monitor, 27*(6), 28.

Chesno, F. A., & Kilmann, P. R. (1975). Effects of stimulation intensity on sociopathic avoidance learning. *Journal of Abnormal Psychology, 84,* 144–151.

Chitayat, D. (1993, February). Presentation to the Fifth International Interdisciplinary Congress on Women, University of Costa Rica, San Jose, Costa Rica.

Chomsky, N. (1980). Rules and representations. *Behavioral and Brain Sciences, 3,* 1–16.

Chomsky, N. (1991). Linguistics and cognitive science. In A. Kasher (Ed.), *The Chomskyan turn.* Cambridge, MA: Blackwell.

Chronicle of Higher Education (1992, March 18). Pp. A35–A44.

Cimons, M. (1996). Social pressures impede women's health. *APA Monitor, 26*(3), 39–40.

Cinciripini, P. M., Cinciripini, L. G., Wallfisch, A., Haque, W., & Van Vunakis, H. (1996). Behavior therapy and the transdermal nicotine patch. *Journal of Consulting and Clinical Psychology, 64,* 314–323.

Clark, D. M., and others. (1997). Misinterpretation of body sensations in panic disorder. *Journal of Consulting and Clinical Psychology, 65,* 203–213.

Clark, L. A., Watson, D., & Mineka, S. M. (1994). Temperament, personality, and the mood and anxiety disorders. *Journal of Abnormal Psychology, 103,* 103–116.

Clarke-Stewart, K. A. (1990). "The 'effects' of infant day care reconsidered." In N. Fox & G. G. Fein (Eds.), *Infant day care* (pp. 61–86). Norwood, NJ: Ablex.

Clarke-Stewart, K. A. (1991). A home is not a school: The effects of child care on children's development. *Journal of Social Issues, 47,* 105–123.

Clay, R. A. (1996a). Beating the "biological clock" with zest. *APA Monitor, 27*(2), 37.

Clay, R. A. (1996b). Older men are more involved fathers, studies show. *APA Monitor, 27*(2), 37.

Clay, R. A. (1997). Meditation is becoming more mainstream. *APA Monitor, 28*(9), 12.

Clement, J. (1991). Nonformal reasoning in experts and in science students. In J. Voss, D. Perkins, & J. Siegel (Eds.), *Informal reasoning and education.* Hillsdale, NJ: Erlbaum.

Clkurel, K., & Gruzelier, J. (1990). The effects of active alert hypnotic induction on lateral haptic processing. *British Journal of Experimental and Clinical Hypnosis, 11,* 17–25.

Coe, C. (1993). Cited in Adler, T. (1993). Men and women affected by stress, but differently. *APA Monitor, 24*(7), 8–9.

Cohen, L. A. (1987, November). Diet and cancer. *Scientific American,* pp. 42–48, 53–54.

Cohen, R. (1996). Cited in Clay, R. A. (1996). Beating the "biological clock" with zest. *APA Monitor, 27*(2), 37.

Cohen, S., Evans, G. W., Stokols, D., & Krantz, D. S. (1986). *Behavior, health, and environmental stress.* New York: Plenum.

Cohen, S., Tyrrell, D. A. J., & Smith, A. P. (1993). Negative life events, perceived stress, negative affect, and susceptibility to the common cold. *Journal of Personality and Social Psychology, 64,* 131–140.

Cohen, S., & Williamson, G. M. (1991). Stress and infectious disease in humans. *Psychological Bulletin, 109,* 5–24.

Cohn, E. G. (1990). Weather and violent crime. *Environment and Behavior, 22,* 280–294.

Cohn, L. D., Macfarlane, S., Yanez, C., & Imai, W. K. (1995). Risk-perception: Differences between adolescents and adults. *Health Psychology, 14,* 217–222.

Coie, J. D., and others. (1993). The science of prevention. *American Psychologist, 48,* 1013–1022.

Coleman, L. (1990). Cited in Goleman, G. (1990, August 2). The quiet comeback of electroshock therapy. *The New York Times,* p. B5.

Coleman, M., & Ganong, L. H. (1985). Love and sex role stereotypes. *Journal of Personality and Social Psychology, 49,* 170–176.

Collaer, M. L., & Hines, M. (1995). Human behavioral sex differences: A role for gonadal hormones during early development? *Psychological Bulletin, 118,* 55–107.

Collier, G. (1994). *Social origins of mental ability.* New York: Wiley.

Comas-Diaz, L. (1994, February). Race and gender in psychotherapy with women of color. *Winter roundtable on cross-cultural counseling and psychotherapy: Race and gen-*

der. New York: Teachers College, Columbia University.

Compas, B. E., Haaga, D. A. F., Keefe, F. J., Leitenberg, H., & Williams, D. A. (1998). Sampling of empirically supported psychological treatments from health psychology: Smoking, chronic pain, cancer, and bulimia nervosa. *Journal of Consulting and Clinical Psychology, 66,* 89–112.

Condon, J. W., & Crano, W. D. (1988). Inferred evaluation and the relation between attitude similarity and interpersonal attraction. *Journal of Personality and Social Psychology, 54,* 789–797.

Cools, J., Schotte, D. E., & McNally, R. J. (1992). Emotional arousal and overeating in restrained eaters. *Journal of Abnormal Psychology, 101,* 348–351.

Coon, H., Fulker, D. W., DeFries, J. C., & Plomin, R. (1990). Home environment and cognitive ability of 7-year-old children in the Colorado Adoption Project. *Developmental Psychology, 26,* 459–468.

Cooney, J. L., & Zeichner, A. (1985). Selective attention to negative feedback in Type A and Type B individuals. *Journal of Abnormal Psychology, 94,* 110–112.

Cooney, N. L., Litt, M. D., Morse, P. A., Bauer, L. O., & Gaupp, L. (1997). Alcohol cue reactivity, negative-mood reactivity, and relapse in treated alcoholic men. *Journal of Abnormal Psychology, 106,* 243–250.

Coons, P. M. (1994). Confirmation of childhood abuse in child and adolescent cases of multiple personality disorder and dissociative disorder not otherwise specified. *Journal of Nervous and Mental Disease, 182,* 461–464.

Coons, P. M., Bowman, E. S., & Pellow, T. A. (1989). Post-traumatic aspects of the treatment of victims of sexual abuse and incest. *Psychiatric Clinics of North America, 12,* 325–327.

Cooper, J. R., Bloom, F. E., & Roth, R. H. (1991). *The biochemical basis of neuropharmacology.* New York: Oxford University Press.

Cooper, M. L., & Orcutt, H. K. (1997). Drinking and sexual experience on first dates among adolescents. *Journal of Abnormal Psychology, 106,* 191–202.

Corey, L., & Holmes, K. K. (1996). Therapy for HIV infection—What have we learned? *New England Journal of Medicine, 335,* 1142–1144.

Corter, J. E., & Gluck, M. A. (1992). Explaining basic categories: Feature predictability and information. *Psychological Bulletin, 111,* 291–303.

Cose, E. (1997, February 17). Getting past the myths. *Newsweek,* pp. 36–37.

Cousins, N. (1979). *Anatomy of an illness as perceived by the patient.* New York: W. W. Norton.

Cowley, G. (1996, September 16). Attention: Aging men. *Newsweek,* pp. 68–77.

Cox, M. J., Owen, M. T., Henderson, V. K., & Margand, N. A. (1992). Prediction of infant-

father and infant-mother attachment. *Developmental Psychology, 28,* 474–483.

Craik, F. I. M., & Lockhart, R. S. (1972). Levels of processing. *Journal of Verbal Learning and Verbal Behavior, 11,* 671–684.

Craik, F. I. M., & Watkins, M. J. (1973). The role of rehearsal in short-term memory. *Journal of Verbal Learning and Verbal Behavior, 12,* 599–607.

Cramer, R. E., McMaster, M. R., Bartell, P. A., & Dragna, M. (1988). Subject competence and minimization of the bystander effect. *Journal of Applied Social Psychology, 18,* 1133–1148.

Crawford, H. J., & Barabasz, A. (1993). Phobias and fears: Facilitating their treatment with hypnosis. In J. Rhue, S. Lynn, & I. Kirsch (Eds.), *Clinical handbook of hypnosis.* Washington, DC: American Psychological Association.

Crawford, H. J., Brown, A. M., & Moon, C. E. (1993). Sustained attentional and disattentional abilities: Differences between low and highly hypnotizable persons. *Journal of Abnormal Psychology, 102,* 534–543.

Creamer, M., Burgess, P., & Pattison, P. (1992). Reaction to trauma. *Journal of Abnormal Psychology, 101,* 452–459.

Crews, D. (1994). Animal sexuality. *Scientific American, 270*(1), 108–114.

Crick, F., & Koch, C. (1997). The problem of consciousness. *Scientific American mysteries of the mind, Special Issue Vol. 7,* No. 1, 18–26.

Crick, N. R., & Dodge, K. A. (1994). A review and reformulation of social information-processing mechanisms in children's social adjustment. *Psychological Bulletin, 115,* 74–101.

Crowe, R. A. (1990). Astrology and the scientific method. *Psychological Reports, 67,* 163–191.

Croyle, R. T., Smith, K. R., Botkin, J. R., Baty, B., & Nash, J. (1997). Psychological responses to BRCA1 mutation testing. *Health Psychology, 16,* 63–72.

Crusco, A. H., & Wetzel, C. G. (1984). The Midas touch: The effects of interpersonal touch on restaurant tipping. *Personality and Social Psychology Bulletin, 10,* 512–517.

Culbertson, F. M. (1997). Depression and gender. *American Psychologist, 52,* 25–31.

Cunningham, M. R., Shaffer, D. R., Barbee, A. P., Wolff, P. L., & Kelley, D. J. (1990). Separate processes in the relation of elation and depression to helping. *Journal of Experimental Social Psychology, 26,* 13–33.

Curfman, G. D. (1993a). The health benefits of exercise. *New England Journal of Medicine, 328,* 574–576.

Curfman, G. D. (1993b). Is exercise beneficial—or hazardous—to your heart? *New England Journal of Medicine, 329,* 1730–1731.

Curran, P. J., Stice, E., & Chassin, L. (1997). The relation between adolescent alcohol use and peer alcohol use. *Journal of Consulting and Clinical Psychology, 65,* 130–140.

Curtis, R. C., & Miller, K. (1986). Believing another likes or dislikes you: Behavior making the beliefs come true. *Journal of Personality and Social Psychology, 51,* 284–290.

Damaged gene is linked to lung cancer. (1996, April 6.) *The New York Times*, p. A24.

Danforth, J. S., and others (1990). Exercise as a treatment for hypertension in low-socioeconomic-status Black children. *Journal of Consulting and Clinical Psychology, 58,* 237–239.

Daniel, M. H. (1997). Intelligence testing: Status and trends. *American Psychologist, 52,* 1038–1045.

Darley, J. M. (1993). Research on morality. *Psychological Science, 4,* 353–357.

Darley, J. M., & Latané, B. (1968). Bystander intervention in emergencies: Diffusion of responsibility. *Journal of Personality and Social Psychology, 8,* 377–383.

Darwin, C. A. (1872). *The expression of the emotions in man and animals.* London: J. Murray.

Davey, L. F. (1993, March). *Developmental implications of shared and divergent perceptions in the parent-adolescent relationship.* Paper presented at the biennial meeting of the Society for Research in Child Development, New Orleans.

Davidson, J. R., & Foa, E. G. (1991). Diagnostic issues in posttraumatic stress disorder. *Journal of Abnormal Psychology, 100,* 346–355.

Davis, J. H., Tindale, R. S., Nagao, D. H., Hinsz, V. B., & Robertson, B. (1984). Order effects in multiple decisions by groups. *Journal of Personality and Social Psychology, 47,* 1003–1012.

Davis, K. L., Kahn, R. S., Ko, G., & Davidson, M. (1991). Dopamine in schizophrenia. *American Journal of Psychiatry, 148,* 1474–1486.

DeAngelis, T. (1993). It's baaack: TV violence, concern for kid viewers. *APA Monitor, 24*(8), 16.

DeAngelis, T. (1994). Educators reveal keys to success in classroom. *APA Monitor, 25*(1), 39–40.

DeAngelis, T. (1995a). Firefighters' PTSD at dangerous levels. *APA Monitor, 26*(2), 36–37.

DeAngelis, T. (1995b). Mental health care is elusive for Hispanics. *APA Monitor, 26*(7), 49.

DeAngelis, T. (1996). Women's contributions large; recognition isn't. *APA Monitor, 27*(4), 12–13.

DeAngelis, T. (1997a). Body-image problems affect all groups. *APA Monitor, 28*(3), 44–45.

DeAngelis, T. (1997b). Abused children have more conflicts with friends. *APA Monitor, 28*(6), 32.

DeCasper, A. J., & Prescott, P. A. (1984). Human newborns' perception of male voices. *Developmental Psychobiology, 17,* 481–491.

Decline in smoking levels off and officials urge a tax rise. (1993, April 2). *The New York Times,* p. A10.

DeFries, J. C., Plomin, R., & LaBuda, M. C. (1987). Genetic stability of cognitive development from childhood to adulthood. *Developmental Psychology, 23,* 4–12.

de Jong, P. F., & Das-Smaal, E. A. (1995). Attention and intelligence. *Journal of Educational Psychology, 87,* 80–92.

De La Cancela, V., & Guzman, L. P. (1991). Latino mental health service needs. In H. F. Myers and others (Eds.), *Ethnic minority perspectives on clinical training and services in psychology* (pp. 59–64). Washington, DC: American Psychological Association.

Delahanty, D. L., and others. (1996). Time course of natural killer cell activity and lymphocyte proliferation in response to two acute stressors in healthy men. *Health Psychology, 15,* 48–55.

Delgado, J. M. R. (1969). *Physical control of the mind.* New York: Harper & Row.

Denmark, F. L. (1994). Engendering psychology. *American Psychologist, 49,* 329–334.

DePaulo, B. M. (1992). Nonverbal behavior and self-presentation. *Psychological Bulletin, 111,* 203–243.

DeRubeis, R. J., & Crits-Christoph, P. (1998). Empirically supported individual and group psychological treatments for adult mental disorders. *Journal of Consulting and Clinical Psychology, 66,* 37–52.

DeValois, R. L., & Jacobs, G. H. (1984). Neural mechanisms of color vision. In I. Darian-Smith (Ed.), *Handbook of physiology* (Vol. 3). Bethesda, MD: American Physiological Society.

Devine, P. G. (1989). Stereotypes and prejudice. *Journal of Personality and Social Psychology, 56,* 5–18.

Devine, P. G., & Zuwerink, J. R. (1994). Prejudice and guilt: The internal struggle to overcome prejudice. In W. J. Lonner & R. Malpass (Eds.), *Psychology and culture.* Boston: Allyn & Bacon.

DiClemente, C. C., and others (1991). The process of smoking cessation. *Journal of Consulting and Clinical Psychology, 59,* 295–304.

DiLalla, D. L., Carey, G., Gottesman, I. I., & Bouchard, T. J., Jr. (1996). Heritability of MMPI personality indicators of psychopathology in twins reared apart. *Journal of Abnormal Psychology, 105,* 491–499.

DiLalla, D. L., & Gottesman, I. I. (1991). Biological and genetic contributors to violence— Widom's untold tale. *Psychological Bulletin, 109,* 125–129.

Dill, C. A., Gilden, E. R., Hill, P. C., & Hanselka, L. L. (1982). Federal human subjects regulations. *Personality and Social Psychology Bulletin, 8,* 417–425.

Dindia, K., & Allen, M. (1992). Sex differences in self-disclosure. *Psychological Bulletin, 112,* 106–124.

Dix, T. (1991). The affective organization of parenting. *Psychological Bulletin, 110,* 3–25.

Docherty, N. M., and others (1996). Working memory, attention, and communication disturbances in schizophrenia. *Journal of Abnormal Psychology, 105,* 212–219.

Dockery, D. W., and others (1993). An association between air pollution and mortality in six U.S. cities. *New England Journal of Medicine, 329,* 1753–1759.

Doctors tie male mentality to shorter life span. (1995, June 14). *The New York Times,* p. C14.

Dodge, K. A., Price, J. M., Bachorowski, J., &

Newman, J. P. (1990). Hostile attributional biases in severely aggressive adolescents. *Journal of Abnormal Psychology, 99,* 385–392.

Doherty, K., Militello, F. S., Kinnunen, T., & Garvey, A. J. (1996). Nicotine gum dose and weight gain after smoking cessation. *Journal of Consulting and Clinical Psychology, 64,* 799–807.

Dollard, J., Doob, L. W., Miller, N. E., Mowrer, O. H., & Sears, R. R. (1939). *Frustration and aggression.* New Haven, CT: Yale University Press.

Donnerstein, E. I., & Wilson, D. W. (1976). Effects of noise and perceived control on ongoing and subsequent aggressive behavior. *Journal of Personality and Social Psychology, 34,* 774–781.

Doob, A. N., & Wood, L. (1972). Catharsis and aggression. *Journal of Personality and Social Psychology, 22,* 236–245.

Drapkin, R. G., Wing, R. R., & Shiffman, S. (1995). Responses to hypothetical high risk situations. *Health Psychology, 14,* 427–434.

Drobes, D. J., & Tiffany, S. T. (1997). Induction of smoking urge through imaginal and in vivo procedures. *Journal of Abnormal Psychology, 106,* 15–25.

Dubbert, P. M. (1992). Exercise in behavioral medicine. *Journal of Consulting and Clinical Psychology, 60,* 613–618.

Duckitt, J. (1992). Psychology and prejudice. *American Psychologist, 47,* 1182–1193.

Dugan, K. W. (1989). Ability and effort attributions. *Academy of Management Journal, 32,* 87–114.

Dumas, J. E., & LaFreniere, P. J. (1993). Mother-child relationships as sources of support or stress. *Child Development, 64.*

Dunning, J. (1997, July 16). Pursuing perfection: Dancing with death. *The New York Times,* p. C11.

Dweck, C. (1997). Paper presented to the meeting of the Society for Research in Child Development. Cited in Murray, B. (1997). Verbal praise may be the best motivator of all. *APA Monitor, 28*(6), 26.

Eagly, A. H. (1995). The science and politics of comparing women and men. *American Psychologist, 50,* 145–158.

Eagly, A. H., Ashmore, R. D., Makhijani, M. G., & Longo, L. C. (1991). What is beautiful is good, but . . . *Psychological Bulletin, 110,* 109–128.

Eagly, A. H., & Chaiken, S. (1993). *The psychology of attitudes.* Fort Worth: Harcourt Brace Jovanovich.

Eagly, A. H., & Steffen, V. J. (1984). Gender stereotypes stem from the distribution of men and women into social roles. *Journal of Personality and Social Psychology, 46,* 735–754.

Ebbinghaus, H. (1913). *Memory: A contribution to experimental psychology.* (H. A. Roger & C. E. Bussenius, Trans.). New York: Columbia University Press. (Original work published 1885).

Edwards, R. (1995). American Indians rely on

ancient healing techniques. *APA Monitor, 26*(8), 36.

Egeth, H. E. (1993). What do we *not* know about eyewitness identification? *American Psychologist, 48,* 577–580.

Eisenberg, N., Cialdini, R. B., McCreath, H., & Shell, R. (1987). Consistency-based compliance: When and why do children become vulnerable? *Journal of Personality and Social Psychology, 52,* 1174–1181.

Eisenberger, R., & Cameron, J. (1996). Detrimental effects of reward: Reality or myth? *American Psychologist, 51,* 1153–1166.

Ekman, P. (1980). *The face of man.* New York: Garland.

Ekman, P. (1993a). Facial expression and emotion. *American Psychologist, 48,* 384–392.

Ekman, P. (1993b). Cited in D. Goleman (1993, October 26). One smile (only one) can lift a mood. *The New York Times,* p. C11.

Ekman, P. (1994). Strong evidence for universals in facial expression. *Psychological Bulletin, 115,* 268–287.

Ekman, P., and others (1987). Universals and cultural differences in the judgments of facial expressions of emotion. *Journal of Personality and Social Psychology, 53,* 712–717.

Ekman, P., Levenson, R. W., & Friesen, W. V. (1983). Autonomic nervous system activity distinguishes among emotions. *Science, 221,* 1208–1210.

Ellickson, P. L., Hays, R. D., & Bell, R. M. (1992). Stepping through the drug use sequence. *Journal of Abnormal Psychology, 101,* 441–451.

Ellis, A. (1977). The basic clinical theory of rational-emotive therapy. In A. Ellis & R. Grieger (Eds.), *Handbook of rational-emotive therapy.* New York: Springer.

Ellis, A. (1993). Reflections on rational-emotive therapy. *Journal of Consulting and Clinical Psychology, 61,* 199–201.

Ellis, L. (1990). Prenatal stress may effect sex-typical behaviors of a child. *Brown University Child Behavior and Development Letter, 6*(1), pp. 1–3.

Ellis, L., & Ames, M. A. (1987). Neurohormonal functioning and sexual orientation. *Psychological Bulletin, 101,* 233–258.

Ellsworth, P. C., Carlsmith, J. M., & Henson, A. (1972). The stare as a stimulus to flight in human subjects. *Journal of Personality and Social Psychology, 21,* 302–311.

Emde, R. (1993). Cited in Adler, T. (1993). Shy, bold temperament? It's mostly in the genes. *APA Monitor, 24*(1), 7, 8.

Engel, J. (1996). Surgery for seizures. *New England Journal of Medicine, 334,* 647–652.

Engels, G. I., Garnefski, N., & Diekstra, R. F. W. (1993). Efficacy of rational-emotive therapy. *Journal of Consulting and Clinical Psychology, 61,* 1083–1090.

Erikson, E. H. (1963). *Childhood and society.* New York: W. W. Norton.

Eron, L. D. (1982). Parent-child interaction, television violence, and aggression of children. *American Psychologist, 37,* 197–211.

Eron, L. D. (1993). Cited in DeAngelis, T. (1993). It's baaack: TV violence, concern for kid viewers. *APA Monitor, 24*(8), 16.

Espenshade, T. (1993). Cited in Barringer, F. (1993, April 25). Polling on sexual issues has its drawbacks. *The New York Times,* p. A23.

Esterling, B. A., Antoni, M. H., Kumar, M., & Schneiderman, N. (1993). Defensiveness, trait anxiety, and Epstein-Barr viral capsid antigen antibody titers in healthy college students. *Health Psychology, 12,* 132–139.

Estes, W. K. (1972). An associative basis for coding and organization in memory. In A. W. Melton & E. Martin (Eds.), *Coding processes in human memory.* Washington, DC: Winston.

Etaugh, C., & Rathus, S. A. (1995). *The world of children.* Fort Worth: Harcourt Brace.

Evans, G. W., Jacobs, S. V., & Frager, N. B. (1982). Behavioral responses to air pollution. In A. Baum & J. E. Singer (Eds.), *Advances in environmental psychology* (Vol. 4). Hillsdale, NJ: Erlbaum.

Eysenck, H. J., & Eysenck, M. W. (1985). *Personality and individual differences.* New York: Plenum.

Fallon, A. E., & Rozin, P. (1985). Sex differences in perceptions of desirable body shape. *Journal of Abnormal Psychology, 94,* 102–105.

Fantz, R. L. (1961). The origin of form perception. *Scientific American, 204*(5), 66–72.

Farrell, A. D., Camplair, P. S., & McCullough, L. (1987). Identification of target complaints by computer interview. *Journal of Consulting and Clinical Psychology, 55,* 691–700.

Fazio, R. H. (1990). Multiple processes by which attitudes guide behavior. In M. P. Zanna (Ed.), *Advances in experimental social psychology.* San Diego, CA: Academic Press.

FDA approves second drug for Alzheimer's. (1996, November 27). *The New York Times,* p. C8.

Feder, B. J. (1997, April 20). Surge in the teenage smoking rate left the tobacco industry vulnerable. *The New York Times,* pp. A1, A28.

Fehr, B., & Russell, J. A. (1991). The concept of love viewed from a prototype perspective. *Journal of Personality and Social Psychology, 60,* 425–438.

Feingold, A. (1992a). Gender differences in mate selection preferences. *Psychological Bulletin, 112,* 125–139.

Feingold, A. (1992b). Good-looking people are not what we think. *Psychological Bulletin, 111,* 304–341.

Feingold, A. (1994). Gender differences in personality: A meta-analysis. *Psychological Bulletin, 116,* 429–456.

Feshbach, S. (1994). Nationalism, patriotism, and aggression. In L. R. Huesmann (Ed.), *Aggressive behavior.* New York: Plenum.

Festinger, L. (1957). *A theory of cognitive dissonance.* Evanston, IL: Row, Peterson.

Festinger, L., & Carlsmith, J. M. (1959). Cognitive consequences of forced compliance. *Journal of Abnormal and Social Psychology, 58,* 203–210.

Festinger, L., Riecken, H. W., Jr., & Schachter, S. (1956). *When prophecy fails.* Minneapolis: University of Minnesota Press.

Fibel, B., & Hale, W. D. (1978). The generalized expectancy for success scale—A new measure. *Journal of Consulting and Clinical Psychology, 46,* 924–931.

Field, T. M. (1991). Young children's adaptations to repeated separations from their mothers. *Child Development, 62,* 539–547.

Finn, P. R., and others. (1997). Heterogeneity in the families of sons of alcoholics. *Journal of Abnormal Psychology, 106,* 26–36.

Fischer, K. W., Shaver, P. R., & Carochan, P. (1990). How emotions develop and how they organize development. *Cognition and Emotion, 4,* 81–127.

Fisher, C. B., & Fyrberg, D. (1994). Participant partners. *American Psychologist, 49,* 417–427.

Fiske, S. T. (1993). Controlling other people: The impact of power on stereotyping. *American Psychologist, 48,* 621–628.

Fitzgibbon, M. L., Stolley, M. R., & Kirschenbaum, D. S. (1993). Obese people who seek treatment have different characteristics than those who do not seek treatment. *Health Psychology, 12,* 342–345.

Flack, J. M., and others (1995). Panel I: Epidemiology of minority health. *Health Psychology, 14,* 592–600.

Flavell, J. H., Miller, P. H., & Miller, S. A. (1993). *Cognitive development* (3rd ed). Englewood Cliffs, NJ: Prentice-Hall.

Flor, H., & Birbaumer, N. (1993). Comparison of the efficacy of electromyographic biofeedback, cognitive-behavioral therapy, and conservative medical intervention in the treatment of chronic musculoskeletal pain. *Journal of Consulting and Clinical Psychology, 61,* 653–658.

Flor, H., Fydrich, T., & Turk, D. C. (1992). Efficacy of multidisciplinary pain treatment centers. *Pain, 49,* 221–230.

Foa, E. B., Franklin, M. E., Perry, K. J., & Herbert, J. D. (1996). Cognitive biases in generalized social phobia. *Journal of Abnormal Psychology, 105,* 433–439.

Follette, W. C. (1996). Introduction to the special section on the development of theoretically coherent alternatives to the DSM system. *Journal of Consulting and Clinical Psychology, 64,* 1117–1119.

Ford, E. S., and others (1991). Physical activity behaviors in lower and higher socioeconomic status populations. *American Journal of Epidemiology, 133,* 1246–1256.

Foster, G. D., Wadden, T. A., Vogt, R. A., & Brewer, G. (1997). What is a reasonable weight loss? Patients' expectations and evaluations of obesity treatment outcomes. *Journal of Consulting and Clinical Psychology, 65,* 79–85.

Fowler, R. D. (1992). Solid support needed for animal research. *APA Monitor, 23*(6), 2.

Fowler, W., Ogston, K., Roberts-Fiati, G., & Swenson, A. (1993, February). *The long term development of giftedness and high competencies in children enriched in language during infancy.* Paper presented at the Esther Katz Rosen Symposium on the Psychological Development of Gifted Children, University of Kansas.

Fox, R. (1996). Cited in Seppa, N. (1996). APA releases study on family violence. *APA Monitor, 26*(4), 12.

Frankel, K. A., & Bates, J. E. (1990). Mother-toddler problem solving. *Child Development, 61,* 810–819.

Franzoi, S. L., & Herzog, M. E. (1987). Judging physical attractiveness. *Personality and Social Psychology Bulletin, 13,* 19–33.

Freedman, D. (1994). *Brainmakers.* New York: Simon & Schuster.

Freedman, D. X. (1993, August 8). On "Beyond wellness." *The New York Times Book Review,* p. 6.

Freedman, J. L., & Fraser, S. C. (1966). Compliance without pressure: The foot-in-the-door technique. *Journal of Personality and Social Psychology, 4,* 195–202.

Freeman, M. S., Spence, M. J., & Oliphant, C. M. (1993, June). *Newborns prefer their mothers' low-pass filtered voices over other female filtered voices.* Paper presented at the annual convention of the American Psychological Society, Chicago.

Freud, S. (1927). A religious experience. In *Standard edition of the complete psychological works of Sigmund Freud, Vol. 21.* London: Hogarth Press, 1964.

Friedman, M., & Ulmer, D. (1984). *Treating Type A behavior and your heart.* New York: Fawcett Crest.

Friedman, M. A., & Brownell, K. D. (1995). Psychological correlates of obesity. *Psychological Bulletin, 117,* 3–20.

Friedman, R. C., & Downey, J. I. (1994). Homosexuality. *New England Journal of Medicine, 331,* 923–930.

Friman, P. C., Allen, K. D., Kerwin, M. L. E., & Larzelere, R. (1993). Changes in modern psychology. *American Psychologist, 48,* 658–664.

Frisch, R. (1997). Cited in Angier, N. (1997). Chemical tied to fat control could help trigger puberty. *The New York Times,* pp. C1, C3.

Fritsch, G., & Hitzig, E. (1870). On the electrical excitability of the cerebrum. In G. von Bonin (Ed.), *Some papers on the cerebral cortex.* Springfield, IL: Charles C. Thomas. (1960).

Frodi, A. M., Macauley, J., & Thome, P. R. (1977). Are women always less aggressive than men? A review of the experimental literature. *Psychological Bulletin, 84,* 634–660.

Furedy, J. J. (1990, July). *Experimental psychophysiology and pseudoscientific polygraphy.* Symposium at the 5th International Congress of Psychophysiology, Budapest, Hungary.

Furumoto, L. (1992). Joining separate spheres—Christine Ladd-Franklin, woman-scientist. *American Psychologist, 47,* 175–182.

Galambos, N. L. (1992, October). Parent-adolescent relations. *Current Directions in Psychological Science,* 146–149.

Galambos, N. L., & Almeida, D. M. (1992). Does parent-adolescent conflict increase in early adolescence? *Journal of Marriage and the Family, 54,* 737–747.

Galassi, J. P. (1988). Four cognitive-behavioral approaches. *The Counseling Psychologist, 16*(1), 102–105.

Gallagher, R. (1996). Cited in Murray, B. (1996). College youth haunted by increased pressures. *APA Monitor, 26*(4), 47.

Gallucci, W. T., and others. (1993). Sex differences in sensitivity of the hypothalamic-pituitary-adrenal axis. *Health Psychology, 12,* 420–425.

Gallup, G. H., & Newport, F. (1991). Belief in paranormal phenomena among adult Americans. *Skeptical Inquirer, 15*(4), 137–146.

Garcia, J. (1981). The logic and limits of mental aptitude testing. *American Psychologist, 36,* 1172–1180.

Garcia, J. (1993). Misrepresentation of my criticism of Skinner. *American Psychologist, 48,* 1158.

Garcia, J., Brett, L. P., & Rusiniak, K. W. (1989). Limits of Darwinian conditioning. In S. B. Klein & R. R. Mowrer (Eds.), *Contemporary learning theories: Instrumental conditioning theory and the impact of biological constraints on learning.* Hillsdale, NJ: Erlbaum.

Garcia, J., & Koelling, R. A. (1966). Relation of cue to consequences in avoidance learning. *Psychonomic Science 4,* 123–124.

Gardner, H. (1983). *Frames of mind.* New York: Basic Books.

Garfinkel, R. (1995). Cited in Margoshes, P. (1995). For many, old age is the prime of life. *APA Monitor, 26*(5), 36–37.

Garland, A. F., & Zigler, E. (1993). Adolescent suicide prevention. *American Psychologist, 48,* 169–182.

"Gateway to madness." (1997, March 29). *The New York Times,* p. 18.

Gauthier, J., Côté, G., & French, D. (1994). The role of home practice in the thermal biofeedback treatment of migraine headache. *Journal of Consulting and Clinical Psychology, 62,* 180–184.

Gayle, H. D., and others (1990). Prevalence of human immunodeficiency virus among university students. *New England Journal of Medicine, 323,* 1538–1541.

Gaziano, J. M., and others (1993). Moderate alcohol intake, increased levels of high-density lipoprotein and its subfractions, and decreased risk of myocardial infarction. *New England Journal of Medicine, 329,* 1829–1834.

Gazzaniga, M. S. (1995). Consciousness and the cerebral hemispheres. In M. S. Gazzaniga (Ed.), *The cognitive neurosciences.* Cambridge, MA: MIT Press.

Gazzaniga, M. S. (1997), Cited in Gorman, J. (1997, April 29). Consciousness studies: From stream to flood. *The New York Times,* pp. C1, C5.

Geen, R. G., Stonner, D., & Shope, G. L. (1975). The facilitation of aggression by aggression. *Journal of Personality and Social Psychology, 31,* 721–726.

Geiger, H. J. (1996). Race and health care. *New England Journal of Medicine, 335,* 815–816.

Gelman, D. (1994, April 18). The mystery of suicide. *Newsweek,* pp. 44–49.

Gelman, R., & Baillargeon, R. (1983). A review of some Piagetian concepts. In J. Flavell & E. Markman (Eds.), *Handbook of child psychology.* New York: Wiley.

Gentry, J., & Eron, L. D. (1993). American Psychological Association Commission on Violence and Youth. *American Psychologist, 48,* 89.

George, J. M. (1991). State or trait: Effects of positive mood on prosocial behaviors at work. *Journal of Applied Social Psychology, 76,* 299–307.

Gerstner, L. V., Jr. (1994, May 27). Our schools are failing. Do we care? *The New York Times,* p. A27.

Geschwind, N., & Galaburda, A. M. (1987). *Cerebral lateralization: Biological mechanisms, associations, and pathology.* Cambridge, MA: Harvard University Press.

Getzels, J. W., & Jackson, P. W. (1962). *Creativity and intelligence.* New York: Wiley.

Gibbs, N. (1991, June 3). When is it rape? *Time,* pp. 48–54.

Gibson, E. J., & Walk, R. D. (1960, April). The visual cliff. *Scientific American, 202,* 64–71.

Gibson, M., & Ogbu, J. (Eds.). (1991). *Minority status and schooling.* New York: Garland.

Gigerenzer, G., Hoffrage, U., & Kleinbölting, H. (1991). Probabilistic mental models. *Psychological Review, 98,* 506–528.

Gigone, D., & Hastie, R. (1997). Proper analysis of the accuracy of group judgments. *Psychological Bulletin, 121,* 149–167.

Gilbert, S. (1996, August 28). More men may seek eating disorder help. *The New York Times,* p. C9.

Gilbert, S. (1997, June 25). Social ties reduce risk of a cold. *The New York Times,* p. C11.

Gilbert, S. J. (1981). Another look at the Milgram obedience studies. *Personality and Social Psychology Bulletin, 7,* 690–695.

Gilligan, C. (1982). *In a different voice.* Cambridge, MA: Harvard University Press.

Gilligan, C., Lyons, P., & Hanmer, T. J. (Eds.). (1990). *Making connections.* Cambridge, MA: Harvard University Press.

Gilligan, C., Rogers, A. G., & Tolman, D. L. (Eds.). (1991). *Women, girls, and psychotherapy.* New York: Haworth.

Gilligan, C., Ward, J. V., & Taylor, J. M. (1989). *Mapping the moral domain: A contribution of women's thinking to psychological theory and education.* Cambridge, MA: Harvard University Press.

Gillis, A. R., Richard, M. A., & Hagan, J. (1986). Ethnic susceptibility to crowding. *Environment and Behavior, 18,* 683–706.

Gillis, J. S., & Avis, W. E. (1980). The male-taller norm in mate selection. *Personality and Social Psychology Bulletin, 6,* 396–401.

Gilovich, T. (1983). Biased evaluation and persistence in gambling. *Journal of Personality and Social Psychology, 44*, 1110–1126.

Ginsburg, G., & Bronstein, P. (1993). Family factors related to children's intrinsic/extrinsic motivational orientation and academic performance. *Child Development, 64*, 1461–1474.

Glaser, R., and others (1991). Stress-related activation of Epstein-Barr virus. *Brain, Behavior, and Immunity, 5*, 219–232.

Glaser, R., and others (1993). Stress and the memory T-cell response to the Epstein-Barr virus. *Health Psychology, 12*, 435–442.

Gleason, J. B., & Ratner, N. B. (1993). Language development in children. In J. B. Gleason & N. B. Ratner (Eds.), *Psycholinguistics*. Fort Worth: Harcourt Brace Jovanovich.

Gleitman, H., Rozin, P., & Sabini, J. (1997). Solomon E. Asch (1907–1996). *American Psychologist, 52*, 984–985.

Glenn, S. S., Ellis, J., & Greenspoon, J. (1992). On the revolutionary nature of the operant as a unit of behavioral selection. *American Psychologist, 47*, 1326–1329.

Glover, J. A., Ronning, R. R., & Bruning, R. H. (1990). *Cognitive psychology for teachers.* New York: Macmillan.

Godden, D. R., & Baddeley, A. D. (1975). Context-dependent memory in two natural environments: On land and underwater. *British Journal of Psychology, 66*, 325–331.

Gold, D. R., and others (1996). Effects of cigarette smoking on lung function in adolescent boys and girls. *New England Journal of Medicine, 335*, 931–937.

Goldman, J. A., & Harlow, L. L. (1993). Self-perception variables that mediate AIDS-preventive behavior in college students. *Health Psychology, 12*, 489–498.

Goldman, K. (1993, June 1). Jordan & Co. play ball on Madison Avenue. *The Wall Street Journal*, p. B9.

Goldman-Rakic, P. S. (1992). Working memory and the mind. *Scientific American, 267*(3), 110–117.

Goldman-Rakic, P. S. (1995). Cited in Goleman, D. (1995, May 2). Biologists find site of working memory. *The New York Times*, pp. C1, C9.

Goldsmith, H. H. (1993). Cited in Adler, T. (1993). Shy, bold temperament? It's mostly in the genes. *APA Monitor, 24*(1), 7, 8.

Goleman, D. J. (1995a, March 28). The brain manages happiness and sadness in different centers. *The New York Times*, pp. C1, C9.

Goleman, D. J. (1995b, May 2). Biologists find site of working memory. *The New York Times*, pp. C1, C9.

Goleman, D. J. (1995c). *Emotional intelligence.* New York: Bantam Books.

Goleman, D. J. (1996a, May 28). Evidence mounting for role of fetal damage in schizophrenia. *The New York Times*, pp. C1, C3.

Goleman, D. J. (1996b, November 19). Research on brain leads to pursuit of designer drugs. *The New York Times*, pp. C1, C3.

Gomez, J., & Smith, B. (1990). Taking the home out of homophobia: Black lesbian health. In E. C. White (Ed.), *The Black women's health book*. Seattle: Seal Press.

Goodman, L. A., Koss, M. P., Fitzgerald, L. F., Russo, N. F., & Keita, G. W. (1993). Male violence against women. *American Psychologist, 48*, 1054–1058.

Goodwin, F. K., & Jamison, K. R. (1990). *Manic-depressive illness.* New York: Oxford University Press.

Gordon, C. M., & Carey, M. P. (1996). Alcohol's effects on requisites for sexual risk reduction in men. *Health Psychology, 15*, 56–60.

Gorman, J. (1997, April 29). Consciousness studies: From stream to flood. *The New York Times*, pp. C1, C5.

Gortmaker, S. L., and others. (1993). Social and economic consequences of over-weight in adolescence and young adulthood. *New England Journal of Medicine, 329*, 1008–1012.

Gottesman, I. I. (1991). *Schizophrenia genesis.* New York: Freeman.

Gottfried, A. E., Fleming, J. S., & Gottfried, A. W. (1994). Role of parental motivational practices in children's academic intrinsic motivation and achievement. *Journal of Educational Psychology, 86*, 104–113.

Grady, D. (1997a, January 21). Brain-tied gene defect may explain why schizophrenics hear voices. *The New York Times*, p. C3.

Grady, D. (1997b, May 21). Exercise may not curb depression. *The New York Times*, p. C11.

Granberg, D., & Brent, E. (1983). When prophecy bends. *Journal of Personality and Social Psychology, 45*, 477–491.

Greene, B. (1993). African American women. In L. Comas-Diaz & B. A. Greene (Eds.), *Women of color and mental health*. New York: Guilford.

Greene, B. (1994). Ethnic-minority lesbians and gay men. *Journal of Consulting and Clinical Psychology, 62*, 243–251.

Greenfield, S. A. (1995). *Journey to the center of the mind.* New York: W. H. Freeman.

Greeno, C. G., & Wing, R. R. (1994). Stress-induced eating. *Psychological Bulletin, 115*, 444–464.

Greist, J. H. (1984). Exercise in the treatment of depression. *Coping with mental stress.* Washington, DC: National Institute of Mental Health.

Griffin, E., & Sparks, G. G. (1990). Friends forever. *Journal of Social and Personal Relationships, 7*, 29–46.

Grodstein, F., and others. (1997). Postmenopausal hormonal therapy and mortality. *New England Journal of Medicine, 336*, 1769–1775.

Gross, J. J., & Levenson, R. W. (1997). Hiding feelings. *Journal of Abnormal Psychology, 106*, 95–103.

Grove, W. M., and others (1991). Familial prevalence and coaggregation of schizotypy indicators. *Journal of Abnormal Psychology, 100*, 115–121.

Gruber-Baldini, A. L. (1991). *The impact of health and disease on cognitive ability in adulthood and old age in the Seattle Longitudinal Study.* Unpublished doctoral dissertation, Pennsylvania State University.

Gruder, C. L., and others (1993). Effects of social support and relapse prevention training as adjuncts to a televised smoking-cessation intervention. *Journal of Consulting and Clinical Psychology, 61*, 113–120.

Grush, J. E. (1980). The impact of candidate expenditures, regionality, and prior outcomes on the 1976 Democratic presidential primaries. *Journal of Personality and Social Psychology, 38*, 337–347.

Guilford, J. P. (1988). Some changes in the structure-of-intellect model. *Educational and Psychological Measurement, 48*, 1–4.

Guisinger, S., & Blatt, S. J. (1994). Individuality and relatedness. *American Psychologist, 49*, 104–111.

Guralnik, J. M., Land, K. C., Blazer, D., Fillenbaum, G. G., & Branch, L. G. (1993). Educational status and active life expectancy among older Blacks and Whites. *New England Journal of Medicine, 329*, 110–116.

Guthrie, R. V. (1990). Cited in Korn, J. H., Davis, R., & Davis, S. F. (1991). Historians' and chairpersons' judgments of eminence among psychologists. *American Psychologist, 46*, 789–792.

Haaf, R. A., Smith, P. H., & Smitley, S. (1983). Infant response to facelike patterns under fixed trial and infant-control procedures. *Child Development, 54*, 172–177.

Haaga, D. A. F., & Davison, G. C. (1993). An appraisal of rational-emotive therapy. *Journal of Consulting and Clinical Psychology, 61*, 215–220.

Haber, R. N. (1969). Eidetic images. *Scientific American, 220*, 36–55.

Haber, R. N. (1980). Eidetic images are not just imaginary. *Psychology Today, 14*(11), 72–82.

Haley, W. E., and others. (1996). Appraisal, coping, and social support as mediators of well-being in Black and White caregivers of patients with Alzheimer's disease. *Journal of Consulting and Clinical Psychology, 64*, 121–129.

Hall, C. S. (1984). "A ubiquitous sex difference in dreams" revisited. *Journal of Personality and Social Psychology, 46*, 1109–1117.

Hall, G. C. I. (1997). Cultural malpractice: The growing obsolescence of psychology with the changing U.S. population. *American Psychologist, 52*, 642–651.

Hall, G. C. I., & Barongan, C. (1997). Prevention of sexual aggression. *American Psychologist, 52*, 5–14.

Hall, J. A., and others (1990). Performance quality, gender, and professional role. *Medical Care, 28*, 489–501.

Halperin, K. M., & Snyder, C. R. (1979). Effects of enhanced psychological test feedback on treatment outcome. *Journal of Consulting and Clinical Psychology, 47*, 140–146.

Halpern, D. F. (1989). *Thought and knowledge.* (2nd ed.). Hillsdale, NJ: Erlbaum.

Halpern, D. F. (1997). Sex differences in intelligence: Implications for education. *American Psychologist, 52,* 1091–1102.

Halpern, D. F., Hansen, C., & Riefer, D. (1990). Analogies as an aid to understanding and memory. *Journal of Educational Psychology, 82,* 298–305.

Hamer, D., and others. (1993). Cited in Henry, W. A. (1993, July 26). Born gay? *Time,* pp. 36–39.

Hamm, N. M., Baum, M. R., & Nikels, K. W. (1975). Effects of race and exposure on judgments of interpersonal favorability. *Journal of Experimental Social Psychology, 11,* 14–24.

Haney, D. Q. (1997, September 30). AIDS virus resisting new drugs. *Daily Record,* pp. A1, A10.

Haney, M., and others (1994). Cocaine sensitivity in Roman high and low avoidance rats is modulated by sex and gonadal hormone status. *Brain Research, 645*(1–2), 179–185.

Harkins, S. (1987). Social loafing and social facilitation. *Journal of Experimental Social Psychology, 23,* 1–18.

Harlow, H. F. (1959). Love in infant monkeys. *Scientific American, 200,* 68–86.

Harlow, H. F., Harlow, M. K., & Meyer, D. R. (1950). Learning motivated by a manipulation drive. *Journal of Experimental Psychology, 40,* 228–234.

Harlow, H. F., & Zimmermann, R. R. (1959). Affectional responses in the infant monkey. *Science, 130,* 421–432.

Harnishfeger, K. K., & Bjorklund, D. F. (1990). Children's strategies. In D. F. Bjorklund (Ed.), *Children's strategies* (pp. 1–184). Hillsdale, NJ: Erlbaum.

Harris, G. T., Rice, M. E., & Quinsey, V. L. (1994). Psychopathy as a taxon. *Journal of Consulting and Clinical Psychology, 62,* 387–397.

Hashimoto, N. (1991). Memory development in early childhood. *Journal of Genetic Psychology, 152,* 101–117.

Hasselhorn, M. (1992). Task dependency and the role of typicality and metamemory in the development of an organizational strategy. *Child Development, 63,* 202–214.

Hauser-Cram, P., Pierson, D. E., Walker, D. K., & Tivnan, T. (1991). *Early education in the public schools.* San Francisco: Jossey-Bass.

Hawkins, S. A., & Hastie, R. (1990). Hindsight: Biased judgments of past events after the outcomes are known. *Psychological Bulletin, 107,* 311–327.

Hayes, P. (1993). Cited in Chartrand, S. (1993, July 18). A split in thinking among keepers of artificial intelligence. *The New York Times,* p. E6.

Hayes, S. C. (Ed.). (1989). *Rule-governed behavior.* New York: Plenum.

Hays, K. F. (1995). Putting sport psychology into (your) practice. *Professional Psychology: Research and Practice, 26,* 33–40.

Heatherton, T. F., Mahamedi, F., Striepe, M., Field, A. E., & Keel, P. (1997). A 10-year longitudinal study of body weight, dieting, and eating disorder symptoms. *Journal of Abnormal Psychology, 106,* 117–125.

Hegarty, M., Mayer, R. E., & Monk, C. A. (1995). Comprehension of arithmetic word problems. *Journal of Educational Psychology, 87,* 18–32.

Heingartner, A., & Hall, J. V. (1974). Affective consequences in adults and children of repeated exposure to auditory stimuli. *Journal of Personality and Social Psychology, 29,* 719–723.

Heller, D. A., de Faire, U., Pedersen, N. L., Dahlén, G., & McClearn, G. E. (1993). Genetic and environmental influences on serum lipid levels in twins. *New England Journal of Medicine, 328,* 1150–1156.

Helmes, E., & Reddon, J. R. (1993). A perspective on developments in assessing psychopathology. *Psychological Bulletin, 113,* 453–471.

Helms, J. E. (1992). Why is there no study of cultural equivalence of standardized cognitive ability testing? *American Psychologist, 47,* 1083–1101.

Helson, R., & Moane, G. (1987). Personality change in women from college to midlife. *Journal of Personality and Social Psychology, 53,* 176–186.

Henkin, W. A. (1985). Toward counseling the Japanese in America. *Journal of Counseling and Development, 63,* 500–503.

Hensley, W. E. (1981). The effects of attire, location, and sex on aiding behavior. *Journal of Nonverbal Behavior, 6,* 3–11.

Hepper, P. G., Shahidullah, S., & White, R. (1990, October 4). Origins of fetal handedness. *Nature, 347,* 431.

Hepworth, J. T., & West, S. G. (1988). Lynchings and the economy. *Journal of Personality and Social Psychology, 55,* 239–247.

Herbert, T. B., & Cohen, S. (1993). Depression and immunity. *Psychological Bulletin, 113,* 472– 486.

Hergenhahn, B. R. (1997). *An introduction to the history of psychology* (3rd ed.). Pacific Grove, CA: Brooks/Cole.

Herrmann, D. J. (1991). *Super memory.* Emmaus, PA: Rodale.

Herrnstein, R. J., & Murray, C. (1994). *The bell curve: Intelligence and class structure in American life.* New York: Free Press.

Hershey, D. A., Walsh, D. A., Read, S. J., & Chulef, A. S. (1990). Relationships between metamemory, memory predictions, and memory task performance in adults. *Psychology and Aging, 5,* 215–227.

Herzog, D. B., Keller, M. B., & Lavori, P. W. (1988). Outcome in anorexia and bulimia nervosa. *The Journal of Nervous and Mental Disease, 176,* 131–143.

Hewitt, P. L., Flett, G. L., & Ediger, E. (1996). Perfectionism and depression. *Journal of Abnormal Psychology, 105,* 276–280.

Hilgard, E. R. (1994). Neodissociation theory. In S. J. Lynn & J. W. Rhue, *Dissociation: Clinical, theoretical, and research perspectives.* New York: Guilford Press.

Hilton, J. L., & von Hippel, W. (1996). Stereotypes. *Annual Review of Psychology, 47,* 237–271.

Hilts, P. J. (1995, May 30). Brain's memory system comes into focus. *The New York Times,* pp. C1, C3.

Hobfoll, S. E., Jackson, A. P., Lavin, J., Britton, P. J., & Shepherd, J. B. (1993). Safer sex knowledge, behavior, and attitudes of inner-city women. *Health Psychology, 12,* 481–488.

Hobfoll, S. E., Ritter, C., Lavin, J., Hulsizer, M. R., & Cameron, R. P. (1995). Depression prevalence and incidence among inner-city pregnant and postpartum women. *Journal of Consulting and Clinical Psychology, 63,* 445–453.

Hobson, J. A. (1992). Cited in Blakeslee, S. (1992, January 7). Scientists unraveling chemistry of dreams. *The New York Times,* pp. C1, C10.

Hoffman, C., & Hurst, N. (1990). Gender stereotypes. *Journal of Personality and Social Psychology, 58,* 197–208.

Hogan, R., Curphy, G. J., & Hogan, J. (1994). What we know about leadership. *American Psychologist, 49,* 493–504.

Holahan, C. J., & Moos, R. H. (1990). Life stressors, resistance factors, and psychological health. *Journal of Personality and Social Psychology, 58,* 909–917.

Holahan, C. J., & Moos, R. H. (1991). Life stressors, personal and social resources, and depression. *Journal of Abnormal Psychology, 100,* 31–38.

Holahan, C. J., Moos, R. H., Holahan, C. K., & Brennan, P. L. (1995). Social support, coping, and depressive symptoms in a late-middle-aged sample of patients reporting cardiac illness. *Health Psychology, 14,* 152–163.

Holland, J. L. (1996). Exploring careers with a typology. *American Psychologist, 51,* 397–406.

Hollinger, L. M., & Buschmann, M. B. (1993). Factors influencing the perception of touch by elderly nursing home residents and their health caregivers. *International Journal of Nursing Studies, 30,* 445–461.

Hollingshead, A. B., & Redlich, F. C. (1958). *Social class and mental illness.* New York: Wiley.

Hollon, S. D., Shelton, R. C., & Loosen, P. T. (1991). Cognitive therapy and pharmacotherapy for depression. *Journal of Consulting and Clinical Psychology, 59,* 88–99.

Holmes, D. S. (1984). Meditation and somatic arousal reduction. *American Psychologist, 39,* 1–10.

Holmes, T. H., & Rahe, R. H. (1967). The social readjustment rating scale. *Journal of Psychosomatic Research, 11,* 213–218.

Holyoak, K., Koh, K., & Nisbett, R. E. (1989). A theory of conditioning. *Psychological Review, 96,* 315–340.

Honan, W. H. (1996, April 11). Male professors keep 30% lead in pay over women, study says. *The New York Times,* p. B9.

Honorton, C. (1985). Meta-analysis of psi

Ganzfeld research. *Journal of Parapsychology, 49,* 51–91.

Honorton, C., and others. (1990). Psi communication in the Ganzfeld. *Journal of Parapsychology, 54,* 99–139.

Honts, C., Hodes, R., & Raskin, D. (1985). *Journal of Applied Psychology, 70*(1).

Hopper, J. L., & Seeman, E. (1994). The bone density of female twins discordant for tobacco use. *New England Journal of Medicine, 330,* 387–392.

Horn, J. M. (1983). The Texas adoption project. *Child Development, 54,* 268–275.

Horney, K. (1967). *Feminine psychology.* New York: W. W. Norton.

Howard, L., & Polich, J. (1985). P300 latency and memory span development. *Developmental Psychology, 21,* 283–289.

Howard-Pitney, B., LaFramboise, T. D., Basil, M., September, B., & Johnson, M. (1992). Psychological and social indicators of suicide ideation and suicide attempts in Zuni adolescents. *Journal of Consulting and Clinical Psychology, 60,* 473–476.

Hubel, D. H., & Wiesel, T. N. (1979). Brain mechanisms of vision. *Scientific American, 241,* 150–162.

Huesmann, R. (1993). Cited in DeAngelis, T. (1993). It's baaack: TV violence, concern for kid viewers. *APA Monitor, 24*(8), 16.

Huesmann, L. R., Eron, L. D., Klein, R., Brice, P., & Fischer, P. (1983). Mitigating the imitation of aggressive behaviors by changing children's attitudes about media violence. *Journal of Personality and Social Psychology, 44,* 899–910.

Huesmann, L. R., & Miller, L. S. (1994). Long-term effects of repeated exposure to media violence in childhood. In L. R. Huesmann (Ed.), *Aggressive behavior.* New York: Plenum.

Hultquist, C. M., and others. (1995). The effect of smoking and light activity on metabolism in men. *Health Psychology, 14,* 124–131.

Humphrey, L. L. (1986). Family dynamics in bulimia. In S. C. Feinstein and others (Eds.), *Adolescent psychiatry.* Chicago: University of Chicago Press.

Hunt, M. (1993). *The story of psychology.* New York: Anchor Books.

Huxley, A. (1939). *Brave new world.* New York: Harper & Row.

Hyde, J. S., Fennema, E., & Lamon, S. J. (1990). Gender differences in mathematics performance. *Psychological Bulletin, 107,* 139–155.

Hyde, J. S., & Linn, M. C. (1988). Gender differences in verbal ability. *Psychological Bulletin, 104,* 53–69.

Hyde, J. S., & Plant, E. A. (1995). Magnitude of psychological gender differences. *American Psychologist, 50,* 159–161.

Hyman, R. (1994). Anomaly or artifact? Comments on Bem and Honorton. *Psychological Bulletin, 115,* 19–24.

Ironson, G. (1993). Cited in Adler, T. (1993). Men and women affected by stress, but differently. *APA Monitor, 24*(7), 8–9.

Isabella, R. A. (1993). Origins of attachment: Maternal interactive behavior across the first year. *Child Development, 64,* 605–621.

Isay, R. A. (1990). Psychoanalytic theory and the therapy of gay men. In D. P. McWhirter, S. A. Sanders, & J. M. Reinisch (Eds.) *Homosexuality/heterosexuality* (pp. 283–303). New York: Oxford University Press.

Isomura, T., Fine, S., & Lin, T. (1987). Two Japanese families. *Canadian Journal of Psychiatry, 32,* 282–286.

Izard, C. E. (1984). Emotion-cognition relationships and human development. In C. E. Izard, J. Kagan, & R. B. Zajonc (Eds.), *Emotions, cognition, and behavior.* New York: Cambridge University Press.

Izard, C. E. (1990). Facial expression and the regulation of emotions. *Journal of Personality and Social Psychology, 58,* 487–498.

Izard, C. E. (1994). Basic emotions, relations among emotions, and emotion-cognition relations. *Psychological Bulletin, 115,* 561–565.

Jackson, J. (1993). Human behavioral genetics, Scarr's theory, and her views on interventions. *Child Development, 64,* 1318–1332.

Jacob, T., Krahn, G. L., & Leonard, K. (1991). Parent-child interactions in families with alcoholic fathers. *Journal of Consulting and Clinical Psychology, 59,* 176–181.

Jacobs, T. J., & Charles, E. (1980). Life events and the occurrence of cancer in children. *Psychosomatic Medicine, 42,* 11–24.

Jacobson, N. S., & Addis, M. E. (1993). Research on couples and couples therapy *Journal of Consulting and Clinical Psychology, 61,* 85–93.

Jacobson, N. S., & Hollon, S. D. (1996). Cognitive-behavior therapy versus pharmacotherapy. *Journal of Consulting and Clinical Psychology, 64,* 74–80.

Jacobson, N. S., and others. (1996). A component analysis of cognitive-behavioral treatment for depression. *Journal of Consulting and Clinical Psychology, 64,* 295–304.

Jacox, A., Carr, D. B., & Payne, R. (1994). New clinical-practice guidelines for the management of pain in patients with cancer. *New England Journal of Medicine, 330,* 651–655.

James, W. (1890). *The principles of psychology.* New York: Henry Holt.

James, W. (1904). Does "consciousness" exist? *Journal of Philosophy, Psychology, and Scientific Methods, 1,* 477–491.

Jamison, K. R. (1997). Manic-depressive illness and creativity. *Scientific American mysteries of the mind, Special Issue Vol. 7,* No. 1, 44–49.

Janerich, D. T., and others. (1990). Lung cancer and exposure to tobacco smoke in the household. *New England Journal of Medicine, 323,* 632–636.

Janis, I. L. (1982). *Groupthink* (2nd ed.). Boston: Houghton Mifflin.

Janos, P. M. (1987). A fifty-year follow-up of Terman's youngest college students and IQ-matched agemates. *Gifted Child Quarterly, 31,* 55–58.

Janowitz, H. D., & Grossman, M. I. (1949). Effects of variations in nutritive density on intake of food in dogs and cats. *American Journal of Physiology, 158,* 184–193.

Janus, S. S., & Janus, C. L. (1993). *The Janus report on sexual behavior.* New York: Wiley.

Jeffery, R. W. (1991). Population perspectives on the prevention and treatment of obesity in minority populations. *American Journal of Clinical Nutrition, 53,* 1621S–1624S.

Jemmott, J. B., and others (1983). Academic stress, power motivation, and decrease in secretion rate of salivary secretory immunoglobin A. *Lancet, 1,* 1400–1402.

Jensen, M. P., & Karoly, P. (1991). Control beliefs, coping efforts, and adjustment to chronic pain. *Journal of Consulting and Clinical Psychology, 59,* 431–438.

Jensen, M. P., Turner, J. A., & Romano, J. M. (1994). Correlates of improvement in multidisciplinary treatment of chronic pain. *Journal of Consulting and Clinical Psychology, 62,* 172–179.

Johnson, B. T., & Eagly, A. H. (1989). Effects of involvement on persuasion. *Psychological Bulletin, 106,* 290–314.

Johnson, G. (1995, June 6). Chimp talk debate: Is it really language? *The New York Times,* pp. C1, C10.

Johnson, K. W., and others (1995). Panel II: Macrosocial and environmental influences on minority health. *Health Psychology, 14,* 601–612.

Johnson, W., Emde, R. N., Pannabecker, B., Stenberg, C., & Davis, M. (1982). Maternal perception of infant emotion from birth to 18 months. *Infant Behavior and Development, 5,* 313–322.

Johnston, L. D., O'Malley, P. M., & Bachman, J. G. (1996). National survey results on drug use from the Monitoring the Future Study, 1975–1995. National Institute on Drug Abuse, 5600 Fishers Lane, Rockville, MD 20957; US-DHHS, Public Health Service, National Institutes of Health.

Joiner, T. E., Heatherton, T. F., Rudd, M. D., & Schmidt, N. B. (1997). Perfectionism, perceived weight status, and bulimic symptoms. *Journal of Abnormal Psychology, 106,* 145–153.

Jones, E. E. (1990). *Interpersonal perception.* New York: W. H. Freeman.

Jones, J. L., & Leary, M. R. (1994). Effects of appearance-based admonitions against sun exposure on tanning intentions in young adults. *Health Psychology, 13,* 86–90.

Jones, M. C. (1924). Elimination of children's fears. *Journal of Experimental Psychology, 7,* 381–390.

Jordan, J. V., Kaplan, A. G., Miller, J. B., Stiver, L. P., & Stiver, J. L. (Eds.). (1991). *Women's growth in connection.* New York: Guilford.

Jorgensen, R. S., Johnson, B. T., Kolodziej, M. E., & Schreer, G. E. (1996). Elevated blood pressure and personality. *Psychological Bulletin, 120,* 293–320.

Judd, C. M., & Park, B. (1988). Out-group homogeneity. *Journal of Personality and Social Psychology, 54*, 778–788.

Just, N., & Alloy, L. B. (1997). The response styles theory of depression: Tests and an extension of the theory. *Journal of Abnormal Psychology, 106*, 221–229.

Kail, R. (1990). *The development of memory in children* (3rd ed.). New York: W. H. Freeman.

Kail, R. V., & Salthouse, T. A. (1994). Processing speed as a mental capacity. *Acta Psychologica, 86*, 199–225.

Kamin, L. J. (1995). Behind the curve [Review of *The Bell Curve: Intelligence and Class Structure in American Life*]. *Scientific American, 272*, 99–103.

Kandel, E. R., & Hawkins, R. D. (1992). The biological basis of learning and individuality. *Scientific American, 267*(3), 78–86.

Kane, J. M. (1996). Schizophrenia. *New England Journal of Medicine, 334*, 34–41.

Kaplan, S. J. (1991). Physical abuse and neglect. In M. Lewis (Ed.), *Child and adolescent psychiatry* (pp. 1010–1019). Baltimore: Williams & Wilkins.

Karasek, R. A., and others (1982). Job, psychological factors and coronary heart disease. *Advances in Cardiology, 29*, 62–67.

Karoly, P., & Ruehlman, L. S. (1996). Motivational implications of pain. *Health Psychology, 15*, 383–390.

Katz, M. H., & Gerberding, J. L. (1997). Postexposure treatment of people exposed to the human immunodeficiency virus through sexual contact or injection-drug use. *New England Journal of Medicine, 336*, 1097–1100.

Katzell, R. A., & Thompson, D. E. (1990). Work motivation. *American Psychologist, 45*, 144–153.

Kaufman, J., & Zigler, E. (1989). The intergenerational transmission of child abuse. In D. Cicchetti & V. Carlson (Eds.), *Child maltreatment* (pp. 129–150). Cambridge: Cambridge University Press.

Kazdin, A. E. (1993). Adolescent mental health. *American Psychologist, 48*, 127–141.

Keefe, F. J., Dunsmore, J., & Burnett, R. (1992). Behavioral and cognitive-behavioral approaches to chronic pain. *Journal of Consulting and Clinical Psychology, 60*, 528–536.

Keen, S. (1991). *Fire in the belly*. New York: HarperCollins.

Keesey, R. E. (1986). A set-point theory of obesity. In K. D. Brownell & J. P. Foreyt (Eds.), *Handbook of eating disorders*. New York: Basic Books.

Keil, J. E., and others (1993). Mortality rates and risk factors for coronary disease in Black as compared with White men and women. *New England Journal of Medicine, 329*, 73–78.

Keinan, G. (1987). Decision making under stress. *Journal of Personality and Social Psychology, 52*, 639–644.

Keita, G. P. (1993, February). Presentation to the Fifth International Interdisciplinary Congress on Women, University of Costa Rica, San Jose, Costa Rica.

Kellerman, J., Lewis, J., & Laird, J. D. (1989). Looking and loving: The effects of mutual gaze on feelings of romantic love. *Journal of Research in Personality, 23*, 145–161.

Kelley, H. H., & Michela, J. L. (1980). Attribution theory and research. *Annual Review of Psychology, 31*, 457–501.

Kellman, P. J., & von Hofsetn, C. (1992). The world of the moving infant. In C. Rovee-Collier & L. P. Lipsitt (Eds.), *Advances in Infancy Research* (Vol. 7). Norwood, NJ: Ablex.

Kelly, G. A. (1955). *The psychology of personal constructs, Vols. 1 & 2*. New York: W. W. Norton.

Kelly, I. W., Culver, R., & Loptson, P. J. (1989). Astrology and science. In S. K. Biswas and others (Eds.), *Cosmoperspectives*. Cambridge: Cambridge University Press.

Kelman, H. C. (1997). Group processes in the resolution of international conflicts. *American Psychologist, 52*, 212–220.

Kemeny, M. E. (1993). Emotions and the immune system. In B. Moyers, *Healing and the mind*. New York: Doubleday.

Kemeny, M. E., Weiner, H., Taylor, S. E., Schneider, S., Visscher, B., & Fahey, J. L. (1994). Repeated bereavement, depressed mood, and immune parameters in HIV seropositive and seronegative gay men. *Health Psychology, 13*, 14–24.

Kenrick, D. T., & MacFarlane, S. W. (1986). Ambient temperature and horn honking. *Environment and Behavior, 18*, 179–191.

Kessler, D. A. (1995). Nicotine addiction in young people. *New England Journal of Medicine, 333*, 186–189.

Kiecolt-Glaser, J. K. (1993). Cited in Adler, T. (1993). Men and women affected by stress, but differently. *APA Monitor, 24*(7), 8–9.

Kihlstrom, J. F., Glisky, M. L., & Angiulo, M. J. (1994). Dissociative tendencies and dissociative disorders. *Journal of Abnormal Psychology, 103*, 117–124.

Kilborn, P. T. (1995, March 16). Women and minorities still face "glass ceilings." *The New York Times*, p. A22.

Kilshaw, D., & Annett, M. (1983). Right- and left-hand skill: Effects of age, sex, and hand preferences showing superiors in left-handers. *British Journal of Psychology, 74*, 253–268.

Kimble, D. P. (1992). *Biological psychology* (2nd ed.). Fort Worth: Harcourt Brace Jovanovich.

Kimble, G. A. (1994). A frame of reference for psychology. *American Psychologist, 49*, 510–519.

Kimerling, R., & Calhoun, K. S. (1994). Somatic symptoms, social support, and treatment seeking among sexual assault victims. *Journal of Consulting and Clinical Psychology, 62*, 333–340.

Kinderman, P., & Bentall, R. P. (1997). Causal attributions in paranoia and depression. *Journal of Abnormal Psychology, 106*, 341–345.

Kinnunen, T., Doherty, K., Militello, F. S., & Garvey, A. J. (1996). Depression and smoking cessation. *Journal of Consulting and Clinical Psychology, 64*, 791–798.

Kinnunen, T., Zamansky, H. S., & Block, M. L. (1994). Is the hypnotized subject lying? *Journal of Abnormal Psychology, 103*, 184–191.

Kinsey, A. C., Pomeroy, W. B., & Martin, C. E. (1948). *Sexual behavior in the human male*. Philadelphia: W. B. Saunders.

Kinsey, A. C., Pomeroy, W. B., Martin, C. E., & Gebhard, P. H. (1953). *Sexual behavior in the human female*. Philadelphia: W. B. Saunders.

Kintsch, W. (1994). Text comprehension, memory, and learning. *American Psychologist, 49*, 294–303.

Kirsch, I., Montgomery, G., & Sapirstein, G. (1995). Hypnosis as an adjunct to cognitive-behavioral psychotherapy. *Journal of Consulting and Clinical Psychology, 63*, 214–220.

Kleinke, C. L. (1977). Compliance to requests made by gazing and touching experimenters in field settings. *Journal of Experimental Social Psychology, 13*, 218–223.

Kleinke, C. L. (1986). Gaze and eye contact. *Psychological Review, 100*, 78–100.

Kleinke, C. L., & Staneski, R. A. (1980). First impressions of female bust size. *Journal of Social Psychology, 110*, 123–134.

Kleinmuntz, B., & Szucko, J. J. (1984). Lie detection in ancient and modern times. *American Psychologist, 39*, 766–776.

Klepinger, D. H., and others (1993). Perceptions of AIDS risk and severity and their association with risk-related behavior among U.S. men. *Family Planning Perspectives, 25*, 74–82.

Klesges, R. C., and others (1997). How much weight gain occurs following smoking cessation? *Journal of Consulting and Clinical Psychology, 65*, 286–291.

Klorman, R., Brumaghim, J. T., Fitzpatrick, P. A., Borgstedt, A. D., & Strauss, J. (1994). Clinical and cognitive effects of methylphenidate on children with attention deficit disorder as a function of aggression/oppositionality and age. *Journal of Abnormal Psychology, 103*, 206–221.

Klosko, J. S., Barlow, D. H., Tassinari, R., & Cerny, J. A. (1990). A comparison of alprazolam and behavior therapy in treatment of panic disorder. *Journal of Consulting and Clinical Psychology, 58*, 77–84.

Klüver, H., & Bucy, P. C. (1939). Preliminary analysis of functions of the temporal lobe in monkeys. *Archives of Neurology and Psychiatry, 42*, 979–1000.

Knight, G. P., Fabes, R. A., & Higgins, D. A. (1996). Concerns about drawing causal inferences from meta-analyses: An example in the study of gender differences in aggression. *Psychological Bulletin, 119*, 410–421.

Knight, M. (1994). Darwinian functionalism. *The Psychological Record, 44*, 271–287.

Kobasa, S. C. O. (1990). Stress-resistant personality. In R. E. Ornstein & C. Swencionis (Eds.), *The healing brain* (pp. 219–230). New York: The Guilford Press.

Kobasa, S. C. O., Maddi, S. R., Puccetti, M. C., & Zola, M. A. (1994). Effectiveness of hardiness, exercise, and social support as resources against illness. In A. Steptoe & J. Wardle (Eds.), *Psychosocial processes and health* (pp. 247–260). Cambridge, England: Cambridge University Press.

Kohlberg, L. (1969). *Stages in the development of moral thought and action.* New York: Holt, Rinehart and Winston.

Kohlberg, L. (1981). The philosophy of moral development. San Francisco: Harper & Row.

Köhler, W. (1925). *The mentality of apes.* New York: Harcourt Brace World.

Kolata, G. (1996, August 27). Gene therapy shows first signs of bypassing arterial blockage. *The New York Times*, p. C3.

Kolata, G. (1997, February 24). With cloning of a sheep, the ethical ground shifts. *The New York Times*, pp. A1, B8.

Kolko, D. J., & Rickard-Figueroa, J. L. (1985). Effects of video games on the adverse corollaries of chemotherapy in pediatric oncology patients. *Journal of Consulting and Clinical Psychology, 53*, 223–228.

Koocher, G. P. (1991). Questionable methods in alcoholism research. *Journal of Consulting and Clinical Psychology, 59*, 246–248.

Korn, J. H., Davis, R., & Davis, S. F. (1991). Historians' and chairpersons' judgments of eminence among psychologists. *American Psychologist, 46*, 789–792.

Kosonen, P., & Winne, P. H. (1995). Effects of teaching statistical laws on reasoning about everyday problems. *Journal of Educational Psychology, 87*, 33–46.

Koss, M. P. (1993). Rape. *American Psychologist, 48*, 1062–1069.

Koss, M. P., Gidycz, C. A., & Wisniewski, N. (1987). The scope of rape. *Journal of Consulting and Clinical Psychology, 55*, 162–170.

Kosslyn, S. M. (1994). *Image and brain.* Cambridge, MA: The MIT Press, a Bradford Book.

Kramer, P. D. (1993). *Listening to Prozac.* New York: Viking.

Krantz, D. S., Contrada, R. J., Hill, D. R., & Friedler, E. (1988). Environmental stress and biobehavioral antecedents of coronary heart disease. *Journal of Consulting and Clinical Psychology, 56*, 333–341.

Krosnick, J. A. (1989). Attitude importance and attitude accessibility. *Personality and Social Psychology Bulletin, 15*, 297–308.

Kubiszyn, T. (1996). Cited in Murray, B. (1996). Task force defines psychology's role in schools. *APA Monitor, 26*(4), 34.

Kübler-Ross, E. (1969). *On death and dying.* New York: Macmillan.

Kuczaj, S. A., II (1982). On the nature of syntactic development. In S. A. Kuczaj, II (Ed.), *Language development: Vol. 1. Syntax and semantics.* Hillsdale, NJ: Erlbaum.

Kumanyika, S. (1996). Improving our diet—Still a long way to go. *New England Journal of Medicine, 335*, 738–740.

Kupfer, D. J., & Reynolds, C. F. (1997). Management of insomnia. *New England Journal of Medicine, 336*, 341–346.

Lackner, J. M., Carosella, A. M., & Feuerstein, M. (1996). Pain expectancies, pain, and functional self-efficacy expectancies as determinants of disability in patients with chronic low back disorders. *Journal of Consulting and Clinical Psychology, 64*, 212–220.

Lacks, P., & Morin, C. M. (1992). Recent advances in the assessment and treatment of insomnia. *Journal of Consulting and Clinical Psychology, 60*, 586–594.

LaFramboise, T. (1994). Cited in DeAngelis, T. (1994). History, culture affect treatment for Indians. *APA Monitor, 27*(10), 36.

Lakka, T. A., and others (1994). Relation of leisure-time physical activity and cardiorespiratory fitness to the risk of acute myocardial infarction in men. *New England Journal of Medicine, 330*, 1549–1554.

Lamb, M. E., & Baumrind, D. (1978). Socialization and personality development in the preschool years. In M. E. Lamb (Ed.), *Social and personality development.* New York: Holt, Rinehart and Winston.

Lamb, M. E., Sternberg, K. J., & Prodromidis, M. (1992). Nonmaternal care and the security of infant-mother attachment. *Infant Behavior and Development, 15*, 71–83.

Lambert, W. E. (1990). Persistent issues in bilingualism. In B. Harley and others (Eds.), *The development of second language proficiency.* Cambridge, England: Cambridge University Press.

Lambert, W. E., Genesee, F., Holobow, N., & Chartrand, L. (1991). *Bilingual education for majority English-speaking children.* Montreal: McGill University.

Lang, A. R., Goeckner, D. J., Adesso, V. J., & Marlatt, G. A. (1975). Effects of alcohol on aggression in male social drinkers. *Journal of Abnormal Psychology, 84*, 508–518.

Lang, P. J., & Melamed, B. B. (1969). Case report: Avoidance conditioning therapy of an infant with chronic ruminative vomiting. *Journal of Abnormal Psychology, 74*, 1–8.

Lang, S. S., & Patt, R. B. (1994). *You don't have to suffer.* New York: Oxford University Press.

Langer, E. J., Rodin, J., Beck, P., Weinan, C., & Spitzer, L. (1979). Environmental determinants of memory improvement in late adulthood. *Journal of Personality and Social Psychology, 37*, 2003–2013.

Larrick, R. P. (1993). Motivational factors in decision theories. *Psychological Bulletin, 113*, 440–450.

Larson, R., & Richards, M. H. (1991). Daily companionship in late childhood and early adolescence. *Child Development, 62*, 284–300.

Larson, R. K. (1990). Semantics. In D. N. Osherson, & H. Lasnik (Eds.), *An invitation to cognitive science: Language* (Vol. 1). Cambridge, MA: The MIT Press, a Bradford Book.

Lashley, K. S. (1950). In search of the engram. In *Symposium of the Society for Experimental Biology* (Vol. 4). New York: Cambridge University Press.

Latané, B., & Dabbs, J. M. (1975). Sex, group size, and helping in three cities. *Sociometry, 38*, 180–194.

Lau, M. A., Pihl, R. O., & Peterson, J. B. (1995). Provocation, acute alcohol intoxication, cognitive performance, and aggression. *Journal of Abnormal Psychology, 104*, 150–155.

Laumann, E. O., Gagnon, J. H., Michael, R. T., & Michaels, S. (1994). *The social organization of sexuality.* Chicago: University of Chicago Press.

Lawton, C., & Morrin, K. (1997). Cited in Azar, B. (1997). Environment can mitigate differences in spatial ability. *APA Monitor, 28*(6), 28.

Lazarus, R. S., DeLongis, A., Folkman, S., & Gruen, R. (1985). Stress and adaptational outcomes. *American Psychologist, 40*, 770–779.

Lazarus, R. S., & Folkman, S. (1984). *Stress, appraisal, and coping.* New York: Springer.

Leary, W. E. (1991, October 22). Black hypertension may reflect other ills. *The New York Times*, p. C3.

Leary, W. E. (1995, May 2). Billions suffering needlessly, study says. *The New York Times*, p. C5.

Leary, W. E. (1997, January 14). Researchers investigate (horrors!) nicotine's potential benefits. *The New York Times*, p. C3.

Le Bon, G. (1960). *The crowd.* New York: Viking. (Original work published 1895)

LeBow, M. D., Goldberg, P. S., & Collins, A. (1977). Eating behavior of overweight and nonoverweight persons in the natural environment. *Journal of Consulting and Clinical Psychology, 45*, 1204–1205.

Lederberg, A. R., & Mobley, C. E. (1990). The effect of hearing impairment on the quality of attachment and mother-toddler interaction. *Child Development, 61*, 1596–1604.

LeDoux, J. E. (1994, June). Emotion, memory, and the brain. *Scientific American, 270*, 50–57.

LeDoux, J. E. (1997). Emotion, memory, and the brain. *Scientific American mysteries of the mind, Special Issue Vol. 7, No. 1*, 68–75.

Lee, C. C., & Richardson, B. L. (1991). *Multicultural issues in counseling.* Alexandria, VA: AACD.

Lefcourt, H. M., & Martin, R. A. (1986). *Humor and life stress.* New York: Springer-Verlag.

Lefcourt, H. M., Miller, R. S., Ware, E. E., & Sherk, D. (1981). Locus of control as a modifier of the relationship between stressors and moods. *Journal of Personality and Social Psychology, 41*, 357–369.

Lefcourt, H. M. (1997). Cited in Clay, R. A. (1997). Researchers harness the power of humor. *APA Monitor, 28*(9), 1, 18.

Lefley, H. P. (1990). Culture and chronic mental illness. *Hospital and Community Psychiatry, 41*, 277–286.

Leibowitz, H. W. (1996). The symbiosis between

basic and applied research. *American Psychologist, 51,* 366–370.

Leigh, B. C. (1993). Alcohol consumption and sexual activity as reported with a diary technique. *Journal of Abnormal Psychology, 102,* 490–493.

Leigh, B. C., & Stall, R. (1993). Substance use and risky sexual behavior for exposure to HIV. *American Psychologist, 48,* 1035–1045.

Leitenberg, H., & Henning, K. (1995). Sexual fantasy. *Psychological Bulletin, 117,* 469–496.

Lenneberg, E. H. (1967). *Biological foundations of language.* New York: Wiley.

Leor, J., Poole, K., & Kloner, R. A. (1996). Sudden cardiac death triggered by an earthquake. *New England Journal of Medicine, 334,* 413–419.

Lerman, C. (1997). Psychological aspects of genetic testing. *Health Psychology, 16,* 3–7.

Lerman, C., and others. (1997). Incorporating biomarkers of exposure and genetic susceptibility into smoking cessation treatment. *Health Psychology, 16,* 87–99.

Leutwyler, K. (1997). Depression's double standard. *Scientific American mysteries of the mind, Special Issue Vol. 7,* No. 1, 53–54.

Levine, I. S., & Rog, D. J. (1990). Mental health services for homeless mentally ill. *American Psychologist, 45,* 963–968.

Levine, S. R., and others (1990). Cerebrovascular complications of the use of the "crack" form of alkaloidal cocaine. *New England Journal of Medicine, 323,* 699–704.

Levinson, D. J., Darrow, C. N., Klein, E. B., Levinson, M. H., & McKee, B. (1978). *The seasons of a man's life.* New York: Knopf.

Levinson, D. J. (1996). *The seasons of a woman's life.* New York: Knopf.

Lewin, T. (1995, December 7). Parents poll shows higher incidence of child abuse. *The New York Times,* p. B16.

Lewinsohn, P. M., Rohde, P., & Seeley, J. R. (1994a). Psychosocial risk factors for future suicide attempts. *Journal of Consulting and Clinical Psychology, 62,* 297–305.

Lewinsohn, P. M., and others (1994b). Adolescent psychopathology: II. Psychosocial risk factors for depression. *Journal of Abnormal Psychology, 103,* 302–315.

Lewis, P. H. (1995, August 21). Planet Out: "Gay global village" of cyberspace. *The New York Times,* p. D3.

Lewis-Fernández, R. & Kleinman, A. (1994). Culture, personality, and psychopathology. *Journal of Abnormal Psychology, 103,* 67–71.

Lieber, C. S. (1990). Cited in Barroom biology: How alcohol goes to a woman's head (January 14). *The New York Times,* p. E24.

Liebert, R. M., Sprafkin, J. N., & Davidson, E. S. (1989). *The early window* (3rd. ed.). New York: Pergamon.

Linden, W., Chambers, L., Maurice, J., & Lenz, J. W. (1993). Sex differences in social support, self-deception, hostility, and ambulatory cardiovascular activity. *Health Psychology, 12,* 376–380.

Linville, P. W., Fischer, G. W., & Salovey, P. (1989). Perceived distribution of the characteristics of in-group and out-group members. *Journal of Personality and Social Psychology, 57,* 165–188.

Lips, H. (1993). *Sex and gender* (2nd ed.). Mountain View, CA: Mayfield.

Lipsey, M. W., & Wilson, D. B. (1993). The efficacy of psychological, educational, and behavioral treatment. *American Psychologist, 48,* 1181–1209.

Lochman, J. E. (1992). Cognitive-behavioral intervention with aggressive boys. *Journal of Consulting and Clinical Psychology, 60,* 426–432.

Lochman, J. E., & Dodge, K. A. (1994). Social-cognitive processes of severely violent, moderately aggressive, and nonaggressive boys. *Journal of Consulting and Clinical Psychology, 62,* 366–374.

Loftus, E. F. (1983). Silence is not golden. *American Psychologist, 38,* 564–572.

Loftus, E. F. (1993a). The reality of repressed memories. *American Psychologist, 48,* 518–537.

Loftus, E. F. (1993b). Psychologists in the eyewitness world. *American Psychologist, 48,* 550–552.

Loftus, E. F. (1994). Conference on memory, Harvard Medical School. Cited in D. Goleman (1994, May 31). Miscoding is seen as the root of false memories. *The New York Times,* pp. C1, C8.

Loftus, E. F. (1997). Cited in Loftus consulting in Oklahoma City bombing trial. *APA Monitor, 28*(4), 8–9.

Loftus, E. F., & Ketcham, K. (1994). *The myth of repressed memory.* New York: St. Martin's Press.

Loftus, E. F., & Loftus, G. R. (1980). On the permanence of stored information in the brain. *American Psychologist, 35,* 409–420.

Loftus, E. F., & Palmer, J. C. (1973). Reconstruction of automobile destruction. *Journal of Verbal Learning and Verbal Behavior, 13,* 585–589.

Loftus, G. R. (1983). The continuing persistence of the icon. *Behavioral and Brain Sciences, 6,* 28.

Loftus, G. R., & Loftus, E. F. (1976). *Human memory.* Hillsdale, NJ: Erlbaum.

Lohr, J. M., & Staats, A. (1973). Attitude conditioning in Sino-Tibetan languages. *Journal of Personality and Social Psychology, 26,* 196–200.

"Longer, healthier, better." (1997, March 9). *The New York Times Magazine,* pp. 44–45.

Lopez, S., & Hernandez, P. (1986). How culture is considered in evaluations of psychopathology. *Journal of Nervous and Mental Diseases, 176,* 598–606.

Lore, R. K., & Schultz, L. A. (1993). Control of human aggression. *American Psychologist, 48,* 16–25.

Lorenz, K. Z. (1981). *The foundations of ethology.* New York: Springer-Verlag.

Lowe, M. R., and others. (1996). Restraint, dieting, and the continuum model of bulimia nervosa. *Journal of Abnormal Psychology, 105,* 508–517.

Luborsky, L., Barber, J. P., & Beutler, L. (1993). Introduction to special section. *Journal of Consulting and Clinical Psychology, 61,* 539–541.

Luchins, A. S. (1957). Primacy-recency in impression formation. In C. I. Hovland (Ed.), *The order of presentation in persuasion.* New Haven, CT: Yale University Press.

Ludwick-Rosenthal, R., & Neufeld, R. W. J. (1993). Preparation for undergoing an invasive medical procedure. *Journal of Consulting and Clinical Psychology, 61,* 156–164.

Lundeberg, M. A., Fox, P. W., & Puncochar, J. (1994). Highly confident but wrong. *Journal of Educational Psychology, 86,* 114–121.

Lurie, N., and others (1993). Preventive care for women? *New England Journal of Medicine, 329,* 478–482.

Lydiard, R. B., Brawman, A., Mintzer, O., & Ballenger, J. C. (1996). Recent developments in the psychopharmacology of anxiety disorders. *Journal of Consulting and Clinical Psychology, 64,* 660–668.

Lykken, D. T. (1982). Fearlessness. *Psychology Today, 16*(9), 20–28.

Lykken, D. T. (1996). Cited in Goleman, D. (1996, July 21). A set point for happiness. *The New York Times,* p. E2.

Lykken, D. T., McGue, M., Tellegen, A., & Bouchard, T. J., Jr. (1992). Emergenesis: Genetic traits that may not run in families. *American Psychologist, 47,* 1565–1577.

Maas, J. W., and others. (1993). Studies of catecholamine metabolism in schizophrenia/psychosis—I. *Neuropsychopharmacology, 8,* 97–109.

Maccoby, E. E. (1990). Gender and relationships. *American Psychologist, 45,* 513–520.

Maccoby, E. E., & Jacklin, C. N. (1974). *The psychology of sex differences.* Stanford, CA: Stanford University Press.

MacDonald, K. (1992). Warmth as a developmental construct. *Child Development, 63,* 753–773.

Macfarlane, J. A. (1975). Olfaction in the development of social preferences in the human neonate. In M. A. Hofer (Ed.), *Parent-infant interaction.* Amsterdam: Elsevier.

Mack, D., & Rainey, D. (1990). Female applicants' grooming and personnel selection. *Journal of Social Behavior and Personality, 5,* 399–407.

MacKenzie, T. D., Bartecchi, C. E., & Schrier, R. W. (1994). The human costs of tobacco use. *New England Journal of Medicine, 330,* 975–980.

Mackie, D. M., & Worth, L. T. (1989). Processing deficits and the mediation of positive affect in persuasion. *Journal of Personality and Social Psychology, 57,* 27–40.

Mackie, D. M., Worth, L. T., & Asuncion, A. G. (1990). Processing of persuasive in-group messages. *Journal of Personality and Social Psychology, 58,* 812–822.

Maher, B. A., & Maher, W. B. (1994). Personality and psychopathology. *Journal of Abnormal Psychology, 103,* 72–77.

Maier, N. R. F., & Schneirla, T. C. (1935). *Principles of animal psychology.* New York: McGraw-Hill.

Maier, S. F., Watkins, L. R., & Fleshner, M. (1994). Psychoneuroimmunology. *American Psychologist, 49,* 1004–1017.

Malgady, R. G., Rogler, L. H., & Costantino, G. (1990). Hero/heroine modeling for Puerto Rican adolescents. *Journal of Consulting and Clinical Psychology, 58,* 469–474.

Malinosky-Rummell, R., & Hansen, D. H. (1993). Long-term consequences of childhood physical abuse. *Psychological Bulletin, 114,* 68–79.

Manber, R., & Bootzin, R. R. (1997). Sleep and the menstrual cycle. *Health Psychology, 16,* 209–214.

"Man transmits HIV with kiss." (1997, July 11). *USA Today,* p. 3D.

Marecek, J. (1995). Gender, politics, and psychology's ways of knowing. *American Psychologist, 50,* 162–163.

Marenberg, M. E. and others (1994). Genetic susceptibility to death from coronary heart disease in a study of twins. *New England Journal of Medicine, 330,* 1041–1046.

Margoshes, P. (1995). For many, old age is the prime of life. *APA Monitor, 26*(5), 36–37.

Markman, H. J., Renick, M. J., Floyd, F. J., Stanley, S. M., & Clements, M. (1993). Preventing marital distress through communication and conflict management training. *Journal of Consulting and Clinical Psychology, 61,* 70–77.

Markus, H., & Kitayama, S. (1991). Culture and the self. *Psychological Review, 98*(2), 224–253.

Marteau, T. M., Dundas, R., & Axworthy, D. (1997). Long-term cognitive and emotional impact of genetic testing for carriers of cystic fibrosis. *Health Psychology, 16,* 51–62.

Martin, J. E., and others. (1997). Prospective evaluation of three smoking interventions in 205 recovering alcoholics. *Journal of Consulting and Clinical Psychology, 65,* 190–194.

Martin, R. A., & Lefcourt, H. M. (1983). Sense of humor as a moderator of the relation between stressors and moods. *Journal of Personality and Social Psychology, 45,* 1313–1324.

Martin, S. (1994). Music lessons enhance spatial reasoning skills. *APA Monitor, 27*(10), 5.

Marx, E. M., Williams, J. M. G., & Claridge, G. C. (1992). Depression and social problem solving. *Journal of Abnormal Psychology, 101,* 78–86.

Maslow, A. H. (1970). *Motivation and personality* (2nd ed.). New York: Harper & Row.

Matefy, R. (1980). Role-playing theory of psychedelic flashbacks. *Journal of Consulting and Clinical Psychology, 48,* 551–553.

Matlin, M. (1996). *The psychology of women* (3rd ed.). Fort Worth: Harcourt Brace College Publishers.

Matlin, M. (1997). *Cognition* (4th ed.). Fort Worth: Harcourt Brace College Publishers.

Matlin, M. W., & Foley, H. J. (1995). *Sensation and perception* (4th ed.). Boston: Allyn & Bacon.

Matthews, K. (1994). Cited in Azar, B. (1994). Women are barraged by media on "the change." *APA Monitor, 25*(5), 24–25.

Matthews, K., and others. (1997). Women's Health Initiative. *American Psychologist, 52,* 101–116.

Matus, I. (1996.) Cited in Clay, R. A. (1996). Beating the "biological clock" with zest. *APA Monitor, 27*(2), 37.

Mazzella, R., & Feingold, A. (1994). The effects of physical attractiveness, race, socioeconomic status, and gender of defendants and victims on judgments of mock jurors. *Journal of Applied Social Psychology, 24*(15), 1315–1344.

McCall, R. (1997). Cited in Sleek, S. (1997). Can "emotional intelligence" be taught in today's schools? *APA Monitor, 28*(6), 25.

McCann, I. L., & Holmes, D. S. (1984). Influence of aerobic exercise on depression. *Journal of Personality and Social Psychology, 46,* 1142–1147.

McCarley, R. W. (1992). Cited in Blakeslee, S. (1992, January 7). Scientists unraveling chemistry of dreams. *The New York Times,* pp. C1, C10.

McCauley, C., Woods, K., Coolidge, C., & Kulick, W. (1983). More aggressive cartoons are funnier. *Journal of Personality and Social Psychology, 44,* 817–823.

McClelland, D. C. (1958). Methods of measuring human motivation. In J. W. Atkinson (Ed.), *Motives in fantasy, action, and society.* Princeton, NJ: Van Nostrand.

McClelland, D. C. (1965). Achievement and entrepreneurship. *Journal of Personality and Social Psychology, 1,* 389–392.

McCrae, R. R. (1996). Social consequences of experiential openness. *Psychological Bulletin, 120,* 323–337.

McCrae, R. R., & Costa, P. T., Jr. (1997). Personality trait structure as a human universal. *American Psychologist, 52,* 509–516.

McDermott, D. (1997, May 14). Yes, computers *can* think. *The New York Times,* p. A21.

McDougall, W. (1904). The sensations excited by a single momentary stimulation of the eye. *British Journal of Psychology, 1,* 78–113.

McDougall, W. (1908). *An introduction to social psychology.* London: Methuen.

McGovern, T. V. (1996). Cited in Murray, B. (1996). Psychology remains top college major. *APA Monitor, 27*(2), 1, 42.

McGovern, T. V. (1989). Task force eyes the making of a major. *APA Monitor, 20*(7), 50.

McGovern, T. V., Furumoto, L., Halpern, D. F., Kimble, G. A., & McKeachie, W. J. (1991). Liberal education, study in depth, and the arts and sciences major—psychology. *American Psychologist, 46,* 598–605.

McGovern, T. V., & Reich, J. N. (1996). A comment on the *Quality Principles. American Psychologist, 51,* 251–255.

McGowan, R. J., & Johnson, D. L. (1984). The mother-child relationship and other antecedents of childhood intelligence. *Child Development, 55,* 810–820.

McGrath, E., Keita, G. P., Strickland, B. R., & Russo, N. F. (1990). *Women and depression.* Washington DC: American Psychological Association.

McIntosh, H. (1996). Solitude provides an emotional tune-up. *APA Monitor, 26*(3), 1, 10.

McKeachie, W. (1994) Cited in DeAngelis, T. (1994). Educators reveal keys to success in classroom. *APA Monitor, 25*(1), 39–40.

McNally, R. J. (1990). Psychological approaches to panic disorder. *Psychological Bulletin, 108,* 403–419.

McNally, R. J., & Eke, M. (1996). Anxiety sensitivity, suffocation fear, and breath-holding duration as predictors of response to carbon dioxide challenge. *Journal of Abnormal Psychology, 105,* 146–149.

McTiernan, A. (1997). Exercise and breast cancer. *New England Journal of Medicine, 336,* 1311–1312.

Mead, M. (1935). *Sex and temperament in three primitive societies.* New York: Dell.

Meade, V. (1994). Psychologists forecast future of the profession. *APA Monitor, 25*(5), 14–15.

Meichenbaum, D. (1993). Changing conceptions of cognitive behavior modification. *Journal of Consulting and Clinical Psychology, 61,* 202–204.

Meichenbaum, D., & Jaremko, M. E. (Eds.). (1983). *Stress reduction and prevention.* New York: Plenum.

Meier, B. (1997, June 8). In war against AIDS, battle over baby formula reignites. *The New York Times,* pp. A1, A16.

Meltzoff, A. N. (1997). Cited in Azar, B. (1997). New theory on development could usurp Piagetian beliefs. *APA Monitor, 28*(6), 9.

Meltzoff, A. N., & Gopnik, A. (1997). *Words, thoughts, and theories.* Cambridge, MA: MIT Press.

Melzack, R. (1980). Psychological aspects of pain. In J. J. Bonica (Ed.), *Pain.* New York: Raven Press.

Melzack, R. (1990). Phantom limbs and the concept of a neuromatrix. *Trends in Neurosciences, 13,* 88–92.

Melzack, R. (1997). Phantom limbs. *Scientific American mysteries of the mind, Special Issue Vol. 7,* No. 1, 84–91.

Mendez, M., and others (1992). Disturbances of person identification in Alzheimer's disease. *Journal of Nervous & Mental Disease, 180,* 94–96.

Merluzzi, T. V., & Martinez Sanchez, M. (1997). Assessment of self-efficacy and coping with cancer. *Health Psychology, 16,* 163–170.

Metcalfe, J. (1986). Premonitions of insight predict impending error. *Journal of Experimental Psychology: Learning, Memory, and Cognition, 12,* 623–634.

Mevkens, F. L. (1990). Coming of age—The chemoprevention of cancer. *New England Journal of Medicine, 323,* 825–827.

Meyer, T. (1997). Americans are getting fatter. Associated Press; America Online.

Meyers, A. W., and others (1997). Are weight concerns predictive of smoking cessation? *Journal of Consulting and Clinical Psychology, 65,* 448–452.

Michael, R. T., Gagnon, J. H., Laumann, E. O., & Kolata, G. (1994). *Sex in America: A definitive survey.* Boston: Little, Brown.

Michaelson, R. (1993). Tug-of-war is developing over defining retardation. *APA Monitor, 24*(5), 34–35.

Michels, R., & Marzuk, P. M. (1993a). Progress in psychiatry. (Part 1). *New England Journal of Medicine, 329,* 552–560.

Michels, R., & Marzuk, P. M. (1993b). Progress in psychiatry. (Part 2). *New England Journal of Medicine, 329,* 628–638.

Mikesell, R. H., Lusterman, D., & McDaniel, S. (Eds.). (1995). *Family psychology and systems therapy.* Washington, DC: American Psychological Association.

Milgram, S. (1963). Behavioral study of obedience. *Journal of Abnormal and Social Psychology, 67,* 371–378.

Milgram, S. (1974). *Obedience to authority.* New York: Harper & Row.

Milgram, S. (1977). *The individual in a social world.* Reading, MA: Addison-Wesley.

Miller, G. A. (1956). The magical number seven, plus or minus two: Some limits on our capacity for processing information. *Psychological Review, 63,* 81–97.

Miller, J. L. (1990). Speech perception. In D. N. Osherson, & H. Lasnik (Eds.), *An invitation to cognitive science: Language* (Vol. 1). Cambridge, MA: The MIT Press, A Bradford Book.

Miller, J. L. (1992). Trouble in mind. *Scientific American, 267*(3), 180.

Miller, M. E., & Bowers, K. S. (1993). Hypnotic analgesia. *Journal of Abnormal Psychology, 102,* 29–38.

Miller, M. F., Barabasz, A. F., & Barabasz, M. (1991). Effects of active alert and relaxation hypnotic inductions on cold pressor pain. *Journal of Abnormal Psychology, 100,* 223–226.

Miller, N. B., Cowan, P. A., Cowan, C. P., Hetherington, E. M., & Clingempeel, W. G. (1993). Externalizing in preschoolers and early adolescents. *Developmental Psychology, 29,* 3–18.

Miller, N. E. (1969). Learning of visceral and glandular responses. *Science, 163,* 434–445.

Miller, N. E. (1995). Clinical-experimental interactions in the development of neuroscience. *American Psychologist, 50,* 901–911.

Miller, N. E., & Dollard, J. (1941). *Social learning and imitation.* New Haven, CT: Yale University Press.

Miller, S. M., Shoda, Y., & Hurley, K. (1996). Applying cognitive-social theory to health-protective behavior: Breast self-examination in cancer screening. *Psychological Bulletin, 199,* 70–94.

Miller, T. Q., Smith, T. W., Turner, C. W., Guijarro, M. L., & Hallet, A. J. (1996). A meta-analytic review of research on hostility and physical health. *Psychological Bulletin, 119,* 322–348.

Mills, C. J. (1992). Academically talented children: The case for early identification and nurturance. *Pediatrics, 89,* 156–157.

Milner, B. R. (1966). Amnesia following operation on temporal lobes. In C. W. M. Whitty & O. L. Zangwill (Eds.), *Amnesia.* London: Butterworth.

Mindell, J. A. (1993). Sleep disorders in children. *Health Psychology, 12,* 151–162.

Mineka, S. (1991, August). Paper presented to the annual meeting of the American Psychological Association, San Francisco. Cited in Turkington, C. (1991). Evolutionary memories may have phobia role. *APA Monitor, 22*(11), 14.

Mischel, W., & Shoda, Y. (1995). A cognitive-affective system theory of personality. *Psychological Review, 102,* 246–268.

Moliterno, D. J., and others (1994). Coronary-artery vasoconstriction induced by cocaine, cigarette smoking, or both. *New England Journal of Medicine, 330,* 454–459.

Money, J. (1987). Sin, sickness, or status? Homosexual gender identity and psychoneuroendocrinology. *American Psychologist, 42,* 384–399.

Montemayor, R., & Flannery, D. J. (1991). Parent-adolescent relations in middle and late adolescence. In R. M. Lerner, A. C. Petersen, & J. Brooks-Gunn (Eds.), *Encyclopedia of adolescence.* New York: Garland.

Moore, R. Y. (1995). Vision without sight. *New England Journal of Medicine, 332,* 54–55.

Morales, E. (1992). Latino gays and Latina lesbians. In S. Dworkin & F. Gutierrez (Eds.), *Counseling gay men and lesbians.* Alexandria, VA: American Association for Counseling and Development.

Moreland, R. L. & Zajonc, R. B. (1982). Exposure effects in person perception: Familiarity, similarity, and attraction. *Journal of Experimental Social Psychology, 18,* 395–415.

"More research needed on medical use of marijuana." (1997). *APA Monitor, 28*(4), 9.

Morin, C. M., Kowatch, R. A., Barry, T., & Walton, E. (1993). Cognitive-behavior therapy for late-life insomnia. *Journal of Consulting and Clinical Psychology, 61,* 137–146.

Morris, W. N., Miller, R. S., & Spangenberg, S. (1977). The effects of dissenter position and task difficulty on conformity and response conflict. *Journal of Personality, 45,* 251–256.

Moscovitch, M. (1994). Conference on memory, Harvard Medical School. Cited in Goleman, D. (1994, May 31). Miscoding is seen as the root of false memories. *The New York Times,* pp. C1, C8.

Moser, C. G., & Dyck, D. G. (1989). Type A behavior, uncontrollability, and the activation of hostile self-schema responding. *Journal of Research in Personality, 23,* 248–267.

Moyers, B. (1993). *Healing and the mind.* New York: Doubleday.

Mullen, B., and others (1987). Newscasters' facial expressions and voting behavior of viewers. *Journal of Personality and Social Psychology, 53.*

Muñoz, R. F., Hollon, S. D., McGrath, E., Rehm, L. P., & VandenBos, G. R. (1994). On the AHCPR *Depression in Primary Care* guidelines: Further considerations for practitioners. *American Psychologist, 49,* 42–61.

Murray, B. (1996a). Psychology remains top college major. *APA Monitor, 27*(2), 1, 42.

Murray, B. (1996b). Virtual classrooms draw cheers, fears. *APA Monitor, 27*(2), 40–41.

Murray, B. (1997a). America still lags behind in mathematics test scores. *APA Monitor, 28*(1), 44.

Murray, B. (1997b). Teaching today's pupils to think more critically. *APA Monitor, 28*(3), 51.

Murray, C. (1995). *"The Bell Curve* and its critics." *Commentary, 99*(5), 23, 28.

Murray, H. A. (1938). *Explorations in personality.* New York: Oxford University Press.

Murtagh, D. R. R., & Greenwood, K. M. (1995). Identifying effective psychological treatments for insomnia: A meta-analysis. *Journal of Consulting and Clinical Psychology, 63,* 79–89.

Muslim Women Bridging Culture Gap. (1993, November 8). *The New York Times,* p. B9.

Myers, L. B., & Brewin, C. R. (1994). Recall of early experience and the repressive coping style. *Journal of Abnormal Psychology, 103,* 288–292.

Nadol, J. B., Jr. (1993). Hearing loss. *New England Journal of Medicine, 329,* 1092–1102.

National Center for Health Statistics (1996, March.). News Releases and Fact Sheets. *Monitoring Health Care in America: Quarterly Fact Sheet.*

National Institute of Mental Health. (1982). *Television and behavior: Ten years of scientific progress and implications for the eighties.* Washington, DC: National Institute of Mental Health.

National Institute of Occupational Safety and Health. (1990). *A proposal: National strategy for the prevention of psychological disorders.* Draft paper provided to the U.S. Senate Appropriations Subcommittee on Labor, Health and Human Services, and Education and Related Agencies by NIOSH.

Neisser, U. (1993). Cited in Goleman, D. J. (1993, April 6). Studying the secrets of childhood memory. *The New York Times,* pp. C1, C11.

Neisser, U. (1997a). Never a dull moment. *American Psychologist, 52,* 79–81.

Neisser, U. (1997b). Cited in Sleek, S. (1997). Can "emotional intelligence" be taught in today's schools? *APA Monitor, 28*(6), 25.

Neisser, U., Boodoo, G., Bouchard, T. J., Jr., Boykin, A. W., Brody, N., Ceci, S. J., Halpern, D. F., Loehlin, J. C., Perloff, R., Sternberg, R. J., & Urbina, S. (1996). Intelligence: Knowns and unknowns. *American Psychologist, 51,* 77–101.

Nelson, K. (1973). Structure and strategy in learning to talk. *Monographs for the Society for Research in Child Development, 38* (Whole No. 149).

Nelson, K., Hampson, J., & Shaw, L. K. (1993). Nouns in early lexicons: Evidence, explanations, and implications. *Journal of Child Language, 20,* 228.

Nevid, J. S., Rathus, S. A., & Greene, B. A. (1997). *Abnormal psychology in a changing world* (3rd ed.). Englewood Cliffs, NJ: Prentice Hall.

Nevid, J. S., Rathus, S. A., & Rubenstein, H. (1998). *Health in the new millennium.* New York: Worth.

Newlin, D. B., & Thomson, J. B. (1990). Alcohol challenge with sons of alcoholics: A critical review and analysis. *Psychological Bulletin, 108,* 383–402.

Newman, F. L., & Howard, K. I. (1991). Introduction to the special section on seeking new clinical research methods. *Journal of Consulting and Clinical Psychology, 59,* 8–11.

Newman, J., & McCauley, C. (1977). Eye contact with strangers in city, suburb, and small town. *Environment and Behavior, 9,* 547–558.

Newman, R. (1994). Prozac: Panacea? Psychological steroid? *APA Monitor, 25*(4), 34.

Newport, E. L. (1994). Cited in Senior, J. (1994, January 3). Language of the deaf evolves to reflect new sensibilities. *The New York Times,* pp. A1, A12.

Nides, M. A., and others. (1995). Predictors of initial smoking cessation and relapse through the first 2 years of the lung health study. *Journal of Consulting and Clinical Psychology, 63,* 60–69.

NIMH. See National Institute of Mental Health.

Nolen-Hoeksema, S. (1991). Responses to depression and their effects on the duration of depressive episodes. *Journal of Abnormal Psychology, 100,* 569–582.

Nolen-Hoeksema, S., Morrow, J., & Fredrickson, B. L. (1993). Response styles and the duration of depressed mood. *Journal of Abnormal Psychology, 102,* 20–28.

Norris, F. H., & Kaniasty, K. (1994). Psychological distress following criminal victimization in the general population: Cross-sectional, longitudinal, and prospective analyses. *Journal of Consulting and Clinical Psychology, 62,* 111–123.

Norvell, N., & Belles, D. (1993). Psychological and physical benefits of circuit weight training in law enforcement personnel. *Journal of Consulting and Clinical Psychology, 61,* 520–527.

Novick, L. R., & Coté, N. (1992). The nature of expertise in anagram solution. In *Proceedings of the Fourteenth Annual Conference of the Cognitive Science Society.* Hillsdale, NJ: Erlbaum.

O'Brien, C. P. (1996). Recent developments in the pharmacotherapy of substance abuse. *Journal of Consulting and Clinical Psychology, 64,* 677–686.

ODEER (1994). See Office of Demographic, Employment, and Educational Research.

Office of Demographic, Employment, and Educational Research (1994). Summary report doctorate recipients from United States universities. Washington, DC: American Psychological Association.

Ogbu, J. U. (1993). Differences in cultural frame of reference. *International Journal of Behavioral Development, 16,* 483–506.

Okazaki, S. (1997). Sources of ethnic differences between Asian American and White American college students on measures of depression and social anxiety. *Journal of Abnormal Psychology, 106,* 52–60.

Olds, J. (1969). The central nervous system and the reinforcement of behavior. *American Psychologist, 24,* 114–132.

Olds, J., & Milner, P. (1954). Positive reinforcement produced by electrical stimulation of the septal area and other regions of the rat brain. *Journal of Comparative and Physiological Psychology, 47,* 419–427.

O'Leary, A. (1990). Stress, emotion, and human immune function. *Psychological Bulletin, 108,* 363–382.

Olson, S. L., Bates, J. E., & Kaskie, B. (1992). Caregiver-infant interaction antecedents of children's school-age cognitive ability. *Merrill-Palmer Quarterly, 38,* 309–330.

Ortega, D. F., & Pipal, J. E. (1984). Challenge seeking and the Type A coronary-prone behavior pattern. *Journal of Personality and Social Psychology, 46,* 1328–1334.

Ouimette, P. C., Finney, J. W., & Moos, R. H. (1997). Twelve-step and cognitive-behavioral treatment for substance abuse. *Journal of Consulting and Clinical Psychology, 65,* 230–240.

Paffenbarger, R. S., Jr., Hyde, R. T., Wing, A. L., & Hsieh, C. C. (1986). Physical activity, all-cause mortality, and longevity of college alumni. *New England Journal of Medicine, 314,* 605–613.

Paffenbarger, R. S., Jr., and others (1993). The association of changes in physical-activity level and other lifestyle characteristics with mortality among men. *New England Journal of Medicine, 328,* 538–545.

Pagan, G., & Aiello, J. R. (1982). Development of personal space among Puerto Ricans. *Journal of Nonverbal Behavior, 7,* 59–68.

Paikoff, R. L., & Collins, A. C. (1991). Editor's notes: Shared views in the family during adolescence. In R. L. Paikoff & A. C. Collins (Eds.), *New Directions for Child Development* (Vol. 51). San Francisco: Jossey-Bass.

Pajares, F., & Miller, M. D. (1994). Role of self-efficacy and self-concept beliefs in mathematical problem solving. *Journal of Educational Psychology, 86,* 193–203.

Papini, D. R., & Roggman, L. A. (1992). Adolescent perceived attachment to parents in relation to competence, depression, and anxiety. *Journal of Early Adolescence, 12,* 420–440.

Papousek, M., Papousek, H., & Symmes, D. (1991). The meanings of melodies in motherese in tone and stress languages. *Infant Behavior and Development, 14,* 415–440.

Pappas, G., Queen, S., Hadden, W., & Fisher, G. (1993). The increasing disparity of mortality between socioeconomic groups in the United States, 1960 and 1986. *New England Journal of Medicine, 329,* 103–109.

Pardes, H., and others (1991). Physicians and the animal-rights movement. *New England Journal of Medicine, 324,* 1640–1643.

Parker, J. G., & Herrera, C. (1996). Interpersonal processes in friendship: A comparison of abused and nonabused children's experience. *Developmental Psychology, 32,* 1025–1038.

Patrick, C. J., Bradley, M. M., & Lang, P. J. (1993). Emotion in the criminal psychopath: Startle reflex modulation. *Journal of Abnormal Psychology, 102,* 82–92.

Patterson, D. R., & Ptacek, J. T. (1997). Baseline pain as a moderator of hypnotic analgesia for burn injury treatment. *Journal of Consulting and Clinical Psychology, 65,* 60–67.

Patterson, G. R. (1993). Orderly change in a stable world: The antisocial trait as a chimera. *Journal of Consulting and Clinical Psychology, 61,* 911–919.

Patterson, M. L. (1991). Functions of nonverbal behavior in interpersonal interaction. In R. S. Feldman & B. Rime (Eds.), *Fundamentals of nonverbal behavior.* Cambridge, England: Cambridge University Press.

Pavlov, I. (1927). *Conditioned reflexes.* London: Oxford University Press.

Pedersen, N. L., Plomin, R., McClearn, G. E., & Friberg, L. (1988). Neuroticism, extraversion, and related traits in adult twins reared apart and reared together. *Journal of Personality and Social Psychology, 55,* 950–957.

Penfield, W. (1969). Consciousness, memory, and man's conditioned reflexes. In K. H. Pribram (Ed.), *On the biology of learning.* New York: Harcourt Brace Jovanovich.

Penn, D. L., Corrigan, P. W., Bentall, R. P., Racenstein, J. M., & Newman, L. (1997). Social cognition in schizophrenia. *Psychological Bulletin, 121,* 114–132.

Penn, N. E., Kar, S., Kramer, J., Skinner, J., & Zambrana, R. E. (1995). Panel VI. Ethnic minorities, health care systems, and behavior. *Health Psychology, 14,* 641–648.

Penner, L. A., Thompson, J. K., & Coovert, D. L. (1991). Size overestimation among anorexics: Much ado about very little? *Journal of Abnormal Psychology, 100,* 90–93.

Perls, F. S. (1971). *Gestalt therapy verbatim.* New York: Bantam.

Perrett, D. I. (1994). *Nature.* Cited in Brody, J. E. (1994, March 21). Notions of beauty transcend culture, new study suggests. *The New York Times,* p. A14.

Perry, D. G., & Bussey, K. (1979). The social learning theory of sex differences. *Journal of*

Personality and Social Psychology, 37, 1699–1712.

Peterson, E. D., and others. (1997). Racial variation in the use of coronary-revascularization procedures. *New England Journal of Medicine, 336,* 480–486.

Peterson, L. R., & Peterson, M. J. (1959). Short-term retention of individual verbal items. *Journal of Experimental Psychology, 58,* 193–198.

Petraitis, J., Flay, B. R., & Miller, T. Q. (1995). Reviewing theories of adolescent substance use. *Psychological Bulletin, 1995,* 67–86.

Petrie, T. A., & Diehl, N. S. (1995). Sport psychology in the profession of psychology. *Professional Psychology: Research and Practice, 26,* 288–291.

Pettingale, K. W., and others (1985). Mental attitudes to cancer. *Lancet, 1,* 750.

Petty, R. E., Cacioppo, J. T., Strathman, A. J., & Priester, J. R. (1994). To think or not to think: Exploring two routes to persuasion. In S. Shavitt & T. C. Brock (Eds.), *Persuasion* (pp. 113–147). Boston: Allyn & Bacon.

Phillipson, E. A. (1993). Sleep apnea. *New England Journal of Medicine, 328,* 1271–1273.

Phinney, J. S. (1996). When we talk about American ethnic groups, what do we mean? *American Psychologist, 51,* 918–927.

Phinney, J. S., Chavira, V., & Williamson, L. (1992). Acculturation attitudes and self-esteem among high school and college students. *Youth and Society, 23*(3), 299–312.

Piaget, J. (1963). *The origins of intelligence in children.* New York: W. W. Norton.

Pihl, R. O, & Peterson, J. B. (1992). Etiology. *Annual Review of Addictions Research and Treatment, 2,* 153–175, p. 155.

Pihl, R. O., Peterson, J. B., & Finn, P. (1990). Inherited predisposition to alcoholism. *Journal of Abnormal Psychology, 99,* 291–301.

Pike, K. M., & Rodin, J. (1991). Mothers, daughters, and disordered eating. *Journal of Abnormal Psychology, 100,* 198–204.

Pilkonis, P. (1996). Cited in Goleman, D. J. (1996, May 1). Higher suicide risk for perfectionists. *The New York Times,* p. C12.

Pillard, R. C. (1990). The Kinsey Scale: Is it familial? In D. P. McWhirter, S. A. Sanders, & J. M. Reinisch (Eds.) *Homosexuality/Heterosexuality: Concepts of sexual orientation* (pp. 88– 100). New York: Oxford University Press.

Pillard, R. C., & Weinrich, J. D. (1986). Evidence of familial nature of male homosexuality. *Archives of Sexual Behavior, 43,* 808–812.

Pinker, S. (1990). Language acquisition. In D. N. Osherson, & H. Lasnik (Eds.), *An invitation to cognitive science: Language* (Vol. 1). Cambridge, MA: The MIT Press, a Bradford Book.

Pinker, S. (1994a). *The language instinct.* New York: William Morrow.

Pinker, S. (1994b, June 19). Building a better brain. *The New York Times Book Review,* pp. 13–14.

Pinpointing chess moves in the brain. (1994, May 24). *The New York Times,* p. C14.

Pion, G. M., Mednick, M. T., Astin, H. S., Hall, C. C. I., Kenkel, M. B., Keita, G. P., Kohout, J. L., & Kelleher, J. C. (1996). The shifting gender composition of psychology. *American Psychologist, 51,* 509–528.

Plomin, R., DeFries, J. C., McClearn, G., & Rutter, M. (1997). *Behavioral genetics* (3rd ed.). New York: W. H. Freeman.

Plous, S. (1996). Attitudes toward the use of animals in psychological research and education. *American Psychologist, 51,* 1167–1180.

Plutchik, R. (1984). A general psychoevolutionary theory. In K. Scherer & P. Ekman (Eds.), *Approaches to emotion.* Hillsdale, NJ: Erlbaum.

Polivy, J., Zeitlin, S. B., Herman, C. P., & Beal, A. L. (1994). Food restriction and binge eating. *Journal of Abnormal Psychology, 103,* 409–411.

Pollack, W. S. (1996). Cited in Clay, R. A. (1996). Older men are more involved fathers, studies show. *APA Monitor, 27*(2), 37.

Pomerleau, O. F., Collins, A. C., Shiffman, S., & Pomerleau, C. S. (1993). Why some people smoke and others do not. *Journal of Consulting and Clinical Psychology, 61,* 723–731.

Pope, K. S. (1996). Memory, abuse, and science: Questioning claims about the false memory syndrome epidemic. *American Psychologist, 51,* 957–974.

Popkin, B. M., Siega-Riz, A. M., & Haines, P. S. (1996). A comparison of dietary trends among racial and socioeconomic groups in the United States. *New England Journal of Medicine, 335,* 716–720.

Porter, R. H., Makin, J. W., Davis, L. B., & Christensen, K. M. (1992). Breast-fed infants respond to olfactory cues from their own mother and unfamiliar lactating females. *Infant Behavior and Development, 15,* 85–93.

Posner, M. I., & Raichle, M. E. (1994). *Images of mind.* New York: W. H. Freeman.

Poussaint, A. (1990, September). An honest look at Black gays and lesbians. *Ebony,* pp. 124, 126, 130–131.

Powch, I. G., & Houston, B. K. (1996). Hostility, anger-in, and cardiovascular reactivity in White women. *Health Psychology, 15,* 200–208.

Powell, E. (1996). *Sex on your terms.* Boston: Allyn & Bacon.

Price, L. H., & Heninger, G. R. (1994). Lithium in the treatment of mood disorders. *New England Journal of Medicine, 331,* 591–598.

Putallaz, M., & Heflin, A. H. (1990). Parent-child interaction. In S. R. Asher & J. D. Coie (Eds.), *Peer rejection in childhood.* New York: Cambridge University Press.

Putnam, F. W., Guroff, J. J., Silberman, E. K., Barban, L., & Post, R. M. (1986). The clinical phenomenology of multiple personality disorder: Review of 100 recent cases. *Journal of Clinical Psychiatry, 47,* 285–293.

Quattrone, G. A. (1982). Overattribution and unit formation. *Journal of Personality and Social Psychology, 42,* 593–607.

Raichle, M. E. (1994). Visualizing the mind. *Scientific American, 270*(4), 58–64.

Rakowski, W. (1995). Cited in Margoshes, P. (1995). For many, old age is the prime of life. *APA Monitor, 26*(5), 36–37.

Rapoport, K., & Burkhart, B. R. (1984). Personality and attitudinal characteristics of sexually coercive college males. *Journal of Abnormal Psychology, 93,* 216–221.

Rappaport, N. B., McAnulty, D. P., & Brantley, P. J. (1988). Exploration of the Type A behavior pattern in chronic headache sufferers. *Journal of Consulting and Clinical Psychology, 56,* 621–623.

Rathus, S. A. (1973). A 30-item schedule for assessing assertive behavior. *Behavior Therapy, 4,* 398–406.

Rathus, S. A., & Fichner-Rathus, L. (1997). *The right start.* New York: Longman.

Rathus, S. A., Nevid, J. S., & Fichner-Rathus, L. (1997). *Human sexuality in a world of diversity* (3rd ed.). Boston: Allyn & Bacon.

Ratner, N. B., & Gleason, J. B. (1993). An introduction to psycholinguistics. In J. B. Gleason & N. B. Ratner (Eds.), *Psycholinguistics.* Fort Worth: Harcourt Brace Jovanovich.

Redd, W. H., and others (1987). Cognitive/attentional distraction in the control of conditioned nausea in pediatric cancer patients receiving chemotherapy. *Journal of Consulting and Clinical Psychology, 55,* 391–395.

Reid, P. T. (1994). The real problem in the study of culture. *American Psychologist, 49,* 524–525.

Reid, T. R. (1990, December 24). Snug in their beds for Christmas Eve: In Japan, December 24th has become the hottest night of the year. *The Washington Post.*

Reinke, B. J., Holmes, D. S., & Harris, R. L. (1985). The timing of psychosocial changes in women's lives. *Journal of Personality and Social Psychology, 48,* 1353–1364.

Reis, H. T., and others. (1990). What is smiling is beautiful and good. *European Journal of Social Psychology, 20,* 259–267.

Reiser, M. (1992). *Memory and mind and brain.* New York: Basic Books.

Renninger, K. A., & Wozniak, R. H. (1985). Effect of interest on attentional shift, recognition, and recall in young children. *Developmental Psychology, 21,* 624–632.

Repetti, R. L. (1993). Short-term effects of occupational stressors on daily mood and health complaints. *Health Psychology, 12,* 125–131.

Rescorla, R. A. (1988). Pavlovian conditioning: It's not what you think it is. *American Psychologist, 43,* 151–160.

Resnick, H. S., Kilpatrick, D. G., Dansky, B. S., Saunders, B. E., & Best, C. L. (1993). Prevalence of civilian trauma and posttraumatic stress disorder in a representative national sample of women. *Journal of Consulting and Clinical Psychology, 61,* 984–991.

Resnick, M., and others (1992, March 24). *Journal of the American Medical Association.* Cited in Young Indians prone to suicide, study finds. *The New York Times,* March 25, 1992, p. D24.

Rest, J. R. (1983). Morality. In P. H. Mussen, J. Flavell, & E. Markman (Eds.), *Handbook of child psychology: Vol. 3. Cognitive development.* New York: Wiley.

Reynolds, A. G. (1991). The cognitive consequences of bilingualism. In A. G. Reynolds (Ed.), *Bilingualism, multiculturalism, and second language learning.* Hillsdale, NJ: Erlbaum.

Rice, M. E., Quinsey, V. L., & Harris, G. T. (1991). Sexual recidivism among child molesters released from a maximum security psychiatric institution. *Journal of Consulting and Clinical Psychology, 59,* 381–386.

Rich, C. L., Ricketts, J. E., Thaler, R. C., & Young, D. (1988). Some differences between men and women who commit suicide. *American Journal of Psychiatry, 145,* 718–722.

Richardson, D. C., Bernstein, S., & Taylor, S. P. (1979). The effect of situational contingencies on female retaliative behavior. *Journal of Personality and Social Psychology, 37,* 2044–2048.

Richardson, P. H., & Vincent, C. A. (1986). Acupuncture for the treatment of pain. *Pain, 24,* 15–40.

Richman, J. (1993). *Preventing elderly suicide.* New York: Springer.

Riggio, R. E., & Woll, S. B. (1984). The role of nonverbal cues and physical attractiveness in the selection of dating partners. *Journal of Social and Personal Relationships, 1,* 347–357.

Rilling, M. (1996). The mystery of the vanished citations: James McConnell's forgotten 1960s quest for planarian learning. *American Psychologist, 51,* 589–598.

Rinn, W. E. (1991). Neuropsychology of facial expression. In R. S. Feldman & B. Rime (Eds.), *Fundamentals of nonverbal behavior.* Cambridge, England: Cambridge University Press.

Robbins, C., & Ehri, L. C. (1994). Reading storybooks to kindergartners helps them learn new vocabulary words. *Journal of Educational Psychology, 86,* 54–64.

Robins, C. J., & Hayes, A. M. (1993). An appraisal of cognitive therapy. *Journal of Consulting and Clinical Psychology, 61,* 205–214.

Robinson, N. M. (1992, August). *Development and variation: The challenge of nurturing gifted young children.* Paper presented at the meeting of the American Psychological Association, Washington, DC.

Rodriguez, N., Ryan, S. W., Kemp, H. V., & Foy, D. W. (1997). Posttraumatic stress disorder in adult female survivors of childhood sexual abuse: A comparison study. *Journal of Consulting and Clinical Psychology, 65,* 53–59.

Rogers, C. R. (1951). *Client-centered therapy.* Boston: Houghton Mifflin.

Rogers, D. E., & Ginzberg, E. (1993). *Medical care and the health of the poor.* Boulder, CO: Westview Press.

Rose, J. S., Chassin, L., Presson, C. C., & Sherman, S. J. (1996). Prospective predictors of quit attempts and smoking cessation in young adults. *Health Psychology, 15,* 261–268.

Rose, R. J. (1995). Genes and human behavior. *Annual Review of Psychology, 46,* 625–654.

Rosenbaum, M., Leibel, R. L., & Hirsch, J. (1997). Obesity. *New England Journal of Medicine, 337,* 396–407.

Rosenberg, J., Perlstadt, H., & Phillips, W. R. (1993). Now that we are here: Discrimination, disparagement, and harassment at work and the experience of women lawyers. *Gender & Society, 7,* 415–433.

Rosenblatt, R. (1994, March 20). How do tobacco executives live with themselves? *The New York Times Magazine,* pp. 34–41, 55, 73–76.

Rosenfeld, A. (1995). Cited in Collins, C. (1995, May 11). Spanking is becoming the new don't. *The New York Times,* p. C8.

Rosenthal, A. M. (1994, March 15). The way she died. *The New York Times,* p. A23.

Rosenthal, E. (1993a, March 28). Patients in pain find relief, not addiction, in narcotics. *The New York Times,* pp. A1, A24.

Rosenthal, E. (1993b, July 20). Listening to the emotional needs of cancer patients. *The New York Times,* pp. C1, C7.

Ross, C. A., Joshi, S., & Currie, R. (1990). Dissociative experiences in the general population. *American Journal of Psychiatry, 147,* 1547–1552.

Ross, L., & Nisbett, R. E. (1991). *The person and the situation.* New York: McGraw-Hill.

Ross, M. J., & Berger, R. S. (1996). Effects of stress inoculation training on athletes' postsurgical pain and rehabilitation after orthopedic injury. *Journal of Consulting and Clinical Psychology, 64,* 406–410.

Rossouw, J. E., and others (1990). The value of lowering cholesterol after myocardial infarction. *New England Journal of Medicine, 323,* 1112–1119.

Rothbart, M. K., & Ahadi, S. A. (1994). Temperament and the development of personality. *Journal of Abnormal Psychology, 103,* 55–66.

Rothbaum, B. O. (1995). *American Journal of Psychiatry.*

Rothbaum, B. O., Foa, E. B., Riggs, D. S., Murdock, T., & Walsh, W. (1992). A prospective examination of post-traumatic stress disorder in rape victims. *Journal of Traumatic Stress, 5,* 455–475.

Rotheram-Borus, M. J., Koopman, C., & Haignere, C. (1991). Reducing HIV sexual risk behaviors among runaway adolescents. *Journal of the American Medical Association, 266,* 1237–1241.

Rotheram-Borus, M. J., Trautman, P. D., Dopkins, S. C., & Shrout, P. E. (1990). Cognitive style and pleasant activities among female adolescent suicide attempters. *Journal of Consulting and Clinical Psychology, 58,* 554–561.

Rothman, A. J., & Salovey, P. (1997). Shaping perceptions to motivate healthy behavior. *Psychological Bulletin, 121,* 3–19.

Rotter, J. B. (1990). Internal versus external control of reinforcement. *American Psychologist, 45,* 489–493.

Royce, R. A., Seña, A., Cates, W., Jr., & Cohen, M. S. (1997). Sexual transmission of HIV. *New England Journal of Medicine, 336,* 1072–1078.

Rozin, P., & Fallon, A. (1988). Body image, attitudes to weight, and misperceptions of figure preferences of the opposite sex. *Journal of Abnormal Psychology, 97,* 342–345.

Rule, B. G., Taylor, B. R., & Dobbs, A. R. (1987). Priming effects of heat on aggressive thoughts. *Social cognition, 5,* 131–143.

Russo, A. (1996). Cited in Azar, B. (1996). Training is enhanced by virtual reality. *APA Monitor, 26(3),* 24.

Rüstemli, A. (1986). Male and female personal space needs and escape reactions under intrusion: A Turkish sample. *International Journal of Psychology.*

Rutkowski, G. K., Gruder, C. L., & Romer, D. (1983). Group cohesiveness, social norms, and bystander intervention. *Journal of Personality and Social Psychology, 44,* 545–552.

Rutter, M. (1997). Nature-nurture integration. *American Psychologist, 52,* 390–398.

Rychlak, J. F. (1997). *In defense of human consciousness.* Washington, DC: American Psychological Association.

Rymer, R. (1993). *Genie: An abused child's flight from silence.* New York: HarperCollins.

Saarni, C. (1990). Emotional competence. In R. Thompson (Ed.), *Nebraska Symposium on Motivation: Vol. 36. Socioemotional development.* Lincoln: University of Nebraska Press.

Saccuzzo, D. (1994, August). Coping with complexities of contemporary psychological testing: Negotiating shifting sands. G. Stanley Hall lecture presented at the annual meeting of the American Psychological Association, Los Angeles.

Sadalla, E. K., Kenrick, D. T., & Vershure, B. (1987). Dominance and heterosexual attraction. *Journal of Personality and Social Psychology, 52,* 730–738.

Sadalla, E. K., Sheets, V., & McCreath, H. (1990). The cognition of urban tempo. *Environment and Behavior, 22,* 230–254.

Sadker, M., & Sadker, D. (1994). *How America's schools cheat girls.* New York: Scribners.

Sadowski, C., & Kelley, M. L. (1993). Social problem solving in suicidal adolescents. *Journal of Consulting and Clinical Psychology, 61,* 121–127.

Salgado de Snyder, V. N., Cervantes, R. C., & Padilla, A. M. (1990). Gender and ethnic differences in psychosocial stress and generalized distress among Hispanics. *Sex Roles, 22,* 441–453.

Sanders, G. S. (1984). Effects of context cues on eyewitness identification responses. *Journal of Applied Social Psychology, 14,* 386–397.

Sandman, C., & Crinella, F. (1995) Cited in Margoshes, P. (1995). For many, old age is the prime of life. *APA Monitor, 26(5),* 36–37.

Sanna, L. J., & Shotland, R. L. (1990). Valence of anticipated evaluation and social facilitation.

Journal of Experimental Social Psychology, 26, 82–92.

Santee, R. T., & Maslach, C. (1982). To agree or not to agree: Personal dissent amid social pressure to conform. *Journal of Personality and Social Psychology, 42,* 690–700.

Sarbin, T. R., & Coe, W. C. (1972). *Hypnosis.* New York: Holt, Rinehart and Winston.

Sarter, M., Berntson, G. G., & Cacioppo, J. T. (1996). Brain imaging and cognitive neuroscience. *American Psychologist, 51,* 13–21.

Saxe, L. (1991a). Lying. *American Psychologist, 46,* 409–415.

Saxe, L. (1991b). Science and the CQT polygraph. *Integration of Physiological and Behavioral Sciences, 26,* 223–231.

Scarr, S., & Kidd, K. K. (1983). Developmental behavior genetics. In M. Haith & J. J. Campos (Eds.), *Handbook of child psychology.* New York: Wiley.

Scarr, S., & Weinberg, R. A. (1976). IQ test performance of Black children adopted by White families. *American Psychologist, 31,* 726–739.

Scarr, S., & Weinberg, R. A. (1977). Intellectual similarities within families of both adopted and biological children. *Intelligence, 1,* 170–191.

Scarr, S., & Weinberg, R. A. (1983). The Minnesota adoption studies: Genetic differences and malleability. *Child Development, 54,* 260–267.

Schachter, S. (1959). *The psychology of affiliation.* Stanford, CA: Stanford University Press.

Schachter, S., & Latané, B. (1964). Crime, cognition, and the autonomic nervous system. In D. Levine (Ed.), *Nebraska Symposium on Motivation.* Lincoln: University of Nebraska Press.

Schachter, S., & Singer, J. E. (1962). Cognitive, social, and physiological determinants of emotional state. *Psychological Review, 69,* 379–399.

Schafer, J., & Brown, S. A. (1991). Marijuana and cocaine effect expectancies and drug use patterns. *Journal of Consulting and Clinical Psychology, 59,* 558–565.

Schafran, L. H. (1995, August 26). Rape is still underreported. *The New York Times,* p. A19.

Schaie, K. W. (1993). The Seattle Longitudinal Studies of adult intelligence. *Current Directions, 2,* 171–175.

Schaie, K. W. (1994). The course of adult intellectual development. *American Psychologist, 49,* 304–313.

Schaie, K. W., & Willis, S. L. (1991). Adult personality and psychomotor performance. *Journal of Gerontology: Psychological Sciences, 46,* P275–284.

Schaller, M., & Maas, A. (1989). Illusory correlation and social categorization. *Journal of Personality and Social Psychology, 56,* 709–721.

Schenker, M. (1993). Air pollution and mortality. *New England Journal of Medicine, 329,* 1807–1808.

Schiffman, H. (1990). *Sensation and perception.* New York: Wiley.

Schmidt, N. B., Lerew, D. R., & Trakowski, J. H. (1997). Body vigilance in panic disorder. *Journal of Consulting and Clinical Psychology, 65,* 214–220.

Schneider, B. H., & Byrne, B. M. (1987). Individualizing social skills training for behavior-disordered children. *Journal of Consulting and Clinical Psychology, 55,* 444–445.

Schneider, W., & Bjorklund, D. (1992). Expertise, aptitude, and strategic remembering. *Child Development, 63,* 461–473.

Schotte, D. E., Cools, J., & Payvar, S. (1990). Problem-solving deficits in suicidal patients. *Journal of Consulting and Clinical Psychology, 58,* 562–564.

Schreiber, G. B., et al. (1996). The risk of transfusion-transmitted viral infections. *New England Journal of Medicine, 334,* 1685–1690.

Schuckit, M. A. (1996). Recent developments in the pharmacotherapy of alcohol dependence. *Journal of Consulting and Clinical Psychology, 64,* 669–676.

Schulz, R., & Heckhausen, J. (1996). A life span model of successful aging. *American Psychologist, 51,* 702–714.

Schutte, N. S., Malouff, J. M., Post-Gorden, J. C., & Rodasts, A. L. (1988). Effect of playing videogames on children's aggressive and other behavior. *Journal of Applied Social Psychology, 18,* 454–460.

Schwartz, M. W., & Seeley, R. J. (1997). Neuroendocrine responses to starvation and weight loss. *New England Journal of Medicine, 336,* 1802–1811.

Schwartz, R. M., & Gottman, J. M. (1976). Toward a task analysis of assertive behavior. *Journal of Consulting and Clinical Psychology, 44,* 910–920.

Schwarz, N., Bless, H., & Bohner, G. (1991). Mood and persuasion. In M. Zanna (Ed.), *Advances in experimental social psychology* (Vol. 24). New York: Academic Press.

Schweinhart, L. J., & Weikart, D. P. (Eds). (1993). *Significant benefits: The High/Scope Perry Preschool Study through age 27.* Ypsilanti, MI: High/Scope Press.

Scott, J. (1994, May 9). Multiple personality cases perplex legal system. *The New York Times,* pp. A1, B10, B11.

Scruggs, T. E., & Mastropieri, M. A. (1992). Remembering the forgotten art of memory. *American Educator, 16*(4), 31–37.

Segal, N. (1993). Twin, sibling, and adoption methods. *American Psychologist, 48,* 943–956.

Seligman, M. E. P. (1995). The effectiveness of psychotherapy: *The Consumer Reports* study. *American Psychologist, 50,* 965–974.

Seligman, M. E. P. (1996, August). Predicting and preventing depression. Master lecture presented to the meeting of the American Psychological Association, Toronto.

Selye, H. (1976). *The stress of life* (Rev. ed.). New York: McGraw-Hill.

Selye, H. (1980). The stress concept today. In I. L. Kutash, and others (Eds.), *Handbook on stress and anxiety.* San Francisco: Jossey-Bass.

Senior, J. (1994, January 3). Language of the deaf evolves to reflect new sensibilities. *The New York Times,* pp. A1, A12.

Seppa, N. (1996). APA releases study on family violence. *APA Monitor, 27*(4), 12.

Seppa, N. (1997a). Young adults and AIDS: "It can't happen to me." *APA Monitor, 28*(1), 38–39.

Seppa, N. (1997b). Sexual harassment in the military lingers on. *APA Monitor, 28*(5), 40–41.

Seta, J. J. (1982). The impact of comparison processes on coactors' task performance. *Journal of Personality and Social Psychology, 42,* 281–291.

Shadish, W. R., & Ragsdale, K. (1996). Random versus nonrandom assignment in controlled experiments. *Journal of Consulting and Clinical Psychology, 64,* 1290–1305.

Shadish, W. R., and others (1997). Evidence that therapy works in clinically representative conditions. *Journal of Consulting and Clinical Psychology, 65,* 355–365.

Shavitt, S. (1990). The role of attitude objects in attitude functions. *Journal of Experimental Social Psychology, 26,* 124–148.

Shaywitz, B. A., and others (1995). Sex differences in the functional organization of the brain for language. *Nature, 373,* 607–609.

Sheehy, G. (1976). *Passages.* New York: Dutton.

Sheehy, G. (1995). *New passages: Mapping your life across time.* New York: Random House.

Shepherd, J., and others. (1995). Prevention of coronary heart disease with pravastatin in men with hypercholesterolemia. *New England Journal of Medicine, 333,* 1301–1307.

Sheppard, J. A., & Strathman, A. J. (1989). Attractiveness and height. *Personality and Social Psychology Bulletin, 15,* 617–627.

Shepperd, J. A. (1993). Productivity loss in performance groups. *Psychological Bulletin, 113,* 67–81.

Sher, K. J., & Trull, T. J. (1994). Personality and disinhibitory psychopathology: Alcoholism and antisocial personality disorder. *Journal of Abnormal Psychology, 103,* 92–102.

Sher, K. J., Wood, M. D., Wood, P. K., & Raskin, G. (1996). Alcohol outcome expectancies and alcohol use. *Journal of Abnormal Psychology, 105,* 561–574.

Sherif, M., Harvey, O. J., White, B. J., Hood, W. R., & Sherif, C. W. (1961/1988). *The Robbers Cave experiment: Intergroup conflict and cooperation.* Middletown, CT: Wesleyan University Press.

Sherman, R. A. (1997). *Phantom pain.* New York: Plenum.

Shiffman, S., and others. (1997). A day at a time: Predicting smoking lapse from daily urge. *Journal of Abnormal Psychology, 106,* 104–116.

Shneidman, E. S. (1985). *Definition of suicide.* New York: Wiley.

Shumaker, S. A., & Hill, D. R. (1991). Gender differences in social support and physical health. *Health Psychology, 10,* 102–111.

Silverstein, L. B. (1991). Transforming the debate about child care and maternal employment. *American Psychologist, 46,* 1025–1032.

Simons, A. D., Angell, K. L., Monroe, S. M., & Thase, M. E. (1993). Cognition and life stress in depression. *Journal of Abnormal Psychology, 102*, 584–591.

Simons, A. D., Gordon, J. S., Monroe, S. M., & Thase, M. E. (1995). Toward an integration of psychologic, social, and biologic factors in depression. *Journal of Consulting and Clinical Psychology, 63*, 369–377.

Simons, R. L., Whitbeck, L. B., Conger, R. D., & Chyi-In, W. (1991). Intergenerational transmission of harsh parenting. *Developmental Psychology, 27*, 159–171.

Simpson, M., & Perry, J. D. (1990). Crime and climate. *Environment and Behavior, 22*, 295–300.

Simpson, M. L., Olejnik, S., Tam, A. Y., & Supattathum, S. (1994). Elaborative verbal rehearsals and college students' cognitive performance. *Journal of Educational Psychology, 86*, 267–278.

Skinner, B. F. (1938). *The behavior of organisms: An experimental analysis.* New York: Appleton.

Skinner, B. F. (1948). *Walden Two.* New York: Macmillan.

Skinner, B. F. (1957). *Verbal behavior.* New York: Appleton.

Skinner, B. F. (1972). *Beyond freedom and dignity.* New York: Knopf.

Skinner, B. F. (1983). Intellectual self-management in old age. *American Psychologist, 38*, 239–244.

Slaven, L., & Lee, C. (1997). Mood and symptom reporting among middle-aged women: The relationship between menopausal status, hormone replacement therapy, and exercise participation. *Health Psychology, 16*, 203–208.

Sleek, S. (1994). Bilingualism enhances student growth. *APA Monitor, 25*(4), 48.

Sleek, S. (1995a). Group therapy. *APA Monitor, 26*(7), 1, 38–39.

Sleek, S. (1995b). Rallying the troops inside our bodies. *APA Monitor, 26*(12), 1, 24–25.

Sleek, S. (1996). Side effects undermine drug compliance. *APA Monitor, 26*(3), 32.

Slobin, D. I. (1983). Crosslinguistic evidence for basic child grammar. Paper presented at the biennial meeting of the Society for Research in Child Development, Detroit.

Sloman, S. A. (1996). The empirical case for two systems of reasoning. *Psychological Bulletin, 119*, 3–22.

Smetana, J. G., Yau, J., Restrepo, A., & Braeges, J. L. (1991). Conflict and adaptation in adolescence. In M. E. Colten & S. Gore (Eds.), *Adolescent stress: Causes and consequences.* New York: Aldine deGruyter.

Smith, G. F., & Dorfman, D. (1975). The effect of stimulus uncertainty on the relationship between frequency of exposure and liking. *Journal of Personality and Social Psychology, 31*, 150–155.

Smith, M. L., & Glass, G. V. (1977). Meta-analysis of psychotherapy outcome studies. *American Psychologist, 32*, 752–760.

Smith, R. E., Smoll, F. L., & Ptacek, J. T. (1990). Conjunctive moderator variables in vulnerability and resiliency research. *Journal of Personality and Social Psychology, 58*, 360–370.

Smith, S. M., Glenberg, A. M., & Bjork, R. A. (1978). Environmental context and human memory. *Memory and Cognition, 6*, 342–355.

Smoke rises. (1993, December 27). *The New York Times*, p. A16.

Snyder, M., & DeBono, G. (1989). Understanding the functions of attitudes. In A. R. Pratkanis and others (Eds.), *Attitude structure and function.* Hillsdale, NJ: Erlbaum.

Snyder, M., Grether, J., & Keller, K. (1974). Staring and compliance: A field experiment on hitchhiking. *Journal of Applied Social Psychology, 4*, 165–170.

Snyderman, M., & Rothman, S. (1987). Survey of expert opinion on intelligence and aptitude testing. *American Psychologist, 42*, 137–144.

Snyderman, M., & Rothman, S. (1990). *The I.Q. controversy.* New Brunswick, NJ: Transaction Publishers.

Solomon, E. P., Berg, L. R., Martin, D. W., & Villee, C. (1993). *Biology* (3rd ed.). Philadelphia: Saunders College Publishing.

Sommers-Flanagan, J., & Sommers-Flanagan, R. (1995). Intake interviewing with suicidal patients. *Professional Psychology: Research and Practice, 26*, 41–47.

Sorenson, S. B., & Rutter, C. M. (1991). Transgenerational patterns of suicide attempt. *Journal of Consulting and Clinical Psychology, 59*, 861–866.

Southern, T., & Jones, E. D. (1991). *The academic acceleration of gifted children.* New York: Teachers College Press.

Sperling, G. (1960). The information available in brief visual presentations. *Psychological Monographs, 74*, 1–29.

Sperry, R. W. (1993). The impact and promise of the cognitive revolution. *American Psychologist, 48*, 878–885.

Spiegel, D., & Cardeña, E. (1991). Disintegrated experience. *Journal of Abnormal Psychology, 100*, 366–378.

Spinhoven, P., Labbe, M. R., & Rombouts, R. (1993). Feasibility of computerized psychological testing with psychiatric outpatients. *Journal of Clinical Psychology, 49*, 440–447.

Spitzer, R. L., Gibbon, M., Skodol, A. E., Williams, J. B. W., & First, M. B. (1989). *DSM-III-R casebook.* Washington, DC: American Psychiatric Press.

Spreat, S., & Behar, D. (1994). Trends in the residential (inpatient) treatment of individuals with a dual diagnosis. *Journal of Consulting and Clinical Psychology, 61*, 43–48.

Sprecher, S., Sullivan, Q., & Hatfield, E. (1994). Mate selection preferences. *Journal of Personality and Social Psychology, 66*(6), 1074–1080.

Springer, S. P., & Deutsch, G. (1993) *Left brain, right brain* (4th edition). New York: Freeman.

Squire, L. R. (1993). Memory and the hippocampus. *Psychological Review, 99*, 195–231.

Squire, L. R. (1994). Cited in Pool, R. *The dynamic brain.* Washington, DC: National Academy Press.

Squire, L. R. (1996, August). Memory systems of the brain. Master lecture presented to the meeting of the American Psychological Association, Toronto.

Stacy, A. W. (1997). Memory activation and expectancy as prospective predictors of alcohol and marijuana use. *Journal of Abnormal Psychology, 106*, 61–73.

Stacy, A. W., Bentler, P. M., & Flay, B. R. (1994). Attitudes and health behavior in diverse populations. *Health Psychology, 13*, 73–85.

Stacy, A. W., Newcomb, M. D., & Bentler, P. M. (1991). Cognitive motivation and drug use. *Journal of Abnormal Psychology, 100*, 502–515.

Stampfer, M. J., and others (1991). A prospective study of cholesterol, apolipoproteins, and the risk of myocardial infarction. *New England Journal of Medicine, 325*, 373–381.

Staples, S. I. (1996). Human responses to environmental noise. *American Psychologist, 51*, 143–150.

Stasser, G., Taylor, L. A., & Hanna, C. (1989). Information sampling in structured and unstructured discussion of three- and six-person groups. *Journal of Personality and Social Psychology, 57*, 67–78.

Steele, C. M. (1994, October 31). "Bizarre black IQ claims abetted by media." *San Francisco Chronicle*, Editorial page.

Steele, C. M. (1996, August). The role of stereotypes in shaping intellectual identity. Master lecture presented to the meeting of the American Psychological Association, Toronto.

Steele, C. M. (1997). A threat in the air: How stereotypes shape intellectual identity and performance. *American Psychologist, 52*, 613–629.

Steele, C. M., & Aronson, J. (1995). Cited in Watters, E. (1995, September 17). Claude Steele has scores to settle. *The New York Times Magazine*, pp. 44–47.

Steele, C. M., & Josephs, R. A. (1990). Alcohol myopia. *American Psychologist, 45*, 921–933.

Steinberg, L. (1996). *Beyond the classroom.* New York: Simon & Schuster.

Steinberg, L., Brown, B. B., & Dornbusch, S. M. (1996). Ethnicity and adolescent achievement. *American Educator, 20*(2), 28–35.

Steinberg, L., Dornbusch, S. M., & Brown, B. B. (1992a). Ethnic differences in adolescent achievement. *American Psychologist, 47*, 723–729.

Steinberg, L., Lamborn, S. D., Dornbusch, S. M., & Darling, N. (1992b). Impact of parenting practices on adolescent achievement: Authoritative parenting, school involvement, and encouragement to succeed. *Child Development, 63*, 1266–1281.

Steinbrook, R. (1992). The polygraph test—A flawed diagnostic method. *New England Journal of Medicine, 327*, 122–123.

Steiner, M., et al. (1995). Fluoxetine in the treatment of premenstrual dysphoria. *New England Journal of Medicine, 332,*

Sternberg, R. J. (1985). *Beyond IQ: A triarchic theory of human intelligence.* New York: Cambridge University Press.

Sternberg, R. J. (1988). Triangulating love. In R. J. Sternberg & M. J. Barnes (Eds.), *The psychology of love.* New Haven, CT: Yale University Press.

Sternberg, R. J. (1997a). What does it mean to be smart? *Educational Leadership, 54,* 20–24.

Sternberg, R. J. (1997b). The concept of intelligence and its role in lifelong learning and success. *American Psychologist, 52,* 1030–1037.

Sternberg, R. J., & Davidson, J. E. (1994). *The nature of insight.* Cambridge, MA: The MIT Press, a Bradford Book.

Sternberg, R. J., & Lubart, T. I. (1995). *Defying the crowd: Cultivating creativity in a culture of conformity.* New York: Free Press.

Sternberg, R. J., & Lubart, T. I. (1996). Investing in creativity. *American Psychologist, 51,* 677–688.

Sternberg, R. J., Wagner, R. K., Williams, W. M., & Horvath, J. A. (1995). Testing common sense. *American Psychologist, 50,* 912–927.

Sternberg, R. J., & Williams, W. M. (1997). Does the Graduate Record Examination predict meaningful success in the graduate training of psychologists? *American Psychologist, 52,* 630–641.

Stevenson, H. W., Lee, S. Y., & Stigler, J. W. (1986). Mathematics achievement of Chinese, Japanese, and American children. *Science, 231,* 693–699.

Stier, D. S., & Hall, J. A. (1984). Gender differences in touch. *Journal of Personality and Social Psychology, 47,* 440–459.

Stokols, D. (1992). Establishing and maintaining healthy environments. *American Psychologist, 47,* 6–22.

Stout, D. (1996, October 18). Direct link found between smoking and lung cancer. *The New York Times,* pp. A1, A19.

Straube, E. R., & Oades, R. D. (1992). *Schizophrenia.* San Diego: Academic Press.

Strauss, M. (1995). Cited in Collins, C. (1995, May 11). Spanking is becoming the new don't. *The New York Times,* p. C8.

Strollo, P. J., & Rogers, R. M. (1996). Obstructive sleep apnea. *New England Journal of Medicine, 334,* 99–104.

Strom, J. C., & Buck, R. W. (1979). Staring and participants' sex. *Personality and Social Psychology Bulletin, 5,* 114–117.

Strom, S. (1993, April 18). Human pheromones. *The New York Times,* p. V12.

Strupp, H. H. (1996). The tripartite model and the *Consumer Reports* study. *American Psychologist, 51,* 1017–1024.

Study finds smaller pay gap for male and female doctors. (1996, April 11). *The New York Times,* p. B9.

Stunkard, A. J., Harris, J. R., Pedersen, N. L., & McLearn, G. E. (1990). A separated twin study of the body mass index. *New England Journal of Medicine, 322,* 1483–1487.

Stunkard, A. J., & Sørensen, T. I. A. (1993). Obesity and socioeconomic status. *New England Journal of Medicine, 329,* 1036–1037.

Sue, S. (1991). In J. D. Goodchilds (Ed.), *Psychological perspectives on human diversity in America.* Washington, DC: American Psychological Association.

Sue, S., & Okazaki, S. (1990). Asian-American educational achievements. *American Psychologist, 45,* 913–920.

Suinn, R. A. (1982). Intervention with Type A behaviors. *Journal of Consulting and Clinical Psychology, 50,* 933–949.

Suinn, R. A. (1995). Anxiety management training. In K. Craig (Ed.), *Anxiety and depression in children and adults* (pp. 159–179). New York: Sage.

Suls, J., Wan, C. K., & Costa, P. T., Jr. (1995). Relationship of trait anger to resting blood pressure. *Health Psychology, 14,* 444–456.

Susser, E. S., & Lin, S. P. (1992). Schizophrenia after prenatal exposure to the Dutch Hunger Winter of 1944–1945. *Archives of General Psychiatry, 49,* 983–988.

Sutker, P. B. (1994). Psychopathy: Traditional and clinical antisocial concepts. In D. C. Fowles, P. B. Sutker, & S. H. Goodman (Eds.), *Progress in experimental personality and psychopathology research* (pp. 73–120). New York: Springer.

Suzuki, L. A., & Valencia, R. R. (1997). Race-ethnicity and measured intelligence: Educational implications. *American Psychologist, 52,* 1103–1114.

Sweeney, P. D., & Gruber, K. L. (1984). Selective exposure. *Journal of Personality and Social Psychology, 46,* 1208–1221.

Szasz, T. S. (1984). *The therapeutic state.* Buffalo, NY: Prometheus.

Tabor, M. B. W. (1996, August 7). Comprehensive study finds parents and peers are most crucial influences on students. *The New York Times,* p. A15.

Tailoring treatments for alcoholics is not the answer. (1997). *APA Monitor, 28*(2), 6–7.

Tangney, J. P. (1990). Assessing individual differences in proneness to shame and guilt. *Journal of Personality and Social Psychology, 59,* 102–111.

Tanzi, R. E. (1995). A promising animal model of Alzheimer's disease. *New England Journal of Medicine, 332,* 1512–1513.

Taub, A. (1993, April 8). Narcotics have long been known safe and effective for pain. *The New York Times,* p. A20.

Taylor, H. (1993). Cited in Barringer, F. (1993, April 25). Polling on sexual issues has its drawbacks. *The New York Times,* p. A23.

Taylor, S. E. (1990). Health psychology: The science and the field. *American Psychologist, 45,* 40–50.

Télégdy, G. (1977). Prenatal androgenization of primates and humans. In J. Money & H.

Musaph (Eds.), *Handbook of sexology.* Amsterdam: Excerpta Medica.

Teller, D. Y., & Lindsey, D. T. (1993). Motion nulling techniques and infant color vision. In C. E. Granrud (Ed.), *Visual perception and cognition in infancy.* Hillsdale, NJ: Erlbaum.

Tharp, R. G. (1991). Cultural diversity and treatment of children. *Journal of Consulting and Clinical Psychology, 59,* 799–812.

Thase, M. E., & Kupfer, D. J. (1996). Recent developments in the pharmacotherapy of mood disorders. *Journal of Consulting and Clinical Psychology, 64,* 646–659.

Thompson, C. P., & Cowan, T. (1986). The neurobiology of learning and memory. *Science, 233,* 941–947.

Thompson, L. A., Detterman, D. K., & Plomin, R. (1991). Associations between cognitive abilities and scholastic achievement. *Psychological Science, 2,* 158–165.

Thompson, R. A. (1991a). Attachment theory and research. In M. Lewis (Ed.), *Child and adolescent psychiatry.* Baltimore: Williams & Wilkins.

Thompson, R. A. (1991b). Infant daycare. In J. V. Lerner & N. L. Galambos (Eds.), *Employed mothers and their children* (pp. 9–36). New York: Garland.

Thoresen, C., & Powell, L. H. (1992). Type A behavior pattern. *Journal of Consulting and Clinical Psychology, 60,* 595–604.

Thune, I., Brenn, T., Lund, E., & Gaard, M. (1997). Physical activity and the risk of breast cancer. *New England Journal of Medicine, 336,* 1269–1275.

Thurstone, L. L. (1938). Primary mental abilities. *Psychometric Monographs, 1.*

Thurstone, L. L., & Thurstone, T. G. (1963). *SRA primary abilities.* Chicago: SRA.

Tolchin, M. (1989, July, 19). When long life is too much. *The New York Times,* pp. A1, A15.

Tolman, E. C., & Honzik, C. H. (1930). Introduction and removal of reward, and maze performance in rats. *University of California Publications in Psychology, 4,* 257–275.

Tomes, H. (1993). It's in the nation's interest to break abuse cycle. *APA Monitor, 24*(3), 28.

Torgersen, S. (1983). Genetic factors in anxiety disorders. *Archives of General Psychiatry, 40,* 1085–1089.

Triandis, H. C. (1990). Cross-cultural studies of individualism and collectivism. In J. J. Berman (Ed.), *Nebraska Symposium on Motivation, 1989. Cross-cultural perspectives.* Lincoln: University of Nebraska Press.

Triandis, H. C. (1994). *Culture and social behavior.* New York: McGraw-Hill.

Triandis, H. C. (1995). *Individualism and collectivism.* Boulder, CO: Westview Press.

Triandis, H. C. (1996). The psychological measurement of cultural syndromes. *American Psychologist, 51,* 407–415.

Trickett, P. K., Aber, J. L., Carlson, V., & Cicchetti, D. (1991). Relationship of socioeconomic status to the etiology and developmental sequelae of physical child abuse. *Developmental Psychology, 27*, 148–158.

Trimble, J. E. (1991). The mental health service and training needs of American Indians. In H. F. Myers and others (Eds.), *Ethnic minority perspectives on clinical training and services in psychology* (pp. 43–48). Washington, DC: American Psychological Association.

Trobst, K. K., Collins, R. L., & Embree, J. M. (1994). The role of emotion in social support provision. *Journal of Social and Personal Relationships, 11*, 45–62.

Trujillo, C. (Ed.). (1991). *Chicana lesbians: The girls our mothers warned us about.* Berkeley, CA: Third Woman Press.

Tsui, A. S., & O'Reilly, C. A., III. (1989). Beyond simple demographic effects. *Academy of Management Journal, 32*, 402–423.

Tucker, J. S., Friedman, H. S., Wingard, D. L., & Schwartz, J. E. (1996). Marital history at midlife as a predictor of longevity. *Health Psychology, 15*, 94–101.

Tulving, E. (1985). How many memory systems are there? *American Psychologist, 40*, 385–398.

Tulving, E. (1991). Memory research is not a zero-sum game. *American Psychologist, 46*, 41–42.

Turner, A. M., & Greenough, W. T. (1985). Differential rearing effects on rat visual cortex synapses: I. Synaptic and neuronal density and synapses per neuron. *Brain Research, 329*, 195–203.

Turner, S. M., Beidel, D. C., & Jacob, R. G. (1994). Social phobia: A comparison of behavior therapy and atenolol. *Journal of Consulting and Clinical Psychology, 62*, 350–358.

Tversky, A., & Kahneman, D. (1982). Judgment under uncertainty. In D. Kahneman, P. Slovic, & A. Tversky (Eds.), *Judgment under uncertainty: Heuristics and biases.* New York: Cambridge University Press.

Uchino, B. N., Cacioppo, J. T., & Kiecolt-Glaser, J. K. (1996). The relationship between social support and physiological processes. *Psychological Bulletin, 119*, 488–531.

Ukestad, L. K., & Wittrock, D. A. (1996). Pain perception and coping in female tension headache sufferers and headache-free controls. *Health Psychology, 15*, 65–68.

Upstream (1997, June 21). People: Charles Murray. Upstream@cycad.com.

USBC (U.S. Bureau of the Census). (1995). *Statistical abstract of the United States* (115th ed.). Washington, DC: U.S. Government Printing Office.

U.S. Congress (1983, November). *Scientific validity of polygraph testing* (OTA-TM-H-15). Washington, DC: Office of Technology Assessment.

Vaillant, G. E. (1994). Ego mechanisms of defense and personality psychopathology. *Journal of Abnormal Psychology, 103*, 44–50.

Valenstein, E. S. (1986). *Great and desperate cures.* New York: Basic Books.

Valentiner, D. P., Foa, E. B., Riggs, D. S., & Gershuny, B. S. (1996). Coping strategies and posttraumatic stress disorder in female victims of sexual and nonsexual assault. *Journal of Abnormal Psychology, 105*, 455–458.

Van Brunt, L. (1994, March 27). About men: Whites without money. *The New York Times Magazine*, p. 38.

Vandell, D. L., & Corasaniti, M. A. (1990). Child care and the family. In K. McCartney (Ed.), *New Directions for Child Development* (Vol. 49, pp. 23–37. San Francisco: Jossey-Bass.

Vandenbergh, J. G. (1993). Cited in Angier, N. (1993, August 24). Female gerbil born with males is found to be begetter of sons. *The New York Times*, p. C4.

VandenBos, G. R. (1996). Outcome assessment of psychotherapy. *American Psychologist, 51*, 1005–1006.

Venables, P. H. (1996). Schizotypy and maternal exposure to influenza and to cold temperature. *Journal of Abnormal Psychology, 105*, 53–60.

Vernberg, E. M., La Greca, A. M., Silverman, W. K., & Prinstein, M. J. (1996). Prediction of posttraumatic stress symptoms in children after Hurricane Andrew. *Journal of Abnormal Psychology, 105*, 237–248.

Vernon, S. W., and others. (1997). Correlates of psychologic distress in colorectal cancer patients undergoing genetic testing for hereditary colon cancer. *Health Psychology, 16*, 73–86.

Visintainer, M. A., Volpicelli, J. R., & Seligman, M. E. P. (1982). Tumor rejection in rats after inescapable or escapable shock. *Science, 216*(23), 437–439.

Vitousek, K., & Manke, F. (1994). Personality variables and disorders in anorexia nervosa and bulimia nervosa. *Journal of Abnormal Psychology, 103*, 137–147.

Von Békésy, G. (1957, August). The ear. *Scientific American*, pp. 66–78.

Voyer, D., Voyer, S., & Bryden, M. P. (1995). Magnitude of sex differences in spatial abilities. *Psychological Bulletin, 117*, 250–270.

Wachtel, P. L. (1994). Cyclical processes in personality and psychopathology. *Journal of Abnormal Psychology, 103*, 51–54.

Wadden, T. A., and others. (1997). Exercise in the treatment of obesity. *Journal of Consulting and Clinical Psychology, 65*, 269–277.

Wade, N. (1997, April 1). Artificial human chromosome is new tool for gene therapy. *The New York Times*, C3.

Wagner, B. M. (1997). Family risk factors for child and adolescent suicidal behavior. *Psychological Bulletin, 121*, 246–298.

Wagner, R. K. (1997). Intelligence, training, and employment. *American Psychologist, 52*, 1059–1069.

Walk, R. D., & Gibson, E. J. (1961). A comparative and analytical study of visual depth perception. *Psychological Monographs, 75*(15).

Walker, L. E. A. (1993). Cited in Mednick, A. (1993). Domestic abuse is seen as worldwide "epidemic." *APA Monitor, 24*(5), 33.

Walsh, M. R. (1993, August). Teaching the psychology of women and gender for undergraduate and graduate faculty. Workshop of the Psychology of Women Institute presented at the meeting of the American Psychological Association, Toronto, Canada.

Watkins, C. E., Jr., Campbell, V. L., Nieberding, R., & Hallmark, R. (1995). Contemporary practice of psychological assessment by clinical psychologists. *Professional Psychology: Research and Practice, 26*, 54–60.

Watkins, M. J., Ho, E., & Tulving, E. (1976). Context effects on recognition memory for faces. *Journal of Verbal Learning and Verbal Behavior, 15*, 505–518.

Watson, J. B. (1913). Psychology as the behaviorist views it. *Psychological Review, 20*, 158–177.

Watson, J. B. (1924). *Behaviorism.* New York: W. W. Norton.

Watson, J. B., & Rayner, R. (1920). Conditioned emotional reactions. *Journal of Experimental Psychology, 3*, 1–14.

Weaver, T. L., & Clum, G. A. (1995). Psychological distress associated with interpersonal violence: A meta-analysis. *Clinical Psychology Review, 15*, 115–140.

Webb, W. (1993). Cited in Adler, T. (1993). Sleep loss impairs attention—and more. *APA Monitor, 24*(9), 22–23.

Weber, R., & Crocker, J. (1983). Cognitive processes in the revision of stereotypic beliefs. *Journal of Personality and Social Psychology, 45*, 961–977.

Wechsler, D. (1975). Intelligence defined and undefined. *American Psychologist, 30*, 135–139.

Weekes, J. R., Lynn, S. J., Green, J. P., & Brentar, J. T. (1992). Pseudomemory in hypnotized and task-motivated subjects. *Journal of Abnormal Psychology, 101*, 356–360.

Wegner, D. M. (1979). Hidden Brain Damage Scale. *American Psychologist, 34*, 192–193.

Weidner, G., Boughal, T., Connor, S. L., Pieper, C., & Mendell, N. R. (1997). Relationship of job strain to standard coronary risk factors and psychological characteristics in women and men of the Family Heart Study. *Health Psychology, 16*, 239–247.

Weinberg, R. A., Scarr, S., & Waldman, I. D. (1992). The Minnesota Transracial Adoption Study: A follow-up of IQ test performance at adolescence. *Intelligence, 16*, 117–135.

Weiner, B. (1991). Metaphors in motivation and attribution. *American Psychologist, 46*, 921–930.

Weiner, K. (1992). Cited in Goleman, D. J. (1992, January 8). Heart seizure or panic attack? *The New York Times*, p. C12.

Weisinger, H. (1990). *The critical edge.* New York: Harper & Row.

Weisz, J. R., Sweeney, L., Proffitt, V., & Carr, T. (1993). Control-related beliefs and self-reported depressive symptoms in late childhood. *Journal of Abnormal Psychology, 102,* 411–418.

Welch, K. M. A. (1993). Drug therapy of migraine. *New England Journal of Medicine, 329,* 1476–1483.

Wells, G. L. (1993). What do we know about eyewitness identification? *American Psychologist, 48,* 553–571.

Weniger, B. G., & Brown, T. (1996). The march of AIDS through Asia. *New England Journal of Medicine, 335,* 343–345.

Wentzel, K. R. (1994). Relations of social goal pursuit to social acceptance, classroom behavior, and perceived social support. *Journal of Educational Psychology, 86,* 173–182.

Werner, C. M., Brown, B. B., & Damron, G. (1981). Territorial marking in a game arcade. *Journal of Personality and Social Psychology, 41,* 1094–1104.

Westerman, M. A. (1990). Coordination of maternal directives with preschoolers' behavior in compliance-problem and healthy dyads. *Developmental Psychology, 26,* 621–630.

Wetzler, S. E., & Sweeney, J. A. (1986). Childhood amnesia. In D. C. Rubin (Ed.), *Autobiographical memory.* New York: Cambridge University Press.

Wheeler, M. A., Stuss, D. T., & Tulving, E. (1997). Toward a theory of episodic memory: The frontal lobes and autonoetic consciousness. *Psychological Bulletin, 121,* 331–354.

Whisman, M. A., Miller, I. W., Norman, W. H., & Keitner, G. I. (1991). Cognitive therapy with depressed inpatients. *Journal of Consulting and Clinical Psychology, 59,* 282–288.

Whitaker, M. (1995, October 16). Whites v. Blacks. *Newsweek,* pp. 28–35.

White, J. L., and others (1994). Measuring impulsivity and examining its relationship to delinquency. *Journal of Abnormal Psychology, 103,* 192–205.

White, J. L., & Nicassio, P. M. (1990, November). The relationship between daily stress, pre-sleep arousal and sleep disturbance in good and poor sleepers. Paper presented at the annual meeting of the Association for the Advancement of Behavior Therapy, San Francisco.

Whitehead, W. E. (1994). Assessing the effects of stress on physical symptoms. *Health Psychology, 13,* 99–102.

Whorf, B. (1956). *Language, thought, and reality.* New York: Wiley.

Widiger, T. A., & Costa, P. T., Jr. (1994). Personality and personality disorders. *Journal of Abnormal Psychology, 103,* 78–91.

Widiger, T. A., and others (1996). DSM-IV antisocial personality disorder field trial. *Journal of Abnormal Psychology, 105,* 3–16.

Wiens, A. N., & Menustik, C. E. (1983). Treatment outcome and patient characteristics in an aversion therapy program for alcoholism. *American Psychologist, 38,* 1089–1096.

Wilcox, V. L., Kasl, S. V., & Berkman, L. F. (1994). Social support and physical disability in older people after hospitalization. *Health Psychology, 13,* 170–179.

Wilder, D. A. (1990). Some determinants of the persuasive power of in-groups and out-groups. *Journal of Personality and Social Psychology, 59,* 1202–1213.

Williams, J. E., & Best, D. L. (1994). Cross-cultural views of women and men. In W. J. Lonner & R. Malpass (Eds.), *Psychology and culture.* Boston: Allyn & Bacon.

Williams, L. (1992, February 6). Woman's image in a mirror: Who defines what she sees? *The New York Times,* pp. A1, B7.

Williamson, D. A., Cubic, B. A., & Gleaves, D. H. (1993). Equivalence of body image disturbances in anorexia and bulimia nervosa. *Journal of Abnormal Psychology, 102,* 177–180.

Willoughby, T., Wood, E., & Khan, M. (1994). Isolating variables that impact on or detract from the effectiveness of elaboration strategies. *Journal of Educational Research, 86,* 279–289.

Wills, T. A., McNamara, G., Vaccaro, D., & Hirky, A. E. (1996). Escalated substance abuse. *Journal of Abnormal Psychology, 195,* 166–180.

Wilson, B. (1997). Cited in Seppa, N. (1997). Children's TV remains steeped in violence. *APA Monitor, 28*(6), 36.

Wilson, G. T. (1993). Cited in O'Neill, M. (1993, September 29). Diet sabotage: The new battle of the sexes. *The New York Times,* pp. C1, C6.

Wilson, G. T., & Fairburn, C. G. (1993). Cognitive treatments for eating disorders. *Journal of Consulting and Clinical Psychology, 61,* 261–269.

Wilson, R. S. (1983). The Louisville twin study: Developmental synchronies in behavior. *Child Development, 54,* 298–316.

Wink, P., & Helson, R. (1993). Personality change in women and their partners. *Journal of Personality and Social Psychology, 65,* 597–606.

Winkleby, M., Fortmann, S., & Barrett, D. (1991). Social class disparities in risk factors for disease. *Preventive Medicine, 19,* 1–12.

Winner, E. (1997). Exceptionally high intelligence and schooling. *American Psychologist, 52,* 1070–1081.

Winson, J. (1997). The meaning of dreams. *Scientific American mysteries of the mind, Special Issue* Vol. 7, No. 1, 58–67.

Wissow, L. S. (1995). Child abuse and neglect. *New England Journal of Medicine, 332,* 1425–1431.

Woloshyn, V. E., Paivio, A., & Pressley, M. (1994). Use of elaborative interrogation to help students acquire information consistent with prior knowledge and information inconsistent with prior knowledge. *Journal of Educational Psychology, 86,* 79–89.

Wolpe, J. (1990). *The practice of behavior therapy* (4th ed.). New York: Pergamon.

Wolpe, J., & Lazarus, A. A. (1966). *Behavior therapy techniques.* New York: Pergamon Press.

Wolpe, J., & Plaud, J. J. (1997). Pavlov's contributions to behavior therapy: The obvious and the not so obvious. *American Psychologist, 52,* 966–972.

Wolraich, M. L., and others (1990). Stimulant medication use by primary care physicians in the treatment of attention-deficit hyperactivity disorder. *Pediatrics, 86,* 95–101.

Wood, J. M., & Bootzin, R. R. (1990). The prevalence of nightmares and their independence from anxiety. *Journal of Abnormal Psychology, 99,* 64–68.

Wood, J. M., Bootzin, R. R., Rosenhan, D., Nolen-Hoeksema, S., & Jourden, F. (1992). Effects of the 1989 San Francisco earthquake on frequency and content of nightmares. *Journal of Abnormal Psychology, 101,* 219–224.

Worchel, S., & Brown, E. H. (1984). The role of plausibility in influencing environmental attributions. *Journal of Experimental Social Psychology, 20,* 86–96.

Wren, C. S. (1997, June 3). One of medicine's best-kept secrets: Methadone works. *The New York Times,* p. C3.

Wu, C., & Shaffer, C. R. (1987). Susceptibility to persuasive appeals as a function of source credibility and prior experience with the attitude object. *Journal of Personality and Social Psychology, 52,* 677–688.

Wulfert, E., & Wan, C. K. (1993). Condom use: A self-efficacy model. *Health Psychology, 12,* 346–353.

Yoder, J. D., & Kahn, A. S. (1993). Working toward an inclusive psychology of women. *American Psychologist, 48,* 846–850.

Young, T., and others (1993). The occurrence of sleep-disordered breathing among middle-aged adults. *New England Journal of Medicine, 328,* 1230–1235.

Youngblade, L. M., & Belsky, J. (1992). Parent-child antecedents of 5-year-olds' close friendships. *Developmental Psychology, 28,* 700–713.

Zagorski, M. G. (1997). Cited in Leary, W. E. (1997, January 14). Researchers investigate (horrors!) nicotine's potential benefits. *The New York Times,* p. C3.

Zahn-Waxler, C., & Kochanska, G. (1990). The origins of guilt. In R. A. Thompson (Ed.), *Nebraska Symposium on Motivation: Vol. 38. Socioemotional development.* Lincoln: University of Nebraska Press.

Zajonc, R. B. (1968). Attitudinal effects of mere exposure. *Journal of Personality and Social Psychology, Monograph Supplement 2*(9) 1–27.

Zajonc, R. B. (1980). Compresence. In P. Paulus (Ed.), *The psychology of group influence.* Hillsdale, NJ: Erlbaum.

Zane, N., & Sue, S. (1991). Culturally responsive mental health services for Asian Americans. In H. F. Myers and others (Eds.), *Ethnic minority perspectives on clinical training and services in psychology* (pp. 49–58). Washington, DC: American Psychological Association.

Zigler, E. (1995). Modernizing early childhood intervention to better serve children and families in poverty. Master Lecture delivered to the meeting of the American Psychological Association, New York, August 12.

Zigler, E., Abelson, W. D., Trickett, P. K., & Seitz, V. (1982). Is an intervention program necessary to improve economically disadvantaged children's IQ scores? *Child Development, 53,* 340–348.

Zigler, E., Taussig, C., & Black, K. (1992). Early childhood intervention: A promising preventative for juvenile delinquency. *American Psychologist, 47,* 997–1006.

Zimbardo, P. G. (1997). What messages are behind today's cults? *APA Monitor, 28*(5), 14.

Zimbardo, P. G., LaBerge, S., & Butler, L. D. (1993). Psychophysiological consequences of unexplained arousal. *Journal of Abnormal Psychology, 102,* 466–473.

Zinbarg, R. E., & Barlow, D. H. (1996). Structure of anxiety and anxiety disorders. *Journal of Abnormal Psychology, 105,* 181–193.

Ziv, T. A., & Lo, B. (1995). Denial of care to illegal immigrants. *New England Journal of Medicine, 332,* 1095–1098.

Zuckerman, M. (1980). Sensation seeking. In H. London & J. Exner (Eds.), *Dimensions of personality.* New York: Wiley.

Zuckerman, M. (1992). What is a basic factor and which factors are basic? Tumbles all the way down. *Personality and Individual Differences, 13,* 675–681.

Zuger, A. (1997a, June 10). "Morning after" treatment for AIDS. *The New York Times,* pp. C1, C3.

Zuger, A. (1997b, August 19). Removing half of brain improves young epileptics' lives. *The New York Times,* p. C4.

Literary Acknowledgments

Allyn & Bacon: (Table 13.1) Gender Role Stereotypes Around the World, from "Cross-Cultural Views of Women and Men" by J. E. Williams and D. L. Best, in *Psychology and Culture*, eds. W. J. Lonner and R. Malpass, © 1994 by Allyn & Bacon. Reprinted by permission.

American Psychological Association: (Table 14.1) Students' Reasons for Seeking Counseling from B. Murray, in "College Youth Haunted by Increased Pressures" *APA Monitor*, 26(4), 1996, p. 47. Copyright © 1996 by the American Psychological Association. Reprinted with permission.

American Psychological Association: (Questionnaire) "Will You Be a Hit or Miss? The Expectancy for Success Scale," from "The Generalized Expectancy for Success Scale—A New Measure" by B. Fibel and W.D. Hale, in *Journal of Consulting and Clinical Psychology*, 46, 1978, pp. 924–931, p. 931. Copyright © 1978 by the American Psychological Association. Reprinted with permission.

American Psychological Association: (Table 1.2) Percentage of Doctoral Degrees Awarded to Women in Various Major Fields and Professions, by G.M. Pion, from "The Shifting Gender Composition of Psychology: Trends and Implications for the Discipline," *American Psychologist*, 51, 1996, pp. 509–528. Copyright © 1996 by the American Psychological Association. Reprinted with permission.

Harvard University Press: Two poem excerpts by Emily Dickinson from *The Poems of Emily Dickinson*. Reprinted by permission of the publishers and the Trustees of Amherst College from *The Poems of Emily Dickinson*, Thomas H. Johnson, ed., Cambridge, Mass.: The Belknap Press of Harvard University Press, Copyright © 1951, 1955, 1979, 1983 by the President and Fellows of Harvard College.

Human Resources Institute: (Questionnaire) "How Long Will You Live? The Life-Expectancy Scale," from *Lifegain*, by Robert F. Allen and Shirley Linde, ©1986. Reprinted by permission of Human Resources Institute, 115 Dunder Road, Burlington, VT 05401, (www.healthyculture.com).

Liveright: The lines from "since feeling is first," copyright 1926, 1954, © 1991 by the Trustees for the E.E. Cummings Trust. Copyright © 1985 by George James Firmage. Poem excerpt from *Complete Poems: 1904–1962* by E.E. Cummings. Edited by George J. Firmage. Reprinted by permission of Liveright Publishing Corporation.

McGraw-Hill: (Questionnaire) The Social Readjustment Rating Scale, by Peggy Blake et al., from *Self-Assessment and Behavior Change Manual*, © 1984, pp. 43–47. Reprinted with permission from The McGraw-Hill Companies.

National Academy Press: (Figure 1.1) Recipients of Doctorates in the Various Subfields of Psychology, from *Summary Report 1994: Doctorate Recipients from United States Universities*, Office of Scientific and Engineering Personnel National Research Council, National Academy Press, Washington, DC. Note: For data on psychology, engineering, the neurosciences, and the computer, life, mathematical, physical, and social sciences, the data are from the National Science Foundation (1988) and Ries and Thurgood (1993a). For education and the humanities, the data are from Harmon (1978), Syverson (1982), and Ries and Thurgood (1993a). The data on dentistry, law, medicine, and veterinary medicine are from Snyder (1988) and Snyder and Hoffman (1994).

New York Times: (Table 11.2) "Criticism: The Good and the Bad" from "A Criticism Primer" by Daniel Goleman, in the *New York Times*, September 16, 1990. Copyright © 1990 by The New York Times Co. Reprinted by permission.

New York Times: (Figures 5.34 and 5.35) Based on "Language of Deaf Evolves to Reflect New Sensibilities" by Jennifer Senior, illustrated by Megan Jaegerman, in the *New York Times*, January 3, 1994. Megan Jaegerman/New York Times Permissions.

Rafael Javier: (Essay excerpt) "Machismo/Marianismo Stereotypes and Hispanic Culture" by Rafael Javier. Reprinted by permission of the Center for Psychological Services and Clinical Studies, St. John's University, Jamaica, NY.

W.W. Norton: (Table 4.1) Erikson's Stages of Psychological Development, from *Childhood and Society* by Erik H. Erikson. Copyright 1950. © 1963 by W.W. Norton & Company, Inc., renewed © 1978, 1991 by Erik H. Erikson. Reprinted by permission of W.W. Norton & Company, Inc.

Warner Bros.: Lyric excerpt from "Summertime" by George Gershwin, Dubose and Dorothy Heyward, and Ira Gershwin. All rights for U.S. and Canada administered by Warner-Tamarlane Publishing Corp. All rights reserved. Used by permission. WARNER BROS. PUBLICATIONS, INC., Miami, FL 33014.

Wiley: Brief Version of Sensation Seeking Scale, from "Sensation Seeking" by M. Zuckerman, in *Dimensions of Personality*, eds. H. London and J. Exner, © 1980. Reprinted by permission of Wiley & Sons, Inc.

A

AAUW. *See* American Association of University Women (AAUW)
Abbey, A., 649
Abeles, N., 74, 145, 147, 385
Aber, J.L., 124
Abramowitz, A.J., 267
Abramowitz, J.S., 626
Ackerman, P.L., 360
Addis, M.E., 618
Ader, D.N., 23, 41
Ader, R., 539
Adeyemo, S.A., 324
Adler, A., 436
Adler, D.N., 542
Adler, T., 198, 213
Agras, W.S., 535, 544, 588
Ahadi, S.A., 124, 570
AIDS Hotline, 504
Aiello, J.R., 670
Ainsworth, M.D.S., 117–118, 398
Akhtar, N., 414
Albert Ellis Institute, 615
Aldag, R.J., 662
Alkateeb, M., 658–659
Allen, F., 536
Allen, J.P., 124
Allen, L., 21
Allen, M., 439, 476
Allen, R.F., 148
Allen, W., 230
Alloy, L.B., 568, 570
Allport, G.W., 440
Almeida, D.M., 138
Alston, J.H., 17
Altman, J., 652
Amabile, T.M., 331, 333
American Association of University Women (AAUW), 456, 472, 473
American Psychiatric Association, 220, 624
American Psychological Association, 28, 59, 61, 272, 622
Ames, M.A., 492
Andersen, B.L., 541, 544, 547
Anderson, C.A., 668
Anderson, J.R., 325
Anderson, R., 512
Andrews, B., 569
Angell, M., 540, 549
Angier, N., 97, 137, 314, 549
Annett, M., 88
Annunziata, J., 618
Antonuccio, D., 628
Appel, L.J., 544
Apter, T., 142
Archer, J., 97, 476, 477
Aristotle, 9, 57
Arnold, D.H., 345

Aronson, J., 381
Asch, S.E., 656–657
Ashton, R., 216
Atkinson, R.C., 287, 305
Audrain, J.E., 227
Avis, W.E., 483
Ayanian, J.Z., 541
Ayllon, T., 607
Azar, B., 43, 56, 75, 99, 109, 123, 190, 221, 225, 329, 332, 442, 443, 529, 538, 545, 547, 549, 620

B

Babcock, J.C., 618
Babinski, J., 367
Bach, G.R., 634n
Bachman, J.G., 220
Bachrach, L.L., 578
Baddeley, A., 290, 309
Baddeley, A.D., 302
Baenninger, M.A., 476
Bagatell, C.J., 92
Bahrick, H.P., 305
Bailey, J.M., 491
Baillargeon, R., 132
Baker, L.A., 380
Bal, D.G., 541
Ballo, D.A., 373
Baltes, P.B., 149, 385
Bandura, A., 21, 135, 271, 272, 273, 444, 448, 523, 563, 605, 606
Banks, M.S., 113
Banks, S.M., 338, 639
Baquet, C.R., 541
Barabasz, A., 235
Barbaree, H.E., 494
Barboza, D., 586
Barchoff, H., 497
Bard, P., 422
Barlow, D.H., 557, 560, 606, 620
Barnett, W.S., 384
Barnum, P.T., 62, 63
Baron, R.A., 413, 642, 647, 663, 664, 665, 668, 669, 670
Barongan, C., 494
Barr, C.E., 581
Barringer, F., 351, 504
Barsalou, L.W., 322
Bartek, S.E., 636
Bartoshuk, L.M., 193, 194
Basen-Engquist, K., 220
Bashore, T.R., 417
Basic Behavioral Science Task Force, 19, 21, 22, 161, 209, 270, 373, 420, 454, 455, 523, 562, 622, 647
Bates, J.E., 118
Baucom, 621
Bauer, P.J., 309

Baum, A., 102, 562
Baumeister, R.F., 583, 584
Baumgardner, A.H., 649
Baumrind, D., 120–121, 122, 387
Bearak, B., 659
Beauchamp, G.K., 193, 194
Beck, A.T., 574, 613–614, 621
Becker, L.B., 541
Behar, D., 621
Békésky, G. von, 190
Bell, A.G., 186
Bell, A.P., 491
Bell, P.A., 668
Belle, D., 569
Belles, D., 537, 573
Belsky, J., 118, 123, 124
Bem, D.J., 202
Bem, S.L., 397, 469, 470–471, 474, 475, 480
Benbow, C.P., 376
Benight, C.C., 523
Benson, H., 233, 544
Benson, P.L., 666
Bentall, R.P., 571
Berenbaum, H., 514
Berger, K.S., 149
Berger, R.S., 198, 199
Berke, R.L., 101
Berkowitz, L., 273, 414
Berliner, D., 194
Bernstein, I.L., 549
Bernstein, W.M., 485
Berquier, A., 216
Best, D., 470, 471
Betancourt, H., 541
Bevan, W., 453
Bexton, W.H., 406
Bianchi, S.M., 439, 473
Binet, A., 15, 367, 598
Binswanger, L., 450
Birbaumer, N., 199
Bjork, D.W., 255
Bjorklund, D.F., 131, 132, 300, 476
Blake, P., 517
Blakeslee, S., 186, 194, 215, 382, 541
Blanchard, E.B., 535, 543, 562, 621
Blass, T., 654
Blatt, S.J., 140, 438, 439, 522, 570, 620, 665
Block, J., 443
Bloom, B.L., 458, 558
Bloom, L., 304, 347
Blum, D., 78
Bly, R., 439
Boden, M.A., 330
Bogen, J., 88
Bond, R., 455, 657
Boneau, C.A., 23

Bootzin, R.R., 216, 218
Boskind-White, M., 589
Boss, M., 450
Boston Women's Health Book Collective, 495
Bouchard, T.J., Jr., 379, 380
Bower, G.H., 302, 422
Bowers, K.S., 236
Bowes, J.M., 481
Bowlby, J., 117, 118, 398
Boyatzis, R.E., 53, 54
Boyd-Franklin, N., 622
Brach, P., 594
Bradley, E.J., 414
Bradley, R.H., 383
Brandt, H., 358
Bransford, J.D., 304
Braun, B.G., 564
Bray, R.M., 660
Bremner, W.J., 92
Brent, E., 408
Brewer, C.L., 310
Brewin, C.R., 43, 431
Bridges, K., 418
Bridgwater, C.A., 638
Broberg, A., 123
Broca, P., 86
Brody, J.E., 95, 143, 229, 342, 400, 538, 541, 543, 548, 549, 577
Brody, N., 360
Brokaw, T., 639, 640
Bronstein, P., 410
Brown, B., 276
Brown, B.B., 652
Brown, E.H., 669
Brown, G.W., 569
Brown, L.S., 569
Brown, M., 227
Brown, R., 299, 301
Brown, S.A., 221
Browne, A., 41
Browne, M.W., 63
Brownell, K.D., 400, 401, 402
Brownell, W.E., 188
Brownlee-Duffeck, M., 523
Bruck, M., 296
Bryant, W.C., 151
Buchanan, B., 510, 552
Buchanan, C.M., 138
Buchanan, R.W., 74, 578, 580, 581, 582
Buck, R.W., 653
Bucy, P., 80
Budd, L.S., 261
Buffone, G.W., 537, 573
Bullock, M., 275
Burke, E., 4
Burkhart, B.R., 494
Burman, B., 528
Burnette, E., 352

Burns, D.D., 620
Burns, R., 486
Burnstein, E., 662
Burt, M., 493
Buschmann, M.B., 652
Bushman, 56
Buss, D.M., 476
Bussey, K., 479
Butler, R., 140, 146, 147
Byrne, B.M., 609
Byrne, D., 642, 647, 663, 664, 665, 668, 669, 670
Byrnes, J., 475

C
Cacioppo, J.T., 420
Calhoun, K.S., 495
Califano, J.A., 227
Calkins, M.W., 17
Cameron, J., 333
Campbell, J., 360
Campbell, N., 483
Campos, J.J., 115
Cannistra, S.A., 504
Cannon, W.B., 422, 529
Cantor, J., 273
Cappella, J.N., 485
Cardeña, E., 564
Carey, G., 97, 563
Carey, M.P., 223
Carling, P.J., 598
Carlsmith, J.M., 407, 408
Carlson, J.G., 416, 418
Carmichael, L.L., 295
Carpenter, W.T., Jr., 74, 578, 580, 581, 582
Carroll, K.M., 54, 620
Carstensen, L., 149
Case, R., 132
Castelli, W., 536, 544
Cattell, R.B., 377, 441
Caulfield, M., 543
Cavaliere, F., 350, 351
Ceci, S.J., 296
Celis, W., 494
Centers for Disease Control (CDC), 228, 229, 505, 541, 546, 575, 577
Cepeda-Benito, A., 228
Cerletti, U., 627
Chadwick, P.D.J., 621
Chagall, M., 214
Chaiken, S., 636, 637, 639
Chan, C., 490
Charcot, J.M., 367, 598
Charles, E., 545
Chassin, L., 221
Chesney, M.A., 507, 546
Chesno, F.A., 584
Chitayat, D., 41
Chomsky, N., 349–350
Chronicle of Higher Education, 372
Church, C., 586
Churchill, W., 399
Cicchetti, D.V., 373

Cimons, M., 541
Cinciripini, P.M., 228
Clark, D.M., 561
Clark, K.B., 18
Clark, L.A., 442, 571
Clark, M.P., 18
Clarke-Stewart, K.A., 38, 123
Clay, R.A., 144, 233
Cleaver, R., 632
Clement, J., 327
Clkurel, K., 235
Clum, G.A., 566
Cochran, J., 339
Coe, C., 532
Coe, W.C., 237
Cohen, L.A., 541
Cohen, R., 144
Cohen, S., 514, 529, 533, 539, 667
Cohn, E.G., 668
Cohn, L., 138, 139
Coie, J.D., 538, 539
Coleman, L., 627
Coleman, M., 474
Collaer, M.L., 478, 492
Collier, G., 50
Collins, A.C., 139
Comas-Diaz, L., 570, 622
Condon, J.W., 485
Connelly, J., 514
Cools, J., 401, 403
Coon, H., 102, 380, 382
Cooney, J.L., 522
Cooney, N.L., 228
Coons, P.M., 566
Cooper, 56
Cooper, J.R., 571
Cooper, M.L., 223
Corasaniti, M.A., 123
Corey, L., 507
Corkin, S., 309
Corter, J.E., 299
Cose, E., 339
Costa, P.T., Jr., 441, 442, 582, 584
Coté, N., 326, 327
Cousins, N., 525
Cowan, T., 299
Cowley, G., 143, 144
Cox, M.J., 118
Craik, F.I.M., 297, 302
Cramer, R.E., 665
Crano, W.D., 485
Crawford, H.J., 235, 236
Creamer, M., 519, 562
Crenshaw, T., 501
Crews, D., 98, 478, 491
Crick, F., 98, 208
Crick, N.R., 414, 584, 650
Crinella, F., 150
Crocker, J., 637
Crowe, R.A., 63
Croyle, R.T., 545
Crusco, A.H., 652
Culbertson, F.M., 569
cummings, e.e., 343
Cunningham, M.R., 664
Curfman, G.D., 536, 544

Curran, P.J., 221
Curtis, R.C., 485
Curtis-Christoph, 621

D
Dabbs, J.M., 666
Damasio, A., 57
Damasio, H., 57
Danforth, J.S., 544
Daniel, M.H., 367
D'Arcangelo, A., 167, 168
Darley, J.M., 664, 665
Darwin, C., 11, 97, 245, 414, 420
Das-Smaal, E.A., 320
Davey, L.F., 138
Davidson, J.E., 328
Davidson, J.R., 562
Da Vinci, L., 87
Davis, J.H., 661
Davis, K.L., 582
Davis, R., 15
Davis, S.F., 15
Davison, G.C., 621
Dean, G., 63
DeAngelis, T., 17, 18, 124, 273, 274, 310, 561, 586, 588, 589, 622
DeBono, G., 636
DeCasper, A.J., 115
DeFries, J.C., 101
De Jong, P.F., 320
De La Cancela, V., 623
Delahanty, D.L., 532
Delgado, J., 85
Democritus, 9
DeNeve, K.M., 668
Denmark, F.L., 21
DePaulo, B.M., 651
DeRubeis, 621
Descartes, R., 396
Deutsch, G., 88
Deutsch, R.M., 634n
DeValois, R.L., 170
Devine, P.G., 643, 644
Diana, Princess of Wales, 299
Dickinson, E., 57, 396
DiClemente, C.C., 523
Diehl, N.S., 8
DiLalla, D.L., 97, 101, 563, 584
Dill, C.A., 60
Dindia, K., 439, 476
Dix, T., 121
Docherty, N.M., 578
Dockery, D.W., 668
Dodge, K.A., 414, 415, 584, 650
Doherty, K., 228
Dollard, J., 252, 663
Donnerstein, E.I., 667
Doob, A.N., 414
Dorfman, D., 638
Dornbusch, S., 276
Downey, J.I., 492
Drapkin, R.G., 401, 403
Drobes, D.J., 227
Dubbert, P.M., 544
Duckitt, J., 643, 644

Dugan, K.W., 413
Dumas, A., 40
Dumas, J.E., 122
Dunning, J., 588
Dweck, C., 410
Dyck, D.G., 522

E
Eagly, A.H., 471, 475, 636, 637, 639, 642
Ebbinghaus, H., 15, 304, 305, 306
Edwards, R., 624
Egeth, H.E., 296
Ehri, L.C., 345
Eisenberg, N., 641
Eisenberger, R., 333
Eke, M., 561
Ekman, P., 418, 420, 422, 424
Elenteny, K., 476
Eliot, G., 145
Ellickson, P.L., 223
Ellis, A., 521–522, 534, 535, 613, 614, 615, 621
Ellis, L., 492
Ellsworth, P.C., 653
Emde, R., 100, 380
Engel, J., 88
Engels, G.I., 621
Erikson, E.H., 20, 116–117, 139, 140, 141, 151, 436–437, 438
Eron, L.D., 138, 273, 274
Escher, M.C., 172, 178
Escobar, C.M., 384
Espenshade, T., 44
Esterling, B.A., 539
Estes, W.K., 301
Etaugh, C., 265, 479
Evans, G.W., 668
Eysenck, H.J., 440, 441

F
Fairburn, C.G., 613, 627
Fallon, A.E., 484
Farrell, A.D., 558
Fazio, R.H., 636
Fechner, G.T., 10, 15, 157, 158, 305
Feder, B.J., 228
Fehr, B., 321
Feingold, A., 476, 642
Feshbach, S., 414
Festinger, L., 392, 397, 407, 408
Fibel, B., 447
Fichner-Rathus, L., 494, 496
Field, S., 565
Field, T.M., 38, 123
Finn, P.R., 222
Fischer, K.W., 418
Fisher, C.B., 60
Fiske, D., 441
Fiske, S.T., 413, 488, 644
Fitzgibbon, M.L., 400
Fitz-Roy, R., 97
Flack, J.M., 540
Flannery, D.J., 138
Flavell, J.H., 131, 132, 134, 135

Fleming, I., 562
Flor, H., 198, 199
Foa, E.B., 562
Foa, E.G., 562
Foley, 190
Folkman, S., 528
Follette, W.C., 557
Ford, E.S., 542
Foster, G.D., 402
Fowler, R.D., 61
Fowler, W., 376
Fox, R., 412
Frankel, K.A., 118
Frankl, V., 450
Frantz, R., 114
Franzoi, S.L., 483
Fraser, S.C., 640
Freedman, D., 366
Freedman, D.X., 442
Freedman, J.L., 640
Freeman, A., 621
Freeman, M.S., 115
Freud, A., 437
Freud, S., 15, 16, 19, 29, 37, 43,
    109, 135–136, 209–210,
    214, 215, 227, 236, 252, 294,
    308–309, 342n, 367, 394,
    414, 430–435, 436–437,
    438, 451, 478–479, 481, 559,
    563, 598, 599–602
Friedman, M., 526, 527, 544
Friedman, M.A., 401
Friedman, R.C., 492
Friman, P.C., 23
Frisch, R., 137
Fritsch, G., 85
Frodi, A.M., 477, 480
Fromm, E., 20
Fry, R., 517
Fuchs, 223
Fuller, S.R., 662
Furedy, J.J., 417
Furumoto, L., 17
Fyrberg, D., 60

G
Gage, P., 57
Gagnon, J.H., 45, 46
Galaburda, A.M., 88
Galambos, N.L., 138
Galassi, J.P., 605
Galileo, 29
Gallagher, R., 515
Gallucci, W.T., 531
Gallup, G.H., 63
Galton, F., 377, 440
Galvani, L., 71
Ganong, L.H., 474
Garcia, J., 248, 257, 377
Gardner, H., 362–363
Garfinkel, R., 149
Garland, A.F., 138
Gauthier, J., 543
Gaziano, J.M., 223
Gazzaniga, M.S., 85, 87, 88, 208
Geen, R.G., 414

Geiger, H.J., 540
Gelman, D., 574
Gelman, R., 132
Genovese, K., 664, 665
Gentry, J., 138
George, J.M., 664
Gerberding, J.L., 507
Gerstner, L., Jr., 274–275
Geschwind, N., 88
Gesell, A., 109
Getzels, J.W., 332
Gibson, E.J., 115
Gibson, M., 454
Gigerenzer, G., 340
Gigone, D., 661
Gilbert, S., 529, 532, 538, 586,
    588
Gilbert, S.J., 654
Gilligan, C., 133, 136, 140, 438
Gillis, A.R., 670
Gillis, J.S., 483
Gilmore, G., 583
Gilovich, T., 649
Ginsburg, G., 410
Glaser, R., 538
Glass, G.V., 621
Gleason, J.B., 342, 345, 348
Gleitman, H., 645
Glenn, S.S., 256
Glover, J.A., 269
Gluck, M.A., 299
Goddard, H.H., 377
Godden, D.R., 302
Gold, D.R., 228, 229
Goldman, J.A., 340, 505
Goldman, K., 639
Goldman, R., 338
Goldman-Rakic, P.S., 57, 85, 290,
    297
Goldsmith, H.H., 97, 101
Goleman, D.J., 58, 85, 365, 424,
    580, 626
Goodall, J., 47, 48
Goodenough, F., 377
Goodman, L.A., 41
Goodnow, J.J., 481
Goodwin, F.K., 571
Gopnik, A., 131
Gordon, C.M., 223
Gorman, J., 208
Gortmaker, S.L., 400
Gottesman, I.I., 581, 584
Gottfried, A.E., 383, 410
Gottman, J.M., 640
Grady, D., 75, 230
Graham, M., 449
Granberg, D., 408
Gray, T., 587
Greene, 263
Greene, B., 456, 489, 490, 491,
    622, 623, 624
Greenfield, S.A., 76
Greeno, C.G., 401
Greenough, W.T., 312
Greenwood, K.M., 216
Greist, J.H., 537, 573

Griffin, E., 485
Grodstein, F., 143
Grossman, M.I., 399
Grove, W.M., 581
Gruber, K.L., 640
Gruber-Baldini, A.L., 385
Gruder, C.L., 529
Grush, J.E., 638
Gruzelier, J., 235
Guilford, J.P., 362
Guisinger, S., 140, 438, 439,
    665
Guralnik, J.M., 540, 549
Guthrie, R.V., 17
Guzman, L.P., 623

H
Haaf, R.A., 115
Haaga, D.A.F., 621
Haber, R.N., 289, 290
Haddad, Y., 658
Haines, P.S., 402
Hale, W.D., 447
Haley, W.E., 529
Hall, C.S., 476
Hall, G.C.I., 494, 622
Hall, G.S., 10
Hall, J., 248
Hall, J.A., 652
Hall, J.V., 638
Hall, S.M., 542
Halperin, K.M., 62
Halpern, D.F., 324, 475
Halpern, J.A., 326
Hamer, D., 488, 491
Hamm, N.M., 638
Haney, D.Q., 507
Haney, M., 221
Hansen, D.H., 124
Harkins, S., 660
Harlow, H.F., 119–120, 407
Harlow, L.L., 340, 505
Harnishfeger, K.K., 132
Harris, G.T., 583
Harris, Z., 349
Hashimoto, N., 132
Hasselhorn, M., 300
Hastie, R., 340, 661
Hatfield, E., 416, 418
Haughton, E., 607
Hauser-Cram, P., 384
Hawkins, R.D., 313, 314
Hawkins, S.A., 340
Hayes, A.M., 621
Hayes, P., 366
Hayes, S.C., 269
Hays, K.F., 8, 536, 573
Heatherton, T.F., 586
Heckhausen, J., 149
Hefflin, A.H., 122
Hegarty, M., 324
Heggestad, E.D., 360
Heidegger, M., 449
Heingartner, A., 638
Heller, D.A., 100
Helmes, E., 458

Helmholtz, H. von, 170, 190
Helms, J.E., 377
Helson, R., 140, 142, 145
Hemingway, E., 569
Heninger, G.R., 627
Henning, K., 476
Hensley, W.E., 666
Hepper, P.G., 88
Hepworth, J.T., 644
Herbert, T.B., 539
Hergenhahn, B.R., 308, 414, 438,
    555
Hering, E., 170
Hernandez, P., 21, 455
Herrera, C., 124
Herrmann, D.J., 310
Herrnstein, R., 378, 379
Hersen, 573
Hershey, D.A., 327
Herzog, D.B., 588
Herzog, M.E., 483
Hewitt, P.L., 570, 577
Hilgard, E.R., 237
Hill, D.R., 569
Hilton, J.L., 643
Hilts, P.J., 85, 312, 313
Hinckley, J., 554
Hines, M., 478, 492
Hippocrates, 440
Hitler, A., 654
Hitzig, E., 85
Hobfoll, S.E., 505, 570
Hobson, J.A., 213, 214
Hodges, L.F., 606
Hoffman, C., 471
Hogan, H.P., 295
Hogan, R., 412
Hogarth, W., 178, 180
Holahan, C.J., 522, 523, 529
Holland, J.L., 443, 460, 461
Hollinger, L.M., 652
Hollingshead, A.B., 580
Hollon, S.D., 621, 628
Holmes, D.S., 233, 537
Holmes, K.K., 507
Holmes, T.H., 515
Holyoak, K., 246
Homburger, T., 437
Honan, W.H., 473
Honorton, C., 202
Honzik, C.H., 270
Hopper, J.L., 229
Horn, J.M., 380
Horney, K., 20, 436
Houston, B.K., 544
Howard, K.I., 620
Howard-Pitney, B., 575
Hubel, D., 160
Huesmann, L.R., 272, 273, 275
Hull, C., 256, 394
Hultquist, C.M., 227
Humphrey, L.L., 589
Hunt, M., 133, 349, 408, 665
Hurst, N., 471
Hutchins, R.M., 27
Huxley, A., 100

Hyde, J.S., 475
Hyman, R., 202

I

Innocent VIII, 555, 556
Ironson, G., 562
Isabella, R.A., 118
Isay, R.A., 491, 624
Isomura, T., 623
Izard, C.E., 418

J

Jacklin, C.N., 480
Jackson, J.F., 387
Jackson, P.W., 332
Jacob, T., 60
Jacobs, G.H., 170
Jacobs, T.J., 545
Jacobson, N.S., 613, 618, 621
Jacobson-Kram, P., 618
Jacox, A., 198, 548
James, W., 10–11, 15, 16, 17, 18, 24, 29, 206, 208, 286, 288, 298, 394, 397, 409, 421, 424, 439, 572
James I, 227
Jamison, K.R., 568, 569, 571
Janerich, D.T., 229
Janis, I.L., 662
Janos, P.M., 375
Janowitz, H.D., 399
Janus, C.L., 489
Janus, S.S., 489
Jaremko, M.E., 534
Javier, R.A., 471n
Jeffery, R.W., 544
Jemmott, J.B., 538
Jennings, P., 639, 640
Jensen, C.D., 198
Jensen, M.P., 199
Johnson, B.T., 636
Johnson, D.L., 383
Johnson, G., 341
Johnson, K.W., 542
Johnson, S.B., 23, 41
Johnson, V.E., 498–499, 624
Johnson, W., 419
Johnston, L.D., 220, 222, 227
Joiner, T.E., 589
Jones, E.D., 376
Jones, E.E., 646
Jones, G.H., 17
Jones, J.L., 639
Jones, M.C., 252, 254
Jordan, J.V., 140, 438
Jordan, M., 639
Jorgensen, R.S., 543
Josephs, R.A., 223
Josephson, W.D., 273
Judd, C.M., 644
Jung, C., 409, 436, 440
Just, N., 570

K

Kahn, A.S., 41
Kahneman, D., 337

Kail, R.V., 132
Kamin, L.J., 379
Kandel, E.R., 313, 314
Kane, J.M., 626
Kaniasty, K., 515
Kaplan, S.J., 124
Karasek, R.A., 544
Karoly, P., 197, 198, 199
Kasparov, G., 366
Katz, M.H., 507
Katzell, R.A., 412
Kaufman, J., 124
Kazdin, A.E., 138
Keech, M., 392, 408
Keefe, F.J., 198, 199
Keen, S., 439
Keesey, R.E., 399
Keil, J.E., 543
Keinan, G., 662
Keita, G.P., 41
Kellerman, J., 653
Kelley, H.H., 649
Kelley, M.L., 575
Kellman, P.J., 113
Kelly, G.A., 396
Kelly, I.W., 63
Kelman, H.C., 650
Kemeny, M.E., 525, 539
Kenrick, D.T., 668
Kessel, F., 453
Kessler, D.A., 221, 227
Ketcham, K., 308
Khan, W., 658
Kidd, K.K., 101
Kiecolt-Glaser, J.K., 519
Kihlstrom, J.F., 566
Kilborn, P.T., 473
Kilmann, P.R., 584
Kilshaw, D., 88
Kimble, D.P., 197, 199, 399
Kimble, G.A., 24, 63, 208, 210, 213, 367, 393
Kimerling, R., 495
Kinderman, P., 571
Kinnunen, T., 227, 228, 237
Kinsey, A.C., 42, 44
Kintsch, W., 4
Kipp, K., 476
Kirkley, B.G., 588
Kirsch, I., 235
Kitayama, S., 455
Kleinke, C.L., 652, 653
Kleinman, A., 21, 456
Kleinmuntz, B., 417
Klepinger, D.H., 546
Klesges, R.C., 227
Klett, S., 587
Klock, C., 606
Klorman, R., 226
Klosko, J.S., 563
Klüver, H., 80
Knight, M., 68
Kobasa, S., 525
Koch, C., 208
Kochanska, G., 583
Koelling, R.A., 248

Koffka, K., 13, 16
Kohlberg, L., 133–136, 438
Köhler, W., 13, 14, 16, 328
Kolata, G., 101, 102, 103, 231
Kolko, D.J., 198, 547
Koocher, G.P., 60
Korn, J.H., 15, 16
Kosonen, P., 335
Koss, M.P., 41, 492, 494, 495, 501
Kosslyn, S.M., 312
Kramer, H., 556
Kramer, P.D., 442
Krantz, D.S., 544
Krosnick, J.A., 636
Kubiszyn, T., 6
Kübler-Ross, E., 150–151
Kuczaj, S.A., II, 346, 348
Kulik, J., 299
Kumanyika, S., 402
Kupfer, D.J., 217, 218, 626, 627, 628
Kwan, M., 525
Ky, K., 382

L

Lackner, J.M., 523
Lacks, P., 218
Ladd-Franklin, C., 17
LaFramboise, T., 622, 624
LaFreniere, P.J., 122
Lakka, T.A., 544
Lamb, M.E., 121, 123
Lambert, W.E., 351, 352
Landon, A., 39
Lang, A.R., 54, 56, 59, 61
Lang, P.J., 267
Lang, S.S., 225, 549
Lange, K.G., 421, 424
Langer, E.J., 147
Larrick, R.P., 662
Larson, R., 138
Larson, R.K., 353, 355
Lashley, K.S., 312
Latané, B., 584, 665, 666
Lau, M.A., 56
Laumann, E.O., 45, 46, 143, 485, 488, 489
Lawton, C., 476
Lazarus, A.A., 536
Lazarus, R.S., 422, 514, 528
Leary, M.R., 639
Leary, W.E., 227, 230, 541, 542, 543
Le Bon, G., 663
Leborgne, 86
Lederberg, A.R., 118
LeDoux, J.E., 314, 416
Lee, C., 573
Lefcourt, H.M., 518, 525
Lefley, H.P., 624
Leibowitz, 5
Leigh, B.C., 223
Lenneberg, E.H., 350
Leor, J., 544
Lerman, C., 102, 545

Leutwyler, K., 569
Levine, I.S., 598
Levine, L., 382
Levine, S.R., 227
Levinson, D., 140, 142
Lewin, T., 124, 473
Lewinsohn, P.M., 529, 572, 574, 577
Lewis, P.H., 490
Lewis-Fernández, R., 21, 456
Lieber, C.S., 222
Liebert, R.M., 273
Lin, S.P., 581
Linde, S., 148
Linden, W., 529
Lindsey, D.T., 113
Linn, M.C., 475
Linville, P.W., 644
Lips, H., 376
Lipsey, M.W., 621
Lishman, B., 121
Liu, H., 3, 466
Lo, B., 541
Lochman, J.E., 415, 584, 650
Lockhart, R.S., 302
Loftus, E.F., 236, 290, 294, 295, 296, 297, 308, 431
Loftus, G.R., 294
Lohr, J.M., 637
Lopez, S., 21, 455
López, S.R., 541
Lore, R.K., 411
Lorenz, K.Z., 120, 121
Lowe, C.F., 621
Lowe, M.R., 589
Lubart, T.I., 330
Luborsky, L., 619, 620
Luchins, A.S., 323, 646
Luchins, E.H., 323
Ludwick-Rosenthal, R., 198, 528
Lundeberg, M.A., 340
Lurie, N., 541
Lydiard, R.B., 625, 626
Lykken, D.T., 97, 101, 584
Lyons-Ruth, K., 118

M

Maas, A., 644
Maas, J.W., 582
Maccoby, E.E., 475, 480
MacDonald, K., 121
Macfarlane, J.A., 116
MacFarlane, S.W., 668
Mack, D., 412
MacKenzie, T.D., 227
Mackie, D.M., 639, 640
MacPhillamy, D.J., 572
Maeder, G., 659
Maher, B.A., 63, 440
Maher, W.B., 63, 440
Maier, N.R.F., 328–329
Malgady, R.G., 623
Malinosky-Rummell, R., 124
Manber, R., 218
Manke, F., 588
Marecek, J., 475

Marenberg, M.E., 543
Margolin, G., 528
Margoshes, P., 149
Markman, H.J., 618
Markus, H., 455
Marshall, W.L., 494
Marteau, T.M., 102
Martin, 628
Martin, J.E., 228
Martin, N., 56
Martin, R.A., 525
Martinez Sanchez, M., 548
Marx, E.M., 569
Marx, K., 220
Marzuk, P.M., 563, 571, 575, 582
Maslach, C., 640, 657
Maslow, A.H., 20, 395–396, 449, 450, 451
Massaro, S., 227
Masters, W.H., 498–499, 624
Mastropieri, M.A., 297
Matefy, R., 231–232
Matlin, 190
Matlin, M., 23, 326, 333, 336
Matthews, K., 22, 41, 143
Matus, I., 144
May, R., 20
Mayer, J., 364
Mazzella, R., 642
McCall, R., 365
McCann, I.L., 537
McCarley, R.W., 213
McCauley, C., 670
McClelland, D.C., 409–410
McConnell, J.V., 314
McCrae, R., 441, 442
McDermott, D., 366
McDonald, F.J., 135
McDougall, W., 288, 394
McGovern, T.V., 9, 24, 28, 59
McGowan, R.J., 383
McGrath, E., 569
McIntosh, H., 332
McKeachie, W., 4
McNally, R.J., 561, 563
McNeill, D., 301
McTiernan, A., 223, 548
Mead, M., 397
Meade, V., 650
Meichenbaum, D., 534, 562, 563, 613
Meier, B., 504
Melamed, B.B., 267
Meltzoff, A.N., 131, 398
Melzack, R., 197
Mendez, M., 74
Menustik, C.E., 607
Merluzzi, T.V., 548
Mesmer, F.A., 235
Metcalfe, J., 327
Mevkens, F.L., 549
Meyer, T., 400
Meyers, A.W., 227
Michael, R.T., 45, 46, 485
Michaels, S., 45, 46
Michaelson, R., 373

Michela, J.L., 649
Michelangelo, 87
Michels, R., 563, 571, 575, 582
Mikesell, R.H., 618
Milgram, S., 34–37, 40, 48, 52, 56, 59, 60, 61, 654–655, 670
Miller, 656
Miller, G., 292
Miller, J.L., 209, 353, 355
Miller, K., 485
Miller, L.S., 272, 273
Miller, M.D., 448
Miller, M.E., 236
Miller, M.F., 235, 237
Miller, N.B., 121
Miller, N.E., 5, 233–234, 399, 663
Miller, S.M., 444n, 523
Miller, T.Q., 544
Mills, C.J., 376
Milner, B.R., 309
Milner, P., 80
Mindell, J.A., 219
Mineka, S., 562, 563
Mischel, W., 21, 444, 445, 523, 539
Moane, G., 140, 142
Mobley, C.E., 118
Moliterno, D.J., 227
Mondale, W., 639
Money, J., 478, 488, 491
Moniz, A.E., 628
Montemayor, R., 138
Moore, R.Y., 161
Moos, R.H., 522, 523
Morales, E., 489
Moreland, R.L., 638
Morgan, C., 409, 462
Morgan, R., 495
Morin, C.M., 217, 218
Morrin, K., 476
Morris, W.N., 658
Moscovitch, M., 313
Moser, C.G., 522
Moyers, B., 198, 199, 512
Mozart, W.A., 382
Mudd, S.A., 304
Mullen, B., 639
Munch, E., 215
Muñoz, R.F., 628
Murray, B., 24, 28, 268n, 274, 514
Murray, C., 378–379
Murray, H., 462
Murray, H.A., 409
Murtagh, D.R.R., 216
Myers, H.F., 542
Myers, L.B., 431

N
Nadol, J.B., Jr., 190, 191
National Center for Health Statistics, 539, 543
National Institute of Mental Health (NIMH), 273
National Institute of Occupational Safety and Health, 471

Neisser, U., 47, 312, 360, 363, 365, 372, 379, 384, 385, 475
Nelson, K., 345
Neufeld, R.W.J., 198, 528
Nevid, J.S., 42, 60, 146, 222, 228, 229, 230, 400, 402, 548, 580, 609
Newlin, D.B., 222
Newman, F.L., 620
Newman, J., 670
Newman, R., 442
Newport, E.L., 192
Newport, F., 63
Newton, I., 161
Nicassio, P.M., 218
Nides, M.A., 529
Niloff, J.M., 504
NIMH. See National Institute of Mental Health (NIMH)
Nisbett, R.E., 448
Nolen-Hoeksema, S., 570, 620
Norris, F.H., 515
Norvell, N., 537, 573
Novick, L.R., 326, 327
Nowicki, 530

O
Oades, R.D., 581
O'Brien, C.P., 222, 225, 227, 228, 626
Oddbert, H.S., 440
Office of Demographic, Employment, and Educational Research (ODEER), 6, 18
Ogbu, J., 454
Okazaki, S., 372, 373, 455
Olds, J., 80
O'Leary, A., 532
O'Leary, S.G., 267
Olivier, L., 272
Olson, G., 56
Olson, S.L., 122, 382
O'Malley, P.M., 220
Orcutt, H.K., 223
O'Reilly, C.A., II, 413
Ouimette, P.C., 223

P
Paffenbarger, R.S., Jr., 536, 537
Pagan, G., 670
Paikoff, R.L., 139
Pajares, F., 448
Palmer, J.C., 295, 296
Palmer, M.T., 485
Papini, D.R., 138
Papousek, M., 115
Pappas, G., 540, 549
Pardes, H., 61
Park, B., 644
Parker, J.G., 124
Patrick, C.J., 584
Patt, R.B., 225, 549
Patterson, 583
Patterson, D.R., 199
Patterson, G.R., 274
Patterson, M.L., 650

Pavlov, I., 12, 13, 15, 244–246, 249–250, 250–252, 260
Pedersen, N.L., 563
Penfield, W., 294
Penn, D.L., 579
Penn, N.E., 540, 622
Penner, L.A., 588
Penrod, S., 658
Perls, F., 603
Perret, D.I., 483
Perry, D.G., 479
Perry, J.D., 668
Pesjack, M., 517
Peterson, E.D., 541
Peterson, J.B., 405
Peterson, L.R., 293
Peterson, M.J., 293
Petraitis, J., 221
Petrie, T.A., 8
Pettingale, K.W., 549
Petty, R.E., 637
Phillipson, E.A., 218
Phinney, J.S., 22, 456
Piaget, J., 15, 19, 109, 125–131, 284, 296, 353, 396, 438
Picasso, P., 87, 331
Pihl, R.O., 222, 405
Pike, K.M., 589
Pilkonis, P., 575
Pillard, R.C., 491
Pinel, P., 598, 599
Pinker, S., 86, 346, 347, 349, 350, 352, 353, 355
Pion, G.M., 23
Plant, E.A., 475
Plath, S., 569
Plato, 9
Plaud, J.J., 254, 604
Plomin, R., 97
Plous, S., 61
Plutchik, R., 418
Polivy, J., 589
Pollack, W.S., 144
Pomerleau, O.F., 221
Pope, K.S., 308
Popkin, B.M., 402
Porter, R.H., 116
Posner, M.I., 58
Powch, I.G., 544
Powell, E., 494, 495, 497
Powell, L.H., 522, 544
Prescott, P.A., 115
Price, L.H., 627
Ptacek, J.T., 199
Putallaz, M., 122
Putnam, F.W., 566

Q
Quattrone, G.A., 637

R
Ragsdale, K., 619
Rahe, R.H., 515
Raichle, M.E., 58, 59, 86
Rainey, D., 412
Rakowski, W., 150

Rapaport, K., 494
Rapp, P.E., 417
Rappaport, N.B., 543
Rather, D., 513, 639, 640
Rathus, S.A., 42, 78, 93, 94, 98, 143, 144, 265, 468, 479, 489, 494, 496, 608, 621
Ratner, N.B., 342, 345, 348
Rauscher, F., 382
Ray, M., 172
Rayner, R., 209, 252, 253
Reagan, N., 63
Reagan, R., 63, 554, 639
Redd, W.H., 198, 548
Reddon, J.R., 458
Redlich, F.C., 580
Reid, P.T., 21
Reid, T.R., 469
Reinke, B.J., 142, 145
Reis, H.T., 484
Reiser, M., 214
Renninger, K.A., 290
Repetti, R.L., 514
Rescorla, R.A., 246, 252, 270, 396, 407
Resnick, H.S., 562
Resnick, M., 575
Rest, J.R., 135
Reston, J., 198–199
Reynolds, A.G., 351
Reynolds, C.F., 217, 218
Rhine, J.B., 202
Rice, M.E., 607
Rich, C.L., 574
Richards, M.H., 138
Richardson, D.C., 480
Richardson, P.H., 199
Richman, J., 575
Rickard-Figueroa, J.L., 198, 547
Riecken, H., 408
Riggio, R.E., 484, 485
Rilling, M., 314
Ringgold, F., 440
Robbins, C., 345
Robins, C.J., 621
Robinson, N.M., 376
Rodin, J., 402, 589
Rodriguez, N., 562
Rog, D.J., 598
Rogers, C., 20, 449, 451–453, 456, 602, 603
Rogers, R.M., 219
Rogers, W., 637
Roggman, L.A., 138
Rooney, A., 400
Roosevelt, E., 452
Roosevelt, F.D., 39
Rorschach, H., 462
Rorschach, U., 462
Rose, J.S., 229
Rose, R.J., 97, 387, 571
Rosenbaum, M., 400
Rosenberg, J., 473
Rosenblatt, R., 228
Rosenfeld, A., 260
Rosenthal, 664

Rosenthal, E., 225, 547
Ross, C.A., 566
Ross, L., 448
Ross, M.J., 198, 199
Rossouw, J.E., 543
Rothbart, M.K., 124, 570
Rothbaum, B.O., 562, 606
Rotheram-Borus, M.J., 546, 575, 577
Rothko, M., 167, 169
Rothman, B.O., 338
Rothman, S., 377, 387
Rotter, J.B., 21, 525
Rousseau, J.-J., 472
Royce, R.A., 504, 505
Rozin, P., 484
Ruehlman, L.S., 197
Rule, B.G., 414
Rush, 614
Russell, J.A., 321
Russo, A., 606
Rüstemli, A., 476
Rutkowski, G.K., 665
Rutter, C.M., 577
Rutter, M., 97, 584
Rychlak, J.F., 208, 210
Rymer, R., 44

S

Saarni, C., 651
Saccuzzo, D., 458
Sadalla, E.K., 485, 670
Sadker, D., 445
Sadker, M., 445
Sadowski, C., 575
Salgado de Snyder, V.N., 456
Salovey, P., 338, 364
Salthouse, T.A., 132
Sanchez, J., 17
Sanders, G.S., 296
Sandman, C., 150
Sanna, L.J., 660
Santayana, G., 108
Santee, R.T., 640, 657
Sarbin, T.R., 237
Sarter, M., 58
Satre, J.-P., 449
Saxe, L., 416, 417
Scarr, S., 101, 380, 384, 385
Schachter, S., 408, 411, 422–423, 424, 584, 665
Schafer, J., 221
Schafran, L.H., 492
Schaie, K.W., 385
Schaller, M., 644
Schapiro, M., 390
Schenker, M., 668
Schiffer, C., 483
Schiffman, H., 197
Schmidt, N.B., 561
Schneider, B.H., 609
Schneider, W., 300
Schneirla, T.C., 328
Schotte, D.E., 575, 577
Schreiber, G.B., 505
Schuckit, M.A., 223, 225

Schultz, L.A., 411
Schulz, R., 149
Schumann, R., 569
Schutte, N.S., 273
Schwartz, M.W., 401
Schwartz, R.M., 640
Schwarz, N., 640
Schwarzenegger, A., 366
Schweinhart, L.J., 384
Scott, J., 554
Scruggs, T.E., 297
Sechenov, I., 245
Seeley, R.J., 401
Seeman, E., 229
Segal, N., 102
Seligman, M.E.P., 570, 620
Selye, H., 513, 529
Senior, J., 191
Seppa, N., 124, 497, 505
Seta, J.J., 660
Seurat, G., 168, 169
Shadish, W.R., 619, 620
Shaffer, C.R., 636
Shakespeare, W., 0, 2, 3, 29, 213n, 417, 578, 596n, 599, 613
Shannon, E., 113
Shapiro, M., 0
Shavitt, S., 636
Shaw, G., 382
Shaw, G.B., 400
Shaywitz, B.A., 478
Sheehy, G., 140, 141, 142, 149
Shepherd, J., 544
Sheppard, J.A., 483
Shepperd, J.A., 661
Sher, K.J., 221, 583, 584
Sherman, R.A., 197
Sherif, M., 642
Shiffman, S., 227
Shiffrin, R., 287
Shimomura, R., 240, 428
Shneidman, E., 151, 576
Shoda, Y., 444, 445, 523, 539
Shotland, R.L., 660
Shumaker, S.A., 569
Siega-Riz, A.M., 402
Silverstein, L.B., 122
Simon, T., 367
Simons, A.D., 518, 569, 571, 621
Simons, D.L., 32
Simons, R.L., 124
Simpson, M., 668
Simpson, M.L., 298
Simpson, N.B., 338
Simpson, O.J., 299, 338–340
Singer, J.E., 422–423, 424
Sizemore, C., 43, 565
Skinner, B.F., 12–13, 15, 16, 147, 255–258, 260, 262, 269, 348–349, 444
Slaven, L., 573
Sleek, S., 350, 549, 616, 627
Slobin, D.I., 345, 346
Sloman, S.A., 321, 335
Smetana, J.G., 138
Smith, G.F., 638

Smith, J. Quick-to-See, 154, 318
Smith, M.L., 621
Smith, P.B., 455, 657
Smith, R.E., 518
Smith, S.M., 302
Snarey, J.R., 134
Snyder, C.R., 62
Snyder, M., 636, 666
Snyderman, M., 377, 387
Socrates, 9, 19
Solomon, E.P., 98, 165, 170, 193
Sommers-Flanagan, J., 575
Sommers-Flanagan, R., 575
Sorensen, S.B., 577
Sorensen, T.I.A., 400
Southern, T., 376
Spain, D., 439, 473
Sparks, G.G., 485
Sparrow, S.S., 373
Spearman, C., 361
Sperling, G., 288–289
Sperry, R.W., 19, 57
Spiegel, D., 564
Spinhoven, P., 558
Sporer, S.L., 304
Spreat, S., 621
Sprecher, S., 476–477
Sprenger, J., 556
Springer, S.P., 88
Squire, L.R., 80, 309, 313, 315
Staats, A., 637
Stacy, A.W., 221, 405, 636
Stall, R., 223
Stampfer, M.J., 543
Staples, S.I., 667
Stasser, G., 661
Steele, C.M., 223, 379, 381
Steele, S., 381
Steffen, V.J., 471
Steinberg, L., 138, 275–276, 373, 382
Steinbrook, R., 417
Steinem, G., 473
Steiner, M., 95
Stern, W., 368
Sternberg, R.J., 50, 292, 328, 330, 331, 360, 363–364, 486
Stevens, A., 663
Stevenson, H.W., 372
Stewart, M.W., 518
Stier, D.S., 652
Stokols, D., 538, 539
Stout, D., 229
Strathman, A.J., 483
Straube, E.R., 581
Strauss, M., 124, 261
Strickland, 530
Strollo, P.J., 219
Strom, J.C., 653
Strom, S., 194
Strupp, H.H., 619
Stunkard, A.J., 400
Sue, S., 17, 372, 373, 622, 623
Sugarman, R., 660
Suinn, R., 526
Suls, J., 543

Susser, E.S., 581
Sutker, P.B., 583
Suzuki, L.A., 371, 382
Swaim, 221
Sweeney, J.A., 308
Sweeney, P.D., 640
Szasz, T.S., 559
Szucko, J.J., 417

T

Tabor, M.B.W., 275
Takahira, S., 475
Tanford, S., 658
Tangney, J.P., 584
Tanzi, R.E., 74
Taub, A., 225
Taylor, H., 44
Teller, D.Y., 113
Tennyson, A. Lord, 569
Terman, L., 367, 375–376
Tharp, R.G., 415
Thase, M.E., 626, 627, 628
Thompson, C.P., 299
Thompson, D.E., 412
Thompson, G.D., 172
Thompson, L.A., 380
Thompson, R.A., 118, 123
Thomson, J.B., 222
Thoreau, H.D., 572
Thoresen, C., 522, 544
Thorndike, E.L., 255
Thune, I., 548
Thurstone, L., 441
Thurstone, L.L., 361
Thurstone, T.G., 361
Tiffany, S.T., 227
Tolman, E.C., 270–271
Tomes, H., 415
Torgersen, S., 563
Toulouse-Lautrec, H. de, 489
Triandis, H.C., 454, 455
Trickett, P.K., 124
Trobst, K.K., 665
Trujillo, C., 490
Trull, T.J., 583, 584
Tsui, A.S., 413
Tucker, J.S., 518
Tulving, E., 283
Turlington, C., 483
Turner, A.M., 312
Turner, S.M., 254
Tversky, A., 337
Twain, M., 14

U

Uchino, B.N., 528, 538
Ukestad, L.K., 199, 542
Ulmer, D., 526, 527, 544
U.S. Bureau of the Census, 42, 122
Upstream, 379

V

Vaillant, G.E., 518, 566
Valencia, R.R., 371, 382
Valenstein, E.S., 628
Valenteiner, D.P., 529
Van Brunt, L., 644
Vandell, D.L., 123
Vandenbergh, J.G., 478
VandenBos, G.R., 620
Van Kammen, D.P., 582
Vasarely, V., 178, 179
Venables, P.H., 582
Vernberg, E.M., 529
Vernon, S.W., 545
Vincent, C.A., 199
Visintainer, M.A., 547
Vitousek, K., 588
Von Hippel, W., 643
Von Hofsten, C., 113
Voyer, D., 475

W

Wachtel, P.L., 571
Waddell, T., 206
Wadden, T.A., 401, 402
Wade, N., 103
Wagner, R.K., 124, 360, 577
Walk, R.D., 115
Walker, L.E.A., 415
Wallace, A.R., 97
Walsh, M.R., 23
Walter, A.A., 295
Wan, C.K., 504
Wapner, G.B., 66
Ward, W.S., 198
Washburn, M.F., 17
Watkins, C.E., Jr., 369, 458, 463
Watkins, M.J., 297, 301
Watson, J., 98
Watson, J.B., 11–12, 15, 16, 20, 21, 29, 208, 209, 252, 253, 254, 418, 443–444
Watters, E., 381

Weaver, T.L., 566
Webb, W., 213
Weber, E.H., 158–159
Weber, R., 637
Wechsler, D., 365, 369–370
Weekes, J.R., 236
Wegner, D.M., 62
Weidner, G., 41
Weikart, D.P., 384
Weinberg, R.A., 380, 384, 385
Weiner, B., 246, 269
Weiner, K., 561
Weinrich, J.D., 491
Weisinger, H., 413
Weisz, J.R., 570
Welch, K.M.A., 543
Welles, O., 272
Wells, G.L., 296
Wentzel, K.R., 267
Werner, C.M., 652
Wertheimer, M., 13, 16, 172
West, S.G., 644
Westerman, M.A., 122
Wetzel, C.G., 652
Wetzler, S.E., 308
Wheeler, M.A., 315
Whisman, M.A., 621
Whitaker, M., 339
White, J.L., 218, 583
White, W.C., 589
Whitehead, W.E., 519
Whitman, W., 71n, 407
Whorf, B., 354
Widiger, T.A., 442, 582, 583, 584
Wiens, A.N., 607
Wiesel, T., 160
Wilcox, V.L., 529
Wilder, D.A., 639
Williams, J., 470, 471
Williams, L., 456, 586, 588
Williams, R., 352
Williams, W.M., 331, 363
Williamson, D.A., 588
Williamson, G.M., 529
Willis, S.L., 385
Willoughby, T., 4, 310
Wills, T.A., 223
Wilson, B., 272, 273
Wilson, D.B., 621
Wilson, D.W., 667
Wilson, G.T., 613, 627

Wilson, R.S., 380
Wing, R.R., 401
Wink, P., 145
Winkleby, M., 542
Winne, P.H., 335
Winner, E., 376
Winson, J., 212
Wissow, L.S., 123
Wittrock, D.A., 199, 542
Wolfe, W.B., 437
Woll, S.B., 484, 485
Woloshyn, V.E., 4, 297
Wolpe, J., 254, 536, 604, 605, 621
Wolraich, M.L., 226
Wood, J.M., 216
Wood, L., 414
Woodward, J., 565
Woody, E.Z., 236
Woolf, V., 569
Worchel, S., 669
Worth, L.T., 640
Wozniak, R.H., 290
Wren, C.S., 225
Wright, E., 382
Wu, C., 636
Wulfert, E., 504
Wundt, W., 10, 15, 16, 305

Y

Yoder, J.D., 41
Yogi, M.M., 232, 233
Young, S., 87, 88
Young, T., 168, 170, 219
Youngblade, L.M., 118

Z

Zagorski, M.G., 230
Zahn-Waxler, C., 583
Zajonc, R.B., 422, 638, 660
Zane, N., 623
Zeichner, A., 522
Zigler, E., 124, 138, 381, 384
Zimbardo, P.G., 424, 659
Zimmerman, R.R., 119–120
Zinbarg, R.E., 560
Ziv, T.A., 541
el-Zoghbi, M., 659
Zuckerman, M., 405, 443
Zuger, A., 86, 506
Zuwerink, J.R., 643

A

AA. *See* Alcoholics Anonymous (AA)
Abnormal behavior. *See* Psychological disorders
Abnormalities. *See also* Developmental psychology
  developmental, 108
  genetic and chromosomal, 112
A–B problem, 636
Absolute threshold, 157
Abstinence syndrome, 221
Abstraction, 358
Abuse. *See* Child abuse
Academic ability, creativity and, 331–332
Academic achievement, culture, ethnicity, and, 274–276
Acceptance stage, dying and, 151
Accessibility, 636
Accidents, to brain, 57
Accommodation, 125
Acculturation, 106
  machismo/marianismo and, 472
  psychotherapy and, 623
  and self-esteem, 456
Acetylcholine (ACh), 73–74, 75
  Alzheimer's disease and, 314
  memory and, 314
  neurotransmitters and, 73–74, 75
ACh. *See* Acetylcholine (ACh)
Achievement
  academic, 274–276
  intelligence and, 49
  motivation and, 409–413
Acoustic code, 285
  nonsense syllables and, 304
Acquired drives, 394
Acquisition trials, 250
Acrophobia, 560
ACTH. *See* Adrenocorticotrophic hormone (ACTH)
Action potential, 72
Activating effects, of sex hormones, 491
Activation, of reticular activating system (RAS), 215
Activation-synthesis model, 214–215
Activity, sensory stimulation and, 404–406
Activity theory, of aging, 149
Actor-observer effect, 647
Acupuncture, 156, 198–199
Acute stress disorder, 562
Adaptation, 97
  dark, 165
  light, 165–166
  negative, 161
  sensory, 160–161

Addiction, 221n. *See also* Dependence
Additive color mixtures, 168
Adenine, 98
ADH. *See* Antidiuretic hormone (ADH)
Adipose tissue, 401
Adolescence, 117, 136–137. *See also* Substance abuse
  alcohol use during, 223
  eating disorders and, 586–589
  physical development in, 137–138
  social and personality development in, 138–139
Adoptee studies, 102
  anxiety disorders and, 563
  intelligence and, 380–381, 384–385
Adoption, alcohol-related problems and, 221–222
Adrenal cortex, 90, 96
Adrenal glands, 92, 96
Adrenaline, 90, 92
  memory and, 314
  self-efficacy expectations and, 523, 605
  sexual orientation and, 492
Adrenal medulla, 90, 96
Adrenocorticotrophic hormone (ACTH), 92, 96
Adult development, 140–151
  in late adulthood, 145–151
  in middle adulthood, 141–145
  in young adulthood, 140–141
Advertising, 637–640
Aerobic exercise, 536
Afferent neurons, 71
Affiliation motivation, 411
African Americans. *See also* Ebonics
  health of, 540–541
  intelligence and, 387
  intelligence testing and, 371–372, 381
  as psychologists, 17–18, 352
  psychotherapy and, 622
  in sexual behavior study, 45
  sexual orientation and, 489, 490
  Simpson verdict and, 339
  stereotype vulnerability of, 381–382
  suicide and, 574, 575
Afterimages, 168
Age. *See also* Adolescence; Adult development; Aging; Children; Late adulthood
  isolation of older women, 146
  poverty among older women, 146
  smoking and, 229
  suicide and, 574

Age-30 transition, 140–141
Age regression, 236
Aggression, 15. *See also* Obedience; Sexual coercion
  biological perspective on, 413–414
  cognitive perspective on, 414–415
  gender and, 40, 477, 480
  learning perspectives on, 415
  motivation and, 411–415
  psychodynamic perspective on, 414
  sociocultural perspective on, 415
Aggressive behavior, media violence and, 272–274
Aging. *See also* Age; Late adulthood
  Alzheimer's disease and, 74
  death, dying, and, 150–151
  gender and, 146
  intelligence and, 385
  psychosocial views of, 147–149
  successful, 149–150
  theories of, 147
Agoraphobia, 560
Agreeableness, 441
"Aha" experience. *See* Insight
A.I. *See* Artificial intelligence
AIDS (acquired immune deficiency syndrome), 501, 502, 504–505
  ethnicity and, 540–541
  health psychology and, 546
  hotline for, 507
Air pollution, 668
Alarm reaction, 528, 529–531, 532
Alcohol and alcoholism, 220, 222
  A–B problem and, 636
  cancer and, 548
  effects of, 54–56, 223
  ethics in research about, 59–60, 61
  ethnicity and, 222–223
  gender and, 222–223
  population studied for, 41
  reasons for drinking, 224
  treatment of, 223–225
Alcoholics Anonymous (AA), 223–224
Algorithms, 325
All-or-none principle, 73
Alpha waves, 211. *See also* Biofeedback training (BFT)
Altered states of consciousness, 210
  drugs and, 219–222
Altruism, 665–666
Alzheimer's disease, 74
  acetylcholine and, 314
  nicotine and, 230

Amacrine cells, 163
Ambiguous, 183
American Association of Sex Educators, Counselors and Therapists, 501
American Association on Mental Retardation, 373
American Polygraph Association, 417
American Psychiatric Association
  DSM of, 557, 559
  sexual orientation and, 624
American Psychological Association, 10
  ethics code of, 61
  music, spatial task performance, and, 382
American Sign Language (ASL), 96, 190, 191–193, 342n
Amnesia
  anterograde, 309
  dissociative, 308
  infantile, 308–309
  posthypnotic, 236
  retrograde, 309–312
Amniocentesis, 112
Amniotic sac, 111
Amphetamines, 74, 226
Amplitude, 186
Amygdala, 80–81
Anaerobic exercise, 536
Anal-expulsive traits, 435
Anal fixations, 435
Analgesic drugs, 197
Analogies, 326
Analogous colors, 168–169
Anal-retentive traits, 435
Anal stage, 434
Analytical psychology, 436
Anatomy of an Illness (Cousins), 525
Anchoring and adjustment heuristic, 337
  Simpson trial verdict and, 339
Androgens, 110, 492
Androgyny, 469
Anger, 416. *See also* Rage
Anger stage, dying and, 150
Animals
  behaviorism and, 11
  behavior of, 3
  brain and, 80
  classical conditioning with dogs, 270
  communication by, 97, 341, 342
  ethics in research with, 61
  Gestalt psychology and, 14
  hormones in, 18
  insight experiments and, 328–329
  latent learning, cognitive maps, and, 270–271

observing behavior of, 47, 48
Pavlov's research with, 12, 244–246, 251, 270
reinforcement experiments and, 12–13
Skinner's research with, 255–256, 257–258
in Thorndike's law of effect research, 255
Animism, 127, 128
Anorexia nervosa, 542, 585–589
ANS. *See* Autonomic nervous system (ANS)
Anterograde amnesia, 309
Antianxiety drugs, 627
Antibodies, 533
Antidepressants, 626–627
Antidiuretic hormone (ADH), 91
Antigens, 533
Antipsychotic drugs, 625–626
Antisocial personality disorder, 583
Anxiety, systematic desensitization and, 605
Anxiety disorders, 560–563, 590
APA. *See* American Psychological Association
Apes. *See also* Chimpanzees; Gorillas; Monkeys
communication by, 341
Aphasia, 86
Apnea, 218–219
Appearance. *See* Physical appearance
Applied research, 5
Appraisal of worker performance, 413
Approach-approach conflict, 519, 520
Approach-avoidance conflict, 519, 520
Aptitude, 458
Aptitude tests, 46, 47
Archetypes, 436
Arguments
assumptions in, 25
errors in, 29
Aromas, 668. *See also* Smell
Arousal
emotions, lie detection, and, 416–417
lowering, 535
media violence and, 273
sexual, 498
Artificial intelligence, 366
Artificialism, 127, 128
Asch study, 656–657
Asian Americans
alcohol use and, 223
IQ testing and, 372–373
as psychologists, 17
psychotherapy and, 622–623
in sexual behavior study, 45
sexual orientation and, 489–490

ASL. *See* American Sign Language (ASL)
Assertive behavior, depression and, 573
Assertiveness training, 609, 610
Assimilation, 225
Association
conditioning through, 244–245
for memory improvement, 310–311
Association areas, 85
Astrology, 63
Asylums, 597–598
Atkinson-Shiffrin model, of memory, 287
Attachment, 116, 117–120
day care and, 123
Attachment-in-the-making phase, 118
Attention, selective, 132
Attention-deficit/hyperactivity disorder, 226
Attitude-discrepant behavior, 407–408
Attitudes, 635–644, 645
A–B problem and, 636
cognitive appraisal and, 637
defined, 636
origins of, 637
persuasion and, 637–641
prejudice and, 641–644, 645
Attraction, 482–492
love and, 486–488
Attribution, 646
dispositional and situational, 647
Attributional styles, 570–571
Attribution process, 646
factors contributing to, 649–650
Attribution theory, 646–650
actor-observer effect and, 647
fundamental attribution error and, 647
international conflict resolution and, 650–651
self-serving bias and, 649
Audience, persuasion and, 640
Auditory nerve, 188. *See also* Hearing
Authoritarian parents, 120, 121
Authoritative parents, 120, 121, 122
Authority. *See also* Obedience
obedience studies (Milgram) and, 34–37, 653–655
perception of legitimate, 654
Autokinetic effect, 176
Automaticity, 132
Autonomic nervous system (ANS), 82–83
Autonomy stage, 116–117
Availability heuristic, 337
Simpson trial verdict and, 339
Average, defined, A1
Aversive conditioning, 607

Avoidance, 612
staring and, 652, 653
Avoidance-avoidance conflict, 519, 520
Avoidance learning, 267
Avoidant personality disorder, 583
Awareness, direct inner, 209
Axon, 69–70
AZT, 507

B
Babbling, 344–345, 347, 348–349
Babinski reflex, 113
Backward conditioning, 248
Bacterial vaginosis, 502
Barbiturates, 226
Bargaining stage, dying and, 151
Barnum effect, 62
Basilar membrane, 188
Bassa language, linguistic-relativity hypothesis and, 354
BEAM. *See* Brain electrical activity mapping (BEAM)
Beauty, attraction and, 482–483
Bedlam, origins of term, 597, 598
Bed-wetting, 219
bell-and-pad treatment for, 253
Behavior. *See also* Animals; Learning; Social behavior
aggressive, 272–274
aging and, 147
animal, 3
attitude-discrepant, 407–408
biology and, 68–69
of chimpanzees, 47, 48
contemporary view of, 18–23
controlling, 4
Darwin and, 11
discriminatory, 642
gender-appropriate, 265
genetics and, 97
group, 659–666
health and, 510
human, 2–3
learning and, 243
motives and, 393
operant, 256
psychology as study of, 12
psychotherapy and, 597
strategies aimed at, 612
Type A, 521, 522, 524, 526–527
Type B, 524
units of, 256
Behavioral dependence, 220–221
Behavioral factors, in health and illness, 539
Behavior genetics, 96, 97, 99
Behaviorism, 11–14, 16, 21, 443–444, 449
choice and, 20
learning and, 243, 443–444
Behavior modification. *See* Behavior therapy
CHD and, 544

Behavior of Organisms, The (Skinner), 256
Behavior-rating scales, 458
Behavior rehearsal, 609
Behavior therapy, 604–611, 612, 616
aversive conditioning and, 607
effectiveness of, 621
operant conditioning procedures and, 607–610
rational emotive, 615
self-control methods and, 611, 612
Beliefs, irrational, 521–522
Bell-and-pad treatment, for bed-wetting, 253
Bell Curve, The (Herrnstein and Murray), 378–379, 381, 384, 385
Bell-shaped (normal) curve, A9
Bennies (Benzedrine), 226
Benzodiazepines, 563, 625
BFT. *See* Biofeedback training (BFT)
Bias
in performance appraisal, 413
volunteer, 42
Bilingual education, 350
Bilingualism, 350–351. *See also* Ebonics
Bimodal distribution, A5
Binet-Simon scale, 367
Binocular cues, 180–181
Biofeedback, 199
Biofeedback training (BFT), 233–235, 265–266, 609–610
Biological clock, pregnancy and, 141
Biological dependence, 221
Biological psychologists, 68
Biological risk factors, for schizophrenia, 580–581
Biological theories, 18–19. *See also* Biological therapies; Biology
on aggression, 413–414
on anxiety disorders, 563
on depression, 571–574
on health and illness, 539
of substance abuse and dependence, 221–222
Biological therapies, 625–629
drug therapy, 625–627
effectiveness of, 628
electroconvulsive therapy, 627
for personality disorders, 442
psychosurgery, 628
Biological variables, 4
Biology. *See also* Brain; Developmental psychology; Endocrine system; Heredity
aging and, 147
alcoholism and, 223
behavior and, 68–69
gender-typing and, 478

of learning, 314
of memory, 312–315
Biopsychology, sexual orientation and, 491
Bipolar cells, 163, 164
Bipolar disorder, 568–569
lithium and, 627
Birds, communication by, 342
Bisexuals, 488
BITCH (Black Intelligence Test of Cultural Homogeneity), 352
Black Dialect. *See* Ebonics
Black English. *See* Ebonics
Blinds, 53–54
Blind spots, 164
Blood pressure. *See* Hypertension
B lymphocytes, 505
Body language, 604, 650–653
touching and, 652
Body shape. *See also* Eating disorders
attractiveness and, 483–484
cancer and, 548
Bottom-up processing, 175
Boys. *See also* Gender; Males; Men
sexual development in, 137–138
Brain, 78–81. *See also* Central nervous system; Nervous system
amygdala and, 80–81
biological perspective and, 18
cerebellum and, 78
cerebral cortex and, 83–89
cerebrum and, 81
drug therapy and, 626
gender-typing and, 478, 481
hindbrain, 78
hypothalamus and, 80
limbic system and, 80, 81
medulla and, 78
memory and, 312–315
parts of, 79
research methods and, 57–59
reticular activating system and, 78–79
sensitive periods and, 350
thalamus and, 80
Brain electrical activity mapping (BEAM), 19
Brainstorming, 333–334
Brain waves, 12
Brave New World (Huxley), 100
Breast cancer, 548–549
Brightness (value), 166
Brightness constancy, 183
Broca's aphasia, 86, 87
Buffers, obedience and, 655
Bulimia nervosa, 542, 589
Bystander effect, 664–666

C
CA. *See* Chronological age (CA)
Cancer, 544–549
Candidiasis, 502

Cannon-Bard theory of emotion, 421, 422, 424
Carcinogens, smoking and, 548
Careers
gender polarization and, 473
psychological tests for, 459–460
in psychology, 28
Case study, 43, 55
CASPER, 558
Catastrophize, 521
Catatonic schizophrenia, 579
Catch 30s, 141
Catharsis, 414, 600
Catholicism. *See also* Religion
and sexual behavior, 45
CAT scan, 58
Cause, and effect, 51
CD4 cells, 505
Cells, 163. *See also* Neurons
bipolar, 163
glial, 69
taste, 194
Centering, 128
Central nervous system, 77–81. *See also* Nervous system
brain, 78–81
spinal cord, 77–78
Cerebellum, 78
Cerebral cortex, 68, 81, 83–89
geography of, 83–85
handedness and, 87–88
hemispheres of, 86–87
language and, 86
split-brain experiments and, 88–89
thought and, 85
Cerebrum, 81
Chain breaking, 612
CHD. *See* Coronary heart disease (CHD)
Chemical substances. *See* Hormones; Neurotransmitters
Chemotherapy, 547–548
Chicago. *See* University of Chicago
Child abuse, 123–124
repression of memories and, 308
Child psychology, 10
Child rearing. *See* Parenting
Children. *See also* Developmental psychology
day care and, 122–123
Piagetian theory and, 19
Chimpanzees. *See also* Animals; Monkeys
communication by, 97
observing behavior of, 47, 48
research with, 14
Chinese Americans. *See* Asian Americans
Chlamydia, 502, 504
Choice, 20
Choleric, 440
Cholesterol. *See* Serum cholesterol

Chrionic villus sampling (CVS), 112
Chromosomes, 98–99, 110
abnormal development and, 112
sexual orientation and, 491
Chronological age (CA), 368
Chunks, 291–293
Cigarettes, 227–229
aversive conditioning and, 607
human diversity and smoking, 229
nicotine benefits and, 230
quitting smoking, 228
Circadian rhythm, 210–211
Circle of emotions, 418
Circular explanations
self-actualization and, 453
of trait theory, 443
City life, crowding and, 670
Clairvoyance, 201–202
Classical conditioning, 242, 244–254, 274
applications of, 252–254
contingency theory and, 269–270
defined, 246
discrimination and, 251–252
extinction and, 249–250
generalization and, 250–251
higher-order conditioning and, 252–254
Pavlov and, 244–246
spontaneous recovery and, 250
taste aversion and, 248–249
types of, 247–248
Classification, of psychological disorders, 557–559
Classroom
discipline in, 267
virtual, 268
Claustrophobia, 560
Clear-cut-attachment phase, 118
Client-centered therapy, 602–603
Cliff experiment, 115
Climacteric, 143
Clinical psychologists, 6
Clinical scales, 459
Clinic judgments, validity of, 620
Clitoris, 499
Cloning, 100–101
Closure, 172
Cocaine, 74, 226–227, 626
Cochlea, 188
Cochlear implants, 191
Cocktail party effect, 209
Codes, memory and, 285
Cognitive abilities, men and women compared, 475–476
Cognitive appraisal, 519, 637
Cognitive appraisal theory of emotions, 422–424
Cognitive behavioral therapy, 621
Cognitive development, 125–136
information-processing approaches to, 131–136
in late adulthood, 147

Cognitive-developmental theory, 19, 125–131
Cognitive-dissonance theory, 392, 407–408
Cognitive factors, in learning, 269–276
Cognitive maps, 270–271, 329
Cognitive theories, 19, 396–397, 398
on aggression, 414–415
on anxiety disorders, 562–563
contingency theory and, 269–270
defined, 18
on depression, 570–571
of emotion, 422–424
learning and, 243
motivation and, 396–397
Cognitive therapies, 613–615, 616
behavioral, 621
effectiveness of, 621
Cognitive triad, 614
Coke, 227
Collective unconscious, 436
Collectivism, vs. individualism, 455
College students
rape and, 494
sexual harassment and, 497
Color
hue and, 161
psychological dimensions of, 166–169
Color blindness, 171, 172
Color constancy, 182–183
Color discrimination, 113
Color vision, 166
theories of, 169–171
Color wheel, 166
Common fate, 174, 175
Commonsense theory of emotion, 421, 424
Communication. *See also* Language
by apes, 97, 341
global, 56
Community mental health movement, 598
Companionate love, 486
Competencies, 444, 445–446
Competing responses, 612
Complementary colors, 166, 167–168
Componential intelligence, 363, 364
Compulsion, 560, 561
Computerized axial tomography (CAT). *See* CAT scan
Computers
artificial intelligence and, 366
diagnosis by, 558
Computer science, information processing and, 19
Concept, 321
prototypes and, 321–322

Conclusions, critical thinking about, 25
Concordance rate, 563
Concrete-operational stage, 129
Conditional positive regard, 451
Conditioned reflexes, 244–246
Conditioned responses (CRs), 245
Conditioned stimulus (CS), 246
Conditioning. *See also* Classical conditioning; Operant conditioning
aversive, 607
Watson on, 209
Conditions of worth, 451–452
Conductive deafness, 191
Cones, 163, 164, 165
Confidential information, 60
Conflict, 519–520
parent-adolescent, 138–139
social, 644, 645
Conflict resolution. *See also* Attribution theory
with Gestalt therapy, 603–604
international, 650–651
Conformity, 656–659
Asch study of, 656–657
groupthink and, 662–663
among Muslim women, 658–659
Conscientiousness, 441
Conscious, 209, 431
Conscious experience, 453
Consciousness, 206
biofeedback and, 233–235
brain and, 57
defined, 208–210
depressants and, 222–226
drugs and, 219–222
hallucinogenics and, 230–233
hypnosis and, 235–237
meditation and, 233
memory and, 288
sleep, dreams, and, 210–219
stimulants and, 226–229
Consensus, 649
Conservation, 128, 130
Consistency, 649
Consumer psychologists, 8
Consummate love, 486, 488
Context, Gestalt and, 13–14
Context-dependent memory, 301–302
Contextual intelligence, 364
Contiguity, 270
Contingency theory, 269–270
Continuity, in vision, 174, 175
Continuity theory, of aging, 149
Continuous reinforcement, 262–263
Control groups, 53
Conventional level, 134
Convergence, 180, 181
Convergent thinking, 331
Conversion disorder, 567
Cooing, 344, 347
Cool colors, 167

Coping
for cancer patients, 549
with pain, 198–199
with stress, 534–537
Cornea, 162
Coronary heart disease (CHD), 543–544
Corpus callosum, 81
hemispheres and, 87
Correlation, 49–52, 55
Correlational evidence, 25, 518
Correlational method, 49–52
Correlational relationships, 51
Correlation coefficient, A9
Correlation coefficients, 49, 51
Cortex. *See also* Cerebral cortex memory and, 312
Corticosteroids, 92
Cortisol, sexual orientation and, 492
Counseling. *See also* specific therapies
students' reasons for seeking, 514
Counseling psychologists, 6
Counterconditioning, 254, 266, 605
Couple therapy, 618
Covert reinforcement, 612
Covert sensitization, 612
Creative self, 436
Creativity, 330–334
and academic ability, 331–332
brainstorming and, 333–334
factors affecting, 332–334
Crime victims, posttraumatic stress disorder among, 562
Critical period, 120
Critical thinking, 24–29
about pseudoscience, 62–63
in research, 38–39
about self-help books, 25–26
Cross-cultural perspectives. *See* Cultural bias; Culture; Ethnicity; Stereotypes
Crowding, 669–670
CRs. *See* Conditioned responses (CRs)
Crying, 344, 347
CS. *See* Conditioned stimulus (CS)
Cuento therapy, 623–624
Cults, 659–660
Cultural bias, in intelligence tests, 352, 377
Culture, 21. *See also* Gender roles
academic achievement and, 274–276
gender-schema theory and, 480–481
health and, 541
learning and, 240
menstruation and, 93
physical appearance and, 482–483
psychotherapy and, 622

Culture-Fair Intelligence Test (Cattell), 377, 378
Culture-free intelligence tests, 377–378
Cumulative recorder, 258
Curare, 73–74
Current cognitions, 613
Curve. *See* Normal curve
CVS. *See* Chrionic villus sampling (CVS)
Cyberbabes, 586–587
Cybersex, 196
Cycles
circadian rhythm and, 210–211
in problem solving, 323–324
Cytosine, 98

D

Daily hassles, 514
life changes, health problems, and, 515–518
Dani people, linguistic-relativity hypothesis and, 355
Dark adaptation, 165
Darwinian theory, 97, 99
Date rape. *See* Rape
Day care, 122–123
Deafness, 190–191
Death and dying, 150–151
Debriefing, 61
Decentration, 129
Deception, and ethics in research, 60–61
Decibels, 186, 667
ratings of familiar sounds, 187
Decision making
brain and, 85
framing effect and, 337–339
in groups, 661
heuristics in, 339–340
judgment and, 335–341
overconfidence and, 340
Deductive reasoning, 334
"Deep Blue," 366
Deep-sleep disorders, 219
Defense mechanism, 433
Deindividuation, 663–664
Delayed conditioning, 247
Delayed reinforcers, 259
Delirium tremens, 221
Delta waves, 212
Delusions, 578–579
Dendrites, 69, 73
Denial, 433
Denial stage, dying and, 150
Density, 669–670
personal space and, 670–671
Deoxyribonucleic acid. *See* DNA
Dependence
causal factors in, 221–222
on marijuana, 231
substance abuse and, 220–221
Dependent variables, 53
Depersonalization disorder, 565–566
Depolarization, 72

Depressants, 220, 222–226
Depression, 416, 568
alleviating, 572–573
assertive behavior and, 573
biological theories on, 571–574
bipolar disorder and, 568–569
cognitive theories on, 570–571
exercise and, 573
learning theories on, 570
major, 568
noradrenaline and, 571
psychodynamic theories on, 570
suicide and, 574–577
women and, 569–570
Depression stage, dying and, 151
Deprivation, of REM sleep, 213
Depth cues, 115
Depth perception, 177–181
binocular cues and, 180–181
monocular cues and, 177–180
shadowing and, 178–179
Descriptive statistics, A1–A7
frequency distribution and, A2–A4
measures of central tendency and, A4–A5
measures of variability and, A5–A7
Desensitization, 161, 604–605
systematic, 254
Despair, ego integrity vs., 147–149
Developmental psychologists, 7
Developmental psychology, 10
adolescence and, 117, 136–137
adult development and, 140–151
cognitive development and, 125–136
controversies in, 108–109
goals of, 108
moral development and, 133–136
physical development and, 113–116
prenatal development and, 109–113
social development and, 116–124
Deviation IQ, 370
Dexies, 226
Diabetes, 91
Diagnosis, by computer, 558
Diagnostic and Statistical Manual (DSM), 557. *See also* DSM-IV
Dialogue, 603
Dichromats, 171
Diet, cancer and, 548
Dieting. *See also* Eating disorders metabolism and, 401
Difference threshold, 158–159
Diffusion of responsibility, 661
Dimensions, perception of, 178–179
Direct inner awareness, 209

Discipline. *See also* Child abuse; Parenting
in classroom, 267
Discrimination, 251–252, 641
Discrimination training, 251
Discriminative stimuli, 262
Disease. *See also* Cancer; Health
aging and, 146
Disengagement theory, of aging, 149
Disgust, 416
Disinhibition, media violence and, 273
Disorganized schizophrenia, 579
Displaced, 435
Displacement, 342, 433
in memory theory, 292, 293, 294
Dispositional attributions, 647
Dissimilarity, 643–644, 645
Dissociation, hypnosis and, 237
Dissociation theory, 236
Dissociative amnesia, 308, 564
Dissociative disorders, 564–566, 590
Dissociative fugue, 564
Dissociative identity disorder, 554, 555, 564
Dissonant tones, 186
Distancing, of adolescents, 138
Distinctiveness, 649
Distress, irrational beliefs and, 521–522
Divergent thinking, 331
Diversity, 22. *See also* Culture; Ethnicity
ethnic groups in research and, 41
of psychologists, 17–18
psychotherapy and, 621–625
samples and populations representing, 39–42
women in research and, 41
Divided-brain experiment. *See* Split-brain experiments
Dizygotic (DZ) twins, 100, 380
DNA, 98
genetic screening and, 102–103
Dogs. *See also* Animals
classical conditioning with, 270
Pavlovian research with, 12, 244–246, 251
Dopamine, 74, 75, 626
Dopamine theory, of schizophrenia, 581–582
Double-blind studies, 54
Double helix, 98
Down syndrome, 98, 112, 374
Draw-A-Person test (Goodenough), 377
Dream analysis, 601
Dreams, 15, 213–216
consciousness and, 210–219
Levinson's concept of, 140
nightmares and, 215–216
in psychodynamic theory, 604

REM sleep and, 213–214
sleep and, 213–216
symbols in psychodynamic theory, 215
theories of content of, 214–215
unconscious and, 214
Drinking. *See* Alcohol and alcoholism
Drive for superiority, 436
Drive-reduction theory, 256, 394–395
Drives, 393, 394–395
hunger and, 399–403
primary, 398
Drugs. *See also* Alcohol and alcoholism; Drug therapy
altering consciousness through, 219–222
for anxiety disorders, 563
depressants and, 222–226
hallucinogenics and, 230–233
HIV and use of, 505
for personality disorders, 442
psychoactive, 219, 231, 232
stimulants and, 226–229
studies of, 54
Drug therapy
antianxiety drugs, 625
antidepressants, 626–627
antipsychotic drugs, 625–626
lithium, 627
DSM. *See Diagnostic and Statistical Manual* (DSM); DSM-IV
DSM-IV, 557
multiaxial classification system of, 559
Duncker candle problem, 330
Dying. *See* Death and dying
DZ twins. *See* Dizygotic (DZ) twins

E

Ear, 187–188, 189. *See also* Hearing
vestibular sense and, 200
Eardrum, 188
Early childhood stage, 117
Eating disorders, 542, 585–590
gender and, 588–589
theoretical views of, 589–590
types of, 585–589
Ebbinghaus' curve of forgetting, 306
Ebonics, 352–353
Echoic memory, 290
ECT. *See* Electroconvulsive therapy (ECT)
Education
bilingual, 350
gender polarization and, 472–473
IQ and, 378, 379, 384
objective of, 27
smoking and, 229
young adulthood and, 140
Educational psychologists, 7

EEG. *See* Electroencephalograph (EEG)
Effect, cause and, 51
Efferent neurons, 71
Effort justification, 407–408
Ego, 432–433, 438
Ego analyst, 602
Egocentrism, 127, 128
Ego identity, 140, 437
role diffusion and, 138–139
Ego integrity, vs. despair, 147–149
Egyptians, ancient, brain and, 57
Eidetic imagery, 289–290
Ejaculation, 499
premature, 500
Elaboration likelihood model, 637–638
Elaborative rehearsal, 298
Elderly. *See* Age; Aging
Electra complex, 435, 438, 478–479
Electrical stimulation of the brain (ESB), 57
Electrochemical impulses, 71–73
Electroconvulsive therapy (ECT), 627
Electroencephalograph (EEG), 58, 211, 610
Electromagnetic spectrum, 162
Electromyograph (EMG), 234
Elements of Psychophysics (Fechner), 10
Embarrassment, 416
Embryo, 109, 111–112. *See also* Cloning
Embryonic stage, 110
EMG. *See* Electromyograph (EMG)
Emotion, 416, 444. *See also* Motivation
ANS and, 83
arousal, lie detection, and, 416–417
Cannon-Bard theory of, 421, 422, 424
cognitive appraisal theory of, 422–424
commonsense theory of, 421, 424
expression of, 419
feeling and, 420–421
immune system and, 525
James-Lange theory of, 421–422, 424
number and source of, 418–419
Plutchik's theory of, 418
Schachter-Singer study of, 422–424
theories of, 420–424
Emotional intelligence theory, 364–365
Empathic understanding, 603
Empirical scales, 459
Empirical science, 34, 63. *See also* Research

Employment, for psychologists, 28
Empty love, 486
Empty-nest syndrome, 144–145
Encoding, 285, 291
levels-of-processing model and, 302–304
social-cognitive theory and, 446–447
strategies for, 446–447
Encounter groups, 617–618
Endocrine system, 68–69, 89–95
adrenal glands and, 92, 96
defined, 90
hypothalamus and, 90, 96
menstruation and, 93–95, 96
pancreas and, 91–92, 96
pituitary gland and, 90–91, 96
stress and, 531
testes, ovaries, and, 92–93, 96
thyroid gland and, 92, 96
Endometriosis, 94
Endomorphins, 75
Endorphins, acupuncture and, 199–200
English language, linguistic-relativity hypothesis and, 354
Engram, memory and, 312
Environment. *See also* Environmental psychology; Nature
adult intellectual functioning and, 385
aging and, 147
health, illness, and, 539
intelligence and, 379, 381–385
language development and, 348
Environmental psychologists, 7
Environmental psychology, 666–671
aromas, air pollution, and, 668
crowds and, 669–670
noise and, 667
personal space and, 670–671
temperature and, 667–668
Epilepsy, 88
Epinephrine. *See* Adrenaline
Episodic memory, 283
Erikson's psychosocial development stages, 116–117
Erogenous zone, 434
Eros, 434
ESB. *See* Electrical stimulation of the brain (ESB)
ESP. *See* Extrasensory perception (ESP)
Esteem needs, 396
Estrogen, 93
Ethical Principles of Psychologists and Code of Conduct (APA), 61
Ethics
in animal research, 61
obedience studies and, 34–37
in psychological research and practice, 59–61
Ethics review committees, 60

Ethnicity, 21, 22. *See also* Race
  academic achievement and, 276
  alcoholism and, 222–223
  health and, 540–541
  intelligence and, 371–373, 387
  life expectancy and, 146–147
  of psychologists, 17
  psychotherapy and, 621–624
  and research populations, 41
  in research samples, 42
  in sexual behavior study, 45
  sexual orientation and, 489–491
  smoking and, 229
  suicide rates by, 574, 575
Eustress, 513
Evaluation, social, 333
Evaluation apprehension, 660–661
Evidence, critical thinking about, 25
Evolution theory, 11
  Darwin and, 97, 99
Excitation of neurons, 73
Excitement phase, of sexual response cycle, 499
Exemplars, 321–322
Exercise, 536–537
  cancer and, 548
  depression and, 573
  pregnancy and, 110
  weight control and, 402
Exhaustion stage, 532
Existentialism, 20, 449
Expectancies, 444, 447–448
  scale of, 446–447
Experience, 20
  adult intellectual functioning and, 385
  openness to, 441
Experiential intelligence, 363–364
Experiment(s), 3, 52, 55
  in psychotherapy, 619–620
Experimental groups, 53
Experimental method, 52–56
Experimental psychologists, 7–8
Expertise, and problem solving, 326–327
Exploration, manipulation and, 406–407
Extinction, 605
  in classical conditioning, 249
  in operant conditioning, 260
Extinction curve, 249
Extinction trials, 250
Extrasensory perception (ESP), 201–203
Extraversion, 441
Eye, 162–166. *See also* Vision
  blind spots in, 164
  parts of, 163
  saccadic movements of, 288
Eyewitness testimony, long-term memory and, 296
Eysenck's personality dimensions, 440, 441

F
Facial expressions
  emotion and, 419
  facial-feedback hypothesis, 420
Factor analysis, 361
Factor theories of intelligence, 361–362
Family, academic achievement and, 275–276
Family therapy, 618
Fantasy, achievement motivation and, 409–410
FAP. *See* Fixed-action pattern (FAP)
Farsighted, 182
Fat cells, obesity and, 401
Fathers, older, 141
Fatuous love, 486
Fear, 416
  anxiety disorders and, 563
  conditioning for overcoming, 266
Fear appeal, 638–639
Fear-reduction methods, in behavior modification, 604–607
Feature detectors, 160
Feedback, 609
  facial, 420
Feeling-of-knowing experience, 301
Feelings, 20. *See also* Emotion
  emotion and, 420–421
  psychotherapy and, 597
Females. *See also* Gender; Girls; Women
  gender stereotypes of, 470
  individuality vs. relatedness and, 439
Female sexual arousal disorder, 500
Feminine behavior. *See* Gender roles; Gender-typing
Feminist psychotherapy, 624
Festinger's theory of motivation, 397
Fetal stage, 112–113
Fetus, 109
Fight-or-flight reaction, 528
Figure-ground perception, 13–14, 172
File-drawer problem, 202
First impressions, 645–646, 648
First-shift rule, 661
Fissures, 81
Five-factor model, 441–443
Fixation, 434
  anal, 435
  pregenital, 435
Fixation time, 114–115
Fixed-action pattern (FAP), 120, 394
Fixed-interval scallop, 263
Fixed-interval schedule, 263
Fixed-ratio schedule, 264
Flashbacks, 232–233
Flashbulb memories, 298–299

Flexibility, creativity and, 332
Flooding, 254, 266
Fluency, creativity and, 332
Food. *See* Hunger; Weight control
Food and Drug Administration, 54
Foot-in-the-door technique, 640–641
  obedience and, 654–655
Forced-choice format tests, 458
Forebrain, 78, 80
Forensic psychologists, 8
Forgetting, 304–312. *See also* Amnesia; Memory
  Ebbinghaus' curve of, 306
  infantile amnesia and, 308–309
  interference theory and, 307–308
  measuring, 305–307
  repression and, 308
Formal-operational stage, 130
Fovea, 165
Frames of reference, 451, 603
Framing effect, 337–339
  Simpson trial verdict and, 339
Fraternal twins. *See* Dizygotic (DZ) twins
Free association, 600–601
Frequency theory, 190
Freudian psychology. *See* Freud's theory of psychosexual development; Psychoanalysis
Freud's theory of psychosexual development, 431–435
Frontal lobe, 83, 84
Frustration and Aggression (Dollard and others), 252
Functional analysis, 610
Functional fixedness, 330
Functionalism, 10–11, 16
Functional (fast) MRI, 59
Fundamental attribution error, 647

G
GABA. *See* Gamma-aminobutyric acid (GABA)
Gamma-aminobutyric acid (GABA), 563
Ganglion cells, 163, 164
Gardner's theory of multiple intelligences, 362–363
GAS. *See* General adaptation syndrome (GAS)
Gate theory, 197–198, 199
Gauche, handedness and, 87–88
Gay males, 488, 624. *See also* Homosexuals; Sexual orientation
Gazing, 653
Gender, 21, 22–23, 466. *See also* Attraction; Gender-typing; Sex organs; Sexual coercion; Sexuality
  aggression and, 40
  aging and, 146
  alcoholism and, 222–223
  altrusim and, 666

cognitive abilities and, 475–476
  eating disorders and, 588–589
  of fetus, 112
  health and, 541–542
  moral development and, 135–136
  psychological differences in, 474–477
  sexual orientation and, 488–489
  smoking and, 229
  social behavior and, 476–477
  suicide rates by, 574
  young adulthood differences by, 140
Gender-appropriate behavior, 265
Gender identity, 478
Gender polarization, 469–474
  costs of, 472–474
Gender roles, 469. *See also* Gender-typing
  stereotypes of, 470
Gender schema, 397
Gender-schema theory, 480–481
Gender-typing, 478–482. *See also* Gender; Gender roles; Sexual orientation
  biological influences on, 478
  psychological influences on, 478–482
General adaptation syndrome (GAS), 528, 529–532
Generalization, 250–251
Generalized anxiety disorder, 560, 561
Generalizing, 39
Generativity vs. stagnation, 141–142
Genes, 18–19, 98–99
  abnormal development and, 112
  handedness and, 88
Genetic code, 98
  memory and, 314
Genetics, 96, 97. *See also* Heredity
  cloning and, 100–101
  intelligence and, 379–381
  and personality disorders, 584
  schizophrenia and, 581
Genetic screening, 102–103
Genie studies, 44
Genital herpes, 503, 504
Genital stage, 435
Genital warts, 503, 504
Genius, Terman studies of, 375–376
Genome, 102
  Human Genome Project and, 102–103
Genuineness, 603
German language, 343
Germany, Milgram studies and atrocities in, 48
Germinal stage, 110

Gestalt psychology, 13–14, 16
  perceptual organization and, 172–175
  therapy and, 603–604
g factor, 361
Giftedness, 375–376
Girls. See also Females; Gender; Women
  sexual development in, 137
Glands
  ducts and, 90
  endocrine system and, 89–95
Glial cells, 69
Global research, 56
Goals, realistic, 452
Gonorrhea, 503
Gorillas. See also Animals
  communication by, 97
Graduate Record Exams, creativity and, 331
Grammar, 343
Grammar school stage, 117
"Grandma's method," 612
Grasp (palmar) reflex, 113
Gray matter, 78
Greeks
  brain and, 57
  hysteria and, 567
  philosophers, 9
Grief, 416
Group(s). See also Ethnicity
  control, 53
  experimental, 53
Group behavior, 659–666
  altruism, bystander effect, and, 664–666
  deindividuation and, 663–664
  group decision making and, 661
  groupthink and, 662–663
  mob behavior and, 663
  polarization effect, "risky shift," and, 661–662
  social facilitation and, 660–661
Group intelligence tests, 370–371
Group therapies, 615–618
  couple therapy and, 618
  encounter groups and, 617–618
  family therapy and, 618
Groupthink, 662–663
Growth. See Physical development
Growth hormone, 91
Growth hormone-releasing factor (hGRF), 90
Guanine, 98

H
Habits, 10–11
Habituation, media violence and, 273
Hallucinations, 578–579
  drugs and, 221
Hallucinogenics, 230–233
Halo effect, 413
Hammer of Witches, The (Innocent VIII), 555
Handedness, 87–88

Hanunoo language, linguistic-relativity hypothesis and, 354
Harassment. See Sexual harassment
Harris polls, 44
Hashish, 231
Headaches, 542–543
Head Start programs, 384
Health. See also Disease; Health psychology
  behavior patterns and, 510
  marijuana, 231
  nicotine and, 230
  obesity and, 400
  sociocultural factors in, 539–542
  stress and, 50
Health psychologists, 8, 546, 547–548
Health psychology. See also Health; Multifactorial approach; specific illnesses
  defined, 512–513
  multifactorial approach and, 538–549
  stress and, 513–538
  in 21st century, 546
Hearing, 115, 185–193, 201
  absolute threshold of, 158
  brain and, 83
  deafness and, 190–193
  ear and, 187–188, 189
  loudness and, 185, 186–187
  overtones, timbre, and, 187
  perception and, 189–190
  pitch and, 158, 185, 186
Heart attacks, and physical activity, 537
Heart disease. See Coronary heart disease (CHD)
Heaven's Gate group, 659–660
Height, attractiveness and, 483
Helper T cells, 505n
Hemispheres, 81, 86–89
  specialization of, 87
Hepatitis, 504
Heredity, 69, 96–103. See also Genetics
  handedness and, 88
  intelligence and, 379–381
  language development and, 348
  obesity and, 400–401
  physical traits and, 97
  in schizophrenia, 581
  sexual orientation and, 491
  of social behaviors, 97
  traits and, 440
Hering-Helmholtz illusion, 184
Heritability, of intelligence, 380
Heroin, 225
Herpes, genital, 503
Hertz (Hz), 186
Heterosexuals, 488
Heuristics, 325
  anchoring and adjustment, 337
  availability, 337

  in decision making, 339–340
  judgment, decision making, and, 336
  representativeness, 336
hGRF. See Growth hormone-releasing factor (hGRF)
Hierarchies, 321, 605
  of long-term memory, 299–301
Hierarchy of needs, of Maslow, 396, 398
Higher education, gender polarization and, 472–473
Higher-order conditioning, 252–254
Hindbrain, 78
Hippocampus, 74, 80
  amnesia and, 309
  memory and, 315
Hippocrates' personality types, 440, 441
Hispanic Americans
  acculturation, self-esteem, and, 456
  IQ testing and, 372
  machismo/marianismo and, 471–472
  as psychologists, 17
  psychotherapy and, 623
  in sexual behavior study, 45
  sexual orientation and, 489–490
Histogram, A3
History of psychology, 9–18
  ranking of figures in, 15
  schools of, 16
HIV (human immunodeficiency virus), 504–505, 507
Holland's types, 460–461
Holophrases, 345
Home, intelligence and, 382–383
Homeostasis, 395
Homosexuals, 488, 624
  ethnicity and, 489–491
  gay organizations and, 490
  Planet Out and, 490
Homunculus, 57
Hopi language, linguistic-relativity hypothesis and, 354
Horizontal cells, 163
Hormones, 18, 90
  endocrine system and, 89–95
  manopause and, 143, 144
  memory and, 314
  menopause and, 143
  PMS and, 95
  sex, 478
  sex differentiation and, 110
Horoscopes, 63
Hostility, 527
Hotline
  AIDS, 507
  suicide, 576
Hue, 161, 166
Human behavior. See Behavior
Human diversity. See Culture; Diversity

Human factors psychologists, 8
Human Genome Project, 102–103
Humanism, 20, 449
Humanistic-existential theories, 20
  evaluation of, 453
  Maslow and self-actualization, 451
  on personality development, 449–454, 457
  Rogers' self theory, 451–453
Humanistic-existential therapies, 602–604, 616
  client-centered therapy, 602–603
  gestalt therapy, 603–604
Humanistic theory, 395–396
Human research, ethics in, 59–61
Humor. See Sense of humor
Humors, Hippocrates on, 440
Hunger, 399–403
  obesity and, 400–401
  theories about, 4
  weight control and, 402–403
Hunter's notch, 191
Hydrocarbons, 229
Hyperglycemia, 91
Hypermnesia, 236
Hyperphagic, 399, 400
Hypertension, 543
Hyperthyroidism, 92
Hypnagogic state, 212
Hypnosis, 235–237
  pain and, 198–199
  theories of, 236–237
  trance state and, 210
Hypoactive sexual desire disorder, 500
Hypochondriasis, 567
Hypoglycemia, 92
Hypothalamus, 80, 90, 96
  hunger and, 399–400
Hypothesis, 37–38
Hypothyroidism, 92
Hysteria, 567

I
Iconic memory, 289
  and saccadic eye movements, 290
Id, 437, 438
Identical twins. See Monozygotic (MZ) twins
Identification, 434
  gender-typing and, 478, 480
Identity crisis, 437
Illness. See also Health; Mental health; Stress
  cancer and, 544–549
  multifactorial approach to, 538–539
Illusions
  of movement, 176
  visual, 183–184
Imagery, eidetic, 289–290
Immediate reinforcers, 259

Immune system
emotions and, 525
stress and, 532–538
Imprinting, 120
Impulses, 15
neural, 71–73
Incentives, 393
Incest taboo, 435, 468
Incubation, 329–330
Independence, in adolescence, 138
Independent variables, 52–53
Indiscriminate attachment, 118
Individualism, vs. collectivism, 455
Individuality, vs. relatedness, 438–439
Individual psychology, 436
Inductive reasoning, 334–335
Industrial psychologists, 8
Infantile amnesia, 308–309
Infants. *See also* Children; Developmental psychology
infancy stage and, 117
Infatuation, 486
Infer, A10
Inferential statistics, A9–A10
Inferiority complex, 436
Infertility, 504
Infinite creativity, 342
Inflammation, 533
Inflections, 343
Information, as biofeedback reinforcement, 265
Information processing, 19, 131, 644, 645. *See also* Memory
approaches of, 131–136
cognition and, 19
Information transfer, 56
Informed consent, 60
Inheritance. *See* Genetics; Heredity
Inhibition of neurons, 73
Initial-preattachment phase, 118
Inkblot test. *See* Rorschach tests
Inner ear, 188
Insanity, 554, 555
Insight, 14, 327–328, 613
Insomnia, 216–218
Instinct, 394, 397–398
attachment as, 120
Instinct theory, 394
Instrumental competence, 120–121
Insulin, 91
Intelligence, 360. *See also* Intelligence tests
abstraction and, 358
and achievement, 49
adoptee studies and, 380–381, 384–385
artificial, 366
determinants of, 378–387
deviation, 370
education and, 384
enhancing functioning, 386
environment and, 379, 381–385

environment and adult functioning, 385
ethnicity and, 387
extremes of, 373–376
factors in functioning of children and adults, 386
factor theories of, 361–362
Gardner's theory of multiple intelligences, 362–363
gender and, 475
genetic influences on, 379–381
giftedness and, 375–376
heredity and, 379–381
language and, 355
measurement of, 367–373
mental retardation and, 373–375
parenting styles and, 382–383
socioeconomic and ethnic differences in, 371–373
spatial reasoning and, 382–383
Sternberg's triarchic theory of, 363–364
theories of, 360–365
twin studies and, 380
variations in scores, 371
Intelligence quotient (IQ), 367–369. *See also* Intelligence
race and, 387
Intelligence tests, 46, 47. *See also* Intelligence; Intelligence quotient (IQ)
creativity and, 331–332
cultural biases of, 352
culture-free, 377–378
group tests, 370–371
individual, 367–370
Stanford-Binet, 367–369
traits measured by, 377–378
Wechsler and, 365, 369–370
Intensity, of color, 167
Interest inventories, 460
Interference, 307–308
proactive, 307–308
retroactive, 307
Intergroup contact, 642
Interneuron, 77
Interpersonal attraction. *See* Attraction
Interpersonal skills, emotional intelligence and, 365
Interposition, 178, 179
Interpretation, 601
Interviews, 44
Intimacy, 141
isolation and, 141
love and, 486–488
Intrapersonal skills, emotional intelligence and, 365
Introspection, 9
Introversion-extraversion, 440
Inuit peoples, linguistic-relativity hypothesis and, 354
Invariant sequence, of language development, 349

IQ. *See* Intelligence quotient (IQ)
Iris, 162
Irish Americans, alcohol use and, 222–223
Irrational beliefs and thoughts, 521–522
controlling, 534–535
pain and, 199
Isolation
intimacy and, 140
of older women, 146

J

James-Lange theory of emotion, 421–422, 424
Japanese Americans. *See also* Asian Americans
World War II detention of, 240
Jealousy, 416
Jewish Americans. *See also* Culture; Ethnicity; Stereotypes
alcohol use and, 223
jnd. *See* Just noticeable difference (jnd)
Jobs. *See* Employment
Job satisfaction, enhancing, 412–413
Job-strain model, 545
John Hopkins University, behaviorism at, 12
Joy, 416
Judgment, decision making and, 335–341
Just noticeable difference (jnd), 158–159

K

K complex, 212
Kinesthesis, 200, 201
Kinsey studies, 44
Kinship studies, 99–102
adoptee studies, 102
intelligence and, 379–380
twin studies, 99–101
Kohlberg's theory of moral development, 133–136

L

La belle indifférence, 567
Laboratory, 48
Laboratory observation, 48, 55
Laboratory science, psychology as, 10
LAD. *See* Language acquisition device (LAD)
Lang study. *See* Alcohol and alcoholism
Language, 341–344. *See also* Language development
basic concepts of, 342–344
cortex and, 86
linguistic-relativity hypothesis and, 354–355
morphology and, 342
phonology and, 342
psychotherapy and, 622

semantics and, 343–344
syntax and, 343
thought and, 320–321, 353–355
Language acquisition device (LAD), 349–350
Language development, 344–353
bilingualism and, 350–351
complex, 346–347
Ebonics and, 352–353
learning theories and, 348–349
milestones in, 347
nativist theory of, 349–350
syntax and, 345–346
theories of, 347–351
vocabulary and, 345
Late adulthood, 117, 145–151
ethnicity and, 146–147
gender and, 146
Latency stage, 435, 438
Latent content, 601
Latent learning, cognitive maps and, 270–271
Lateral hypothalamus, 399–400
Law of effect, 255
L-dopa, 74
Learned helplessness, 570
Learning, 240. *See also* Learning theories
behaviorism and, 12
biology of, 314
classical conditioning and, 242–243, 244–254, 274
cognitive factors in, 269–276
culture, ethnicity, and, 274–276
defined, 243
memory and, 280
operant conditioning and, 242–243, 254–269, 274
programmed, 269
punishment and, 35–36
rote, 292
social, 644, 645
Learning curve, 249
Learning disabilities, handedness and, 88
Learning theories, 21
on aggression, 415
on anxiety disorders, 562
behaviorism and, 443–444
on depression, 570
on dissociative disorders, 566
evaluation of, 448–449
language development and, 348–349
on personality development, 443–449, 457
on personality disorders, 584
on schizophrenia, 580
sexual orientation and, 491
social-cognitive theory and, 444–448
Left brain. *See* Hemispheres
Lens, 162
Lenses of Gender, The (Bem), 469

Lesbians, 488, 624. *See also* Homosexuals; Sexual orientation
Lesions, 58
Leukocytes, 532, 533
Levels-of-processing model, of memory, 302–304
Libido, 434, 437
Lice, pubic, 503
Lie detection, emotion and, 416–417
Life changes, 515–518
  positive vs. negative, 518
Life cycle. *See* Lifespan
Life expectancy, scale of, 148
Lifespan, 106, 140, 145. *See also* Developmental psychology
  ethnicity and, 146–147
  gender and, 146
Light, 161. *See also* Eye; Vision
  additive and subtractive color mixtures and, 168
Light adaptation, 165–166
Liking, 416, 486. *See also* Attraction; Love
Limbic system, 80, 81
  memory and, 315
Linguistic-relativity hypothesis, 354–355
Listening to Prozac (Kramer), 442
Literacy, emotional, 365
Lithium, 627
"Little Albert" experiment (Watson and Rayner), 209, 252
"Little Hans" study (Freud), 252
Lobes. *See also* Brain
  of brain, 83
Lobotomy. *See* Prefrontal lobotomy
Locus of control, 525–528
  scale of, 530
Long-term memory (LTM), 19, 287, 294–302
  accuracy of, 294–296
  context-dependent memory and, 301–302
  and eyewitness testimony, 296
  flashbulb memory and, 298
  hierarchical organizational structure of, 299–301
  tip-of-the-tongue phenomenon in, 301
  transferring information to short-term memory, 297–298
  volume of information stored in, 297
Loudness, 186–187
  perception of, 189–190
Love, 486–488
  romantic, 486, 488
  scale, 487
Love and belongingness needs, 396
Love triangle. *See* Triangular model of love
LSD, 231–232

LTM. *See* Long-term memory (LTM)
Lynching, mob behavior and, 663

M
MA. *See* Mental age (MA)
MacArthur Longitudinal Twin Study, 380
Machismo/marianismo, 471–472
Magnetic resonance imaging. *See* MRI
Maintenance method, 350
Maintenance rehearsal, 285, 297
Major depression, 568
Majority-wins scheme, 661
Major tranquilizers, 625–626
Maladaptive behavior, 11
Male erectile disorder, 500
Male menopause. *See* Manopause (male menopause)
Males. *See also* Boys; Gender; Men
  gender stereotypes of, 470
  individuality vs. relatedness and, 438–439
Malingering, 564
Manic-depressive disorder. *See* Bipolar disorder
Manic phase, 568
Manifest content, 601
Manipulation, exploration and, 406–407
Manopause (male menopause), 143–144
Mantras, 232, 233
MAO inhibitors. *See* Monoamine oxidase (MAO) inhibitors
Marianismo. *See* Machismo/marianismo
Marijuana, 230–231, 626
  benefits of, 230
  psychoactive effects of, 231
Marriage, adult intellectual functioning and, 385
Masculine behavior. *See* Gender roles; Gender-typing
Maslow's hierarchy of needs, 396, 398
Mastery, 142
Masturbation, 438, 468
Matching hypothesis, and attraction, 484, 485
Mate selection, gender and, 476–477
Maturation, 109
Maturational theorists, 109
Mean, A4–A5
Meaning, semantic memory and, 284
Means-end analysis, 325
Measurement. *See also* Tests and testing
  errors in, 44
  of intelligence, 367–373
  of personality, 458–463
Median, A4–A5

Mediation, for memory improvement, 310
Media violence, observational learning and, 272–274, 275
Meditation, 232, 233
Medulla, 78
Memories of Childhood #2 (Mesa-Bains), 280
Memory, 280. *See also* Alzheimer's disease; Amnesia; Forgetting
  acetylcholine (ACh) and, 314
  biology of, 312–315
  brain and, 85
  defined, 286
  echoic, 290
  eidetic imagery and, 289–290
  encoding and, 284
  episodic, 283
  forgetting and, 304–312
  iconic, 289, 290
  improving, 310–311
  information processing and, 19
  levels-of-processing model of, 302–304
  long-term, 294–302
  metamemory and, 132–133
  procedural, 284
  processes of, 284–286
  as reconstructive, 295
  retrieval in, 286
  semantic, 284
  sensory, 288–290
  short-term, 290–294
  stages of, 286–302, 303
  state-dependent, 302
  storage in, 285
Memory trace, 288
Men. *See also* Attraction; Boys; Gender; Males; Sexual coercion
  aging and, 146
  cognitive abilities of, 475–476
  machismo and, 471–472
  moral development in, 135–136
  social behavior of, 476–477
  young adulthood and, 140
Menarche, 137
Menopause, 143. *See also* Manopause (male menopause)
Menstruation, 137. *See also* Menopause
  menstrual cycle and, 93–94
  premenstrual syndrome (PMS) and, 94–95
Mental age (MA), 367, 368
Mental deterioration, in Alzheimer's disease, 74
Mental disorders. *See* Psychological disorders
Mental health, community movement in, 598
Mental hospitals, 598
Mental processes, controlling, 4

Mental retardation, 98, 373–375
  causes of, 374–375
  levels of, IQ, and adaptive behaviors of, 375
Mental sets, 327
  incubation and, 329–330
Mescaline, 232
Mesmerization. *See* Hypnosis
Message, persuasive, 638–639
Meta-analysis, 620–621
Metabolism, 92
  dieting and, 401
Metamemory, 132–133, 285
Metaqualone, 226
Methadone, 225
Method of constant stimuli, 157
Method of loci, 311
Method of savings, 306
Midbrain, 78–79
Middle adulthood, 117, 141–145
  new parents in, 141
Middle Ages, psychological disorders during, 555
Middle ear, 188
Middlescence, 142–143, 149
Midlife crisis, 142
Midlife transition, 142
Migraine headache, 542–543
Milgram studies, 480, 654–655. *See also* Obedience
  reasons for following orders in, 655
  at Yale University, 34–37
Military, conformity in, 656
Minnesota adoption studies, 384–385
Minnesota Multiphasic Personality Inventory (MMPI), 458–462
Minority groups. *See also* specific groups
  aging and, 146–147
  psychotherapy and, 621–625
  in research samples, 42
Minor tranquilizers, 625
MMPI. *See* Minnesota Multiphasic Personality Inventory (MMPI)
Mnemonic devices, for memory improvement, 284, 311
Mob behavior, 663
Mode, A5
Model, 261
Modeling, 266, 444–445, 606–607
Moniliasis, 502
Monkeys. *See also* Animals
  amygdala of, 80–81
  communication by, 97
  research with, 14, 61
Monoamine oxidase (MAO) inhibitors, 627
Monocular cues, 177–180
Monolingual children, bilingual children and, 350

Monozygotic (MZ) twins, 100, 379–380
Mood disorders, 568–577, 590
Moral development theory, 133–136
Morality. *See* Ethics
Moral judgment, of preoperational children, 129
Moral principle, 434
Moral traits. *See* Traits; Trait theories
Moro reflex, 113
Morphine, 225
Morphology, 342
Mothers, older, 141
Motion, illusions of, 176–177
Motion parallax, 181
Motivation, 393–394. *See also* Emotion
    achievement and, 409–411
    affiliation and, 411
    aggression and, 411–415
    cognitive theory and, 396–397
    drive-reduction theory and, 394–395
    emotion and, 390
    evaluation of theories of, 397–398
    fantasies and, 409–410
    humanistic theory and, 395–396
    hunger and, 399–403
    instinct theory and, 394
    sociocultural perspectives on, 397
    stimulus motives and, 404–407
    weight control and, 402
Motives, 393
    stimulus, 404–407
Motor cortex, 85
Motor development, 114
Movement, perception of, 175–176
MRI, 58–59
Müller-Lyer illusion, 184
Multifactorial approach, 538–549
    to cancer, 544–549
    to coronary heart disease, 543–544
    to headaches, 542–543
    human diversity and, 540–542
    to schizophrenia, 581
Multiple approach-avoidance conflict, 519, 520
Multiple intelligences theory, 362–363, 375
    music studies and, 382–383
Multiple personality disorder. *See* Dissociative identity disorder
Muscular dystrophy, 112
Music, intelligence and, 382–383
Muslim women, conformity among, 658–659
Mutism, 579
Myelin, 71
Myotonia, 499

N
Narcolepsy, 218
Narcotics. *See* Drugs
National AIDS Hotline, 507
National Health and Social Life Survey (NHSLS), 45, 46
National Institute of Mental Health, 626
National Institute on Alcohol Abuse and Alcoholism, 225
National Institute on Child Health and Human Development, day care and, 123
Native Americans, 318. *See also* Culture; Ethnicity
    alcohol use and, 222
    IQ testing and, 372
    as psychologists, 18
    psychotherapy and, 624
    in sexual behavior study, 45
    sexual orientation and, 489, 490–491
Nativist theory, of language development, 349–350
Naturalistic observation, 47, 48, 55
Natural science, psychology as, 11–12
Nature, nurture and, 99–102, 108–109
Nearsighted, 182
Necker cube, 174
Needs, 393
    humanistic theory and, 395–396
Negation, in Ebonics, 353
Negative correlation, 50
Negative instances, 322
Negative reinforcement, 259, 566n
    punishments and, 261
Neoanalysts, 20
Neodissociation, 236
Neonate, 113. *See also* Infants
Nervous system, 68, 76–83
    autonomic (ANS), 82–83
    central, 77–81
    peripheral, 77, 81–83
Neural impulse, 71–73
Neural level, memory and, 312–313
Neurons, 68, 69–76
    afferent and efferent, 71
    anatomy of, 70
    cells in eye as, 163
    makeup of, 69–71
    myelin and, 71
    neurotransmitters and, 69, 73–76
    synapse and, 73
Neuroses. *See* Psychological disorders
Neuroticism, 440, 441, 571
Neurotransmitters, 69, 70, 73, 626
    acetylcholine (ACh), 73–74, 75
    anxiety disorders and, 563
    dopamine, 74, 75

endorphins, 75
    memory and, 314
    noradrenaline, 74
    serotonin, 75
NHSLS. *See* National Health and Social Life Survey (NHSLS)
Nicotine, 227–229
    benefits of, 230
Nicotinic cholinergic receptors, 230
Nightmares, 215–216
Noise
    environmental psychology and, 667
    hearing and, 187
    signal-detection theory and, 187
Nonconscious processes, 210
Nongonococcal urethritis (NGU), 502
Non-rapid-eye-movement (NREM) sleep, 211–212
    dreams and, 214
Nonsense syllables. *See also* Forgetting
    memory and, 304
Nonspecific factors, 620
Noradrenaline, 74, 75, 92, 563
    depression and, 571
    neurotransmitters and, 74
Norepinephrine. *See* Noradrenaline
Normal curve, A7–A8, A9
Norms, social, 656
NREM sleep. *See* Non-rapid-eye-movement (NREM) sleep
Nurture, nature and, 99–102, 108–109
Nutrition, PMS and, 94–95

O
Obedience. *See also* Conformity
    to authority, 653–655
    ethical issues in studying, 60–61
    gender and, 480
    Milgram studies and, 34–37, 40, 48, 52, 654–655
Obesity, 400–401
    psychological factors in, 401
    weight control and, 402–403
Objective responsibility, 129
Objective sensations, 10
Objective tests, of personality, 458–462
Object permanence, 126
Observation, 20
    case study and, 43
    laboratory, 48
    methods of, 42–49
    naturalistic, 47
    survey and, 44
    testing and, 46–47
Observational learning, 271–274, 444–445, 479–480. *See also* Observation
    media violence and, 272–274, 275

Obsession, 560, 561
Obsessive-compulsive disorder, 561
Occipital lobe, 83, 84
Occupations, trait theory and, 443, 460–461
Odor discrimination, 115–116
Odors, 193
    impact of, 668
Oedipus complex, 435, 438
    gender and superego development, 135–136
    gender-typing and, 478–479
    personality disorders and, 583
    sexual orientation and, 491
Office of Technology Assessment (OTA), polygraph and, 417
Older adults. *See* Late adulthood
Olfactory, 193
Olfactory membrane, 193
Olfactory nerve, 193
On Death and Dying (Kübler-Ross), 150–151
"One-trial learning," 263
Operant, 256
Operant behavior, 256
Operant conditioning, 242, 254–269, 274, 607–610
    applications of, 265–269
    assertiveness training and, 609
    biofeedback training and, 609–610
    discriminative stimuli in, 262
    extinction in, 260
    fear and, 266
    reinforcers vs. rewards and punishment in, 260–262
    schedules of reinforcement in, 262–265
    Skinner and reinforcement, 255–258
    social skills training and, 609
    spontaneous recovery in, 260
    successive approximations and, 608
    Thorndike and law of effect, 255
    token economies and, 607–609
    types of reinforcers, 258–260
Operational definitions, 38
Ophthalmoscope, 170
Opiates, 225
Opioids, 225
Opponent-process theory, 170
Opportunistic diseases, 504
Optic nerve, 163
Oral stage, 434
Organization
    hierarchies and, 321
    in long-term memory, 299–301
Organizational psychologists, 8
Organizing effect, of sex hormones, 491
Organ of Corti, 188, 190
Orgasm, 468
    in sexual response cycle, 499

Orgasmic disorder, 500
Originality, creativity and, 332
Osteoporosis, 143
OTA. *See* Office of Technology Assessment (OTA)
Outer ear, 188
Out-group. *See* Actor-observer effect; Prejudice
Out magazine, 490
Oval window, 188
Ovaries, 92–93, 96
Overconfidence, decision making and, 341
Overextension, 322, 345
Overregularization, 346, 347
Overtones, 187
Ovum, 110
Oxytocin, 91

P

Pain, 197–200. *See also* Biofeedback training (BFT); Cancer
acupuncture and, 198–199
coping with, 198–199
gate theory and, 197–198
hypnosis and, 198–199
perception and control of, 156–157
phantom limb pain, 197
sensation of, 197–200
stress and, 199
Paired associates, 305
Palmar reflex, 113
Pancreas, 91–92, 96
Panic disorder, 560, 561
Paranoid personality disorder, 582
Paranoid schizophrenia, 578, 579
Parasympathetic ANS, 83
Parenting. *See also* Adoptee studies; Adoption
intelligence and, 382–383
older parents and, 141
styles of, 120–122
Parietal lobe, 83, 84
Parkinson's disease, 74
nicotine and, 230
Partial reinforcement, 262–263
Partial-report procedure, 288
Passive smoking, 229
Pathogens, 513, 533
Pavlovian conditioning, 244–246, 251. *See also* Classical conditioning
Pavlovian model, 12
PCP. *See* Phencyclidine (PCP)
Peace, conflict resolution and, 650–651
Peers, academic achievement and, 276
Pelvic inflammatory disease (PID), 94
Perception, 13–14, 154
defined, 157
depth, 177–181
extrasensory, 201–203

Gestalt psychology and, 172–175
hypnosis and, 236
of loudness and pitch, 189–190
of movement, 175–177
sensation, virtual reality, and, 196
signal-detection theory and, 159–160
social, 645–653
visual, 171–184
Perceptual constancies, 182–183
Perceptual development, 113–116
Perceptual organization, 171–175
Performance, competencies and, 445
Performance anxiety, 501
Performance assessment, 369, 370
Period of the ovum, 110
Peripheral nervous system, 77, 81–83
autonomic nervous system and, 82–83
Permissive parents, 120, 121
Personal factors, creativity and, 332–333
Personality, 428, 429
Adler and, 436
Allport and trait approach to, 440
brain damage and, 57
development in adolescence, 138–139
Erikson and, 436–437
Freud's theory of psychosexual development and, 431–435
health, illness, and, 539
Hippocrates and trait approach to, 440
Horney and, 436
humanistic-existential perspective on, 449–454
Jung and, 436
learning perspective on, 443–449
Maslow and, 449, 450, 451
measurement of, 458–463
psychic structure and, 432–434
psychodynamic perspective on, 430–439
Rogers and, 449, 451–453, 456
sociocultural perspective on, 454–457
stress and, 518
trait perspective on, 439–443
Personality disorders, 582–584, 590
biological treatments for, 442
theories of, 583–584
types of, 582
Personality measurement
for career determination, 460–461
objective tests for, 458–462
projective tests for, 462–463
tests and, 46, 62
Personality psychologists, 7

Personality research, fantasy in, 410
Personality tests. *See* Personality measurement
Personal space, 670–671
Personnel tests, 460
Person variables, 444, 445
Perspective, 177
Persuasion, 637–641
persuasive message and, 638–639
Personality, Eysenck's personality dimensions and, 440, 441
PET scan, 58, 59
Phagic, 400
Phallic stage, 435, 438
Phallic symbols, 601
Phallocentric bias, 438
Phencyclidine (PCP), 232
Phenothiazines, 74
Phenylketonuria, 374
Pheromones, 194, 394
Philosophy. *See* Greeks
Phi phenomenon, 177
Phobias, 560
behavior therapy and, 605
theoretical views on, 562–563
Phonemes, 342, 345
Photoreceptors, 163
rods and cones as, 165
Physical activity. *See* Exercise
Physical appearance
attraction and, 482–486
first impressions and, 645–646, 648
Physical development, 113–116
adolescence and, 117, 136–137, 136–139
of adults, 140–151
in late adulthood, 147
perceptual development and, 113–116
reflexes and, 113
Physical environment, 666–667
Physical events, 10
Physical illness. *See* Health
Physical traits. *See* Traits; Trait theories
Physiological drive, 393
hunger as, 399
Physiological needs, 393, 395
Piagetian cognitive-developmental theory, 19
language development and, 353–354
Piaget's cognitive-developmental theory, 125–131
PID. *See* Pelvic inflammatory disease (PID)
Pigeon project, 255–256, 257
Pitch, 158, 159, 186
perception of, 189–190
Pituitary gland, 90–91, 96
Placebo, 53, 54
Placebo effect, 200
Placement, worker motivation and, 412

Placenta, 111
Place theory, 190
Planet Out, 490
Plateau phase, of sexual response cycle, 499
Pleasure center, 80, 233
Pleasure principle, 432
Plutchik's theory of emotions, 418
PMS. *See* Premenstrual syndrome (PMS)
Polarization, 72
gender, 469–474
Polarization effect, 661–662
Polling
Harris polls and, 44
techniques of, 39
Pollution
air, 668
noise and, 667
Polygon, A3–A4
Polygraphs, 417
Ponzo illusion, 184
Population, 39, A1
samples and, 39–42, A12
Positive correlation, 49, 50
Positive instances, 322
Positive regard, 451–453
Positive reinforcers, 259
Positive vs. negative life changes, 518
Positron emission tomography (PET). *See* PET scan
Postconventional level, 134
Posthypnotic amnesia, 236
Posthypnotic suggestion, 236
Posttraumatic stress disorder (PTSD), 560, 561–562
Poverty
health and, 542
of older women, 146
Practical intelligence, 364
Praise, in classroom discipline, 267
Precognition, 201
Preconscious, 209, 431
Preconventional level, 133–134
Predictability, of stressors, 525–526
Predispositions, genetic, 538
Prefrontal lobotomy, 628
Pregenital fixations, 435
Pregnancy
aging and, 141
exercise during, 110
Prejudice, 640–644, 645
combating, 642–643
discrimination and, 641
sources of, 643–644, 645
stereotypes and, 641–643
Prelinguistic vocalization, 344–345
Premature ejaculation, 500
Premenstrual syndrome (PMS), 94–95
Prenatal development, 109–113
Preoperational stage, 127–129

Presbyopia, 182
Preschool stage, 117
Pressure, 195–196, 201
Prevention, of STDs, 506
Primacy effect, 291, 645
Primary colors, 168
Primary drives, 394, 398
Primary mental abilities, 361
Primary reinforcers, 260
Primary sex characteristics, 93
Prism, 161
Proactive interference, 307–308
Problems, understanding of, 324–325
Problem solving, 322–330
  algorithms and, 325
  analogies and, 326
  approaches to, 323–326
  brain and, 85
  expertise and, 326–327
  factors affecting, 326–330
  functional fixedness and, 330
  heuristics and, 325
  incubation and, 329–330
  insight and, 327–328
  mental sets and, 327
  perception and, 13
Procedural memory, 284
Productivity, enhancing, 412–413
Progesterone, 93
Programmed learning, 269
Programmed senescence, 147
Progressive relaxation, 535–536, 605
Projection, 433
Projective tests, 462–463
  Rorschach, 462
  Thematic Apperception Test (TAT), 462–463
"Project Pigeon," 255–256, 257
Prolactin, 91
Protease inhibitors, 507
Prototypes, concepts and, 321–322
Proximity, 174
Prozac, 442
Pseudomemories, hypnosis and, 236
Pseudoscience, critical thinking about, 62–63
Psi communication, 201, 203
Psychedelic, 231
Psychiatrist, 6
Psychic structures, 438
  of personality, 432–434
Psychoactive substances, 219, 231, 232
Psychoanalysis, 15–16, 16, 431–432, 599–601
  dream analysis in, 601
  free association and, 600–601
  modern, 601
Psychoanalytic theory, 432
Psychobiologists, 68
Psychodynamic theories, 15, 19, 20
  Adler and, 436
  of aggression, 414

on anxiety disorders, 562
case studies and, 43
on depression, 570
on dissociative disorders, 566
dream symbols in, 215
Erikson and, 436–437
evaluation of, 437–439
Freud's theory of psychosexual development and, 431–435
gender-typing and, 478–479, 481
Horney and, 436
Jung and, 436
of personality development, 430–439, 457
on personality disorders, 583–584
on schizophrenia, 580
sexual orientation and, 491
of substance abuse and dependence, 221
Psychodynamic therapies, 599–602, 616
  modern, 601
  psychoanalysis as, 599–601
Psychokinesis, 201
Psycholinguistic theory, 349
Psychological androgyny, 469
Psychological dependence, 221
Psychological disorders, 552, 554–555
  anxiety disorders, 560–563
  classification of, 556–560, 557–559
  defined, 555–556
  dissociative disorders, 564–566
  eating disorders, 585–590
  mood disorders, 568–577
  personality disorders, 582–584
  schizophrenia, 577–582
  somatoform disorders, 567
Psychological hardiness, 523–525
Psychological influences, on gender-typing, 478–482
Psychological needs, 393
Psychological principles, 597
Psychological tests, 46–47
Psychologists
  activities of, 5–8
  diversity of, 17–18
Psychology. See also Ethics; specific fields
  behaviorism, 11–14, 16
  contemporary perspectives of, 18–23
  critical thinking and, 24–29
  defined, 2–3
  doctorates in subfields of, 6
  as field, 28
  functionalism, 10–11, 16
  Gestalt, 13–14, 16
  history of, 9–18
  psychoanalysis, 15–16
  as science, 3–5
  structuralism and, 10, 16
Psychomotor retardation, 568

Psychoneuroimmunology, 533
Psychophysical relationship, 158
Psychophysicists, 157
Psychosexual development
  Freud on, 109, 431–435, 438
  stages of, 434–435
Psychosocial development, Erikson on, 116–117, 437
Psychosocial views of aging, 147–149
Psychosurgery, 628
Psychotherapy, 594. See also Counseling
  behavior therapy, 604–611, 612
  biological therapies and, 625–629
  cognitive therapies, 613–615
  defined, 596–597
  drugs and, 442
  effectiveness of, 620–621
  ethnicity and, 621–624
  feminist, 624
  group therapies, 615–618
  history of, 597–598
  and human diversity, 621–625
  humanistic-existential, 602–604
  for personality disorders, 442
  psychoanalysis as, 15
  psychodynamic therapies, 599–602
  research problems in, 619–620
  sex, 501
  sexual orientation and, 624
  virtual reality and, 606
PTSD. See Posttraumatic stress disorder (PTSD)
Puberty, 109, 137
  sex glands and, 93
Pubic lice, 503
Public behaviors, 12
Punishment
  law of effect and, 255
  learning and, 35–36
  moral development theory and, 133–136
  in operant conditioning, 260–262
  reinforcers and, 260–262
Pupil, 162
Pure research, 5
Purposes (functions), of behavior, 11
Puzzle box, of Thorndike, 255

Q

Questionnaires, 44

R

Race. See also Ethnicity
  health and, 540–541
  intelligence and, 378–379
  IQ and, 387
  Simpson trial verdict and, 339–340
  sociocultural factors, self, and, 456

Rage. See also Anger
  amygdala and, 80–81
Random sample, 42, A10
Range, A5–A6
  defined, A1
Rape, 492–497
  college students and, 494
  myths about, 493, 497
  preventing, 495
  reasons for, 494
Rapid-eye-movement (REM) sleep, 211–212
  deprivation of, 213
  dreams and, 213–214, 215
  nightmares and, 216
Rapid flight of ideas, 568
Rapid smoking, 607
RAS. See Reticular activating system (RAS)
Rathus Assertiveness Schedule, 608, 609
Rational emotive behavior therapy (REBT), 615
Rationalization, 433
Rational thought, 9
Reaction formation, 433
Reaction time, 147
Reality principle, 433
Reality testing, 462
Reasoning, 334–335
  deductive, 334
  inductive, 334–335
  moral, 133–136
Rebound anxiety, 625
REBT. See Rational emotive behavior therapy (REBT)
Recall, forgetting and, 305
Recency effect, 291, 646
Receptor cells, 188
Reciprocal determinism, 444
Reciprocity, and attraction, 484, 485
Recognition, forgetting and, 305
Recruitment, worker motivation and, 412
Reflection, 4–5
Reflex(es), 78, 113, 244
  conditioned, 244–246
  spinal, 77
Reflex arc, 77
Refractory period, 73
  of sexual response cycle, 500
Regression, 236, 433
Rehearsal, 609. See also Memory
  elaborative, 298
  levels-of-processing model and, 302–304
  maintenance, 285, 297
Reinforcement, 12–13, 255–258, 612
  continuous, 262–263
  in language development, 348
  schedules of, 262–265
  strategies aimed at, 612

Reinforcers
  rewards, punishments, and, 260–262
  types of, 258–260
Relatedness, vs. individuality, 438–439
Relationships. *See also* Sexual coercion
  gender and, 476
  gender polarization and, 474
  for memory improvement, 310
Relaxation, 535–536
Relaxation response, 232, 233
Relaxation training, 199, 605
Relearning, 306–307
Releasers, 394
Reliability, of tests, 47
Religion, sexual behavior and, 45
Remote Associates Test, 333
REM sleep. *See* Rapid-eye-movement (REM) sleep
Rent (musical), 505
Repetition, memory and, 310
Replication, 39
Representativeness heuristic, 336
  Simpson trial verdict and, 339
Repression, 210, 294, 431, 433
  forgetting and, 308
Research
  on effectiveness of therapy, 620–621
  ethical issues in, 59–61
  global, 56
  on psychotherapy, 619–620
Research methods, 3
  for brain studies, 57–59
  correlation as, 49–52
  critical assessment of, 25
  Milgram studies and, 34–37
  observation methods as, 42–49
  pure and applied, 5
  samples, populations, and, 39–42
  scientific method and, 37–39, 52–56
Resistance, 432, 601
Resistance stage, 532
Resolution phase, of sexual response cycle, 500
Response. *See also* Operant conditioning; Sexual response
  stimuli and, in classical conditioning, 246–247
Response cost, 612
Response prevention, 612
Response sets, 459
Responsibility
  diffusion of, 661
  objective, 129
Resting potential, 72
Retardation. *See* Mental retardation
Reticular activating system (RAS), 78–79, 215
Reticular formation, 80
Retina, 163, 165

Retinal disparity, 180–181
Retrieval, in memory, 286
Retroactive interference, 307
Retrograde amnesia, 309–312
Reuptake, 74
Reverse transcriptase, 507
Reversibility, 129
Rewards, in operant conditioning, 260, 261–262
Rhesus monkeys, amygdala of, 80–81
Rh incompatibility, 112
Ribonucleic acid (RNA), memory and, 314
Right brain. *See* Hemispheres
Risky shift, 662
Ritalin, 226
RNA. *See* Ribonucleic acid (RNA)
Robbers Cave experiment, 642
Rods, 163, 164, 165
Role diffusion, ego identity and, 138–139
Role models, gender-typing and, 479
Role playing, hypnosis and, 236
Roles. *See also* Gender; Gender-typing
  gender, 469
  in young adulthood, 140
Role theory, of hypnosis, 236, 237
Roman Catholicism. *See* Catholicism
Romantic love, 486, 488
Rooting, 113
Rorschach tests, 462, 463
Rote learning, 292
Rote maintenance rehearsal, 310
Roy G. Biv (mnemonic device), 161
Rubin vase, 173–174

S

Saccadic eye movements, 288
  iconic memory and, 289
Safety needs, 395
Sales. *See* Advertising; Persuasion
Sample, 39, A12
  defined, A1
  populations and, 39–42
  random and stratified, 42
Sanguine, 440
SAT. *See* Scholastic Assessment Test (SAT)
Satiety, 399
Saturation, of color, 166, 167
SBIS. *See* Stanford-Binet Intelligence Scale (SBIS)
Scales. *See* specific scales
Schachter-Singer study of emotion, 422–424
Schedules of reinforcement, 262–265
Schema, 294–296
Scheme, 125
  social decision, 661
Schizoid personality, 582–583

Schizophrenia, 19, 554, 555, 577–582, 590
  biological risk factors for, 580–581
  catatonic, 579
  disorganized, 579
  dopamine and, 74, 581–582
  genetics and, 581
  heredity and, 581
  learning theories on, 580
  multifactorial approach to, 581
  nicotine and, 230
  paranoid, 578
  psychodynamic theories on, 580
  psychological disorders on, 577–582
  sociocultural theories on, 580
  theoretical views of, 579–581
  types of, 579
Schizotypal personality disorder, 582
Scholastic Aptitude Test, 372
Scholastic Assessment Test (SAT), A8
School psychologists, 6
Schools of psychology, 16
Science
  empirical, 34
  psychology as, 3–5, 10
Scientific method, 37–39. *See also* Research methods
Scripts, gender-typing and, 480–481
Seattle Longitudinal Study, 385
Second adulthood, 141, 142, 149
Secondary colors, 168
Secondary reinforcers, 260
Secondary sex characteristics, 93, 137
Second language. *See* Bilingualism
Security, 120
Sedative, 627
Selection factor, 38
Selective attention, 132
  consciousness as, 209
Selective avoidance, 640
Selective exposure, 640
Self
  consciousness and, 219
  sociocultural factors and, 456
Self-actualization, 395, 396, 450, 453
  Maslow and, 451
Self-awareness, 20, 365
Self-concept, 451
  sociocultural factors and, 456
Self-control methods, 610, 612
Self-efficacy expectations, 448, 452, 523, 605
Self-esteem, 451–453
  acculturation and, 456
  enhancing, 452
  sociocultural factors and, 456

Self-help books, critical thinking about, 25–26
Self-improvement, 452
Self-insight, 432
Self-knowledge, 9
Self-monitoring, 609
Self-regulatory systems, 448
Self-reporting, 44
Self-serving bias, 649
Self theory, of Rogers, 451
Semantic codes, 285
Semanticity, 342, 344
Semantic memory, 284
Semantics, 343–344
Semicircular canals, 200
Seminal fluid, 499
Sensation, 154
  absolute threshold and, 157–158
  defined, 157
  difference threshold and, 158–159
  feature detectors and, 160
  of pain, 197–200
  perception, virtual reality, and, 196
  sensory adaptation and, 160–161
  signal-detection theory and, 159–160
  skin senses and, 195–200
  stimuli and, 157–158
  of temperature, 197
  vestibular sense and, 200
Sensation-seeking scale, 405
Sense of humor, 525
Senses, 9. *See also* Hearing; Kinesthesis; Pressure; Sensation; Smell; Taste; Touch; Vestibular sense; Vision
  development of, 114–116
  "sixth," 194
Sensitive period, in linguistic theory, 350
Sensitization, 160–161, 612
Sensorimotor coordination, 113
Sensorimotor stage, 126–127
Sensorineural deafness, 191
Sensory adaptation, 160–161
Sensory awareness, consciousness as, 208–210
Sensory deprivation, 404
Sensory information, brain and, 85
Sensory memory, 287, 288–290
Sensory receptors, 195–196
Sensory register, 288
Sensory stimulation, activity and, 404–406
Sensory thresholds, 157
Sentences, 345
Sequence, invariant, of language development, 349
Serial-position effect, 291
Series, in problem solving, 323

Serotonin, 75, 563, 626
  depression and, 571
  memory and, 314
  PMS and, 95
Serotonin-uptake inhibitors, 627
Serum cholesterol, 543
SES. *See* Socioeconomic status
  (SES)
Sex, gender and, 476
Sex characteristics, secondary, 137
Sex chromosomes, 98
Sex hormones, 92–93
  gender-typing and, 478, 481
  sexual orientation and, 491–492
Sex organs, differentiation of, 110
Sex therapy, 501
Sexual abuse, forgetting, 308
Sexual behavior
  Kinsey studies and, 44
  survey of, 45
Sexual coercion, 492–498
Sexual dysfunctions, 498, 500–501
Sexual gratification, in psychosex-
  ual development, 434–435
Sexual harassment, 497
  resisting, 496
Sexual impulses, 15
Sexuality, 468–469. *See also*
  Freud's theory of psychosex-
  ual development; Gender;
  Psychoanalysis
  arousal and, 498
  manopause and, 143, 144
  menopause and, 143
  pheromones and, 194
  sexual response and, 498–501
  virtual sex and, 196
Sexually transmitted diseases
  (STDs), 469, 501–507
  listing of, 502–503
  preventing, 506
Sexual orientation, 488–489
  ethnicity and, 489–491
  origins of, 491–492
  psychotherapy and, 624
Sexual response
  cycle, 498, 499–500
  reflexes and, 78
"s" factors, 361
Shades, of color, 167
Shadowing, 178–179
Shape constancy, 183
Shaping, 264–265
  language development and, 349
Shona language, linguistic-
  relativity hypothesis and, 354
Short-term memory (STM), 19,
  287, 290–294
  interference in, 293–294
  transferring information to
  long-term memory, 297–298
Sickle cell anemia, 112
Sight
  brain and, 83
  physical development and, 113
Signal-detection theory, 159–160

Signed English, 342n
Signing, 96
Similarity, 174
Simultaneous conditioning, 247
Sinister, handedness and, 87–88
Situational attributions, 647
Situational variables, 4, 445
"Sixth sense," 194
Size constancy, 177, 182
Skill memory, 284
Skin, 195
Skin contact, in attachment, 119
Skinner box, 256–258
Skinner's reinforcement research,
  255–258
Skin senses, 195–200
  absolute threshold of touch
    and, 158
  pain and, 197–200
  temperature and, 197
  touch, pressure, and, 195–196
Sleep, 210–213
  and dreams, 213–216
  functions of, 213
  insomnia and, 216
  stages of, 211–212
Sleep cycles, 212
Sleep disorders, 217–219
Sleep spindles, 212
Sleep terrors, 219
Sleepwalking, 219
Smell, 193, 201
  absolute threshold of, 158
Smoking. *See also* Cigarettes
  aversive conditioning and, 607
  cancer and, 548
Snellen Chart, 181
Snow, 227
Social awareness, 365
Social behavior
  aggression and, 477
  inheritance of, 97
  mate selection and, 476–477
  men and women compared, 476
  sex, relationships, and, 476
Social categorization, 644, 645
Social-cognitive theory, 21, 444
  on anxiety disorders, 562
  competencies and, 445–446
  emotions and, 448
  encoding strategies and,
    446–447
  expectancies and, 447–448
  gender-typing and, 479–480,
    481
  observational learning and,
    444–445
  self-regulatory systems, plans,
    and, 448
Social comparison, obedience and,
  654
Social comparison theory, 411
Social conflict, 644, 645
Social decision schemes, 661
Social development, 116–124
  in adolescence, 138–139

Social evaluation, creativity and,
  333
Social facilitation, 660–661
Social influence, 653–659
  conformity and, 655–659
  obedience to authority and,
    653–655
Socialization, 265
  gender-typing and, 480
  obedience and, 654
Social learning, 644, 645
  in female aggressiveness, 480
Social Learning and Imitation
  (Miller and Dollard), 663
Social-learning theorists, 16n
Social-learning theory. *See* Social-
  cognitive theory
Social norms, 656
Social perception, 645–653
  attribution theory and,
    646–650
  body language and, 650–653
  first impressions and, 645–646,
    648
  primary and recency effects,
    645–646
Social psychologists, 7
Social psychology, 632, 634–635
  attitudes and, 635–644, 645
  defined, 635
  environmental psychology and,
    666–671
  group behavior and, 659–666
  prejudice and, 640–644, 645
  social influence and, 653–659
  social perception and, 645–653
Social readjustment rating scale,
  516–517
Social skills training, 609
Social support, 528–529
Sociobiological perspective, on
  aggression, 413–414
Sociobiologists, 97
Sociocultural factors
  in health and illness, 539–542
  in sexual behavior survey, 45, 46
Sociocultural theories, 21–23
  acculturation, self-esteem, and,
    456
  on aggression, 415
  evaluation of, 456–457
  individualism vs. collectivism
    and, 455
  on personality development,
    454–457
  on schizophrenia, 580
  and self, 456
Socioeconomic class, intelligence
  and, 371–373, 378
Socioeconomic status (SES), 21
  adult intellectual functioning
    and, 385
  health and, 542
  smoking and, 229
Somatoform disorders, 567, 590
Somatosensory cortex, 84–85

Sound. *See also* Ear; Hearing;
  Language; Phonemes
  decibel ratings of, 187
  locating, 188
Sound waves, 185, 186
Space
  crowding and, 669–670
  personal, 670–671
Spatial abilities. *See* Visual-spatial
  abilities
Spatial reasoning, music studies
  and, 382–383
Specificity, 636
Specific phobia, 560
Spectrum, visible, 161–162
"Speed" (amphetamines), 74, 226
Sphincter, 113
Spina bifida, 112
Spinal cord, 77
Spinal reflexes, 77
Split-brain experiments, 88–89
Spontaneous recovery
  in classical conditioning, 250
  in operant conditioning, 260
Sports psychologists, 8
Stability-instability, 440
Stages of memory. *See* Memory
Stage theorists, 109
Stagnation, generativity vs.,
  141–142
Standard deviation, A5, A6, A11
Standardized tests, 458
Stanford-Binet Intelligence Scale
  (SBIS), 367–369
Staring, 653
  avoidance and, 652
Startle (Moro) reflex, 113
State-dependent memory, 302
Statistically significant differ-
  ences, A10–A12
Statistics, 9
  correlation coefficient, A9
  defined, A1
  descriptive, A1–A7
  inferential, A9–A12
  normal curve, A7–A8, A9
STDs. *See* Sexually transmitted
  diseases (STDs)
Stereotypes, 637, 641–643
  gender, 469, 470
  of women, 485
Stereotype vulnerability, intelligence tests and, 381–382
Sternberg's triarchic theory,
  363–364
Steroids, 90
Stimulants, 220, 226–229
Stimulation, adult intellectual
  functioning and, 385
Stimulus, 244. *See also* Piaget's
  cognitive-developmental theory; Skinner's reinforcement
  research
  behavioral strategies and, 612
  choice and, 20
  control of, 612

discriminative, 262
hierarchy of, 605
and responses, in classical conditioning, 246–247
sensory memory and, 288
sensory response to, 159–160
visual, 115
Stimulus motives, 398, 404–407
STM. *See* Short-term memory
Storage
in brain, 313–315
information processing and, 19
of memories, 285
Stranger anxiety, 118
Strange situation method, 117–118
Stratified sample, 42
Stream of thought, memory and, 288
"Street smarts," 364
Strength of attitudes, 636
Stress
adrenal glands and, 92
and cancer, 545–547
coping with, 534–537
defined, 513–514
endocrine system and, 531
general adaptation syndrome (GAS) and, 529–532
health and, 50
immune system and, 532–538
job-strain model and, 545
in Milgram studies, 37
pain and, 199
psychological moderators of, 522–529
sources of, 514–522
suicide and, 575
Strictness, in parenting, 122
Stroboscopic motion, 176
Structuralism, 10, 16
Stupor, 579
Subject experiences, 20
Subjective feelings, 10
Subjective moral judgment, 229
Subjective values, 444
Sublimation, 433
Subordination, in hierarchical organization, 300
Substance abuse, 626. *See also* Alcohol and alcoholism; Drugs
causal factors in, 221–222
dependence and, 220–221
Subtractive color mixtures, 168
Successive approximations, 264, 608, 612
Suggestibility, hypnotic, 235, 236
Suicide, 574–577
prevention of, 576–577
Superego, 434, 438
in men and women, 135–136
Superiority, drive for, 436
Super Memory (Herrmann), 310
Superordination, in hierarchical organization, 299–300

Support groups, 658
Suppression, 210
Surrogate mothers, attachment and, 119–120
Survey method, 3, 44, 55
Survival of the fittest, 11
Sympathetic ANS, 83
Synapse, 73
memory and, 312–315
Synaptic cleft, 73
Syntax, 343
development of, 345–346
Syphilis, 503, 504
Systematic desensitization, 254, 604–605
Systematic interaction, 596–597
Systematic random search algorithm, 325

T
T4 cells, 505n
Talents, multiple intelligences theory and, 362–363
Target population, 40
Taste, 193–195, 201
absolute threshold of, 158
Taste aversion, 248
Taste buds, 194
Taste cells, 194
Taste discrimination, 116
TAT. *See* Thematic Apperception Test (TAT)
Tay-Sachs disease, 112
Technological factors, in health and illness, 539
Technology, virtual classroom and, 268
Telegraphic speech, 345, 347
Telepathy, 201, 202
Temperature, 197
environmental psychology and, 667–668
Temporal lobe, 83, 84
Tension. *See* Relaxation
Tension headache, 542
Terman studies of genius, 375–376
Terminals, 69–71
Tertiary colors, 168
Testes, 92–93, 96
Testosterone, 92–93
sexual orientation and, 491
Test-retest reliability, 47
Tests and testing, 46–47, 55. *See also* Intelligence tests; Measurement; Research; Scientific method
creativity and, 331–332
cultural biases in, 352
for genetic and chromosomal abnormalities, 112
of intelligence, 367–373
personality measurement and, 458–463
Texture gradient, 180
Thalamus, 80
memory and, 315

"Thanatopsis" (Bryant), 151
Thematic Apperception Test (TAT), 409, 410, 462–463
Theory, 37
defined, 3–4
Theory of social comparison, 411
Therapy. *See* Psychotherapy; specific therapies
Theta waves, 211–212
Thinking, 320
convergent, 331
creativity and, 330–334
critical, 24–29
decision making and, 335–341
divergent, 331
judgment and, 335–341
language and, 320–321
perception and, 13
problem solving and, 322–330
reasoning and, 334–335
Thirties, age-30 transition and, 140–141
Thorndike's law of effect, 255
Thought
cortex and, 85
language and, 353–355
psychotherapy and, 597
Three Faces of Eve, The (movie), 565
Thrush, 502
Thymine, 98
Thyroid gland, 92, 96
Thyroxin, 92
Timbre, 187
Time out, 261
Time urgency, 526–527
Tints, of color, 167
Tip-of-the-tongue (TOT) phenomenon, 301
TM. *See* Transcendental meditation (TM)
Token economies, 266–267, 607–609
Tolerance, for drugs, 221
Top-down processing, 175
TOT. *See* Tip-of-the-tongue (TOT) phenomenon
Total immersion method, 350
Touch, 116, 195–196, 201. *See also* Skin senses
absolute threshold of, 158
Touching, 652
Trace conditioning, 247
Training, worker motivation and, 412
Traits, 439–440
careers and, 461
genetic influences on, 97
Trait theories
evaluation of, 443
of Eysenck, 440, 441
five-factor model and, 441–443
Hippocrates to present, 440, 441
on personality development, 439–443, 457
on personality disorders, 584

Trance, 210
hypnosis and, 235–237
Tranquilizers, 625–626
Transcendental Meditation (TM), 232, 233
Treatment, 52
Triangular model of love, 486–488
Triarchic theory of intelligence, 363–364
Trichomoniasis, 503
Trichromatic theory, 170
Trichromats, 171
Tricyclic antidepressants, 627
Trust versus mistrust stage, 116, 117
Truth-wins scheme, 661
Trying 20s, 140
Tuning fork, 185
Twenties, development during, 140–141
Twin studies, 99–101
IQ and, 379–380
sexual orientation and, 491
Two-point threshold, 195–196
Two-thirds majority scheme, 661
Two-way immersion, 350
Type A behavior, 521, 522, 524
alleviating, 526–527
Type B behavior, 524

U
Ultrasound, 112
Umbilical cord, 111
Unconditional positive regard, 451, 603
Unconditioned response (UR), 246
Unconditioned stimulus (US), 246
Unconscious, 15, 20, 210, 431
collective, 436
dreams and, 214
repression and, 294
Understanding, of problem, 324–325
Universities. *See* College students
University of Chicago, behaviorism and, 11
Unobtrusive observation measures, 47
Uplifts, 514
Uppers, 226
UR. *See* Unconditioned response (UR)
US. *See* Unconditioned stimulus (US)

V
Vaccination, 533n
Vaginismus, 500
Validity, of tests, 47
Validity scales, 47, 459
Value (color), 166
Values
obedience and, 655
psychotherapy and, 622
Variable-interval schedule, 263

Variable-ratio schedule, 264
Variables
  independent and dependent, 52–53
  persona and situational, 445
Vasocongestion, 499
Vasopression, memory and, 314
Ventromedial nucleus (VMN), 399
Verbal assessment, 369
Verbal Behavior (Skinner), 348
Verbs, in Ebonics, 352–353
Vested interest, 636
Vestibular sense, 200, 201
Victimization by prejudice, 644, 645
Victims, bystander effect, altruism, and, 666
Video games, cyberbabes and, 586–587
Vineland Adaptive Behavior Scales, 374
Violence
  effects on women, 41
  media, 272–274, 275
Virtual classrooms, 268
Virtual reality, 196, 606
Visible light, 161
Visible spectrum, 161–162
Vision, 201
  absolute threshold of, 158
  color blindness and, 171
  color vision, 166–171
  depth perception and, 177–181
  eye and, 162–166
  light and, 161
  movement perception and, 175–177

perceptual, 184
perceptual constancies and, 182–183
perceptual organization and, 172–175
problems in perception and, 181–182
visual illusions and, 183–184
Visual acuity, 181–183
Visual code, 285
Visual cortex, memory and, 312
Visual discrimination, cliff experiment and, 115
Visual illusions, 183–184
Visual perception, 171–184
Visual-spatial abilities, gender and, 474, 475–476
VMN. *See* Ventromedial nucleus (VMN)
Vocabulary, 347
  development of, 345
Vocalization, prelinguistic, 344–345
Vocational Preference Inventory (Holland), 461
Volley principle, 190
Volunteer bias, 42
Vomeronasal organ, 194

W

Waking state, consciousness as, 210
Walden Two (Skinner), 444
Warfare, conflict resolution and, 650–651
Warm colors, 167
Warts, genital, 503

Wavelength, of light, 167
Waxy flexibility, 579
Wear-and-tear theory, 147
Weber's constant, 158, 159
Wechsler intelligence scales, 369–370
  Adult Intelligence Scale, 370
Weight. *See* Body shape; Weight control
Weight control, 402–403
Wernicke's aphasia, 86, 87
Western personality theories, individuality vs. relatedness and, 438–439
When Prophecy Fails, 392
White Americans
  IQ testing and, 372
  Simpson verdict and, 339
White matter, 78
White noise, 187
White people, intelligence and, 387
Whole-report procedure, 288
Whorfian hypothesis, 354
Wish fulfillment, 601
Witchcraft, 554
Withdrawal reflex, 113
Witnesses, long-term memory and, 296
Women. *See also* Attraction; Females; Gender; Girls; Mothers; Sexual coercion
  aging and, 146
  alcohol and, 222
  careers of, 473
  cognitive abilities of, 475–476
  depression and, 569–570

eating disorders and, 588–589
effects of violence on, 41
feminist psychotherapy and, 624
isolation of, 146
marianismo and, 471–472
moral development in, 135–136
Muslim, 658–659
personality disorders and, 583–584
poverty among, 146
as psychologists, 17, 28
rape and, 492–497
in research, 41
social behavior of, 476–477
stereotypes of, 485
superego in, 135–136
violence and, 41
weight control and, 402–403
work and, 41
young adulthood and, 140
Work, women and, 41
Working memory, 290. *See also* Short-term memory
Workplace, sexual harassment in, 497

Y

Yale University. *See also* Milgram studies
Yeast infection, 502
Young adulthood, 117, 140–141
Young-Helmholtz theory, 170, 190

Z

Zener cards, 202
Zygote, 109